Y0-BBY-544

CULTURAL ANTHROPOLOGY

Second Edition

Nancy Bonvillain

Bard College at Simon's Rock

Prentice Hall

Boston   Columbus   Indianapolis   New York   San Francisco   Upper Saddle River
Amsterdam   Cape Town   Dubai   London   Madrid   Milan   Munich   Paris   Montreal   Toronto
Delhi   Mexico City   Sao Paulo   Sydney   Hong Kong   Seoul   Singapore   Taipei   Tokyo

Planet Friendly Publishing
✔ Made in the United States
✔ Printed on Recycled Paper
Learn more at www.greenedition.org

At Pearson Education we're committed to producing books in an earth-friendly manner and to helping our customers make greener choices. Manufacturing books in the United States ensures compliance with strict environmental laws and eliminates the need for international freight shipping, a major contributor to global air pollution.

And printing on recycled paper helps minimize our consumption of trees, water and fossil fuels. The text of *Cultural Anthropology, Second Edition*, was printed on paper made with 10% post-consumer waste, and the cover was printed on paper made with 10% post-consumer waste. According to Environmental Defense's Paper Calculator, by using this innovative paper instead of conventional papers, we achieved the following environmental benefits:

Trees Saved: 34 • Air Emissions Eliminated: 3,749 pounds
Water Saved: 12,241 gallons • Solid Waste Eliminated: 2,030 pounds

For more information on our environmental practices, please visit us online at www.pearsonhighered.com/difference

VP, Editorial Director: Leah Jewell
Editor in Chief: Dickson Musslewhite
Publisher: Nancy Roberts
Editorial Assistant: Nart Varoqua
Editor in Chief, Editorial Development: Rochelle Diogenes
Senior Development Editor: Gerald Lombardi
Director of Marketing: Brandy Dawson
Senior Marketing Manager: Laura Lee Manley
Marketing Assistant: Pat Walsh
Managing Editor: Maureen Richardson
Project Manager: Marianne Peters-Riordan
Copy Editor: Heather McElwain
Proofreader: Heather Mann
Senior Operations Supervisor: Mary Ann Gloriande
Operations Specialist: Maura Zaldivar
Senior Art Director: Nancy Wells
Art Director: Anne Bonanno Nieglos
Interior and Cover Designer: Ximena Tamvakopolous
AV Project Manager: Maria Piper
Manager, Visual Research: Beth Brenzel
Photo Researcher: Teri Stratford, Susanna Lesan

Manager, Rights and Permissions: Zina Arabia
Image Permission Coordinator: Nancy Seise and Cynthia Vincenti
Manager, Cover Visual Research & Permissions: Karen Sanatar
Cover Art: Row 1: Dorling Kindersley © Jamie Marshall, Hougaard Malan\istockphoto.com, Patrick Laverdant\istockphoto.com, Bill Grove\istockphoto.com; Row 2: Rita Ariyoshi\PacificStock.com, Paul Liebhardt\Paul W. Liebhardt, Martin Harvey\CORBIS All Rights Reserved, Kazuyoshi Nomachi\CORBIS All Rights Reserved; Row 3: Robert Fried\robertfriedphotography.com, Ted Wood\Getty Images Inc. - Stone Allstock, Image Bank\Getty Images, Graham Monro\Photolibrary.com; Row 4: Mayumi Terao\istockphoto.com, Fuat Kose\istockphoto.com, Blue Jean Images\Getty Images, Inc., Robert Churchill\istockphoto.com
Media Director: Brian Hyland
Senior Media Editor: David Alick
Media Project Manager: Diane Lombardo
Full-Service Project Management: Jill Traut
Composition: Macmillan Publishing Solutions
Printer/Binder and Cover Printer: Courier Companies, Inc.

 DK Maps designed and productioned by DK Education, a division of Dorling Kindersley Limited, 80 Strand, London WC2R ORL. DK and the DK logo are registered trademarks of Dorling Kindersley Limited.

This book was set in 10/11.5, New Baskerville.

Credits and acknowledgments borrowed from other sources and reproduced, with permission, in this textbook appear on appropriate page within text (or on page 485).

Copyright © 2010, 2006 Pearson Education, Inc., publishing as Prentice Hall, 1 Lake St., Upper Saddle River, NJ 07458. All rights reserved. Manufactured in the United States of America. This publication is protected by Copyright, and permission should be obtained from the publisher prior to any prohibited reproduction, storage in a retrieval system, or transmission in any form or by any means, electronic, mechanical, photocopying, recording, or likewise. To obtain permission(s) to use material from this work, please submit a written request to Pearson Education, Inc., Permissions Department, 1 Lake St., Upper Saddle River, NJ 07458

Library of Congress Cataloging-in-Publication Data

Bonvillain, Nancy.
 Cultural anthropology / Nancy Bonvillain. – 2nd ed.
  p. cm.
 Includes bibliographical references and index.
 ISBN-13: 978-0-205-68509-7 (pbk.)
 ISBN-10: 0-205-68509-9 (pbk.)
 1. Ethnology. I. Title.
 GN316.B67 2010
 306–dc22
                              2009018810

10 9 8 7 6 5 4 3 2 1

Prentice Hall
is an imprint of

www.pearsonhighered.com

Student Edition
ISBN 10: 0-205-68509-9
ISBN 13: 978-0-205-68509-7
Exam Edition
ISBN 10: 0-205-68980-9
ISBN 13: 978-0-205-68980-4

BRIEF CONENTS

1 WHAT IS ANTHROPOLOGY? 1

2 THE NATURE OF CULTURE 19

3 STUDYING CULTURE 44

4 LANGUAGE AND CULTURE 67

5 LEARNING ONE'S CULTURE 93

6 MAKING A LIVING 127

7 ECONOMIC SYSTEMS 154

8 KINSHIP AND DESCENT 180

9 MARRIAGE AND THE FAMILY 208

10 GENDER 239

11 EQUALITY AND INEQUALITY 275

12 POLITICAL SYSTEMS 301

13 CONFLICT AND CONFLICT RESOLUTION 327

14 RELIGION 352

15 THE ARTS 383

16 COLONIALISM AND CULTURAL TRANSFORMATIONS 407

17 LIVING IN A GLOBAL WORLD 433

CONTENTS

Special Features   xi

Preface   xiv

1 WHAT IS ANTHROPOLOGY?   1

PREVIEW   2

THE STUDY OF HUMANITY   3
  The Concept of Culture   4
  A Holistic Perspective   4
  A Comparative Perspective   5

THE FOUR SUBFIELDS OF ANTHROPOLOGY   6
  Cultural Anthropology   6
  Linguistic Anthropology   10
  Archaeology   11
  Biological Anthropology   13

APPLIED ANTHROPOLOGY   15

CHAPTER SUMMARY   17 • KEY TERMS   18 • REVIEW
QUESTIONS   18 • MyAnthroLab EXERCISES   18

2 THE NATURE OF CULTURE   19

PREVIEW   20

WHAT IS CULTURE?   20

CHARACTERISTICS OF CULTURE   22
  Culture Is Shared   22
  Culture Is Learned   24
  Culture Is Adaptive   26
  Culture Is Integrated   28
  Culture Is Based on Symbols   30
  Culture Organizes the Way People Think
  About the World   30

CULTURE CHANGE   33
  Internal Culture Change   33
  External Culture Change   36

GLOBAL CULTURE   38

CHAPTER SUMMARY   42 • KEY TERMS   43 • REVIEW
QUESTIONS   43 • MyAnthroLab EXERCISES   43

3 STUDYING CULTURE   44

PREVIEW   45

ANTHROPOLOGY AND THE EXPLANATION
OF CULTURAL DIVERSITY   46
  Evolutionism   46
  Empiricism   47
  Functionalism   48
  Modern Theoretical Perspectives: An Overview   48
  Materialist Perspectives   48
  Structuralist Perspectives   50
  Interpretive Anthropology   50
  Conflict Perspectives and the Analysis of Culture
  and Power   51

ETHNOGRAPHY AND FIELDWORK   51
  Cross-Cultural Comparisons   52
  Ethnohistorical Research   53
  Ethnographic Fieldwork   53
  Doing Fieldwork   54
  Anthropological Research in Urban Societies   57

THE ANTHROPOLOGY OF ANTHROPOLOGY   61
  Labeling Issues in Anthropology   62
  Ethical Issues in Anthropology   62

CHAPTER SUMMARY   65 • KEY TERMS   65 • REVIEW
QUESTIONS   66 • MyAnthroLab EXERCISES   66

4 LANGUAGE AND CULTURE   67

PREVIEW   68

WHAT IS LANGUAGE?   68

THE COMPONENTS OF LANGUAGE   70
  Phonology: The System of Sounds   70
  Morphology: The Structure of Words   71
  Syntax: The Structure of Sentences   71
  Semantics: The Study of Meaning   71

NONVERBAL COMMUNICATION   73

LINGUISTIC ANTHROPOLOGY   75
  Linguistic Relativity   75
  Language, Culture, and Society   78
  The Study of Language Speakers   78

Language and Dialects 78

Language and Gender, Class, and Race 80

African American English 81

ETHNOSEMANTICS 84

Componential Analysis 84

Cultural Presuppositions 85

Ethnography of Communication 85

PROCESSES OF LANGUAGE CHANGE 87

Creoles, Pidgins, and Lingua Francas 87

Historical Linguistics 88

Loanwords 88

CHAPTER SUMMARY 91 • KEY TERMS 92 • REVIEW
QUESTIONS 92 • MyAnthroLab EXERCISES 92

5 LEARNING ONE'S CULTURE 93

PREVIEW 94

THE PROCESS OF ENCULTURATION 95

Becoming a Human Being 96

Child Rearing 97

INFORMAL AND FORMAL LEARNING 103

Learning Skills and Values 103

Learning Behavioral Expectations 104

Age and Gender Socialization 106

Rites of Passage 109

Schooling 110

PSYCHOLOGICAL ANTHROPOLOGY 116

Culture and Personality Traits 116

Culture and Self-Concept 118

Culture and Cognition 119

DEVIANCE AND ABNORMAL BEHAVIOR
IN CROSS-CULTURAL PERSPECTIVE 121

Responses to "Mental Illness" 121

Culture-Specific Psychological Disorders 122

CHAPTER SUMMARY 125 • KEY TERMS 125 • REVIEW
QUESTIONS 126 • MyAnthroLab EXERCISES 126

6 MAKING A LIVING 127

PREVIEW 128

ECONOMIC ANTHROPOLOGY 128

UNDERSTANDING HUMAN SUBSISTENCE
PATTERNS 129

Foraging Versus Food Production 129

Ecosystem, Adaptation, and Carrying Capacity 130

Subsistence and Settlement Pattern 131

Subsistence and Population 131

Subsistence, Work, and Division of Labor 131

Subsistence and Social Relations 131

FORAGING 132

Ecological Factors 132

Optimal Foraging 133

Population Factors 133

Social and Cultural Factors 134

Land, Labor, and Production in Foraging
Societies 137

PASTORALISM 138

Combined Subsistence Strategies 139

Land and Labor in Pastoralist Societies 139

Nomadic Pastoralism 140

HORTICULTURE 144

Impacts of Sedentism and Surpluses 144

Slash-and-Burn Horticulture 144

Gender Allocation of Work 145

AGRICULTURE 147

Intensive Agriculture and Crop Variety 149

SUBSISTENCE AND CULTURE CHANGE 150

CHAPTER SUMMARY 152 • KEY TERMS 152 • REVIEW
QUESTIONS 152 • MyAnthroLab EXERCISES 153

7 ECONOMIC SYSTEMS 154

PREVIEW 155

ANALYZING ECONOMIC SYSTEMS 156

Allocating Land and Resources 156

Producing Goods 157

Organizing Labor 157

Distributing and Exchanging Products
and Services 160

MARKET ECONOMIES AND CAPITALISM 164

IMPACTS OF COLONIAL EXPANSION,
INDUSTRIALISM, AND GLOBALIZATION 166

Colonialism and the Exploitation of Labor 167

Industrial Economies 168

Industrial Agriculture 169

Social Consequences of Capitalism
and Industrialism 173

COMPARING SUBSISTENCE STRATEGIES 176

CHAPTER SUMMARY 178 • KEY TERMS 179 • REVIEW
QUESTIONS 179 • MyAnthroLab EXERCISES 179

8 KINSHIP AND DESCENT 180

PREVIEW 181

KINSHIP SYSTEMS 181
Bilateral Descent 183
Unilineal Descent 184

MATRILINEAL AND PATRILINEAL SYSTEMS 185
Prevalence of Matrilineal and Patrilineal Descent 185
Matrilineal and Patrilineal Societies Compared 186
Influence and Inheritance in Unilineal Descent Groups 187
Other Forms of Unilineal Descent 189

UNILINEAL DESCENT GROUPS 190
Lineages 190
Exogamy and Endogamy 191
Clans 192
Phratries and Moieties 195

PATTERNS OF RELATIONSHIPS 198

PATTERNS OF CHANGE 199

KINSHIP TERMINOLOGY SYSTEMS 201
The Eskimo and Hawaiian Systems 202
The Crow, Omaha, and Sudanese Systems 203

CHAPTER SUMMARY 206 • KEY TERMS 207 • REVIEW QUESTIONS 207 • MyAnthroLab EXERCISES 207

9 MARRIAGE AND THE FAMILY 208

PREVIEW 209

DEFINING MARRIAGE AND FAMILY 210

FAMILIES AND IDEAL TYPES 212
Nuclear Families 212
Extended and Joint Families 213

ENDOGAMY, EXOGAMY, AND THE INCEST TABOO 216
Effects of Exogamy on Social Organization 216
Effects of Endogamy on Social Organization 217

FORMS OF MARRIAGE 218
Polygyny and Polyandry 218
Explanations of Polygyny 219

"Ghost Marriage" and Other Adaptive Forms 220
Same-Sex Marriage 221

MARRIAGE AS ALLIANCE AND ECONOMIC EXCHANGE 222
Bridewealth and Brideservice 222
Dowry 223

MARRIAGE AS A RITE OF PASSAGE 225

PATTERNS OF RESIDENCE AFTER MARRIAGE 228
Matrilocal and Patrilocal Residence 228
Avunculocal Residence 228
Bilocal and Neolocal Residence 229
Correlates of Residence Patterns 229

WIDOWHOOD AND DIVORCE 232
The Levirate and Sororate 232
Divorce 232

CHAPTER SUMMARY 236 • KEY TERMS 237 • REVIEW QUESTIONS 237 • MyAnthroLab EXERCISES 238

10 GENDER 239

PREVIEW 240

SEX AND GENDER 240
Evolutionary Perspectives 241
The Cultural Construction of Gender Identity 243
Gender and Sexuality 244
Gender and Homosexuality 245

GENDER ROLES AND RELATIONS 248
Division of Labor by Gender 248
Gender and Status 250

GENDER AND SUBSISTENCE 253
Foragers and Gender 254
Gender in Pastoral Societies 256
Gender in Horticultural Societies 257
Gender in Agricultural States 259
Industrialism, Postindustrialism, and Gender 260

GLOBALIZATION AND GENDER 266
Women's Roles in Urban and Rural Economic Development 268
Women in Changing Socialist States 269
Impacts of Ideology on Gender Constructs 270

CHAPTER SUMMARY 273 • KEY TERMS 273 • REVIEW QUESTIONS 274 • MyAnthroLab EXERCISES 274

11 EQUALITY AND INEQUALITY 275

PREVIEW 276

EQUALITY, INEQUALITY, AND SOCIAL STRATIFICATION 277
Egalitarian Societies 278
Ranked Societies 278
Stratified Societies 279
Explaining Social Stratification 282

CASTE AND CLASS 284
Determinants of Class 284
Social Class and Language 286
Slavery 287

RACE AND ETHNICITY 287
Race as Caste 288
Race in the United States 288
Race in Brazil 291
Ethnic Identity 291

CLASS, RACE, ETHNICITY, AND IDEOLOGY IN AMERICAN SOCIETY 296

CHAPTER SUMMARY 299 • KEY TERMS 300 • REVIEW QUESTIONS 300 • MyAnthroLab EXERCISES 300

12 POLITICAL SYSTEMS 301

PREVIEW 302

POLITICAL ANTHROPOLOGY 302

TYPES OF POLITICAL ORGANIZATION 303
Bands 303
Tribes 306
Confederacies 308
Chiefdoms 310

CHARACTERISTICS OF STATE SOCIETIES 317

INTERNAL POLITICAL CHANGE AND STATE SOCIETIES 322

CHAPTER SUMMARY 325 • KEY TERMS 325 • REVIEW QUESTIONS 326 • MyAnthroLab EXERCISES 326

13 CONFLICT AND CONFLICT RESOLUTION 327

PREVIEW 328

EVOLUTIONARY PERSPECTIVES ON CONFLICT 329

AVOIDING CONFLICT 330
Politeness 331
Channeled Aggression 331
Role of Reciprocity in Conflict Avoidance 334

WITCHCRAFT AND RITUAL IN CONFLICT RESOLUTION 334

PATTERNS OF FAMILY AND COMMUNITY CONFLICT 336
Family Violence 336
Conflicts in Bands and Tribes 337
Blood Vengeance and the Feud 338

PATTERNS OF CONFLICT BETWEEN GROUPS 339
Warfare 339
Impacts of Globalization on Warfare 340
Warfare in State Societies 344

CHAPTER SUMMARY 350 • KEY TERMS 350 • REVIEW QUESTIONS 351 • MyAnthroLab EXERCISES 351

14 RELIGION 352

PREVIEW 353

WHAT IS RELIGION? 354

SPIRIT BEINGS AND FORCES 356
Animism and Animatism 356
Gods and Heroes 356
Ancestors, Ghosts, and Demons 357
Mana, Totems, and Taboos 357

RELIGIOUS PRACTITIONERS 359
Mediums, Diviners, and Healers 359
Shamans and Priests 360

RELIGIOUS PRACTICE 361
Sacred and Secular Rituals 361
Prayer and Sacrifice 362

Rites of Passage   364

Healing or Curing   366

Magic and Witchcraft   368

THE ORIGINS AND FUNCTIONS OF RELIGION   370

Explaining the World   370

Solace, Healing, and Emotional Release   371

Social Cohesion   371

Social Control   371

Economic Adaptation   372

RELIGION AND CULTURE CHANGE   373

Revitalization Movements   374

Cargo Cults   374

Role of Founders in Buddhism, Christianity, and Islam   375

Religion and Globalization   376

CHAPTER SUMMARY   380 • KEY TERMS   381 • REVIEW QUESTIONS   381 • MyAnthroLab EXERCISES   382

15   THE ARTS   383

PREVIEW   384

WHAT IS ART?   385

CULTURAL AESTHETICS   386

BODY ART   388

ORIGINS AND FUNCTIONS OF ART OBJECTS   389

THE ARTS OF SOUND AND MOVEMENT   394

ORAL LITERATURE AND WRITTEN TEXTS   396

ART AND GLOBALIZATION   399

Art and Identity   399

Art in the Global Economy   400

Art and Tourism   401

CHAPTER SUMMARY   405 • KEY TERMS   406 • REVIEW QUESTIONS   406 • MyAnthroLab EXERCISES   406

16   COLONIALISM AND CULTURAL TRANSFORMATIONS   407

PREVIEW   408

EUROPEAN COLONIALISM   409

Colonialism Defined   409

Types of Colonies   410

THE EUROPEAN SLAVE TRADE   411

Slavery in Africa   411

Slavery in the Americas   413

TRADE AND SETTLEMENT IN NORTH AMERICA   413

The Fur Trade   414

Westward Expansion and Depopulation   414

SPANISH COLONIZATION IN THE AMERICAS   415

Spanish Landholding in the Colonies   417

Mining Quotas   418

Intermarriage   418

The Mission System   418

AGENTS OF DIRECTED CULTURE CHANGE   418

Missionaries   419

Schoolteachers   419

Government Officials   420

A Cash Economy   420

JUSTIFICATIONS FOR COLONIAL RULE   421

White Man's Burden   421

A Sacred Trust   422

The Reservation System   422

REACTIONS OF INDIGENOUS PEOPLES TO EUROPEAN COLONIZERS   424

Trade Goods and Gods   425

Guns and Other Technological Wonders   426

Native Resistance and Retaliation   427

GLOBALIZATION IN THE POSTCOLONIAL ERA   428

CHAPTER SUMMARY   431 • KEY TERMS   432 • REVIEW QUESTIONS   432 • MyAnthroLab EXERCISES   432

17 LIVING IN A GLOBAL WORLD   433

PREVIEW   434

MIGRATION   436

Rural-to-Urban Migration   436

Transnational Migration   439

ETHNOGENESIS AND ETHNIC IDENTITIES   440

Transnationalism   441

Nationalism and Pluralism   442

Genocide? The Case of Rwanda   444

Reactions Against Pluralism   445

Globalization and Cultural Identities   446

A Global Identity?   446

CULTURAL MINORITIES IN A GLOBAL WORLD   447

United States and Canada   447

Mexico and *Indigenismo*   449

Brazil and the "Indian Problem"   451

Costs of Economic Development in Ecuador and Bolivia   454

Developments in Africa   455

LEGAL RIGHTS AND INTERNATIONAL RECOGNITION   458

ECOTOURISM AND INDIGENOUS LANDS   460

CHAPTER SUMMARY   463 • KEY TERMS   463 • REVIEW QUESTIONS   463 • MyAnthroLab EXERCISES   464

GLOSSARY   465

REFERENCES   473

CREDITS   485

INDEX   487

SPECIAL FEATURES

CASE STUDY

- Environment, Adaptation, and Disease: Malaria and Sickle-Cell Anemia in Africa and the United States 14
- Daughter from Danang 24
- Maladaptive Adaptations: Kuru and Mad Cow 27
- Consequences of Cultural Integration: Women and Work in the United States 29
- Life in Riverfront: A Midwestern Town Seen Through Japanese Eyes 60
- Ebonics: Language and Politics 82
- Sleeping Arrangements in Two Cultures 100
- Language and Interaction in Japan 105
- The Education of Aztec Children 111
- A Foraging Society: The Dobe Ju/'hoansi 134
- A Pastoral Society: The Basseri, Nomadic Pastoralists of Iran 141
- A Farming Society: The Kaluli of Papua New Guinea 146
- Child Laborers Today 158
- The Potlatch: An Example of Negative Reciprocity 160
- A Patrilineal Society: The Ganda of Uganda 194
- Two Matrilineal Societies: The Mohawks and the Trobriand Islanders 196
- A Wedding in Nepal 225
- Residence in Rural North India and Western Borneo 230
- Marriage and Divorce among the Kpelle of Liberia 234
- Two-Spirits: A Third Gender 246
- Male Dominance in Traditional Chinese Culture 261
- The Samoans: A Ranked Society 279
- Out-Groups of Japan 289
- Ethnic Identity in the United States 294
- A Band Society: The Tiwis of Northern Australia 305
- Age-Linked Associations in Tribal Societies: The Hidatsa and the Maasai 308
- The Inca of Peru and Ecuador 321
- Conflict Avoidance Strategies in Japan 331
- Conflict Resolution among the Semai of Malaysia 332
- Pomoan (California) and Sambian (Papua New Guinea) Warfare 341
- Making Contact with the Spirit World 363
- Puberty Rites Among the Apache and the Suku 365
- Pigs for the Ancestors 372
- Yoruba Art 387
- Tourists Among the Toraja 403
- Lakota Trade and the Consequences of Change in Economic Production 416
- Captive Societies of Australia and Tasmania 423
- Labor Migration in Mexico 438
- Ethnic Identity in Sudan 441
- Papua New Guinea's Customary Law 458

xii   Special Features

CULTURE CHANGE

- Documenting Changes in the Lives of Australian Aborigines   52
- Changing Norms in Language Use in the United States   79
- Changing Attitudes Toward Childhood and Child Care in the United States   101
- Transformations of Nuer Economy and Society   142
- Deforestation, Environmental Change, and Resource Sustainability   170
- Cheyenne Descent   200
- The Changing American Family   213
- Dowry in India   223
- Transformation of Gender Status in a Foraging Society   255

- Transformation of American Work in the Twentieth Century   263
- Caste in India   284
- Globalization and the Transformation of a Tongan Chiefdom into an Island State   315
- Reestablishing Traditional Methods of Dispute Resolution   342
- The Development of Religious Denominations   377
- Diné Art Responds to Market Forces   401
- Impacts of the European Slave Trade on African States   412
- Impacts of Indonesian State Expansion   443

CONTROVERSIES

- What Are the Limits of Cultural Relativism?   8
- How Do Anthropologists Present Knowledge About the People They Study?   63
- Is There Such a Thing as National Character?   120
- Explaining the Incest Taboo   217

- Is Male Dominance Universal?   252
- Origins of the State   319
- Interpreting "Art": The Case of Inca Quipus   393
- Who "Owns" the Past? NAGPRA and American Anthropology   450

IN THEIR OWN VOICES

- Extinction in a Nutshell   11
- *Hamlet* and the Tiv   34
- Notes from the Field in Morocco   56
- Honoring Native Languages   76
- Going to School in Ake, Nigeria   114
- An Inupiaq Whaler's Wife   136
- "Free to Do as You Like"   162
- Wedding Songs from North India   188
- "I Hear That I'm Going to Get Married!"   226
- Tsetsele Fantan on Women and AIDS in Botswana   267

- The Souls of Black Folk   292
- Constitution of the Iroquois Confederacy   312
- Testimony from South Africa's Truth and Reconciliation Hearings of 1998   346
- Macumba, Trance and Spirit Healing   369
- Artists Talk About Art   390
- Nelson Mandela on the Struggle Against Apartheid in South Africa   427
- Viktor Kaisiepo on the International Decade of the World's Indigenous People   457

ANTHROPOLOGY APPLIED

- Cultural Survival   16
- Development Anthropology   41
- Anthropology on Trial in the Amazon   64
- Languages Lost and Found   90
- The Ethnobotany of Psychotropic Substances   124
- Interpreting Economic Activity from Archaeological Remains   151
- Economic Anthropologists and Consumer Behavior   177
- Linkages Genealogy Projects   205

- Anthropologists as Expert Witnesses   235
- Advocacy for Women   272
- Working Against Human Trafficking   298
- Anthropologists and the NGOs   324
- Legal Anthropology   349
- Medical Anthropology and Ethnomedicine   379
- Ethnomusicology   404
- Establishing the Xingu National Park   430
- FUNAI Anthropologists   462

Cultural Anthropology, Second Edition, is intended to introduce students to the concepts and methods that anthropologists bring to the study of cross-cultural diversity. It focuses on understanding how cultural practices and beliefs develop, how they are integrated, and how they change. The goal of this book is consistent with one of the goals of most anthropology teachers, to excite students about the world in which we all live. Although much in people's behaviors and attitudes differs throughout the world, much also unites us. The book therefore provides a global view of humanity's many facets. It takes a traditional approach in chapter organization, focusing on various aspects of societal organization and expression. It also makes central the role of cultural change, processes of adaptation and transformation that are integral to all societies. In addition to learning about other peoples, anthropology as a discipline and a framework of analysis has the potential to help students appreciate the cultural patterns underlying their own behaviors, beliefs, and attitudes. This book attempts to present the voices of the peoples who anthropologists often study. Through these voices, and through analyses of indigenous and marginalized people today, students may come to understand the global processes that affect us all.

An important feature distinguishing this text is its thorough focus on culture change, derived both from internal processes of adaptation and innovation as well as from external forces through contact with other peoples. The context of contact is critical, of course. In some cases, contact is friendly and benign, each group exchanging ideas, practices, and material goods as equals. In other cases, contact occurs between groups that are unequal in their power and ability to control their own lives and exert control over others. In focusing on change, this text highlights the notion that the societies and cultures that people develop are dynamic systems, adapted to new situations and invigorated by new ideas.

The focus on culture change is carried into the discussions of global trends, whether these are the processes of past colonial expansion or of modern globalization. These two kinds of processes are interrelated because modern globalization has resulted from the legacies of colonial expansion. These issues are discussed throughout the book, culminating in the final two chapters.

FORMAT OF THE BOOK

The book consists of seventeen chapters covering the breadth of the discipline of cultural anthropology. The first three chapters lay the groundwork for the study of human culture. Chapter 1 (What Is Anthropology?) presents the basic outline of the field of anthropology, describing its development, exemplifying its various subdisciplines, and introducing some of its basic theoretical questions. Chapter 2 (The Nature of Culture) discusses some universal characteristics of culture and describes how human societies are organized to meet people's needs. It also introduces a key focus of this text, namely understanding that cultures are dynamic systems of behavior and belief, ever changing and adjusting to internal and external forces. Chapter 3 (Studying Culture) takes a closer look at the specific methodologies that anthropologists have developed to analyze cultural behavior and build theories to explain both similarities and differences found throughout the world. It offers an array of theoretical perspectives used to analyze culture. It also takes readers into the experience of fieldwork, a hallmark of anthropological research.

The next two chapters describe the systems of language and socialization basic to all human societies. Chapter 4 (Language and Culture) introduces topics in the structure of language but concentrates on the complex relationships between language and other aspects of culture. Chapter 5 (Learning One's Culture) addresses the various perspectives that different societies take about the ways that parents and families raise their children and teach them the norms and values of their communities.

Following these sections, the text proceeds with discussions of specific topics within cultural anthropology. Chapters 6 (Making a Living) and 7 (Economic Systems) focus on subsistence practices, ways of making a living, and patterns of production and exchange. Chapters 8 (Kinship and Descent) and 9 (Marriage and the Family) describe the various systems of kinship found throughout the world, detailing different patterns of reckoning descent and forming marriages and families. In Chapter 10 (Gender), we look closely at issues of gender, attempting to understand the conditions under which egalitarian gender relationships and attitudes are sustained as well as the conditions under which inequality between men and women is established. Chapter 11 (Equality and Inequality) also considers issues of inequality in the realm of social stratification, analyzing social segmentation on the basis of caste, class, race, and ethnicity. Chapter 12 (Political Systems) furthers this discussion in the analysis of political systems, including ways of establishing leadership, arriving at group decisions, and settling disputes both within a community and between communities. This last topic is continued in Chapter 13 (Conflict and Conflict Resolution), a unique chapter that takes a detailed look at the reasons for conflict and the methods of conflict resolution in different types of societies.

Chapters 14 (Religion) and 15 (The Arts) focus on various aspects of expressive and symbolic culture. Chapter 14 is concerned with the ways that people express religious beliefs and organize religious practice. It relates these beliefs and practices to other aspects of social, economic, and political life. Chapter 15 is concerned with aesthetic values and their embodiment in artistic production.

Finally, Chapters 16 (Colonialism and Cultural Transformations) and 17 (Living in a Global World) are directly concerned with themes of cultural change that permeate the text and are addressed in every chapter. Chapter 16 focuses on the processes of cultural transformation emanating from European colonization beginning in the sixteenth century, although the dynamics of colonial and imperial control both predate and follow European dominance. In the final chapter of the book, we look at recent global trends influencing the lives of indigenous peoples in the twenty-first-century and discover how these trends have local manifestations.

SPECIAL FEATURES

In addition to the focus on change, the text is tied together by a number of features of content and style. Each chapter begins with a narrative, usually a sacred or secular story that dramatizes important themes discussed in the chapter.

In Their Own Voices boxes feature the words of indigenous peoples whose lives are discussed in the text.

Case Study features provide extended discussions that enable students to understand complex relationships among various practices.

IN THEIR OWN VOICES

Extinction in a Nutshell

In September 1992, Dune Lankard and Marie Smith Jones of Alaska were interviewed about their involvement in an unsuccessful lawsuit against the Eyak Corporation to stop it from clear-cutting on lands sacred to the Eyak people. Dune Lankard is part-Eyak and has served on the board of the Eyak Corporation. Marie Smith Jones was the chief of the traditional elders council, established to protect the remaining heritage of the Eyaks. She died in January 2008.

In answer to the question, What factors have led to the extinction of the Eyak people? Dune Lankard said:

From 1889 to about 1915, a couple of events took place that were very destructive to our way of life and our people. In the late 1890s, five canneries were built in the Copper River Delta area. The Eyaks' livelihood and subsistence lifestyle was drastically changed because the cannery work-

The population of our people prior to the canneries being built was over 300; we were diminished to 50 by about 1920. The final event that wiped out many of our people was the 1918 flu.

Now, Marie is the last full-blooded Eyak Indian on the face of the earth. If Marie were white, this would not be happening. It would be a whole different ballgame then. People would be really concerned that a race of people is being destroyed. But we are just another Indian clan to a lot of people, so they are not taking this seriously. I believe that when Marie does pass on, there will probably be books written about her, maybe even a movie, like "The Last of the Mohicans"—"The Last of the Eyaks." By then it will already be a done deal. And it is so sad.

We were the last "founded," or rediscovered, tribe in North America and we are the first language and race of Alaskan Indians that will be wiped off the face of the earth

CASE STUDY

A Foraging Society: The Dobe Ju/'hoansi

A close look at a nomadic foraging society provides insight into the cultural characteristics common to many such societies. Although the specific features of the environment and adaptation of the Ju/'hoansi of Botswana and Namibia are unique, the cultural correlates of their social life and attitudes are like those of other foraging peoples.

The Ju/'hoansi live in the hot, dry Kalahari Desert. The Dobe are a group of Ju/'hoansi who, in the 1960s and 1970s, numbered about 400 and lived by foraging in 3,000 square miles of semidesert terrain. Unlike most foraging peoples, who congregate in larger groups when resources were abundant and disperse into smaller groups when resources were scarce, the Ju/'hoansi reversed this pattern, settling around permanent water holes during the dry season and dispersing during the rainy season when water was more available. Dry-season camps generally consisted of eight to fifteen huts, housing twenty to fifty people. Population had to be kept small to avoid straining the resources around the permanent water holes. Rainy season settlements, located near seasonal and secondary water sources, varied in size from three to twenty huts (Lee 2003, 32).

Each camp had a core group of residents, usually siblings or cousins, with other residents related by blood or marriage to members of the core group. Camp composition was kept balanced. If a persistent imbalance emerged between numbers of males and females, for example, some families would move to another camp. Families would also move if the num-

CULTURE CHANGE

THE CHANGING AMERICAN FAMILY

Family types are responsive to changes in productive modes and general social values. In the United States, the percentage of family units conforming to the idealized model of husband, wife, and children has declined since the mid-twentieth century. The idealized nuclear family model is itself a product of economic needs and adjustments made during the nineteenth and twentieth centuries as capitalist and industrial production dominated North American society. Other kinds of family units have now become more common. The number of blended families, based on remarriages and the combining of children from previous marriages, has also increased.

Growing rates of divorce have also increased the number of single-parent households. As women have gained more economic independence, the financial need to remarry after divorce or the death of a spouse has declined. More people also never marry. Many households consist of a man and woman involved in a long-term relationship who choose not to marry. Such couples may or may not have children. Another less common but not unusual type of household consists of two people of the same gender who share a sexual relationship, economic responsibilities, and other attributes of family life such as child rearing.

ANTHROPOLOGY APPLIED

Cultural Survival

Cultural anthropologists sometimes help indigenous communities improve their economic conditions, adapt to change, and preserve their traditions. They help communities find ways to use their resources productively while protecting their environment and cultural heritage. Some anthropologists have also helped protect indigenous peoples' indigenous rights.

Cultural Survival is an organization founded by anthropologists that promotes the rights, voices, and visions of indigenous peoples around the world. The organization deals with conflict and migration, cultural preservation, improvement of health care, indigenous economic enterprises, law and self-determination, and the preservation of natural resources. Its initiatives include publications to publicize issues and share news, indigenous curricula, fair trade stores and exchanges such as the Coffee Alliance, legal defense, and an indigenous action network.

Not all applied anthropology concerns native peoples and their cultural survival, however. Some cultural anthropologists advise government agencies and private companies on

CONTROVERSIES

Explaining the Incest Taboo

The origins of the incest taboo are much debated. One theory proposes that the incest taboo arose out of an instinctive aversion toward sexual relations within the nuclear family. However, incest occurs fairly widely in human societies, so avoiding it is not instinctual. Another biological theory suggests that the incest taboo is a learned, cultural response to the possible biological consequences of inbreeding, which can increase the incidence of undesirable or harmful (as well as desirable and beneficial) genetic traits in a population. This theory assumes that ancestral humans understood the relationship between mating and the variability of traits in their population, and that this cultural adaptation then spread to all human societies through diffusion or contact to become a universal element of culture or, alternatively, that human societies in different areas independently invented an incest taboo.

A theory championed by anthropologist Bronislaw Malinowski, based on the work of Sigmund Freud, focused on the

between siblings. Sibling marriage occurred among the monarchs of ancient Peru, Egypt, and Hawaii but was not defined as incest. Marriage between a brother and sister at the highest level of the state consolidated power and minimized struggles over succession. However, sibling marriage was not permitted among ordinary citizens.

Many anthropologists favor understanding the incest taboo as a means of ensuring survival by forcing people to make alliances with others outside the nuclear family. This "marry out or die out" theory emphasizes that marriage within a small unit will over time lead to the isolation and genetic homogeneity of the group, which makes the unit more vulnerable to population loss or even extinction. Mating outside the nuclear family reduces this risk and also creates social alliances and bonds of reciprocity with other people that can be critical in times of scarcity and other dangers to survival.

We may never know why the incest taboo started, but the fact that it is universal indicates its importance. All these theo-

GLOBALIZATION

Culture contact, a major force in the process of globalization, leads to several strategies and consequences of culture change, including acculturation, assimilation, and reactive

---

Culture Change features present material focusing specifically on the ways that culture is transformed. They stress the interconnections among material change, behavioral practices, and ideology, demonstrating the complex interactions that result from change.

Anthropology Applied boxes have been expanded and highlight the roles that anthropologists play in applying theory and knowledge to practical concerns.

Controversies boxes present differing opinions about key theoretical or research topics.

Global Icons contribute to and strengthen the emphasis on culture change and situate cultural transformations in their global context.

Finally, the book contains pedagogical features including a margin glossary and marginal notes, preview and summary questions, critical thinking questions, and both section reviews and chapter summaries. These features help students focus on significant ideas and concepts presented in each chapter.

NEW TO THIS EDITION

This second edition contains many new sections, expansions of material in previous sections, and updates on statistical information throughout the chapters. The new case studies or culture change boxes include Daughter from Danang (Chapter 2; explaining enculturation); a Mayan sacred narrative on Popol Vuh (Chapter 6); The Kaluli, farmers of Papua New Guinea (Chapter 6); Economic Transformation of the Nuer (Chapter 7); Deforestation, Environmental Change, and Resource Sustainability (Chapter 7); Matrilineal Societies: The Mohawks and the Trobriand Islanders (Chapter 8); Residence in Rural North India and Western Borneo (Chapter 9); The Samoans: A Ranked Society (Chapter 11); Sambian Warfare (Chapter 13); Making Contact with the Spirit World (Chapter 14).

New sections include material on the urban Hausa (Chapter 3); Igbo trade (Chapter 7); gender evolution (Chapter 10); gender in pastoral societies (Chapter 10); and Melanesian songs (Chapter 15).

MyAnthroLab. MyAnthroLab is a state-of-the-art interactive and instructive online resource that incorporates video, animation, assessment, and additional readings in the form of case studies and ethnographies. MyAnthroLab activities have been integrated into every chapter of *Cultural Anthropology, Second Edition,* in the following ways:

The MyAnthroLab icon appears at the end of the Case Study and In Their Own Voices features. This icon directs students to specific activities in MyAnthroLab that enhance the material they just read.

MyAnthroLab activities are found in end-of-chapter materials. These activities include videos, interative animations, audio programs, and suggestions for research papers. In addition, suggestions are made for students to read specific case studies and ethnographies that relate to concepts found in the chapter; these additional readings are included in the MyAnthroLibrary section of MyAnthroLab.

myanthrolab EXERCISES

To complete the following exercises and activities, you must log in to www.myanthrolab.com and select your current textbook.

1. In the **Explore** tab of Chapter 8, click on the *NPR Audio Programs Broadcast* tab and go to *Theme 20: Marital Residence and Kinship.* Listen to one of the programs in this section and complete the short answer exercise that accompanies the program.
2. In the **Practice** tab, click on *Activities* and complete the *Kinship Patterns* animation.
3. In the **Research Tools** section on the home page, click on the *Research Navigator*™ link and enter the

Anthropology database to find relevant and recent scholarly and popular press publications. For this chapter enter the following keywords: *kinship system, matrilineal, patriarchy, lineage,* and *totem.*

4. Enter the **MyAnthroLibrary** section on the home page to read more about topics and cultures that are discussed in this chapter. Suggested readings include:

   Varieties of Marital Relationships by Lewellyn Hendrix

   Nandi: From Cattle-Keepers to Cash-Crop Farmers by Regina Smith Ololer

SUPPORT FOR INSTRUCTORS AND STUDENTS

This book is accompanied by an extensive learning package to enhance the experience of both instructors and students.

 MyAnthroLab is an interactive and instructive multimedia site designed to help students and instructors save time and improve results. It offers access to a wealth of resources geared to meet individual teaching and learning needs of all instructors and students. Combining an e-book, video, audio, multimedia simulations, research support, and assessment, MyAnthroLab engages students and gives them the tools they need to enhance their performance in the course. Please see your Pearson sales representative for more information about **MyAnthroLab** or visit the website at www.myanthrolab.com.

Instructor's Resource Manual with Tests (0-205-68510-2)   For each chapter in the text, this valuable resource provides a chapter outline, preview questions, lecture topics, research topics, and questions for classroom discussion. In addition, test questions in multiple-choice and essay formats are available for each chapter; the answers are page-referenced to the text. For easy access, this manual is available within the instructor section of MyAnthroLab for *Cultural Anthropology, Second Edition,* or at www.pearsonhighered.com

MyTest (0-205-68523-4)   This computerized software allows instructors to create their own personalized exams, to edit any or all of the existing test questions, and to add new questions. Other special features of this program include random generation of test questions, creation of alternate versions of the same test, scrambling question sequence, and test preview before printing. For easy access, this software is available within the instructor section of MyAnthroLab for *Cultural Anthropology, Second Edition,* or at www.pearsonhighered.com

PowerPoint Presentation for Cultural Anthropology (0-205-68991-4)   These PowerPoint slides combine text and graphics for each chapter to help instructors convey anthropological principles in a clear and engaging way. In addition, Classroom Response System (CRS) In-Class Questions allow for instant, class-wide student responses to chapter-specific questions during lectures for teachers to gauge student comprehension. For easy access, they are available within the instructor section of MyAnthroLab for *Cultural Anthropology, Second Edition,* or at www.pearsonhighered.com

***Strategies in Teaching Anthropology* (0-13-603466-7)**   Unique in focus and content, this book focuses on the "how" of teaching anthropology across all four fields and provides a wide array of associated learning outcomes and student activities. It is a valuable single-source compendium of strategies and teaching "tricks of the trade" from a group of seasoned teaching anthropologists, working in a variety of teaching settings, who share their pedagogical techniques, knowledge, and observations.

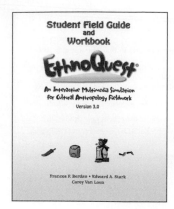

Student Field Guide and Workbook

EthnoQuest®

An Interactive Multimedia Simulation for Cultural Anthropology Fieldwork

Version 3.0

Frances F. Berdan • Edward A. Stark
Carey Van Loon

EthnoQuest® (0-13-185013-X)   This interactive multimedia simulation includes a series of ten ethnographic encounters with the culture of a fictional Mexican village set in a computer-based learning environment. It provides students with a realistic problem-solving experience and is designed to help students experience the fieldwork of a cultural anthropologist. Please see your Pearson sales representative for more information about **EthnoQuest®**.

ACKNOWLEDGMENTS

I wish to thank the many people who contributed ideas, time, and support to this project. The encouragement and advice of Nancy Roberts, publisher of anthropology at Prentice-Hall, is especially appreciated and acknowledged. I also wish to thank development editors Gerald Lombardi and Susanna Lesan, whose advice and constructive criticism were instrumental in shaping the text. The final stages of production were ably managed by Marianne Peters-Riordan, aided by the skillful photo research of Teri Stratford.

In addition, I wish to acknowledge, with thanks, a faculty development grant from Bard College at Simon's Rock that provided for a number of student research assistants, especially Clara Gordon and Andy Harris, who helped identify and collect sources for some of the new sections and for statistical updates. Andy also revised the index for this edition. I thank Bard College at Simon's Rock for their support and the assistants for their perseverance.

Finally, I would like to thank the reviewers whose careful reading and valuable suggestions aided me in refining this revision. Responsibility for the final version is, of course, my own.

For their constructive reviewing of the first edition, I would like to thank the following:

Diane Baxter, *University of Oregon*
John Beatty, *Brooklyn College*
Ann Louise Bragdon, *Northwest College – Houston Community College System*
Vaughn M. Bryant, *Texas A&M University*
Andrew Buckser, *Purdue University*
Ratimaya Bush, *Wright State University*
Gregory R. Campbell, *The University of Montana*
Erve Chambers, *University of Maryland*
Wanda Clark, *South Plains College*
Samuel Gerald Collins, *Towson University*
Karla L. Davis, *University of South Florida*
William W. Donner, *Kutztown University*
Charles O. Ellenbaum, *College of DuPage*
Blenda Femenias, *Brown University*
Carol Hayman, *Austin Community College*
Dorothy Hodgson, *Rutgers*
David E. Jones, *University of Central Florida*
Barry D. Kass, *State University of New York – Orange County*
Theresa Kintz, *Wilkes University*
Joshua S. Levin, *Community College of Southern Nevada*
Susan R. Martin, *Michigan Tech University*
Geoffrey G. Pope, *William Patterson University*
Kevin Rafferty, *Community College of Southern Nevada*
Frank A. Salamone, *Iona College*
Jsh Schendel, *University of Tennessee*
Wesley Shumar, *Drexel University*
Susan R. Trencher, *George Mason University*

For suggestions for the second edition, I would like to thank the following:

John Ambenge, *Middlesex Community College*

Michael Angrosino, *University of South Florida*

Christina Beard-Moose, *Suffolk County Community College*

Vaughn M. Bryant, *Texas A&M University*

Samuel Gerald Collins, *Towson University*

Molly Doane, *University of Illinois at Chicago*

William W. Donner, *Kutztown University*

Louis Forline, *University of Nevada, Reno*

Renee Garcia, *Saddleback College*

Ellen S. Ginsburg, *Massachusetts College of Pharmacy and Health Sciences*

Jon Hageman, *Northeastern Illinois University*

Barbara Jones, *Brookdale Community College*

Susan R. Martin, *Michigan Technological University*

Derek Maxfield, *Capital Community College*

Chrisy Moutsatsos, *Iowa State University*

Richard Scaglion, *University of Pittsburgh*

Angela M. Siner, *University of Toledo*

James Todd, *Modesto Junior College*

Susan R. Trencher, *George Mason University*

Cassandra White, *Georgia State University*

Herbert Ziegler, *Chesapeake College*

WHAT IS ANTHROPOLOGY?

- What are the core concepts of anthropology?
- How does anthropology overlap with other fields?
- What two perspectives do anthropologists use to study cultures?
- What is globalization? How can the concepts of culture contact and culture change help us understand globalization?
- What are the four subfields of anthropology? How is the study of culture integrated into each subfield?
- How is cultural relativism different from ethical relativism?
- What is applied anthropology? What contributions can applied anthropologists offer other fields?

There were villagers at the Middle Place and a girl had her home there . . . where she kept a flock of turkeys.

At the Middle Place they were having a Yaaya Dance . . . and during the first day this girl . . . stayed with her turkeys taking care of them. . . . it seems she didn't go to the dance on the first day, that day she fed her turkeys . . . and so the dance went on and she could hear the drum.

When she spoke to her turkeys about this, they said, "If you went it wouldn't turn out well: who would take care of us?" That's what her turkeys told her.

She listened to them and they slept through the night.

Then it was the second day of the dance and . . . with the Yaaya Dance half over she spoke to her big tom turkey:

"My father-child, if they're going to do it again tomorrow why can't I go?" she said. "Well if you went, it wouldn't turn out well." That's what he told her. "Well then I mustn't go."

. . . The next day was a nice warm day, and again she heard the drum over there.

Then she went around feeding her turkeys, and when it was the middle of the day, she asked again, right at noon. "If you went, it wouldn't turn out well . . . our lives depend on your thoughtfulness," that's what the turkeys told her.

"Well then, that's the way it will be," she said, and she listened to them.

But around sunset the drum could be heard, and she was getting more anxious to go. . . .

She went up on her roof and she could see the crowd of people. It was the third day of the dance.

That night she asked the same one she asked before and he told her, "Well, if you must go, then you must dress well. . . .

"You must think of us, for if you stay all afternoon, until sunset, then it won't turn out well for you," he told her. . . .

The next day the sun was shining, and she went among her turkeys and . . . when she had fed them she said, "My fathers, my children, I'm going to the Middle Place. I'm going to the dance," she said. "Be on your way, but think of us. . . ." That's what her children told her.

She went to where the place was, and when she entered the plaza . . . , she went down and danced, and she didn't think about her children.

Finally it was mid-day, and . . . she was just dancing away until it was late, the time when the shadows are very long.

The turkeys said, "Our mother, our child doesn't know what's right."

"Well then, I must go and I'll just warn her and come right back and whether she hears me or not, we'll leave before she gets here," that's what the turkey said, and he flew . . . along until he came to where they were dancing, and there he glided down to the place and . . . sang,

"Kyana tok tok Kyana tok tok."

The one who was dancing heard him.

He flew back to the place where they were penned, and the girl ran all the way back. When she got to the place where they were penned, they sang again, they sang and flew away. . . .

When she came near they all went away and she couldn't catch up to them.

Long ago, this was lived. . . .

From *Finding the Center: Narrative Poetry of the Zuni Indians.* 2nd edition translated by Denis Tedlock, reprinted by permission of The University of Nebraska Press. ©1999 by Denis Tedlock.

"The Girl Who Took Care of the Turkeys" is a Zuni narrative. A Native American people who live in what is now New Mexico, Zunis traditionally supported themselves by farming. They also kept domesticated turkeys, whose feathers they used to make ceremonial gear. In the story, the young girl uses kin terms when addressing the turkeys to indicate her close bonds with them.

You may have noticed similarities between this Zuni story and the European story of Cinderella. In both, the central character is a young woman who wants to go to a dance but is at first dissuaded or, in Cinderella's case, prevented from doing so. Eventually, she does attend, but is warned that she must be sure to return home early. In both stories, the girl stays past the appointed time because she is enjoying herself. The Zuni and European stories, however, differ in both outcomes and details.

The European folk-tale, Cinderella, has been retold countless times. In this musical version by Rodgers and Hammerstein, the cast includes Brandy, Whitney Houston, and Whoopi Goldberg.

The similarities and differences between these stories are no coincidence. Zunis first learned the Cinderella story from white settlers in the 1880s and transformed the tale to fit their circumstances, values, and way of life. This is an example of *selective borrowing* that takes place when members of different cultures meet, share experiences, and learn from one another. Global influences have accelerated borrowing over the last five centuries.

The Zunis reverse the ethical standing of the story's characters. Cinderella, who yearns to go to the ball, is a virtuous and long-suffering servant to her wicked family. The Zuni girl is also a caretaker for her family, the flock of turkeys (whom she significantly addresses as "father" and "child"), but she is not a figure of virtue. On the contrary, to go to the dance, she has to neglect her duties, threatening the turkeys' well-being.

And what happens? Cinderella marries the prince and emerges triumphant, but disaster befalls the Zuni girl. The European story of individual virtue and fortitude rewarded has become a Zuni story of moral failing and irresponsibility to one's relatives and dependents.

The differences between Europeans and Zunis fit into a constellation of features that define Zuni and European culture—the languages they speak, how they feed and shelter themselves, what they wear, the material goods they value, how they make those goods and distribute them among themselves, how they form families, households, and alliances, and how they worship the deities they believe in. This concept—culture—is central to the discipline of anthropology in general and to cultural anthropology, the subject of this book, in particular.

THE STUDY OF HUMANITY

Anthropology, broadly defined, is the study of humanity, from its evolutionary origins millions of years ago to its present worldwide diversity. Many other disciplines, of course, also focus on one aspect or another of humanity. Like sociology, economics, political science, psychology, and other behavioral and social sciences, anthropology is concerned with how people organize their lives and relate to one another in interacting, interconnected groups—**societies**—that share basic beliefs and practices. Like economists, anthropologists are interested in society's material foundations—how people produce and distribute food and other goods. Like sociologists, anthropologists are interested in how people structure their relations in society—in families, at work, in institutions. Like political scientists, anthropologists are interested in power and authority: who has them and how they are allocated. And, like psychologists, anthropologists are interested in individual development and the interaction between society and individual people.

Also, anthropologists share an interest in human evolution and human anatomy with those in the biological sciences. They share an interest in the past of peoples and communities with historians. As the discussion of the Zuni story that opens suggests, they share an interest in how people express themselves with students of literature, art, and music. And they are interested in the diversity of human philosophical systems, ethical systems, and religious beliefs.

Although anthropology shares many interests with other disciplines, the following key features distinguish it as a separate area of study:

- A focus on the concept of culture
- A holistic perspective
- A comparative perspective

anthropology
The study of humanity, from its evolutionary origins millions of years ago to its current worldwide diversity.

societies
Populations of people living in organized groups with social institutions and expectations of behavior.

Cultural anthropologists seek to explain people's thoughts and behaviors in terms of their culture or way of life.

These features are the source of anthropology's insights into both common humanity and the diversity with which that humanity is expressed.

The Concept of Culture

Anthropology is unique in its focus on the role of **culture** in shaping human behavior. We examine this important concept in detail in Chapter 2. For now, we can define culture as the learned values, beliefs, and rules of conduct shared to some extent by the members of a society and that govern their behavior with one another and how they think about themselves and the world. Culture can be broadly divided into **symbolic culture**—people's ideas and means of communicating those ideas—and **material culture**—the tools, utensils, clothing, housing, and other objects that people make or use.

A Holistic Perspective

Unlike other behavioral and social sciences, anthropology views cultures from a **holistic perspective**—as an integrated whole, no part of which can be completely understood in isolation. How people arrange rooms in their homes, for example, is related to their marriage and family patterns, which in turn are related to how they earn a living. Thus, the single-family home with individual bedrooms that became the norm in America's suburbs in the twentieth century reflects the value Americans place on individualism and the nuclear family—husband, wife, and their children. These values, in turn, are consistent with an economy in which families are dependent on wage earners acting individually and competitively to find employment. Thus, a holistic perspective that considers the interconnections among factors that contribute to people's behavior helps us understand the kinds of homes in which they live.

Anthropologists, then, attempt to understand all aspects of human culture, past and present. They are interested in people's economic lives and in learning about the food they eat, how they obtain their food, and how they organize their work. They also study people's political lives to know how they organize their communities, select their leaders, and make group decisions. And they investigate people's social lives to understand how they organize their families—whom they marry and live with, and to whom they consider themselves related. Anthropologists also study people's religious lives to learn about the kinds of deities they worship, their beliefs about the spirit world, and the ceremonies they perform.

Anthropologists understand that cultural norms and values guide but do not dictate people's behavior. They also know that people often idealize their own practices, projecting

culture
The learned values, beliefs, and rules of conduct that are shared to some extent by the members of a society, and that govern their behavior with one another.

symbolic culture
The ideas people have about themselves, others, and the world, and the ways that people express these ideas.

material culture
The tools people make and use, the clothing and ornaments they wear, the buildings they live in, and the household utensils they use.

The ubiquity of electronic music developed in Japan and Korea is an example of global cultural exchange.

beliefs about what they do even though their actual behavior may differ from those ideals. For example, when workers are asked about their job responsibilities, they may talk about official procedures and regulations even though their daily work is more flexible and unpredictable.

A Comparative Perspective

The juxtaposition of the Cinderella story and the Zuni narrative of "The Girl Who Took Care of the Turkeys" is a small example of anthropology's comparative perspective at work. Comparing the two stories opens a window onto the contrasting values of Zuni and European cultures and increases our understanding of each.

Anthropology is fundamentally comparative, basing its findings on cultural data drawn from societies throughout the world and from throughout human history. Anthropologists collect data about behavior and beliefs in many societies to document the diversity of human culture and to understand common patterns in how people adapt to their environments, adjust to their neighbors, and develop unique cultural institutions. This **comparative perspective** can challenge common assumptions about human nature based solely on European or North American culture. For example, as you will learn in Chapter 9, marriage and family take many different forms worldwide. Only through systematic comparison can we hope to determine what aspects of marriage and family—or any other aspect of culture, for that matter—might be universal (found in all human societies) and which aspects vary from society to society.

The Comparative Perspective and Culture Change. The comparative, or "cross-cultural," perspective also helps people reexamine their own culture. Cultures are not static. They change in response to internal and external pressures. Anthropology's comparative perspective is a powerful tool for understanding **culture change.** Because this concept is so important, each subsequent chapter of this textbook contains a special feature on culture change.

The Comparative Perspective and Globalization. The comparative perspective also allows anthropologists to evaluate the impact of globalization. **Globalization** is the spread of economic, political, and cultural influences across a large geographic area or many different societies. Through globalization, many countries and communities are enmeshed in networks of power and influence that extend far beyond their borders, exchanging goods and services, forms of entertainment, and information technologies. Although all countries can contribute to globalization in principle, dominant countries have more control over the flow of goods and services and exert more influence over other societies in practice. However, no one country or region of the world currently controls the process of globalizing. Rather, many powerful countries contribute to globalization.

Globalization has occurred in the past when states and empires expanded their influence far beyond their borders. However, one of the distinctions of globalization today is the speed with which it is transforming local cultures as they participate in a worldwide system of interconnected economies and polities. These influences are also changing other aspects of culture, including family structures, religious practices, and aesthetic forms. Along with the export of products and technologies, rapid communications and information systems also spread attitudes and values throughout the world, including capitalist cultural practices, consumerism, cultural icons, and media and entertainment. Finally, globalization is uneven, both in the degree to which goods and services are exchanged in different places and in the way it creates inequalities as well as similarities.

Chapter 2 will further explore cultural transformation and globalization, and their causes and consequences, and they will be considered in depth in Chapters 16 and 17. Culture change is not, however, a recent phenomenon. Cultures are not and never were static systems. Indeed, changes in beliefs and practices help to strengthen societies and to endow them with the resilience to survive. Therefore, change and stability are not opposite processes. They depend on one another. That is why we highlight examples of cultural transformations throughout this text.

holistic perspective
A perspective in anthropology that views culture as an integrated whole, no part of which can be completely understood without considering the whole.

comparative perspective
An approach in anthropology that uses data about the behaviors and beliefs in many societies to document both cultural universals and cultural diversity.

culture change
Changes in peoples' ways of life over time through both internal and external forces.

globalization
The spread of economic, political, and cultural influences throughout a very large geographic area or through a great number of different societies. Through globalization, many countries and local communities are enmeshed in networks of power and influence far beyond their borders, exchanging goods and services, forms of entertainment, and information technologies.

GLOBALIZATION

Culture contact and culture change, such as occurred between the Europeans and Zuni, underlie the phenomenon of globalization. Globalization is a major theme of this textbook. The symbol that appears here and elsewhere throughout this textbook calls your attention to globalization-related issues.

What signs of globalization do you see in your immediate surroundings—for example, in your clothes, cars, and information or communications technologies?

REVIEW —◉ Anthropology focuses on the study of all aspects of being human. It has many concepts and subjects in common with other behavioral and social sciences, and with biological sciences. Core concepts include culture, culture change, and globalization. Three characteristics differentiate anthropology from other fields: the concept of culture, the holistic perspective, and the comparative perspective.

THE FOUR SUBFIELDS OF ANTHROPOLOGY

Almost since it emerged as an academic discipline in the late nineteenth century, anthropology in North America has encompassed four subfields, each with its own focus, methodologies, and theories: cultural anthropology, linguistic anthropology, archaeology, and biological (or physical) anthropology. Each subfield also has branches or interest areas (see Figure 1.1). Table 1.1 identifies some of the many kinds of work anthropologists perform.

Cultural Anthropology

Cultural anthropology is, as the term implies, the study of culture—any cultural behavior and especially people's ways of life. The work of cultural anthropologists centers on **ethnology,** building theories to explain cultural processes based on the comparative study of societies throughout the world. The method they use to gather these data is called **ethnography,** a holistic, intensive study of groups through observation, interview, and participation.

To conduct ethnographic research, anthropologists do "fieldwork," that is, they live among the people they are studying to compile a full record of their activities. They learn about people's behaviors, beliefs, and attitudes. They study how they make their living, obtain their food, and supply themselves with tools, equipment, and other products. They study how families and communities are organized, and how people form clubs or associations, discuss common interests, and resolve disputes. And they investigate the relationship between the people and larger social institutions—the nations they are part of and their place in the local, regional, and global economies.

Collecting ethnographic information is a significant part of the preservation of indigenous cultures. It contributes to the fund of comparative data cultural anthropologists use to address questions about human cultural diversity. These questions—such as how people acquire culture, how culture affects personality, how family structures and

cultural anthropology
The study of cultural behavior, especially the comparative study of living and recent human cultures.

ethnology
Aspect of cultural anthropology involved with building theories about cultural behaviors and forms.

ethnography
Aspect of cultural anthropology involved with observing and documenting peoples' ways of life.

FIGURE 1.1
Subfields of Anthropology

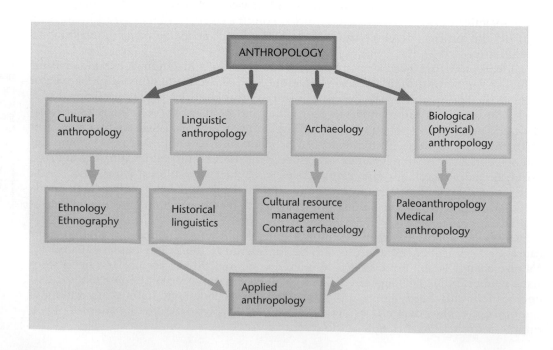

TABLE 1.1   CAREER OPPORTUNITIES IN THE FOUR SUBFIELDS OF ANTHROPOLOGY

Field	Definition	Examples
Cultural Anthropology	The study of human culture	Ethnographer Ethnologist Museum curator University or college professor International business consultant Cross-cultural researcher
Linguistic Anthropology	The study of language	International business consultant Diplomatic communications worker Administrator Ethnographer Domestic communications worker University or college professor
Archaeology	The study of past cultures	Cultural resource management worker Museum curator University or college professor State archaeologist Historical archaeologist Zoo archaeologist Environmental consultant
Biological (Physical) Anthropology	The study of human origins and biological diversity	Primatologist Geneticist University or college professor Medical researcher Genetic counselor Forensic specialist Government investigator Human rights investigator Biomedical anthropologist

gender roles vary, the role of art and religion, and the impact of global economic forces on local cultures—are the subjects of the chapters of this textbook.

In anthropology's early years, cultural anthropologists primarily studied non-Western societies, particularly traditional, **indigenous societies**—peoples who were once independent and have occupied their territories for a long time but are now usually minority groups in larger states. These early researchers favored societies in regions of the world that the West's expanding influence had left relatively unaffected or, like the native societies of southern Africa or North and South America, had been overwhelmed and transformed by conquest. The idea was that a small, comparatively homogeneous society could serve as a kind of laboratory for understanding humanity. Over the years, cultural anthropologists have challenged this view, however, and globalization has all but ended cultural isolation. Today, cultural anthropologists are likely to do an ethnographic study of, say, a small town in the American Midwest, Somali refugees adapting to life in Minnesota, Americans participating in a hospice program, changing political systems in Afghanistan, or life in a prison.

indigenous societies
Peoples who are now minority groups in state societies but who were formerly independent and have occupied their territories for a long time.

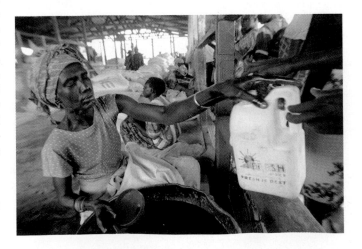

Cultural anthropologists study how refugees like these Somali Bantu adapt to American life and how American communities adapt to refugees.

CONTR⬤VERSIES

What Are the Limits of Cultural Relativism?

The controversial practice of female genital mutilation (FGM) or female circumcision, prevalent in twenty-eight countries in Africa and found in other regions as well, illustrates the uneasy relationship between cultural relativism and concern for individual human rights. FGM removes part or all of the external genitals of prepubescent girls. The procedure varies but usually entails the removal of the clitoris. In some areas, particularly in southern Egypt, Sudan, Somalia, Ethiopia, and Mali, it also includes *infibulation*—the stitching closed—of the vagina, leaving only a tiny opening for the passage of urine and menstrual blood. The United Nations Division for the Advancement of Women suggests that at least 100 million women living today have been subjected to FGM, whereas the World Health Organization (WHO) puts the number at more than 132 million women and girls in Africa alone, estimating also that about 2 million procedures are performed annually (Ras-Work 2006; Almroth et al. 2005). Although FGM is now sometimes performed in hospitals, local midwives usually complete the procedure, working with crude tools and without anesthesia on girls who are typically between 5 and 11 years old.

The two most common names by which the practice is known—female genital mutilation and female circumcision—reflect opposing attitudes toward it. Calling the practice *female circumcision* equates it with male circumcision, which is also debated but more widely accepted. The term *female genital mutilation* was introduced by the United Nations Inter-African Committee (IAC) on Traditional Practices Affecting the Health of Women and Children, a group established to help end the practice. This term reflects "the cruel and radical operation so many young girls are forced to undergo" involving "the removal of healthy organs" (Armstrong 1991, 42).

Although its exact origin is unknown, FGM predates both Christianity and Islam, and occurs among peoples of both faiths and among followers of traditional African religions. It is most common, however, in predominantly Islamic regions of Africa and is associated with strongly patriarchal cultures—that is, cultures that stress the subordination of women to male authority.

Medical risks for girls undergoing the procedure reportedly include pain, shock, loss of bladder and bowel control, and potentially fatal infections and hemorrhaging (Gruenbaum 1993). Infibulation in particular can have serious, painful, long-term consequences. Defenders of the procedure claim that there is no reliable evidence of its increasing a girl's risk of death or of excessive rates of medical complication. Opponents claim that FGM reduces a woman's capacity for sexual pleasure and that infibulation makes sexual intercourse and childbirth painful.

Groups who practice FGM defend it on cultural grounds. In their views, infibulation helps ensure a woman's premarital chastity and her sexual fidelity to her husband while increasing his sexual pleasure. Some prominent African women, such as Fuambai Ahmadu, an anthropologist from Sierra Leone, defend the practice. On the basis of her research, Ahmadu (2000, 304–05) views it as an emotionally positive validation of womanhood. In her interviews, African women reported that the practice did not diminish their sexual drive, inhibit sexual activity, or prevent sexual satisfaction, and that it did not adversely affect their health or birthing. The women looked forward to carrying on the tradition and initiating their younger female relatives into the pride of womanhood. Other local observers, such as Olayinka Koso-Thomas (1992),

ethnocentrism
The widespread human tendency to perceive the ways of doing things in one's own culture as normal and natural and that of others as strange, inferior, and possibly even unnatural or inhuman.

cultural relativism
An approach in anthropology that stresses the importance of analyzing cultures in that culture's own terms rather than in terms of the culture of the anthropologist. This does not mean, however, that all cultural behavior must be condoned.

Two important concepts—ethnocentrism and cultural relativism—influence the anthropological approach to ethnography and cross-cultural research. **Ethnocentrism** refers to the tendency for people to see themselves as being at the center of the universe. They perceive their own culture's way of doing things (making a living, raising children, governing, worshipping) as normal and natural and that of others as strange, inferior, and even unnatural or inhuman. Governments, for example, often ethnocentrically justify their economic and military dominance over other peoples by claiming the natural superiority of their culture. The ancient Romans, Chinese, Aztecs, Incas, and others similarly held themselves superior to the people they conquered.

In the nineteenth and early twentieth centuries, many Europeans assumed they represented the highest form of civilization, and ranked other societies beneath them according to how closely they approached middle-class European appearance, practices, and values. Early anthropologists, hardly immune to this pervasive ethnocentrism, developed evolutionary schemes that ranked people on a scale of progress from "savagery" to "civilization," with middle- and upper-class Europeans at the top.

To counter the influence of ethnocentrism, cultural anthropologists try to approach cultures from the viewpoint of **cultural relativism.** That is, they try to analyze a culture in terms of that culture, rather than in terms of the anthropologist's culture. This a physician from Sierra Leone, oppose the practice for its brutality, its dangerous consequences, and its role in perpetuating the subordination of women.

Some anthropologists, citing cultural relativism and the ideal of objectivity, do not support outside organizations that pressure African, Middle Eastern, and Indonesian governments to abolish FGM. Although they don't condone the procedure, they prefer to hope for change from within. Other anthropologists point out that, although cultural relativism may help us understand a culture on its own terms, it can also help us understand how cultural beliefs reinforce inequalities by convincing people to accept practices that may be harmful and demeaning as natural.

Recent medical studies indicate multiple harmful effects of FGM. Research carried out by the WHO in six African countries concluded that, compared to women who have not had FGM, " . . . deliveries to women who have undergone FGM are significantly more likely to be complicated by cesarean section, postpartum hemorrhage, tearing of the vaginal wall, extended maternal hospital stay, and inpatient perinatal death [infant mortality]" (WHO 2006, 1,835). The study was conducted in hospitals, and outcomes for women who give birth at home might be even more negative because emergency medical treatment would not be available. Another medical study of women in Sudan reported that women who had undergone the most extensive types of FGM were the most likely to be infertile (Almroth et al. 2005, 390). Because fertility in women is highly valued, particularly in patriarchal cultures, the finding that FGM is a significant cause of infertility might be an effective argument against the procedure.

Many anthropologists, together with health workers, women's rights advocates, and human rights organizations, oppose FGM and are working to end it with some success. In 1995, a United Nations–sponsored Conference on the Status of Women declared FGM to be a violation of human rights. In 1996, the U.S. Board of Immigration Appeals, ruling that FGM is a form of persecution, granted political asylum to a young woman from Togo who feared returning to her native country because she would be forced to undergo the procedure as a prelude to her arranged marriage (Dugger 1996 A1; B2).

In response to campaigns against FGM, sixteen African governments have outlawed it, and others have taken steps to limit its severity and improve the conditions under which it is performed (Ras-Work 2006, 10). These initiatives have not eradicated FGM. Still, recent reports indicate that some women who specialize in the procedure have decided not to continue performing it. For example, a grassroots organization called Womankind Kenya has persuaded influential practitioners to join their cause. Among the arguments they use are teachings from the Koran that some imams interpret as opposing FGM (Lacey 2004). The Inter-African Committee of the United Nations is also organizing around the issues of religion, sponsoring conferences of Muslim and Christian religious leaders to speak out against FGM (Ras-Work 2006). Outreach programs are also training practitioners in other work, and are promoting messages about women's worthiness and the value of their bodies.

● CRITICAL THINKING QUESTIONS

Are there universal human rights? Who defines those rights? What are the benefits and risks of intervening in other people's ways of life?

principle is central to cultural anthropology. For example, in the nineteenth century, native peoples of the Pacific Northwest of North America engaged in rituals, called potlatches, which included feasting and giveaways of large amounts of food and personal and ceremonial property. Missionaries and officials in the United States and Canada considered these activities harmful, wasteful, and illogical because they contradicted Euro-American values that stress the importance of accumulating and saving wealth. But anthropologists came to understand the economic and social significance of potlatches to the native peoples. We will discuss the meaning of potlatches in more detail in Chapter 7, but for now note that they effectively redistributed food and other goods to all members of a community. These displays of generosity also raised the social standing of the hosts.

Although cultural anthropologists usually take for granted the need to embrace cultural relativism in their work, there is debate about the extent to which it is possible to apply the principle. Anthropologists, like everyone else, are products of their own society. No matter how objective they try to be, their own cultural experience inevitably colors how they interpret the behavior of people in other cultures. Anthropologists need to acknowledge the potential effect of their own attitudes and values on the kinds of research problems they formulate and how they interpret other people's behavior.

GLOBALIZATION

Globalization has included the spread of Western beliefs and values codified as laws on human rights.

With the spread of English and other languages of business, globalization has endangered native languages as well as the ways of life those languages express.

Do you use words among friends that you would never use in a job interview, in class, or with children? What does your use of language reveal about your relationships to the people you address?

Although cultural relativism requires anthropologists to try to understand other cultures on that culture's terms, it does not require them to abandon their own ethical standards or to condone oppressive practices. Cultural relativism, in other words, is not the same as **ethical relativism,** the acceptance of all ethical systems as equivalent to each other. Nevertheless, anthropologists have different views on the applicability of cultural and ethical relativism, as the Controversies feature on pp. 8–9 illustrates.

Linguistic Anthropology

Linguistics, the study of language, is a separate academic discipline independent of anthropology. However, language is a key concern of anthropology. Not only is it a defining feature of all cultures, language is also the primary means by which we express culture and transmit it from one generation to the next.

Linguistic anthropology, discussed in more detail in Chapter 4, shares with linguistics an interest in the nature of language itself, but with an added focus on the interconnections among language, culture, and society. To gain insight into social categories, for example, linguistic anthropologists might investigate how people use language in different social contexts. Do people use a formal style of speech in one situation and an informal style in another? Do they vary words, pronunciation, and grammar in different social contexts? Do they speak differently to relatives and nonrelatives, friends and strangers, males and females, children and adults?

Some linguistic anthropologists study the languages of indigenous peoples to document their grammars and vocabularies. This is critical work because increasing globalization has led to the advancement of English and other languages of business. In their attempts to keep pace with the new world order, native peoples are losing their traditions, and their languages are becoming extinct.

Many indigenous peoples are under pressure to abandon their own languages and adopt the official languages of the countries in which they find themselves. For example, in the United States and Canada, many indigenous languages have only a few speakers because of the intense pressures brought upon native peoples to use English or French in place of their own languages. These social and political factors began under European colonialism, but they have continued in Canada. However, dozens of programs run by indigenous Americans and Canadians, and assisted by linguists, are now documenting and teaching indigenous languages, so that they can be maintained and revitalized.

Linguistic anthropologists also document how language changes over time within a culture. And they are witnesses to how the expanding influence of a few globally spoken languages has reduced the number of indigenous languages spoken in the world. Endangered languages also include Western languages as well, such as Gaelic, Breton (spoken in France), and Yiddish.

Other linguistic anthropologists specialize in **historical linguistics.** Their work is based on the premise that people who speak related languages are culturally and historically related, descended from a common ancestral people. By looking at the relationships among languages in a large area, historical linguists can help determine how people have migrated to

ethical relativism
The belief that all rights and wrongs are relative to time, place, and culture, such that no moral judgments of behavior can be made.

linguistic anthropology
The study of language and communication, and the relationship between language and other aspects of culture and society.

historical linguistics
The study of changes in language and communication over time and between peoples in contact.

When she died in 2008, Marie Smith Jones was the last speaker of Eyak, a Na-Dene language of Alaska.

IN THEIR OWN VOICES

Extinction in a Nutshell

In September 1992, Dune Lankard and Marie Smith Jones of Alaska were interviewed about their involvement in an unsuccessful lawsuit against the Eyak Corporation to stop it from clear-cutting on lands sacred to the Eyak people. Dune Lankard is part-Eyak and has served on the board of the Eyak Corporation. Marie Smith Jones was the chief of the traditional elders council, established to protect the remaining heritage of the Eyaks. She died in January 2008.

In answer to the question, What factors have led to the extinction of the Eyak people? Dune Lankard said:

From 1889 to about 1915, a couple of events took place that were very destructive to our way of life and our people. In the late 1890s, five canneries were built in the Copper River Delta area. The Eyaks' livelihood and subsistence lifestyle was drastically changed because the cannery workers placed nets five miles off-shore, funneled the fish into the canneries and blocked off the traditional salmon runs. So the Eyaks became dependent on the canneries for survival. And at the same time that they were taking the entire run, they were dynamiting streams. They basically wiped out our way of life.

When whites moved into the area and built the canneries, they brought alcohol. The canneries brought in a cheap Chinese labor force and the Chinese brought in opium. Just think about the destruction, about what can happen when the alcohol is mixed with the drugs: there is rape, there is violence, there is the abuse of Indian women.

Shortly after that, the railroad was built, right over the top of the last Eyak village site in Cordova. Then the government schools came in, the public schools that allowed only white children. Some of the Eyak children were shipped away to boarding schools in Oregon, some never to return.

The population of our people prior to the canneries being built was over 300; we were diminished to 50 by about 1920. The final event that wiped out many of our people was the 1918 flu.

Now, Marie is the last full-blooded Eyak Indian on the face of the earth. If Marie were white, this would not be happening. It would be a whole different ballgame then. People would be really concerned that a race of people is being destroyed. But we are just another Indian clan to a lot of people, so they are not taking this seriously. I believe that when Marie does pass on, there will probably be books written about her, maybe even a movie, like "The Last of the Mohicans"—"The Last of the Eyaks." By then it will already be a done deal. And it is so sad.

We were the last "founded," or rediscovered, tribe in North America and we are the first language and race of Alaskan Indians that will be wiped off the face of the earth when Marie dies. We were recognized as a tribe by anthropologists in 1933 and now, 60 years later, we are facing extinction. So more than anything, we want people to learn from this sad story and grasp its meaning so it never happens again.

**Explore more at
www.myanthrolab.com**

From *Multinational Monitor Online*, "Stewards to Shareholders: Eyaks Face Extinction" by Dune Lankard et al. © 1992 by Essential Information. Reproduced with permission of Essential Information in the formats of Textbook and Other Book via Copyright Clearance Center.

● CRITICAL THINKING QUESTION

How does Dune Lankard's story illustrate the perspectives that cultural anthropology can bring to the study of people and their ways of life?

---

arrive in the territories they now occupy. For example, the Apaches in New Mexico, the Navajos in Arizona, and the Hupas of northern California all speak related languages, which are, in turn, related to a family of languages known as Athabascan. Most Athabascan speakers occupy a large area of western Canada and Alaska. These linguistic ties suggest that the Hupas, Navajos, and Apaches are all descended from Athabascan groups that migrated south from Canada.

By studying how people have borrowed words and grammatical patterns from other languages, historical linguists can also gain insight into how groups have interacted over time. Combined with archaeological evidence, these kinds of analyses can produce a rich picture of the historical relationship among peoples who otherwise left no written records, contributing to our understanding of the processes of culture change.

Archaeology

Archaeology is the study of material culture. Its methods apply to both historic cultures, those with written records, and prehistoric cultures, those that predate the invention of

archaeology
The study of past cultures, both historic cultures with written records and prehistoric cultures that predate the invention of writing.

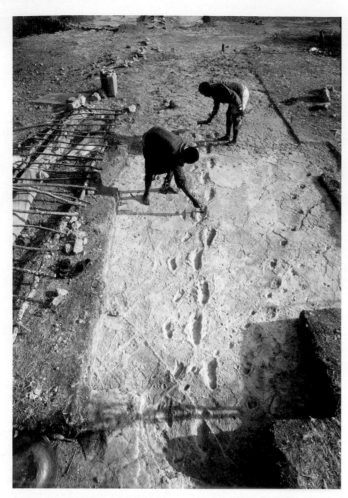

These 3.6-million-year-old tracks of hominids walking through an ash fall from a distant volcanic eruption in Tanzania are the first evidence of fully bipedal locomotion in ancient humans.

writing. Archaeologists have also applied their methods to living societies, a subfield called ethnoarchaeology, with sometimes surprising results.

Unlike cultural anthropologists, who can observe and talk to living people, archaeologists rely mostly on evidence from material culture and the sites where people lived. Such evidence includes, among many other things, the tools that people made and used, the clothing and ornaments they wore, the buildings they lived and worked in, the remains of the plants and animals they relied on, and how they buried their dead.

This kind of evidence can reveal how people lived in the past. The remains of small, temporary encampments, for example, might indicate that the people who used them foraged their food. If the encampment had a lot of stone debris, it was likely used as a workshop for making stone tools. A settlement with permanent dwellings near farmable land and irrigation canals would have been inhabited by agriculturalists.

Judging from the density of settlements and household refuse like fragments of pots, archaeologists can estimate the population of a region at a particular time. The size and distribution of dwellings in a settlement or region can reveal aspects of a society's social structure. If a few of the houses in a settlement are much larger than most others, if they contain many more objects than other dwellings, especially luxury items, archaeologists can conclude that some people were wealthier than others. In contrast, if all of the houses are more or less the same size and contain similar types and amounts of possessions, archaeologists can infer that all of the people lived in more or less the same fashion and were probably of equal status.

Skeletal remains can provide similar clues to social structure. Archaeologists working at a site in Peru called Chavín de Huántar, which flourished from around 800 B.C. to 200 B.C., found evidence from skeletons that the people living close to the site's center ate better than those who lived on its margins. This evidence, combined with similar findings from other sites, suggests that Chavín society was becoming more stratified—that is, divided into classes (Burger 1992a; 1992b).

Archaeologists can also tell us about people's relationships with members of other communities. In much of the world, indigenous trading networks supplied people with goods and products not found in their own territories. Archaeologists can reconstruct these trading networks by studying the distribution of trade goods in relation to their place of origin. Similar evidence also can trace migrations, warfare, and conquest.

Written records add enormously to our understanding of the past, but they do not replace the need for archaeology. Archaeology provides a richer understanding of how people lived and worked than do documents alone. People write and keep records about what is important to them. Because the elite members of a society are usually those who are literate, the historical record is more likely to reflect their interests and points of view than that of poor and marginal people. Archaeology can help correct those biases. In 1991, construction in lower Manhattan in New York City uncovered the five-acre African Burial Ground containing the remains of 10,000 to 20,000 enslaved and free African Americans. Archaeologists were able to determine the diets, health, and causes of death of many of the people buried there, documenting the role slavery played in New York City in the early eighteenth century, a feature of urban life previously not well known (Encyclopedia of New York State 2008).

Archaeological methods can help address important issues in contemporary societies. In the 1970s, the archaeologist William Rathje founded the Arizona Garbage Project to study what Americans throw away and what happens to this refuse. Rathje defined archaeology as the discipline that learns from garbage (Rathje and Murphy, 1992). Among

What might an analysis of refuse reveal about life in a dormitory?

the surprising findings, fast-food packaging actually makes up less than 1 percent of the volume of American landfills, contrary to popular opinion and the estimates of experts. Compacted paper takes up the most space.

Archaeology's great chronological depth—from humanity's origins millions of years ago to twenty-first-century landfills—makes it particularly suited to study culture change. Theories of culture change are one of the discipline's main concerns. For example, many archaeologists are interested in the processes that led to the first cities thousands of years ago, and with them the first state—societies with centralized governments, administrative bureaucracies, and inequalities of wealth and power.

Biological Anthropology

Biological, or **physical, anthropology** is the study of human origins and contemporary biological diversity. In the popular imagination, the study of human origins, or **paleoanthropology,** is probably the most visible face of biological anthropology. Paleoanthropologists seek to decipher the fossil record—the usually fragmentary remains of human forebears and related animals—to understand human evolution. Paleoanthropologists have also turned to the science of genetics and the study of DNA for clues to human origins.

Humans are primates; we belong, in other words, to the same order of animals that includes monkeys and apes. DNA evidence indicates that we share a common ancestry with gorillas and chimpanzees—our closest living relatives—and that our evolutionary line separated from theirs in Africa between 5 million and 8 million years ago. Working from fossil evidence, paleoanthropologists are reconstructing the complex course of human evolution. They study changes in the environment in which our ancestors emerged millions of years ago to understand the adaptive benefits of the physical changes they underwent. They study the size and structure of teeth to learn about our ancestors' diets. And they study the distribution of fossils worldwide to learn how and when our ancestors migrated out of Africa and populated most of Earth.

Once humans began to create clothes, shelters, and tools appropriate for environments from the Arctic to the tropics, they no longer depended exclusively on their physical characteristics for survival. With language and more complex social organization, they could enhance group survival. Thus, paleoanthropologists are particularly interested in clues to the emergence of human culture. Here their interests and methods overlap with those of archaeologists as they excavate sites looking for evidence of early toolmaking in association with fossils.

Some physical anthropologists study nonhuman primates to gain insight into the nature of our own species. The primatologist Jane Goodall, for example, spent years observing the behavior of chimpanzees in the wild, and her discoveries about their social behavior have a bearing on the origins of our own social behavior. Goodall also found that chimpanzees can make and use rudimentary tools.

In addition to human origins and primate social behavior, physical anthropologists also study the interaction of biology, culture, and environment to understand humanity's current biological diversity. For example, the Inuit, an indigenous people of Arctic Canada, have developed ways to clothe and shelter themselves to survive in their harsh environment, but they also appear to have a greater rate of blood flow to their bodily extremities in response to cold than other people do (Itoh 1980; McElroy and Townsend 1989, 26–29). Indigenous inhabitants of the Andes Mountains in South America have a greater than average lung capacity, which is an adaptation to the low oxygen of their high-altitude environment. And people from regions rich in dairy products are genetically adapted to digest milk easily, whereas adults from regions where milk is not a traditional part of the diet are not. These lactase-deficient adults get sick when they drink milk. Skin color also is in part an adaptation to climatic conditions and exposure to sun, as darker skin has a higher content of melanin, a

GLOBALIZATION

The global spread of humans was made possible by the evolution of the capacity for culture and the development and spread of the first tool traditions.

biological, or **physical, anthropology**
The study of human origins and contemporary biological diversity.

paleoanthropology
The study of the fossil record, especially skeletal remains, to understand the process and products of human evolution.

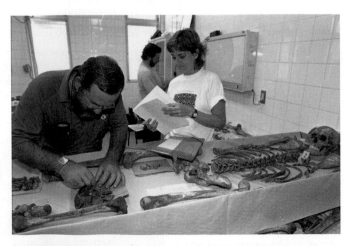

Paleoanthropologists analyze fossil skeletal material or otherwise preserved human remains to learn about ancient populations and their ways of life.

medical anthropology
A discipline that bridges cultural and biological anthropology, focusing on health and disease in human populations.

substance that protects against overabsorption of the sun's harmful ultraviolet rays (Rensberger 2001, 83). We discuss the social significance and interpretation of skin color further in Chapter 12.

The subfield of **medical anthropology** focuses on health and disease in human populations. Medical anthropologists investigate the susceptibilities or resistances of populations to specific diseases. They also trace the spread of diseases within a population and from one population to another. Before the arrival of the first Europeans and Africans in South and North America in the sixteenth and seventeenth centuries, for example, smallpox, measles, and other infectious diseases were unknown. As a result, Native Americans, unlike the newcomers, had no natural immunity to the diseases. The results were catastrophic; once exposed to the diseases, millions of Native Americans died.

In contrast to the vulnerabilities of indigenous peoples of the Americas, some populations have advantageous resistances to diseases endemic in their areas, as the following Case Study investigates.

CASE STUDY

Environment, Adaptation, and Disease: Malaria and Sickle-Cell Anemia in Africa and the United States

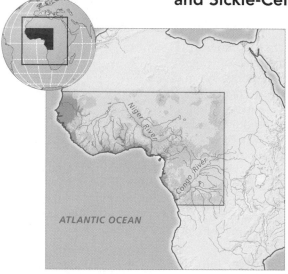

ATLANTIC OCEAN

What does this analysis of sickle-cell anemia and malaria suggest about the relationships between biological and cultural factors in human health?

Study of the incidence of two diseases, malaria and sickle-cell anemia, demonstrates how the processes of biological adaptation and culture change can interact to affect human health.

Sickle-cell anemia is a genetic disease that causes red blood cells to have a sickle shape rather than their normal disk shape. Sickled cells cannot hold and transport oxygen normally. Because the disease can be fatal in those who have inherited the recessive gene from both parents, one might expect that the sickle-cell trait would naturally die out in a population. However, individuals who carry one dominant and one recessive copy of the gene survive and also happen to have immunity from another disease—malaria. Malaria is an infectious disease spread by the *Anopheles* mosquito. Both diseases are extremely debilitating and potentially fatal. And both are endemic to West Africa, the ancestral homeland of most African Americans.

The genetic trait that causes sickle-cell anemia probably evolved in human populations in West Africa about 2,400 years ago (Edelstein 1986). At the time, dense forests covered much of West Africa. The inhabitants had lived for millennia by hunting and collecting wild plants. The *Anopheles* mosquito was present; however, because it breeds in unshaded pools of standing water, the mostly shady conditions of the forest kept its numbers in check.

Around 2,000 years ago, however, farming peoples from East Africa began to filter into West Africa, displacing the indigenous population and clearing forestlands for their fields.

By not transporting oxygen properly and clogging organs, sickled red blood cells cause lifelong, potentially life-threatening health problems for people with this genetic disorder.

This created the open areas with standing pools of water in which the *Anopheles* mosquito thrives (Foster and Anderson 1978). As farming spread, so did malaria. As the human population and its cattle herds increased, so did the mosquito population and malaria.

Those who inherit the sickle-cell gene from one parent gain some resistance to malaria, which lessens the severity of the infection. As a result, the sickle-cell gene has spread in malaria-stricken areas. An estimated 30 percent of West African farmers carry the gene. The lowest incidence of the gene is among those who live in still-forested peripheral areas of West Africa, where the *Anopheles* mosquito and malaria are also less prevalent.

The adaptive advantage of the sickle-cell trait, then, is high in populations that live in areas where malaria is prevalent but is less for those who live where the disease is less common. In the United States, where malaria is rare, people of West African descent have higher rates of the sickle-cell gene than do non-Africans, but their rates are much lower than among West Africans today.

If the cultural practice of farming helped spread malaria in West Africa, diet may contribute to the adaptive advantage of the sickle-cell gene. Common crops grown in Africa and the West Indies, including cassava (manioc), yams, sorghum, millet, sugarcane, and lima beans, reduce the severity of the symptoms of sickle-cell anemia because they contain chemical compounds that interfere with the sickling of the red blood cells. This may explain why a lower percentage of Africans suffer from sickle-cell anemia than do African Americans, even though more West Africans have the sickle-cell gene. A study revealed that Jamaicans with sickle-cell anemia had relatively mild symptoms when they lived in Jamaica

Explore more at
www.myanthrolab.com

and ate a Jamaican diet, but experienced more severe symptoms when they migrated to the United States or Britain and changed their eating habits (Frisancho 1981).

Anthropology has four subfields: cultural anthropology, linguistic anthropology, archaeology, and biological (or physical) anthropology. Because we all are prone to be ethnocentric, cultural anthropologists adopt the method of ethnography and the perspective of cultural relativism to avoid being judgmental of other cultures. The work of linguistic anthropologists and archaeologists sheds light on culture change, and subdisciplines such as medical anthropology combine biological and cultural anthropology.

APPLIED ANTHROPOLOGY

Applied anthropology intersects with and draws from the four major subfields. Indeed, many anthropologists regard applied anthropology as a fifth subfield of anthropology. Applied anthropologists employ anthropological understandings and perspectives to work outside traditional academic settings. For example, some biological anthropologists work as **forensic anthropologists,** applying their knowledge of human anatomy to help solve crimes. Working for police departments, the Federal Bureau of Investigation (FBI), and other law enforcement agencies, forensic anthropologists can help determine the cause of death by examining a victim's remains and the physical evidence found at a crime scene. Forensic anthropologists' knowledge of skeletal anatomy, blood types, and biochemical markers in the blood can also help identify a victim and provide leads to suspects. Forensic anthropologists have also been asked to study human remains for evidence of human rights abuses that occur during wars and civil conflicts.

Many government agencies, such as the FBI's behavioral science unit Violent Criminal Apprehension Program (ViCAP), employ forensic anthropologists. Forensic anthropologists and archaeologists also work for the Central Identification Laboratory—Hawaii (CILHI). Members of CILHI have traveled to Vietnam and Korea to find the remains of downed airplanes in attempts to identify people missing in action (MIAs) from the Vietnam and Korean wars. Forensic anthropologists also helped identify remains of victims of the terrorist attacks on the World Trade Center in New York City.

Applied archaeology has grown with federal and state laws that protect archaeological sites and materials, which has led to the creation of the field of **cultural resource management (CRM).** Laws now require archaeological surveys in advance of many highway and other construction projects to assess their impact on archaeological sites. The need for these assessments has given rise to **contract archaeology,** in which archaeologists are hired to do this kind of research.

applied anthropology
An area of anthropology that applies the techniques and theories of the field to problem solving outside of traditional academic settings.

forensic anthropologists
Biological anthropologists who analyze human remains in the service of criminal justice and families of disaster victims.

cultural resource management (CRM)
The application of archaeology to preserve and protect historic structures and prehistoric sites.

contract archaeology
The application of archaeology to assess the potential impact of construction on archaeological sites and to salvage archaeological evidence.

Cultural Survival

Cultural anthropologists sometimes help indigenous communities improve their economic conditions, adapt to change, and preserve their traditions. They help communities find ways to use their resources productively while protecting their environment and cultural heritage. Some anthropologists have also helped protect indigenous peoples' indigenous rights.

Cultural Survival is an organization founded by anthropologists that promotes the rights, voices, and visions of indigenous peoples around the world. The organization deals with conflict and migration, cultural preservation, improvement of health care, indigenous economic enterprises, law and self-determination, and the preservation of natural resources. Its initiatives include publications to publicize issues and share news, indigenous curricula, fair trade stores and exchanges such as the Coffee Alliance, legal defense, and an indigenous action network.

Not all applied anthropology concerns native peoples and their cultural survival, however. Some cultural anthropologists advise government agencies and private companies on how to overcome resistance from indigenous and rural communities to policies and projects that benefit national governments and private concerns but threaten indigenous rights and resources.

⊙ CRITICAL THINKING QUESTION

How can anthropological research affect public policy, private enterprise, and advocacy for indigenous peoples?

Archaeologists' findings about the past can also be used to solve contemporary problems. Archaeologists working around Lake Titicaca in the Andes of South America, for example, discovered an ancient and productive method of cultivation that had fallen into disuse. They helped reintroduce this method to local farmers, which substantially increased their yields.

Some linguistic anthropologists apply their skills to preserve indigenous languages. They may work with native speakers to prepare dictionaries, grammars, and other aids for use in language classes and schools. Their work helps indigenous communities counter the rapid decline in the number of people who speak local languages. Collecting data from speakers of endangered languages is a fieldwork priority for linguistic anthropologists.

Cultural anthropologists complete applied anthropology work in nonacademic settings, such as government agencies, nongovernment organizations, charitable foundations, and private companies. Some help shape the policies of city, state, and federal agencies that deliver services to local communities; for example, they may advise on the best ways to contact different populations in a community to deliver services. These may be health care services, such as vaccinations, legal aid services, or preschool and other educational opportunities for children. Cultural anthropologists work in research firms and think tanks to solve social problems. They also help communities, companies, and organizations to resolve management disputes and conflicts. They help resolve labor and workplace issues and work for courts to develop and implement alternative sentencing programs for offenders.

Anthropologists may act as advocates and testify in courts to support native claims to land or other benefits or rights, and may help indigenous people present their history and culture from a native perspective. Cultural Survival, for example, helps Amerindians in Ecuador, Peru, and Brazil protect their interests in the face of globalization.

Medical anthropologists may help preserve traditional medical practices and pharmaceuticals, and encourage practitioners of both traditional and Western medicine to understand the physical and psychological benefits of both medical models for developing treatment procedures that combine both forms of medicine.

Anthropologists who work for industries and corporations analyze workplace interactions to suggest improvements in the working environment and worker productivity. Anthropologists may provide sensitivity training for American businesspeople planning to meet overseas with their foreign counterparts. Anthropologists even study consumer habits to help companies increase sales or develop new products and services. For example, Canon employed a team of anthropologists to study the kinds of pictures and notes that families create and affix to their walls and refrigerators. The company used the findings to develop Canon Creative software, which allows families to make their own greeting cards, posters, and T-shirts, and thus increased printer sales (Hafner 1999).

GLOBALIZATION

Anthropology-based advocacy centers on protecting and preserving the native cultures of small-scale societies that share these goals from the impacts of globalization.

How might Western pharmaceutical companies employ the services of anthropologists?

REVIEW

Applied anthropology is the practical use of all four subfields of anthropology outside academia. Applied anthropology includes forensic anthropologists, workers in cultural resource management, contract archaeologists, and linguistic and cultural anthropologists. All applied anthropologists use their training in other fields of anthropology.

CHAPTER SUMMARY

The Study of Humanity

- Anthropology is the study of humanity, from its evolutionary origins millions of years ago to today's worldwide diversity of peoples and cultures.

- Three features distinguish anthropology from other social sciences: a focus on the concept of culture, a holistic perspective, and a comparative perspective.

- Culture is the constellation of learned values, beliefs, and rules of conduct that members of a society share. Culture change and globalization are important subjects of anthropological research.

- Anthropology's holistic perspective focuses on culture as an integrated whole, the various features and patterns of which can only be understood in relation to one another.

- Anthropology's comparative perspective is based on cultural data drawn from societies throughout the world and from throughout human history, documenting the diversity of human culture in an attempt to understand common patterns in peoples' adaptations to their environments and their unique cultural institutions.

The Four Subfields of Anthropology

- Cultural anthropology is the comparative study of living and recent cultures. Cultural anthropologists use ethnographic fieldwork and the perspective of cultural relativism.

- Linguistic anthropology is the study of language in its cultural and historical context. It includes the study of languages of indigenous peoples, language change, and the relationships between language and other aspects of culture, thought, and belief.

- Archaeology is the study of past cultures. Archaeologists study historic cultures with written records and prehistoric cultures whose lives can be inferred from material artifacts, settlement patterns, and remains of foods and tools.

- Biological anthropology is the study of human origins, using the fossil record to understand human evolution. Some biological anthropologists study biological diversity of contemporary human populations.

Applied Anthropology

- Applied anthropology intersects with and draws from all of the major subdisciplines in anthropology to study and help solve contemporary problems in communities, government, and businesses.

KEY TERMS

anthropology   3
societies   3
culture   4
symbolic culture   4
material culture   4
holistic perspective   4
comparative
   perspective   5

culture change   5
globalization   5
cultural anthropology   6
ethnology   6
ethnography   6
indigenous societies   7
ethnocentrism   8
cultural relativism   8

ethical relativism   10
linguistic
   anthropology   10
historical linguistics   10
archaeology   11
biological, or physical,
   anthropology   13
paleoanthropology   13

medical anthropology   14
applied anthropology   15
forensic
   anthropologists   15
cultural resource
   management (CRM)   15
contract archaeology   15

REVIEW QUESTIONS

1. What features distinguish anthropology from other social and behavioral sciences? Why are the concepts of culture and culture change important in anthropology?

2. Why is globalization a major concern in anthropology today? How does culture change relate to globalization?

3. Why does anthropology use the holistic and comparative perspectives?

4. How does each of the four subfields of anthropology seek to fulfill anthropology's mission?

5. How do cultural anthropologists conduct research? What are some of the goals they try to achieve?

6. Why is cultural relativism important in studying other cultures? How does cultural relativism differ from ethical relativism?

7. What can linguistic anthropologists and archaeologists learn about symbolic and material culture?

8. How do diseases like sickle-cell anemia and malaria highlight the relationship between biology and culture?

9. How can research in each of the subfields of anthropology help solve problems and make policy?

PEARSON myanthrolab EXERCISES

To complete the following exercises and activities, you must log in to www.myanthrolab.com and select your current textbook.

1. In the **Explore** tab of Chapter 1, choose two of the *Careers Videos* to watch. Which one did you find the most interesting? Why?

2. While you are still in the **Explore** tab, click on the *Fields of Anthropology* animation to see a variety of career options that are available with an anthropology degree.

3. In the **Research Tools** section on the home page, click on the *Research Navigator*™ link and enter the Anthropology database to find relevant and recent scholarly and popular press publications. For this chapter enter the following keywords: *ethnography, linguistic anthropology, ethnocentrism,* and *medical anthropology.*

4. Enter the **MyAnthroLibrary** section on the home page to read more about topics and cultures that are discussed in this chapter. Suggested readings include:

Are Ethnographies "Just-So" Stories? by E. Paul Durrenberger

The Research Process by Susan C. Weller

THE NATURE
OF CULTURE

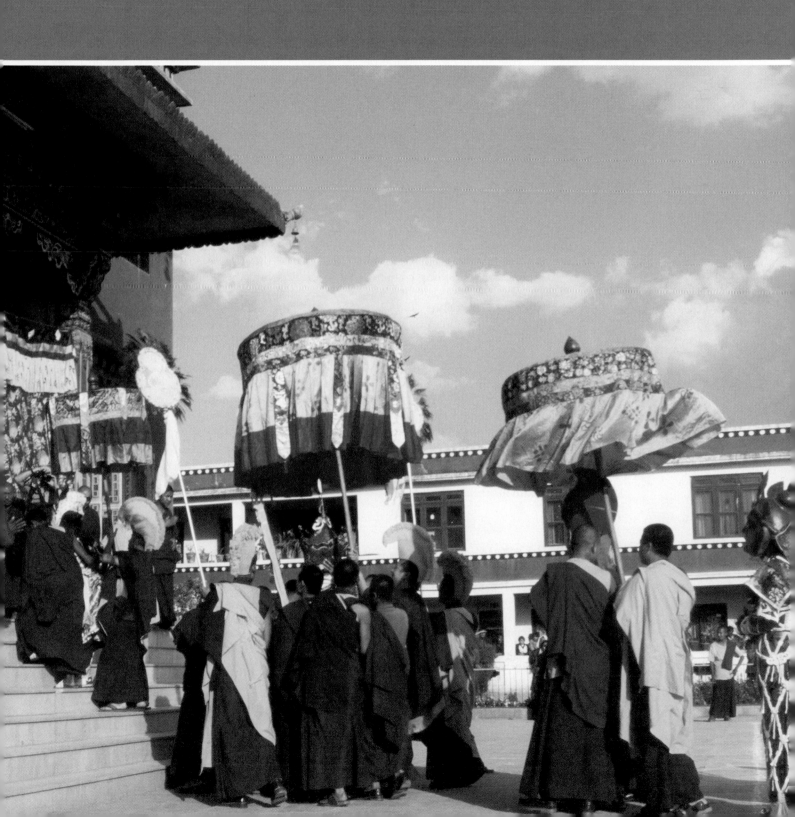

- What is culture? What features are usually included in definitions of culture?

- What elements of culture are regarded as universal, and why?

- How can members of a society both share and not share culture?

- How is culture learned and transmitted?

- How can culture be both adaptive and maladaptive?

- What are some forces of cultural integration?

- How is culture based on symbols?

- How do cultures change from within and through contact?

- What are the dynamics of global culture change today?

At the beginning there was on the earth only a single man; he had neither house nor tent, for at that time the winter was not cold, and the summer was not hot; the wind did not blow so violently, and there fell neither snow nor rain; the tea grew of itself on the mountains, and the flocks had nothing to fear from beasts of prey. This man had three children, who lived a long time with him, nourishing themselves on milk and fruits. After having attained to a great age, this man died. The three children deliberated what they should do with the body of their father, and they could not agree about it; one wished to put him in a coffin, the other wanted to burn him, the third thought it would be best to expose the body on the summit of a mountain. They resolved then to divide it into three parts. The eldest had the body and arms; he was the ancestor of the great Chinese family, and that is why his descendants have become celebrated in arts and industry, and are remarkable for their tricks and stratagems. The second son had the breast; he was the father of the Tibetan family, and they are full of heart and courage, and do not fear death. From the third, who had inferior parts of the body, are descended the Tartars, or simple and timid, without head or heart, and who know nothing but how to keep themselves firm in their saddles.

From David L. Snellgrove and Hugh Richardson, *A Cultural History of Tibet.* © 2003 Orchid Press, reprinted by permission of the publisher.

This Tibetan narrative, describing the origin of the Tibetan people and two ethnic groups who live near them, tells us much about Tibetan attitudes toward themselves and other peoples. These attitudes are part of the core of Tibetan culture; that is, Tibetans' understanding of the world, its origins, and the people who inhabit it. In the beginning, the story depicts the world as an idyllic, peaceful place, without harsh weather and hardship. The Tibetans and their neighbors descend from the same founder. But the story also tells us what qualities the Tibetans believe differentiate them from others. They praise the Chinese for their arts and accomplishments but disapprove of their trickery. They are disparaging and condescending toward the Tartars. And they think of themselves as people of courage and kindness.

The narrative also gives us information about burial practices. Each brother advocated a method of burial that is practiced in different societies around the world: interment in the ground, cremation, and exposure to the elements. These practices are aspects of culture, how people organize their lives. The story thus provides insight into features of Tibetan culture. We learn about how Tibetans view themselves and their neighbors, how they think about their relationships with other groups, and some practices they engage in. In this chapter, we will explore what culture is and how cultural practices and attitudes change.

WHAT IS CULTURE?

Chapter 1 proposed a basic definition of culture: the behaviors, values, and attitudes shared by a group of people. This chapter expands on this definition. Although defining what culture is may sound like a simple task, anthropologists have struggled to define and specify culture since the late nineteenth century, when anthropology was established as a discipline. The British social anthropologist Edward Tylor was the first to attempt a formal definition. Writing in *Primitive Culture* in 1871, he stated, "Culture is that complex whole which includes knowledge, belief, art, morals, law, custom, and any other capabilities and habits acquired by man as a member of society."

Tylor's definition captures several significant features that most definitions of culture include today. It focuses on the holistic quality of culture ("that complex whole") and embraces all the activities, attitudes, and beliefs of human beings. Significantly, these are traits people "acquire." That is, people's attitudes, beliefs, and ways of acting are learned

To what extent is culture shared? For example, what could you say about "American" attitudes toward self and others and "American" ways of organizing life?

rather than inherited, instinctual, or automatic. Finally, Tylor stressed that people acquire culture "as a member of society." People live and interact with other people, learning skills and attitudes from them, and in turn transmitting their knowledge and beliefs to others.

Since Tylor, anthropologists have expanded on and refined the definition of culture innumerable times. By the 1950s, Alfred Kroeber and Clyde Kluckhohn had collected more than one hundred definitions, and all differ according to their focus and the theoretical orientation that underlies them (Kroeber and Kluckhohn 1952). Nevertheless, all the definitions include statements about human behavior and activities in families, groups, and communities, and about people's selectively shared knowledge, attitudes, values, and beliefs.

Cultural knowledge refers to the information people have that enables them to function in their social and physical environments. Some of this information is practical—how to make a living, what kinds of clothes to wear and shelters to build, and so on. Other cultural knowledge is less obvious—for example, people share knowledge about the world, why people do the things they do, what a person can expect from others, and so on. This kind of cultural knowledge is expressed in people's attitudes, values, and beliefs, including ethical values about what is right and wrong and what is proper and improper behavior. Cultural knowledge thus includes religious beliefs and scientific theories about the past, the world, people and their origins, and people's relationships to plants, animals, and the natural world.

The cultural knowledge of these Sami includes everything there is to know about reindeer, living in the Arctic, and coping with citizenship in the modern state society of Norway.

cultural knowledge
Information that enables people to function in their society and contributes to the survival of the society as a whole.

In addition to cultural knowledge, social and cultural skills are included in the definition of culture, such as the activities and practices that people engage in to obtain their food, clothe and shelter themselves, and make or procure goods needed for their households. Cultural behaviors include the ways that people organize themselves to provide leadership, make decisions, and carry out communal activities. In all societies, people need to develop modes of subsistence and economic exchange, methods of social control and conflict resolution, and principles of leadership and governance. They need to organize families and provide for child care and socialization. Other aspects of culture, such as religion and artistic expression, are also part of the human experience. People share similar basic societal needs with members of other societies, but the strategies and institutions they develop to satisfy or cope with those needs vary.

Thus, people in all societies have their own specific thoughts (cultural knowledge) and behaviors (cultural skills) that vary from group to group. Although each culture is unique, any culture also shares similarities with others. In today's world, cultural influences are spreading in the context of a global culture that includes ways of organizing economies, purchasing goods and services, and communicating through the arts, travel, and the Internet. Elements of this global culture emanate from many parts of the world. Although Europe and the United States provide powerful centers for this global culture, economic, political, and artistic influences also come from Asia, Africa, and Latin America as well.

What is global culture? This question is widely debated among social scientists. What thoughts, behaviors, tools, and skills do you identify as making up today's global culture?

REVIEW

Culture includes cultural knowledge (people's ideas, attitudes, beliefs, and values) and cultural skills (people's activities and behaviors for living and organizing their lives). People's thoughts and behaviors are mutually reinforcing. Some aspects of culture deal with concrete knowledge, such as what food to eat, how to build a shelter, and what clothes to wear. Other aspects of culture deal with abstract ideas, such as how people are expected to behave, what attitudes are appropriate in given situations, and value systems. Concrete and abstract components of culture and their behavioral analogs are present in all human societies. At the same time that each culture is unique, a developing and expanding global culture also spreads economic, political, and aesthetic influences throughout the world.

cultural models
Shared assumptions that people have about the world and about the ideal culture.

norms
Sets of expectations and attitudes that people have about appropriate behavior.

CHARACTERISTICS OF CULTURE

Although each culture is unique, a number of characteristics in their organization and functioning are universal. To begin, any culture is a product of a group of people who share and transmit some basic attitudes and assumptions about the world. In addition, aspects of culture tend to interrelate and function together with some consistency to form a coherent system of behaviors and beliefs. Through their cultures, people adapt to their life situations and to changes in their social and physical environments. What do we mean when we say that culture is shared, learned, adaptive, and integrated?

Culture Is Shared

Humans are by nature social creatures; that is, we do not live as individuals alone. Rather, we live with other people in families, households, and communities of various sizes and relationships. The way we behave, our attitudes about right and wrong, our ideas about the world we live in are all formed through our interactions with others. We do not act alone, and we do not have ideas all to ourselves. Together with these other people, we are societies. As defined in Chapter 1, a society is a group of people who live within an acknowledged territory, who could potentially interact with one another, and who share certain practices and values. Societies are held together by social structures that organize family life, means of making a living, and ways of arriving at decisions and establishing methods of leadership.

To say that culture is shared is not to say that all members of a particular society have exactly the same attitudes and do exactly the same things in the same way. Rather, the general principles of culture are shared. For example, not all Americans vote or believe that voting is efficacious, but most would staunchly defend everyone's right to vote. Thus, voting is included in the broad cultural conception of legitimate governance in the United States.

Societies can function as groups to minimize conflicts because their members agree about the basic parameters of living. If this were not so, people would not be able to coordinate their activities or agree on what to do next. And even though they might speak the same language, they would not be able to accurately interpret each other's meanings and intentions if they did not share basic cultural assumptions about the world. These shared assumptions, or **cultural models,** form a background ideology in terms of which behavior becomes relatively coherent and consistent.

Despite cultural models, there are disagreements and conflicts within any community. In all communities, some people are more fully committed to general societal norms than others. Societal **norms** are sets of commonly held expectations and attitudes that people have about appropriate behavior. Although these norms are generally held to be valid within each culture, not everyone acts in accordance with them.

Deviance from expected and appropriate behavior occurs in every community. Some types of deviance are tolerated whereas others are not. In fact, behavior that may be considered deviant within a community as a whole may be a marker of identity for a particular group. For example, body piercings or tattooing might violate adult conceptions of beauty, but teenagers may engage in these physical alterations to conform to youthful standards. Violent behavior such as assault and murder are deviant acts that are not tolerated in most societies. Other kinds of violence that occur within the family, though, such as spousal abuse, may be tolerated, even if not condoned.

People occupying different social roles and statuses may hold opposing views about the existing social order and prevailing cultural norms. For example, age may be a factor in the way people organize their lives and in the kinds of attitudes that they hold. Younger and older people have different experiences and different frames

This young woman was photographed in traditional Burkina Faso garb with her aunt.

of reference. Opposing activities and norms for older and younger people may be relatively stable, though; that is, as younger people age, they adopt the lifestyles and norms of their elders. Differences between the young and the old may also signal ongoing social and culture change, if young people introduce new ways of living as they replace their elders through the normal aging process.

Gender differences are another common source of distinctions in people's activities and attitudes. Issues of gender will be explored in depth in Chapter 10, but here we can note that gender is a complex cultural concept through which people assign particular roles and convey particular attitudes. Gender as a social construct differs from sex, which is a biological attribute. In most societies, women and men usually have certain specific tasks that they fulfill in their homes and communities. The relationships between men and women in the family and in the public sphere influence the ways they experience their lives. For example, men and women are likely to have different ideas about their rights and responsibilities, depending on which gender is the dominant decision maker and authority in the household. Women who have the major share of the household and child-rearing responsibilities may feel burdened and restricted, or they may feel challenged and fulfilled. In societies that sanction violence against women and permit men to abuse their wives, women's experience of household life certainly contrasts sharply with men's.

In the diverse society of Bolivia, this peasant woman of the Andes does not fully share the same culture as her counterpart in La Paz, the capital.

Like differences in age and gender, other status differences in society result in incomplete sharing of culture. Such differences also may be a source of social tension and cultural disagreement. For example, members of elite groups may reap greater economic and social benefits from the way in which society is structured than do members of marginalized or oppressed groups. Although differences of experiences, attitudes, and opinions vary within all societies, such differences are likely to be sharper in complex heterogeneous societies than in small, relatively homogeneous ones where people interact more personally with one another. Class, race, or ethnicity may segment large societies, creating group cultural distinctions in how people organize their lives. In addition, people who belong to different religions may apply different philosophical orientations and moral principles to their daily lives.

Thus, members of different groups in stratified societies may have different attitudes and values. For example, when economists and politicians in the United States tell us that the economy is booming, this does not mean that everyone is doing well. The wealthy and those who own shares on the stock market experience an economic boom very differently from workers whose factories have been relocated abroad, or from people on welfare. Thus, a culture is not fully shared in a diverse society.

In addition to differences derived from distinct social roles and statuses, some societies contain groups that participate in identifiable subcultures. A **subculture** is a group of people who think of themselves, and are thought of by others, as different in a significant way from the majority of people living in the society. Members of subcultures interact more frequently among themselves than with "outsiders," and share attitudes and practices that distinguish them from other groups.

In complex, multiethnic societies, including American society, ethnic groups may comprise subcultures, especially if members have allegiance to their native country, use their native language, and observe ethnic food, preferences, and family relations. Some occupational groups may also function as subcultures. For example, police officers may work and socialize together, have shared vocabulary, and share expectations of life patterns, cooperation, and mutual aid.

subculture
A group whose members and others think of their way of life as different in some significant way from that of other people in the larger society.

Hasidic families are an American urban subculture among many in New York City. Their subculture is distinguished through ethnic background and religious beliefs and practices.

People can acquire any culture if they are raised in it, just as people can learn any language.

enculturation

Process of learning one's culture through informal observation and formal instruction.

All of these sources of difference modify our understanding of culture as a constellation of shared behaviors and beliefs. Still, when people interact within the same society, they must share some basic premises about social order and social values. If they did not, community cohesion would disintegrate, and the groups within the society would separate.

Culture Is Learned

Culture is transmitted from generation to generation and is learned mainly in childhood and during maturation. We learn not only our behavior but also our attitudes and values. The ability to acquire culture in this way makes humans highly adaptable to different cultural environments. Humans are born with a potential to learn whatever knowledge and skills are practiced in their communities. They do this through the process of **enculturation**—learning one's culture through informal observation and formal instruction, beginning in earliest childhood. Children learn the culture that they are exposed to, as the Case Study, "Daughter from Danang" illustrates. We all can acquire any culture if we are raised in it, just as most people can learn any language. Through these processes of exposure and learning, people acquire their culture and transmit it to others. Chapter 5 further explores the topic of enculturation.

CASE STUDY

Daughter from Danang

Mai Thi Hiep was born in Danang, Vietnam, in 1968. She was the daughter of a Vietnamese mother and an American soldier who had abandoned Hiep's mother when she became pregnant. In 1975, her Vietnamese mother, troubled by the chaos of war, participated in "Operation Babylift," an American government program that placed racially mixed children from Vietnam for adoption in the United States, wanting to protect her child and expecting her to be returned later. Hiep's mother also feared reprisals from Vietnamese angered by the U.S. intervention in Vietnam.

At age seven, Hiep was sent to the United States where a single woman adopted her. Hiep became Heidi and grew up in the small town of Pulaski, Tennessee. Heidi recalls that her adoptive mother advised her not to tell people that she was Vietnamese because of the racial climate in Pulaski. Heidi learned to think of herself as American. She forgot her native language quickly because she had no other Vietnamese people to speak with, and acquired all of the tastes and attitudes of American teenagers. By 1997, Heidi had married an American serviceman and became the mother of two young daughters.

Heidi longed to reconnect to her birth mother and to her Vietnamese family. By an odd coincidence, Heidi and her mother were contacting various agencies at about the same time, trying to find one another. Heidi located her mother and arranged for Heidi to visit her family in Danang. Before the trip, Heidi spoke of "going home." It was " . . . going to be so healing for us. It would make all those bad memories [of war and separation] go away."

Reuniting with her Vietnamese family was deeply moving, but Heidi found the sights and sounds of Vietnam strange. She was shocked by the poverty of people on the streets and of her own family. At the first dinner, she did not know the etiquette of how to eat (dipping food from common plates into sauces rather than the American custom of placing a quantity of food on one's own plate), and was not used to the spiciness of the cooking. Within a few days, more problems surfaced. Heidi's mother never left her alone, holding her hand as they walked through the streets, touching and hugging her whenever she could. Although Heidi began to " . . . feel a little smothered," she was also a little "jealous" of the "love and unity" characteristic of Vietnamese kinship ties.

Her mother asked Heidi to help a sister who was extremely poor. Heidi gave her money, but when her sister asked for more, Heidi felt "insulted . . . I didn't come here to be anybody's salvation, I came here to be reunited." This was not what she had imagined. She wanted to "escape back to the world I feel comfortable in." For Heidi, love and asking for financial support were incompatible needs but to her Vietnamese kin, asking for money didn't lessen the integrity of their love.

Before Heidi's departure, their final meeting revealed the stark contrasts between Heidi's expectations and those of her family. Her brother began to talk about their mother's advancing age and her need for material and emotional support. He said that, for twenty-two years, " . . . we, your siblings, have been taking care of our mother. We hope that now you will assume your filial responsibility toward her," meaning to send money monthly. Again, Heidi was shocked, but her mother understood her negative reaction to this direct request for financial help: "What does she know about the Vietnamese notion of love and emotion? She's used to living in a different way." Heidi's brother added, "We are trying to understand your situation and we hope you'll try to understand ours. . . . As a Vietnamese, I thought what I said was normal." Although saddened by her family's situation, Heidi could not respond the way they expected. "It's not how I wanted it to be."

From a cultural perspective, the complex, conflicting expectations of both Heidi and her Vietnamese relatives were understandable and appropriate, given the cultural contexts in which each lived and the attitudes and values that they learned. Although Heidi was born Vietnamese, she had become an American. Because her family remembered her as the child known as Hiep, they expected her to conform to their own system of values. Heidi interpreted her family's expectations through the lens of American culture because most of her socialization had been in the United States.

This story demonstrates how cultural learning molds people to regard their society's practices and values as normal and natural. Understanding other people's reactions from their own perspective requires insight and empathy.

PEARSON
myanthrolab

Explore more at
www.myanthrolab.com

From *Daughter from Danang*, PBS American Experience. Directed by Gail Dolgin and Vicente Franco. © 2003 PBS.

Although most human cultural behavior is the result of learning, this behavior is also influenced by inherited drives as well as acquired needs. People must fulfill important physical and survival needs, just like all living creatures. People need to eat, drink, sleep, eliminate body wastes, and engage in sexual activity. And, like other primates, people also need to interact with one another to obtain food and protection. Culture intervenes and influences the ways in which people satisfy these needs.

For example, each culture has attitudes about what kinds of foods are edible and suitable for human consumption. People do not eat everything that is edible in their environment; they select some foods and reject others, expressing these choices as preferences and prohibitions, or **taboos.** In the United States and Canada, most people consider eating insects distasteful, but many peoples of Australia, Asia, Mexico, and Africa consider insects as a delicacy. The Maasai of Kenya and northern Tanzania drink the blood of their cattle. Koreans farm puppies for meat. Religion-based food taboos of Muslims, Hindus, and Jews further illustrate the mediation of survival needs through culture. Further, people also have norms about how many meals to have, when to eat them, and which foods to eat at each meal.

Although all people need to sleep, they normally do so at a culturally prescribed time and place. No matter how tired you are at work, it would probably be inappropriate to lie down on the floor or your desk to sleep. People follow culturally prescribed rules about where and when to eliminate body wastes. Most people are taught not to urinate or defecate in public under any circumstances, for example. In fact, doing so may be a criminal offense. All cultures also have norms about when and how to satisfy sexual urges appropriately. These norms include strong taboos that prohibit sexual relations between parents and their children and between siblings.

Societies enculturate children in culturally specific ways. In many societies, children are expected to learn skills informally by observation and imitation. That is, they watch

How many meals do you eat in a day, and at what times? What kinds of foods do you eat at each meal? If you ate eggs at different mealtimes, how might you prepare them differently for each meal, and why? What do your answers to these questions reveal about your cultural norms and values?

taboos
Norms specifying behaviors that are prohibited in a culture.

cultural core
Practices by which people organize their work and produce food and other goods necessary for their survival.

and observe their parents or other elders and learn by trying to do the same thing. Adults may offer guidance, but, for the most part, the child learns by doing and is an active participant in the process. This type of learning takes place in all communities in some contexts, but training and education also take place in formal settings such as schools in some societies.

Casual observation of others as they interact informally also plays a role in enculturation. Through observation, children learn attitudes: They hear what people have to say about themselves and others, and what they think of other people's behavior. They listen to people express their beliefs about the world. Through these conversations and interactions, children learn what is valued and what is criticized by members of the community. In these contexts, they thus gain a sense of personal identity as well as a sense of the world and their place in it.

Culture Is Adaptive

When anthropologists say that culture is adaptive, they are usually referring to behaviors and beliefs that respond to environmental constraints and opportunities that ensure a community's survival. People must adapt to their environment, and culture is their chief mechanism of adaptation. Because of their capacity for adaptation, humans can survive in nearly any environment. Further, people can modify their environments and create artificial ones to enhance survival. Cultural adaptations often involve technological innovation and the elaboration of material culture. For example, people living on islands or along coasts construct rafts, canoes, and boats to cross rivers, bays, and oceans, and people everywhere make a vast array of tools and equipment to help them obtain food and perform other kinds of subsistence tasks. The tools and practices that enable people to satisfy their survival and adaptation needs make up what is called a **cultural core**.

Although adaptation through culture is a fundamental and universal process, not all cultural practices are adaptive. Some practices may be maladaptive or have unintended negative consequences as circumstances change. Sometimes, solving one problem may lead to new, unforeseen problems.

The archaeological record gives us some clues about how agricultural techniques that turned out to have unforeseen negative consequences contributed to the decline of several large and prosperous ancient cultures in both the Eastern and Western Hemispheres. For example, Sumer in ancient Mesopotamia (what is now southern Iraq) had developed large city-states by 3000 B.C. The Sumerian economy was based on intensive farming, made possible by extensive irrigation systems that channeled water from the Tigris and Euphrates rivers to fields. Sumerian farmers produced a greater yield of crops than farmers in the region produce today (Sasson 1995).

Over time, crop yields declined. One reason for the eventual fall of Sumerian civilization was that intensive irrigation increased salinization, or salt content, in the soil. As the land deteriorated, Sumer was no longer able to support large populations without a decline in living standards (Peregrine 2003).

The Industrial Revolution provides a more recent example of unintended negative consequences. Industry's ability to supply millions of people with an ever-increasing amount and variety of products has led to pollution, contamination, and overexploitation of natural resources and nonrenewable energy resources. Many practices like the heavy reliance on chemical fertilizers and pesticides commonly used in industrial agriculture are maladaptive in the long run, although they may increase productivity in the short term.

Thus, the idea that culture is adaptive needs to be considered in context. That is, a particular practice may be adaptive in one situation but not in another. For instance, farming techniques used in temperate climates to increase crop yields may be counterproductive in the Amazon rain forest because the topsoil there is too thin and relatively infertile to sustain them. This is exactly what is happening in parts of the Amazon today, where environmentally inappropriate farming techniques are harming the long-term viability of the soil (Schmink and Wood 1992).

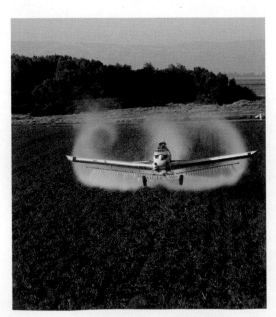

This cropduster's payload is carefully regulated because chemical fertilizers may contaminate food and deplete land productivity in the long term.

CASE STUDY ●

Maladaptive Adaptations: Kuru and Mad Cow

In 1910, a new disease appeared among the South Fore (pronounced For´ray), a farming people of New Guinea. This progressive disease, called *kuru* (meaning "trembling" or "fear" in the Fore language), affects the central nervous system and slowly leads to complete physical incapacitation and death. Victims gradually become unable to sit or walk unaided, focus their eyes, speak clearly, or even swallow. Death usually occurs six to twelve months after the onset of symptoms, although some people may survive as long as two years.

☐ South Fore People

Investigation of the spread of kuru during the 1950s led to suspicion that it correlated with ritual cannibalism by women. In Fore society, as elsewhere in New Guinea, women are the primary farmers, growing sweet potatoes, yams, and other vegetables. They also care for the domesticated pigs each household keeps. Men clear the fields and hunt, but do little farm labor. Women live in small huts with their children and pigs, and men reside communally in a "men's house," eating and sleeping away from their families. Fore culture emphasizes concepts of pollution and danger, against which rituals serve as antidotes. This includes the belief that women pose a threat to male strength and vitality. Men and women also participate in different social and ceremonial activities.

In the early 1900s, South Fore women began practicing cannibalism as part of their mourning ceremonies when a female relative died. This ritual involved eating the brains and body parts of the deceased kin. According to anthropologist Shirley Lindenbaum (1979), this practice had some adaptive value because it provided needed protein, particularly for women. As the population increased and more land came under cultivation, sources of animal protein had declined. In addition, men had access to more high-quality protein than women because they claimed greater rights to the pigs. They believed that other sources of protein, such as insects, frogs, and small mammals, were not only unfit for men but might threaten their health and vigor. Thus, women may have turned to cannibalism to secure more protein.

When a South Fore woman died, her female relatives dismembered her body and ate it. Some of the meat was given to children of either sex, but adult men rarely ate it because of the belief that contact with women (and, logically, eating their flesh) was dangerous and polluting. The Fore did not associate cannibalism with kuru, but they were alarmed by the high incidence of the disease, particularly among women. They attributed kuru to sorcery, a common cause of illness and death in their belief system. When someone died of kuru, kinspeople tried to identify the evildoer, usually accusing someone who might have had reason to wish the victim harm.

Between 1957 and 1968, when the disease was at its height, about 1,000 people died in the South Fore population of 8,000. The fact that nearly all the deaths were of adult women added to the social and economic burden, because women produced the crops, tended the pigs, and gave birth. In some villages, nearly half of the adult female deaths and nearly all of the deaths of children between ages 5 and 16 were due to kuru (Foster and Anderson 1978).

The riddle of kuru was not solved until the late 1960s, when the anthropologist-virologist Carlton Gajdusek discovered that the disease was transmitted by a prion, the same kind of agent responsible for mad cow disease. Prions, slow-acting proteins that attack and destroy brain tissue, remain dormant for years after they are ingested and eventually cause progressive damage to the brain. Thus, when South Fore women and children ate the brains of their female relatives, they unknowingly ingested the cause of their own deaths. The incidence of kuru began to decline after the Australian colonial administration in New Guinea persuaded the Fore to give up ritual cannibalism.

The Fore had adopted a maladaptive practice. Similarly, the spread of mad cow disease in Britain in the 1980s and 1990s resulted from a procedure that seemed financially beneficial in the short term but ultimately proved disastrous. Companies began to use bonemeal derived from sheep brains as cheap protein filler for cattle feed. However, some of the bonemeal was infected with a disease called scrapie, caused by agents of the family of prions similar to those that caused kuru. When cattle ate the infected bonemeal, they developed symptoms similar to those manifested by the Fore.

Once mad cow disease became known and its source identified, more than 140,000 cows in Britain had to be slaughtered to prevent the disease from spreading. In 1996, some people in Britain who died of a prion-caused disease now identified as Creutzfeldt-Jakob disease were thought to have become sick after eating beef infected with mad cow disease. As a consequence, more British cattle were slaughtered to stem a potential epidemic. The European Union banned the export of British beef from 1996 to 1999, and nearly half of the country's 11 million cattle were destroyed. Some British cattle imported into Canada and the United States also were destroyed.

The U.S. Department of Agriculture now bars importation of cattle and many cattle by-products from Britain and most other European nations. The Food and Drug Administration has also banned the use of beef proteins or hormonal extracts from cattle organs in medicines, dietary supplements, and cosmetics. The economic loss to the European and Canadian cattle industry has been disastrous. Using cheap sheep brains to fatten cattle ended up costing millions of dollars and many lives.

What are some other examples of "maladaptive" adaptations in today's world?

Mad cow disease, like kuru among the Fore, demonstrates that people sometimes engage in practices that seem to make sense when first introduced but have consequences in the long term that are maladaptive and even life-threatening. These two syndromes are vastly different in their cultural causes, one stemming from religious beliefs and the other driven by the economic motive to cut costs. However, they share a similar process, namely, that seemingly sensible behavior often has unforeseen and dangerous consequences.

PEARSON

Explore more at
www.myanthrolab.com

Culture Is Integrated

Cultural integration refers to the observation that people's practices and beliefs form a relatively coherent and consistent system. Cultures are not simply random collections of activities but, instead, are patterned and interrelated in systematic ways. For example, behaviors that take place in one domain, such as political organization, tend to be compatible with and support behaviors taking place in other domains, such as family organization. Anthropologists recognize that terms such as *economy, social organization, family organization,* and *government* are not discrete, separable units of activity but are closely intertwined. For example, economic activities are usually integrated with, affect, and are affected by other kinds of activities. The work of obtaining food and other goods and services is often performed by people who occupy particular social roles and statuses. Gender roles may assign men and women different kinds of work in contributing to their household economies. Also, social norms or, in complex societies, laws enacted by legislators and policies formulated by political agencies tend to be consistent with particular economic consequences and to reinforce particular economic goals.

The shared ways that people organize their lives are major integrating factors. In some societies, religious beliefs permeate and guide all aspects of daily life. Religion then becomes an overarching, integrative system of beliefs and practices. People in societies integrated by religion might perform daily rituals to bless and safeguard themselves and their families; they may recite prayers when hunting or planting crops to ensure success; and they may ask for spirit protection when engaging in any dangerous activity. People in

cultural integration
Tendency for people's practices and beliefs to form a relatively coherent and consistent system.

these societies believe that the human and spiritual realms are not separable but that spiritual forces are omnipresent and continually affect their lives.

Naturally, not all aspects of cultural behavior and belief are internally consistent or integrated with all others. Humans and their experiences are not so neat and tidy. Nevertheless, cultural systems as wholes tend toward consistency. A consequence of this consistency and integration is that change in one societal domain causes change in others (see "Women and Work in the United States," for example).

CASE STUDY ◉

Consequences of Cultural Integration: Women and Work in the United States

In the United States, changes in women's participation in paid employment have affected both their roles in other spheres of life and the prevailing attitudes about men and women (Fox and Hesse-Biber 1984). Women's rates of employment began to rise significantly during World War II, as a consequence of the nation's military and economic policies. As millions of men entered the armed forces, millions of jobs necessary to support the economy and the war effort were left vacant. Public policy encouraged women to do their patriotic duty by working in factories and offices, where they had previously met resistance and discrimination. The banner of women's rights, which had won American women the right to vote in 1920, was raised again.

After the war, many women returned to exclusively domestic roles, but others remained in the work force, partly for personal reasons and partly to improve their family's standard of living.

Also, work outside the home gave women a degree of financial equality with their husbands. Women's economic gains contributed to rising rates of divorce because wives could sometimes afford to leave unhappy marriages, and husbands could leave if they felt that their ex-wives could be at least partially self-supporting (Costello et al. 1998). In intact families, greater financial equality as well as the greater amount of time that women spent outside the home contributed to shifting the roles of husbands toward some household and child-care responsibilities.

By the late twentieth century, the percentage of marriages that ended in divorce had risen, and the social stigma formerly associated with divorce had all but disappeared. Also, women's paid employment and opportunities to make prominent contributions in public arenas had expanded. Today, more legislators, governors, and heads of government agencies are women. Women's leadership roles in religion have also broadened; many Protestant and Jewish denominations ordain women ministers and rabbis. More women have advanced educational degrees and are more accepted in formerly male-dominated occupations and professions, such as law and law enforcement, the military, and the building trades.

Changes in women's roles have also affected how men think about themselves and their work. Husbands now expect their wives to contribute to household incomes. And work roles for men have become more flexible. A father could be a stay-at-home Dad if his wife's work brought in more money than his or if he simply preferred that role. And society has become more accepting of men working in certain jobs traditionally associated with women, such as nursing and elementary school teaching.

Thus, within a mere fifty years, changes in one societal sphere in the United States led to changes both in other spheres and in people's thoughts and behaviors. These multiple and interrelating effects illustrate how cultural integration can lead to cultural transformation.

Explore more at
www.myanthrolab.com

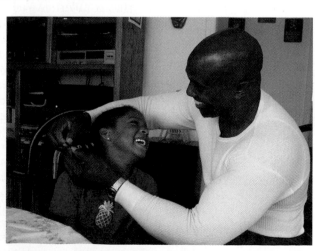

Changes in the roles and status of women in American society have affected men's lives as well as the society as a whole.

Culture Is Based on Symbols

People's behaviors and understanding of the world are based on meanings expressed through symbols. A **symbol** is a sound or object that represents or stands for an idea, event, meaning, or sentiment. Language is a pervasive and powerful symbol system. Words in any language are just sequences of sounds, but each sequence is a symbol of something other than the sounds themselves. The collection of sounds in each word in this sentence, for instance, stands for some arbitrarily assigned meaning.

Symbols permeate human culture in ways other than language. Objects, art, and artistic performances may represent powerful cultural ideas and attitudes. The colors and designs of national flags, for instance, come to be associated with complex levels of meaning. People can understand those meanings by examining the contexts of flag use, the way people talk about their national colors, and the way people react to them. Flags are used to symbolically represent a country, a territorial and cultural unit differentiated from all other similarly organized territorial and cultural units. Flags take on additional associations, demonstrated by the emotional reactions they can trigger in observers. People may use their country's flag in ways that show their attitudes and political beliefs. For example, in the United States, after the al Qaeda attack on 9/11, flag pins became necessities for many political figures and represented a show of support for the "war on terror" that the United States undertook.

Religion, too, is a domain filled with symbolic meanings. Believers invest tremendous importance in objects considered to have religious significance. Ordinary objects and substances used in rituals take on sacred properties. Books, cups, images, pieces of cloth or wood, or foodstuffs can be symbols of beliefs and can evoke powerful emotions and dramatize sacred actions. Symbolic culture thus includes both sacred and secular meanings and all the ways in which those meanings are communicated.

Culture often is expressed in symbolic interaction between individuals using verbal and nonverbal language. Thus, language can also be used to challenge basic assumptions encoded in ordinary speech. For example, a dialect of Caribbean immigrants and their descendants in Great Britain, called Afro-Lingua, focuses on the ways that standard English transmits common cultural assumptions about race in the uses and meanings that associate *white* with "good" and *black* with "bad." For example, in common English expressions, "a black day" means a day when things go drastically wrong, and "a black sheep" means an outcast family member (Bones 1986, 46). Afro-Lingua speakers might refer to "a white day" and "a white sheep" in equivalent contexts. In addition, Afro-Lingua also changes syllables in some English words to highlight cultural and political meanings: the word *politics* is transformed into *politricks,* and *oppression* becomes *downpression* (Wong 1986, 119).

Humor is another form of symbolic cultural communication. For example, Western Apache communities in New Mexico have a repertoire of joke routines that ridicule Anglos by imitating and exaggerating their intrusive, domineering communicative styles (Basso 1979). Apaches find these Anglo communication styles insensitive at best or offensive. Scorned behaviors include making direct eye contact with or staring at interlocutors, touching another person while talking to him or her, calling casual acquaintances "friend," and asking intrusive, personal questions. Through their informal comic routines, Apaches share the opposite norms and values.

Both the changes in English expressions used by speakers of Afro-Lingua and the joking routines of Western Apaches demonstrate the ways that symbolic behavior can be used to challenge dominant values. Through symbolic practices, people can forge their unity with others and can simultaneously develop and transmit messages of resistance. Afro-Lingua speakers defy commonplace notions of race and power; Western Apaches resist communicative norms imposed on them by dominant Anglo society.

Culture Organizes the Way People Think About the World

Through exposure to cultural symbols, enculturation, and the acquisition of shared cultural concepts, people develop ways of thinking about themselves, their lives, other people, and the world. These underlying shared concepts become so ingrained that they are taken for granted, assumed to be true. People understand them as natural and commonsense. These are **naturalized concepts,** ideas thought to be essential and to exist in nature.

What emotional reactions can images of national flags stir? How has the American flag been used to display both positive and negative feelings about the U.S. government or its policies?

GLOBALIZATION

Afro-Lingua is a language that was created to symbolically challenge the basic assumptions encoded in the ordinary speech of European colonizers of the Caribbean.

What would you learn about cultural communication from studying in your workplace or dorm?

symbol
A word, image, or object that stands for cultural ideas or sentiments.

naturalized concepts
Ideas and behaviors so deeply embedded in a culture that they are regarded as universally normal or natural.

These Chinese and American children are forming group identities based on symbiotic culture.

All societies have a core of naturalized ideas, based on societal norms. For example, in most capitalist societies, it is taken for granted that people want to own property and obtain wealth. It is assumed that people are naturally competitive and want to continually acquire more property, own larger and more expensive houses, and have unlimited access to possessions. Yet, people in these societies generally may not understand that their attitudes and values about property and wealth stem from the kind of economic system they live in. Models of gender are also deeply naturalized in people's behaviors and attitudes. We come to believe that men's and women's roles and value are derived from qualities, feelings, and needs inherent in women and men rather than understanding that these gender models are largely derived from culture. In other words, people who lack an anthropological perspective think that their attitudes and values are natural and universal rather than products of their culture. Thus, naturalized concepts orient people's thinking about themselves and the world, forming a background ideology that gives meaning to people's behaviors and attitudes. To the extent that they shape the way we view other cultures, they are also a source of ethnocentrism.

Although all cultures have fundamental organizing concepts, these principles may be challenged from within the society. In all societies, members of different subcultures or subgroups hold alternative and conflicting values. Alternative views may be discussed and debated in the context of mutual respect or they may erupt in more contentious challenges, in what some observers refer to as **culture wars**. Expressions of antipathy between conservatives and liberals over many social policy issues in the United States, such as gun control, abortion rights, gay rights, and immigration policy, are examples of so-called culture wars.

On the other hand, individuals and groups engaging in practices with underlying meanings that conflict with prevailing assumptions and norms may be participants in a **counterculture**—an alternative culture model. Members of a counterculture view themselves as in active opposition to dominant cultural themes and values. For example, the hippies of the 1960s openly rejected prevailing puritanical attitudes toward sex, the materialism of contemporary society, and the militaristic policies of the government as it escalated the war in Vietnam.

Challenges to widely recognized assumptions often come from members of groups that are marginalized or oppressed, or who hold different **worldviews** than those of the dominant groups or elites. For example, apartheid, South Africa's dominant racist cultural ideology until the 1990s, was imposed by a powerful white minority that had inherited power through colonial rule. That rule was challenged by the majority of black South Africans, who eventually overturned that ideology and rebelled against the government that oppressed them. Black South Africans asserted not only their political rights but also their right to replace the cultural model of white supremacy with one of racial equality. Thus, many political movements seek more than a reordering of social and political forces. They also seek the institutionalization of new cultural models as organizing principles in their society.

What are some examples of culture wars in U.S. society today? What are some examples of countercultures in U.S. history?

culture wars
Internal disagreements in a society about cultural models or about how society or the world should be organized.

counterculture
An alternative cultural model within a society that expresses different views about the way that society should be organized.

worldview
A culture-based, often ethnocentric way that people see the world and other peoples.

TABLE 2.1 CHARACTERISTICS OF CULTURE

Culture Is Shared	Behavior, attitudes, and ideas are formed through interaction with others. **Norms:** Sets of expectations and attitudes that people have about appropriate behavior. **Subculture:** A group whose members interact more frequently among themselves and share attitudes and practices that are distinct from others.
Culture Is Learned	Culture is acquired rather than inherited. **Enculturation:** The learning of one's cultural behaviors, attitudes, and values.
Culture Is Adaptive	Aspects of behavior and belief are responses to environmental constraints and the need to ensure a community's survival. **Cultural core:** Basic practices that function to satisfy people's adaptive needs.
Culture Is Integrated	Practices and beliefs that form a relatively coherent and consistent system. **Cultural model:** Comprehensive shared ideas about the ideal culture.
Culture Is Based on Symbols	People's behavior and understanding of the world are based on meanings expressed through language, art, and symbolic objects. **Symbols:** Words, images, or objects that stand for cultural ideas or sentiments.
Culture Organizes the Way People Think About the World	**Naturalized concepts:** Ideas and behaviors so deeply embedded in a culture that they are regarded as universally normal or natural. **Worldview:** The culture-based, often ethnocentric way that people see the world and other peoples. **Counterculture:** Alternative cultural model within a society that expresses opposition to dominant social and political views.

culture contact
Direct interaction between peoples of different cultures through migration, trade, invasion, or conquest.

syncretism
Process by which a cultural product is created when people adapt a cultural item selectively borrowed from another culture to fit their existing culture.

Similarly, through symbolic culture, some segments of a society might resist the official culture or offer an alternative cultural model. In the Middle East and North Africa, women's challenges to the ideology of male dominance often take the form of poetry and song, a low-risk context for expressing discontent. Bedouin women, for example, recite poetry and compose songs expressing their longings for love and respect. Song lyrics express passion and joy in attentions they receive from clandestine lovers (Abu-Lughod 1986; 1990). Artistic genres thus permit women to verbalize private feelings that run contrary to accepted norms of female deference and modesty.

Table 2.1 summarizes the characteristics of culture as it is defined in this chapter. This section then closes with a story in the In Their Own Voices section on pages 34–35, about an anthropologist's field experience that highlights the challenges of understanding cultures as unique collections of symbols and meanings.

REVIEW — ⦿ Characteristics of culture include the fact that it is shared. Individuals who belong to a culture share assumptions about the world and develop cultural models and societal norms and taboos that define how one should and should not behave. Members of different subcultures in a society share culture differently. Culture is also learned through enculturation. We are enculturated both formally and informally through social interactions with other members of society. Culture is adaptive in that people change their culture when needed or when influenced to change. The knowledge, skills, and tools people use to survive and adapt are referred to as the cultural core. Culture is integrated—that is, aspects of culture are interconnected and mutually reinforcing. Thus, cultural integration means that change in one aspect of culture leads to changes in other aspects. The existence of culture wars and countercultures within a society illustrates, however, that cultures are not rigidly integrated, that alternative cultural models coexist. Culture is based on symbols, and language is the most important symbol system people use. Symbolic objects and symbolic communication are used in diverse contexts, such as religion and humor. Culture influences the way people organize their experience and their worldview. They use naturalized concepts to apply their cultural assumptions to other people's ways of life.

CULTURE CHANGE

Cultures are dynamic systems that respond to societal and historical changes from numerous sources. Some sources of culture change are internal, emerging from new practices and attitudes, technological innovations, or adaptations to the consequences of earlier practices. Other sources of culture change are external, emerging as people borrow ideas or artifacts from their neighbors or from people with whom they interact through migration, trade, or other contacts. Some borrowings take place in friendly interactions during **culture contact,** but others are forced on people, as in conquest or foreign intervention.

Cultural changes stimulated by external culture change then typically undergo further change through internal processes. As the Zuni story you read in Chapter 1 showed, people usually adapt outside cultural borrowings to their own cultures. They may borrow only parts of a cultural item, whether a story or a way of organizing economic activity, and combine those parts with items that already exist in their cultural repertoire. For example, in the realm of religion, people often combine elements of their traditional beliefs with those that they learn from external sources as a consequence of culture contact. This process, called **syncretism,** is seen in religions such as Santeria, which combines traditional Afro-Caribbean beliefs in magic and witchcraft with Roman Catholicism. Spanish colonizers in the Caribbean derisively called this religion of the Yoruba—and other Bantu slaves from Nigeria, Senegal, and the Guinea Coast—Santeria, "Way of the Saints."

Anthropologists have other terms to describe the kinds of internal change that take place following culture contact, depending on the power relations between peoples and the extent of change. **Assimilation** occurs when a less numerous and less powerful group changes its ways to blend in with the dominant culture. In assimilating, people abandon or modify their prior beliefs and practices and adopt the cultural repertoire of the dominant population. For example, immigrants may voluntarily change their national and cultural identities by assimilating the language and culture of their new country. Assimilation is also sometimes forced on people by a dominant culture, especially in the context of conquest and colonization.

A group's adjustment to living within another, more dominant, culture while at the same time maintaining its original cultural identity is called **acculturation.** For example, many Native Americans in the United States and Canada adopt many features of dominant American culture such as the economic and political systems, but maintain their own languages, family systems, and religious beliefs. The term **cultural pluralism** describes a stratified society that contains many diverse cultural groups who ideally live together equally and harmoniously. Other complex changes that occur through combinations of external and internal processes include economic transformations, such as **modernization,** based on industrialism and a market economy.

Internal Culture Change

Early anthropologists, such as Edward B. Tylor, believed that cultures evolve through various stages, from a simpler and more primitive state to a complex and more culturally advanced state. To Tylor and his nineteenth-century contemporaries, middle-class Euro-American culture represented the pinnacle of this **cultural evolution,** which other

GLOBALIZATION

Culture contact, a major force in the process of globalization, leads to several strategies and consequences of culture change, including acculturation, assimilation, and reactive adaptation.

assimilation
Process by which a less numerous and less powerful cultural group changes its ways and cultural identity to blend in with the dominant culture.

acculturation
Process by which a group adjusts to living within a dominant culture while at the same time maintaining its original cultural identity.

cultural pluralism
Condition in a stratified society in which many diverse cultural groups ideally live together equally and harmoniously without losing their cultural identities and diversity.

modernization
Complex culture change, both internal and external, based on industrialism and a transnational market economy.

cultural evolution
Belief of early anthropologists that cultures evolve through various stages from a simpler and more primitive state to a complex and more culturally advanced state.

Aboriginal star singer Archie Roach, shown here with Ruby Hunter, was a member of Australia's "Stolen Generation." Roach was put into a Salvation Army Home at age three and then fostered out to three different white families.

IN THEIR OWN VOICES

Hamlet and the Tiv

An anthropologist's effort to explain Shakespeare's Hamlet to Tiv villagers in central Nigeria illustrates how far both the anthropologist and the Tiv culture shape the way they think about the world. When Laura Bohannan lived among the Tiv, they were a farming people living in small villages. Village life centered on groups of families related through men, with fathers, sons, and brothers forming the core of households. After marriage, women moved from their families to live with their husband's relatives. Men prepared fields for planting, but women planted seeds, weeded the plants, and harvested crops. In addition to their families, men depended on their age-mates—other men of the same age group—for help in times of trouble.

Bohannan was prompted to tell the story of Hamlet because she thought it had a universal meaning that people everywhere would understand in the same way. The Tiv elders also thought the story had universal meaning—but a different one. To both Bohannan and the elders, their particular understanding seemed obvious, showing how powerful cultural assumptions can be. If you need to refresh your memory on what Hamlet is about, read the summary at http://shakespeare.palomar.edu/lambtales/LTHAMLET.HTM. To read the rest of Bohannan's amusing and insightful article, search the Internet for "Shakespeare in the Bush."

The following excerpt expresses the views of both Bohannan and Tiv villagers on the meaning of the play:

I began in the proper style, "Not yesterday, not yesterday, but long ago, a thing occurred. One night three men were keeping watch outside the homestead of the great chief, when suddenly they saw the former chief approach them."

"Why was he no longer their chief?"

"He was dead," I explained. "That is why they were troubled and afraid when they saw him."

"Impossible," began one of the elders. "Of course it wasn't the dead chief. It was an omen sent by a witch. . . ."

Slightly shaken, I continued. "One of these three was a man who knew things"—the closest translation for *scholar*, but unfortunately it also meant *witch*. "So he spoke to the

dead chief saying, "Tell us what we must do so you may rest in your grave," but the dead chief did not answer. . . .

There was a general shaking of heads round the circle. "Had the dead chief no living brothers? Or was this son the chief?" . . .

"He had one living brother who became the chief when the elder brother died. In our country the son is next to the father. The dead chief's younger brother had become the great chief. He had also married his elder brother's widow only about a month after the funeral." . . .

"He did well," the old man beamed and announced to the others, "I told you that if we knew more about Europeans, we could find they really were very like us. In our country also," he added to me, "the younger brother marries the elder brother's widow and becomes the father of his children. Now, if your uncle, who married your widowed mother, is your father's full brother, then he will be a real father to you. Did Hamlet's father and uncle have one mother?"

His question barely penetrated my mind; I was too upset and thrown too far off balance by having one of the most important elements of Hamlet knocked straight out of the picture. Rather uncertainly I said that I thought they had the

---

cultures could naturally and eventually achieve. Others treated the concept of cultural evolution as analogous to biological evolution, claiming that some cultures were naturally superior to others, modeled on the concepts of competition and the survival of the fittest. This faulty reasoning, known as **social Darwinism,** claimed that the wealth and power of Western societies were due to their natural and cultural superiority rather than to the consequences of historical processes. Social Darwinists saw competition between societies as based on similar processes as biological evolution. However, they failed to recognize that particular events and developments in fact contributed to the ability of some societies to dominate others. They also used models of efficiency

social Darwinism
Early belief that cultures compete for survival of the fittest, as in the process of natural selection in biological evolution.

same mother, but I wasn't sure—the story didn't say. The old man told me severely that these genealogical details made all the difference and that when I got home I must ask the elders about it. . . .

Determined to save what I could of the mother motif, I took a deep breath and began again. "The son Hamlet was very sad because his mother had married again so quickly. There was no need for her to do so, and it is our custom for a widow not to go to her next husband until she has mourned for two years."

"Two years is too long," objected the elder's wife. "Who will hoe your farms for you while you have no husband?"

I gave up. . . .

"That night . . . the dead chief again appeared, and . . . Hamlet followed his dead father off to one side. When they were alone, Hamlet's dead father spoke."

"Omens can't talk!" The old man was emphatic. . . .

"It was Hamlet's dead father. It was a thing we call a *ghost*." I had to use the English word, for unlike many of the neighboring tribes, these people didn't believe in the survival after death of any individuating part of the personality. . . .

"Dead men can't walk," protested my audience as one man.

I was quite willing to compromise. "A ghost is the dead man's shadow."

But again they objected. "Dead men cast no shadows."

"They do in my country," I snapped. . . .

"Anyhow," I resumed, "Hamlet's dead father said that his own brother, the one who became chief, had poisoned him. He wanted Hamlet to avenge him. Hamlet believed this in his heart, for he did not like his father's brother." . . .

"Now Hamlet's age-mates," I continued, "had brought with them a famous storyteller. Hamlet decided to have this man tell the chief and all his homestead a story about a man who had poisoned his brother because he desired his brother's wife and wished to be chief himself. Hamlet was sure the great chief could not hear the story without making a sign if he was indeed guilty, and then he would discover whether his dead father had told him the truth. . . . It was true, for when the storyteller was telling his tale before all the homestead, the great chief rose in fear. Afraid that Hamlet knew his secret he planned to have him killed." . . .

This time I had shocked my audience seriously. "For a man to raise his hand against his father's brother and the one

who has become his father—that is a terrible thing. The elders ought to let such a man be bewitched. . . .

I then pointed out that after all the man had killed Hamlet's father.

"No," pronounced the old man, speaking less to me than to the young men sitting behind the elders. "If your father's brother has killed your father, you must appeal to your father's age-mates; they may avenge him. No man may use violence against his senior relatives. . . . But if his father's brother had indeed been wicked enough to bewitch Hamlet and make him mad that would be a good story indeed, for it would be his fault that Hamlet, being mad, no longer had any sense and thus was ready to kill his father's brother."

There was a murmur of applause. Hamlet was again a good story to them, but it no longer seemed quite the same story to me. . . .

The old man made soothing noises. "You tell the story well, and we are listening. But it is clear that the elders of your country have never told you what the story really means. No, don't interrupt! We believe you when you say your marriage customs are different, or your clothes and weapons. But people are the same everywhere; therefore, there are always witches and it is we, the elders, who know how witches work. We told you it was the great chief who wished to kill Hamlet, and now your own words have proved us right. . . .

"Sometime," concluded the old man, "you must tell us some more stories of your country. We, who are elders, will instruct you in their true meaning, so that when you return to your own land your elders will see that you have not been sitting in the bush, but among those who know things and who have taught you wisdom."

Explore more at
www.myanthrolab.com

From Laura Bohannan, "Shakespeare in the Bush," *Natural History* (August/September 1966).

CRITICAL THINKING QUESTION

What Tiv cultural assumptions and values caused them to interpret the story of *Hamlet* differently?

and progress, analogous to biological processes, in their analyses of cultural development and change.

Today, however, evolutionary biologists study the adaptive value of social behavior, cognitive skills, and the capacity for both material and symbolic culture, all of which have contributed to the evolutionary success of the primates, and which all living human groups possess equally. Thus, **culture history** may be a more apt term than cultural evolution for ongoing culture change in which people respond and adapt to their environment and experiences. In adapting, people make themselves. That is, people develop, define, and direct their own cultural and ethnic identities, a process called

What are some problems with applying principles of biological evolution to explanations of culture change?

culture history
Ongoing culture change in which people respond and adapt to their environment.

What do these movie posters suggest about changes in American social and cultural norms over the past 60 years?

ethnogenesis
Ongoing process in which people develop, define, and direct their own cultural and ethnic identities.

inventions
New technologies and systems of knowledge.

innovation
Process by which new technologies and systems of knowledge are based on or built from previous tools, knowledge, and skills.

revolution
Process by which people try to change their culture or overturn the social order and replace it with a new, ideal society and culture.

ethnogenesis (Hill 1992). This concept of culture change views human beings as agents in their own history, continually creating and re-creating the conditions of their lives.

Some changes in societies are not intentional, like ethnogenesis, but result from gradual shifting of public norms and private sentiments. For example, in art and public performance, certain behaviors and language use that were unacceptable in the past have become standard, although not without arousing conflict among some sectors of the population.

Since the 1960s, the content of American films has changed considerably. In previous periods, violence generally was shown only from a distance, and its effects on the human body were not made explicit. Today, the depiction of explicit violence and its effects is commonplace. Nudity and sexual activity also have become routine in American films and videos, and language is not censored as it was in the past. These changes reflect changes in attitudes and values rather than in technology. And these changes are embedded in the wider social and political contexts of the times. The Motion Picture Production Code of the 1930s, which imposed strict limits on language, subject matter, and sexual representation, has been replaced by a rating system identifying film content. Publicized ratings warn potential viewers who do not want themselves or their children exposed to particular content.

Another source of internal culture change is the adaptations that people make by inventing new technologies and skills to better adjust to existing conditions or to deal with new problems. **Inventions** usually are based on previous tools, knowledge, and skills in a process called **innovation.** New environmental challenges and opportunities stimulate innovation and the invention of new adaptive strategies. Some technology-based cultural transformations are so sweeping that they are referred to as revolutions. **Revolution,** in which people try to overturn the social and political order and replace it with a new, ideal society and culture, is another widespread form of internal culture change that has been a part of the history of many state societies.

External Culture Change

Culture change also occurs through culture contact as people migrate, trade, invade, intermarry, or interact in other ways. People learn ideas and skills and borrow tools, foods, clothing, and luxury items from other people with whom they have direct or indirect contact. This process, called **diffusion,** is responsible for the spread of material objects and cultural practices from one place to another.

Diffusion may be local, such as the spread of the invention of blow darts and use of poisons among some native peoples of South America. Diffusion also can be widespread, even global within geographic constraints, such as the invention of agriculture, which spread east and west along certain latitudes over thousands of years, based on the cultivation of diverse kinds of grain. In addition to diffusion, independent invention may account for the appearance of similar cultural traits in different parts of the world. An example is the invention of writing systems, which likely occurred more than once in prehistory among different peoples in the ancient Middle East, Mexico, and China.

Invasion and conquest also are common causes of external culture change. Most early state societies probably developed partly through the process of expanding into neighboring territories and incorporating the peoples (Carniero 1970). Colonization or conquest not only forced indigenous peoples to accept foreign goods and practices but also compelled them to alter many of their cultural practices to conform to their conquerors' ways. The attitudes and values of subject peoples eventually transformed as well to be more consistent with the changes in their behavior. However, subjects of colonial or conquered states are not passive pawns in national and global policies and processes. Rather, indigenous peoples make choices and engage in actions that, in their views, best achieve their goals of maintaining their communities while adapting to their changing conditions. The situations of colonial peoples and their strategies for survival are further explored in Chapters 16 and 17.

The imposition of British colonial rule on the Luo of Kenya in the nineteenth century, for example, led to many interrelated changes in the economic, social, and political systems of that tribal society. The Luo (speakers of the Luo language, today known mainly as the Karivongo) settled in Kenya and Tanzania in the fifteenth or sixteenth century, migrating south from the Sudan. In the Sudan, their economy had been centered on cattle herding but shifted gradually to farming after they arrived in Kenya. This change affected gender relations because men had been primarily responsible for herding the cattle and women were the farmers. Following Luo custom, land was owned communally by groups of relatives headed by men, but women actually controlled the production and distribution of crops resulting from their labor. In the colonial and postcolonial periods, however, women's rights to the land and their economic independence were undermined by British land reforms.

In 1899, the British colonial government imposed policies aimed at consolidating individual holdings that were intentionally scattered in different locations. Traditional Luo patterns of landholding gave individuals use rights in scattered parcels so that they could obtain food resources in different ecological zones. People thus could plant a variety of crops suited to each zone. British authorities did not understand this custom, however; in their view, the traditional system was inefficient. In keeping with European ideals, the British combined landholdings into single parcels, which were registered in the names of male heads of households.

In addition, British colonial authorities imposed hut taxes that had to be paid in cash. To obtain cash for taxes, Luo men as heads of households often had to find wage work away from their local communities. At the same time that taxation was a financial burden, men benefited from colonial policies. Participating in the cash economy gave them access to valuable manufactured goods, and their official status as individual landowners gave them greater power and authority. To raise more cash, Luo men turned land production over from home use to cash crops for export, making families more dependent on more expensive imported food to sustain themselves. The Kenyan government continued these land policies after independence in 1960.

Colonized or conquered peoples have responded to external sources of culture change in diverse ways, including assimilation and acculturation, discussed earlier in the chapter. Another kind of outcome is **reactive adaptation,** in which people react against loss, deprivation, and oppression through passive resistance or violence. Traditional religious leaders and beliefs may play a role in social movements aimed at restoring or revitalizing the traditional culture. A classic example of a **revitalization movement** is the Ghost Dance movement of the North American Plains Indians (Wallace 1956; Mooney 1965). This arose

GLOBALIZATION

Today as in the past, diffusion is a major force in the process of globalization, as concepts, technologies, languages, and symbols spread from one culture to another, aided in part by past conquests and the history of colonization.

diffusion
Spread of ideas, material objects, and cultural practices from one society to another through direct and indirect culture contact.

reactive adaptation
Coping response to loss and deprivation of captive, conquered, or oppressed peoples.

revitalization movement
Type of nonviolent reactive adaptation in which people try to resurrect their culture heroes and restore their traditional way of life.

global culture
A constellation of technologies, practices, attitudes, values, and symbols that spread internationally and enmesh nations and communities throughout the world in networks of power and influence.

in 1889, at a time when native peoples had been forcibly confined to reservations after brutal military campaigns. Most of their land had been taken from them, and measles and smallpox decimated their communities. Reduced to poverty and dependence on rations meagerly handed out by the U.S. government, a spiritual reawakening took place.

Begun by a northern Paiute prophet named Wovoka, the Ghost Dance movement predicted an imminent end to the world during a cataclysmic earthquake, to be followed by the reappearance of Native Americans who had died and the disappearance of white people. Although Wovoka taught the necessity of establishing peace, harmony, and good moral principles, his message was distorted by frightened settlers and government officials who feared an armed uprising of impoverished and beleaguered native people. Performances of the Ghost Dance were banned, and participants were threatened with imprisonment.

Finally, after outlawing the dances and harassing participants, government officials in charge of the Lakota reservations in South Dakota sent Army units to arrest Ghost Dance adherents. The units entrapped more than 300 Lakotas and massacred them at Wounded Knee Creek on December 29, 1890. This final tragedy put an end to Ghost Dance performances. Since then, the message of the Ghost Dance has changed from foretelling the end of American control to focusing on personal improvement and spirituality (Kehoe 1989). Nevertheless, Wounded Knee continues as a potent symbol of U.S. government policies that crushed native peoples and their indigenous cultures.

REVIEW — Culture change can result from either internal or external forces, which usually are mutually reinforcing. Internal culture changes can come about from technological inventions or innovation within a society or can be introduced through culture contact and spread through borrowing, or diffusion. In syncretism, people modify and adapt borrowed items of religious belief and practice to fit their own culture. Culture history and ethnogenesis describe change processes within a society that are self-defining as well as adaptive to both internal and external stimuli. Although the capacity for culture is an important adaptation in human evolution, culture change does not involve cultural evolution, an outdated idea based on beliefs in human progress, racial superiority, and social Darwinism. Outcomes of culture contact include, among others, assimilation and acculturation. Cultural pluralism describes culturally diverse societies in which groups have equal status under the law. Reactive adaptation is an outcome based on unrelieved stresses, often expressed through either violence or spiritual revitalization movements. Sweeping social and culture changes involving both internal and external factors stem from economic and political changes, such as the processes of modernization and revolution.

GLOBAL CULTURE

It is commonplace to hear people say that cultures throughout the world are becoming more similar, that a kind of **global culture** is spreading to all corners of the earth. Global culture "clubs" are springing up on the Internet for people who want to participate actively in this ongoing trend. The term *globalization* can apply to many historical periods when developing states expanded their boundaries, incorporating and transforming neighboring societies. In addition, the spread of proselytizing religions (Christianity, Buddhism, Islam) contributed to fundamental changes in the societies they affected, beyond the domain of religion itself but including social relations, economic and political systems, and aesthetic and ethical values. Today's globalization stems from economic and political processes that have expanded from their original centers in Europe and the United States, as the major capitalist industrialized regions, to many other countries. These processes have affected national governments, urban centers, and the cultures of traditional and indigenous peoples everywhere.

Globalization has multiple and complex cultural consequences, summed up by three concepts: homogenization, polarization, and hybridization (Holton 2000). Proponents of the homogenization theory claim that contemporary globalization is creating a

GLOBALIZATION

Today's globalization stems from economic and political processes that spread their influence through consumerism, the mass media, and information technologies. How should we evaluate the consequences of this globalization?

homogenized world culture dominated by similar values and practices. They stress the influence of Euro-American economic and political forces, associated with cultural values and norms. Multinational companies stimulate consumer buying throughout the world, and Hollywood images create an idealized version of American society. Homogenization also stems from the internationalization of elite classes and interests. In this view, elites from disparate countries identify more with each other than they do with their own compatriots, participating in and promulgating similar values. However, although Western influence is of course significant, homogenization theorists may overstate the global role of Euro-American culture and may understate processes of resistance.

The concept of polarization emerges in part as a reaction to homogenization. That is, the pressure toward homogenization creates antagonisms because members of other societies with different values and practices react against the influence of Euro-American culture and assert their own national and cultural identities. Discussions of polarization tend to focus on a dichotomy of West and non-West, especially centered in the Islamic, Afrocentric, and Confucian worlds (Holton 2000, 147). Resistance to homogenization may be motivated by authentic antiglobalization forces, particularly among indigenous communities, or by the desire to assert alternative globalizing influences.

Finally, the third concept, hybridization, stresses the development of ever-greater variety and vitality through new cross-cultural combinations of cultural elements that result from the worldwide exchange of products, technologies, information, and artistic expression. Hybridization can be fostered by travel, migration, and intermarriage. It also results from exposure to media, especially music and film that promote familiarity with aesthetic forms from other societies. In addition, many migrants are in fact transnational people, going back and forth between their country of origin and their country of settlement for visits to family and friends. These migrants are often active carriers of new forms of cultural expressions from their multiple life contexts. Hybridization is not uniform and allows for local differences in the mixture of cultural forms.

Although culture change is a continual and universal feature of societies, it occurs both locally and globally in the context of "friction" (Tsing 2005, 1) between various societies. And although global interactions have the potential to develop similarities throughout the world, globalizing processes have specific effects on the local level, leading to distinctions in access to products, services, and technologies, and resulting in inequalities in consumption.

Globalizing tendencies are as old as contacts among societies, but the scale and tempo of change has increased dramatically in the last century. The historical origin of contemporary globalization can be traced to European mercantile and colonial expansion of the fifteenth and sixteenth centuries. For hundreds of years, globalization was centered in Europe, especially in Great Britain, France, Portugal, and Spain. In the late nineteenth century, the United States began to influence other regions, particularly Latin America and the Pacific, competing with the European powers. In the mid-twentieth century, after World War II, the centers of world power were concentrated in the United States and the Soviet Union, seen as representing opposing views of economic, political, and cultural orders. After the early 1990s and the dismantlement of the Soviet Union, world power centered in the United States, although several countries in Asia, especially China, Japan, South Korea, and India, as well as the European Union, now exert substantial economic and diplomatic influence. Due in part to the speed of transportation, communication, and information technologies, the influence of capitalist economics and political interests intensified and accelerated throughout the world. However, the cultural and political domination of the West is not uncontested and is countered by Asian economic giants. In addition, cultural influences flow from non-Western countries as Asian and African music, comics, video games, and other items of popular culture are adopted worldwide.

Principal agents of globalization are multinational corporations, which control much of the world's industry and commerce, and the mass media. A global network of finance, manufacture, export, and import has developed, incorporating every nation and many local communities. The prices that farmers receive for their crops are affected by worldwide economic forces through linkages from local to regional, and from national to international networks. Wages received in the manufacturing sector are also connected to worldwide patterns of labor and job availability. National and multinational consumer

As governments, corporations, and the media spread their political, economic, and cultural influences, the traditional ways of life of indigenous peoples like this Tarahumara woman are increasingly threatened.

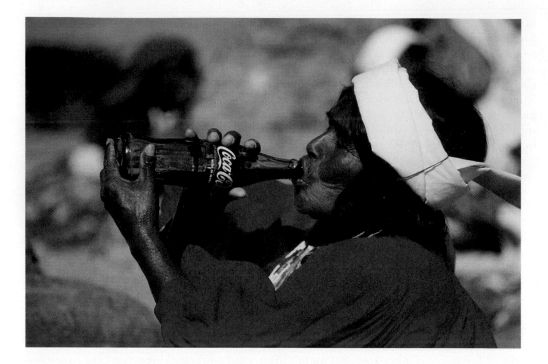

outlets sell their products in nearly every country. Companies such as McDonald's, Coca-Cola, Sony, and Nintendo are icons of global consumerism. Companies and their advertisers create demand for consumer goods through mass communication systems, such as radio, television, the cinema, and the Internet. Although the spread of products, technologies, and information systems seems relentless, these processes are not inevitable but rather are themselves affected by both global and local patterns of consumption and resistance.

Chapters 16 and 17 further explore the long-term effects of colonialism and the efforts of indigenous and local societies to participate in a globalized, modern economy without sacrificing their cultural traditions, natural resources, economic interests, and social welfare (see also the Anthropology Applied feature). Participation remains a challenge, however. Powerful state societies tend to sanction world domination through globalization on the assumptions that technological advances, industrialism, capitalism, environmental exploitation, and democracy are naturally necessary and superior, and that global progress toward those goals is good. Worldwide climate change can be seen as a maladaptive consequence of some of these attitudes. The loss or destruction of other ways of life is seen as sometimes unfortunate but nevertheless inevitable and unavoidable. However, the destruction of indigenous cultures may only be inevitable because the majority of people in the world accept it as such. This too may be a concept that has become naturalized, consistent with profit-oriented notions of progress and development.

Do you think the assumptions used to justify globalization are warranted? Why or why not?

REVIEW —◉ Globalization is a process that historically has had many centers of power as states and empires have expanded their borders and have widened their economic and political influence. However, what is usually referred to today as globalization started in the fifteenth and sixteenth centuries with development of European mercantile capitalism and state expansion affecting African, North and South American, and Asian peoples and nations. Now there are many centers of globalization, carried by a global economy instituted by multinational corporations. Economic and political forces as well as a global culture disseminated by the mass media and information technologies help create similarities in practices and attitudes, but also threaten the loss of traditional ways of life of indigenous societies and cultural diversity among the world's peoples.

Development Anthropology

Development anthropology is a comparatively new branch of cultural anthropology in which anthropologists use their knowledge and skills to help developing countries maneuver through the processes of culture change. Many developing countries want and need help, for example, to balance their economic growth and industrialization with the maintenance of a sustainable environment. Countries also may need help in dealing with the impacts of economic growth and industrialization on their traditional social institutions and systems of social relationships.

The mission statement of the Institute for Development Anthropology (IDA) reflects the goals of developmental anthropologists. The IDA is "an independent, nonpartisan, non-profit, nongovernmental organization with a mission to promote environmentally sustainable development through poverty elimination, equitable economic growth, respect for human rights, gender equity, and cultural pluralism." This is done by applying the comparative and holistic theories and methods of anthropology to "empowering low-income majorities in developing countries." The IDA seeks to enhance the rights of low-income populations to land, natural resources, food, shelter, health, education, income, employment, and participation in democratic and transparent polities. Its activities relate directly to policies involving management and access to productive resources (land, water, forests), credit, employment and enterprise generation, marketing, rural cooperatives, extension programs, resettlement, river-basin development, social forestry, health delivery systems, and education (http://www.developmentanthropology.org/).

As an example of the work that organizations like the IDA do, consider Senegal's decision to permit flooding of the Senegal River valley to sustain traditional riverine economies rather than rely exclusively on damming and irrigation, which would have prevented water from reaching crops and pastures in small landholdings in valleys. The researchers showed that traditional flooding actually made the land more productive than did irrigation. The floodplain could support five to ten times more livestock than irrigated rangeland, and also would sustain the Senegal valley's yield of fish, an important subsistence resource for the people living there.

In 2002, the IDA was awarded a five-year Women in Development research contract, which encompasses projects in women's legal rights; antitrafficking of women and children and antidomestic violence activities; studies on the gender dimensions of population, health, and nutrition; and studies on the gender dimensions of democracy, governance, and the environment. Included under this grant are studies of rural women in central Bolivia; the interplay of ethnicity, gender, class, and caste in Pakistan; the gender dimensions of desertification (the spread of deserts) among pastoralists; and the gender dimensions of water use and water management in central Tunisia.

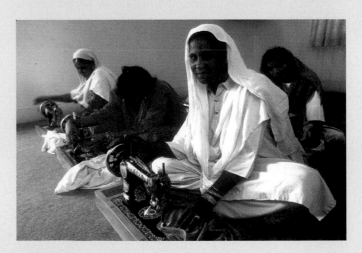

CRITICAL THINKING QUESTION

Based on these examples, how might you define the role of development anthropologists in relation to the forces of globalization at work in the world today?

CHAPTER SUMMARY

What Is Culture?

- Anthropologists use the term *culture* to refer to all of the customs, attitudes, values, and beliefs of members of a society. People acquire these elements of culture in the context of their interactions with others. As members of families, social groups, and communities, people learn what kinds of behaviors are considered appropriate and inappropriate.

Characteristics of Culture

- Several characteristics of culture are fundamental to the way all societies function. Culture consists of behaviors and beliefs that are "shared" by members of the group. If this were not the case, people could not achieve common goals. However, social status, age, gender, race, and ethnicity may create differences in how people's lives are organized and in the attitudes and values they hold.

- Culture is learned. That is, people's behavior is the result of learning, and not instinct. Even when human beings must fulfill critical physical and survival needs, their cultures influence how they satisfy those needs. Many of our attitudes and actions seem natural because our enculturation is so strong.

- Culture is adaptive. That is, people adapt to their environments through cultural means. Human beings can survive in nearly any climate and environment because of the inventions and cultural practices that they develop. However, some practices may become maladaptive over time or not be adaptive in a different context.

- Culture is integrated, forming a relatively coherent and consistent system. Change in one aspect of culture usually leads to changes in other aspects. When cultural traits are borrowed from other peoples, they usually are altered and adapted to fit more closely with the borrower's norms and expectations.

- Culture is symbolic. People's behavior and understandings of the world are based on meanings expressed through symbols. Language is the most obvious and powerful symbolic system, but human beings also use objects and rituals to represent deeply held cultural ideas and attitudes.

- Culture organizes how people think about the world. Through learning and interacting with others, members of a society absorb an array of underlying, taken-for-granted assumptions that help to integrate their activities and beliefs. These concepts become naturalized, so they feel innate and commonsensical rather than acquired. Because all people do not accept the dominant cultural models of their society, these underlying assumptions can be the source of contention, which may, in turn, lead to change.

Culture Change

- Cultures are dynamic systems that change because of internal and external forces. Internal change may take place over time through invention and innovation, leading to new adaptive strategies, customs, technologies, and ideas. Culture history describes the selective record of change in a society, but cultures do not evolve in the same way as species. People define themselves through a process of ethnogenesis. Broad culture changes, such as modernization or revolution, are internal changes that usually are strongly influenced by external forces.

- Culture change also occurs through culture contact. People may borrow traits from other groups. In the process of syncretism, items borrowed through diffusion are modified to fit the existing culture. Culture changes also may be imposed on a society by another society through invasion and conquest. Colonized people are forced to adopt practices and beliefs consistent with those of their rulers.

- When a cultural group is in close contact with a dominant culture, the people may become assimilated or acculturated. Cultural pluralism describes a society with diverse cultural groups who retain their distinctiveness but live side by side on more or less equal terms. In contrast, conquered and oppressed peoples may undergo reactive adaptation to cope with deprivation and loss.

Global Culture

- A global culture, characterized by consumer spending and fueled by advertising by multinational corporations, is spreading to all parts of the world. Although globalization has helped to unify different peoples in a global economy, it may also lead to a loss of cultural and linguistic diversity.

KEY TERMS

cultural knowledge 21	symbol 30	acculturation 33	innovation 36
cultural models 22	naturalized concepts 30	cultural pluralism 33	revolution 36
norms 22	culture wars 31	modernization 33	diffusion 37
subculture 23	counterculture 31	cultural evolution 33	reactive
enculturation 24	worldview 31	social Darwinism 34	adaptation 37
taboos 25	culture contact 33	culture history 35	revitalization
cultural core 26	syncretism 33	ethnogenesis 36	movement 37
cultural integration 28	assimilation 33	inventions 36	global culture 38

REVIEW QUESTIONS

1. How is culture shared? How is it not shared?
2. How does the story of Mai Thi Hiep/Heidi Neville illustrate that culture is learned?
3. What differences with Western culture did the Tiv's reaction to Shakespeare's *Hamlet* illustrate? Why were the Tiv not surprised that Hamlet's mother married his uncle?
4. Why is culture a functionally integrated system? How does the history of women's entry into the labor force in the United States illustrate cultural integration?
5. What are internal and external culture changes?
6. Why do you think anthropologists are concerned by the loss of a language? In what other ways is culture symbolic?
7. How can culture be both adaptive and maladaptive?
8. What are the characteristics and implications of a global culture?

PEARSON myanthrolab EXERCISES

To complete the following exercises and activities, you must log in to www.myanthrolab.com and select your current textbook.

1. In the **Explore** tab of Chapter 2, click on *Videos* and watch the slide show entitled *The Ghost Dance Movement*. Complete the short answer exercise that accompanies the slide show.
2. In that same tab, watch the video about the Luo entitled *Marriage*. Complete the short answer exercise that accompanies the video.
3. In the **Practice** tab, click on *Activities* and complete the *Characteristics of Culture* animation.
4. Enter the **MyAnthroLibrary** section on the home page to read more about topics and cultures that are discussed in this chapter. Suggested readings include:

Family and Household: Who Lives Where, Why Does Is Vary, and Why Is It Important? by Burton Pasternak

Malaysia and "Original People": A Case Study of the Impact of Development on Indigenous Peoples by Robert Knox Dentan, Kirk Endicott, Alberto G. Gomes, M.B. Hooker

3 STUDYING CULTURE

- How did anthropology begin as a discipline? What important figures shaped the development of anthropology?

- What theoretical perspectives do anthropologists bring to their study of cultures?

- What is ethnographic fieldwork? Why is it important in anthropology?

- How do anthropologists use ethnohistories and cross-cultural comparisons in their work?

- Why can the impacts anthropologists have on the people they study be controversial?

Long ago, when the animal people walked the earth, a giant beaver monster lived in Lake Cle Elum, high in the Cascade Mountains. His name was Wishpoosh. [Even though the Lake was full of fish, the monster refused to give any to the other animal people. They appealed to Coyote to save them. With the help of his sisters, Coyote devised a plan. He went to the Lake with a huge spear, and when Wishpoosh tried to stop him from fishing, he drove the spear into the monster's side. In their struggle, Coyote and the monster fell to the bottom of the Lake.]

They fought so hard that they shook the mountains around the Lake and made a great hole in them. The waters of the Lake rushed through this hole, plunged down the mountainside, and soon made a larger lake below, in the Kittitas Valley.

Wishpoosh, still roaring, was carried along with the waters. He tried to drown Coyote, but Coyote hung on. As they tore their way out of the second big Lake, they cut a channel for the Yakima River. As the two fighters plunged down the Yakima River, the waters followed them and made a big lake in the Yakima country. The monster tore through the next ridge and made Union Gap. He plunged eastward across the valley, continuing to dig a channel for the Yakima River as he went. The waters overflowed the new channel and made a big lake in the Walla Walla country.

Then the monster turned sharply toward the west, dragging Coyote after him and cutting the channel of Big River [the Columbia River] as he went. Coyote tried to stop his journey by clutching at the trees and rocks along the shore. But . . . Wishpoosh dragged him on and on. The waters of the lakes followed. . . .

At last they came to the mouth of Big River, where it flows into the ocean. By this time, Coyote was so tired he almost drowned in the waves. [The story continues describing the plan that Coyote uses to kill the beaver monster. Eventually, he succeeds and cuts up the monster's body. . . .]

From Ella Clark, *Indian Legends of the Pacific Northwest*, pp. 172–175. Copyright © 1965 The Regents of the University of California; © renewed 1981 Ella E. Clark. Reprinted by permission.

This story can be interpreted on many levels. One reading of this legend of the Salish and Kootenai peoples may relate to ancient climatic and ecological upheavals in the Pacific Northwest. In this interpretation, the story gives an account of geological events and an explanation of the formation of lakes and rivers resulting from a catastrophic flood that geologists now believe occurred about 12,000 years ago, when an ice dam that had created a huge lake (Lake Missoula) gave way (Deloria 1995). Scientists suggest that, when the lake broke through its natural dam during the last ice age, the water flowed "at a rate 10 times all the rivers on the planet" toward the Pacific Ocean, draining "like a giant bathtub, in as little as 48 hours" (Robbins 2004). According to geologist Dr. Eugene Kiver, the "floods may have happened when people were around. Native Americans have myths about floods" (ibid.).

Stories that seem to parallel actual occurrences suggest the accuracy of people's memories of their past, even though events may be embellished in the rich, poetic language of tradition. **Narratives** may dramatize real events in symbolic form consistent with cultural practices of storytelling. Thus, they may transmit across generations the memories of people who witnessed events that changed their geographic landscape. We will never know whether this Coyote story encapsulates such memories or whether it imagines an explanation for the landscape that existed when the Salish and Kootenai people developed the narrative. Whatever the particular facts, narratives have the power to create and transmit a people's worldview.

Without a writing system, indigenous peoples use storytelling to preserve their history. Collecting and interpreting these stories is one of the methods of cultural anthropology. Anthropologists analyze narratives to identify aspects of cultural identity, social values, moral themes, people's practices and attitudes, and artistic principles and motifs.

Traditional narratives may also be dramatic renditions of historical events. The accuracy of chronologies and events may be uncertain, but **oral traditions** like the story of

narratives
Stories and myths that dramatize actual memories or events in symbolic form consistent with cultural practices of storytelling.

oral traditions
Cultural narratives that have validity as artifacts of culture and experience.

45

What are some oral traditions from your cultural group (such as your family) that you could analyze from an anthropological perspective?

Coyote and Wishpoosh have validity as artifacts of culture and experience. In 1997, for example, the Supreme Court of Canada ruled in a land claims case brought by the Gitksan, an indigenous people of British Columbia, that oral traditions have validity as legal testimony and as records of the past. This chapter further explores the theories and methods involved in the anthropological interpretation of culture.

ANTHROPOLOGY AND THE EXPLANATION OF CULTURAL DIVERSITY

Although the field of anthropology as an academic discipline is only slightly more than a century old, its intellectual roots in Europe go back much farther. Although people everywhere may note cultural differences between themselves and others, anthropology has its roots in the exploration and colonial expansions that originated in Europe in the fifteenth and sixteenth centuries. Explorers, traders, and missionaries, bent on their far-flung journeys of discovery and conquest, often wrote about and commented on the differences they observed in the ways of life of the peoples they encountered.

Europeans wrote many journals, diaries, letters, and memoirs during the first centuries of colonization in North and South America, Africa, Asia, and the Pacific Islands. Although many writers were biased and ethnocentric, they nevertheless often left detailed observations of cultures at the time of contact. For example, Jesuit missionaries wrote detailed accounts about working in North America in the seventeenth century. These men were better educated than most of the explorers and adventurers who preceded and followed them. They were familiar with the scholarly literary and philosophical works of their age. Although critical of many of the practices they described, the Jesuits often were astute observers and recorders. They sometimes judged native customs and attitudes to be superior to the French, for example, such as the people's rules for hospitality and generosity, and their relatively harmonious, noncompetitive community life. In some ways, these missionaries were like anthropologists, both observers and participants in others' lifeways, although of course they had their own goal of converting native peoples to Christianity.

The goal of anthropology as a discipline is to record and account for the great diversity in human cultures. But today there is diversity in anthropology as well, as anthropologists choose different conceptual frameworks to achieve their goals. This section explores a number of perspectives that have been proposed to account for similarities and differences in human societies. These perspectives differ in their focus and in the kinds of theories that they offer to explain human behavior and cultural diversity. A cultural theory is one that attempts to formulate explanations that help us understand why particular practices originate and how they are developed and maintained in particular populations. From an understanding of cultural diversity, some anthropologists also propose theories that can help explain universal trends and processes.

Some approaches in anthropology that were developed in the nineteenth and early twentieth centuries, such as evolutionism, have been discarded as inadequate or incomplete, either because they were unscientific and based on fragmentary and poorly understood data, or because they were based on social attitudes and prejudices that were then prevalent. Nevertheless, the works of some early anthropologists continue to inform aspects of modern inquiry.

Evolutionism

During the Enlightenment of the eighteenth century, European social philosophers, relying on the writings of earlier observers, took a comparative evolutionary perspective, and understood cultural diversity from the point of view of human "progress."

The sixteenth-century Spanish missionary Bartolome de las Casas' description of the effects of colonial life on Native Americans led to humanitarian reforms.

Scholars focused on finding rational, reasoned, and scientific explanations for human differences. They understood that people adapt to their social environments and historical conditions as well as to their physical surroundings, with the goal of progress and the possibility of betterment. Enlightenment philosophers looked for evolutionary trends in the development of human societies. Thus, in **evolutionism,** human differences could be accounted for by different rates of progress, leading to different levels of achievement. Various hypotheses were put forward, demonstrating a progression from stages of primitive culture to civilization. Although these schemes were ethnocentric, using middle-class European culture as a measure of progress, they laid the foundation for nineteenth-century anthropological thinking about sociocultural evolution.

Throughout the nineteenth century, European and American scholars concentrated on developing and refining comparative evolutionary approaches toward understanding the similarities and differences among cultures. The Englishmen Herbert Spencer (1877) and Edward Tylor (1871) and the American Lewis Henry Morgan (1877) proposed models outlining stages of cultural development from the earliest human societies to late nineteenth-century European culture. Both Morgan and Spencer focused on understanding how cultures are integrated and systematized and how the various features of one culture indicate an evolutionary status in comparison with other cultures. For example, Morgan proposed three stages of cultural evolution: savagery, in which people subsist on wild plants and animals; barbarism, in which people start to use agriculture; and civilization, which begins with the invention of writing. Spencer, a social Darwinist, believed that European influence or domination over other peoples was the natural result of evolutionary progress.

Using eighteenth- and nineteenth-century ideas and data, sources that varied widely in their reliability and accuracy, early anthropologists nevertheless advanced the study of human societies by proposing a more thorough analysis of cultural features and their significance for the development of social forms. For example, Morgan first explained the kinship systems of tribes making up the Iroquois Confederacy and the links between a kinship system and the economic system, family organization, and social structure.

Empiricism

Anthropology began to take modern form as a discipline in the late nineteenth and early twentieth centuries with the work of the German-born American Franz Boas (1896), the Polish-born Briton Bronislaw Malinowski (1922), and several others. In this period, fieldwork, rather than "armchair philosophy," became central to the pursuit of knowledge about human cultures. That is, anthropology came to be seen as a scientific inquiry into facts that can be observed directly.

Boas began his career in Germany as a geographer, but on a trip to the Arctic to investigate waters in 1883, he became interested in the indigenous peoples and their cultures. He spent a year living with the Inuit, deepening his appreciation of cultural traits and his conviction that only by living with other people can one truly understand cultural differences. In 1886, Boas traveled to British Columbia to learn about Bella Coola (Nuxalk) culture, and two years later he immigrated to the United States. While studying the Kwakiutl of the Pacific Northwest and their ceremonial life, he became the major figure and driving force in the development of American anthropology. Boas trained many of the most prominent anthropologists of his and the next generation, including Ruth Benedict and Margaret Mead, sending them into the field to collect and archive meticulous data about many different cultures.

Boas consistently stressed the need for **empiricism,** the practice of conducting studies based on direct observation and objective description. He also introduced the concept of cultural relativism, and believed

Margaret Mead's reports about growing up in Samoa and living among the Manus of New Guinea astonished the public.

evolutionism
View held by early social philosophers that human differences can be accounted for by different rates of progress, leading to different levels of cultural achievement.

empiricism
The practice of conducting studies through direct observation and objective description.

that each way of life is a unique adaptation to particular historical conditions, a view that critics referred to as "historical particularism." Boas refuted the earlier theories of cultural evolutionism, criticizing the concepts as being essentially ethnocentric and racist. According to Boas, cultures should be understood and evaluated in their own terms, not in terms of the cultural practices, beliefs, and values of the observer. In his own work and that of his students, Boas stressed the importance of learning the native languages to understand the people's attitudes and beliefs literally in their own terms. Boas's work implicitly questioned Euro-American biases in interpreting other cultures and raised issues that today are concerned with examining the subjectivity of the observer and analyst.

Boas also stressed that similarities and differences should be understood as outcomes of the functions and meanings of cultural traits within a society. He pointed out that the same traits can have different meanings in different cultures. Polygamy, or plural marriage, for example, may occur for different reasons in different societies depending on the cultural context. Marriage rules allowing men to take more than one wife, for instance, may function to signal a man's comparative wealth, power, and prestige; to relieve women of household burdens by providing additional labor; or to ensure that all women can have husbands in societies where women outnumber men.

Functionalism

If you were a functionalist, how would you argue that even negative practices, such as antisocial behavior, can have positive functions for society as a whole?

Functionalism, or the study of the social functions of cultural traits, was a hallmark of the research of Bronislaw Malinowski, whose work especially influenced British social anthropology. Malinowski believed that the social, economic, and political structures of societies were organized to satisfy human needs and that people's diverse institutions and practices have specific functions that address those needs. According to Malinowski, men and women living together in a community develop an "invisible network of social bonds" made up of shared values, attitudes, and practices that "integrate the group into a whole" (1922). All cultural behaviors and artifacts can be explained by understanding their role in maintaining this whole.

Like Boas, Malinowski was dedicated to fieldwork. Malinowski lived with the Trobriand Islanders of the western Pacific in Melanesia, immersing himself in Trobriand culture and language. Like Boas, he also stressed the importance of anthropologists learning the native language of the people they study, because people express their values and attitudes through their language. Malinowski used functionalism to explain his observations of Trobriand life. Students of Malinowski, such as A. R. Radcliffe-Brown and others, applied functionalist interpretations to field data collected among other Pacific Islanders, Africans, and Australian Aborigines. These interpretations are now sometimes criticized for overemphasizing functional stability rather than acknowledging societal change as an ongoing, continuous process.

Modern Theoretical Perspectives: An Overview

One current approach in anthropological theory is to study culture from a materialist perspective, placing technological and economic adaptations at the center of cultural diversity. Another perspective analyzes cultures from a structuralist perspective, emphasizing the role of social structures in fulfilling human needs and integrating social systems. A variation of the structuralist perspective stresses the role of ideas and habits of mind as the sources of diversity. A third orientation, the conflict perspective, places status and power relations at the center of diversity, focusing on how a worldwide system of dominance and subordination, power, and influence operate within and between societies. A fourth perspective is interpretive, with an emphasis on the meanings that people communicate through symbols. Table 3.1 summarizes some of the modern perspectives in anthropological theory.

functionalism
View that cultural traits have social functions that contribute to the smooth operation of the whole society.

materialist perspectives
Explanations of cultural differences that emphasize environmental adaptation, technologies, and methods of acquiring or producing food.

Materialist Perspectives

Materialist perspectives emphasize environmental adaptation, technologies, and methods of acquiring or producing food in the development of culture. Humans adapt to their environments primarily through culture. Humans address the scarcity of resources by developing methods of extracting, exploiting, storing, and processing whatever foods

TABLE 3.1 EXPLAINING CULTURAL DIVERSITY

Materialist Perspectives Marvin Harris	Emphasizes the centrality of environmental adaptation, technology, and methods of acquiring or producing food in the development of culture.
Cultural Ecology	Cultural traits related to the satisfaction of basic human needs form a cultural core that is directly influenced by the physical environment.
Cultural Materialism	All aspects of a society's culture are derived from its economic foundation.
Structuralist Perspectives Claude Lévi-Strauss	Cultural diversity stems from differences in the forms by which people express universal meanings. These forms define and structure their lives and experiences and may serve universal social functions.
Interpretive Perspectives Clifford Geertz	Culture is a unique system of symbols with multiple layers of meaning. Through their behavior, people act out those meanings and communicate them to one another.
Conflict Perspectives	Culture is an expression of power relations within a society and between societies. Distributions of power are linked to distributions of wealth and status and affect gender relations as well as processes such as colonialism.

are available. As you read in Chapter 1, these behaviors, and the satisfaction of other human needs, form a cultural core from which other aspects of society develop and are integrated into a cultural whole. This analytic and explanatory focus in anthropology is called **cultural ecology,** a term introduced by Julian Steward in the 1930s. In societies that depend directly on their environment, ecological factors, such as resources, climate, and topography, have more pervasive effects on cultural development than in societies where people can control and modify their immediate environment.

Another materialist perspective centering on cultural adaptations through economic production is referred to as **cultural materialism,** developed by Marvin Harris (1979). This approach, influenced by the economic views of Karl Marx, gives greatest importance to economic systems and economic relations in the development of culture. Cultural traits can be explained as responses to some economic necessity or benefit. Similarly, people need to organize work in order to produce and exchange foods, other goods, and services. From this basic organization, other features of culture follow. For example, to ensure adequate supplies of resources, people must regulate the size of their communities, increasing or decreasing population growth depending on resource availability. People also must develop methods of arriving at group decisions and controlling behavior to conform to those decisions. Basic economic behaviors and relationships influence how these traits are developed. In other words, what people do ultimately shapes what they believe, rather than the other way around.

Cultural materialism makes a distinction between *subjective* explanations for cultural behavior that are offered by the people engaged in that behavior—**emic** views—and *objective* explanations for cultural behavior that are given by anthropologists or other observers—**etic** views. Cultural materialists claim that people usually are not aware of the underlying adaptive reasons for their actions. Thus, researchers look for explanations of people's behaviors based on observations and other objective criteria developed from an understanding of broad cultural and historical processes.

In his popular book, *Cows, Pigs, Wars and Witches: The Riddles of Culture* (1974), Harris contrasted emic and etic explanations of why Hindus in India do not eat or even kill cows. According to an emic analysis, Hindus do not kill cows because cows are sacred animals, symbolic of "everything that is alive." This is an explanation that a Hindu believer might give. In an etic analysis, however, the meaning of the sacredness of cows is analyzed in the context of the economic needs of farmers in India. For example, Indian farmers use cattle to pull their plows and they use the dung as fuel for cooking fires and

cultural ecology
Field that studies cultures as dynamic wholes based on the satisfaction of human needs through cultural behaviors.

cultural materialism
Explanations of cultural differences as the results of cultural adaptations through economic production.

emic
Subjective, based on insiders' views, as in explanations people have for their own cultural behavior.

etic
Objective, based on outsiders' views, as in explanations of people's behavior by anthropologists or other observers.

From the perspective of cultural materialism, cattle are too important for agriculture to be slaughtered in India.

as insulation in their houses. Harris concluded that cattle are considered "sacred" to protect them from slaughter, because they are vital to Indian farming.

Structuralist Perspectives

Taking a different turn in the analysis of culture, some anthropologists emphasize the centrality of forms and structure in the expression of culture, called **structuralism.** For example, the French scholar Claude Lévi-Strauss used theories from structural linguistics (Saussure 1916) to analyze symbolic expressions of culture in terms of their structures or patterns, in addition to their meanings. His goal was to identify the underlying pattern that all the expressions have in common or the underlying code on which all the expressions are based. Cultures could then be understood in terms of pattern variance.

Lévi-Strauss was interested in explaining why myths from different cultures around the world seem so similar. Treating mythology as a form of language or symbolic communication, he proposed a "principle of opposition" that all myths share, much like novels have a protagonist who engages in some kind of struggle that is somehow resolved. In mythology, heroic struggles involve a contest between opposites, especially between various forms of good and evil, with or without third-party mediation. Myths can be told and retold with elaborations, but the basic structure always stays the same. In this case, understanding cultural differences would involve identifying the particular hero, type of struggle, type of mediation, if any, and type of outcome in each case.

Lévi-Strauss thus essentially developed a theory of the mind, based on structural analysis, to explain cultural differences as variations in basic themes of universal human thinking. He also applied this method to the study of kinship (1949). He was interested in the fact that kinship structures are limited in the number of basic types and are strongly supported by myths and taboos. He looked for a basic unit of kinship that could explain all the variations. For any society requiring a man to marry outside his own hereditary line, for example, Lévi-Strauss identified a cluster of four roles—brother, sister, father, son. These roles structure the exchanges that maintain the circulation of women in the society and establish cooperative relationships or alliances among kin groups. He proposed that marriage is the means through which people, and men in particular, form alliances that promote social cohesion and stability. Marriages forge alliances through a reciprocal exchange between one group that gives women as wives to another group, receiving gifts in return. This sets up patterned relationships between wife givers and wife receivers that over time establish enduring bonds between the groups. Chapters 8 and 9 further explore these topics. Understanding cultural differences in this case would involve identifying and comparing marriage rules, kin roles, forms of exchanges, and forms of alliances. Although Lévi-Strauss is criticized for his focus on men as the primary social actors in these relationships, the perspective of structuralism remains useful today.

Interpretive Anthropology

structuralism
View that cultural differences can be explained by differences in forms or conceptual categories rather than in meanings.

interpretive anthropology
View that cultural differences can be understood as complex webs of meaning rather than through forms.

In contrast to structural-functional analyses, some anthropologists focus on culture as meanings rather than as forms and functions. American anthropologist Clifford Geertz (1973), for example, focuses on mental and cognitive processes in the development and transmission of culture. This kind of analysis, sometimes called **interpretive anthropology,** stresses the multilayered symbolic meanings of people's actions. From this perspective, cultural behavior is the acting out of those meanings.

Geertz developed his theory while working among the Javanese. According to Geertz, "Man is an animal suspended in webs of significance he himself has spun; I take culture to be those webs, and the analysis of it to be therefore not an experimental science in search of law but an interpretative one in search of meaning" (1973, 4–5). Geertz has called culture an "acted document" that is essentially public and therefore observable and analyzable. Doing ethnography, then, is like trying to read or construct a reading from a manuscript. To understand culture, interpretive anthropologists pay close attention to people's expressions of values, attitudes, meanings, intentions, and the felt importance of their actions (9–10). As the collective property of a group, these meanings define cultural differences among groups.

Conflict Perspectives and the Analysis of Culture and Power

Conflict perspectives focus on social problems or social issues in societies, especially those that arise as a result of the distribution of power among groups or social categories. Much of this analysis focuses on the relationship between culture and various forms of social, economic, and political power. Its adherents often use a Marxist framework to analyze how capitalist institutions penetrate and transform indigenous cultures to suit their own needs.

Anthropologist Eleanor Leacock's (1981) pioneering work on the Montagnais and Naskapi in eastern Canada pointed to the role of colonial government in undermining indigenous culture.

One important concern in the analysis of power is the issue of gender, which also plays a role in anthropology. Many anthropological writings (by both male and female anthropologists) have a conceptual male bias. This bias often results in the assumption that male dominance exists (and has existed) in all societies. Reconstructions of indigenous social life prior to European contact tell a different story about the roles of men and women, however. Evidence indicates that, in many societies, especially in communities relying on a hunter-gatherer economy, gender relations were often essentially equal, certainly more equal than after European conquest or colonization led to conformity to a European cultural model. This conformity also led to patterns of leadership and decision-making procedures in small-scale societies that European powers confronted and overwhelmed. Attitudes about communal and family control of land were undermined and altered as notions of private property and individual control of resources became the norm, in keeping with European economic systems. Students of power and colonial control often use conflict perspectives, feminist perspectives, or Marxist frameworks to analyze how indigenous cultures have been transformed.

The discipline of anthropology developed in the nineteenth century; however, some missionaries, explorers, and colonists made detailed accounts of other cultures in the fifteenth and sixteenth centuries. Evolutionism influenced nineteenth-century works by Herbert Spencer, Edward Tylor, and Lewis Henry Morgan. Two important figures in early twentieth-century anthropology are Franz Boas, who called for an anthropology based on cultural relativism and empiricism, and Bronislaw Malinowski, who explained cultural traits from the perspective of functionalism. Anthropologists may also use a materialist perspective (either cultural ecology or cultural materialism), structuralist perspectives and symbolic analyses, or conflict perspectives involving the analysis of culture and power to describe and explain culture. Interpretive anthropology focuses on the interconnectivity, subjectivity, and multiplicity of cultural meanings.

ETHNOGRAPHY AND FIELDWORK

Fieldwork—living with the group under study—remains a hallmark of modern anthropological methods. Writing about fieldwork, Paul Rabinow stated that, "Culture is interpretation. The 'facts' of anthropology, the material that the anthropologist has gone to the field to find, are already themselves interpretations" (1977, 155). These interpretations are in effect translations from one cultural system into another. In the past, most anthropologists worked in societies different from their own, but today many work in their own countries and some even in their own communities. In addition, some anthropologists

conflict perspectives
Understanding cultural differences as a consequence of conflict in the interests and goals of various groups within a society and focusing on issues of power and resistance.

fieldwork
In anthropology, living and interacting with the people or group under study.

CULTURE CHANGE

DOCUMENTING CHANGES IN THE LIVES OF AUSTRALIAN ABORIGINES

Using historical and ethnographic data, Australian ethnohistorians piece together the processes of transformation in the lives of Aborigines before and after the arrival of Europeans on the continent. They base their studies on documents describing interactions between Aboriginal peoples and Europeans, and on the policies carried out by agents of change, such as explorers, missionaries, traders, settlers, and government officials. Maps, photographs, biographies, and oral traditions are other sources of data ethnohistorians use in understanding change.

Ethnohistorians also document how societies invent and reinvent themselves and their cultures in response to internal and external forces. For example, the Aboriginal Family History Project of the South Australian Museum researches Aboriginal genealogies and community histories. The project uses material collected by museum anthropologists, ethnographers, and historians over the past century, but in particular the records of Norman Tindale and Joseph Birdsell, early twentieth-century anthropologists who collected data on Australian Aborigines. The museum's collection includes thousands of photos taken at Aboriginal sites around Australia.

Among many other Australian ethnohistory databases are hundreds of documents that scholars, writers, and community leaders prepared about the Awaba Aborigines of the Lake Macquarie region, housed at the University of Newcastle, including an 1837 translation of The Gospel of St. Mark in Awabakal. Other documents describe the genocide of Aborigines by Europeans and the forced assimilation of survivors, along with the struggles of present-day Aborigines to gain recognition of their claims to land, improve their economic conditions, and preserve their traditional culture.

Australian Aborigines are reinventing themselves today.

focus on secondary analyses of existing data rather than gathering primary data. Two types of studies based on secondary sources are comparisons using databases and ethnologies based on historical documents.

Cross-Cultural Comparisons

cross-cultural comparisons Means of understanding cultural differences and similarities through data analysis rather than direct observation.

In 1949, anthropologists at Yale University founded the Human Relations Area Files (HRAF) to gather in one database and codify all the known cultural facts and details about the world's peoples. HRAF data consist of facts extracted from ethnographies written by anthropologists doing fieldwork in all parts of the world. The collection is divided into five world areas: Africa, Asia, North America, South America, and Oceania. Hundreds of cultural features and practices are coded and cross-referenced for making **cross-cultural comparisons.** Researchers use the HRAF data to find statistical correlations among certain cultural features or to test hypotheses about what cultural facts or forms are likely to be found in association with other facts or forms.

For example, a study by Melvin Ember and Carol Ember (1996) used HRAF data to propose hypotheses about the cultural settings in which couples choose to live near the family of the husband after marriage, in contrast to when couples choose to live near the wife's family. Another HRAF-based study by the Embers (1996) showed a strong correlation among different kinds of violence in societies. Societies that frequently engage in warfare also are more likely to tolerate high levels of violence in other social contexts, such as murder, rape, assault, and domestic abuse.

Although large-scale comparative studies like the Embers's can uncover associations among cultural traits, comparing data that have been collected from numerous ethnographies and articles written by different researchers is difficult. That is, the data may not be comparable. In addition, when gleaned from ethnographies, practices and traits are taken out of their full cultural and historical contexts, which also may make them difficult to compare. Another danger in comparative studies is imputing causality. That is, although certain traits may appear in association, it may not be clear whether they are causally related or whether one trait causes or is an effect of another.

Ethnohistorical Research

A field more concerned with causal relationships in culture change than with comparisons is **ethnohistory,** the reconstruction and interpretation of the history of indigenous peoples from their point of view as well as the points of view of outside observers. Thus, some anthropological work takes place in libraries and archives containing historical records that help researchers learn about past conditions and events relevant to understanding the present lives of the people they are studying. A survey of ethnohistory usually is part of the preparation for conducting fieldwork. Ethnohistorians analyze the processes stemming from historical events and their consequences for changes in indigenous culture. A common focus is the impact of colonialism and conquest on the cultures of colonized peoples.

Ethnographic Fieldwork

Much of the work of anthropology consists of collecting and analyzing information about culture—that is, people's activities, beliefs, and attitudes. As you read in Chapter 1, the reports that result from doing cultural anthropology are called *ethnography* (from the Greek word *ethnos*, meaning "people" or "a division of people"). The methods used in

ethnohistory
Field of study for reconstructing and interpreting the history of indigenous peoples from their point of view as well as the points of view of ethnohistorians.

GLOBALIZATION

Imagine that your e-mails or blogs are among the records on which an ethnohistory of Internet culture is based. What kinds of information would your records provide? How could your records be interpreted to explain changes in Internet culture? How could your records help to document the changes we call globalization?

Anthropologist Elisha Renne (right) confers with professors Dr. Babatunde Agbaje-Williams and Dr. Aderonke Adesanya in Nigeria. Much anthropological field work today takes place in large-scale societies not small indigenous communities.

ethnographic work obviously depend on the kind of data required. Because cultural anthropology is concerned with the complex study of living cultures, anthropologists need to obtain many different kinds of information in many different kinds of settings. Anthropologists' initial fieldwork experiences often set the framework in which their research interests develop and continue throughout their careers. Anthropologists traditionally chose research problems and sites in foreign countries. This is still a common approach, but today many anthropologists work in their own countries, even in their own communities.

Doing Fieldwork

Fieldwork involves a complex process of observing and participating in another culture. As you read in Chapter 1, participant observation is at the core of the fieldwork experience. Anthropologists both observe the activities taking place in the community and participate in them as much as possible and as appropriate. Anthropologists usually live in the community that they are studying, sometimes renting a house or a room in someone else's dwelling. Fieldwork, then, is an ongoing, multifaceted research experience.

Choosing a Problem and Site. Anthropologists begin by choosing a research problem and then the site in which to conduct their study. Most anthropologists do their first research project when they are graduate students. Their interest in a particular subject may develop from an especially exciting course or from an especially stimulating teacher. Some anthropologists have long-standing interests in a particular country or community. Others choose a research site that best suits their theoretical or topical interests. Most graduate students embarking on their first field trip are advised to plan to be on site for about one year. This allows observations during a full annual cycle of economic, social, and ritual activities. Longer field stays are always beneficial but may not be possible for lack of funding.

Doing Preliminary Research. Before fieldwork trips, researchers gather as much information about their subject of study as they can. They read what other anthropologists have written about the topic, attempting to understand the data and the theoretical approaches that others have used in analyzing the problem. To prepare themselves for entering a foreign country or community, they will want to learn as much as they can about the culture, the history, the conditions, and significant current events of that region, as well as the rules for entering and residing in the country. If possible, anthropologists also study the language of the country so that they can communicate directly with the residents. Before setting out for the site, anthropologists often make contact with local people to make sure that their presence in the community will be acceptable.

Arrival and Culture Shock. In the field, researchers must immediately learn new customs, new faces, new foods, new languages, and ways of communicating. This learning is intense because, unlike tourists, anthropologists are immersing themselves in a new way of life in which they will participate. Often, the unstated rules of decorum and etiquette are most easily, and unknowingly, violated. Anthropologists need to be keenly observant, not only of other people's activities but also to the way other people react. By being sensitive to people's reactions, anthropologists can learn much about attitudes, values, and norms. Their experiences also afford them new insights into their own culture, behavior, and beliefs. Nevertheless, doing fieldwork has emotional ups and downs. At the beginning, anthropologists may feel uncertain, fearful, and lonely as they seek acceptance and cooperation. They may also experience **culture shock**—the feeling of being out of place in unfamiliar surroundings, and the feeling of losing one's cultural bearings.

Choosing a Place to Live. Once on site, anthropologists obtain a place of residence, arranging to live in or near a household or renting a dwelling. Living in a household has the advantage of proximity to people through family networks and routine participation in household and community events. Of course, the anthropologists need to find someone willing to be a host, sometimes a difficult task. A disadvantage to staying with a family, however, is that members of a household may try to ally themselves with the

---

Have you ever experienced culture shock? What was the situation? How did you respond to it?

culture shock
Feeling an anthropologist may have at the start of fieldwork of being out of place in unfamiliar surroundings.

anthropologists, against the interests of others in the community, or may try to involve the anthropologists on their side in local social and political networks. In many field locations, anthropologists may have high status among the people they study. In poor and marginalized communities, they may be perceived as rich and powerful. A challenge of fieldwork, then, is to establish good relations without allowing people to use a relationship to gain benefits or advantages over others in the community. Thus, although friendships may develop between an anthropologist and the people in the community, the researcher needs to remain as nonpartisan as possible in village conflicts, disputes, and controversies.

Working in an Unfamiliar Language. As fieldwork begins, anthropologists usually hire an interpreter unless they are fluent in the local language. Learning the field language is clearly desirable, and even necessary, if the anthropologists truly want to learn the kinds of meanings people ascribe to their own behavior. Working through translators is very different from speaking directly to people. Many nuances of meaning and attitudes that are conveyed in language are lost in translation, regardless of the interpreter's skill.

Gathering Data. Once they are established, the anthropologists often survey the village or community or other field site. They may draw a map, situating the site within its local environment and the houses, other structures, farm fields, open spaces, or other areas where people congregate and socialize. A social survey, collecting **qualitative data,** may include information about the composition of households and the relationships between members of nearby houses. From these data, anthropologists learn about family ties and neighborhood networks. Anthropologists sometimes hire assistants to help with these tasks. If assistants come from the village, they can provide a personal connection to other people and help broaden the anthropologist's social network.

Gathering data includes interviewing members of the community. Traditional anthropological methodology includes collecting data concerning kinship, that is, how people trace relationships and descent from generation to generation and among members of the same generation. Combining genealogical information with residence histories that record how long people have resided in which houses allows anthropologists to learn about systems of relationships, people's geographic mobility, and intercommunity relations. It is also traditional to gather data about the ways that people obtain their food, earn a living, and provide themselves and others with goods and services. Economic and social networks may link groups and societies through trade, intermarriage, and friendships.

Anthropologists may collect **quantitative data** such as population trends reflected in births, marriages, and mortality statistics, fluctuations in community size, sources of income, and other statistical measures relevant to their specific studies.

In addition to gathering qualitative and quantitative data, some anthropologists use photography and film as methods of recording the lives and voices of community members. These visual technologies provide dramatic and authentic reflections by the people themselves. However, their use may raise ethical problems, especially around the issue of anonymity. Someone whose image or voice is recorded can obviously be easily identified. In situations of conflict, the personal safety of participants may be jeopardized.

Researchers also gather data through formal interviews and by attending meetings, informal gatherings, religious activities, and other community events. Anthropologists try to participate as much as possible to the extent that their presence is acceptable to community members. Anthropologists need to be sensitive to villagers' attitudes about an outsider's participation in community life. Outsiders may be welcome in some settings but not in others, particularly in sacred or secret activities or in meetings where controversial issues are discussed. Women anthropologists might find their access to certain men's activities limited, and men anthropologists might likewise find their access to certain women's activities restricted. Anthropologists usually want to interview community political officials, religious functionaries, teachers, and doctors for certain kinds of information. It is important, however, not to become overreliant on local authorities, in order to avoid interpretation of village life from the perspective of the local elite. Despite increasing involvement with villagers, researchers usually remain outsiders, except sometimes for those who are themselves indigenous or native to the group they are studying. Some of the best ethnographic accounts are written by native anthropologists.

GLOBALIZATION

The communities in which anthropologists conduct fieldwork are linked to other communities, the nation, and other nations through local, regional, national, and transnational systems of exchange and the global market economy. A farm family in India, for example, might sell produce and handicrafts in regional markets that link ultimately to international export and import markets. Anthropologists must trace these kinds of connections and understand their impacts on people's daily lives.

qualitative data
Information obtained through personal interviews, life histories, observation, and interaction with community members.

quantitative data
Statistical information about population, employment and income figures, census reports on births and mortality, and so on, that reflect trends and processes within a community.

IN THEIR OWN VOICES

Notes from the Field in Morocco

In this excerpt, a member of the "tribe" of anthropologists reflects on his work and his understanding that, from the people's point of view, he is the "Other." In his book, *Reflections on Fieldwork in Morocco*, Paul Rabinow writes about his gradual immersion into the village of Sidi Lahcen, his acceptance by the community, and his understanding of the process of cultural encounters that is fundamental to fieldwork.

After the first several months, my work in Sidi Lahcen was more painstakingly fragmentary and less immediately gratifying. During long, uneventful stretches I struggled with the increasingly imperative need to begin synthesizing my material, formulating specific questions, and searching for ways to answer them.

In the months which followed, I spent a great many hours merely wandering around the village and its fields, engaging in casual talk while sitting around the stores, setting up interviews, waiting for informants, and just being bored. My Arabic was considerably better by this time. I tried to maintain a regular work schedule with Malik [one of Rabinow's key consultants] and several other villagers, but this proved difficult. One particularly trying afternoon when I was cajoling Malik into discussing the local political activity against the French, he became exasperated with my persistent questions and said I was squeezing him like an olive press: if you squeeze too hard, you get the pulp but not the best oil.

After months of consistently self-absorbing activity, I knew I had passed a threshold of acceptance. Slowly and sporadically, I was moving toward the kind of understanding I was seeking. Thus the further along I was, the more I questioned myself as to the state of the data. Particularly toward the end of the stay, I might have to search for weeks for someone who had the knowledge of a specific subject and the willingness to discuss it with me. If I failed to find such a person and convince him to work with me, I was out of luck. There would be

a gap and there was no way to fill it back in Chicago. I awoke each morning with the sense that the material was there if only I could figure out a way to get at it. But as Malik put it, there was only one door open to me—patience, only patience. . . .

Driss ben Mohammed, a jovial, portly, and even-tempered young man, had consistently refused to work as an informant. Over the course of my stay we had come to know each other casually, as time permitted, almost accidentally. Gradually, a certain trust had flowered between us. At its root, I think, was an awareness of our differences and a mutual respect.

Ben Mohammed was not afraid of me (as many other villagers were), nor did he have hesitations about associating with Europeans (although he had had almost no personal contact with them), nor did he seek to profit from my presence (he refused most gifts). Simply, he was my host

Interpreting and Reporting Data. During and after fieldwork, anthropologists reflect on their interactions and the data they have collected. New research questions may arise, new opportunities for observation and participation may present themselves, and new understandings of what has happened may be revealed. Field notes are rewritten as ethnographic accounts and papers, which are published and presented at professional meetings. Sharing the results of research is important in a community of scholars and often leads to new research questions to answer. Anthropological reports are framed within the analytic and theoretical perspectives of the researcher. Other anthropologists may undertake reanalyses of data, focusing on additional questions and employing different theoretical frameworks.

When anthropologists return home after living in the field for an extended period of time and becoming comfortable in a different culture, they often go through a period of

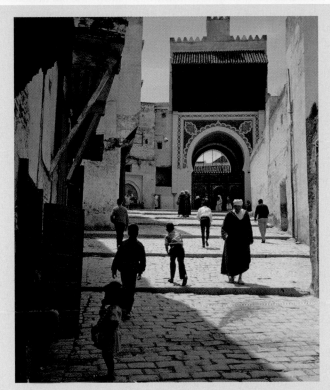

"Culture is interpretation. The 'facts' of anthropology, the material which the anthropologist has gone to the field to find, are already themselves interpretations. . . . The fact that all cultural facts are interpretations, and multivocal ones at that, is true both for the anthropologist and for his informant, the Other with whom he works. His informant (and the word is accurate) must interpret his own culture and that of the anthropologist. The same holds for the anthropologist. Both live in rich, partially integrated, ongoing life worlds. They are, however, not the same. Nor is there any mechanical and easy means of translation from one set of experiences to the other. That problem and the process of translation, therefore, become one of the central arts and crucial tasks of fieldwork. . . . That the communication was often painstaking and partial is a central theme. That it was not totally opaque is an equally important theme. It is the dialectic between these poles, ever repeated, never quite the same, which constitutes fieldwork."

(From Paul Rabinow, *Reflections on Fieldwork in Morocco*, pp. 150–151, 155.)

and treated me with the respect which is supposed to be reserved for a guest, even one who stayed as long as I did.

As time wore on and my friendship with ben Mohammed deepened, I was learning more and more from him. During the last months of fieldwork, when he was home from school and we could spend many of the hot hours together, the field experience, now nearing its completion, reached a new emotional and intellectual depth. Casually, without plan or schedule, just walking around the fields, ripe with grain or muddy from the irrigation water in the truck gardens, we had a meandering series of conversations. Ben Mohammed's initial refusal of informant status set up the possibility of another type of communication. But clearly our communication would not have been possible without those more regularized and disciplined relationships I had had with others. Partly in reaction to the professional situation, we had slipped into a more unguarded and relaxed course over the months. . . .

Explore more at
www.myanthrolab.com

From Paul Rabinow, *Reflections on Fieldwork in Morocco*. Copyright © 1977 The Regents of the University of California via Copyright Clearance Center. Reprinted by permission.

● CRITICAL THINKING QUESTIONS

What parts of this account reveal an anthropologist reporting observations? What parts reveal an individual responding to personal experience? Why are both parts necessary in ethnographic fieldwork?

culture shock, not unlike the culture shock they felt when they first arrived in the field. They may see the behavior of their friends and relatives with new eyes. For a while, they are outside observers of their own culture, once so familiar and taken for granted. Of course, in a short time, they are readily integrated into their own daily lives. The experience of living with other people in another society has profound and lasting meaning. For many, it gives them new insights into their own behavior and their own beliefs.

How could you apply each of the steps described in this section in a fieldwork situation close to home?

Anthropological Research in Urban Societies

When anthropologists conduct research in urban societies, they use many of the same data-collection techniques that they use in rural or isolated communities. Rarely, however, do they study a whole community. Instead, they investigate a specific topic within

urban anthropology
Field that focuses on studying the lives of people living in cities or urban neighborhoods.

survey research
Use of formal questionnaires, administered to a random sample of subjects, eliciting social data that can be analyzed statistically.

a defined subculture or group. For example, some researchers specialize in **urban anthropology,** a field that focuses on studying the lives of people living in cities or urban neighborhoods. Urban anthropologists may analyze a neighborhood association, a particular occupational group, a school setting, a religious network, a health care delivery system, or a senior citizen center. The people in these groups may or may not reside near one another, but they interact frequently in particular areas of their lives.

In conducting this kind of research, anthropologists use data-gathering techniques similar to those sociologists and other researchers use, including survey research. **Survey research** involves the use of formal questionnaires, administered to a random sample of subjects, to elicit social data such as occupation, income, level of education, marital status, participation in clubs and associations, political and religious affiliations, household size, number of computers in the home, and so on. Questionnaires also elicit information about people's attitudes, values, and practices, which are then analyzed and tallied. Survey data provide information about conditions and trends in the community under study, including socioeconomic conditions, social participation, social norms, people's attitudes and opinions, and cultural practices. In survey research, data analysis can emphasize statistical correlations to answer a particular research question, or narrative descriptions to understand the life of the group or community as a whole.

Anthropologists also use participant observation in urban settings. Urban anthropologist Judith Freidenberg (2000) studied elderly Puerto Ricans in New York City's El Barrio (a predominantly Hispanic neighborhood on the Upper East Side of Manhattan). Freidenberg consulted archival and historical records on immigration from Puerto Rico, neighborhood residency, and age and gender distribution of the Puerto Rican community in New York in order to situate her field community within its larger geographic, social, and historical contexts. She gathered statistics on income, occupation, and education to obtain a social and economic profile of the community. Then, before entering the field, she made a survey of neighborhood associations, church groups, after-school programs, and clinics and hospitals to understand the extent of Puerto Rican involvement in community services and networks.

After obtaining enough background information, Freidenberg attended community functions and visited senior centers and health care clinics so that she could get to know the people who used these services and they could get to know her. She then talked with individuals whom she thought would be interested in working with her and began conducting

As an urban anthropologist, how might you go about studying this Puerto Rican community in New York City? What aspects of the culture of this community would you want to try to understand through your study?

in-depth interviews with them. She also accompanied her consultants in their daily activities, such as shopping, attending church, going to the doctor, and visiting with friends.

Over time, Freidenberg gained firsthand knowledge about the people's activities, attitudes, and opinions on a wide range of subjects. By collecting extended **life histories,** she got a fairly complete picture of people's experiences throughout their lives. She was able to understand their perspective on what it means to grow older as immigrants in a large city and to need health care and social services. As years passed, Freidenberg became part of their lives and they part of hers. She used the knowledge she had gained to make policy recommendations about the delivery of medical and social services to the elderly in New York City.

Just as Freidenberg studied elderly Puerto Ricans in New York City, Scott Youngstedt (2004) focused his research on how Hausa migrants to Niamey, the capital of Niger in western Africa, build social networks in their new settings to create or re-create a sense of community and familiarity as they adjust to living far from "home." When new arrivals come to the city, they immediately attempt to locate other people from their hometowns, re-creating the kinds of social support familiar to them from traditional ethics of reciprocity and mutual aid.

In 1960, at the time of Niger's independence, the city had a population of 30,000, approximately 3,600 (or 12 percent) of whom were Hausa. By 2003, slightly more than half of the city's 800,000 residents were Hausa (Youngstedt 2004, 96). Most Hausa migrants to Niamey hope to return to their home villages once they achieve comparative economic success. However, few are able to do so. Few jobs provide steady employment or sufficient salaries to enable workers to save money. Instead, life becomes a struggle to pay for the basic necessities of food and housing. That Hausa and members of other groups continue to be drawn to Niamey indicates the degree of poverty in rural communities. Indeed, a report by the United Nations Human Development Programme in 2002 ranked Niger 173 out of 174 nations studied (Youngstedt 2004, 94).

Hausa men meet daily in coffee shops and public squares where they exchange information about jobs or housing, get news from their hometowns, and debate issues. Youngstedt's interactions with Hausa consultants in these "conversation groups" revealed that the men developed and transmitted their understandings of how the position of their nation in the global economy contributes to creating their own conditions of poverty and disadvantage. Urban studies unveil the complex layers of activities and meanings that connect individuals to one another and to the global contexts in which their lives are situated.

Another topic of research in cities is analysis of occupational groups in their urban and national environments. Florence Babb's research on market women in the city of Huarez in northwestern Peru centered on both the activities of individual traders and the government policies aimed at restricting their work (Babb 1989). Babb's study uncovered the precarious but essential role that tradeswomen render to settled urban populations. For the women, trading provided one of the few income-generating occupations available for people with few or no formal work skills. Marketing is one of the two most common occupations for women in Peru, second only to domestic service. Women are a large majority of the traders throughout the country (Babb 1989, 3). Trading enables women to keep the flexible hours that allow them to fulfill other family responsibilities. Despite the hard work and long hours, most traders make little money. They are increasingly overshadowed by more formal commercial establishments. In addition, men have many more job options because of better education and training.

Peruvian government policies contribute to marginalizing traders, most of whom are members of indigenous communities, in part because their activities are difficult to regulate and their income is difficult to tax. They are also seen as symptoms of economic backwardness. But studies of tradespeople in urban centers, not only in Peru but also throughout Latin America and Africa, demonstrate that they provide a wide range of products including raw and cooked foods, meat, and clothing.

In addition to focusing on particular groups, occupations, and neighborhoods, urban anthropologists may also analyze the cultural and structural linkages among diverse populations within a city. They may also focus on structural linkages between communities, larger urban contexts, and national social and political entities. This focus guided the research of Jagna Sharff (1998), who led a team of three urban anthropologists in a long-term (fifteen-year) research project in a poor, predominantly Hispanic neighborhood on the Lower East Side of New York City.

life histories
A research methodology focusing on collecting narratives of the life experiences of research participants, including their places of residence, work, family composition, social interactions, and roles within their communities.

CASE STUDY

Life in Riverfront: A Midwestern Town Seen Through Japanese Eyes

In their book, *Life in Riverfront: A Middle-Western Town Seen Through Japanese Eyes* (2001), two Japanese anthropologists, Mariko Fujita Sano and Toshiyuki Sano, write about the process of doing ethnography of a foreign culture in a complex, heterogeneous society made up of people of different social classes and ethnic and religious groups. They tell about their expectations before embarking on fieldwork and about their gradual immersion as both observers and participants in community life. The town, located in central Wisconsin, has about 22,000 residents, nearly all of European-American ancestry. Both anthropologists were born and raised in Japan and received PhDs in anthropology from Stanford University in California. They had absorbed stereotypes about "Middle America" that they feared might affect their observations, and were concerned that they might not be readily accepted or trusted in Riverfront, which had few Asian residents: as "foreigners . . . everything that we do would stand out."

The couple also worried about finding a place to live, especially after the owner of the first apartment they looked at asked, "Which church do you go to?" They were afraid that people might be hostile to them because Japan was an enemy of the United States in World War II. Mariko Sano was concerned that "conservative Middle Americans" would think of her as a housewife accompanying her husband, rather than as a well-educated professional. Another preconception that the Sanos brought to Riverfront was that the town would be ethnically uniform. "Although we had known that American society is ethnically diverse, we tended to associate ethnicity with racial minorities such as African Americans, Hispanics, and Asians and tended to see European-American people as a uniform ethnicity" (2001, 1). Yet, Europeans proved equally diverse.

The Sanos imagined Riverfront as a rural community in the midst of farms and open country. They thought that life would be simpler than in a large city, although they really hadn't thought about what "simpler" might mean. They found, of course, that "Middle America" is much more complex than they had anticipated, based on their preconceived notions and stereotypes. They also found that Riverfront is embedded not only in a geographic context but also in an economic and political context of competing interests and identities.

The Sanos combined several research methodologies. They delved into archival material to understand the town's development since its incorporation in 1856. They traced the geographic spread and economic growth of the town and its relationship to a campus in the University of Wisconsin system. They also collected life histories from older residents and used them to "sketch a picture" of life in Riverfront as early as the 1920s and 1930s. They were careful to obtain life histories representative of the various ethnic groups there to ascertain similarities and differences in the immigrant experience. In addition, the Sanos analyzed quantitative statistical data from official census lists dating back to the mid-nineteenth century, detailing population, ethnic and national origin, and residential mobility within the town. The Sanos also volunteered at a senior citizen center, helping to serve meals for elderly townspeople. This activity enabled the Sanos to meet people, establish friendly relations, and contribute to the community. It also gave them opportunities for informal conversations and interviews.

After a year in Riverfront, life changed for the Sanos and their relations with people when Mariko gave birth to their first child. As they point out, "Anthropologists in the field often reach a turning point at which the nature of the relationship with their interviewees changes dramatically. For us, the turning point was the birth of our son." Even before the baby was born, people began to give advice about how to take care of the child, in effect beginning the process of integrating the child into the culture of Riverfront. From being outsiders and strangers, the Sanos became friends and community members, especially to regulars at the senior citizens center. People commented that the child, because of its birth in Riverfront, would be an American.

The Sanos left Riverfront after nearly two years of fieldwork. They returned some twelve years later to see many economic changes, as old industries disappeared and new shopping malls were constructed. Immigrants continued to arrive in town, some from Europe and others from urban and rural American communities. The Sanos realized that these immigrants were much like themselves, arriving in a new place and adapting to its culture. As they conclude, "We have carried on cultural dialogues between 'them' and 'us' and among 'ourselves.'" And they note that these are the same "cultural-dialogical experiences" that all newcomers have, whatever their origins and whatever their purposes.

Explore more at
www.myanthrolab.com

Have you ever been a newcomer? What preconceptions did you bring with you?

The Sharff team collected economic data on income and employment, information on household composition and residence, and social indicators such as health, education, and friendship networks. They opened an office in the neighborhood as headquarters and space for their team to meet together and with community residents. The researchers interacted with people daily, but they framed their research and interpretation of data in terms of a larger picture: the city's economy and national policies affecting poor people. The researchers were untangling the web of economic and political relationships that impacted the daily lives of low-income Hispanics. That web included deindustrialization, leading to loss of employment, and interrelated problems stemming from lack of educational opportunity, cuts in social service spending, neighborhood deterioration, and increased crime and drug use. According to Sharff and her colleagues, the violence in the community resulted from the "violence of poverty" inflicted on poor people by national and local forces beyond their control.

As you can imagine, doing fieldwork in one's own society poses special problems of objectivity. Many anthropologists believe that being completely objective when studying any culture is impossible because all observers bring with them their own learned values, attitudes, and expectations. At the same time, anthropologists need to "know" something about the subjects of study. The challenge, then, is to "learn" about them in a different way, taking account of what they think they already know but looking afresh from an anthropological perspective.

REVIEW

Boas, Malinowski, and other early twentieth-century anthropologists emphasized fieldwork. Ethnohistory and cross-cultural comparisons using databases such as the Human Relations Area Files are examples of anthropological approaches based on records and data rather than on direct observations. When anthropologists do fieldwork, they often write descriptive accounts called ethnographies. Conducting fieldwork involves many steps before even entering the field, at which time most first-time anthropologists experience culture shock. Fieldwork can focus on entire small-scale societies or on subcultures or subgroups within a larger society. Anthropologists also study groups, communities, and institutions within their own societies. Using methods such as interviews and survey research as well as participant observation, researchers in urban anthropology focus on segments of larger societies and their connections with other societies and the world.

THE ANTHROPOLOGY OF ANTHROPOLOGY

The study of anthropology by anthropologists is called **reflexive anthropology.** It has been developed and championed by anthropologists in the tradition of postmodernism. The goal of such studies is to understand cultural impacts on the observations and writings of anthropologists, which must be taken into account in understanding other cultures (Clifford and Marcus 1986).

reflexive anthropology
The anthropology of anthropology, which focuses on the labels that anthropologists use, the impacts of anthropologists on the people they study, and professional ethics.

polyphony
The many voices of people from all the different segments and groups that make up a society; a quality of ethnographic writing today that presents multiple views of a culture.

informed consent
The full disclosure to research participants of the research goals, methods, types of analyses, and reporting procedures.

Labeling Issues in Anthropology

Early anthropologists saw their study populations as "primitive." As a result of colonialism and imperialism, societies were created that often appeared as static, timeless, and "traditional" to later European and American anthropologists, when they were not. Other labels include the terms *non-Western, native,* and *indigenous.*

Today, rather than viewing societies as isolates and ideal types with unique sets of cultural traits, anthropologists investigate how the cultural practices and attitudes of a society relate to processes of globalization, such as modernization and economic development. Many anthropologists look for ways to apply their knowledge and theories to address these contemporary problems. In addition, anthropologists recognize that many voices cooperate and compete in the production of meaning, creating **polyphony**—or the many sounds and voices of people in all segments or groups in a society. In this context, some anthropologists question the choice of voice in the texts that they produce and their own role in the process of presentation (see the Controversies feature).

Ethical Issues in Anthropology

Other issues concerning anthropology relate to the ethics of conducting research involving human subjects. Cultural anthropologists make their living and build their careers by studying other people. They live among them, learn from them, and write about them. As a result, the most important ethical issues they face involve their relationships with and obligations to those people.

The American Anthropological Association, the professional association to which most anthropologists belong, formulated a Code of Ethics, setting out a number of principles that it recommends to its members (American Anthropological Association 1998). The code mandates intellectual honesty, forbidding any falsification or intentional biasing of data. Stage-directing ethnographic film footage would be regarded as unethical, for example. The code also advises that an anthropologist's ethical obligations to the people they study are more important than the pursuit of knowledge or the completion of research projects. Ethical obligations include avoiding harm to or exploitation of the people, and fully disclosing the goals and uses of the research. Anthropologists also must consider the social and political implications of the material that they produce. Finally, the code notes that, although some anthropologists use their research to advocate for the people they study, this is not an ethical responsibility but rather an individual choice. Anthropologists are also guided by federal legal requirements safeguarding the rights of human subjects in any type of research project. These rights include **informed consent,** that is, full disclosure of research goals, research methods, types of analyses, and reporting procedures.

Anthropologists do not agree on their proper roles in relation to the people they study. For some anthropologists, research is an end in itself. People in the community extend their hospitality voluntarily. And although anthropologists should certainly avoid doing anything that they feel may be harmful to the community (in the short or long term), some believe that they have no continuing obligation to the people. Other anthropologists believe that they have ongoing responsibilities to the community, and they lend their help. Anthropologists may be able to collect and analyze documents or testify in court proceedings regarding native territories and indigenous land claims cases. Others can use their training and knowledge to represent native interests in dealings with local and national governments. At the least, anthropologists can present information about the needs of indigenous communities to the public in their writings and in classes. As experts, they can talk to the media, countering negative stereotypes about poor and marginalized peoples. As discussed in Chapter 1, applied anthropologists focus on this goal.

REVIEW — Reflexive anthropology focuses on anthropology itself, the language it uses to describe people, and its impacts on both knowledge and people. Today, many ethnographies are written to reflect polyphony—the many voices of people from all the different segments and groups that make up a society. Concern with the impacts of anthropologists on study populations has led to a professional Code of Ethics for the conduct of anthropology.

CONTR⬤VERSIES

How Do Anthropologists Present Knowledge About the People They Study?

Since the 1960s, anthropologists have questioned their roles as agents of change, as they intentionally or unwittingly facilitate worldwide economic and political processes (Gough 1968). Some anthropologists also side with the people they study against oppressive policies that destroy the people's land and resources or pressure them to abandon their way of life.

Anthropologists interested in the impacts of the researcher's ideologies on other peoples look at the ways groups represent themselves and others, and structure people's ideas about these groups. As people involved in the processes of "writing culture," anthropologists influence the representation of the peoples they study. How do anthropologists write about and present another culture? Often through the construction of the "other" as alien, unusual, different, and exotic. To counteract this tendency, some anthropologists present their findings as a dialogue between themselves and members of the society among whom they have lived. The production of any text, including an ethnography, can be seen as a "dialogic" process with multiple voices and meanings (Bakhtin 1981). In the past, ethnographies tended to present a unified voice in their description of a people's lifeways. Very likely, they contributed to cultural stereotypes and depicted greater conformity, uniformity of opinion, and idealized behavior than actually existed in the society. Deeply contested issues were often glossed over. Because ethnographies focused on a view of culture from the perspective of people with greater prestige and privilege, the voices of marginalized members of communities were muted or unheard.

In addition, because most anthropologists were male in the past, and because they worked primarily with male consultants, ethnographies tended to be told from a male perspective. Women's concerns, lives, and voices were relatively unknown and unheard. Examples of gender bias in ethnological interpretation are common. Writing about the Nuer of southern Sudan, for example, the British social anthropologist E. E. Evans-Pritchard concluded that Nuer family life was "remarkably harmonious on the surface" (1955, 133). Yet his research, based entirely on the testimony of men, disclosed culturally sanctioned wife abuse and the wishes of both husbands and wives (reported by the husbands) for their spouse's death! Not a harmonious picture, even on the surface. More recently, the writings of Napoleon Chagnon (1997) among the Yanomami of Brazil and Venezuela downplay the significance of the violence husbands inflict on women. And many anthropologists overemphasize the male role of hunting in comparison to the female role of gathering. Today, anthropologists pay more attention to looking past their own subjectivity to more fully represent others.

The male bias in anthropology extends to theories about human evolution and cultural origins. For example, since the earliest known tools were found in association with animal bones (dating from about 2 million years ago), and since hunting is assumed to have been primarily a male role, researchers have proposed theories of human development that privilege male inventiveness and initiative while portraying females as passive onlookers to cultural evolution. These conclusions are controversial for many reasons, not the least because there may have been earlier tools made of fiber for use in containers for carrying gathered plant resources, presumably the work of females (Ehrenberg 1989). The point is that although we know quite a bit about physical evolution, we know little about the lives of our earliest ancestors. And as Linda Fedigan (1986) suggests, models of human origins are "symbolic statements about and prescriptions for human nature." They tell us more about the people making the theories than they do about early human populations.

Because of these problems with the ethnographer's voice, some anthropologists are producing "polyphonous" ethnographies with a multitude of voices. Rather than relying on a single, dominant perspective, they give multiple interpretations of activities and opinions from the points of view of people with different roles in the community. The voices of men and women, of the elites and the marginal contribute to a diversity of representations. By focusing on dialogue and polyphony, anthropologists locate culture not only in behavior but also in conversation about behavior, ideas, attitudes, and emotions. Ethnographers also focus on their own issues of power, their relations with communities in their own societies, and their relations with people in the communities they study.

Controversies within the discipline about the role of the anthropologist and the focus of ethnography do not weaken the field but, rather, invigorate it, bringing out issues for thought and dialogue. Anthropology plays a vital role in today's world. It has the tools with which to understand and analyze complex issues of power that structure and confront our world. The theories and methods that anthropologists use provide the knowledge and techniques for understanding people's behavior and how they organize, transmit, evaluate, and express their experiences. Anthropologists can contribute to debates about public policy in national and international arenas. They can help inform people about the value of all cultures.

⊙ CRITICAL THINKING QUESTIONS

How do you think your roles and status as a member of your society might affect your observations of other people? How might they color what you say to an anthropologist interviewing you about your people's way of life?

If you were writing an ethnography of your community, whose voices might you want to represent or include? Why?

ANTHROPOLOGY APPLIED

Anthropology on Trial in the Amazon

In the early twenty-first century, scandal erupted concerning the conduct of anthropologists, other scientists, and journalists working among foragers and horticulturalists in the Amazon River basin in South America during the 1960s. In charges that have not been substantiated to the satisfaction of the academic community, a cultural anthropologist and ethnographic filmmaker was accused of staging events for the camera, interfering with local politics, and inciting native peoples to warfare, partly to support his claim that they were naturally violent (Grossman 2000).

Another problem was the use of weapons—machetes and axes—as trade goods to win the acceptance and confidence of the study population. The use of trade goods to ease contact between peoples is an ancient custom. However, in the hands of native peoples with traditions of intertribal warfare and Stone Age weapons, modern steel tools increased injuries and deaths. The claim also was made that, to test genetic theories, scientists may have intentionally introduced measles in the region, killing an unknown number of native people (Grossman 2000).

These claims may not be true. According to an investigative report by the American Anthropological Association, "These misrepresentations fail to live up to the ethics of responsible journalism even as they pretend to question the ethical conduct of anthropology" (2001). Nevertheless, during the 1970s, attitudes about fieldwork changed as anthropologists became more concerned about native people's rights. A new code of ethics emerged for all social scientists working with human subjects, including the principle of informed consent. Today, the ethics of informed consent require that social scientists explain to their informants how the information they collect will be used—especially how that information could be used against them and what the consequences could be. Thus informed, some groups might reasonably decline to become subjects of study.

In addition, although anthropologists are dependent on the people they research for both information and assistance,

they are trained to avoid acting in ways that may upset the established order in people's social relations, social norms, decision-making processes, and economic exchanges. Thus, anthropologists should not be fully participant observers in family relations, village politics, and intertribal relations. Also, observers must be aware that new, casually introduced technologies can have disastrous consequences. The new ethical standards for social science research reflect the prime directive of medical ethics: "First, do no harm."

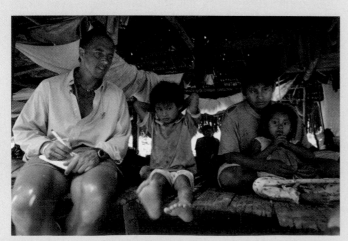

○ CRITICAL THINKING QUESTIONS

Should these ethics apply to native anthropologists studying their own people? Should these ethics apply to workers involved in advocacy and activism for indigenous rights?

CHAPTER SUMMARY

Anthropology and the Explanation of Cultural Diversity

- Although anthropology as an academic discipline is only slightly more than a century old, it has its origins in the colonial expansion of Europe that began in the fifteenth and sixteenth centuries when explorers, traders, and missionaries visited and commented on the peoples and cultures they encountered. During the eighteenth century, European social philosophers consulted the journals and writings of earlier observers. Their evolutionism—proposals about the progress of humankind from one cultural stage to the next—established a basis for anthropological theories.

- The anthropology that emerged in the late nineteenth and early twentieth centuries in the United States and Europe focused on classifying and comparing peoples and cultures throughout the world, attempting to determine their evolutionary relationships to one another. Two important figures were Franz Boas, who championed attention to historical details, empiricism, and cultural relativism, and Bronislaw Malinowski, who contributed the perspective of functionalism. Their work, emphasizing fieldwork and direct interactions with and observations of other cultures, forms the core of anthropology.

- Anthropologists have developed a number of conceptual frameworks to explain human cultures. Materialist perspectives emphasize the centrality of environmental adaptation, technology, and methods of acquiring or producing food. Cultural ecology focuses on how the physical environment directly influences the satisfaction of basic human needs and how people's adaptive behaviors interact with other aspects of culture. Cultural materialists often distinguish between emic explanations of behavior, based on the reasons people themselves offer for what they do, and etic explanations, based on the analysts' observations of people's behavior and other objective criteria.

- Structuralist approaches look at the role of concepts in structuring experiences and relationships. Interpretive anthropologists focus on relationships among meanings in the development and transmission of culture. Conflict perspectives focus on social and cultural inequalities and power relations.

- Some anthropologists emphasize forms of social, economic, and political power in shaping culture. Some of their attention is directed toward anthropology itself, uncovering unstated biases in the field and in the analysis of culture. Today, anthropologists are rethinking notions about "traditional" society and focusing more on the complex ways in which traditional societies reshaped themselves, and were reshaped by the impacts of European expansion and colonial control. Worldwide processes of modernization and globalization also raise issues about how people are enmeshed in economic institutions and political forces beyond their control.

Ethnography and Fieldwork

- The central tool of anthropological research is fieldwork, especially participant observation. Anthropologists live among the people they are studying for an extended time to gain an understanding of their culture from the people's point of view. As participant observers, anthropologists observe and record the communities' activities and participate in them as much as possible and appropriate. Earlier anthropologists focused on small, seemingly isolated indigenous societies. Today, however, many anthropologists work in larger societies, including their own, focusing on specific subcultures or communities.

- In addition to fieldwork, some anthropologists use ethnohistory, researching in libraries and archives to learn about past conditions and events relevant to understanding the lives of the people they are studying. Anthropologists also employ the comparative method in understanding cross-cultural similarities and differences in human cultures.

The Anthropology of Anthropology

- Cultural anthropologists are concerned with ethical issues involving their relationships with the people they study. Some anthropologists become advocates for the communities they have studied, whereas others seek to disseminate information that counters negative stereotypes about poor and marginalized peoples.

KEY TERMS

narratives   45
oral traditions   45
evolutionism   47
empiricism   47
functionalism   48
materialist perspectives   48
cultural ecology   49

cultural materialism   49
emic   49
etic   49
structuralism   50
interpretive
   anthropology   50
conflict perspectives   51

fieldwork   51
cross-cultural
   comparisons   52
ethnohistory   53
culture shock   54
qualitative data   55
quantitative data   55

urban anthropology   58
survey research   58
life histories   59
reflexive anthropology   61
polyphony   62
informed consent   62

REVIEW QUESTIONS

1. How did anthropology become an academic discipline? What were the principal goals of early anthropologists?

2. How did Boas and Malinowski influence the development of anthropology?

3. What main theoretical perspectives do anthropologists use to describe and explain cultural differences and changes?

4. What are the differences between an emic and etic perspective?

5. How might a cultural event be analyzed differently by a conflict theorist and an interpretivist?

6. How do anthropologists prepare for fieldwork? What are the key benchmarks in conducting fieldwork?

7. What are some pitfalls of living and participating in family and community life while doing fieldwork?

8. What is the anthropology of anthropology? What are some issues about the roles of anthropologists and the writing of ethnographies?

myanthrolab EXERCISES

To complete the following exercises and activities, you must log in to www.myanthrolab.com and select your current textbook.

1. In the **Explore** tab of Chapter 3, click on the *NPR Audio Programs Broadcast* tab and go to *Theme 4: Theoretical Approaches to Culture*. Listen to one of the programs in this section and complete the short answer exercise that accompanies the program.

2. In the **Research Tools** section on the home page, click on the *Research Navigator*™ link and enter the Anthropology database to find relevant and recent scholarly and popular press publications. For this chapter enter the following keywords: *urban anthropology, ethnohistory, and cross-cultural.*

3. Enter the **MyAnthroLibrary** section on the home page to read more about topics and cultures that are discussed in this chapter. Suggested readings include:

Glebo: Civilizing the Anthropologist by Mary H. Moran

Morocco: Adolescents in a Small Town by Susan Schaefer Davis

LANGUAGE
AND CULTURE

- What three features distinguish human language from animal communication?
- What are the differences between phonemes and morphemes?
- Why is nonverbal behavior important?
- What did Edward Sapir and Benjamin Whorf contribute to linguistic anthropology?
- What is a dialect? A jargon? How does language relate to gender, class, and race?
- What is an ethnosemantic study of communication?
- How do languages change?
- How can the study of languages help reconstruct their histories and the history of human migrations and contact?

Creator and Changer first made the world in the East. Then he slowly came westward, creating as he came. With him he brought many languages, and he gave a different one to each group of people he made.

When he reached Puget Sound, he liked it so well that he decided to go no further. But he had many languages left, so he scattered them all around Puget Sound and to the north. That's why there are so many different Indian languages spoken there.

These people could not talk together, but it happened that none of them were pleased with the way the Creator had made the world. The sky was so low that the tall people bumped their heads against it. Finally the wise men of all the different tribes had a meeting to see what they could do about lifting the sky. They agreed that the people should get together and try to push it up higher. "We can do it," a wise man said, "if we all push at the same time. We will need all the people and all the animals and all the birds when we push." "How will we know when to push?" asked another. "Some of us live in this part of the world, some in another. We don't all talk the same language. How can we get everyone to push at the same time?"

At last one of them suggested that they use a signal. "When the time comes for us to push, when we have everything ready, let someone shout "Ya-hoh" that means "Lift together!" in all our languages." The day for the sky lifting came. All the people raised their poles and touched the sky with them. Then the wise men shouted "Ya-hoh." Everybody pushed, and the sky moved up a little. They kept on shouting "Ya-hoh" and pushing until the sky was in the place where it is now. Since then, no one has bumped his head against it.

A Snohomish narrative accounting for the diversity of languages.

The Snohomish are an indigenous people of Washington State. Their story seeks to explain the extraordinary diversity of languages spoken in the Pacific Northwest. It also tells how, despite their linguistic (and cultural) differences, the people of the region found a way to cooperate to make the world more to their liking. Unlike in this Snohomish narrative, the creation of different languages in the biblical story of the Tower of Babel stops people from working together, confusing and separating them.

Today, about 6,200 languages are spoken in the world, some by millions of people and some by only several hundred. While 6,200 is a steep decline from the number of languages spoken centuries ago, it still reflects a rich array of linguistic and cultural diversity. Languages are repositories of cultural knowledge and history, and as such, they are integral to personal and group identity.

Language is a fundamental part of human behavior. It is our primary medium for interacting with one another. We use it to convey our thoughts, feelings, intentions, and desires to others. We learn about people through what they say and how they say it; we learn about ourselves through how other people react to what we say; and we learn about our relationships with others through the give-and-take of conversation. In this chapter, you will learn something about the structure of human languages and about how anthropologists study the relationship between language and culture.

Languages are systems of structure and meaning. Although linguists study how the sounds, words, and sentences of a language are organized, it is best to keep in mind that these structures are used to convey meanings. People speak to transmit their thoughts and feelings to others, and they listen to understand the thoughts and feelings of people with whom they interact. Investigating the kinds of meanings conveyed, their social and cultural implications, is central to the work of anthropological linguists.

WHAT IS LANGUAGE?

All animals communicate in some manner, but **language** is unique to humans. Language has three key features that together distinguish it from other forms of animal communication (Table 4.1). First, language is **symbolic.** That is, it is based on symbols—the arbitrary

language
Any form of communication that involves symbols, displacement, and productivity.

symbolic feature
A feature of language based on symbols or on the arbitrary association of sounds with meanings.

TABLE 4.1 THREE KEY FEATURES OF LANGUAGE	
Symbolism	Based on the arbitrary association of sounds with meanings.
Displacement	The ability to communicate about something that is not happening at the moment.
Productivity	The ability to join words in infinite meaningful combinations.

displacement
Ability to communicate about something that is not happening at the moment.

productivity
Ability to join sounds and words in theoretically infinite meaningful combinations.

call systems (signal systems)
Animal communication systems that consist of a relatively small number of sounds to express moods and sensations, like fear, delight, contentment, anger, or pain.

association of sounds with meanings. For instance, the sounds in the word *cat* have no particular association with the animal the word represents. In English, this sound has come to "mean" a particular animal. Even words that speakers think imitate noises (such as the words for the noises animals make) are only stylized approximations. Cats don't really say *meow;* dogs don't really say *bowwow.*

Another feature of language is **displacement,** the ability to communicate about something that is not happening at the moment. Indeed, we use language far more to communicate about events that have already happened in the past or will happen in the future than about what is happening right now. Displacement also permits us to talk about imagined events, or to tell stories, deceive, or lie.

The third feature of language, **productivity,** refers to the fact that every language contains thousands of words that can be combined and recombined to form an infinite number of phrases and sentences. In a sense, nearly every sentence spoken or written is a new sentence because it is a new combination of words.

Many nonhuman animals communicate with **call systems** (or **signal systems**). Unlike human language, these systems consist of a relatively small number of sounds or vocalizations that express moods and sensations, like fear, delight, contentment, anger, or pain. They can be used as warnings, threats, alarms, or requests for attention and affection. Also, research suggests that the calls of some nonhuman primates indicate the direction and location of food sources (Jolly 1985). If so, this demonstrates a limited kind of displacement because the animals are signaling information that is not present at the time. As far as we know, however, even such intelligent animals as chimpanzees and gorillas, our closest primate relatives, do not talk about their plans for the future or reminisce about the past, in the wild at least. Recent research does suggest that, like human beings, nonhuman primates form mental representations of individuals, objects, and spatial relationships when they hear vocalizations (Seyfarth and Cheney 2007).

For decades, researchers have been trying to determine whether chimpanzees and gorillas can learn language. The earliest studies involved trying to teach chimpanzees to pronounce English words. These efforts were doomed because chimpanzees and gorillas are physically incapable of articulating words. They can, however, make intricate hand gestures and can certainly manipulate physical objects. A fascinating series of later studies sought to take advantage of these abilities. In some, chimpanzees and gorillas raised in homelike settings were taught American Sign Language (ASL), the gestural language of the deaf. In other studies, animals were taught to press keys on computers or to manipulate cutout symbols on boards. Many of the animals learned to recognize and use hundreds of words for objects, actions, and feelings. Some even appeared to make up new words by combining words into compounds. The research community is divided on the question of what these studies indicate. Some, especially Roger Fouts (1997), claim that chimpanzees are capable of language-like conceptual formulations, have an understanding of the future, and can use "language" to deceive as well as to express thoughts and feelings. However, although researchers agree that chimpanzees and gorillas have a keen ability to acquire words or rather symbols that represent

How is human communication different from the call and signal systems of nonhuman primates?

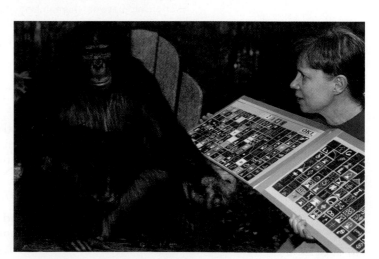

Researchers have developed many techniques for investigating the ability of nonhuman primates to communicate. Here, Dr. Sue Savage Rumbaugh is teaching a chimp named Panibasha to communicate with symbols and signs.

words, there is great disagreement about whether this indicates an understanding of grammatical principles fundamental to human language. For example, the animals seem not to comprehend the significance of the order of "words," a basic feature of all languages. Instead, their ordering of gestures and symbols in "multiword" constructions seems to be random. In addition, research designs have been criticized because some observers of chimpanzee communication efforts may endow the animals' gestures with more meaning than is warranted (Wynne 2008). Perhaps the debate sheds light on the problems of designing studies that attempt to fathom the thinking of another species.

The difference between the natural call systems of nonhuman primates and their abilities in the laboratory may provide some insights into the fascinating but difficult question of the origin of human language. Chimpanzees and gorillas apparently have a rudimentary capacity for understanding and manipulating symbols but seem not to use it in the wild. Presumably, our prehuman ancestors had the same capacity long before they began using language. If this is so, we can look for the origin of human language in conditions that would have made the complex communication it permits advantageous for survival. Displacement, one of the features of language that distinguishes it from call systems, makes communication about the past and future possible. Perhaps language emerged because of our ancestors' need to apply memories and mental representations of past experiences to present and future plans in order to coordinate group activities—to relocate their camps or to plan food-gathering expeditions, for example. Natural selection may have favored ancestors who had these cognitive abilities (Seyfarth and Cheney 2007). Language is also a primary vehicle for the transmission of individual and cultural knowledge. Although we learn from observing other people, we gain most of our knowledge and skills through language, through hearing other people's advice and instruction based on their stored-up memories and experiences.

Nonhuman primates, as already noted, are physically incapable of speech. The emergence of spoken language thus required changes in the physical structure of the mouth and throat. We cannot know exactly when these changes began to occur or when our ancestors first started to use spoken language. Some researchers suggest it may have been about 100,000 to 150,000 years ago. Almost all agree that the people who, some 40,000 years ago, created the earliest known examples of another characteristically human form of symbolic communication—art—were also speaking to one another.

REVIEW — Three principles that characterize human language are arbitrary symbols (association of sounds to specific meanings, with the sounds symbolizing the item being described); displacement (the ability of people to talk about events, people, and objects that are not present); and productivity (the ability to put together sounds and words to form larger words and sentences). To understand the relationship between human language and animal call systems or signal systems, researchers began to teach chimpanzees and gorillas American Sign Language and other methods of communicating.

THE COMPONENTS OF LANGUAGE

Languages consist of sounds, structures, and meanings. When we use language, we produce and understand these elements together as a whole. However, we can learn much about how language works by studying each element separately.

Phonology: The System of Sounds

phonology
Study of sound systems in language, including phonetics and phonemics.

phonetics
Study of the articulation and production of human speech sounds.

phonemics
Analysis of the use of sounds to differentiate the meanings of words.

Phonology is the study of sound systems in language. It includes **phonetics,** the study of human speech sounds, and **phonemics,** the analysis of the use of those sounds to differentiate words. The vocal apparatus with which we produce the sounds, or "phones," of language consists of the lungs, pharynx, larynx, glottis, vocal cords, nose, mouth, tongue, teeth, and lips (see Figure 4.1). As sound is produced, air passes from the lungs through the throat, into the mouth, and then is expelled either through the mouth or nose.

We produce specific sounds by manipulating various parts of the vocal apparatus—for example, by positioning our tongue on our teeth or palate; by closing, opening, or rounding our lips; or by constricting or opening our throats. No language uses the full range of sounds that the human vocal system can produce, but every language organizes the sounds it does use—its phonetic inventory—into a system of phonemes. A **phoneme** is a minimal unit of sound that has no meaning in itself but functions to distinguish one word from another. The contrast between the sounds /p/ and /b/, for example, distinguishes the English word *pit* from the word *bit*. In English, then, /p/ and /b/ are separate phonemes.

You learn to apply the rules for differentiating phonemes unconsciously as you acquire your native language in childhood. These rules are not universal but, instead, operate within each language according to its own patterns. People who speak a second language with a foreign accent are simply applying the pronunciation rules of their native language to the new one.

Morphology: The Structure of Words

Morphology is the analysis of word structure. Words are composed of units of sound and meaning called **morphemes.** Morphemes may be words or sounds that are not words but carry special meanings when attached to words. In English, for example "-s" is a morpheme that attaches to the end of nouns to indicate plural, as in *cats.* Thus, a word may contain combinations of morphemes. The word *inactivity,* for example, consists of the units of meaning, "in-" (meaning "not"), "act" (a verb meaning "to do"), "-ive" (making the verb into an adjective), and "-ity" (making the adjective into a noun).

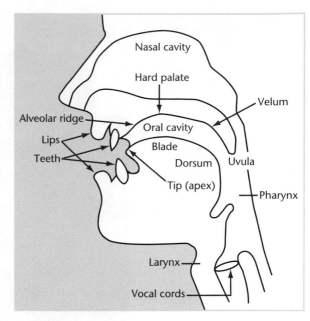

FIGURE 4.1

The Vocal Apparatus (R. Wardhaugh, from *Introduction to Linguistics*, 2/E. © 1977. Reprinted by permission of McGraw-Hill Companies.)

Syntax: The Structure of Sentences

Most talk consists of multiword units—phrases and sentences—not single words spoken in isolation. Every language has rules of **syntax** that govern the ordering of words in phrases and sentences to show their relationship. In English, for example, the subject of a sentence precedes the verb, and the direct object follows it. In the English sentences, "The dog chased the cat" and "The cat chased the dog," all the words are the same, but the meanings are different because of the difference in word order.

Each of the world's languages has its own rules of syntax, and these rules vary greatly. Yet all languages share certain features. In all, for example, sentences may be composed of subject, object, and verb, and in most languages the subject comes before the object. What varies is the position of the verb. In only a few languages does the basic word order place objects before subjects.

Because subjects precede objects in the vast majority of languages, this pattern probably reflects human cognition. People perceive subjects as more important than objects because subjects are more active and in control. That is, subjects initiate, control, direct, or affect actions and events. Objects, on the other hand, are not "doers," but are "receivers" of actions and, therefore, are less cognitively significant or salient. Cognitive salience thus is reflected in linguistic structure.

According to the linguist Noam Chomsky, a number of abstract rules of word order and sentence construction appear to underlie all languages. These common structural features of language reflect a **universal grammar,** part of an innate capacity for language in the human brain. According to this view, the actual syntax of any particular language derives from the basic generic structures of universal grammar. The existence of an innate structure may account for the ease with which children quickly learn to understand and speak their native language (Chomsky 1968).

Semantics: The Study of Meaning

The function of language is to express meaning. We hear language linearly, one word at a time, but we grasp meaning as a unified whole. **Semantics,** or the study of meaning,

phoneme
A minimal unit of sound that differentiates meaning in a particular language.

morphology
The study of the internal structure of words and the combination of meaningful units within the words.

morpheme
A unit of sound and meaning, either a separate word or a meaningful part of a word.

syntax
The rules that generate the combination of words to form phrases and sentences.

universal grammar
Abstract rules that underlie the structure of phrases and sentences in all languages, generally thought to be an innate capacity of human thought.

semantics
Study of systems of meaning in language.

Semantics is the study of how meaning varies with social context. In an informal meal among friends such as these, the formal expression, "Please pass the salt" might seem inappropriate and stuffy.

is complicated because a host of factors contribute to that whole. To begin with, words often carry culturally symbolic freight beyond their specific meaning. To an American, for example, "apple pie" may be more than the name of a particular dessert. It may also conjure up images of home and childhood and a mix of associated values and beliefs.

Words or phrases and sentences also convey interactional meaning that varies with the relationship people have with one another as well as the context in which they are speaking. A husband and wife might call each other "sweetheart" at home, but they are likely to address each other as "Doctor" at work in the same hospital. Finally, utterances can have affective meaning, indicating attitudes of speakers. For example, "John told me about his accomplishments" is a neutral statement of fact, whereas "John boasted about his accomplishments" is implicitly critical of John. The meanings of words and their use in context are powerful signals of people's intentions and reflect social relationships and cultural norms.

Despite these complexities, linguists have tried to develop tools for identifying some basic rules of semantics. One approach is to analyze words in terms of overlapping and contrasting units of meaning. Linguists have abstracted some units of meaning that they claim are universal, developing a kind of universal semantics on the model of the universal grammar of Chomsky and others. Among these, meaning units relevant to nouns are "animate" (contrasted with "inanimate"), "human" (contrasted with "nonhuman"), and "countable" (contrasted with "mass"). Others include the opposition between "male/female" and "adult/nonadult." So, for example, the meaning units that apply to the word *woman* include "animate," "female," "human," "adult," and "countable." Changing one unit—"female"—to "male" defines the closely related word *man*. Similarly, replacing "adult" with "nonadult" gives us *girl* or *boy*.

REVIEW — Humans are genetically predisposed to learning language. Phonology is the study of sound systems in language. Different sounds are made by manipulating the vocal apparatus. Phonology includes phonetics, the study of human speech sounds, and phonemics, the analysis of the use of those sounds to differentiate words. Phonemes are minimal units of sounds that differentiate meanings in words. Morphemes are units of sound and meaning that make up words. Syntax is the rules for word order in phrases and sentences. Universal grammar consists of abstract rules of word order and sentence construction that appear to underlie all languages. Semantics is the study of meaning.

NONVERBAL COMMUNICATION

Human communication is hardly limited to language. We also convey information nonverbally, through gestures, facial expressions, body posture, use of physical space, including distance between speakers, and touch. Some forms of **nonverbal communication** may be universal in that they mean the same thing to everybody, regardless of culture. Some research suggests that we share with other primates certain innate or biologically based signals of enjoyment, distress, threat, and submissiveness, as the photograph on this page suggests (Jolly 1985). Research with chimpanzees indicates similarities between those animals and human beings in the perception and categorization of facial cues expressing emotions (Parr, Walter, and Vick 2007).

In general, the meanings of gestures, expressions, and body postures do not flow from the actions themselves any more than the meanings of words flow from the particular sounds with which they are made. The same gesture may mean one thing in one culture and something entirely different in another. For example, the "A-OK" sign made with the thumb and index finger joined in a circle used by North Americans as a positive gesture, means "zero" or "worthless" in France. In every culture, some nonverbal actions have the status of **emblems**—gestures often substituted for spoken words that are understood to have a specific meaning. Emblems in European and North American cultures include nodding the head to signal assent, or shrugging the shoulders to convey uncertainty. Among the Diné (or Navajo) of the American Southwest, people point out objects or directions by moving their lips slightly forward, a gesture that an Anglo American might not even notice.

Cultural differences in the interpretation of nonverbal behaviors, including **body language,** can lead to cross-cultural misunderstandings. A person from one culture simply may not recognize an emblem or signal used by someone from another culture, in which case no meaning is conveyed. More serious problems can arise when a particular behavior is meaningful to both parties in an encounter, but the meaning is different for each. You may respond inappropriately when confronted with an act you understand one way but the other person intends to mean something else. For example, hand gestures that Americans routinely make to convey positive support can be offensive in other countries. The familiar "thumbs up," meaning "good job," "good luck," or "I'm okay," is interpreted in Bangladesh, Australia, and many Islamic countries as the equivalent of the raised middle finger.

Some gestures have achieved nearly universal meaning through the process of globalization, as different peoples incorporate foreign gestures into their cultural repertoires. One example of this is the peace sign, which is made by extending the index and middle finger, palm-out, to form a "V." The sign originated in wartime Europe as a sign for "Victory!" and implied a coming time of peace. The original meaning has been extended to mean nonviolence, to signal any hard-won success, and to make a gestural "bunny ears" joke at a peer's expense, commonly seen in snapshots. Many cultures around the world have adopted the peace sign along with one or more of its meanings.

A study conducted in Israel suggests how common misunderstandings are in nonverbal as well as verbal **intercultural communication.** A group of students from fourteen different cultural backgrounds viewed videotaped gestures made by recent immigrants to Israel from Ethiopia. The students recognized 85 percent of the

nonverbal communication
Communication through gestures, facial expressions, body posture, use of space, and touch.

emblems
Nonverbal actions with specific meanings that substitute for spoken words.

body language
The meanings people communicate through their posture, stance, movements, expressions, gestures, and proximity to other communicants.

intercultural communication
The communication of meanings between people of different languages and cultures.

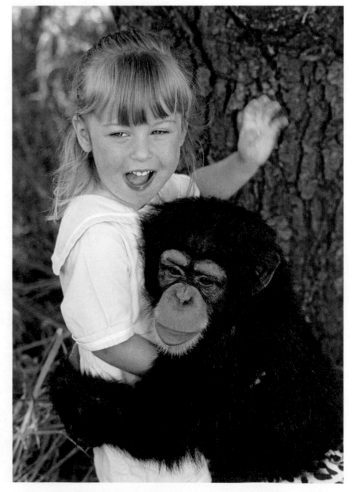

Anthropologists argue that nonverbal communication is not universal and that culture colors our understanding of any gesture or expression.

What roles will gestures and other body language play in the intercultural communication suggested in this photograph? What meanings will the participants' emblematic behaviors express?

GLOBALIZATION

Some gestures, such as the peace sign, have achieved nearly universal meaning through the process of globalization.

gestures as meaningful. However, of the gestures they recognized, they interpreted only 23 percent correctly to mean what the people who made them intended. They were approximately correct about another 7 percent, and misinterpreted entirely the remaining 70 percent of the gestures (Schneller 1988, 158).

In any society, nonverbal behaviors can signal differences in status, just as nonverbal behaviors reveal dominance and subordination among other primate groups. In human societies, cultural attitudes dictate who has higher status and who has lower status. Dominant individuals tend to use broad gestures, such as looking or even staring at others, maintaining serious, unsmiling faces, and taking up large areas of personal space. In encounters between those of nonequal status, subordinates tend to use restricted, small gestures, avert their eyes when looked at, smile frequently, and allow the higher-status person to encroach on their personal space and even to touch them. High-status individuals try to make themselves appear large; low-status individuals try to make themselves small by lowering their heads and keeping their limbs close to their bodies.

Gender inequalities in the United States, for example, are reflected in submissive and dominant nonverbal behaviors that women and men learn as members of their culture. Studies have shown that men are more likely than women to assume a dominant posture, and women are more likely than men to assume a deferential posture. Women typically smile, avert their eyes when looked at, condense their bodies and gestures, avoid encroaching on others' space, and allow intrusions into their own space (Henley 1977; Hall 1984). In studies of mixed-sex interactions, men touched women twice as often as women touched men, men initiated eye contact twice as often with women as women did with men, and women returned smiles of men nearly all the time whereas men returned only two-thirds of the smiles of women (Henley 1977, 115; 164; 176).

REVIEW ─◉ Nonverbal communication includes distance between speakers, facial expressions, body postures (body language), gestures, and touching. Nonverbal communication has a basis in primate evolution, but few actions have universal meaning in human cultures. Every culture has a repertoire of nonverbal communication, called emblems. Cultural differences in nonverbal (and verbal) communication can lead to misunderstandings in intercultural communication. In human societies, culturally defined status differences, such as gender inequality, can be inferred from nonverbal communication that expresses dominance and subordination.

How would you describe the nonverbal interaction between these individuals?

LINGUISTIC ANTHROPOLOGY

Linguistic anthropology investigates connections between language, culture, and worldview. Researchers study the vocabulary and grammar of particular languages to determine how language reflects and is reflected in culture. Linguistic anthropologists are interested in drawing connections between a people's language and their worldview, defined in Chapter 2 as people's perceptions of their environment, their relations with other people and other creatures, and their concepts of time and space. Linguistic anthropology is also concerned with understanding the social dimensions of language use, investigating the ways that social categories such as gender, class, and race influence the use and interpretation of distinctive speech styles. These concerns overlap with the field of **sociolinguistics,** the study of the interplay of social variables such as class, gender, and race on language use.

Linguistic Relativity

The two most influential figures in the early development of linguistic anthropology were Edward Sapir (1884–1939) and his student Benjamin Whorf (1897–1941). Both men studied the languages and cultures of several Native American peoples. Both are also associated with the concept—known as the **Sapir-Whorf hypothesis**—that the language people speak influences the way they think. This basic concept has been developed and expanded in recent decades through the work of linguistic anthropologists who focus on studies of **linguistic relativity,** or the concept that people perceive objects, events, and relationships in time and space based on the grammatical forms provided by their language.

According to Sapir, language affects all human experience to some extent. Vocabulary, in particular, both reflects what is culturally important to a people and at the same time influences what they pay attention to. Speakers give names (words) to important entities and events in their physical and social worlds, and, once named, those entities and events become culturally and individually noticed and experienced. In other words, the relationship between vocabulary and cultural value is bidirectional. Over time, this interdependent process creates and reinforces a unique mental model for each culture. As Sapir noted, "The worlds in which different societies live are distinct worlds, not merely the same world with different labels attached" (1949, 162).

As evidence for this conclusion, Sapir examined the vocabulary of the Paiute people living in semiarid areas of Arizona, Utah, and Nevada. The Paiute, he noted, distinguish fine details of their environment with separate words. Among them are words for (as translated by Sapir) "divide, ledge, sand flat, semicircular valley, circular valley or hollow, spot of level ground in mountains surrounded by ridges, plain valley surrounded by mountains, plain, desert, knoll, plateau, canyon without water, canyon with creek, wash or gutter, gulch, slope of mountain or canyon wall receiving sunlight, shaded slope of mountain or canyon wall, rolling country intersected by several small hill-ridges" (1949, 91).

As Sapir's translation indicates, English can be used to describe each of these features. The Paiute language, however, labels each feature with a separate word and thereby gives it distinctive value. This classification suggests how culturally important these kinds of environmental features are to Paiute speakers but not to English speakers. This contrast is consistent with the differences in the two peoples' ways of living. The Paiute depended on hunting and gathering to obtain their food, and knowledge of and sensitivity to their natural environment

sociolinguistics
Study of the impacts of socioeconomic and cultural factors, such as gender and class, on language and communication within a society.

Sapir-Whorf hypothesis
The assertion that the form and content of language influence speakers' behaviors, thought processes, and worldview.

linguistic relativity
The concept that people perceive objects, events, and relationships in time and space based on the grammatical forms provided by their language.

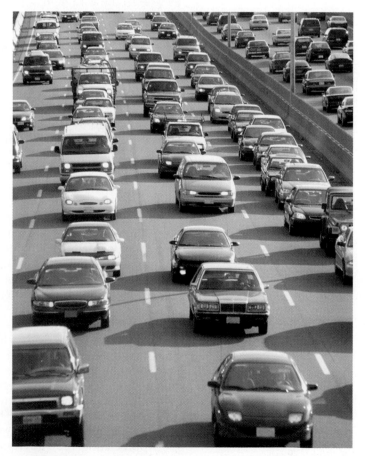

How does the rich American vocabulary for kinds and qualities of automobiles affect our values and how we think about cars?

IN THEIR OWN VOICES

Honoring Native Languages

The Spring 2000 issue of Tribal College Journal and the Summer 2007 issue of Cultural Survival Quarterly focused on efforts by Native American educators and elders to maintain and increase knowledge of indigenous languages by members of their communities. Contributors to the journals expressed their opinions about the types of language revival and maintenance programs suited to their localities and made connections between language and cultural heritage.

Knowing diverse languages is important to the country, to the tribes, and to the individuals. Without the language, ceremonies cannot continue; children cannot communicate with their grandparents; and adults cannot voice their prayers. Some attribute their tribes' social disintegration to the loss of their language and culture. "Our moral imperatives are in the language," said Alan Caldwell, director of the College of the Menominee Nation Cultural Institute in Wisconsin. On the Blackfeet Reservation in Montana, teachers at the Head Start have noticed that children with behavioral problems have been transformed by their experiences in [language] immersion school. By connecting them with their language, the Head Start instructors link the children with their traditional values. The Winnebago Tribal Diabetes Program Director believes that language classes help improve physical and mental health.

Native languages differ from English not just in the words used but also in the concepts conveyed. The common Navajo greeting, Ya'at'eeh, is much more than "Hello, how are you?" To the Diné people, it means, "Everything is good between us," according to Frank Morgan of Diné College. Many common expressions have spiritual connotations, according to Blackfeet Community College language instructor Marvin Weatherwax. In groundbreaking research, Blackfoot language scholars at Red Crow Community College in Alberta are using words and phrases to reconstruct their culture. In the process, they are healing themselves, according to Duane Mistaken Chief. For example, by studying the word Ainna'kowa (to show respect), they learned Ainna'kohsit—to respect themselves.

The Learning Lodge Institute [a project developed by seven tribal colleges in Montana] has the goal of "using education for the teaching of language and culture," said project director Lanny Real Bird. This dual mission is key. All this helps tribal communities reach a larger goal, said Real Bird. It is part of each college's mission to "empower the cultures so they can empower themselves," he said. This means directing "their own education, their own health, their own government. To utilize their own resources." Language instruction is therefore not an exercise in sentimentality but part of a strategy for self-determination.

were crucial to their survival. Similar studies of specialized vocabularies in different languages can provide insights into the cultural attitudes and priorities of the people who speak them.

Like Sapir, Benjamin Whorf was interested in the influence of vocabulary on culture, thought, and behavior. For example, while working for a fire insurance company, he noticed that fires often resulted from confusion over the meaning of words. In some cases, workmen had thrown matches and cigarette stubs into "empty" gasoline drums, even though the drums contained combustible vapors and invisible traces of gasoline. Whorf concluded that the men acted inappropriately because they interpreted "empty" according to its usual meaning of "null and void, negative, inert" (1956, 135).

Whorf also went beyond vocabulary to consider the influence a language's grammatical structures might have on speakers' thoughts and behaviors. Comparing English to the language of the Hopi of Arizona, Whorf noted that, whereas English tenses divide time into three distinct units—past, present, and future—Hopi verbs do not indicate the time of an event. Rather, they focus on the manner or duration of an event. He concluded that, because of these differences, Hopi speakers have different concepts of time, number, and duration than English speakers do (1956). In turn, because of these differences, Hopi speakers and English speakers perceive the world in fundamentally different ways. As Whorf put it, "Concepts of 'time' and 'matter' are not given in substantially the same form by experience to all [people] but depend upon the nature of the language or languages through the use of which they have been developed" (p. 158).

Appreciating the differences in the ways that language expresses and influences speakers' knowledge and attitudes does not, however, imply that any language is superior to any other, only that people adapt their language to fit their environment and culture.

Learning Lodge participants believe language is essential for the survival of tribal cultures. Lanny Real Bird summarized it this way: "Without a language to speak, there is no culture because there are words and expressions unique to particular tribes. They are holy and supernatural. To be translated and used in the context of interpretation of another language would not be possible." And Marvin Weatherwax added that loss of language is more than the loss of words. Instead, "it would be the loss of culture as it is. I cannot teach you culture. Culture is something you have to live. Through the language we can give a part of the culture that can be lived."

Elders involved in the Anishnabe or Ojibwe language program at the Bay Mills Community College in Michigan said that those who cannot speak their own language are only people whose ancestors were Anishnabe; they are no longer Anishnabe themselves. "It's harsh, but I kind of agree with that view" said Tom Peters, who graduated from the Institute this year. Peters views the Anishnabe language as a sacred gift. "Language is the first step to recovering culture. It's authentic culture because the native perspective is not taken out of it." His fellow graduate, Sidney Martin, agrees. "The language means everything. It is the powwow, the culture, the basket making, the values," she said. "It is everything." And according to Doris Boissoneau, a language curriculum developer, "If we are going to call ourselves a Nation with sovereignty rights and inherited rights, we need a language and a culture. The fires have never gone out amongst the Anishnabeg. They have dimmed. The adults and Elders are rekindling the fires, and they will burn even brighter and rekindle the hopes of all Anishnabe."

Language loss has deep consequences for indigenous communities and their systems of knowledge. And this loss has meaning for the entire world community. According to Jacob Manatowa-Bailey, director of the Sauk Language Department for the Sac and Fox Nation in Oklahoma, "When a language dies, the loss to a tribal community—and to the world—is beyond measure. Entire systems of thought, belief, and practice become permanently removed from the storehouse of human knowledge. This is the final stage of a process that has deep historical roots, the culmination of hundreds of years of colonization, assimilation, and genocide. . . . In order to kill a language you must get inside someone's head; you must break their spirit and their mind, not just their body."

**Explore more at
www.myanthrolab.com**

From "Honoring Native Languages, Defeating the Shame," *Tribal College Journal* (Spring 2000). Essays by Marjane Ambler, Paul Boyer, and Jennifer Dale. Reprinted with permission from Tribal College Journal of American Indian Higher Education, www.tribalcollegejournal.org. Copyright © 2000: "The Last Word," *Cultural Survival Quarterly*, vol. 31, summer 2007.

That is, a language with a more elaborate set of words in any one category expressing certain concepts is not superior overall to any other language. Although language may have a role in affecting the way people view the world, it is not strongly deterministic but, rather, consists of indirect links. That is, the words and structures of a language may set guideposts but do not ultimately constrain people's thoughts. Finally, because languages and cultures change all the time, there is no neat fit between a particular element of language and a particular element of culture.

Recent studies in linguistic anthropology attempt to develop experimental designs focusing on memory and perception tasks that can lead to understanding in what ways speakers of various languages use different cognitive resources to classify objects and events. For example, John Lucy (1996) studied the effects of grammatical requirements on memory and sorting tasks with speakers of English and Yucatec, a Mayan language spoken in Mexico. An important distinction between English and Yucatec concerns use of numerals. In English, count nouns (words naming objects or concepts that can be counted) are preceded directly by a word indicating its number (for example, one dog, two cats). In Yucatec, numerals are used in conjunction with a classifier that provides information about the shape, texture, or other material properties of the noun. For instance, the phrase translated from Yucatec as "one candle" is better understood as meaning "one long thin candle" or, even better, as "one long thin wax," with the cultural understanding that wax occurring in a long thin shape is a candle (1996, 50).

To investigate the effect of numeral structure on cognition, Lucy provided speakers of English and Yucatec with sets of three test objects and asked the subjects to classify one of the objects as more like another (for example, "Is item X more like A or more like B?"). Results of this experiment revealed that English speakers classified objects as similar on

What do language maintenance programs in indigenous communities tell us about the relationship between language and culture?

the basis of shape whereas Yucatec speakers classified objects on the basis of their material composition. Further research with young speakers of English and Yucatec indicated that children younger than 7 years tended to classify objects as similar on the basis of shape rather than material, but that Yucatec children shifted to a preference for material as their basis for sorting objects at about the age of 8 years (1996, 51).

Language, Culture, and Society

Most linguistic anthropologists today understand that language influences thought, and at the same time, thought influences language. The idea that language is an intimate part of culture and shapes people's worldviews has influenced efforts to maintain or revive indigenous languages in Hawaii, New Zealand, Australia, North America, and other places. In regions where most native peoples no longer speak the language of their ancestors, community members have developed projects aimed at preventing language loss. Many of these projects are based on the importance of the role of language as an integral part of cultural identity and cultural vitality. In New Zealand, the Maoris have been working to preserve their language, te reo Maori. Revitalization efforts have included *kohanga reo*, literally "language nests," for preschoolers, and radio stations broadcasting in Maori. Nevertheless, by 1995, there were fewer than 10,000 Maori speakers, and of them, only about 14 percent held daily conversations in Maori in their homes. Factors in the continuing endangerment of this language include television, industrialization, intercultural marriages, and the low social status of the language in the eyes of its speakers as well as other New Zealanders.

The Study of Language Speakers

Linguistic anthropologists also study the demographics of specific languages—that is, the frequency, distribution, and range of languages and their variants within a nation, region, or geographic area. This, too, is a concern that overlaps the work of sociolinguists. In pluralistic societies such as the United States, for example, language diversity is common. The United States is a multilingual nation inhabited by numerous immigrants who continue to use their original language on a daily basis in most social interactions. The demographics of language speakers often reveals the history of migration and regional occupation.

Language and Dialects

In all language communities, there are variations in the ways that various groups of people, or people in different regions or even different villages, speak. People in one group may pronounce sounds differently than those in another, use different words for objects or actions, or structure sentences in a distinctive way. Taken together, these differences

GLOBALIZATION

The spread of English throughout the world has led to the development of new "Englishes" (Platt, Weber, and Ho 1984). These English languages are more than dialects because they involve vocabulary, syntax, grammar, and semantics, as well as pronunciations. Other than in the United States, Canada, and the United Kingdom, English is spoken as an official language in Australia, New Zealand, South Africa, India, parts of the Caribbean, the Philippines, and China (Hong Kong).

FIGURE 4.2
Dialect Map of American English (Reprinted by permission of Robert Delaney.)

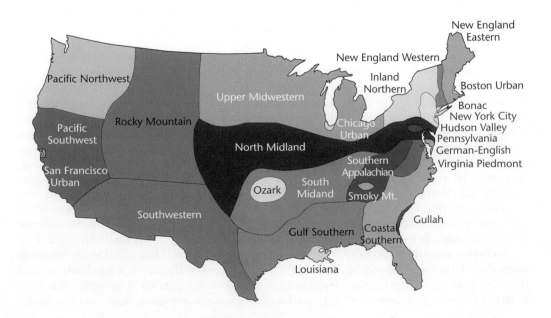

are called **dialects.** In nations with large territories and diverse populations, regional distinctions abound, especially in pronunciation, or *accent*.

Among English speakers in North America, a Canadian accent differs from a U.S. accent, with regional accents prevalent within each country. Similarly, accents differ among English speakers around the world, from Britain to Australia and India. You immediately notice a speaker's accent and can often guess where the person comes from based on it. Similarly, regions may have their own distinctive vocabulary. For example, the word *cabinet* is used in parts of Rhode Island to refer to what other North Americans would call a *milk shake*. Some Americans put items in a *bag*, others in a *sack*. Some call a carbonated sweet drink *pop*, others *soda*, and still others *tonic*. In parts of Pennsylvania, some people say *snicklefritz* when they're talking about a rowdy child. The dialect map in Figure 4.2 shows local dialect variations in each region of the United States.

dialect
A variety of a language spoken by a particular group of people, based on regional differences or social differences such as gender, class, race, or ethnicity.

CULTURE CHANGE

CHANGING NORMS IN LANGUAGE USE IN THE UNITED STATES

In the United States, no federal legislation specifically grants official status to English, but most political leaders support and promote its exclusive use in public domains. This was not always the case, however. From the late eighteenth century through the mid-nineteenth century, many of the country's leading figures saw no reason to discourage the use of other languages, although they thought all Americans should be encouraged to learn English. They understood that different languages express different thoughts and cultural orientations and believed that linguistic diversity strengthened the development and exchange of ideas (Heath 1977). During that period, some states promoted multilingualism by publishing laws in other languages as well as English. Pennsylvania, with its large German-speaking population, published laws in German, and Louisiana, with its large French-speaking population, published laws in French. Some laws affecting Native Americans were printed in their languages.

Official attitudes toward multilingualism changed in the late nineteenth century, and policies promoting or protecting other languages were retracted. This change was prompted by the large influx of immigrants coming into the United States from southern and eastern Europe and the prejudice against them. Educators and public figures promoted the teaching of "correct" Standard English. Many states enacted laws designating English as the only language to be used in schools and mandated fines for teachers who spoke other languages in the classroom. Children were often punished for speaking their native languages in school. The English-only trend accelerated in the twentieth century, particularly during World Wars I and II, when speaking German or Japanese could provoke suspicions of treason. Although the U.S. Supreme Court in 1923 upheld the right of private schools to provide instruction in languages other than English, the ruling did not apply to public schools, which most students attended (Grosjean 1982).

Today, state and local governments determine whether to permit or bar the use of languages other than English as primary modes of communication in schools. A number of organizations actively promote English-only policies and work toward eliminating bilingual education programs in public schools. Some English-only advocates also want to ban the use of public money to disseminate information in other languages to residents, including voter registration information, motor vehicle forms, and health care pamphlets. Twenty-eight states grant some kind of "official" status to English (American Civil Liberties Union 2005; U.S. English, Inc. 2007). English-only state legislation efforts coincide with rising rates of immigration from Spanish-speaking countries in Latin America. However, three states grant official status to two languages: Hawaii (English and Hawaiian Creole), Louisiana (English and French), and New Mexico (English and Spanish).

Despite these pressures, and the de facto official status of English, the United States continues to be a country of linguistic diversity as immigrants from many countries settle here. According to the U.S. Census Bureau, nearly one in five people (19.7 percent) or 55 million residents age 5 and older, spoke a language other than English at home in 2006 (American Community Survey 2007). That was an increase of 23 million people since 1990. About 380 different languages are spoken in the United States, including 155 Native American languages. Table 4.2 lists the most prominent of these.

TABLE 4.2 LANGUAGES OTHER THAN ENGLISH SPOKEN IN THE UNITED STATES

Language	Number of Speakers in 2006
Spanish	34,000,000
Chinese	4,400,000
French	2,700,000
Tagalog	2,700,000
German	2,200,000
Vietnamese	2,200,000
Native American	364,000

According to a government report, about 55.9 percent of the people who spoke a language other than English at home reported they spoke English "very well." Combined with those who spoke only English at home, 91.3 percent of the population age 5 and over had no difficulty speaking English. Spanish speakers increased from 17.3 million in 1990 to 34 million in 2006, and 52.7 percent reported speaking English "very well" (U.S. Bureau of the Census 2007).

The concentration of people with a native language other than English varies nationwide. Only six states have 2 million or more: California (12 million), Texas (6 million), New York (5 million), Florida (3.4 million), Illinois (2.2 million), and New Jersey (2 million). The states with the highest *proportion* of people whose native language is not English are California (42.5 percent), New Mexico (36.5 percent), Texas (33.8 percent), New York (28.8 percent), and Arizona (28.0 percent). The distribution of specific languages also varies. Spanish has by far the most speakers, but French is the most frequently spoken non-English language in Louisiana, Maine, New Hampshire, and Vermont; German is the most frequently spoken in Montana, Minnesota, and North and South Dakota; and Portuguese is first in Rhode Island. The Native American language Yupik dominates in Alaska, and Japanese is the most frequently spoken language in Hawaii.

Surveys of Native American languages indicate that Navajo has the most speakers, with 178,000 who speak it at home, according to 2000 census figures. Other languages with more than 10,000 speakers (according to 1990 data) include Dakota/Lakota, Yupik, Apache, Cherokee, and Pima and Papago (Broadwell 1995, 146–147). In addition, some 17,000 people reported their home language as "Indian" or "American Indian" without mentioning a specific language. Approximately 10,000 people claimed a Native American language as their only language.

Most descendants of immigrants in the United States stop speaking their ancestral languages by the third generation (Fishman 1981). First-generation Americans can usually speak their parents' language because it is used in the home on a regular basis. Second-generation Americans can often understand their ancestral language and converse in a rudimentary way. But by the third generation, any ability to understand or use the language generally disappears. Intermarriage also dissipates an ethnic and linguistic focus on the country of origin. If a husband and wife come from different ethnic groups, English is their only common language. Their children, therefore, will rarely be exposed to the ancestral language of either parent, except perhaps in larger family gatherings. In addition, immigrants and their descendants usually want to assimilate into their new country, abandoning former customs and languages.

Language and Gender, Class, and Race

In addition to region, languages also may vary based on social categories, such as gender, class, and race or ethnicity. The study of such differences is central to the field of sociolinguistics and forms an important part of inquiry in linguistic anthropology. Sociolinguists tend to focus on the social dimensions of language use in large urban societies, whereas linguistic anthropologists investigate these issues among peoples and languages of indigenous communities.

Because gender is a powerful feature of personal and social identity, it is often reflected in language use. Women and men may differ in the frequency with which they use certain pronunciations or words. In both the United States and England, for example, women and girls are more likely to pronounce words ending in "ing"—*running, talking*—according to standard usage, whereas men and boys are more likely to employ colloquial usage, clipping the "ng" sound, as in *runnin'* and *talkin'* (Trudgill 1972). Men also are more likely than women to use profanity and obscenity. In some societies women employ some words or use some sounds that are entirely different from those used by men.

Accent and usage differ with class as well. Middle-class speakers studied in the United States, England, France, and Belgium, for example, tend to use longer sentences and more complex grammatical constructions than working-class speakers (Labov 1972b; Trudgill 1974; Lindenfeld 1969; van den Broeck 1977). Differences in pronunciation, word choice, and grammar often become part of what defines ethnic and racial identities.

In most contemporary countries, one dialect is selected as "standard." There is nothing inherently "better" about this dialect than any others. Rather, its dominance is the result of social, economic, and political factors. Usually, the dialect of a society's elite—the educated, the prosperous, and those in power—becomes the standard. In England, for example, the dialect of English spoken within the geographic triangle linking the cities of London, Cambridge, and Oxford emerged as standard sometime in the fourteenth century. This area was and continues to be Britain's economic and political center. In the United States, upper-class pronunciations often retain the sounds of standard British English, which, in turn, is based on the dialect of upper-class Britons. In Italy, the dialect spoken in Florence, the center of commerce and art in the Renaissance, became the basis of standard Italian.

In every society, once a dialect is recognized as the standard, others become stigmatized and marginalized the more they deviate from it. Standard pronunciation and usage are considered "correct," and other versions are considered "wrong" or "debased." Speakers of the standard dialect gain prestige and respect, whereas speakers of nonstandard dialects are looked down upon. Speakers of nonstandard dialects may look down on themselves as well, thinking that their speech reflects their educational and even moral shortcomings (Bourdieu 1991). These attitudes are transmitted in many settings, especially the schools, the media, and public institutions.

African American Vernacular English (AAVE)
A dialect of English spoken by some, but not all, Americans of African descent.

Ebonics
Another name for African American Vernacular English.

Standard English
Dialect of English chosen as normative, a reflection of the social, economic, and political standing of its speakers.

What are some examples of Briticisms in American English? What are the characteristics of your dialect, and what does that say about who you are?

African American English

In the United States and elsewhere, language use may identify people by race and ethnicity, concepts defined more completely in Chapter 11. Many, but by no means all, African Americans in the United States speak a dialect known as African American English, or **African American Vernacular English (AAVE)** or **Ebonics.** Some speakers use this dialect all the time, whereas others use it only within certain contexts—with family and friends, for example—and speak **Standard English** in other situations—as in school or at work. Individuals also switch from one dialect to the other, depending on the topic under discussion and the attitude and identity of the people with whom they are speaking.

AAVE has patterned rules of phonology, syntax, and semantics equivalent to those of any other language or dialect. Most AAVE rules are identical to those of Standard English, except for a few regularly occurring

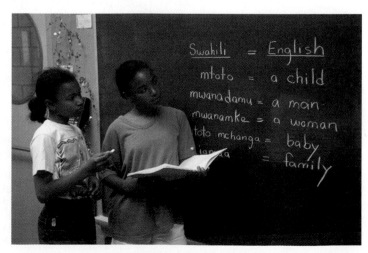

These children probably do not know the West African linguistic origins of some of the words they or their parents may use as speakers of African American Vernacular English (AAVE).

differences. The current consensus among linguists is that some features of AAVE derive from the speech of rural white southerners—itself derived from the Scots-Irish dialect of the region's early white settlers—and that other features, particularly several grammatical rules in the verb system, have their origins in African languages.

Among the most distinctive features of AAVE is the omission of the verb "to be" in the present tense. For instance, "she's smart" becomes "she smart." Other examples are, "He fast in everything he do," "We on tape," and "He always coming over to my house to eat" (Labov, 1972a:67–68). Another prominent feature of AAVE is the use of the verb "to be" to describe an event that occurs over a period of time or one that occurs and is expected to reoccur. The following are some examples (from Labov 1972a; and Baugh 1984):

1. The office be closed on weekends.

2. She say, "Why you be runnin' in the street so much?"

3. But the teachers don't be knowing the problems like the parents do.

Also, in AAVE, "done" is used to mark an action that is completed. For example:

1. The teacher done lost her keys.

2. We done told him 'bout these pipes already.

Finally, AAVE is characterized by a proliferation of negation to mark emphasis and stylistic effect, such as the following:

1. They didn't never do nothing to nobody.

2. He ain't not never gon say it to his face.

3. Didn't nobody see it, didn't nobody hear it!

CASE STUDY

Ebonics: Language and Politics

In December 1996, the school board of Oakland, California, prompted by the poor performance of African American children on tests of reading and language arts skills, passed a resolution to implement a new approach to the teaching of those skills. The goal was to bridge the gap between the vernacular language that many African American children used at home and in the community and the Standard English demanded in the school setting. Teachers were to be trained to appreciate Ebonics/AAVE as a legitimate variant of English, and children were to be instructed in both AAVE and Standard English. The assumption was that children would master basic concepts better if they learned them in their own primary dialect, and this would help them acquire mastery of Standard English.

In one study, AAVE-speaking children in kindergarten and first and second grades took a standard test in reading that had been translated into AAVE. They scored significantly higher than children who took an untranslated version (Williams 1997, 212). Another study involved an AAVE-based reading program, called "Bridge," that had been developed in the 1970s. This program began with reading material written only in the vernacular, then presented texts that were written 50 percent in AAVE and 50 percent in Standard English, and finally switched completely to the standard.

A motivational talk recorded by a young black man introduced students to the program:

> What's happenin', brothers and sisters? I want to tell you about this here program called "Bridge," a cross-cultural reading program. Now I know what you thinkin'. This is just another one of them jive reading programs, and that I won't be needin' no readin' program. But dig it. This here reading program is really kinda different. It was done by a brother and two sisters, soul folk, you know. (quoted in Rickford 1997, 179)

To evaluate the effectiveness of the Bridge approach, children in grades 7 through 12 were tested after 4 months and compared to a group who had not been exposed to the program. Reading scores of the Bridge children increased by a measure of 6.2 months, meaning that they improved more than would be expected for the time period (4 months). In contrast, children in the standard school programs increased only by 1.6 months, less than the increase expected for the 4-month period. The Bridge children not only surpassed children in standard programs but also did better than the norm (4 months' gain for 4 months of instruction) (Rickford 1997, 179). Unfortunately, despite their effectiveness, the publisher discontinued the Bridge readers because of criticism by educators and the media.

The Oakland school board's proposal succumbed to a storm of protest and ridicule. Unfortunately, the board undermined itself by claiming that Ebonics/AAVE was derived from "Niger-Congo African languages" and was "not a dialect of English," although no linguistic evidence supports the claim that AAVE is a separate language. And although AAVE certainly shares features with some African languages, it has complex origins that involve more than a simple affiliation to one particular language family.

These errors gave critics ammunition to oppose the development of special educational programs to serve the needs of African American children. Hoping to counter the barrage of criticism, the Linguistics Society of America voted unanimously in favor of the board, but its support was not widely reported. In the end, Oakland failed to get bilingual education funding and abandoned the program.

What is to be done to teach reading and language skills to children whose home language differs from the standard? Some argue that the dual-language approach is the best answer, whereas others believe that immersion in Standard English is preferable. Black scholars and public figures writing in *The Black Scholar* (1997) and the *Journal of Black Psychology* (1997) argued both points of view.

To gain perspective on this controversy, consider the social context in which AAVE-speaking children may resist learning Standard English. When people elevate a particular language or dialect over another, they convey a message of superiority. Children in countries such as Switzerland, Germany, and Scotland, who grow up speaking a regional dialect, easily learn a standard dialect of their language when they enter school (McWhorter 1997, 12–13). Unlike these European children, however, African American children may confront racial prejudice and social attitudes demeaning to them and to the way they speak. As one commentary concludes, it is important for children to know both AAVE and Standard English and to use them in the appropriate contexts. Appreciating AAVE carries the benefit of a healthy sense of self and pride in their heritage (Smitherman and Cunningham 1997, 230–31).

Other school systems have since tested the Bridge program with greater success. According to William Labov (2004), it has proven to be one of the most useful approaches to improving reading scores for African American children. Its particular strength is that it combines a linguistic and a cultural approach to reading. It employs words and grammatical constructions that are familiar to the children. And it contextualizes language in a cultural background in which the children feel comfortable. Finding techniques that will improve reading scores is especially critical at this time when test scores and linguistic observations point to increasing divergence between AAVE and Standard English.

PEARSON
myanthrolab

Explore more at
www.myanthrolab.com

What do you think is the best approach to the education of AAVE-speaking children, and why?

Serious controversies have arisen in relation to AAVE and the education of African American children. Children who speak AAVE face a host of educational roadblocks. Many teachers regard any nonstandard speech negatively, a bias that colors their judgment of AAVE speakers. Children who have difficulty with Standard English or refuse to use it are sometimes perceived to be hostile, and may even be labeled as learning disabled or mentally handicapped. Because of AAVE's grammatical differences from Standard English, teachers also may have trouble understanding AAVE speakers and misinterpret what they are saying. The children themselves often feel conflict between their desire to succeed in school, which requires them to speak Standard English, and their desire to be accepted by their peers. Other children may ridicule and reject students who speak Standard English and perform well in school. The desire for peer acceptance, combined with the perception that they will never get teachers' approval, may lead children to reject the norms of Standard English.

Some of these issues were raised in a case brought to a federal court in Michigan in 1977. The case arose because of parents' concerns about their children's poor school performance and their feeling that it did not reflect the children's ability but rather a lack of cultural and linguistic understanding between teachers and students. The plaintiffs argued that the local school in Ann Arbor had not taken any remedial action to address their children's educational problems. In 1979, the presiding judge found for the plaintiffs and ordered the Ann Arbor school board to institute procedures to correct teachers' misconceptions about AAVE and to help students better learn the standard language. The judge found that "the language barrier that did exist was in the form of unconscious negative attitudes formed by teachers towards children who spoke African American English, and the reactions of children to those attitudes" (cited in Labov 1982, 193). The school board began instructing teachers about the characteristics of AAVE and developing methods to help children learn the standard language. Despite the findings of the Michigan court, however, attempts to address the use of AAVE in public schools continue to spark controversy (see the Case Study on Ebonics: language and politics on page 82). Fundamental changes in educational systems are often difficult to devise. But, according to Geneva Smitherman (2003), educational approaches should include reinforcing the need for and teaching of the language of wider communication while reinforcing and reaffirming the legitimacy of nonmainstream languages and dialects and promoting mother tongue instruction.

REVIEW ⎯⎯◉ Linguistic anthropology examines the interrelationships between language and culture, for example, how language influences and reflects a culture's worldview. The Sapir-Whorf hypothesis and studies in linguistic relativity argue that language predisposes people to selectively perceive and think about things in certain ways that then affect their behavior and attitudes. Dialects, regional and group distinctions of a language, include differences in pronunciation and vocabulary. They can vary by sex, gender, race, ethnicity, and social class or socioeconomic background. Sociolinguistics is the study of the impacts of socioeconomic and cultural factors on language and communication within a society. Standard dialects, such as Standard English, are usually derived from the versions spoken by social elites. African American Vernacular English (AAVE, also called Ebonics) is a well-known dialect in the United States derived from English spoken by rural white southerners and African languages. AAVE has African loanwords and distinctive grammatical rules for verbs.

ETHNOSEMANTICS

Building on the pioneering foundations of the first half of the twentieth century, linguistic anthropologists have broadened their exploration of the relationship between language and culture. Some continue to study what vocabulary can reveal about the structure of human thought. Others investigate how cultural values and symbols are encoded in words or expressions and are then used by speakers to transmit emotional, attitudinal, and symbolic meanings. Researchers also examine the systems or ways of categorizing words that people use to name people, objects, or forces in their physical and social environments, a field called **ethnosemantics.**

Studies of vocabulary usually focus on the comparative analysis of categories of words or systems of classification, such as words for animals, kinship terms, body parts, colors, or phenomena such as weather. Linguistic anthropologists also study occupational **jargons,** the specialized vocabularies used by people who share specific communication needs relating to their work or some other activity. Philosophy professors, baseball announcers, Web hosts, and thieves are examples of groups that use jargons to communicate.

Componential Analysis

By analyzing similarities and contrasts among the words in a category, you can learn something about what is culturally important to the speakers of a language and how

---

What jargons do you use? How do you use them?

ethnosemantics
Study of culture through people's use of language to categorize and classify people, objects, activities, and experiences.

jargons
Specialized or technical words and expressions spoken by people who share a particular occupation or interest.

they experience their world. This comparative approach, called **componential analysis,** involves isolating components of meaning within the words in a category. The goal is to understand the ethnosemantics, or indigenous systems of meaning, of a culture or group and its members.

For example, take words for animals in English. English has many more words for some animals than it does for others, and these differences reflect differences in cultural interest. English has separate words for horses that specify female and male adults (*mare* and *stallion*), babies (*foal*), female and male juveniles (*filly* and *colt*), and neutered adult males (*gelding*). English has a similarly extensive vocabulary to differentiate age and sex among cattle and other domestic food and draft animals, which historically have played a crucial role in the subsistence and economy of English-speaking peoples. In addition, English has many words for different breeds of these animals. In contrast, other species—chipmunk, otter, and moose, for example—are treated in a more generalized way, with only one term for all members of the class of animals.

Cultural Presuppositions

When people speak, they understand one another because of an array of shared knowledge and assumptions, or **cultural presuppositions,** that mean far more than what words alone convey. Smooth conversation depends on these unstated presuppositions. Without them, people cannot accurately assess how their words are being understood. Americans talking to one another about the World Series, for example, assume they share knowledge that the term refers to professional baseball, that professional baseball teams are organized into leagues, that the teams in a league compete throughout a season to determine the league champions, and that the World Series is the culminating competition between the league champions.

Other cultural presuppositions are more complex and more subtly embedded within language. For example, the language of the Navajo of New Mexico and Arizona reflects different presuppositions about individual self-assertion (Young and Morgan 1987). English has many verbs that express types of coercion: *cause, force, oblige, make, compel, order, command, constrain, must, have to,* and *ought to.* In contrast, the Navajo language lacks such verbs. Rather than saying, "I must go there," a Navajo speaker says the equivalent of, "It is only good that I shall go there." Similarly, whereas English readily expresses the idea that people have a right to impose their will on other creatures, the Navajo language does not. Where an English speaker might say, "I make the horse run," a Navajo speaker would say, "The horse is running for me."

Cultural norms of communicative behavior—the pragmatics of communication—also involve presuppositions. Two casually acquainted North Americans might use a greeting such as "Hi! How are you?" Both parties know that this greeting is a routine social ritual, not a true request for information. The expected response is "Fine, how are you?"—not a detailed account of one's personal problems.

In all cultures, people use language to influence hearers: to convey information, ask questions, persuade, or issue commands. Few words are neutral in their connotations. They have associations that presuppose culturally shared symbolic meanings. Cultural symbols are transmitted through language and obtain their strength because speakers and hearers unconsciously accept the assumptions on which they are based. For example, to promote products, advertisers manipulate the presuppositions associated with such words as *new, bigger,* and *improved.* The word *free* is charged with cultural presuppositions. Repetitive exposure to such use of language reinforces overt and covert cultural messages implied and presupposed by the words.

Ethnography of Communication

Linguistic anthropologists analyze speech behavior and nonverbal communication in their widest cultural and social contexts. Dell Hymes (1974) introduced the term **ethnography of communication** to describe the study of all explicit and implicit norms for communication—verbal and nonverbal—in a particular setting. Included in such a study would be a description of the setting in which the communication occurred, the participants involved, the language they used, the way they communicated (speaking, writing, nonverbal signals),

> **What cultural presuppositions do you and your classmates share about your participation in the course?**

componential analysis
A technique of analyzing the similarities and contrasts among words in a particular category, such as kinship terms or animal names.

cultural presuppositions
Shared knowledge and unspoken assumptions that people have as members of their culture.

ethnography of communication
Study of communication as it occurs within a particular cultural context, considering such features as settings, participants, and participants' attitudes and goals.

An ethnography of communication in a courtroom includes the spatial arrangement of participants (judges, jurors, attorneys, defendants) and their permissible speaking turns.

the genre or form of the communication (conversation, folktale, chant, debate), the topic or subject of the communication, and the attitudes and goals of the participants.

An ethnographic description of communication in an American courtroom, for example, might run like this: The setting, a courtroom, is structured to provide separate seating areas for various categories of participants and to regulate contact between participants. Among the participants are judges, lawyers, defendants, plaintiffs, witnesses, jurors, spectators, and court officials. Participants behave according to their role in the proceedings. The judge, seated on a raised platform at the front of the room and distinguished by special attire, physically dominates the room. The judge controls the communication of the other participants, each of whom has certain obligations to speak or not to speak. Failure to obey the judge may be considered "contempt of court," a legally punishable offense. Only judges, lawyers, and witnesses may speak publicly. Other participants (jurors, spectators, officers) must remain silent. Each type of participant communicates in expected ways. Lawyers may make introductory and concluding statements or ask questions. Witnesses answer questions. Judges make statements, ask questions, and issue commands and rulings.

Topics of discussion in a courtroom are rigidly defined. A trial is intended to resolve a specific issue, and all communication must be relevant to that issue. The goals of participants vary according to their roles in the proceedings. Speakers choose their words, tone of voice, facial expressions, and gestures to accomplish their goals. The judge seeks to appear impartial, lawyers speak and act persuasively or aggressively, defendants may portray themselves as innocent, witnesses appear honest and reliable, and jurors remain silent but convey interest in the speech and behavior of others.

REVIEW — Ethnosemantics, or indigenous systems of meaning, can lead to a better understanding of what is important in a culture. Systems of meaning include jargons, which are specific to certain occupations or activities. Examples of word comparisons using componential analysis include kin terms and terms for animals. The shared knowledge and assumptions that speakers use are cultural presuppositions. The ethnography of communication involves examining all aspects of communication (setting, participants, topics, and goals) to understand language as cultural expression.

PROCESSES OF LANGUAGE CHANGE

Languages change over time. Change sometimes results from processes internal to a language. For instance, a language may gradually eliminate grammatical distinctions, meanings of words may be altered, or the order of words within sentences may change. Evidence of such patterns can be found in the history of English. Old English (the language spoken in the British Isles until about 1066, the year of the Norman invasion from France), had noun endings that indicated whether the noun was a subject or object in a sentence. Modern English nouns lack these markers. However, English retains distinctions between subject and object for pronouns: *I, he, she, we,* and *they* are subjects, whereas *me, him, her, us,* and *them* are objects. *You* can be either subject or object. Modern English is currently undergoing a further loss of the subject-object distinction in the relative pronouns *who* and *whom.* Although the object form *whom* is still used in writing and formal speech, most speakers no longer use it in colloquial and informal contexts. We are, therefore, witnesses to ongoing language change.

Changes in the meanings of words also are commonplace, for example. Modern English speakers often have trouble understanding the works of William Shakespeare because some words that he used have different meanings today, and others have gone out of the language entirely. Some nations try to "freeze" their official national language in time. In the service of linguistic nationalism, France, for example, has a committee in charge of eliminating foreign words from the French language. English is the main influence, with new words and phrases in French such as *le hamburger* and *le blue jeans.*

Language change is constant and natural as new words and expressions are invented or discarded and as vocabularies are elaborated to reflect cultural priorities. Thus, people who are concerned about the "purity" of their language are chasing a phantom. Also, as Edward Sapir pointed out about the relationship between vocabulary and cultural priorities, cultures often change more rapidly than languages. As a result of this "linguistic lag," a specialized vocabulary may not reflect a society's current cultural interests. In time, as linguistic change catches up with culture change, the specialized words are likely to change meaning or to disappear.

Creoles, Pidgins, and Lingua Francas

In addition to internal adjustments, languages also change in response to the influence of other languages because no language is completely isolated from others. External change occurs when peoples with different languages and cultures come into contact, with three possible general results: The languages will remain distinct; one language will become dominant; or the languages will meld into a new language.

One process of language change that results in a new language is creolization, or the creation of creole languages. **Creoles** are languages that combine sounds, grammatical forms, and vocabularies from several different linguistic sources. They arise in situations of close contact and interaction among people who speak different languages. The United States is home to three creole languages, for example, that came into existence in the past several hundred years. The three American creoles are Gullah, Louisiana Creole, and Hawaiian Creole. Gullah (spoken mostly on the Sea Islands off the coast of South Carolina) is derived from various African languages and English. Louisiana Creole is derived from various African languages and French. Hawaiian Creole is a complex mixture of English, Native Hawaiian, and several Asian and Pacific languages.

Creoles often develop from pidgin languages. **Pidgins** are forms of communication made by combining words and constructions from several languages, but they differ from creoles because they are not full languages but, rather, have small vocabularies and simple constructions. They are used for special purposes, especially for trade.

Lingua francas are full languages that are used among numerous peoples who come into contact regularly but who speak distinct languages. Some of these lingua francas are pidgins, such as those that arose to serve the Arab and European slave trades; some are creoles such as Rasta, spoken in Jamaica and other West Indian islands; and others are the regular language of one group that came to be widely used by many other people, such as Swahili, spoken in eastern Africa. More recently, English and French have become international lingua francas.

creoles
Languages that have historic roots as an amalgamation of vocabulary and grammar derived from two or more independent languages.

pidgins
Rudimentary languages that have a simplified grammar and a limited vocabulary.

lingua francas
Languages used in particular areas by speakers of many different languages in order to communicate with each other.

In your experience, what are some examples of new vocabularies that reflect changing cultural priorities?

GLOBALIZATION

Through today's dynamics of globalization, English is now spoken by more than a billion people throughout the world, rivaled only by Chinese. English has become global in three ways: Countries such as Australia and South Africa are dominated by English-speaking inhabitants; countries with few native English speakers nevertheless have English as an official language; and many other countries give priority to English in foreign-language learning.

The Indian film industry produces movies in Hindustani, the lingua franca of north and west India and the language of popular culture in India.

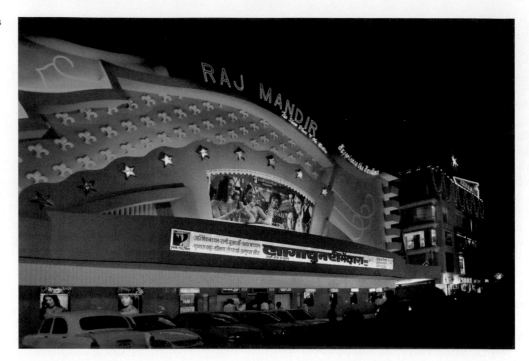

Historical Linguistics

Among groups of people who speak variants of a language, differences between dialects can accumulate to the extent that people no longer understand one another. Thus, mutual intelligibility is a definition of language as shared by its speakers. When people no longer understand one another, new, separate languages emerge. Tracing changes in languages over time and relationships between languages in the past is the goal of historical linguistics.

Over time, people's speech changed into distinct dialects and, ultimately, when speakers could no longer understand one another, into separate languages. Mutual intelligibility is often taken as a test of whether two forms of speech are dialects of the same language or two different languages. By comparing the sounds, vocabularies, and syntax of today's languages, historical linguists can reconstruct the processes that led to change, grouping languages into families descended from a common ancestral form. A **language family,** then, is a group of languages spoken by people who are historically related.

One method for determining the relationships among languages, estimating when they separated, and even reconstructing features of the parent language is to study a core vocabulary of up to 500 words. This core vocabulary consists of words for objects or ideas that every language can be expected to have words for, including pronouns, some numerals, some colors, words for body parts, and common adjectives (such as large, small) and verbs (such as to eat, to sleep). Words with related meanings that are found to share a common heritage are referred to as **cognates.** The English *to pay* and the French *payer* are cognates, for example. English and French are related historically, and both are members of the much larger language family called Indo-European, which also includes languages as diverse as Sanskrit, Hindi, Polish, German, and Norwegian. These languages very likely all started out as one language in central Eurasia an estimated 8,000 to 10,000 years ago.

Loanwords

All languages borrow words from other languages. These **loanwords** are often incorporated into a language when the speakers borrow a new cultural item from another group. The words often name new foods, articles of clothing, tools and other equipment, occupations, or new ideas. Table 4.3 contains a small number of the many thousands of words borrowed into English from a variety of origins, omitting more common sources such as French, Spanish, Italian, and German (Pyles and Algeo 1982, 297–316).

In some cases when people borrow foreign words with meanings similar to words that already exist in the language, they give the words special usage. For example, after the

language family
A group of languages that are historically related, descendants of a common ancestral form.

cognates
Words in different languages that are derived from the same word in their parent language.

loanwords
Words borrowed from one language into another.

TABLE 4.3 LOANWORDS IN ENGLISH

Source	Loanwords
Irish-Gaelic	brogue, leprechaun, shamrock
Scandinavian	muggy, rug, ski
Dutch	boss, cookie, pit (of fruit), sleigh
Yiddish	kibitzer, nebbish, phooey, schlep
Russian	czar, mammoth, tundra, vodka
Turkish	fez, tulip, turban
Arabic	candy, mattress, orange, sugar
Hebrew	cherub, hallelujah, jubilee, kosher
Hindi	bungalow, dungaree, jungle, pajamas
Chinese	tea, kowtow, tycoon
Japanese	hara-kiri, samurai, soya
Pacific languages	bamboo, kangaroo, launch, tattoo
African languages	gorilla, jazz, tote, yam
Native North American languages	bayou, moccasin, moose, pecan
Native Central American languages	chocolate, maize, tomato, potato

TABLE 4.4 ANIMAL TERMS IN ENGLISH

Animal	Meat	French source
Steer	beef	boeuf
Pig	pork	porc
Calf	veal	veau
Sheep	mutton	mouton

Norman invasion of England in 1066, English incorporated the French names of common farm animals to refer to the animals' meat, and the English names were kept for referring to the animals (see Table 4.4).

Similarly, foreign words sometimes have a different connotation than their native equivalents. In English, for example, some words of French origin are considered more formal or polite than their Old English counterparts. In the following pairs, the Old English word is given first, followed by a word whose source is French: smell/odor, sweat/perspiration, eat/dine, dead/deceased, want/desire, look at/regard, go away/depart, come back/return.

Just as English has borrowed thousands of words from foreign sources, other languages have borrowed words from English. And just as English has modified foreign words to fit English sound patterns, so have other languages altered sounds of English words to fit their systems (see Table 4.5).

Language families provide insight into the historical relationships between neighboring and even distant peoples. For instance, if neighboring groups speak unrelated languages, they probably did not always live near one another. They may both have migrated to their current locations from elsewhere, or perhaps one had long residence in the region and the other was a more recent immigrant. If the language spoken by one group of people is related to a language spoken hundreds or even thousands of miles away, both groups have a common ancestor that spoke their one ancestral language.

Relationships between languages are determined by finding regularities in sound shifts between cognates. What regular sound shifts can you identify in the following Indo-European cognates for *father*?

Examples of Indo-European Cognates

father (Modern English)
fader (Middle English)
faeder (Old English)
fader (Swedish, Norwegian, Danish)
vader (Dutch)
vater (German)
pater (Latin)
padre (Spanish, Italian)
père (French)
pai (Portuguese)
pate-r (Greek)
pitar (Sanskrit)
pita- (Hindi)

ANTHROPOLOGY APPLIED

Languages Lost and Found

Closely associated with globalization is the loss of indigenous languages to new languages or to replacement by languages used in business and international politics. The six official languages of the United Nations are Arabic, Chinese, Russian, Spanish, English, and French. The UN conducts most of its business in English and French. Many indigenous peoples and minorities in pluralistic societies are not taught their native languages, but instead focus is on the national or official language to succeed in the larger society.

Globalization thus can lead to language loss, which in turn leads to the loss of cultural content, including people's genealogies, folktales, culture histories, and cultural identities. An estimated 6,800 languages are spoken today. In the last 500 years, 4,000 to 9,000 languages became extinct due to wars, genocide, incorporation of ethnic minorities into majority populations, and bans on native languages use by colonial governments. By the end of the twenty-first century, it is estimated that more than half of the remaining languages will become extinct (Krauss 1992). The 357 languages with fewer than 50 speakers include Sami (Sweden), Birale (Ethiopia), and Menomini (United States). Examples of recently extinct languages are Ubykh (Turkey), Eyak (Alaska), Dalmatian (Albania), and Ainu (Japan).

Linguistic anthropologists, concerned that language loss leads to the loss of culture, have helped indigenous and minority groups document their languages and their stories and implement programs to teach younger generations their native tongue. With the help of anthropologists, Tsalagi (Cherokee) people and others, for example, can learn to speak Tsalagi with language-learning software and games, free MP3 downloads, and other online resources, such as study groups, discussion lists, dictionaries, and texts. The survival of Tsalagi in some form is guaranteed because it is a written language and has a relatively large number of speakers. For some researchers, recording endangered languages and cultures has become a life's work. After the collapse of the Soviet Union in 1991, for example, many multinational teams of linguists and anthropologists raced to Siberia to record rare and disappearing languages such as Itel'men of Kamchatka.

Efforts to reclaim the indigenous Hawaiian language from the brink of extinction are among the best success stories worldwide. By 1980, fewer than 1,000 native residents of Hawaii spoke Hawaiian, and only about 30 of these were younger than 18. Thanks to vigorous programming and funding, language immersion preschool classes were organized beginning in 1984. These were later expanded to include older children (Nettle and Romaine 2000). In 2007, more than 2,300 students were enrolled in classes statewide (Namahoe and Barcarse 2007, 44). In Papua New Guinea, a nation where 823 languages are still spoken, preschool and early education is mandated in the vernacular language of each

region, enabling children to begin their schooling in their native language, with a gradual transition to English (UNESCO 2002). The goal of these programs is speaking fluency, for that is what keeps indigenous languages alive. In Peru, programs are underway to translate works of world literature into Quechua, the language of the Incas. Although Quechua is one of the two official languages of Peru (along with Spanish), its use has been declining. The goal of current endeavors is to develop a "public culture in the language" including books, magazines, and videos, rather than to have its use relegated to home and private contexts. In the words of Demetrio Tupac Yupanqui, a professor and government adviser, "When people communicate in Quechua, they glow" (Romero 2008, A6).

● CRITICAL THINKING QUESTIONS

What languages did your forebears speak? Can you understand, speak, or read those languages? What might you be missing if you cannot?

TABLE 4.5 LOANWORDS FROM ENGLISH		
English Word	Borrowing Language	Loanword
Roof	Spanish (Puerto Rico)	rufo
Police	Swahili (Africa)	polisi
Ruler	Ganda (Africa)	luula
Railway	Ganda (Africa)	leerwe
Thumbtacks	Mohawk (North America)	tamtaks
Christmas	Navajo (North America)	kesmis
Baseball	Japanese	beisuboru
Casual	Tagalog (Philippines)	kazwal

Sources: Puerto Rican Spanish: Zentella 1985, 45; Costa Rican Spanish: Appel and Muysken 1987, 169; Ganda: Halle and Clements 1983, 51; Mohawk: Bonvillain 1978, 37; Navajo: Young and Morgan 1987, 7; Swahili, Japanese: Berlitz 1982, 299–300; Tagalog: Molony 1977, 141–42.

Plotting the distribution of related languages helps to trace the history of migrations, contacts, and conquests among the world's peoples. Although no one knows when or how the first language was spoken or who spoke it, some historical-comparative linguists believe that they might one day be able to reconstruct "protohuman," the first language spoken by the first modern humans.

REVIEW

All languages change. Sounds shift, words change meanings, words are borrowed (loanwords), new words are invented, and languages become extinct. Language change can be both internal and external. Processes of language change that result from culture contact include the creation of pidgins and creoles. Historical linguistics is the comparative study of changes in languages over time and relationships between languages and language families in the past. Divergence of languages is measured by comparing changes in core vocabularies to find cognates, words from different languages with shared sound shifts and similar meanings.

CHAPTER SUMMARY

What Is Language?

- All languages are based on arbitrary symbols for relationships between the sounds of a word and the object, activity, quality, or idea that the word is used to name. Languages are characterized by displacement—that is, the ability to talk about events of the past and the future, not just events that are ongoing at the moment of speech. Languages are productive, in that sounds, words, and sentence constructions can be joined in infinite novel combinations.

The Components of Language

- Talk is achieved through the interdependent components of sounds, words, sentences, and meanings. Although every language is unique, there are some universals, including the human range of phonetic inventories, recurring types of morphological and syntactic constructions, and underlying semantic relationships.

Nonverbal Communication

- Nonverbal communication also consists of both unique and common behaviors. Although some actions may occur in many societies, they are always given culturally specific interpretations.

Linguistic Anthropology

- Linguistic anthropologists investigate associations between language and cultural meaning.

- African American Vernacular English (AAVA) is a variety of speech employed by some people of African ancestry in the United States that diverges from Standard English, although it shares most linguistic rules with it. Controversies over AAVA focus primarily on proposals to incorporate vernacular speech in schools.

- The United States is a complex, multilingual nation with millions of speakers of languages other than English.

Ethnosemantics

- An "ethnography of communication" attempts to uncover all of the rules that connect language to social behavior. Components of any speech interaction include the participants, the code used, the physical and social settings, the topic of conversation, and the goals of the speakers.

Processes of Language Change

- All languages constantly change. Change derives from internal linguistic processes and from contact with other languages. New sounds may be introduced and/or grammatical constructions may be altered. All languages also borrow words from foreign sources.

- When varieties of the same language become so different that people speaking different dialects can no longer understand one another, new languages come into being. A language family consists of languages that are related historically and are the common descendants of an ancestral code.

KEY TERMS

language 68	morpheme 71	Sapir-Whorf hypothesis 75	componential analysis 85
symbolic feature 68	syntax 71	linguistic relativity 75	cultural presuppositions 85
displacement 69	universal grammar 71	dialect 79	ethnography of communication 85
productivity 69	semantics 71	African American Vernacular English (AAVE) 81	creoles 87
call systems (signal systems) 69	nonverbal communication 73		pidgin 87
phonology 70	emblems 73	Ebonics 81	lingua francas 87
phonetics 70	body language 73	Standard English 81	language family 88
phonemics 70	intercultural communication 73	ethnosemantics 84	cognates 88
phoneme 71	sociolinguistics 75	jargons 84	loanwords 88
morphology 71			

REVIEW QUESTIONS

1. What are the connections between language and culture?

2. Why are chimpanzees and other apes unable to communicate verbally? How do they communicate symbolically? What are some differences in primate communication under laboratory conditions and natural settings?

3. What is the difference between a phoneme and a morpheme?

4. What is the Sapir-Whorf hypothesis? How are language and thought connected?

5. Why is nonverbal communication important?

6. What are some internal processes of language change that occur in all languages?

7. How do languages change as a result of cultural contact and globalization?

8. What are the goals and methods of historical-comparative linguistics? How are all human languages ultimately related in space and time?

myanthrolab EXERCISES

To complete the following exercises and activities, you must log in to www.myanthrolab.com and select your current textbook.

1. In the **Explore** tab of Chapter 4, click on *Video* and watch one of the videos available in this section. Complete the short answer exercise that accompanies the video.

2. While in the **Explore** tab of, click on the *NPR Audio Programs Broadcast* tab and go to *Theme 6: Communication and Language*. Listen to one of the programs in this section and complete the short answer exercise that accompanies the program.

3. In the Practice tab, click on *Activities* and complete the *Four Key Features of Language* animation.

4. Enter the **MyAnthroLibrary** section on the home page to read more about topics and cultures that are discussed in this chapter. Suggested readings include:

Altered Paths: Field Research on Luo Language and Culture by Ben G. Blount

Maya of Yucatán: The Sacred in Everyday Life by John R. Sosa

LEARNING ONE'S CULTURE

CHAPTER

5

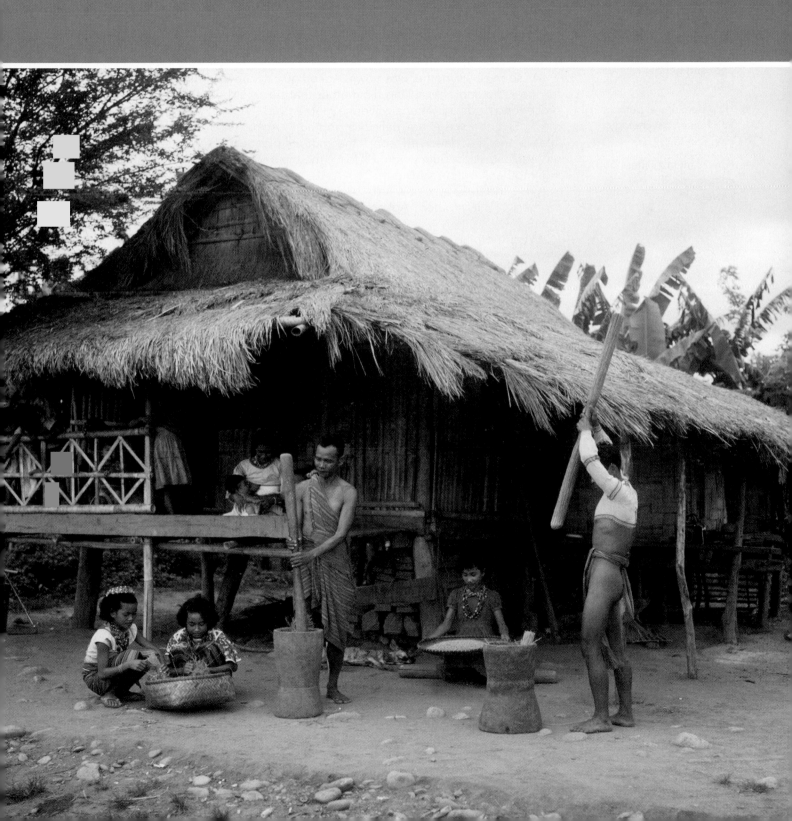

- What is enculturation?

- How do people incorporate children into their society?

- What are the social, cultural, and psychological effects of rites of passage?

- Through what formal and informal means do people learn their culture?

- What social and cultural factors influence a person's age- and gender-related behavior?

- How do culture, personality, and human psychology intersect?

- How is mental illness both culture-specific and universal?

There once lived a widow, Ballingokan, and her son, Agkon. Every morning the rooster would wake up Agkon by crowing:

"Kook-ko-ko-oook! Agkon, come and trap me." Agkon would answer, "Wait, I'll first look for some fibers to make up my snare." The next day, the rooster again jumped on Agkon's window and crowed: "Oo-oo-oo-o! Agkon, come and snare me." And Agkon said, "Wait, I'll get some strings for my snare." On the third day, the rooster flapped his wings loudly and cried out: "O-oo-ook! Agkon, when will you come?"

Agkon ran out, laid his snare with care, and after a few moments it caught a wild fat rooster, which he proudly showed to his mother. "What a nice fat rooster. Now we shall have some nice food," his mother said. . . .

Agkon burned the feathers of the rooster, cut it into pieces, and began to cook it. When it was almost cooked he dropped the ladle. "Mother," Agkon cried, "I dropped the ladle." "Never mind," his mother said as she quickly went out of the house, "I'll pick it up."

As soon as his mother was down, Agkon quickly drew up the ladder. Then he asked for the ladle and after telling his mother that he would eat first and call her later, he proceeded to do so. After a while the mother said, "Agkon, please leave the wings for me." "But the wings are delicious, mother," Agkon said and started to eat them. "Leave me the claws, my son," the mother pleaded. "They are just what I want, mother," he said. "Surely, you will leave me the neck, Agkon." "It is just what I am eating, mother," Agkon said.

Only the head was now left. "Agkon, my son, will you not give the head to your mother?" "But, mother," Agkon answered, "you know very well that I need to eat the brains."

When nothing was left of the rooster, Agkon put back the ladder and the mother wearily went up the steps. She looked at the pot and found a little soup left, which she took, and mashing some rice in it, ate in tears. She decided to revenge herself on her son.

The mother went upstream and after walking for a long time she heard loud weeping and found a family mourning over a man who had been dead [for a long time]. Ballingokan offered to buy the dead man, but the relatives were already happy to have someone take care of the dead so they gladly gave it to her free. She told the Ladag [Dead Man], "I will carry you on my back." The dead man climbed on her back and she brought him to her granary where she covered him with rice. Then going to the house she called her son and said, "There are some ripe bananas in the granary."

Agkon went down and peeped inside the granary where the Ladag caught him and proceeded to eat him. He shouted to his mother, "Mother," he cried, "the Ladag is eating my feet." "That is for the claws of the chicken that you would not share with your mother," the mother answered. "Mother, the Ladag is eating my arms." "But you did not give me the wings either, my child," his mother said. "Now he is eating my breast, mother." "Neither did you share the breast of the rooster with me, my son." "He's beginning to feed on my neck, mother." "Well, you ate the neck of the rooster, Agkon." "Go ahead, Ladag," said the mother, "eat his head."

That night, Balligokan felt lonely; there was no one to talk with. The following day, there was no one to carry fuel, no one to help her. Her loneliness was worse, and feeling sad, she went to the granary to look for any remains of her son. She found a little blood on the floor, which she took, and going to the river began to perform some ritual. She took some water and began to bathe the blood and said, "May I bathe Agkon! May I bathe his hands!" At once his hands were formed. And as she said, "legs, feet, arms," all were formed into a man.

Then the mother and son were reconciled and both resolved to love each other truly. And Agkon said, "Mother, from now on, we shall always eat together!"

Excerpts from Richard Dorson, *Folktales Told Around the World*, pp. 257–259. © 1975. Reprinted by permission of The University of Chicago Press.

This tale from the Kalingga people of the Philippines relates in vivid images the consequences of wrong behavior. Agkon violates cultural rules of how one ought to treat other people, especially one's own mother. As punishment, he is eaten by the Ladag, as his mother wished. But in the end, she brings him back to life because she recognizes that she needs him too. The narrative, therefore, teaches children proper behavior and highlights the economic and social reciprocity that characterizes relationships among kin.

Like language, which is an element of culture, culture as a whole is a symbolic system. As with language, all humans have the capacity to learn any culture, but the specific culture they learn is the one into which they are born and raised. The process by which children acquire their culture is called enculturation, and is similar to **socialization,** the process of learning social norms. This chapter examines how enculturation works, then looks at a related issue, the relationship between culture and individual personality.

THE PROCESS OF ENCULTURATION

Humans are born helpless, too weak and uncoordinated to move on their own. Without speech, they are unable to communicate their thoughts, needs, and wants to others. As a result, infants are completely dependent on adults to be carried, cared for, and fed. Even after they can walk and talk, human children remain dependent on adults. Indeed, humans have the longest period of juvenile dependency of any animal species. Humans don't reach sexual maturity until around the age of 13 or 14, and do not reach full adult maturity until a few years after that.

Many evolutionary pressures account for these characteristics. Infant helplessness probably resulted from a combination of the increasingly large brains of our ancestors and their shift to an upright, or bipedal, posture. Structural changes in the skeleton that made bipedalism possible also favored immature births, before infant head size grew very large. The lengthy period of childhood dependency reflects the human characteristic that a large brain made possible—culture. Whereas other animals depend mostly on their physical adaptations for survival, humans rely on culture. But culture is learned, and learning it—enculturation—takes a long time.

All societies have beliefs and practices surrounding childbirth and maternal and infant care. Ju/'hoansi mothers in Namibia and Botswana are attended by healers when they are in difficult labor. The healers go into a trance (called *kia*) in order to confront the spirits causing harm to mother and child (Katz 1982). These healers lay their hands on the mother's abdomen, transferring healing energy and substance (called *num*) in the hopes of protecting the mother and baby.

After the birth, mother and child often remain in their separate dwelling or room for a prescribed length of time. During that period, the mother may follow similar food, activity, and contact restrictions as she had before the birth. After a set number of days, weeks, or even months, the woman and her child are reincorporated into family and community life. That final transition and reincorporation may be marked by ritualized blessings on both mother and child.

In all societies, the process of enculturation begins as soon as a baby is born and continues into maturity. Infants may be helpless, but they are immediately responsive to the world around them. Gradually, they learn how to communicate through gesture and sound, and they learn how to understand the myriad messages sent their way. Children not only learn to control their muscles, make purposeful actions, and acquire the language and communication practices of their society but, most crucially, they also learn to behave in ways that their culture deems appropriate.

Enculturation is so extraordinarily effective because it takes place primarily through informal, nonexplicit means. Because we learn most of our cultural rules unconsciously, we come to feel that our behavior is natural, a result of our nature rather than our culture. And because we feel that our behavior, attitudes, and values come from our nature, we generally don't question their appropriateness. Instead, we "naturalize" our culture, taking these behaviors and attitudes as part of our nature rather than recognizing their cultural origins. Naturalization of attitudes and behaviors results in unquestioning

socialization
A process similar to enculturation that emphasizes social rather than cultural factors in learning one's culture.

acceptance of cultural norms. The practices that we engage in and the values that we hold become so much a part of our thoughts and feelings that we do not see them as distinct from ourselves. Rather, we see them as forming our very essence as people. We seem to absorb cultural messages without conscious effort, beginning with the great dependency of infancy and continuing through childhood's protracted period of physical and psychological maturation.

Although enculturation is a process begun in earliest childhood, learning one's culture does not end upon adulthood. Rather, people learn throughout their lives, continually acquiring new skills but also continually reshaping and reinforcing attitudes and values. Life's experiences teach new lessons that may encourage people to question old ways of interpreting behavior, or they may strengthen their convictions. Just as maintaining traditions reinforces cultural stability, discoveries and innovations enrich individuals and societies.

Becoming a Human Being

When does human life begin? This question may be familiar because of the heated debate over abortion, but the answer has more cultural variability than the two positions heard frequently in that debate: conception or birth. In many cultures, newborns are not considered human until a few days or even weeks after birth. They are thought instead to occupy some liminal (in-between), transitional, and not fully human state. Not until the end of this period are infants thought of and treated as members of their family and community. This transition to personhood, or **social birth,** is often marked by ritual.

Among the Lohorung Rai of eastern Nepal, babies are introduced to the ancestors when they are 5 (girls) or 6 (boys) days old (Hardman 2000). Until the rite is performed, infants (and their mothers) are thought to be both in danger and dangerous. As yet unprotected by the ancestors, they are vulnerable to harm from evil spirits. This vulnerability and lack of protection make them dangerous to other people, who avoid contact with them. The rite raises the child's ancestral soul and introduces it to the house ancestors, placing it firmly within its family and wider kinship group. Failure to perform the ceremony or to perform it well jeopardizes the child's future health and chances for success.

Zunis of the American Southwest consider newborns to be unripe or soft "as are germinating seeds or unfinished clay vessels" (Cushing 1979, 205). For eight days after birth, babies and their mothers are isolated indoors, away from the sun, until they are sufficiently hardened for safe exposure to "the world of sunlight." At the end of the period of seclusion, the baby's umbilical cord is buried nearby, and the burial site becomes the child's "midmost shrine," connecting it to Earth Mother and the underworld from which the ancestors emerged in primordial times. At sunrise on the eighth day after birth, the baby's paternal grandmother washes the baby's head, puts it in its cradle, places cornmeal in its hands, and takes it out into the dawn air, facing east toward the rising sun. While other female relatives of both parents sprinkle offerings of cornmeal to Sun in the east, the paternal grandmother recites a blessing prayer (Bunzel 1932).

Practices of delayed social birth are generally found in societies that have (or had) high rates of infant mortality. High rates of infant mortality may discourage parental emotional attachment to their child. An infant is most vulnerable right after birth, and the belief that it is not yet fully human can temper parents' grief should it die during this period. For similar reasons, deaths of infants or young children are not marked ritually in any significant way in many cultures. The body is instead disposed of quickly and without ceremony. In contrast, in societies with comparatively low infant mortality rates, social birth may even precede actual birth—for example, in customs such as sending fetal sonograms and holding baby showers.

Beliefs about the humanity of infants also reflect a psychological accommodation to the political and economic circumstances that foster high infant mortality. According to a belief prevalent among impoverished communities in northeastern Brazil, for example, infants who are sickly, weak, and passive are thought to be uninterested in living (Scheper-Hughes 1989; 1992). In other words, in contrast to robust, emotionally engaged infants, sickly infants are thought to *want* to die. They are consequently often ignored, inadequately fed, and little cared for. Those who die are not mourned. A mother's tears are thought to weigh down the infant's angel wings and hinder its ascent to heaven. These

social birth
Social recognition of the transition to personhood.

beliefs may provide comfort to the child's mother, but they also divert attention from the crushing poverty responsible for the region's high infant mortality rate. Rather than a victim of its circumstances, the child becomes an agent in its own demise.

Naming. An important process linked to the recognition of a baby as a social person is naming. In North American societies, a child is usually named at birth or before. Children may be named after a relative or friend of the parents, or they may be given a name from a large stock of familiar names or one that is made up. Some people name a son after the father or, more rarely, a daughter after the mother. Others, such as members of the Jewish faith, never name a child for someone who is living but prefer to name a child after a deceased relative.

In some Native American societies, people often receive new names at various times in their lives, sometimes in hopes of obtaining spiritual powers or protection. For instance, a nineteenth-century Hidatsa woman from North Dakota recounted the reasons for her name change from "Good Way" to "Buffalo-Bird Woman":

> I was a rather sickly child and my father wished after a time to give me a new name. We Indians thought that sickness was from the gods. A child's name was given as a kind of prayer. A new name often moved the gods to help a sick or weakly child. So my father gave me another name, Waheenee-wea, or Buffalo-Bird Woman. My father's gods were birds; and these, we thought, had much holy power. Perhaps the buffalo-birds had spoken to him in a dream. I am still called by the name my father gave me; and, as I have lived to be a very old woman, I think it has brought me good luck from the gods. (Wilson 1981, 8)

Baptism for Christians marks a kind of social birth and functions as an introduction to a social and religious community. In most denominations, baptism ideally takes place as soon as possible after birth, because of the belief that a baptized baby would go to heaven if it were to die. Other theological explanations for infant baptism also exist. Among Baptists and some other groups, however, people are not baptized until they are old enough to understand the significance of the ritual and to make the decision for themselves.

In many societies, the choice of a name is never casual and always carries cultural implications. For example, the Ju/'hoansi of the Kalahari Desert in Botswana and Namibia have an extremely complex naming system. The Ju/'hoansi, who until recently were hunting-and-gathering nomads, have only sixty-seven names, thirty-five for males and thirty-two for females (Lee 2003). A name is assigned systematically to each newborn: a first son is named after his father's father, a second son after his mother's father; a first daughter is named after her father's mother, a second daughter after her mother's mother. Subsequent children are named after their father's and mother's siblings. In contrast to European and North American practice, children can never be named after their own parents, nor can they marry someone with the same name as a parent or sibling.

Child Rearing

In the process of enculturation, once children are named and thought likely to survive, cultural practices begin to teach them the kinds of behaviors and personalities deemed appropriate. Child-rearing practices vary greatly across cultures and across times. Cultural diversity in attitudes toward infants and children and beliefs about what they are capable of are enormous. There are also cultural differences in practices aimed at teaching children and molding them into the kinds of people acceptable in their society.

Attitudes toward children and child-rearing practices are generally consistent with core values prevalent in a society. In societies where competition for economic resources and for social prestige and power is the norm, children are taught to be competitive and to develop a sense of individuality and uniqueness. In societies where adults need to

How were you named, and why? Does your name have any special meaning or carry any special expectations?

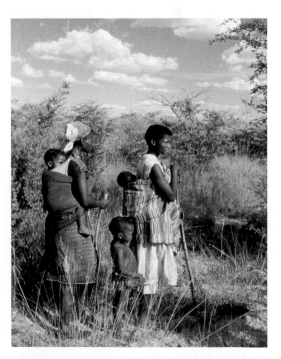

Among the Ju/'hoansi of the Kalahari Desert, children are named for specific relatives according to strict rules. People with the same name are considered to be related regardless of their actual biological connection.

child-rearing practices
Methods used to take care of infants and young children, including ways of feeding, playing with, and carrying, as well as sleeping arrangements.

cooperate economically and to feel part of a network of reciprocal rights and obligations, children are taught to play and work communally. Of course, no society has only one set of values and needs. No matter how competitive an economic and political system may be, people also have to cooperate with others in some endeavors. And no matter how cooperative work and social networks may be, people sometimes compete with one another. However, although children in all cultures need to learn both cooperative and competitive strategies, one type is more dominant than another. As well, although child-rearing attitudes are varied within a society, most parents accept the norms prevalent in their communities because these norms are consistent with environmental constraints or social goals.

Child rearing includes both implicit and explicit messages. Children learn by observing other people, seeing the ways in which they interact, and listening to what people have to say about other people's behavior. Children are also directly instructed about their own behavior. They may be given explicit directions about how to behave in particular circumstances. They may be praised and rewarded for some actions and criticized, punished, or ignored for others. In all cultures, children are taught lessons about behavior and values through storytelling. Sacred narratives and folktales impart fundamental cultural attitudes that children absorb by listening to stories told and retold by respected relatives and elders.

Child-rearing practices are culturally defined techniques for dealing with universal problems relating to the dependency of children. All children need to be fed, carried, and otherwise cared for in order to satisfy their survival needs to eat, eliminate body wastes, and sleep. These strategies both reflect and transmit cultural values and environmental constraints.

Feeding and Weaning. In many traditional societies, mothers nurse their infants for several years, sometimes for as long as three or four years or until another child is born. Babies are fed on demand—allowed to nurse whenever they want. In other societies, even young infants are put on feeding schedules that conform more to the mother's needs than to the child's. In a classic study, John Whiting and Irvin Child (1953) analyzed data reported for fifty-one cultures around the world, and found that about half of the sample was clustered high on a constructed scale of nursing indulgence. Only a few societies had marked restrictions on infant feeding. The lowest rating was given to inhabitants of the Marquesas, an island group in the South Pacific.

The Marquesans believe that frequent nursing makes a child difficult to raise, too willful and disobedient. No other groups were as restrictive as the Marquesans, but an American middle-class sample received a rating of only two points higher than the Marquesans. Whiting and Child point out that some of the worldwide variation can be explained on the basis of allocation of mothers' time. That is, in societies where mothers can rely on other family members to perform household tasks, more time can be spent providing for and catering to a baby's needs. In societies where mothers have numerous other duties, either within their own households or outside the domestic sphere, they have to restrict their child's access to them by necessity.

Both the age at which children are weaned and the weaning process itself vary cross-culturally. In general, weaning tends to take place late and gradually in societies where a child can nurse on demand, whereas weaning tends to take place early and abruptly in societies where nursing or feeding is scheduled. Weaning also takes place later in rural or poor communities, as mother's milk normally is a reliably available source of food. The interrelationships among these practices form an integrated cultural pattern varying from indulgence to restrictions that is consistent with mothers' overall economic duties.

Did you sleep in the same bed or room with your parents or other family members as a child? Why, or why not? At what age were you expected to sleep alone? To drink from a cup? To feed yourself?

Sleeping. Cultural differences are found in sleeping arrangements for infants, young children, and adults. A review of research by psychologists investigating relationships between sleeping arrangements and children's independence reported that only about one-third of American infants slept in the same room as their parents (co-sleeping), and very few slept in their parents' bed (Morelli et al. 1992). Some studies indicate that more than half of infants as young as 2 months of age sleep in rooms separate from their parents, and 98 percent of American infants sleep alone by 6 months of age. This pattern contrasts sharply with that of "most communities around the world," where infants usually sleep in the same bed with their mothers or, if not in her bed, at least in her room.

Data from the United States indicate variation in different cultural and regional groups. African American parents are more likely to allow their children to sleep in their bed or room than are Caucasian parents. And all families in rural communities are more likely to sleep in the same room. American middle-class sleeping arrangements are consistent with child-rearing goals that emphasize independence. In contrast, co-sleeping may help develop interpersonal relationships. Attitudes expressed by people in cultures that routinely practice co-sleeping are especially revealing in their criticism of typical American patterns (see the Case Study). For example, according to studies by T. B. Brazelton, Japanese parents consider American culture to be "rather merciless in pushing small children toward such independence at night" (1990, 7).

Physical and Social Stimulation.   The ways children are held and the degree of contact that they have with caregivers and with other children significantly influence their physical and emotional development. In many cultures, children are in nearly constant contact and involvement with other people, either older siblings or adult caregivers. In many societies, babies and young children are carried in slings on the backs or hips of their caregivers. Because of this constant body contact, they move about just as their caregivers do. The physicality of movement, of walking, bending, straightening, and turning, is a constant part of their daily stimuli. In contrast, in some native cultures of North America, babies were placed in cradleboards and carried around on the mother's back. If the caregivers were indoors, or working or resting outside, they might prop up the cradleboard against a wall or tree, giving the baby a front-facing perspective and enabling the child to be part of the family group and always in visual contact with others. Other societies require babies to spend a good deal of their waking and sleeping hours separated from other people. In cribs, high chairs, and playpens, children may be essentially isolated from the rest of the family group for significant amounts of time.

Efe infants and toddlers are always around adults, whom they see and hear performing numerous activities, learning through observation and interaction. This training leads to a high degree of sensitivity toward others and a "broad array of social skills" (Tronick et al. 1992, 575).

CASE STUDY

Sleeping Arrangements in Two Cultures

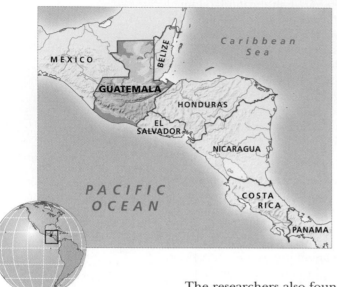

Sleeping arrangements of American middle-class urban families have been contrasted with those of Maya Indians in rural Guatemala (Morelli et al. 1992). Although all fourteen Mayan mothers in the study slept in the same bed with their infants well into the child's second year of life, none of the eighteen American mothers slept in the same bed with their infants regularly, although fifteen had newborns sleeping in a crib near them. As early as 3 months of age, more than half the American babies were sleeping in a separate room, and 80 percent were sleeping alone by the sixth month. The remaining three American families never shared rooms with their newborns. American parents' comments about their practices revealed their concerns with dependency: "I think that he would be more dependent . . . if he was constantly with us like that," and "It was time to give him his own space, his own territory." These attitudes reveal a focus on individuality and self-reliance.

The researchers also found consistencies between sleeping arrangements and nighttime feedings of infants. Mayan mothers allow their babies to nurse on demand during the night as well as during the day. Most of the Mayan mothers reported that they did not have to wake up to feed their babies but merely had to turn toward the child to make the breast accessible. American mothers, in contrast, reported staying awake during nighttime feedings even when they nursed their child. Most of them nursed the babies in a chair in their own or the infant's room, not in the parental bed. These contrasting patterns are consistent with differences in attitudes toward on-demand and scheduled feeding. That is, because American mothers do not sleep in the same bed as their child, they need to interrupt their own sleep to feed their infants and thus strive to keep the baby on a regular schedule. Mayan mothers are not disturbed when sleeping, so they are willing to allow the baby to nurse on demand.

Finally, the researchers drew a connection between sleeping arrangements and bedtime routines. They noted the elaborate bedtime activities such as dressing for bed and storytelling typical of American families and the need to "coax the baby to sleep." In contrast with Mayan patterns, the transition to sleeping was made easily and without formality. The researchers suggest that American families often experience bedtime struggles because of the stress that infants may have about going to sleep without assistance or companionship. This stress results in the child's fear of falling asleep and being alone.

The contrasts between American and Mayan practices reflect differences in each society's attitudes and values. Whereas American parents stress the value of a child's independence and avoid encouraging dependent relationships, Mayan parents stress the importance of interdependence between their children and themselves. Mayan mothers believe that their children learn social rules more quickly, obey their elders' admonitions, and can be trusted not to touch dangerous objects because of the strong bond between mother and child. One Mayan mother commented: "In our community the babies are always with the mother, but with North Americans, you keep the babies apart. Maybe that's why the children here understand their mothers more; they feel close. Maybe U.S. children feel the distance more. . . . If children do not feel close, it will be harder for them to learn and understand the ways of the people around them" (Morelli et al. 1992, 610). In the United States, parents are concerned with fostering independence and self-reliance, in keeping with the society's dominant notions of the importance of individuality. Practices of American parents are also consistent with attitudes about privacy, stressing each person's needs for and rights to private space and concerns.

myanthrolab

Explore more at
www.myanthrolab.com

Research carried out among the Efe, a hunting-and-gathering society of Zaire, increases our understanding of the interrelationships between child-rearing strategies and personality values (Tronick et al. 1992). Observation of Efe children's activities revealed a high degree of interactions with parents, older siblings, community members, and peers. From the very beginning of life, Efe infants (from birth to 4 months of age) spent more than half their time with people other than their mothers, interacting with five or more different people per hour. Although their mothers frequently nursed the children, other women nursed them as well. By the age of 3, they were having social contact with people other than their mothers for about 70 percent of the day. Tronick and coworkers believe that Efe child-rearing practices are enmeshed in economic and social systems that require adults' attention to multiple activities throughout the day. They also reflect the people's value of "sharing and cooperation" and help to enculturate Efe children in this "intensely social society" (1992, 569).

Like every other aspect of culture, child-rearing practices and attitudes toward children are not static but change over time. They may change when people introduce and develop new technologies and ways of living. The possibility of children's contribution to household economies may influence attitudes toward them. In hunting-and-gathering and farming societies, children's dependence on adults may be of much shorter duration than in modern industrial societies. This difference is because, in the former, children can begin to work gathering or producing food when they are fairly young. In contrast, children in modern industrial nations are in schools and in training for their future roles until well into their teens. If they go on to postsecondary education, their financial dependence on their parents may be lengthened.

GLOBALIZATION

Although fully industrialized nations have tended to make child labor illegal, globalization has contributed to the exploitation of child labor in developing countries. Many organizations are working to help countries solve the problems of poverty and child labor in the face of forces of globalization. Education and improvements in living conditions are critical parts of the solution.

CULTURE CHANGE

CHANGING ATTITUDES TOWARD CHILDHOOD AND CHILD CARE IN THE UNITED STATES

Contemporary attitudes toward childhood as a stage of life and toward children and their proper care focus on the uniqueness of each child, their personal needs for development and self-expression, and their central place in family life. Such interpretations of children and home life are radical changes from earlier attitudes in the United States and Europe. According to some historians, medieval European children were thought to be "demonic, animalistic, ill-formed and fragile" with a marked propensity for evil (Hays 1996). Children were also thought of as smaller and less adequate versions of adults (Aries 1962). High infant mortality rates and the demands of labor for mothers and fathers minimized the amount of attention parents could give to children. Children who misbehaved were subject to corporal punishment. Children were also taught their place in a hierarchical household system that mirrored the relationship between subject and king (Hays 1996, 23). Social class, as always, affected these relationships. Wet nurses cared for children of wealthy elites whereas the children of poor people worked hard alongside their parents as soon as they were physically able.

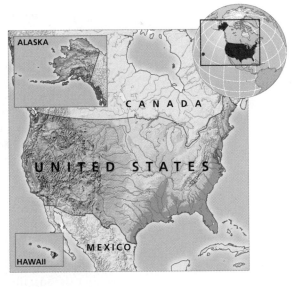

Other historians disagree with this bleak picture and describe the care and concern that parents gave to their children. Medieval children had their own games, toys, and literature (Orme 2002). The lives of poor children were no harsher than those of their parents.

During the seventeenth and eighteenth centuries, the Enlightenment began to influence attitudes toward children among the European bourgeoisie. Children were thought to be innocent and malleable, open to guidance in a loving household. The importance of home life and schooling was stressed. These views did not reach the United States, however, until the nineteenth century. By the 1850s in the United States and Europe, the values of peaceful domesticity held sway. In particular, mothers—and especially those of the middle and upper classes—were responsible for creating home environments that promoted children's physical, intellectual, and moral development, so that they would become successful, competitive men or dutiful women in conformity with nineteenth-century bourgeois expectations.

Ideological emphasis on the maternal role coincided with economic changes that left urban, middle-class women with little opportunity for employment outside the home. A mother's task was now to mold her children's moral character and guide their emotional, behavioral, and cognitive development. Fathers were disciplinarians and models of responsibility, providing the main material support for their wives and children by working in the public domain, a domain increasingly contrasted with the private sphere of the household.

Changes in attitudes toward children and childhood were (and are) consistent with socioeconomic values, the emphasis on competition in the workplace, and the growing consumer culture that fueled capitalist economies. For example, social historians trace a significant shift in attitudes toward envy and deprivation that occurred between the late nineteenth and the early twentieth centuries (Matt 2002). Children in the earlier period were admonished to control their feelings of envy and rivalry, but twentieth-century children were encouraged to be acquisitive and competitive. Family status became reflected in the material well-being and possessions parents could provide for their children and themselves.

By the mid-twentieth century, children were firmly established as the center of the middle-class family. In contrast to earlier times, when children were trained to become proper adults, child care became "expert-guided" and "child-centered," "more emotionally absorbing, labor intensive, and financially expensive." By the 1930s, an estimated 90 percent of middle-class mothers and 65 percent of fathers in the United States read books and manuals on child rearing (Matt 2002). In the second half of the twentieth century, experts inundated parents with advice about children's nutrition, sleeping habits, early instruction, and leisure activities. Every aspect of a child's life and experience has now become the subject of expert opinion and public debate (Hulbert 2003). However, as parents receive more advice, they are also subject to more criticism. They are poised to take both the praise and the blame for their children's behavior because different experts give conflicting advice depending on their social and political orientations. According to some, this multitude of opinion creates anxiety in parents at the very time when the health and welfare of their children are more secure than they ever were (Stearns 2003). Today's children, at least those of middle-class Americans, are privileged: They do little if any work inside or outside the home, their needs are central to the financial consideration of their parents, and they have ample leisure time to do as they choose, within limits of safety.

Finally, in the last quarter of the twentieth century, fathers began to take a more central place in parenting alongside mothers. Fathers today take more direct care for their children and are perceived as potential emotional allies rather than disciplinarians.

Although the constellation of behaviors and values involved in "intensive parenting" is normative in the United States, parents themselves disagree about what children's needs are or how best to satisfy them. In the 1980s, Hays found that, whereas middle-class mothers were apt to negotiate or reason with their children and to give them options, working-class mothers were likely to set rules and seek obedience. These differing approaches reflect different realities. As one working-class mother noted, "Discipline, that's very important to me. Because if children can't respect their own mother and father, they're certainly not going to respect a boss, or an employer, or the law." (Hays 1996).

Our times are fraught with uncertainty in part because rapidly changing technologies provide an ever-growing range of choices in how we obtain information, form and develop relationships, and use our time. In one view, all of these choices and exposures render us "socially saturated" and lead to changes in the very notions of the "self," that is, who we are and how we understand our relationships with others (Gergen 1991). These notions begin in childhood and result from the kinds of familial and community networks and responsibilities that are taken for granted or naturalized within the culture.

REVIEW — Enculturation is the process by which all humans learn their culture. It begins with social birth and naming. In all societies, child-rearing practices meet children's dependency needs and include feeding, weaning, sleeping arrangements, toilet training, and stimulation. Attitudes and values about children and child rearing are adaptive and, therefore, vary culturally and historically.

INFORMAL AND FORMAL LEARNING

Children acquire their culture through both formal and informal means. They learn their future economic and social roles by observing older siblings and the adults in their family. Typically, children play with toys that represent or imitate these roles. In societies with economies based on hunting and gathering, boys play with bows and arrows or other hunting gear, whereas girls play with digging sticks, carrying devices, and dolls. Among herding peoples, children may begin to accompany adults to take animals to pasture. They observe adults working with animals and assist with minor tasks. In some herding societies, such as the Diné (or Navajo) of the American Southwest, boys and girls accompany adult herders as early as the age of 5 or 6, preparing for the herding roles of both men and women. In other cultures, herding activities are restricted to men. For example, among African cattle herders such as the Nuer of southern Sudan, only men and boys who have been initiated are permitted to tend and herd cattle, although women and children usually milk the animals. Therefore, part of a boy's training consists of observing the work of older boys and adult men in anticipation of maturing and assuming adult roles.

In industrial societies, child labor can be efficient in certain settings, but laws regarding children's work vary from country to country. Children are physically capable of doing hand manufacture and working with light and simple machinery before the age of 10. However, many countries outlaw such practices because of ethical stances held by a majority of citizens or by the world community. In countries where child labor is permitted (whether overtly or covertly), children may be apprenticed to their future employers, acquiring manufacturing skills in home and work settings. In postindustrial societies such as the United States, children would be in competition with their parents for jobs, a factor that delays the legal age of paid employment.

Learning Skills and Values

In much of the world, children are trained for their future roles in schools, where they learn to read and write, a prerequisite for most of the jobs that they will attain as adults. Education in formal settings so familiar to North Americans also instills competition and conformity, even though these two values may seem contradictory. Children learn to compete with one another for the attention of the teacher when they raise their hands to answer questions. They compare their grades on tests and in classes with other pupils. They learn the value of individual achievement, feeling pride in their success or shame in their failure. But children also learn to conform to the rigors of obedience to authority, following explicit rules without questioning them as they are taught to respect the culture of institutions.

Cultural values are powerful influences on people's thinking and behavior. Values include norms of behavior, attitudes, and ethics. We manifest our values in how we act toward other people, in what we think about our own and other people's behavior, and in our notions of right and wrong. These values are taught to children in numerous ways. Children observe how people act, and they hear what people say in the course of daily activities. They may listen to discussions of other people's behavior, absorbing the attitudes expressed when someone is either praised or criticized.

Values are also transmitted in more formal settings. Children may be given direct instruction, told what to do and what not to do. They may be told why certain behavior is acceptable and why other behavior is unacceptable. Some actions or thoughts may even be seen as evil, loading negative attributes about people who commit them. Because children

Many agrarian societies use children's labor at an early age to increase the family's productivity and income. Here, a young boy harvests cotton in Nicaragua.

What are some traditional sayings in your culture that teach moral lessons of industriousness, courage in the face of adversity, and other valued personality traits?

(like adults) want to be perceived as appropriate members of their culture, they learn to act in ways viewed positively and avoid negatively viewed behavior.

In some societies, proverbs have a significant role in both private and public discourse. Among the Yorubas of Nigeria, for example, proverbs are used in child rearing, in ordinary conversations between adults, and in public and ceremonial settings. Yoruba proverbs teach proper behavior and transmit cultural wisdom. Examples include "Children are the clothes of men" (that is, a man's most valuable possessions); "A hungry man does not hear sermons"; "Words are like eggs, when they drop, they scatter"; and "You are making love to your thigh" (that is, you are deceiving yourself) (Lindfors and Owomoyela 1973).

Sacred and secular traditional narratives, or **folklore**, convey important lessons about a people's philosophical and ethical principles. The power of the stories comes partly from frequent repetition and social validation. Their power also lies in the artistic and aesthetic appeal of dramatic episodes and heroic characters. The lives of ordinary people can be told and retold, making them larger than life and giving extraordinary meaning to ordinary events. The Philippine narrative that opened this chapter, for example, teaches lessons about the negative consequences of greediness.

folklore
Texts that relate traditional stories, the exploits of cultural heroes and characters handed down from generation to generation.

Narratives can also be used to criticize someone's behavior by repeating stories whose moral lessons are known by everyone in the community. For example, Western Apaches use the telling of "historical tales" about former events that had negative consequences to "alarm and criticize social delinquents . . . , thereby impressing such individuals with the undesirability of improper behavior and alerting them to the punitive consequences of further misconduct" (Basso 1990, 115). The tales are aimed at particular hearers in the group who come to understand that the message in the story is directed at them. They are thus encouraged to think about their behavior and hopefully to profit from the lesson by changing their ways.

Rules of politeness, deference, and status are often inculcated in children through language, through how people speak to them and how they are encouraged to speak.

Learning Behavioral Expectations

In addition to training for their social acceptance and future occupations, children need to learn how to behave when interacting with other people. Children acquire appropriate social expectations and behavior by observing their elders in the household and community. Because language is a key feature of human interactions, children need to know when not to speak, when to speak, and what to speak about. They learn rules of authority and deference. They see how decisions are made, whose voices are heard and whose are silenced, who may exert authority over whom, and who must defer to whom. Children learn the ways in which differences of age, gender, and social standing influence the behavior of others and mold their actions and speech. Through trial and error, they understand what behaviors are appropriate because they are corrected, reprimanded, or punished for transgressing social rules. Children also learn important lessons about social privilege, because they see that certain people are occasionally permitted to violate social norms whereas others are not. These are powerful lessons children learn informally through which they construct themselves as social individuals with specific social identities (see the Case Study).

The telling of stories of personal experience is a pervasive means of conveying attitudes, values and behaviors to children (Miller and Moore 1989). As children hear stories told by adults around them, they learn about the kinds of experiences that people in their societies have, the kinds of interpretations that people give to their own and others' behavior, and the kinds of expectations that they develop about their own lives. As children begin to tell their own stories, their lives become part of the narrative history of their families.

CASE STUDY

Language and Interaction in Japan

A study of child-rearing and language-socialization practices in Japan reveals how children learn culturally appropriate patterns of interaction. *Omoiyari,* or empathy with others, is prized in Japan (Clancy 1986). People are socialized to be sensitive to each other's feelings, attitudes, and needs. They learn to express their own opinions indirectly and ambiguously to avoid conflict and to interpret other people's intentions and opinions from surface clues.

Japanese caregivers instill the virtues of politeness and attentiveness toward others. Adults often explicitly classify behaviors as acceptable or deviant. They correct children's behavior by emphasizing the wishes of other people, especially elders, relatives, or people of higher social status.

In the following exchange, documented in Patricia Clancy's study (1986) of Japanese families, a mother chastises her child for not responding to another adult's questions:

[The child, age 2 years 1 month, is pretending to eat food from a toy dish.]

> ADULT: "Are you eating something? What is in there?"
>
> CHILD: [No response]
>
> MOTHER: "I wonder what could be in there. Older sister is asking: 'What is in there?'"
>
> CHILD: "Pudding."

The mother then repeats the question, this time in the name of Patricia Clancy, whom she refers to as "older sister" to emphasize the child's kin-like obligation to answer the question. Aware of her place in a network of social responsibilities, the child responds.

Because Japanese culture highly values the expression of accommodation and agreement and the avoidance of overt conflict, children are taught to comply with the wishes of others, regardless of their personal inclinations. One mother responded to her two-year-old's refusal to lend a toy to a younger child by admonishing him:

"Do you say 'No!'"? You must lend one to Hirochan, saying, 'Help yourself.' The baby is cute/lovable, isn't he?"

Not only is the mother teaching her child to give in to the wishes of another, but she is also instructing him to make an outright offer of the desired object. Whatever her child's inner feelings, she asks him to agree with her praise of the baby. The mother thus teaches her child that complying with another person's wishes is more important than expressing one's own feelings.

As in all cultures, certain behaviors are considered appropriate whereas deviations from them trigger negative reactions. Japanese mothers often give exaggerated responses to a child's nonconformity:

[The child, 2 years 1 month, was playing hostess and suddenly began pretending to eat one of the toy dishes.]

> MOTHER: "Isn't it strange to do that kind of thing, if you eat a plate? No one eats plates, do they? Who eats plates?"
>
> CHILD: "Maho [child's name] (eats) this."
>
> MOTHER: "You're eating it? Like a beast. It's scary. I don't like it. It's scary, like a monster. I hate monsters."

Here, the mother is essentially saying that violating social norms is "scary" and that people who behave in such ways are hated. This is an important lesson, powerfully transmitted, because it threatens a child's sense of security.

Societies function on the basis of implied principles of consensus and the restraint of conflict. People need to agree implicitly that the open display of too much conflict may be socially disruptive and would impair the cohesion necessary for the viability of groups. This is perhaps most true within families but it is fundamental to any community.

PEARSON
myanthrolab

Explore more at
www.myanthrolab.com

Age and Gender Socialization

Through their socialization, children learn that people's rights and obligations differ depending on their status and the kinds of roles they perform. The term **status** refers to one's place in a hierarchical social order. The factors that determine status vary in different societies, though age and gender are common in most social systems. Older people usually are granted more respect and deference, and children generally have little social standing. In some societies, women and men have relatively equal status, whereas in others, one gender has higher standing. Other factors that may contribute to social status in a particular culture include class, race, ethnicity, and religion.

Social status is a factor within families as well. In familial interactions, children first become aware of different categories of people based on such characteristics as age and gender. In a society stratified by age, gender, and other factors such as class, race, and ethnicity, a child eventually learns that social rights are unequally distributed, that certain types of people have more rights or powers than others. Unequal status within families, then, is a reflection of and reinforces inequality in the larger society. People must learn as children how to order themselves hierarchically as adults. As onlookers and participants, children observe the varied interactions among family members. They formulate conceptions of themselves and of their place in the world according to cultural models that are enacted daily in their households.

Age. On the basis of age, children have restricted rights and limited ability to control others or even to protect themselves from other people's control. Children's lack of power is shown in several ways. First, they rarely contribute to group discussions related to community activities. In families, there is variation from culture to culture and from family to family. In some societies, it would be unthinkable for children to have a say in family decisions, whereas in other societies they might contribute significantly, especially if the discussion relates to an activity that affects them. Older children are more likely to have their opinions heard than younger children.

Second, children's behavior is more directly constrained than is that of adults. As part of the socialization process, children may be verbally reprimanded or physically punished when they violate rules of cultural appropriateness. This process teaches them that some people have the right to comment on and control the behavior of others. The rights of some to control others is one of the earliest lessons children learn.

Third, children have fewer and more restricted conversational rights than adults. For instance, children may be unsuccessful in getting the attention of adults, particularly when the adults are engaged in conversation and interaction with other adults. In a study of middle-class American families, Susan Ervin-Tripp, O'Connor, and Rosenberg (1984) found that when children age 2 to 4½ years tried to get the attention of someone already involved in conversation, they were unsuccessful 94 percent of the time. Older children, age 4½ to 7 years, fared somewhat better but still met with a failure rate of 79 percent. Adults also often interrupt children. Although our cultural stereotypes portray children as talkative and interruptive, laboratory and natural observations of familial interactions demonstrate just the opposite (Gleason 1987). Gender of adults and children is a significant factor in interruption. Research showed that fathers interrupted children more than did mothers, and both parents interrupted daughters more often than sons. Children replicate this gender-differentiated pattern quite early. In a study by Anita Esposito (1979) of children (from 3½ to 4½ years of age) who were observed in male-female encounters, boys interrupted girls twice as frequently as the reverse.

Conversational power is also displayed in the context of giving and receiving commands or instructions. Giving commands is indicative of social rights to control others,

status
The position or rank that one occupies in a group or society that carries certain role expectations.

and the way in which commands are stated also can signal relative social standing. Imperatives ("Sit down!" or "Close the window!") assert power overtly, whereas indirect expressions, questions, and statements of rationales soften the speaker's control and acknowledge the other person's feelings ("Why don't you sit down?" or "Would you please close the window?"). Studies of parent-child interactions indicate that adults consistently issue more commands to children than they receive. Gender difference is manifested in the type of command. For example, Gleason (1987) found that in a study of middle-class urban families, fathers gave imperatives twice as often as did mothers. A total of 38 percent of all fathers' utterances were overt commands. In contrast, mothers tended to make requests with polite constructions and questions.

In addition, some fathers socialize sons into competitive behavior by adding threats or insults to direct imperatives. Commands such as "Don't go in there again or I'll break your head" and references such as "wise guy" or "nutcake" were sometimes addressed to sons. These encounters no doubt serve as training grounds for boys when they interact with other boys in competitive displays and challenges. Later, when they become parents, they may reproduce the same hierarchical status system with their children.

Gender. Gender is a basic aspect of a person's individual and social identity. Children are socialized into their **gender identity** from the earliest age, beginning immediately after birth. Girls and boys may be treated differently and spoken to differently from the very beginning of life. Studies in child development indicate that parents and other caregivers in the United States interact differently with boys and girls. These studies indicate general patterns within populations, but they do not predict any particular interactions between parents and children.

All societies have enormous variability about expected norms and behaviors. However, research indicates that parents in the United States interact more physically with boy babies than with girls, for example. Boys are held, touched, and stimulated more, a pattern that helps them develop stronger muscles and motor behavior. Boys are also handled more roughly than girls. In addition, when boys fuss, parents pay more attention to them than they do to girls. Through these modes of interaction, boys learn to seek attention because they get attention, whereas girls learn to satisfy their own needs (Ember 1981). Fathers in particular tend to handle their sons more roughly than their daughters. As well, boys tend to be physically punished more than girls, especially by their fathers.

Research on expressing aggression suggests cross-sex permissiveness on the part of parents—that is, fathers may permit more aggression from daughters, and mothers may permit more aggression from sons. This pattern may encourage aggressiveness in boys. For example, physical punishment of boys by fathers could result in increased anger, but because sons cannot turn their anger toward their fathers, they displace it in aggressive behavior toward peers. In addition, mothers' greater tolerance for aggression in their sons may increase a boy's aggressive behavior.

Studies also show that girls spend more time playing at home than do boys. They are, therefore, under more adult supervision and are more likely to take on household chores, including helping to care for younger siblings. In contrast, boys interact more with peers. These patterns may also affect aggression. A child is likely to defer to adults and nurture younger children. Girls are more likely to develop these personality and behavior characteristics, therefore, because of their patterns of interaction at home, whereas boys develop more aggressive behavior because of their patterns of interaction both at home and with peers.

In both cases, certain human behaviors are likely to be encouraged and developed (aggression in boys, nurturance in girls) and others inhibited (aggression in girls, nurturance in boys). Patterns of treatment and interaction, therefore, help to mold a child's personality to conform to cultural norms. Females and males are born, but girls and boys (and women and men) are products of enculturation.

Gender Identification. Gender identity is marked in many ways, among them dress and body decoration. A common example is dressing baby boys in blue and baby girls in pink. Clothing styles, hairstyles, and the wearing of jewelry are other visual markers of gender. External modifications of the body are powerful, repetitive indications of one's gender identity and gender differentiation in one's society. Changes in cultural notions of gender may be reflected in changing habits of dress and body ornamentation.

gender identity
The way that people think about themselves in terms of their sex, or how they present themselves as men or women.

How are clothing styles, hairstyles, and jewelry used to challenge gender stereotypes in North America and Europe today?

Naming conventions are nearly universal means of distinguishing males and females. Most cultures bestow different names for boys and girls. In American English, only a handful of names are ambiguous for gender. Some of these, like Leslie and Dana, are older in the language, whereas others, like Kim and Tracey, are newer. Some names that may be used for both males and females have spellings that differentiate the sexes: Frances for girls, Francis for boys; and Sydney for girls, Sidney for boys. English names for girls may refer to flowers (Rose, Iris, Lily), months of the year (April, May, June), and moral virtues (Prudence, Hope). Boys, in contrast, are rarely named for objects or abstractions. Certain sounds in the names also differentiate the genders: English girls' names often end in vowels, whereas boys' names rarely do. Finally, girls' names may be derived from boys' names by addition of "feminine" endings, such as -a, -ine, -ette, for example, Paula, Pauline, Paulette. This process can apply idiosyncratically to any male name, although some are more common than others. The only male name that is derived from a female name is Marion (note the difference in spelling for the girls' name Marian), derived from Mary, a name with religious significance.

Otherwise, to name a boy with a girl's name would be considered highly inappropriate and might have consequences for the carrier. Note, though, that endearing or diminutive forms of some names given to girls are the same as those used for boys: Roberta/Bobby, Geraldine/Jerry, Antoinette/Tony. In addition, boys are more likely to be named for their fathers (John Jr., for example) than girls are to be named for their mothers. This pattern symbolizes and transmits the acknowledgment of kin ties through the male line.

In traditional communities in China and Taiwan, names given to boys and girls are strongly differentiated. Chinese names function as meaningful symbolic markers of men's social distinctiveness and the social nonbeing of women. In a study of naming practices in Hong Kong and Taiwan, Ruby Watson (1986) found that both girls and boys are given personal names based on literary sources, events occurring near the time of the child's birth, or a wish for the child's future. However, boys' names have positive or prestige implications, whereas girls' names more often have negative meanings. For example, an eldest boy might be called "Eldest Luck," but a second or third girl might be named "Too Many" or "Little Mistake." Names with these meanings are not given to all girls, but the fact that the pattern exists indicates negative cultural attitudes toward females. In addition to differences in first names, acquisition of subsequent names also distinguishes males and females. Throughout his life, a man acquires new names that indicate social standing in his household and community and that confer prestige to him, such as a school name given by a teacher, a marriage name selected when he marries, a "courtesy" name that marks economic or social success, and a posthumous name given to honor his life.

Women, in sharp contrast, have only their personal name. Even this name is dropped when a woman marries; rather than acquiring a new marriage name, as men do, a woman becomes known thereafter by kin terms in reference to her husband and children, for example, as "Eldest Luck's wife" or "Too Many's mother." In old age, a woman is simply called "old woman" by everyone except her closest relatives. Finally, a woman's nonbeing is forever memorialized on her tombstone where instead of personal, courtesy, and posthumous names, as are engraved for men, a woman's existence is subsumed under her father's surname and she is listed eternally as "Family of [father's surname]."

Chinese naming patterns are consistent with traditional strong preferences for sons. These preferences go back to ancient times and the establishment of Confucian philosophy, which reinforced the Chinese kinship system. The preference for sons reflects a strongly patrilineal kinship system with inheritance rules in which wealth and property are passed from father to son. In societies where men and women are thought of as equally valuable, parental preferences for girls and boys may be personal but are not generally imbalanced in the society as a whole. In some cultures where people trace their descent and inheritance through women, girls may be preferred. For example, among the Mohawks and other Iroquois nations, parents preferred girls to maintain the family line that in Iroquois culture descended through women. However, children of either sex were equally welcomed and nurtured. The Mohawk pattern of preference was not, therefore, the mirror image of many societies' desires for sons. In numerous cultures, girls are routinely neglected and abused, even killed, because of intense preferences for boys, whereas there are no reported cases of cultures where boys are neglected and abused because of preferences for girls.

Boys and girls learn their future identities as men and women by observing their parents and other household members. They see how men and women treat one another, what they say about one another, and how they respond to one another. They come to understand whether men and women contribute equally to group discussions and decision making. They also see the kinds of work that women and men perform. Through these observations, children absorb attitudes about themselves and about their own worthiness as they prepare for their rights and responsibilities as adults.

One of the ways that children acquire models of gender and social relations is through participation in family interactions. Research conducted by Elinor Ochs and Caroline Taylor (1995) focused on 100 dinnertime conversations among family members. Ochs and Taylor analyzed the content of the conversations, looking especially at which family members introduced the stories, whose activities were discussed, and who commented on the actions described. They found that a majority of the stories were characterized by what they called a "Father knows best" family dynamic in which "father is set up to be primary audience, judge and critic of family members' actions, thoughts and feelings" (p. 99). A majority or 60 percent of the stories focused on the activities of the children, whereas mothers were central in 23 percent of the stories and fathers featured in 19 percent. Because children's activities made up most of the narratives, they became the focus of comments and evaluations by parents. Thus, children's actions and thoughts were most open to others' scrutiny, whereas fathers were talked about the least, making them the least vulnerable to evaluation. Children rarely selected the topic of conversation. They introduced only about one-third of the stories about themselves. Instead, parents (especially mothers) focused the narrative on the child's actions, which could be seen as reinforcing children's lack of privacy and control over information about themselves and the scrutiny of others. Stories were told about children for the fathers' hearing, thereby setting up the father as the "family judge" with the right to evaluate others.

The narrative dynamics of this conversation subtly teaches these children their gender roles and status. Children are socialized into the ideology of unequal gender relations, both because they witness their parents' behavior and because they are chosen as central characters motivating the drama.

Rites of Passage

Enculturation also occurs in linking activities between individuals, represented by their families and their community. Religious teachings and participation in ritual, for example, are powerful means to convey social and ideological principles to children. Myths and folktales transmit practical knowledge, historical information, and symbolic meanings as they are recounted in the informal settings of home and community as well as in the formal contexts of church and school.

In many societies, children undergo critical **rites of passage** as they move from the social role and status of child to those of adult. Other rites of passage occur at other life transitions, such as birth, marriage, and death, which are discussed further in Chapter 14. In the process of preparing for and undergoing rituals marking the transition to adulthood, children may be taught practical arts associated with their future roles. They may also be instructed in knowledge necessary for their roles as parents and spouses, learning their responsibilities, obligations, and rights.

Certain types of rituals and teachings have particular effects on molding the personalities and identities of children approaching adulthood. For example, in many African societies, as well as in Aboriginal Australia, boys undergo intense, prolonged, and frightening **initiation rites** as they approach manhood. The rites are held for groups of boys of the appropriate age once in several years (the number of years varies from culture to

What are some examples of initiation rites and other rites of passage in the United States?

rites of passage
Rituals that mark culturally significant transitions throughout the life cycle, including birth, puberty, marriage, and death.

initiation rites
Rituals that mark a person's transition from childhood to adulthood.

culture). The boys are taken out of their settlements and are subjected to weeks, months, or even years of instruction and preparation for their roles as men.

Among the Kpelle of Liberia, groups initiate boys into a men's secret society called *Poro*. Initiations occur sporadically, perhaps once every ten or fifteen years. Boys are brought from their communities to an isolated bush area for four years. During this time, they are instructed in the knowledge and skills—farming techniques, methods of house building, and craft specialties—needed to function productively in Kpelle society. They also learn various dances, songs, and traditional histories. Finally, they learn how to behave appropriately and how to act with elders and chiefs (Gibbs 1965). Social messages are reinforced by beatings and verbal harassment. Kpelle girls are initiated into a comparable society, called the *Sande*. Both Poro and Sande have complex functions that affect every aspect of Kpelle life, including their social organization, economies, and political and jural systems, in addition to religious and ceremonial domains (Erchak 1977). In the context of education and training, Poro and Sande "bush schools" have primary socialization functions because "the character-molding and enforced conformity learned in these schools shapes the behavior of young Kpelle and weeds out deviants" (Erchak 1977, 61).

A number of physical changes are imposed on boys during their initiation, including circumcision and scarification. Scars formed from cuts made on a boy's back and chest are permanent, visible signs of adult status. Such scars are said to be the teeth marks of a "Great Masked Figure" who embodies a mythic spirit believed to eat the boy at the beginning of the initiation process. According to Kpelle beliefs, a boy dies when he enters the initiation camp and is reborn when the Great Masked Figure disgorges him. He then receives a new name signifying his new status. A boy's childhood name is never used thereafter. Boys who go through their initiation collectively form strong emotional and social bonds with one another. They learn to identify and empathize with the actions and needs of men in their own age cohorts with whom they have been associated in their periods of seclusion and transition. As well, they develop strong bonds of mutual assistance, interdependence, and loyalty that last throughout their lifetimes.

In contrast, some Native American peoples of the North American Midwest and Plains sent young boys (and sometimes girls, too) on lonely, individual quests for visions when they neared adulthood. The overt purpose of the vision quest was the acquisition of a personal spirit guardian who comes to the lonely seeker after periods of isolation (typically four days) in the woods or on the plains. During the quest, the seekers abstain from food and sleep. Guardian spirits thus acquired form a lifelong relationship with the seekers, coming to their aid in visions and dreams and imparting knowledge and comfort.

In addition to the spiritual lessons learned, children also learn the important lessons of endurance, self-control, self-reliance, and courage necessary to survive in harsh conditions. Through their experiences, children learn that they can endure the deprivation of food, water, and sleep. They also learn emotional resilience through the knowledge that they can survive loneliness and fear. These physical and psychological strengths are necessary for survival in nomadic societies where resources are occasionally scarce and difficult to obtain and where weather may be life-threatening.

In many societies, children's initiation ceremonies include instruction in secret ritual and lore. In the Amazon, Australia, and some cultures of central and southern Africa, boys are taught sacred songs that they are told never to reveal to anyone, especially to women and uninitiated children. These rites symbolize the segregation of the genders, fundamental to their society's economic and social roles. The selective transmission of knowledge defines and reinforces gender identity.

Schooling

In many societies, children's enculturation takes place in formal settings of school, where children are taught explicit lessons to acquire practical and intellectual knowledge. In early societies, children of the elites (especially boys) were sent to schools to learn the responsibilities and practical applications of their future administrative or political roles. In early literate societies, elite children were taught to read, write, and do mathematics.

CASE STUDY •

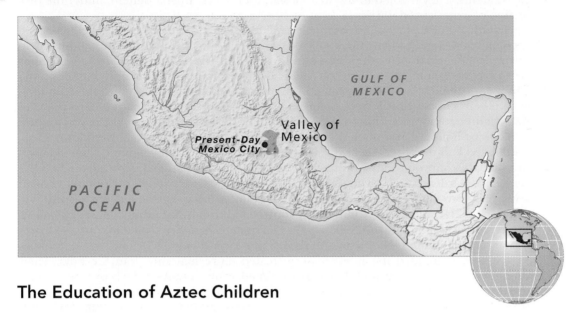

The Education of Aztec Children

The Aztecs developed a large, complex, and wealthy urban society in the Valley of Mexico beginning in the thirteenth and fourteenth centuries. By the fifteenth and sixteenth centuries, they controlled vast territories with more than 5 million inhabitants (Fagan 1984).

Aztec society was organized on the basis of class, wealth, and power. The major social and economic division was between nobles and commoners. The ruler and the nobles owned the land and controlled its resources. Nobles also functioned as government officials, generals, and judges. Commoners worked the land, paid tribute in produce to landowners, performed communal labor organized by the state, and were subject to official regulations.

Aztecs were socialized into their various roles from early childhood. Formal education was one of the means the state used to mold individuals to accept their place in the social order and fulfill their responsibilities. The education of Aztec children was of primary concern to their parents. Boys were under the tutelage of their fathers, and mothers trained their girls. The formalized structure of child care is revealed in the food rations prescribed for children at different ages: a 3-year-old was given half a cake of maize, which was the staple Aztec food, at the main daily meal; children of 4 or 5 years ate one cake; children of 6 through 12 years had a cake and a half; and children of 13 or older were given two cakes. Boys and girls were fed the same amounts of food (Soustelle 1961).

At around age 3 or 4, boys from commoner families began to carry wood from the forests and water from the lakes to their households. They accompanied their fathers to the marketplace. Girls helped their mothers with domestic tasks. When children were between 7 and 13 years old, they learned more difficult tasks. Boys were taught to fish and to maneuver boats; girls helped their mothers spin cotton, weave cloth, and grind maize into meal.

During a child's earliest years, adults treated children with kindness and affection, giving advice and encouragement. However, once the period of more careful supervision began (at about the age of 3), children who misbehaved were treated harshly. Scoldings and physical punishments were meted out to correct errors. A child might be scratched with thorns or forced to breathe the bitter fumes of burning chilies.

Children began formal education between ages 12 and 15. The Aztec educational system included two tracks, one for children who were destined for membership in the bureaucratic and elite classes, the other geared for children of the common people. Schools called *calmecacs* trained the sons and daughters of the elite. These schools were run by priests who themselves had attended such an institution. Education in the *calmecac* prepared children for the priesthood or other high-ranking positions in the state bureaucracy and military. Physical training and hard work were instilled in the students. They learned to use weapons and served on the battlefield, under the protection of experienced warriors.

Training in the *calmecac* was as much psychological and religious as intellectual. Children were awakened when it was still dark and then went alone into the mountains to burn incense and to prick their ears and legs with thorns until they drew blood, actions that were thought to please the gods. They also fasted frequently as a sign of their humiliation and submission to the gods and worked on the lands belonging to the temple to which their school was attached. According to a sixteenth-century Spanish chronicler, an Aztec father admonished his son upon entry to a *calmecac:* "Listen, my son, you are not going to be honored, nor obeyed, nor esteemed. You are going to be looked down upon, humiliated and despised. Every day you will cut agave-thorns for penance, and you will draw blood from your body with these spines and you will bathe at night even when it is very cold. Harden your body to the cold. And when the time comes for fasting do not go and break your fast, but put a good face upon both fasting and penance" (Sahagun 1975, vol. II, p. 222). Children were taught self-control and respect for others, "to speak well, to make proper salutations, and to bow." They learned to read Aztec pictographs and methods of reckoning time. They read and recited poetry and oratory.

Girls who attended the *calmecac* were treated more leniently than the boys. Their training was less rigorous, and they were punished as severely. An elderly priestess taught them etiquette and to value obedience and purity of mind and body. Their practical learning consisted mainly of becoming skilled weavers and embroiderers. Like boys, girls also offered incense to the gods and learned songs and stories about Aztec history. Through these oral traditions, boys and girls acquired their identity as Aztecs and took pride in their culture and history.

A second type of institution, called *telpochcalli,* provided education for children of the commoners. Children at the *telpochcalli* performed physical labor, including sweeping the schoolhouse, cutting wood, repairing ditches and canals, and cultivating lands belonging to the school. These tasks prepared boys for their future economic roles as laborers and for the communal work they would have to do as commoners. Boys in the *telpochcalli* were also trained in the skills of war. In fact, military training was central to the school program. Punishments for misbehavior were sure and harsh.

Two different gods presided over the two systems of education. The god of the *calmecac* was Quetzalcoatl, who was the god of self-sacrifice, penance, learning, discipline, and culture. In contrast, the god of the *telpochcalli* was Tezcatlipoca, the god of war.

The two kinds of educational institutions and the learning they provided exemplified the two contradictory and yet complementary strands of Aztec philosophy. One strand consisted of the ethics of self-control, sacrifice, and dedication to the public good; the other strand emphasized physical prowess, hard work, and the glorification of war in the service of the state. The future leaders of Aztec society were steeped in the cultural traditions of learning, literature, and the arts. They were taught social graces and the burdens and responsibilities of leadership. Punishment for misbehavior by nobles was harsher than that meted out to commoners on the assumption that with privilege came responsibility.

Finally, children of both sexes and all social strata attended a "House of Song" when they were between 12 and 15 years old. These institutions, each one attached to a temple, instructed children in the arts of singing, dancing, and music. Led by elder men and women, the students learned ceremonial songs and sacred narratives of the Aztecan creation and of their ancestors' migrations to central Mexico. Thus, Aztec education gave every child the opportunity to learn and appreciate the history and culture of their people.

PEARSON
myanthrolab

Explore more at
www.myanthrolab.com

Most modern nations have universal education where all children are required to attend school. This principle is consistent with democratic ideals that all people can aspire to have productive, rewarding lives in their societies. However, in practice, children have varying access to schooling in many nations. In many countries in Latin America, Africa, and the Middle East, rates of boys' attendance at school far exceed those of girls. Boys' greater access to education is reflected in statistics compiled by the United Nations on enrollment in schools, especially at higher levels (United Nations, Statistics Division 2007). At the primary school level, girls and boys are about equally likely to attend school in most parts of the world, although boys have an advantage over girls in some countries with marked preference for males. At the secondary level, boys' advantage increases, particularly in the same countries. Unequal opportunities for education result in much lower levels of literacy for women than for men. Even in the developed world, where nearly all of the adult population is literate, girls are somewhat more likely to be illiterate than boys, except in Malta and the United States, where rates of illiteracy for males exceed those for females.

Throughout the rest of the world, however, illiteracy rates for women are higher overall, and the gender discrepancy favoring men is much more marked. Gender discrepancies in illiteracy widen in many Asian, Middle Eastern, and African nations, where women's rates exceed those of men by 20 percent or 30 percent (United Nations 2007). Adult literacy rates affect access to better employment and other economic opportunities. Therefore, the consequences of women's educational disadvantages continue and in fact deepen throughout their lives.

In much of the developing world, girls' school enrollment has increased during the last several decades, but it still falls below that of boys. For example, a study of education in Papua New Guinea revealed that whereas about 70 percent of school-age boys were attending primary schools, only 58 percent of girls were enrolled, despite the government's target of full enrollment for all children (Yeoman 1987). The gender discrepancy in education in Papua New Guinea is the highest of all countries in the Pacific region (UNICEF 2007). Data revealed that for every 100 boys attending primary school, only 80 girls have the same opportunity. Girls' disadvantage increases in secondary school: for every 100 boys, only 65 girls attend school. A significant factor is the attitude of parents, especially fathers, about the status and education of women. Of parents interviewed, 89 percent thought it important for their sons to go to school, but only 56 percent considered education for their daughters to be important.

Research among the Maasai, a pastoral, cattle-herding people of Kenya and Tanzania, documented lower school attendance for girls. This pattern was found both in traditional rural villages and in villages that researchers identified as "modern" because the residents there had greater access to jobs outside the pastoral sphere (Holland 1996). Perhaps counterintuitively, residents of the more modern town were less likely to send their children to school than were residents of the more traditional town. The primary researcher, Killian Holland, suggested that "traditional" parents might be more intent on sending their children to school to seek advantages that might come from schooling and literacy, enabling them to earn incomes outside of the domestic domain. In contrast, residents of the modern towns may realize that educational achievement does not necessarily translate into increased income (1996, 103). Accordingly, "this paradox has to be judged within the context of the perceived world of the Maasai who are a people dealing with a predicament not entirely of their own making. They see the negative aspects of education, the real social and economic costs, and the rare benefits. Quite clearly, the Maasai are struggling with these perspectives, each having its own cogency" (1996, 127–28). Although people with education were likely to report that their schooling had a positive effect on their lives, other members of their families and communities did not generally share in this assessment. Family members were concerned that educated children and relatives did not necessarily share their income and did not necessarily do work that benefited the community as a whole. One trend that is consistent, however, is the lower enrollment of girls in school compared to boys. Many parents in both types of communities reported that education for girls was not only unnecessary but was potentially harmful because "education spoils girls and you get nothing in return from them" (1996, 266). Opinions included fears that educated women would marry men of their own choosing rather than following the advice and direction of their elders; they would leave home and not share their earnings with their families. Of course, some Maasai men and women support the education of their daughters, understanding that women should have equal opportunities for advancement, benefiting themselves and their families.

In addition to gender bias, class, ethnic, and cultural differences may also have an effect on rates of attendance and success in school. Children from different cultural backgrounds may have different expectations about the learning process and about prevailing norms of interactions with others.

GLOBALIZATION

In 2007 the United Nations reported that 20–30 percent of women in many Asian, Near Eastern, and African countries are illiterate, a much higher figure than for men.

IN THEIR OWN VOICES

Going to School in Ake, Nigeria

In this excerpt from his memoir, Ake, The Years of Childhood, Nigerian writer Wole Soyinka recalls his impressions of school in the small town of Ake in western Nigeria, where he grew up in the 1930s and 1940s. Wole Soyinka was awarded the Nobel Prize for Literature in 1986.

Every morning before I woke up, Tinu was gone. She returned about midday carrying a slate with its marker attached to it. And she was dressed in the same khaki uniform as the hordes of children, of different sizes, who milled around the compound from morning till afternoon, occupied in a hundred ways.

At a set hour in the morning one of the bigger ones seized the chain which dangled from the bell-house, tugged at it with a motion which gave the appearance of a dance and the bell began pealing. Instantly, the various jostling, tumbling, racing and fighting pupils rushed in different directions around the school buildings, the smaller in size towards the schoolroom at the further end of the compound where I could no longer see them. The bigger pupils remained within sight, near the main building. They split into several groups, each group lined up under the watchful eye of a teacher. When all was orderly, I saw father appear from nowhere at the top of the steps. He made a speech to the assembly, then stood aside. One member of the very biggest group stepped forward and raised a song. The others took it up and they marched into the school-building in twos, to the rhythm of the song.

It was an unusual song too, since the main song was in English but the chorus was sung in Yoruba; I could only catch the words of the latter:

> B'ina njo ma je'ko
> B'ole nja, ma je'ko

"I am going to school," I announced one day. It became a joke to be passed from mouth to mouth, producing instant guffaws. Mother appeasingly said, "Wait till you are as old as your sister."

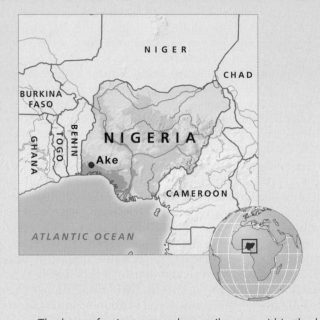

The hum of voices, once the pupils were within the buildings, took mysterious overtones. Through the open windows of the schoolroom I saw heads in concentration, the majestic figure of a teacher who passed in and out of vision, mumbling incantations over the heads of his attentive audience. Different chants broke out from different parts of each building, sometimes there was even direct singing, accompanied by a harmonium. When the indoor rites were over, they came out in different groups, played games, ran races, they spread over the compound picking up litter, sweeping the paths, clipping lawns and weeding flowerbeds. They roamed about with hoes, cutlasses, brooms and sticks, retired into open workshop sheds where they wove baskets, carved bits of wood and bamboo, kneaded clay and transformed them into odd-shaped objects.

Under the anxious eyes of "Auntie" Lawanle, I played by myself on the pavement of our house and observed these varied activities. The tools of the open air were again transformed into books, exercise books, slates, books under armpits, in little tin or wooden boxes, books in raffia bags,

---

The Western model of education is based strongly on the authority of the teacher-adult, question-answer interaction, and individual achievement. Many Native American children are socialized to learn differently, however, and especially to refrain from behavior that isolates their performance in a competitive manner in front of peers. In a comparison of classroom behavior of native children from the Warm Springs Reservation in Oregon with that of nearby nonnative students, Susan Philips (1978) found that native children were extremely reluctant to answer teachers' questions or to speak out in class. In contrast, in situations where they could have individual access to teachers, they were more likely than nonnative students to seek help, initiate questions, and engage in dialogue. The setting, not inherent interest, affected native children's learning.

tied together with string and carried on the head, slung over shoulders in cloth pouches. Directly in front of our home was the lawn, which was used exclusively by girls from the other school. They formed circles, chased one another in and out of the circles, struggled for a ball and tossed it through an iron hoop stuck on a board. Then they also vanished into classrooms, books were produced and they commenced their own observances of the mystery rites.

Tinu became even more smug. My erstwhile playmate had entered a new world and, though we still played together, she now had a new terrain to draw upon. Every morning she was woken earlier than I, scrubbed, fed and led to school by one of the older children of the house.

I got up one morning as she was being woken up, demanded my bath at the same time, ate, selected the clothing which I thought came closest to the uniforms I had seen, and insisted on being dressed in them. I had marked down a number of books on father's table but did not yet remove them. I waited in the front room. When Tinu passed through with her escort, I let them leave the house, waited a few moments, then seized the books I had earlier selected and followed them. Both parents were still in the dining room. I followed at a discreet distance, so I was not noticed until we arrived at the infant school. I waited at the door, watched where Tinu was seated, then went and climbed on to the bench beside her. Only then did Lawanle, Tinu's escort that day, see me. She let out a cry of alarm and asked me what I thought I was doing. I ignored her. The teachers heard the commotion and came into the room. I appeared to be everybody's object of fun. They looked at me, pointed as they held their sides, rocked forward and backwards with laughter. A man who appeared to be in charge of the infant section came in, he was also our father's friend and came often to the house. I recognized him, and I was pleased that he was not laughing with the others. Instead he stood in front of me and asked, "Have you come to keep your sister company?"

"No. I have come to school."

Then he looked down at the books I had plucked from father's table.

"Aren't these your father's books?"

"Yes. I want to learn them."

"But you are not old enough, Wole."

"I am three years old."

Lawanle cut in, "Three years old, Wo? Don't mind him sir; he won't be three until July."

"I am nearly three. Anyway, I have come to school. I have books."

He turned to the class teacher and said, "Enter his name in the register." He then turned to me and said, "Of course you needn't come to school everyday—come only when you feel like it. You may wake up tomorrow morning and feel that you would prefer to play at home."

I looked at him in some astonishment. Not feel like coming to school! The coloured maps, pictures and other hangings on the walls, the coloured counters, markers, slates, inkwells in neat round holes, crayons and drawing books, a shelf laden with modeled objects—animals, human beings, implements—raffia and basket-work in various stages of completion, even the blackboards, chalk and duster. I had yet to see a more inviting playroom! In addition, I had made some vague, intuitive connection between school and the piles of books with which my father appeared to commune so religiously in the front room, and which had constantly to be snatched from me as soon as my hands grew long enough to reach them on the table.

"I shall come everyday," I confidently declared.

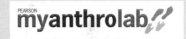

Explore more at
www.myanthrolab.com

From Wole Soyinka, *Aké: The Years of Childhood*, pp. 22–25. Copyright © 1981 by Wole Soyinka. Used by permission of Random House, Inc.

CRITICAL THINKING QUESTION

How does this memoir highlight the perspective that formal education is a privilege?

Studies of working-class African American children in the United States and Afro-Caribbean children in the United Kingdom reveal that the school environment presents difficulties not experienced by middle-class children. Reacting to the demands for conformity to school authorities (teachers and principals) and to middle-class styles of learning and interaction, children from working-class or racially marginalized groups often behave defiantly, insisting on their own norms of action and speech. Sociolinguistic studies in the United States and Britain indicate that such children may reject middle-class standard speech in favor of nonstandard varieties that are distinguished on the basis of both class and race. In such communities, pressure from the peer group often supports nonconformity, noncompliance, and nonachievement. Children who excel in the school setting are sometimes teased, ostracized, or shunned by the social groups of their peers (Labov 1972b; Cheshire 1982; Richmond 1986).

Given the difficulties of children from nonmainstream groups in school settings, some educators advocate developing learning models that are more consistent with learning styles favored by the children themselves. Research aimed at eliciting student preferences pointed to the efficacy of cooperative learning, classrooms where students could participate and talk about their opinions and their feelings, a preference for teachers who expect a high level of work from their students, and an atmosphere that is positive and nonjudgmental (Snow et al. 1996).

REVIEW — Enculturation takes place both informally and formally—for example, through observation, folklore, family interaction, rites of passage (such as initiation rites at puberty), and schooling. Children learn skills, values, behavioral expectations, interactional norms, and role and status based on age and gender. Through enculturation, children develop a gender identity, which strongly affects the way they are perceived and treated in their society.

PSYCHOLOGICAL ANTHROPOLOGY

Although each of us is a unique individual, anthropologists are interested in questions of cross-cultural similarities and differences among people. Some of these questions include the following:

1. Are there psychological differences between human populations, and can those differences be described? What are the causes of such differences?

2. What are the cultural causes and consequences of psychological variations across groups?

3. How do cultural institutions affect individual development?

4. How do sociocultural changes affect individual dispositions, and vice versa?

The field of **psychological anthropology** focuses on cultural factors in the development of personality, people's beliefs and responses to psychological states, and cultural influences on perception and cognition. Although every person is an individual with a unique character and personality, there are overall cultural influences and constraints on the ways that each person's underlying nature is manifested. That is, people are products of both their internal nature and their external experiences as members of a society and culture. Genetic factors that contribute to people's dispositions and feelings are modified and channeled by their culture, by the ideas that parents and other caregivers have about them as children, by their interactions with older and younger family members, and by relations with peers.

Culture and Personality Traits

We think of ourselves as individuals with unique personalities, that is, with particular ways of feeling, thinking, reacting, and meeting needs. People develop their personalities partly in response to the social expectations and cultural models of behavior to which they are exposed. Behaviors and ways of seeing and reacting to the world then become so ingrained and so unconscious that people think of them as part of their nature rather than as a product of culture. Actions and thoughts, expectations for oneself and for others, undergo a process of **naturalization** as a result of the internalization of cultural norms. Thus, personality is, to a large extent, culturally and socially constructed.

Personality can be thought of as consistent patterns of thinking, feeling, and behaving. The way we think, feel, and behave is influenced by complex processes of interaction between innate potentials and exposure to cultural norms and values. It may be that the

psychological anthropology
A subfield of cultural anthropology that studies the psychological motivations of behavior and the personality types prevalent in a society.

naturalization
The process of learning and incorporating attitudes, values, and behaviors so that they seem natural or part of one's nature rather than learned cultural behavior.

personality
A constellation of behavioral traits and dispositions. Some features of personality emerge at birth whereas others are acquired in the process of enculturation and psychological and cognitive growth.

concept of "personality" is a Western cultural construct. Individuals respond to events in their lives differently. Their perceptions, thinking processes, modes of learning, and emotional reactions are distinct.

Cross-cultural research in personality development suggests that cultures and personalities form an integrated, patterned, and adaptive system, suited to the social, economic, and political needs of societies. Put another way, people are molded (and mold themselves) to fit into the cultural contexts in which they live. Different cultures encourage and reward certain personality traits while discouraging and punishing others. Not everyone conforms to the expectations of their society, but most people seek to act in culturally appropriate ways most of the time. Internalized cultural values that affect personality may include, for example, an orientation toward cooperation or competition, an independent or interdependent self-concept, and a focus on a public or a private self.

Cooperation and Competition. Early cross-cultural research on personality tended to focus on traits such as cooperation and competition. In all societies, people exhibit both cooperative and competitive behavior, in different contexts. All cultures, therefore, need to encourage the development of cooperation and competition in particular situations among particular individuals. Behavior must be contextualized. In addition, the labels "cooperation" and "competition" describe sets of behaviors rather than any particular behavior. Finally, competitiveness and cooperativeness are matters of degree rather than absolute qualities.

With these cautions in mind, studies based on experimental testing of children from several countries and from urban and rural areas revealed marked differences in children's willingness to compete or cooperate in achieving tasks (Munroe and Munroe 1975). For example, children in the United States were the least willing to cooperate and continued to compete with one another even when competition led to failure and cooperation would have led to success. American children continued to compete, even after several trials when children should have noticed that, if they had cooperated, they would have been successful. This pattern contrasts with that of urban Mexican children who initially competed but then quickly caught on that cooperation would aid them all and thus changed their strategy. Differences were noted within countries as well. That is, competitiveness was more typical of urban Mexicans than rural Mexicans, urban Israelis than kibbutz children, and urban Canadians than rural Canadians. With contemporary global economic changes, competitive behavior in the workplace and the marketplace has become increasingly normative. People who exhibit these personality traits are more likely to succeed than people who refrain from competing with others.

In contrast, studies of traditional or preindustrial cultures from the anthropological record indicate a common focus on cooperation. Rather than stressing individualistic and competitive goals, these cultures emphasized the interrelationships between people and the groups to which they belong. Strongest links were established with one's kin and a group focus reinforced through child-rearing practices. Children interacted with and learned how to get along with many different people on a daily basis. Older siblings and adults besides their parents cared for them. They saw people engaged in group activities, and they learned the value of cooperation. Personality traits that were encouraged were those of communal responsibility, generosity, and even temper. According to Ruth Bunzel, writing about the Zunis,

> In all social relations whether within the family group or outside, the most honored personality traits are a pleasing address, a yielding disposition, and a generous heart. The person who thirsts for power, who wishes to be as they scornfully phrase it, "a leader of the people" receives nothing but criticism. (1932, 480)

Public Self and Private Self. Cultures vary in their focus on "private self" and "public self" (Triandis 1989). These, too, are labels that refer to sets of attitudes rather than discrete or isolated concepts. People have notions that focus on both their private and public selves, each coming into focus in particular contexts. **Private self** is the feelings and thoughts that involve characteristics and behaviors of the person, whereas **public self** is a person's feelings and thoughts that involve characteristics and behaviors of a "generalized others' view of the self" or of the "collective self".

private self
One's inner feelings and concepts of oneself.

public self
The self that one projects in public, in interactions with others.

self-concepts
Attitudes that people hold about themselves.

independent self
Concepts of individuals as self-contained, independent agents with a focus on their own thoughts, feelings, and achievements.

interdependent self
Concepts of individuals as connected to others, related to other people, with a focus on group needs rather than individual inner feelings, opinions, and attitudes.

How would you describe your personality? What cultural factors influenced the development of your self-concept as a person?

Cultural notions of the private self emphasize self-actualization; cultural notions of the public self emphasize the norms and values of the group. According to Triandis, these divergent emphases on self correlate with societal scale and economic systems. The private self is the focus in large-scale, comparatively affluent societies, where individualism and personal achievement are stressed in the context of social and economic competition. The public self is the focus in smaller, more egalitarian societies, where collectivism and group well-being are stressed. Child rearing in individualistic societies emphasizes personal achievement and the value of standing out, being distinct and different. In contrast, child rearing in collectivist societies emphasizes conformity and fitting in with group norms, especially in public settings.

Culture and Self-Concept

Research suggests that people in different cultures have different ideas of themselves, or **self-concepts.** In an influential review of research, Hazel Markus and Shinobu Kitayama (1991) point to a basic distinction between cultures that have an "independent" view of the self and those with an "interdependent" view of the self. Again, these labels cover constellations of attitudes and societal emphases rather than absolute, discrete differences. In all societies, people have both independent and interdependent concepts, each appropriately displayed in different contexts. Markus and Kitayama characterize the **independent self** view as a primarily Western notion of a person with unique "dispositional attributes . . . detached from context" (p. 225). The **interdependent self** view, in contrast, sees the self as embedded in surrounding context, or "self-in-relation-to-other." These researchers believe that the only universal aspect of self, beyond an awareness of one's physical body, is awareness of internal activity, such as dreams, thoughts, and feelings, which cannot be known directly by anyone else. An inner private self results from this awareness of "unshared experience."

An independent view of the self is individualistic, egocentric, and self-contained, whereas an interdependent sense of self is based on feelings of "connectedness" to others. In cultures where independent views of the self dominate, people are most concerned with their own thoughts and feelings and with their own achievements. In cultures where interdependent views of the self dominate, one's inner feelings, opinions, and attitudes are secondary to the needs of the groups to which one belongs. Group and community consensus and expression of solidarity are valued.

The Mexican girls in this Cinco de Mayo parade are expressing social solidarity and cultural identity through a public event.

Interdependent views of the self are more prominent in some cultures than others. Related values include the importance of respecting other people's feelings and adjusting one's behavior to the needs of the group. Community goals become personal goals as well. People ideally observe other people's behavior for the purpose of deducing their motives and feelings. People in societies with interdependent views of the self express strong needs for affiliation with others.

A person's identity emphasizes one's relationships and one's membership in groups of various kinds, including family and community. In-group and out-group distinctions are likely to be well marked in collectivist societies. People feel great loyalty to their own group (however defined). Self-discipline and emotional restraint may be valued in collectivist societies, whereas self-esteem and personal expression are valued in individualistic societies (Heine et al. 1999). In all cultures, though, people who conform to the expectations of their society, whether for individual accomplishments or for group cooperation, can have feelings of self-regard because they are acting according to cultural models of authenticity and appropriateness. Anthropological studies popular in the 1940s, 1950s, and 1960s focused on these cultural models as examples of **national character.**

national character

A constellation of behaviors and attitudes thought to be characteristic of a modal personality type prevalent in a particular country.

Culture and Cognition

Cross-cultural psychological research raises some important questions about cultural impacts on styles of thinking. Although isolating any one feature as causal is impossible, these questions can be approached from a holistic perspective, viewing cultures as integrated systems of practices, attitudes, and values. Studies with Inuit subjects from Arctic Canada and Alaska and with Kpelle subjects from Liberia illustrate cultural differences in the characteristic ways that people think.

The Inuit have a highly developed ability to make spatial judgments. In tests, subjects were required to sort out the components of their environment, separate an element from its context, and locate themselves accurately in relation to environmental features (Munroe and Munroe 1975, 82). The Inuit also demonstrate a remarkable memory for territorial features. Their success at spatial tasks is consistent with the needs of their economic and settlement patterns. In Arctic terrain, where color and shape are relatively uniform, it takes sophisticated knowledge and judgment to discern and recall significant environmental features. Such knowledge is critical to survival for people who depend on migratory animals for their food sources and who relocate their settlement sites with some frequency.

Inuit child-rearing practices encourage the development of complex spatial abilities. Children have freedom of movement and activity, but the rules that prohibit risky, life-threatening behavior are made clear and are applied consistently. The Inuit language has a rich array of terms that describe location, relations of objects to backgrounds, and relations connecting the speaker to directions, distances, and objects in the environment (Denny 1982). Correlations between hunting-and-gathering economies and spatial acuity are supported by data from Australian Aborigines, who also score high on spatial judgments tests (Segall 1979).

Recall from Chapter 4 that people classify objects and experiences according to different principles. In one study, members of the Kpelle tribe of Liberia were asked to sort twenty objects into categories. The objects included five members of four categories: food, clothing, tools, and utensils (Segall 1979). Rather than sorting into these categories, however, Kpelle subjects sorted into functional groupings. For example, a knife was sorted with an orange, a hoe with a potato. When questioned about their choices, some commented that "was the way a wise man would do things." In response to an experimenter's question, "How would a fool do it?" the subject sorted the objects into "four neat piles with food in one, tools in another, and so on" (Glick 1975, 636).

Additional studies with Kpelle focused on the contextual nature of memory. Kpelle subjects had difficulty remembering objects out of context, but their recall ability improved when they were able to classify them into functional and experiential categories. Recall also increased when items were embedded in folktales (Munroe and Munroe 1975, 87). In addition, Kpelle subjects had a superior ability to estimate quantities of some items but not of others. For example, they were accurate in estimating quantities of rice, their staple food, but not of other substances. Munroe and Munroe suggest that context-bound thought is adaptive in small-scale preindustrial societies, where "categories and processes

CONTR○VERSIES

Is There Such a Thing as National Character?

Research on national character attempted to elucidate personality types prevalent in different cultures. Ruth Benedict's pioneering work, *Patterns of Culture* (1934), characterized tribal groups by what she proposed was an overriding personality type. Working with Native American and Melanesian materials, Benedict attempted to describe contrasting cultures in terms of general, overriding thematic constructs. She suggested that every culture develops a particular configuration of behaviors and beliefs that becomes associated with specific personality types. As illustration, Benedict labeled the Kwakwaka'wakw (or Kwakiutl) of the North Pacific coast of British Columbia as "Dionysian" because of their competitive economic and ritual cycles of feasting (potlatching) and their competitive and boastful personality styles. The Zuni of the American Southwest she referred to as "Apollian" because of their nonaggressive, consensus building, and conformist social ethics. The Dobu Islanders of Melanesia were "paranoid" because of their intense concern of being the target of malevolent witches.

During World War II, Benedict and others attempted to characterize Japanese society, personality, and mentality through handy catchphrases, summed up by the title of her book on the subject, *The Chrysanthemum and the Sword* (1946). Some of these efforts were an attempt to understand Japanese motivations and actions during the war. Studies of Japanese personality focused on the contrast, as perceived by Western observers, between their peaceful, harmonious family life, and serene artistic aesthetic, and their violent militarism. Benedict's work was later criticized for reducing culture and personality to stereotypes.

Although specific personality types may be more or less favored in different cultures, or be more or less adaptive in cultural context and therefore more or less nurtured among children, national character studies overgeneralized personality types and value orientations while overlooking real differences. The concept of national character also risks constructing an "other" that masks the similarities among people.

These studies have lost favor in anthropology. Nevertheless, the tendency to overgeneralize and stereotype particular groups may reemerge in public discourse and social policy. For example, racial or ethnic profiling in criminal investigations, and, most recently, in cases of suspected terrorism, has become highly controversial.

◉ CRITICAL THINKING QUESTIONS

How might governments and power elites use or misuse concepts and attributes of national character? What are recent examples of this?

---

of thought operate with what is immediately relevant—as culturally defined—and this is seldom knowledge for its own sake" (p. 89).

In contrast, cognitive processes that children learn in the United States stress intellectual functioning leading to "more and more flexible and general schemata." This type of thinking is also adaptive. It is adapted to situations of rapid change where people are confronted with numerous types of problems requiring both multitasking and specialized knowledge. Studies indicate that, in all cultures, increased formal schooling correlates with increased success in memory tasks involving abstract concepts and out-of-context items. Intelligence and cognitive styles, too, prove to be adaptive.

Formal education favors decontextualized thinking, which may present difficulties to Kpelle and other children adjusting to the demands of school settings (Rogoff and Morelli 1989). They may find it odd to be expected to answer questions out of context without any perceived need or functional goal. They also may find it odd to provide information to an adult who clearly already has the information being requested.

REVIEW ─ ◉ Culture and a person's internalization of cultural norms, or naturalization, affect personality, self-concepts, and cognitive skills. These are all topics in psychological anthropology. People's personalities and cognitive skills, though highly variable, tend to be fitted or adapted to the culture in which they live. Examples of differences in personality traits include cooperative or competitive tendencies, individualistic or collectivist tendencies, and a focus on the private or public self. This is not to say, however, that societies have a national character distinguished by an overarching specific personality type.

DEVIANCE AND ABNORMAL BEHAVIOR IN CROSS-CULTURAL PERSPECTIVE

deviance
Behaviors that violate cultural norms and expectations.

Societies differ in what is considered normal or abnormal behavior. They also differ in the ways in which abnormal behavior is interpreted and treated. Cultures teach people how to act appropriately in different situations. People learn the behavior expected of them, attuned to the contexts, the people they are interacting with, and the goals that they wish to accomplish. Most people try to act in accordance with the expectations that their cultures teach them, and most people do act appropriately most of the time.

Rules vary from culture to culture, so that what might be considered appropriate behaviors when interacting with relatives, acquaintances, officials, or strangers in one society might be considered rude, unusual, or even "crazy" in another society. In addition, cultures differ in how underlying psychological fears, tensions, and conflicts are manifested. They also contrast in their ways of interpreting people's actions and speech as normal or abnormal and in responding to or treating that behavior. What is considered **deviance** in one culture might be considered powerful in another.

Responses to "Mental Illness"

In the United States, medical interpretations of psychological disorders have gained great currency among experts whose opinions influence the general population. These interpretations lead to treatments that are medical and pharmacological. People with "problems" are advised to take drugs to alleviate their symptoms. Drugs are developed by scientific researchers and prescribed by doctors with increasing frequency. Although these treatments may relieve symptoms, they may not cure underlying problems. Whatever we may think of these modalities, however, they are an improvement over the treatment common in Europe and the United States several centuries ago, when people suffering from anxiety, depression, and hallucinations were isolated in asylums where they were verbally and physically abused (Foucault 1976).

Consider this alternative response to Black Elk, a nineteenth-century spiritual leader of the Oglalas (Neihardt 1961). Beginning when he was a child of 9 years, Black Elk experienced periods of intense anxiety and fear, followed by receiving visual and auditory messages from the spirit realm. These messages were not exclusively for Black Elk but for his community. A modern American physician-psychiatrist might diagnose Black Elk as prone to anxiety attacks or panic disorder and hallucinations, but the Oglalas interpreted his experiences as powerful episodes of contact with the spirit world. Rather than ostracizing, punishing, or medicating him, the Oglalas respected Black Elk as a visionary who could receive messages from the spirit world. Oglala culture gave Black Elk a respected central role in the life of the community.

Research comparing the ways that unusual or deviant behavior is treated in diverse societies uncovers both similarities and differences in specific actions and reactions and underlying attitudes. For example, the Inuit recognize a condition they deem aberrant, called *nuthkavihak*, a word translated as "crazy." It refers to a condition where "something inside the person—the soul, the spirit, the mind—is out of order" (Murphy 1981, 813). Manifestations of this ailment include talking to oneself, screaming at somebody who doesn't exist, believing that a child or husband was murdered by witchcraft when nobody else believes it, believing oneself to be an animal, refusing to eat for fear one will die of it, refusing to talk, running away, getting lost, hiding in strange places, making strange grimaces, drinking urine, becoming strong and violent, killing dogs, and threatening people. Although you may recognize some of these behaviors as deviant or "crazy" in your community, others are highly specific to the Inuit culture and environment.

According to the Yorubas, some people are *were*, a word translated as "insane." Manifestations include hearing voices and trying to get other people to see their source when the other people cannot, laughing when there is nothing to laugh at, talking all the time or not talking at all, asking oneself questions and answering them, picking up sticks and leaves for no purpose except to put them in a pile, throwing away food because it is thought to contain *juju* (sorcery), tearing off one's clothes, setting fires, defecating in public and then touching the feces, taking up a weapon and suddenly hitting someone, breaking things while in a state of being stronger than normal, and believing that an

Do you know anyone who has been diagnosed with a mental illness? What type of treatment has been prescribed for this person?

GLOBALIZATION

Using Western medical models, a study conducted by the World Health Organization in 2001–2003 focused on incidences of psychological disorders in fourteen countries: Belgium, China, Colombia, France, Germany, Italy, Japan, Lebanon, Mexico, the Netherlands, Nigeria, Spain, Ukraine, and the United States. In the findings, untreated panic attacks, phobias, and posttraumatic shock syndrome topped the list everywhere, except in the United States and Ukraine, where untreated mood disorders and depression were most prevalent. The researchers noted that culture-specific disorders, such as attention deficit hyperactivity disorder (ADHD), were not included in the study.

odor is continuously being emitted from one's body. Again, some of these behaviors have analogues in descriptions of psychosis in Western medicine.

Inuit and Yoruba reactions to people with these conditions, which are thought to be incurable, vary with the severity of the symptoms and the danger of the behavior to the sufferer and to others. Such people may be avoided, restrained, or assaulted as the situation warrants. Both the Inuit and the Yorubas also recognize certain emotional and behavioral conditions that disturb the individual and others in the community but are not "insane." According to Jane Murphy, Westerners would describe many of these conditions as instances of anxiety and depression. Inuit and Yoruba treatment theories consider these types of ailments as curable, especially by ritual practitioners, who perform curing ceremonies that alleviate both the symptoms and their cause. However, they also recognize that some people cannot be cured and may suffer lifelong emotional stress.

Finally, the Yorubas and Inuit are aware of people who simply deviate from social norms. Each group focuses on particular aspects of inappropriate behavior that violate their cultural rules of propriety. Yorubas call such people *arankan,* which means a "person who always goes her or his own way regardless of others, who is uncooperative, full of malice, and bullheaded" (Murphy 1981, 821). The Inuit word describing such people, *kunlangeta,* means "the mind knows what to do but the person does not do." In both societies, the negative labels are not applied to people who occasionally act in inappropriate ways, recognizing that all people violate social norms from time to time. Instead, they are used to refer to people who repeatedly offend and violate cultural norms, seemingly without remorse. In both societies, people who behave in these ways are subject to informal means of social control such as gossip, teasing, and reprimands. If their behavior continues, they may be physically punished or even killed. And in both societies, such people are considered social incorrigibles rather than illness sufferers. As a result, rituals or other treatments are not offered to them.

Culture-Specific Psychological Disorders

Researchers have noted specific psychological disorders that occur with some frequency in certain cultures but are rare or absent in others. Such **culture-specific psychological disorders** are named and recognized as aberrant behavior by members of the culture (Yap 1969). Specific reactions to or treatments of such syndromes also may be culture-specific.

In American society, eating disorders such as anorexia and bulimia have relatively high rates of incidence, particularly among young women, although men and women of any age are susceptible. The behaviors are associated with an exaggerated concern with weight and distorted body image. Sufferers who might be very thin see themselves as overweight. The syndromes arise in the context of cultural obsessions with appearance, especially for women, and an obsessive fear of gaining weight, which are linked to emphases on youth and fear of aging. Most Americans do not become anorexic or bulimic in avoiding weight gain but are sympathetic with those who do, because of shared cultural images. Some researchers argue that the majority of women in the United States has some form of eating disorder, even though they may not be anorexic (Bordo 2004). In other societies, these preoccupations might appear to be bizarre in the extreme.

In some Southeast Asian, North African, and Siberian cultures, people may become victims of a syndrome called *latah. Latah* is manifested as a startle reaction, involving trembling, involuntary sudden movements, and overreacting to the behavior of others. People who experience *latah* episodes have difficulty coping with sudden sounds or movements. They become disoriented and extremely anxious. They may have phobic reactions toward common objects and may especially fear worms and certain animals. *Latah* sufferers are particularly vulnerable to repeated episodes after an initial traumatic experience. People in the grip of *latah* usually are not violent, but they may occasionally exhibit aggressive, even homicidal, impulses.

In the Pacific islands and in Indonesia, some people exhibit a syndrome referred to as *amok* (the origin of the English expression "to run amok"). *Amok* is manifested by intense outbursts of rage triggered by relatively simple frustrations of daily life and interactions

culture-specific psychological disorders Psychological disorders that seem to occur with some frequency in certain cultures but are rare or absent in others.

with others. *Amok* sufferers often have amnesia following an episode, not remembering anything that they said or did during the incident. Extreme cases are rare but might include generalized blind rage. In such instances, sufferers may be forcibly restrained.

Among Algonquian peoples of northeastern Canada, people may be afflicted by a syndrome called *windigo.* According to Algonquian beliefs, this disorder is the result of possession by a supernatural being, called *windigo,* a cannibal spirit. Victims of *windigo* manifest depression and anxiety prior to an episode of spirit possession. Algonquian believe that *windigo* can lead to murder and cannibalism if not properly treated, because the victim is in the clutches of the cannibal *windigo* spirit. In traditional communities, shamans treated cases of *windigo,* but if the sufferers became homicidal or cannibalistic, they were more often put to death. Fear of possible starvation during prolonged, intensely cold winters may be an ecological trigger to the development of *windigo,* given its emphasis on eating a forbidden source (another human).

Inuit men are more likely than women to experience "kayak fright." They report feelings of dizziness and paralysis, and are afraid to go out in their boats to hunt on the open seas.

In the Arctic, Inuit may experience a syndrome called *pibloktoq* (or "arctic hysteria") that is manifested by convulsive fits, sobbing, and running around in the cold outdoors without adequate clothing. Women more than men may be prone to episodes of *pibloktoq,* especially after the death of a close relative. Incidents of *pibloktoq* sometimes occur epidemically, one victim setting off the disorder in others.

Some researchers suggest a seasonal and physiological trigger for *pibloktoq* (Wallace 1961; Foulks 1972). Incidents tend to be concentrated toward the end of winter, when sunlight is scarce or absent and people are unable to synthesize vitamin D, a necessary factor in the absorption of calcium. Calcium deficiency may, therefore, be a factor leading to the syndrome and may also result from low amounts of calcium in the Inuit diet. Another possible reason is the disturbance of circadian or daily rhythms that influence many physiological functions, including blood pressure, body temperature, blood sugars, and hemoglobin levels. The rhythms are adjusted to light-dark cycles and are disrupted by the lack of sunlight in the Arctic winters. Lack of synchrony in physiological functioning can disturb the central nervous system, leading to irritability and anxiety. In addition, such factors as isolation, intense cold, and legitimate fears of starvation may contribute to anxiety and depression that are expressed in *pibloktoq.*

Here is a final example of culture-specific psychological disorders: In China and Southeast Asia, some men are gripped by *koro,* an intense and depersonalized fear of the retraction or shrinking of the penis. A man believes that his penis will retract into his abdomen, leading to death. *Koro* panics, which tend to occur as epidemics, may be associated with guilt over real or imagined illicit sexual encounters or over autoerotic thoughts or actions. They can also be triggered by generalized anxiety or by cold. Significant historical and cultural contexts for *koro* include the demands or perceived demands of sex in polygynous households. Husbands may be uncertain about their sexual adequacy or performance in a culture that places high value on the fathering of children to ensure continuation through the male line.

All societies have informal and formal ways of dealing with deviant behavior. For example, people commonly apply informal social sanctions to alert individuals that their violations of social norms are not acceptable. People also define what behavior is regarded as mentally ill. Although people everywhere identify certain behaviors as "insane," some disorders are culture-specific. Many of these disorders have physiological causes, but each society explains them differently based on its system of beliefs and values.

REVIEW

ANTHROPOLOGY APPLIED

The Ethnobotany of Psychotropic Substances

Since prehistory, people around the world have used medicinal and psychotropic substances found in plants. Preserving and passing down botanical knowledge is one of the earliest specializations in human social organization, usually performed by shamans or other spiritual leaders or healers. It is not surprising that humans would have embraced the use of mind-altering substances to enhance religious or spiritual experiences or healing effects. The study of these and other interactions of plants and people is called *ethnobotany*. Medical anthropologists are also interested in this subject. Increasingly, as shamans' and their peoples' ways of life disappear, preserving and passing down ancient botanical knowledge and the species and varieties of medicinal and psychotropic plants fall to ethnobotanists and medical anthropologists.

Psychotropic (or psychogenic) substances, called *entheogens*, may be intoxicating, narcotic, depressant, or hallucinogenic. They may be absorbed through the skin, ingested, or inhaled. In South America, traditional religious sacraments, healing ceremonies, and divination involve the use of liquid or solid tryptamines derived from native plants with high concentrations of alkaloids. Tryptamines include LSD, psilocybin, and other powerful hallucinogens. Administered by shamans, a drink—*ayahuasca*—causes hallucinations in which people, while sweating and convulsing, see jaguars, snakes, and vivid colors (Hill 2002). Depending on the culture,

ayahuasca may be used by everyone in the community, by males only, or by shamans only.

Tryptamines also may be administered as solids, such as ground seeds. The Otomac use a snuff called *yopo*, inhaled nasally through the hollow leg bones of birds. The Waika boil resin from the inner bark of certain trees, which is then dried and ground for use as snuff (Balick and Cox 1996).

Transnational pharmaceutical companies and others compete for access to these and other psychotropic and medicinal plants indigenous to tropical rain forests. Biopiracy, stealing native plants for profit, has become a growing concern in developing countries. Governments have criminalized the use of tryptamine-based entheogens, even in religious contexts. Together, these developments threaten native plants. Fearing the loss of wild plant genomes and heirloom varieties, many ethnobotanists work with other specialists to preserve the species on which modern synthetic drugs are based.

CRITICAL THINKING QUESTIONS

Why do most modern states treat tryptamines as controlled substances? Why might it be important to preserve species and varieties of plants?

CHAPTER SUMMARY

The Process of Enculturation

- Human beings are born helpless and completely dependent on adults. However, infants begin to learn their culture as soon as they are born. They acquire the language of their society and learn to behave in culturally appropriate ways. This process, called enculturation or socialization, takes place primarily through informal means over many years.

- Child rearing differs from place to place and over time. In general, a society's child-rearing practices are consistent with its core values. Child rearing includes implicit messages children absorb as they observe and interact with their family and community.

- Attitudes toward children and child care change over time. In the United States, for example, advice that medical doctors, psychologists, and sociologists give to parents and other caregivers has varied considerably, even in the twentieth century. The advice about how to raise one's child is generally consistent with the economic needs of the nation and with the culture's social values about family, individuality, and gender roles.

Formal and Informal Learning

- Children absorb cultural values, including norms of behavior, attitudes, and ethics, by observing how people act and hearing what they say. Sayings, proverbs, and storytelling are powerful symbolic means of transmitting core cultural values. Children learn how to properly interact with others by observing their elders and interacting with peers, family members, and people of different social roles. Children also learn their place and their social role in their family and community. They learn that factors such as age, gender, and status influence the rights that people have and how they behave.

- Children are also socialized in formal settings such as schools. How schools are organized and give instruction vary cross-culturally. Although today most nations support universal education, children in many nations don't all have equal access to schooling. More boys than girls attend school, resulting in lower rates of literacy among women. Class, ethnic, and racial differences may also affect rates of attendance and a child's success in school. These differences affect people's roles in society and their economic potential and security.

Psychological Anthropology

- Our personalities are largely shaped by environmental factors, including our culture. Personality emerges from the interaction of nature and nurture. Cultural differences in core values lead to differences in the kinds of personality developed in each society. Although all cultures contain and approve of some elements of competitiveness and cooperativeness, cultures differ markedly in the emphasis that they place on one or the other. Many postindustrial societies, including the United States, emphasize individuality and competitiveness, whereas many nonindustrial societies favor the group over the individual and value cooperation more than competition.

- Differences in personality are also reflected in differing cultural concepts of the "self." Some cultures emphasize individual traits, experiences, and accomplishments. Others emphasize a person's relationships with others and membership in groups such as families and communities.

Deviance and Abnormal Behavior in Cross-Cultural Perspective

- Societies differ in what is considered normal or abnormal behavior and in how they interpret and treat abnormal behavior. Cultures also differ in how underlying psychological fears, tensions, and conflicts are manifested. What might be considered deviant behavior in one culture might be considered a sign of spiritual power in another. Anthropologists have isolated culture-specific psychological disorders that seem to occur frequently in certain cultures but are rare or absent in others.

KEY TERMS

socialization 95
social birth 96
child-rearing
  practices 98
folklore 104
status 106

gender identity 107
rites of passage 109
initiation rites 109
psychological
  anthropology 116
naturalization 116

personality 116
private self 117
public self 117
self-concepts 118
independent self 118
interdependent self 118

national character 119
deviance 121
culture-specific
  psychological
  disorders 122

REVIEW QUESTIONS

1. What kinds of beliefs and practices do societies have for managing the physical and social birth of new members? What is the relationship between infant mortality rates and definitions of social birth?

2. What child-rearing tasks must all societies address? How do child-rearing strategies commonly vary?

3. What are some examples of formal and informal modes of enculturation?

4. How does status and inequality within a family reflect status and inequality within a society as a whole?

5. How are age and gender socialization reflected in naming practices?

6. What are some examples of rites of passage? What social and psychological functions do rites of passage serve?

7. How do individuals acquire personality traits in the context of enculturation? What are some examples of cross-cultural differences in personal identity and self-concept?

8. What is national character, and why was it controversial as a concept?

9. What are some examples of the diverse ways in which societies deal with deviant and abnormal behavior?

myanthrolab EXERCISES

To complete the following exercises and activities, you must log in to www.myanthrolab.com and select your current textbook.

1. In the **Explore** tab of Chapter 5, click on *Video* and watch the slide show, *The Changing American Family*. Complete the short answer exercise that accompanies the video.

2. While in the **Explore** tab, watch the video about naming traditions among the Luhya in Kenya. Complete the short answer exercise that accompanies the video.

3. In the **Research Tools** section on the home page, click on the *Research Navigator*™ link and enter the Anthropology database to find relevant and recent scholarly and popular press publications. For this chapter enter the following keywords: *socialization, gender identity, cross cultural,* and *national character.*

4. Enter the **MyAnthroLibrary** section on the home page to read more about topics and cultures that are discussed in this chapter. Suggested readings include:

Andean Mestizos: Growing Up Female and Male by Lauris A. McKee

Norwegians: Cooperative Individualists by D. Douglas Caulkins

MAKING A LIVING

- What is economic anthropology?
- How do the supply and availability of food force people to adapt?
- How does subsistence influence the size of populations and habitation patterns?
- How does subsistence shape people's work, social organization, and social relationships?
- What are some characteristics and examples of foraging and foragers?
- What are some characteristics and examples of pastoralists and horticulturalists?
- What are the benefits and risks of agriculture as a mode of subsistence?
- How can people's subsistence strategies change over time?

H ere, then is the beginning of when it was decided to make human beings, and when what must enter into the flesh of people was sought.

And the Forefathers, the Creators and Makers, who were called Tepeu and Gucumatz said: "The time of dawn has come, let the work be finished, and let those who are to nourish and sustain us appear, the noble sons, the civilized vassals; let humanity appear, on the face of the earth." Thus they spoke.

They assembled, came together and held council in the darkness and in the night; then they sought and discussed, and here they reflected and thought. In this way their decisions came clearly to light and they found and discovered what must enter into the flesh of human beings.

It was just before the sun, the moon, and the stars appeared over the Creators and Makers.

From Paxil, from Cayala, as they were called, came the yellow ears of corn and the white ears of corn.

These are the names of the animals which brought the food: yac (the mountain cat), utiu (the coyote), quel (a small parrot), and hoh (the crow). These four animals gave tidings of the yellow ears of corn and the white ears of corn, they told them that they should go to Paxil and they showed them the road to Paxil.

And thus they found the food, and this was what went into the flesh of created people, they made people; this was their blood; of this the blood of people was made. So the corn entered into the formation of human beings by the work of the Forefathers.

And in this way they were filled with joy, because they had found a beautiful land, full of pleasures, abundant in ears of yellow corn and ears of white corn, and . . . there was an abundance of delicious food in those villages.

The animals showed them the road. And then grinding the yellow corn and the white corn, Xmucane made nine drinks, and from this food came the strength and the flesh, and with this they created the muscles and the strength of human beings.

After that they began to talk about the creation and the making of our first mother and father; of yellow corn and of white corn they made their flesh; of corn-meal dough they made the arms and the legs of human beings.

From Goetz, Deila, and Sylvanus Griswold Morley, *The Book of the People: Popol Vuh. The National Book of the Ancient Quiche Maya.* ©1954 Plantin Press, pp. 104–05. Reprinted by permission.

In this narrative, the Quiche Maya of southern Mexico and Guatemala account for the origin of corn, their subsistence food and ceremonial crop, and acknowledge their dependence on it. The Creators and Makers of earth used this sacred food to form the flesh of human beings, thus forever linking human substance and lives with these foods. The narrative also creates a world of beauty and plenty, in balance and harmony, that allows people to thrive.

ECONOMIC ANTHROPOLOGY

This chapter looks at the many strategies, farming among them, that humans have developed to meet their basic need for food. It also examines the cultural implications of each of these strategies—their influence on everything from population size to social structure. Chapter 7 continues this discussion by examining people's economic systems and systems of exchange.

Economic anthropology focuses on subsistence strategies and economic systems—how people meet their survival needs and make their livings. Meeting survival needs requires resources and the labor and technology necessary to obtain and transform those resources into usable foods and goods. People, therefore, need to develop practices that allow for efficient adaptations to their environments, adjusting their settlement patterns and their populations to the available resources. Economic anthropologists study the ways

economic anthropology Subdiscipline of anthropology that focuses on subsistence strategies and economic systems.

A woman preparing sago, a staple food, in Saidowai, Papua New Guinea.

that people organize their labor, allocate various tasks among members of their communities, and share or distribute goods and services within their settlements as well as with people in other communities or regions. Specific subsistence strategies are generally associated with particular types of social and political life. Economic systems thus influence the ways that other cultural practices develop in order to meet physical and social needs.

Economic anthropology is the study of subsistence strategies—how people meet their basic survival needs—and how those strategies shape their society and culture. Basic subsistence underlies the economic system of a society and influences every other social relationship in that society and people's lives.   **REVIEW**

UNDERSTANDING HUMAN SUBSISTENCE PATTERNS

Everyone must eat to survive, so a fundamental requirement for any cultural group is to feed its members. The way it does so—the way its people make a living—influences and constrains many other cultural traits. There are different **subsistence patterns**—methods of obtaining food—each making different use of available land and resources, each making different use of available labor and energy, and each utilizing a different technology. Other aspects of culture tend to co-occur with particular subsistence strategies. These include the size and permanence of settlements that people establish, the kinds of households that people live in, the ideas that people have about property and ownership, and even the ways that people think of themselves and other people.

Two basic modes of subsistence involve finding food (foraging, or hunting and gathering) and growing food (food production).

Foraging Versus Food Production

Our early ancestors were **foragers,** or hunter-gatherers. They hunted, fished, and collected wild plants, nuts, fruits, and insects. Foraging was humanity's only subsistence strategy for countless millennia until about 10,000 years ago when people living in the Middle East began to herd animals and grow their own crops. Foragers make use of the resources growing wild in their environment.

People who grow crops or manage herds are **food producers.** They transform and manage their environment to obtain their food. The three major types of food production

subsistence patterns
Methods of obtaining food using available land and resources, available labor and energy, and technology.

foragers
Peoples whose subsistence pattern is hunting and gathering.

food producers
Users of a subsistence strategy that transforms and manages the environment to obtain food.

pastoralism
A subsistence strategy focusing on raising and caring for large herds of domesticated animals.

horticulture
A subsistence strategy that focuses on small-scale farming using a relatively simple technology.

agriculture
A subsistence strategy focusing on intensive farming, investing a great deal of time, energy, and technology.

carrying capacity
The number of people who can be sustained by the resources and environment in which they live.

GLOBALIZATION

Anthropologists have studied the globalization of food choices, which are shaped by a vast and increasingly complex global economy. In *Tasting Food, Tasting Freedom: Excursions into Eating, Culture, and the Past* (1996), for example, Sidney Mintz explores the globalization of sugar, tea, chocolate, and the ubiquitous Coca-Cola.

are pastoralism, horticulture, and agriculture. **Pastoralism** involves raising and caring for large herds of domesticated animals as primary subsistence. Horticulture and agriculture are types of farming. Although some people still live by foraging and pastoralism, the forces of globalization are making these ways of life increasingly peripheral. And many people have multiple subsistence strategies based on mixed economies, combining farming, herding, and other methods of food production.

The earliest farming techniques were of the type referred to as **horticulture,** which refers to small-scale farming using a relatively simple technology. Later, intensive farming techniques, or **agriculture,** were developed. Today, agriculture is often combined with industrial processes that eliminate much of the need for human labor. These modes of food production are ideal types and often are combined or practiced in relation to other peoples in trading relationships. The following sections address how these subsistence strategies work.

Ecosystem, Adaptation, and Carrying Capacity

Subsistence techniques vary considerably, in part depending on available resources, climate, and topography. They are developed to satisfy people's needs for food, clothing, and shelter. They must also be adapted to available resources, water, land, and labor supply. Some areas of the world are rich in natural resources whereas others are meager, each presenting an array of possibilities and challenges for human populations.

The **carrying capacity** of any region or environment is the number of people who can be sustained by its resources. Carrying capacity, however, is not a fixed number. Rather, it varies with such factors as subsistence techniques, labor expenditure, and technological development. Some subsistence strategies and technologies are able to extract more resources from the land than others. This means that people can change a region's carrying capacity by changing their way of life. For example, the same region can generally support a bigger population of farmers than of foragers. As farmers work harder to cultivate more land, or develop technologies like irrigation to make their land more productive, they can increase yields and the size of the population that the land can sustain. At some point, however, new limits may eventually be reached, beyond which the productivity of the land can no longer be increased and may, in fact, begin to decline. The resulting problems are something that every society must consider in their subsistence strategies.

Another factor influencing carrying capacity is the resources within an ecosystem that people choose to exploit. People in all cultures make distinctions between the foods that they consider to be edible and those they consider inedible, whether or not they are actually capable of consuming them. For example, different peoples regard different kinds of animals, insects, fish, or plants and seaweeds as inedible or edible because of cultural attitudes.

Communities need to keep their population size within the limits of the carrying capacity of their territory. Their adjustments to their land and resources should be attuned to productivity in bad times in order to be able to sustain their numbers when conditions are not optimal. Different subsistence modes entail different kinds of strategies for adjusting population size to resources and land.

Many aspects of society and culture, including population density, the way people reckon kinship, and the way they organize their communities, may influence and be influenced by the way people feed and shelter themselves. Thus, there are relationships between subsistence and settlement patterns, population factors, division of labor, and other elements of culture. It is also important to keep in mind that people engage in a variety of subsistence modes of production, often shifting over time and interacting with people who practice other modes of subsistence. No subsistence system functions in isolation or in a timeless way unaffected by the forces of culture change.

Culture as much as biology dictates the foods we choose to eat. Many foods that most North Americans would consider unfit to eat—such as insects, grubs, or snakes—may be delicacies elsewhere in the world.

Subsistence and Settlement Pattern

Subsistence strategies tend to be related to particular types of settlement patterns. The term **settlement pattern** refers to the way people distribute themselves in their environment: where they locate their dwellings, how they group dwellings into settlements, and how permanent or transitory those settlements are. Foragers, for example, tend to live in small settlements that fluctuate in size and location, depending on the seasonal availability of plants, animals, and water.

Foragers are usually mobile. They do not have fixed, permanent settlements but, rather, move from camp to camp to secure resources in different places at different times of the year. Pastoralists also tend to relocate their settlements throughout the year, although their movements may be more predictable than those of foragers. Pastoralists often alternate between two or three locations during the year, making use of familiar available grazing lands for their animals. The size of pastoral settlements varies significantly. Some are quite small, numbering less than 100 people, whereas others may be in the hundreds or even thousands.

In contrast to foragers and pastoralists, farmers often establish relatively permanent settlements. Horticulturalists might move among their gardens and groves or relocate to more fertile fields. Many farmers live in small, scattered villages and may change location every generation or so when their farmland becomes depleted of nutrients. Agriculturalists might live in large, permanent towns or cities.

Subsistence and Population

The number of people living in a community depends on the resources available and the strategies used to extract them. Foraging communities tend to have relatively few people. Some may number no more than a few dozen, whereas others may number into the hundreds. The variation in community size depends on the scarcity or abundance of resources. In places with more resources, larger populations may congregate; places of scarcity support fewer people. In most foraging societies, community size fluctuates throughout the year, depending on the availability of resources. People come together when resources are available to support them and disperse when resources dwindle. Food producers tend to have larger populations than foragers. The security afforded by producing one's own food, along with the possibility of producing surpluses, enables larger populations to concentrate in one settlement.

Subsistence, Work, and Division of Labor

Different subsistence strategies involve different kinds of work, allocated to different people. In foraging societies, most work is assigned according to gender. In general, men do most of the hunting and fishing, and women do most of the gathering of food from plants. However, these patterns are rarely rigid. Instead, in practice, the roles of men and women overlap so that men may participate in gathering and women may assist in hunting and fishing. In farming societies, the heavy work of clearing fields is usually assigned to men. Thereafter, there are no hard-and-fast rules cross-culturally. In some cultures, women are the principal farmers, whereas men are in others. Age is also a factor in allocating work. In foraging societies, young children may contribute by gathering wild plants; in farming societies, they may help plant and weed fields and harvest crops.

Subsistence and Social Relations

Modes of subsistence affect people's interpersonal and intergroup relationships. To some extent, all societies have subsistence strategies that result in greater or lesser equality among individuals and social groups because of the way that resources are allocated. Societies also differ in their emphasis on greater or lesser cooperation or competition in producing and consuming resources and placing greater or lesser value on **reciprocity**—principles of mutual gift giving and material support.

settlement pattern
The way people distribute themselves in their environment, including where they locate their dwellings, how they group dwellings into settlements, and how permanent or transitory those settlements are.

reciprocity
Principles of mutual gift giving.

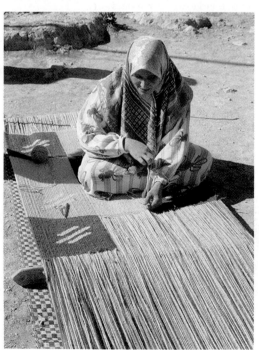

Bedouin women of the Bani Hamida tribe in Jordan weave traditional carpets for international trade. Weaving is women's work in this society.

Societies also differ in having more or less effective systems for **redistribution**—the gathering together and then reallocation of food and resources to ensure everyone's survival. In addition, the economies of all societies have **leveling mechanisms**—practices designed to equalize access to food, resources, and wealth or to prevent the concentration of wealth in too few hands, again to ensure general survival of the larger group.

> **REVIEW** ⊙ Subsistence patterns are broadly divided into foragers and food producers. Pastoralism, horticulture, and agriculture are three forms of food production. People's subsistence strategies depend in part on the carrying capacity of the environment they occupy, which, in turn, affects their settlement pattern, population size, and movements within a territory. The greater the carrying capacity, the more people an environment can support. Subsistence strategies also shape and are expressed in people's social relationships and systems of exchange.

FORAGING

What foraging have you done? How might your practices differ if your foraging was for subsistence rather than recreation?

redistribution
The gathering together and then reallocation of food and resources to ensure everyone's survival.

leveling mechanisms
Cultural practices designed to equalize access to food, resources, and social prestige through a community so that no one individual can amass greater wealth or greater prestige than other people.

nomads
People who do not have permanent homes but travel to sources of food as the food becomes seasonably available.

Foragers depend on nature to supply them with resources, although they need to develop technologies and techniques to exploit those resources. Foraging societies once existed in all parts of the world, but today very few people, if any, remain dependent exclusively on a food-collecting subsistence strategy. Over many centuries, foraging societies have been transformed into food producers, either because they adopted new subsistence techniques on their own, in response to environmental or internal social change, or because they were forcibly absorbed by expanding agricultural or industrial societies.

Foraging survived longest in environments that have proven inhospitable to other subsistence strategies. The indigenous foraging peoples of the Canadian and Alaskan Arctic, for example, until recently lived off the scarce resources of a region that is extremely cold for most of the year. At another extreme, the indigenous foragers of the Kalahari Desert in southeast Africa depended on the limited resources of an extremely hot and dry environment. Now, however, the indigenous people even of these regions have become enmeshed in the national economies of the countries within whose borders they live; they no longer rely exclusively on foraging, and most of their members have abandoned foraging entirely. Nearly throughout the world, foraging has become a marginalized way of life.

Ecological Factors

Because they depended on widely dispersed and relatively scarce resources, most foragers were **nomads**. They had to travel to particular sources of food as the food became seasonally available. In some cases, seasonal migration meant frequent relocations; in other cases, seasonal migration meant only a few relocations. The more abundant and concentrated a region's resources, the less a foraging group had to move to exploit them. In some rare cases, such as in the Pacific Northwest of North America, resources were so concentrated and abundant that the people were able to live in permanent settlements. The need of most foragers to exploit a wide variety of plants and animals added interest and novelty to their diets and supplied a well-balanced assortment of nutrients. Exceptions to this foraging diet included the diet of people like the Inuit, which consisted almost exclusively of meat and fish because of the scarcity of vegetation in the Arctic.

To successfully exploit the resources available to them, foragers needed an intimate knowledge of their environment. They had to be familiar with the life cycles and properties of the plants and animals they depended on and adjust their own migrations to coincide with their seasonal availability. In arid environments, they also had to know where and when

Inuit foragers developed a complex and sophisticated technology to help them survive in a harsh environment. Here an Inuit hunter uses a dog sled team to help him travel and carry back the seals and walrus that he catches.

they could find fresh water. This crucial knowledge was gathered from experience and, along with critical skills such as fire making, transmitted from generation to generation.

Optimal Foraging

Some researchers have suggested that human foraging behavior can be understood through analogies with the foraging behavior of other animals (MacArthur and Pianka 1966; Stephens and Krebs 1986). They use decision theory to predict the behavior of "optimal foragers," people with perfect knowledge of their environment, of the survival benefits of particular food resources, and of the relative risks involved in pursuing particular food resources. **Optimal foraging theory** might be used to explain why labor is expended in certain pursuits but not in others. However, although this theory offers some intriguing insights, it may reduce human behavior to biological processes and ignore the intervention of culture. Cultural practices respond to environmental constraints and develop to ensure individual and societal survival, but they respond to cultural values and attitudes as well.

A common misconception is that foraging requires constant labor in the pursuit of food. Observations of the Ju/'hoansi of the Kalahari, however, suggest that they spent considerably less time in subsistence activities than do people living in farming or industrial societies (Lee 2003, 56). As Table 6.1 indicates, the Ju/'hoansi workweek—including foraging for food, making and repairing tools, and food preparation and other household maintenance—averaged only 42.3 hours.

Although men spent more time and energy in subsistence work than did women, women provided the bulk of the calories (56 percent) in the Ju/'hoansi diet (Lee 1982, 40). Women were more productive than men because success in hunting is appreciably lower than success in food collecting. On average, men killed one animal for every four days of hunting. And on average, women gathered enough plants, fruits, insects, and nuts in a few hours' work several times a week to feed everyone in a camp each night.

Population Factors

Most foraging societies had to keep their numbers low to avoid literally eating themselves out of their territories. In addition, the size of settlements—the number of people living together—usually varied according to the seasonal availability of resources. Generally, people tended to congregate in seasons of abundance and disperse in smaller groups in seasons of scarcity. When families migrated from one location to another, parents had to carry infants and small children, yet another incentive to limit family size.

Because the availability of resources varied from year to year, as well as within the year, the ideal population size for a foraging society would not exceed their region's carrying capacity in a bad year. Failure to keep population in check could result in starvation and malnourishment, which would leave survivors with long-term physical and psychological damage, devastated by the loss of family and fearful for the future.

Foragers adopted a variety of strategies to curb population growth. These included ritually prescribed periods of sexual abstinence before, during, or after certain ceremonies or in conjunction with cleansing or purifying rites. In addition, women in many foraging societies (as in many other types of indigenous societies) often nursed their children for many years. Women are less fertile when they are nursing than when they aren't. Reinforcing this contraceptive effect, many foraging societies (like many societies

What are the implications of foraging for the accumulation of material culture? What kinds of social relations would foraging tend to foster?

optimal foraging theory
Application of animal studies and decision theory to human foraging.

TABLE 6.1 AN ESTIMATED JU/'HOANSI WORKWEEK			
	Subsistence Work	Tool Making/ Fixing	Housework	Total Workweek
Men	21.6	7.5	15.4	44.5
Women	12.6	5.1	22.4	40.1
Average both sexes	17.1	6.3	18.9	42.3

generally) had taboos or restrictions on the sexual activity of nursing mothers. Some indigenous peoples knew of plants and other natural substances that may have some contraceptive or abortive effects. Finally, when all else failed, many societies permitted infanticide as a response to the need to limit population growth. Taken together, these strategies could not control fertility completely, but that was rarely a necessary goal. Rather, they helped to stabilize population growth over time.

Social and Cultural Factors

Foraging peoples tended not to accumulate much property. For nomadic peoples, having many possessions is a burden because they have to carry them whenever they move. Foraging peoples were rarely interested in claiming land as property. Because they could not control the resources on which they relied, ownership of land would be futile and counterproductive because it would tie people to a particular location. Instead, subsistence based on foraging required territorial flexibility. Ownership of land contradicts that principle of flexibility and might potentially stifle the freedom of movement foragers needed to survive.

CASE STUDY

A Foraging Society: The Dobe Ju/'hoansi

A close look at a nomadic foraging society provides insight into the cultural characteristics common to many such societies. Although the specific features of the environment and adaptation of the Ju/'hoansi of Botswana and Namibia are unique, the cultural correlates of their social life and attitudes are like those of other foraging peoples.

The Ju/'hoansi live in the hot, dry Kalahari Desert. The Dobe are a group of Ju/'hoansi who, in the 1960s and 1970s, numbered about 400 and lived by foraging in 3,000 square miles of semidesert terrain. Unlike most foraging peoples, who congregate in larger groups when resources were abundant and disperse into smaller groups when resources were scarce, the Ju/'hoansi reversed this pattern, settling around permanent water holes during the dry season and dispersing during the rainy season when water was more available. Dry-season camps generally consisted of eight to fifteen huts, housing twenty to fifty people. Population had to be kept small to avoid straining the resources around the permanent water holes. Rainy season settlements, located near seasonal and secondary water sources, varied in size from three to twenty huts (Lee 2003, 32).

Each camp had a core group of residents, usually siblings or cousins, with other residents related by blood or marriage to members of the core group. Camp composition was kept balanced. If a persistent imbalance emerged between numbers of males and females, for example, some families would move to another camp. Families would also move if the number of children in a camp became too large for the adults to care for them.

Women's main subsistence activity was to gather wild foods. The Dobe region has more than 100 edible varieties of plants, roots, fruits, and nuts. Gathered foods accounted for approximately 70 percent of the Ju/'hoansi diet. Men's primary subsistence task was hunting (Lee 1982, 40). Individual men tracked and hunted small animals, but larger animals, especially antelope and giraffe, were usually hunted by groups of men.

The Ju/'hoansi valued meat. It provided a more concentrated source of protein and calories than plant food, making it important to people who expended a lot of energy in their daily activities. Given the relatively low success rate in hunting, meat was also a scarce resource, and scarcity contributed to its desirability. Perhaps most important, however, meat had great social value. Whereas gathered foods were usually consumed within the

gatherer's household, meat was distributed throughout a camp and even among residents of other camps.
A successful hunt provided the opportunity for feasting and the display of proper etiquette in distributing
portions to kin and neighbors. As among the Inuit of
the Arctic, the distribution of meat had great social
significance, as recounted in an ethnography of the
Ju/'hoansi by Richard Lee:

> Distribution is done with great care, according to a
> set of rules, arranging and rearranging the pieces
> for up to an hour so that each recipient will get
> the right proportion. Successful distributions are
> remembered with pleasure for weeks afterwards,
> while improper meat distributions can be the cause
> of bitter wrangling among close relatives. (2003)

In 2006, the High Court in Botswana granted the Ju/'hoansi the right to
return to their homelands in the Kalahari Game Reserve, from where they
had been expelled by the Botswana government. The woman here is
celebrating that victory.

The Ju/'hoansi had leveling mechanisms to prevent
successful hunters from gaining disproportionate
wealth, status, and authority over others. For example,
"ownership" of a kill went not to the hunter who shot it
but to the owner of the fatal arrow. Arrows were given
to hunters through reciprocity—gift exchanges called
hxaro. A person could give a present to anyone and thereby establish a relationship based on
future reciprocity. When a man went hunting, he might use arrows that he made himself as
well as arrows that one or more of his *hxaro* partners had given him. Prestige accrued to the
arrow owner, who supervised the distribution of meat.

A second leveling mechanism was the practice of "insulting the meat." A successful
hunter did not immediately bring his kill into camp. Instead, he left it a distance outside
and returned alone. He would then announce his deed and persuade other men to
come and see. When the group arrived at the kill site, they made derogatory comments
about the animal and voiced annoyance at the hunter for bothering them with such an
insignificant kill. The hunter was expected to join in insulting the meat and ridiculing
himself. The Ju/'hoansi were well aware of the "leveling" purpose of these social rituals.
An elder hunter explained:

> When a young man kills much meat, he comes to think of himself as a chief or a big man,
> and he thinks of the rest of us as his servants or inferiors. We can't accept this. We refuse
> one who boasts, for someday his pride will make him kill somebody. So we always speak of
> his meat as worthless. In this way we cool his heart and make him gentle. (2003)

Economic and political changes have transformed the Ju/'hoansi's lives since the
1960s. Modern technology, wage work, and incorporation into nation states have affected
their society. Governments have taken most of their traditional lands. These changes
occurred over a relatively short time. Most Ju/'hoansi in Botswana and Namibia today
live in sedentary villages where subsistence is based on farming and herding. Men do this
work, whereas women mainly do domestic tasks and occasionally forage for wild
foods (Draper 1975, 101–03). In addition, many Ju/'hoansi men and women are now
employed for wages in nearby towns. Some men work as far away as the gold mines in
South Africa (Lee 2003, 159–60). Notions of private ownership of property by individuals
have become incorporated into Ju/'hoansi ethics. Men separately own goats and cattle in
Ju/'hoansi herds. The male heads of households are also said to "own" houses, and
wealthier men are even "owners" of a village (Lee 2003, 98). Because the property that
constitutes wealth is identified more with men than with women, men are endowed with
greater status. Thus these economic changes have also affected gender roles and values.

Despite these changes, many Ju/'hoansi are trying to negotiate with local and
national authorities to maintain some control over their traditional territories. Some of
the most successful initiatives involve resource management plans. In conjunction with
the Community-Based Natural Resource Management
office in Botswana, Ju/'hoansi are developing programs
that combine subsistence (foraging and farming) with
tourism and resource conservation (Hitchcock and
Biesele 2002).

PEARSON
myanthrolab

Explore more at
www.myanthrolab.com

IN THEIR OWN VOICES

An Inupiaq Whaler's Wife

As elsewhere among foraging peoples, work roles among the Inuit and Inupiaq of Arctic Canada and the United States were generally allocated according to gender. Men were the primary hunters whereas women collected birds' eggs, fished, cooked, made clothing, and performed other domestic tasks. However, among some Arctic peoples, daughters as well as sons learned to hunt (Blackman 1989; Bodenhorn 1993). Inuit families hoped for at least one son and one daughter who could fulfill the complementary subsistence tasks associated with each sex. In Alaska, families sometimes adopted children to balance the size and gender composition of their households (Bodenhorn 1988). Alternatively, parents with only boys or girls might train one child to do both men's and women's tasks (D'Anglure 1984). Because of their knowledge of the full range of Inuit subsistence skills, these individuals were valued as spouses.

Inuit villagers from Kaktovik, Barter Island, Alaska participate communally in hunting, butchering, and distributing the meat from a bowhead whale.

In Alaska, whale hunting often involved a crew of men working under a leader, called *umialik*, who owned a boat and hunting equipment and recruited the crew. The men in a whaling crew were a cohesive social group, forming relationships with one another that were second in closeness only to those with their families (Spencer 1984).

Sadie Brower Neakok was an Inupiaq woman living in Barrow, Alaska. She died on June 18, 2004, and was praised in the U.S. Senate for her work as the first woman to serve as a magistrate in the state of Alaska. Daughter of a native mother and an Anglo father, she was raised in both traditional and nontraditional ways. From her mother, Sadie learned to hunt and fish. And from her father, a whaler, she learned the importance of education in the "outside" world. Sadie grew up to be a social worker and magistrate in Barrow. She married an Inupiaq man and accompanied him on hunting trips. In this excerpt from her life history, Sadie

Social etiquette in foraging societies was often based on the principle of communal sharing. Sharing the meat of large animals was a critical way of distributing resources and making sure that everyone in the community had the same chances of surviving. People in foraging societies depended on one another in times of need, and sharing food is a way of symbolizing community interdependence just as it ensures everyone's well-being. In such societies, people understood the needs of others to be just as important as their own needs. What is good for all is good for each one. They also understood that the people whom they help feed one day might help feed them the next.

Most foraging societies were characterized by social equality. Foragers generally believed that all people have equal rights to resources, equal rights to social respect and prestige, and equal rights to a decent standard of living. In foraging societies, there was usually little differentiation among families in terms of possessions, wealth, housing, and equipment. Similarly, there was usually little differentiation among people in terms of social standing except as a reflection of individual differences in intelligence, skill, and

Brower Neakok: An Inupiaq Woman, *Sadie describes women's contributions to whale hunting.*

Being a whaler's wife is just as much work as preparing to go out with a crew. You have to see that they all have warm clothing. So your husband buys all the fur. In the olden days, it was caribou hides, ruffs, fur socks, fur pants. We didn't have down clothing, so everything was made out of caribou hide or reindeer hide and sealskin for waterproof boots. New clothing is made every year because it's tradition.

If you want a good skin on your husband's boat, you have to hire several women to sew together six or seven ugruk hides with waterproof seams and stretch them over a frame. . . . The sewers also have to know how to make the thread; it's braided from caribou leg sinew, and then the part where you put the needle [i.e., eye of the needle] is made from the back sinew.

Nate [Sadie's husband] has been a whaling captain for quite a while. And in his time, I guess he has gotten about five whales. The last one was in 1984. And you could see him cutting it up, measuring it for the various parts that go to certain people.

The fluke area is for the whaling captain, and then there's a belt of about eighteen to twenty inches wide, which is for the captain's pleasure. It's up to the captain whether he wants to sell it; he talks with his crew whether they want a share of it for their own consumption or to sell it. And the captain's part is set aside by itself, to give to people at the whale catch celebration—Nalukataq time—and Thanksgiving and at Christmastime. We cut it up in thirds for all the people. That's a lot of work, cutting it up. You have to feed the whole town; that's the custom.

Everybody enjoyed our whale. There are so many people in town now—even our whites have acquired the taste of fresh maktak and meat, and they mingle in with our people— and feeding some three and four thousand in one day out of that whale, by 10:00 P.M. we were all in.

Then you do it all over again at Nalukataq time. You have to cut up meat and maktak and put it into containers to age. You cook the heart, and the kidney, and the intestines at Nalukataq time. Oh, it's a lot of excitement when it happens. Then there's the blanket toss and the dances, but it's not like the old days anymore. People didn't work in those days when I was young. Now we have to wait till everybody gets off work to serve our big portions of whale. It starts at five.

As far back as I can remember, in the old tradition, women were out there on the ice with the men. They could go out and hunt with the menfolk; they would cook for them, or sew, or tend to their men's needs out there. But we are shying off from that today. There's not very many women who would go out and stay out there, but Nate gives our girls a chance to be out there.

When you're a whaling captain's wife, your part is just as important as the men's because you're entrusted with keeping your husband's crewmen out there comfortable and fed. You're in charge of all their care, preparing their food. . . . When the boats start chasing a whale, all you do is just listen to see who is catching it. It gets so exciting, like you are inside of the boat yourself. It's an exciting event when your crew gets a whale, a lot of work, but when all the women's work of feeding the whole town is done, then you feel like you have shared in the whale catch.

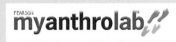

Explore more at
www.myanthrolab.com

From Margaret Blackman, *Sadie Brower Neakok: An Inupiaq Woman*, pp. 209–16. © 1989. Reprinted by permission of the University of Washington Press.

● CRITICAL THINKING QUESTION

What does Sadie Brower Neakok's story suggest about the work roles of Inupiaq women and men?

---

personality. Only a few foraging societies had significant distinctions of wealth and social standing.

Finally, in many foraging societies, people had religions that included the belief that animals, plants, and some objects had souls similar to the souls of human beings. Animals were understood to be capable of thought and speech. Foraging peoples also performed rituals aimed at securing successful hunting.

Land, Labor, and Production in Foraging Societies

In most foraging societies, land and resources were generally available to all members of the group. A "group" might be defined as a family, a larger kin group, a local community, or a dispersed population that considered themselves the inhabitants of a particular territory. Each type of group tended to have certain territories and resource sites that its members utilized on a repeated basis, following usually unstated customs. Everyone acknowledged by tacit agreement everyone's customary rights to a usual territory. Individual control or ownership of land and resources was absent, but kin groups or a recognized social group might claim land or expect that their rights to land and resources would prevail. Adjustments in the balance among people, land, and resources were made informally.

Although foragers usually had open access to land, they might allocate certain key resources to specific groups. For example, among the Ju/'hoansi of the Kalahari, water is the scarcest and most valuable resource. Water holes were owned or controlled by two or three individuals related through kinship (usually siblings or cousins). Owners held access to water holes, but they were not the exclusive users. Other people might make claims to the water through their relationships to the owners, either by blood or marriage. Individuals who needed access to water owned by relatives made a direct request. When a claim was made, access had to be granted. Therefore, although in principle only a few people owned the water holes, the rights to use the water were widely dispersed throughout the community. No one was left without the right to have water, an obvious necessity for survival.

Similarly, among Native American foragers of California, such as the Wintus, Yokuts, Maidus, Yanas, and Miwoks, separate kinship groups owned acorn groves. The acorns and their products were important food staples. However, ownership did not entail exclusive usage rights. If another group of people entered one's territory and came upon one's acorn groves, it was customary for them to ask formal permission of the owners before exploiting the resource. Formal requests for permission to use one's acorn groves had to be granted. The asking and granting of permission was automatic but symbolized one group's right to ownership and the entire community's reciprocal interdependence.

As another example, among foragers of the Pacific Northwest, salmon were the primary and most prized food resource. Particular kin groups owned streams where salmon spawned. Such groups also owned berry patches and other abundant food sites. Members of the kinship group who claimed them and were acknowledged as owners exclusively exploited the salmon streams and berry sites. However, as you read on, you'll learn that the fish and fruit were distributed in a much wider network that included many families belonging to the same community and even to families in other communities.

REVIEW ──◉ Foragers share hunting and gathering as a subsistence strategy. They are nomadic, moving seasonally as resources become available. Optimally, foraging gets the most or best food for the least investment of time and energy, but cultural factors also play a role in foraging. Foragers typically have egalitarian relationships, cooperate in getting food, share food across kin groups, and do not own land or resources individually.

PASTORALISM

Pastoralism is a way of life that centers on the herding and care of domesticated animals. A very broad term, it applies to people dependent on diverse animals in diverse environmental and social contexts who exploit their animals for various products—rarely just for their meat and in some cases not even for food. Pastoralism differs from simple animal husbandry, which is the keeping of domesticated animals. It is a way of life in which a people's economy, settlement patterns, and social systems are adapted to large-scale herding. So, for example, American farm families in rural communities are not pastoralists by virtue of keeping a small number of chickens, cows, and horses. In contrast, pastoral families in Africa, the Middle East, and Asia may own hundreds of cows, sheep, goats, horses, or camels whose needs for grazing land and water determine people's daily routines and seasonal movements.

Like farming, pastoralism allows people some control over their food sources. Perhaps by about 9,000 years ago, people in the Middle East were keeping domesticated sheep and goats. Pigs were domesticated in southeastern China at about the same time. African peoples domesticated cattle as early as 9,500 years ago. Andean peoples in Peru began to domesticate animals by 7,000 years ago, keeping alpaca and llamas for their meat and wool. They also kept guinea pigs. In North and Central America, people domesticated dogs and turkeys.

Pastoral nomads of Mongolia, like other horse-herding peoples, have a mixed economy that reflects the power of basic modes of subsistence such as pastoralism to shape peoples' ways of life and daily activities.

Combined Subsistence Strategies

Rarely, if ever, has pastoralism been a self-contained subsistence strategy. Some pastoralists combined herding with foraging, others with small-scale farming, and still others traded for food with their settled farming neighbors. Like foraging, pastoralism is rarely the central economic strategy of any people today. Most pastoralists have adopted farming, wage work, or trade as their primary mode of making a living. It has become increasingly difficult for pastoralists to keep control of a large enough territory in which to graze their animals, as the pressure on land has increased with population growth and national economic policies.

> What different patterns might you predict for relationships between pastoralists of the ranges and farming peoples of the valleys?

Middle Eastern sheep and goat herders like the Basseri of Iran drank milk from their animals and processed it into butter, cheese, and yogurt. They also traded milk, wool, and other animal products for grains and other crops from their farming neighbors.

The sheepherding Diné (Navajo) kept their animals mostly for their wool, used for weaving into blankets and clothing for household consumption and for sale. In the past, the Diné obtained food primarily through farming, hunting, and gathering plant foods. Horse pastoralists, such as the Cheyenne, Lakota, and Crow, who dominated the North American Plains until the late nineteenth century, used their animals for transportation, warfare, and to hunt the great herds of bison that roamed the plains. They also had a complex intertribal trade network, often traveling great distances by horse to exchange bison meat and hides for farm produce.

Land and Labor in Pastoralist Societies

Pastoralists' strategies for organizing and controlling land and resources differ significantly from those of foragers because, in pastoralist societies, individuals or groups controlled, and even owned, land and resources such as domesticated animals. Pastoralist societies closely regulate and manage rights to use land to ensure that the animals have enough forage. Sometimes, herds may put excessive strain on lands and resources because of overgrazing. To prevent overgrazing, pastoralists take their herds to different grazing areas throughout the year. Pastoralists make total use of their animals and allocate these crucial resources according to rules of ownership and control. Among the Diné, livestock is tended as a family herd on family land. In pastoralist societies, domesticated animals become objective measures of wealth as a consequence of individual ownership, and inequalities of wealth and competitive status seeking can arise based on the size of herds.

The division of labor by gender varies in pastoralist societies but is generally not as egalitarian as in foraging societies. Men and boys generally tend to the animals while women and children do related tasks, such as milking, dressing skins, and watching over animals. Among some pastoralists, people of any age and either gender may assist with herding animals to and from grazing lands.

Pastoralists may accumulate some surpluses, based on surpluses of animals. The more animals a family owns, the more animals they may feel they need for both herd size and all the products derived from animals (hides, furs, bone) that can be used for many purposes, including the manufacture of clothing, tools, and utensils. The animals and the products crafted from them become important items in trading networks, enabling families to obtain other foods, goods, and services.

Nomadic Pastoralism

The diversity in subsistence strategies among pastoralists is associated with a variety of settlement patterns. Some pastoralists, like the Basseri, were nomadic, changing locations frequently as they led their herds to new pastures, a practice known as **transhumance,** or seasonal movements of people in search of available grazing land. Others, like the Nuer, maintained a year-round home base from which they led their herds to nearby pastures.

Despite their variety of subsistence strategies and settlement patterns, most pastoralists shared a common self-concept as pastoralists, constructing their social and personal identities around herding. Certain cultural features are commonly associated with pastoralism. For example, because pastoralists needed access to land for grazing and seasonal control over access to specific areas, they tended to define and defend their territories more vigorously than foragers. Some pastoralists, such as the Bantu-speaking peoples of southern Africa and the native peoples of the North American Plains, used the strategies of raiding and warfare to defend their territories and to expand into the grazing lands occupied by others. Nomadic pastoralists might be satisfied with customary rights to graze their animals on some defined but not necessarily exclusive territory. They might be content to share their grazing lands with other people, negotiating occasional or seasonal usage. Sedentary pastoralists, on the other hand, might require permanent and exclusive access to particular tracts of land. These tracts might be under the ultimate control of large kin groups or under individual ownership.

Population density varied in pastoral societies, depending on the size and quality of grazing lands and herds. Unlike foraging societies, measuring and accumulating wealth and property, especially in the form of animals, has been a major feature of pastoralism. Because animals are easily countable and their numbers increased by breeding, pastoral peoples generally measured wealth by the size of a family's or individual's herds or flocks. In addition, because animals or products derived from them (meat, hides, wool) can be traded for other goods, herds represent both present and future wealth. In some pastoral societies, wealth in animals became the basis for differentiating people in terms of social status. People with larger herds had higher social standing, prestige, and influence than others. In this context, competition was a successful adaptive strategy. In most nomadic pastoralist societies, systems of descent and inheritance typically follow in the male line because men are usually the owners of most, if not all, of the animals in the herds.

Nomadic pastoralists, like nomadic foragers, are limited in the amount of property they can acquire because of the difficulties of transporting many possessions from one location to another. In contrast, sedentary pastoralists are able to build up their stores of goods, keeping extra clothing, household utensils, and tools beyond the amount necessary for their survival. Along with notions of private property in animals, competition among individuals and families may be reflected in the desire to accumulate goods and to raise one's standard of living over that of others.

Despite a focus on ownership and competition, pastoralists maintained values of reciprocity and expressed generosity and hospitality, especially sharing with relatives. Social norms calling for generosity acted as a leveling mechanism, ensuring that richer families shared some of their wealth with poorer families.

Why did pastoralism as a subsistence mode favor competition over cooperation?

---

transhumance
The practice among pastoralists of moving to new pastureland on a seasonal basis.

CASE STUDY ◦

A Pastoral Society: The Basseri, Nomadic Pastoralists of Iran

Pastoralists in the Middle East herded sheep and goats and traded animal products for grains with settled farmers (Barth 1964). The Basseris, numbering about 16,000, were nomadic pastoralists living in southern Iran, until recently. Today, most Basseris have given up their traditional lifestyle, principally because the Iranian government, like national governments elsewhere, found nomadic peoples difficult to control and discouraged pastoralism.

Central governments and their economic planners also view pastoralism as an outmoded way of life that retards national economic development. This attitude is based more on ideology than fact. The Basseris' traditional way of life was an efficient use of sparse resources and territories. Their territory—about 300 miles long and 50 miles wide—contains mountains, deserts, and plains. Rainfall is light, occurring mainly in the winter. Precipitation, often in the form of snow, is heaviest in the mountains, which, as a result, are richest in vegetation. The rest of Basseri territory is dry with only sparse grasses.

Basseris shared their territory with other pastoral peoples. Each group had its own migration route and schedule, however, so that two or more groups were never at the same pastureland at the same time of year. Each route and schedule—called the *il-rah*, or "tribal road"—was the collective property of the group that followed it. Groups, not individuals, thus controlled access to pastureland.

Basseris moved frequently—on average once every three days—among the pasturelands on their route. Their winter pastures were in the low-altitude southern part of their region, where snowfall is relatively light. As spring approached, they moved to middle-altitude pastures; in summer, they headed to high-altitude pastures that are snow-covered at other times of the year. In the fall and spring, they moved nearly every day, whereas they might stay in one location for days in the summer and winter. Each day's trek took about three hours. The sheep and goats were led from camp first. Usually about thirty or forty families traveled and camped together. In the winter, large groups dispersed to avoid overburdening pastureland.

A Basseri family usually consisted of a couple and their children. Each family had its own tent and flock. A family required about 100 sheep and goats to sustain itself. Boys and men herded the animals to their daily grazing areas. Although girls sometimes led the animals on migratory treks, they generally did not herd when their families stayed in the same location for several days. Families with many animals and few able-bodied sons might hire boys to work for them. One shepherd could usually handle about 300 or 400 sheep and goats. People kept donkeys as pack animals and mounts for women and children. Men rode horses. Camels carried heavy loads.

Milk and milk products from their animals, such as butter, buttermilk, sour milk, and cheese, were the basis of the Basseri diet. Men and women, usually in a group, did the milking. The animals were milked at least once a day. Women prepared foods derived from the milk. Basseris rarely slaughtered adult sheep and goats to eat, but they did eat excess lambs and kids to keep their herds from growing unsustainably large. They used wool and hides for clothing, tent coverings, and bags. They also traded hides, wool, and goods made from animal products to people in settled farming communities for grains, fruit, vegetables, and cash.

The Basseris had complex relations with their neighbors in these communities. During lean years, some Basseris took seasonal jobs in towns to earn money for clothing, tools, and other goods. Some Basseris amassed enough wealth to buy land, which they leased to farmers, receiving money or produce as rent.

PEARSON
myanthrolab

Explore more at
www.myanthrolab.com

CULTURE CHANGE ●

TRANSFORMATIONS OF NUER ECONOMY AND SOCIETY

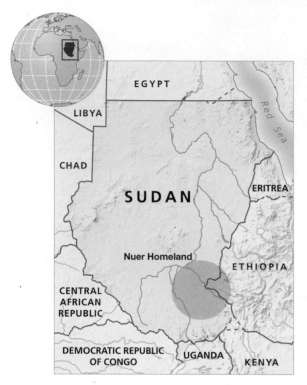

The Nuer, a pastoral and farming people of the Southern Sudan, have been written about extensively since the 1930s when the British social anthropologist, E. E. Evans-Pritchard began to live among them and study their cultural patterns. In his writings on Nuer subsistence, Evans-Pritchard (1940; 1951; 1956) emphasized their self-identities as pastoralists even though farming supplied most of their calories. Still, in the past, the lives of the Nuer, especially the men, revolved around the care of their cattle. Boys were socialized to expect to be cattle herders, to value their livestock, and to form bonds of identity and affection with individual animals that they owned. Nuer social norms rigidly distinguished men's from women's work. Men (including boys of about 15 or older who had been ritually initiated into manhood) were responsible for herding cattle. They also fished and did some hunting. Women, girls, and young boys were responsible for milking the cattle twice a day. Women also grew millet, maize, and vegetables.

Cattle camps were located away from the domestic dwellings where women and children, including boys too young to care for cattle on their own, lived. Spatial configurations of the villages and the cattle camps therefore served as boundary markers between the lives of men and initiated boys and those of women, girls, and young boys.

In the 1930s, the British colonial penetration into Nuer territory increased, and economic conditions for the Nuer began to deteriorate. Diseases decreased their cattle herds. Some Nuer were therefore reluctantly drawn into a trading system, exchanging hides for grain. Some men also obtained wage work, mostly in construction. However, although the British tried to persuade Nuer to sell their cattle, most people resisted because cattle represented more than just a commodity to them. The British government devised strategies to extract cattle from Nuer owners. They confiscated cattle in payment of fines levied by local courts, and chiefs, installed by the British, demanded cattle as tribute (Hutchinson 1996, 65).

In the late 1940s, officials held auctions to dispose of cattle taken as court-imposed fines. Nuer were able to purchase cattle, especially economically valuable heifers, and replenish their herds. Because buyers had to pay for auctioned cattle with cash, interested Nuer had to obtain money. Most did so by selling oxen. And the British wanted the oxen because of their value on the meat market (Hutchinson 1996, 66–67). To the Nuer, money was not a goal in and of itself, but rather was the means to purchase cattle. In other words, they sold cattle (oxen) to get money necessary to buy cattle (heifers).

In the 1960s more wage work became available. Most young Nuer men seeking employment migrated north to Khartoum, the capital of Sudan. There they worked in construction and infrastructure support. Many thousands of jobs were also available on cotton plantations that developed rapidly along the upper Nile River. Through these endeavors, Nuer men obtained money that they could use to purchase more cattle. They could thus increase their herds without selling any animals.

In 1963, shortly after achieving independence, Sudan erupted in civil war. This war pitted southern Sudanese, who were mostly Christians and animists and whose goal was secession from the Arab- and Muslim-dominated north, against the more heavily armed forces of the central government control. The fighting undermined the stability of Nuer economies, disrupting the markets for importing grain and exporting cattle. Many Nuer living in Khartoum and other northern cities returned to the south to find their cattle herds raided by soldiers on both sides. Villages were abandoned. This civil war ended with an agreement in 1972 that paved the way for renewed employment and reestablishment of cattle markets. Nuer men took over local commercial networks, previously dominated by northern traders. To obtain funds to set themselves up as traders and storekeepers, people sold cattle. Thus began a pattern of converting cattle into money (Hutchinson 1996, 72).

However, although the Nuer seemed to be equating money and cattle, not all cattle could be properly converted into money, and not all money could go to buy cattle. This lack of mutual convertibility was due to differences in the uses of cattle and in the origins of money. In traditional Nuer society, cattle were circulated among families when prospective husbands gave cattle to the kin of their intended wives and as payments from the family of a killer to the family of the victim. Cattle were also sacrificed to honor the spirits at life cycle rituals and times of social or psychic stress. Cattle used for these purposes could not be bought with money that came from sources the Nuer deemed disrespectful. For example, money earned for work considered demeaning or dirty (for example, custodial or servant work) could not be converted into cattle for marriage exchanges, payments for murder, or sacrifice (Hutchinson 1996, 83–84). Cattle bought with money obtained in these ways were thought likely to die or harm anyone who ate their meat.

Finally, attitudes toward collective rights of families and larger kinship groups began to emphasize individual ownership of cattle and control of money from work or trade. However, this shift does not apply equally in all contexts. Cattle that are received in marriage or ritual exchanges continue to be thought of as owned collectively by the family, but cattle purchased for money earned through one's own work can be thought of as individually owned. Attitudinal changes therefore are a consequence of the transformation of economic systems and of underlying economic and social principles. In the words of Deng Gatluak, an eastern Nuer man, "Before everyone used to hoe together, eat together, and go to war together. But now that's all over; today, everyone wants to get ahead. . . . Today everyone seems to want to get ahead by him/herself" (Hutchinson 1996, 39).

Today, the lives of the Nuer have drastically changed. Caught up as victims of more civil wars that raged in the 1990s, some 200,000 Nuer became refugees in camps in Ethiopia and Kenya (Holtzman 2000). About 4,000 Nuer were permitted to emigrate to the United States in the mid-1990s. Most of them now reside in Minnesota, where they have maintained a strong sense of community and Nuer identity, focusing on kinship and on affiliation with Christian churches.

Even the lives of Nuer who remain in Africa have been radically transformed. Many remain in refugee camps in Kenya under the auspices of the United Nations. Others returned to Southern Sudan, only to find their homes destroyed. Those who stayed in Sudan throughout the civil war have also altered their traditional cultures. Fundamental to many of these changes have been the erosion of the pastoral way of life and the centrality of cattle (Hutchinson 1996). Although cattle remain significant in marriage and ceremonial exchanges, the animals have lost some of their traditional symbolic value. As people repeatedly told anthropologist Sharon Hutchinson, "Cattle are no longer as important as they once were."

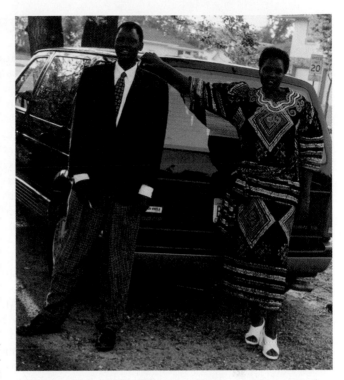

These Nuer focus on the challenges of living as immigrants in the United States, where a pastoral way of life is not possible.

Pastoralists depend on the animals they herded for their subsistence needs. Animals are also the basis of wealth. Some pastoralists practice transhumance, moving herds to different pasturelands as they become seasonally available for grazing. Control of grazing land and rights in a herd are major concerns in pastoralist societies.

REVIEW

surplus
Food and other goods that are produced at a level greater than that needed for survival.

sedentary communities
Settlement pattern involving long-term, permanent settlements.

slash-and-burn (swidden) cultivation
A farming technique for preparing new fields by cutting down trees and bushes and then burning them to clear the land and enrich the soil with nutrients.

HORTICULTURE

Horticulture and agriculture are two types of farming that are not always easily distinguished. The term *horticulture* refers to small-scale farming with a relatively simple technology consisting of digging sticks, hoes, and other handheld tools. The term *agriculture* refers to large-scale farming and the use of more complex technology, which can include draft animals, for example. Intensive agriculture involves irrigation systems and extensive exploitation of land and labor. Some farming peoples may be horticulturalists and others agriculturalists; still others may combine both kinds of farming.

In contrast to foragers and pastoralists, farmers generally require secure access to and control over specific plots of land. In some farming societies, a group of relatives owns or controls land as a collective unit. In others, individuals may own land for their own benefit and that of their immediate families. Because farming requires regular access to land, farming communities tend to be stable. Agriculturalists in particular usually live in fully sedentary communities. Among horticulturalists, there may be more variation. Some are permanently settled, whereas others may shift locations from one season to the next, residing near their fields during the planting season and living elsewhere, perhaps near foraging sites, at other times. Weather conditions may also dictate changes in location. So, for example, many African horticulturalists live in different settlements during the rainy and dry seasons. When there is no rainfall, people live close to the few flowing rivers, but they move to higher ground in the rainy season.

Because they live in stable settlements, farmers can accumulate more property than can foragers or nomadic pastoralists. Their houses may be more substantial because erecting a large, solid house is worth people's efforts if the house is to be their permanent dwelling. Farm families may own forms of property other than land, such as herds, ornaments, tools, and household goods. Households measure their relative wealth according to the quantity of such goods they possess. At the same time, many farming societies limit the accumulation of wealth by encouraging people to redistribute surplus food and property to needier community members.

Impacts of Sedentism and Surpluses

Horticulturalists tend to live in relatively small settlements of from one or several hundred to several thousand people. Settlements may be sedentary, depending on the amount of surplus generated. Farmers regularly try to produce more food than they need for any one season to have enough to sustain themselves in years of drought, during crop failure for any reason, or in the event of flooding. **Surplus** means food and other goods that are produced at a level greater than that needed for survival. Farmers usually produce enough surplus to last one or two years of bad times. In **sedentary,** or stable, **communities,** people develop methods for preserving and storing surplus produce, but their techniques rarely yield great abundance. Therefore, they need to control population size with strategies like those used by foragers: periods of sexual abstinence, lengthy periods of breast-feeding, and the use of contraceptives, abortion, and infanticide.

Slash-and-Burn Horticulture

The tasks involved in farming include preparing fields or gardens for cultivation, planting, weeding, and harvesting. The most strenuous of these is preparing new fields for cultivation. Many horticulturists, especially those who live in tropical forest areas, use **slash-and-burn,** or **swidden, cultivation** to accomplish this task. Once an area of land is selected for planting, men cut down and burn trees and bushes, which

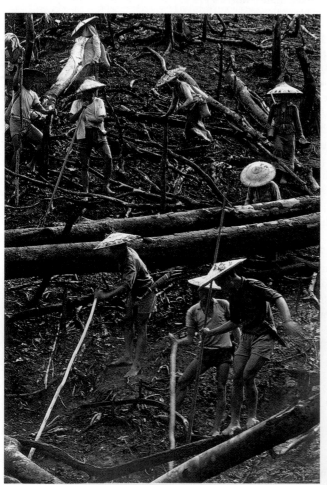

Swidden farmers in Borneo transform forests on marginal mountain slopes into palm groves for producing rattan, used in caning and weaving.

both clears the land and enriches the soil with nutrients. Farmers usually rotate their fields, allowing some to remain fallow intermittently to restore their fertility. Others may relocate from every few years to a generation or so, when the fields around a settlement become depleted of nutrients. Relocating villages and selecting new fields is a strategy that works only when population densities are low and land is readily available.

Gender Allocation of Work

In horticulture societies, gender allocation of work typically calls for men to do the heavy work of clearing forests and woodlands to make new fields. In some societies, men continue as the primary workers, whereas women are the farmers in others. In other societies, both men and women do farmwork, growing the same or different crops.

Among the Pueblo peoples of the American Southwest such as the Zunis and Hopis, both men and women grow crops, although they employ different methods and work in different types of farmland. Zuni men plant, weed, and harvest crops in the fields surrounding their villages. Some work was traditionally carried out individually, whereas other tasks were done collectively, usually by a group of relatives consisting of fathers, their unmarried sons, and their resident sons-in-law. Before marriage, men worked the land controlled by their mothers; after marriage, they worked on land under the direction of their wife's mother.

Because of the difficulty of farming in an arid environment, the people developed a system of floodwater irrigation that made best use of available water from rainfall and from the small Zuni River and a few nearby springs. When a man cleared new land for planting, he built small dams and canals with mud walls to direct water from rainfall and overflowing streams. The walls were constructed by packing mud over a row of stakes made of branches, rocks, sticks, and earth.

In contrast to men's work, women grew some produce in "waffle gardens" along the banks of the Zuni River. Waffle gardens were divided into small square or rectangular cells surrounded by low mud walls that helped conserve water and protect the plants from wind. Women watered their plants by hand, using ladles to distribute water brought from the river or from nearby wells in water jars.

Farming families are able to utilize the labor of their children at early ages. Young children can plant seeds, weed gardens, and pick fruits and vegetables. Some people may become part-time specialists, making pottery, baskets, canoes, houses, and other items. By bartering or selling their products, artisans and other part-time specialists may free themselves from some subsistence work. Horticultural societies produce surplus crops as a buffer against hunger and starvation in years of low yield. Farmers produce surpluses by intensifying their labor and maximizing the land's productivity. People prevent the overburdening of land and its fertility by rotating their crops or relocating every generation or so. Social norms calling for hospitality and generosity contribute to the redistribution of surpluses so that no one goes hungry.

Among the Yanomamo of the Orinoco River basin of Brazil and Venezuela, men are the principal farmers. They clear and prepare fields and plant and harvest crops. Principal crops include plantain, manioc, and sweet potatoes. Men also grow tobacco, used for chewing, and cotton, used to make yarn for weaving hammocks. Men also hunt and fish. In effect, men provide all the food for the family. Women's work, which includes food preparation and child care, is entirely domestic. Their work is considered secondary to men's work, and they have a correspondingly low status in Yanomamo society (Chagnon 1997).

In contrast, among the Jivaros of Peru, women were responsible for planting, and tending and harvesting crops, notably manioc, sweet potatoes, and squash. These crops, supplemented by fish and game that men provided, supplied the bulk of the Jivaro diet (Meggers 1971). Women were also responsible for performing the garden rituals that ensure good crops. The Jivaro valued these tasks, and Jivaro women still have a higher status in their society than Yanomamo women do in theirs.

In some West African societies, both men and women perform horticultural work, but they plant different crops. Among the Igbos of Nigeria, for example, tasks are strongly demarcated according to gender. Men traditionally plant yams, considered to be the staple crop. Rice, introduced into the region in the 1950s, is the only plant that both men and women grow. Women plant and harvest all other crops, including manioc, cocoyams,

GLOBALIZATION

The expansion of slash-and-burn farming into tropical rain forests in Indonesia and the Amazon region contribute to global deforestation, but on a smaller scale than commercial lumbering. Deforestation alters climate and weather patterns and contributes to global warming.

maize, beans, and okra. Women also weed their husbands' yam gardens. Even when work has a collective focus, tasks are demarcated according to gender. For example, men harvest yams, but women and children carry the yams to the household yam barn (Ottenberg 1965; Ottenberg and Ottenberg 1962). Other subsistence and household activities are likewise allocated according to gender. Both men and women fish, but in different places: men in nearby rivers, women in ponds and streams.

In some horticultural societies, especially in sub-Saharan Africa, farming is combined with pastoralism. Horticulturists may keep domesticated animals for meat. For example, indigenous peoples of the Melanesian Islands of the western Pacific cultivate yams and other food crops and also keep pigs. Pigs, however, are not grazing animals like cattle, sheep, or goats. They eat the same foods as humans. Melanesian horticulturalists, as a result, grow crops to feed both themselves and their pigs. As the pig population grows, the effort to feed them becomes increasingly burdensome. Eventually, the pig population grows so large that it triggers a round of ceremonials accompanied by pig sacrifices and feasts. The pig population plummets and the cycle begins anew (Rappaport 2000).

CASE STUDY

A Farming Society: The Kaluli of Papua New Guinea

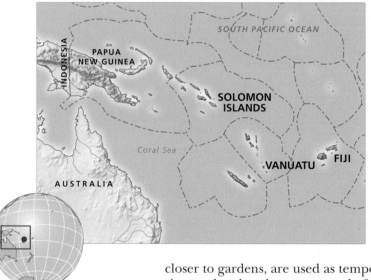

The Kaluli are a farming people who live in a plateau region covered by rain forest and criss-crossed by streams and rivers. Temperatures average in the mid-80s F throughout the year. Seasonal variation is based on precipitation: a dry season (March to November) and a rainy season (December to February) (Gratton 1991, 101). Kaluli lands are dotted with small villages built on ridges where the forest cover is less dense. In the 1980s, the Kaluli had approximately twenty villages. Each village generally contains one large longhouse and several smaller dwellings. Farmland is nearby. Residence in a longhouse follows principles of descent through men. A longhouse, therefore, is typically inhabited by a group of related men, their wives, children, and unmarried sisters. Each contains about fifteen families (Feld 1990, 5). The smaller houses, located closer to gardens, are used as temporary dwellings during harvesting periods. Most marriages take place between people from different villages. Women move from their natal settlements to that of their husband. People are therefore affiliated with several villages, either through ties of birth or marriage.

The Kaluli currently number more than 2,000. This figure represents a sharp decline from their numbers before contact with European colonial agents in the early twentieth century. An estimated 25 percent of the Kaluli died in the 1940s from measles and influenza epidemics (Gratton 1991, 101).

The Kaluli practice slash-and-burn or swidden farming. All the men of the village work together when new fields are needed. Gardens are used until the soil becomes depleted and the yield diminishes. Then new lands are prepared and planted. Rights to land follow principles of descent through men. Men are allocated land based on their membership in a kinship group. They can claim rights to specific portions of land and of groves of sago palms if they continue to use it. If left unused for more than a generation, the land will be reassigned to another man in the group. Rights to use land are most often passed from father to son. However, brothers of the deceased and the sons of a man's sister may also have a claim.

Men cooperate in planting the gardens and in building dams on the rivers and streams. Once the seeds are planted, women are responsible for weeding the gardens. All able members of the household usually harvest the crops together. Like those of other New Guinea peoples, the Kaluli's primary crops include bananas, pandanus (a root crop), sweet potatoes, breadfruit (a starchy seedless fruit), sugarcane, and green vegetables.

The staple of their diet, however, is a wild food that grows along the streams. Wild sago, from sago palms, is eaten daily. Men split the sago palm and grind up the core. Women process and cook the sago.

Kaluli also consume fish and animal resources that are abundant in their environment. Both men and women easily obtain these in casual fishing or hunting. When larger game is needed for ceremonial occasions or trade, groups of men hunt wild pigs and cassowaries (flightless birds) in the dense forests. These expeditions may take days and are nearly always successful due to the abundance of wildlife.

Finally, women in each household keep a few domesticated pigs. The pigs are eaten on ceremonial occasions, especially marriages and funerals, but they are also cooked for guests as a sign of hospitality and respect. Taking advantage of the abundance of their environment, the Kaluli diet is varied and rich in nutrients.

Today, many Kaluli men supplement subsistence activities by working for wages on plantations that grow tea, coffee, and copra or for government agencies as custodians or porters (Schieffelin 1990, 2).

PEARSON
myanthrolab

Explore more at
www.myanthrolab.com

REVIEW

In horticultural societies such as the Kaluli and Yanomamo, people keep small animals, cultivate food trees, and plant gardens with staple crops. Sedentism—living in one place—requires small populations sustained on surpluses from horticultural production. Work is allocated by gender and age. Slash-and-burn (swidden) horticulture is a destructive process that involves a constant round of abandoning depleted land and bringing new land under cultivation.

AGRICULTURE

The subsistence strategy called agriculture originated in the Middle East about 12,000 years ago. At that time, the region's climate was gradually drying, prompting people to concentrate near rivers, where resources remained plentiful. Over time, people learned to control their supplies of food by planting their own crops and domesticating their own animals (dogs, sheep, goats, and cattle). They began growing grains that could sustain large populations. The earliest crops were wheat and barley. Once farming proved productive, more people settled in the region and learned the new techniques. Others acquired the skills and moved to outlying areas, gradually spreading farming knowledge to other communities. Similar processes led to the independent emergence of farming in several other regions of the world, including the Indus Valley of Pakistan, the Yellow River Valley of China, the Nile Valley of Egypt, Mexico, and the Andean region of South America. Recent radiocarbon dating suggests that some of these areas may have developed farming nearly as early as in the Middle East. For example, domesticated squash seeds that date to about 10,000 years ago have been discovered in both northern Peru and Mexico (Dillehay et al. 2007).

Archaeologists have proposed a variety of explanations for the origin of farming. Some suggest that increasingly concentrated populations exceeded the capacity of the fertile regions to sustain a foraging existence, while declines in wild vegetation also discouraged people from dispersing into surrounding environments (Binford 1971; Flannery 1973). Another theory suggests that some people in foraging societies began to accumulate surpluses of storable foods to sponsor feasts and thereby raise their social status. As their desire for larger surpluses grew, they began to control and augment their accumulation of foods by

This irrigation and flood-control system in Szechuan, China, is one of the oldest surviving man-made engineering projects in the world.

FIGURE 6.1
Consequences of Food Production

PEOPLE WERE ABLE TO PLANT, HARVEST, PRESERVE, AND STORE MORE FOOD.

Increase in surplus ⟶ increase in population ⟶ increase in accumulation of material culture

Use of grains to feed babies and young children ⟶ decline in lactation ⟶ increase in fertility ⟶ increase in population

Increase in population ⟶ increase in food production ⟶ pressure on the environment

Dependence on intensive agriculture ⟶ sedentary populations ⟶ crowding in urban centers

Dependence on grains ⟶ malnutrition ⟶ vulnerability to drought and famine

Large sedentary urban populations ⟶ decline in health standards ⟶ rapid spread of disease

How would you compare the benefits and costs of food production as a subsistence strategy?

protecting and then producing their own crops (Bender 1978). These theories are not mutually exclusive. Several factors operating together may have led to the beginnings of plant and animal domestication.

Archaeologists are more certain about the consequences of food production (see Figure 6.1). We know that populations increased rapidly and became sedentary because of the ability to control the growth of crops, to plant more crops, and to harvest, preserve, and store greater surpluses. Reliance on grains also allowed women to nurse their babies for shorter periods of time because young children could be given cereals to eat. And fertility levels rose with the decline in lactation, leading to greater increases in population size and greater crowding of population centers.

Another result of food production was a general decline in health standards (Diamond 1995). Studies of the bones and teeth of members of early farming communities indicated signs of malnutrition, probably resulting from an overdependence on only a few sources of food rather than the more typical varied range of the foraging diet. And diseases spread more rapidly among sedentary farming people.

In addition, permanent settlements made possible by farming permitted people to accumulate an increasing number and variety of material possessions.

Agricultural production employs interrelated techniques of intensification. Specialized technology, sophisticated land-use strategies, and labor inputs result in more reliable production techniques that result in larger crop yields. Agriculturalists use plows, often pulled by horses or oxen, to turn the earth and increase the area they can cultivate productively in a certain period of time. Early agriculturists in the Middle East, China, and Central and South America built extensive, permanent irrigation systems to deliver water to outlying fields. In mountainous regions, they built terraces to increase the surface area available for farming on steeply sloping terrain. People in swampy areas piled up earth (berms) to create fertile artificial islands. Because of their heavy investments in labor and infrastructure, agriculturalists maintain permanent, fully sedentary communities.

These two characteristics of agricultural societies—permanent settlements, called sedentism, and an intensive investment in labor and technology—likely emerged together in a complex and dynamic process of change. Investment of labor and material in agricultural production set the stage for permanent settlements, and permanent settlements created conditions conducive to increasing investments in labor and technology. As labor and technology intensified, the energy expended per acre increased, leading to greater yields and the accumulation of larger surpluses. These surpluses helped support an ever-growing sedentary population. The more food there was, the more people could be supported, and the more people there were, the more food could be produced.

Furthermore, unlike in foraging and pastoral societies, where most subsistence work required adult strength, skill, and judgment, agricultural societies could make productive use of the labor of young children. Thus, large families were a premium. The result was a relaxation of the birth-control practices that limited population in foraging and pastoral societies. On the contrary, agricultural societies encouraged fertility, an attitude that might be incorporated into religious doctrines that specifically encouraged women to have many children.

This dynamic set the stage for increasing population size. Eventually, however, population size would come up against the carrying capacity of a particular region at a particular level of technology. In other words, at some point, increasing the amount of labor available (by increasing population) would fail to result in increased yields. As it reached that point, an agricultural society would have to develop new, more productive agricultural technologies or secure more land. New technologies were not always readily available, however, and expanding into new territory ultimately brought a society into conflict with its neighbors.

Among the Inca and other Andean farmers of Peru and Ecuador, ownership of land was vested in a collective group of relatives, whereas in India, an individual owns each parcel of land. Private individual ownership usually permits owners to sell their land, a practice impossible in most horticultural societies. The importance of ownership and control is demonstrated in patterns of inheritance in which children or other designated relatives receive the land belonging to their parents or other kin. Large-scale agrarian states also tend to foster competition among individuals and families, reflected in the goal of accumulating surpluses and consuming them within the household.

In many agrarian states, the central government may organize the redistribution of surpluses so that everyone can be maintained at some minimum level of subsistence. In addition to humanitarian goals, maintaining the population is essential in state societies to forestall dissatisfaction that might lead to rebellion. The Inca state developed an efficient system of redistribution in which district chiefs collected farm produce and woven cloth from people in their territory. Some goods were channeled into the households of chiefs and other state elites, but a portion was stored in large regional granaries and warehouses. Chiefs dispensed these goods to needy members of their communities.

A common pattern in agrarian societies is for land to be concentrated in the hands of a few. Nonwealthy individuals and families lose their control of land through misfortune—illness, poor crops, or other disaster. Motivated by values that promote competition and the accumulation of surplus, wealthier landowners enlarge their acreage by buying land from those less fortunate. Over time, a large part of the population may become landless. Landless people then hire themselves out as laborers on other people's land. In one system, called *sharecropping*, they work the land and pay rent to the landlord, either in money or as part of their harvest. Competition and accumulation of wealth lead to economic exploitation in both agricultural and industrial societies as well as in mixed or transitional economies.

A hallmark of settled, large-scale, state societies with mixed economies is the appearance of full-time specialists. Specialists, rather than doing subsistence work, instead produce tools, utensils, or crafts, or they become state functionaries, working as traders, soldiers, or government officials. Because these specialists do not perform subsistence work, they must be supported by the extra work of others. Intensive agriculture and industrial agriculture increase farm output that can be traded or sold to nonsubsistence workers. Surplus outputs may also be taken from farmers in the form of tribute or taxation to support nonproducers or state functionaries. In modern states, the percentage of people working as specialists has greatly increased, while the percentage of people producing food or working in food-delivery systems has greatly decreased.

Intensive Agriculture and Crop Variety

Throughout the centuries, new inventions and technological advances have contributed to a tremendous growth in agricultural productivity. **Intensive agriculture** involved the use of the plow, draft animals, and irrigation. As worldwide population increased exponentially in recent centuries, however, the growth of cities has reduced the amount of land under cultivation. The dilemma of more people to feed on less land has so far been solved by the application of industrial processes to agriculture. In much of the world, preparing fields, planting seeds, fertilizing, weeding, and harvesting have become highly mechanized. Work once done by people is now done by machinery with only minimal human participation and direction. In the United States, less than 3 percent of the population works in agriculture. In countries with less developed industrial and technological

intensive agriculture
Application of technology and intensive labor to farming, such as the plow and irrigation.

sectors, the proportion is higher but has been declining everywhere. Fewer workers and less land must now produce food for more people.

One consequence of intensive agriculture has been a limited number of crops and varieties of crops. For example, in native North America, farming peoples such as the Iroquois in the Northeast and the Pueblo nations of the Southwest grew more than a dozen varieties of corn. Now, only a few types of corn, selected for yield and resistance, are grown. This process of limiting diversity to maximize efficiency is potentially danger-ous. Different varieties of a crop often supply a different mix of nutrients, so limiting crop diversity limits nutritional variety. Furthermore, some varieties may be susceptible to diseases and infestations to which other varieties are immune. As a result, decreased crop diversity can increase the risk of catastrophic crop failure. We cannot know what needs future generations might have that a now-lost plant variety might have met. We will dis-cuss one form of intensive agriculture, industrial agriculture, in detail in Chapter 7.

REVIEW — Agricultural societies have larger populations and greater division of labor, along with more centralization and wider disparity of wealth and power. Intensive agriculture involves the use of draft animals, fertilizers, and irrigation to farm on a large scale. Industrial agriculture, or agribusiness, involves the mechanization of farmwork on an even larger scale and scientific interventions in food production.

Food production based on agriculture permits greater accumulation of surplus, which sustains larger sedentary populations in villages and urban centers. Craft specialization, ownership of land and resources, social inequalities, and public health problems are among the many consequences of agriculture as a mode of subsistence.

SUBSISTENCE AND CULTURE CHANGE

No society is locked into a particular subsistence pattern. All are in a dynamic relation-ship with the environment and with other societies and are subject to change from both internal processes and external sources. A change in the environment might force a change in subsistence strategy, a change in population, the invention of a new technol-ogy, or changing patterns of trade with neighboring societies. Subsistence strategies may also change as a result of borrowings from other peoples, either through peaceful trade or through forced elimination of traditional patterns and their replacement by foreign methods of economic production and work as a result of conquest and colonization.

Environmental change or relocation to a different area may compel people to rely on different kinds of foods or different subsistence strategies. Foragers may have their terri-tories diminished because of incursions or invasions by farming or herding peoples and therefore abandon their traditional ways of life, adopting farming themselves or working for wages on other people's farms or ranches. Technological developments may also affect subsistence strategies. For example, as industrial techniques have led to improve-ments in agricultural productivity, fewer farmworkers can produce enough food for many more people, freeing up a large labor force to work in other sectors.

Indigenous societies throughout the world have become increasingly involved in regional, national, and international economic networks in the global economy. Many of their traditional patterns have been altered. In some cases, they have been able to sell their products widely through commercial outlets. Others have found wage employment in locally expanding production and manufacturing. Even in earlier historical periods, the economies of societies that were conquered or colonized were altered as a result of both direct and indirect pressures from the dominant societies. As addressed in Chapter 12, as state societies expanded, they transformed the lives of the peoples whose land they have taken. Although this process is as old as the history of state societies, its rate and consequences have accelerated in the last several centuries. Chapter 7 will address the issues of changing economic systems, and Chapters 16 and 17 will focus on global issues.

REVIEW — Economic anthropologists also study changes in people's subsistence due to environmental or population changes and cultural contact, as well as the effects of those changes on society and culture.

ANTHROPOLOGY APPLIED

Interpreting Economic Activity from Archaeological Remains

Cultural anthropology helps interpret archaeological sites, and vice versa. For example, archaeological remains often contain information about diet, health, and economic activities. Craft specialization, for example, indicates that a population had enough food to support people who did not contribute directly to subsistence. Craft specialization is widespread in agricultural societies, and signs of it in an archaeological site are evidence that the people had a subsistence base as farmers.

Evidence of craft specialization is found at the archaeological site of Huánuco Pampa, Peru, a provincial capital of the Inca. Through excavations there, archaeologists Craig Morris and Donald Thompson (1985) found a compound of fifty buildings containing thousands of distinctive ceramic jars and spindle whorls. The buildings were manufacturing and

storage sites, as well as housing for artisans. Using ethnohistorical records, Morris determined that the finds were associated with beer-making and cloth production.

A special class of women, called *aklla* (or *aclla*), worked for the Inca state and were segregated from the rest of the society. They were the "chosen women," or girls, who might be sacrificed to the sun god in bad times. Awaiting their possible fate, they lived and worked together in special houses making and preserving beer and weaving cloth.

⊙ CRITICAL THINKING QUESTIONS

What signs of an agricultural economy other than craft specialization might you expect to find at Huánuco? What kinds of remains might you expect to find in archaeological sites of people using other modes of subsistence? For example, what evidence of subsistence activities and material culture might you find among prehistoric pastoralists or foragers?

CHAPTER SUMMARY

Economic Anthropology

- Economic anthropology focuses on subsistence strategies and economic systems—how people meet their survival needs and make their living.

Understanding Human Subsistence Patterns

- Subsistence strategies include methods that people use to obtain food. People need to develop techniques to adapt to their environment, exploit available resources, or produce their own food. Subsistence strategies affect and are affected by environmental conditions, such as topography, climate, and available plants and animals. The techniques that people use have an impact on population size, settlement patterns, and household composition.

Foraging

- Foraging is a subsistence strategy that depends directly on plants and animals available in the environment. Foragers collect wild plants, fruits, nuts, and seeds and hunt animals and fish. Foragers require a large territory for subsistence. Most foragers are nomadic and live in relatively small communities so as not to overburden their environment.

Pastoralism

- Pastoralism is a subsistence strategy that centers on the herding and care of large numbers of domesticated animals. Some pastoralists are nomadic, moving frequently as they take their animals to new pasturelands. Others retain a home base and make daily excursions to graze their animals. Most pastoralists live in communities of no more than several hundred.

In most pastoralist societies, individuals own animals, although the animals may be cared for in a collective herd.

Horticulture

- Horticulture is a subsistence strategy based on growing crops. Horticulture is small-scale farming, using handheld tools and relatively simple technology. Farmers need to remain near their fields during the planting season. Some horticulturalists live in permanent villages whereas others shift their locations in different seasons. Their settlements usually number from several hundred to at most several thousand. Horticulturalists generally produce enough surplus to last a year or two beyond their minimum requirements.

Agriculture

- Agriculture is a form of food production based on permanent settlement; large-scale farming using complex technology; and the storage, distribution, and trade of large surpluses. Agriculture arose independently in different parts of the world based on different kinds of domesticated plants and animals. Increases in population and food supply were offset by problems of poor nutrition and the spread of disease in urban centers that grew up around centers of agriculture.

Subsistence and Culture Change

- Subsistence strategies change in response to environmental changes, population migration, and cultural contact between peoples.

KEY TERMS

economic
  anthropology   128
subsistence patterns   129
foragers   129
food producers   129
pastoralism   130

horticulture   130
agriculture   130
carrying capacity   130
settlement pattern   131
reciprocity   131
redistribution   132

leveling mechanisms   132
nomads   132
optimal foraging
  theory   133
transhumance   140
surplus   144

sedentary
  communities   144
slash-and-burn (swidden)
  cultivation   144
intensive agriculture   149

REVIEW QUESTIONS

1. What do economic anthropologists study?
2. What are the essential differences between foraging and food production? Which is more costly in terms of time, effort, and calories? Which is more costly in terms of short-term survival?
3. What is carrying capacity, and how do people adapt to this subsistence constraint?

4. How do modes of subsistence influence settlement patterns? How is nomadism an example of settlement pattern adaptation?
5. How do subsistence modes influence population size, density, composition, and distribution?
6. How do subsistence modes influence a society's division of labor by age, gender, skill, and social status?

7. How do peoples' systems of roles and statuses both reflect and reinforce their subsistence?

8. What ecological, demographic, and sociocultural factors characterize foraging?

9. What is the theory of optimal foraging? How can foraging be combined with horticulture to increase survival rates?

10. What ecological, demographic, and sociocultural factors characterize pastoralism?

11. Why do many pastoralist societies avoid using their animals for food?

12. What are the impacts of greater sedentism and production of surpluses among some pastoralists and horticulturalists?

13. How does swidden farming work as a subsistence strategy? What are its advantages and disadvantages?

14. What are the chief characteristics of agriculture as a subsistence strategy?

15. How do subsistence patterns change over time? How can changes in subsistence cause other changes in a people's way of life?

myanthrolab EXERCISES

To complete the following exercises and activities, you must log in to www.myanthrolab.com and select your current textbook.

1. In the **Explore** tab of Chapter 6, click on *Video* and watch one of the videos available in this section. Complete the short answer exercise that accompanies the video.

2. While in the **Explore** tab, click on the *NPR Audio Programs Broadcast* tab and go to *Theme 8: Food and Production.* Listen to one of the programs in this section and complete the short answer exercise that accompanies the program.

3. In the **Practice** tab, click on *Activities* and complete the *Consequences of Food Production* animation.

4. Enter the **MyAnthroLibrary** section on the home page to read more about topics and cultures that are discussed in this chapter. Suggested readings include:

Were Early Agriculturalists Less Healthy than Food Collectors? by Mark Nathan Cohen

Kalahari San: Sometime Hunter-Gatherers by Edwin N. Wilmsen

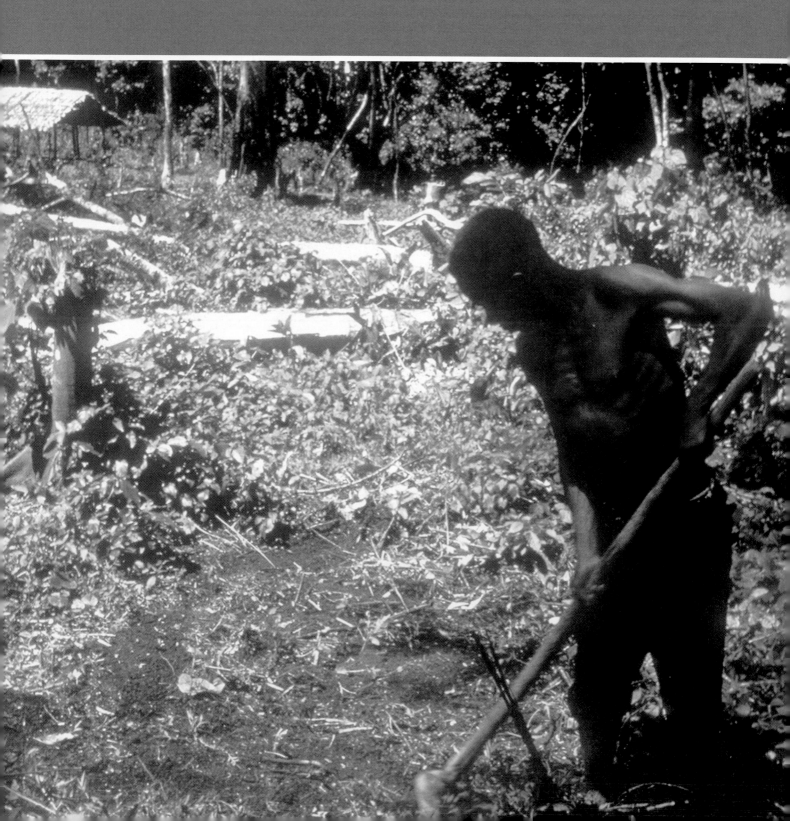

Three men went into the forest: one was the Cultivator, the other the Trapper, the third the Gatherer-of-Honey. Arriving in the forest, they asked themselves: "how shall we build our houses?" They said: "you, the Cultivator, build your house in the middle of the three hills." The Trapper built his house on a hill, the Gatherer-of-Honey built his on a hill. No sooner had they finished building their houses then the Cultivator had already finished growing plants behind his house. The Trapper asked the Gatherer-of-Honey to make a blood pact with him, stating that they should not make such a pact with the Cultivator. Having finished making friendship, and having killed game, the Trapper went with the meat to his friend. They did not show it to the Cultivator. The following day, the Gatherer-of-Honey passed with a jar of honey to bring to his friend the Trapper. They did not give anything to the Cultivator. And so it was every day; they made things pass at the entrance of the village of this one, the Cultivator. He said to himself that his children alone would die of hunger.

This Harvester, this Cultivator, went to sow discord between the two friends. He called in a loud voice, "you man of the rodents Mikii, you the Trapper, it is you will kill my children, never again bring rodent Mikii here at my house." The Cultivator also set out to the village of the Gatherer-of-Honey calling, "you Gatherer-of-Honey, it is the flies that you bring here that cause my children to be sick; also it is my rodents Mikii, which you eat, that makes you fatter." On his side, the Trapper reflected much, stating that so then his friend had just insulted him; on his side the Gatherer-of-Honey also thought that his friend had just insulted him. Having heard that, the Trapper and the Gatherer-of-Honey . . . met in the valley at the Cultivator's. Arriving there, they questioned each other.

One said, "you yelled to me that it was my rodents Mikii who are the reason why your children have caught the kwashiorkor, yes my rodents Mikii!" And the other said, "you yelled that because of me your children have their throat obstructed by larvas of bee." The one denied and the other denied, both at the same time. At this time, the Cultivator . . . took to dancing and singing:

I, the instigator Cultivator.
I just finished placing in discord those who are two.

The two friends understood, having heard the manner in which this Cultivator had placed them in discord, one against the other. Having considered that, they made a pact of friendship with the Cultivator. As such, the three became friends among each other; and they began to give meat, honey, and agricultural products, all of them giving to one another mutually.

That is why a man should never refuse the mark of friendship because the mark of friendship is a thing capable of saving the family group.

Excerpts from Richard Dorson, *Folktales Told around the World*, pp. 384–85. © 1975. Reprinted by permission of The University of Chicago Press.

In this narrative, the Nyanga of Central Africa dramatize the three significant elements in their economic system: hunting, gathering, and farming. They express the interdependence of these subsistence strategies and the importance of trade and exchange in binding a community together.

Chapter 6 described the subsistence strategies of foraging, pastoralism, horticulture, and agriculture. This chapter analyzes economic systems involving issues of the production, distribution, and consumption of foodstuffs and other goods and services. As you will learn, cultural features, such as population growth, emphasis on accumulating wealth, and status differences within a community are interrelated with others aspects of economic systems.

- What is an economic system? How is it integrated into a culture?
- What are the different types of economic exchange?
- How do different economic systems allocate land and resources?
- How is surplus related to the different subsistence modes?
- How is specialization related to the different subsistence modes?
- Why is the theory of surplus value in a capitalist economy important?
- How has industrialization affected economies and cultures?
- What are the characteristics of postindustrial societies and of today's global economy?

consumption
The use of subsistence resources, including outcomes of production.

economic system
Cultural methods of allocating natural resources, the means of exploiting the resources through technology, the organization of work, and the production, distribution, consumption, and exchange of goods and services.

ANALYZING ECONOMIC SYSTEMS

Societies organize subsistence strategies to utilize their land and resources efficiently. Available land must be distributed among members of the community. People need to agree about methods of exploiting their resources so that everyone has at least a minimal share to survive. People also need to know how to organize their work, taking account of differences in age, gender, and skill, as well as whatever other social variables are considered significant (such as class, race, or ethnicity). Societies must also have methods of distributing food, goods, and services within and among their communities. Rarely do people consume all and only what they produce individually. Instead, they share with others or exchange their products or services for other products or services. Patterns of **consumption,** therefore, are also affected by cultural norms. In some communities, all members have similar opportunities to consume or avail themselves of resources and goods and services. In other communities, though, levels of consumption may vary considerably. Taken together, these various factors constitute an **economic system.**

Anthropologists understand economies and economic systems holistically. They try to situate features of land, resource use, and labor organization in the context of people's adaptation to their environment. They also try to delineate the ways that land, resources, and labor are interrelated with other features of culture, including social and political systems. Put another way, economic systems consist of practices that organize people's activities of production, distribution, and consumption.

Subsistence strategies constitute an important but not exclusive factor in economic systems. Food-obtaining techniques are central to economies, but other factors, such as production of utilitarian and luxury goods, distribution and exchange of products, and specialization of work and services, are also important aspects of economic systems. Thus, for example, different modes of subsistence generally are correlated with different principles on which economic systems are organized. Subsistence strategies that focus on foraging, pastoralism, or farming tend to have different ways of allocating land and resources, organizing labor, producing goods, and distributing or exchanging products and services.

Allocating Land and Resources

What do you own, and how did you come to own it? Do you control the redistribution of what you own?

Different subsistence modes tend to foster different attitudes about land rights and access to natural resources. Foragers' concepts of open access to the lands and resources in their territories and to the lands' resources are especially useful for nomadic peoples, who rely on their ability to exploit available resources seasonally. Their occupation of territory is occasional and temporary rather than permanent. Pastoral peoples may also extend rights to exploit all available land in their territory to graze their herds. However, some pastoral societies limit access to land to particular groups on either a seasonal or permanent basis. Farming peoples need to make claims to specific parcels of land that they cultivate. Among some farming peoples, land is permanently owned by an individual. In others, land may be reallocated from time to time, depending on inheritance rules and the size and composition of households living in the same area. Finally, in industrial and postindustrial societies, individuals, groups, and states own land and resources and other means of subsistence and production.

As a way of allocating resources, ownership varies in different types of societies. Ownership may be vested in a community as a whole or in individuals. Among nomadic foraging peoples, individuals rarely have rights to exclusive ownership and control of land and resources. Ownership of land tends to be most formalized among farming peoples, who expend a great deal of labor readying their fields for planting and need specific acreage to produce sufficient food.

In Vietnam rice farming has become women's work as men have left farming for wage jobs. Here, peasants near Danang irrigate their fields with wooden paddlewheels.

Producing Goods

In addition to subsistence products, people also need other goods to ensure their survival and well-being. Systems of **production** provide clothing, shelter, tools, utensils, and weapons. People also want decorative items to adorn their bodies and their residences. Their religious practices require ritual objects, costumes, and other paraphernalia for ceremonial use. In some societies, people within a household may make all of the various types of equipment that their family requires. In others, some people develop the skills and arts that enable them to become part-time or full-time specialists in the production of specific types of goods. Specialists engage in some types of exchange in which they either sell their products or exchange them for other goods and services.

Different types of subsistence strategies are more or less likely to produce surpluses. When surpluses arise, societies use different ways to dispose of them. Sometimes people keep surpluses on hand for use when supplies are low. At other times and in other circumstances, surpluses may be traded or sold so that the producers can obtain goods or services that they require but do not make themselves. Surplus, therefore, is tied to patterns of distribution and exchange. In general, nomadic peoples obtain little in the way of surplus goods because of the inconvenience of carrying more than basic necessities when moving from one camp to another. Sedentary peoples, in contrast, prefer producing a certain amount of surplus to protect themselves against lean years.

In addition, surpluses serve social functions. Surplus farm produce or manufactured goods can be distributed by the wealthy to those less fortunate, stabilizing social networks and enhancing the prestige of the givers. Surplus goods can be distributed in ritual contexts, such as celebrations of births, marriages, and funerals. Finally, in state societies, surplus wealth may be appropriated through taxation to support the various functions of government and public services.

Organizing Labor

Societies allocate the labor of their members to productive tasks through division of labor. Work roles are assigned minimally on the basis of age and gender. In addition, certain individuals may specialize in craft production or other arts and skills. Men and women may be assigned different but complementary tasks. Elderly people usually retire from direct productive work, depending on the ability of the family or society to support them, although their advice may be sought because of their knowledge and experience. Young children are assigned household and subsistence tasks consistent with their physical and cognitive maturation as well as the type of economy. Whereas farm families depend on children's labor, children in industrial societies typically are prevented from competing with their parents for jobs and wages. These norms often are codified as laws. The legal age of work in the United States, for example, is 14. Nevertheless, children are widely exploited as sources of labor in the world today.

Labor and Specialization. **Specialization of labor** based on skill, talent, or training is a common feature of many societies. All societies have some degree of labor specialization within households as well. In addition, communities may value individuals skilled at making certain kinds of tools, utensils, or crafts. Others may seek to acquire their high-quality, unique, or effective products or services. In some societies, part-time specialists accumulate income from their work. The more skilled the artisans, the more compensation they may receive because others especially prize their work. In other societies, labor specialization involves full-time specialists. These people do not participate in direct subsistence activities but instead exchange their labor and skill for food and goods obtained through the labor of others. Depending on the system of exchange and relationships between people, these products may be given away, exchanged, traded, purchased, or sold.

production
System of extracting resources and utilizing labor and technology to obtain foods, goods, and services.

specialization of labor
System of allocating work in which different people perform different tasks.

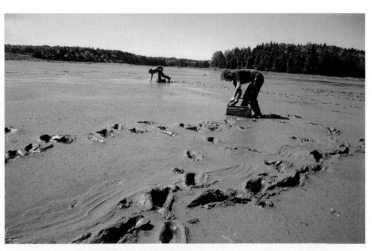

These clam diggers belong to a maritime community in New England and are among the few who are granted commercial licenses each year to exploit this easily overburdened resource.

CASE STUDY

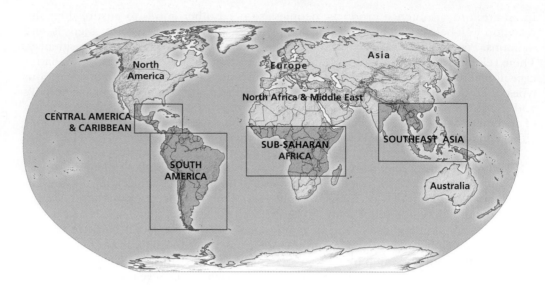

Child Laborers Today

The exploitation of child labor is an international concern. According to a report issued in 2006 by the International Labour Organization (ILO), children who work are divided into four categories: "children at work in economic activity," "child laborers," "children in hazardous work," and "children in unconditional worst forms of child labor." "Children at work in economic activity" is a broad category that encompasses most productive activities that children perform, including all market production (paid work) and some types of nonmarket production (unpaid work), such as producing goods for one's own use. Work may be in the formal sector (especially factory work) or the informal sector (street vendors, construction) and may involve legal or illegal activities.

"Children at work in economic activity" includes children who work in a market-oriented establishment that a relative in the same household operates. It also includes children who are domestic workers in someone else's household, but it excludes children who do the same chores in their own households without pay. The ILO estimates that some 317 million children between the ages of 5 and 17 "work in economic activity." Of these, about 196 million are under the age of 14.

Boys and girls are equally likely to be engaged in economic activities. For children younger than 14, there are no significant gender differences; however, for children ages 15 through 17, more boys than girls are engaged in economic activities, perhaps because many girls in developing countries are married or doing unpaid work in their own households by age 15.

The largest numbers of children engaged in economic activity are found in the Asia-Pacific region (127.3 million), followed by sub-Saharan Africa (48 million), and Latin America and the Caribbean (17.4 million). In terms of the ratio of working to nonworking children, sub-Saharan Africa has the highest ratio of child workers. There, about 29 percent of children younger than 15 are engaged in economic activities. In developed countries, only about 2 percent of children below the age of 15 are economically active.

The second ILO category, "child laborers," refers to child workers under the internationally agreed minimum ages for specific kinds of work, but any working child younger than 12 or 13 is considered a laborer. Children between the ages of 12 and 14 may also be classified as "child laborers" if they do light work for more than 14 hours per week. The ILO defines "light work" as work that is not harmful to children's physical development and health and does not interfere with their education. By this definition, an estimated 166 million child laborers are under age 15. Here, too, boys are more likely than girls to be child laborers, particularly in the older age group (15 to 17), where 57 percent are boys.

The third ILO category, children engaged in "hazardous work," is defined as "any activity or occupation that has, or leads to, adverse effects on the child's safety, health (physical or mental), and moral development." Hazardous work may also refer to excessive workloads or long or intense periods of work, even if the work itself is not hazardous. Some examples of hazardous work for children are mining, construction, working with heavy machinery, exposure to pesticides, and work underwater, at dangerous heights, or in confined spaces.

The ILO estimates that nearly 126 million children work in hazardous situations. This figure accounts for somewhat less than half the total number of economically active children but more than two-thirds of the world's child laborers. For all age groups, slightly more than half of boys and somewhat less than half of girls were working in hazardous conditions.

The final category, "children in unconditional worst forms of child labor," includes human trafficking, forced and bonded labor, armed conflict, prostitution and pornography, and criminal activities. A United Nations survey issued in 2002 reported that about 8.4 million children are in this category worldwide. About 1.2 million children are trafficked to and from all regions of the world. Boys are more often trafficked for forced labor (especially in commercial farming), petty crimes, and the drug trade, whereas girls are likely to be trafficked for commercial sexual exploitation and domestic service.

An estimated 5.7 million children are engaged in forced and bonded labor. About 5.5 million of these reside in the Asia-Pacific region, although Africa and Latin America also have many. Some 300,000 children, mostly boys, are forced to serve in wars, mostly in Africa and the Asia-Pacific region. About 1.8 million children in all regions of the world are engaged in prostitution and pornography. Both tourists and domestic clients exploit child prostitutes. Finally, about 600,000 children are engaged in illicit activities, including petty crimes and especially the production and trafficking of drugs.

Rates of child labor reported in 2006 indicate declines of about 11 percent worldwide from previous surveys. The decline was sharpest in Latin America, with somewhat narrower decreases in Asia and no decrease in sub-Saharan Africa. ILO officials attribute the worldwide decline to efforts by the United Nations and member countries to address the problems of child laborers. The lack of decline in sub-Saharan Africa, however, can be attributed to the devastating effects of HIV/AIDS on the adult population, forcing children to support their families.

PEARSON myanthrolab

Explore more at
www.myanthrolab.com

Labor and Social Status. The relationship between labor and social status is reflected in relative contributions to subsistence, which affect social prestige and influence. For example, in societies where men have higher social status than women and perform most of the subsistence work, their higher social standing may be attributed to their contributions to their households as producers. In contrast, women's lesser social standing may result from their relatively minor contributions to the food supply. Performing a major share of productive work does not necessarily translate into social prestige or power, as in the case of slavery. In the Caribbean and the southern United States, for instance, African slaves in the eighteenth and first half of the nineteenth centuries were the primary subsistence workers and also produced most of the crops intended for external trade. However, they clearly did not benefit from their labor in terms of greater social prestige. The determinants of social power stem more from control over labor and the right or authority to exert control, manage productive forces, and distribute the products. For example, monarchs, nobles, and other members of elite classes control and benefit from the labor of others. Finally, in many large-scale industrial societies, some people accumulate wealth and power from the labor of others and do little or no productive work themselves.

generalized reciprocity
The exchange of goods and services without keeping track of their exact value, but often with the expectation that their value will balance out over time.

balanced reciprocity
Exchange of goods and services of a specified value at a specified time and place.

potlatch
Ceremonial feast, characteristic of indigenous Pacific Northwest coast societies, during which hosts distributed to guests a great deal of food and goods that had been accumulated over many months or years.

Distributing and Exchanging Products and Services

Once goods, whether foodstuffs or manufactures, are produced, they enter into patterns of distribution and consumption. Because societies are organized on principles of interdependence in cooperation and competition, individuals must always be connected to others in networks of distribution. Systems of exchange include reciprocity, defined in Chapter 6 as giving and taking "in kind" between individuals and families, as in simple spontaneous gift exchange. Reciprocity can be far from simple, however. Networks of reciprocal relations may be complex and of long standing. For example, in the Trobriand Islands of Melanesia, complicated patterns of interisland trade linked people through the exchange of ritual items (necklaces and armbands), as well as food and other goods.

Types of Reciprocity. Members of families and households may be intertwined in recurring series of exchanges, a type of distribution called generalized reciprocity. In **generalized reciprocity,** goods and services are exchanged, but the value of the products or services given and received is not exactly or objectively calculated. There may be an expectation that goods and services will be given and received frequently and will have approximately equivalent worth, but the frequency and the amount of value are not specified. Many exchanges between parents and children, for example, are examples of generalized reciprocity. Distribution of food in some societies likewise involves principles of generalized reciprocity, as in the exchanges of foraging peoples such as the Inuit and Ju/'hoansi. Through generalized reciprocity, all families become both givers and receivers of food over time.

Some exchanges are characterized by **balanced reciprocity,** in which exchanges more closely specify the value and the time at which an exchange will take place. The mutual giving and receiving of gifts at birthdays or religious holidays and the informal exchanges of clothing or objects are examples of balanced reciprocity. Balanced reciprocity characterizes exchanges between people of equal social status who are not kin.

CASE STUDY

The Potlatch: An Example of Negative Reciprocity

An unusual example of negative reciprocity, called the **potlatch,** was prevalent in indigenous societies of the Pacific Northwest coast. The Kwakwaka'wakw (known previously as the Kwakiutl) now live on reserves and in communities in British Columbia, Canada. They formerly were a cultural and linguistic group made up of approximately thirty independent "tribes" that each occupied a separate territory. They were foragers, but not nomadic. An abundance of wild resources, especially fish and other sea products, land animals, plants, fruits, and berries allowed the Kwakwaka'wakw to live in permanent villages containing hundreds of residents.

People of highest status constituted the informal leadership of kin groups and villages. Chiefs received portions of animal, fish, and plant products obtained by members of their group and were usually exempt from subsistence tasks. Chiefs organized cooperative activities, such as house building, but individuals acting alone did most hunting and fishing. Chiefs were also representatives of their lineages in the system of potlatching or feasting that served to validate people's social standing.

Potlatches (from the Chinookan word for "to give") were feasts to which relatives, community members, and high-ranking chiefs were invited. They were held to celebrate life-cycle transitions (birth, naming, puberty, marriage, death), the building of new houses, and the naming of new chiefs. As part of the potlatch, the host, who had accumulated goods over many months or even years, gave food and gifts to the invited guests. High-ranking chiefs also received gifts such as bowls, dishes, and ceremonial objects. The host sought to distribute more wealth than other hosts had given out at potlatches. By doing this, the host raised and secured his social standing. However, the system was inherently competitive, so that the next time around, hosts who had been guests at one potlatch would attempt to outdo the generosity of the previous host to regain the highest social position.

Giving more than receiving might appear to be the reverse of negative reciprocity, but in this case a different kind of reward was being negotiated. Hosts gave away material goods in exchange for greater social prestige. Helen Codere (1950) gives perhaps one of the best definitions of the potlatch:

> "Potlatching" is more than any single potlatch. The public distribution of property by an individual is a recurrent climax in an endless series of cycles of accumulating property—distributing it in a potlatch—being given property—again accumulating and preparing. The whole potlatch system is a composition of these numerous individual potlatch cycles.

In addition to its social and symbolic value, the potlatch cycle thus served economic functions. In days of feasting, food was distributed along with blankets and other surplus wealth. People of high status could recirculate these goods when they hosted potlatches, but lower-ranking people used them in their domestic consumption. This system of exchange maintained the entire society.

Explore more at
www.myanthrolab.com

Balanced and generalized reciprocity are similar in their social basis and principle of equivalence; for example, items or services given or received are roughly equal in value. Furthermore, in addition to distributing food and material items, reciprocal exchanges are symbolic affirmations of social relationships. By exchanging goods and services, people enact their mutual interdependence.

A third type of reciprocity, **negative reciprocity,** characterizes exchanges in which some parties receive more than they have given. Negative reciprocity is rarely found within families or among members of small communities but is typical of trade or market exchanges in which the goal is profit. Negative reciprocity is common between strangers or enemies. However, negative reciprocity may occur among people in the same community who operate on the principle of competition. Trade exchanges called barter may be based on negative reciprocity. In **barter,** people trade a product they have in excess to obtain an item they need but do not produce themselves. Capitalist economic systems are based on negative reciprocity. For example, manufacturers and providers of services strive to sell their goods at prices that exceed the costs of producing those goods.

negative reciprocity
Exchange of goods and services in which each party seeks to benefit at the expense of the other, thus making a profit.

barter
An exchange of products in which one person gives one type of product in exchange for another type of product.

Have you ever bartered services or products?

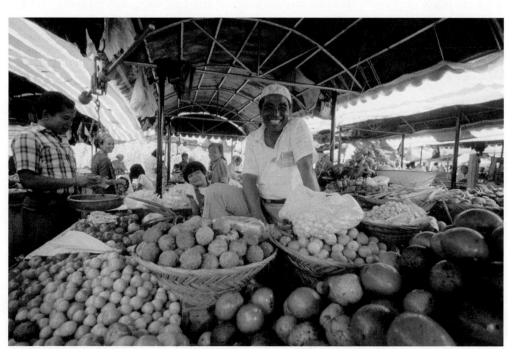

In Sumatra, horticulturalists still barter for manufactured goods, especially hunting tools, or even for tourists' personal objects.

IN THEIR OWN VOICES

"Free to Do as You Like"

In this excerpt from his autobiographical novel, Fragments of Memory: A Story of a Syrian Family, *Hanna Mina describes the plight of sharecroppers in his homeland, bound to and dependent on landlords who extract most of the profits from the farmers.*

Ever since February, Mother had been gathering the hen eggs with great care. We were living and working as day laborers in a field belonging to the village *mukhtar* [headman]. It was a small field, empty except for mulberry trees. Our only duty was raising silkworms during the silk season. It was a raw deal that Father had contracted with the *mukhtar*. . . . He didn't succeed here either but he was forced into it. . . . He had to find shelter somewhere, so he agreed to take the abandoned field. The *mukhtar* opened a page for us in his debt ledger. The first thing he put down in it, against the account of the silk harvest, was five kilos of mixed sorghum and barley, a few meters of unbleached cotton and a few articles like salt, oil, kerosene and soap. He also advised Father to be a faithful share cropper who knows his obligations and pays his debts. Father raised his hand to his forehead and then placing it over his heart said, "At your service, Mr. Elias!". . .

Our house was a rectangle built of unbaked clay bricks, divided into two parts by a wall. One part was for animals, the other for living in. Since we possessed no animals, that part remained empty. Hens that relatives had generously bestowed upon Mother ran around and pecked there. In one corner we piled up firewood and dung, and in another near a small window high in the wall was a hearth made of stones and clay.

Father began, with the help of the family, the cultivation of the land and the care of the mulberry trees by borrowing a neighbor's animal. Before the work was finished, a messenger arrived from the *mukhtar* asking for Father. So he went only to be told that he must work in his fields first and that Mother must

work in the *mukhtar*'s house. Father raised his hand to his forehead, lowered it and placing it over his heart said, "At your service, Mr. Elias!"

Although the parents worked hard as sharecroppers, their precarious situation worsened because synthetic silk made in India undersold natural silk. The landlord shut down silkworm production, forcing sharecroppers to leave.

So we bundled up the belongings we had left, and our parents went to inform the *mukhtar* that we were leaving.

We could have left covertly at night or in the early morning without our departure arousing anyone's attention or interest. The surrounding houses were empty, the mulberry groves were being cut down and burned or their trunks gathered for wood. The paths were filled with columns of travelers on the

Redistributive Networks. The Pacific Northwest coast potlatch is an example of a system of redistribution. In **redistributive networks,** an organizer collects produce and other goods and then distributes them to community members or guests at a large public gathering. The occasions for redistribution are many. Ceremonial events, especially those marking rites of passage (birth, marriage, death), may provide the context for redistribution by the host to the guests, as in the potlatch. Political events, such as installations of chiefs in Melanesia and Polynesia, are occasions for redistribution as the new leaders or their relatives provide giveaways displaying their generosity and at the same time attracting loyal followers. In some early states that had agriculture as an economic base, such as the Inca, central governments collected surplus produce and other goods, stored them in granaries and warehouses, and distributed them to needy people in times of poor harvests or other catastrophe.

In contemporary societies, state governments organize networks of redistribution. One of the state's functions is to collect taxes, now paid in money, from its citizens to fund and support public projects and programs. In theory, the value of these monies is returned

redistributive networks
Economic systems in which an organizer amasses food and other goods and then distributes to community members or guests at large public gatherings.

In this 1960s photograph, a family and their neighbors in Balakan, Azerbaijan, reel silk by hand from silkworm cocoons they have harvested from their mulberry trees. Craft specialization in transitional economies is risky for landless families because their income is dependent on a stable market in which to sell their product—but market forces are beyond their control.

backs of animals or in carts drawn by donkeys or cows. The fathers who lacked these means carried their things on their backs, dragging their children along, fleeing from hunger, fear, and thieves, traveling together to be safe from highway robbers who lay in wait for them in the valleys and the foothills of the mountains.

It was possible for us, in this state of collective emigration, this mutual dissolution of contracts to forsake our mud hut and the mulberry grove, empty except for the whistling wind, and flee the whole village without letting anyone know and without anyone asking about us. But our oldest sister was with the *mukhtar*. Considering her to be payment for the debt, he had tightened his watch over her since learning that Father had returned and that we were on the point of leaving since it had become impossible for us to stay on.

Father's lengthy beseeching diatribe, Mother's tearful entreaties, and requests from those who were acquainted with our circumstances and sympathized with us, were of no avail. The *mukhtar* spurned them all. He would not give us anything to eat and could not cope with us remaining hungry. We were of no use to him as *fellahin* [peasant farmers]. So he made it known that we were free to leave, but as far as our sister was concerned, he would keep her until we paid our debt.

"You're free to do as you like!" said the *mukhtar*. The landowners had said that before him, and he said it to other *fellahin* beside us. The sweet word "freedom" had become frightening, meaning no money, no food and no concern for the unpredictable destiny of the families who had lived on raising silkworms. The arrival of artificial silk was finishing off them and the silkworms together.

Therefore the word "free" became an odious term to the *fellahin*, who came from their fields seeking aid from the owners of the fields. As a consequence, they rejected this term, bringing up the matter of their servitude being in exchange for certain conditions, among which was the stipulation that they should be sustained until winter was over and the growing season arrived.

Explore more at
www.myanthrolab.com

From Hanna Mina, *Fragments of Memory: A Story of a Syrian Family*, pp. 19–20, 88–89. © 1993. Reprinted by permission of the Center for Middle Eastern Studies, the University of Texas at Austin.

CRITICAL THINKING QUESTIONS

Why were Hanna and his family not really free to do as they wanted? What patterns in agricultural societies lead to social inequality?

to citizens in public services such as road construction, water supplies, schools, justice systems, and defense. In practice, however, systems of redistribution based on taxation are often flawed or work imperfectly as leveling mechanisms. For example, in the United States, the progressive income tax was developed to allocate people's tax burdens more equitably so that wealthier people paid a higher percentage of their income in taxes than poorer people. The wealthiest people have many ways to reduce their tax liability, however, so poorer people shoulder a disproportionately higher tax burden.

Markets and Trade.   Another form of redistribution is **trade,** in the form of either barter or market exchange. As defined previously, barter is the exchange of goods between individuals, each one supplying the other with produce, crafts, or other items. People who engage in barter usually know one another. In some cases, they may establish relatively formalized and permanent trading relationships, visiting one another's communities from time to time and exchanging their goods. Market exchange, on the other hand, is usually impersonal and is based, in principle, on fixed prices for goods. However, people

trade
System of exchange in which goods are exchanged for either other goods or for money.

Many subsistence farmers in Africa use simple technologies to cultivate their fields. Here, a girl in Zimbabwe uses a digging stick to plant and weed her crops.

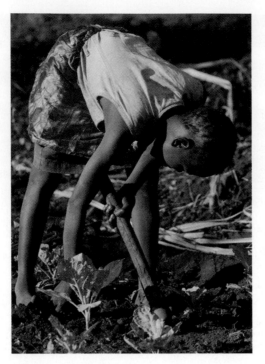

buying and selling in local and regional markets in many societies frequently haggle over prices in an attempt to reach a compromise between the seller's desire to get as much as possible for the goods and the buyer's desire to pay as little as possible.

In West African societies, local and regional markets function to redistribute farm products and crafts among villagers who themselves lack mobility to obtain a variety of goods. For example, among the Igbos of Nigeria, women are the principal local traders, bringing their own and their husbands' products to market (Njoku 1990). Some women are part-time traders, combining their own farm labor and their commercial activities. Part-time traders usually live in rural areas where they have access to land. Other women are full-time specialists, working in markets in urban areas. They are buyers and sellers, purchasing farm goods and other products from people in rural areas and then selling them in town markets. Some urban traders employ assistants to travel to the villages to buy produce. Finally, foreign goods enter local and urban markets through the work of large-scale importers and exporters. Most of these traders are men.

The modern Igbo system of market exchange is partially financed by credit associations. Some of these are based on kinship whereas others bring together unrelated traders who form credit unions (Njoku 1990, 106–07). In one type of savings club, each member contributes a fixed amount of money at specific times (for example, on market day). Then the full amount of money collected each time is given to each member of the club in rotation. In addition, money is available to members for emergencies. Some savings clubs lend money to members, charging rates of interest for a fixed loan. Women traders sometimes organize together to protect their rights and to support one another with loans and credit.

REVIEW — An economic system involves interdependent systems of production, consumption, allocation of land and resources, organization and specialization of labor, and exchange. In systems of exchange-based generalized reciprocity, people exchange goods and services of unequal or unfixed value. In balanced reciprocity, equal exchanges are sought. In negative reciprocity, people expect to get more than they give. Systems of exchange also include redistributive networks, barter, trade, and market transactions.

MARKET ECONOMIES AND CAPITALISM

A **market economy** is a system of allocating goods and services and determining prices on the basis of market forces, such as supply and demand. Thus, items in short supply with high demand cost more to buy. In contemporary societies, buying and selling of goods and services is negotiated through a system of money exchange. Money, whether in the form of paper, coin, precious metals, gems, or other material object, is endowed with a specific value. Societies might have special-purpose money, such as cowrie shells, of fixed value that can be exchanged only for certain commodities, or tokens or tickets good only for a particular event on a particular day. In contrast, market economies rely on all-purpose money that can be exchanged for any product or service at any time. This money is portable, durable, divisible, abstract, and universal. Its value is calculated independently of any particular exchange, therefore, and can be used as a measure of worth in any exchange of goods, services, and labor. Money can even be used to "commodify" (make into a **commodity** to be bought and sold) essentially noneconomic things, such as people, their talents, and events in their lives. Market economies are based on these principles of measurement of the value of goods and services. Markets as physical places for the exchange of

market economy
Economic system in which products are traded in impersonal exchanges between buyers and sellers using an all-purpose currency.

commodity
A product that can be sold or traded in return for money or other products.

products, such as in local or regional markets, may exist in societies with all kinds of subsistence strategies, even including foraging, simple farming, or pastoralism.

Capitalism is both an economic system based on money and markets and an ideology based on the private and corporate ownership of the means of production and distribution. Means of production include land, money, factories, and the like, collectively called **capital**. Economies based on capitalism must grow to survive, and growth is based on profits from buying and selling in diverse markets. The greatest profits are made in free markets that are unrestricted by industries or governments, and the greatest growth occurs as profits are accumulated and reinvested in businesses. Thus, capitalist economies favor business interests and state expansion for the purposes of acquiring new capital, including land, raw materials, and inexpensive labor.

Capitalism as an ideology-based economic system arose in Europe beginning in the sixteenth century, based on the principles of private property, individual rights, free trade, profit, and the amassing of wealth. By amassing wealth in the form of money, some people are able to gain control of the means of production and can then use this control to accumulate even greater wealth. The capitalist mode of production differs in many significant ways from modes of production in traditional indigenous societies. In contrast to economic relations in kin and community-based societies, capitalist economic relations are impersonal and institutionalized. According to Karl Marx, these relations are facilitated through the exchange of money, which although seemingly abstract and neutral, ". . . actually conceals, instead of disclosing, the social character of private labor, and the social relations between individual producers" (1967, 76).

Capitalist production is characterized by the following three fundamental attributes (Plattner 1989):

1. Workers do not control the means of production; they cannot by themselves produce the goods they need for survival. In contrast to subsistence farmers and artisans, workers in capitalist production are dependent on the owners of factories or industries that organize and produce goods and services.

2. Workers gain access to the means of production only through working for wages. According to the classic Marxist paradigm, because of this relationship, capitalist societies are divided into two basic classes: owners of the means of production (capitalists) and workers (proletariat). While some discussions of capitalism describe workers as "free" in the sense that they can sell their labor independently of kinship or other constraints, they are not free in that their lack of capital forces them to work for wages.

3. Workers produce value that is greater than the wage paid to them. This **surplus value** is retained by the owners of capital and contributes to their profit (above the costs of maintaining the means of production). In contrast to economic systems that strive for balance and stability in labor output and the benefits reaped, capitalist systems strive for continual increases in profits and rates of growth. Capitalists raise profits by increasing the scale of production, purchasing more machinery, increasing the efficiency of production, investing in new technology, finding inexpensive labor, and increasing labor output.

Cultural beliefs and values support the principles and practices by which economic systems operate. Ideological constructs that support capitalism include the idea that benefits accruing to owners are "natural" and legitimate. Owners deserve their wealth because they plan ahead, take risks, make sacrifices, and work hard. In contrast, people who are poor are seen as undeserving. Poverty, which actually results from fundamental

Here, a Senegalese woman wears a traditional headpiece made of cowrie shells. For centuries, West Africans used cowrie shells from the Indian Ocean as currency.

GLOBALIZATION

Today, farm products enter into complex systems of transportation and delivery to national and worldwide markets. Some of the profits reaped from sale of produce are reinvested in newer technologies that permit the production of even greater surpluses, a cycle of profit and growth consistent with the principles of capitalist economic production.

capitalism
An economic mode of production in which the goal is to amass wealth in the form of money to gain control over the means of production and then use this control to accumulate even greater wealth.

capital
Land, money, factories, and the like that support and supply the materials needed for production.

surplus value
The amount of value that workers produce in capitalist production that is greater than the wage paid to them.

What values, beliefs, and practices support the type of economic system in which Tokyo thrives?

social and economic inequalities, is presented as the consequence of an individual's personal failings—lack of intelligence, laziness, or even moral deficiencies. Through formal and informal enculturation and the reinforcement of political and religious beliefs, most members of capitalist societies learn to accept their "proper" roles without question. Members of elite classes expect to be privileged, to have wealth, and to exert social and political power; in turn, members of lower classes accept their comparative disadvantage.

REVIEW — ● A market economy is based on supply and demand and the use of money and other capital as mediums of exchange. A good, service, idea, or even a person is treated as a commodity to be bought and sold. In capitalism, workers are dependent on owners to organize and produce goods and services, sell their labor for wages or salaries, and produce a surplus value that the owners retain as profit. Capitalism is based on private property and profits from the buying and selling of commodities in free markets.

IMPACTS OF COLONIAL EXPANSION, INDUSTRIALISM, AND GLOBALIZATION

The growth of capitalism depended on the exploitation of land, labor, natural resources, and raw materials. Beginning in the fifteenth century, European explorers, traders, soldiers, missionaries, and settlers traveled throughout the world in an effort to acquire new territories, resources, markets, and souls. Each colonial power had its specific goals but all shared a common purpose and worldview, that is, to expand their national wealth and power. In the process, they had to control and conquer other lands and peoples.

Through **colonialism,** conquered or dominated peoples were incorporated into European economic systems as extractors of resources. In North America, native peoples became enmeshed in trading networks directed by Dutch, French, British, and Russian merchants, delivering animal furs in exchange for manufactured goods. In Mexico, Central and South America, and the Caribbean, indigenous peoples were forced to work on plantations and in mines operated by Spanish and Portuguese owners. In Africa, people were extracted as resources to be bought and sold along with gold and ivory.

colonialism
Policies in which countries establish colonies in distant places to exploit their resources and labor, and possibly to establish settlements of their own citizens abroad.

Many millions of other people died from warfare, overwork, and disease as the direct and indirect casualties of European colonial expansion.

In Asia, European expeditions met powerful, centralized, and well-organized states that they were not able to defeat militarily. Instead, Europeans developed trading networks that brought resources and products to Asia from colonies in other parts of the world. In exchange, they obtained Asian luxury items to sell in Europe. Some indigenous peoples in all parts of the world readily and even enthusiastically welcomed European traders, wanting to acquire manufactured goods and luxury items. They willingly supplied the merchants with the resources, products, and people so much sought after in European and world markets. The participation of many other indigenous peoples was not voluntary, however.

European economic expansion was closely connected with nation building. Governments controlled much of the trade, directly or through state-appointed merchant organizations, and pursued policies of political and military intervention to promote and protect their economic interests. These policies often led to military invasions and wars of conquest, followed by the establishment of direct colonial rule. Far-flung empires were established, with European powers competing to acquire colonial possessions. The French and British claimed much of North America, for example, and the British claimed India.

As colonial control spread throughout the world, capitalism and market economies were introduced to peoples whose subsistence strategies were based on foraging, pastoralism, and horticulture. Because economic systems are integrated with other aspects of culture, changes in work and landholding practices caused by colonialism and trade stimulated political, social, and ideological transformations as well. These processes of globalization increased cultural connections throughout the world. Chapters 16 and 17 will address these topics further.

GLOBALIZATION

The Europeans needed to develop markets to sell goods manufactured in Europe and to expand markets for materials extracted from their colonies. This dynamic produced the complex economic system that we refer to as globalization.

Colonialism and the Exploitation of Labor

Slavery was the most extreme form of colonial exploitation of labor of indigenous peoples. Slavery deprived the victims of all rights to determine their own labor, forced them to produce goods directed by their owners, and expropriated all their products to be distributed and consumed according to the wishes of their masters. In the eighteenth and first half of the nineteenth centuries in the Caribbean and southern United States, the economic value produced by slaves fueled the growing wealth of these regions but did not benefit the workers themselves. From the beginning of the slave trade in the fifteenth century until its end in the nineteenth century, some 10 million Africans were forcibly sent to the Americas (Wolf 1982). Although the vast majority of slaves in the Americas were taken from Africa, native peoples were also systematically enslaved. For example, in the mid-eighteenth century, the Spanish colonizers of what became California rounded up indigenous inhabitants and forced them to live and work at mission sites, growing grains, fruits, and vegetables for the consumption of the Spanish settlers (Jackson and Castillo 1995). They also raised livestock and produced textiles intended for local and regional sale. When the United States government took control of California, it disbanded the missions, but the practice of kidnapping and enslaving native children and adults continued. By the time the practice ended in 1867, more than 4,000 Indian children had been taken (Castillo 1978, 109).

Spanish and Portuguese settlers used forced native labor to work on plantations in Central and South America prior to the importation of slaves from Africa. Native workers also mined silver, gold, and other metals. In Australia, New Zealand, and the Pacific Islands, colonial regimes forced indigenous peoples to work on plantations under European control.

Another means of controlling indigenous labor was the imposition of colonial taxes, for example, mandatory **poll taxes,** or head taxes. Because taxes had to be paid in cash, people were compelled to seek wage employment in the European-controlled economic sectors in their countries—in mines, plantations, or service and construction jobs—or they grew crops for cash, removing land from subsistence farming. Their crops thus entered national and international markets under the control and distribution of colonial powers.

Ideologies that supported these practices focused on perceived benefits to the native peoples. In the words of a member of the British Parliament, speaking in 1906, "Under all circumstances the progress of natives toward civilization is only secured when they shall be convinced of the necessity and dignity of labor; and therefore I think that everything we reasonably do to encourage the natives to work is highly desirable"

poll taxes
Taxes levied on households.

industrialism
The use of machines to produce products and foods.

(Joseph Chamberlain, quoted in Wellington 1967, 250). In 1934, another British official stated, "As the natives were often reluctant to leave their homes, a little gentle pressure was brought to bear upon them with the introduction of a poll tax. This measure quite effectively stimulated their desire for earning the white man's money" (Eiselen 1934, 71). Comments such as these show how colonial powers were able to rationalize the economic exploitation of colonized peoples.

Industrial Economies

Colonialism led to the spread of capitalism and market-based economies, which increasingly relied on the mass production of commodities. Merchants, desiring to increase their profits and to find new markets for their goods, promoted the invention of new technologies that would increase productivity. Demand for mass-produced goods also encouraged new technologies and the development of the factory system, a hallmark of **industrialism,** the use of machinery to produce goods. In Europe and the United States in the late eighteenth century, innovations in production began a process that transformed agricultural societies into industrial nations.

Industrial production began in Great Britain as an outgrowth of cottage piecework in the making of textiles and clothing. Women traditionally wove woolen cloth and made garments for their families, in keeping with a domestic division of labor between men and women in a farm household. Gradually, women began to produce surplus cloth and garments for sale to merchants, who bought up the products and sold them in regional and then national markets. Initially, women were paid to produce the cloth and garments in their homes. Eventually, cottage piecework shifted to factories, whose owners hired workers and directed their labor on site, away from homes and household duties. In some cases, entire families were hired to work in the factories. However, to fulfill domestic and child-care responsibilities, many married women dropped out of the labor force.

By 1820, manufacturing incorporated complex machinery and new sources of energy. These innovations enabled workers to create more products in the same amount of time, and machine production replaced handwork. Labor patterns shifted. The employment of children became inefficient because they could not operate heavy or complicated equipment. In addition, public disclosure of children's illnesses and injuries caused by

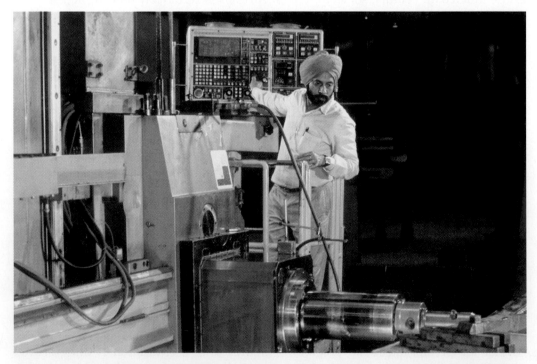

This industrial employee in northern India is performing work that a preindustrial counterpart would have done at home without the aid of machines.

long working hours and unsafe conditions led to demands for legal protections against the abuse of children. Consequently, men and young women remained the primary factory employees.

In the United States, one of the first industries to develop was textile manufacturing. In Massachusetts mill towns, for example, young women from farm families worked to help their families buy a growing number of commodities, such as shoes, household utensils, and tools. Unmarried daughters were available for factory jobs because their labor was not as critical to agricultural production on the family farm as that of sons.

By the use of machines and powerful energy sources (coal, steam, electricity) to produce goods, industrial processes have vastly increased the efficiency and growth of commodity production. Increased production makes higher levels of consumption possible, and consumption creates demand, which, in turn, fuels more production. That is, the more goods that are produced, the greater the demand; and the greater the demand, the more goods are produced. Our attitudes about consumption are shaped by this cycle, which reflects the needs of a capitalist economy. We are given every incentive to consume and to believe that we need to consume more. In other words, demand is artificially created and maintained through an ideology that promotes the acquisition of material goods as the means of achieving pleasure and progress.

Industrial Agriculture

Industrial agriculture is characterized by six general features (Bartlett 1989): (1) increased use of complex technology, leading to increased replacement of human labor with machinery and increased use of fossil fuels as sources of energy in production; (2) increased role of state agencies in farm production policies; (3) a tendency toward competition among producers; (4) specialization of crop production; (5) overproduction of farm products; and (6) increased interdependence between farm units and the corporations that control machinery, sales, processing, and transport.

Mechanization has become part of nearly all agricultural processes, from planting to weeding and harvesting. Many small farmers cannot afford to invest in all of the new machinery available and, therefore, are threatened by large, corporate-run farms, or agribusinesses. Chemicals are also increasingly expensive, putting a strain on the budgets of small farmers. They pose a threat as well in the contamination of water and the destruction of ecosystems. Chemical use also harms farmworkers. A study carried out in the 1980s showed that corn farmers in Iowa and Nebraska had a 44 percent to 63 percent greater risk of leukemia than the general population (Bartlett 1989). Furthermore, agricultural chemicals are potentially harmful to anyone who consumes the food treated with chemicals. The industrial conditions under which poultry and livestock are grown and slaughtered can result in outbreaks of illness from dangerous bacteria like *Salmonella* and *Escherichia coli*. The use of antibiotics in the poultry and livestock industries contributes to the emergence of immune strains of those same bacteria (ibid.).

Genetic engineering and irradiation of foods have become standard, but controversial, processes. Genetic engineering modifies the genetic codes inherent in the foods to produce strains that have particular market advantages, such as more even textures or tougher skins on fruits and vegetables so that they will not be bruised in transport from fields to stores. According to the Centers for Disease Control, ionizing irradiation eliminates disease-causing bacteria and parasites. Although some people favor these processes, others fear potential danger because of the manipulation of genetic codes for foodstuffs and the introduction of possibly harmful substances.

Energy usage has increased significantly in industrial agriculture. For example, although 2.2 pounds (1 kilogram) of breakfast cereal provides 3,600 calories of food energy, 15,675 calories are required to produce and transport that 1 kilogram (Bartlett 1989). The processes involved in growing, packaging, processing, and transporting food, in other words, expend far more energy than the food provides in calories.

Industrial production of farming has led to a decline in the number of varieties of crops. For example, by the 1990s, ". . . only six varieties of corn accounted for 46 percent of the crop, nine varieties of wheat made up half of the wheat crop, and two types of peas made up 96% of the pea crop" (Union of Concerned Scientists 2008). In addition, as an example of the influence of market forces, more than half of the land throughout the entire world that is planted with potatoes is devoted to growing only one variety of potato,

industrial agriculture
Application of industrial technology and chemicals to farming for increased productivity.

What do you think about your role as a consumer in a capitalist economy?

Does your local store sell irradiated or genetically engineered foods? Do you think these foods should be labeled accordingly?

Industrial agriculture, using complex machinery, increasingly replaces labor intensive production techniques used by family farmers.

the one utilized by McDonald's. The declining number of varieties of foods has a nutritional cost in narrowing the range of vitamins, minerals, and other dietary essentials. In addition, it makes large segments of the productive system vulnerable to pests that might destroy specific crops. Increased pesticide use is then a technological response that also carries dangers to the consumers and the environment.

The U.S. government influences agricultural production by implementing tax laws that favor capital investment over labor. Tax benefits are provided for investments in farming technology and research. The government also directly subsidizes agricultural research that leads to increased mechanization, genetic engineering of plants, and other scientific processes. And government programs subsidize the production (and overproduction) of particular crops. Intense capital investment and competition have led to a sharp drop in the number of farms in the United States. Government programs also encourage the integration of plant and animal production. For example, most of the corn grown in the United States goes to feed livestock. Thus, promoting the consumption of meat also aids farmers who grow corn.

In many parts of the world, industrial agriculture undermines the stability of subsistence farming. In Africa and Latin America, household farming for subsistence has become precarious, as owners of large plantations have succeeded in putting pressure on local farmers to sell their land. Smallholders are caught in the bind of needing cash to buy clothing, household goods, equipment, and food. As their household economies become insecure, people need to obtain cash either through employment or sale of their land. Employment is difficult to find in rural communities, so many people opt to leave their homes, temporarily or permanently, and migrate to towns and cities to find jobs. However, rampant urban growth, especially in developing regions of the world, has led to the spread of slums, deteriorating health conditions, and increasing rates of urban crime.

CULTURE CHANGE

DEFORESTATION, ENVIRONMENTAL CHANGE, AND RESOURCE SUSTAINABILITY

Throughout human history, economic activities that people have undertaken to survive have affected their environments and resources. Even foraging peoples affect the resources they use. Farmers have more sustained techniques of environmental modification. Swidden farming utilizes slash-and-burn strategies to clear fields and enrich the soil. Intensive agriculturalists modify the land even more to extract ever-increasing yields from it. Environmental change resulting from human occupation is, therefore, nothing new. However, the scope and rapidity of change today are unprecedented and frequently negative, destroying environmental equilibrium and resources, threatening the survival of indigenous communities, and potentially leading to worldwide shortages of food and other resources. For example, Michael Williams (2003) reports that the rate of global loss of forest cover was only 1.94 percent per year between 1700 and 1849, jumping to 11.52 percent per year by 1950, and increasing again to 15.10 percent per year in 1995 (2003, 396). Until the early twentieth century, most forest loss occurred in temperate climates, but since then, the decline in tropical regions has far outpaced temperate losses.

Many factors contribute to environmental degradation. The sheer growth in human populations puts

Clearcutting for commercial timber results in deforestation that can have widespread environmental and economic consequences.

added stress on land and resources. The intensification of industrial agriculture, turning vast amounts of acreage into production of foods and other crops, has led to the loss both of land for subsistence farming and of animal and plant species. Oil, mineral, and timber companies are also major contributors to environmental exploitation, particularly to deforestation and water pollution.

The effects of these processes are especially evident in tropical countries that have been used for centuries as sites of resource extraction. The desire for their products has grown since the mid-twentieth century as consumer demands have broadened and deepened. Consumerism in the United States was the principal catalyst for this increase, but more recently, worldwide consumption is responsible for the exploitation of tropical resources. Richard Tucker (2007) identifies the production of sugarcane and bananas in the Caribbean, coffee in South America, rubber and timber extraction in the tropical rain forests, and cattle ranching in Latin America as the major culprits. Throughout much of the twentieth century, multinational corporations exploited tropical resources with little or no environmental safeguards. Middle-class and elite affluence accelerated during this period without concern for ecological consequences in distant lands (Tucker 2007, 218).

By the 1970s, unrestrained deforestation led to the strengthening of conservation groups whose alarm began to reach a worldwide audience. Governments in many newly independent tropical countries also used conservation rhetoric as an argument to manage their own resources. However, postcolonial governments have often formulated policies that, although sounding protective, in fact exploit resources to the point of causing ecological damage. For example, the Indonesian government has promoted the policy of turning natural forests into forest plantations that produce specific types of trees for timber exports (Peluso 1992, 5). However, the government allows multinational corporations that have little regard for sustainability to extract these woods even though international conventions outlaw trade in woods that have not been "sustainably harvested" (Intrator 2007, 27). The land rights of indigenous peoples and their access to forest resources are routinely ignored. Indonesian government agencies that control the extraction of forest resources allot contracts to companies and receive revenue from their operations. Local residents have no say in this system (Peluso 1992, 10). In Indonesia, and in Central and South America, state forest management is often linked to national development plans that view indigenous subsistence strategies as obstacles to affluence. However, indigenous communities continue to occupy some of these forests. On the Indonesian island of Java alone, 6,000 "forest villages" are located in or adjacent to state forests (Peluso 1992, 23).

The Amazonian region has become representative of global deforestation. The Amazon basin encompasses parts of Brazil, Peru, Bolivia, Colombia, Ecuador, and Venezuela (in descending order of acreage). Deforestation in the region has multiple interrelated causes. In Brazil, colonial settlement began the destructive process along coastal forests to establish plantations for sugar, cotton, cocoa, and coffee in the 1500s (Williams 2003, 464). In the latter half of the twentieth century, peasants seeking land for farming and cattle ranching invaded the Amazon. Here, as elsewhere, rural poverty and deforestation are intertwined. Governments encouraged settlement and economic development to improve the standards of living of some of their poorest citizens.

Timber companies are also responsible for forest loss in the Amazon. Between 1970 and 1990, between 8.2 percent and 9.6 percent of the forested area there had been cut (Williams 2003, 480). Rates of clearing continue to destroy the Amazon forests with no effective safeguards.

Deforestation also contributes to climate change. Loss of trees leads to declines in rainfall, causing droughts and land erosion. Forest clearing also releases carbon into the atmosphere, which increases temperatures (Williams 2003, 430–34).

In some tropical countries, indigenous resistance to state control is manifested both in acts of sabotage and in the growth of organizations to promote sustainable resource management. As a result, governments have begun to work with local communities to develop systems of "social forestry" that take into account local knowledge and needs for sustainable development. However, indigenous communities have only limited participation in planning and implementing these programs.

Opposition to central state management of resources is not simply because of opposition to development. Indeed, indigenous communities may favor development to improve their standards of living (Kirsch 2006; 2007). However, they may want guarantees that their resources, particularly the quality of the land and water, are sustained rather than degraded. For example, complex issues of development and sustainability have arisen in Papua New Guinea in communities near the Ok Tedi gold and copper mine that began operating in 1984. By the late 1980s, particulate pollution from the mine was destroying trees and gardens. By 2007, more than one billion metric tons of finely ground metal tailings had been released into the Ok Tedi River (Kirsch 2007, 305). The affected area of rain forest currently comprises more than 579 square miles and is expected to more than double (Kirsch 2007, 308). The government of Papua New Guinea supports the operation of the mine, the source of 18 percent of the country's foreign exchange revenue (Kirsch 2007, 309).

The Yonggum people, indigenous inhabitants of the region, protested against the mining company because of the harm done to their subsistence. Their goal is containment and proper disposal of mine tailings, not closure of the mine, because they favor the economic jobs and revenues the mine can provide. The Yonggum understand the struggle in terms of principles of reciprocity and responsibility and the dire consequences of failed relationships (Kirsch 2006, 25). For them, the rain forest is a world full of communication between themselves and the animals with whom they share it. Indeed, they believe people can assume the shape and knowledge of animals (ibid.). The Yonggum's concepts of sustainability, therefore, are intertwined with social and religious practices and values.

Conflicts between state agencies and indigenous peoples also occur over traditional subsistence practices. For example, for centuries, subsistence farmers have used fire to clear fields for planting and to control invasive species. These practices are particularly effective in the African savanna, but in Zambia, for instance, the state views fire as destructive, an attitude it inherited from colonial authorities (Eriksen 2007). In tropical and savanna drylands, however, fire and other natural factors such as drought actually support and encourage the coexistence of multiple types of vegetation. By shaping their natural environment through fire, Zambians increase their subsistence base, providing land for planting, vegetation for animals, and weed control (Eriksen 2007, 23).

In some regions, reviving indigenous practices can reclaim lands that have been deforested and eroded. For example, Mixtec farmers in Oaxaca, Mexico, are slowly reclaiming their land by planting trees, building terraces of stone walls on the hillsides, and digging ditches along the slopes of the hills to capture rainwater. They are also planting corn, beans, and squash together in native fashion, a practice that improves the nutrient content of the soil and reduces insect pests. Since beginning this project, the Mixtec have tripled or quadrupled their yield (Malkin 2008).

An important and frequently overlooked issue in environmental degradation is access to potable water. As industrial development, resource extraction, and mining move further into forests, waterways become polluted from runoff and waste products. Indigenous strategies for sustainable supplies of clean water are defenseless against these new pollutants (Lutz 2006), which threaten the health of the people and their subsistence in their own lands.

The World Summit on Sustainable Development, held in 2002, affirmed international conventions linking "environmental degradation, poverty reduction, indigenous rights, and access to education, health services and employment" (Carter 2008, 63). To make these linkages real, governments committed themselves to working with local communities when planning and implementing development schemes. Anthropologists and other social scientists can participate by carrying out research in communities affected by the environmental and economic consequences of development projects. This research can reveal how indigenous peoples see the projects and advocate for their concerns, so that local participation is meaningful and effective (Carter 2008, 64).

In many countries, indigenous peoples are working out agreements with governments to gain recognition of rights to resources and to continue and develop sustainable economies. These initiatives are especially significant in Bolivia, Peru, and Colombia, where indigenous lands are being demarcated and protected (Aylwin 2007, 14–15). Although the pace of demarcation is not always swift, the policies at least establish principles that can form the basis of meaningful negotiation and action.

Social Consequences of Capitalism and Industrialism

Social inequalities increase in capitalist economies based on industrialism. This raises the question of whose needs are satisfied by socioeconomic systems. Unlike in foraging, pastoral, or horticultural economies, the needs of some people in a capitalist economy are satisfied much more than those of others. Another question is to what extent the general affluence of capitalist economies compared to other kinds of economies gives people more leisure and security, as is commonly believed. Anthropologists have tried to answer this question. For example, in a comparison of middle-class French people and members of the Machiguenga society in Peru, Allen Johnson (1978) points out that horticulturalists like the Machiguenga spend less time in subsistence work and have more leisure time than workers in modern industrial nations. Johnson compared the ways in which French and Machiguenga people spend their time in production (of goods and services), in consumption (using consumption goods, as in eating and leisure activities), and free time (idleness, rest, and chatting). Johnson found that French men spent more time in production than any other group while Machiguenga women spent the least time producing. Machiguenga men and French women spent about the same amount of time in production, less than French men but more than Machiguenga women. In addition, French people spent far more time in consumption than the Machiguenga, about three to five times as much, in fact. In contrast, the Machiguenga had much more leisure time than did the French.

Johnson and others have also pointed out that people's ideas about their needs and satisfactions are subjective and culturally constructed. For example, although North Americans and Europeans consume more goods and services than any other group, they often feel a shortage of time. Consumption provides pleasure and excitement, but people sometimes do not enjoy it because they feel pressed for time, needing to keep busy schedules, and cram as much as possible in a day. Time itself is treated as a commodity. In English, metaphors for time as a commodity include "spending time," "saving time," "having time for [something]" (Lakoff and Johnson 1980).

Consumerism, which is the culture of consumption, has grown among all economic classes in all parts of the world. The expansion of consumer credit enables people without cash on hand to accumulate household and personal possessions that represent a lifestyle above their means. The extent of consumer debt in the United States

consumerism
Culture of consumption of goods and services.

GLOBALIZATION

Western consumerism has infiltrated developing countries (Dannaeuser 1989). In Latin America, Asia, and Africa, Western-style shopping malls satisfy the demands of the rising numbers of the middle class. Products with the greatest demand include home appliances, TVs, computers, and other electronic equipment.

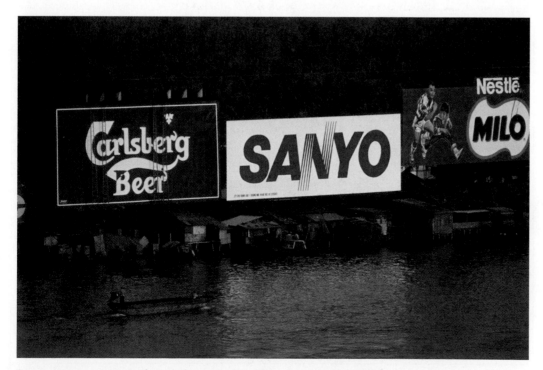

By creating a perception of need, these advertisements in Vietnam contribute to overspending and debt.

and elsewhere reveals the power of culturally constructed demand, including the desire to display the trappings of wealth and prestige. For example, American households carry about $8,000 in credit card debt annually. In 2003, American consumers spent an average of 43 percent more than they earned. According to the Federal Reserve, U.S. consumer debt in 2007 stood at $2.5 trillion, or more than $20,000 per household, not including mortgage debt (Federal Reserve 2008). Consumer debt grew at a rate of 5.5 percent annually. The U.S. national debt was also the highest in history that year.

An important difference in consumer spending between the developed and developing countries is the fact that the developed countries have a strong, domestic industrial base, whereas most of the developing world lacks national industries. Therefore, spending in the developing world pays primarily for imported goods, which tend to be more expensive. Developing countries often lack the capital and infrastructure to develop strong domestic industries, and so become dependent on other nations for production and distribution of products to their citizens. Local economies may be undermined as a result, as rural subsistence farmers and artisans are put out of business by imported and mass-produced goods.

In the past 100 years, a dramatic shift has taken place in the types of work that people do. A century ago, the vast majority of people in the world worked in the agricultural sector, either owning or working on a farm. Today, only a small fraction of the population in many countries works in agriculture, as Tables 7.1 and 7.2 show.

In Table 7.1, "agriculture" includes all farming for commercial purposes as well as full-time subsistence farmers; "industry" refers to heavy industry; and "services" includes secretarial, sales, and information occupations. The figures show that (1) participation in farming is lowest in the wealthiest regions with the highest standards of living—developed economies and Europe; (2) conversely, participation in farming is highest in the poorest regions—Africa and Asia; (3) levels of industrial production are in an inverse relationship with farming—where farming is high, industrial production is low, and where farming is low, industrial production is high; and (4) service employment is highest in the wealthiest regions. Table 7.2 indicates that countries deriving higher percentages of their gross domestic product from agriculture tend to have higher rates of poverty. Of course, government policies also influence poverty rates.

GLOBALIZATION

In a new trend, service jobs are now being exported, or outsourced, from countries like the United States to countries in the developing world, where labor costs are less. As service industries and information technologies increase, heavy industry declines as an economic past, prompting some analysts to refer to Western nations as "postindustrial."

TABLE 7.1 PERCENT OF POPULATION INVOLVED IN THREE ECONOMIC SECTORS 2007			
	Agriculture	Industry	Services
World	34.4	22.7	42.9
Developed economies and European Union	3.9	25.0	71.1
Central, South Europe (non-EU)	19.5	25.4	55.1
East Asia	38.6	27.0	34.4
Southeast Asia and Pacific	44.8	18.8	36.4
South Asia	48.2	21.8	30.0
Latin America and Caribbean	17.1	22.6	60.3
Middle East	17.3	24.8	57.9
North Africa	33.1	22.7	44.2
Sub-Saharan Africa	62.5	10.1	27.4

Source: International Labor Organization, Global Employment Trends, Econometric Models, December, 2008.

TABLE 7.2 PERCENTAGE OF GROSS DOMESTIC PRODUCT (GDP) IN THREE ECONCOMIC SECTORS

Continent	Country	%GDP Agriculture	%GDP Industrial	%GDP Service	Poverty Rate
Africa	Chad	40	14	46	64
Africa	Egypt	17	32	51	23
Africa	Liberia	60	10	30	80
Africa	Rwanda	40	20	40	70
Africa	Zimbabwe	28	32	40	60
Asia	Bangladesh	30	18	52	36
Asia	India	25	24	51	35
Asia	Mongolia	36	22	42	40
Asia	Vietnam	25	35	40	47
Europe	Belgium	1	26	73	4
Europe	Poland	4	37	59	18
Europe	Romania	14	33	53	45
Europe	Ukraine	12	26	62	50
North America	Costa Rica	12	31	57	21
North America	El Salvador	12	28	60	48
North America	Haiti	32	20	48	80
North America	Mexico	5	27	68	27
North America	United States	2	18	80	13
South America	Brazil	9	29	62	17
South America	Chile	8	38	54	22
South America	Colombia	19	26	55	55
South America	Ecuador	14	36	50	50
South America	Paraguay	28	21	51	36

Source: National Council of Economic Education, 2008. www.econedlink.org. All rights reserved. For more information, visit www.councilforeconed.org or call 1-800-338-1192.

Native peoples across the world became enmeshed with European market economies beginning in the fifteenth century. Through colonialism and trade, the exploitation of native lands, resources, labor, and coercive practices such as poll taxes and the mission system, capitalist and industrial economies gradually came to dominate the growing present-day global economy. Industrial agriculture and manufacturing have replaced foraging, horticulturalism, and pastoralism in most regions of the world. Industrialism increases efficiency and productivity through the use of machines and automation. Increases in production lead to greater wealth, and increases in consumption and consumerism further stimulate economic growth. Over the past 100 years, service industries have replaced agriculture and industrial manufacturing as the dominant economic sector in wealthy postindustrial societies.

REVIEW

COMPARING SUBSISTENCE STRATEGIES

We tend to think that, because of its ability to feed so many billions of people, modern industrial agriculture is superior to all earlier subsistence strategies. However, as discussed in Chapter 6, other strategies have their advantages as well as disadvantages. Foragers do not have exclusive ownership of land and resources. Division of labor is based on age and gender, though men and women often share the same tasks. Labor specialization in foraging societies is at the household level, with individuals doing craftwork for the family. Among nomadic foragers, surpluses, when they occur, are consumed and shared with the group to reinforce social ties.

Foraging societies had the advantage of access to a complex and varied diet from resources growing wild in different ecological niches. For example, the Ju/'hoansi ate about 100 kinds of plants, fruits, and nuts in a yearly foraging cycle. Offsetting this advantage, however, was their vulnerability to malnutrition or starvation in years of severe drought or other environmental disaster. Moreover, foragers' dietary variety usually came at a price—the need to move constantly. Nomadism puts a premium on good health because it is hard for the frail, sick, and elderly to relocate frequently. It also puts a burden on pregnant women and parents with young children. The need for mobility also prevents the accumulation of surpluses of clothing, shelter, and tools and utensils.

The physical activity required by a nomadic lifestyle has health benefits of its own. The kinds of infectious diseases that plague people living in close quarters in settled communities were rare or absent among nomadic peoples. As they moved, they left behind their garbage and bodily waste—another source of disease. The small community size characteristic of foraging societies had the advantage of minimizing pressure on resources and reducing interpersonal tensions. The need to limit household size, however, may have been a burden because of the need for aggressive birth control.

Pastoralists put more stake in the idea of land and animal ownership. Grazing land may be owned by a collective (a family or group), with individuals owning or having rights to the animals. Wealth and prestige are counted by the size of one's herd, so there really is no surplus. Division of labor is variable, but everyone's work addresses the care and herding of the animals and secondary production using animal products.

In horticultural societies, families or kin groups own and allocate land. Men clear fields, cut trees, and burn brush. The division of labor for other subsistence tasks varies from society to society. Part-time artisans are paid in goods or food. Horticultural surpluses are stored against famines and disasters and are redistributed to those in need.

Horticulture solves some of the problems of foraging. Farming provides people with a stable source of food. Rather than relying on the fluctuating bounty of nature, people grow their own crops. The security of horticulturalists is not absolute, however, because drought, insect infestation, flooding, or other natural disasters may wipe out a season's produce. For these reasons, horticulturists try to obtain surpluses to rely on in bad years. Pastoralists solve the uncertain success of hunting by maintaining their own herds of animals. In contrast, hunters and fishers may or may not find the game they seek. However, pastoralists must invest more labor and resources in maintaining their herds than foragers do in hunting.

In most agricultural societies, individuals own and control land. Surpluses are more common and may be hoarded or used to pay tribute or taxes to state governments, which redistribute surpluses to those in need. Surpluses also support full-time specialists, who do nonagricultural work in arts, crafts, occupations, and professions.

Intensive agriculturists solve many of the problems engendered by other subsistence strategies, but they also create additional difficulties. They solve the problems of nomadism by establishing sedentary communities, but settled life also has problems. Sedentary farmers usually have a much less varied diet than foragers or people who utilize a mixed horticultural and foraging strategy. The more limited variety of crops and foods potentially leads to the kinds of diseases that result from the lack of certain nutrients. Sedentary communities are also more vulnerable to epidemic diseases. With many people confined to one place, their communities are subject to festering tensions or open conflicts between groups and individuals. Agriculturists do, however, have a striking advantage in that they are able to use increasing numbers of people to produce larger surpluses and, therefore, they have access to a secure supply of food except in times of natural catastrophe. This often comes

ANTHROPOLOGY APPLIED

Economic Anthropologists and Consumer Behavior

Methods of cultural anthropology include ethnographic observation, interviews, and recording qualitative (as well as quantitative) information about human behavior. Anthropologists are also trained in cross-cultural research. For these reasons, companies hire anthropologists to do consumer research, especially to reveal the cultural and social patterns that shape consumer behavior.

People's cultural identities, beliefs, and values, as well as their environmental influences, shape their economic behavior. Anthropologists can see through the "other's" eyes to find insights that companies can use to increase their sales. Anthropologists also analyze brands, conduct focus groups, and write employee and customer ethnographies.

For example, economic anthropologists might help a company test a new product, enter a new market by appealing to an ethnic group or other demographic, decide on the right interface for selling products online, analyze a wedding registry for consumer preferences, observe shoppers in a new setting, gather information on customer satisfaction or loyalty, predict trends in technologies for the home, or identify how

people make shopping decisions, such as whether to buy organic produce (http://www.ethno-insight.com/). Anthropologists also do market research for pharmaceutical firms, professional sports teams, and companies like Pizza Hut and Coca-Cola (http://www.ethnographic-solutions.com/).

Anthropologists who work for corporations are also concerned with the cultural, material, and health and safety impacts that products and services have on consumers, company employees, and communities. In addition, they analyze the sustainability of economic growth and development in relation to people's physical, social, and cultural environments.

○ CRITICAL THINKING QUESTION

In applied anthropology, what might be some concerns in balancing the goals of corporations with anthropological perspectives?

at the cost of backbreaking labor, however. Agriculturists work harder and longer than do horticulturists, pastoralists, or foragers.

The relaxation of population-control mechanisms in some agricultural societies results in rapid population growth and problems of overpopulation. As a consequence, more labor is available, but more labor is also required to feed larger populations. This process leads to greater burdens on the land and creates needs for more land for farming and living space. In addition, numerous pregnancies and births create burdens on mothers' health and increase the risks of maternal death.

Industrial agriculture solves some problems of supply. Through industrial techniques, farm output has increased enormously. There is now the ability to feed everyone in every country, but many people continue to go hungry and to die of malnutrition because of the uneven distribution of food. The complex reasons are partly economic and partly political. But industrial agriculture has also created unforeseen problems in its overreliance on harmful chemicals in food growing and processing.

REVIEW — Modes of subsistence can be compared and contrasted in terms of how they affect the quality of human life in relation to security, food supply, diet, living space, living conditions, labor burdens, health risks, and life expectancies.

CHAPTER SUMMARY

Analyzing Economic Systems

- Economic systems include strategies for allocating land, resources, and labor. People everywhere need to produce, distribute, and consume foods and other goods. They obtain their resources from their land through various modes of production. Different cultures allocate land and resources in different ways.

- Societies need to allocate the labor of their members to productive tasks. Work roles are often assigned to people on the basis of age and gender. How gender affects work roles varies in different cultures.

- Economic exchanges occur among family members, friends, traders, and other members of communities. Exchanges between family members or other familiars are usually of the type called generalized reciprocity, where no immediate return is expected, whereas exchanges between other members of communities are called balanced reciprocity, where there is usually a mutual exchange of goods. Exchanges between strangers, especially in the marketplace, are characterized by negative reciprocity, where all parties try to receive more value than they give.

- Systems of exchange also include redistributive networks, barter, trade, and market transactions.

Market Economies and Capitalism

- Market economies are based on the buying and selling of commodities of fixed value, depending on supply and demand and using standardized mediums of exchange.

- Capitalist economic production is based on the desire by owners of the means of production to increase their profit. In capitalist production, workers must sell their labor for a wage to owners of institutions that produce goods and services. Workers produce "surplus value": the value of the goods they produce by their labor is greater than the wage paid to them. This surplus value becomes profit for the owners. Capitalist economic systems are geared toward an ever-increasing rate of profit. Unlike traditional indigenous subsistence economies, capitalist production is inherently unstable.

Impacts of Colonial Expansion, Industrialism, and Globalization

- In the fifteenth century, European powers began a process of economic and colonial expansion aimed at expropriating resources and labor from indigenous lands and peoples. In this process of globalization, which was not confined to Europeans, resources and trade items were incorporated into a worldwide economic system that led to the growth and concentration of wealth in Europe. This wealth and desire for even greater profits motivated the development of industrialization.

- In complex agrarian and industrial societies, systems of distribution have developed to circulate foods and other goods from direct producers to those who do not produce food. Members of elite classes in particular benefit from the distribution of goods. Some segments of society are not able to control at least some of the products of their labor.

- Postindustrial societies increasingly rely on consumerism and the provision of information and services to the global economy rather than goods.

Comparing Subsistence Strategies

- In most foraging societies, all members of the community generally have access to land and resources. In pastoral societies, individuals or families control or own land and especially animals. In horticultural and agricultural societies, individuals or family groups own

land. Intensive farming increases the need to retain permanent and individual control of land.

- In foraging, pastoral, and horticultural societies, most people, given characteristics of gender and age, perform similar subsistence work. However, in complex agricultural and industrial societies, economic life is characterized by labor specialization. In the past century, the percentage of people engaged in producing food has declined everywhere.

KEY TERMS

consumption   156
economic system   156
production   157
specialization
   of labor   157
generalized
   reciprocity   160

balanced reciprocity   160
potlatch   160
negative reciprocity   161
barter   161
redistributive
   networks   162
trade   163

market economy   164
commodity   164
capitalism   165
capital   165
surplus value   165
colonialism   166
poll taxes   167

industrialism   168
industrial
   agriculture   169
consumerism   173

REVIEW QUESTIONS

1. What social behaviors are part of any society's economic system? How do anthropologists view economic systems?

2. How do systems of exchange relate to modes of subsistence?

3. What are the different types of reciprocity? Why is balanced reciprocity seen in foraging groups? How is the potlatch an example of negative reciprocity?

4. How do foragers, pastoralists, horticulturalists, and agriculturalists allocate land and labor?

5. How are economic concepts, such as ownership, integrated with other cultural systems, such as kinship, social status, political power, and ideology?

6. What is a market economy? How does capitalism affect production, distribution, and consumption?

7. Which changes in economic systems lead to social inequality?

8. How were indigenous peoples brought into European economies? How did colonialism affect those peoples and their economies?

9. Why do capitalist economies depend on ever-increasing consumerism?

PEARSON myanthrolab EXERCISES

To complete the following exercises and activities, you must log in to www.myanthrolab.com and select your current textbook.

1. In the **Explore** tab of Chapter 7, click on *Video* and watch the video on *Specialization*. Complete the short answer exercise that accompanies the video.

2. While in the **Explore** tab of, click on the *NPR Audio Programs Broadcast* tab and go to *Theme 14: Economy*. Listen to one of the programs in this section and complete the short answer exercise that accompanies the program.

3. In the **Research Tools** section on the home page, click on the *Research Navigator*™ link and enter the

Anthropology database to find relevant and recent scholarly and popular press publications. For this chapter enter the following keywords: *subsistence strategies, colonialism,* and *reciprocity*.

4. Enter the **MyAnthroLibrary** section on the home page to read more about topics and cultures that are discussed in this chapter. Suggested readings include:

Variation in Economy by Richard E. Blanton

Miskito: Adaptations to Colonial Empires, Past and Present by Mary W. Helms

KINSHIP AND DESCENT

Whereas I, Joseph Mygatt, of Hartford upon the River and in the jurisdiction of Connecticut in New England, have in the behalf of my son Jacob and at his request made a motion to Mrs. Susanna Fitch, in reference to her daughter Sarah Whiting, that my said son Jacob might with her good liking have free liberty to endeavor the gaining of her said daughter Sarah's affection towards himself in a way of marriage: . . . I will pay thereupon unto my said son as his marriage portion the full sum of two hundred pounds sterling. . . . And I do further engage for the present to build a comfortable dwelling house for my said son and her daughter [Jacob's bride-to-be, Sarah] to live in by themselves. . . . And [I] also give them therewith near the said house one acre of ground planted with apple trees and other fruit trees, which said house, land, and trees shall be and remain to my said son as an addition for his marriage portion, before mentioned, and to his heirs and forever. . . . And I do further promise and engage that at the day of my death I shall and will leave unto him my said son and his heirs so much estate besides the dwelling house, ground, and trees. . . . I do hereby engage and bind over my dwelling house and all my lands and buildings in Hartford. . . . And I do further engage that my daughter Mary's portion of one hundred pounds being first paid to her, I will leave to my said son and his heirs forever my whole estate at the day of my death, he [Jacob, his son] paying to my wife during her natural life twelve pounds a year, and allowing to her a dwelling entire to herself in the two upper rooms and cellar belonging to my now dwelling house, with the going of half the poultry and a pig for her comfort in each year during her said life; also allowing her the use of half the household stuff during her life, which she shall have power to dispose of to Jacob or Mary at her death. . . . And lastly I do engage that the whole benefit of the Indian trade shall be to the sole advantage of my son Jacob, and do promise that I will during my life be [an] assistant and helpful to my said son in the best ways I can, both in his trading with the Indians, his stilling, and otherwise, for his comfort and advantage.

Excerpts from "Marriage Settlement of Jacob Mygatt, of Hartford, Connecticut," cited in *Remarkable Prividences 1600-1700*, edited by John Demos. © 1972. Reprinted by permission of George Braziller.

● What is descent, and why is it significant in organizing human relationships?

● What types of descent are found in human cultures?

● What kinds of kin groups do the various descent rules create?

● How do different unilineal descent rules affect people's interrelationships?

● How do kinship systems interrelate with other aspects of culture?

● How and why do kinship systems change?

● What terms do people use to classify their kin?

● How do kin terms reveal the type of kinship system people have?

This marriage contract for Jacob Mygatt and Sarah Whiting was written on November 27, 1654, in Hartford, Connecticut. It reveals a complex array of concerns common to all human societies: Among the people you live with, to whom do you owe the greatest loyalty and support? Who among them might you marry? What will happen to your dependents when you die? How will they support themselves? How will your property be divided and distributed, and to whom? Universally, these and other questions are resolved through kinship systems. This chapter compares the various ways that people define their relatives and reckon their kinship.

KINSHIP SYSTEMS

In all societies, people have ways of organizing their relationships with other people, especially their primary relationships with kin. As children, our earliest and most influential interactions are with our parents, siblings, and other relatives. We rely on our families for all of our survival needs. Our families feed us, clothe us, and provide our shelter. They also help us adjust to the world around us, teaching us the behavior and attitudes that our culture expects, and they provide emotional support in both good times and bad.

Many of our relatives continue as important economic and emotional supports throughout our lives. Even as adults, we can turn to our kin in networks of reciprocity, asking for aid in times of need. In turn, we may be asked to respond to their requests when they are in need. We may align ourselves with our relatives when they are engaged

kinship system
System of determining who one's relatives are and what one's relationship is to them.

consanguines
People related by blood.

affines
People related through marriage.

fictive kin
Unrelated individuals who are regarded and treated as relatives.

rules of descent
Social rules that stipulate the nature of relationships from one generation to another.

bilateral descent
Principle of descent in which people think of themselves related to both their mother's kin and their father's kin at the same time.

unilineal descent
Principle of descent in which people define themselves in relation to only one side, either their mother's side or their father's side.

in disputes with others. We may expect loyalty from our kin when we are in conflict with neighbors or other community members. During personal or family crises, we may expect emotional support from our relatives. Together we celebrate happy occasions such as births and marriages, and we mourn the deaths of our kin.

In industrial societies, friends, colleagues, comembers of clubs, and other nonrelatives also function significantly to give us companionship and support. In most societies, however, kinship relations permeate people's daily lives and mold their identity and their sense of themselves. In societies or communities characterized by cohesive social systems, family members may be united in dense, complex networks. They may perform important functions in the absence of the formal institutions that regulate and organize economic, political, and religious life in industrial societies. People identify themselves not just as individuals, but as members of kinship groups.

A **kinship system** consists of connections between people by "blood," marriage, or adoption, and the beliefs and practices by which people regard and treat one another as relatives. The people may be genetically related (**consanguines,** "related by blood") or related by marriage (**affines**), or they may not be related at all. Many kin groups include adopted kin and **fictive kin,** unrelated individuals who are regarded and treated as relatives. Thus, the notion of kinship is essentially a social and symbolic idea, not based on universal objective criteria.

Among foragers, pastoralists, and horticulturalists, kinship relations were the primary regulators of social and economic life. Through kin relations, people organized their households, allocated work roles, controlled land and other property in common, made decisions affecting the group, and carried out ritual functions. In agrarian societies, kinship relations generally continued to be paramount in organizing and integrating communities, but new patterns of interaction also emerged. Gradually, as state societies developed, specialists and state institutions took over many of the functions carried out by kinship groups. The state regulated intergroup trade, established formal procedures for making decisions and settling disputes, and set up institutions to carry out some social functions, replacing the critical roles of kinship groups. In postindustrial societies, people may live apart from their relatives, and all of the functions of kin groups can be fulfilled through public or private institutions. Thus, fundamental differences exist between those societies where people's lives center around their kin and where social, economic, and political functions are integrated with kinship groups and those societies

This family reunion, held at Monticello in Virginia in July 2004, celebrates the kinship of descendants of Thomas Jefferson and the African slave Sally Hemings. Some relatives at this event met each other for the first time.

where ties among kin are looser and less intense and where formal institutions provide social, economic, and political functions.

Kinship systems are organized around rules of marriage (the subject of Chapter 9) and **rules of descent,** which stipulate the nature of relationships from one generation to another. Although the notion of kinship is subjective, there are a limited number of ways in which people trace descent and organize kinship groups. Two fundamental organizing principles are bilateral descent and unilineal descent. In societies with **bilateral descent,** people think of themselves as related to both their mother's kin and their father's kin at the same time (*bilateral* means "two sides," from *bi* meaning "two" and *lateral* or "side"). In **unilineal descent** systems, people define themselves in relation to only one side, either their mother's or their father's (*unilineal* means "one line," from *uni* meaning "one" and *lineal* or "line").

Bilateral Descent

Organizing one's relatives according to the principle of bilateral descent creates a large, potentially limitless group of people to whom one may claim relationship. People usually do not interact with everyone in this large kinship group. Rather, they tend to know, socialize with, and depend on a smaller group of relatives within the wider network. This smaller group of bilateral relatives is called a **kindred** (see Figure 8.1).

Reckoning one's kin through bilateral descent is common in industrial societies, but it is also found in many small foraging societies. Kindreds are adaptive in both kinds of cultures, but for different reasons. In foraging societies, bilateral descent allows people to make claims on a wide group of people for economic assistance and emotional support. This strategy is adaptive, especially when resources are scarce. In times of need, people may ask relatives for aid, based on the principle of reciprocity. At different times, people are both givers and receivers of support. They are at an advantage if they can call on the help of many others in times of need. They are also likely to be asked for help, but having diffuse reciprocal networks is an efficient and reliable adaptive strategy in the long run.

Bilateral descent is also adaptive for people in modern industrial countries, where it functions to loosen kinship ties. Thus, the same system of descent can have different outcomes and serve different purposes, depending on people's needs as they adapt to specific ecological, social, and economic conditions. Although bilateral descent provides a large number of people with reciprocal obligations and responsibilities, it also creates a loosely organized kin group without definite social limits or boundaries. By loosening kinship ties, people establish greater individual autonomy, freeing themselves from claims that other people might make on them. Individuals and small family units can advance themselves economically, accumulate more wealth, and raise their standards of living if fewer people can make claims on them for support. Thus, capitalist societies favor bilateral descent because of the focus on individual achievement and accumulation of personal wealth. However, although autonomy and independence can free people from obligations, they may also have the consequence of social isolation and may limit the number of people from whom a person might seek aid in times of need.

The functions of bilateral descent are different in foraging and industrial societies because of both cultural context and cultural history. Although a particular cultural behavior may be adaptive, its advantage can be understood only within the society and

kindred
Kinship group consisting of known bilateral relatives with whom people interact, socialize, and rely on for economic and emotional assistance.

> **What rule of descent is followed in your family? What is the name for the type of kin group formed by this rule?**

GLOBALIZATION

The increasing prevalence of bilateral descent in the world today is partly an outgrowth of the adaptive functions of bilateral descent groups in industrial societies and partly a result of the globalization of culture based on Euro-American power and influence.

FIGURE 8.1
A Kindred. A group of people, traced through bilateral descent, related to the brother and sister shown at the bottom row, center.

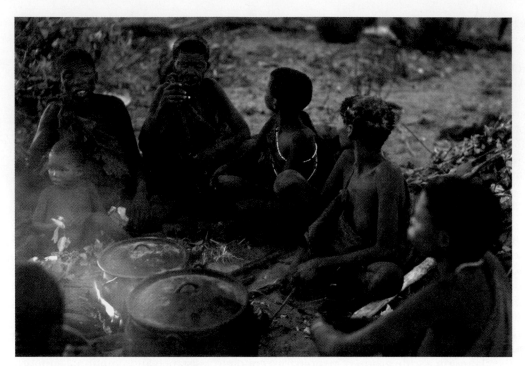

Here, members of a G/wi band in Botswana gather around a cooking fire. Like other peoples of the Kalahari, the G/wi reckon their kinship bilaterally.

circumstances. That is why a particular strategy, in this case, bilateral descent, can be advantageous in different societies for different reasons.

In historical context, bilateral kin groups in industrial societies reflected changing economic and social conditions favoring individual achievement and personal advancement. These conditions tended to weaken kin ties. Nevertheless, both the poor and the wealthy can benefit from membership in bilateral kin groups. Carol Stack's research in African American urban families (1975) and Rhoda Halperin's study of rural Kentuckians (1990) demonstrate that low-income people and people living in rural areas tend to maintain large networks of kin, which diversifies and widens their possibilities of support in times of need. The very wealthy, meanwhile, can shelter their money in trusts distributed among their kin (Marcus 1992). They also rely on one another for political support based on shared interests and goals.

Unilineal Descent

Unilineal descent has two principal forms: matrilineal and patrilineal (see Figures 8.2 and 8.3). Other variants, discussed later in this chapter, are far less common. In both forms, kinship is traced through descendants on one side only, either through the mother or the

FIGURE 8.2

Matrilineal Descent. Brown triangles and circles are ego's kin group. Diagrams of kinship terminology systems use the following conventions: Circles represent females, triangles represent males, horizontal lines link siblings, vertical lines link generations, and equal signs link husband and wife. Abbreviations used to designate kin in a kin diagram are M = mother, F = father, Z = sister, B = brother, D = daughter, S = son, H = husband, and W = wife. Using combinations of these symbols, anthropologists can describe all kin relations in any kinship system.

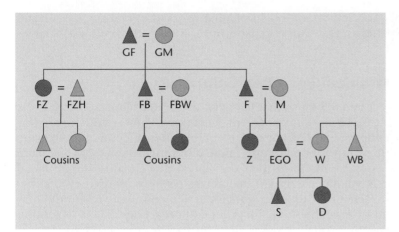

FIGURE 8.3
Patrilineal Descent. Brown circles and triangles are in ego's kin group.

father. However, they differ in the side through which descent is traced or the side chosen for affiliations, or even whether both sides may be taken into account. In **matrilineal** societies, people reckon descent through their mothers. That is, children belong to the kinship group of their mother. In **patrilineal** societies, people reckon descent through their fathers, so that children belong to the kinship group of their father.

A kinship system consists of the beliefs and practices by which people regard and treat each other as relatives. The people may be genetically related (consanguines) or related by marriage (affines). They may also be unrelated, adopted, or fictive kin. Rules of descent stipulate the nature of kin relationships from one generation to another. Two ways that people trace their descent are bilateral descent (tracing relationships through both parents and both sets of their parents) and unilineal descent (tracing relationships through either the mother's kin or the father's kin). Bilateral descent groups are called kindreds.

MATRILINEAL AND PATRILINEAL SYSTEMS

Although people in unilineal systems belong to one particular line of descent, social bonds with people belonging to other kinship groups are also recognized. For example, in patrilineal systems, children belong to the father's kin group but still know that they are also related to people on the mother's side. Nevertheless, people feel the strongest ties to members of their own group, in this case, the father's.

Prevalence of Matrilineal and Patrilineal Descent

Of known cultures whose kinship systems were organized on principles of unilineal descent, the great majority were patrilineal. Possibly only about 15 percent were matrilineal (Aberle, 1961, 663). Matrilineal societies were concentrated among peoples whose economies were based on horticulture, especially those where women were responsible for the farmwork. Because women were the primary subsistence workers and helped one another with both child care and farmwork, they benefited from the existence of stable and cooperative units. Tracing descent through women in such societies stressed the communal and permanent bonds among women and between women and their children, especially their daughters. Most horticultural societies were patrilineal, however, even those that relied on women's labor.

The proportion of matrilineal societies was highest among horticulturalists of West Africa and native North America (Aberle 1961, 665). Patrilineal societies were most prevalent among nomadic foragers and pastoralists, who rely on men's cooperative labor.

> If your kinship system were matrilineal, who would be in your kin group? Who would be your closest relatives if your kinship system were patrilineal?

matrilineal
Descent system in which kinship group membership and inheritance pass through the female line.

patrilineal
Descent system in which kinship group membership and inheritance pass through the male line.

patriarchy
Social system in which men occupy positions of social, economic, and political power from which women are excluded.

Although subsistence plays an important role in shaping patterns of kinship, it is not sufficient to explain these patterns. Exceptions to patterns show that other cultural variables are involved.

Matrilineal and Patrilineal Societies Compared

A comparison of Figures 8.2 and 8.3 shows that the structure of matrilineal descent is the mirror image of the structure of patrilineal descent. In practice, however, there are several important differences between them, particularly in the kinds of bonds people maintain with their own kinship group after marriage. These differences stem from one main cause: In matrilineal societies, women bear their own lineal descendants; in patrilineal societies, women bear the lineal descendants of the men into whose group they marry.

In patrilineal systems, particularly those in which married couples live with the husband's family, women tend to leave their own kin group after marriage. Their separation is in part residential because they usually move to their husband's household, and in part structural and psychological. The intensity of a woman's separation from her own kin group and incorporation into her husband's group varies among patrilineal cultures. Separation is strongest in societies where men control descent, inheritance, and social power. Such societies are said to be patriarchal. In patriarchal societies, women typically lose much contact with and support from their own relatives. **Patriarchy**—rule or dominance by men in social, economic, and political life—is not the same as patrilineality—descent traced through men. One term refers to power and the other to descent.

In contrast, in patrilineal societies with greater gender equality, women may maintain strong emotional bonds with their families, especially with parents and siblings, even if they change residence after marriage. For instance, among the Tewa of New Mexico, daughters leave their natal family when they marry, but emotional ties to their kin remain strong. Women continue to visit their relatives often, to participate in family rituals and other important events, and to take part in discussions about matters of communal interests. In times of conflict with her husband or in-laws, a woman can also expect that her family members will be her allies.

In patrilineal systems, it is in the interests of kin groups to establish secure marital ties because a patrilineal descent group obtains its children through marriage. That is, through marriage, a man is able to claim the children his wife bears. For this reason, divorce tends to be difficult to obtain. The couple's relatives may exert pressure on both husband and wife to remain in an unhappy union. Even where divorce is possible, some social criticism attaches to the couple after divorce, especially to the wife.

These conditions, common in patrilineal systems, are absent in matrilineal societies or appear in different form and function. Matrilineal kinship groups obtain new members (children) from women of their own group, so the marriage tie is often not as intense or secure. Divorce may be more easily obtained by either spouse and carries less social stigma, if any.

In parts of rural India that are strongly patriarchal, once a woman marries and moves to her husband's household, she cannot expect emotional or financial support from her birth family.

Although matrilineal societies have practices and attitudes that support women, none is matriarchal in the sense that some patrilineal societies are patriarchal. That is, there are no known examples of societies in which women exclusively control descent, inheritance, and social and political power. There are also no societies in which men's voices are silent and their interests are ignored. Issues of relationships between men and women in a society are discussed more fully in Chapter 10.

In matrilineal systems, especially those in which married couples reside with the wife's kin, men often have split loyalties. Their identification with and integration into their wife's household may be rather loose, particularly in the early years of marriage. Men often maintain strong emotional, economic, and ritual ties to their family of birth. They may function as representatives of their natal family to outsiders and may have important decision-making roles within it.

Influence and Inheritance in Unilineal Descent Groups

Matrilineal descent groups characteristically differ from patrilineal descent groups in several important ways (Schneider 1961). For instance, matrilineal descent groups depend for their continuity and operation on retaining control over both male and female members. In contrast, women are peripheral members of their own patrilineal descent groups because they bear children for their husbands' group. In matrilineal systems, women give birth and care for future members of their own kin groups. Men retain interests in their descent groups through ties that are not completely severed when they marry. They may continue to have some control over resources allotted to their kin group. They may be required to give economic support to their mothers and especially to their sisters. They may also play a role in the upbringing of their sisters' children, who, by virtue of descent, are members of their kin group (their own children belong to the kinship group of their wives, the children's mothers).

For example, among the Trobriand Islanders of Melanesia, men are responsible for supplying their sisters (and their sisters' husbands) with yams (Weiner 1976; 1988). Although men tend the yam gardens, the "owner" of the produce is the man's sister. A man begins planting a yam garden for his daughter with the understanding that one of her brothers will take over the responsibility and continue to supply her and her family with yams after she marries. A man also assumes the role of authority and disciplinarian to his sisters' children rather than to his own because his sisters' children are members of his own matrilineal kin group.

Inheritance rules are strongly related to rules of descent. In societies with matrilineal descent, for example, resources and property are inherited through women. However, men may still control the allocation and disposition of resources, so that inheritance passes from one man to another within the matrilineal kin group. In such societies, the role of the mother's brother is enhanced because inheritance passes from one's mother's brother to one's sister's son. For example, among the matrilineal peoples of the Pacific Northwest of North America, such as the Tlingit, resources that matrilineal kin groups own and men use are passed from a man to his sister's son rather than to his own son.

Thus, matrilineal descent groups do not require the statuses of father and husband. Because of the matrilineal descent rule, children belong to the kin group of their mother. Women do not need to be married, and the identity of the father is not relevant to descent. In contrast, in patrilineal systems, the statuses of father and husband are critical in the determination of descent and the legitimacy of the offspring. Marriage is necessary for men because a man as husband claims the status of father to his wife's children through marriage. Marriage is also necessary for women in patrilineal systems because, through marriage, a woman's child may claim membership in a kin group and thus be granted legitimacy.

The institutionalization of strong, lasting, intense ties between husband and wife may not be compatible with the maintenance of matrilineal descent groups. In matrilineal societies, women's loyalties remain primarily with their own kin group and not with their husband. Men's loyalties, on the other hand, are split between the kin group of their wife and children and the kin group of their own family of descent. Men often are needed by their own kin group to perform economic, ritual, and political functions, and thus remain identified with and loyal to that group. In contrast, as noted earlier in this chapter, women in patrilineal societies may lose all or most attachments to their own kin group, and once married, they no longer have economic obligations to their family of origin.

The matrilineal Diné of the American Southwest recognize a man's continuing bonds and responsibilities to his natal family, especially to his mother and sisters. His integration into his wife's household is gradual and limited. His role in decision making in his own household is only slowly recognized and remains limited in scope. In contrast, the patrilineal

inheritance rules
Rules for the passage of land, wealth, and other property from one generation to the next.

These Trobriand Islanders are sorting yams from a patch that their father planted for their sister. A brother's responsibility is to supply his sister and her husband with yams.

IN THEIR OWN VOICES

Wedding Songs from North India

The poignancy of women's separation from their kin is vividly dramatized in North India at the moment of departure, when a newly married woman first leaves her natal home in the company of her husband and his male kin. Both men and women are apt to shed tears at the sight of the heavily veiled young woman being carried to a waiting vehicle. The women of the bride's village sing "departure songs" at the doorway. Many of these songs are commentaries on the fragile position of a woman in her husband's household and on her relationships with her blood relatives and her in-laws.

1. Refrain [bride's kin speaking]

   Dear girl, today you have left your father's house, today you have become "other".

   The streets in which you spent your childhood have today become "other".

[Bride speaking]

   My grandfather cries, my grandmother cries, the whole family cries.

   My younger brother cries, your sister born from the same mother has left and gone away.

[Verses are repeated with bride speaking, using different kin terms]

2. Two water pots are on my head.

   A beautiful golden pendant is on my forehead.

   Call me back quickly, Mother.

   Beg with folded hands.

   My heart is not here in my husband's mother's house.

   My heart is not here with this foreign man.

   Call me back quickly, Mother.

   Beg with folded hands.

   My friends still played with dolls together.

   But I went off to my in-law's house.

   Call me back quickly, Mother.

   Beg with folded hands.

[The first verse is repeated a number of times, changed only by the substitution of the names of other ornaments worn by married women.]

Explore more at www.myanthrolab.com

From Gloria Goodwin Raheja and Ann Grodzins Gold, *Listen to the Heron's Words: Reimagining Gender and Kinship in North India.* © 1994. The Regents of the University of California Press. Reprinted by permission.

● CRITICAL THINKING QUESTION

What do these songs suggest about the positions of women in their husbands' households?

Yanomamo of the Amazonian rain forests of Brazil and Venezuela emphasize men's control over their own households, wives, and children.

The bonds that may develop between children and their father may compete with the authority of the children's matrilineal descent group. Thus, in matrilineal systems, fathers may develop strong, intense, and lasting emotional bonds with their children, but their authority over their children is usually weak. Instead, men in the mother's kinship group, especially the mother's brothers, tend to exert authority over the child. The Diné and the Trobriand Islanders exemplify this pattern. In both groups, men are affectionate toward their own children but are not authority figures for them.

In matrilineal descent groups, the emotional investment of the father in his own children may be a source of strain because he owes his primary allegiance to the children of his own kin group, namely, his sister's children. In patrilineal descent groups, emotional ties between the mother and her children may be a source of strain. Because of children's early bonds with their mothers and a mother's affection for her children, children may not always identify with their father's group. Indeed, in strongly patrilineal societies, a mother and her children may form intense emotional ties as a buffer or refuge against the father's control. Nevertheless, these emotional ties do not directly threaten the father's dominant position as head of household.

In matrilineal societies, strong bonds between fathers and their children might threaten the mother's authority and the important position of other men in the children's matrilineal descent group. Men and women in the father's kinship group also play important roles, however. Among the Zuni of the American Southwest, for example, a baby's father's mother performs critical birth ceremonies honoring and protecting the child (Gill 1982). Immediately after a baby is born, its paternal grandmother comes to the home and recites protective prayers. She then bathes the baby, rubs ashes on its body, and remains with the mother and child for eight days. At sunrise on the eighth day, after washing the baby's head and sprinkling it with cornmeal, she takes the baby out to greet the rising sun, again reciting protective prayers.

In Japan, mothers encourage the development of strong, enduring emotional bonds, called *amae*, with their children, especially their sons.

Women also play an important role in funerals. At the end of life, the sister of a deceased's father has the responsibility of preparing the body for burial. She bathes the body, rubs cornmeal on it, and dresses it in new clothes, thus preparing the deceased for the journey to the afterworld.

The ritual participation of men's relatives dramatizes the connections between people and their paternal kin in a matrilineal system. Table 8.1 compares matrilineal and patrilineal descent groups in terms of the cultural and relational characteristics discussed in this section.

Other Forms of Unilineal Descent

Although most societies with unilineal descent trace kinship through either matrilineal or patrilineal principles, some societies reckon descent according to both patrilineal and matrilineal principles. In this system, called **double descent,** people belong to kinship groups of both mother and father. This system differs from bilateral descent because it is based on the existence of strongly delineated kinship groups. Some kinds of property

double descent
Kinship principle in which people belong to kinship groups of both their mother and father.

	Continuity	Status of Father and Husband	Strength of Marital Bond	Male Authority	Father-Child Relationship	Kin-Group Relationship
TABLE 8.1 A COMPARISON OF CULTURAL CHARACTERISTICS IN MATRILINEAL AND PATRILINEAL DESCENT						
Matrilineal Descent Groups	Women bear their own descendants and are crucial members of their descent group.	Not required.	Weak	Weak in marital household, but often strong in sister's household.	Strong emotional bond, little authority.	Father's kin group retains important ceremonial functions.
Patrilineal Descent Groups	Women bear their husbands' descendants and are secondary members of their own descent group.	Required for legitimacy of offspring.	Strong	Strong in marital household.	Great authority.	Mother's kin group relinquishes attachments and obligations.

parallel descent
Kinship principle in which descent and inheritance follow gender-linked lines so that men consider themselves descended from their fathers and women consider themselves descended from their mothers.

ambilineal descent
Principle of descent in which individuals may choose to affiliate with either their mother's or their father's kinship group.

lineage
A set of relatives tracing descent from a known common ancestor.

might be inherited along matrilineal lines and other kinds patrilineally. For example, the Yako of eastern Nigeria have a double descent system in which property is divided into patrilineal and matrilineal ownership (Fox 1984, 135). Patrilineal descent groups own farmland and grazing pastures whereas matrilineal descent groups own cattle and other livestock. People inherit these two different kinds of resources, one permanent and inalienable and the other consumable, from each of their parents.

The Inca of Peru had a system of **parallel descent,** in which descent and inheritance followed gender-linked lines, so that men considered themselves descended from their fathers, and women considered themselves descended from their mothers (Silverblatt 1987). Inheritance of property and rights to use land typically followed these parallel lines as well. That is, men inherited from their fathers, and women inherited from their mothers. Parallel descent and inheritance created strong gender identity and solidarity. Principles of parallel descent made sibling bonds important in kinship unity. Inheritance could flow through men from a mother's brother to sister's son and through women from a father's sister to brother's daughter.

Finally, some peoples have systems of **ambilineal descent,** in which individuals may choose to affiliate with either their mother's kinship group or with their father's group. People make this decision based on a strategic consideration of the territory, wealth, and social prestige of each group they are eligible to join. In societies of the South Pacific where such systems operate, people can affiliate only with one group during their lifetime, but their offspring may choose a different affiliation. In societies with ambilineal descent, as in the Pacific Northwest of North America, a person could make claims to be a member of multiple descent groups. For example, among the Kwakwaka'wakw (or Kwakiutl) of British Columbia, people could inherit material and ceremonial wealth, as well as access to food resource sites, through claims to multiple kin groups.

REVIEW ◉ Unilineal descent rules include matrilineal (reckoned through one's mother's line), patrilineal (reckoned through one's father's line), ambilineal (reckoned through either parent's line), parallel descent (reckoned by women through their mothers and by men through their fathers), and double descent (reckoned through both one's mother's line and one's father's line). A patriarchy is any society, especially one organized by patrilineal descent, in which men have dominant power and authority. Inheritance rules generally follow principles of descent.

UNILINEAL DESCENT GROUPS

Unilineal descent systems usually organize people into more structured groupings than are formed by bilateral descent rules. Four kinds of unilineal descent groupings are lineages, clans, phratries, and moieties. Some cultures have all four types; others have only one or two. All have in common a focus on lineal descent, following either the mother's or the father's line, so that the specific descent group may be a matrilineage or patrilineage, or a matriclan or patriclan, respectively.

Lineages

What do you know about the history of your descent group? How is this knowledge preserved?

The smallest kinship unit is a **lineage,** or a set of relatives tracing descent from a known common ancestor. In a matrilineal system, a matrilineage may consist of a female ancestor, her sons and daughters, her daughters' children, and her daughters' daughters' children. A patrilineage may consist of a male ancestor, his sons and daughters, his sons' children, and his sons' sons' children. The depth of lineages varies in different cultures. In some societies, people know the names of their lineage members for only a few generations, whereas people may have a known depth of nine or more generations in other societies. In some West African societies, the names and deeds of lineage members are memorized and passed on by word of mouth from generation to generation, in some cases covering 200 years or more. Written records create greater time depth. The Old Testament of the Bible, for example, contains a chronology of ancient patrilineages.

Among the Kwakwaka'wakw of British Columbia, lineages are named groupings that control access to resource sites such as ocean coastline, salmon streams, berry patches, and other foraging locations. Lineages also own ceremonial objects such as masks, crests, sacred songs, and dances. Each lineage has a founder shrouded in myth and a story of origin from an animal ancestor. Although membership in a lineage follows principles of descent, individuals can choose to affiliate with the group of their mother, father, or one of their grandparents. In the past, choices were made as they might best advance a person's social position. So, for instance, if one's maternal grandfather were a renowned chief, a person would choose to affiliate with his lineage. This is an example of the way that people can manipulate their positions in systems with ambilineal descent.

Siblings belong to the same patrilineage or matrilineage, depending on the descent rule in effect. New lineages are formed after the death of the senior parent. At that time, surviving sons in patrilineal systems and surviving daughters in matrilineal systems establish themselves as the heads of new groups. In societies where seniority contributes to one's social standing and prestige, sibling order determines the relative status of each new lineage. That is, an individual who is a member of the lineage of an elder son has higher status than an individual who is a member of the lineage of a younger son.

Exogamy and Endogamy

As mentioned previously, lineages have corporate functions in some societies. That is, they hold land in common, apportioning land and resources to member households. They may have formal procedures for selecting leaders and settling disputes among members or with members of other lineages. They also regulate marriage, forbidding unions between certain members. Most unilineal kin groups practice **exogamy,** or marrying out. In exogamy, people cannot marry members of their own lineage or clan but must forge alliances with members of other groups. Lineages and clans are usually exogamous.

A less common marriage rule is **endogamy,** or marrying in, as in parallel cousin marriage, for example. A **parallel cousin** is one's mother's sister's child or one's father's brother's child. In parallel cousin marriage, one of these sets of children would be one's preferred marriage partners—the mother's sister's children in a matrilineage and the father's brother's children in a patrilineage. Parallel cousin marriage is prevalent among Middle Eastern Arab societies with patrilineal descent. In patrilineal systems, brothers belong to the same patrilineage or patriclan, and descent is traced through men. Thus, through the endogamy rule, it is desirable for the children of brothers to marry. This "patrilateral" parallel cousin marriage conserves wealth within the patriclan. Thus, land, wealth, and resources stay within the kinship group rather than being dissipated or fragmented through inheritance among a wider group of claimants. Endogamous marriage patterns also solidify and strengthen bonds between brothers and avert conflicts over inheritance.

The opposite of a parallel cousin is a **cross-cousin:** one's mother's brother's child or one's father's sister's child. In cross-cousin marriage, these children would be preferred as one's marriage partners. As in parallel cousin marriage, this form of endogamy functions to strengthen a unilineal descent group and to concentrate resources within it. Figure 8.4 shows the types of cousins. Notice that cross-cousins are related through

exogamy
Marriage principle in which people cannot marry members of their own lineage or clan but instead must forge alliances with members of other groups.

endogamy
Marriage principle in which people marry members of their own group.

parallel cousin
A child of one's mother's sister or of one's father's brother.

cross-cousin
A child of one's mother's brother or of one's father's sister.

Does your kinship system distinguish between cross-cousins and parallel cousins?

FIGURE 8.4
Distinctions between parallel and cross-cousins.

Cross-cousins | Parallel cousins | Brother | Sister | Parallel cousins | Cross-cousins

Father's sister's husband | Father's sister | Father's brother's wife | Father's brother | Father | Mother | Mother's sister | Mother's sister's husband | Mother's brother | Mother's brother's wife

clans
Named groups of people who believe that they are relatives even though they may not be able to trace their actual relationships with all members of their group.

matriclans
Clans formed through descent and inheritance from women of their group.

patriclans
Clans formed through descent and inheritance from men of their group.

totem
An animal or plant believed by a group of people to have been their primordial ancestor or protector.

opposite-sex siblings (father's sister, mother's brother), whereas parallel cousins are related through same-sex siblings (father's brother, mother's sister).

Clans

Many cultures with unilineal descent organize their members into clans. **Clans** are named groups of people who believe that they are relatives, although they may not be able to trace all the actual relationships with clan members. Clans differ from lineages in this feature. That is, members of lineages can trace their exact relationship to all other members of the same lineage, but members of clans, which are much larger kin groups, can trace relationships only to close relatives.

Clans recruit new members through the birth of children. **Matriclans** obtain new members from women of their group (a child belongs to the clan of its mother), whereas **patriclans** recruit new members from men of their group (a child belongs to the clan of its father). Depending on the size of a society, clan size may range from several hundred members to many thousands. Although clan members cannot know all their relatives, because clans are named groups, members can always determine if strangers are related to them by asking them to identify their clan.

The conventions for naming clans vary cross-culturally. In some societies, clans are named after animals or plants; in others, they are named for locations. Where clans are named after animals, people often have beliefs about some mythic connection between the originators of the clan and the animal for which they are named. The origin myth might describe how the clan animal saved the human ancestors from some calamity or mated with the human ancestor to found the clan.

In some societies, clans are totemic. A **totem** is an animal or plant with a special spiritual connection to the members of its clan. Ritual prohibitions, or taboos, mark the relationship between clan animals and members of the kinship group. For example, people may not hunt or eat the animal that is their totem. By observing taboos, people express their respect for their ancestors. Totems also identify people in terms of their eligibility for marriage. In societies with clan exogamy, for example, two people with the same totem would not be allowed to marry.

Australian Aborigines believe that in mythic times, human ancestors had encounters with animals who endowed them with spiritual knowledge. The people honored these relationships by naming themselves after their animal protectors.

Thus, clans, like lineages, not only establish and organize relatives but also regulate social relations, especially marriage. Clans usually are exogamous, that is, people cannot marry someone belonging to their own clan. Such a marriage would be considered incestuous. Marriage rules may also preclude people from marrying into the clan of either parent. For example, according to marriage restrictions among the matrilineal Diné, people cannot marry someone of their own clan or father's clan, even though people are not members of their fathers' groups by rules of matrilineal descent. An even wider proscription bars people from marrying anyone whose father is a member of one's own father's clan. These rules may be a reflection of an early Diné pattern of bilateral descent that prevailed before their arrival in the Southwest and the change from a nomadic foraging society to one based on semisedentary farming. According to bilateral principles, one's mother's and one's father's relatives are treated the same.

In some cultures, lineages and clans have corporate functions, owning or controlling land and resources in common. Lineages and clans have continuity independently of their specific membership at any one time. Their structures and functions are perpetual, and their membership is continually replenished with the births of new members. Lineages and clans also usually regulate marriage, favoring some unions or forbidding others between members of the same or related groups. Other social functions of unilinear kin groups vary from culture to culture, such as making communal decisions, settling disputes, selecting leaders, and performing ritual obligations.

The Diné talk about clan relations by saying that people are "born in" or "born to" their mothers' clan and "born for" their fathers' clan. Therefore, two people who are "born for" the same clan are not permitted to marry. According to the Diné view, such a marriage would be incestuous. The importance of Diné clan membership is also reflected in the etiquette of self-introductions. When introducing themselves to another person, the Diné first identify their mother's clan and then mention their father's clan. These identifications precede a statement of one's personal name. This practice reflects the importance of situating oneself within a network of kin. Kinship relationships are the most critical influences on one's social being.

In addition to social features, clans often have corporate functions. In some societies, these functions may be similar to those of lineages, whereas in others, they may be more highly structured and formalized. Clan members may hold land in common, apportioning fields or resource sites to their members individually or by household. Clan-held territory can be periodically reapportioned to adjust to changes in resources as well as to changes in the size of households.

Clans usually have structured means of decision making and problem solving. They have recognized leaders who may be informally selected by public opinion and consensus or formally chosen by representatives of households or lineages. Such leaders have various functions in different societies. In some, they may serve as spokespersons for their clan when interacting with similarly structured groups. They may meet with leaders of other clans to make decisions that affect the whole community, to resolve interclan disputes, and to act as a unified body when dealing with outsiders. Clan leaders may also adopt strategies to help foster community cohesion and cooperation by exhorting members to behave properly and to help one another.

In some societies, clans and lineages are organized in a complex hierarchical structure in which different levels of the hierarchy have different social or political functions. Several peoples in Sudan, for instance, were organized into clans composed of **segmentary lineages,** hierarchically ranked according to the number of generations they encompassed. The Nuer, for example, were organized into about twenty patrilineal clans (Evans-Pritchard 1955; Sahlins 1961). Each clan was subdivided into four levels of lineage segments. The first subdivision was into large units, called maximal lineages. Each maximal lineage was segmented into smaller groups, called major lineages, and these were divided into still smaller groups, called minor lineages. Finally, the smallest segment, referred to as a minimal lineage, consisted of a group of relatives descended from a common great-grandfather or great-great-grandfather. In other words, a minimal lineage had a depth of four or five generations. Members of these smallest segments interacted frequently, lived near one another, and shared resources in times of need. Seniority in a lineage conferred influence and prestige. Lineage segments could temporarily become allies in times of conflict, but there was no established

Does your descent group have corporate functions?

segmentary lineages
Lineages organized in a hierarchical structure, ranked according to the number of generations they encompass.

leadership beyond the smallest lineage and no permanent structure that united them. However, when disputes arose, the parties concerned could appeal for support to members of structurally similar units in wider and wider networks. Therefore, the segmentary system was a flexible solution to the problem of resolving disputes within and between the twenty clans.

CASE STUDY

A Patrilineal Society: The Ganda of Uganda

The Ganda are a horticultural people who live in small villages of between thirty and eighty homesteads. Homesteads contain several huts, and the Ganda use yards between huts for socializing and tending domesticated animals. Most households consist of husband and wife, although some men have more than one wife. Co-wives usually reside in the same household, each having her own bedroom, but women sometimes have separate huts within the homesteads. Some men establish residences for their several wives in separate villages. In any case, women leave their natal village when they marry to live with their husband. The marital bond tends to be unstable today, although in the past, men had greater authority and control over their wives (Southwold 1965, 105).

The people's principal subsistence crop is bananas or plaintains, but they also grow sweet potatoes, yams, peanuts, and a variety of leafy vegetables, roots, and fruits. Men clear the fields for planting, but women do most of the subsistence farmwork. In the past, men hunted and fished to supplement the diet, but today people keep domesticated animals. They also obtain money by growing cotton and coffee for the export market.

Ganda society is organized around membership in clans and lineages. Descent is patrilineal, so children belong to the lineage and clan of their father. Clans are exogamous, husband and wife belonging to different kinship groups. There currently are forty-eight named clans (Southwold 1965, 95). Each clan is associated with particular animals thought to have a special relationship to the members who are not permitted to kill or eat their animal totem. Each clan is composed of several lineages, organized in a hierarchy of segments, or "segmentary lineages." There are four levels of segmentary organization: a clan; a segment of a clan is called a *ssiga;* a segment of a *ssiga* is called *mutuba;* and a segment of a *mutuba,* the smallest segment, is called *lunyiriri.*

In daily life, one's patrilineal kin are prominent in social interactions and share economic and personal responsibilities toward one another. People secure rights to use land and plant their gardens on the basis of membership in patrilineal clans. Men obtain these rights through descent from their fathers. Women obtain rights to gardens through marriage. That is, a woman plants her crops on her husband's land. After marriage, a man chooses his place of residence from among the villages in which he has rights through patrilineal affiliation, selecting acreage in clan-controlled territory.

Men prefer to marry women from villages other than their own to expand their network of relatives and allies. They also prefer to make a new homestead near more distant kin rather than live in their father's or their wife's father's village (Southwold 1965, 96). Ganda men wish to establish their independence from their fathers and also to avoid conflict with their brothers. Ties to other male relatives provide men with the aid and allegiance they expect from kin. Families may move to new villages if their needs or inclinations change.

Ganda clans have a number of corporate functions. Each clan and lineage has a leader who is responsible for administering his group. A council of the heads of subordinate lineage segments assists him. They settle disputes after hearing testimony from both sides. Decisions made by councils can be appealed to the council of the next higher segment in the lineage and clan hierarchy.

In the past, final appeals could be made to the highest authority or king, called *kabaka.* The corporate nature of clans is demonstrated in formal obligations that each clan owed to the *kabaka*. For example, clan members supplied bark cloth to the *kabaka* and herded his cattle. They also performed services for the *kabaka*'s mother, a person of great authority and prestige in her own right. And each clan provided boys to serve in the king's household.

Today the king's power has diminished, although he remains an honored and influential figure in Uganda. Clan councils and clan members supervise the activities of their group. If anyone commits an offense, the clan settles disputes and punishes its members. In the past, a clan could also suffer collective punishment, including the execution of all of its members, if one of its chiefs committed an offense against the *kabaka*.

Clans and lineage segments also own land in common. Each clan has an allotted territory in which its members have a right to live. Prominent members also have a right to be buried in clan territory. Residence on clan land is complicated because each clan owns territory in several areas. Therefore, people may make claims to diverse pieces of residential land, adjusting their needs to available acreage. People also base their decisions on the qualifications of political leaders who control each territory, choosing to affiliate where they might seek an advantage. Personal and political allegiance, then, contributes to settlement patterns as much as kinship connections do (Southwold 1965, 102).

In earlier times, clans controlled the distribution and inheritance of movable property from a deceased male clansman to his successor. The successor was formally chosen and ceremonially installed, taking the place of the deceased in kinship networks. He adopted the deceased's name and was called by kin terms appropriate to the deceased. He also received most of the dead man's property. Succession was inherited through kinship, but a man's eldest son was not eligible. In fact, there was a preference to bypass a man's sons altogether and instead choose a more distant patrilineal relative. This preferential pattern dispersed kinship ties and created linkages with more distant relatives, broadening one's alliances. The traditional rules of succession were changed in the late nineteenth century, so that a man's son could succeed him. Today, father to son inheritance is preferred. The practice of making wills setting out a person's wishes for the inheritance of his property has reduced clan power. Still, clan leaders influence the process through their prestige.

Collective principles underlying clan organization include the obligation to be hospitable to all members of one's clan. Men who move to new villages could expect to receive banana shoots from their resident clansmen to start their gardens. People are expected to be helpful to clansmen in economic difficulty or to help pay a fine for some offense that a clansman committed. Similarly, clansmen had the obligation of avenging an injured or murdered member of their group. Thus, clan membership remains fundamental in defining one's identity, organizing social relations, restricting marriage choices, and promoting ethics of hospitality and collective responsibility.

Explore more at
www.myanthrolab.com

Phratries and Moieties

Clans may combine to form larger organized kinship units, such as phratries and moieties. **Phratries** are groups of linked clans that usually are exogamous: in a phratry, people cannot marry someone belonging to a clan associated with their own clan. The phratry may or may not be named. Unlike clans, phratries rarely have corporate functions. In a phratry system, there are always three or more linked groups.

Like phratries, **moieties** are groups of linked clans, but they differ in that there are only two of them. A moiety system divides a society into two halves (*moiety* comes from the French word meaning "half"). Thus, in such a system, all clans are apportioned into two groups. Like clans and phratries, moieties are usually exogamous, although people in some cultures can marry within their moiety even though they cannot marry within their clan. Moieties generally are named groups. They may or may not have corporate functions such as owning land, resource sites, and other property communally. In some societies, moieties may have ceremonial functions.

phratries
Groups of linked clans that are usually exogamous.

moieties
Groups of linked clans that divide a society into two halves, usually exogamous.

CASE STUDY ●

Two Matrilineal Societies: The Mohawks and the Trobriand Islanders

THE MOHAWKS

The Mohawks are one of the member nations of the Iroquois Confederacy. Organized on kinship principles of lineage, clan, and moiety (Bonvillain 2001, 69–70), Mohawk descent is reckoned matrilineally so that children belong to the lineage and clan of their mothers. Until about 200 years ago, the ideal was for members of a matrilineage to live together. A household typically consisted of an elder woman, her husband, their daughters and daughters' families, and the couple's unmarried sons. Each nuclear group of parents and children had its own quarters within a large house separated by bark partitions. If a woman survived to be elderly, she might live to have great-grandchildren and be the head of a lineage of four generations. In other cases, a lineage might have a three- or only a two-generation depth. The deeper the lineage, the more respected was its leading woman.

Mohawk society is divided into three matrilineal clans named after animals: Bear, Wolf, and Turtle. In former times, clans practiced exogamy, stipulating that people could not marry members of their own clan. These rules created linkages between kinship groups through marriage alliances. Today, restrictions on marriage choices have largely been abandoned. However, Mohawks who want their marriage ceremony performed in the indigenous Iroquois religion now known as the Longhouse Religion must belong to different clans.

Mohawk clans controlled and distributed farmland to their members. Land was held in common but was allocated and farmed by lineages working collectively. The leading woman of the matrilineage was said to own land, not as her personal property but as collective control. Women in the household were given portions of land that they planted and harvested. Finally, clans owned the large communal houses in which their members lived. Today, the corporate functions of clans have disappeared, and land is owned individually as a result of European and American influences. Most households consist of parents and children, although some grandparents may reside with the basic family group. Private property and individual economic pursuits have largely replaced the collective labor of clan relatives.

Mohawk clans continue to have leaders, both women and men. Leading clan women, now usually referred to as clan mothers, are chosen informally through recognition of their intelligence, sound advice, and personal charisma. They lead by example and play a central role in protecting Mohawk lands, culture, and language. Clan mothers select the men who serve as clan chiefs. The women make their choices based on a man's intelligence, good judgment, even temper, and charisma. Clan chiefs represent their groups in community meetings and at meetings with representatives from the other Iroquois nations.

The Mohawk nation is divided into two moieties. The Wolf and Turtle clans form one moiety and the Bear Clan is the other. Like clans, moieties were formerly exogamous. They have mainly ceremonial functions, the most important of which is to prepare and conduct funerals for members of the opposite group. This custom reflects the Mohawk belief that people from the deceased's clan or moiety are too overcome by grief to be able to conduct a proper rite. Viewed as a feature of social structure, the reciprocal exchange of funerary duties symbolizes and enacts the mutual interdependence and unity of all members of the Mohawk nation.

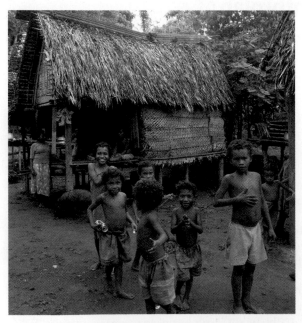

Children in the village of Kulukwekela on Kiriwina, the major island in the Trobriand Islands chain.

Iroquois Territory

Present-Day New York State

St. Lawrence River

Lake Champlain

Lake Ontario

Mohawk Homeland

Hudson River

THE TROBRIAND ISLANDERS

The Trobriand Islanders, inhabiting a chain of islands off the coast of New Guinea, have a kinship system based on matrilineal descent, assigning children to the descent group of their mothers. Trobrianders are divided into four named exogamous clans, each associated with various plants, animals, and fish (Malinowski 1929). People belonging to the same clan consider themselves kin and believe that they share personality traits. However, clans do not function as corporate groups and have no collective obligations. Even though people of the same clan should not marry each other in principle, such unions do take place without serious negative consequences (Weiner 1976, 51). In place of the clan, the "dala" (what Malinowski referred to as a "subclan") is the unit that is the focus of social, economic, and political activities. Sexual relations within the dala are forbidden. Each dala has a sacred narrative of origin from a female ancestor who, along with her brother, emerged from inside the earth.

Each original pair then had to find land for themselves and their dala descendents. Currently, all land is owned by a particular dala, including a village or more often a hamlet surrounded by farmland. Each dala also owns protective magic that ensures the fertility of its fields. Malinowski reported that members of dalas have a right by descent to reside in the hamlet associated with their group. However, not all people live in their ancestral village. Couples, however, often reside in the dala settlement of the husband. The Trobriand system of residence in the husband's ancestral dala is sometimes referred to as "avunculocal," but, although men move to the place where their mother's brother resides, they do not actually move into his household but instead set up a separate dwelling for their own family. Although resident dala members do not live in the same household, they cooperate in economic and ceremonial activities.

In practice, most men, however, remain in their father's hamlet, bringing their wife to live there. Weiner found that the only men who predictably moved to their mother's brother's hamlet were those who were positioned to become headman of the settlement (1976, 42). The difference in reports of residence patterns by Malinowski and Weiner (1976; 1988) may reflect either the contrast between idealized patterns and actual practices or changes over time, since Weiner's research took place fifty years after that of Malinowski. Weiner, though, does assert the absolute right of dala members to be buried in dala land regardless of where one resided during one's lifetime (1976, 43).

Trobriand men have to contribute to the support of their married sisters and sisters' children. When a man matures, he is allocated land to plant fields of yam, sweet potatoes, taro, bananas, and coconuts (Malinowski 1935). About 50 percent of the harvest is usually given as "urigubu" to his married sister's husband, but is intended for the support of the sister and her children. By principles of matrilineal descent, a man is not a member of the same kinship group as his own children but rather belongs to the group of his sister and her children. Urigubu symbolizes the claims that women have to the productive fields their dala controls, even though they do not live in those settlements. It further symbolizes the ties between sisters and brothers, that is, children of the same mother and members of the same kinship group. Sisters therefore have claims both to food and to the labor of their brothers. In this relationship, one sister is paired with one brother, not necessarily in order of seniority. If one sister has several brothers, the eldest is responsible for urigubu, although younger brothers are expected to contribute. If one brother has several sisters, he may rely on sisters' sons to help, but if none are old enough to do so, he will be responsible to provide for them all.

Each dala is ranked in relation to all others, not only to others within its own clan but to other dala in the three remaining clans as well. Each dala has a leader or "headman," usually the eldest male of the eldest lineage in the group. He is also generally the hamlet leader because his dala is localized in that settlement. Upon his death or retirement, the position of headman is passed to younger brothers in order of seniority or to a sister's son. Headmen allocate farmland to resident members of the dala and initiate the planting and harvesting cycles each year. They also have ceremonial duties to protect and enhance the fertility of their land. Finally, all the village households give them gifts of food, which are used as urigubu payments to the husband of the headman's sister and are redistributed to villagers and members of other communities in celebratory feasts.

Kinship plays a further role in territorial organization. The whole of Trobriand territory is divided into a number of districts (Malinowski 1929). Each district is led by a chief, the headman of the highest-ranking dala in that region. Chiefs are the only men allowed to have more than one wife. Typically, the chief's wives are sisters of the headmen of each village in his district. Because all men owe urigubu to their sisters' husbands, the headman of each village must deliver food to the district chief. The chief distributes this food to villages throughout his district in ceremonial feasts, thus enhancing his status through displays of generosity.

Men's power in Trobriand society is based on their control of land and of the statuses of hamlet headman and district chief. They exchange gifts of yams and ceremonial wealth. Women's power is based on their roles in the continuity of the dala and of dala identity. Through reproduction, women give birth to the future members of the dala and thus ensure its immortality. At the end of life, women's centrality is enacted through elaborate mortuary practices and exchanges of valuables (Weiner 1976; 1988). When a death occurs, rituals last for months. Exchanges of yams, products of male labor, are part of some of these rituals. But the most elaborate ceremonies focus on the exchange of women's valuables, such as skirts woven of banana leaves. One of the most prominent exchanges is that between a woman and the wife of the brother from whom she and her husband receive urigubu. Additional exchanges focus on other kinship relationships including acknowledging the father and father's sister of the deceased. Although these individuals are not members of the deceased's dala, ceremonial gifts to them symbolize a wider unity of kin and community.

Mohawk and Trobriand kinship systems exemplify different types of matrilineal societies. In Mohawk society, women are central figures in kinship groups and in the economic and social activities of the household. Men and women share decision making and work out a consensus on public policy. In Trobriand society, men occupy major positions of prestige and productivity whereas women preserve the continuity of kinship groups through birth and death.

Explore more at
www.myanthrolab.com

REVIEW   Four levels of descent organization are lineages (relatives who trace descent from a known common ancestor), clans (groups of people who believe but do not know that they are relatives), phratries (groups of linked exogamous clans), and moieties (two groups of linked clans that divide the society). Depending on the unilineal descent rule in effect, a lineage may be a matrilineage or a patrilineage, and a clan may be a matriclan or a patriclan. Segmentary lineages are subdivisions of lineages that are hierarchically ranked. Most unilineal kin groups practice exogamy, or marrying outside of one's lineage or clan, which broadens kin ties. Clan membership and marriage eligibility are often defined through the use of totems and taboos. Forms of endogamy, or marrying in, are parallel cousin marriage (one's mother's sister's children or one's father's brother's children are preferred marriage partners) and cross-cousin marriage (one's mother's brother's children and father's sister's children are preferred). Endogamy keeps resources within a kin group rather than broadening kin ties.

GLOBALIZATION

Within the past century, the economies of preindustrial peoples worldwide changed from subsistence activities to wage work, and the production of food and goods for cash and export to national and international markets. How have these changes transformed people's kinship behavior and relationships?

PATTERNS OF RELATIONSHIPS

In addition to establishing structured groupings of relatives, kinship systems also define and enforce expected behaviors among kin. Members of every society share ideas about appropriate attitudes and actions between any set of individuals, especially relatives. For example, we may be taught to be respectful of our elders and gentle with younger siblings. We learn how to behave with our relatives, what to say to them, and what not to say to them. We learn our rights with respect to them, and we learn what obligations we owe them. We learn that we must behave with respect, deference, and obedience toward some relatives, whereas we can exert influence and authority over others. With some relatives, we learn to comply with their wishes and acknowledge their dominance in other ways. With others, we may joke, tease, and act informally.

As with other social rules, or norms, there is great cross-cultural variation in the types of behaviors prescribed between relatives, and there may be variation within a society as well. Factors of gender, age, and class may have effects on people's attitudes and actions. The more homogeneous a society is, the more likely people will agree about appropriate behavior, whereas heterogeneous, or pluralistic, societies may have less consensus. Still, we can recognize general social values even if we do not behave in accordance with them as individuals.

Two common patterns that anthropologists observe in many cultures are avoidance relationships and joking relationships. Some societies focus on relationships of avoidance or respect. Gary Witherspoon (1972), writing about the Diné, also refers to this behavior as "bashfulness." In some societies, **avoidance relationships** characterize the relationship between parents-in-law and their sons-in-law or daughters-in-law. For example, among the Diné, a man does not speak directly to his mother-in-law and avoids being alone with her. If he needs to make a request of her, he asks his wife to intercede on his behalf. He defers to his mother-in-law, complies with her wishes and requests, and makes himself helpful and cooperative.

This kind of behavior is fairly common between men and their mothers-in-law in matrilineal societies. In such societies, men usually leave their natal homes when they marry and take up residence with or near their wife's kin. Circumspect, deferential, and "bashful" behavior helps minimize potential conflict that may exist between a man and his mother-in-law in matrilocal households. A new husband does nothing that could be interpreted as a challenge to her authority or of anyone else in the household. After many years in a stable marriage, a husband's behavior may be modified and he may begin to assert himself more with his wife's relatives. Eventually, he may take on leadership roles in the household.

Avoidance and respectful behavior on the part of a daughter-in-law toward her father-in-law is especially expected in patrilineal societies, where the married couple lives with the husband's kin. In this situation, a daughter-in-law lives in a household dominated by her father-in-law. Here, too, avoidance behavior mitigates any potential conflict. Rarely would a daughter-in-law have authority in such a household, but rather the potential conflict might concern the emotional allegiance of her husband, their son. The wife acts with deference and respect to avoid forcing the husband to choose sides between her and his parents. In strongly patriarchal societies, daughters-in-law are expected to be acutely aware of their subordinate status and act with extreme deference and obedience to their husbands' parents.

The pattern of **joking relationships** between certain sets of relatives involves reciprocal joking, teasing, and playfulness. Joking may take the form of flirtation, sexual innuendo, and even explicit sexual remarks. This type of behavior is found most commonly between certain kinds of cousins, as between cross-cousins in societies in which cross-cousin marriage is preferred. Joking behavior may also be common between individuals and their spouses' same-sex sibling. For example, a woman may joke with her husband's brother, and a man may joke with his wife's sister. In many cultures, these in-laws are potential spouses. They may be preferred marriage partners in the event of the death of one's own husband or wife. So, joking relationships between some types of relatives (cross-cousins, spouse's siblings) acknowledge the potential sexual or marital relationship that might be established between the individuals.

avoidance relationships
Patterns of behavior between certain sets of kin that demonstrate respect and social distance.

joking relationships
Patterns of behavior between certain sets of kin that involve reciprocal joking, teasing, and playfulness, sometimes taking the form of flirtation and sexual innuendo.

Do you have avoidance relationships and joking relationships among your kin?

All societies identify specific behaviors as appropriate for specific sets of relatives. Two common patterns of relationship are avoidance relationships and joking relationships. In patrilineal societies, bashful behavior and avoidance are common for daughters-in-law toward their fathers-in-law, whereas these are seen with sons-in-law toward their mothers-in-law in matrilineal societies. In some cultures, avoidance may also be prescribed for siblings. In some societies, joking relationships are common among cross-cousins, spouse's siblings, or others who may be potential sexual or marital partners.

PATTERNS OF CHANGE

One would think that the way we reckon our kin would be a permanent feature of our culture. As you have read, however, even kinship systems respond to changes in the way people make their living or adapt to their environment. One pattern of change, for example, involves shifts from matrilineal descent to other rules of descent, based on changes in men's and women's subsistence roles. Forces of cultural contact and change also bring about changes in the way people reckon their kin, identify their kin group, and interact with relatives.

CULTURE CHANGE ●─────────────────────────

CHEYENNE DESCENT

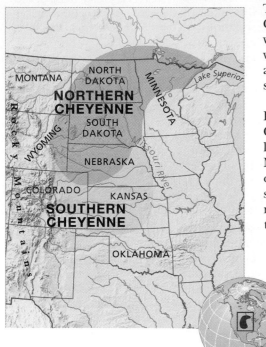

The Cheyenne currently reside on two reservations. The Northern Cheyenne live in Montana and the Southern Cheyenne share a reservation with the Arapaho in Oklahoma. These lands are the last refuge of people with a complex history, which reveals how changes in economic systems and adaptations to one's environment affect social life, even systems of descent (Eggan 1966).

The Cheyenne originally lived in the woodlands surrounding the Great Lakes in what is now Minnesota. When the French explorer René-Robert Cavelier, Sieur de La Salle encountered them in 1680, the Cheyenne were living in small villages with perhaps 200 or 300 residents along the upper Mississippi River west of Lake Michigan and Lake Superior. Their economy was based on foraging. Women gathered wild rice that grew along the shores of lakes and in marshes, and many other plants, tubers, fruits, and nuts. Men caught fish in lakes and rivers, hunted deer and small animals in the dense woodlands, and caught waterbirds.

It is likely that their social systems revolved around families and kinship groups organized by principles of bilateral descent, consistent with the usual practice of foraging peoples in the northern woodlands. These patterns are adaptive for situations of resource flexibility and nomadic settlement.

The Cheyenne began to leave this region in the late seventeenth century because of conflict with neighbors who were being pushed westward by British and French traders and settlers. By the early 1700s, the Cheyenne had settled in eastern North Dakota in the northern prairies. There, borrowing from other native peoples in the region, they began to grow some of their own crops, especially corn, beans, squash, and tobacco. They also adopted the descent systems of the nearby Mandans and Hidatsas. Like them, the Cheyenne began to trace descent through matrilineal kinship ties in which children belong to the kin group and clan of their mother, and couples reside with the wife's family after marriage.

The Cheyenne soon began to trade buffalo hides and deerskins for manufactured goods with French merchants who had opened a post in southern Manitoba. Then, sometime after 1750, the Cheyenne obtained horses from other native peoples, such as the Crow. The horses made an enormous difference in the Cheyenne economy, enabling people to travel farther to hunt and trade and to more easily transport their possessions.

By the late 1700s, conditions on the prairies worsened. Native peoples from the East and Midwest were pushing into the central prairies because Europeans and American colonists were taking more and more land. As eastern peoples moved westward, they came into Cheyenne territory, competing for the region's natural resources. By the early nineteenth century, the Cheyenne were building settlements west of the Missouri River on the plains of South Dakota. They spread west and south, expanding their territory to the Rocky Mountains. There, the Cheyenne established a way of life different from the one they left behind on the prairies. They no longer lived in permanent villages, but moved their camps several times each year. They no longer planted crops. Instead, they hunted animals, especially buffalo, and gathered wild plants. They also more fully utilized horses for hunting and as beasts of burden (Jablow 1950).

As a consequence of the changes in their economy and settlement patterns, Cheyenne social systems were also transformed. The need to maximize alliances, to widen one's network of kin, and to be able to shift membership in local and territorial units, which their new way of life required, led to the disappearance of matrilineal clans and the reemergence of bilateral descent.

Nevertheless, the Cheyenne continued to live in groups of households of families linked by relationships through women, and couples continued to reside with the wife's family after marriage. Each nuclear family resided in its own lodge, but groups related through women generally built their dwellings near one another. Such residential groupings often consisted of an elder couple, their unmarried children, married daughters, and the daughters' husbands and children. These family groupings also shared resources and foraging tasks. Men hunted together and provisioned the coresidential group. Most of the men working together were unmarried brothers still living with their parents or the brothers-in-law brought in after marriage to daughters of the group. Women worked with their sisters and daughters, gathering wild foods and sharing cooking and child care.

A bilateral system allows for an emphasis on generations rather than on lines of descent. That is, whereas unilineal descent separates members of a generation according to their degrees of descent from specific ancestors, bilateral descent focuses on similarities among the members of each generation across lines of descent. The kinship terms that the Cheyenne used emphasized these generational relations, as well as the social equivalence of people. For example, kin terms made no distinction between siblings and cousins other than by relative age (Hoebel 1978), and only elder siblings were distinguished by gender. Rather than referring only to a small set of relatives, the Cheyenne system extended the concept of family to many people.

When studying changes in kinship systems, we can see how sensitive these systems are as indicators of cultural transformation. Principles of kinship reckoning are consistent with other cultural practices. When behavior changes, kinship systems respond by altering the way that kin groups are organized. Changes may come from internal dynamics within a society as people adjust to their environments and develop and transmit new ways of living. They may also come from external sources when societies come into contact with others, either learning and adopting new systems voluntarily or being forced to adapt to more powerful peoples.

Patterns of change in kinship systems are based on the functions of kin groups in relation to environmental adaptations. Foragers tend to develop bilateral descent rules, for example. Kinship also changes in response to cultural adaptations. For example, people may adopt the kinship system of another people with whom they come into contact.

KINSHIP TERMINOLOGY SYSTEMS

Cross-cultural comparisons of categories of kin terms (words used to identify relatives) can sometimes reveal basic similarities and differences in worldview and experience. For example, people's social relations can be inferred from their kin terms. North Americans generally use the following words for relatives: grandmother, grandfather, mother, father, aunt, uncle, sister, brother, cousin, daughter, son, niece, nephew, granddaughter, grandson. Analysis of these words reveals systematic meanings. First, North Americans distinguish between generations: grandmother/mother/daughter/granddaughter. Second, they note the sex of relatives: mother/father, sister/brother. Third, they distinguish between direct or lineal relatives and collateral relatives (those who may have a common ancestor but are not lineally related): mother/aunt, son/nephew. These three sets of contrasts—of generation, sex, and lineality—define the features of their kin that are meaningful to North Americans.

Other cultures may select other aspects of kinship relationships to emphasize, revealing different priorities through a different set of contrasts. Differences in kinship terminology are not merely linguistic, but they reflect societal attitudes toward one's relatives. Individuals called by each kin term are understood to stand in particular social relationships and to have certain rights and obligations. The meanings of words, then, reflect one's social universe.

The Cheyenne, discussed in the Culture Change study, called siblings and cousins by the same kin term, using separate terms only for elder brother and elder sister. Younger

What are the names of the people you regard as members of your kindred? How are they related to you?

The Cheyenne used a system of naming relatives called the Iroquois system, which is based on the criteria of generation and age.

siblings of both sexes were called by the same term, a fact that further indicates the importance of seniority in Cheyenne society. Relatives in one's parents' generation were called by terms that distinguished between paternal and maternal relatives and between the genders. The same term was used for one's father, father's brothers, and his male cousins, whereas another term was used for one's mother's brother and mother's male cousins. A parallel set of terms was used for female relatives. Grandparents were distinguished only by gender—one term for all the men and another for all the women. The terms used for one's children were extended to the children of one's same-sex siblings and cousins. So, for example, a woman used the same kin terms for her son and daughter and the children of her sisters and female cousins. A man used these terms for his son and daughter and for the children of his brothers and male cousins. A different set of names was used for children of one's opposite-sex siblings and cousins. On the generational level of one's grandchildren, all related children were called by the same term regardless of gender or relationship.

The Cheyenne pattern of naming kin is an example of a type of **kinship terminology system** known as the Iroquois system. There are six types of terminological systems, and all people worldwide have a system of kin terms that fits one of these types. Each type is named for the culture in which it was first described. Kinship terms are more than just words for people, however; they define types of relationships. The **Iroquois system,** for example, emphasizes the difference between one's parents' same-sex siblings (MZD, MZS, FBD, FBS) and parents' opposite-sex siblings (MBD, MBS, FZD, FZS). As Figure 8.5 shows, one's parents are classed with their siblings of the same sex, and parallel cousins are classed with one's own siblings. Separate names for cross-cousins identify them as potential marriage partners. Children of anyone whom one calls mother and father are called sister and brother.

The Eskimo and Hawaiian Systems

The Eskimo and Hawaiian types of kinship terminology systems make the least distinctions among kin. The **Eskimo system** focuses on distinctions between the nuclear family and all other types of relatives and on gender distinctions. This system is likely to be associated with bilateral descent and is prevalent in both industrial and foraging societies.

As Figure 8.6 shows, the Eskimo system has separate terms for mother, father, sister, and brother. Siblings of one's parents are distinguished by gender, but whether they are related through one's mother or one's father is ignored. Relatives of one's own

kinship terminology system
System of terms used to address and refer to relatives.

Iroquois system
Kin terms that emphasize the difference between one's parents' same-sex siblings and parents' opposite-sex siblings, classifying parallel cousins with one's own siblings.

Eskimo system
Kin terms making distinctions between the nuclear family and all other types of relatives and on gender.

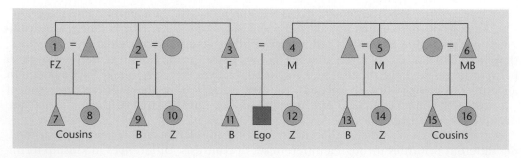

FIGURE 8.5

Iroquois Kinship System. According to the Iroquois system of kinship terminology, the father's brother (2) is called by the same term as the father (3); the mother's sister (5) is called by the same term as the mother (4); but the people numbered 1 and 6 have separate terms for themselves. Those people numbered 9-14 are all considered siblings, but 7, 8, 15, and 16 are cousins.

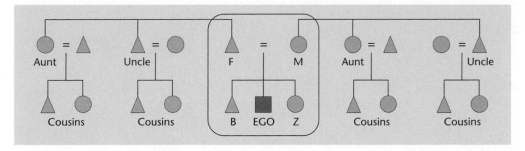

FIGURE 8.6
Eskimo Kinship System. The Eskimo system of kinship terminology emphasizes the nuclear family. Ego's father and mother are distinguished from ego's aunts and uncles, and siblings from cousins.

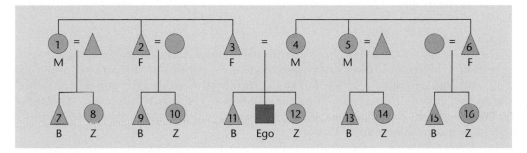

FIGURE 8.7
Hawaiian Kinship System. Ego calls the men numbered 2 and 6 by the same term as father (3) and the women numbered 1 and 5 by the same term as mother (4). All cousins of ego's own generation (7–16) are considered brothers and sisters.

generation outside of the nuclear family are all called by the same term: cousin. There are separate terms for one's own children and the children of one's siblings, based on gender: daughter, son; niece, nephew. And children of one's cousins are also called cousin, although some speakers may note different degrees of relationship.

The Eskimo system of terminology distinguishes among kin primarily by generation and gender. It highlights a distinction between the nuclear family and other relatives, but whether they are related through the mother or father is irrelevant. These terms are consistent with a social system that centers on the nuclear family as an independent, mobile, and potentially self-sustaining unit.

The **Hawaiian system,** in contrast, has even fewer terms than the Eskimo system because it makes distinctions only of generation and gender. For this reason, it is sometimes referred to as a generational system. As Figure 8.7 shows, all male relatives of the parental generation are called father and all females are called mother. Similarly, all male relatives of one's own generation are called brother and all females of one's generation are called sister. Sons and daughters include one's children and the children of anyone that one calls brother or sister.

The Hawaiian system is found in many societies of the Pacific and among speakers of Malayo-Polynesian languages. It is often associated with ambilineal descent, in which people can choose to affiliate with the kinship group of either their mother or father. In the Hawaiian system, marriage with cousins is impossible because all cousins are classified as siblings.

The Crow, Omaha, and Sudanese Systems

The Crow system is similar to the Iroquois system for the parental generation (see Figure 8.5). That is, father and father's brother are called by the same term and mother's brother is named separately; similarly, mother and mother's sister are called by the same term and father's sister is named separately. As Figure 8.8 shows, parallel cousins are called by sibling terms.

Hawaiian system
Kin terms making distinctions only of generation and gender.

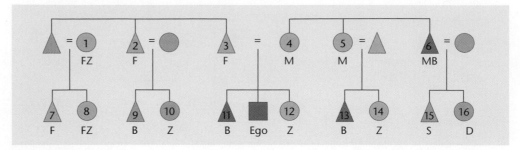

FIGURE 8.8
Crow Kinship System. The Crow system is obverse of the Omaha system. Those numbered 4 and 5 are merged under a single term, as are 2 and 3. Ego's parallel cousins (9, 10, 13, and 14) are considered siblings, whereas the mother's brother's children are equated with the children of a male ego and his brother.

The **Crow system** is used by some matrilineal peoples. Its key feature is that it extends the terms for father and father's sister to include cross-cousins on the paternal side—that is, the children of father's sister—and then continues the terms for father and father's sister in the female paternal line. Thus, the children of the father's sister are called father and father's sister. The effect of the Crow system is that it distinguishes descendants in the female line on one's father's side.

The Crow system also extends the terms for son and daughter to include cross-cousins on the maternal side, the children of one's mother's brother. That is, the children of one's mother's brother are called son and daughter. So, although one's cross-cousins are of the same biological generation as oneself, these relatives are given terms otherwise applied to one's own children.

The **Omaha system** follows the same principles as the Crow system except that it applies the generational skewing pattern to the descendants of one's mother's brother instead of one's father's sister. The Omaha system is found in some patrilineal societies where its purpose is to identify descendants of male members of the maternal side of the family.

Both the Crow and Omaha systems have a generational skewing pattern that focuses on lineal relatives not in one's own clan. So, in the matrilineal Crow system, the father's sister and her descendants are singled out because these are the people in one's father's clan. Similarly, in the patrilineal Omaha system, the mother's brother and his descendants are singled out because these are the people in one's mother's clan.

In the **Sudanese system,** which is rare, all kinship relationships are given separate terms. There are separate terms for members of the nuclear family, a distinctive word for mother's brother and another for father's brother, and separate words for mother's sister and for father's sister. Parallel cousins and cross-cousins are called by different terms. The Sudanese system allows individuals to negotiate their relationships with others and to affiliate with either side of their family, depending on their circumstances or personal inclinations.

Crow system
Kin terms used by some matrilineal peoples that extend the term for one's father and father's sister to include cross-cousins on the paternal side.

Omaha system
Kin terms used by some patrilineal peoples that extend the term for one's mother and mother's brother to include cross-cousins on the maternal side.

Sudanese system
Kin terms that give separate words for all kin relationships.

REVIEW ──◉ Kinship terminology system refers to how relatives are classified. It identifies a specific kind of relationship and the rights and obligations that that relationship entails. In the Eskimo system, which generally uses bilateral descent, the nuclear family is distinguished from other relatives. The Hawaiian system makes distinctions with gender and generation, and is often associated with ambilineal descent. The Iroquois system distinguishes between one's parent's same-sex and different-sex siblings and also between parallel cousins and cross-cousins. The Crow system, used in matrilineal societies, is similar to the Iroquois system except for the terminology referring to cousins. The Omaha system, found in patrilineal societies, is similar to the Crow system, with maternal cross-cousins called "mother" and "mother's brother" and paternal cross-cousins called "son" and "daughter." The Sudanese system is unique in that every individual has a distinct term. Differences in kin terms reflect differences in people's social systems.

Linkages Genealogy Projects

When doing ethnography in the field, cultural anthropologists gather kinship data for the people they are among. Then they link these data into a local genealogy. This information tells anthropologists who people are and how they relate to one another. As you have seen from this chapter, understanding a society's kinship system is also a key to understanding how people organize their communities, subsistence activities, and leadership. Kin relations are the building blocks of human social organization. But what can ethnographic and historical genealogies of particular people tell us about what it takes to build self-sustaining human communities?

Linkages is an international network of researchers concerned with assessing how economic development and culture change affect populations. These researchers create database sets of recorded kinship data and track long-term changes. The

researchers hope to show how knowledge of kinship must be taken into account when planning social policy and economic change. The knowledge gained from large-scale, long-term comparisons of kin networks may also help local communities participate more effectively in changes that affect their lives and cultural ecologies.

The data sets that Linkages maintains are diverse; among them are Alyawarra kin networks in Australia; kinship in Tlaxcala, Mexico; genealogies of U.S. presidents; Muslim elites in an Indonesian village; Old Testament patriarchs; Mbuti Pygmies of the Ituri Rainforest of Africa; genealogical censuses for band societies; and many others (for example, !Kung of Africa, Chechu of India, Ainu of Japan, Vedda and Semang of Indonesia, and Inuit of North America). Affiliates of Linkages around the world have established long-term field sites for tracking changes in kinship. Data are displayed in maps and graphs generated by special software, such as Large Network Analysis and Genealogical Information Manager. Studies on such a large scale have been made possible only though recent advances in computer technology and the Internet (http://eclectic.ss.uci.edu/~drwhite/linkages/linkages.html).

⊙ CRITICAL THINKING QUESTIONS

What do you know about your families' genealogies? How far back do they go? How might information about long-term changes in your networks of kin contribute to Linkages's goals?

CHAPTER SUMMARY

Kinship Systems

- In every society, people have systems for tracing descent and organizing kinship groups to which they belong.

Bilateral Descent

- In many cultures, people consider themselves related to both their mother's and their father's families. In such systems of bilateral descent, the most significant kin group is that of the kindred, a loosely defined network of relatives who interact on a regular basis and acknowledge mutual rights and obligations. Systems of bilateral descent are commonly found in foraging societies and in modern industrial nations. Bilateral descent is adaptive in societies where mobility is a premium. In small-scale foraging societies, people can make claims in a wide network of kin in times of scarcity and need, whereas people in modern industrial countries can loosen their kin ties to promote their economic independence.

Matrilineal and Patrilineal Descent

- In unilineal descent, people acknowledge relationships on either only their mother's (matrilineal) or their father's (patrilineal) side. Unilineal descent is common in farming and pastoral societies. About 15 percent of unilineal groups are matrilineal; the remainder are patrilineal.

- A few societies have (or had) systems of double descent, in which people could belong to kinship groups of both their mother and father. In systems of parallel descent, men were considered descended from their fathers and women from their mothers. Finally, systems of ambilineal descent allow people to affiliate with either their mother's or their father's kin group.

Unilineal Descent Groups

- Unilineal descent systems usually organize people into structured groupings of related people. The smallest such unit is a lineage, a specific set of relatives that trace descent from a common ancestor. A matrilineage consists of a female ancestor, her children, her daughters' children, her daughters' daughters' children, and so on. A patrilineage consists of a male ancestor, his children, his sons' children, his sons' sons' children, and so on.

- Many cultures with the unilineal descent organize their members into clans, named groups of people who believe they are relatives but cannot trace their actual relationship with all members of their clan. Whereas members of lineages can prove their common descent from a specific ancestor, members of clans stipulate or claim relationship. Clans also often forbid marital or sexual unions between their own members. Clans also often have corporate functions such as holding land in common and apportioning fields or resource sites to their members. They may choose leaders who speak for their group and have methods of making decisions and settling disputes.

- Phratries are groupings of linked clans that serve primarily to regulate marriage by forbidding unions between members. Moieties are even larger groupings, dividing the society as a whole into two groups or halves. Typically, people cannot marry members of their own moiety. Moieties are usually named groups that may have corporate and ceremonial functions and control land, resource sites, and other property.

Patterns of Relationships

- Kinship groups sometimes have preferences for the kind of marriage that their members may make. Clans are often exogamous, their members marrying people of other groups. Endogamy, in contrast, is a preference for marriage with a member of one's own group. In some societies, there are preferences for marrying particular types of cousins, either cross-cousins or parallel cousins. Marriage patterns tend to be consistent with other rules that organize social groups.

- Members of every society share ideas about what is deemed appropriate between any set of relatives. Some societies highly structure behaviors between certain relatives. At one end of the behavioral spectrum, some people are in a "joking" relationship, allowing them to tease one another and make critical or sexual remarks, whereas at the other end, people may be in an "avoidance" relationship, barring them from teasing or criticizing but instead encouraging them to be "bashful," avoiding eye contact, and refraining from speaking directly to or even being alone with a dominant person.

Patterns of Change

- Kinship changes as a result of changes in people's economic systems. Globalization also causes people to change how they reckon their descent and their rules for inheritance and kin relations.

Kinship Terminology Systems

- Kinship terminologies are words that people use to refer to and address their relatives. Worldwide there are a small number of such sets of terminologies. Kinship terms are labels that symbolize relationships, including the rights and obligations that relatives have for one another. The kinds of systems used reveal the kinds of distinctions that people make about which relatives are similar in status and relationship.

KEY TERMS

kinship system 182
consanguines 182
affines 182
fictive kin 182
rules of descent 183
bilateral descent 183
unilineal descent 183
kindred 183
matrilineal 185
patrilineal 185

patriarchy 186
inheritance rules 187
double descent 189
parallel descent 190
ambilineal descent 190
lineage 190
exogamy 191
endogamy 191
parallel cousin 191
cross-cousin 191

clans 192
matriclans 192
patriclans 192
totem 192
segmentary
  lineages 193
phratries 195
moieties 195
avoidance
  relationships 199

joking relationships 199
kinship terminology
  system 202
Iroquois system 202
Eskimo system 202
Hawaiian system 203
Crow system 204
Omaha system 204
Sudanese system 204

REVIEW QUESTIONS

1. What is bilateral descent? What are some cultural correlates of this descent rule in societies that practice it?

2. What are the two types of unilineal descent? With what kinds of societies is unilineal descent associated?

3. How would you compare and contrast the descent groups that are created by the application of descent rules? How are kindreds different from lineages?

4. What are the distinctions among lineages, clans, phratries, and moieties?

5. What patterns of relationships among kin group members do anthropologists observe?

6. How, and why, do kinship systems change?

7. What are the six methods of classifying relatives? What are the distinguishing characteristics of each?

8. How are kinship systems and rules of descent functionally interrelated with other social systems, such as economic and political systems?

PEARSON myanthrolab EXERCISES

To complete the following exercises and activities, you must log in to www.myanthrolab.com and select your current textbook.

1. In the **Explore** tab of Chapter 8, click on the *NPR Audio Programs Broadcast* tab and go to *Theme 20: Marital Residence and Kinship*. Listen to one of the programs in this section and complete the short answer exercise that accompanies the program.

2. In the **Practice** tab, click on *Activities* and complete the *Kinship Patterns* animation.

3. In the **Research Tools** section on the home page, click on the *Research Navigator*™ link and enter the

Anthropology database to find relevant and recent scholarly and popular press publications. For this chapter enter the following keywords: *kinship system, matrilineal, patriarchy, lineage,* and *totem.*

4. Enter the **MyAnthroLibrary** section on the home page to read more about topics and cultures that are discussed in this chapter. Suggested readings include:

Varieties of Marital Relationships by Lewellyn Hendrix

Nandi: From Cattle-Keepers to Cash-Crop Farmers by Regina Smith Ololer

MARRIAGE AND THE FAMILY

A woman had an only son who became grown up and had not been married yet. She wanted to find him a bride, but he always told her, "Later, not now. . . ." One day his mother said to him, "Listen, my son, I've grown old and become tired of household work. You must get married before I die."

He said to her, "Well! Find me a good girl from a good house."

She . . . found him a girl from one of the most notable houses in their town and he married her.

When the wedding [party] was over and after seven days or so, he went back to his shop to work, while his mother stayed with his wife. "Listen, in this house [you] don't open what is closed or close what is opened, nor uncover what is covered or cover what is uncovered, nor unwrap what is wrapped or wrap what is unwrapped, nor unfold what is folded or fold what is unfolded. Do you understand?"

The girl, his wife, said, "Yes."

Days passed with things like that. His mother is everything in the house; his wife works all day while his mother orders her around. When the man returns home, his mother would set the dinner for him and if he would say "[Let us] call [his wife] to eat with me," his mother would answer him, "This can't be. She is still new in the house. She would get bold with us. Wait for a few more days."

After a few more days her son would say, "Let her come and eat with me."

His mother would say, "She hasn't been broken to our house yet. She does not need to eat for she has been eating all day."

He would say to his mother, "May God extend his grace upon us. Let her eat as much as she wants," and [he] used to eat only until he was half-full and leave some of the best food to his wife. His mother would hide it and would give her only hard bread and water.

The girl grew sicker and weaker by the day. Whenever her husband asked her, "What is the matter with you?" she would answer, "Nothing."

One day he said to one of his friends at the store, "By God, my wife is becoming sick. Every day she is getting thinner and paler. I am afraid she doesn't want me. Ever since she set foot in my house, she doesn't speak to me, and she is always sad."

His friend said to him, "I'll tell you what to do to see whether she wants you and wants to stay in your house, or whether she hates you and would like to return to her father's house. After dinner swear by God that she joins you and your mother for the coffee, then break wind. If she laughs at you, she doesn't care for you and you should send her back to her father's home. If she doesn't, then she is ill."

That same day after the man ate his supper and thanked his God, he said to his mother, "Call [his wife] to have coffee with us." He swore by God, and his mother went to call her. As they were drinking their coffee, he broke wind. His mother laughed, but his wife didn't and kept on drinking until she finished her cup. . . .

The following day he told his friend about what had happened. His friend said to him, "Your wife is hungry. Your mother is starving your wife."

He built a new house for his wife and moved out of the old one and got his mother a servant.

Excerpts from Richard Dorson, *Folktales Told around the World,* pp. 166–168. © 1975. Reprinted by permission of the University of Chicago Press.

———————

This narrative from Iraq tells of the conflict and tensions between a new bride and her mother-in-law. In the story, the young husband is beset with divided loyalties. His respect for his mother is tempered by his concern for his wife. The wife is obedient and deferential to the older woman. The narrative raises issues of power for women in patrilineal and patriarchal households. The mother tries to exert power over her daughter-in-law, but in the end she has less authority than her son because he is the man, the recognized head of the family. He chooses to protect his wife's interests and allies himself with her.

- How do anthropologists define marriage and family?
- What are the characteristics of nuclear and extended families?
- How do residency patterns relate to other aspects of a culture?
- How do marriage rules extend kinship while observing incest taboos?
- What are some theories about the origins of the incest taboo?
- How is marriage a rite of passage?
- What are some social functions of marriage?
- What forms of marriage are known to exist?
- How is marriage a form of political alliance and economic exchange?

household
A group of people occupying a common dwelling.

family
A married couple or other group of adult kinfolk who cooperate economically and in the upbringing of children, and all or most of whom share a common dwelling.

This Iraqi family unit was formed not only through rules of descent but also through marriage rules. The family unit at the household level consisted of a man, his widowed mother, his wife, any children borne by his wife, and the man's unmarried siblings. This chapter explores marriage and the family and how they interrelate with other elements of culture in a society.

Kinship systems and family arrangements are basic elements in all societies. They are among the topics of central concern in anthropology because they help structure people's daily lives and lay the foundations for how they are integrated into their communities. However, societies differ greatly in how families are formed, about who constitutes a family, and about the rights and obligations of family members toward one another. As we shall see, variations in family organization are not random but are consistent with economic and social needs. Thus, different types of families are preferred in different types of societies.

DEFINING MARRIAGE AND FAMILY

People are social beings. We live together in groups, work with others, and form emotional bonds with other people. Although some individuals live alone at any given time in every society, most people live with others during all or most of their lives. Most people who live together are members of families. In everyday speech, we use the word *family* casually to refer to our relatives without specifying how we are related to these people. Even anthropologists do not agree on a single or concise definition of family.

Anthropologists tend to make a distinction between family and household, although people often use the two words interchangeably. A **household** refers to a group of people occupying a common dwelling. The Iraqi man, his wife, and his mother are members of a household. The term *homestead* refers to multiple dwellings occupied by related and interacting people.

As you read in Chapter 8, members of families are related either through descent (consanguines) or marriage (affines). For example, one's grandparents, parents, aunts and uncles, siblings, children, and cousins are all consanguineous relatives, whereas one's spouse and all the people called in-laws are affinal relatives. North Americans differ in the ways they apply the word *family* to many of these relatives. Some people use the word to encompass all their relations, but others restrict the term to refer to close relatives with whom they interact regularly.

A useful starting definition of **family** is one given by anthropologist Kathleen Gough (1975, 52). She defines the family as a "married couple or other group of adult kinfolk who co-operate economically and in the upbringing of children, and all or most of whom share a common dwelling." In this definition, a family is more than just a couple. Gough's definition includes several important features of family, stressing the cooperative links among members who share social and economic responsibilities. On this basis, the Iraqi man, his wife, and his mother constitute a family.

There are other definitions of family, however, and family members need not occupy the same household. Some members of polygynous families may occupy different households within an area. In addition, although marriage is the most common bond that creates families, marriage itself is not a required component of family. Heterosexual or gay couples that are not married also constitute families. The single-parent family of parent and child is perhaps the smallest family unit (Fox 1984).

Although issues of family composition, family life, and "family values" are controversial in the current climate of North American social and political discourse, the American Anthropological Association has taken a strong position supporting the legitimacy and

...oommates share a household. Unlike family households, ...es typically do not share all economic resources and have no ...ns of mutual obligations or an enduring relationship.

viability of all family types. In its statement, issued in 2003, the association said the following:

> More than a century of anthropological research on house-holds, kinship relationships, and families, across cultures and through time, provide no support for the view that either civilization or viable social orders depend upon marriage as an exclusively heterosexual institution. Rather, a vast array of family types can contribute to stable and humane societies.

The family is a basic unit of economic cooperation and stability. Members of families usually perform at least some-what different economic tasks, a pattern that highlights the interdependent relationships among family members. They also pool all or at least some of their resources for the sur-vival of the group.

These indigenous Mexican families in Tzintzuntzan are celebrating the Day of the Dead.

The family serves social needs as well, providing members with companionship, emotional support, and assistance. Fam-ilies also function in the propagation and survival of society. They provide the context for biological reproduction and for the training and enculturation of children. Families function universally as vehicles for socialization into expected roles and goals of their own or adopted children. Children learn what is appropriate by observing adults and by overt learning and practicing skills for roles they will assume as adult women and men. In the context of their families, children learn their gender identity and their role in households and communities. Through observa-tion of social relations between their parents or among all adults in their households, they learn whether men and women have equal rights to contribute to discussions and decision making. They also deduce social rights through the ways that conflicts are resolved. Girls and boys also learn whether they can expect emotional and economic support from their natal kin groups once they reach adulthood and form their own families.

In addition, families are decision-making groups. Members of families consult with one another, make decisions together, and may function as political units with others in their communities to establish and provide leadership. In some societies, positions of leadership are inherited within families. Everywhere, inheritance of property and the transmission of cultural knowledge take place within family units.

All societies contain units recognized as families, but there are differences in the ways in which families are formed. Throughout the world, most families are formed through marriage. *Marriage* is another word that we use casually with reference to a union between a man and a woman, but anthropologists have not settled on an uncontested definition of marriage. There is even some debate in the field about whether marriage and the family are universal constructs. Still, even if we accept that marriage is a recognized social status in most, if not all, cultures, there are differences in the ways that marriages are contracted and in the relationships between the spouses.

Marriage is generally understood as a socially recognized, enduring, stable bond between two people who each have certain rights and obligations toward one another. These rights and obligations vary from culture to culture, but are likely to include some common features. For example, married partners have the right to expect to have a sexual relation-ship with each other, although the number of partners may vary. In plural marriages, for example, a person may have more than one spouse. In most societies, husbands and wives have obligations to assist one another in rearing children and providing for their house-hold. They share economic resources and provide shelter, clothing, and household equip-ment. Marriage also establishes bonds between groups of kin (the wife's relatives and the husband's relatives), who also have rights and obligations toward one another.

Through marriage, men and their kinship groups may claim rights to children. For this reason, as pointed out in Chapter 8, there is a fundamental difference in the empha-sis on marriage in patrilineal groups, where descent and inheritance are traced through men, and matrilineal groups, where they are traced through women. In matrilineal soci-eties, kinship groups obtain new members when the women of the group give birth to chil-dren. A mother's child automatically becomes a member of her own kin group, whether she is married or not. In contrast, patrilineal kinship units cannot obtain children from their own women because a child does not belong to its mother's kin group but to its

Based on your experience in your family, what are some specific expressions of the functions of the family as a social institution?

What do you think might be some sources of disagreements about the definitions of marriage and family?

marriage
A socially recognized, stable, and enduring union between two adults that publicly acknowledge their rights and obligations and form a new alliance between kin groups.

father's. In this case, marriage serves the purpose of securing a stable relationship between men and women from outside their kin group. Marriage also provides for the establishment of what Kathleen Gough calls "social fatherhood." **Social fatherhood** may or may not be the same as biological paternity. One's social father is the man who fulfills the responsibilities of parenting, just as stepparents and adoptive parents are social parents.

REVIEW A family is a group of people related by blood or by marriage who live together, raise children, and share economic and other social responsibilities. A household consists of relatives and, often, nonrelatives who live together and share economic responsibilities. In all societies, enculturation of children and the inheritance of property and status take place within families. In most societies, families are formed through marriage, a public acknowledgment of a couple's commitment and a new alliance between kin groups. Marriage enables men in patrilineal societies to add children to their kin group, whereas children in matrilineal societies are automatically in their mother's group. Marriage also allows for social fatherhood.

FAMILIES AND IDEAL TYPES

Anthropologists differentiate between one's family of orientation (the family one grows up in) and one's family of procreation (the family one founds as an adult). In addition, anthropologists have long used a classification of ideal family types that is generally descriptive of different family structures. Many real families diverge from these types in some way or to some degree. Nevertheless, the types are useful because they broadly correlate with other aspects of culture. The nuclear family, extended family, joint family, and single-parent family are some of these types.

Nuclear Families

Among nomadic foragers and members of industrial societies, most families are of the type that anthropologists call "nuclear." A **nuclear family** consists of one or both parents and their children, although another relative, such as a grandparent or an unmarried sibling of one of the parents, may reside in the same household for a time. The nuclear family is the characteristic family form of societies with bilateral descent, which, as discussed in Chapter 8, are typically either foraging or industrial societies.

A nuclear family structure provides certain benefits. For instance, it has the advantage of mobility. The relatively small number of people in a nuclear family unit can easily separate themselves from the larger community in which they live. In foraging societies, nuclear families aid in survival in conditions of scarcity. If there are insufficient resources to support a large group, nuclear families can go their own way, dispersing into a large territory and exploiting meager resources. In industrial societies, nuclear families allow for economic independence and promote the loosening or weakening of wider kinship bonds. This pattern is advantageous for societies where competition and individual advancement are goals.

Comparatively, small families are an advantage for people in both foraging and industrial societies. Family size is limited among foragers in order not to exceed the carrying capacity of the environment. In addition, infants and young children need to be carried when traveling, which favors the spacing of births. Because foragers lack grains and animal milk as foods for babies, mothers nurse their children for as many as three or four years. Therefore, closely spaced children have a low chance of survival. As well, frequent pregnancies and deliveries have a negative impact on the health and long-term survival of mothers. In industrial societies, small nuclear families have the mobility necessary for leaving larger kin groups and moving from job to job and region to region. Distant relatives are unlikely to make claims for assistance, and if they do, families can easily avoid contact with them or deny their requests for aid. Small families are an advantage because dependent children are

social fatherhood
The status of a man who fulfills the responsibilities of parenting, a role that may or may not be the same as biological paternity.

nuclear family
Family consisting of parents and their children.

This Japanese nuclear family is enjoying a day out.

economic liabilities in modern industrial economies where work requires strength, stamina, and skilled training and where laws forbid or restrict child laborers.

Nuclear families risk social isolation. Family reunions in industrial societies may be seen as equivalent to seasonal gatherings of larger kin units among nomadic foragers. **Single-parent families** in industrial societies are formed as the result of divorce or the death of a spouse and parent. Others develop when the parents do not marry or live together. In the United States, most single-parent households consist of mother and children. According to U.S. Census statistics for 2000, 12 percent of all households were headed by a single mother and 4 percent had a single father as head. Single-parent households, especially those headed by women, are more likely to have incomes near or below the poverty line. Their economic difficulties stem from a common problem of nuclear families: Economic independence accrues only to people with resources and jobs. For people with meager incomes, the isolation of single-parent families increases the difficulty of seeking support from kin. In contrast, in extended family systems, people who lose or lack a spouse can rely on a large network of relatives for assistance.

This four-generation extended Polish family, grouped around their 96-year-old matriarch, is characterized by vertical ties between generations.

Extended and Joint Families

Family systems based on an extended family principle are more common worldwide. Extended family arrangements are especially prevalent in farming and pastoral economies. **Extended families** consist of three or more generations of people, extending the family vertically. Typically, an extended family unit is composed of an elder parent or couple, their unmarried children, some of the married children, and the children's spouses and children. As you read in Chapter 8, rules of descent determine which adult married children remain with the parents. That is, in patrilineal systems where descent and inheritance are traced through men, more often the sons remain with their parents, whereas daughters leave home after marriage to reside with their husbands' families. In matrilineal societies, daughters remain with their parents after marriage, but married sons leave to join their wives' families.

single-parent family
Family consisting of one parent (either mother or father) and her or his children.

extended family
Family formed with three or more generations, for example, parents, children, and grandparents.

CULTURE CHANGE

THE CHANGING AMERICAN FAMILY

Family types are responsive to changes in productive modes and general social values. In the United States, the percentage of family units conforming to the idealized model of husband, wife, and children has declined since the mid-twentieth century. The idealized nuclear family model is itself a product of economic needs and adjustments made during the nineteenth and twentieth centuries as capitalist and industrial production dominated North American society. Other kinds of family units have now become more common. The number of blended families, based on remarriages and the combining of children from previous marriages, has also increased.

Growing rates of divorce have also increased the number of single-parent households. As women have gained more economic independence, the financial need to remarry after divorce or the death of a spouse has declined. More people also never marry. Many households consist of a man and woman involved in a long-term relationship who choose not to marry. Such couples may or may not have children. Another less common but not unusual type of household consists of two people of the same gender who share a sexual relationship, economic responsibilities, and other attributes of family life such as child rearing.

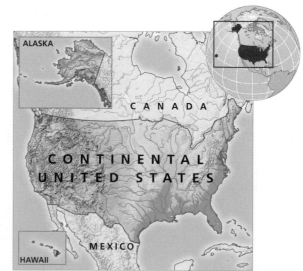

Census statistics indicate changes in U.S. household composition, marital status, and numbers of children over the last several decades. Tables 9.1 through 9.4 present some of the relevant data.

As the figures in Table 9.1 indicate, the percentages of people "Never married" and "Divorced" have risen between 1980 and 2006, whereas the percentage of people "Married" has declined.

The size of families has also decreased between 1980 and 2006. More couples are having fewer children than in the past. Indeed, the number of childless couples has increased, as Table 9.2 demonstrates.

TABLE 9.1 MARITAL STATUS OF THE U.S. POPULATION, 1980–2006 (AS PERCENTAGE OF TOTAL, BY SEX)

	1980		1990		2000		2006	
	Male	Female	Male	Female	Male	Female	Male	Female
Never Married	27.3	21.1	32.1	22.5	32.3	23.4	28.6	22.0
Married	67.1	64.3	60.9	62.4	59.7	60.7	59.9	58.5
Widowed	1.6	7.1	1.5	6.5	1.6	6.5	2.5	9.9
Divorced	4.0	7.6	5.5	8.5	6.4	9.3	9.1	11.6

Source: U.S. Census Bureau, *Statistical Abstract of the United States, 2001,* Table 49; *2006,* Table 55.

TABLE 9.2 NUMBER OF CHILDREN PER HOUSEHOLD

Number of Children	1980	1990	2000	2006
No children	48%	51%	52%	53%
One child	21	20	20	20
Two children	19	19	18	18
Three or more children	12	10	10	9

Source: U.S. Census Bureau, *Statistical Abstract of the United States, 2001,* Table 58; *2003,* Table 71; *2006,* Table 67. Table 9.3 shows that the composition of households also changed from 1990 to 2006.

TABLE 9.3 COMPOSITION OF HOUSEHOLDS

Type of Household	1990	2000	2006
Family Household	71%	69%	68%
Married couple family	56	53	51
Single father	3	4	4
Single mother	12	12	12
Nonfamily Household	29	31	32
Living alone	25	26	27
Males	10	11	11
Females	15	15	15

Source: U.S. Census Bureau, *Statistical Abstract of the United States, 2001,* Table 53; *2006,* Table 60.

TABLE 9.4 NUMBER OF PEOPLE PER FAMILY				
Size of Family	1980	1990	2000	2006
Two people	39%	42%	44%	45%
Three people	23	23	22	23
Four people	21	21	20	19
Five people	10	9	9	9
Six people	4	3	3	3
Seven or more people	3	2	2	2

Source: U.S. Census Bureau, *Statistical Abstract of the United States, 2003*, Table 67; *2006*, Table 68.

The number of cohabiting unmarried couples has also increased. In 1980, there were 1,589,000 such couples, but by 2000, there were 4,486,000 unmarried couples, and the number rose to 5,966,106 by 2006 (U.S. Census Bureau, *Statistical Abstract of the United States, 2001*, Table 52; *2006*, Table 62).

Finally as Table 9.4 indicates, the number of people per family has declined since 1980.

More families with children consist of single parents. In 1990, 71.9 percent of all families with children contained two parents; by 2005, the percentage had dropped to 67.4 percent. In 2005, mothers headed 26.4 percent of all families with children whereas fathers headed 6.2 percent (U.S. Census Bureau, *Statistical Abstract of the United States*, Table 63). In addition, although the actual numbers remain small, the growth of stay-at-home fathers reflects changes in gender expectations. In 2006, of all married couple families with children under 15 years old, 24.3 percent had stay-at-home mothers while .7 percent had stay-at-home fathers. This represents a more than doubling of stay-at-home fathers since 1995 (U.S. Census Bureau, *Statistical Abstract of the United States*, Table 64).

Census figures also indicate a sharp increase in the number of same-sex households between 1990 and 2006. This may reflect both real growth in same-sex households and a greater likelihood that their members self-report. In 2006, 776,943 households consisted of same-sex partners. Of these, 413,095 were male couples and 363,848 were female couples (U.S. Census Bureau, *Statistical Abstract of the United States, 2006*, Table 62). Although same-sex marriages are legal in Massachusetts, Connecticut, and then Iowa and Vermont in 2009, the U.S. Census Bureau reclassifies legally married same-sex couples as "unmarried, same-sex partners" in compliance with the Defense of Marriage Act.

Data reveal that 70 percent of all children live with two parents (Roberts 2008). Although this is a decline from the 85 percent in 1970, it is still a sizable majority. Approximately 65 percent of all children live with two married parents, and about 60 percent live with their biological mother and father. In 2004, 23 percent of children lived with their mother only (up from 11 percent in 1970). The figures on children and household composition have remained fairly steady since 1990, indicating that the familial effects of social changes of the 1960s and 1970s have leveled off. Only 4 percent of the nation's children live in households without either parent, and about 2 percent are living with their grandparents only. There are marked disparities in children's experiences for different racial and ethnic groupings; for example, 87 percent of Asian children, 78 percent of non-Hispanic white children, 68 percent of Hispanic children, but only 38 percent of African American children live with two parents.

All of these data are consistent with quantitative and qualitative studies soliciting Americans' attitudes toward marriage and family life. Several large-scale research projects from the 1960s through the late 1990s reveal that, although most Americans ". . . value marriage, children, and family life, these institutions are now much more voluntary and less obligatory . . . leading to more individual freedom in these areas" (Thornton and Young-DeMarco 2001, 1031). Examples of these shifts include more acceptance of divorce, of unmarried couples living together, and of unmarried women having children.

A family that is extended laterally rather than vertically is referred to as a joint family, which is much less common. A **joint family** typically consists of siblings who combine their families to share work and resources, such as two or three brothers, their wives, and their children.

Extended and joint family systems have the advantage of establishing a more or less stable group of people who can share resources, household tasks, and subsistence work, and provide emotional support and material aid. However, because many people live together, conflicts may develop. Intergenerational tensions may arise because of the authority of the eldest couple over their adult children, or sibling rivalry may develop in a joint family compound. Conflicts over authority, inheritance, and loyalty are common. In addition, extended and joint family systems may lead to social difficulties for in-marrying spouses. Women moving in with their husbands' kin, for example, may face demanding mothers-in-law. Economic cooperation and interdependence is a prominent feature of extended and joint families. For this reason, people in industrial societies may form this type of family unit on a temporary or permanent basis when they are unemployed or otherwise lack resources.

> **Which ideal type best characterizes your family? What are some benefits and challenges of life in this type of family in relation to the larger culture?**

REVIEW Ideal family types include nuclear, single-parent, extended, and joint families. A nuclear family consists of parents and their offspring and occasionally another relative. Single-parent families have a mother or a father and children. Women head most single-parent families. Extended families consist of parents, their unmarried children, married children and their spouses, and their grandchildren. Joint families extend the family unit horizontally among siblings rather than vertically across generations.

ENDOGAMY, EXOGAMY, AND THE INCEST TABOO

As discussed in Chapter 8, marriage serves as a means of extending kinship within a particular group (*endogamy*) or extending kinship to other groups (*exogamy*). All societies ban marriage—and condemn sexual relations—within the nuclear family, particularly between parents and children and also, with very few exceptions, between brothers and sisters. This ban is referred to as the **incest taboo.** The incest taboo is essentially a rule of nuclear family exogamy, forcing people to marry outside their families. The incest taboo is universal, but beyond the nuclear family the "forbidden" relatives are different in different societies. For example, one set of cousins is preferred for marriage in some societies, whereas other sets of cousins are forbidden under the incest taboo.

Effects of Exogamy on Social Organization

The marriage rules of endogamy and exogamy are predicated on the incest taboo. Both exogamy and endogamy reflect and reinforce the structure and organization of a society, the subject of Chapter 11. For example, village exogamy is the norm in societies in which people contract marriages with residents of other villages. Through intervillage marriages, people create alliances over a broader geographic area, thereby widening their networks of allies and supporters. In areas of frequent warfare, such marriages also give some protection against raids because people are less likely to attack villages where they have relatives.

In addition, some stratified societies practice exogamy, stipulating that members of identifiable social groups or strata need to marry outside their own group or **class,** a social grouping whose membership is usually based on a combination of birth and achievement. For example, the Natchez of the south-central United States were divided into two major classes—nobles and commoners. These groups had different, unequal access to resources, services, and power. The nobility consisted of three graded ranks: Suns,

joint family
Family consisting of siblings with their spouses and children, sharing work and resources.

incest taboo
A ban on sexual relations or marriage between parents and their children and between siblings.

class
Social grouping usually determined on the basis of a combination of birth and achievement.

caste
Social grouping whose membership is determined at birth and is generally inflexible.

CONTR○VERSIES

Explaining the Incest Taboo

The origins of the incest taboo are much debated. One theory proposes that the incest taboo arose out of an instinctive aversion toward sexual relations within the nuclear family. However, incest occurs fairly widely in human societies, so avoiding it is not instinctual. Another biological theory suggests that the incest taboo is a learned, cultural response to the possible biological consequences of inbreeding, which can increase the incidence of undesirable or harmful (as well as desirable and beneficial) genetic traits in a population. This theory assumes that ancestral humans understood the relationship between mating and the variability of traits in their population, and that this cultural adaptation then spread to all human societies through diffusion or contact to become a universal element of culture or, alternatively, that human societies in different areas independently invented an incest taboo.

A theory championed by anthropologist Bronislaw Malinowski, based on the work of Sigmund Freud, focused on the origin of the incest taboo as a response to the need to lessen sexual competition within the nuclear family unit. This psychological theory might account in part for the ban on sexual relations between parents and their children, which would strain the marriage bond between husband and wife. However, it does not explain the near-universal prohibition on marriage between siblings. Sibling marriage occurred among the monarchs of ancient Peru, Egypt, and Hawaii but was not defined as incest. Marriage between a brother and sister at the highest level of the state consolidated power and minimized struggles over succession. However, sibling marriage was not permitted among ordinary citizens.

Many anthropologists favor understanding the incest taboo as a means of ensuring survival by forcing people to make alliances with others outside the nuclear family. This "marry out or die out" theory emphasizes that marriage within a small unit will over time lead to the isolation and genetic homogeneity of the group, which makes the unit more vulnerable to population loss or even extinction. Mating outside the nuclear family reduces this risk and also creates social alliances and bonds of reciprocity with other people that can be critical in times of scarcity and other dangers to survival.

We may never know why the incest taboo started, but the fact that it is universal indicates its importance. All these theories add interesting dimensions and clues to the debate.

● CRITICAL THINKING QUESTION

Which theory or combination of theories about the origin of the incest taboo do you favor, and why?

Nobles, and Honored Persons. Descent was matrilineal. The chief was the highest ranked member of the highest ranked matrilineage, the Suns. The Suns were never able to consolidate their power and wealth, however, because the Natchez social system required that all members of the nobility practice class exogamy. That is, they had to marry commoners. The Sun matrilineage was perpetuated through children of Sun women who were Suns themselves, but children of Sun men, including children of the Great Sun, were not members of that chiefly lineage. The children and more distant relatives of Sun men became Nobles and Honored Persons, whose male children were commoners through membership in their mothers' lineage. On the other hand, children of male commoners became members of the nobility if their fathers married noble women. Commoners could also raise their status through exemplary services to the nation, such as serving in the military, which raised wives' status as well (Bonvillain 2001, 132–33).

Effects of Endogamy on Social Organization

Many stratified societies also practice endogamy, in which people marry within their class or rank to maintain social, economic, and political distinctions. Endogamous marriages solidify and preserve the privilege of elites by consolidating wealth and power. Recall the examples of parallel cousin marriage and cross-cousin marriage, described in Chapter 8.

A strong form of endogamy occurs in caste systems (described further in Chapter 11). **Caste** is an ascribed social category identifying a group by status or by occupation. At birth, people automatically become members of the caste

Brahmans, like the one in this photograph, are the highest of four main castes identified in ancient Hindu sacred writings.

GLOBALIZATION

Increases in rates of multiracial marriage and in numbers of mixed-race children in many parts of the world can be seen as an extension of the process of globalization. In many countries, including the United States, interethnic marriage also contributes to the spread of English.

of their parents and remain in that caste throughout life. In India, for example, people traditionally must marry other members of their own caste. Caste exogamy (marrying someone of another caste) is, in principle, forbidden, although it does occur.

Informal class endogamy is widespread in stratified societies, simply because people with similar backgrounds tend to associate with one another and marry within their group. Members of the same class tend to socialize together, attend the same schools, live in the same neighborhoods, perform the same social activities, and so on. Therefore, even in the absence of a strong marriage rule, proximity and informal sanctions against marrying down tend to lead to class endogamy. Other marriage preferences that follow informal social norms include the tendency for people in pluralistic societies to marry within their own racial or ethnic group and to choose partners who speak the same language and observe the same religion.

REVIEW — The universal incest taboo is a general ban against sexual relations between individuals within a nuclear family. Explanations for its origins include biological and psychological explanations and hypotheses based on cultural adaptations to survival factors. Marriage rules affect the organization of a society. Examples of impacts of endogamy on social systems include the caste system of India, alliances created through cross-cousin marriage, and class systems with preferential marriage based on shared membership in a social, racial, or ethnic group.

FORMS OF MARRIAGE

Marriage rules define the forms that marriages can take, and these forms vary. For example, norms concerning the number of spouses that can constitute the marital unit differ in different societies. In most societies, marriage is a union between two people—**monogamy.** However, in some societies the marital unit may consist of three or more people—**polygamy,** or plural marriage. Monogamy is the most common form of union today, even in societies where plural marriages are possible. Societies that permit remarriage after the death of a spouse or divorce practice **serial monogamy,** meaning that a person can be married to only one person at a time, although individuals may have two or more spouses during their lifetime.

Polygyny and Polyandry

There are two forms of polygamy. **Polygyny** is marriage between a man and two or more women, and **polyandry** is marriage between a woman and two or more men. Polygyny is far more common than polyandry as a form of plural marriage, but most couples live in monogamous unions, even in societies where plural marriages are possible. A common type of polygyny is a pattern in which a man marries two or more sisters, usually wedding one first and the other years later. This system is called **sororal polygyny.** Sororal polygyny has the advantage of minimizing potential conflicts between wives because the women have close emotional and supportive bonds as sisters. When co-wives are not related, they may have tensions between them, each vying for favoritism from their common husband to benefit themselves and their children. Different societies favor different kinds of residence patterns for plural marriages. In some, the entire unit of husband and several wives lives together in one dwelling. In others, each wife of a polygynous homestead has a separate hut for herself and her children.

Polyandry may also take several forms. In some cases, a woman may marry unrelated men whereas, in others, several brothers may be married to the same woman, a form called fraternal polyandry. The best documented examples of polyandry occur in South Asia, especially in India, Tibet, and Nepal. Polyandry has also been reported elsewhere in the past, including among the Inuit of Arctic Canada and the Iroquois of New York State.

Polyandrous marriages may occur in societies where there are shortages of women. For example, in some communities in the Indian Himalayas and Chinese Tibet, such as the Nyinba and the Pahari, brothers may jointly contract for a wife. This fraternal polyandry permits all men to be married, and also promotes economic cooperation among brothers for their mutual benefit. Rather than fragmenting a family's property through inheritance

monogamy
Marriage rule that stipulates a union between two people.

polygamy
Marriage in which the marital unit consists of three or more people.

serial monogamy
Marriage pattern that stipulates that a person can be married to only one person at a time, although individuals may have two or more spouses during their lifetime. Subsequent marriages may be formed after the death of one spouse or after divorce.

polygyny
Marriage between a man and two or more women.

polyandry
Marriage between a woman and two or more men.

sororal polygyny
Marriage between a man and two or more women who are sisters.

by numerous and possibly conflicting heirs, polyandrous unions solidify wealth, property, and social status and raise people's overall standard of living (Levine 1988). However, the shortage of women in Nyinba society derives from social attitudes that devalue females. Because sons are preferred, they are better fed and cared for than are daughters. The neglect of females leads to higher rates of infant and child mortality, resulting in a gender imbalance. Currently, in traditional Nyinba communities, the sex ratio is 118 men to 100 women (Stone 2006, 201). Polyandry permits all men to marry while at the same time limiting population growth, an adaptive strategy in a region of scarce resources.

Finally, Nyinba men are often away from their households pursuing economic activities. Men's work includes herding their households' animals, especially goats and sheep. They are also involved in trading grains and other products, traveling from Tibet into northern India (Stone 2006, 195). Polyandry ensures that households will likely have at least one man at home to accomplish male economic tasks.

Explanations of Polygyny

Polygyny develops in different societies for different reasons. Care must therefore be taken in interpreting its meanings and functions depending on the cultural and historical contexts in which polygyny occurs. In communities where women significantly outnumber men, polygyny helps correct imbalances in the sex ratio. Among the Innu of eastern

In this West African family, each co-wife has her own hut, which she occupies with her children.

Canada in earlier centuries, for example, polygyny, limited to two or three wives, ensured marriage for all women in a society with a scarcity of men. Male mortality rates were comparatively higher than female mortality rates because of the dangers for men in hunting and warfare. After lecturing the Innu about the evils of plural marriage, the seventeenth-century French Jesuit missionary Paul LeJeune observed: "Since I have been preaching among them that a man should not have more than one wife, I have not been well received by the women; for, since they are more numerous than the men, if a man can only marry one of them, the others will have to suffer. Therefore this doctrine is not to their liking" (Thwaites 1906, vol. 12, p. 165). In the case of the Innu, polygyny prevented population decline by maintaining an effective rate of reproduction.

Polygyny occurs in some strongly patriarchal societies in which women are viewed as property and a source of status. Men who can afford to support a greater number of wives and dependents are seen to have greater wealth, power, and prestige in their communities. Historically, hereditary high chiefs of polygynous Central African kingdoms boasted hundreds of wives and concubines. In pre-Communist imperial China, wealthy men measured their status and good fortune in the number of wives they accumulated. Daughters became mediums of exchange between men seeking to form alliances with each other.

Polygyny also develops as an adaptation to economic needs or goals because of the important economic roles women serve. For example, as the economy of the Plains Indians shifted to dependence on the buffalo by the middle of the nineteenth century, men wanted to obtain the economic services of more than one wife because women were responsible for tanning the buffalo hides and thus turning a raw product into a marketable item. To advance themselves in trade networks that were supplied by the labor of women, men wanted several wives.

In some farming societies, polygyny serves the purpose of supplying additional labor of women and their children. For example, among the Tswana and Herero, two cattle-herding and horticultural societies of southern Africa, men with more than one wife were able to accumulate greater farm surpluses because of women's key roles as subsistence farmers. Also, the more wives a man had, the more children he acquired. His children raised his social standing because they contributed to the growth of his patrilineage and patriclan. A man's sons helped care for his cattle, and his daughters brought cattle to the family as wedding gifts from their husbands' kin.

Men living in foraging societies may reap benefits from the labor of more than one wife. Among the Tiwi of Australia, men want to have several wives because the Aboriginal foraging economy centers on the collection of wild plant resources, work that women generally do. As one Tiwi reported, "If I had only one or two wives I would starve, but with

GLOBALIZATION

The shared practice of polygyny fostered the rapid spread of patriarchal Arab culture and Islam to African nations. It is well known that culture change occurs more rapidly and more completely when peoples in contact share basic cultural characteristics such as forms of marriage and family.

ghost marriage
Marriage practice among the Nuer of Sudan in which a widow marries her dead husband's brother and in which the children ensuing from the second marriage are said to be the children of the first, dead husband.

my present ten or twelve wives I can send them out in all directions in the morning and at least two or three of them are likely to bring something back with them at the end of the day, and then we can all eat" (Hart and Pilling 1960, 34).

Tiwi husbands benefit from polygyny both economically and socially. A man with several wives can accumulate enough food surplus to give to others, raising his prestige by his generosity. Australian Aborigine men also value their wives because of their desire to have many children, a condition of marriage. The Tiwi traditionally practiced reciprocal polygyny, with men sometimes agreeing to marry each other's sisters or each other's daughters.

"Ghost Marriage" and Other Adaptive Forms

Cultures demonstrate a great deal of variety in the ways that people think of sexual relations, marriage, and family. Marriage might even be entirely symbolic and not involve procreation. Yet, even in rare forms of marriage, principles of descent, patterns of residence and household composition, and ways of establishing bonds with others form systems of relationships and meaning that integrate individuals into families and communities.

In some African societies with patrilineal descent, marriages can be contracted in ways that emphasize the importance of descent and the continuity of patrilineal kin groups. Among the Nuer, for example, if a married man died without sons, one of his younger brothers married his widow. The children of the new couple, though, were considered heirs of the deceased (Evans-Pritchard 1955). Nuer **ghost marriage** thus permitted an elder brother to maintain his patrilineage even after his death. In Nuer society, seniority in a lineage was an important criterion for determining relative social status, so allowing descent to follow from an elder sibling, dead or alive, was a strategic practice. In this way, children born to the younger brother but claimed by the dead older brother would have seniority over members of junior lineages.

Another Nuer marital option was allowed when a lineage failed to produce a male heir. In that event, a woman in the lineage could take the role of husband and be married to another woman. The woman who became a husband refrained from having sex because husbands cannot conceive. The "wife" conceived by having sex with a chosen man from any lineage other than her own. The children borne to the "wife" belonged to the "husband's" lineage, thus supplying the line with heirs (Evans-Pritchard 1955, 108).

In marriages between women, the woman who acted as husband was transformed into a legal man. As a "man," she could receive bridal payments given in marriages for her kinswomen, and she could inherit cattle from her father. She could also be compensated with cattle if her "wife" had an adulterous affair without her consent. Nuer practices of marriage between women and "ghost marriage" both create social fatherhood for the purpose of securing the continuation of patrilineages.

In another rare form, the matrilineal Kwakwaka'wakw (Kwakiutl) of British Columbia developed a marriage option that created daughters for men who had none. Such a strategy was necessary because status, wealth, and named titles were transmitted from men to men through women. In practice, men needed daughters because wealth and titles passed from a father to his daughter's children. To accommodate men who had no daughters, several types of marriage could be arranged. According to George Hunt, a Kwakiutl chief, a man "turned the left side of his son's body into a woman and gave ['her'] the name belonging to the oldest daughter of his line" (quoted in Boas 1966, 55). Then another man proposed marriage to the first man's "daughter." After they were married, the first man was able to acquire the titles belonging to "her" lineage and could pass these on to children whom he had with a subsequent wife. If a man had no children at all, according to Hunt, "the father may call his foot or one side of his body, his daughter. The marriage ceremony is performed as though these were the women married, and the names are transferred in the usual manner." This was called "taking hold of the foot" (Boas 1897, 359). These marital options allowed for the transmission of wealth and status in a society where man controlled wealth but the wealth passed through women.

The Nayar, a matrilineal people living in Kerala, South India, had concepts of marriage that differ from most peoples' (Gough 1961; Mencher 1965). Although contemporary Nayar no longer practice these marriage options, they demonstrate possible human options. Nayar kinship centers on matrilineal relatives, organized into matrilineal descent and residence groups called *taravad*. The *taravad* consists of sisters and brothers, the sisters' children, the sisters' daughters' children, and so on, all descended from a female ancestor. They hold land and other property in common, managed by the senior man. They also care collectively for children born to their female members. In the past, shortly before a girl reached puberty, she was married to a man chosen by her family. After the marriage ceremony, the couple stayed together for three days. If they wanted, they were permitted to have sexual intercourse but that was not a requirement. On the fourth day, they separated and need not ever see each other again. The man and woman had no social or economic responsibilities toward one another and did not live together. However, bond between them was symbolized when the man died because the woman honored him in mourning ceremonies.

Thereafter, the man and woman had a succession of lovers over the years. These unions were referred to as "joining together" (Stone 2006, 143). A lover acknowledged and legitimized his sexual relationship with a particular woman by giving her gifts three times a year for as long as the liaison lasted. Children produced from these unions belonged to the *taravad* of the mother, and her family took responsibility for the economic care of children. Fathers had no economic obligations for their children, but establishment of paternity was critical to the social standing of mother and child. Her "husbands" publicly declared themselves possible fathers of a child by giving gifts to the mother and to the midwife who assisted in the birth.

Today, distinctive Nayar marriage practices have largely disappeared, replaced by monogamous marriages and nuclear family residence patterns. Although matrilineal kinship groups continue to delineate relationships for some people, the Nayar have shifted toward patrilineal preferences consistent with the loss of property rights previously held by matrilineal groups because contemporary wage work, especially performed by men, has led to the separateness and mobility of the family unit.

The Na, an ethnic group of Yunnan province in southern China, do not recognize marital ties or obligations at all (Hua 2001). Households consist of siblings and the children of female members. Men or women can propose sexual encounters, termed "visits," but they always take place at night in the woman's house. They have no mutual obligations or rights and do not expect to have exclusive sexual access to one another. Nor do they contribute to a joint household. Children belong to the kin group of the mother, but they do not acknowledge paternity or social fatherhood. Instead, children are raised by their mother and her male and female kin.

Same-Sex Marriage

Although most marriages in most cultures are unions between men and women, some societies allow marriage between individuals of the same sex. This is not the same as the **same-sex marriages** practiced by the Nuer, in which a woman is legally defined as a man for purposes of marriage to another woman. In this case, the couple does not have sexual relations. Rather, the female wife has sex with a man in order to bear children for her female husband.

Same-sex marriage was an option in many Native American societies as late as the early decades of the twentieth century. Especially in cultures of the Great Plains, the Southwest, and California, two women or two men might marry, have sexual relations, and share household and family responsibilities. These people, now often referred to as "Two-Spirits," were publicly recognized as forming legitimate couples. Chapter 10 discusses in greater detail the Two-Spirits and their roles in their communities.

In North America today, growing numbers of lesbian and gay couples advocate for the right to marry in ceremonies that have legal standing. Advocates note that same-sex couples fulfill all of the same obligations and responsibilities toward one another, as do heterosexual couples. They share their resources, make joint decisions, and make commitments to exclusive sexual relationships. Many also raise children together. Opponents of lesbian and gay marriage claim that the traditional cultural concept of marriage, based on religious precepts, applies only to the union of one man and one

same-sex marriage
Marriage between two men or two women.

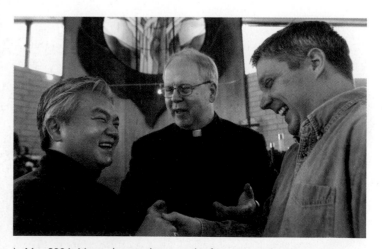
In May 2004, Massachusetts became the first state to legalize gay marriage. California followed in 2007, but a voter referendum in 2008 banned the legal sanctioning of gay marriages. Pictured here is a couple preparing to marry in Los Angeles.

bridewealth
Presents given by the husband's family to the wife's kin before, during or after the wedding ceremony.

woman. Growing tolerance for homosexual marriages in the United States and Canada is a measure of social and culture change. In the United States, Vermont was the first state to permit the legal recognition of civil unions between homosexuals, so long as they did not call it "marriage." In 2004, Massachusetts became the first state to legalize same-sex marriage, not simply to recognize same-sex civil unions, followed in 2008 by California and Connecticut. However, in 2008, voters in California approved a ballot initiative banning same-sex marriages. Then in 2009, Vermont, Iowa, and Maine recognized same-sex marriages. The issue remains deeply controversial. In 2003, the Supreme Court of Canada ruled that Canadian marriage laws allow homosexuals to wed. Belgium, the Netherlands, Norway, Spain, South Africa, and Sweden also allow same-sex couples to marry.

REVIEW ———◉ Monogamy is the marriage of one man and one woman, either for life or for a given time (serial monogamy). Polygamy, or plural marriage, can be in two forms: polygyny or polyandry. Polygyny is marriage between one man and two or more women. Marriage between a man and two or more sisters is called sororal polygyny. Explanations for the development of polygyny relate to population sex ratios, the status of women, and economic adaptations. Polyandry, marriage between one woman and two or more men, often brothers, is rarer. Other rare forms of marriage include ghost marriages, foot marriages, and same-sex marriages.

MARRIAGE AS ALLIANCE AND ECONOMIC EXCHANGE

The relationship established through marriage is not only social but economic as well. Each spouse usually has certain obligations to the other and to their children to supply basic needs such as food, clothing, and shelter. The economic factor in marriage may also be expressed through exchanges of goods and services prior to, during, or after marriage rites. In most Native American cultures, gifts were mutually exchanged before and during a marriage ceremony. Relatives of the bride and groom gave each other foods, clothing, and ornaments as a sign of their mutual respect and support.

Bridewealth and Brideservice

In some places, substantial gifts may be given, not mutually by both sides, but more often by one side to the other. In patrilineal societies, for example, **bridewealth** is given from the husband's group to that of the wife. Among the Nuer and most of the cattle-herding societies of eastern Africa, bridewealth was primarily in the form of cattle. In the plains of North America, people gave horses as bridewealth. The number of cattle or horses given was taken to be a reflection of the wealth and prestige of the husband's kin and an indication of the esteem in which they held the bride and her family. Offering too little, then, could be an insult.

In societies where a married couple lived with the husband's kin, the transfer of goods from the husband's group to that of the wife was symbolic compensation for the woman's loss to her family. Bridewealth was also recognition that, after the wedding, the husband's family benefited from the bride's labor while her own kin would be deprived of it. In addition, bridewealth was a means of legitimizing the couple's children and their membership in the husband's patrilineal group. Bridewealth typically was returned if a couple divorced, so the wife's kin often had a large stake in discouraging the dissolution of the marriage.

Patterns and amounts of bridewealth payments may change as societies undergo economic and social transformations. For example, among the Nuer of the Southern Sudan, the number of cattle expected as gifts from the husband's family to that of

Some of these Botswana cattle may become bridewealth for sons from the owner's family to give to the parents of their prospective wives.

the wife has fluctuated in the last 50 years in response to conditions that affected the size of herds. When drought or cattle diseases decimated herds, the number of cattle given as bridewealth declined. During the first civil war in Sudan, which lasted from 1963 until 1972, bridewealth rates also declined sharply (Hutchinson 1996, 81). Thereafter, the expected number of cattle increased in the 1980s during a period of relative stability.

A second change in bridewealth practices among the Nuer was the introduction of money. Although some families are willing to accept some money, cattle remain the preferred tokens of bridewealth. As the Nuer say, "Money has no blood" (Hutchinson 1996, 74).

Finally, some young Nuer men now attempt to free themselves from family ties by purchasing cattle for their own bridewealth payments with funds that they have earned from work. This is a significant break with past practices where the circulation of cattle among families in bridewealth payments secured and symbolized larger social bonds, linking individuals to the support networks of their kin who contributed cattle for their bridewealth payments and linking families to other kinship groups.

In another form of gift giving related to marriage, called **brideservice,** men are obligated to perform services for their wife's parents. A period of brideservice may predate the marriage ceremony, or the period may extend for many years after marriage. During this period, the future or newly married husband contributes his labor to his parents-in-law. Depending on the subsistence strategies employed, he may give all or a portion of animals he has caught and help with planting and harvesting crops. In addition, the husband may help construct his parents-in-law's dwellings, fetch wood or water, and perform other domestic tasks.

Dowry

In some societies, the bride's family rather than the groom's family gives goods of value. These gifts are given to the newly married couple and/or to the husband's kin prior to or upon the marriage. This type of exchange is called **dowry.** Dowries are prevalent in some patriarchal cultures that stress the prestige of men and their families. In theory, dowries are a kind of insurance that protects the interests of a wife in a patrilineal and patriarchal society. In practice, however, dowry wealth is often appropriated by the husband and his family.

brideservice
A period of months or years before or after marriage during which the husband performs labor for his wife's parents.

dowry
Gifts given by the wife's family to the married couple or to the husband's kin before, during, or after the wedding ceremony.

CULTURE CHANGE

DOWRY IN INDIA

Dowry was the traditional marital exchange in India. A woman's family had to present wealth in jewelry, fine cloth, and money to the husband's family before the marriage took place. The amount of wealth given was an indication of both the bride's status and the esteem of the husband's kin. Wealthy parents gave a lot of property, but even poor families tried to collect as many valuables as they could so as not to shame their daughter and themselves.

The economic burden of dowry contributed to a preference for sons over daughters because girls were a financial liability whereas boys brought in dowry wealth when they married. Thus, the custom of dowry contributed to female infanticide and the neglect of the health of daughters in India and Bangladesh. However, dowry was not the only factor involved in preferences for sons and the consequences of such preferences. Rather, a constellation of behaviors and attitudes place value on men and undermine the worth of women: kinship based on patrilineal descent and inheritance, subsistence strategies emphasizing intensive agriculture done primarily by men, and male control over land.

Although outlawed by the Dowry Prohibition Act (1961, amended in 1984 and 1986), a husband's family often still demands specific amounts of cash or goods to contract a marriage (Ghadially and Kumar 1988, 175). Young men of high status, good education, and favorable employment prospects command large sums. Dowry demands are often made after a marriage is contracted and even after a wedding.

The deaths of young wives whose families have not satisfied the dowry demands of their in-laws have led to controversy. Of a registered 179 "unnatural deaths" of young married women in Delhi between 1981 and 1982, 12 percent to 16 percent were reportedly dowry-related (Ghadially and Kumar 1988, 167). In two-thirds of these cases, young women committed suicide; their in-laws murdered the remaining third. The families involved were of all social classes, educational levels, and occupations.

Ghadially and Kumar (1988) also report that, in the Indian state of Maharashtra, dowry deaths rose from 120 in 1984 to 211 in 1985, an increase of 64 percent. By the mid-1990s, dowry deaths, including bride burnings, had climbed to an estimated 5,800 incidents a year. Many "unnatural deaths" of women are classified as "kitchen/cooking accidents" and "stove bursts," a common method of killing unprofitable daughters-in-law. Retaliation against wives whose families fail to meet dowry demands takes many forms, from verbal abuse to beatings, burns, hanging, poisoning, and strangulation.

A disturbing finding in studies of dowry abuse and death is that the wife's parents are sometimes aware of the violence perpetrated against their daughter but tell her to endure her situation rather than stir controversy that would sully her family's reputation.

Dowry and the related mistreatment and deaths of women gave impetus to the birth of the feminist movement in India. Beginning in 1979, women's groups staged public protests to publicize the issue of dowry harassment. As a result, many families of abused daughters came forward to give testimony and ask for redress. In 1980, the government mandated police investigation of the death of any woman who had been married less than five years at the time of her death. In 1983, legislation made "cruelty to a wife a cognizable, non-bailable offense" and stipulated that "cruelty" included both mental and physical harassment (Kumar 1995, 68). Cases reported as suicides (frequently involving death by dousing and burning) could be investigated as "abetment to suicide," shifting the burden of proof to the woman's husband and his family, and women who died within seven years of marriage had to have autopsies.

The latest studies, however, indicate increases in dowry demands. For example, the All India Democratic Women's Association surveyed 10,000 people in eighteen of India's twenty-six states and found "an across-the-board increase in dowry demands" (Brooke 2003). Government statistics report that, in 2001, husbands or in-laws angry over small dowries killed nearly 7,000 women. In 2003, a well-publicized case brought the issue of dowry demands to national attention. A bride called police on her wedding day when her father refused to pay her in-laws an additional $25,000 they demanded, and a scuffle broke out. The husband eventually served fourteen days in jail for violating laws against dowry (Brooke 2003). Government statistics indicate that dowry deaths rose 46 percent from 1995 to 2005 (Government of India 2006, 171).

In Europe, from medieval times until well into the nineteenth century, well-to-do families bestowed dowries on their daughters when they married. The ability to give large amounts of money, property, and annual incomes was a sign of a family's wealth, enhancing their prestige as well. In turn, fathers who could afford handsome dowries could bargain for wealthy and powerful sons-in-law. Through marriage exchanges of dowries for husbands with property and status, men acquired a host of affinal relatives as personal and political allies. The legacy of the European dowry system is preserved today in the custom of collecting fine clothes and linens in a bridal hope chest.

Marriages are economic transactions, but they are also occasions for celebration. What is celebrated is not simply the union of two people, but the alliances formed between two families, lineages, or clans. When marriage takes place between a man and a woman who come from different villages, the wedding may symbolize extended networks and alliances between two communities.

REVIEW   As well as creating alliances among families and larger social units, marriage has important economic functions, and economic exchange is a common feature of marriage arrangements. Gifts are exchanged in many societies to represent the new economic obligations the spouses now have to one another and their in-laws. Bridewealth, found in patrilineal societies, consists of forms of wealth or objects of value given to the bride's family by the groom's family. Brideservice consists of work that the groom does for his in-laws. In the dowry system, the family of the bride pays or promises to pay wealth to the family of the groom in exchange for the marriage of their daughter.

CASE STUDY

A Wedding in Nepal

In larger communities and settled populations, especially where lineages are important kinship, economic, and political units, marriages may be complex, lengthy procedures. Among the Lohorung Rai of eastern Nepal, marriage involves a ten-step process (Hardman 2000). The most complex aspect of the marriage is the negotiation between the families of the intended husband and wife. These negotiations underscore the social and economic as well as spiritual alliances created between two families, their clans, and their villages.

Most Lohorung Rai marriages are arranged when the boy and girl are young, beginning with a gift of liquor brought from the boy's kin to the girl's parents. The boy's emissaries recount his good qualities and those of his family. The girl's family often refuse the initial request, returning the gift to the boy's relatives, and several trips may be needed before the girl's parents drink the liquor and tell the boy's relatives how much meat they will need to distribute to their kin.

Subsequently, the boy's kin bring more gifts to those of the girl. Eventually, they present the final gift of a live pig, some rice, and liquor to the girl's kin. This final gift, referred to as a "ransom," marks the formal betrothal of the couple and commits the families to the marriage. The wedding, lasting all night, takes place at the bride's home. The groom proceeds there accompanied by his cousin (father's sister's son). The rite not only celebrates a marriage but also marks the transition of a male from boyhood to manhood.

At this Nepalese wedding, the bride's relatives accept gifts of gold, clothing, and jewelry that symbolize the marriage.

After the wedding, the bride accompanies her husband to his parents' home, but the following day she returns to her own parents' home, bringing additional gifts from her husband's family. She returns to her husband's home sixteen days later but remains for only a few days, not finally taking up residence there for perhaps a year. Several years later, usually after the birth of her first child, she returns to her parents' home for a final rite of separation, receiving gifts from her brothers.

The lengthy and complex Lohorung Rai marriage process not only solidifies an alliance between two families but also symbolizes and enacts the difficulty of a young woman's separation from her family in a society where postmarital residence is in the husband's locality and usually involves village exogamy. The woman's family demonstrates their reluctance to lose her by hesitating to accept the initial gifts, and she shows her reluctance to leave by repeatedly returning to her parents' home.

PEARSON
myanthrolab

Explore more at
www.myanthrolab.com

MARRIAGE AS A RITE OF PASSAGE

For individuals, families, kin groups, and communities, marriages are crucial rites of passage. Because of the importance of the alliances formed by marriage, one's parents or other relatives arrange marriages, especially first marriages, in many societies. A proposal of marriage may be made from one side or the other, although it is more common worldwide for

IN THEIR OWN VOICES

"I Hear That I'm Going to Get Married!"

Florence Edenshaw Davidson, a Haida woman from Vancouver Island, British Columbia, Canada, was 14 when her parents told her that she would be married to Robert Davidson. As was proper in this matrilineal society, Robert's kin made the proposal to Florence's parents. Her father deferred to his wife's brother (Florence's mother's brother), who was a senior member of Florence's matriclan. These are Florence's recollections about how she came to be married to her husband.

I was still going to school yet when several people came into my dad's house to propose for my husband-to-be. I was wondering what was going on when all these people came in. The women all belonged to C'al'lanas, my husband's tribe [lineage], and the men all belonged to my husband's dad's tribe, Stl'ang'lanas, except for my husband's brother. They were all streaming in and I didn't know what was going on . . .

"Don't say anything when I tell you something," my mother said to me. "Those who came in last week proposed to you." I didn't know what to say. Propose! Why? I thought. I was just a kid yet. I didn't know what to say and mother advised me not to say anything about the proposal because they were high-class [y'a Yet] people . . .

"They want you to marry Robert Davidson." "Did you say yes?" I asked her. "No, your dad sent them to your uncle [Florence's mother's brother]. Your dad says he's got nothing to do with it; it has to go through your uncle. You have more respect for your uncle than for us," she told me. "That's the only brother I have." "You're going to make me marry," I said. "Yes, you're going to marry him." "I'm not going to marry him," I said. "Don't say that, Florence, he's a real prince [y'a Yet]."

It bothered me so much. . . . Every day I bothered my mother. "I'm not going to marry that old man. I'm not. If you make me marry him, summertime I'll run away. You won't see

me again." My mother didn't say anything. . . . My dad didn't say a word to me about it. Finally, my mother said, "Don't say anything dear. Your uncle thinks it's best for you to marry him. He's a prince. He's going to respect you all your life and if you don't want to marry him you're going to feel bad all your life. He belongs to clever people; you're not going to be hard up for anything. We need a young man's help, too. You must remember that. We belong to chiefs too and you're not supposed to talk any old way. You have to respect yourself more than what you worry about." . . . I made up my mind not to say anything much as I disliked it.

From Margaret Blackman, *During My Time: Florence Edenshaw Davidson, A Haida Woman*, pp. 95–96. © 1982. Reprinted by permission of the University of Washington Press.

This couple married through mutual consent after declaring their love for one another, and their families were the last to know about their plans.

the future husband's kin to approach the family of the intended wife. This is true whether the people follow patrilineal or matrilineal rules of descent.

A proposal of marriage may be a simple, short process, or it may be a long, drawn-out, ritualized exchange of greetings, proposals, counterproposals, and gift exchanges before the hoped-for marriage is finally settled upon. Among the Lohorung Rai of Nepal, for example, the marriage proposal process may take many years to accomplish. After the husband's family makes the initial contact, numerous exchanges of refusal and counterproposal follow before a final date is set for the wedding.

Arranged marriages symbolically emphasize the fact that such unions are not simply relationships between a woman and a man but are more

And these are the recollections of James Sewid, a Kwak-waka'wakw man from Alert Bay, British Columbia. He, too, was married when he was nearly 14 to a girl he knew only by sight.

And that's when the big day came. . . . I had been out late that night to a dance with my friends and when I came in I lay down on the couch. That was when I heard Jim and Mary Bell talking about me to Ed and Rachel Whanock and my mother and stepfather. One of them was saying, "You might as well go and see her parents because I think he should get married because we don't want him running around like this.". . . I lay there and pretended that I was sleeping and pretty soon my grandparents walked out. So as soon as they had gone I got up and said to my stepfather, "Let's go take a walk. It's pretty warm in here." . . . When we got outside . . . I asked him, "What was going on in there? I heard the people talking about me." "Well," he said, "you're going to get married." "Well," I said, "I can't get married! I'm too young!" "Oh that's all right," he said. "We'll look after you. I think it is the best way for you, to get married now, because if you're not going to get married now you might go haywire." "Well," I said, "who is this girl anyway?" And just then we happened to be passing by the house where Moses Alfred lived, and David said, "It is the girl that lives here." I didn't know what to say. I used to see her around the village but I didn't know her.

Well, it was the Indian custom for someone to go to the parents of the girl and ask their consent. That is where my grandparents had gone that night when they walked out of the house. So I just waited for the answer that this girl's parents would give to the old people who went to talk with them. I was careful after that not to listen anymore because I didn't like to butt in on what was going on. A few days after that I was alone with my mother. . . . I said to her, "I hear that I'm going to get married. You know that I'm too young to get married." "Oh, no!" she said. "Don't talk like that. We want

you to get married. You are going to marry Flora Alfred. It has already been arranged with her parents and it's all right. Now you have to go and see the minister so it can be announced in the church and published in the band." "Well," I said, "I don't think I should get married. It isn't that I don't want to get married, but what am I going to do if I have children?" "Well," my mother said, "we'll look after you some."

After that I went to see my old grandmother, Lucy. She had already heard about it. I went in and sat down and said, "Well, they say I'm going to get married." "Yes," she said, "I heard about that and I think it's a wonderful thing. I would really like to see it. I want to see you get married and have children before I die. . . ." Well, that is what made me kind of give in. I didn't want to get married but of course . . . I had no business to try and argue or anything like that because I knew that the older people knew what was right for me; that's what I figured. I never did like to argue with anybody that was older than me but I always liked to respect what they said to me.

Explore more at
www.myanthrolab.com

From James Spradley, *Guests Never Leave Hungry: The Autobiography of James Sewid, a Kwakiutl Indian,* pp. 66–67. © 1972. Reprinted by permission of Yale University Press.

Although both Florence and James voiced reservations about their arranged marriages, especially concerning their young age and fears about taking on adult responsibilities, they gave up in the interests of their families. As it turned out, they both had long and loving relationships with their spouses.

● CRITICAL THINKING QUESTIONS

Would you be willing to have your family arrange your marriage? Why, or why not?

---

fundamentally alliances between families. Each side measures their own worthiness in relation to the social standing and resources of the other side. Their willingness to promote a marital union is an indication of their trust in their future affines.

Weddings are rites of passage in which the participants change their status from single to married. In societies without arranged marriages, preparation for marriage usually involves some form of **courtship,** in which a couple tests their attraction and compatibility as well as the acceptability of their union to others who are important in their lives. Mate selection is the common goal of courtship, and weddings mark the passage from courtship to marriage. The bases on which people choose their mates may include personal compatibility, desired personality traits, likelihood of reliability and economic contributions, and physical attraction. In most societies, the Western concept of romantic love is not a prerequisite for courtship or marriage, although these feelings may develop when people begin to live together, adjusting to one another and sharing their lives.

arranged marriages
Marriages that are arranged by the parents or other relatives of the bride and groom.

courtship
Period prior to marriage when a couple tests attraction to and compatibility with each other.

In small-scale societies, especially among foraging and horticultural peoples, a wedding ceremony is usually a simple affair. Among the Mohawk, a young man's family traditionally proposed a marriage to the family of the intended bride, or a couple announced their plans to marry. Before the wedding, the couple separately presented gifts to their future mothers-in-law. The future husband gave his bride's mother a gift of deer meat, and the future bride gave her husband's mother a gift of cornbread. These presents were symbolic of the economic roles of men as hunters and women as farmers, thus representing the interdependence of spouses and households.

A Mohawk wedding involved a feast sponsored by the bride's family for relatives, clan members, and villagers. The father of the bride made a formal announcement of the couple's marriage and bestowed the family's approval. Then followed speeches from a number of respected elder guests who exhorted the couple to behave properly, responsibly, and kindly to each other.

REVIEW — Weddings are rites of passage that publicly confirm the changes in marital and kinship status of the participants. Societies that place high value on kinship and community relations often have arranged marriages. In others, individuals choose their own marriage partners. Weddings also extend the alliance and economic transaction functions of marriage.

PATTERNS OF RESIDENCE AFTER MARRIAGE

The elaborate Nepalese wedding process described in the Case Study is partly a result of postmarital residence patterns that call for a bride to separate herself from her relatives. In all societies, newly married couples follow norms dictating where they should live. They may live with or near the husband's or the wife's family; they may alternate their residences between families; or they may establish a place of their own apart from any of their relatives. Their choice may depend on factors such as the amount of resources available or the composition of existing households. Societies vary in the patterns of postmarital residence that they encourage. Particular postmarital **residence rules** are often associated with different descent systems and specific economic strategies.

Matrilocal and Patrilocal Residence

residence rules
Rules that stipulate where a couple will reside after their marriage.

matrilocal residence
Pattern for residence after marriage in which the couple lives with or near the wife's family.

uxorilocal
Living with or near the wife's parents.

patrilocal residence
Pattern of residence after marriage in which the couple lives with or near the husband's relatives.

virilocal
Living with or near the husband's parents.

avunculocal residence
Patterns of residence after marriage in which the couple lives with or near the husband's mother's brother.

Arrangements in which a married couple lives with or near the wife's family are termed **matrilocal residence.** Usually (but not always), matrilocal residence is associated with matrilineal descent. That is, societies that reckon descent matrilineally usually prefer that couples live with the wife's family. Because children resulting from marriage belong to the lineage of the mother, matrilocal residence ensures that kin group members remain together. Matrilocal households typically consist of an elder couple, their daughters, their daughters' husbands and children, and their unmarried sons. Married sons live with their wives' kin. This kind of residence pattern is also called **uxorilocal**—living with the wife's family.

Patrilocal residence refers to arrangements in which a married couple lives with or near the husband's family. Patrilocal residence usually occurs in societies that reckon descent patrilineally. Because children resulting from marriage belong to the father's lineage, patrilocal residence creates stable, interacting groups of patrilineally related kin. Patrilocal households, therefore, consist of an elder couple, their sons, their sons' wives and children, and their unmarried daughters. Married daughters live with their husbands' relatives. This kind of residence pattern is also called **virilocal**—living with the husband's family.

Avunculocal Residence

In some societies with matrilineal descent and inheritance, an arrangement called **avunculocal residence** is preferred (from the Latin word *avunculus* meaning "mother's brother" and origin of the English word *uncle*). In these cases, a married couple lives with the husband's mother's brother. Avunculocal residence is found in societies where inheritance follows matrilineal descent but in which men hold wealth, property, and social status. According to rules of matrilineal descent, a man's wealth and status cannot be passed to his own son because his son is a member of his wife's kinship group, not his own. Wealth, therefore, passes from a man to his sister's son. From the inheritor's point of view, a man gains wealth and status from his mother's brother. Avunculocal residence establishes a residential and emotional bond between a man and the person from whom he will inherit.

Bilocal and Neolocal Residence

In **bilocal residence,** married couples live alternately with the husband's and the wife's families. Bilocality has the advantage of flexibility, adapting residence to economic and resource conditions. When resources are scarce, couples can make adjustments by relocating from one household to another. Bilocal patterns are also adaptive in realigning living arrangements depending on the composition of households. That is, if households grow too large by the addition of in-marrying spouses and their children, then some people can leave and align themselves with their spouse's kin.

In societies with **neolocal residence,** a married couple establishes a new household independently of the residence of either the husband's or the wife's kin. Such systems typically are found in industrial and postindustrial societies, where couples tend to form new households immediately after marriage or within a year or two. Neolocal residence has the feature of independence, another reflection of the loosening of kinship bonds advantageous in capitalist economies. Neolocal residence separates people from larger kinship groups, allowing them to ignore claims from relatives who might want to share their resources.

Correlates of Residence Patterns

Among foragers, postmarital residence tends to be fairly diverse. Although couples generally live with relatives, the choice of the wife's or husband's family depends on the composition of the households, the availability of resources, and personal preferences. According to Kathleen Gough (1975), approximately 60 percent of foraging societies tended to live patrilocally, whereas 16 percent to 17 percent preferred matrilocal residence. The remaining 15 percent to 17 percent were bilocal, choosing location with the family of either spouse. In farming societies with unilineal descent systems, postmarital residence tends to be consistent with principles of descent. Societies with matrilineal descent usually prefer matrilocal residence, whereas those with patrilineal descent prefer patrilocal residence. In societies whose economies are based on intensive agriculture, descent is nearly always patrilineal, and residence is nearly always patrilocal. The patterns

bilocal residence
Patterns of residence after marriage in which the couple alternates between living with the wife's kin and the husband's kin.

neolocal residence
Pattern of residence after marriage in which the couple establishes a new, independent household separate from their relatives.

> What residence rule is observed in your culture? Are there different historical patterns in residence that relate to people's cultures of origin?

Like the Yanomamo of the Amazon, the Dani of the New Guinea highlands were patrilineal horticulturalists who engaged in frequent internal warfare.

internal warfare
Warfare between closely situated villages or communities.

external warfare
Warfare that takes place at some distance from home communities, requiring warriors' absence from their homes for extended periods of time.

are consistent with men's primary responsibility for farming and their control over the allocation and use of land.

Residence patterns have been observed to correlate with other cultural patterns. For example, in a classic study, anthropologists found that in societies with frequent **internal warfare,** household groups are likely to be organized patrilocally (Ember and Ember 1971). Internal warfare is characterized by frequent raiding among neighboring or nearby settlements. Because men act as warriors who defend their households and communities against the threat of attack by others, living near male relatives they trust is advantageous for them. In contrast, **external warfare,** fought against people from other societies, does not favor a particular residence rule, though external warfare that takes warriors away from home for extended periods may shift economic burdens to women in a way that favors matrilocal residence.

The Iroquois of North America and the Yanomamo of South America provide contrasting examples of the connection between types of warfare and postmarital residence patterns. Iroquois society was based on matrilineal descent, with people organized into matriclans. Iroquois economy centered on horticulture, an occupation for women, supplemented by hunting and fishing provided by men. By the seventeenth and eighteenth centuries, men were involved in frequent and prolonged external warfare with Europeans and with other native peoples, spending many months away from home. Matrilocal residence, the traditional preferred pattern, was strengthened by men's absence from home communities. In contrast, the Yanomamo reckon descent patrilineally. They are horticulturalists whose subsistence is provided nearly entirely by men. Yanomamo men engage in frequent internal warfare, raiding neighboring villages and defending their own homes against attacks by others. Consistent with the Embers's predictions, postmarital residence is strongly patrilocal.

REVIEW — Residence rules tend to ensure that people belonging to the same kin group remain close to one another. Matrilocal patterns, in which the couple lives with or near the wife's parents, are common in matrilineal societies. Patrilocal patterns, in which the couple lives with or near the husband's parents, is common in patrilineal societies. In avunculocal residence, the couple moves in with the husband's mother's brother. Bilocal residency allows the couple to live with either the husband's or wife's family, depending on the resources available. Neolocal residency allows the couple to establish their own independent household.

CASE STUDY

Residence in Rural North India and Western Borneo

RURAL NORTH INDIA

Households consist of large extended or joint families. Village economies center on farming, although villagers may have other occupations. Descent follows patrilineal principles, that is, people belong to the kinship group of their father. Parents arrange marriages. Men typically marry in their early twenties to women in their teens. Girls may be betrothed as young children. Postmarital residence is generally patrilocal. Residential groups, therefore, consist of a couple, their sons and sons' families, and their unmarried daughters. Women move to their husbands' homes upon marriage and have infrequent contact with their own kin. Because girls usually marry shortly after puberty, a wife's subordination is based on age as well as gender. She is thus easily dominated by her husband and especially by his mother. As many researchers have noted, Indian wives often experience their greatest difficulties from their mothers-in-law rather than their husbands (Chitnis 1988).

The domination by mothers-in-law is due, in part, to the uncertain quality of relationships between spouses. Rarely are newlywed couples acquainted before marriage, and unions are arranged without consent from either the bride or the groom. Once married, couples have little interaction. The husband is himself young and lives under his father's authority. As a subordinate in his father's household, he takes care not to shift away from his first allegiance to his parents. Because wives are perceived as potentially destabilizing to established familial order, married sons refrain from showing too much affection or even concern for them, especially early in their married life. Couples rarely interact publicly or have extended conversation when other family members are present. A wife thus spends most of her time with other women in the household. These women, unmarried daughters and in-marrying wives, are all under the supervision of the elder woman. A new daughter-in-law is typically met with some hostility by her husband's mother and sisters. As a result, authoritative statuses are immediately established and reinforced.

WESTERN BORNEO

Iban of Western Borneo

The Iban are rice farmers living along rivers in Western Borneo, especially in the province of Sarawak, Malaysia. Their social system centers on an autonomous unit called a "bilek" or family whose members are related through bilateral ties. The bilek controls land collectively and owns ritual property. Members of the family work cooperatively in economic tasks, especially but not limited to farming the rice fields that supply their basic subsistence. The bilek also owns and occupies a section of the longhouse dwelling that typifies Iban society. An Iban settlement contains one longhouse that is structurally divided into several apartment-like units. Most longhouses contain between ten and twenty bilek units (Freeman 1970, 184).

A bilek itself consists of three generations: an elder couple, one of their married sons or daughters, his or her spouse and children, and the elder couple's unmarried children. Siblings have equal rights as to who will remain with their parents. The Iban show no preference based on gender or seniority. Decisions about where a new couple resides are made on the basis of personal choice and negotiation about access to resources. The son or daughter who remains has full rights to bilek land and other property whereas sons or daughters who leave to reside with the families of their spouses give up their ancestral rights and instead gain access to the land and property of their spouse's family. That is, residence, not genealogy alone, confers social, economic, and ritual rights.

When more than one sibling and spouse claim the natal bilek unit, one of the siblings will eventually leave and set up his own bilek unit (with spouse and children), beginning the process of descent and affiliation anew. Looked at as a structure over time, the bilek family persists, but its members change as generations succeed generations and as siblings unite and then separate to form their own families.

The separate families that together occupy a longhouse form a community distinct from similar communities. Longhouses are dispersed at irregular intervals along river banks (Freeman 1970, 184). They are the residential bases of a community. The residents have ritual responsibilities toward one another and ensure their collective well-being through the proper performance of rituals. Each longhouse has a headman who can help resolve disputes and advise residents on appropriate behavior in keeping with customs and beliefs. When a headman dies or retires, any male resident of the longhouse can succeed him. The choice is made by community consensus.

A few closely related families form the core of the longhouse. The other resident families can claim ties to one of the core groups through either blood or marriage. Indeed, although marriages between siblings are banned, marriage between first or second cousins is preferred because it ". . . constantly reinforces the network of cognatic ties linking individual Iban, and kin" (Freeman 1970, 190). However, people

levirate
Marriage preference rule in which a widow marries her deceased husband's brother.

sororate
Marriage between a widower and his deceased wife's sister.

are free to choose their own spouse. Relationships between husband and wife are based on mutual respect and equality. Although women's and men's economic and ritual roles are distinct, they treat each other and are viewed by others as equals.

Finally, the core group of families in each longhouse generally remains stable until the death of an elder couple leads to fragmentation. However, other families may move to another longhouse in cases of serious conflict. Because people have consanguineous or affinal ties to many other communities, relocation is usually easy.

Today, the Iban (also known as "Dayak") are an indigenous minority within Malaysia, dominated by ethnic Malays who differ in their language, religion, and cultural practices. Many Iban have been educated in British and American schools. They have used their education to advance the rights of their people. Nearly half of the 1.4 million inhabitants of Sarawak are Iban. Another quarter are Moslem Malays, and most of the remainder are ethnic Chinese (Crossette 1987). According to Iban anthropologist, James Masing, the Iban are attempting to strengthen their own communities and identities: "Our priority now is to organize the Dayak community and make them a strong political force" (Crossette 1987).

Explore more at
www.myanthrolab.com

WIDOWHOOD AND DIVORCE

All societies have strategies intended to preserve kin ties, marriage bonds, and household units. All cultures have patterns of beliefs and behaviors for dealing with widows and orphans, for example, and for regulating divorce and remarriage. These cultural patterns reveal the underlying principles of kinship, marriage, and family that are most important in a society. For example, the importance of family alliances is highlighted by marriage preference patterns that anthropologists refer to as "levirate" and "sororate."

The Levirate and Sororate

In the levirate and sororate marriage patterns, if a spouse dies, the deceased's family of origin supplies a younger sibling to marry the surviving spouse. So, for example, in the **levirate,** if a husband dies, his (usually younger) brother will marry the surviving widow. In the **sororate,** a younger sister of a deceased wife will marry the surviving widower. These kinds of marriages symbolically stress family alliances because they say in effect that once two families are joined through marriage, maintaining the established alliance is in the families' interests. Because the death of a husband or wife potentially disrupts the bond between families, a sibling of the deceased spouse perpetuates the alliance by marrying the survivor. The "ghost marriage" of the Nuer is a type of levirate because a younger brother marries the widow of his elder brother. It differs from the more common pattern only in that children of the subsequent union are considered the offspring of the dead brother.

Divorce

Societies vary in their views about the dissolution of marriages. In some societies, divorce is a common outcome of an unhappy union, whereas in others, it rarely occurs because of social or religious restrictions. In some societies, either husband or wife may seek divorce; in others, only one of the parties (usually the husband) may initiate a breakup of the marriage. The ways in which marriages are dissolved also vary across cultures.

In general, matrilineal societies have more lenient attitudes toward divorce than do patrilineal societies because of the differences in principles of descent and the resulting claims that kinship groups have over children. Nearly universally (although there are exceptions), young children continue to live with their mothers after a divorce. Because children belong to the kin group of their mother in matrilineal societies,

In Saudi culture, children belong to the father, his patrilineage, and his patriclan.

divorce does not cause a contradiction between location and kinship. In contrast, the dissolution of a marriage in patrilineal societies causes a problem because patrilineal descent groups are able to make claims over children produced by the wives of their male members through marriage. In addition, patrilineal societies generally exert more control over women's sexual behavior than do matrilineal societies because they need to establish paternity to ensure a child's legitimate place in the father's kinship group.

Foraging and horticultural societies often have flexible attitudes toward divorce, regardless of the type of descent system in their culture. In native North America, for example, with few exceptions, either husband or wife could initiate a breakup of their marriage. Divorce was fairly common, especially in the early years of a marriage and especially if the couple had no children. Acceptable grounds for divorce included adultery, failure to provide or fulfill domestic obligations, or simply personal incompatibility. Few societies had formal procedures for divorce. Rather, the couple would separate, each returning to his or her natal family, or the in-marrying spouse would leave. A divorce could be the result of a joint decision by husband and wife, or one or the other could initiate it.

In some Native American societies, there were publicly recognized ways to signal one's wishes for divorce. For example, among both the Mohawk and the Diné, two matrilineal, matrilocal societies, if a woman wanted a divorce, she might remove her husband's personal belongings from the house when he was away and place them outside. When the husband returned, he would collect his belongings and go back to the home of his mother or sister. If the husband initiated the divorce, he would simply take his possessions and leave. No social stigma was attached to either husband or wife after a divorce.

Among the Lakota and some other peoples of the Great Plains, both parties could jointly agree upon a divorce. However, a man had a public way of signaling his wishes to end their marriage that was not available to a woman. He would beat a drum at a warrior society dance and proclaim that he wished to "throw away [his] wife" (Hassrick 1964, 130). Through this strategy, a man not only ended his marriage but publicly humiliated his wife as well. Although men did not suffer social criticism if their marriages ended, divorced women were shamed.

There are economic deterrents to divorce. For example, exchanges of bridewealth tend to lessen rates of divorce. The husband's kinship group does not favor divorce because a couple's children, although belonging to the husband's kin group in patrilineal societies, usually stay with their mother and therefore leave the husband's household if divorce occurs. A wife's family may also be reluctant to sanction a divorce because when couples break up, the wife's kin must return the goods that they received as bridewealth. Therefore, they may pressure an unhappy wife to remain with her husband. Conflicts over bridewealth and its return in cases of divorce may result not only in the end of family alliances but lead to interfamilial tension and conflict.

In extreme patriarchal societies, such as in some villages in India, in prerevolutionary China, and in many Middle Eastern nations, women rarely have the right to divorce, whereas men are free to break up their marriages, usually on grounds of their wives' disobedience, laziness, or adultery. In some societies, a woman's failure to produce sons might also be a cause for divorce. In such cases, great social criticism is heaped on a divorced woman and on her family as well, although little if any criticism is leveled at the husband.

In some cultures, religious beliefs are used to strongly condemn and even outlaw divorce. Today, Roman Catholicism, Islam, and Orthodox Judaism place barriers to the breakup of marriages. In these belief systems, people have no right to dissolve a union because a marriage was sanctified in the wedding ceremony. In strict Islamic and Orthodox Jewish communities, it is very difficult for women to initiate divorce, but men may seek divorce in religious councils if they cite acceptable grounds.

The levirate and the sororate marriage patterns maintain alliances between families after the death of a spouse. Marriage is not only a relationship but also an economic obligation to the other party. Patrilineal societies generally have more strict rules concerning divorce than do matrilineal societies.

REVIEW

CASE STUDY

Marriage and Divorce among the Kpelle of Liberia

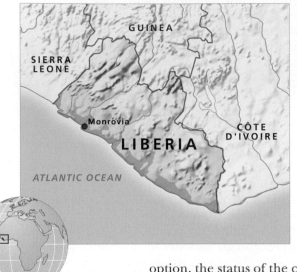

Marriage patterns among the Kpelle, a farming society, provide several options of payment and service that lead to differences in the strength of bonds between couples and the rights that a man exercises over his children (Gibbs 1965). The idea and standard form of marriage involves transfer of bridewealth from a husband's kin group to that of his wife. It permits a husband and his lineage to claim children produced by the marriage. A second form involves performance of brideservice rather than payment of bridewealth. In this type of marriage, a couple resides with the wife's family for a fixed time agreed upon by the parties concerned. During this period, the husband performs labor for his in-laws. Children born to the couple during the years of service belong to the wife's lineage rather than to the husband's. Once the period of brideservice is completed, the children become members of the father's patrilineage.

A third marital option is "male concubinage." In this option, the status of the couple is ambiguous. It involves an economic and sexual union between a poor man and one of the wives of a chief or wealthy man. Although the woman remains the legal wife of the patron, her relationship with the client is publicly recognized and sanctioned. Such a marriage enables a poor man who would otherwise have few marital prospects to marry and ally himself with the wealthy person. A wealthy man who is either already a chief or wishes to become one can gain the political support of a dependent client. Because the client and patron's wife farm land the patron controls, the latter obtains products of their labor that he can sell for cash or distribute to others and thereby gain their support as well. Finally, because the woman remains the legal wife of the patron, children born to the client couple belong to the patron's lineage rather than to that of their biological father.

Kpelle marriages, then, are basically differentiated in terms of the legal status of women and the rights that husbands and their lineages may claim over a woman's children. If a woman is a full legal wife, that is, in a standard marriage with payment of bridewealth, her children belong to her husband's patrilineage. If a woman's legal status is in transition, as during the period of brideservice, her children belong to her patrilineage and her husband cannot claim them. And if the woman is the legal wife of a patron even though she lives with another man, her children belong to the patron.

Although marriage is the usual and preferred state for adults, rates of divorce are "moderately high" (Gibbs 1965). Divorces are granted by formal courts under the jurisdiction of local chiefs. Proceedings involve public hearings to determine the party at fault. Women usually initiate divorce, in part because the initiator usually ascribes blame, and men are reluctant to be publicly criticized for ending their marriages. Even though women are characteristically blamed for failed marriages, their request for divorce is usually granted. A man who wishes a divorce may mistreat his wife, so that she will seek a formal divorce in court. In this manipulative manner, he obtains his objective but is not publicly faulted.

Kpelle divorce benefits both wife and husband in an unhappy marriage. A wife who seeks to divorce is given her freedom and thus is personally satisfied. A husband, whether or not he wants to be divorced, receives the return of bridewealth that he had given to his wife's kin when he married, and retains rights as father to his children, including the privilege of receiving bridewealth for his daughters when they marry.

This description of Kpelle practices remains accurate for those in relatively isolated villages. However, in areas where economic transformations have affected subsistence patterns, marriage and divorce have also changed. In traditional villages, household farming, especially of rice, is the basis of subsistence. In villages close to main roads or larger towns, some people also produce cash crops whereas others work in towns and cities. Both cash crops and wage work provide money to purchase food and other

Anthropologists as Expert Witnesses

Testifying in court is not associated with cultural anthropology. However, cultural anthropologists are often called to testify in cases involving possible cultural misunderstandings on issues ranging from landownership to family law and child custody. They also testify as expert witnesses in cases about tribal rights, criminal investigation, and forensic science.

In her article "Infighting in San Francisco: Anthropology in Family Court, Or: A Study in Cultural Misunderstanding," anthropologist Barbara Jones (1998) outlines a custody dispute in which she was an expert witness. The dispute was between a mother seeking custody and the father, with whom the child was living. The mother had remarried a fourth time, was pregnant, and planned to leave the country. The father was single but closely tied to an extended family network. A psychologist, hired by the court and assumed to be unbiased, examined

both households and concluded that the mother should have sole custody of the child. Jones believed that the psychologist did not understand the benefits that the father and his extended family could offer the child.

She told the court that the child had been interacting almost daily with loving grandparents, cousins, aunts, and uncles. The father had also hired a full-time nanny to care for his daughter while he worked. Contrary to the psychologist, Jones concluded that the father's extended family provided greater benefits to the child than the mother's situation would allow.

● CRITICAL THINKING QUESTION

What perspectives do anthropologists have that might make them valuable contributors to legal cases?

goods previously produced in the household. These changes have affected bridewealth payments. Previously, a prospective husband and his family often needed to spend years accumulating the goods or funds needed for bridewealth. If they did not have the funds themselves, they needed to borrow from others, thus becoming clients financially and socially of people more prosperous than themselves. Men are now often able to amass bridewealth while they are relatively young and are therefore less dependent on other members of their families, including their parents. This has loosened family ties.

Women can also benefit from changed circumstances. Young women can postpone marriage and maintain their independence by selling crops they have grown or other goods in markets in towns, or through wage work, even though women have fewer jobs available than do men. Older women who are divorced or widowed can decide not to remarry if they have independent sources of income. Studies conducted in the 1970s document the beginnings of trends still operative today; for example, women residing in "modern towns" are more likely to "marry later, divorce more often, and remarry less frequently" than women living in traditional villages (Bledsoe 1976, 380).

Conversations with Kpelle living in small villages or larger towns revealed complicated attitudes toward marriage and divorce. Although young men and women favored the severing of responsibilities toward their elders, exemplified for men by amassing their own bridewealth payments and for women by postponing marriage, older men and women regretted the breakdown of family obligations that had kept younger people dependent on them. In Bledsoe's view, ". . . the distinction between the old and the young is probably more important in understanding individuals' goals and strategies in African societies, than the distinction between men and women" (1976, 387). Men and women have, however, used different strategies to reach their goals.

PEARSON
myanthrolab

Explore more at
www.myanthrolab.com

CHAPTER SUMMARY

Defining Marriage and Family

- Families serve economic and social functions. Members of families usually reside together and provide for biological reproduction and the training and enculturation of children. Families provide people with companionship, emotional support, and assistance, and are the basic unit of economic cooperation and interdependence. Families, particularly households, work together to complete the daily tasks necessary for survival. They are also decision-making groups. In many societies, families perform religious functions and rituals that celebrate significant events in members' lives.

- Marriage is the most common way in which families are formed. Marriage is a socially recognized, enduring, stable bond between people who each have certain rights and obligations with respect to one another. Husbands and wives can expect to have an exclusive sexual relationship and assist one another in raising children and in provisioning their household. Through the marriage bond, men are able to claim "social fatherhood" by establishing themselves as the husband of the mother.

Families and Ideal Types

- Although the family is a universal cultural construct, the types of families found in different kinds of societies vary. Nuclear families consist of parents and their children, whereas extended families usually contain at least three generations. Nuclear families are often found in industrial societies, which stress economic independence, and in many foraging societies, because they are adaptive to survival when resources are scarce.

- Extended families are more common in farming and pastoral societies. They have the advantage of perpetuating the social unit, sharing resources and work, and providing emotional support and material aid.

- Family types are responsive to changes in productive modes and general social values. In many countries, the idealized model of husband, wife, and children has declined, as has the number of children per household.

Endogamy, Exogamy, and the Incest Taboo

- The incest taboo universally forbids marriage between parents and their children and between siblings. In some societies, it also forbids marriage between other relatives.

- Theories about the origin of the incest taboo include an instinctual revulsion and aversion toward sexual relations within the nuclear family, the biological consequences of inbreeding, a reduction in the fitness of a population through genetic homogeneity, a response to the need to diminish sexual competition within the nuclear family unit, and a means of forcing people to make alliances with others.

Forms of Marriage

• Different societies allow people to have different numbers of spouses at any one time. Marriage between one man and one woman is called monogamy; marriage between more than two people is called polygamy. Polygyny is the marriage between one man and two or more women. Polyandry is the marriage between one woman and two or more men.

Marriage as Alliance and Economic Exchange

• Marriage often involves an economic exchange. Bridewealth is a gift the husband or his family gives to the family of his intended wife. Brideservice requires the husband to perform some service for his wife's parents. Dowry is the economic goods or wealth the bride's family gives to the new couple or to the husband's kin.

Marriage as a Rite of Passage

• Marriages may be arranged by parents or by the couple themselves through courtship. The marriage cere-

mony publicly sanctions marriage and symbolizes the rights and duties of couples to each other and to their families.

Patterns of Residence After Marriage

• In some societies, a married couple resides with or near the husband's relatives (patrilocal residence). In others, they reside with or near the wife's kin (matrilocal residence). In bilocal residence, married couples live alternately with the husband's and the wife's families. In societies with matrilineal descent and inheritance, a couple may live with the husband's mother's brother (avunculocal residence). In neolocal residence, couples establish a new household, separate from either group of kin.

Widowhood and Divorce

• Marriage preference patterns, called levirate and sororate, emphasize marriage as an alliance between families. In the levirate, a deceased husband's brother (usually younger) marries the surviving widow; in the sororate, a younger sister of the deceased wife marries the surviving widower.

KEY TERMS

household 210	class 216	same-sex marriage 221	patrilocal residence 228
family 210	caste 217	bridewealth 222	virilocal 228
marriage 211	monogamy 218	brideservice 223	avunculocal residence 228
social fatherhood 212	polygamy 218	dowry 223	bilocal residence 229
nuclear family 212	serial monogamy 218	arranged marriages 226	neolocal residence 229
single-parent family 213	polygyny 218	courtship 227	internal warfare 230
extended family 213	polyandry 218	residence rules 228	external warfare 230
joint family 216	sororal polygyny 218	matrilocal residence 228	levirate 232
incest taboo 216	ghost marriage 220	uxorilocal 228	sororate 232

REVIEW QUESTIONS

1. What definition of marriage would cover all the marriage types discussed in this chapter?

2. How is subsistence related to family forms? How can changes in marriage and family reflect adaptations to changes in subsistence?

3. How do endogamy and exogamy affect a society's social organization?

4. What are some hypotheses about the origins of the incest taboo?

5. What are the benefits of polygamous marriages? What are the drawbacks?

6. What are common forms of political and economic exchange in marriage, and what types of kinships are associated with those forms?

7. How are postmarital residence patterns related to kinship? How are residence rules related to women's and men's status in a society?

8. What are some reasons that marriages are arranged? Why is divorce discouraged in arranged marriages?

9. How are levirate and sororate different? Why do societies have these practices?

myanthrolab EXERCISES

To complete the following exercises and activities, you must log in to www.myanthrolab.com and select your current textbook.

1. In the **Explore** tab of Chapter 9, click on *Video* and watch the video on *Africa Polygamist Wives*. Complete the short answer exercise that accompanies the video.

2. In the **Explore** tab of Chapter 9, click on the *NPR Audio Programs Broadcast* tab and go to *Theme 19: Marriage and Family*. Listen to one of the programs in this section and complete the short answer exercise that accompanies the program.

3. In the **Research Tools** section on the home page, click on the *Research Navigator*™ link and enter the Anthropology database to find relevant and recent scholarly and popular press publications. For this chapter enter the following keywords: *caste, extended family, nuclear family,* and *courtship.*

4. Enter the **MyAnthroLibrary** section on the home page to read more about topics and cultures that are discussed in this chapter. Suggested readings include:

Konda Valley Dani: Marriage, Politics, and War by Denise O'Brien

Nayars: Tradition and Change in Marriage and Family by N. Prabha Unnithan

GENDER

- What is the difference between sex and gender?

- How do gender roles and gender relations vary across cultures?

- How does subsistence strategy relate to gender roles and relationships?

- How do gender constraints relate to a culture's ideological system?

- How does male dominance or gender equality affect a society?

- What global factors affect women's participation in the work force?

- How have ideologies affected gender constructs in the industrial and postindustrial eras?

A man and a woman were once making a hard journey through the bush. The woman had her baby strapped upon her back. . . . They had nothing to eat with them, and as they traveled on they became very hungry. Suddenly, . . . they came upon a herd of bush cows grazing quietly.

The man said to the woman, "You have the power of transforming yourself into whatever you like; change now to a leopard and capture one of the bush cows, that I may have something to eat and not perish." The woman . . . said, "Do you really mean what you ask, or are you joking?" "I mean it," said the man, for he was very hungry.

The woman untied the baby from her back, and put it upon the ground. Hair began growing upon her neck and body. She dropped her loincloth; a change came over her face. Her hands and feet turned into claws. And, in a few moments, a wild leopard was standing before the man, staring at him with fiery eyes. The poor man was frightened nearly to death and clambered up a tree. . . . When he was nearly to the top, he saw that the poor little baby was almost within the leopard's jaws, but he was so afraid, that he couldn't make himself come down to rescue it.

When the leopard saw that she already had the man . . . full of terror, she ran away to the flock of cattle to do for him as he had asked her to. Capturing a large young heifer, she dragged it back to the foot of the tree. The man, who was still as far up in its top as he could go, . . . begged the leopard to transform herself back into a woman.

Slowly, the hair receded, and the claws disappeared, until finally, the woman stood before the man once more. But . . . he would not come down until he saw her take up her clothes and tie her baby to her back. Then she said to him, "Never ask a woman to do a man's work again."

From Roger D. Abrahams, *African Folktales*, pp. 148–49. © 1983 by Roger D. Abrahams. Used by permission of Pantheon Books, a division of Random House, Inc.

This narrative of the leopard woman from Liberia shows attitudes about the proper work of women and men and the dangers of violating social norms about gender. This chapter explores the cross-cultural study of gender and gender relations, about which every human society has something to say. People's norms for gender behavior vary widely, yet common patterns exist. These patterns of thought and behavior relate in part to the way people make their living and the ideologies that support those ways.

SEX AND GENDER

gender
The roles that people perform in their households and communities and the values and attitudes that people have regarding men and women.

sex
Biological differences between males and females.

gender construct (gender model)
The set of cultural assumptions about gender roles and values and the relations between the genders that people learn as members of their societies.

As anthropologists use the word, **gender** refers to the roles that people perform in their households and communities and the values and attitudes that people have regarding men and women. Thus, gender is a cultural category. Gender is not the same as **sex,** which is a biological category. That is, females and males are born, but women and men are products of their culture's definitions of how females and males should act.

The term *gender identity* refers to how people internalize and enact those attitudes and expectations that are associated with their gender category. Gender identity is conveyed, for example, by how people dress, walk, and speak. And it is shown by the activities that people engage in and the attitudes they have about themselves and others. The term **gender construct (gender model)** refers to the set of cultural assumptions about gender roles and values and the relations between the genders that people learn as members of their societies. Unlike sex, gender is in every way "culturally constructed."

People in every culture maintain and transmit ideas about the roles that are appropriate for women and men to fill, the rights they have in relation to one another, and the values associated with their activities. These gender constructs are based in part on sex differences between males and females, but they vary widely across cultures. In many societies, however, the contrasting activities of men and women are constrained by the reproductive role that is exclusive to women. For example, engaging in physically stressful or dangerous activities during childbearing and nursing is difficult for women.

Evolutionary Perspectives

Anthropologists have sometimes looked to the evolutionary and archaeological records to explore the origins of gendered roles and behaviors. What can we learn about our earliest hominid ancestors? What data can we use to develop models of hominid and human behavior?

Based on DNA evidence, biological anthropologists suggest that the ancestors of humans and nonhuman primates such as chimpanzees and gorillas diverged some 5 or 6 million years ago (Zihlman 1981, 85–86). Complex adaptations deriving from climatic changes in southern and eastern Africa led

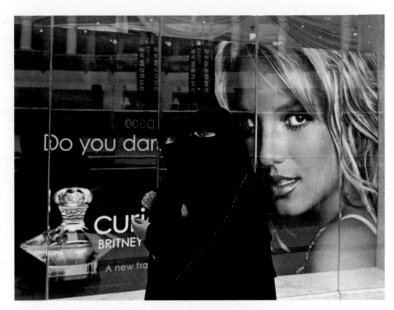

Gender identity is signaled in many ways, including one's attire and presentation of self. This street scene in Dubai, United Arab Emirates, contrasts the burkhas of Muslim women with an advertisement featuring Britney Spears.

to species differentiation and the exploitation of distinct ecological zones. Fossil evidence indicates that the hominid ancestors of modern humans (the australopithecines) were established by about 3.5 million years ago. These creatures were small by modern standards but were markedly different from other primates, principally because they could walk upright. Among the critical adaptations they had undergone were changes in the knees, allowing them to lock to support extended legs, the development of arches in the feet to support body weight and shift balance from heel to toe in walking, and repositioning the spine and pelvis to support upright posture.

The skeletal features distinguishing hominid males and females had also evolved. Nonhuman primate species have different degrees of sexual dimorphism. Some species have relatively slight differences in height, weight, and structural features between males and females whereas these differences are marked in others. A general decline in sexual dimorphism in human evolution was due to the dual factors of decreases in male body size and increases in female stature (Hager 1991, 48). The significant contrasts in the size and shape of the female and male pelvis, a critical factor in human evolution, began about 2 million years ago. This adaptation was interrelated with the enlargement of the brain. As cognitive complexity increased, presumably to process information and solve problems, the brain itself became bigger. This growth eventually posed dangers to pregnant females because their infants' heads would be too large to pass through the pelvic opening without endangering the mother's life. Adaptive changes in the size and positioning of the female pelvis responded to these dangers, allowing for safe births. However, human babies also had to adapt, so that their muscular coordination at birth now is relatively undeveloped compared to other mammals and even other primates. They are therefore dependent on adult caregivers for a long time. This dependency had critical consequences for the development of social bonds, especially between mother and child but also with other family and community members.

Although scientists have learned much about the physical structure of early hominids, they know little about how they lived. The first direct evidence of cultural patterns comes from about 2 million years ago with the manufacture and use of stone tools. Although there is controversy about how these earliest tools were used, they are often found along with animal bones (McBrearty and Moniz 1991, 72). Some bones have cut marks made by stone tools, and stone hammers may have been used to smash bones to extract the marrow.

The association of tools and animal bones has led some researchers to emphasize the significance of meat eating and therefore of hunting in the development of human culture. However, it is not clear that early hominids obtained their meat by hunting. Nonhuman primates, and presumably some early hominid groups, obtained meat by scavenging as often as by hunting. Hominids probably used both techniques, and the archaeological record supplies no clear evidence that distinguishes hunting from scavenging.

Still, despite a lack of supporting data, anthropologists have theorized that the dietary emphasis on hunting privileged males as the major agents of human cultural advances. Because males are assumed to have been the primary hunters in early hominid groups, they are also assumed to have invented tools and weapons, artifacts considered the hallmarks of humanity, differentiating us from other primates. From these assumptions, early hominid males are represented as using their intelligence and skills to provide food for themselves and others. In contrast, females are represented as passive recipients of meat provided by males and as leading relatively sedentary lives at home bases where they cared for their offspring and for sick or elderly members of the group. In this model, males shaped human culture, supplying women and children with necessary resources (Zihlman 1981, 75).

This "man-the-hunter" model is a modern manifestation of assumptions that first became popular through the works of Charles Darwin in the mid- and late nineteenth century and reflect the cultural practices and attitudes prevalent in Europe at that time. When twentieth-century anthropologists revisited questions of human cultural origins, they again privileged "man the hunter" as the key to human development that differentiates us from other primates. However, it is crucial not to impose contemporary attitudes and constructs on hominid ancestors living hundreds of thousands, if not millions, of years ago. The model of "man the hunter" as the primary actor in human origins and agent of cultural innovation and progress is a projection backward into history and prehistory of contemporary constructs of gender.

Despite their seeming logic, models of "man the hunter" are based on questionable or even faulty assumptions. First, hominid species evolved about 2 million years before evidence of stone tool use. Although it has been suggested that bipedalism (walking on two feet) was an adaptation to the need to see prey animals over tall savanna grasses and to throw simple weapons at them, structural changes allowing bipedalism evolved millennia before stone tools were being made. According to Margaret Ehrenberg (1989, 42), bipedalism more likely developed because early hominid mothers had to carry their infants because the infants were unable to cling to their mothers as earlier primate young had. Infants could not cling because the hominid loss of body hair left the baby nothing to cling to and because changes in the feet did not permit gripping.

In addition, stone tools were not necessarily the first kind of tools that hominids invented. Other types of tools made from plant fibers might have been used at earlier stages of development, but because they disintegrated and have not become part of the fossil or archaeological record, they have therefore not influenced theories about human cultural origins. Indeed, some researchers suggest that the earliest tools were artifacts used to dig for plants because gathering preceded hunting as a strategy for resource exploitation (Ehrenberg 1989, 46). Furthermore, early inventions probably focused on containers and devices to carry infants, young children, and gathered foods. Females probably invented these devices and taught others how to make them because females are the primary caregivers of children in all species of primates.

Moreover, no clear evidence supports assumptions about the importance of meat eating in the diet of early hominids. Early hominid teeth were adapted for an omnivorous diet, and we have no way of knowing the percentages of plants, seeds, and meat they ate (Fedigan 1986, 52). Unlike the connection between meat-eating and stone tools, evidence of plants or seeds in the diet would not be preserved because of the impermanence of these foods and of wooden or fiber tools used to process or transport them. Hominid front teeth were smaller and their back teeth larger and flatter than nonhuman primates, indicating an adaptation to chewing fibrous foods. And although the canine teeth of nonhuman male primates are typically much larger than those of females, male and female hominids had similar-sized canines, perhaps indicating decreased emphasis on male dominance and aggression.

Furthermore, although there is evidence of the association between stone tools and animal bones, we do not know all of the uses to which early hominids put these tools. The earliest tools have been called "scrapers" or "choppers," but their actual function is unclear. The wear patterns on some of them indicate that they were used for a number of different functions such as processing meat, plants, and hides, but many may have been used for other purposes (McBrearty and Moniz 1991, 76; Ehrenberg 1989, 46).

The "man-the-hunter" construct emphasizes male dominance behavior. Hominid males and their human descendents are seen as protectors of dependent females and children. However, this too is impossible to verify. Although male dominance is a feature of many, but not all, nonhuman primate groups, its role in human evolution is unknown. Some researchers, especially those in sociobiology, emphasize the importance of dominant males in selecting mates and therefore in transmitting their genes to future generations. Other theorists question the centrality of dominance in mate selection. Zihlman (1981), for example, notes that, in most species, the sex investing the greatest amount of energy and time in offspring chooses mates and therefore has the greatest influence on gene flow (1981, 88). Given this observation, what kind of mate would a female favor if she were looking forward to years of caring for dependent children? Zihlman has suggested that such females would select mates who are "sociable" and "willing to share food and protect them and their offspring" (1981, 91). Smuts (2001) cites comparative evidence from nonhuman primate studies indicating that females mate with males who are cooperative and nonaggressive. Data from observations of chimpanzees also find that females do not mate with aggressive males (Ehrenberg 1989, 49). Such evidence leads Ehrenberg to conclude that hominid females probably preferred sociable and friendly males. Furthermore, Lancaster and Whitten (1993) agree that sharing is both a behavior and an attitude that distinguishes human beings from all other primates. Through sharing and cooperation, people forge bonds of mutual interdependence. These ethics are the foundations of human families and community life.

During periods of early human evolution, female roles combined reproduction, food procuring, and social responsibilities. Males also gathered plant foods, at first primarily for themselves following the primate pattern. Gradually, traits of sharing and cooperation were favored as females selected mates and established pair bonds. As a result, males' emotional investments in their children increased (Zihlman 1981, 93). Indeed, rather than hunting providing the template for human society, hunting patterns may have been built on behaviors developed in gathering and sharing plant resources.

Although we do not know how social roles developed in the evolutionary or prehistoric past, researchers have suggested theories that account for the development of the role of fathers in social interaction with their children. Male involvement with children may have developed from men's hunting and sharing the meat with their wives and children (Lancaster 1983; Mackey 1985). Other theories emphasize the evolutionary trends toward greater dependency of infants and young children due to larger brain size and the consequent need for birth earlier in the developmental process (Smuts 1985; Hewlett 1991). Hewlett suggests that the critical factor in the evolution of the role of fathers was the kind of male-female relationship that developed early in human evolution. As social bonds among our earliest hominid ancestors (the australopithecines) were strengthened between a male and female pair, associated with ongoing and consistent sexual relations, males formed bonds with offspring, essentially the offspring of the female with whom they mated. Males provided meat and offered protection, primarily to their female mate, but their offspring benefited indirectly from the male's investment in the female (Hewlett 1991, 160). Later, transmission of cultural knowledge based on experience became another feature of fathers' involvement with their children.

The Cultural Construction of Gender Identity

Gender as a social or cultural construct is a primary aspect of one's personal and social identity. It develops in earliest socialization through the ways that a baby is handled, treated, and spoken to. **Cultural constructs** are models of behavior and attitudes that a particular culture transmits to its members. These constructs are shared beliefs and values that become taken for granted as guiding principles. Childhood learning teaches appropriate behavior and molds personality to conform to cultural norms. Girls and boys learn skills and attitudes that make them functioning members of their community. In addition, most (but not all) cultures use two sets of personal names, one appropriate for females and one appropriate for males. In Chapter 5, we discussed the importance of naming in constructing a person's social and gender identity.

cultural constructs
Models of behavior and attitudes that a particular culture transmits to its members.

transvestism
Dressing in the clothes usually worn by members of the opposite gender.

Ideological messages about women's and men's places in their families and communities and about their social value may be conveyed through religious beliefs and practices, language, and daily interactions between men and women in their families, communities, and wider social arenas. Rights to make decisions, to speak, and to participate in particular activities reflect cultural valuations and privileges allocated to people. In our discussion of language (see Chapter 4), we considered examples of the differences in how English-speaking women and men use language not only to communicate their ideas and feelings but also to transmit their gender identity. For example, we noted that women tend to be more polite, deferential, and attentive to others, whereas men tend to be more assertive and interruptive when speaking with others.

One universal expression of gender identity is the signaling of gender differences by bodily adornments and comportment. For example, men and women generally wear different kinds of clothing or jewelry. They may fashion their hair in different styles or use body decorations such as tattoos or makeup. In North American and European countries, pants have only been considered appropriate attire for women since the middle of the twentieth century. Even so, styles, colors, and designs used for women's clothing may differ from those commonly used for men. Moreover, although wearing garments styled like men's pants and shirts may be acceptable for women, wearing dresses and skirts is not at all acceptable for men in most American settings. It was not until 1995 that **transvestism,** or cross-dressing to look and act like someone of the opposite gender, was removed from the official list of mental illnesses.

Other kinds of gender-differentiating behavior are subtler and less conscious but just as powerful. Social presentation includes dynamics of walking, sitting, and general body posture. Speech styles employed by women or men are also often distinct. Nonverbal communication, such as gestures, smiling, eye contact, and touch, may be differentially employed.

Gender and Sexuality

Although we commonly think of sexual feelings and practices as part of our nature, they are also shaped by culture. Our culture teaches us what kinds of sexual feelings and practices are "normal" or "natural" and what kinds are "deviant." We learn who are appropriate sexual partners, when and where sexual relations are appropriate, and the proper ways to engage in sex. With few exceptions, these expectations are culturally constructed.

As discussed in Chapter 8, all societies institute some form of the incest taboo that bans sex between members of the nuclear family and certain other relatives. Many societies also set an appropriate age to begin sexual relations. In the United States, for example, it is illegal for an adult to have sex with someone younger than 16, a crime called statutory rape. This obviously does not mean that no one under the age of 16 has sex, but it does formalize cultural attitudes and criminalize specific behaviors. American society also has gender-based attitudes about the relative ages of men and women engaging in consensual sex. In many "normal" couples, a man may be fifteen or twenty years older than the woman, but it is rare to hear of a couple in which a woman is significantly older than the man. One reason may have to do with reproductive potential. That is, an old man can still have children with a young woman, but a young man cannot have children with a much older woman. Nevertheless, negative attitudes about younger men who choose much older women reveal cultural values about both sex and gender.

Another cultural element in attitudes about sexuality is the accepted relationship between sex and marriage. In American society, public discourse regards sex between unmarried people as inappropriate or less appropriate than sex between a husband and wife. Actual practice contradicts public morality, but the fact that political and religious leaders are reluctant to condone sex outside of marriage indicates the strength of underlying cultural constructs.

In this ancient symbol of yin (femaleness) and yang (maleness), the light area represents the greater sunlight of the summer solstice, which is associated with maleness; the dark area represents the greater moonlight of the winter solstice, associated with femaleness.

In contrast, it is considered normal and natural that unmarried people engage in sex in many other societies. In some societies, proving one's ability to conceive is a prerequisite for marriage. And although no society encourages extramarital sexual activities, the punishment for adulterers varies widely and is not severe everywhere. In addition, patriarchal societies often have double standards about these issues. Men are permitted and even encouraged to have premarital sexual experiences, whereas women are taught to remain chaste before marriage. In some patrilineal societies, a woman's virginity is a prerequisite for marriage, and adultery may be more severely punished if committed by a woman than by a man. In some Islamic countries, adultery is a capital offense for both partners. In others, only the woman is singled out for punishment. In 2003, for example, a divorced Nigerian woman, Amina Lawal, was condemned to death by stoning by an Islamic court for bearing a child out of wedlock; the man, who denied he was the father, received no punishment. However, an appeals court acquitted and released Lawal later that year, in large part because of international pressure.

Gender and Homosexuality

Attitudes about homosexuality are a further reflection of cultural learning. Judeo-Christian-Islamic teachings consider homosexuality a violation of natural law. Many nations dominated politically by religious thinking have laws that criminalize homosexual conduct and institute policies that discriminate against homosexuals. As recently as 1986 in the United States, the U.S. Supreme Court, in *Bowers* v. *Hardwick*, upheld the right of the state of Georgia to make private sexual relations between consulting adult homosexuals a crime punishable by imprisonment. This ruling was superseded, however, in 2003. Attitudes about homosexuality are continuously debated in many countries, most recently over gay marriage and gay people in ministry. In 2003, the Episcopal Church installed an openly gay priest, Gene Robinson, as bishop of New Hampshire, setting off a controversy that led to Anglican dioceses in Africa and Latin America threatening to break from the central Church in Britain.

Antihomosexual attitudes are far from universal. In India, for example, Hindu belief regards homosexuality as one of the possible expressions of human desire. Mystic stories portray both heterosexual and homosexual experience as natural and joyful. In addition, the pantheon of Hindu deities includes some who are sexually ambiguous, combining aspects of maleness and femaleness, or who transform themselves from one gender into the other. Finally, some Indian male homosexuals and transvestites adopt the role of *hijras*, people thought of as "neither man nor woman" (Nanda 1990). Although *hijras* are sometimes feared and ridiculed, they are also considered sacred, combining and mediating between female and male aspects believed to exist in all humans.

> Why do you think that third gender roles such as the *hijras* exist?

As another example, the Etoro and several other horticultural societies in New Guinea insist on male homosexual activity to ensure a man's physical growth and enhance his physical and spiritual strength. According to Etoro beliefs, people have a kind of spirit essence called *hame* that is needed to develop and maintain one's energy and vitality. At birth, only a small amount of *hame* is placed in a child, not enough to protect it for a long, healthy life. So, as people mature, they must try to augment their store of *hame* or life force. They must also protect it from potential sources of depletion, and one of the major causes of depletion is heterosexual intercourse. Men protect themselves from depleting their *hame* by avoiding sexual intercourse with women during periods associated with farming and trading cycles, estimated by anthropologist Raymond Kelly (1976) to amount to between 205 and 260 days per year. Protection against depletion is not enough, however, because the Etoro also believe that boys lack semen, which contains *hame*. Youths can acquire *hame* only by receiving semen from adult men. Boys orally consume a man's semen after manipulating his penis to the point of ejaculation.

In contrast to men, women are thought (at least by men) to have a limited amount of *hame*, thus explaining their relative weakness compared to men. Kelly did not collect women's beliefs about *hame*, however, because "a male anthropologist cannot develop an informant relationship with a female" (p. 47). Although Etoro men claimed that "only the women know what the women do," they believe that women engage in some form of homosexual activity through which adult women may transmit menstrual blood to young girls to initiate their reproductive capacity.

CASE STUDY

Two-Spirits: A Third Gender

Although the division of humans into two gender categories is the most common cultural pattern, other possibilities exist. For example, many native cultures in North America recognized a third gender category. The concept of a third gender was based on separating the social being (the gender category) from the biological body (the facts of sex). The third gender was a social concept that included biological males and females who assumed social roles other than (or sometimes in addition to) the roles usually associated with their sex. This third gender was a distinct gender category, different from woman and man. Western observers formerly misused the term **berdaches** to refer to third-gender individuals in a derogatory way.

According to documentary evidence reviewed by Charles Callender and Lee Kochems (1983), 113 native North American societies provided a third gender status as a possibility for their members. Lack of mention of third genders, now often called **Two-Spirits,** in other cultures does not necessarily mean that they were absent. Rather, Euro-American observers may not have noted their existence. In any case, third genders were well established in most of North America. Callender and Kochems find no correlation between types of social or economic systems and the use of third genders, except that Two-Spirits were least likely in societies that relied heavily on hunting.

People became Two-Spirits as a result of personal inclination, spiritual calling, or parental selection. A young girl or boy might take an interest in the occupations and demeanors usually displayed by members of the opposite gender. Parents thereafter trained the child in the subsistence skills appropriate to the child's chosen role. Among some groups, parents who had no sons might choose a daughter to learn hunting skills as a son would.

A more common mode of recruitment was to receive a spiritual calling through a vision or dream. Dreaming to assume the third gender gave both spiritual and social validation to a male's or female's gender transformation. Two-Spirits who came to their status through a spiritual calling were often thought to have extraordinary powers to heal and to foretell the future.

A Two-Spirits' social role was formally validated with rituals that publicly marked their special status. Among the Kaska of Yukon Territory, the parents of a female Two-Spirit tied a bear's dried ovaries to her belt to protect her from becoming pregnant when she reached the age of 5. At puberty, female Two-Spirits of the Cocopa had their noses pierced like men rather than tattoos on their chins like women. Among the Mohave, a male Two-Spirit participated in a public ceremony in which he was led into a circle surrounded by an audience and a singer when he was about 10 years old. When the singer sang initiation songs, the Two-Spirit danced as women did and was proclaimed an *aylha* (Two-Spirit) after the fourth dance. The Two-Spirit was then ritually bathed, given a woman's skirt, and announced a new woman's name.

Two-Spirits typically performed economic duties usually appropriate to the opposite sex, sometimes in addition to those associated with their biological sex. Female Two-Spirits were hunters and trappers. Male Two-Spirits worked as farmers (where economies included horticulture) and were trained in domestic skills, such as sewing, embroidery, and cooking.

Although male Two-Spirits generally did not participate in warfare, they joined war parties in some societies, either as fighters or carriers of supplies. Among the Cheyenne, they accompanied war expeditions, serving as healers of the wounded and guardians of scalps obtained in battle. They also had charge of the Scalp Dances that followed raids. Some female Two-Spirits became famous for their military skills.

Two-Spirits were often more prosperous than other members of their community. Their ability to perform both women's and men's work gave them economic advantages.

berdaches

Male Two-Spirits in some Native American societies who adopted some of the economic and social roles of women.

Two-Spirits

In Native American societies, males who adopted some of the social and economic roles of women, and females who adopted some of the social and economic roles of men.

In some societies, Two-Spirits had unique sources of income because they performed ritual functions specifically assigned to them. For example, Lakota Two-Spirits received horses in return for bestowing secret, spiritually powerful names on children. In several California groups, Two-Spirits were responsible for burial and mourning rituals. In societies such as the Diné, Cheyenne, and Omaha, they were often paid for resolving conflicts between spouses or arranging liaisons and marriages (Williams 1986, 70–71).

One of the consistent features of third-gender tradition was that members wore clothing and hairstyles associated with their chosen social role rather than with their biological sex. This demonstrates that gender distinctions are given both symbolic and practical value. In a literal as well as figurative sense, people wear the markings of the gender with which they are associated. Some Two-Spirits changed their clothing to reflect the gender identity of the work. For instance, Western Mono Two-Spirits wore men's clothing when hunting and women's dress when gathering, and male Osage and Miami Two-Spirits wore men's clothing when they joined war expeditions but dressed like women when they returned home. Deceased male Zuni Two-Spirits were buried in women's dress and men's trousers (Williams 1986, 454).

This drawing from the 1800s shows Sac and Fox warriors competing to attract the attention of a male Two-Spirit. (Smithsonian American Art Museum, Washington, DC/Art Resource, NY)

The social and sexual lives of Two-Spirits were consistent with their gender roles. Sexual activity and marriage usually involved relationships with members of the opposite social gender. That is, female Two-Spirits had sexual relations with and might marry women, and male Two-Spirits had sexual relations with and might marry men. Two-Spirits were often highly desired mates because of their prosperity, productive skills, and spiritual knowledge. According to recorded accounts, they had little difficulty marrying and establishing successful households. The wives of female Two-Spirits sometimes had children fathered by men but claimed by the Two-Spirit husband in an expression of social fatherhood. In some societies, Two-Spirits might marry either men or women. Significantly, Two-Spirits never married other Two-Spirits because two people with the same social gender could not marry.

Native Americans did not view sexual relations between Two-Spirits and their mates as either homosexual or heterosexual because Two-Spirits were not men or women. They were a distinct third gender. Symbolic transformation made gender, not biological sex, the important factor. Two-Spirits' sexual activity, like all their behavior, was seen as private and specific to them as members of a distinct third gender. Native American worldview extended this privacy to all sexual activity, including homosexuality and heterosexuality.

Gender equality is a prerequisite for the respect and high status conferred on Two-Spirits because it meant that neither males nor females gave up or acquired social prestige by abandoning roles usually associated with their sex and instead assuming other roles. Euro-American observers did not understand this underlying gender equality, however. They could not understand why males chose not to identify as men, interpreting this choice as a voluntary decline in status. In contrast to Euro-American values, males in most Native American societies did not give up dominance by abandoning men's roles because men's roles did not include rights to dominate. Most examples of men's dominance over women occurred in native societies that contact with European and American traders, officials, and missionaries had already transformed.

By the late nineteenth and early twentieth centuries, the number of Two-Spirits declined due to voluntary or forced adoption of Euro-American attitudes and practices. These insisted on only a two-category system of gender, denigrated males who dressed like women or assumed women's roles, and proclaimed homosexuality to be a violation of natural and divine laws. Agents of the U.S. and Canadian governments who supervised native reservations tried to force male Two-Spirits to wear men's clothing and short hair.

The following are the words of a Lakota religious leader speaking of events that occurred in the 1920s:

> When the people began to be influenced by the missions and the boarding schools, a lot of them forgot the traditional ways and the traditional medicine. Then they began to look down on the *winkte*, Two-Spirits, and lose respect. Some changed their ways and put on men's clothing. But others, rather than change, went out and hanged themselves. (quoted in Williams 1986, 182)

Explore more at
www.myanthrolab.com

Female Two-Spirits were also forced to abandon their social and sacred roles. Despite decades of concerted social and ideological pressures, however, Two-Spirits continue to exist in some Native American societies.

REVIEW   Gender, cultural constructs that refer to the roles people perform in their households and communities, differs from sex, which is a biological category. Gender identity is expressed in clothing, makeup, personal names, speech, nonverbal communication, economic roles, and how people are enculturated into appropriate behaviors for men and women. Attitudes and practices concerning homosexual and heterosexual sexual behavior are also culturally constructed. Gender constructs also include third gender roles, such as Two-Spirits and berdaches, people who are biologically male or female but take on the cultural and economic roles of the opposite gender.

GENDER ROLES AND RELATIONS

In all societies, certain behaviors and activities are deemed appropriate for women and others for men, with some overlap for both genders. Constellations of behaviors that are culturally associated with each gender are referred to as **gender roles.** Gender roles include the kind of work typically assigned to men and women, the familial roles that people play, the positions of leadership at home or in the community, and the ritual practices in which they engage. In some societies, women's and men's roles may be quite distinct with little overlap, whereas gender roles may be flexible in other societies.

Men and women carry out their gender roles in relation to one another, interacting in their households and their communities in nearly every aspect of life. Even in activities in which women and men are separated from each other, same-gender groups usually act in a way that is mindful of the other group. Coming-of-age rituals for girls and boys, for example, may be organized around gender differences.

Gender relations consist of interactions between men and women, which may reflect differences in the relative status, prestige, and power of women and men. In some societies, gender equality generally prevails. Women and men are thought of as equal, having the same rights to respect, autonomy, and independence. Although men and women may have different roles in their households and communities, their work and activities are equally valued and socially rewarded. In other societies, the genders are not considered equal, and some degree of male dominance prevails. Men are thought of as superior to women, as more capable, intelligent, or spiritually endowed. Men occupy more prestigious roles in their societies as leaders and decision makers. In their homes, men may have control over the activities of their wives. Extreme forms of male dominance may be reflected in physical abuse and rape. These behaviors tend to be more acceptable in strongly patriarchal societies, where men hold positions of authority and power to the exclusion of women. As mentioned in Chapter 8, there are no known examples of matriarchal societies in which women have exclusive power.

Division of Labor by Gender

As mentioned in Chapters 6 and 7, some form of division of labor by gender influences the range of daily work that an individual carries out in all societies. Men's and women's work is often complementary, both contributing to the maintenance of their households by providing food, shelter, clothing, and necessary equipment. There is a great deal of

gender roles
Constellations of rights, duties, attitudes, and behaviors that are culturally associated with each gender.

gender relations
Norms of interaction between men and women, which may reflect differences in the relative status, prestige, and power of women and men.

TABLE 10.1 TASKS AND GENDER	
Tasks Usually Performed by Women	**Tasks Usually Performed by Men**
Gathering plants, seeds, fruits, nuts	Hunting animals
Caring for children	Fishing as a primary responsibility
Caring for the sick and elderly	Herding large animals
Keeping up dwellings	Clearing fields for planting
Making clothing	Conducting warfare
	Conducting long-distance trade
Variable Gender Assignment or Cooperative Tasks	
Hunting small animals	Making crafts: pottery, basketry, tools
Fishing as a secondary resource	Building houses
Herding small animals	Conducting local trade
Planting/harvesting crops	

cross-cultural variation in the allocation of work according to gender, but certain patterns tend to be found in most societies. Table 10.1 summarizes some of these frequent associations between tasks and gender.

Inferences about division of labor by gender can be made from data concerning nonhuman primate behavior and traditional foraging societies whose cultural patterns are well documented. Such data led Lila Leibowitz to postulate that a division of labor was not necessary when human ancestors engaged in "unspecified and undifferentiated" production (1983, 123). Our early hominid ancestors, like modern nonhuman primates (chimpanzees and gorillas, for example), spent their days in the same pursuits. They moved from one resource site to another, gathered and ate fruits and plants, and socialized together. Male and female tasks were not differentiated except for childbearing, nursing, and caring for the young, all obviously female responsibilities. However, at some point in our ancestral past, a division of labor developed when people began to engage in more specialized economic techniques, requiring more complex skills and learning. A division of labor was efficient because it allowed different people to learn different sets of skills, enabling them to specialize, refine, and deepen their knowledge and proficiency.

A division of labor based on gender contributed to coordinating a group's activities, due to the fact that women were restricted in their mobility because of their reproductive roles. That is, unlike other mammals whose young are able to walk and feed themselves fairly soon after birth, human infants remain dependent on adults for a protracted period of many years. As a consequence, caregivers are limited in their own activities. Pregnancy, childbearing, and nursing limit women's ability to travel during significant periods of their lives. Travel becomes more burdensome and also more dangerous to a mother's and child's survival. In almost all cultures, women are allotted the care of infants and young children. Presumably as an extension of these duties, women generally perform other caretaker activities, such as preparing family meals and caring for the sick, disabled, or aged individuals within the household.

The division of labor based on gender is also an efficient allocation of human resources and energy in cultures where different kinds of labor require different outputs of energy and strength. Furthermore, it is efficient to teach people skills they are going to use during most of their lives. Skills needed to recognize and utilize edible plants, roots, herbs, and fruits or to track, locate, and kill animals require many years of careful instruction and practice. Therefore, specialization by gender and other factors such as age is efficient and provides for the survival of all.

As mentioned in Chapter 6, women in foraging societies gather wild plants, fruits, and nuts and may also hunt small animals. In contrast, hunting and trading, which may require a man to be absent from the home settlement for days, are typically the work of men.

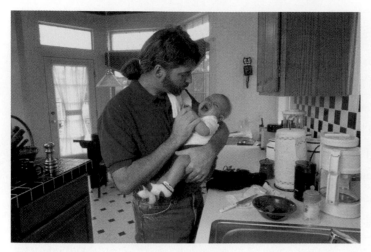

What socioeconomic and sociocultural changes in the United States permitted the changes in gender roles that this photograph represents?

Anthropologists extrapolate from these data to make assumptions about the lives of prehistoric peoples.

In addition to considerations of energy and mobility, foraging societies may assign home-based activities to women and external hunting and traveling to men because of the need to protect women against possibilities of accidents and deaths that might occur away from local settlements (Friedl 1975, 135). Because the survival and continuity of a community depend on the successful reproductive life of women, protecting them from unnecessary danger is adaptive. At the same time, cooperative labor may include both men and women within a community. For example, communal hunting and farming might involve adults and youths of both genders.

In addition, gender roles change as economic and material factors change (for example, when foragers become agriculturalists). Cultural forms arise in specific conditions and are changeable when those conditions no longer obtain. Although gender roles may have arisen because women and men have different reproductive functions and different energy and mobility requirements, the adaptive basis of earlier division of labor by gender is lost when productive work is historically transformed and can be performed equally well by women or men. However, more than economic and material factors are involved. For example, in modern industrial societies, most jobs can be accomplished equally well by women or men, but many jobs are held predominantly by one gender or the other. Men or women equally could be brain surgeons or typists, but most brain surgeons are men and most typists are women. Therefore, we need to explain gender roles in noneconomic terms as well.

One explanation is the social organization of households. As mentioned in Chapter 8, all societies structure households on the basis of families, regardless of family composition and household organization. Economic cooperation helps sustain family units because members perform different kinds of work that complement each other's tasks, becoming interdependent in providing basic necessities. Households are established and maintain stability on this basis, so the gender division of labor remains a convenient method of organizing household production even when it is no longer an economic necessity.

Another explanation is that attitudes about work and its association with gender are part of the background ideologies that members of a society take for granted. These beliefs and attitudes are naturalized and thought of as human nature rather than understood as endowments of one's culture. Ideological processes, then, contribute to the maintenance of a gender division of labor, regardless of economic or other considerations.

One aspect of these ideologies is the evaluation of some work roles as inherently more attractive or fitting for men and others as inherently more appropriate and appealing to women. For example, women are thought to make good nurses because they have an innate desire to be nurturing. They also make good elementary school teachers because they like to work with children, an extension of their motherly roles. Men, in contrast, are thought to make good leaders and heads of corporations because they are innately assertive and like to be in control. Nurturance and dominance, however, are learned behaviors. Nevertheless, positive judgments become associated with the proper performance of one's gender roles, whereas people who resist assuming their culturally prescribed gender identities are negatively viewed.

Gender and Status

Gender roles are complicated by the fact that work and other tasks assigned to men and women may not be considered equivalent or equally valuable. In theory, gender relations may be characterized on a continuum from approximate equality to the complete domination of members of one gender by members of the other. In practice, whenever there is gender domination, as in strongly patriarchal societies, it is always the domination of women by men.

Gender equality refers to a constellation of behaviors, attitudes, and rights that support the autonomy of both women and men. In a gender-equal society, women and men may have different economic, social, and political roles but the rewards given to them are roughly similar. For example, in Mohawk communities, women did most of the farmwork and household tasks while men hunted, fished, and traded. Although their activities were distinct, their work and contributions to their households were equally valued. Both men and women could hold positions of prestige and influence in their communities. Gender equality is more likely to exist in foraging and small horticultural societies, where all individuals make important contributions to subsistence and where hierarchical leadership is absent or minimal.

These Orthodox Jewish men are praying at the Wailing Wall in Jerusalem. Women are not permitted to pray at the same section of the wall as men.

In contrast, gender inequality refers to denial of autonomy and equal rights to one group of people based on their gender. Gender inequality tends to be most marked in large-scale societies with strong economic specialization, where social and political stratification affects the allocation of rights and privileges among social categories, including class and gender. In patriarchal societies, such as in India, Pakistan, and many Middle Eastern countries, women generally do not occupy positions of authority and are restricted in many of their daily activities. In these and other male-dominated societies, men contribute most of the productive labor that supports their families. They make most of the important decisions that affect their families, and they serve their communities as political or religious leaders.

Cultural values and social rewards mold people's attitudes about themselves and their relations to others. In societies where male dominance is pervasive, men learn to disvalue women and to assume rights to control women's activity. Women in these cultures learn to disvalue themselves and accept male domination. These gender models are often conveyed nonconsciously and go unquestioned. They are automatically accepted and followed and thus strengthened in the society.

In all societies, ideological constructs support and perpetuate existing ways of living. For example, as discussed in Chapter 14, religion often provides explanations and justifications for existing social relations. Religious beliefs sanction the status and roles of women and men, explaining divine origins for personal freedoms or restrictions, for differences in the prestige or power of men and women, and for the rights and obligations that they have. Myths of creation may give greater or lesser prominence to male or female deities, justifying the social value of human women and men (Sanday, 1981). For example, religious practice affects gender by allowing or restricting the ability of men and women to perform rituals. Barring women from sacred roles limits their status and prestige.

How does a religion with which you are familiar define the status and roles of women and men?

Even in societies that restrict women's public participation, however, women nevertheless have some power and informally control much of what happens in their households. Women's lives are sometimes described as focused on the "domestic sphere" and men's lives taking place in the "public sphere." This distinction may be fitting for some societies, especially large-scale agrarian or industrial states where labor tasks are highly specialized and gender roles are rigidly defined. But the distinction loses its value when applied to small-scale foraging or horticultural societies (Lamphere 2001). In these societies, there is little differentiation between a public and private domain. Most activities take place communally, often out in the open or indoors in dwellings inhabited by multiple family groups. Much work requires the cooperative efforts of men and women. Although these societies certainly have gender distinctions as well, a demarcation of domains is generally less rigid.

Women are sometimes able to exert influence, even in the most rigidly segregated communities, through direct personal religious experiences. In Ethiopia, for example, women may be possessed by spirits known as *zars*, whose presence is manifested through ecstasy and out-of-body experiences. Women who are possessed by spirits must attend a communal ceremony in the company of other afflicted individuals. At these rituals, held regularly about once every month, healers cure the women in an atmosphere of festivity and abandon (Boddy 2001). In addition to the ritual functions of *zar* beliefs, afflicted women have the

gender equality
A constellation of behaviors, attitudes, and rights that support the autonomy of both women and men.

gender inequality
The denial of autonomy and equal rights to one group of people based on their gender.

male dominance
A constellation of behaviors and attitudes that grant men access to roles of prestige and reward and deny the same to women.

CONTR⊙VERSIES

Is Male Dominance Universal?

Anthropologists long maintained that, in all societies, the status of women was at least to some extent subordinate to that of men (Friedl 1975, 7; Rosaldo 1974, 17). In other words, although women's status varied from society to society, in no society were they fully men. But are there (or were there) genuinely equal or superior to egalitarian societies? From the data, it seems that the answer is yes. But this is a complex issue, for several reasons. One is that there has been a long history of Western male bias in reporting behavior and beliefs in non-Western cultures (Leacock 1981, 17; Rohrlich-Leavitt, Sykes, and Weatherford 1975, 110–11). Explorers, missionaries, soldiers, and travelers in European colonization of the Americas, Africa, Asia, and the Pacific were almost exclusively men, who interpreted the cultures of native peoples through their own ethnocentric worldviews.

Later observers, including anthropologists, economists, and historians, were also predominantly men. Notwithstanding their supposed objectivity, they brought with them, as all people do, biases and frames of reference dominant in their own cultures. They usually asked for the opinions of men, partly because interacting with women was difficult for a foreign man, but also partly because male investigators considered men's opinions to be more significant than those of women. As Joseph Lafitau, a French observer of Native American cultures, commented in 1724, "authors who have written on the customs of the Native Americans concerning the rights and status of women have formed their conceptions, in this as in everything else, on European ideas and practices" (1974, 344).

Colonial contact also often swiftly and dramatically altered traditional gender relations by transforming indigenous cultures (Leacock 1981; Etienne and Leacock 1980; Gailey 1987; Wolf 1982). Emphases on external trade rather than household production and consumption undermined women's contributions and enhanced male control over resources. As a result, the allocation of productive roles changed.

Rapid realignments of indigenous political formations to meet colonizers' demands often accompanied changes in production. Among the Iroquois, for example, British, French, and American officials dealt only with male chiefs, ignoring the authority and opinions of women. As described in Chapter 12, however, among the Iroquois, female heads of matrilineal clans chose men of their group as leaders and appointed spokespersons to voice their opinions in council meetings.

Also, in Africa, the European colonizers bypassed female chiefs and warriors in favor of male leaders. Among the Igbo of Nigeria, for example, villages traditionally had a male leader for men and a female leader for women, but British officials undermined the power of the female leaders. Changes in political organization following European colonization usually enhanced the public prestige of men and increased their control over their localities and families.

⊙ CRITICAL THINKING QUESTIONS

How could changes in gender relations caused by colonialism be interpreted as proof of the theory of universal male dominance? Why would that interpretation be wrong?

GLOBALIZATION

Beginning in the fifteenth century, European explorers and colonizers directly and indirectly altered the gender roles, status, and relations of people in the societies with which they came into contact. Europeans imposed their own cultural beliefs and attitudes on those peoples, devaluing women and regarding men as dominant.

Would you say that gender equality exists in the United States? How would you defend your answer?

opportunity to socialize together away from the control and supervision of their fathers or husbands. *Zar* spirits may possess any individual, but their most frequent targets are married women. It has been hypothesized that, in the context of a male-dominated society, *zar* beliefs and practices provide married women with an outlet for frustrations, a release from restrictions imposed upon them, and an escape from household responsibilities (Lewis 1989).

In societies with gender equality, men and women are equally able to occupy positions of prestige and authority in their communities. Both contribute to making decisions that affect themselves and their families, and their rights to act independently and autonomously are equally respected. Gender equality does not necessarily mean that women and men do the same kinds of work or have the same social roles and responsibilities but that their contributions are equally valued. In addition, attitudes about males and females reflect positive evaluations. In family and personal life, women and men have the same opportunities and rights. Attitudes toward male and female sexuality are comparable. If premarital sex is permitted for men, it is permitted for women as well. If men can initiate divorce, women may also end their unhappy marriages.

Although the status of men is generally secure in most societies, the status of women varies greatly across cultures. Anthropologists attempt to explain this variability by drawing attention to economic, structural, and ideological factors. A basic feature of society and influence on gender status is the productive contribution that women and men make to their household and community economies. Ownership or control over resources interrelates with participation in economic production. As well, risk taking in hunting and warfare further influences the relative status of men and women.

In general, women's status is higher in societies where their labor contributes the major share of food that their families consume. For example, among foragers such as the Ju/'hoansi of Namibia and Botswana, the plants, roots, and nuts that women gather make up about 70 percent of the people's yearly caloric intake (Lee 2003). Significantly, women's social rights are also respected and their independence is secure. In contrast, in foraging societies such as the Inuit of the Alaskan and Canadian Arctic, where the percentage of food obtained by women's direct labor is relatively low, women's status is correspondingly lower.

In farming societies, a generally consistent relationship can be seen between the amount of farmwork that women do and their social and political rights. For example, among the northeastern Iroquois, women's labor (planting and harvesting crops) supplied most of the food that people ate, supplemented by meat and fish that the men brought in. In addition to their direct labor, women controlled the allocation of land through the matrilineages that they headed. They also controlled the distribution of food to families within their kinship groups. All these responsibilities in production and distribution gave women a secure basis for their high social status. In contrast, among the farming and hunting peoples of the Amazon region in South America, women's relatively low status can be understood partly as consistent with their minor roles in obtaining food, as men do most of the planting, hunting, and fishing.

As addressed in Chapter 7, historical evidence shows that when relations of production are transformed in a way that limits women's participation, then women's social and political rights become restricted and their social value declines. Recall from Chapter 9 that patterns of postmarital residence also play a role in women's security and independence. Matrilocal societies provide women with continued emotional support from their kin, whereas patrilocal residence patterns remove women from their kin groups and the support they can provide when conflicts arise. In addition, social and political complexity and the patterns of community leadership also affect gender status.

The degree and type of warfare in a region also influence gender constructs. Success in warfare usually confers social prestige on men. However, men's ability to translate their military achievements into control over women in their communities is in part related to the frequency of warfare and to characteristics of warfare. Where warfare is frequent and directed against distant enemies, warriors are absent from home for long periods of time and are less able to dominate the households they leave behind. Women in these societies have higher status. Warfare directed against nearby settlements, however, creates conditions in which warriors can extend their military dominance to other aspects of social life, including gender dominance. Furthermore, frequent internal warfare endangers noncombatants, affirming men's roles as defenders and protectors.

REVIEW

In some societies, gender roles are more segregated than in others. Gender roles strongly affect gender relations. Societies exhibit either gender equality or gender inequality, which usually means male dominance. All societies have some division of labor by gender, which allows people to specialize in a few skill areas rather than having to master all the survival skills of their culture. All societies also have cooperative labor. Gender division of labor reflects biological, economic, and cultural realities. Women's status in a society is based in part on the importance of their roles in the production of goods or provision of food; on their importance as householders, depending on the type and frequency of warfare; and on their access to kin support based on postmarital residence patterns.

GENDER AND SUBSISTENCE

As mentioned, modes of subsistence relate to gender roles, gender status, and gender relations. Foraging societies tend to have gender equality and egalitarian gender relations, except where men's economic or political roles are critical to the survival of the group, a situation that favors male dominance. Horticultural, pastoral, and agricultural societies tend to have greater gender inequality, depending on the control of subsistence resources and other factors, with the likelihood of some degree of male dominance. This pattern, however, varies considerably. Industrial societies, with economies built on agricultural bases, tend to retain ideological male dominance while gradually enlarging economic opportunities for women and extending legal and institutional equalities to both genders.

Foragers and Gender

In many foraging bands, women's and men's interdependent contributions to their households were (and in some cases still are) reflected in equality of social relations and social status. However, among others, male dominance is apparent. We can compare two foraging societies, the Ju/'hoansi of southern Africa and the Inuit of the North American Arctic, to understand similarities and differences. Both these small, nomadic societies were traditionally organized around bilaterally related kin groups. Economic roles were defined according to gender, but flexibility and overlap were also found. The productive labor of both women and men was essential for survival and was socially recognized and rewarded. Formal political structures and formalized leadership were absent. Settlements were politically and economically autonomous.

In Ju/'hoansi and Inuit societies, marriages are usually monogamous, although polygyny and polyandry occur infrequently. Initial postmarital residence is matrilocal, providing a young wife with support from her kin until children are born and her marriage becomes stable. Divorce, though, is common, particularly in the early years of marriage, and can be initiated by either spouse. Fathers in both cultures take an active role in child care and are affectionate and playful with their children. In general, attitudes toward premarital sexual activity are permissive for both girls and boys. And, although adultery is not condoned, its only punishment is gossip and criticism. Despite these similarities, important differences in the two cultures help us understand the conditions under which egalitarian gender relations are maintained and, conversely, some of the conditions that promote male dominance.

In contrast to Ju/'hoansi society, where annual caloric intake consisted mainly of plant products, the Inuit diet was almost exclusively based on meat and fish. Because men supplied these resources primarily, their labor was seen as more directly producing conditions for survival. Women's contributions, although substantial and essential, were seen as supplements. An emphasis on male labor among the Inuit led to preferences for patrilocal residence following an initial period with the wife's kin. Camp affiliation was commonly based on kinship bonds among men. Collective male labor was essential for many economic pursuits, especially among coastal peoples engaged in hunting sea animals.

These Mbuti Pygmy women live in a foraging society in the Ituri rain forest in Congo in Central Africa. In Mbuti society women are valued artists and have greater gender equality than women have in groups that live in more hostile environments.

CULTURE CHANGE

TRANSFORMATION OF GENDER STATUS IN A FORAGING SOCIETY

The role of subsistence in gender constructs can be seen clearly in well-documented cases of culture change. Economic and political changes among the Inuit, for example, have significantly affected gender roles, relationships between women and men, and cultural evaluation of the genders. Trade with Europeans, Canadians, and Americans encouraged Inuit men to spend more time and energy trapping animals for furs instead of subsistence hunting. Men who engaged in trade could accumulate valued manufactured goods, especially items related to men's work, such as fishing nets, metal fishhooks, guns, ammunition, steel traps, modern boats, and outboard motors (Graburn 1969, 129–30). As Arctic economies focused on trapping, families congregated near trading posts, becoming more dependent on the goods and foods they received in exchange for furs. In the twentieth century, Canadian and U.S. authorities accelerated this relocation by establishing administrative offices, schools, and nursing stations in settled villages.

Inuit

Inuit attitudes toward ownership changed. Formerly, anyone in the area shared land and resources. Later, trapping lines and the animals they snared were considered individual property. Because inspecting trapping lines and retrieving animals were done individually rather than collectively, cooperation in most economic activities became unnecessary. Emphases on individual property and accumulation of wealth enhanced the status of young men who were successful trappers.

After World War II, the pace of change throughout the Artic accelerated. Towns grew through consolidation of neighboring communities, influx of people from distant camps, and natural population increases. Exploration for oil, particularly in Alaska, by transnational corporations created numerous jobs, and thousands of nonnatives immigrated to the region (Chance 1990).

Today wage work is available to some Inuit women and men, often in gender-linked occupations. Men typically are employed in construction, mining, building maintenance, and work at Canadian and U.S. military bases. Women work in service jobs and as nurse's aides, teachers, and school aides. Since the 1980s, however, women have joined men in technical, managerial, and professional fields (Bodenhorn 1993, 184). Both men and women also gain income from skilled craftwork, including sculpture, painting, and basketry. Wage-earning work has increased the economic independence of contemporary Inuit women, leading to gender equality.

The Inuit situation contrasted with that of Ju/'hoansi economies. Ju/'hoansi hunters were respected and socially rewarded, but Ju/'hoansi women were also recognized for contributing to and controlling the major food supply. The Inuit division of labor that required men to leave their camps for individual or collective hunting resulted in the physical separation of men and women. Primary social interactions were with members of one's own gender. In contrast, physical and social separation of women and men was not common among the Ju/'hoansi. Conversational and interactional groupings form casually without regard to gender.

The conditions under which men pursued their economic roles added to their prestige because of the risks involved. The Arctic environment presents severe constraints, and a man's efforts, however skilled and fearless the hunter, were likely to fail. Daily risks to survival, compounded by the likelihood of failure, encouraged hunters to attempt to establish some control over their situation. Their religious beliefs revolved around ritualized precautions, taboos, and prayers to forestall disaster. The greater risks they took were rewarded with greater social prestige. Arctic survival depended on men's ability to control resources in dangerous situations involving violent acts against large, aggressive animals (Sanday 1981). This control extended to dominance over women. In a society where interpersonal aggression was condemned and where cooperative, friendly, and hospitable behavior was preferred, men were permitted to act violently toward women. Wife beating and rape were not uncommon (Briggs 1982).

Gender in Pastoral Societies

Anthropological studies of pastoralist societies, especially in Africa, have emphasized their patriarchal social and political organization. Men control access to land and herds. They own the animals, particularly cattle, that form the basis of subsistence and of ideology. That is, the people think of themselves as pastoralists centering on male pursuits, male interests, and male norms. For example, to be a Maasai (cattle herders of Kenya and Tanzania), is to be a pastoralist. Maasai men, therefore, fit this ideal, but Maasai women are marginalized because they are not herders. If women do partake in the self-conception of Maasai, it is as wives of men and mothers of sons, who they socialize into the male-centered ideal.

Although persuasive, this portrayal of pastoral societies is problematic. One problem concerns male bias in the analysis—most of the anthropologists who first described East African pastoral societies were men. A second problem concerns the historical transformations of pastoral societies resulting from European colonial influences. These transformations have become the focus of critical study to uncover earlier cultural practices and norms and to understand the processes that have shaped contemporary pastoral societies.

For example, in the late 1800s, when German colonial authorities first entered Maasai territory in what was then called Tanganyika, Maasai familial and community roles were distinguished by gender, but both men and women had autonomy in their own spheres. Women and men could achieve respect by their oratorical skills, generosity, and other personality traits (Hodgson 1999, 45). Subsistence responsibilities were allocated by gender. Women took care of calves, sheep, and goats, milked the cows, distributed milk within their households, and traded surplus milk. Young boys herded the goats and sheep. Adult men and older boys herded the cattle and decided where and when to graze the animals. Although their roles were separate, husbands and wives cooperated in deciding whether to slaughter, trade, or give away the animals. Women as well as men could give cattle and other animals to other people. After marriage, a husband gave some cattle to his wife as "house-property" under her control (Hodgson 1999, 47). Finally, women traded animals (mostly goats and sheep), milk, and hides to neighboring farming peoples to obtain grain and other crops.

Men held the major public political roles, as heads of lineages, ceremonial leaders, and members of village councils. Women could contribute to group decisions either indirectly through their husbands and sons or directly by speaking at meetings. Both men and women participated in negotiations for the marriages of their sons and daughters, and both could benefit from the cattle received as bridewealth when their daughters married.

German authorities sought to "pacify" indigenous groups to make the territory safe for European settlement. When the British replaced the Germans in 1920, after World War I, government intervention increased, affecting Maasai economic activities, leadership, and religious practices, and consequently also traditional gender roles.

Colonial authorities sought out Maasai elders who they thought could help them control the military impulses of younger men. The elders took this opportunity to increase their power.

British agents also contributed to the marginalization of Maasai women by restricting and regulating trade in ways that favored men. Men were enticed or coerced into the growing cash economy. They were considered "heads of households" and forced to pay taxes. To pay these taxes, however, men had to obtain cash by selling cattle, which increasingly became commodities to be bought and sold in the marketplace, or by working for wages. Because the British considered men the owners of cattle, the rights of women to share in the control of animals were diminished. To raise taxes, the British also began to regulate the casual, small-scale trade carried on by women. Once trade came under government supervision, men were privileged because of their greater familiarity with cash transactions. Finally, British authorities initiated programs aimed at economic "development." Men were taught new techniques of animal care and health to improve their stock.

As a consequence of these colonial policies, Maasai men gained economic and political centrality, excluding women from shared control over resources and from family and community decision making. Therefore, contemporary gender norms and attitudes that privilege Maasai men in most domains of life are an outgrowth of cultural transformations first initiated by colonial processes and then used by men to benefit themselves as a group.

Studies of other African pastoralist societies document complexities of gender roles and relations, not neatly subsumed under assumptions of patriarchy. Among the Turkana of Kenya, a mixture of patrilateral and matrilateral patterns prevails (Broch-Due 2000). Although kin-group membership follows patrilineal descent and postmarital residence is typically patrilocal, houses and their contents are the property of women. In polygynous households, each wife has her own dwelling. Her children reside with her, viewing her as the central node in their familial relationships. Mothers' houses are also the sites of ceremonial activities for births, marriages, and deaths. Women can also inherit property.

Residence compounds pass through different cycles, some of which are patrifocal and some matrifocal. The male focus centers on the senior male, his wife or wives, and his control of the cattle herd. The female focus centers on the senior female, usually an elder grandmother, her daughters-in-law and their children. Because husbands are usually much older than wives, women usually outlive their husbands and become the center of a growing household. When the grandmother dies, the household eventually splinters into new core groups, each composed of one of the elder woman's sons and his wife or wives. Then, when the senior man dies, the focus shifts to his wife. This view of the changing household unveils the complementarity of gender in cyclical patterns.

Attitudes about kinship also reflect Turkana ideologies of gender. For them, kinship is not based on relations forged by sex but rather on those forged by eating together (Broch-Due 2000, 171). In this realm, too, women are central because they milk the cows and allocate the milk. Women therefore control the physical flow of milk whereas men control the social flow of cattle, given and received in bridewealth.

Turkana social and political prestige revolves more around issues of seniority than of gender. The numbers of cattle necessary for bridewealth have increased as people have moved into a cash economy. But bridewealth still must be given in cattle, so that access to herds has become increasingly competitive. Younger men who cannot secure enough cattle may never be able to contract suitable unions. Elder men have therefore monopolized both their access to cattle and their ability to marry. The age difference between husbands and wives has consequently widened, leading to more rapid cyclical changes from patrifocal to matrifocal households.

The conversion of many communities to Islam has also affected women's roles in Africa. For example, among the Boorana of northern Kenya, men viewed their conversion to Islam as a link to other Africans living under colonialism. The height of the conversions took place in the 1930s when British control over the region intensified (Aguilar 2000, 253). Women were less drawn to Islam because many of its practices and values undermined their autonomy. Previously monogamous, Boorana men began to follow the Islamic pattern of polygynous marriages, which Boorana women opposed. In addition, Muslim husbands could divorce their wives if the woman failed to bear a child without questioning whether infertility was in fact due to the wife or the husband. Social stigma also made remarrying or finding households that would accept them difficult for divorced women, so the number of single-person households grew.

Today, Boorana women have begun to regain their centrality in their households, as owners of the dwelling and its contents and as keepers of Boorana identity and customs. Many younger men are abandoning Islam for indigenous traditions. Women are contributing to this change through their traditional ritual practices and their ability to communicate with the spirit world.

Gender in Horticultural Societies

In horticultural societies, control over the distribution of produce and goods influences gender status. In societies that are generally egalitarian, women exert their rights to make decisions concerning economic activities. In Iroquoian economies, for example, women performed most of the farmwork, including planting and tending crops and harvesting. In addition, women gathered a wide assortment of fruits, nuts, and roots and were responsible for domestic tasks and child care. Men's subsistence roles included hunting and fishing to supplement the basic plant diet. Trading with other native peoples for animal skins and utilitarian and luxury articles was also the work of men (Thwaites 1906, 15–155). Both women's and men's work was highly valued, socially recognized, and rewarded.

Women were not only responsible for food production but also controlled distribution of both the food and the resources that their husbands and sons contributed. This control over resources was a crucial factor in Iroquoian women's high status in their households and communities (Brown 1975, 236; Bonvillain 1980, 50). In addition to allotting food for daily consumption, women collected and distributed supplies for public feasts and ceremonial occasions (Lafitau 1974, 318). Their economic roles in household production and as resource distributors were thus extended into public domains.

Household organization centered around matrilineal clans that formed the basis of Iroquoian kinship. Matrilocality was the preferred residence pattern, so a house typically consisted of an elder woman, her husband, their daughters and daughters' families, and the couple's unmarried sons.

Iroquoian behaviors and attitudes related to sexuality and marriage reflected the independence and autonomy of women and men. People freely chose to engage in sexual relationships and to form marriages. Marriages were monogamous. Violence against women in the form of wife beating or rape was unheard of (Bonvillain 1980).

Iroquoian women's prestige was strengthened through many features of their roles within clans. Senior women of matrilineages composing each clan had responsibility for overseeing domestic tasks performed in their households and for allocating farmland to their kinswomen (Lafitau 1974, 69). Clan mothers chose lineage and clan chiefs from among prominent men in their kin groups. Thus, both men and women made important, socially valued contributions to their society and had ultimate control over their own behavior.

In contrast, among the Igbo of Nigeria, both men and women contribute to subsistence through their farm labor, but men control land and resources. Patrilineal kinship groups communally hold land. The elders of the patrilineage allocate land to each male member as needed (Njoku 1990). Preferred postmarital residence is patrilocal, consolidating bonds between fathers and sons and between brothers. Men occupy most major decision-making and influential roles in political life. However, women dominate village and regional trade. Therefore, although Igbo culture contains overtly expressed attitudes of male superiority, Igbo tradeswomen control market exchanges and benefit both economically and socially from their expertise in this sphere of life. Women trade their own farm products and crafts as well as those goods made by their husbands. Women's control over local trade is key to their ability to establish a high degree of autonomy in a culture that otherwise is dominated by men.

Igbo subsistence is based on horticulture. Tasks are strongly demarcated according to gender. Men plant yams considered to be the staple crop. Men also plant cassava, another root crop. Rice, a product introduced in the early twentieth century, is the only crop both men and women grow. Women plant and harvest all other crops, including maize, melons, okra, and varieties of beans (Njoku 1990, 53). These plants are interspersed among the yams and cassavas. Women also weed their husbands' yam gardens. Even when work has a collective focus, tasks are performed according to gender. For example, men harvest yams, but women and children carry the yams to the household yam barn (Ottenberg 1965, 7; Ottenberg and Ottenberg 1962, 119). A man's social prestige depends in part on the output of his yam gardens. Men whose gardens produce a great excess of yams beyond his family subsistence needs has the right to take the title of Eze-ji ("yam king") (Njoku 1990, 54). His children then can take yam-related names, indicating the respect shown to their father.

Other subsistence and household activities are likewise allocated according to gender. Men obtain fish from nearby rivers; women fish in ponds and streams. Men make bamboo frames for houses, women collect and carry mud for house walls; men put mud on the frames, women smooth it when dry. Gender differentiation is extended to craft production as well: Women are potters and men make mats (Ottenberg 1965, 9–10).

Most Igbo women engage in trade, as do the women of a majority of cultures throughout West Africa. Men also trade, but their participation was traditionally less extensive than that of women. Women's marketing expertise encompasses men's products as well because women usually sell agricultural products grown by their husbands in addition to those in their own domain. Most Igbo women are not full-time traders but engage in marketing as an extension of their roles in agricultural production. However, some women do engage in more complex trading activities, functioning as intermediaries and buying from local producers and reselling produce in regional markets. Others buy in large quantity from markets and then resell to villagers who do not go to market (Ukwu 1969, 177). Through these various efforts, women function as catalysts for wide redistributive networks.

Tradeswomen's husbands avoid interfering with their activities or making too many demands on their labor. Successful women have the income and prestige to manage on their own and, therefore, are able to leave an abusive or domineering husband. If divorced or widowed, successful tradeswomen do not feel compelled to remarry because they know that they can support themselves and their children.

In contrast to the Iroquois and Igbo, among the Yanomamo of Amazonia, women are excluded from direct productive work. This exclusion is then used as justification for their social subordination. Yanomamo culture sanctions men's dominance over women in every feature of ideology and practice (Chagnon 1973;

Many West African women are prominent traders, supplying their families and communities with produce and crafts., as shown in this market in Nombori, Mali.

1997). Settlement patterns, social systems, subsistence activities, and village leadership are all dominated by men. These conditions of Yanomamo society have been strongly influenced by economic changes as a result of culture contact (Kellman 1982), a subject taken up further in Chapters 16 and 17.

Residence patterns are patrilocal, based on affiliation among patrilineal kin. Marriages are usually arranged by men, a father giving his daughter to be wed to a man with whom he wishes to forge an alliance. Young girls, often as young as 8 or 9 years old, are married to men in their 20s or 30s. Polygyny is common and desired by all men but not economically possible for everyone. A man may contract multiple marriages through establishing alliances with several men who have daughters. Men also obtain wives by capture when raiding other villages.

Prestige in Yanomamo culture is principally based on success in two roles held exclusively by men: warrior and shaman, a type of ritual practitioner who makes contact with the spirit world and performs ceremonies to heal the sick and protect warriors. Successful warriors also function as influential village leaders. Warfare is common and is characterized by raids against nearby villages with the aim of killing as many inhabitants as possible. Young women, however, are often captured and brought back to become wives.

Although men are more likely than women to die as the result of raiding, there is still a relative lack of women in most communities because of the practice of female infanticide, a dramatic reflection of the unworthiness of females. This artificially created scarcity of women is a motivation for warfare, giving men the opportunity to capture a wife from a neighboring village (Harris 1974). Warfare creates a dangerous situation for noncombatants, enhancing men's status in their role as defenders. Thus, men's success is rewarded by both high social prestige and the subordination of women. Women's subordination is demonstrated by frequent violence in the form of beatings and rapes.

Finally, in an area of scarce resources, practices may develop in order to disperse populations (Siskind 1973). The scarcity of women, created by female infanticide and polygyny, helps limit population growth and also generates conditions of warfare conducive to forcing people to relocate away from centers of conflict.

Gender in Agricultural States

Agrarian states are complex societies with centralized political systems that maintain some degree of control over local areas within the state. They have economies based on intensive farming and produce surpluses that are used to support a ruling elite. These communities have marked segmentation of the population into classes that occupy different positions in society, and have different kinds of occupations and different standards of living. Many such societies are (or were) characterized by male dominance in gender relations. As in other types of societies, however, the degree of male dominance

gender gap
The difference in wages and income earned by men and women for comparable work.

cult of domesticity
A constellation of beliefs popular in the late nineteenth and early twentieth centuries that promoted the notion that women were, by nature and biology, suited to the domestic tasks of nurturing and caring for their husbands and children.

GLOBALIZATION

Culture change through government mandate is a force in the process of globalization. As in the case of China, central governments that have unified or expanded their countries through revolution or territorial conquest often have the power to compel obedience to laws that affect gender and other relationships.

varies widely, depending on economic, political, and historical factors, as well as on patterns of kinship, marriage, and family.

Industrialism, Postindustrialism, and Gender

In Europe and the United States of the late eighteenth century, innovations in productive modes began a process that transformed agricultural societies into industrial nations. Industrialization began in the manufacture of textiles, using mainly women's labor for the first several decades and then marginalizing women as manufacturing became fully established as the dominant productive mode. During the early nineteenth century, the independent self-sufficiency of farming families was gradually eroded by the need to purchase commodities. At the same time, transformations of production in manufacturing resulted in owners hiring workers for the burgeoning industrial sector. These two processes coalesced in the growth of industrial production.

Textile manufacture, centered in Massachusetts, was one of the first industries to develop in the United States, as it had been in Great Britain as well. Manufacturing began in the early 1800s and became well established by the 1820s. Young women, the daughters of farmers, constituted the bulk of mill operators. Unmarried daughters were available for outside employment because their direct productive contribution to their families was not as critical as that of sons. In the farming economy, daughters generally helped in farmwork and housework, but sons were central to agricultural production because they, along with their fathers, contributed the major share of labor on the farms.

American women's participation in mill work began to decline by the 1840s, when working conditions in the mills deteriorated due to competition from abroad and the desire of mill owners to cut costs. Women at mills in Lowell, Massachusetts, went on strike in the 1830s, but their efforts to protect their jobs and improve work conditions failed because the owners were able to find immigrant, especially Irish, women and men willing to work for lower wages. Except for textiles, native-born men also made up a large percentage of the work force in the growing industries of the northeastern and central states (Goldfield et al. 2004). However, they, too, faced competition from immigrant workers willing to work for lower pay.

Women were marginalized in the industrial sector through intersecting links between gender segregation in employment and unequal pay. Some occupations were considered appropriate for women and others for men. For example, industrial jobs requiring operation of large, heavy machinery were open to men, whereas women were employed in industries that relied on handwork and small machinery that produced such items as soap, hats, and cigars (Hartmann 1979). Even where both men and women worked in the same industry, they were differentiated according to specialization. In the manufacture of boots and shoes, for instance, men were employed as cutters and finishers, and women were stitchers and sewers (Matthaei 1982, 189).

In addition, women generally received lower wages than did men, even when both performed the same jobs. This differential in pay, or **gender gap,** as it is now called, was—and is—often masked by the segregation of work and workplaces. Men's social dominance can then be justified by the fact that they earn more money than do women. Paying women lower wages was justified by an ideology that women were only interested in working until they married and would leave the labor force to become wives and mothers.

In the early and mid-nineteenth century, a cultural construct currently referred to as the **cult of domesticity** became popular and justified separation of the genders, relegating women to the domestic sphere. Its popularity grew throughout the nineteenth century and remains in one form or another as a gender construct in American society. According to this cultural ideal, separate roles and domains are appropriate for women and men. Men provide material support for their families; women are suited to perform domestic tasks. Married women

Mill life reproduced the patriarchal relations that existed in households. Men controlled the organization of production, whereas young, unmarried women labored as subordinate workers.

CASE STUDY ●

Male Dominance in Traditional Chinese Culture

Patriarchal gender relations were developed through millennia of Chinese history. To underpin political and military power, China's ruling classes adopted philosophies that supported state control. The thoughts of Confucius (551–479 B.C.) and his disciples were especially influential. A cornerstone of Confucianism is the notion of "filial piety" that ordains obedience to one's social superiors. Thus, all Chinese owed obedience to the emperor, sons to their fathers, and women to their husbands.

Male dominance was manifested in numerous social, economic, political, and religious spheres. Households consisted of members of patrilineages, headed by the eldest male. His wife, unmarried children, and married sons and their wives and children were all under his authority. The rule of a head of household was potentially harsh, involving culturally sanctioned beatings of wives and children. Because postmarital residence was patrilocal, wives could rarely depend on their relatives for support in conflicts with their in-laws (Wolf 1974, 158). A wife was subordinate within her husband's household, especially when young and not yet the mother of sons to carry on her husband's lineage.

Mothers-in-law often acted as "surrogates for male authority" (Diamond 1975, 376). Although subordinate to their own husbands, they asserted authority over their sons' wives who had few, if any, allies in their husbands' households. In keeping with notions of filial piety, a man's allegiance was first and foremost to his parents. His wife could not depend on him for social support. Women began to receive deferential treatment after they reached middle or old age and had adult sons. Sons were a woman's main allies, and mothers could attempt to control their sons through strong emotional bonds (Wolf 1974, 168). Sons gravitated toward their mothers' emotional warmth in contrast to the authoritarian relationship they had with their fathers.

A marked preference for sons reflected patriarchal attitudes. Sons were necessary for the social, material, and spiritual well-being of their parents. Through sons, patrilineages maintained their continuity. The division of labor was gender assigned and contributed to the preference for sons over daughters. China was an agricultural country, and although peasant women did work in the fields at harvest time, men were primarily responsible for agricultural production. Women's work was usually confined to domestic tasks.

Women living in prosperous households seldom left the home. The Chinese word for wife, *neiran*, literally means "inside person" (Croll 1982, 224). By keeping his wife in the home, a man demonstrated his wealth and that he did not need her to work in the fields. Thus, women's economic dependence on men reinforced their social subordination (Wong 1974, 234).

Fathers arranged marriages without consulting the bride or groom. Girls generally were married in their late teens but were often betrothed as children. These betrothals solidified alliances between men. Girls' chastity before marriage was essential to maintain the honor of the girl and that of their families, but men had no premarital restrictions and frequented brothels to gain sexual experience (Wong 1974, 236–37). This double standard was another instance of male privilege.

Customs about divorce further discriminated against women. Only husbands could initiate divorce, often because of a wife's disobedience or failure to produce a son (Wong 1974, 234). Divorce shamed a woman but carried no stigma for a husband.

Ideally, widows were not supposed to remarry, but poor men who were unable to find suitable wives sometimes sought them (Wong 1974, 236). Widows often agreed to such unions to escape the social stigma and economic hardships of widowhood.

The practice of foot binding symbolized restrictions on girls and women in traditional Chinese society. The feet of young girls at age 4 or 5 were tightly bound with cloth, so that their toes curled under their feet. As the girls grew to adulthood, their feet became

With four sons, this traditional Chinese family has a strong future. Families depended on sons for labor and crucial religious functions.

deformed, and normal walking was impossible. Adult women took tiny, faltering steps on feet as small as three inches long (Wong 1974, 232). Only among the very poor, where women's agricultural labor was necessary for family survival, did daughters escape this practice.

In the early twentieth century, some customs began to change because of the influence of Chinese intellectuals and administrators, as well as British and French imperial agents (who had defeated the Chinese in a series of nineteenth-century wars). Although men certainly dominated British and French societies, their influences improved women's status in China. For instance, foot binding was outlawed in 1902, although the ban was widely ignored until the 1950s, when the new Communist government eliminated it.

After coming to power in 1949, the Chinese Communists attempted to transform social and familial relationships between women and men. The Marriage Law of 1950 declared that the "New-Democratic marriage system is based on the free choice of partners, on monogamy, on equal rights for both sexes, and on the protection of the lawful interests of women and children" (quoted in Wong 1974, 242). Additional laws banned child-marriage and dowry.

However, patriarchal attitudes continue in a preference for sons, even in the face of government reforms and programs for population control. To limit population growth, the Chinese government began a "One-Child Certificate Program" in 1979. A couple that pledge to have only one child receive cash bonuses, preferential housing, job assignments, and educational opportunities for their child. According to a 1986 study conducted by Fred Arnold and Liu Zhaoxiang (1986), 37 percent of Chinese couples with one child enrolled in the program, but a disparity exists between those with one son and those with one daughter. Sixty percent of holders of one-child certificates have sons; only 40 percent have daughters (Arnold and Liu 1986, 227–28). The Population and Family Planning Law allows a couple to have a second child if both mother and father were themselves the only child in their natal families (Hu 2002). Rural couples may also have a second child if the first child is a girl. This provision recognizes the importance of sons' labor to farm families and is aimed at protecting the life of a first-born girl because without it, parents might be tempted to eliminate their daughter. Some families, however, use prenatal ultrasound to learn the sex of an unborn fetus and abort a female child. Moreover, wealthier families sometimes prefer to pay the large fines imposed on couples who violate the law, leading to disparities in family size between rich and poor. The government is therefore considering imposing higher fines on wealthier families. However, after a devastating earthquake hit China in 2008, couples whose only child was either killed or seriously injured were allowed to have another child (Jacobs 2008).

The one-child program has reduced population growth, a matter of critical importance in China. In 1985, the natural growth rate was 15.73, but it had fallen to only 5.89 by 2005 (China Statistical Yearbook 2005). However, the gender disparity is troubling and has consequences for future opportunities of men and women.

PEARSON
myanthrolab

Explore more at
www.myanthrolab.com

who joined the labor force as an economic necessity were told that they were neglecting their proper duties to nurture their husbands and children by working outside the home. Husbands of working women were similarly made to feel derelict in their duty. Because the ideal man was one who supported his wife and children, a man whose wife worked was less than a real man.

Labor leaders also used these attitudes to restrict women's involvement in wage work as competition between employed women and men intensified at the beginning of the twentieth century. Although ostensibly dedicated to bettering conditions for all workers, most unions in the nineteenth and early twentieth centuries discriminated against women, barring them from membership or relegating them and their interests to auxiliary status (Berch 1982). When men were faced with competition from women, who often were willing to work for lower wages, unions had two possible responses: They could advocate equality of pay for all workers, to remove the financial incentive for employers to hire women rather than men; or they could advocate restrictions on women's employment as a strategy for maintaining men's advantages. They chose the latter course.

In another response to competition from women workers, labor leaders and public figures advocated enactment of "protective legislation" to protect women from harmful conditions on the job. Hours for women were decreased, night work in some occupations was forbidden, and exposure to dangerous chemicals, materials, or machinery was banned. But the same protections were not extended to men. Although the rules protected women from dangers on the job, they carried hidden costs, rendering women less attractive as employees and, therefore, hurting their chances of being hired.

Despite strong pressures to keep women in the home, some women sought to obtain higher education and to participate in the work force, spurring social changes in gender roles and expectations. Their political activism also increased. As early as the mid-nineteenth century, women sought political rights equal to men. Organizing at the Seneca Falls (New York) Convention in 1848, Elizabeth Cady Stanton and Lucretia Mott (later joined by Susan B. Anthony) issued a Declaration of Sentiments and Resolutions modeled on the U.S. Declaration of Independence calling for equal rights for women (Sapiro 1986). The women's suffrage movement culminated in 1920, in ratification of the Nineteenth Amendment to the U.S. Constitution, which gave women the right to vote.

CULTURE CHANGE

TRANSFORMATION OF AMERICAN WORK IN THE TWENTIETH CENTURY

Many factors came together to change the economic and social roles of men and women in the twentieth century. New demands for workers, rising standards of living, and growing awareness of inequalities all led to increased participation of women in paid employment. During World War I (1914–1918), women replaced men who had joined the military, obtaining jobs that had previously been barred to them and including managerial positions and jobs in heavy industry. Patterns of employment among women also changed. As white women were increasingly hired as office workers, teachers, saleswomen, and telephone operators, black women moved into domestic and service occupations (Amott and Matthaei 1991).

After the war, many women remained in the work force to help support their families as inflation rose, real wages fell, and the demand for consumer goods increased. Many mothers also worked to support children through college.

The years of the Great Depression, beginning in 1929 and lasting through the 1930s, witnessed another cycle of shifts in employment. Millions of men lost jobs in industry and construction. To give work to men, many people, including wives of unemployed men, attacked married working women, and states passed laws barring their employment.

The Depression was followed by World War II (1939–1945). Millions of men entered the military, leaving millions of jobs unfilled. Women again heeded the patriotic call to join the work force. Job opportunities for all women improved. Black women worked in industries that had previously been closed to them (Bose 1987, 279). The numbers of married working women increased, and women with young children entered public labor. After the war, men again pushed women out of work or at least out of the positions they had occupied during the war. Many women, though, remained in the work force, motivated by necessity and personal interest.

TABLE 10.2 LABOR FORCE PARTICIPATION FOR MOTHERS WITH YOUNG CHILDREN				
Mothers with Children 14–17	Mothers with Children 6–13	Mothers with Children 3–5	Mothers with Children Under 3	Mothers with Infants Under 1
79.6%	73.0%	64.2%	57.0%	55.8%

Workers from different social categories have fed each increase in women's employment. At first, most women workers were young and unmarried. Then immigrant women, single and married, entered the work force. Married, native-born women entered and stayed in paid employment in large numbers in the 1940s. Subsequently, most married working women were older women whose children had grown up. Since the 1960s, however, working mothers with young children have taken jobs in addition to their domestic responsibilities (Fox and Hesse-Biber 1984, 27–28).

Today, costs of living make it necessary for married women and for mothers to earn money. Thus, the two-worker family has become commonplace. In addition, many mothers are single, either because of divorce or of never having married. Many women also choose to pursue a career or escape the social isolation of their homes.

By 2008, about 70.6 percent of women aged 20 to 64 were in the labor force, as were 83.2 percent of men (U.S. Bureau of the Census, 2008 American Community Survey), with the highest levels of employment for men and women between the ages of 25 and 55.

Most women with children of all ages were in the labor force in 2008 (U.S. Department of Labor). That is, about 70 percent of mothers with children under the age of 18 were working. This is a large increase since 1975, when only 47 percent of mothers with children under 18 were working. The increase comes primarily from mothers with young children. However, those with younger children tended to work fewer hours than those with older children. Table 10.2 gives the data for labor force participation rates and employment rates for mothers of children under age 18 (U.S. Department of Labor 2008).

Labor force participation rates for married women with children under the age of 18 grew steadily in the second half of the twentieth century but leveled off in the 1990s. Since 1997, labor force participation and employment rates for mothers have slightly declined for all categories of women. Although the educational levels of these mothers had no effect on the rate of decrease, their husbands' earnings did. Women whose husbands' earnings were in the top 20 percent and in the bottom 20 percent were more likely to stay at home than women whose husbands' incomes were in the middle range (Cohany and Sok 2007, 15). Racial and ethnic differences also affected whether married mothers with young children are likely to have paid employment. African American mothers were the most likely to work outside the home, at a rate of 65 percent. Most white (58 percent) and Asian mothers (51 percent) were also in the labor force. In contrast, only about one third (34 percent) of Hispanic mothers sought employment (Cohany and Sok 2007, 12). Finally, married mothers born in the United States were more likely than immigrant mothers to be in the labor force (59 percent compared to 35 percent).

Although the number of women in paid employment has grown, discrimination in wages and lack of access to some jobs still hinder their equality as workers, even though the wage gap has narrowed in most occupations. As Table 10.3 shows, women are paid, on average, less than men in all occupations and for all age cohorts. When salaries are compared for women and men with comparable education and years of experience, the gender gap remains. Although the gender gap in pay exists for all races, African American and Hispanic women's wages are closer to those of men of their own group than is true for whites. African American women earn 91 percent of African American men's wages, and Hispanic women's wages are about 88 percent of Hispanic men's earnings. However, these data reflect the relatively lower wages of nonwhite men rather than higher wages of nonwhite women.

Women continue to face occupational segregation in the types of jobs for which they are hired. Table 10.4 gives percentages of women in selected occupations.

Women who remain at home and fulfill the traditional ideal of domestic roles are involved in the important work of social reproduction. **Social reproduction** entails the care

Why is housework devalued? What role does household labor play in statistics about the productivity of the American economy?

social reproduction
The care and sustenance of people who will be able to contribute productively to society.

TABLE 10.3   WOMEN AS A PERCENTAGE OF WORKERS IN SELECTED OCCUPATIONS

Occupation	Women as % of Total (2006)
Total	46.34%
Management, professional, and related occupations	50.56%
Management, business, and financial operations occupations	41.85%
Professional and related occupations	56.90%
Service occupations	57.34%
Sales and office occupations	63.27%
Sales and related occupations	49.05%
Office and administrative support occupations	75.40%
Natural resources, construction, and maintenance occupations	4.75%
Farming, fishing, and forestry occupations	22.06%
Construction and extraction occupations	3.07%
Installation, maintenance, and repair occupations	4.63%
Production, transportation, and material moving occupations	22.82%
Production occupations	30.39%
Transportation and material moving occupations	14.84%

Source: Current Population Survey, U.S. Department of Labor, U.S. Bureau of Labor Statistics

TABLE 10.4   OCCUPATION AND MEDIAN EARNINGS FOR MEN AND WOMEN

Occupation	% Men	% Women	Men's Median Earnings	Women's Median Earnings
Management	62.8	37.2	65, 010	46, 256
Business and financial	45.8	54.2	57, 513	41, 384
Computer and mathematical operations	72.2	27.8	65, 914	55, 816
Architecture and engineering	85.5	14.5	64, 653	49, 418
Life, physical, and social science	55.4	44.6	55, 719	44, 334
Community and social services	38.7	61.3	35, 468	32, 007
Legal occupations	49.7	50.3	100, 000	46, 008
Education and library occupations	26.4	73.6	42, 487	31, 338
Arts, entertainment, sports, and media	52.6	47.4	38, 939	27, 731
Health care practitioner and technical occupations	25.7	74.3	67, 475	41, 687
Health care support occupations	11.8	88.2	22, 906	19, 761
Law enforcement workers	80.0	20.0	50, 078	40, 271
Food preparation and serving occupations	43.6	56.4	13, 702	10, 483
Sales and related occupations	50.7	49.3	37, 874	17, 006
Office and support occupations	25.9	74.1	28, 166	25, 266
Farming, fishing, forestry	79.7	20.3	17, 940	11, 405
Construction	97.0	3.0	30, 238	22, 258
Transportation and moving	84.3	15.7	27, 752	17, 312

Source: U.S. Bureau of the Census, 2006 American Community Survey.

and sustenance of people who will be able to contribute productively to society. Necessary tasks include obtaining and preparing food, maintaining the physical premises of the home, purchasing clothing and other material goods, tending family members when they are ill, and planning and supervising the education of children. However, the worth of labor contributed by stay-at-home wives and mothers is socially devalued, reflected, for example, in the phrase "just a housewife," which women themselves often use as a self-definition. However, the work of social reproduction that such women perform is vital to society and to the economic system. Although nonemployed wives are perceived as dependent on their husbands, husbands also depend on their wives. Just as men contribute their wages to support their families, women contribute their unpaid labor to family survival.

REVIEW — Relationships between subsistence and gender relations depend on the allocation of power, control of resources, and other factors. Some forager and horticultural societies had gender equality, whereas others have male dominance. Agrarian societies were generally male dominated. Industrialism changed gender relations. Segregation and a gender gap (unequal pay) developed in factory work. More women have entered the American work force in the twentieth century. Unemployed women who stay at home came to be seen as nonproductive, an attitude contributing to the subordination of women.

GLOBALIZATION AND GENDER

Agricultural and industrial development programs sponsored by national governments or international agencies aim to strengthen economies, raise living standards, and improve health in impoverished rural communities. Development theory emphasizes the importance of modernizing in technology, agricultural production for trade, and industrialization dependent on a mobile labor force. When measured by gross national product (GNP), median family or household income, and longer life expectancy, advances can be demonstrated, but researchers still question the impact of economic development on different sectors of the population.

When the differential effects of development on men and women were first systematically explored, evidence suggested that modernization contributed to a decline in women's status, especially in Africa and Asia (Boserup 1970). In Africa, landownership has passed from the collective control of kinship groups to individual control, increasingly concentrated in the hands of men. As land utilization has changed from an emphasis on subsistence to production for trade in national and global markets, women have seen their role in subsistence farming diminished. As their centrality in family production shrinks, their status has also declined. In Asia, mechanization and technological advances in farming have tended to favor male farmworkers.

An additional element in weighing the changes in women's status is their role in social reproduction and the gender division of labor in the household. The domestic labor that women do helps support family members and makes their participation in agriculture or industry possible. Policy planners and analysts of economic development often ignore this element (Beneria and Sen 1986). Furthermore, in societies where attitudes about gender limit women's ability to participate in work outside the home, their social status declines as societal value is placed on wage-earning activities.

Women's actual contributions to the world economy are often distorted and rendered invisible because of the inadequacy of research and statistics on labor force participation in the public sphere and because women's economic contributions in the home are ignored. Productive work or "active labor" is generally interpreted as participation in income-earning activities. Because much of women's work is in subsistence agriculture, home craft production, or the "informal" labor sector in urban environments (peddling, domestic service), their economic contributions are often seriously underestimated. In addition, census classifications of workers according to their "main"

GLOBALIZATION

European colonization had a significant impact on gender roles and attitudes. European traders preferred to deal with men and thus ignored or subverted the economic contributions of women. Missionaries affected gender relations directly and indirectly by redefining marriage and family in terms of European principles. Colonizers also tended to legitimate men's political authority and diminish women's public political roles.

IN THEIR OWN VOICES

Tsetsele Fantan on Women and AIDS in Botswana

In this address from a 2003 conference on Botswana's Strategy to Combat HIV/AIDS, Tsetsele Fantan, from the African Comprehensive HIV/AIDS Partnership, discusses the cultural constraints affecting HIV/AIDS prevention and treatment programs in Botswana. She mentions attitudes about sex, marriage, and women's roles that hamper the effectiveness of these programs. And she emphasizes the need to involve men and women to achieve change. Africa is the continent hardest hit by HIV/AIDS. In Botswana, 67 percent of HIV-infected people ages 16 to 49 are women. Women are also the principal caretakers for AIDS sufferers in their households. And because eight out of ten farmers are women, their illness and death from AIDS affect their entire communities.

Globally, women are exposed to HIV transmission because of four main vulnerabilities: the social/cultural context, economic subordination, sexual subordination, and the female biological makeup. As far as the social/cultural context in Botswana is concerned, boys and girls are socialized differently, predominantly along traditional norms that emphasize female subordination throughout the lifecycle. This is also emphasized when young women get married. We remind them that they need to honor and obey. This becomes extremely difficult when women are abused in marriage because as they go to uncles and aunts for counsel, they are reminded of their marriage vows. This gender power differential is compounded by age differences.

As far as economic subordination is concerned, poverty does force some women to adopt economic strategies, survival strategies, such as transactional sex. As far as sexual subordination is concerned, women are expected to have one lifetime partner, while male deviation is condoned, generally expected, or even encouraged. Women are also vulnerable to coerced sex, including rape and other sexual abuse, both inside and outside of the family, including marital rape. Young women and girls are increasingly targeted by older men seeking safe and/or subservient sexual partners, or just sexual adventure.

In addition to all the education that is being given about HIV and AIDS, I would like to mention three areas where I believe work needs to be done. The first is a need to redefine traditional gender images. There is an urgent need to redefine images of masculinity and femininity through culturally relevant public education, and this is an area where the media can play a very important role. We need to emphasize the role of men, not only as breadwinners, but as ensuring the protection of the health of themselves and their families. We need to clearly articulate the imperative for men to change attitudes and behaviors in a nonthreatening way. We need transformational programs that acknowledge that men are partners in the fight against HIV and AIDS. Secondly, we need to engage men in the empowerment of women. We need to recognize and come to terms with the realities of women in Botswana, and the realities of our social circumstances in Botswana, and recognize that women's empowerment cannot be realized without full involvement and engagement of the men. We therefore need to develop initiatives, innovative community-based programs that empower grassroots men to work with women. We need to develop programs that assist men and women to effectively negotiate for space, recognition, and acknowledgment of each other. To develop targeted programs for men that utilize informal, traditional structures, led by traditional and opinion leaders in the districts.

We need to develop gender and culturally sensitive programs and support services that address the vulnerability of women to HIV and AIDS. We need to develop women's entrepreneurial skills, as well as giving them or facilitating their access to credit, because acquiring skills without the capital to start a business which has a market will not change much.

Attitudes and practices that are deeply rooted in culture are unlikely to change in the short term. Programs to address this will require long-term commitment from development partners. Local traditional leaders must be empowered to advocate for and effect these changes at the community level. This should be done through proper dialogue. We need to identify and liberate the positive aspects of culture for gender-sensitive prevention initiatives. Lastly, we need to make sure that the valuable elements in our culture must be preserved and passed on to the next generation.

Explore more at
www.myanthrolab.com

From Center for Strategic and International Study HIV/AIDS Task Force, Botswana's Strategy to Combat HIV/AIDS, Empowering Women and People Living with HIV/AIDS, November 12, 2003. Reprinted by permission of the Center for Strategic & International Studies, Washington D.C.

CRITICAL THINKING QUESTIONS

What aspects of traditional culture encourage the spread of HIV/AIDS among women in Botswana? What features of traditional culture can best prevent this spread?

occupation tend to ignore women's economic contributions because they are classified as home workers without detailing their specific contributions to subsistence and also to extra household income such as making foods or crafts for sale. Finally, development programs often focus on the generation of work itself rather than on the reasons that women are not qualified, rooted in their lack of training and education because of discriminatory attitudes.

Women's Roles in Urban and Rural Economic Development

In some countries, industrial development favors women's employment in certain sectors. For example, in Malaysia, Singapore, and Taiwan, national and multinational corporations have established factories, especially in electronics and garment assembly, which employ mainly young women. According to some estimates, about 80 percent of workers in light manufacturing plants worldwide are women between the ages of 13 and 25 (Moore 1988, 100). In Singapore, labor force participation rates for women have increased dramatically since the government embarked on rapid industrialization, providing tax incentives to foreign investment and curtailing labor union organizing (Wong 1986, 208). By 1995, women's economic activity rate had risen to 51 percent (United Nations, Division for the Advancement of Women 2000). Factories in Malaysia have also increased the wage-earning opportunities of young women (Ong 1983). There, and in other Asian and Latin American countries, rural women leave their homes to improve their skills and chances of economic advancement. Their needs are especially acute in the context of increasing poverty in the countryside and the resulting dislocation. In the decade of the 1970s alone, shortly after the government began its industrialization program, the number of Malay women factory workers increased dramatically, from about 1,000 to more than 60,000 (Ong 1983, 429).

Young women benefit from their job opportunities by earning an income that gives them some economic independence and greater status in their families. They also escape the intense control traditionally exerted over them in their households, and they meet friends and socialize in the industrial centers. The wages they earn are higher than available in other jobs. However, the companies take advantage of the workers' poverty, lack of skills, and few alternative opportunities, paying them relatively low wages and offering few benefits.

Today, economic development increasingly affects small, relatively isolated communities. For example, the Pacific islands of Melanesia and Polynesia have become incorporated into national and global export networks. The production of copra (dried coconut) as a cash crop on the Melanesian island of Vanuatu (formally called New Hebrides) has gradually involved villagers in globalization while also maintaining a diversified subsistence and cash economy (Rodman 1993). The people of Vanuatu first became involved in coconut production in the 1930s, but by the early 1980s, world prices for copra declined, and the local market collapsed. At that time, the Vanuatu government sponsored a fisheries development program to diversify sources of income and employment.

The shift from copra to fishing has had an impact on gender relations and contributions to household economies. Although most land under copra production was owned or controlled by men, both men and women worked cooperatively in the fields. The fisheries industries, however, tend to recruit men because deep-water fishing is an occupation reserved to men. Still, women continue some traditional roles by marketing the fish locally. In addition, although people have become involved in the global economy, they have also continued subsistence farming, fishing, and craft production. Melanesian women have thus been able to maintain much of their traditional status and equality.

In Polynesia, Tahitian women have also been able to retain or even enhance their status in the context of economic change because cultural values supporting

Women in street markets throughout the Andes, as shown here in Pisac, Peru, sell many kinds of produce, prepared foods, and crafts.

gender equality have remained intact. Local governments initiated agricultural development projects oriented toward growing potatoes and green vegetables. These programs are largely successful, involving both men and women by granting financial support and technological training to all. By the early 1990s, approximately 43 percent of potato farmers were women (Lockwood 1997, 511–12). Women's involvement in farming represented a break with the traditional division of labor that had limited women to performing domestic tasks. But they were able to use their customary access to communal land and their new access to government programs to produce crops for export. In addition, women's crafts, such as woven mats, hats, and quilts, have become major income-generating occupations, allowing women's economic contributions to be seen as central to the welfare of their families. Women's rights are protected by the traditional view that people control the products of their labor and the income received.

Women in Changing Socialist States

Most socialist nations have made great strides in a relatively short time in increasing women's participation rates in paid employment. Full employment is an underlying principle both for national economic growth and social equality of all citizens. Universal education has helped women acquire the necessary skills and training for industrial and professional occupations. However, serious discrepancies remain between the wages received by men and women for comparable work. For example, women agricultural workers in four socialist societies (the former Soviet Union, China, Cuba, and Tanzania) are concentrated in less skilled, nonspecialist, low-paying, and low-prestige jobs (Croll 1986). Women's contributions to total economy are minimized by the official definitions of "economically active" that omit family subsistence production, a sector in which women are concentrated (Kruks and Wisner 1989). Furthermore, women often perform the major share of household responsibilities, leading to the "double day" typical of women in many industrial societies.

Although women work in all sectors of the industrial and professional economy, occupations in which women are concentrated tend to have low prestige. Although most socialist governments officially advocate policies aimed at combating discrimination against women, in varying degrees they all fail to recognize the critical link between public production and social or household reproduction. Women's roles in their households make entering the public work force as equals more difficult for them.

The fragility of the advances made by women in socialist countries in terms of economic participation, legal protections, and social equality is demonstrated by changes that have taken place in the former Soviet Union and Eastern Europe since the collapse of the socialist systems at the beginning of the 1990s. In the former Soviet Union, for instance, a market system has, among other things, resulted in drastic reductions in employment. Although all sectors of the economy have experienced declines, women have suffered disproportionately. For example, in 1993, approximately 70 percent of people officially listed as unemployed were women (Waters and Posadskaya 1995, 353). In addition, men are nearly twice as likely as women to hold positions of authority in both public and private organizations and enterprises, except in the fields of health care and education, professions long dominated by women (Russian Federation State Statistics Service 2006). Even in fields with numerical majorities of women, men are often found in positions of authority. Because of fears of population decline and falling birth rates (so low that Russia now experiences a negative birth rate), pressure on women to become full-time mothers and housewives has increased considerably. The resurgence in defining women as childbearers and homemakers indicates that changes in social attitudes necessary to protect advances in women's status have not been realized.

A further indicator of the fragility of women's status in the former Soviet Union is the fact that women's political representation on the national level has plummeted. In the 1980s, women constituted approximately 33 percent of the deputies in the Supreme Soviet (the highest government body in the USSR) and approximately 50 percent or more in lower-level government organizations. After the elections of 1991, however, women accounted for only 5.6 percent of national deputies and were even less represented in regional and local governing bodies (Waters and Posadskaya 1995, 352–53). Similar dramatic declines in women's political representation and increases in unemployment rates have occurred throughout Eastern Europe.

Norway and Sweden have the highest percentage of women in elected parliaments (about 40%). Pictured here are leaders of three of Norway's major parties: Kristen Halvorsen, leader of the Socialist Party, Jens Stoltenberg of the Labour Party; and Aslaug Haga of the Centre Party.

Impacts of Ideology on Gender Constructs

Ideological influences can be seen clearly in the history of American women's participation in the labor force. Since the nineteenth century, each increase in women's participation evoked an ideological attack by supporters of patriarchal values. At first these attacks focused on beliefs about the divine and innate origins of the gender division of labor. Following World War II, ideological bias socialized men and women to want to do different kinds of work. Interest in popular psychology spread the ideas that men were inherently aggressive and driven to competition and domination, whereas women were passive, docile, and wanted to be dominated. It was widely believed that attempts to behave in ways that contradicted one's innate gender roles were not merely futile but also produced warped, destructive personalities.

Mothers' responsibility for their children's mental health became paramount. A mother's job, then, consisted of selfless devotion to the interests of her children. Mothers who, by poverty or through divorce or widowhood, were compelled to work outside the home received some sympathetic understanding, but middle- and upper-class women who sought professional careers were thought to be selfish and destructive.

Attitudes change to reflect realities, and a reality today is that a majority of households is composed of people in quite different circumstances than the earlier cultural ideal. Couples who both work, unemployed husbands, separated or divorced people, widows or widowers, single parents, and unmarried people living alone constitute a larger percentage of households. Table 10.5 presents data on various types of family composition, indicating a trend toward both fewer married-couple families and fewer households with nonemployed wives (Ries and Stone 1992, 253).

Government statistics thus indicate that, in 2000, 77 percent of American households consisted of a married couple. Of these, more than half of the wives were in the paid labor force. Therefore, less than one-third of all American households consisted of a husband and nonemployed wife. According to figures released by the U.S. Department of Labor for 2001, 59 percent of married-couple families were supported by the incomes of both husband and wife. This figure shows an increase from 1967, when only 44 percent of married-couple households had incomes from both spouses (U.S. Department of Labor 2001).

TABLE 10.5 TYPES OF FAMILY COMPOSITION, 1970–2006					
Type	1970	1980	1989	2000	2006
Married-couple families	86.7	81.7	79.2	77.0	75.2
Wife in paid labor force	—	41.0	45.7	51.0	—
Wife not in paid labor force	—	40.0	33.5	22.0	—
Male householders, no spouse present	2.4	3.2	4.4	5.0	6.6
Female householders, no spouse present	10.9	15.1	16.5	17.0	18.2

Sources: From U.S. Bureau of the Census, cited in Ries and Stone (1992, 253); U.S. Bureau of the Census (2000; 2006).

As women's roles have been transformed, men's roles have also changed. Husbands are no longer the sole supporters of their families, relieving them of an intense economic and psychological burden. They no longer need to feel that their wives and children are completely dependent on their incomes but can look to their wives for support as well. Some men have taken on the role of "house-husband" or "stay-at-home dads," adopting many of the caretaking responsibilities formerly identified with mothers. This new alignment of roles within the households frees both men and women and enables them to do what suits them best as individuals. Another change has been around issues of child custody in cases of divorce. Courts are no longer automatically granting custody to mothers but instead are weighing multiple factors in their decisions, sometimes assigning custody to fathers.

Although gender roles and relations in any given culture can be analyzed at specific historical periods, it is crucial to understand the forces of change that transform people's behavior and their concepts about themselves and others. The possibility of change always exists, and this is what makes culture a dynamic rather than a static system. Gender relations can become more or less equal or hierarchical, depending on the specific context and operative forces experienced by members of each social category.

The relations between ideology and behavior are extremely complex. Although ideological systems develop in response to structural conditions, changes in these structural conditions usually occur much more rapidly than do changes in the ideological constructs that validate them. People's beliefs may continue despite changes in the contexts that produced them. Therefore, people sometimes have difficulty accepting a new social order and new social concepts.

Additional difficulties in changing ideologies derive from the fact that ideological constructs are often embedded in powerful systems of religious teachings and in attitudes expressed through daily interactions. Individuals usually experience their own behavior as "normal" and "natural" rather than as motivated and mediated by cultural constraints. They are, therefore, largely unaware of the underlying rationales influencing their actions and responses.

Analyses of gender roles and constructs in societies throughout the world demonstrate the diversity of possibilities of human life. People are not forever bound by traditional beliefs and practices. They can accept changes in their actions and they can adopt new ideological concepts relevant to their own experience. Just as we can uncover and understand the transformative dynamics that have occurred in the past, we can also witness and appreciate changes occurring in the present and into the future.

REVIEW

Cultural ideologies are used both to maintain and change gender constructs. Ideological attacks on working women in the United States were designed to discourage participation, just as later ideological inducements encouraged participation during wartime. Contact with Europeans influenced many indigenous groups to adopt more patriarchal or male-dominant ideologies and behaviors. In other instances, European contact improved the status of women. Ideological frameworks create, maintain, and change gender roles and constructs that a society considers acceptable. Behavior usually changes before ideology does.

ANTHROPOLOGY APPLIED

Advocacy for Women

Anthropologists work in organizations that champion women's rights, economic independence, and quality of life. For example, anthropologists conduct and report research on the impacts of economic development on women as well as on their households and communities. Women have been found to play an important role in the economies of developing countries as both producers and consumers, even in strongly patriarchal societies that tend to ignore women's contributions outside the home.

International organizations involved in advocacy for women include, for example, the Women's Environment and Development Organization (WEDO), the International Center

for Research on Women, and the Women's Rights Project of EarthRights International. Through the efforts of organizations such as EarthRights International, rural Burmese women were able to address the United Nations about human rights abuses against women in their country. They reported on their dislocation, forced labor, abandonment, and abuse related to the construction of the Burma-Bangladesh-India natural gas pipeline. The International Fund for Agricultural Development (IFAD), another example, is concerned with ending poverty for rural people. IFAD attempts to strengthen the roles of women in their communities by ensuring that they serve as advisers in projects and as intermediaries between women's organizations and the government. IFAD also attempts to involve both women and men in the outcomes of development projects, thus avoiding the tendency for these initiatives to favor men's interests.

IFAD contends that gender inequality helps perpetuate poverty. To break the cycle of poverty, IFAD attempts to increase women's access to resources (including food, water, and education) and enable them to attain political positions. IFAD also seeks to involve men in the new roles of women because women need the support of men to become empowered to change their roles and status. The idea is that, with equal access to resources, women and men in poverty can help each other and their society.

◉ CRITICAL THINKING QUESTIONS

How does gender inequality perpetuate poverty? As a cultural anthropologist, how might you determine if goals like those of IFAD are viable?

CHAPTER SUMMARY

Sex and Gender

- Gender is a cultural construct that assigns an identity and appropriate roles to people based partly on sexual differences and partly on cultural beliefs about sex and behavior. Gender models make use of sexual differences between males and females, but cultures vary in the roles that women and men perform, the rights they have in relation to each other, and the values associated with their activities. People learn their gender identity from their earliest socialization in infancy through their childhood, learning appropriate behavior and molding personality to conform to cultural norms. Females and males are born, but women and men are products of their culture.

- Most cultures organize their concepts of gender into a dual division of man and woman. However, some cultures allow males and females to identify as a third gender with different roles and behaviors.

- Our culture shapes our sexual feelings and practices and teaches us what is "normal" and what is "deviant." We learn who are appropriate sexual partners, and when, where, and how it is appropriate to have sexual relations. Attitudes about the relationship between sex and marriage and about homosexuality also reflect cultural learning. Some societies view homosexuality as unnatural, sinful, or criminal; others regard it as an expression of human desire.

Gender Roles and Gender Relations

- In all societies, gender influences work. Women's work always includes caring for young children and performing household tasks. Men's work always includes hunting and warfare. Men, women, or both may perform other economic activities, such as farming. Like other elements of culture, gender roles change as economic and material factors change.

- Gender equality is likely in foraging societies where all individuals contribute to subsistence and where hierarchical leadership and control are minimal. In other societies, male dominance may be reflected in men's control over access to resources, economic production and distribution, decision making and leadership, and ritual activity. The most intense male dominance tends to occur in agricultural states. However, in male-dominated societies, women may have independence and power in some spheres of life.

- Some anthropologists suggest that some form of male dominance exists in all societies. Others point to societies in which women and men have or had equal rights and privileges. Rapid culture change brought about by European colonization enhanced men's status and power.

Gender and Subsistence

- Egalitarian relationships develop among foragers and in industrial and postindustrial societies. In the United States, women were central to the industrializing economy. Many women entered the workforce outside the home during World Wars I and II. Although there is a "gender gap" in pay between men and women, more than half of women with children of all ages were in the work force by 1996.

Globalization and Gender

- Globalization has affected men and women differently. Women often lose their central roles as subsistence farmers when land is taken out of household production and dedicated to growing crops for national and global trade. Multinational corporations build light manufacturing plants that employ young, unmarried women at low pay.

- Most socialist and former socialist societies promoted women's participation in production and equal rights. However, working women remain burdened by a "double day," combining paid employment with household responsibilities. Women's unemployment has been disproportionately high in Eastern Europe and the former Soviet Union as socialist economies have changed to a free market. In most countries, women constitute only a small fraction of elected officials or appointed administrators with decision-making powers.

Impacts of Ideology on Gender Constructs

- Despite the significant contributions of women to U.S. economic development and to their families, ideological pressures continue to undermine gender equality. Some people promote the nineteenth-century "cult of domesticity," claiming that men and women are suited for different roles because of their biological needs, psychological orientations, and social wants. Men are supposedly inherently aggressive and assertive whereas women are innately nurturing and passive. However, many other people support the goal of gender equality.

KEY TERMS

gender 240	cultural constructs 243	gender roles 248	male dominance 251
sex 240	transvestism 244	gender relations 248	gender gap 260
gender construct (gender model) 240	berdaches 246	gender equality 251	cult of domesticity 260
	Two-Spirits 246	gender inequality 251	social reproduction 264

REVIEW QUESTIONS

1. What are cultural constructs? How are they used to define gender in societies?

2. What are some economic roles typically undertaken by women, and how are those roles different from those of men?

3. What is a third gender identity? How do third gender concepts relate to sexuality and homosexuality?

4. How do production, postmarital residence, and warfare patterns affect the status of women?

5. How are gender roles and relations related to subsistence strategies?

6. How did gender relations among the Ju/'hoansi, Inuit, Iroquois, and Chinese change as a result of both external contact and internal change?

7. How do ideologies affect changes in gender constructs?

PEARSON myanthrolab EXERCISES

To complete the following exercises and activities, you must log in to www.myanthrolab.com and select your current textbook.

1. In the **Explore** tab of Chapter 10, click on *Video* and watch the slide show on *Gender*. Complete the short answer exercise that accompanies the video.

2. While in the **Explore** tab of Chapter 10 click on the *NPR Audio Programs Broadcast* tab and go to *Theme 17: Sex, Gender, and Culture*. Listen to one of the programs in this section and complete the short answer exercise that accompanies the program.

3. In the **Research Tools** section on the home page, click on the *Research Navigator*™ link and enter the Anthropology database to find relevant and recent scholarly and popular press publications. For this chapter enter the following keywords: *gender, gender roles, male dominance,* and *globalization and gender.*

4. Enter the **MyAnthroLibrary** section on the home page to read more about topics and cultures that are discussed in this chapter. Suggested readings include:

Women's Movements and Feminism in a Transnational World by Florence E. Babb

Yap: Changing Roles of Men and Women by Sherwood G. Lingenfelter

EQUALITY AND INEQUALITY

- What is social stratification? How does inequality arise in human societies?
- What are three basic types of social organization? How do they work?
- How do caste and class systems differ as two forms of stratified societies?
- What are some determinants and indicators of social standing in stratified societies?
- How are societies stratified by gender, race, and ethnicity?
- Why is the concept of race controversial?
- How and why do people create, accept, maintain, reject, and change their ethnic identities?
- How do ideologies reinforce systems of stratification?
- What does an anthropological perspective of class, ideology, ethnicity, and race indicate about American society?

On a bright Sunday morning some peasants sat . . . chatting about their affairs.

The village shopkeeper . . . began to boast that he . . . had been in the lord's own chambers.

One of the peasants, the poorest of the lot, . . . scoffed.

"Pooh, that's nothing. I could dine with the lord if I wanted to."

"What—you? Dine with the lord? Never in all your life!" cried the rich shopkeeper. . . .

They argued on until the poor man said:

"Let us lay a wager. If I dine with the lord, I win your black and your bay; if I do not, I shall work three years for you for nothing."

The shopkeeper was mighty pleased.

"Very well, I bet you my black and my bay with a calf thrown in for good measure. Let these good men stand witness."

And they shook hands on it before the witnesses.

The poor man went to the lord.

"I should like to ask you in secret—what might be the price of a gold nugget the size of my cap?"

The lord said nothing. He just clapped his hands.

"Ho, there! A drink for this man and myself! Be quick about it. And serve us dinner, too. Sit down, sit down, my man, make yourself at home. Help yourself to all that is on the table!"

The lord treated the poor man as he would an honored guest, and all the time he was agog with impatience. There was nothing he wanted so much as to lay hands on that gold nugget.

"Now, my man, go quickly and fetch the nugget. I will give you a sack of flour and a piece of silver for it."

"But I haven't got any nugget. I was just asking what a nugget the size of my cap would be worth."

The lord flew into a rage.

"Get out, you fool!"

"How can I be a fool when you yourself have treated me as such an honored guest and the shopkeeper owes me two horses and a calf for this same dinner?"

And the peasant went home happy as a lark.

From Alex Alexander, *Russian Folklore: An Anthology in English Translation*, pp. 216–18. © 1975. Belmont, CA: Norland Publishing.

In this Russian tale, differences in wealth and status are at the center of the narrative. Peasants are generally looked down on because of their poverty, but the peasant prevails by his wit. The story can also be read as a form of resistance to the dominant ideology in prerevolutionary Russia, which granted privileges to some and disadvantages to others. Although poor, the peasant outsmarts the rich shopkeeper and the lord. This story, then, subverts the prevailing system of inequality.

"Four score and seven years ago our fathers brought forth, upon this continent, a new nation, conceived in liberty, and dedicated to the proposition that all men are created equal." This is the opening sentence of the Gettysburg Address by President Abraham Lincoln, one of the most famous and most quoted excerpts from American oratory. But the world of 1863 was not the world implied in this speech. Presumably Lincoln meant that the founders of the United States intended to establish a nation where all people were free. But the United States in its beginnings was a country with slavery and founded on land appropriated from indigenous peoples. In contrast, an ideology of equality, stated in the Declaration of Independence, in Lincoln's Gettysburg Address, and in countless political speeches ever since, has permeated American public discourse for centuries. Through this discourse, people come to believe in an equality of opportunity that did not, and does not, exist.

EQUALITY, INEQUALITY, AND SOCIAL STRATIFICATION

In previous chapters, we encountered societies in which everyone has equal access to resources, livelihood, and respect. We also encountered societies in which access to resources, livelihood, and respect is given more to some people than to others. The first type of system, based on principles of equality among members of communities, is called egalitarian. The second type, based on social, economic, and political inequality, is called stratified. In this chapter, we are particularly concerned with systems of social and political inequality.

Before beginning, though, several important distinctions must be made clear. Although people in egalitarian societies have equal access to resources and to positions of prestige and respect, all people are not equal in ability. Individuals everywhere differ in that some have more talent, intelligence, skill, or valued personality traits than others. And, of course, those people with more desirable characteristics are more respected, appreciated, and liked than those people lacking such positive traits. Nonetheless, everyone may make use of the group's resources, secure subsistence, and live a decent life more or less comparably to other people in their community.

In contrast, some people in stratified societies achieve positions of respect, influence, and power that grant them privileges and opportunities denied to others. We will be examining the bases on which stratified societies make social distinctions and the differing rewards and benefits available to some.

Three categories of culturally valued resources are wealth, power, and prestige (Fried 1967). **Wealth** refers to economic resources, whether in land, goods, or money. **Power** refers to the ability to exert control over the actions of other people and to make decisions that affect them. **Prestige** is a social resource that is reflected in other people's good opinions, in their respect, and in their willingness to solicit and to listen voluntarily to one's advice. According to Max Weber (1968; 1981), prestige, or honor as he called it, is central to the establishment and maintenance of status. Weber related honor to the notion of personal charisma. People strive to be well thought of because they then can influence other people. In stratified societies, prestige is linked to wealth and power. Because social values emphasize the worthiness of accumulating wealth, wealthy people are considered successful and are looked to as models to emulate. Prestige, then, built on wealth, can be used to obtain and exercise power.

Another set of terms relevant to our discussion of egalitarian and stratified societies has to do with various statuses and roles. Some of these are achieved and some are ascribed. An **achieved status** is one that people attain on the basis of their own efforts and skills. An **ascribed status** is one that a person occupies simply by birth or through a culturally determined right. In our society, leadership is an achieved status; we elect our mayors, governors, and presidents, presumably because of their abilities. In monarchies, leadership is an ascribed status; a king occupies his position simply because he is the eldest son of the previous king.

Finally, the distinctions among societies are not absolute, discrete types but, rather, form a continuum from egalitarian to stratified. Many societies contain elements of both, combining principles of equality in certain contexts with principles of inequality in other contexts. Indeed, there is a type of society, called ranked, that exhibits characteristics of both. **Ranked societies** differentiate individuals or, more usually, kinship groups along a continuum from lowest to highest, based partly on achieved status and partly on ascribed status. The benefits of high rank are primarily social rather than economic or political. People of high rank have prestige and respect but they do not have a living standard significantly better than that of people of lower rank, although there may be some

wealth
Economic resources, whether in land, goods, or money.

power
The ability to exert control over the actions of other people and to make decisions that affect them.

prestige
A social resource reflected in others' good opinions, respect, and willingness to be influenced.

achieved status
A social position attained by a person's own efforts and skills.

ascribed status
A social position that a person attains by birth. A person is born into an ascribed status.

ranked societies
Societies in which people or, more usually, kinship groups are ordered on a continuum in relation to each other.

What is an example of one of your achieved statuses? What is an example of one of your ascribed statuses?

In any stratified society, wealth, power, and prestige confer privileges. Here, King Leruo Tshekedi Molotlegi of Bafokeng in South Africa rides in a donkey cart at his coronation to symbolize his pledge not to personally profit from the mineral riches of his country.

Have you been a member of a ranked social organization? How would your experience compare with living in a ranked society?

differences in the size or decoration of their houses or in the amount of their clothing and ornaments. Although people of high rank may have influence in their communities, they do not have the power to control the activities of others. Still, high-ranking people may be able to exert wider influence than others and therefore be able to have their voices heard in economic and political domains. However, they cannot force others to comply with their wishes.

Egalitarian Societies

Egalitarian societies are ones in which all people have equal access to valued resources. Everyone has available land and natural resources to supply the food that they need to survive. Everyone can achieve positions of respect and influence. Although people may seek the advice of respected individuals, no one is able to exert control or dominance over other people. Egalitarian social systems are usually found in cultures with economies based on producing for subsistence and use rather than to accumulate large surpluses and wealth. Small foraging societies tend to be egalitarian in their social and ethical principles. Many horticultural societies are also egalitarian. This does not mean, however, that such societies have no forms of inequality. There are the inequalities of intelligence, skill, and personality that render some people more respected and influential than others. There are also attribute inequalities, such as age and gender, which may affect one's position in the household and society. Older people may be consulted and asked for their opinions about personal or community matters because of their greater experience in life.

The importance of age may be reflected within the household as well. Some of the authority and influence of parents derives from their age as well as from their genealogical relationship to their children. In some societies, the importance of seniority among siblings may be reflected in kinship terms that distinguish older and younger siblings and in behavior where younger siblings act deferentially toward their elders.

In addition, gender may be a factor in the respect and authority that people exert. If men and women are thought of as equal, both have influential roles in family and community decision making, conflict resolution, and group action. In male-dominated societies, however, men's opinions have paramount weight in these matters, and women's voices are muted. Other kinds of inequalities derived from kinship relationships may exist as well. Heads of lineages or clans may have important, decisive roles, certainly within their families and often in wider social contexts. In some societies, lineage or clan leaders may form village or district councils to discuss matters of community concern.

Despite all of these possible forms of inequality, "status tends to be individual or situational rather than categorical" (Berreman 1989, 8). That is, peoples' prestige and influence are based primarily on their personal qualities and relationships. Finally, people with influence do not use their advantages for personal material gain. The reward for being respected, skilled, and charismatic is social prestige, not wealth or power.

In egalitarian societies, social ethics stress generosity, hospitality, cooperation, and loyalty. People are expected to share resources and to aid one another in household and community work. Coupled with responsibilities to kin and community members, individual autonomy and the rights of all men and women to make decisions and act independently are valued. Coercion of others, either within households or in camps, is not tolerated and, given the strong negative reactions against such behavior, it is rarely attempted. Group leadership tends to be diffuse, flexible, and dependent on personal qualities and skills. People look for advice to those who are intelligent and successful in the particular endeavor requiring assistance or consultation—for example, skilled hunters are consulted regarding hunting. However, a man's or a woman's influence is temporary, fitted to the given occasion. Advice, therefore, is sought among local "experts," but such people cannot exert authority or control. Decisions are made jointly by all involved.

Ranked Societies

In systems of rank, every person—or, more accurately, every lineage or kin group—has a different position in the social hierarchy. Each rank is ordered in relation to all others. People of higher ranks have more social prestige than people of lower ranks, but they do not have significantly greater wealth or power. Their rewards are social, manifested in the respect given to them and the influence allowed them. If people follow their advice and

egalitarian societies
Societies in which all members have equal access to valued resources, including land, social prestige, wealth, and power.

direction, it is only because they have earned respect by their intelligence, behavior, and sound judgment. Ranked positions are established and maintained through a complex interplay of economic resources, political alliances, personal demeanor, and charisma, all leading to the formation of people's opinions of others.

Ranked systems are not static. Indeed, they are inherently extremely dynamic, even potentially volatile types of social organization. People can raise their status by their behavior and achievement and by the support of their relatives. But one's status can also fall. To move up the metaphoric "ladder of success," people have to mobilize public opinion because public opinion legitimates one's place in the system. People attempt to increase their economic wealth, forge alliances and attract dependents or clients, and act in ways that convey self-respect and conform to social norms of personality and attractiveness. To be successful and achieve these results, people need the support of their kin. Because of the competitive nature of ranked systems, competition within the family might prove disruptive if family members vied with one another for access to rank. Therefore, many such systems include the rule of primogeniture, or inheritance by seniority, so that the eldest child has the privilege of representing the family by occupying a position of rank. (In some societies, only men may hold rank; in others, women or men might occupy status positions.)

Stratified Societies

In **stratified societies,** people do not have equal access to valued resources. Because of their ability to accumulate all three elements of culturally valuable resources—wealth, power, and prestige—in stratified societies, some people have more economic resources than others. They have more land, food, and possessions, and their standard of living is superior to that of other people. Some people have more power than others, and they are able to exert control over the actions of other people by making decisions that affect them with or without their consent. As a consequence of having more wealth and power, they also have more social prestige. People respect them and regard them with envy. In stratified societies, some wealth, power, and prestige accrue to people because of their achievements, hard work, and personal characteristics. However, some of their good fortune comes to them because of their birth. They are the children of wealthy and powerful people. Prestige, wealth, and power, therefore, are both ascribed and achieved.

> **stratified societies**
> Societies in which people have differential access to valued resources, including land and property, social prestige, wealth, and political power.

CASE STUDY

The Samoans: A Ranked Society

The Samoan Islands are in the Pacific Ocean about halfway between Hawaii and New Zealand. The islands are divided into two groups: Western Samoa, an independent nation since 1961, and American Samoa, a territory under United States jurisdiction since 1904. The two groups of islands share most practices and systems of organization.

Samoan subsistence centers on farming, especially coconuts, taro (a starchy tuber), and breadfruit. Both women and men participate in farming, although men do the heavy work of clearing fields. The principal source of protein comes from ocean fish and shellfish, but domesticated pigs are eaten on ceremonial occasions. Kinship groups hold land communally, under the stewardship of family leaders who allocate individual plots for each family. Farm work, however, is generally carried out collectively by the appropriate members of the household, considering age and gender roles.

Samoan social and political life is organized around a system of stratification called "rank." In ranked societies, kinship groups are ordered in terms of prestige, influence, and privilege. In Samoa, the most important units of affiliation are the household, the extended family, and the village (Holmes and Holmes 1992, 28). Households generally consist of a leading man, his wife, their children, and additional relatives possibly including elderly parents, siblings, and siblings of the parents. People have the right to claim residence with relatives by either blood or affinal ties. Such flexibility allows people to make strategic decisions about individual affiliation. A newly married couple may live with either the husband's or wife's family, possibly depending on the number and gender of siblings already living in the household, on personal affection, or on the status of the household head. The size of households usually varies from ten to twenty individuals.

Members of extended families may live together in one household or in several different dwellings. The heads of extended families have titles, called "matai," derived from ancient or mythological times. They are ranked relative to one another depending on their association with mythical beings or venerable historical personages. There are two types of matai titles: Chief and Talking Chief. Some extended families have claim to Chief titles whereas others claim Talking Chief titles.

The position of matai is held by a man, chosen by all the adult members of the extended family that he represents. Ordinarily, a man holds this position for life, but someone who loses favor may be demoted, or an elderly matai may retire. The successor is chosen at a public meeting at which anyone who wishes may speak in support of a candidate. Discussions may last weeks. Although present, candidates do not participate in the deliberations. Good character, generosity, intelligence, hard work, dedication to the family, and oratorical skills are favored traits. If a son of the former chief has these qualities, he is a likely, although not assured, successor, but if not, the field is open to other candidates.

Successors to the position of matai are celebrated in a family ritual involving drinking "kava," a beverage made from kava root, steeped in water. It is the Samoans' ceremonial beverage, drunk on a variety of celebrations. The new matai is given the honor of drinking "first kava," a mark of prestige and respect. Later, the matai is formally installed at a meeting of the village council of chiefs, composed of all of the matai of the extended families represented in the village. There, he also drinks first kava and gives an elaborate speech full of metaphor and imagery. Each of the other chiefs in order of their rank answers the speech. Seating arrangements at the council meetings and other official occasions also indicate relative rank.

The new matai's first obligation is to provide a feast for the community. To amass the quantities of food and gifts of bark cloth for the feast, he must mobilize his extended family to work harder to supply these goods. They are willing to do so because their own status rises and falls with that of their matai. This feature of social organization is also the essence of a ranked society.

In addition to the extended family as a unit, the Samoans recognize internal branches derived from the sons and daughters of the first founder. The sons were the originators of male branches whereas the daughters were originators of female branches. In principle, members of male branches are more likely to be chosen as matai, but members of female branches also have claims. Furthermore, to balance their privileged social position, members of male branches have special responsibilities toward members of the female branches, owing them respect and performing services when called on (Holmes and Holmes 1992, 30). Although women are not named as matai, they have significant voices collectively and individually in choosing successors to the title. A woman's birth and marriage determine her own status. That is, daughters of titled fathers or wives of titled men have prestige in their communities. However, the respect that is due a particular woman also derives from her own character, intelligence, oratorical skills, and ability to manipulate the system of status in her favor.

Matai have numerous responsibilities, including overseeing communal land, settling disputes among members of the extended family, and representing the family on the village council of chiefs and at other public functions. Although matai have high social status, they work in the fields alongside other family members. Each matai has an assistant who helps plan daily activities and communicates the matai's decisions to the relevant people. Chiefs and Talking Chiefs have different roles. Each group (Chiefs and Talking Chiefs) is divided into three grades: High Chiefs, Chiefs, and Between-the-Posts Chiefs. The High Chiefs have titles closely associated with gods or culture heroes. They serve as heads of village councils and settle disputes arising between village residents. They receive the largest share of food and other gifts at ceremonial feasts hosted by other matai. Chiefs are heads of large extended families that have influence and stature. Between-the-Posts Chiefs (so named because, in council houses, they sit between the end posts reserved for more distinguished members) are holders of titles that have been created recently to acknowledge special service or abilities of individual men. Chiefs within each group are also internally ranked according to their origins and accomplishments.

Talking Chiefs are skilled orators who sometimes function as speakers for High Chiefs on special occasions. They also represent their villages in intervillage meetings and rituals. When an important delegation is sent to another village, the emissaries are accompanied by a Talking Chief who makes elaborate speeches and is greeted in turn by a resident Talking Chief.

In ranked societies, as in all systems of social stratification, the privilege and status of elites depends on the existence of a large group of untitled people or commoners. In Samoa, untitled men in each village may participate in a voluntary association called "aumaga." This group has both economic and ceremonial functions. The men perform collective labor for the village, clearing fields, building houses, repairing paths, and fishing. When the village council of chiefs meets, men from the aumaga prepare and serve the food and kava. They perform the same functions on ceremonial occasions. They also carry out and enforce council decisions. The internal organization of the aumaga is similar to that of the village council of chiefs. It is an internally stratified group, with a leader (often a son or close relative of a High Chief) and members ranked according to principles similar to the ranking of chiefs.

Unmarried women may join an association called "aualuma." In the past, these women served mainly ceremonial functions, but today they work primarily in public health, child care, and other community services (Holmes and Holmes 1992, 42). Like the men's organizations, the aualuma is headed by the wife of one of the High Chiefs or Talking Chiefs. She leads group meetings, plans activities, and assigns work to members.

Although matai have social privileges due their high rank in a stratified system, Samoan society is also based on egalitarian ethics. A matai who abuses his position or becomes arrogant and ignores the sentiments of his relatives is likely to be demoted. People who disagree with the decisions of the matai can leave and affiliate with another household in which they have rights by blood or marriage. The prestige of a matai falls if the number of people in his household declines. Therefore, untitled people have many ways to influence a matai's reputation. Just as the status of untitled people depends on the rank of their matai, his status depends on their good favor.

The Samoan system of social stratification continues today to order relations among people in village life. Changes in the system have, of course, taken place throughout Samoa, especially in larger towns. Even in the villages, however, there have been moves toward individual control over farmland. Although most land is still held communally under the stewardship of the matai, nuclear families can gain access to small plots of land. The qualities that make a man a likely successor to the title of matai have also changed. Education and/or job experience in the United States enables young men to advance more rapidly than would have been possible in the past. Untitled men with job skills are encouraged to work in the United States for brief periods so that they can send money to their families and the matai. These gifts demonstrate the donor's generosity and hard work, important assets for a future matai. The position of matai remains crucial, not only to leadership in the extended family, but also as a necessary qualification for election to the Samoan Senate, one of the two island-wide legislative bodies (the other is the House of Representatives whose members may be either titled or untitled).

The traditional "aumaga" of untitled young men continues to have ceremonial functions, but its role in mobilizing cooperative labor has declined. Especially in rural villages, many young men migrate to the larger towns or to the United States (mostly to Hawaii or West Coast states) to find employment. The "aualuma" association of unmarried women has largely disappeared, its collective social welfare functions taken over by women's associations that include unmarried, married, and widowed women. Because of traditional gender roles and attitudes, women are less likely to migrate to the United States, but those who do send money home to their families. Although most Samoan immigrants have low incomes by American standards, the money they send back to Samoa has a significant impact both in purely financial terms and in contributing to the prestige of their families.

PEARSON
myanthrolab

Explore more at
www.myanthrolab.com

social stratification
Division of society into two or more groups, or strata, that are hierarchically ordered.

elites
Members of a social group in a stratified society who have privileges denied to the majority of the population.

GLOBALIZATION

Systems of stratification based on the control of capital and the concept of social mobility have spread throughout the world as a consequence of globalization. Stratification based on class membership is rapidly replacing other forms of stratification, as well as ranked and egalitarian societies.

Social stratification refers to a division of society into two or more groups, or strata, that are hierarchically ordered in relation to each other. Within each stratum, members are all more or less of equal social standing. Although there are differences among individuals in stratified systems, people in the same stratum have equivalent opportunities, privileges, and similar standards of living, at least when compared to people in other strata.

One of the significant features of all systems of stratification is that the highest group is usually, if not always, a numerical minority. Why, then, are the majority of people willing to accept a system that does not benefit them? There are many and complex explanations. One reason is that the elite group controls the means of forcing compliance with their wishes. Because the **elites** control social, economic, and political resources, they are in a position to use political (and often military) power against those who resist their control. However, the use of force is costly, not just in economic terms. When force is used against people, especially if they constitute the majority of the population, they will likely sooner or later rebel against a system that disadvantages them. So, instead, social attitudes and beliefs are developed to induce conformity. People are taught to believe that the system they live in is just. If not entirely just, it is at the least legitimate.

There are many ways of creating and transmitting such attitudes or ideologies. Religious teaching, for example, is an effective means of instilling obedience to the rulers. People may be taught that the deities chose their leaders or that the system they live in has divine approval. Or they may be pacified by the hope that divine beings favor them, an idea conveyed by the biblical phrase "The meek shall inherit the Earth." In addition, social ideologies transmit the notion that elites are more capable, more intelligent, and in other ways superior to common people. Common people absorb these ideologies through their socialization and through exposure to public discourse that elites control.

Thus, for example, many fail to see that poverty and wealth are part of the structure of our society. They fail to see that our capitalist economic system depends as much on the existence of poverty as it does on the existence of wealth. The wealth of some people depends on the labor of other people, many of whom work for low wages. In addition, the existence of a group of unemployed and underemployed people exerts a downward pressure on all wages because more people are wanting work than jobs are available. This situation leads to competition among workers for jobs and creates a situation where even low-paying jobs become attractive.

Explaining Social Stratification

Social stratification is a characteristic of complex state societies. Among other traits, states have economies based on intensive agricultural production, resulting in a large surplus. This surplus can be used to support ever-growing populations and to free some people from agricultural work. Labor specialization develops so that some people work as farmers, others as artisans, traders, soldiers, or government officials. States are also characterized by unequal access to resources. Some people accumulate more goods, land, and other property than others. Rather than distributing their wealth to community members in need, they use their property for themselves, raising their standard of living and living better than people with fewer resources. Over time, inequalities in standards of living become entrenched as children of wealthy parents are born with advantages and opportunities lacking to the children of poor people. (Characteristics of state societies are discussed further in Chapter 12.)

Several types of explanations are offered to explain the existence of stratification. Functional analyses emphasize the fact that different sectors of the population perform different roles in society. Rewards are given to those people who are more capable and hardworking than others. In functionalism, people

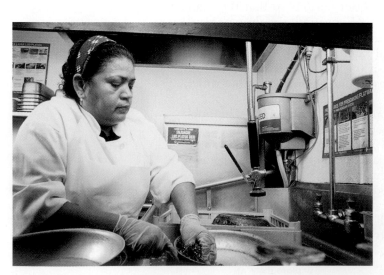

This woman is one of many working poor who earn minimum wages in the United States.

who are leaders, traders, and officials, performing important functions for the community as a whole, are acknowledged and permitted to accumulate wealth, social prestige, and power. These benefits are believed to be just compensation for their societal contributions.

Although there is merit in this argument, because it points out the various roles of different people in systems of economic specialization, it fails to take into account several important factors. People with wealth are not necessarily more capable than others. Some people inherit their wealth without any effort or achievement of their own. Also, some leaders are incompetent. In monarchies where the eldest son of the king automatically becomes the next ruler, there is no guarantee that the person so promoted is the most capable. Hard work does not necessarily translate into wealth, prestige, and power. As an extreme example, African slaves in the United States and the Caribbean certainly contributed great effort and often gave their lives in the production of wealth, but received no benefit at all from their work. The value of their labor was extracted and used by their owners. In modern societies as well, the hard work and long hours of, for example, factory workers, secretaries, and nurses are not reflected in luxurious standards of living.

A second set of explanations for social stratification emphasizes the conflicts between members of different strata or classes. These analyses, following Karl Marx, focus on the processes that create groups in opposition to each other. Members of different classes have different class interests. They develop a consciousness of their class and strive to protect and expand their interests. Members of elite classes try to influence economic and political policies that will benefit themselves. Although members of lower classes may also try to influence leaders to implement policies that will aid them, they are generally less successful, in part because the leaders tend to come from or identify with the elites.

These explanations focus on societies as dynamic systems. They emphasize the processes of struggle between members of opposing groups. Through these struggles, societies can be transformed. Then new types of group formation and new types of opposition and conflict lead to further series of changes and adaptations. Of course, although complex societies are composed of groups with different, often conflicting, interests and goals, societies also attempt to build consensus and foster cooperation among groups. Therefore, functional and Marxist explanations for social stratification both offer insights that can be useful in analyzing societal structures and processes.

Karl Marx explained social stratification as an outgrowth of class conflict over the control of resources and wealth.

How might a functionalist or a Marxist explain homelessness in a stratified society such as the United States?

REVIEW — ⊙ Societies become stratified through the unequal distribution of wealth, power, and prestige, which attach to the different ascribed statuses (inherited) and achieved statuses (acquired) in a society. In ranked societies, different groups are ranked hierarchically on the basis of both ascribed and achieved statuses. Egalitarian societies provide equal access to resources, whereas some individuals and groups in stratified societies have more resources and others less. Structuralism, functionalism, Marxism, and other theoretical perspectives offer alternative explanations for social stratification.

CASTE AND CLASS

A caste is a social group whose membership is hereditary. Castes are endogamous. That is, people must marry within their caste, and their children are also members of the same group. Thus, caste is an ascribed status with automatic, involuntary, and unchanging membership and identity. Separation on the basis of caste may be manifested by restrictions on living spaces, occupation, style of dress, and demeanor. In caste systems, each group is assigned a particular order of prestige relative to the others on a scale from lowest to highest. Unlike rank, caste order cannot change.

Determinants of Class

Systems of class are also ways of grouping people in a hierarchical order. Whereas castes are differentiated according to the sole criterion of ancestry, class may be defined in various ways. One way to talk about class is to talk about economic factors, primarily income,

CULTURE CHANGE ⊙ ——————————————————————————

CASTE IN INDIA

In India, there are hundreds of discrete castes (called *jati*), all ranked in relation to one another (Koller 1982). The caste system unifies constituent groups into four large groupings (called *varna*), each containing numerous castes that are perceived to be similar in their origin, function, and especially in their ritual purity. Members of the highest varna, called the Brahmins, were traditionally the priests and scholars. The second-highest category is the Kshatriyas, who were the warriors. The merchants and traders constitute the third varna, called Vaishyas. The fourth varna are the Shudras, or artisans, carpenters, blacksmiths, barbers, farmers, and menial workers. Finally, a fifth group ranks below all the others: the untouchables. Untouchables are considered ritually impure, fit to do only the most menial work, such as cleaning toilets. According to Hindu beliefs, a member of one of the higher castes can become ritually polluted by touching or being touched by an untouchable.

Caste in India is an example of a comparatively closed system of stratification. Although some social mobility is possible, people are traditionally born into a particular caste and remain in it throughout their lives. Rural villages are often divided into caste neighborhoods, and occupations are determined by caste. In the most traditional contexts, people can do little, if anything, to change their circumstances. Even if people move to another community and do not reveal their heredity, their ways of talking and behaving would probably be telltale signs of their ancestry and, by implication, caste identity.

The behavior of people in different castes is a barrier to social interactions, acting as boundary markers. People belonging to different castes should not eat together or have sexual relations with one another. Members of higher castes may avoid taking food offered by members of lower castes. Higher-caste people are more likely to be vegetarians and not drink alcohol. Members of different castes may have different ways of speaking, including pronunciation and choice of words. The most stringent restrictions concern untouchables. In villages, untouchables must reside in their own section and cannot drink from wells used by the higher castes.

The most prestigious group, the Brahmins, is considered ritually pure. They need to maintain their purity through social distance. But Brahmins are not necessarily wealthy. For example, they may work as cooks in restaurants because members of all castes may eat food touched by the highest group.

Indian castes also have economic functions. High-caste people cannot perform important subsistence and productive functions for themselves because of the polluting nature of these activities, such as working with wood or making pottery. Lower-caste people provide these goods and services in

Hindus revere many deities, including the god Shiva, here represented at Shiva Temple in Gangaikonda Cholapuram, India.

return for food, clothing, and money. Over the years, a permanent and stable relationship between patron and client may provide for an exchange of goods and services between the two parties. This relationship may pass to the descendants of the originators, continuing important economic exchanges through the generations. Both groups thus receive significant benefits.

Caste economic relationships are both divisive and integrating. They are divisive because people are restricted to performing caste-specific economic roles, but they are integrating because they create necessary interdependence among people of different castes. However, despite the advantages of stability and security lower-caste people obtain from their patrons, the system as a whole stigmatizes them and takes more from them than it gives. As in any system of social stratification, higher-ranked people benefit most.

Finally, Indian castes were intimately associated and intertwined with political power. The structures of caste functioned in villages and regional territories to both segment and articulate various kinship groups and residential communities. They formed the basic structure of political alliances and control. British colonial administrators ignored and obliterated much of the political significance of caste. By reinventing caste significance as primarily ritual, the British pretended that India lacked "genuine politics," in effect providing a rationale for British control (Dirks 2001).

The system of caste in India is less static than it is often described, however. Since India's independence in 1947, laws have loosened restrictions on caste behavior. People belonging to different castes can now legally marry and cannot be prosecuted for engaging in sexual relations. Family and community opinion, however, still often frowns on such unions. It is illegal to discriminate against untouchables. Indeed, certain jobs and a percentage of openings in universities must be reserved for members of the lower castes. And all people have the right to vote, a right that carries with it the potential, if exercised, to improve the economic and social position of the lower castes.

In modern India, especially in the cities, caste ranking is not immutable. Upward mobility for the caste as a group is possible if members have achieved wealth and prestige. Upward mobility pertains to the group; it is not a narrowly individual process. However, striving for upward mobility does not necessarily undermine the system of stratification. It merely changes the ordering of groups rather than challenges the legitimacy of the social principles on which the system is based. Over time, fluidity in caste may fundamentally challenge the system. Untouchables are especially vocal opponents of the system, calling for laws that ban discrimination. Thousands have converted from Hinduism to Buddhism or Christianity to protest the injustices of caste hierarchies. In northwest India, a group called the Guijars, traditionally nomadic shepherds, wants the government to classify them as a "lower-caste group" to enable them to qualify for government benefits and job opportunities (Johnston 2008).

These Saudi royals experience privilege in their living standards, health, and the control they have over other people.

education, and occupation. These factors tend to go together, so that people with the highest incomes usually have the most advanced education and the most prestigious jobs. However, cases can easily be cited that contradict this general tendency, such as occupations requiring advanced education but earning lower incomes than other occupations with lower educational requirements. In this economic meaning of class, the groups are not closed, discrete units but, rather, are categories differentiated along a continuum. These categories form social layers or strata that are ranked in relation to one another. There are no absolute boundary markers between them; they differ only in relative terms.

Unlike caste, class is an achieved status because the criteria for determining class membership are subject to achievement by individuals as well as to change. Also, unlike caste, where a person's identity is rigidly determined, the factors used to determine class membership are less easily and less consistently specified. Also unlike the fixed and closed nature of caste, systems of class are open and allow for mobility from one group to another. Class **mobility** may be either upward or downward.

How does your social class influence your life experiences? How does your culture reinforce the class system of which you are a part?

Another way of talking about class is to talk about relations of production. In this Marxian sense of class, there are two contrasting groups—the group that owns the means of economic production and controls the distribution of products and the group that does not own the means of production. These two groups, or classes, can be simplified as owners and workers. Owners control production and distribution and profit from the productive labor of others, and workers sell their labor to the owners for a wage. In modern corporate capitalism, the distinction between owners and workers is more complicated than was true in the late nineteenth century, when Karl Marx developed his insights about the European capitalist economic system.

In North American discourse on class, there are strong pressures against public discussion of class interests and underlying class conflicts. Rather, we are led to believe that anyone can grow up to be president. Nevertheless, members of different classes, however defined, occupy different places in society, and their life experiences are fundamentally different.

Social Class and Language

Class differences are revealed and reinforced by patterns of language use. When we speak, we consciously and unconsciously use forms (pronunciations, words, grammar) that identify who we are. People can immediately tell something about us—where we come from, how old we are, what gender we are, and what social group we belong to. Our class, race, and ethnicity are some of the social factors that we reveal when we speak. When we hear other people speak, we make judgments about them based on their language.

Although all speakers may employ both the standard and nonstandard forms, middle-class speakers use the standard forms more frequently, and lower-class speakers more often use the nonstandard forms. In the United States and Great Britain, instead of the standard pronunciation of "thing" and "the," lower-class speakers might say "ting" and "de," replacing the "th" sound with "t" or "d" (Labov 1966, 1972b; Trudgill 1974, 1983). Class-related variations in these sounds are documented in the English language in both Great Britain and the United States as early as the seventeenth century.

Research in Belgium conducted by Jef van den Broeck (1977) also showed differences in the speech of working-class and middle-class speakers. Van den Broeck discovered that middle-class and working-class speakers showed no significant differences in sentence complexity in informal situations, but a marked distinction in formal contexts. In formal situations, middle-class speakers used more complex constructions than in informal situations, but working-class formal grammar was less complex than working-class informal

mobility
A principle that people can move from membership in one social group to another.

style. Van den Broeck suggested that, in formal situations, middle-class speakers want to distinguish their style from that of the working class. They use linguistic mechanisms as an "act of conspicuous ostentation, a marker of social distance." Working-class speakers, on the other hand, may reflect through their speech their feelings of relative powerlessness in formal situations.

Slavery

Slavery, the most extreme form of stratification, is an ascribed status. People become slaves either by being born into slavery or by being captured in warfare or slaving raids. Slavery is thus forced upon a person, either

A group of slaves gather under a tree as they wait for freedom in southern Sudan.

through accident of birth or through the deliberate actions of others. The slave group, like castes and classes, is endogamous. Slaves usually marry other slaves, not necessarily because of their preferences but because nonslaves are unwilling to marry them. Slavery generally entails the loss of a person's independence and autonomy. At the least, slaves work at the direction and the behest of their owners. They cannot control their own labor, and they do not benefit materially from the goods that they produce. In addition, slaves cannot leave and find homes and work elsewhere. With low social status, slaves cannot hope to achieve any position of prestige or influence in their society, except within the community of other slaves. Social attitudes attribute negative qualities to slaves. They are thought to be inferior and incapable of valued achievements.

The quality of a slave's life varies across cultures. We are familiar from the history of the United States with a form of slavery in which slaves had no rights of any kind. In other societies with slavery, the life of a slave was not necessarily much different from that of ordinary people. For example, among the Kwakwaka'wakw and other indigenous societies of the Pacific Northwest, slaves lived in the homes of their owners, ate the same kind of food, and wore the same kind of clothing. They usually performed menial tasks and suffered the indignity of low social status, but they could be ransomed by their relatives and returned to their own communities.

Societies may be stratified by caste—a hierarchical, hereditary, endogamous, closed system of social strata defined by occupation and concepts of religious purity. Societies may also be stratified by class—a hierarchy of social strata based mainly on achieved economic status, in which people may be upwardly or downwardly mobile but tend to marry within their own group. Class membership typically is identified by lifestyle and the use of language. Slavery is an extreme form of social stratification, based on ascribed status, in which people are defined and treated as commodities.

RACE AND ETHNICITY

Like caste and class, **race** is a social, not a biological, category. There are no absolute biological differences among people that would allow for an objective categorization of human beings into discrete, nonoverlapping groups. Rather, so-called racial distinctions focus on a particular set of external physical traits that are then used to identify different "races." In the United States and elsewhere, these traits most especially include skin color, hair color and texture, and facial features. However, it is obvious that all of these characteristics appear in human populations on a continuum. The classification, labeling, and valuing of these differences as races are entirely arbitrary.

slavery
An ascribed status forced on a person upon birth or through involuntary servitude.

race
A cultural category that groups people according to so-called racial distinctions.

In the process of constructing race as a cultural category, people are identified as belonging to different "races" based on supposed biological differences. Social ideologies are then developed to justify the system. The next step associates certain constellations of behavior with each group. So, for example, members of one race are said to be more intelligent, more honest, more capable than members of another race. These associations and the social foundation on which they are based privilege some groups and disadvantage others. The group that controls the social, economic, and political structures of the society thinks of itself as superior and of different others as inferior. Whether a majority or minority of the population, the group in power has the ability to control the ideological grounds on which the social order rests.

Race as Caste

In its artificiality, race is very much like caste. In both systems, particular groups are said to have separate ancestral origins, thus explaining their appearance, behavioral characteristics, and place in society. Both caste and race are ascribed statuses, and both are closed systems. Like castes, racial groups tend to be endogamous because people usually marry members of their own race. In some racialist societies, marriage between members of different races is legally forbidden but, even where there are no legal boundaries to intermarriage, people generally choose to marry members of their own group for a number of social and emotional reasons. In the United States in 2006, for example, only 3.8 percent of married couples were of different racial backgrounds. The U.S. Bureau of the Census reports that 0.7 percent of married couples consisted of a white partner and an African American partner, 3.0 percent consisted of a white partner and a partner who was neither white nor African American, and a final 0.2 percent of married couples consisted of an African American partner married to someone of a race other than white or African American (U.S. Census Bureau, Statistical Abstract of the United States, 2008, Table 59). Finally, race is like caste in the attribution of purity to superior groups and impurity to inferior groups who are often thought of as "unclean" in some ways. Contact between the races is thought to pollute those of higher status. For example, in some southern American states, African Americans were legally barred from drinking from the same public water fountains as whites, from using the same restrooms, and from sitting in the same sections on buses and trains. Although these laws were repealed in the 1950s and 1960s, their underlying symbolism has not been entirely eradicated in some communities.

Race in the United States

In the United States, the races are ordered in a hierarchy that is arbitrary and culturally derived. Attitudes toward members of the different races are learned and transmitted without any basis in fact, although holders of these attitudes believe that they are factually true. In addition, races tend to be endogamous, partly because people tend to live near, go to schools with, and socialize with people of their same racial background, but also because of lingering attitudes about racial separation. According to the U.S. Bureau of the Census, reporting for the year 2000, there were 3.1 million interracial couples, accounting for 6 percent of all married couples. About 7.3 million Americans (3 percent of the population) identified themselves as being of two or more races (Navarro 2008, A15). Although it is true that many workplaces are racially mixed, occupational stratification often contributes to boundaries between the races. Attitudes toward members of the disadvantaged groups are fraught with negative stereotypes and prejudice. These attitudes are no doubt changing, but members of disadvantaged races are still burdened by unfair treatment, lack of equal opportunity, and a marginalized role in public life.

These Amerasian children of mixed descent would be regarded as outcasts in their home countries in Southeast Asia.

CASE STUDY

Out-Groups of Japan

The Japanese believe they belong to a homogeneous racial and cultural group. They believe that they are physically similar to each other and look different from other Asians. They also believe that "Japanese" is an identity that is ascribed and cannot be acquired. As George De Vos and Hiroshi Wagatsuma state, "In the Japanese mind only those born of Japanese parents are genetically Japanese—nobody can become a Japanese" (1995, 268). People who are not defined as "Japanese" face overt and covert discrimination even though their ancestors may have lived in Japan for thousands of years.

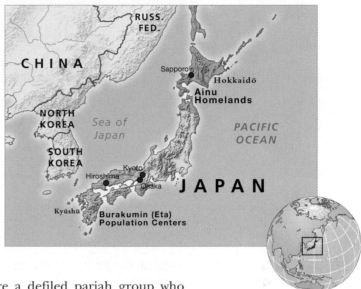

According to De Vos and Wagatsuma, about 4.5 percent of the population in Japan belongs to "minority" groups. Some are Japanese citizens, but others are denied citizenship. The largest minority group socially defined as "not Japanese" are the 3 million Burakumin, descendants of an ancient group of outcasts. In the traditional stratified social system, the Burakumin were a defiled pariah group who ranked below the four classes of Japanese. The official name of the Burakumin, called eta, is written with characters meaning "full of filth." Their traditional occupations included work considered ritually polluting, such as slaughtering animals, disposing of the dead, and making musical instruments (containing leather and other animal products). The Burakumin, literally "village people," originally lived in separate villages, but now they may also live in certain urban neighborhoods. Despite no supporting evidence, most Japanese believe that the Burakumin are racially distinct.

The Buraku community is as heterogeneous as any other in a modern state. Class distinctions exist, based principally on occupation and income. Some Burakumin work in their traditional occupations, but others own land and property. Some members accept their minority status and identify as Burakumin, but others attempt to "pass," principally by learning new occupations and changing their residence. However, changing one's residential identity is not simple in Japan because official records list all past addresses, and teachers and employers, among others, can investigate them.

In the past, the Burakumin were the only Japanese to eat meat, in violation of Buddhist principles, but now many Japanese eat meat. As a self-conscious marker of identity, some Burakumin wear a distinctive sandal called *setta zari*. Otherwise, Japanese consider Buraku dress to be "careless," a negative characteristic in Japan. Finally, Buraku speech is generally more "informal" and "less refined" than that of the general population. Most Burakumin work in their own communities, employed by or working with relatives or people familiar to them. But many are unemployed or underemployed and rely on government assistance. A high rate of endogamy exists within the Buraku community because of both their own preferences and the prejudices among other Japanese.

Because the Burakumin physically look just like ordinary Japanese, they can "pass" in public simply by avoiding the dress styles and speech patterns considered identity markers. Middle-class Burakumin have stronger pressures to pass than do poor people because they hope to give their children educational and financial advantages that would allow them to become white-collar and professional workers. The major impediment to "passing" is the record of residence that betrays one's origin.

Japanese have negative stereotypes about the Burakumin. They are considered impulsive, volatile, hostile, and aggressive. Because polite behavior and an even-tempered demeanor is so highly regarded in Japan, the behavior attributed to the Burakumin is especially disvalued. The Burakumin also demonstrate less conformity and deference to authority than ordinary Japanese. The Burakumin tolerate and may even reward deviant behavior, especially toward authority figures, as a reaction to the discrimination they experience. Finally, the Burakumin are more open about engaging in and talking about

The Ainu, descendants of the indigenous people of ancient Japan (pictured here at a Thanksgiving festival), live in a few small villages on the northern island of Hokkaido, where they were driven when Japan invaded their territory.

sexual activity than is acceptable in Japan. That some Burakumin behave in ways that they know most Japanese criticize may be an example of a subversive challenge to dominant ideologies.

Interviews with officials in the city of Kobe revealed that the small Buraku minority contributed disproportionately to the number of cases brought before the courts because of family problems and delinquency. Partly because of real criminal problems and partly because of negative stereotypes, ordinary Japanese claim to be fearful of the Burakumin. Other cultures with hierarchical social systems often have similar attitudes. Disadvantaged groups frequently bear the brunt of derogatory suspicions and fears that undermine their own self-esteem and serve to justify the majority's discrimination against them.

Other groups, supposedly distinguished racially from the Japanese, also face discrimination. Okinawans, Taiwanese, and Koreans are considered foreigners even though they have lived in Japan for generations. The ancestors of some of these groups were forced to come to Japan by the Japanese army. Most are not Japanese citizens and live in urban ghettos. Koreans in particular are thought to be "inherently uncouth and uncivilized." Because of the discrimination they face, many Koreans in Japan are poor. Rather than being considered victims of discrimination, they are seen as deserving the negative attitudes toward them. To become citizens, some people of Korean or Taiwanese ancestry have hidden their origins by taking Japanese names. As in other cultures with racial or ethnic discrimination, children of mixed marriages are considered tainted and impure.

The 200,000 Ainu are an indigenous people, native to the northern Japanese island of Hokkaido. Until 2008, the Japanese government refused to recognize them as a separate ethnic group (Makino 2008). As a result of discrimination, Ainu are more than three times more likely to live on welfare than other Japanese. They also have low educational levels and substandard housing.

Another group of people who face negative attitudes are the *hibakusha,* survivors of the atomic bombs that the United States dropped on Japan in 1945 during World War II. These victims are considered "irrevocably contaminated" because of their illnesses and deformities. Children of marriages or sexual relationships between Japanese women and American soldiers stationed in Japan during the U.S. occupation also face discrimination. According to De Vos and Wagatsuma, "More than any other minority group in Japan, offspring of Japanese and non-Asian foreigners are maliciously stereotyped in mass media, including popular literature, films, and comic books."

Attitudes about race in Japan are similar to those in the United States. So-called minority groups are thought to be physically different from the majority population no matter how erroneous this assumption and no matter how little evidence supports it. Negative personality traits and behavior are attributed to them, again with little supporting evidence. The poverty in which disadvantaged and stigmatized groups live actually results from discrimination but is used to prove their lack of merit and justify the negative stereotypes about them.

Explore more at
www.myanthrolab.com

It is apparent to most North Americans that racial groups in the United States are ordered hierarchically with "white" as the privileged group. Stating that whites are privileged does not mean that all white people live well and have power. Clearly, this is not the case. Many white people are poor, unemployed, undereducated, and endure many kinds of hardships. Most white people lack social and political power because they, like members of the minority groups, do not control the means of producing wealth and influence. However, although individual whites suffer from poverty and lack of opportunity, their suffering is based on class, not race. Poor whites are marginalized in a class system that disadvantages them, but poor African Americans, Native Americans, and Hispanics are marginalized by both class and race, compounding their structural powerlessness. The antagonism that pervades and obscures issues of class and race surfaces in attitudes toward affirmative action programs, for example. Working-class and middle-class whites who oppose affirmative action are expressing an anger that stems from competitive relations underlying capitalist economies, turned instead toward people who are even more disadvantaged than they.

Despite the successes of social movements, there are still barriers between racial groups. One reason is the reluctance of North Americans to acknowledge issues of class. Of course, although most members of the highest classes are white, there are wealthy African Americans, Hispanics, and Native Americans. Focusing attention on race helps hide distinctions of class that account for much of the disadvantage experienced by many members of minority groups. In addition, racial antagonisms are used to create barriers to the formation of multiracial interest groups based on class. Members of privileged groups benefit from a system that pits poor people against one another based on race, each group believing that its problems are caused by members of other racial groups rather than by members of other classes, even within their own racial group.

Although racial categorization springs from and is connected to issues of control and oppression, "race" identity can also be a means of mobilizing and countering oppression. In the words of Manning Marable:

> "Race" for the oppressed has come to mean an identity of survival, victimization and opposition to those racial groups or elites which exercise power and privilege. What we are looking at here is not an ethnic identification or culture, but an awareness of shared experience, suffering and struggles against the barriers of racial division. These collective experiences, survival tales and grievances form the basis of an historical consciousness . . . this sense of racial identity is both imposed on the oppressed and yet represents a reconstructed critical memory of the character of the group's collective ordeals. Definitions of "race" and "racial identity" give character and substance to the movements for power and influence among people of color. (1995, 365)

Race in Brazil

In Brazil, there is the same mix of races as in the United States, with people whose ancestry stems from indigenous groups, Africa, and Europe. However, there is not the same rigidity of categories, and there is much greater public recognition of multiracial ancestry. Brazilians employ some 500 different labels to identify a person's race, many more than the dual division of black/white that dominates U.S. racial discourse (Harris 1970). Not everyone knows and uses all of these labels, but in a study of a small village in northeastern Brazil, about forty different racial terms are used (Kottak 1999). Most of these terms make fine distinctions about skin color, hair color and texture, eye color, eye shape, shape of the nose, and shape of the lips. The same person might describe himself or someone else using different labels in different contexts. The terms selected are based on comparisons with other people present, for example, whether someone were lighter or darker, had lighter, darker, or redder hair, and so on. People in the village also disagree about the proper labels to use for specific individuals.

Although the Brazilian system might appear to be more flexible, a hierarchy of race-based privilege exists nonetheless. This system is also more flexible than that in the United States, but the wealthiest and most powerful elites, whether measured in economic or political terms, tend to be light-skinned and/or of European ancestry. In fact, the distribution of wealth in Brazil is even more unequal than that in the United States. The gap between rich and poor in income, education, standard of living, and social and political power is enormous (Andrews, 1992). In general, the ranks of the poor are made up largely of nonwhites.

Ethnic Identity

Like race, **ethnicity** is a social category. Its definition includes a complex mix of ancestry, culture, and self-identification. Ethnicity is largely based on a "shared cultural heritage" (Berreman 1989). This heritage may include language, religion, family and household structure, preferences for foods and clothing, and a general perspective

ethnicity
Social category based on a complex mix of ancestry, culture, and self-identification.

IN THEIR OWN VOICES

The Souls of Black Folk

W.E.B. DuBois was born in Great Barrington, Massachusetts, in 1868. He received his undergraduate degree from Fisk College and his PhD in sociology from Harvard University. Having grown up in western Massachusetts, DuBois was shocked at the overt racism that he experienced when he went to college in the South. He taught school for several years in Georgia, where he again confronted bigotry. In this excerpt from his book, The Souls of Black Folk (1903), DuBois writes about the lives and destinies of two men, one black and one white.

The white folk of Altamaha, Georgia voted John a good boy,—fine plough-hand, good in the rice-fields, handy everywhere, and always good-natured and respectful. But they shook their heads when his mother wanted to send him off to school. "It'll spoil him,—ruin him," they said. But full half the black folk followed him proudly to the train station.

Up at the Judge's they too had a John—a fair-haired, smooth-faced boy, who had played many a long summer's day to its close with his darker namesake. "Yes, sir! John is at Princeton, sir," said the Judge every morning as he marched down to the post-office. "Showing the Yankees what a Southern gentleman can do," he added.

Thus in the far-away Southern village the world lay waiting for the coming of two young men, and dreamed in an inarticulate way of new things that would be done and new thoughts that all would think. And yet it was singular that few thought of two Johns,—for the black folk thought of one John, and he was black; and the white folk thought of another John, and he was white. And neither world thought the other world's thought, save with a vague unrest.

John grew slowly to feel almost for the first time the Veil that lay between him and the white world; he first noticed now the oppression that had not seemed oppression before, differences that erstwhile seemed natural, restraints and slights that in his boyhood days had gone unnoticed or been greeted with a laugh. He felt angry now when men did not call him "Mister," he clenched his hands at the "Jim Crow" cars, and chafed at the color-line that hemmed in him and his.

It left John sitting so silent and rapt that he did not for some time notice the usher tapping him lightly on the shoulder and saying politely, "Will you step this way, please, sir?" A little surprised, he arose quickly at the last tap, and, turning to leave his seat, looked full into the face of the fair-haired young man. For the first time the young man recognized his dark boyhood playmate, and John knew that it was the Judge's son. The White John started, lifted his hand, and then froze into his chair; the black John smiled lightly, then grimly, and followed the usher down the aisle.

[When John arrived back in his segregated hometown, he applied for a job teaching at a school for Black children.]

The Judge plunged squarely into the business. "You've come for the school, I suppose. You know I'm a friend to your people. I've helped you and your family. Now I like the colored people, and sympathize with all their reasonable

and worldview. In small homogeneous societies of the type that anthropologists formerly studied, all members of the group shared their basic cultural heritage. But in modern, complex societies, where people of many different backgrounds are united within the same nation, cultural differences can be significant. Ethnicity, as a social category, is a feature of such societies. In many modern nations, ethnic groups are ranked relative to one another. Some groups have higher status, and therefore greater privilege and power, than others.

Ethnicity, unlike race and caste, is not an entirely closed or ascribed status. Although ethnicity is based on ancestry, it is also based on identification with a cultural group. For example, if a person is a recent immigrant in another country, his or her ethnic identity is automatically assigned, but if that person is the child or descendant of immigrants, there may be more flexibility in that person's identity. Under most circumstances, people who are not themselves immigrants may choose to either retain or abandon the cultural traits that identify them as members of a particular ethnic group. The process of relinquishing one's cultural heritage is called assimilation. Immigrants may want to positively identify with their new country, but they may also want to distance themselves from the social stigma attached to their immigrant status. Contrasting ethnicity and race in the United States, Gerald Berreman points out that "the American 'melting pot' works for ambitious ethnic groups because they can assimilate by relinquishing their heritage; it aspirations; but you and I both know, John, that in this country the Negro must remain subordinate, and can never expect to be the equal of white men. In their place, your people can be honest and respectful; and God knows, I'll do what I can to help them. But when they want to reverse nature, and rule white men, and marry white women, and sit in my parlor, then, by God! We'll hold them under if we have to lynch every Nigger in the land. Now, John, the question is, are you, going to accept the situation and teach the darkies to be faithful servants and laborers as your fathers were?"

"I am going to accept the situation, Judge Henderson," answered John, with a brevity that did not escape the keen old man. He hesitated a moment, and then said shortly, "Very well,—we'll try you awhile. Good-morning."

[As a teacher, John instructed his students well, teaching them to read and write but also teaching them to think about their lives and the world in which they lived.]

"John, this school is closed. You children can go home and get to work. The white people of Altamaha are not spending their money on black folks to have their heads crammed with impudence and lies. Clear out! I'll lock the door myself."

The great brown sea lay silent. The air scarce breathed. The dying day bathed the twisted oaks and mighty pines in black and gold. There came from the wind no warning, not a whisper from the cloudless sky. There was only a black man hurrying on with an ache in his heart, seeing neither sun nor sea, but starting as from a dream at the frightened cry that woke the pines, to see his dark sister struggling in the arms of a tall and fair-haired man.

He said not a word, but, seizing a fallen limb, struck him with all the pent-up hatred of his great black arm; and the body lay white and still beneath the pines, all bathed in sunshine and in blood. John looked at it dreamily, then walked back to the house briskly, and said in a soft voice, "Mammy, I'm going away—I'm going to be free."

He leaned back and smiled toward the sea, whence rose the strange melody, away from the dark shadows where lay the noise of horses galloping, galloping on. With an effort he roused himself, bent forward, and looked steadily down the pathway.

Amid the trees and in the dim morning twilight he watched their shadows dancing and heard their horses thundering toward him, until at last they came sweeping like a storm, and he saw in front that haggard white-haired man, whose eyes flashed red with fury. Oh, how he pitied him,—pitied him,— and wondered if he had the coiling twisted rope. Then, as the storm burst round him, he rose slowly to his feet and turned his closed eyes toward the Sea.

And the world whistled in his ears.

Explore more at
www.myanthrolab.com

From W.E.B. DuBois, *The Souls of Black Folk*, pp. 246–63.
© 1903/1995 Signet Classics.

CRITICAL THINKING QUESTIONS

What contrasts does DuBois draw here? What does he conclude about race relations in the United States?

does not work for race groups because their status is an unalterable consequence of birth that they cannot relinquish (i.e., are not allowed to relinquish), and hence they cannot assimilate (this is the very essence of racism)" (1989, 16).

In some contexts, ethnic identification is irrelevant and not thought about; in other situations, ethnicity may be a key feature of one's personal identity. In multiethnic nations undergoing rapid social change, identifying with and asserting one's ethnicity may be an important means of group formation. In Africa, for example, the search for identity has complex meanings attached to different ethnic symbols, depending on the contexts and frames of reference used. According to Victor Uchendu (1995), the search for an African identity takes place on four contrasting planes: continental, racial, national, and tribal. A continental-wide identity as "African" contrasts Africa with other continents. As Uchendu observed, "Continental identity became an instrument for decolonization and a weapon for post independence international diplomacy" (p. 129). Racial identity contrasts black Africans with other groups living on the continent, that is, Arabs and whites. National identity refers to the quest for the formation of a cohesive identity within a given country. This goal is often problematic in Africa because of the artificial national boundaries created by colonial European powers for their own interests. Finally, the search for tribal identity takes place within the newly independent and emerging multiethnic African nations.

GLOBALIZATION

Pan-Africanism refers to various movements in Africa that have sought to define African ethnic, racial, and transnational identity at the continental level. Starting in 1900, these movements had the common goal of unifying Africans against colonialism and colonial influences. The great diversity of peoples and interests prevented that unity. In 1963, the Organization of African Unity (OAU) was founded as a forum for discussing problems in Africa and achieving shared goals. In 2002, the OAU was replaced by the African Union (AU), modeled on the European Union (EU).

CASE STUDY

Ethnic Identity in the United States

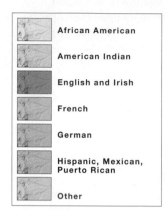

African American

American Indian

English and Irish

French

German

Hispanic, Mexican, Puerto Rican

Other

Because of their growing numbers, particularly since the mid-twentieth century, people of Spanish origin or ancestry, variously referred to (and self-referred) as Hispanic or Latino, have received prominent attention (Fears 2003). Some members of this group, especially in the Southwest, are the descendants of Spaniards who settled in North America in the 1600s, but most are immigrants or descendants of recent immigrants from Mexico, the Caribbean, and Central and South America rather than from Spain. However, "Hispanic" is clearly an ethnic, not racial, label because Hispanic people may be white, black, or Native American.

Recent federal census questionnaires reflect the complexity of categories of race and ethnicity. In the 2000 census, respondents were asked to identify their "race" and were given the option of choosing "one or more" of these identifications: White; Black, African-American, or Negro; American Indian or Alaska Native; Asian Indian; Chinese; Filipino; Japanese; Korean; Vietnamese; Native Hawaiian; Guamanian or Chamorro; Samoan; Other Asian; Other Pacific Islander; Some Other Race. People were also asked to state whether they were "Spanish/Hispanic/Latino." If they responded affirmatively, they were then asked to identify their "group" from among the following: (1) Mexican, Mexican-American, Chicano; (2) Puerto Rican; (3) Cuban; (4) Other.

Census Bureau statistics, compiled in 2001, revealed the following percentage makeup of the U.S. population: white: 70 percent; Hispanic: 13 percent; African American: 12.7 percent; Asian: 4 percent; Native American: 0.9 percent. For the first time, Hispanics outnumbered African Americans. The Hispanic population experienced the fastest growth, increasing at a rate of nearly 5 percent since the 2000 census. This growth is a result of high fertility rates and increased immigration. Both the absolute numbers and percentage of Hispanics are projected to continue to rise.

Similar counting procedures are not used for Native Americans. In fact, the government's practice of categorizing many respondents with mixed Indian ancestry as whites, African Americans, or Hispanics undercounts native peoples. According to Jack Forbes (1990), a more accurate assessment of the number of people with Indian ancestry should include people with "Hispanic" identification, as well as the 30 percent to 70 percent of African Americans who report to be part Indian. In the 1990 census, the official native population stood at 1.9 million, but the U.S. census reported nearly 8 million people with Native American ancestry by the year 2000. The large growth in the reported number can be accounted for by changes in census questionnaires and counting people who claimed either Native American identity or ancestry.

In the census of 2000, 7.3 million Americans (3 percent of the total population) chose two or more identities. The number of biracial and multiracial individuals will continue to grow. According to the census reports, 41 percent of people identifying as mixed race were under 18 years of age (Navarro 2008).

PEARSON
myanthrolab

Explore more at
www.myanthrolab.com

Until the 1960s and 1970s, when African nations won their independence from their European colonizers, African peoples did not identify as "African," even though Europeans identified them as such. Self-identifications were tribal and ethnic. Today, people choose from among numerous possibilities for self-identification based on circumstances. For example, "Nigerian students in London or New York are more likely to identify themselves as African than as Nigerian unless the situation clearly indicates that identification of country is expected or required. To another Nigerian, they are most likely to identify themselves with state or region; if they are speaking to a co-ethnic, they are likely to name the provincial or administrative headquarters to which they belong. Thus, identity is likely to change as the frame of reference changes" (Uchendu 1995, 131).

Ethnic allegiance also has different meanings in rural and urban settings. According to Uchendu, tribal identity is paramount in rural Africa because "the tie to the tribal, communal, or lineage land, often phrased in the idiom of filial loyalty to ancestors, is still an important social and economic asset" (p. 129). Although such ties are not significant in urban areas, ethnic loyalty may be advantageous in the context of "the competition for jobs, the uneven distribution of government patronage, and the insecurity of urban employment" (p. 129). Through ethnic identification, a person can claim membership in a cohesive community that provides economic, social, and emotional support.

In many countries, the inherent stratification of ethnic groups in relation to each other can come to crisis in times of economic and political stress. In these situations, ethnic groups can be pitted against one another in struggles for prestige and power. Loyalty to one's ethnic group then becomes a paramount factor in taking sides, only exacerbating underlying tensions and furthering the processes of ethnic identification and conflict.

Just such a crisis developed in the 1980s and 1990s in the former Yugoslavia. Although the causes of the breakup of Yugoslavia need much more study and reflection, political leaders on all sides used long-standing ethnic animosities to gain support in their own identifiable ethnic enclaves. According to Mary Kay Galliland (1995), most of the people residing in a "midsize town" in eastern Croatia on the border with Bosnia were "relatively unconcerned about ethno-national identity" during the 1980s (p. 201), thinking of themselves primarily as citizens of the unified country of Yugoslavia. Their primary concerns were economic: food shortages, inflation, and lack of jobs and housing. After the death of the longtime Yugoslav president, Josip Broz (known as Tito), in 1982, the government instituted an austerity program aimed at limiting imports and increasing exports to gain hard currency needed to repay Yugoslavia's large debts to Western nations. The government also rationed domestic products, such as gasoline, coffee, and laundry detergent (p. 206). The basic Yugoslav currency, the dinar, was devalued, resulting in a precipitous decline in real wages as prices soared. Shortages of many foods and domestic products also became widespread. All of these conditions contributed to feelings of uncertainty and instability.

Each group saw itself as victims of economic and political policies promulgated by other groups. According to Galliland, "Serbs [a minority in Croatia] blamed Croats for their own lack of economic development; the Western portion of the former Yugoslavia, they said, had gained at Serbian expense. Croats turned the argument around; they had been supporting the less-developed regions with the products of their own hard work. Worse, they had also been paying for a growing military and corrupt [federal Yugoslav] government bureaucracy heavily dominated by Serbs" (1995, 203).

As tensions mounted and incidents of interethnic violence occurred, nationalist politicians and the media contributed to the "production of fear" that characterized much of Yugoslav discourse. Although the causes of the violence are complex, ethnic nationalism clearly played a role in solidifying group identity and creating rigid boundaries among the various ethnic groups. By culturally constructing groups in opposition to each other, people came to see themselves and their group as distinct from all others. In addition, people began to speak more openly about the past, redefining the past as they talked about it. No longer did they remember Yugoslavian unity but instead recalled incidents that provided reasons for distrust and animosity. Although throughout much of the postwar period these memories were not considered important, they were lying beneath the surface, "waiting to be called into action, if the times were right, if someone wanted to make use of them, and if the means of communication were available" (Galliland 1995, 216). Nationalist Serbian and Croatian political leaders tapped into this reservoir of memory, exploiting it to mobilize followers and gain power. But, by intensifying people's fears, political leaders unleashed a wave of hatred and violence that ended by destroying a nation and creating new reasons for people to distrust one another.

REVIEW ⊙ Race is a social, not a biological classification. Race and ethnic identity are culturally constructed and are stratified differently in different societies. Racial or ethnic minorities may be viewed negatively and experience discrimination. Ethnicity is based on identification with a cultural or ethnic group.

CLASS, RACE, ETHNICITY, AND IDEOLOGY IN AMERICAN SOCIETY

As in other stratified societies, the system of inequality in the United States that grants privilege to members of some groups and denies opportunities to others is supported by ideological beliefs that members of high-status groups, whether based on class, race, or ethnicity, deserve their advantages. In contrast, it is believed that members of low-status groups are responsible for their plight because of their lack of motivation and initiative. However, some hope of achievement and advance is held out to less privileged people in order to diminish their anger and resistance. Many people are nurtured by the "American Dream," convinced that if they work hard enough and are sensible and practical, they can achieve a better standard of living for themselves and their children.

The dream of the rewards of hard work, elusive though it may be for most people, is based on the fact that class, at least theoretically, is a social ordering that allows for mobility. The hope of upward class mobility helps alleviate the burdens of class disadvantage and blunts potential anger on the part of the lower-class people who might otherwise challenge the legitimacy of the system. Issues of class and class interests are also masked behind an ideology of equality. Even to talk about class may be considered disruptive and antagonistic, especially in political campaigns and media rhetoric.

However, it is clear that members of the upper classes act in their class interests. They may not talk about their identity as a class, at least not publicly, because to do so would violate the ideology of classlessness that makes up the American Dream. However, their actions in formulating economic and political policies do indicate their awareness of class solidarity. Even the trend toward living in gated communities translates class segregation into architecture. In contrast, members of the middle and lower classes generally do not understand their social position as part of the structure of a hierarchical social order. Those that do perceive it as temporary, amenable to change if they persist.

There are, in addition, other difficulties in uniting as a class. Among these are antagonisms that develop between members of groups defined in ways other than by class, such as race, ethnicity, and gender. These three factors are employed as part of the hierarchical structure to divide members of nonelite classes to keep them from recognizing and acting on their common interests.

Talking about race is also perceived as divisive. Much of the popular discourse on race focuses on the

To what extent and in what ways are you upwardly mobile? In what circumstances could you become downwardly mobile, and what are your chances of this?

The election of Barak Obama to the presidency of the United States in 2008 generated discussion of biracial identity. In this photo, Obama is shown with his maternal grandparents, Madelyn and Stanley Dunham.

partial successes of the civil rights movement of the 1950s and 1960s that led to passage of legislation mandating equal treatment and recognition of the civil rights of all Americans. One can point to vigorous programs to end segregation in schools, to bar the most overt forms of racial discrimination, and to redress underrepresentation of nonwhites in many occupations through affirmative action policies. Nonetheless, these programs and policies have not created full racial equality. Members of nonwhite groups remain disadvantaged in terms of income, employment, quality of education and health care services, and political representation. However, race was supposed to be eliminated in the vocabulary of a "color-blind" society, proven so by the fact that some African Americans could achieve wealth and status (Baker 1998).

Despite the hope of upward class mobility, most people do not experience improvements in their class standing. Indeed, some members of the middle and upper classes experience downward mobility. As the work of Katherine Newman (1989) has documented, since the 1980s in the United States, a large but largely unpublicized number of Americans have been catapulted from comfortable and rewarding lifestyles after they lost their jobs. Newman found that people "fall from grace" for a variety of reasons. Some lose jobs as well-paid executives or managers in large corporations when the firms "downsize." Others lose jobs in factories when the plants move to "more profitable and business-friendly" regions of the United States or to foreign countries in a trend toward outsourcing that is becoming increasingly frequent, with dire economic consequences for many North American workers. Still others are fired when they participate in strikes. When plants close down or workers in small communities go out on strike, the economic effects can be disastrous to more than just the people immediately involved. Whole communities may suffer when residents no longer have money to spend in stores, restaurants, and local entertainment.

The extent of downward mobility is much greater than most Americans realize. The true picture certainly does not square with the mythology of the American Dream that many people adhere to. And it doesn't square with media coverage of the U.S. economy. Newman uses several indices to measure downward mobility. People who experience a decline in income or are employed in a job having less prestige or status than their previous jobs can be victims of downward mobility. In a national survey taken every year by the National Opinion Research Center, approximately 25 percent of respondents claimed that their financial situation in the 1980s had worsened during the year they were questioned (Newman 1989, 21). Federal statistics indicate that individual real income (adjusted for inflation) declined 14 percent between 1972 and 1982. The rate of decline accelerated so that between 1978 and 1982, 56 percent of the population was falling behind inflation, a clear indicator that their standard of living declined. Economic decline affects families in all socioeconomic groups. Many families experiencing downward mobility are not just "sliding" but are actually "plunging." In the 1970s, studies indicated that nearly one-third of the American population experienced a drop in family income of 50 percent or more (p. 23).

Job loss affects all economic sectors but is most severe in manufacturing and heavy industry. Plant closings often occur to save money by relocating to areas of the country that are less heavily unionized (especially the South) or to foreign countries where wages are lower and job protection is nearly absent. The plight of displaced industrial workers is compounded by general economic trends resulting in the decline of manufacturing in the United States. In addition, managers and professional, technical, and administrative workers have also been displaced in high numbers. Women have a harder time finding new jobs than do men. African Americans and Hispanics have longer periods of unemployment than do whites. Using government statistics, Newman concluded that job displacement in the 1980s caused nearly 6 million people to become downwardly mobile (p. 27).

Finally, divorce has a deleterious effect on women's income and is often the catalyst that propels them into a downward economic spiral. Divorced women with children, particularly when they have little or no continued financial support from their husbands, usually

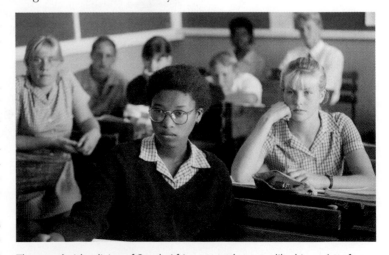

The apartheid policies of South Africa created a caste-like hierarchy of whites and blacks. After the collapse of the régime in 1992, schools, such as this one in Cape Town, were desegregated.

ANTHROPOLOGY APPLIED

Working Against Human Trafficking

In both government and nongovernment organizations, anthropologists are among those combating international human trafficking. Human trafficking includes buying and selling women and children into indentured servitude or slavery, illegally transporting migrants, and marketing body parts. The United Nations and national governments publish reports on the effectiveness of measures against human trafficking. In the summer of 2004, the U.S. State Department's report on human trafficking named ten countries—including Sudan, Myanmar, and North Korea—as among the world's most negligent in protecting human rights. Forty-two other nations, including Japan, had inadequate measures against human trafficking. Japan is a destination for Asian, Latin American, and East European women and children trafficked for forced labor and sexual exploitation by the *yakuza*, Japan's organized

crime groups. Other countries in this group include Russia, Thailand, Vietnam, the Philippines, Pakistan, India, Zimbabwe, Greece, Mexico, and Peru (Sakajiri 2004).

Anthropologists may combat human trafficking in different ways. For example, anthropologists working for HimRights (International Institute for Human Rights, Environment and Development), a watchdog organization, in Nepal conduct preventive educational campaigns and help monitor border crossings to detect and report suspected trafficking and protect Bhutanese and Tibetan refugees. They may help rescue and repatriate trafficked people. They also provide data for the region to the United Nations Commission on Human Rights.

In addition, human rights work often involves surveillance (or observation) and documentation, which are the skills of an ethnographer. The underworld trafficking of human organs for transplants was exposed largely through "undercover ethnography." This kind of work, which raises ethical issues for anthropologists and the medical profession, led to the discovery of an extensive network of "outlaw surgeons, kidney hunters, and transplant tourists" buying and selling human body parts (Scheper-Hughes 2004).

◉ CRITICAL THINKING QUESTIONS

Why is anthropologist involvement in human rights work controversial? What are arguments for and against undercover ethnography?

experience downward mobility. Many divorced women who were not working at the time of their divorce have great difficulty finding employment. Even those who work do not earn as much money as their husbands and therefore cannot support themselves and their children at their previous standard of living.

People who experience downward mobility suffer socially and psychologically in addition to their economic losses. They may have to give up spacious houses and a comfortable lifestyle. They may lose their friends because they can no longer afford to socialize in the ways they had in the past. Economic problems may put strains on marriages, resulting in separation and divorce. People also feel ashamed because of what they perceive to be their lack of success. They feel that they have not lived up to their own and others' expectations.

Although people who experience downward mobility are actually disadvantaged by a hierarchical social system, there are many ways that social ideologies about the American Dream blunt people's awareness of class as a major determinant of their lives and their opportunities. Rather than becoming angry at a system that not only tolerates inequality but is in fact built on necessary inequality, they feel disappointed and ashamed. Rather than understanding their predicament as part of the integral structure of capitalist economies, they make a judgment about their personal deficiencies.

GLOBALIZATION

A dark side of globalization today is widespread trafficking of women and children for the sex trade and illicit trade in human body parts for transplants. These and other transborder crimes feed on a global service economy.

REVIEW

Social, political, economic, educational, and religious ideologies serve to justify and maintain a society's system of social stratification. Thus, people learn to believe that social inequalities are normal or necessary. Furthermore, ideologies influence people's sentiments and behaviors, so that people readily believe in things that are not true and act on those beliefs.

CHAPTER SUMMARY

Equality, Inequality, and Social Stratification

- Societies differ in respect to people's access to resources, livelihood, respect, and prestige. In egalitarian societies, all individuals have equal access to resources and equal likelihood of achieving respect and prestige. Although people's different skills and talents are rewarded, no one is denied opportunities for achievement. Foraging societies and some horticultural societies are likely to be egalitarian.

- In social systems based on rank, individuals and kinship groups occupy different positions in the social hierarchy. Each position is ranked in relation to all others. High rank confers advantages. In some ranked systems, high-ranking individuals are freed from subsistence activities and are supported by the productive work of others. High-ranking individuals are awarded prestige and influence and wield political influence as leaders of kinship groups and territorial units. Despite the privileges of rank, no one is denied a basically decent standard of living. In fact, high-ranking people have the responsibility of distributing goods to members of their kin groups.

- In stratified societies, people are differentiated on the basis of attributes they have at birth. These differences allow some people to have greater access to resources, wealth, and positions of prestige, influence, and power than other people. Granting privileges and opportunities to some people effectively denies them to others. Many traditional agrarian societies and all modern industrial states are highly stratified. Unlike systems of rank, some people in stratified societies may go hungry and be poorly clothed and housed. The gap in the standard of living between rich and poor may be wide.

Caste and Class

- A caste is a closed social group whose membership is hereditary, that is, people born into a particular caste and remaining so for life. Caste membership is an ascribed status. The various castes are ordered hierarchically from highest to lowest in a fixed order. Mobility is impossible. Members of higher castes have rights and privileges denied to members of lower castes. They have better standards of living, greater opportunities for achievement, and are more likely to occupy positions of influence and power.

- Some stratified systems are organized into classes rather than castes. Class systems are, at least theoretically, based on achievement, including education, occupation, and income. However, in practice, people whose parents are wealthier and are in higher classes have greater access to education and thus to higher incomes and occupations. In addition, although mobility is theoretically a characteristic of class systems, most people remain more or less constant in their social position. Downward mobility is as likely as upward mobility.

Race and Ethnicity

- Race is a social construct, focusing on a particular set of external physical traits but having no biological basis as separate, discrete categories. Physical traits that are used to demarcate the races, including skin color, hair color and texture, and facial features, appear in human populations on a continuum, not as consistent markers of groups. But race, once identified on the basis of physical characteristics, becomes projected onto social and personal behavior. The races are then ranked hierarchically. The dominant social group ascribes negative qualities to groups it considers inferior.

- Ethnicity is a feature of cultural identification. Cultural traits that often define group membership include language, residence, food, dress, and body ornamentation. Ethnicity is an ascribed status in that people are born into a cultural group. It is also an achieved status because people can choose either to identify with their ethnic group of origin or assimilate into the mainstream society.

Class, Race, Ethnicity, and Ideology in American Society

- In the United States, an ideology coalescing around the American Dream obscures the actual facts of the structure of class and class privilege. Although elites who control government policies act in the interests of their class, barriers hinder class consciousness among disadvantaged groups. People blame themselves, for their disadvantages instead of recognizing that a hierarchical system imposes a position on them. People also feel that their low position in the socioeconomic system is temporary, amenable to change if they try harder to achieve. Other barriers that divide people include racial, ethnic, and gender differences.

KEY TERMS

wealth 277
power 277
prestige 277
achieved status 277

ascribed status 277
ranked societies 277
egalitarian societies 278
stratified societies 279

social stratification 282
elites 282
mobility 286
slavery 287

race 287
ethnicity 291

REVIEW QUESTIONS

1. What core concepts are used to analyze systems of social stratification?
2. How are egalitarian, ranked, and stratified societies different?
3. What are three basic theoretical explanations for systems of social stratification?
4. How is caste different from class? What role does social mobility play in caste and class societies?

5. How can ideologies be used to socialize conformity to the social order, to reinforce the system of social stratification, and to challenge the system?
6. How does language reveal class membership? What else indicates social class?
7. How are race and ethnicity social constructs? How are race and ethnicity a form of caste?

PEARSON myanthrolab EXERCISES

To complete the following exercises and activities, you must log in to www.myanthrolab.com and select your current textbook.

1. In the **Explore** tab of Chapter 11, click on *Video* and watch one of the videos in this section. Complete the short answer exercise that accompanies the video.
2. While in the **Explore** tab of Chapter 11 click on the *NPR Audio Programs Broadcast* tab and go to *Theme 15: Social Stratification*. Listen to one of the programs in

this section and complete the short answer exercise that accompanies the program.

3. Enter the **MyAnthroLibrary** section on the home page to read more about topics and cultures that are discussed in this chapter. Suggested readings include:

Origins of Social Inequality by Elizabeth M. Brumfiel

Is There Caste Outside of India? By Morton Klass

POLITICAL SYSTEMS

- ● What do political anthropologists study?

- ● What are the five main types of political organization in human societies? How are they different?

- ● Why and how do political systems change?

- ● What are the origins and characteristics of states?

Long ago, a girl named Short Woman lived with her parents and her brother on the plains at a distance from a large Cheyenne camp. One day the father, named Bull Looks Back, killed his wife and deserted his two young children. The children wandered about for a time trying to find the main camp to seek shelter and food. Finally, they came upon the camp and entered a lodge. There they were told that they were the children of Bull Looks Back, who was then also in the camp. When the father heard that his children had arrived, he said aloud: "Those monstrous children of mine killed their own mother and ate her flesh. That is why I left them. They should be staked to the ground and abandoned."

And so the people did as he said. The girl and boy were bound by leather ropes and left to die on the plains. But a dog approached at nightfall and chewed on the straps binding the girl. When she got free, she untied her brother and both ran swiftly away. They were met by a stranger who told them that the girl had a power to kill buffalo by looking at them. At first she did not believe the stranger's words, but when a large herd of buffalo appeared, she looked up and they all fell dead.

After she butchered the animals, the girl told a crow to carry some meat to the Cheyenne camp where she and her brother had been abandoned. She said to the crow: "Tell those people the meat is from the children they left on the plains to die." The people then understood that the children were alive and that the girl had special powers.

Then the girl sent for the people to come to her. She told them, "We are going to make chiefs. You know I have been accused of killing my mother. That is not true. Now, we shall make chiefs, and hereafter we shall have a rule that if anyone kills a fellow tribesmember they shall be ordered away from one to five years, whatever the people shall decide."

The girl chose the first chiefs. She told them, "You will swear that you will be honest and care for all the tribe."

The girl told the chiefs how they should act and gave them a pipe of peace to smoke. She taught them songs and prayers to guide and protect them. Then she said, "My brother and I will leave this earth. We may go up into the heavens. Yet I shall always be working for the people. I may be a star."

From E. Adamson Hoebel, *The Cheyennes: Indians of the Great Plains*, 2/E, pp. 45–49. © 1978. Reprinted with permission of Wadsworth, a part of Cengage Learning. www.cengage.com/permissions

---

In this narrative, the Cheyenne of the American Plains tell the story of the founding of their system of tribal governance. It tells of the creation of the Council of 44 chosen from the ten Cheyenne bands (Hoebel 1978). Members served ten-year terms. They met only during the summer, when the Cheyenne nation gathered for communal buffalo hunts. Council members settled internal disputes and organized the hunts. The members of the council were selected because they were men of judgment and good character. The story also relates that wrongdoers were banished from their communities, a punishment that might have severe consequences because other bands would be reluctant to take in strangers or people suspected of antisocial behavior. Systems of leadership and decision making are mechanisms that help unify and integrate community members into a cohesive society.

POLITICAL ANTHROPOLOGY

In every society, indeed, in every social group, actions need to be planned, decisions need to be made, and procedures for organizing group activities need to be drawn up. Societies differ in the ways in which people organize their interactions and integrate themselves into a cohesive community. In every society and in every social group, different people have different roles to play. Some people have more influence than others when group decisions have to be made and assume leadership responsibilities when actions have to be undertaken. These features of society are the components of each group's **political organization.** Political systems, then, include procedures for making decisions, organizing group actions, choosing leaders, and settling disputes both within the group and with other groups. All societies have some form of political organization, but not all have formal governments familiar to people living in modern states.

Political anthropology studies these cultural dynamics. Political anthropologists focus on the mechanisms people use to solve the basic problems that confront them as a group. Although every person has individual interests and needs, social groups are formed on principles of cohesion, sharing, and reciprocity. People know that no matter what their individual inclinations, they need to adjust their actions in ways that enable their group to survive and thrive. Political anthropologists are concerned with understanding these mechanisms and with analyzing how they develop and are implemented. They are interested in understanding differences in the degree of influence, authority, or

Political disputes may erupt in violence when negotiations fail to resolve underlying conflicts. Car bombs, such as this one on April 18, 2007 in Baghdad, Iraq are deadly symptoms of such unresolved conflicts.

power that leaders may wield in different types of society. Of course, not everyone in any community agrees with group goals or conforms to group wishes. So political anthropologists also study the ways that community decisions are reached and conflicts are resolved. In this chapter, we examine questions of community organization and leadership; in the next, Chapter 13, we will be concerned with conflict and conflict resolution.

Political anthropology studies political organization—the roles and processes that societies have for making decisions, mobilizing action, choosing leaders, settling disputes, and enforcing social norms.

TYPES OF POLITICAL ORGANIZATION

It has become commonplace to describe political systems in a four-part typology of band, tribe, chiefdom, and state. This typology, introduced by Elman Service (1962), is based on distinguishing different kinds of sociopolitical organization in terms of types of leadership, societal integration and cohesion, decision-making mechanisms, and degree of control over people. Although the typology might seem to make too sharp distinctions among societies, it is a useful tool in discussing cultural differences. It is important to remember, though, that few societies are ideal "types," but, rather, there are features within them that overlap from one set in the typology to another. It is best to think of the types as constellations of varying features rather than as overgeneralized, absolute cases. The different sociopolitical types of societies tend to co-occur with particular kinds of subsistence activities, economic modes, settlement patterns, and kinship systems.

Bands

Bands are generally small, loosely organized groups of people. Their leaders are selected on the basis of personal qualities and skills. They lead by example and influence but lack authority to enforce their opinions on the community. Decision making is relatively informal and open to the participation of all competent members. Until a few centuries ago, band societies could be found in many parts of the world, but, by the middle of the twentieth century, the remaining band societies were located only in marginal areas of the world, such as the Arctic, the desert regions of Africa and Australia, and the dense forests of South America (see Table 12.1). Bands generally have (and had) relatively small populations. The smallest groups have perhaps only twenty-five to fifty people, whereas larger bands might have as many as several hundred members. Individual settlements were generally dispersed throughout a wide territory; consequently, population densities were low.

political organization
The ways in which societies are organized to plan group activities, make decisions affecting members of the group, select leadership, and settle disputes both within the group and with other groups.

political anthropology
The study of the ways that communities plan group actions, make decisions affecting the group, select leadership, and resolve conflicts and disputes both within the group and with other groups.

bands
Small, loosely organized groups of people held together by informal means.

TABLE 12.1 EXAMPLES OF BAND SOCIETIES

Americas	Europe	Africa	Asia	Pacific
Netsilik of Arctic Circle	Lapp (Saami) of northern Scandinavia	Mbuti (Pygmies) of Congo Basin	Ainu of Japan	Tiwi of Australia
Inuit of eastern Canada			Chenchu of India	
Apache (historical) of western United States		Ju'/hoansi of Botswana	Semang (Negritos) of Malaysia	
Mi'kmaq of Nova Scotia			Vedda of Sri Lanka	
Ojibwe of Great Lakes region, United States and Canada				
Yahgun of Tierra del Fuego				

Most bands relied on foraging as their primary, if not exclusive, subsistence strategy. Consistent with foraging, bands were nomadic, utilizing various resource sites within a familiar territory. Today, some bands are seminomadic, moving their settlements between several relatively fixed locations on a yearly basis. Bands are often no more than territorial units, occupying common territory that may be well defined or that may be only vaguely delineated in relation to other comparable groups.

Bands are held together by informal means. Families or households are the significant units of the band. Membership within one band rather than another is generally based on kinship ties, through either descent or marriage, to other people in the group. Choice of band membership may also be based on loyalty to and approval of the band's leader. But band leadership is also informal. It is based on the personal abilities of the leader, including intelligence, subsistence skills, charismatic personality traits, and in some cases spiritual knowledge. The leader contributes as much, and in some cases more, to the band's subsistence than anyone else. He (or she, although most leaders of bands are men) lives no differently than other members of the band and receives no financial economic rewards.

The reward of leadership is prestige. Leadership also carries with it greater responsibilities because the leader is thought to be responsible for the well-being of the group. Although the band's success increases the prestige of its leader, the band's failure is similarly attributed to the leader's weakness or faults. A leader who proves unsuccessful risks losing his position. The band members will simply choose another among themselves to be the leader or will leave the settlement and relocate to another group. Band leaders, therefore, have only influence, not power. That is, they can use their oratorical skills to persuade people to remain with them and to follow their advice, but they have no means of enforcing their decisions. In fact, in many band societies, leaders who even attempt to control the actions of others would immediately disqualify themselves as leaders. Authority roles tend to be limited to the family, and even in that context, the authority of parents over children or of one spouse over the other is generally weak.

Other features of band societies are not necessarily components of a sociopolitical system but derive from the kind of subsistence and production generally found in bands. So, for example, the small size of settlements follows from the principle of carrying capacity—that is, the number of people that can be supported by the land and its resources (see Chapter 6). In addition, notions of private property are generally weak or absent. Land is never individually owned but is understood to be the common domain of band members. In some bands, specific resources or resource sites may be controlled by kinship groups but never by individuals. People in band societies do not accumulate significant surpluses of resources or personal possessions. These concepts about land and property derive from a foraging economic system and a nomadic or seminomadic settlement pattern. Band societies, and foraging societies generally, are usually egalitarian in their social system. Their egalitarian ethics are reflected in people's equal access to resources, equal potential access to prestige, and generally equal gender relations.

CASE STUDY

A Band Society: The Tiwis of Northern Australia

The Tiwis are indigenous foragers living on Bathurst and Melville islands, off northern Australia. Both islands have rivers, marshlands, extensive coastlines, dense forests, and abundant natural resources. Until recently, the Tiwi obtained their food by hunting, fishing, and gathering wild plants. Most of their diet was derived from the vegetable foods that the women gathered. Men did most of the hunting and fishing.

Tiwi camps consisted of a number of related families or one large family. If the camp contained more than one family unit, the groups were usually related through men. During the rainy season, November through April, people needed protection against the heavy rains. They built small dwellings made of wooden poles covered with bark. In the dry season, May through October, dwellings were made with leaf-covered branches tied together to give shade.

Households were the basic social units. Households hunted and gathered food for their group together. Households and camps were linked informally into larger units or bands of about 100 members, although people did not necessarily identify with the same band from year to year, and households within a band might disperse to exploit seasonal resources.

Band membership and residence overlapped. Every adult owned land, usually where they were born and lived. But land was not divided into individual parcels. Rather, a particular area, now referred to as a "country," was owned collectively (Goodale 1971). All of the owners of a particular country were communally responsible for its well-being, including its physical and spiritual protection. Women and men inherited landholding rights from their fathers. People could hold land through their fathers in several countries if the father had lived and was buried in a place other than his own land. Since 1976, when Tiwis were officially recognized as the legal owners of their land, the Tiwi Land Council regulates and registers the owners of countries and holds them responsible for protecting the land.

The Tiwi kinship system is based on membership in matrilineal clans. All clans are linked into four larger units, or phratries, that are exogamous—that is, a person cannot marry someone belonging to a clan in one's own phratry. Clans and kinship groups generally have informal leaders. These people, usually men, have influence in their families and communities because of their intelligence, skills, and sound judgment. Although every man in theory can aspire to high status, men with large families have advantages because of the loyalty and support of their kin.

Men enlarged their families, and, therefore, their influence, by marrying more than one wife. Prestige and leadership were thus intertwined with marriage customs. In traditional Tiwi society, all females had to be married from birth to death. Girls were betrothed immediately upon their birth, sometimes even before birth. Fathers arranged their daughters' marriages to men with whom they wished to form an alliance. The men were usually in their twenties or thirties and had shown promise by their hunting skills and personality. The actual marriage ceremony did not take place until the girl reached puberty, but the future son-in-law supplied his future in-laws with meat, rendered other aid, and acknowledged his father-in-law's influence. Fathers were also guaranteed support in their old age. Thus, fathers used their daughters to gain economic support and social prestige.

Given the age difference between a wife and her first husband, women were usually widowed one or more times. Immediate remarriage was expected. Often, a middle-aged or elderly widow would marry a much younger man who had been unable to contract a

tribes
Societies with some degree of formalization of structure and leadership, including village and intervillage councils whose members regularly meet to settle disputes and plan community activities.

favorable marriage. An older woman's extensive kinship relations could help her young husband. Eventually, he could marry other women and form alliances with their fathers.

Tiwi women also could aspire to positions of influence and prestige in their families and communities. A woman gained prestige and authority as she aged and accumulated a large family. So men's and women's leadership intertwined. No one wielded absolute control over anyone else, however, and no one's position of authority was automatic. Rather, leadership and influence were available to all community members and could be manipulated by the most skilled and intelligent.

PEARSON
my**anthrolab**

Explore more at
www.myanthrolab.com

Comparatively, there is less violence in band societies. Because of the informal links between band members and the instability of group composition, people can react to disputes by leaving the band and joining another. Tensions that might otherwise erupt in violence can be relieved by the departure of a party to a dispute. Violence between bands in neighboring territories is also infrequent because there is little to fight over. Land and resources are not owned and surpluses are not amassed, so conflicts over property have no basis. As well, because bands are widely dispersed within a large territory, even personal conflicts with neighbors are unlikely to arise.

Tribes

Tribes differ from bands in the degree of structure and organization contributing to group cohesion and community integration. Tribal societies may have more formalized organizational procedures than those found in bands. For example, they may have highly structured councils with greater authority whose members meet and deliberate regularly. In addition to their roles as influential advisory bodies, councils may have some coercive powers in some contexts. Tribal chiefs with enforcement powers may be selected in more formal ways than the casual and informal recognition of band leaders. However, the powers of tribal chiefs and councils are limited by the underlying egalitarian social ethics prevalent in most tribal societies. Often there are structured ways to ignore or depose leaders who try to exert too much authority. Like leveling mechanisms that prevent overcentralization of wealth, structured ways to ignore or depose leaders are leveling mechanisms that prevent overcentralization of power. Examples of tribes are given in Table 12.2.

A number of cultural correlates tend to be associated with tribes, although subsistence patterns vary considerably. Some tribes have economies based on foraging, some on pastoralism, and still others on horticulture. Many tribal societies have mixed economies, combining resources derived from foraging, farming, and animal herding.

Settlement patterns and sizes vary as well. Some tribal groups are fully sedentary, remaining in stable villages for many years. Farmers are especially likely to be sedentary, locating near their fields. Some farmers, though, shift locations, alternating between two or more residences each year. Foragers and pastoralists are less likely to remain in stable settlements due to the necessity of gathering wild plants, hunting animals, or finding grazing land for their animals. Sedentary villages may consist of many hundreds of people, whereas less permanent settlements tend to be much smaller.

Regardless of size, tribal societies often have mechanisms to unite the group at certain times of the year or at regular intervals. At those times, larger concentrations of people congregate to socialize, discuss issues of common interest, trade with one another, and celebrate religious occasions through group ritual. For example, the Cheyenne communal buffalo hunts referred to in the opening narrative took place every year in the summer and brought together large groups of people to hunt, perform rituals, socialize, plan group actions, and exchange products and gifts.

By 1900, Mi'kmaq families in Nova Scotia like this one had transformed many traditional practices.

TABLE 12.2 EXAMPLES OF TRIBAL SOCIETIES

Americas	Europe	Africa	Asia	Pacific
Penare of Venezuela	Scottish clans (historical)	Berbers of the western Sahara	Bani Khalid of Saudi Arabia	Dani of New Guinea
Kayapo and Yanomamo of Brazil	Druids of France (historical)	Kababish of northern Sudan	Munda of India	Marquesans (Tahiti island group)
Blackfeet of Montana	Celts of Eastern Europe (historical)	Samburu and Maasai of Kenya	Hmong of Southeast Asia	
Hidatsa of North Dakota		Amhara of Ethiopia	Miao of China	
Cheyenne of the Great Plains		Ibo of Nigeria		
Passamaquoddy of Maine				

Intergroup trade is common in tribal societies. People exchange foods and specialized handcrafts with others to obtain resources not found in their own territories or not produced by their own artisans. Well-established trading networks can carry resources and other goods over many hundreds if not thousands of miles, either through long-distance trade or through local and regional exchanges.

Concepts of territoriality and private property tend to be more significant in tribal than in band societies. Farming and pastoral people delineate commonly recognized boundaries encompassing their territories. Status differentiation based on wealth occurs in some tribal cultures. However, great imbalances in wealth and standards of living do not develop because the values of generosity and hospitality counter tendencies toward accumulation. People aspiring to positions of prestige and influence must cooperate with others and generously give away whatever surpluses they may have. People are especially obligated to help and support their kin materially as well as emotionally. In tribal societies, networks of kin are the primary arena of social action and social responsibility.

Kinship relations in tribal societies are usually organized according to some unilineal principle, either patrilineal or matrilineal. However, some tribal societies reckon descent bilaterally. Where they exist, unilineal kinship groups, such as patriclans, are often corporate political bodies, controlling access to land and resources. Kinship groups may become differentiated on the basis of the amount or value of the resources they control. Some social inequality may arise as members of some kin groups have higher status than members of other groups. Although kinship is the most important factor in organizing social interactions and responsibilities, many tribal societies also develop non-kin sociopolitical **associations** that link people in a community on the basis of shared interests and skills. These associations may have social, economic, ritual, or military functions. Membership may be voluntary or it may be assigned on the basis of specific criteria. Membership may also be temporary or permanent. By drawing members from diverse kinship groups, associations integrate or ally people on a basis other than kinship and descent. Modern state societies also have such associations, such as political clubs, religious groups, and hobby groups.

Some tribal societies have a system of age grades or age sets, associations of people of a similar age. An **age grade** is an assigned sociopolitical association—a grouping of people of more or less similar ages who are given specific social functions. Members of the same age grade consider themselves to have a kin-like relationship. They are expected to aid one another in times of need, to share resources when necessary, and to give one another emotional support. When disputes arise between members of different age grades, the members of each are expected to rally behind their own. Although their functions are very different, modern state societies also have age groups, as in school categories, for example, freshmen, seniors, or the Class of 2006.

associations
Sociopolitical groups that link people in a community on the basis of shared interests and skills.

age grade (age set)
A sociopolitical association of people of more or less similar age who are given specific social functions.

confederacy
A form of political organization in which tribes and bands join together under common leadership to face an external threat.

Confederacies

In some tribal societies, formal systems of leadership and decision making may develop that link separate tribes into political systems aimed at coordinating activities and arriving at decisions that affect all members. People may choose leaders and then set and follow procedures for decision making. In such societies, intertribal unity is an important goal and an important factor in the people's survival. A well-organized political apparatus may develop in response to perceived external threats. A form of political organization in which tribes and bands join together under common leadership to face an external threat is referred to as a **confederacy.** A prime example is the Iroquois, a group of five distinct but closely related indigenous nations living in what is now New York State, Vermont, and the Canadian provinces of Québec and Ontario. The Iroquois developed a highly structured confederacy that created internal unity and protection from external threats.

The five nations that came to be known as the Iroquois (Mohawk, Oneida, Onondaga, Cayuga, and Seneca) came together in a league or confederacy to preserve peace among members and to act as a unified body in dealing with other nations, either in peace or war. On the whole, these goals were achieved, although internal conflicts were not unknown. The founding of the Iroquois Confederacy predated the arrival of Europeans in North America. Although some historians and anthropologists assume a fourteenth- or fifteenth-century origin, Iroquois datekeepers contend that the confederacy began much earlier. Using the arguments of the datekeepers, archaeological data, astronomical data of the eclipses, and historical sources, researchers have dated the League's origin to 1142 (Mann and Fields 1997).

Employing the kinship metaphor of family, the confederacy was symbolized as a great longhouse, stretching from east to west across Iroquois territory. In this longhouse, the Mohawk were referred to as "Keepers of the Eastern Door" and the Seneca were "Keepers of the Western Door," reflecting their geographic locations as the easternmost and westernmost nations. Leadership was vested in clan heads, their advisers, and respected elders. Clan chiefs were men chosen by leading women of their group. Chiefs ideally retained their office for life, but if a chief's behavior was deemed inappropriate or contradicted local opinions, he could be demoted and replaced by another of his clan. Each chief had assistants or advisers, men and women who also could be demoted if their behavior was considered unacceptable.

GLOBALIZATION

Many indigenous peoples established confederacies prior to the globalization stimulated by the colonial era. The earliest written records report confederations for commerce and war. However, many confederacies sprang up as defensive measures against the spread of European dominance and control. Today, independent states in Central America, the Caribbean, and West Africa, for example, have established political confederacies to further regional economic interests.

CASE STUDY

Age-Linked Associations in Tribal Societies: The Hidatsa and the Maasai

The Hidatsa were a farming people who resided in present-day central North Dakota. Their kinship system was organized around matrilineal clans and moieties. Membership in households revolved around a stable core of lineally related women. Kinship informed most daily interactions, but non-kin associations also figured prominently in village life.

Most adults belonged to age-grade societies that had social, economic, and ceremonial functions. Both men and women began their participation in the age-grade system in their early teens and proceeded from one age grade to the next until they retired in old age. The age-grade system united individuals across families, clans, and moieties. Members aided one another and presented food and gifts to relatives of a deceased age-mate. Certain women's and men's societies were linked as "friends," and their members gave reciprocal aid and assisted in rituals and feasts.

People advancing to an appropriate age group because of their age and achievements collectively purchased membership in it. The relationship between the buyers and sellers was phrased as one between parent and child (mother/daughter, father/son). Purchase of membership included transfer of spirit powers and sacred objects associated with the group. Women gained spirit powers directly from the previous holders, but men needed the assistance of their wives to finalize the transfer. As part of the ritual of purchase, wives of the buyers invited the sellers to have sexual intercourse with them in the belief that the elder men passed their spirit power to the woman in the sex act and that she later transferred it to her husband when they had intercourse.

Twelve age-grade societies existed for men and four for women. Most of the male societies were connected to military participation. The Black Mouths, one of the major male associations, served as police, enforcing decisions of the village council of elders. Black Mouths also attempted to arbitrate disputes and dissuade victims of assaults or the kin of a murdered relative from exacting blood revenge. Because of the Black Mouths' community control functions, the Hidatsa considered it crucial that men not be advanced to the society until they were mature and showed sound judgment. Consequently, most Black Mouths were between 30 and 45 years old (Bowers 1992). Members of the most senior male age grade, called the Bull Society, formed the council of elders, who made decisions about community matters and chose village leaders. The Bull Society also had the important task of performing "buffalo calling" rituals of renewal and thanksgiving for the buffalos.

The most prominent of the women's associations were the Goose Society and the White Buffalo Cow Society. The Goose Society was composed of mature women, usually between ages 30 and 40. Members performed planting rites in the spring when the first waterbirds appeared, celebrating the renewal of the earth and the fertility of crops. They also performed dances during the summer whenever villagers so requested. Their aid was sought during droughts to bring rain and protect crops. The Goose Society also performed rituals at the time of the fall migration of waterbirds in thanks for successful harvests. The eldest women's association was the White Buffalo Cow Society. When the people moved to their winter settlements, members performed rituals to attract buffalo near the camps, so that they could be caught easily during that difficult season.

Each Hidatsa village had a council composed of mature men who were beyond the age of membership in the Black Mouth Society. Anyone could speak at council meetings, but the influence of the participants varied with their ages and achievements. Still, consensus was the paramount goal. Representatives of all households in the village were asked to express their opinions before important decisions were made. For decisions to have weight, approval by all households was critical. If a unanimous decision could not be reached, the matter was dropped.

Village councils chose a mature man to be the village leader, alternating between a summer and a winter incumbent. Fortunate occurrences during any leader's term of office, such as successful buffalo hunts, victorious raids, the appearance of buffalo near the camp in winter, and the good health and fortune of the community, were all attributed to the leader's practical and spiritual abilities. Failures were attributed to his lack of power. Generosity, intelligence, even temper, and compassion were critical requisites for being chosen for leadership. Spirit power was also a necessary adjunct to civil and military success. However, as one assumed greater responsibilities, spirit powers eventually waned. In fact, the more responsibilities one had, the greater was the loss of spirit power. These beliefs limited people's remaining in office for any length of time. Power sharing thus reflected the egalitarian basis of Hidatsa society.

The Maasai, cattle herders living in Kenya and Tanzania, have a system of age sets that organize military, political, and ritual life for men (Spencer 1988). Passing from one named age set to another is automatic upon reaching the proper age and achievements. Men collectively move from one group to the next from the time they are teenagers.

Boys undergo ritual circumcision in preparation for entering the youngest age set. Thereafter, each subsequent "graduation" to the next age set requires a ritual of initiation. The first age set is that of the warriors or "murran." As murran, young men learn the skills of warfare and cattle raiding. They live together in a murran village where they form close, lifelong bonds. They learn to depend on and help one another. Murran may wear distinctive clothing and adornments, emphasizing their youthfulness and vigor (Spencer 1993, 141). The murran stage usually lasts about fifteen years. Then the murran participate in a ceremony of transition to the next group where they retire from active military engagement. They are then eligible to marry. Because of the delay in marriage, Maasai husbands are markedly older than their wives who tend to marry in their teenage years.

The third stage of a Maasai male's lifecycle comprises the elders who function as village political and religious advisers and leaders. Their interests contrast with those of the murran. In fact, Maasai society is organized around a gerontocracy, leadership and power vested in elders who advance their group interests (Spencer 1993). The system of age sets with the restrictions on marriage for young men means that elders can live polygynously, marrying several women and thereby creating alliances with their wives' families that contribute to their political support. The power of individual elders wanes when the next set of murran advance into elderhood, pushing the previous elders into retirement.

In recent years, the Maasai age-set system has changed significantly because the governments of Kenya and Tanzania have banned cattle raiding and warfare, the traditional functions of the murran. Young men in the murran set have difficult adjustments to make. Many young Maasai men do not become murran, and some who do never reside in separate murran villages (Spencer 1993, 150). However, by tradition, they are too old to live with their mothers but not yet considered eligible to marry. Tension between young men and elders remains because the elders control property, especially cattle, that constitute the bridewealth necessary to solidify a marriage.

Although Maasai women do not belong to age sets, women function prominently in their relationships with men. Mothers of murran often accompany their sons to the murran villages, supporting and enhancing their sons' reputations. Principles of seniority order the status of women as well as men. Older women, especially the mothers of sons, gain prestige and authority, not only among women but also in the community at large. Women may act collectively to humiliate an elder man who violates social, and especially sexual, norms and may destroy his property (Spencer 1993, 154). Women, therefore, play roles as spectators of and commentators on the behavior of the murran and the elders.

Explore more at
www.myanthrolab.com

Political integration and expression of public opinion took place in councils that were structured by territory and by social identity. Three types of councils were held in villages: those of the elder men (including but not limited to clan chiefs), those of women, and those of young men. Members of each council deliberated together and eventually came to a unanimous opinion concerning the matter at hand. Then each group chose a speaker, who presented the group's decisions in a unified meeting. Chiefs delegated one of their members to speak for them; women and young men appointed representatives who made their opinions publicly known. These representatives were often chosen among prominent senior men, but a woman or a young man was the selected delegate in some cases. If decisions varied, further discussion was necessary in *caucus* (a word of Native American origin referring to a meeting for the purpose of achieving consensus). The process of deliberation and consensus was repeated in tribal (or national) and confederacy forums, finally arriving at a universally accepted position.

Chiefdoms

Chiefdoms are stratified societies organized by kinship, although the degree of difference among the various strata varies cross-culturally (see Table 12.3). They have structured methods of choosing leaders from within kin groups. These leaders, or chiefs, perform both political and economic functions. Chiefs and their families have higher status than other people. In some chiefdoms, they are not markedly distinguished from other people except in their social prestige, whereas in other chiefdoms, higher status people have economic, social, and political privileges. In all cases, however, higher status chiefs and their families have authority but not power. That is, because of their position, chiefs have some ability to control economic production and labor and the distribution of resources. However, their position and influence depend on the voluntary compliance of members of their kin groups and communities. Chiefs cannot coerce other people, whether relatives or nonrelatives, to do their bidding. They can only advise, cajole, encourage, and request the labor and support of others, and they lead more by example and goodwill than by control.

chiefdoms
Stratified societies organized
by kinship.

TABLE 12.3 EXAMPLES OF CHIEFDOMS

Americas	Europe	Africa	Asia	Pacific
Timucuan of Florida	Mycenae of Middle Bronze Age, Greece	Ashanti of Ghana	Buyeo of Manchuria (prior to Chinese conquest)	Trobriand Islanders (Boyowans)
Natchez of the Mississippi Valley		Bamileke of Cameroon		Tongan Islanders
Olmecs of Mexico (historical)		Zulu of South Africa		Maoris of New Zealand
Kwakwaka'wakw of British Columbia				Tikopians and Tahitians of Polynesia

Despite the marked stratification in chiefdom societies, ethics of egalitarian relationships underlie daily interactions and community activities. Although the chief and chief's family are privileged, notions of equality and the responsibility of kinspeople to one another remain strong. These ethics are demonstrated in the redistributive networks and functions of the chief. Chiefs know very well that they owe their position to the voluntary loyalty of their kin and others in the community. They solidify their support through their generosity, through attending to emergency needs of members of their community, and by showing respect and consideration to all. In essence, then, chiefs are embedded in kinship networks and are burdened with the responsibilities and obligations that come from expectations of reciprocity and fair treatment.

In contrast to band and tribal societies where leadership is diffuse and spontaneous, chiefdoms have some centralization of authority. However, this centralization does not extend to the whole society but, rather, to local kinship groups such as lineages and clans. There are, therefore, many chiefs in a chiefdom, not one paramount leader, and each chief owes primary allegiance to his or her kin group. Chiefs usually are chosen by seniority. In some, the eldest child of either gender ascends to the position of chief when the incumbent dies. In other chiefdoms, succession is not automatic. A person aspiring to the position of chief needs the requisite skills, intelligence, and personality traits as well as the support of kin. In some parts of the world, particularly in Melanesia and Polynesia, chiefs are sometimes referred to as "Big Men." A Big Man earns his prestige and status by maneuvering within his kin group, displaying generosity by sponsoring pig feasts and other redistributions, and forming strategic alliances with other high-status and influential people.

With only a few exceptions, chiefdom economies are based on farming, either horticulture (gardens and groves) or agriculture (fields). The aboriginal chiefdoms of the Pacific Northwest in Canada and the United States were exceptional because their economies were based on foraging. However, like the farming chiefdoms, they were able to amass a surplus because of the abundance of natural resources in their environment. This points out an important characteristic of chiefdoms: They are surplus-producing economies, able to extract or produce more than enough food for their subsistence.

The distribution of surplus goods, both in food and material items, is the special prerogative of chiefs in such societies. As heads of their lineages and clans, chiefs redistribute resources among their members and throughout their local communities. They arrange and host feasts periodically, celebrating harvests, successful hunts, and ceremonial

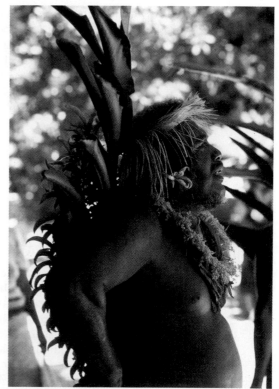

Tikopian society is ranked with chiefs having the highest status. Chiefs of patrilineages (*maru*) are elders directly descended from lineage ancestors, whereas clan chiefs (*ariki*) are descended from the common ancestor of the lineages (Firth 1970).

IN THEIR OWN VOICES

Constitution of the Iroquois Confederacy

The Iroquois Confederacy was founded by two great leaders as an organization dedicated to establishing peace among the five original member nations—the Mohawk, Oneida, Onondaga, Cayuga, and Seneca. The two leaders, one known as the Peacemaker and the other named Hayonhwatha, devised the plan and then brought it to the council of each nation for consideration. The following is an excerpt from the founding narrative of the Iroquois.

The Peacemaker then said, "My junior brother, your mind being cleared and you being competent to judge, we now shall make our laws and when all are made we shall call the organization we have formed the Great Peace. It shall be the power to abolish war and robbery between brothers and bring peace and quietness."

Hayonhwatha [Hiawatha, a historical figure but not the subject of the poem by Henry Wadsworth Longfellow] then said, "What you have said is good, I do agree."

Then the Peacemaker said, "My younger brother, we shall now propose to the Mohawk council the plan we have made. We shall tell our plan for a confederation and the building of a house of peace. It will be necessary for us to know its opinion and have its consent to proceed."

The plan was talked about in the council and the Peacemaker spoke of establishing a union of all the nations. He told them that all the chiefs must be virtuous men and be very patient. Then the speaker of the Mohawk council said, "You two, the Peacemaker and Hayonhwatha, shall send messengers to the Oneida and they shall consider the plan."

When the tomorrow of the next year had come, there came the answer of the Oneida council, "We will join the confederation."

So then the Mohawks sent two messengers to Onondaga asking that the nation consider the proposals of the Peacemaker. The next year when the midday came and the Onondaga council sent messengers who said, "We have decided that it would be a good plan to build the fire and set about it with you." So then at the same time the Peacemaker and Hayonhwatha sent messengers to the Cayuga nation and the answer was sent back. The next year at midsummer the Cayugas sent their answer and they said, "We do agree with the Peacemaker and Hayonhwatha."

Now the Senecas were divided and were not agreed because there had been trouble between their war chiefs, but messengers were sent to them but the Senecas could not agree to listen and requested the messengers to return the next year. So when the messengers returned the councils did listen and considered the proposals. After a year had passed they sent messengers to say that they had agreed to enter into the confederacy.

The Peacemaker requested some of the Mohawk chiefs to call a council, so messengers were sent out among the people and the council was convened.

The Peacemaker said, "I, with my co-worker, have a desire to now report what we have done on five successive midsummer days, of five successive years. We have obtained the consent of five nations. These are the Mohawks, the Oneidas, the Onondagas, the Cayugas and the Senecas. Our desire is to

events such as marriages or deaths. They might also host feasts that celebrate victorious raids or sporting competitions. In preparation for feasts, chiefs encourage their kinspeople to work hard to produce surplus crops and to amass large stores of foods. Then entire communities and sometimes neighboring villages as well are invited to the feasts. The visitors receive part of the bounty of goods produced and collected by the host lineage or clan. They thus benefit economically and also bear witness to the generosity of the chief. The potlatch, described in Chapter 7, is a classic example of the redistributive functions of chiefs and the complex meanings of the feasts that they sponsor.

Because of their role at the center of redistributive networks, chiefs and their close kin have access to strategic resources not available to other people. In some chiefdoms, the chief and chiefly families do not benefit at all economically from their position. They work just as hard as other members of the community. In other chiefdoms, the chiefs and their kin are able to retain a disproportionate amount of surplus brought in for feasting occasions. They use this surplus, both of foods and goods, for their own economic and social benefits. Their standard of living is higher or more elaborate than that of other people in the community. Their houses are larger, their clothing and ornaments finer, and their foods more exotic. In addition to economic benefits, chiefs and their kin use their access to strategic resources to attract followers. Through their redistribution of goods and their generosity in both formal and informal contexts, chiefs secure the loyalty of their followers.

form a compact for a union of our nations. Our next step is to seek out Adodarhoh [an Onondaga chief]. It is he who has always set at naught all plans for the establishment of the Great Peace.

Now the Peacemaker addressed the council and he said, "I am the Peacemaker and with me is my younger brother. We two now lay before you the laws by which to frame the Ka-ya-neh-renh-ko-wa or the Great Peace. The titles shall be vested in certain women and the names shall be held in their maternal families forever." All the laws were then recited and Hayonhwatha confirmed them.

Therefore the council adopted the plan.

Then the Peacemaker himself sang and walked before the door of Adodarhoh's house. When he finished his song he walked toward Adodarhoh and held out his hand to rub it on his body and to know its inherent strength and life. Then Adodarhoh was made straight and his mind became healthy.

The Peacemaker addressed the three nations. He said, "We have now overcome a great obstacle. It has long stood in the way of peace. Now indeed may we establish the Great Peace."

"Before we do firmly establish our union each nation must appoint a certain number of its wisest and purest men who shall be rulers, Rodiyaner. They shall be the advisers of the people and make the new rules that may be needful. These men shall be selected and confirmed by their female relations in whose lines the titles shall be hereditary."

So then the women of the Mohawks brought forward nine chiefs who should become Rodiyaner and one man as war chief.

So then the women of the Oneidas brought forward nine chiefs who should become Rodiyaner, and one man who should be war chief.

So then the Onondaga women brought forward fourteen chiefs who should become Rodiyaner, and one man who should be war chief.

The Peacemaker then said: "Now, today in the presence of this great multitude I disrobe you and you are not now covered by your old names. I now give you names much greater." Then calling each chief to him he said: "I now place antlers on your head as an emblem of your power. Your old garments are torn off and better robes are given you. Now you are Royaner, each of you.? You must be patient and henceforth work in unity. Never consider your own interests but work to benefit the people and for the generations not yet born. You have pledged yourselves to govern yourselves by the laws of the Great Peace. All your authority shall come from it."

Then did the Peacemaker repeat all the rules which he with Hayonhwatha had devised for the establishment of the Great Peace. Then in the councils of all the Five Nations he repeated them and the Confederacy was established.

**Explore more at
www.myanthrolab.com**

From Arthur C. Parker, *Parker on the Iroquois: The Constitution of the Five Nations*, edited and with an introduction by William N. Fenton, pp. 24–29. © 1968. Reprinted by permission of Syracuse University Press.

CRITICAL THINKING QUESTION

What principles of leadership and decision making guided the creation of the Iroquois Confederacy and the Great Peace?

Although chiefs and their families are privileged economically and socially, their position is inherently unstable. Chiefs compete with one another for followers in attempts to solidify and expand their spheres of influence. These underlying tensions create competition because each chief and chiefly lineage continuously has to reinforce their position in the face of competitors.

A number of other cultural correlates are associated with chiefdom societies. Concepts of territoriality and landownership tend to be well developed. The boundaries between neighboring chiefdoms are usually marked and recognized by both residents and outsiders. Ownership or control of other resources is also strongly identified. Some property might be deemed private and individual, and other types might be considered a communal heritage of kinship groups as collective bodies. Where property is held communally, the chief becomes its guardian and titular owner (owner by title). Most chiefdoms have fully sedentary settlements with economies based on farming or pastoralism. Populations tend to be larger than in band or tribal societies. Methods of economic production allow for the accumulation of surpluses that can be used to support a growing population.

People in chiefdoms tend to have a strong sense of belonging not only to their own kinship group but to wider political and social associations as well. This sense of identity may promote rivalry and competition. Rivalry may be friendly, expressed in competitive sporting events, or, in some cases, lead to raiding and warfare. Warfare tends to occur more frequently

Maori men performing a traditional dance for war.

in chiefdoms than in band and tribal societies. The goals of warfare may involve factors relatively rare or unknown in band or tribal warfare, such as the goal of economic gain by looting or confiscating enemy property. Warfare may also include raiding for captives. Warfare in chiefdoms also tends to be more deadly than in band or tribal groups, as killing one's enemies becomes a goal.

An important function of the chief is as a mediator in disputes. Conflicts within a lineage or clan are often brought to the chief for advice and mediation. Some chiefdoms have councils of leaders that intervene to settle disputes between people belonging to different kinship groups. Ultimately, the chief or the council has only an advisory function, lacking the ability or power to force their decisions on adversaries in a dispute.

Chiefs and their families may be associated with ritual and spirit power. They may function as leaders of ceremonies that help bind members of the community together. In some chiefdoms, the chief may be thought to possess special spirit powers or even to be a descendant of divine beings. Religious beliefs, discussed further in Chapter 14, therefore, can be seen to enhance the status and authority of the chief. Among the Maori of New Zealand, for example, *mana* is a kind of power and knowledge derived from the spirit world that can be controlled and manipulated by human beings and human action (Mataira 2000). People demonstrate their control of *mana* by success and achievements. Chiefs, who have the highest status and greatest success, are assumed also to have greater control of *mana*.

In some chiefdoms of Polynesia, including Tikopia and Tahiti, contact with a chief's powerful *mana* could cause harm to an ordinary person. Commoners, therefore, were not permitted to approach a chief too closely, to look at him directly, or to speak to him without an intermediary. Such beliefs isolated the chief from ordinary people. Although separation between chiefs and commoners was phrased as necessary for the protection of the commoners' well-being, the chief was protected from contact with and the demands of ordinary people. Through these processes, religious beliefs serve to mystify the person of the chief and to render his actions and statements beyond the questioning of common people.

Tongan chiefs often embraced the new opportunities for acquiring wealth and power made available through European trade. The Tongans were not passive victims of colonization but active participants in a new kind of society.

CULTURE CHANGE ●—

GLOBALIZATION AND THE TRANSFORMATION OF A TONGAN CHIEFDOM INTO AN ISLAND STATE

The Tongans are islanders of the South Pacific. In former times, they were organized into a highly stratified and complex chiefdom. Their social system was based on ranking in which no two individuals were of equal rank. Three principles determined an individual's status relative to others: (1) seniority—an older person outranked a younger; (2) gender—a man outranked a woman; and (3) sisterhood—a sister outranked her brother (Gailey 1987b). This could lead to variable ranking between, for example, an older woman and a younger man or an older brother and a younger sister. Actual determination of rank was open to maneuvering and personal claims.

The Tongan system divided the populace into two primary social strata: chiefs and non-chiefs. These two groups had different relationships to land and different roles in subsistence. Land was controlled by paramount chiefs, who then allocated portions to lower or district chiefs. Chiefs were guardians of the land.

Chiefs had prestigious titles through membership in high-ranking lineages. Succession to a title was ideally awarded to a chief's oldest son, but other men could make rival claims based on kinship with the previous chief's sister and on their wealth, ability, and charisma. Descent through a sister was especially important if the prior chief had no surviving children. Because sisters were of higher status than brothers, a chief's sister's son outranked his brother's sons. But claims through sisterhood could be made even against a chief's own sons, particularly if the sister were senior to the deceased chief.

Chiefly people obtained food and goods from the work of others. Chiefs commanded collective labor by men, who farmed the chief's fields, and by women, who produced mats, bark cloth, and other valuables. Although most rights and obligations in Tongan society stemmed from kinship relations, the right of chiefly people to obtain support from commoner households reflected their dominance over non-kin.

Two groups functioned as buffers between chiefs and commoners. *Matapules* included artisans, warriors, administrators, and attendants to chiefs. They were internally ranked, depending on what job each performed. Attendants and administrators oversaw cooperative work for the chiefs and summoned assemblies of commoners to advise them of chiefs' directives. *Mu'as* were offspring and descendants of intermarriages between chiefs' families. They watched over young members of chiefs' families to ensure that the youths conformed to norms of public etiquette and morality. Although high rank brought privileges, it also incurred obligations to act in a suitable manner.

Chiefly people used marital alliances to consolidate high rank. At the highest levels, among paramount chiefs, marriage between a brother and sister was the most direct form of exclusion of counterclaims. This violation of the usual incest prohibitions set the chiefs apart from the rest of the population, but it also solidified alliances and consolidated wealth. Another strategy that the most powerful chiefs used to secure their dominance and exclude rivals was to marry their sisters to foreigners. By such marriages, the chiefs simultaneously forged alliances with other leaders and eliminated competition from their sisters' sons, who instead became chiefs in their fathers' communities.

Seeds of political and social transformation were inherent in the Tongan chiefdom, as chiefs vied for power and control. However, contact with Europeans accelerated change and channeled cultural shifts in particular directions. Among the consequences, men's authority over women's social, economic, and political claims increased.

Tongans first encountered European traders and explorers in the seventeenth century. Chiefs were keenly interested in trade with the British. They especially wanted to obtain firearms. Guns intensified Tongan disputes over succession to chiefly titles,

In Tonga today, the processing of coconut into copra is the only significant industry.

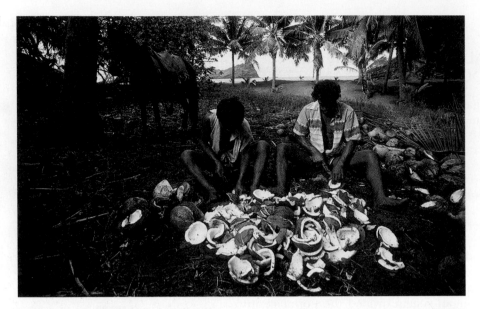

disputes that sometimes led to warfare. By the mid-nineteenth century, reasons for warfare widened to include quests for land (Gailey 1987b). These struggles transformed the Tongan political system from a chiefdom into a **kingdom,** which became institutionalized in 1845, when a paramount chief named Taufa'ahau assumed the title of king.

Coconut oil, traditionally processed by women, was an important trade item because Europeans used it to light lamps and manufacture soap. Women's production of coconut oil increased to fill demand, and their importance in commerce enhanced their status (Gailey 1980). The economic value of coconut oil was consistent with Tongan systems that privileged products made by women, collectively called *koloa,* over products made by men, called *nguae* (Gailey 1987b). However, after the mid-nineteenth century, the market for coconut oil declined. Instead, Europeans wanted copra (dried coconut meat), which was traditionally processed by men. The shift to trade in copra began a realignment of Tongan beliefs about the inherent value of women's and men's products.

As copra production increased, men spent less time doing other subsistence and domestic tasks. Women had to engage in work that carried low status, such as farming and cooking, rather than producing *koloa,* valuables used in social, economic, political, and ritual contexts. Women also occasionally helped in copra production (men's work) to amass a greater supply. Although this increased the household incomes of women, it further altered the traditional division of labor.

Women's work was also affected by the importation of European manufactured cotton and wool cloth, replacing traditional bark cloth, one of the most highly valued *koloa* items. Because cotton cloth was purchased with cash, men's access to money from copra production changed Tongan concepts of value. A dual process of material replacement and ideological change thus undermined women's wealth.

Economic changes and political changes went hand in hand. Codification of laws and enactment of a constitution in the mid-nineteenth century solidified the state's power and men's authority over women. New laws also granted land-use rights individually to men as heads of their households. After the establishment of the Tongan kingdom, Tongan land was owned by the king, who allocated its use to men. Inheritance of land rights passed patrilineally from father to son. Laws abolished the traditional right, called *fahu,* of a sister to the labor and products of her brother and his children. This shift resulted in women's dependence on their husbands, because other means of support were eliminated. In addition, a woman could no longer inherit chiefly titles from her father unless she was the firstborn child with no brothers. Even in this case, if her father had a brother, his claim took precedence.

Thus, historical transformations stemming both from internal competition and external pressures from British colonial authorities benefited men of the chiefly stratum. Women lost rights relative to chiefly men, and the economic and political autonomy of non-chiefly people of both genders declined.

kingdom
A centralized political organization with the king as the paramount leader.

Foraging societies tended to form small, mobile, loosely defined bands. Leadership was informal, temporary, and consensual in bands. The political organization of tribes, whether horticultural, agricultural, or pastoral, was based on kin groups such as clans, which might be ranked. Tribal people also formed groups that crosscut kin ties, based on associations such as warrior societies or age grades. Confederacies were bands and tribes that joined together for mutual benefit. Chiefdoms were stratified societies based on kinship and the inheritance of social status. Chiefs were chosen more formally and served as the heads of redistributive networks. Chiefdoms became kingdoms when power and authority came to be inherited through a single paramount chief.

CHARACTERISTICS OF STATE SOCIETIES

States are centralized social and political systems with formal governments organized into a hierarchical structure of authority. Ultimate authority and power rest with the head of state, whether called a president, a king, or an emperor. The head of state delegates responsibilities to advisers and assistants. State government systems include procedures for formally selecting leaders. In **republics,** presidents and prime ministers are elected by some segment of the citizenry for a set period of time. In some republics, officeholders may seek reelection for an additional term or terms, whereas in others, they are barred from succeeding themselves. Factors of age and gender may affect a person's right to vote.

In kingdoms, or monarchies, the successor to the king or queen is chosen by traditional patterns of inheritance, usually **primogeniture.** The eldest child, or more often the eldest son, automatically becomes the next monarch upon the death of the previous holder of that title. Monarchies and republics also differ in that the kings or queens in monarchies, once installed, remain in the position until death or voluntary abdication.

Based on principles of sovereignty, or self-rule, state systems usually demarcate their territory and divide it into jurisdictions or districts and subdistricts. The size and complexity of these units vary considerably, but often each unit has some degree of independence and coordination of functions. Each territorial unit is administered by officials chosen locally or delegated by central authorities. These officials are in charge of implementing government policies in their regions, acting as conduits for central powers and sometimes as intermediaries between local residents and state officials. The larger the unit over which they have control, the greater their power and prestige. Thus, states are based on political unification, often with a national identity, and the centralization and delegation of power within a sovereign territory. Expanding state societies become **empires,** enlarging their territory and power through conquest.

State societies have much larger populations than bands, tribes, or chiefdoms, and continuous population growth leads to the development of labor specialization. Unlike other types of societies where all members, given characteristics of age and gender, perform at least some direct subsistence work, many people in state societies do not engage in economic production. Some people work as artisans and craft specialists making pottery, baskets, clothing, woodwork, and all manner of necessary tools, equipment, and utensils. Other people obtain these goods either in exchange for money or for barter with foods and other resources.

In addition, state societies have the need for many different kinds of officials and bureaucrats who help organize and run projects that involve many people. Some of these are public works projects, such as construction and maintenance of roads, water delivery systems, and other infrastructure. Some bureaucrats keep track of the populace, taking census and collecting tribute or taxes. Other people work for the state as members of a police force that controls the resident population, or as a military force that defends the state from its enemies and conducts offensive warfare to expand the borders or influence of the state. Still other specialists work in commerce, facilitating the flow of raw materials, foods, and manufactured goods from one area of the state to another, as well as to other states. And some members of society are full-time religious practitioners, conducting private and public rituals. Finally, some segments of the state society do no work at all but are fully supported by the labor of others.

Labor specialization intersects with systems of social stratification. All states are hierarchically stratified societies in which some people have greater access than other people to

GLOBALIZATION

Imperialism is the empire-building process by which expanding state societies gain more land and resources and control more labor, either directly through conquest or indirectly through power and influence. Imperialism has been a major contributing factor in the process of globalization that we see today.

states
Highly organized, centralized political systems with a hierarchical structure of authority.

republics
State societies with elected rather than inherited leadership.

primogeniture
A system of inheritance of leadership in which the eldest child (usually the eldest son) automatically inherits the position of leadership from his or her parent.

empires
States expanded into larger units through conquest and the occupation or annexation of new territories.

How is the society of the United States stratified? What ideologies support your status in this system?

property of all kinds and to other strategic social and economic resources. States are divided into at least two strata: elites and commoners. Elites make up a minority of the population but reap disproportionate wealth and disproportionately occupy positions of social prestige and political power (Mills 1956). Elites have important economic functions in society but rarely enter the labor force as workers. They are sustained directly or indirectly by the tribute, rents, and taxes that commoners pay. For example, elites may own land that peasant workers farm, receiving part of the harvest as tribute. State societies usually develop urban areas where populations are concentrated. These urban centers become the seats of centralized government functions. Cities are the sites of monumental architecture that celebrate the power of the state. Large buildings house government and administrative offices. Wealth is displayed in the size and opulence of homes.

Just as in chiefdoms where chiefs manage and organize redistributive networks, elites in state societies control the production and distribution of foods and other resources for consumption. However, unlike chiefs, elites retain the majority of surplus, improving their standard of living as a class whereas other people live in situations of comparative disadvantage. The degree of inequality between elites and commoners varies in different states. The greater the disparity in wealth, the greater the likelihood that elites will exert control over commoner classes, as commoners may come to resent the fact that the elite lifestyle is supported by their own labor. Therefore, as noted in Chapter 11, ideologies arise in state societies that legitimate the status and privileges that elites receive.

In addition to ideological control, state societies have mechanisms of force that can be brought to bear on an unruly populace. Laws are codified and standardized that regulate behavior and declare certain actions criminal offenses punishable by state authorities. Court systems determine the guilt or innocence of individuals accused of crimes and punish those deemed guilty. A police force is used as an agent of **social control,** an informal or formal mechanism in society through which people's actions are controlled and social norms or laws are enforced. In the codification of rules of conduct and in the punishment of wrongdoing, the state replaces kinship groups as the regulators of social behavior. These and other characteristics of state societies are itemized in Figure 12.1.

In bands, tribes, and chiefdoms, social relations are enmeshed in networks of kin. People's behavior conforms to the principles of reciprocity and ethical standards valued among relatives. In state societies, however, kinship groups lose their control over members and are replaced by mechanisms of the state. Anonymous and depersonalized procedures

social control
Informal and formal mechanisms in society through which people's actions are controlled and social norms or laws are enforced.

FIGURE 12.1
Features of state society

- Centralized government
- Hierarchical structure of authority
- Bureaucratic administrative functions
- State control of redistributive services
- Territorial districts
- Labor specialization
- Social stratification, class and status differentiation
- Urbanization, monumental architecture
- State control of law and punishment
- State monopoly over military force, used internally as police and externally as an army
- Regulation of social relations, marriage, and family
- Delineation of rights and obligations of citizenship
- Integrative networks of communication and transportation
- Ideological support through religious and social ideologies

CONTR⊙VERSIES

Origins of the State

Many theories have been suggested for the origin of the state. One of the most widely accepted theories is that offered by Robert Carneiro (1970). According to Carneiro, a critical factor in state development is what he calls *environmental circumscription*. Under certain circumstances, economies expand and intensify production in territories that are limited by natural barriers, such as mountains, oceans, or deserts. The problem people face in such circumstances is the natural limitation on access to more land as populations increase. This theory of state origins is related to theories about the interrelationship between population growth and economic production. As you may recall from Chapter 6, surplus food and population growth are intertwined. As people produce more food, they can support larger families and communities. As more people are available to work, they can produce even larger surpluses, leading to more population growth. This cycle of rising economic production and population can continue until it threatens to surpass the carrying capacity of the land. At that point, they must develop new methods of increasing production and obtain additional land.

Where people have enough land, they can convert it into fields. But, according to Carneiro, when natural surroundings curtail access to additional land, competition among neighboring peoples may lead to raiding and warfare. Unlike warfare in band, tribal, and even chiefdom societies, warfare in developing state societies is aimed at confiscating land and controlling its inhabitants. These inhabitants may be forced out of their original territory or reduced to the status of captives, slaves, or indentured workers.

The processes that lead to increased production, population growth, and the need for new land are never-ending. State societies, therefore, are unstable. As populations grow, land shortages intensify, leading to renewed cycles of expansion, competition, and war. The more intense and rapid these cycles are, the greater the need for centralization and control over economic and political functions. Successful states continue to expand beyond their original boundaries as they move into the territories of smaller independent societies. As they do so, they confiscate land and disrupt the inhabitants' lives by incorporating them into the expanding state society under the control of the central authorities. Such expanding states may become *empires*.

Carneiro's theory of state origins also addresses the fact that states have been established in areas without environmental circumscription. According to Carneiro, states may arise where natural resources are concentrated in a relatively small area, and where land elsewhere is poor. Therefore, people congregate, and populations grow in these small areas of resource abundance. High population densities may also lead to the development of state societies without environmental circumscription.

An earlier theory about state origins is the *hydraulic hypothesis*, proposed by Karl Wittfogel (1957). According to this theory, states originated in certain environments near rivers when institutions arose to organize the construction of large-scale irrigation systems. Wittfogel, therefore, saw state organization as responding to the internal need for increasing agricultural production as populations increased. Whereas Carneiro emphasizes the political and military pursuit of wealth, Wittfogel stresses the structural bureaucratic mechanisms that help organize communal activities in large populations. These theories emphasize different aspects of state functioning. However, the hydraulic hypothesis does not account for the existence of either productive irrigation without state control, for example, in early Mesopotamia and Peru (Adams 1982), or state bureaucracies before the development of large irrigation systems (Johnson 1973).

⊙ CRITICAL THINKING QUESTIONS

How does Carneiro's theory interrelate population and environment? How does the hydraulic hypothesis explain the emergence of states?

---

and personnel replace individual and personalized loyalties and affections. The loosening of the bonds of kinship is a slow process that is never complete, for people in all societies have responsibilities and loyalties to their kin, as well as to other people and other entities. In state societies, powerful extended family systems continue to thrive, especially among the ruling classes. Networks of kin among the elites help solidify their power and maintain their distinctiveness.

The state, through its police force and court system, supervises decision making and sanctioning. Individuals are deemed solely responsible for their actions, whereas kin groups are collectively responsible for the behavior of their members in bands and tribal societies. State governments assume the right to enforce decisions that they make in the name of the society at large. These decisions affect internal functioning, law and order, and procedures that regulate many of the activities of private citizens. Other decisions affect external relations with other societies. The existence of capital punishment is an example of the state's

All the characteristics of a state society described in this section can be seen in the Inca Empire of South America. Here, the ruins of Machu Picchu mark one of the last sacred outposts of the Inca.

How is terrorism a factor in the maintenance and expansion of modern states today?

terrorism
Acts of violence perpetrated by private citizens against groups within their own country or against a foreign country without the cover and sanction of a state-declared war.

theocracies
Societies ruled by religious leaders, in which the social order is upheld through beliefs in its divine origin or sanction.

monopoly on power. It demonstrates that only the state can legally kill.

In external relations, the state also monopolizes rights to conduct warfare against others. Private citizens cannot legitimately take up arms against a foreign country without the cover and sanction of a state-declared war. In fact, we now label such behavior **terrorism.** According to the U.S. Federal Bureau of Investigation, terrorism is "the unlawful use of force against persons or property to intimidate or coerce a government, the civilian population or any segment thereof, in the furtherance of political or social objectives" (U.S. Department of Justice 1999). From their origin and throughout their history, states specialized in warfare. Unlike band and tribal societies, where raiding and warfare were carried out for personal honor, revenge, prestige, or ritual goals, wars in state societies are undertaken to conquer neighboring peoples and to incorporate them and their territories into the expanding state population.

The state also regulates social relations concerning marriage and the family. Through religious sanction and state rules, the state determines eligibility for marriage, grounds for divorce, and the legitimacy of children. The state thus intervenes in personal and familial relations and decisions. States also determine procedures for extending citizenship to new members and regulating their rights and obligations. People may be assigned particular work to perform and tribute or taxes to be paid. Privileges of citizens may include the right to some level of support in times of need, protection against foreign invaders or domestic disorder, and access to training or education. Obligations of citizens to the state may include contributing to communal efforts and obeying authorities. In some early states, officials organized a complex system of public warehouses that kept stores of foods and other necessities to dispense to the populace if crops failed. States vary considerably in their provisions for social welfare.

States are integrated through networks of communication and transportation. The larger the population and territory, then the more likely that complex systems of record keeping and notation will develop. Specialist bureaucrats are trained to keep track of the settlements and movements of populations within the territory, tribute and taxes collected, public labor organized and expended, and services required and rendered. Routes of trade and commerce also link urban centers with one another and rural villages to regional and urban markets. Networks of long-distance trade transport products and resources throughout the state. Regional specializations, therefore, develop, enabling each locality to become efficient producers of foods and other goods in their territory.

State systems are often supported by religious ideology. A unifying state religion may develop that legitimates and rationalizes the system, including its social inequalities. A trained and specialized priesthood may ally itself with civil authorities, both groups benefiting from their consolidation of power. Religious specialists may define right and wrong, encourage obedience to authority, and claim divine origin or sanction for the political system. Many early states were **theocracies,** ruled by religious leaders or by rulers thought to be divine or divinely sanctioned to rule.

REVIEW States are centralized social and political systems with hierarchical formal governments that replace or supersede kin groups in many social functions. Theories of the origins of states include environmental conscription, in which states arose through a mutually reinforcing spiral of economic production and population growth within a territory, and the hydraulic hypothesis, in which states developed to ensure the regulation of intensive agriculture through irrigation. State societies are stratified, with ruling elites exercising power and authority. States enforce formal systems of social control and regulate warfare. Terrorism includes acts of war that are not state sanctioned. State systems are justified through ideologies and religious teachings. Many early states were theocracies.

CASE STUDY

The Inca of Peru and Ecuador

The Incas developed a complex, multiethnic, centralized agricultural empire, growing out of indigenous Andean cultures centered around Cuzco, Peru. The Incas were members of two dominant kinship groups that gradually increased their wealth and power over others, eventually transforming Andean cultures into a hierarchical state society. The Inca state expanded in the fifteenth century to encompass an estimated 6 million people living in what are now Peru and Ecuador. The empire grew by incorporating and transforming local cultures. The social and political features of Inca society are consistent with the general patterns of agricultural societies. Villages, towns, and cities were permanent and varied in size, depending on their location and importance to the Inca Empire. Major cities contained thousands of inhabitants. Social and economic roles were highly differentiated and specialized. People were also segmented according to social status and power.

Inca Empire

The Inca state was headed by a supreme ruler, or emperor, who maintained his power through a complex network of agents, bureaucrats, armies, and priests. These people ensured that local communities fulfilled elite demands. Administrative power was exclusively a male domain. The emperor chose most of his closest advisers and aides from among the men in his lineage. Succession to the throne was not rigid, but the emperor usually selected one of his sons to be his successor.

The ruler's wife, known as *coya*, or "queen," was his own sister. Marriage between a brother and sister at the highest level of state consolidated power and minimized struggles over succession. Marriage between siblings was absolutely forbidden to all except the emperor and *coya*. The *coya* had both economic and administrative influence. She owned land and could dispose of its produce, but she redistributed some of the surplus delivered to her, holding huge public feasts as demonstrations of her generosity. *Coyas* had special lands that they used to grow new crops (Silverblatt 1978). Also, they occasionally governed from Cuzco in the absence of their husbands.

Local kinship groups called *ayllus* controlled Andean land. An *ayllu* consisted of people living within a particular territory. It was a corporate entity and allocated land to households. *Ayllu* leaders periodically reassigned allotments to adjust to changes in household composition. Land was apportioned to male heads of households on the basis of family size. Each married man received one measure (*tupu*) of land for himself and his wife. He received an additional *tupu* for each of his sons, one-half *tupu* for each daughter. When a son married, he was allotted the portion of land originally given to his father on his behalf. In most cases daughters relinquished their share of land upon marriage (Silverblatt 1978; 1980).

Both men and women, working singly or together, performed agricultural work. They cultivated more than forty species of plants (Rowe 1950), depending on altitude, climate, and topography. Basic crops were potatoes, maize, grains, berries, chilies, squash, beans, peanuts, tomatoes, and coca. People also kept domesticated animals, especially llamas, alpacas, dogs, guinea pigs, and ducks. Guinea pigs supplied most of their meat. Foraging and hunting were relatively unimportant.

Communal rights to resources within an *ayllu* were recognized and enacted through redistribution of foods and goods to community members. A family or individual in need received aid from others. This system of redistribution was based on egalitarian ethics and limited individuals' accumulation of wealth.

However, although all people had rights to resources and sustenance, some individuals were of higher social status than others. These people, known as *curacas*, constituted a governing body (Silverblatt 1980, 153). Although there were women *curacas*, it is uncertain whether they had only economic privileges or whether they also had decision-making and leadership roles (Silverblatt 1987, 16–18). In return for goods received from common people, *curacas* were obligated to be generous to those in need.

Common people also had to perform other kinds of labor, known as *mita* service. Men were enlisted to construct and maintain public works projects, such as palaces, temples, forts, irrigation systems, and roads. Some men were conscripted into army units. Others were trained from childhood to serve as runners in an elaborate postal system, carrying messages throughout the empire. Women were compelled to spin and weave cotton and wool cloth.

Households, not individuals, paid tribute in labor or goods to the Inca elite. Each household had collective responsibility to fulfill its obligations. Work was assigned within a household depending on individuals' availability and skills. Although men and women performed different kinds of work, flexibility was possible when people were called to state service or when illness or absence required a shift in tasks.

Although Inca society was highly stratified and power rested exclusively with the upper class, chiefly generosity was expected. To ensure basic survival, the state maintained granaries and warehouses from which *curacas* could obtain supplies for *ayllus* in times of famine. These goods were derived from surpluses originally taken by elites from the labor of commoners. The Inca system reveals the ethics of reciprocity underlying social relationships and uniting people in kin-based societies. As in other state societies, these ethics were kept alive even as the Inca extended their empire.

Explore more at
www.myanthrolab.com

INTERNAL POLITICAL CHANGE AND STATE SOCIETIES

State societies are the largest, most complex, and highly centralized political systems. The first states arose in the Middle East in Mesopotamia around 8,000 years ago. Other states developed slightly later in the Nile region of Egypt. States also arose independently in the Indus River valley of India, in China, in Mesoamerica (Mexico and Guatemala), and in the Andes of Peru. Today, state societies exist everywhere, replacing other kinds of society and dominating the world scene.

Political systems also change through internal processes. State societies, for example, change through revolution and factionalism, the tendency for groups to split into opposing parties over political issues, often a cause of violence and a threat to political unity. Disagreements about community actions occur in all societies, but they can lead to entrenched **factionalism** as various interest groups vie for control of decision-making and leadership roles. If a powerful faction can assert its will, this can lead to fundamental social changes. For example, in the early 1900s, two contentious factions developed in the Hopi community of Oraibi in Arizona over whether to participate in federal educational programs for Hopi children. Some people believed that knowledge of the English language and American culture would benefit the Hopi, but others feared that any but the most tangential contacts with American culture would lead to the destruction of Hopi lifeways.

Conflicts between these two factions grew increasingly bitter, eventually spilling into other issues and even dividing family groups. Finally, in 1906, the Hopi in Oraibi decided that they could not all live together in the same community. Using the quasi-ritualistic means of a "tug-of-war" across a line etched in the dirt, the two sides dramatized their inability to coexist. The group who lost (called the "Hostiles," because of their opposition to American assimilationist policies) was forced to leave, later founding a new village, Hotevilla. The faction known as the "Friendlies" remained at Oraibi and continued their more accommodating approach toward American cultural innovations (Titiev 1992). Today, the two groups have achieved more cooperation toward community goals, although disagreements reemerge from time to time about policies affecting internal development and direction, as well as about attitudes toward outsiders.

In societies where people are linked with many others through ties of kinship, marriage, and social association, factionalism may be disruptive but rarely leads to violence within communities. However, in state societies, factionalism can lead to armed conflict. In our contemporary world, we find many examples of internal disputes escalating into civil war. In many of these cases, ethnic or religious differences become highlighted, although the fundamental issues in contention are usually economic inequalities and/or political power struggles. For example, the breakup of the former Yugoslavia in 1992 was exacerbated by dredging up ethnic and religious rivalries of centuries past. The genocidal campaigns in

factionalism
The tendency for groups to split into opposing parties over political issues, often a cause of violence and a threat to political unity.

Rwanda in 1994 also turned on ethnic differences, although political and economic rights and privileges underlay the ethnic conflicts. Finally, the fighting between Shiite and Sunni groups in Iraq and between various Palestinian factions in the occupied territories of Israel/Palestine are additional manifestations of the tenuous nature of some modern states and the tendencies for disagreements over political and economic policies to erupt in violence in such circumstances.

In large stratified societies, political change can come about as a result of rebellion and revolution. These are complex processes that take different forms in different contexts. In colonial situations, residents of the colonies may eventually decide that they no longer want to live under foreign domination. They may rebel in wars of independence to oust their rulers. A successful rebellion may enable indigenous people to return to some form of traditional life. Or the colonists themselves may rebel against their country of origin to set up an independent nation. For example, the American Revolution was a revolution in its focus on eliminating what had come to be seen as a foreign, distant power controlling people in the colonies. It was revolutionary in its transformation from a monarchy to a republic with ultimate power in the hands of elected officials. The French Revolution of 1789 had the additional goal of overturning a whole social system, eliminating the class privileges of wealthy and aristocratic elites. These goals were never fully met, demonstrating how difficult it is to break completely with the past.

King Mohammed VI of Morocco addressing the United Nations General Assembly in 2004. He began his reign in 1999 pledging political and economic reforms.

In the twentieth century, new movements for social and political change occurred in many places in the world. The Mexican Revolution of 1910 and the Russian Revolution of 1917 were attempts to change the stratified social systems that created economic and political inequalities. Following the end of World War II, many countries in Africa that Europeans had colonized gained their independence. These movements were successful both because of internal resistance to colonial control and external pressure from growing international anticolonialism. Internal and external forces of cultural change are discussed further in Chapters 16 and 17.

More recently, movements for internal democratic change have also taken root worldwide as people in stratified societies with great imbalances in wealth and power have attempted to claim a more equitable share of their country's resources. Elites do not give up their power and privilege easily, however. They may resist openly by using the police force at their disposal to put down revolutionary movements or by using the legal apparatus to arrest and punish leaders and participants. They may also resist by ideological means, claiming the moral authority and legitimacy of the prevailing system. In the end, movements for social and political change succeed when supported by a large and dedicated segment of the population. The civil rights movement in the United States in the 1950s and 1960s and the antiapartheid struggles in South Africa in the 1970s and 1980s eventually won fundamental political transformations, despite strenuous opposition from those in power.

Today, the crises in the Middle East have spawned movements for social and political change within many countries in the region. Middle Eastern monarchs have implemented or begun to talk about steps toward democratization of their political processes. For example, King Mohammed VI of Morocco, installed in 1999, has broadened citizens' access to political participation and given more power to elected representatives in an attempt to respond to people's desire for a voice in their own society. And King Fahd bin Abdul Aziz of Saudi Arabia, head of one of the most autocratic governments in the world, has hinted at the possibility of reforms to allow more popular participation. These governments are responding to forces of globalization that have begun to affect their own citizenry and, perhaps, to fears of the spread of Islamic fundamentalism, which feeds on deep popular resentment.

GLOBALIZATION

Some political anthropologists trace the spread of Euro-American political concepts and institutions. These concepts, such as democracy, and institutional behaviors, such as elections, tend to accompany the economic influences of those regions on world cultures. Political ideas and behaviors also may be forced on other people through conquest or other dominating influence.

Internal patterns of change in political systems include factionalism, in which groups split over issues and vie for power, as well as revolution, in which citizens rebel against their rulers.

REVIEW

ANTHROPOLOGY APPLIED

Anthropologists and the NGOs

NGOs—nongovernmental organizations—include charities, research institutes, churches, professional associations, and advocacy or lobby groups. These private organizations may be international, national, or community-based. They often work with governments and with international umbrella organizations such as the United Nations. NGOs may defend a particular cause, such as land rights or refugee resettlement, or design and implement large economic development programs. Most NGOs serve people in disadvantaged or developing countries, based on values of social justice (http:// library.duke.edu/research/subject/guides/ngo_guide/).

Oxfam, CARE, and Save the Children are international public charities. Private-sector NGOs include the Mennonite Central Committee and World Vision, a Christian relief organization. Partners in Health (PIH) is a Boston-based international professional organization that serves people in poor countries. PIH medical teams, working with anthropologists

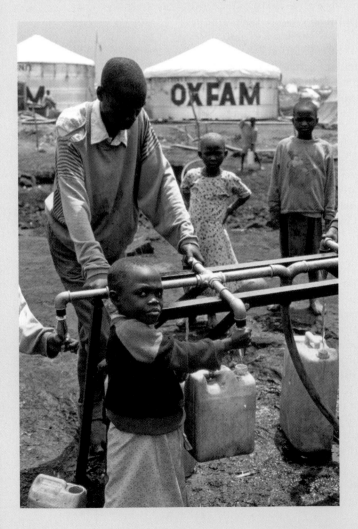

and local community leaders, treat people with HIV in Haiti and people with drug-resistant tuberculosis in Peru (Castro 2004).

Because of the focus on development and social justice for disadvantaged groups in poor countries, anthropologists play key roles in NGOs. They conduct research, advise organizations, protect the interests of aid recipients and their communities, and serve as liaisons or mediators (Hursey 2001). Because of their training, anthropologists know to question the cultural assumptions and power structures that restrict people's access to health care, education, housing, and so on. They also have the background to understand how NGOs, as transnational carriers of culture, act as instruments of globalization.

◉ CRITICAL THINKING QUESTIONS

How might recipients of NGO aid find "strings attached"? How should negative impacts of globalization be balanced with the needs for help that NGOs meet?

CHAPTER SUMMARY

Political Anthropology

- Political anthropology focuses on how societies select their leaders, make decisions affecting the group, provide community functions and services, and resolve conflicts. These cultural mechanisms help integrate a community and direct relations with other communities.

Types of Political Organization

- Bands are small, loosely organized groups of people. Communities in band societies are usually relatively small and dispersed throughout a wide territory. Bands are held together by informal means. Membership in a band is typically based on kinship ties. Band leadership is based on the abilities of the leader. Such leaders have influence but cannot control the actions of others. Bands are usually egalitarian societies.

- Tribal societies are more structured, organized, and cohesive than bands. Tribal societies may have more formalized procedures for making decisions and selecting leaders with limited power to enforce their decisions.

- Voluntary associations and age-grade or age-set organizations are common in tribal societies. Members of the same age grade consider themselves to have a kin-like relationship.

- Some tribal societies link themselves in confederacies. A confederacy is a formal, well-organized political structure to counteract external threats. Confederacies have formal procedures to select leaders, debate issues, make decisions, and plan and execute actions.

- Chiefdoms are stratified societies organized by kinship. Within chiefdoms, the chiefs and their families have the most prestige, authority, and privileges but not power. Their position and influence depend on voluntary compliance of their kin groups and communities. In chiefdoms, there is no paramount leader. Chiefs owe primary allegiance to their kin groups.

Although chiefly rank may be inherited, aspirants need skills and personality traits to be appropriate heirs.

- Chiefs are often the centers of redistributive networks. They redistribute by hosting feasts.

Characteristics of State Societies

- State societies are the largest, most complex, and highly centralized political systems. In every part of the world, states have replaced other types of societies.

- State governments are hierarchical. State government systems include procedures for formally selecting leaders and their assistants. States usually divide their territory into districts and have economic systems characterized by labor specialization. States are stratified societies in which some people have greater access to property and resources than others.

- State societies promulgate ideologies that legitimate the status and privileges that elites receive. States also have mechanisms of force to maintain the status quo. States have law codes and monopolize the right to control and punish wrongdoers and conduct warfare.

Internal Political Change and State Societies

- States are inherently expansionist because their elites want to increase their wealth and power. State conquest always has cultural components as basic systems of family organization, economic relationships, and religion change to conform to the practices and beliefs of the conquerors.

- States may also be transformed from within as interest groups or factions compete. Reform or revolutionary movements may develop in response to perceived inequalities and injustices or to effect more fundamental changes. Although states resist revolutions, some revolutionary movements like the wave of post-World War II decolonization have proven to be unstoppable. Global movements toward democratization have also more recently gained momentum.

KEY TERMS

political
organization 303
political
anthropology 303
bands 303

tribes 306
associations 307
age grade
(age set) 307
confederacy 308

chiefdoms 310
kingdom 316
states 317
republics 317
primogeniture 317

empires 317
social control 318
terrorism 320
theocracies 320
factionalism 322

REVIEW QUESTIONS

1. How might a political anthropologist study factionalism or domestic terrorism in a state society?
2. How are bands, tribes, chiefdoms, confederacies, and states different?
3. What roles do kinship and associations play in each type of political system?
4. Are bands, tribes, chiefdoms, confederacies, and states steps in the development of political systems? If so, how? What determines which form of political organization a society is likely to have?
5. Why are state societies characterized by social stratification?
6. How have colonization and globalization affected sociopolitical systems?
7. How do political systems change?

PEARSON myanthrolab EXERCISES

To complete the following exercises and activities, you must log in to www.myanthrolab.com and select your current textbook.

1. In the **Explore** tab of Chapter 12 click on the *NPR Audio Programs Broadcast* tab and go to *Theme 24: Politics*. Listen to one of the programs in this section and complete the short answer exercise that accompanies the program.
2. In the **Practice** tab, click on *Activities* and complete the *Trends in Political Organization* animation.
3. In the **Research Tools** section on the home page, click on the *Research Navigator*™ link and enter the Anthropology database to find relevant and recent scholarly and popular press publications. For this chapter enter the following keywords: *tribes, empires,* and *political anthropology.*
4. Enter the **MyAnthroLibrary** section on the home page to read more about topics and cultures that are discussed in this chapter. Suggested readings include:

Bulgaria: Anthropological Corrections to Cold War Stereotypes by Gerald W. Creed

Political Participation by Marc Howard Ross

CONFLICT AND CONFLICT RESOLUTION

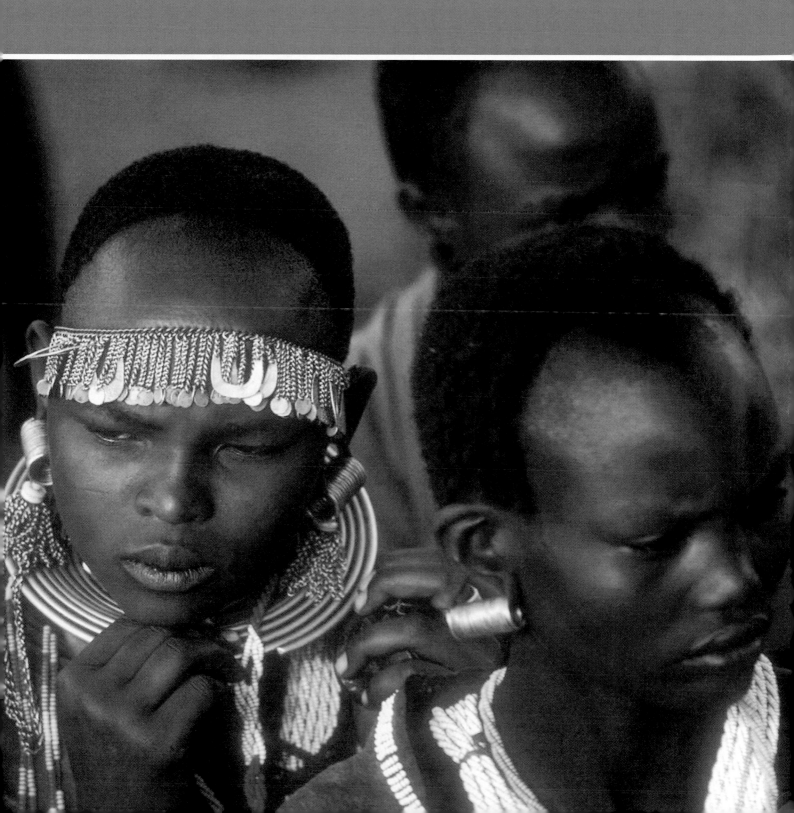

- Why do primates engage in aggression and conflict?
- How do individuals and societies prevent, avoid, or reduce conflict?
- What are the sources, goals, and expressions of conflict in and among groups within a society and between societies?
- What measures or mechanisms do people have for mediating and resolving conflicts?

There was once a time of great famine, and Tortoise, like everyone else, was busy seeking food for his children. He bought much maize and made up a good load. On his way home he came to a fallen tree lying across the road, and he could not get over it. He walked up and down along the trunk of the tree, and at last his load slipped off and fell down the other side. Just then a monitor lizard . . . seeing the load, exclaimed—"Well look what I have found." Tortoise . . . said to him, "That's mine—it just slipped off my head and fell on this side." Monitor Lizard replied, "I don't know about that; all I know is that I picked it up. Finders keepers, losers weepers." Tortoise said, "Let us go to the elders and have them judge what to do."

When they came to the elders, Tortoise explained what happened. . . . The elders said to Tortoise, "You know that the finder of such things is permitted to keep them. That is our rule." So Tortoise went his way, and Monitor took up what he had "found" and carried it to his children.

Now, it happened one day that Tortoise and his companions went hunting, and they made a fire to lure prey into their trap. In the grass that they had set on fire, Monitor was sleeping. He woke up and ran here and there, and found a small hole in which to hide, but his tail stuck out of it. Tortoise, seeing Monitor's tail exposed, put out his hand and seized it, saying, "Finders keepers, losers weepers."

Monitor said, "You have got hold of my tail, my friend, let me alone." Tortoise said, "I did not touch your tail, I have found something to which I am entitled, a beautiful sword." Monitor begged, "My friend, this is my tail, you cannot claim it as a spoil." Tortoise said to him, "Let us go to the elders." When they arrived, Monitor said, "I was running away from a fire and I entered a small hole, but my tail was outside; then this person came along and said, 'It is a sword,' and I said, 'It is my tail,' but he would not listen." Tortoise said, "Today you are surprised. Lately you took my food gathering, and you thought nothing of it." Monitor said, "It was only food I took that day. Wait, my friend, I will fetch what I took." Tortoise said, "Today is today." The elders said to Monitor, "Give your companion his sword." Monitor said, "But it is not a sword, it is my tail." They said, "Give it to him," and the tail was cut off. Tortoise said, "Cut it high up, that I may have a good handle." So Monitor's tail was cut off, and given to Tortoise, and half-way home he threw it away, saying, "I only wanted to be even with him." Monitor wriggled and died. If a person does harm to one another, he should remember what may happen to him another day.

From Roger Abrahams, *African Folktales*, pp. 147–48. © 1983 by Roger D. Abrahams. Used by permission of Pantheon Books, a division of Random House, Inc.

In this story, the Bondei people of Tanzania dramatize the conflicts that arise when people think only of their own interests and fail to acknowledge the rights of others. It also describes social norms or rules that people affirm when they want to justify their own behavior. The story also highlights the critical role of mediators in settling disputes or resolving conflicts.

All societies, communities, and even families have the potential for conflict over issues of daily life, household responsibilities, or roles within communities. Such conflicts may arise in any family and be settled quickly and amicably. Disputes within communities may be about interpersonal issues or rights to property and other resources. These problems also may be settled amicably, but their resolution may involve more complex negotiations and mediation. Conflicts occur between communities or, in the modern context, between nations. Such conflicts can lead to protracted antagonisms and even warfare. However, families, communities, and societies have methods to avoid conflict in some situations and resolve those conflicts that do arise.

Societies differ about what causes conflict and in how they settle disputes and reestablish peace or harmonious relationships. Societies also differ in their mechanisms for applying sanctions that influence or control people's behavior. **Positive sanctions** are recognition or rewards, either as material benefits or social prestige, granted to people who behave according to social norms. **Negative sanctions** are formal or informal

positive sanctions
Recognition and rewards for observing social norms.

negative sanctions
Punishments for offending social norms.

methods of discouraging people from behaving improperly. **Informal sanctions** include teasing, ostracizing, or gossiping about wrongdoers. **Formal sanctions** consist of fines and other punishments meted out by leaders or other legal authorities or systems of adjudication, such as village councils, juries, and judges. Thus, norms and sanctions establish the basis of social order.

EVOLUTIONARY PERSPECTIVES ON CONFLICT

Evolutionary biologists and psychologists have recognized the origins of behaviors that help animals avoid conflict and restore peace after incidents of open aggression. In primate groups, social hierarchies are established, usually along lines of sex and age. Males and females learn their place through socialization into their groups. However, the **dominance hierarchies** are inherently unstable. Although some animals seem to accept their position in the hierarchy, others vie for prominence and attempt to oust the dominant male or female from their positions of leadership. One of the ways that conflict can be avoided is for subordinate animals to demonstrate acceptance of their position in the hierarchy through the display of submissive gestures and actions.

Primate gestures of dominance and subordination have certain similarities to human behavior. Studies of nonverbal communication demonstrate that, in encounters between two socially unequal people, the subordinate person smiles more, averts the eyes when looked at by the dominant person, and attempts to take up less space by contracting the body and lowering the head. Subordinate people also get out of the path of dominant people, giving way to them on the street or in any enclosed space. All of these behaviors seek to avoid conflict by signaling one's acceptance of subordinate status.

However, despite mechanisms that minimize aggression, conflicts occasionally arise. Although conflict within a primate group is disruptive of the social unit while it occurs, the aggression does not do permanent damage to the group's cohesion. Studies of our close primate relatives, the chimpanzees, reveal patterned behavior that occurs immediately after conflict has erupted and taken its course. Animals who have just been involved in aggressive actions with one another may kiss, hold out a hand, or embrace, accompanied by submissive vocalizations. These are practices that Frans de Waal refers to as **postconflict reconciliation** (2000:17). De Waal also observed behaviors that he calls "consolation" between a recipient of aggression and a third individual. In addition, de Waal suggests that some common primate behaviors, such as mutual grooming and body contact, function to reduce aggression and promote interpersonal and group stability.

Studies such as those of de Waal and his associates bring into question models of primate behavior that focus on aggression and competition. Instead, they stress the critical importance of shared interests to create solidarity among members of a stable social group. Avoidance of aggression is then only partly explained as an outcome of weighing

informal sanctions
Rewards and punishments expressed through praise, ridicule, gossip, and the like.

formal sanctions
Rewards and punishments administered by persons in authority, the state, or the law.

dominance hierarchies
In primate groups, social hierarchies established on the basis of sex and age.

postconflict reconciliation
Patterned behavior that occurs immediately after conflict has erupted and taken its course, to restore some measure of social harmony.

In what ways is your post-conflict reconciliation behavior similar to that of chimpanzees?

Primate gestures of submission include crouching to make oneself relatively small, baring one's teeth in a smiling facial expression, and avoiding a dominant animal. The chimpanzee on the right is clearly signaling submission.

According to evolutionary psychologists and primatologists, how might this fight have been avoided? How does the boys' aggression toward one another affect their social group? How can their conflict be resolved and future aggression prevented?

the risks of injury to oneself. Chimpanzees and other primate species may avoid aggression also because of the importance of cooperation and the risk of the social damage that conflict would cause.

Seen in this light, aggression and the avoidance of conflict are both enmeshed in their social context. **Conflict avoidance** has the positive value of maintaining social harmony. Behaviors characterized as reconciliation and consolation have the effect of restoring and repairing social relationships. The greater the value that individuals attach to their relationships, the less likely that disagreements and disputes will erupt into open conflict. When they do, reconciliatory behavior helps repair those relationships critical to personal and community stability. De Waal poses a central paradox that emerges in the study of primate social behavior: the need to "integrate fully the vertical (hierarchical) and horizontal (affiliative networking) dimensions of social organization" (2000, 30). As we shall see, this paradox also exists among humans and is critical to an understanding of conflict and conflict resolution in human societies.

> **REVIEW** — ⊙ Social norms and sanctions—informal and formal, positive and negative—establish the basis of social order, but conflicts arise in all primate groups and societies. Using an evolutionary perspective, we can see the roots of conflict and conflict resolution in primate dominance hierarchies and behaviors associated with dominance and subordination, postconflict reconciliation, and conflict avoidance. Both aggression and the avoidance of conflict are mediated through social and cultural contexts.

AVOIDING CONFLICT

In human societies, people develop ways to express disagreement while avoiding open conflict. In some societies, the emphasis on deferring to others, not stating one's opinions directly, and generally shunning people who are angry are efficient means of lessening the possibilities of conflict and creating social harmony within families or small communities. In his overview of conflict management strategies, Douglas Fry (2000) lists a number of cultural prevention mechanisms that are both social and psychological. One technique is self-control and restraint in the expression of anger.

Among many groups living in small settlements, people learn to control the expression of strong negative feelings. They learn that negative feelings, including anger, envy, and jealousy, can be socially disruptive, especially when everyone has frequent face-to-face interaction with everyone else in the community. In such societies, group mechanisms develop to squelch negative emotions from continuing and becoming dangerous. These mechanisms of social control include teasing people who act inappropriately, gossiping about their behavior, or avoiding the people—giving the "cold shoulder." Negative sanctions confront people about their disruptive behavior and encourage them to act according to social norms. These informal sanctions are especially effective in small communities where people interact frequently. Being teased, gossiped about, or avoided in such contexts can be psychologically painful, a constant reminder of one's inappropriate actions and of the negative view in which one is held by community members.

conflict avoidance
Prosocial behaviors, such as reconciliation, consolation, politeness, or apology, to repair social relationships without aggression.

peacemakers
Individuals with a specialized social role of preventing conflict from erupting into dangerous combat.

Another technique of conflict management in Fry's list is to control aggression once it erupts, preventing it from becoming too dangerous. For example, among the Ju/'hoansi of the Kalahari Desert in Namibia, if two people are engaging in verbal abuse, others quickly intervene and try to distract the disputants (Lee 2003). If the verbal abuse escalates into pushing and shoving, onlookers immediately disengage the people by pulling them apart and trying to calm them down. In Ju/'hoansi camps, disagreements rarely escalate beyond the stage of pushing and shoving except in situations where alcohol is involved.

The Ju/'hoansi techniques are related to another of Fry's conflict prevention measures: the intervention of **peacemakers.** In the Ju/'hoansi case, nearly everyone in the community is a potential "friendly peacemaker," attempting to squelch a conflict from erupting into dangerous combat.

Still another conflict prevention technique is what Fry refers to as "attention to the satisfaction and needs of others." In many societies, people develop personalities that exhibit values emphasizing the importance of keeping other people happy or satisfied. They focus on sharing and supporting other people, not only in economic terms but in emotional terms as well. Toleration of other people's behavior, even if unpleasant or provocative, also contributes to maintaining peaceful, if not entirely harmonious, relationships. In this category, one could include linguistic and nonverbal means of conveying politeness or **deference** to others.

Politeness

Politeness consists of a constellation of words and actions that demonstrate people's consideration of the feelings of others and deference to their wishes and needs. The cultural mechanisms through which one expresses politeness vary considerably. Every language has polite words or expressions and polite ways of phrasing one's thoughts. Every culture also has its norms about how politeness is shown and about who deserves to be the recipient of polite behavior (Brown and Levinson 1987).

Politeness strategies function to mute antagonisms and avoid overt hostility by affirming common bonds and recognizing another person's rights and feelings. In addition to techniques that calm or pacify the other person, an individual who has committed a social wrong or has erupted in anger can prevent further antagonism and conflict by showing remorse or apologizing. Apologies function to maintain or reestablish rapport between participants. They are occasioned by actions that are perceived to have negative effects on others and for which speakers take responsibility.

Channeled Aggression

In some societies, specific social mechanisms help prevent conflict or channel aggressive behavior in socially acceptable forms. An example of channeled aggression is the Inuit practice of men challenging each other to **song duels** to vent their anger and jealousy without resorting to physical combat. Sexual jealousy was a common precipitating factor in song duels. Men who were competing as suitors for a particular woman engaged in a public display of verbal wit. The two men faced each other in front of an audience consisting of community members. They took turns beating on a drum while composing insulting and derisive songs about their opponent. The audience typically reacted with laughter to both contestants.

deference
Nonthreatening verbal and nonverbal behaviors that convey respect or subordination to others.

politeness strategies
Behaviors designed to mute antagonisms and avoid overt hostility by affirming common bonds and recognizing another person's rights and feelings.

song duels
Inuit contests in which conflict is expressed and resolved through public response to music.

CASE STUDY ●────────────────────────────────────

Conflict Avoidance Strategies in Japan

In the words of the influential sociologist Erving Goffman, a speaker, by apologizing, "splits [him-/herself] into two parts, the part that is guilty of an offense and the part that dissociates itself from the delict [offense] and affirms a belief in the offended rule" (1971, 143). Naturally, what counts as a deed or intent necessitating an apology depends entirely on cultural models of offensive or regrettable behavior. For example, Japanese social norms require apologies in more situations than would be expected in Western societies. According to Florian Coulmas (1981), citing the Japanese sociologist Sugiyama Lebra, Japanese people are highly conscious of their effects on others and are concerned not to infringe others' rights and needs. They strive not to embarrass themselves or those listening. Japanese not only frequently apologize for offenses, they also "line other speech acts such as greetings, offers, thanks with an apologetic undertone." In fact, a common utterance, *sumimasen* (literally: "this is not the end" or "it is not finished"), can be translated as either "I'm sorry" or "Thank you" and is used to express apology or gratitude. In contexts such as leaving someone's home, where a Westerner might say, "Thank you for a wonderful evening," a Japanese guest often says the equivalent of "I have intruded on you" (literally: "disturbance have done to you"). As in Western societies, Japanese speakers typically respond to apologies with polite "downgraders," for example, "No, no, don't mention it."

Japanese norms require explicit recognition of people's effects on one another in the form of apology for actual or implicated intrusions, disturbances, and infringements. Apologies are perceived as polite, considerate, and deferential according to Japanese models of social rights. Serious breaches and formal situations invoke more elaborate apologies.

PEARSON
myanthrolab

Explore more at
www.myanthrolab.com

According to Inuit social etiquette, the man who bested his rival in the song duel was rewarded with marriage to the woman in dispute. Although these contests provided a safe venue for open hostility between the men involved, they may or may not actually have settled the issue at hand. The woman might decide not to marry the victor. And the emotions revealed and dramatized during the song duel may have been so strong that they led to actual violence at a future date. But the social mechanism was aimed at alleviating the conflict and stopping it from escalating to violence.

According to Iranian cultural norms, parent-child relationships are imbued with special expectations whose violation, particularly if perpetrated by the child, lead to practices called *qahr* and *ashti* (Behzadi 1994). The parent who feels hurt or somehow slighted by the child conveys *qahr*, an intention to withdraw from further interaction until the rift is mended. *Qahr* indirectly expresses a constellation of complex feelings of hate, anger, dislike, and hurt and at the same time evokes in the other person another complex set of feelings of guilt, shame, regret, compassion, and love. Recipients of *qahr* are prompted to correct their behavior and seek reconciliation. They may do this directly to the person offended or through intermediaries. The cultural practice of *ashti* is this stage of mediation and reconciliation. The word itself can also be used to mean "to end a war," "to compromise with someone," and "to forget disappointment and resentment about someone" (Behzadi 1994, 322). The successful use of *qahr* and *ashti* depends on people's sensitivity to interpersonal signals that are not directly stated, especially in family relationships or close friendships where people expect others to respond appropriately without overt cues.

> **In your culture or group, what are some examples of ways that aggression may be channeled to avoid conflict?**

CASE STUDY

Conflict Resolution among the Semai of Malaysia

The Semais are a farming people who live in mountainous regions of the Malay Peninsula. Numbering about 1,500, the Semais live in small villages or bands of around 100 people that are politically autonomous. Semai society is based on an egalitarian social system. No one can exert power or compel others to do something against their wills. In addition, Semai men and women are considered equal. Gender roles are not rigidly defined, so that men and women do whatever work is necessary in the household and the fields. Semais believe that the social personalities of men and women are the same, making for no differences in the emotional attributes or intellectual abilities of the two genders. Although everyone is considered to have the same rights and opportunities, a headman, usually a man recognized by the community for his intelligence, oratorical abilities, and judgment, has moral authority. Although men are usually chosen as headmen, women can also occupy the role.

Semais make a significant distinction between kin and non-kin and between members of their band and outsiders (Robarchek 1997). In-group members, whether in one's kin group or band, give one another support, nurturance, and security. Outsiders are viewed with suspicion and fear.

The Semai perception of human relations is mirrored in the dichotomies they impose on the universe as a whole. The known and familiar are considered helpful and supportive, but the unknown is fraught with danger. Semais also make a distinction between protective spirits that are considered to be kin or like kin and malevolent spirits that are the source of misfortune, illness, and death.

Human beings, therefore, must be ever alert against malevolent spirits. They protect themselves by reciting prayers, avoiding dangerous places or actions, and carrying out rituals that guard against misfortune and death. In this context of danger and unpredictability, Semais look to their relatives and fellow band members for security and protection. They are bound together in strong networks of reciprocal aid and support. People can also call on their protective spirits for aid.

The values of Semai social living center on nurturance, both in the form of material aid, emotional support and affiliation, and the maintenance of harmonious relationships among relatives and community members. According to Semai ethics, "goodness" is characterized by helping, giving, and sharing, and "badness" by anger, quarreling, and fighting (Robarchek 1997, 53). Therefore, people who are helpful, generous, and cooperative are good; those who are angry and violent are bad.

In this social and ethical climate, conflict is, by definition, bad and threatens the stability of Semai society. When psychologist Clayton Robarchek asked Semai to finish a sentence beginning "more than anything else, he/she is afraid of . . . ," the most common response was "a conflict (more common than evil spirits, tigers, and death combined)" (1997, 54).

When conflict does erupt, or threatens to, Semais have a formal mechanism to limit it. The entire community attends a meeting, called a *becharaa'* to air grievances and allow all parties to voice their concerns and opinions. In principle, kinship groups are likely to support their own members in disputes; rather than be divisive, this "taking sides" integrates the community because Semais reckon descent bilaterally. Most people are related to many other people within the settlement through blood or marriage, so individuals are likely to have relatives on both sides of the dispute. Therefore, settling conflicts amicably and quickly is to the advantage of all community members. People are held responsible for creating problems for their relatives and are thus under pressure to avoid conflict or settle it without disruption.

At the beginning of the *becharaa'*, people congregate in the headman's house and discuss mundane events but not the dispute itself. After a while, an elder member of one of the disputants' kin groups delivers a long oration about the importance of community interdependence and harmony. Other prominent people give similar speeches emphasizing the importance of unity and the need to resolve the dispute quickly.

At that point, the disputants take turns arguing their case, stating facts, explanations, justifications, and accusations against one another. Following these presentations, relatives of the principal disputants argue for their own kin. Then any other interested members of the community may offer interpretations and opinions. Displays of anger or strong emotion during these proceedings are considered highly inappropriate.

The *becharaa'* may last for several days and nights. The hosting headman provides food for all in attendance. People sleep for short intervals and then rejoin the discussion. The *becharaa'* continues "until finally a point is reached where there is simply nothing left to say" (Robarchek 1997). Then the headman delivers a summary and consensus of the community, discusses the guilt of one or both of the disputants, offers alternatives to how they should have behaved, and admonishes them never to repeat their offending actions or words. Fines may be imposed on one or both of the principals. Finally, elders of both kin groups admonish their relatives against improper behavior and again stress the importance of community cohesion and harmony.

As Robarchek points out, the Semai *becharaa'* deals with the affective, substantive, and social components of conflict. By talking, retalking, and, one might say, overtalking the issues, an emotional catharsis and release is achieved for the disputants. At the end of the *becharaa'*, participants are no doubt physically and emotionally exhausted. The nearly endless talk dissipates the emotional aspects of conflict. The substantive issues of the conflict are also talked over endlessly until "there is nothing more to say." Every angle is examined in minute detail. Finally, the repetitive emphasis at the beginning and end of the *becharaa'* on the importance of community, cohesion, and harmonious social relationships addresses the social content of disputes.

Explore more at
www.myanthrolab.com

Role of Reciprocity in Conflict Avoidance

In some societies, it is expected that antagonisms and conflicts will surface in the context of specific occasions, giving people opportunities to vent feelings of anger, rivalry, and envy in a culturally controlled manner. For example, among the Torajas, a farming and livestock-raising people of South Sulawesi, Indonesia, anger and strong negative emotions are avoided in most daily contexts, but they are likely to arise at ritual occasions when sacrificed animals are butchered and distributed to the participants. According to Toraja etiquette, the person who distributes meat must pay heed to the relative status and prestige of the recipients (Hollan 1997). However, because relative status and prestige in Toraja society are flexible and inherently unstable, the meat distributor may inevitably hurt the feelings of some of the recipients who believe that they should have received larger or more prestigious shares than other recipients. A person's expression of anger or resentment in such contexts is considered normal, even predictable.

Outside these ritualized contexts, however, the overt expression of anger is considered dangerous and threatening to community stability. When disputes over other issues arise, they are handled through a number of intersecting cultural norms that are aimed at avoiding or at least limiting the intensity and scope of conflict. Incidents that may stir anger and lead to disputes often involve people's feelings of having been shamed. Such incidents include a spouse's adultery or failure to fulfill domestic responsibilities. In addition to spousal concerns, people are vigilant about making or receiving requests for resources or services from other villagers. People are careful about making requests of others because of the shame involved in being turned down. They are also hesitant to grant requests because they worry that their offer will not be reciprocated at some future time when they are in need. In essence, these interpersonal matters hinge on the principle of reciprocity, defined in Chapters 6 and 7 in the context of economic exchange. In any context, reciprocity refers to the expectation that people can depend on one another for material and emotional support. Among the Torajas, additional conflicts may arise over resources, particularly land. The most intense disputes, some leading to physical aggression, arise over disputes involving land.

To counteract conflict and limit community damage, Toraja culture transmits critical values and patterns of behavior. People learn to avoid others with whom they have disputes or even potential conflict. Confronting another individual directly is highly inappropriate. The Torajas believe that, when conflicts and anger erupt in ritualized contexts such as ceremonial meat distributions, the anger that is revealed should not be carried over into any other daily context. In addition, people who are the targets of someone's anger must not appear to hold a grudge against the person expressing hostility. Furthermore, Torajas believe that a person should refrain from showing anger even if it is legitimate anger caused by a wrong committed by another. According to Douglas Hollan, "A person who publicly berates or humiliates someone for being a thief is criticized more than the act of theft itself" (1997, 64). Finally, if disputes arise, village elders act as mediators to resolve conflicts. They lecture the parties about proper behavior and restore at least the appearance of social harmony.

> **What are the main sources of conflict in your family, group, or community? What do you do to counteract conflict and limit damage?**

REVIEW — Human strategies for avoiding conflict, in addition to systems of social control, include special roles for peacemakers, deference, and reciprocity. Deferential behavior includes politeness and apologies. Societies also have socially accepted or ritualized ways of channeling aggression and procedures for settling grievances and disputes.

WITCHCRAFT AND RITUAL IN CONFLICT RESOLUTION

In some societies, rituals may provide the means of avoiding or resolving conflicts and breaches of proper behavior. For example, among the Taitas, a farming and cattle-herding people of Kenya, anger is dealt with in a complex ceremony that links anger with illness.

Negative emotions, especially anger, are thought to be one of the most common causes of illness. However, the angry person is not the one who becomes ill. Rather, the person at whom the anger is directed suffers misfortune or illness. If a person has been slighted, insulted, or wronged by someone else, the person who has been wronged naturally becomes angry and resentful. The Taitas believe that, although anger may be justifiable and legitimate, unresolved and brewing anger is what is most likely to cause illness.

When a person becomes ill, a diviner asks for those who feel they might be the cause of the patient's illness to come forward because of the anger the person harbors toward the patient. It is no shame to come forward because an admission of responsibility helps solidify community values and restore individual and social harmony. Finally, a person admits anger toward the patient and agrees to participate in a ritual cure. During the cure, the angry person "casts out anger" (Harris, 1986). This person ritually takes in a mouthful of water and then spits it out while calling blessings and good fortune upon the sick person. Through this dramatic enactment of anger and its expulsion, the patient and the person causing the illness are reunited and reconciled.

Because the ritual takes place publicly, it also enacts and dramatizes the importance of understanding and forgiveness. Both parties have behaved badly; the sick person is judged to have wronged the person who harbors the anger, and the angry person has violated social norms by holding grudges. And although the anger is understandable and legitimate, it needs to be expelled so that both the community and the patient can be healed. Thus, Taita rituals emphasize the importance of restoring community and interpersonal harmony.

Beliefs about **witchcraft** may function both as methods of social control and as channels for anger toward others. Witchcraft beliefs include the notion that people can use spirit powers to cause harm to others, leading to illness, misfortune, and death. Belief in witchcraft serves to control anger in a complex interplay of fears of being both a target of witches and a target of accusations of witchcraft. That is, in most societies with witchcraft practices and beliefs, people attempt to control angry outbursts and demonstrations of interpersonal antagonisms because they fear that they might offend, knowingly or unknowingly, a person who practices witchcraft. The witch has the power to retaliate and cause misfortune, illness, or death. But people also attempt to control their anger and jealousies because an angry, jealous person is likely to be accused of being a witch. These are informal sanctions controlling or responding to people's behavior.

In a study of witchcraft accounts given by respondents from the Cibecue settlement of the Western Apache in Arizona, Keith Basso (1989) recounts the ways in which occurrences of misfortune are attributed to the action of witches and the ways that accusations are used to channel anger and hostilities between community members. People who become ill after being the target of someone's angry outburst often accuse the latter of being a witch and having caused them harm. Such an accusation is difficult to shake off unless the accused person can excuse the behavior by claiming drunkenness and therefore lack of control or responsibility for words spoken.

In addition, accusations sometimes come from men directed at their mothers-in-law. Apache society is matrilineal, and postmarital residence is frequently matrilocal, a pattern even more prominent in the past. Whether or not the married couple lives with the wife's family, a woman's mother continues to have influence over her daughter's actions.

In the current context of changing norms about household structure and gender roles, men sometimes resent what they consider to be interference from their mothers-in-law in their conjugal relationship. Acknowledging the strong ties between mother and daughter, however, married men often feel that they cannot directly challenge the mother-in-law's authority. Accusing the woman of witchcraft accomplishes the goal of criticizing her in a traditional way, that is, through witchcraft accusations. The elder woman can counter the accusation by stressing her kindness, responsibility, and adherence to sound ethical principles, noting her generosity and helpfulness to the couple and their children as well as her general good character. Still, whether or not community consensus believes the accusation, it allows the son-in-law a way to channel his anger and give it at least temporary voice.

witchcraft
A belief system that functions as a mechanism of social control by channeling anger toward others.

This !Kung Ju/'hoansi man, N!eisi n!a, throws discs to divine the future in Botswana.

REVIEW ——⊙ Through religious or spiritual beliefs and practices, people ritually treat feelings of anger and aggression that underlie conflict. Witchcraft is a powerful mechanism of social control because people fear being accused of it as much as they fear being its victims.

GLOBALIZATION

A result of globalization is that many international nongovernmental organizations have arisen to address problems of family and community conflict. For example, the International Women's Rights Action Watch (IWRAW) and the International Child Abuse Network (ICAN) monitor and report on the status of women and children, respectively; university-affiliated programs such as the Sustainable Community Network (SCN) and the Center for International Development and Conflict Resolution (CIDCR) help communities and regions to resolve conflicts. Appreciating cultural similarities and understanding cultural differences are essential to these efforts.

PATTERNS OF FAMILY AND COMMUNITY CONFLICT

Although there are many cultural-specific and individual causes of conflict, there also are some overall general patterns in the content of disputes. Within families, disputes may arise over personal preferences and styles of interaction. Arguments may arise over the proper course of action when decisions have to be made. When parents arrange marriages for their children, parents as well as their children whose lives are being affected can have obvious possibilities of disagreement. Such conflicts tend to be worked out through the give-and-take of conversation, deference to others, and respect due certain family members because of their status and authority.

In societies with polygynous or polyandrous marriages, jealousies can be aroused by any favoritism shown by the central spouse to the wives or husbands. Co-wives or co-husbands in plural marriages may compete with one another and harbor resentments if they perceive that they have been unfairly treated or slighted. But co-spouses often get along well, finding friendship and mutual support with work and emotional stress. Particularly in patrilineal, patrilocal households, co-wives may become allies, aiding one another with housework, child care, and emotional support.

Women who marry into patrilocal households may be well positioned to function as peacemakers in situations of intergroup conflict. For example, a study of peacemaking roles among the Somali highlights women's strategic ability to act as intermediaries and negotiate resolution of conflict that occurs between members of their own clan and that of their husband (Elmi, Ibrahim, and Jenner 2000). Somali society, a pastoral people living in Somalia, has a social life based on membership in patrilineal clans. Members of families may have disagreements about land use, animal ownership, and other familial matters. Women can carry messages back and forth between the parties in the dispute, based on their traditional patterns of visiting their own families while living primarily with the family of their husband. In patrilocal societies, women have a significant stake in maintaining friendly relations between their two families. Because women in Somali society do not have central structural roles in political systems, they are seen as neutral participants. It could be argued that women's marginality makes them ideal intermediaries in disputes. Women's ability to help settle disputes may also derive from the fact that they are situated in the middle of overlapping networks in contrast to men's position within one specific lineage or clan. Women's networks can therefore be seen as building horizontal relationships, again in contrast to men's more vertical and dense involvements within their clans.

Family Violence

In patriarchal family structures in India and elsewhere (see Chapter 9), young wives marrying into patriarchal households often face verbal and physical abuse from their mothers-in-law and other senior relatives while they are being integrated into the husband's family. Women in such situations must live with a great deal of resentment, anger, and shame caused by the treatment they receive and by their own powerlessness. The potential for domestic violence is greatest in strongly patriarchal societies. A jealous husband or rejected suitor in Pakistan may seek revenge against a woman by throwing acid on her face and body, disfiguring her and making her ineligible for either infidelity or

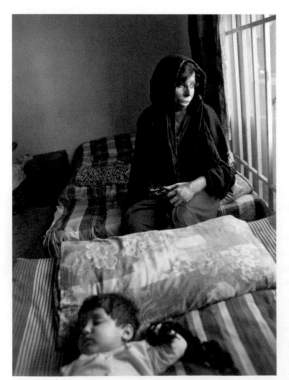

This Pakistani woman sought refuge in a women's shelter after her husband burned her.

marriage. In India, in a phenomenon known as "dowry death," young brides may be murdered, set ablaze by their husbands or in-laws, who then arrange for another marriage with another dowry. Reform movements to modernize law codes in these countries address these and other "traditional" crimes against women. (These issues are addressed further in Chapter 10.)

In societies where property is valued and accumulated, siblings may compete to establish themselves as preferred heirs, especially if the society has no automatic rules of inheritance. Again, with rural India as an example, brothers may try to curry favor with the father, hoping to inherit the largest or best-located section of family landholdings. Because conflict among brothers is considered inappropriate and violates the ethics of family solidarity, their wives are often blamed for causing friction in the household. The women are already in a vulnerable social position, having moved away from their parental home, so they are easy scapegoats.

Families, and especially kin groups organized as lineages and clans, often have both informal and formal mechanisms for dealing with disputes among members. The heads of families and the heads of lineages or clans are aware of conflicts among their members and have the authority to mediate and resolve disputes. Lacking coercive power to have their judgments enforced, they can nonetheless influence the parties concerned to follow their advice because of the prestige of their position.

As previously described, women in Somali society can use their influence informally to help resolve disputes between their own clans and that of their husband. Even when interclan conflicts erupt into actual physical violence, women can help restore peace and harmonious relationships by acting as ". . . conduits of information, carrying messages of peace and offers of negotiation and reconciliation to the opposing clans" (Elmi, Ibrahim, and Jenner 2000, 123). Once a conflict is resolved, women may help arrange marriages between the children of former opposing clans as "concrete symbols of the cessation of hostilities and the renewal of peaceful relationships" (ibid.).

In traditional, relatively small communities, disputes may be settled in different ways, depending on the relationship between the people involved. Within families, disagreements are often worked out by advice from other family members, especially senior men and women in the household or in the clan. Disagreements tend to arise within families over personal matters. In societies where land is owned communally, people do not argue or disagree over inheritance of property or over rights to use communal territory.

Conflicts in Bands and Tribes

In foraging band societies, conflicts over property are unlikely to emerge because individuals usually do not own land and other resources. The conflicts that do arise tend to be caused by jealousies, often of a sexual nature. Disputes or antagonisms may surface between rivals for a person's affections or between suitors hoping to marry the same woman. Such jealousies may lead to physical assaults, but this rarely happens in most band societies. Instead, people may attempt to use magical means such as witchcraft and harmful spells to deter or injure rivals.

In tribal societies, in addition to conflicts with personal motivations, people may engage in disputes over property. Where individuals own land and other valuable resources, people may accuse others of theft or destruction of property. Even where kinship groups control land and resources communally, outsiders may make accusations of trespass onto kin-owned resources.

In some tribal societies, social etiquette regulates the behavior of neighbors and even of strangers in other people's territories. For example, among the Eastern Pomos, a foraging society of northern California, residents of villages or members of kinship groups communally owned certain resource sites. Villages owned hunting territories in surrounding areas and marked off their borders by twisting the branches of oak trees. In addition, some trees, said to belong to particular families, were marked in an identifiable design that everyone in the village recognized. Landings on lakes from which people fished were also the property of individual families and were so marked. Coastal Pomos owned sections along the streams that flowed to the sea, but no part of the ocean shoreline was considered private property.

vengeance
Aggression against others based on the principle of revenge.

blood feud
Ongoing conflict between kin groups or communities, based on vengeance.

Any claim to property was publicized throughout the community. However, if a family's resource areas were unproductive in any given year, they might ask permission to gather plants or to hunt and fish in areas claimed by a relative or neighbor. Such requests were customarily granted. Pomos, therefore, recognized individual or communal claims to land and resources, but the needy could make use of the resources to sustain themselves in hard times. Taking resources from someone else's land was not considered theft as long as permission had been requested and granted. This social etiquette forestalled the likelihood of a dispute arising over resources.

In many tribal societies, a council of village elders mediates disputes. Membership in these councils may be determined by lineage or clan affiliation, or the members can be drawn from any segment in the village. Leaders tend to be selected on the basis of community consensus because of their intelligence, success, sound judgment, and moral character.

Blood Vengeance and the Feud

In tribal societies where the stakes of conflict are high, specific people may function as mediators and employ a combination of interpersonal and ritual skills. For example, among the Nuers, a cattle-herding and farming people of southern Sudan, conflicts over cattle frequently arose over the rightful ownership of the animals. Cattle raiding was not uncommon, leading to accusations and counteraccusations. There was always the danger that these conflicts could lead to physical violence and even to murder. Once a kinsman was murdered, his kin group was responsible for seeking revenge by killing either the original antagonist or another member of his kinship group. One revenge killing would then necessitate another round of **vengeance** on the part of the kinship group of the next victim, leading to a series of killings and eventually to a state of **blood feud.**

The Nuers instituted a process to forestall the escalation of a conflict to murder and blood feuds. Certain men functioned as "leopard-skin chiefs." They were ritual practitioners who controlled spirit powers that could be used against any person who failed to comply with their advice in a conflict. But essentially the leopard-skin chiefs were mediators who functioned as intermediaries between the two rival kinship groups. Because they belonged to neither of the antagonists' kinship group, they were not identified as allies of anyone involved but, rather, were objective negotiators. They went from one group to another and back again, carrying messages and demands. Their role was to negotiate a settlement, usually a payment in cattle between the two disputing parties. In cases of murder, a leopard-skin chief attempted to convince the kin group of the murdered man to accept reparations as settlement for the crime rather than to seek bloody revenge.

Nuer and Dinka Chiefs at a market in Thiet, Sudan while attending a peace conference between the two groups.

Although leopard-skin chiefs had no power to enforce their decisions, except for the threat of supernatural harm, their advice was generally taken after protracted negotiations. These mediators were skilled orators, able to persuade people to come to agreements that were in the interest of the entire community. The lengthy negotiations allowed the wronged kinship group to save face by initially putting up a stiff resistance. In the end, however, they came around to accepting the leopard-skin chief's advice for the good of restoring social harmony in the community.

Family conflict tends to arise from tensions in marital, co-wife, and in-law relationships. Domestic violence against women is widespread in some societies. Conflicts over property and land are more common in chiefdoms and states than in bands or tribes. Tribal conflicts include raiding, vengeance, and blood feuds among kin groups. These communities have special bodies to try to prevent bloodshed.

PATTERNS OF CONFLICT BETWEEN GROUPS

As discussed, many indigenous communities traditionally had both informal and formal means of resolving disputes. Village leaders, usually informally selected through community consensus, helped mediate disputes by appealing to all parties concerned and stressing the importance of community harmony and stability. Through both private and public efforts, leaders typically tried to create a climate in which mediation and agreement could be successful. However, community leaders had no coercive powers; they could not enforce their opinions or decisions on people. Rather, they were skilled orators with powers of persuasion and personal charisma.

If conflicts continued and the parties refused to come to a negotiated settlement, a person had the option of leaving the band or village and joining another group. Because band and village membership was flexible, people could decide to take up residence elsewhere. Because kinship was a fundamental organizing principle, people often had relatives in several communities, and people related by blood or marriage were obligated by the ethics of kinship support to provide assistance and hospitality to one another.

If disputes arose between different villages, the leaders attempted to resolve the disputes through mediation and negotiation. When these efforts failed, disputes continued to fester, sometimes leading to physical assault or murder. Then a spate of revenge killings could ensue, leading to blood feuds and prolonged antagonism. Conflicts could escalate into raiding and warfare between communities in different tribes. Because these conflicts are between different groups acting as collective units rather than as individuals, they tend to be more deadly, escalating into warfare when diplomacy fails.

Warfare

Armed aggression and hostilities between groups can occur anywhere, but the causes and character of **warfare** vary in different types of societies. In warfare, armed and organized fighters attack specified enemies with the intent of causing injury or death and possibly destroying property or the means of sustenance, thus harming survivors as well. Warfare is least likely and least destructive in bands than in any other kind of society. The reasons are multiple and interrelated. People in nomadic bands usually do not have a strong sense of territorial ownership and control, so fighting over land and resources is not likely. Because nomadic peoples do not have many possessions, they have little desire to raid neighbors for their property, though raiding sometimes occurs between groups belonging to different bands. Blood feuds may develop following the murder of a member of one band by an outsider as the victim's relatives seek revenge against the assailant and his band. Although such hostile actions can lead to cycles of raiding and killing, the number of people affected is relatively few. And though the death of any one individual is a loss to the person who dies and is deeply mourned by the person's relatives, such practices are not necessarily disruptive on a societal level.

In tribal societies, raiding and warfare may exact a deadlier toll on the population and be more disruptive. Motives for hostilities may include trespass on tribal territory

warfare
Armed aggression and hostilities between groups.

The Eagle Dance, shown here, might be performed to welcome back Choctaw warriors. (George Catlin [1796–1872]. "Eagle Dance, Choctaw," oil on canvas, 191/2 × 271/2 in. Gift of Mrs. Joseph Harrison, Jr. Smithsonian American Art Museum, Washington, DC. Photo Credit: Smithsonian American Art Museum, Washington, DC/Art Resource, NY)

for the purpose of exploiting tribal resources. Killings and revenge counterkillings are also contributing factors. Because of the ways in which tribal societies are organized, and because of their communal orientation, raiding and warfare generally do not have economic motives. Although some property may be stolen in a raiding expedition, and captives may be brought back to the home community, tribal warriors rarely have the goal of ousting their enemies from territory and taking over lands and resources in a sustained manner. Territorial expansion is also not a likely goal of tribal warfare because of relatively low population densities and consequent lack of need for additional lands.

Tribal warfare generally involves relatively few fighters. The organization of the war expedition tends to be based on voluntary association. Men may join in the war if they agree with the goals and if they perceive the leadership and organization to be sound. They may also leave the war party if they object to the leader's tactics.

Both the Pomo and Sambia examples (see Case Study) demonstrate common patterns in tribal societies. They had no standing armies; rather, volunteers joined a war party because of their own inclinations and goals. The reasons for a conflict were primarily social and ritual, especially seeking revenge for previous wrongs done to the community. In some tribal societies, such as the Pomo, once the conflict ended, the principal goal was restoration of harmonious relationships rather than humiliation and subjugation of the losers. In others, however, such as the Sambia, reconciliation after serious intertribal warfare was unusual because of lingering antagonisms resulting from the overt eruption of violence.

Impacts of Globalization on Warfare

Throughout time, technological, material, and organizational inequality between peoples has led to rapid social and culture change. Beginning in the sixteenth century, for example, European contact contributed to both greater unity and greater conflict among indigenous peoples. European technology made that conflict more lethal, and European technological superiority in warfare made overall conquest likely.

Prior to European contact, most Native American societies lacked formal mechanisms of dispute management in conflicts between different tribes. Perhaps the most formalized system was that of the Iroquois Confederacy, which was founded to eliminate conflicts among five nations. The arrival of Europeans at first prompted the Iroquois Confederacy to compete with other native groups for access to trade and influence. For

GLOBALIZATION

Traditional native approaches to conflict resolution were transformed as peoples were contacted and then overwhelmed by European colonizers. Fatalities increased in feuds and raids as bands and tribes replaced their wooden and stone arrows with iron and steel weapons and guns. Causes of warfare also changed from personal or group revenge to economic and political motives as groups vied with each other for access to trade and later fought to hold on to their remaining territories.

more than a century, the Iroquois were able to expand their domain of power through skillful negotiation and military prowess, reaching as far south as the Carolinas and as far west as Lake Superior. But then the growing population and military might of the United States led to the confederacy's loss of influence and power shortly after the American Revolution. Elsewhere on the continent, the presence of Europeans stimulated open hostilities and warfare among Native Americans. The cultural contexts of warfare, tactics, and goals also changed.

CASE STUDY

Pomoan (California) and Sambian (Papua New Guinea) Warfare

Among the Pomos of northern California, war might erupt when trespassers gathered resources or hunted in another group's territory without permission. More often, such conflicts were motivated by the desire for revenge for an alleged poisoning death of a community member. Any man might organize a group of followers to go to war. War leaders were temporary figures chosen for their military skills but were not universally admired. They were referred to as "good bad men" (Loeb 1926, 200).

Pomo battles with neighboring tribes usually entailed confrontations between the two groups organized into lines of about 100 warriors each, standing about 30 yards apart. They shot arrows, threw stones, and hurled insults at one another but did not engage in direct contact. Women and boys sometimes accompanied the warriors and assisted by resupplying them. The battle might end as soon as anyone was seriously wounded, but fighting always ceased at night. Raids against an enemy village generally resulted in higher casualties than in the formal line battles.

The rituals practiced once a conflict ended reflected the Pomoan attitude toward war as a sometimes necessary but unfortunate breach in social harmony. Chiefs of the victorious party brought a peace offering of clamshell beads collected from their villagers to the community of their defeated foe. Negotiations were prefaced by sending a messenger to the enemy village, often a person related to them through marriage. When the chief arrived, he made a formal speech apologizing for the suffering that had been caused. The chief of the defeated village accepted the reparation and made a speech voicing hope that peace would be restored. The beads received from the victors were divided among the families who had lost men in battle. Through these procedures, the former foes were reconciled. And, significantly, the victorious community paid damages to the losers as compensation for the deaths that they had caused.

Warfare in many New Guinean societies was directly related to concepts of masculinity. Boys were socialized into aggressive behavior, especially after their initiation into adulthood. Masculine ideals focused on strength and power, diametrically opposed to weakness and subordination. These ideals were played out in several kinds of violent confrontations. For example, among the Sambia of Papua New Guinea, three types of warfare occurred, differing in scale and deadliness (Herdt 2006, 33). The least deadly were ritualized "bow fights" or "little fights" that involved men from neighboring hamlets who stood on opposite hillsides surrounding a valley and threw arrows at one another. Each village could probably provide about ten warriors. The goal in these fights was to impress opponents with one's strength and daring. Men usually sided with their own hamlet, but they might fight on the other side depending on personal loyalties and ties to in-laws. Serious injuries or deaths were inadvertent and were interpreted as the victim's own fault. Common expressions in these cases were, "He stood in front of my arrow," or "He found my arrow" (Herdt 2006, 34).

Sometimes, "little fights" escalated into "big fights." These involved men from numerous villages. Instead of ritualized arrow throwing from a distance, men ambushed their enemies or raided villages. Noncombatants (women, children, and elderly people) might be victims. Religious practitioners used magic to safeguard the warriors and harm their enemies. As conflicts escalated, each side mobilized supporters (relatives, in-laws, allies) to aid them,

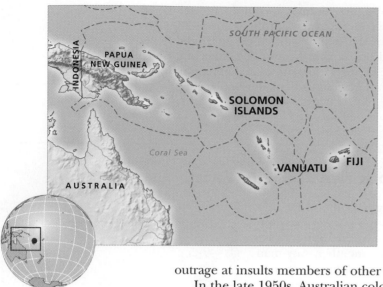

perhaps rallying an additional twenty-five fighters. In protracted fights, more than a dozen men might be injured, and some were killed. Eventually, a truce ceremony might end the open conflict, but the antagonisms created might also lead to future violence because Sambia ethics demanded that family members avenge a killing of one of their own.

The most deadly type of conflict was intertribal warfare. Warriors carried out surprise raids against enemy villages. In addition to killing enemy warriors, Sambia fighters sometimes captured women to take back as wives. Other women and children might be killed. The goal was to inflict as much harm and destruction as possible, killing many, if not all, inhabitants of enemy villages and burning their houses. These raids were prompted by long-standing grievances, desire to avenge deaths, and outrage at insults members of other tribes supposedly made.

In the late 1950s, Australian colonial administrations began to pacify the Sambia Valley. When attempts at persuasion seemed to fail, colonial authorities rounded up Sambia men, forced them to give up their weapons, and sent forty to prison (Herdt 2006, 41). By 1964, indigenous warfare had ended. Because warfare was bound up with concepts of masculinity, the forced end of fighting was particularly humiliating.

PEARSON
myanthrolab

Explore more at
www.myanthrolab.com

The increase in the incidence of warfare was due to two interrelated processes. First, as France, Britain, the Netherlands, and Spain engaged in wars against each other both in Europe and in their colonial adventures, the European powers attempted to forge alliances with various native groups to aid their own governments. When the Europeans fought each other, their native allies became embroiled in these conflicts. When Indians fought with and for their European partners, they were fighting against both European enemies and the tribes with whom those enemies were linked. New animosities, therefore, developed between native groups.

CULTURE CHANGE

REESTABLISHING TRADITIONAL METHODS OF DISPUTE RESOLUTION

After the establishment of the United States, the American army forcibly settled native groups on reservations, and the federal government imposed its laws and procedures on them. Traditional systems of leadership were bypassed, and federal legislation overrode traditional systems of conflict resolution and mediation. The Major Crimes Act in 1885 allowed federal courts to claim jurisdiction over Native Americans who committed seven specific crimes: murder, manslaughter, rape, assault with intent to kill, arson, burglary, and larceny on reservations. Until that time, tribal courts where they existed had dealt with Native Americans who committed these crimes on their own reservations (Bacheller 1997, 10).

In 1976, the Indian Crimes Act added an additional seven crimes to be dealt with by federal courts: kidnapping, assault with intent to commit rape, assault with a dangerous weapon, assault resulting in serious bodily injury, robbery, incest, and statutory rape (sexual intercourse with a female under age 16) (French 2003, 58–59). Any Native American accused of one of these crimes is tried and sentenced in federal courts. On reservations where a tribal court system operates, the tribal court has jurisdiction over lesser crimes. On reservations that lack their own court system, federal authorities deal with accused offenders.

Some indigenous peoples in North America are returning to traditional practices. Tribes across the country have reinstituted *banishment* for chronic wrongdoers (Kershaw and Davey 2004). Formerly, individuals who committed wrongs, assaulted people repeatedly, or violated other social rules might be exiled, forced to leave their own villages. Sometimes another community took them in, but if their history were well known, no other group was likely to accept them, fearing that the offenders might cause more trouble. Now some tribes are returning to the imposition of banishment, usually as a last resort, especially for drug or alcohol abuse (*Indian Time* 2003). Few other avenues are open to tribal courts for repeat offenders, as federal laws only permit tribal courts to impose sentences of no longer than one year in jail and no more than a $5,000 fine. Some tribal councils see banishment as an effective means of dealing with nonnatives who are causing trouble on the reservation.

As part of efforts by Native Americans to reestablish traditional practices in their communities, the Diné (Navajo) reintroduced its peacemaker processes of conflict resolution. American-style systems of justice were forced upon the Diné in 1892, about twenty-five years after they had been released from four years of virtual incarceration in an army base at Fort Sumner, New Mexico in 1868. For about ninety years, therefore, the Diné were under federal guidelines for adjudicating both criminal and civil offenses. The U.S. model of justice is essentially adversarial, where a court divorced a person accused of wrongdoing from the social network of community judges. In this legal process, each side argues its own point of view, contradicting or explaining facts introduced by its adversary. The court's decision renders a defendant guilty or not guilty of the offense.

These procedures, and the moral theory on which they are based, contradict traditional Diné ethics. In the Diné view, conflicts disturb the harmony that should exist within a person, between one person and others, with the environment, and with spirit world. In 1982, the Diné nation established its Navajo Peacemaker Court to coexist with the American-style adversarial system (French 2003). According to Robert Yazzie, chief justice of the Navajo Nation, the Anglo-American court system is a "vertical system of justice where judges possess a tremendous amount of power to affect human lives, either to harm them or bring goodness to them. This vertical system relies on coercion to control and force people to do and not do something. . . . In the adversarial system the goal is to punish wrongdoers and teach them a lesson" (1992, 2).

Yazzie contrasts this system of justice with the horizontal system of the Diné Peacemakers: "Traditionally, Navajos used a peacemaker to mediate disputes. Peacemakers help preserve ongoing relationships, within both immediate and extended families. The parties settled their disputes in a forum where they could talk and settle their problems by consent. In this way harmony was restored" (1992, 3).

The Navajo goals of peacemaking differ markedly from those of the Anglo-American system of crime and punishment. According to Yazzie,

> In the peacemaker process, the mediator aims at one goal, and one goal only—restoring true justice among individuals, families and the larger community and society. This is done by allowing the wrongdoer and the victim "to talk things out." Navajos have always believed that the more individuals are restored to harmony, the more the family, community, and society will live and function in a harmonious fashion. The ultimate goal of the Peacemaker process is to restore the minds, physical being, spirits, and emotional well-being of all people involved. (1992, 4)

The Navajo government set out procedures governing the Peacemakers and their duties and powers. Peacemakers may call people to meetings if they consider that those individuals might contribute to understanding or resolving the problem. However, the Peacemakers have no power to force individuals to participate or accept a resolution (French 2003).

The Diné nation is divided into eighty-four districts or chapters. Residents of each chapter elect a representative to the tribal council. Each chapter also has at least one officially recognized Peacemaker. Although anyone can be nominated and selected, Peacemakers are generally intelligent, influential members of their communities who have shown sound judgment and solid moral character.

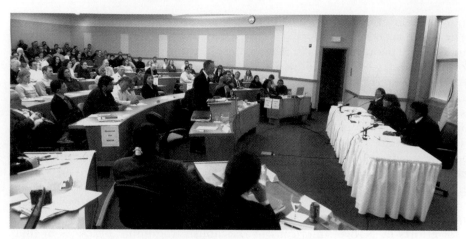

Today Diné Peacemakers are mediators whose goal is to reach agreement among contending parties. Here Chief Justice Robert Yazzie of the Navajo Supreme Court speaks about Navajo culture and law before hearing oral arguments.

The Peacemaker Court convenes whenever people ask for assistance from the court for problems in their family or community. Although any type of issue or dispute may be brought for mediation, the Peacemaker Court manual emphasizes its use for everyday problems, such as those arising between spouses, married couples and their in-laws, parents and children, and neighbors. The court is not formally established to handle serious criminal offenses, such as murder, assault, and rape, but it may serve a purpose in such situations, according to Chief Justice Yazzie. He notes that the Diné and other native peoples of North America formerly had community-oriented systems of justice and conflict resolution where perpetrators of violent crimes could be compelled to pay compensation to the relatives of the person harmed. Some groups are experimenting with these traditional procedures to determine if they are still effective today.

A second reason for the growth of intertribal conflict was the emergence of competition over land and resources. By the mid-seventeenth century, European powers sought land for settlement in addition to their earlier goals of obtaining trade goods and resources from North America. As the Europeans expropriated Indian land and resources, native groups competed to hold on to their territories. As they lost access to their lands, people competed for the remaining land and resources, often through direct confrontation and warfare. Wars in the northeast and southeast increased from the early seventeenth until the late eighteenth century. As trade and European settlement moved steadily westward in the eighteenth and nineteenth centuries, Indians along the Mississippi River and its tributaries were affected. Intense wars of survival pitted native groups against one another. By the mid-nineteenth century, inhabitants of the Great Plains also saw their territories crowded by Euro-American settlers and other Indians fleeing west from the sprawling conflicts in their own homelands.

Unlike most early warfare, wars of later centuries were primarily generated by economic motives or the need to defend one's own community from invaders. Native warfare changed not only in frequency and motive but also in tactics. Warriors began to destroy the homes and fields of their enemies, leaving survivors with no means to sustain themselves. The goal of annihilating one's enemies or forcing them to flee in order to take land and resources was rare before the Europeans brought fundamental transformations in warfare.

Warfare in State Societies

In state societies, warfare has primarily economic and political goals. As discussed in Chapter 12, state societies are usually born through warfare and depend on armed combat or indirect pressure to compel neighboring groups to come under the jurisdiction of the expanding state society. States expand both territorially and politically by enlarging their spheres of influence and control. The major means of accomplishing this expansion is through armed conflict or the threat of war.

The organization of warfare in state societies differs fundamentally from warfare in other types of cultures. State societies have standing armies composed of men (in some cases, also women) who are either part-time or full-time specialists. Fighters sometimes volunteer for that role, but they may be compelled to join the armed services in other cases. Warfare in state societies is organized and controlled by full-time leaders who plan the military campaigns and have absolute control over the soldiers and operations of battle. Unlike band or tribal warriors, state soldiers have little discretion in their actions. They must follow the lawful orders of their superior officers. The entire operation is structured hierarchically, in keeping with the hierarchical nature of all government functions in state societies. In some state societies, monopoly on the use of force is exerted internally as well as by the use of capital punishment to control internal enemies or violators of law.

Again, unlike band and tribal warfare, the goals of state warfare are either the total annihilation of the enemy or its humiliation into surrender and submission. The victorious side may confiscate land and other property belonging to the loser. The inhabitants of the defeated communities may be forced to capitulate to the winners, becoming citizens of an expanding state but as a subjugated people. In contrast to some tribal societies, such as the Pomos, the loser pays tribute or reparations to the winner.

Not all wars end decisively but may instead have a negotiated end that gives some advantages or concessions to both sides. In modern warfare, losers are usually permitted some face-saving options so that their economic and political losses and their public humiliation do not breed deep resentment against the winners. Such seething resentment might be counterproductive from the winner's perspective because it might turn the losers into perpetual resistors against the winner's control and influence. After World War I, the German government felt that provisions of the Treaty of Versailles were humiliating, providing one of the complex causes of the rise of extreme nationalist and fascist sentiment that led to Nazism and to World War II.

Even though many countries in the world today spend large sums of money on armaments, both in absolute terms and relative to other spending, there are several exceptional examples of countries that control military spending and the influence of the military on their government. Following World War II, both the Japanese and the German governments restricted the use of military forces following their defeat and humiliation in the world community. The Japanese constitution does not permit the country's soldiers to fight in wars outside of the territory of Japan. The purpose of the military is exclusively defensive. In Germany, laws also limit the roles of German soldiers to defensive operations within Germany or to strictly peacekeeping functions abroad.

The small Central American country of Costa Rica abolished its army in 1948. Its constitution, written in 1949, expressly prohibits the creation of an army. Remarkably, Costa Rica has survived as a demilitarized state without civil unrest or discord, although surrounded by neighbors such as Honduras, El Salvador, and Nicaragua, where civil war, repressive government action, and external military involvement have destabilized the countries for several decades (Arias 1997). The example of Costa Rica is an exception, however, in today's world.

Despite efforts to develop international mechanisms to resolve disputes through peaceful means, many armed conflicts continue to erupt throughout the world. And although every continent has been a battleground, some regions have seemingly intractable problems. In Africa since 1990, for example, civil wars over control of the central governments have broken out in Liberia, Sierra Leone, Ivory Coast, Rwanda, and Burundi. A long, ongoing war over resources, especially diamonds, is causing havoc in the Democratic Republic of Congo. In all of these conflicts, civilians have been killed and tens of thousands of survivors have been routed from their homes. In North Africa, civil wars and struggles for internal regional independence have shattered Algeria, Morocco, Ethiopia (Eritrea), and Sudan. Many of these struggles can be interpreted, at least in large part, as the legacy of colonialism and the outcome of a history of slavery. European colonial agents imposed on the borders of many African countries, carving up a vast continent rich in people and resources. After independence, conflicts erupted internally over power and over the control of wealth derived from mineral resources and crop production for export. The current situation of violence demonstrates the complexity of history and its contemporary legacies.

In the Middle East, the Israeli-Palestinian crisis continues unabated. Both sides accuse the other of terrorist acts against civilians. Both sides also refuse to compromise on key

IN THEIR OWN VOICES

Testimony from South Africa's Truth and Reconciliation Hearings of 1998

Following the end of apartheid in South Africa, the newly elected government, led by the African National Congress (ANC), established the Truth and Reconciliation Commission to confront and help resolve past tragedies with the goal of uncovering the causes of racial violence and unify the country. The commission held hearings in 1998, to determine whether individuals who had committed politically motivated racial killings and assaults during the decades of civil war deserved amnesty. People requesting amnesty had to testify at the hearings, confess their crimes, explain their motivations, and express remorse. On the basis of this testimony, putting great weight on the person's sincerity and insights into their crimes, the commission decided whether the person deserved amnesty.

The commission was established because South Africans decided that revenge against the perpetrators of racial crimes would create division and hostility for generations to come. As one of the commission's members said, "It is natural to want revenge but we need to rebuild a nation."

In the first of these excerpts, a black South African discusses his role in killing Amy Biehl, an American who was in South Africa working in the antiapartheid movement. In the second excerpt, two white policemen discuss their role in killing four members of the ANC. The questioners are all members of the commission.

Testimony of Ntobeko Ambrose Peni, one of the men who killed Amy Biehl

MR BRINK: You had absolutely no idea of what Amy Biehl's political views were, isn't that the situation?

MR PENI: I did not know.

MR BRINK: And your evidence here was that you participated in this murderous attack because the aims of your organisation was to bring back land to the African people, now what I want to know is, how would the killing of an unarmed, defenceless woman possibly help you to achieve that aim?

MR PENI: We believed that the minority White people ruling the country would realise that we wanted our land back. We also believed that they were going to give up this land back to the African people.

MR BRINK: Is it your evidence that by murdering, in the most brutal fashion, Amy Biehl, the African people would get their land back?

MR PENI: Yes it's my evidence.

First of all I would like to rectify something, gender was not significant. Our aim was to attack each White person and go forward.

JUDGE WILSON: But it was not the aim of the PAC [Pan Africanist Congress] at that time to kill every White person they saw, was it?

MR PENI: It could not happen that every person be killed, but there was one slogan: 'One Settler, one bullet'.

JUDGE WILSON: Do you agree it was not the policy of the PAC to kill White persons on sight, which is what you did on this afternoon, do you agree with that?

MR PENI: It is true that the PAC could not have killed everybody that they saw, however, the PAC was aware that killing each White person the land would come back to the African people.

MR BRINK: Mr Peni, isn't it the position that on that dreadful afternoon you were involved in a mindless, savage attack on

points of disagreement, although it is clear that the only way to reach a lasting peace is mutual recognition of each other's legitimate claims for security and autonomy. The war being waged by Israelis and Palestinians also has a destabilizing effect on both the region and the world. The growth and intensity of Islamic fundamentalism can be traced, in part, to the geopolitics of the Israeli-Palestinian conflict and the perceived role of the United States as a staunch ally of Israel.

Members of some Islamic fundamentalist factions conduct campaigns within Middle Eastern countries, attempting to undermine the governments and establish regimes this young woman, and that it was not politically motivated at all?

MR PENI: Our killing Amy Biehl had everything to do with politics.

Testimony of Mr. Du Plessis, a security police officer, who helped set up and kill the Cradock 4, members of the African National Congress

MR BOOYENS: Did you have anything personal against any of these four persons?

MR DU PLESSIS: I can state this unequivocally, absolutely not.

MR BOOYENS: To the extent that you were involved in the fact that they lost their lives ultimately, why were you involved?

MR DU PLESSIS: Because I felt or had the opinion that it would prevent the anarchy, that it would disempower the state of anarchy. . . . They were definitely members of the ANC. I don't have precise facts about their activities any more, but I know that they were all buried under the flag of communism.

MR BOOYENS: Very well. And for which reason did you personally become involved in these matters?

MR DU PLESSIS: In this case I received an order to become involved. I also felt that it would be the only way to attempt to stop the onslaught.

MR BOOYENS: Mr Du Plessis, today it is almost 15 years since what happened. How do you feel now about what happened?

MR DU PLESSIS: One is indeed sorry and I am speaking for myself that a person as a result of one's job, was compelled to such steps.

For us who believed in the struggle of the National Party, we also believed that if the ANC/SACP [South African Communist Party] alliance were to take over, it would signify the end of the white in Africa.

Right or wrong, that is what we believed. It is a great pity that two political parties such as the NP and the ANC could not sit down and discuss this matter and sort it out. And as a result, some of us and some of them died in the struggle.

I am sorry, especially for the families. I am sincerely sorry, not only for the sake of the families, but for the families of the members of the Security Branch to which we had to give orders.

CHAIRPERSON: Do I understand correctly that if it had not been for the nature of the work, that none of this would have happened?

MR DU PLESSIS: I was placed in a situation where I believed that this was the only way out. If I had been in a different position, perhaps I would have regarded the situation differently and believed something different, but I can tell you in all earnesty that that is what I believed to be the only viable solution.

Testimony of Mr. Taylor, another of the policemen

MR POTGIETER: Was it wrong if black people demanded human rights?

MR TAYLOR: Mr Chairperson, if you can give the opportunity to answer the question fully. It wasn't a question of the whole black population of South Africa, it was about the activation of radicals and mass activities and this demand for human rights was about the question of housing, schools, accommodation, books, to vote etc., etc. In other words it was part of the whole liberation struggle, yes. And I wish to reiterate that is how I thought and believed in 1985.

MR POTGIETER: And you thought it was wrong?

MR TAYLOR: Yes.

MR POTGIETER: But now you think it's right?

MR TAYLOR: Of course.

You must remember that if I have to admit, at that time I had been indoctrinated, I was politicised and for me all of these things were part of the struggle to overthrow the government and at time I thought that way and I felt that way.

The circumstances and the climate of that time, the feelings among the people, all these things have changed and we can see it now in 1998 that everything has changed.

Explore more at
www.myanthrolab.com

From South African government website: www.doj.gov.za/trc/trc_frameset.htm.

● CRITICAL THINKING QUESTIONS

What do these testimonies have in common? Do you agree that events must be interpreted in their historical and cultural contexts? Is public discussion an effective means of postconflict reconciliation?

dominated by conservative religious authorities. Some of these countries have moderate leadership (Jordan, Egypt), and others are ruled by autocratic monarchs (Saudi Arabia). Although al Qaeda is not solely a religious fundamentalist organization, it effectively recruits among such groups because of its anti-American stance.

Underlying many Middle Eastern conflicts is the geopolitics of oil, because of world dependence on oil as a principal energy source. Oil-rich countries, whether in the Middle East, Asia, or South America, are able to affect the economies of nations that rely on their supplies by lowering or raising output, thus influencing prices on the world market.

Rescue workers search for survivors in the collapse of the World Trade Center in New York City on September 11, 2001.

GLOBALIZATION

In modern times, as weaponry has become increasingly sophisticated and deadly—nuclear warfare and biological warfare—and as wars have embroiled larger numbers of countries, international efforts have been directed at establishing formal mechanisms for conflict resolution. The United Nations and the World Court, formed after World War II, are two international groups that mediate conflicts.

This in turn leads to political reactions by world powers, which try to control the oil-producing governments so that officials will make decisions beneficial to them.

Mixed in with these issues is the desire to control the proliferation of nuclear weapons. Although all the permanent members of the United Nations Security Council (United States, Britain, France, Russia, and China) have had nuclear weapons for decades, they lead the effort to prevent other nations from acquiring them. Other countries resent this stance, which they see as a hypocrisy. Many developing nations believe that attitudes about the proliferation of nuclear weapons discriminate against them. These reactions persist and cloud the basic issue of the danger posed to all peoples by the very existence of nuclear weaponry and the threats to use them.

Internal disputes and civil wars can damage societies for generations, leaving animosities and desires for revenge. In South Africa, for example, decades of clandestine and then open armed struggle of blacks and progressive whites were waged against apartheid laws that curtailed the legal rights of the majority blacks, forced residential and occupational segregation, and left most blacks in dire poverty. These struggles were met with the full military force of the government until the authorities recognized that the end of their power was inevitable. In 1992, Nelson Mandela, a leading member of the African National Congress, was sworn in as the first president elected after all South Africans were granted the right to vote. The new government understood that it needed to confront the conflicts of its past to resolve disputes and arrive at peaceful reconciliation. It did not ignore the past injustices directed at the majority blacks, but it also did not ignore the legitimate claims of the minority whites.

South Africa today is a very different country than it was before 1992. The majority black population has equal legal rights and full representation in governing institutions. The African National Congress is the country's major political party, winning most local and national elections. However, problems of economic justice continue. The majority of blacks are still poor, living in substandard housing, lacking adequate educational and medical services, and suffering high rates of unemployment. Despite government attempts, racial animosities continue to plague the country, especially in the countryside where black farmers and rural residents live in poverty with little hope of immediate improvement. White farmers fear that they will be the targets of racially motivated attacks. Although these fears are perhaps exaggerated, they are based on real occurrences. And in both rural and urban areas, rates of violent crime are among the highest in the world. Rape and domestic violence against women are especially frequent crimes, with rates that are again among the highest worldwide. The efforts of the government sometimes fail because of a lack of resources and because of the damaging legacies of racial tension and economic and political injustice.

REVIEW —⊙ Conflict between groups includes warfare, which varies among different societies. Intertribal warfare is waged by voluntary warrior societies. Societies may mediate conflict and prevent war through political marriage, banishment, or adjudication. Chiefdoms and states may wage war to conquer people, annex territory, or control resources using standing armies. Warfare has spread through globalization.

ANTHROPOLOGY APPLIED

Legal Anthropology

Applied legal anthropology touches all aspects of law, especially international human rights, indigenous rights, and intercultural criminal law. Anthropologists serve as expert witnesses in court cases involving human remains, cultural artifacts, and cultural beliefs and practices. Anthropologists with law degrees serve as tribal public defenders and represent tribal governments or other indigenous groups in disputes with national governments. Such disputes may involve natural resources, treaties, sovereign immunity, jurisdiction, zoning, family law, land claims, commercial rights, environmental protection, religious freedom, criminal justice, and contract violation.

Sometimes justice is hard to obtain. In the mid-1990s, investigations began into the U.S. government's intentional exposing of people to radiation during the 1950s and 1960s, including some Inupiat in Alaska, Navajo uranium miners in

Nevada, and Marshall Islanders whose home, Bikini Atoll, is still off limits to them because of nuclear testing there. In one case, anthropologists assisted seventy Inupiat of the original eighty-four subjects who participated in an iodine-131 experiment without their knowledge. The suit against the government called for them to receive health care services to which they otherwise would not have access (www.eh.doe.gov/ohre/roadmap/). A presidential commission established in 1995 to investigate the procedures of the Inupiat study concluded that the amount of iodine-131 that participants in the study were given was within acceptable medical limits and that therefore ". . . the subjects were not harmed. . . . From an ethical perspective . . . aspects of this study, especially the informed consent process, were flawed even by 1950s standards, and thus the Alaskan Natives who participated were wronged" (Department of Defense 2008, 47).

Also in the 1990s, legal anthropologists assisted the Tonggom, Wopkaimin, and other peoples of Papua, New Guinea, in bringing suit against Broken Hill Proprietary (BHP), Australia's biggest mining corporation—and won. For more than a decade, BHP's copper and gold mine had released mine tailings and waste into the headwaters of the Ok Tedi and Fly rivers, polluting the water, killing or driving off subsistence species, and forcing people to relocate. The case drew international attention. In 1996, BHP settled out of court, agreeing to clean up the river, pay affected villages $28.6 million, and close the mine by 2010. In 2002, the company transferred its 52 percent equity in the mine to the newly created Papua New Guinea Sustainable Development Program Company (Ghazi 2004).

◉ CRITICAL THINKING QUESTIONS

What knowledge and skills can legal anthropologists bring to issues of social justice? Why do indigenous peoples need their services?

CHAPTER SUMMARY

Evolutionary Perspectives on Conflict

- In all societies, communities, and families, conflicts may occur over issues of daily life, household responsibilities, or roles within communities. Disputes within communities may be about interpersonal issues or rights to property and other resources. Conflicts may also occur between communities or nations. Such conflicts can lead to protracted antagonisms and even to warfare. There are, therefore, mechanisms to avoid or resolve conflicts. Societies differ in what they consider to be causes of conflict and in how they settle disputes and reestablish peace or harmonious relationships.

- Evolutionary biologists and psychologists study the primate origins of behaviors that help avoid conflict and restore peace after open aggression between animals. One way that conflict is avoided is for subordinate animals to display submission. Postconflict animal reconciliation behavior includes approaching one another, holding out a hand, and embracing to reassure the other animals. Mutual grooming and body contact reduce aggression and promote interpersonal and group stability.

Avoiding Conflict

- In human societies, people develop means of expressing disagreement while avoiding open conflict. Deference to others or stating one's opinion indirectly and politely create social harmony while managing disagreement. Self-control and restraint are positive personality traits that help avoid conflict. Informal sanctions such as teasing, gossiping about, or ostracizing wrongdoers also squelch disruptive behavior. Conflict management may take the form of control of aggressive behavior once it erupts. Peacemakers may intervene when disputes arise.

Witchcraft and Ritual in Conflict Resolution

- In some societies, social mechanisms help prevent conflict or channel aggressive behavior in socially acceptable forms. Beliefs in witchcraft may also channel aggressive impulses and control people's behavior, because angry or aggressive people may either become the target of witchcraft or be accused of being witches.

Patterns of Family and Community Conflict

- Within families, conflicts may erupt over personal preferences and styles of interaction. People may also disagree about household responsibilities, marriage choices, and community involvement. In societies that value property, siblings may compete over inheritance.

- In societies where the stakes of conflict are high, people may function as mediators to resolve disputes before they become deadly. Such conflicts may lead to attacks, counterattacks, and revenge, resulting in killings and blood feuds. Mediators may be appealed to because of their skill as orators and ability to persuade people to come to agreements that are in the interest of the entire community.

Patterns of Conflict Between Groups

- When conflicts erupt between communities, societal mechanisms may develop to negotiate a settlement that avoids or lessens hostility. Although armed aggression and hostilities between groups can occur anywhere, the causes and character of warfare vary among societies. Warfare is least likely and least destructive in nomadic bands. In tribal societies, raiding and warfare may be deadlier and more disruptive. Tribal warfare generally involves relatively few fighters.

- In state societies, warfare has primarily economic and political goals. Indeed, state societies are usually born through warfare and generally depend on armed conflict or other coercion to expand. State societies have standing armies made up of people who are either part-time or full-time specialists. The goals of state warfare are either the total annihilation of the enemy or its submission. In modern warfare, losers are usually permitted face-saving options, so that their losses and public humiliation do not breed deep resentment.

- Despite efforts to develop international mechanisms to resolve disputes peacefully, armed conflicts continue to erupt. Internal disputes and civil wars can damage societies for generations after they have ended. Some governments have limited their military spending, eliminating standing armies altogether, or instituting formal mechanisms for resolving disputes. International organizations sometimes help disputing parties arrive at peaceful reconciliations within countries that have been devastated by civil wars and internal antagonisms.

KEY TERMS

positive sanctions 328	dominance hierarchies 329	peacemakers 330	witchcraft 335
negative sanctions 328	postconflict	deference 331	vengeance 338
informal sanctions 329	reconciliation 329	politeness strategies 331	blood feud 338
formal sanctions 329	conflict avoidance 330	song duels 331	warfare 339

REVIEW QUESTIONS

1. Is aggressive behavior human nature? Are there universal features in all human societies that lead to conflict?

2. How do primates avoid conflict? How do they structure conflict? How do they reconcile following conflict?

3. What are the social contexts of conflict in primate societies? What is the adaptive value of both conflict and conflict avoidance?

4. What are some informal and formal mechanisms of social control in human societies?

5. How do saving face, politeness, apology, and channeled aggression avoid conflict?

6. How are principles of kinship duty and reciprocity involved in both conflict avoidance and aggressive conflict?

7. How can witchcraft function as a system of social control?

8. What are some ethnographic examples of family and community conflict and conflict resolution strategies?

9. How are conflicts between groups different from conflicts within groups? How do patterns of conflict differ between bands, tribes, and states?

10. How does conflict lead to warfare? How can warfare lead to culture change?

myanthrolab EXERCISES

To complete the following exercises and activities, you must log in to www.myanthrolab.com and select your current textbook.

1. In the **Explore** tab of Chapter 13, click on *Video* and watch the slide show on *Native Justice: The Diné Peacemakers*. Complete the short answer exercise that accompanies the slide show.

2. In the **Research Tools** section on the home page, click on the *Research Navigator*™ link and enter the Anthropology database to find relevant and recent scholarly and popular press publications. For this chapter enter the following keywords: *witchcraft, dispute resolution,* and *family violence.*

3. Enter the **MyAnthroLibrary** section on the home page to read more about topics and cultures that are discussed in this chapter. Suggested readings include:

Family Violence by Gerald M. Erchak

Abelam: Giant Yams and Cycles of Sex, Warfare, and Ritual by Richard Scaglion

The surface of the fourth world was unlike the surface of any of the lower worlds. For it was a mixture of black and white. The sky above was alternately white, blue, yellow, and black, just as it had been in the worlds below. But here the colors were of a different duration. As yet there was no sun and no moon; as yet there were no stars.

When they arrived on the surface of the fourth world, the exiles from the lower worlds saw no living thing. But they did observe four great snow-covered peaks along the horizon around them. One peak lay to the east. One peak lay to the south. One peak lay likewise to the west. And to the north there was one peak.

It was now evident to the newcomers that the fourth world was larger than any of the worlds below.

Twenty-three days came and went, and twenty-three nights passed and all was well. And on the twenty-fourth night the exiles held a council meeting. They talked quietly among themselves, and they resolved to mend their ways and to do nothing unintelligent that would create disorder. This was a good world, and the wandering people meant to stay here, it is said.

[Eventually the gods or "Holy People" gave the people instructions about how to prepare themselves to live in the fourth world. The Holy People promised to give them advice and to teach them to live properly.]

Proceeding silently the gods laid one buckskin on the ground, careful that its head faced the west. Upon its skin they placed two ears of corn, being just as careful that the tips of each pointed east. Over the corn they spread the other buckskin, making sure that its head faced east.

Under the white ear they put the feather of a white eagle. And under the yellow ear they put the feather of a yellow eagle. Then they told the onlooking people to stand at a distance.

So that the wind could enter.

Then from the east the white wind blew between the buckskins. And while the wind thus blew, each of the Holy People came and walked four times around the objects they had placed so carefully on the ground. As they walked, the eagle feathers moved slightly. Just slightly. So that only those who watched carefully were able to notice. And when the Holy People had finished walking, they lifted the topmost buckskin. And lo! The ears of corn disappeared.

In their place there lay a man and there lay a woman.

The white ear of corn had been transformed into our most ancient male ancestor [First Man] and the yellow ear of corn had been transformed into our most ancient female ancestor [First Woman].

It was the wind that had given them life: the very wind that gives us our breath as we go about our daily affairs here in the world we ourselves live in. When this wind ceases to blow inside of us, we become speechless. And we die.

In the skin at the tips of our fingers we can see the trail of that life-giving wind. Look carefully at your own fingertips. There you will see where the wind blew when it created your most ancient ancestors out of two ears of corn, it is said.

From Paul Zolbrod, *Diné Bahané: The Navajo Creation Story*, pp. 45–51. © 1984. Reprinted by permission of the University of New Mexico Press.

- What is religion?
- What perspectives do anthropologists take in studying religion?
- What types of spirit entities and powers or forces do people believe in?
- How do religious practitioners reflect their society and culture?
- What are the main types of religious practice?
- What are some psychological, social, and cultural sources and functions of religion?
- How do religions help maintain the social order? How do they both instigate and reflect culture change?

Creation stories from various cultures express different ideas about how people were given life and relate to their physical and social universe. The stories express different worldviews about themselves and their relationships with their environment, other people, and the spirit world. The narrative told by the Diné (or Navajo) describes the physical environment in which the people come to be. It is a world surrounded by four sacred mountains. This environment is also the fourth world in which people now live. The fact that it is the fourth world surrounded by four sacred mountains is no coincidence. Four is the sacred number for the Diné and for most Native Americans. When

religion
Thoughts, actions, and feelings based on belief in the existence of spirit beings and supranormal (or superhuman) forces.

the people emerged into this fourth world, they saw that it was beautiful and well formed. The three previous worlds had also been beautiful and well formed, but the people had made those worlds dangerous and frightening by their own behavior. Because of their lying, adultery, and greed, they had rendered their worlds uninhabitable. Through their own wrongdoings, they created worlds of disorder. Now, arriving in the fourth world, they hoped, as the narrative says, "to do nothing unintelligent," so that they could live in peace and harmony.

The gods, called the "Holy People," created First Man and First Woman out of ears of corn, the most potent and sacred of all Diné symbols of life. These sacred ears of corn, white symbolizing maleness and yellow symbolizing femaleness, came to life through the breath of wind that animates all living things. The narrative is an origin story, explaining why we breathe and why our fingertips have whirls.

The Diné story sets out a physical and moral landscape for the people to live in. They learn the importance of proper behavior, of goodness, so that the inherent harmony of the world can be maintained. Disorder comes through wrong behavior, whereas harmony, balance, and order come through ritual and right thinking. The story ties the people to a specific place, giving explanations for their surroundings and linking them to an ancient and sacred past.

WHAT IS RELIGION?

Religion is thoughts, actions, and feelings based on beliefs in the existence of spirit beings and supranormal (or superhuman) forces. It includes constellations of beliefs and practices about the spirit world and its relationship to everyday existence. Religious beliefs and practices also give people ways to contact spirit beings and forces to show them honor and respect, as well as to invoke their blessings and protection.

Spirits may be thought to inhabit a realm different from our own, or they may be ever-present, although usually unseen. People believe that the spirit world, whether visible or invisible, is connected in some ways to humans, influencing the course of human life and the outcome of human activities. To obtain the help of spirit beings and to harness spirit forces, people perform rituals that convey their desires and intentions.

Although we often speak of the spirit world as "supernatural," this term may be misleading and not fitting for all cultures. People in some cultures believe that the spirit realm is ever-present as part of their natural world and informs their daily lives in significant ways. For them, the spirit world and spirit forces are not distinct from, but rather are intertwined with, everyday life.

Religion includes both beliefs and practices. Beliefs are a people's ideas about the spirit world, the kinds of beings and forces that have spirit power, and the ways in which the universe is created and continues to be. Religions also embody worldviews that teach people ethical values and attitudes. Sacred rituals also dramatize people's beliefs and allow them to actively express those beliefs. Through ritual action and speech, people make contact with the spirit world and manipulate spirit power for their own purposes.

Anthropologists analyze religious beliefs and rituals using etic and emic perspectives, reviewing objective

The "Creation of Adam" shows the bearded figure of God touching the finger of the first man. In the book of Genesis from the Judeo-Christian-Islamic tradition, the first humans are created in the image of God and instructed to "replenish the earth," so that people will live in every habitable place, not one specific locale as in the Diné story. (Michelangelo, "The Creation of Adam," 15-08-1512. Fresco, ceiling (restored), Sistine Chapel, The Vatican, Rome. Photograph © Nippon Television Network Corporation, Tokyo)

Hindu worshipers carry a statue of the elephant-headed god, Ganesha, through the streets of Mumbai, India. Ganesha, the god of wisdom, prosperity, and good fortune, is celebrated in an annual festival.

conditions and subjective experiences. What do people's beliefs and practices mean for them? How do people interpret their world and their experience? How does participating in rituals affect them, and what meanings do they ascribe to the rituals? Also, how are people's religious beliefs and practices consistent with other aspects of their culture? How do people's economies and modes of subsistence influence the meanings and actions of their rituals, for example? How do their political systems or systems of social stratification frame the ways they structure their beliefs about the spirit world?

Variations in religious practices and beliefs sometimes correlate with other aspects of society. In egalitarian, stateless societies, for example, relationships between deities or spirit beings tend to be egalitarian as well. Just as all individuals have more or less equal access to economic resources and social prestige, they also have the potential to acquire spirit powers. In contrast, people in societies with hierarchical social structures are more likely to believe in the existence of a ranked pantheon of deities. The Greek and Roman gods and goddesses are a good example of such a system. Zeus (in Greece) or Jupiter (in Rome) stood at the apex of a pyramidal structure of power. Each was allied with a spouse, Hera and Juno, respectively, with whom they formed a conjugal unit, a reflection of the household structure of ancient Greece and Rome.

Monotheistic religions with their single supreme deity reflect political systems having central supreme leaders—a king or emperor. In the past, rulers of these societies were thought to be divine or to derive their authority directly from a god. Thus, many of the first state societies are referred to as theocracies, literally, governments by god. The relationships of gods and their activities are thus metaphors for ways of life on earth but on a more heroic, larger-than-life scale.

Religious behavior is both practical and symbolic. Performing rituals is doing something to achieve practical results, but these actions also have symbolic meanings. **Religious speech**—invocations, prayers, prophecies, songs of praise, curses—is a powerful means

religious speech
Invocations, prayers, prophecies, songs of praise, and curses that are powerful means of transmitting messages about the world and also creating the world.

These gospel singers illustrate the concept of religious speech.

of transmitting messages about the world, and it creates the world as well. Religious speech attempts to change a state of being, to exert agency or control over people or over events or natural phenomena. Through both speech and action, people express their ideas about causality, about how things happen and how human and other powers affect the world.

Religious beliefs are subject to change and respond to change in the social system, partly because of their underlying ambiguity and mystery. The mystery stems from the impossibility of proof, replaced instead by the certainty of faith. Ambiguity arises in religious speech, in which messages are layered with meanings. These messages must be interpreted and reinterpreted. In reinterpreting religious messages, people refer to their wants and needs to weave together a meaningful philosophy of life.

In what ways does your life philosophy reflect the religious and secular values of your society?

REVIEW ⎯⊙ Religion is thoughts, actions, and feelings based on beliefs in the existence of god(s), spirit being(s), or supernatural force(s). Religious beliefs and practices give people ways to contact such beings or forces, to honor and respect them, and to invoke their blessings and protection. Anthropologists use comparison and cultural relativism to analyze religious beliefs and behaviors. Religions tend to reflect the structure of the societies in which they arise.

SPIRIT BEINGS AND FORCES

Spirit beings and forces have extraordinary, more-than-human, powers. They typically are eternal or indestructible; they know more than an ordinary person can know; and they are able to act in ways that humans cannot. Thus, people seek contact with them to gain their protection and aid. Spirits may have the shape of animals, humans, or other unusual forms and may change their shape at will. Sometimes they imbue inanimate objects with special powers. A supernatural force may be a vague spirit essence that pervades the universe.

Animism and Animatism

One common, nearly universal form that spirit takes is the soul. Souls are the eternal aspect of living things. In some belief systems, such as Judaism, Christianity, and Islam, only human beings have souls. But in many cultures, people believe that animals and plants— all living things—have souls as well. The soul is seen as the animating aspect of living things. It gives life to the body that it inhabits. When the body dies, the soul leaves and exists eternally in some other form or in a nonmaterial state. The belief in souls and the spirit essences of all living things is called **animism.** In some belief systems, what we might think of as inanimate objects may be endowed with spirit essence as well. For example, people with animistic beliefs might ascribe consciousness and personality to a thunderstorm, a tree, or a rock. In some societies, people believe that an impersonal spiritual force exists that can manifest itself in people, animals, or inanimate objects. This belief is sometimes called **animatism.** For example, a person's success or good fortune are signs of one's access to this impersonal force just as one's failures result from the absence of spiritual force.

Gods and Heroes

Some religious traditions have many spirit beings in human form—gods—with specific attributes, powers, and functions. Belief in numerous deities, called **polytheism,** is widespread throughout the world. In Hinduism, with its hundreds of millions of followers, as well as in the belief systems of small subsistence societies numbering in the hundreds, polytheistic spirit worlds are inhabited by multitudes of beings, each with a name, identity, genealogy, history, and domain of influence. In contrast, in **monotheistic religions** people believe in one supreme deity who has powers and knowledge that affect all aspects of life. In addition, there may be other, lesser spirit beings and important mortal heroes as well.

animism
Belief in the existence of souls.

animatism
Belief that all things are endowed with some spirit form or essence.

polytheism
Belief in the existence of numerous deities that have specific attributes, powers, and functions.

monotheistic religions
Belief systems that hold to the existence of one supreme deity who has powers and knowledge that affect all aspects of life.

Ancestors, Ghosts, and Demons

Other types of spirit beings include the spirit forms of deceased ancestors. Ancestral spirits have a particular connection to their living descendants, who honor them through prayer and ritual. In return, the spirits bestow blessings, health, and good fortune on their surviving kin. If people fail to perform the rituals, ancestor spirits can bring illness and misfortune.

After a death in Japan, especially of a man, the eldest son prepares a mortuary tablet that commemorates his father (Morioka 1984). These tablets are kept in a household altar for at least several generations. They are honored and given offerings from time to time in commemorative rituals. Eventually, the tablets of the eldest ancestor may be retired, either buried or broken and discarded. This ritual or ceremony is sometimes referred to as **ancestor worship.** In the past, reflecting Japan's patrilineal descent and patriarchal society, tablets for women usually were discarded after only one or two generations, but tablets for men were kept for a longer time. Today, however, a bilateral principle governs ancestor worship, and mothers and grandmothers are honored along with fathers and grandfathers. Any member of the family, not just the eldest son, can carry out the rituals. These changes reflect shifts in Japanese household composition from extended family to nuclear family forms.

Among the Ju/'hoansi of the Kalahari, ancestral spirits, called *gangwasi,* are thought to cause illness and misfortune. People are wary of their ancestral spirits, avoiding contact with them in the night and hoping to be spared misfortune. They periodically perform dances to prevent ancestral spirits from attacking them and causing harm. Most important is treating people right while they are alive so that their spirit will not seek out offenders to harm them after death.

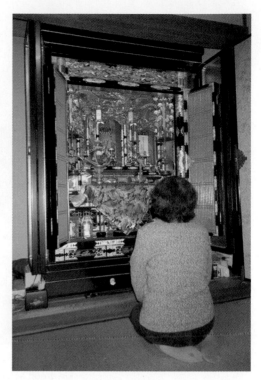

This Japanese woman honors a dead ancestor by presenting offerings at an altar in her home.

The Hopis of Arizona believe that ancestral spirits join the kachinas, powerful beings that bring rain. When people die, their spirits become mist and clouds that return to the people in the form of rain, helping to sustain crops in an arid environment. Hopis view themselves as eternally linked in cycles of life and death, and they pray to and honor their ancestors so that they will be blessed with rain. Representational wooden carvings of spirits, called kachina dolls, are conduits to the spirit world.

In many cultures, people believe that deceased individuals may return or appear in the form of ghosts. Ghosts may have human shape, or they may be only shadows. Ghosts may be welcomed or feared, and they may return to the living to cause mischief or harm or to transmit messages of great importance. In some societies, ghosts are cast as demons. Among New Guinea natives, for example, village compounds must be ritually protected against wandering demons.

> **How are ghosts viewed in American popular culture today?**

Mana, Totems, and Taboos

In addition to or instead of believing in spirit beings, many people believe in the existence of a pervasive spirit power. This power or essence endows people, animals, other living things, and possibly inanimate objects with special qualities or powers. This force has its own name in every culture, but is often referred to as **mana,** from Polynesian languages where it was first described, in the anthropological literature on religion. A belief in mana is a form of animatism. Having mana gives a person special knowledge and power or an object special properties and qualities. Perfectly grown yams may be said to have mana, for example. Spirit powers are sometimes held in talismans or fetishes to give the wearer good luck. A rabbit's foot held or worn for luck, for example, is an expression of animatism.

In some cultures of Australia and the Pacific Northwest of North America, people believe that they are the descendants of spirit beings or ancestors, a belief called **totemism.** Totemic ancestors may have human or animal form. From ancient times, they gave protection or lifesaving advice to human beings in need or in danger. Thus, they are the primordial protectors of the people. Ancestral totems may also be identified as the actual progenitors of the present-day people. In either case, people owe them gratitude and

ancestor worship
Belief in the importance of ancestors as they affect the lives of their survivors, protecting their descendants in return for rituals of honor performed to show them respect.

mana
A force, power, or essence that endows people, animals, other living things, and possibly inanimate objects with special qualities or powers.

totemism
Belief system in which people believe they are descendants of spirit beings.

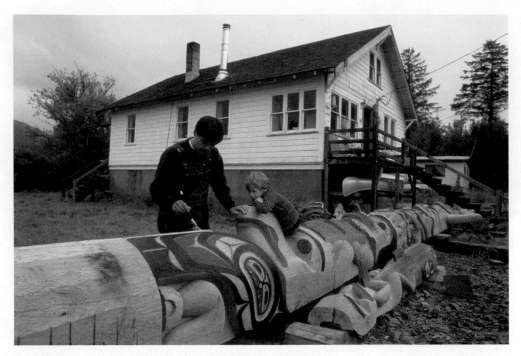

The familiar totem poles of some Pacific Northwest Native American groups depict the record of a kin group and its relationship with its spirit ancestor—in the form of a mammal, bird, or other animal.

respect and perform rituals in their honor so that they will continue to receive protection and guidance.

Totemism celebrates the solidarity of social groups. Australian Aborigines believe that each clan is descended from a specific animal in the mythic past or "the Dreaming" (Hume 2000). At some time in an earlier realm of existence, the mythic animal ancestor was transformed into a human being and continues to be connected to its human descendants. The descendants honor their animal ancestor, or totem, by performing rituals in its honor and by refraining from eating its flesh. The totemic figure functioned to unite Aborigines, who, because of their nomadic lifestyle and dispersed populations, rarely came into sustained contact. Spirit links among people have survival value because they create bonds of mutual acknowledgment, interdependence, and obligations to extend hospitality and share resources.

Spirit forces and beings are dangerous if contacted in the wrong way, in the wrong place, or at the wrong time. Some spirits inhabit particular locales that may be dangerous if entered without spiritual protection. Objects used in rituals may also be dangerous if touched or used when a person is not prepared. Societies that believe in these dangers may have organizations, known as **secret societies,** that control the special places or the use of special objects. For example, among Australian Aborigines and Amazonian Indians, only men may touch special musical instruments or ritual objects. If women come into contact with these objects, they may be seriously harmed or even killed by the spirit forces associated with them. Even to hear the sounds of the music or the singing of the men may be dangerous to women.

Restrictions such as these are called taboos. A taboo object or place is one that can cause harm if contacted or entered. Its danger derives from its power. A dangerous person, object, or place may not be regarded as evil, however, because spirit power in itself is neither positive nor negative. Rather, the use to which the power is put renders it good or bad. Individuals may use their spirit powers to become healers, fortune-tellers, or other ritual practitioners, serving their communities in important ways. Others, however, may seek to acquire spirit powers to do harm.

An example of taboos is seen in rituals surrounding pregnancy and birth. In many cultures, expectant mothers, and sometimes their husbands as well, avoid eating certain foods or engaging in certain kinds of activities. Many of these restrictions are geared toward ensuring a safe pregnancy and easy delivery. Inuit parents were not to tie their belts

secret societies
Organizations that control the use of special objects used in religious rituals.

tight lest the placenta strangle the baby during birth. Haida mothers refrained from eating sticky substances, such as salmon eggs, to ensure a smooth and quick delivery.

Pregnancy taboos symbolize the dangers of pregnancy and birth and the uncertainty of outcomes. Through taboos, people express their fears and their desires to control essentially unpredictable events. In addition, taboos allow people to explain both positive and negative results. If the birth goes well and the baby is healthy, parents can feel that their behavior contributed to the happy occasion. However, if the baby is sickly or dies, parents can find the reason for their misfortune by recalling taboos that they failed to observe.

REVIEW

Spirit beings and forces include gods, ancestors, ghosts, demons, totems, mana, souls, and spirit powers that may be evidenced in good or bad luck. Animism is belief in souls, and animatism is the belief that animals, plants, and inanimate objects are endowed with souls or personalities and have spiritual powers. Some religions are monotheistic (with one god) whereas others are polytheistic (with many gods). In totemism, people trace their descent from animal ancestors and observe ritual taboos to protect the ancestral spirits. Spiritual power, such as mana, may be positive or negative, depending on how it is used. Potentially dangerous or contaminating spiritual power may be managed through secret societies or taboos. Religious rituals and religious speech often are aimed at giving people agency or control over forces and events that affect their lives. Shared religious beliefs and practices also contribute to people's social solidarity.

RELIGIOUS PRACTITIONERS

Most religions have individuals or groups who function as either part-time or full-time specialists or practitioners. Sometimes people receive a calling from the spirit world to become a religious specialist. The calling could be received in a dream, a waking vision, or an omen or sign. Some societies believe that particular individuals inherit spiritual abilities from one generation to the next. In other cases, a person decides to become a religious practitioner because of interests, experiences, or wishes to benefit the community through ritual practice. Some people may be drawn to ritual practice because of its creative and aesthetic qualities that give outlet for artistic expression through music, song, dance, and drama. Religious specialists may enlist others to take the training necessary to become a practitioner. Mediums, healers, shamans, diviners, and priests are all religious practitioners.

Mediums, Diviners, and Healers

Mediums are believed to have special gifts that enable them to make contact with the spirit world and with spirit beings or spirits of the dead. They usually establish a direct relationship with a particular spirit or group of spirits. Through rituals they perform, mediums become conduits or channels between ordinary people and the contacted spirit beings. They often conduct these rituals in a state of trance—an altered state of consciousness in which they are not fully conscious of their surroundings. Trance states can be achieved through various means, including meditation or mental concentration; once in a trance, mediums can pass messages between individuals and members of the spirit world.

Diviners have the power to predict the future through messages and omens they receive and interpret from the spirit world. They use various divination techniques to obtain the spirit's guidance or answers to specific questions or problems. For example, they may recognize patterns or designs that tell a story, as in reading tea leaves or tarot cards. In some African societies, diviners roll chicken bones to read a person's fortune or examine animal entrails to predict a family's best course of action. In some Central American societies, diviners tell fortunes by throwing corn kernels into a bowl and finding meaning in the pattern the kernels make. In North America, native diviners threw fruit pits to read patterns in the way they fell. Diviners may also look at the stars or gaze into water to retrieve omens and warnings.

Healers are religious practitioners who acquire spirit power to heal. They can diagnose the spirit cause of illness and effect cures through the performance of rituals.

How do mediums and diviners practice in your society or community today?

mediums
People having special gifts to make contact with the spirit world, often in a state of trance.

diviners
People with the power to predict the future through messages and omens from the spirit world.

healers
Religious practitioners who acquire spirit power to diagnose the spirit cause of illness and effect cures.

shamans
Part-time religious practitioners who make contact with the spirit world through prayer, ritual, and trance.

priests
Full-time religious practitioners who lead a religious organization and officiate at rituals but are not expected to be able to communicate directly with the spirit world.

In North America, many people heed the advice of "faith healers," some of whom have large followings of enthusiastic believers. Traditional healers usually have some practical knowledge of human anatomy and physiology, pharmacology, and pharmaceutical substances in their environment. Healers may use this practical knowledge in their cures in addition to religious rituals. In some societies, healers may be suspected of sometimes using their control of spirit powers to cause harm rather than to cure illness. As discussed in Chapter 12, beliefs and practices of sorcery or witchcraft constitute powerful sources of social control.

Ritual healers are usually called in to treat a patient when the illness is protracted or life-threatening. The following account, related in 1918 by a Fox woman, describes her experience with a healer called to assist her in the difficult birth of her first child:

> When that woman [the healer] came, she at once boiled some medicine. After she had boiled it, she said: "Let her sit up for a while. You must hold her so that she will not fall over." After I was made to sit up, she spat upon my head; and she gave me the medicine to drink. After she had given me the medicine, she began singing. She started to go out singing and went around the little lodge singing. When she danced by where I was, she knocked on the side. "Come out if you are a boy," she would say. And she would again begin singing. When she danced by she again knocked the side. "Come out if you are a girl," she would say again. After she sang four times in a circle, she entered the lodge. And she gave me medicine to drink. "Now it will be born. She may lie down." Lo, sure enough, my baby was born. (Michelson 1920, 319)

Shamans and Priests

Shamans are part-time religious practitioners who contact the spirit world through ritual, prayer, and trance. They may use masks that represent spirit beings. Shamans are similar to mediums in many respects, except that they may not channel with a particular spirit being. Rather, they enter trance states to receive visions and messages from the spirit realm. Their work tends to be on behalf of the community as a whole. Shamans may also perform healing rituals or rituals seeking spirit protection, advice, and support. Ecstatic experience, whether through trance, visions, or dreams, is central to the way that shamans make contact with the spirit world. Shamanism may be quite ancient in the origins of religions (Goodman 1990).

Some societies have full-time religious practitioners called **priests,** who lead religious organizations and officiate at rituals but are not necessarily expected to be able to communicate directly with gods or the spirit world. The category of priest includes spiritual and ritual leaders of formally institutionalized religions with places of worship, such as churches, mosques, or congregations, including ministers, rabbis, and mullahs, in addition to Roman Catholic or Greek Orthodox priests. Priests work on behalf of their religious organization, as well as their community and its members. Priests often preside at rites of passage, such as those that mark birth, puberty, marriage, and death.

This female shaman, or *mudang,* in Korea is summoning the spirit world to promote harmony, heal, bring messages to the living, or appease the dead.

Religious practitioners include mediums, healers, diviners, shamans, and priests. Mediums enter trance states to communicate between individuals and the spirit world; diviners tell the future or enter trance states to receive omens or advice from the spirit world. Healers use both spiritual and practical means to treat illness. Priests are full-time specialists who work for religious organizations and lead congregations in religious ceremonies and rituals. Unlike shamans, priests are not expected to have spirit power or communicate directly with divine beings.

REVIEW

RELIGIOUS PRACTICE

Religious practices, or **rituals,** are demonstrations of belief, putting belief into action. Rituals may be formal and public with many well-rehearsed participants and performers. They may also be informal and private, carried out by individuals or small groups. Rituals, including those involving religious speech, play a central role in most religions. They are the means by which believers make contact with the gods or spirit world; express honor and respect for spirit beings; obtain blessings, health, prosperity, or success; and achieve particular personal or communal goals. Rituals also can have specific ends, such as purification (spiritual cleansing), sanctification (making something sacred), veneration (worshipping something), or absolution (giving spiritual forgiveness). Individual rituals may be linked together in a ceremonial, a series of interconnected rituals.

Rituals usually involve the visual and performing arts. The aesthetic impact and spiritual meaning of rituals transport participants to a mental, emotional, and spiritual state of being that is different from their ordinary lives. Participants may adorn themselves with special clothing, masks, or face and body painting. They typically employ special objects made with precious metals, or such objects may be carved, painted, or decorated with jewels, feathers, or stone in designs that incorporate religious symbols. Religious art and iconography (the meaning of symbols and design) thus reveal people's aesthetic values. Rituals also involve poetic language and the arts of music, song, and dance, the subjects of Chapter 15.

Sacred and Secular Rituals

Secular life is full of rituals or ritualized activities, but these are not the same as sacred rituals. **Sacred rituals** are dedicated to the spirit realm and the expression of religious

rituals
Activities, including religious speech, ceremonies, and behaviors, that are demonstrations of belief.

sacred rituals
Activities, places, or objects that are connected to the spirit realm and are imbued with power.

The Nuna and Bwa peoples of Burkina Faso use wooden painted animal masks and dances to make the spirit world come alive, as the butterfly dancer shows here.

Devotee offering prayer flags in Thimphu, Bhutan. The flags carry Buddhist sacred texts and symbols.

faith. Secular rituals may also be important culturally. For example, secular holidays such as Independence Day (in the United States) and Canada Day (in Canada) are times to display national symbols such as flags, sing national songs, and hear patriotic speeches. Sporting events may also be marked by ritualized protection, such as wearing team insignia or colors and cheering. The players may practice personal rituals to bring success, such as wearing good-luck gear in the game. These behaviors and attitudes involve magical thinking not unlike practices associated with religious beliefs, but their purpose is secular rather than spiritual.

In many societies, seasonal or annual rituals with both sacred and secular elements are held to celebrate the earth's bounty. Celebrations serve both as a thanksgiving for the past year's plants and animals and as a request to the spirits for renewed generation and continued supplies. These are examples of **rites of renewal,** also called rites of intensification.

Prayer and Sacrifice

Prayer is both a private and a public ritual. Through **prayer,** believers transmit messages to the spirit beings or to particular deities or ancestors. Prayers are meant to honor the spirits, ask favors of them, or win future blessings. Some religions emphasize the memorization and correct verbatim repetition of prayers. Without correct recitations, prayers may not be effective. Other religions permit or encourage private prayers that individuals make up as they pray.

Believers also transmit messages to the spirit realm through the **sacrifice** of offerings that honor spirit beings by giving up something important. Offerings may consist of foods that the deities are thought to prefer or valuable objects. People may also fast, refrain from sleep, or subject themselves to some kind of ordeal as a kind of sacrifice. Offerings may also include animals given in rituals of blood sacrifice in which the animals are slaughtered. Societies where people keep domesticated animals may use their stock in sacrificial offerings.

Blood sacrifice centers on the killing of a valuable domesticated animal, but some societies practiced human sacrifice. Perhaps the best-known example was the human sacrifice performed by the Aztecs in central Mexico in the fifteenth and sixteenth centuries. Aztecs believed that the sun god (also the war god), called Huitzilopochtli, needed to be fed so that he would have the energy to travel across the sky from sunrise to sunset every day. He was nourished on human blood from daily sacrifices. This practice eventually contributed to the downfall of the Aztec Empire: As the need for more sacrificial victims increased, the priesthood demanded sacrifices from defeated groups forcibly incorporated into the expanding Aztec state. Those groups thus became even more hostile toward the Aztec state and aided the Spanish invasion of the Aztec Empire in the early sixteenth century.

rites of renewal
Rituals performed with the goal of renewing the bounty of the earth.

prayer
Religious speech or thought through which believers transmit messages to spirit beings.

sacrifice
Offerings made to spirit beings to show gratitude and honor.

In the Sun Dance, young North American Plains Indian warriors like the one pictured here sacrificed small parts of their bodies in honor of their spirit protectors.

CASE STUDY

Making Contact with the Spirit World

Religious practice includes rituals that enable people to contact the spirit world. These rituals may be personal and private or public communal demonstrations of belief. Prayer is the most personal method of attempting to contact the spirit world. Through prayer, believers convey their thoughts, feelings, hopes, and worries. The purpose of prayer is both cathartic and practical. The cathartic element comes about from the relief that people feel in the act of prayer, allowing themselves to express feelings and fears. Prayer is also aimed at achieving practical goals such as healing an illness in oneself or family members, gaining prosperity, or obtaining spiritual knowledge. Prayer attempts to establish a relationship with the spirit world through words and thoughts. But how can people know if their messages have been received? In some belief systems, a spirit being might communicate directly with a believer through visual or auditory contact. In others, a person might receive a symbolic or mysterious message that would have to be interpreted. Such messages might occur in dreams, visions, signs, or omens that are so obscure or mundane that a specialist has to interpret them.

Certain religious practitioners specialize in seeking out and deciphering messages from the spirit realm. They may do this for an entire community, or they may interpret signs or omens for individuals. For example, oracles have skills that enable them to understand the hidden meanings of ordinary objects and patterns. Oracles employ their skills in response to questions. They may interpret past events or advise about future options. For example, a parent might request advice about whether a child's marriage will be favorable; a person might wonder whether a dwelling he or she wants to build is in a location that will bring health or misfortune; or someone might ask whether a visit will turn out well. Oracles are not consulted lightly. Their advice is sought when danger and disruption threaten social relations or familial or community stability.

Once consulted, oracles use their spiritual gifts to foresee the future. They might do this by entering a state of trance or altered consciousness that allows them to get in touch with another realm of existence and meaning. Oracles may also use techniques of divination, reading the signs ordinary objects make. Some oracles cut open sacrificed animals such as goats or chickens to see whether the form or color of internal organs convey positive or negative messages.

Although divination may appear to lead to random results, successful oracles are intimately familiar with their clients' circumstances and have keen understanding of social networks and relationships. The actions people take as a result of an oracle's advice, therefore, fit well with accustomed and appropriate behavior consistent with community norms.

In some societies, ordinary people may make direct contact with the spirit world through trance or heightened awareness of the spirit realm. People may acquire this ability spontaneously and without training. Messages or visions may appear to them while awake or sleeping. They may find objects that have special meaning and can be used for protection and "good luck." These objects may appear mundane but are representations of spirit contact.

The most direct form of communication with the spirit realm is through possession in which a spirit being invades a person's body, taking over some of that person's physical and cognitive functions. The spirit may then speak through the person's mouth, imparting messages or simply expressing a state of being in an unknown language. In some belief systems, spirit possession happens spontaneously whereas a person in other systems may consciously seek it out. However initiated, the experience can be both fearful and cathartic, from the close contact with extraordinary power. The experience is transformative, changing a person's sense of self.

In addition, people in many indigenous societies who participate in rituals are thought to be in close contact with spirit powers. They may be privileged to understand and partake of a realm of knowledge outside ordinary experience. For example, when dancers put on costumes and masks that represent spirit beings, they are not merely impersonating the spirits but they actually become transformed into those beings, even if only temporarily.

PEARSON
myanthrolab

Explore more at
www.myanthrolab.com

puberty rites
Rituals performed to mark the passage of an individual from childhood to adulthood; also called initiation rites.

funerary rites
Rituals performed to mark a person's death and passage to the afterworld.

As an ethnographer, how might you describe a puberty rite, funerary rite, or other rite of passage that you have observed?

Rites of Passage

As discussed in Chapter 5, people in most societies perform rituals to celebrate socially significant transitions in an individual's life cycle. Such rites of passage are typically conducted to mark birth, puberty, marriage, and death. Rituals may also mark other aspects of the life cycle, such as naming or initiation into an association. According to anthropologist Arnold van Gennep (1961), rites of passage ritualize three aspects of change in life status: separation, transition, and reincorporation. That is, individuals separate from their families, learn new knowledge and skills, and return to their communities as new people. Let us apply this model to two rites of passage: puberty rites and funerary rites.

Puberty Rites. Van Gennep's model can be applied to **puberty rites,** also called initiation rites, which celebrate the transition from childhood to adulthood. In some cultures, puberty rites are held for only girls or only boys; in others, both boys and girls receive ritual recognition. The Jewish and Christian faiths have rituals that mark a child's growth and maturation. The Jewish bar mitzvah (for boys) and bat mitzvah (for girls) incorporate the child into the adult community of believers. In the Christian ceremony of confirmation, children pledge themselves to their faith and join the congregation of their own volition. Children are usually around 10 or 11 years old when they are confirmed, an age associated with cognitive maturation. In some Christian denominations, christening marks religious as well as social birth, baptism consecrates the person in the faith, and confirmation welcomes the individual into the community of believers. The Western Apaches of New Mexico and the Sukus of Zaire conduct elaborate ceremonies when girls and boys, respectively, reach puberty (see the Case Study).

Funerary Rites. Funerals, or **funerary rites,** mark the final stage of life and are usually solemn. Death rituals serve purposes both for the living and the dead. According to many belief systems, the proper performance of a funeral allows the soul of the deceased to depart in peace. At death, the soul, which is the activating, invigorating, life-giving aspect of a person, leaves the body and eventually travels to the afterworld. Usually, though, the soul does not make its final journey until after the funeral. If the funeral is not properly conducted, the soul may never be fully released. It may hover near the living or wander aimlessly, possibly causing mischief and harm.

Hindu funeral rites in India end in an above ground cremation of the deceased on a funeral pyre.

After a death, relatives or hired specialists usually cleanse, decorate, and dress the body in special clothes. After a set number of days, the funeral takes place. Cultures vary widely in the degree of elaboration of funerals and the amount of time spent on them. For example, foragers spend less time and resources on funerals than people in settled populations. In some cultures, funerals are a time for the display of solidarity or interdependence among kin. For example, Mohawk funerals were arranged and conducted not by members of the deceased's own clan and moiety but by people belonging to the opposite moiety. Mohawks thought that close relatives of the deceased were too overcome by grief to be bothered with funeral details; the exchange of roles also symbolized interdependence, unity, and societal balance. In some societies, the treatment of the dead depends upon characteristics such as gender, age, and status. Among the Turkana pastoralists of Kenya, people have different burial sites (Broch-Due 2000, 176, 178–179). A married man is

Cave art like this from Acacus National Park, Libya, may have expressed magical beliefs. The ancient painters drew pictures of animals that they wanted to hunt.

buried in his household's goat corral at the center of his homestead. This placement symbolizes his role as the head of household and emphasizes his central economic contributions. Married women are buried in their night huts, the dwelling where they conceived and gave birth to most of their children, emphasizing their roles as mothers. Children, teenagers, and unmarried adults are not buried but rather their bodies are left outside the borders of the camp, in the bush to the west, the direction of "badness." Finally, in stratified societies, the burials of high-status and wealthy individuals are more elaborate than those of commoners. The deaths of high status people are ritually commemorated for longer periods of time.

CASE STUDY

Puberty Rites Among the Apache and the Suku

The Western Apaches associate girls' puberty with themes of fertility and power. The ritual occasioned by a girl's first menstruation, or menarche, is thought to benefit both her and her entire community (Basso 1970). The name of the ritual, *nai'es*, or "preparing her," "getting her ready," signifies one of its themes. It readies the pubescent girl for adulthood and motherhood. Preparations for the ceremony, always held in the summertime, begin immediately after menarche. The girl's parents choose a woman as sponsor for their daughter. The sponsor must not belong to the girl's matrilineal clan or that of her father. Thereafter, the sponsor and the girl's parents establish a lasting reciprocal bond, aiding one another as if they were kin.

The *nai'es* ceremony is a public event that everyone in the community attends. It begins shortly after sunrise, a time considered spiritually powerful. The rite consists of eight phases, each highlighting a different theme or activity believed to endow the girl with spiritual and material benefits. In the first phase, she dances on a public dance ground to attract supernatural powers from a deity known as Changing Woman, a symbol of fertility and benevolence. Apaches believe that the girl is transformed into Changing Woman and acquires her qualities and powers during puberty rites.

The next to last phase is one of "blessing her." The young girl and her sponsor dance in place and are blessed by each person at the ceremony.

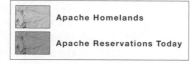

Apache Homelands

Apache Reservations Today

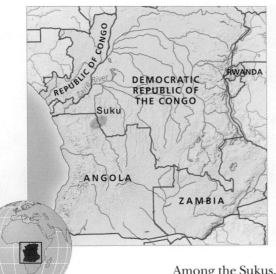

Anyone may request aid from the powers of Changing Woman that reside in the girl. Basso (1970, 68) recorded specific requests made at one rite, including:

> To have a good crop of corn and beans
> To make my sick wife get better
> My cattle, to get fat for sale time
> To cure my daughter
> Rain
> My son in Dallas learning to be a barber, not get into any trouble

The ritual ends when the girl shakes out the buckskin blanket on which she has been dancing and then throws it toward the east, the sacred direction of the rising sun, and then toward each of the other three cardinal directions. The spiritual powers of Changing Woman remain in the girl's body for four more days during which time she can cure illness or bring rain.

Among the Sukus, a farming people of southwestern Congo, boys traditionally undergo a circumcision rite in groups when they are between 10 years and 15 years old (Kopytoff, 1961). The ritual takes place in the summertime, the dry season. Following their circumcision, the boys are taken to a ceremonial hut outside the village, where they remain for weeks. In the past, the seclusion lasted months; today, it is shortened so that the boys can return to school in September. During the summer, the initiates are taught ritual songs and dances and receive rough physical and verbal treatment from the elder men who are charged with the boys' training. At the end of seclusion, the boys go to the river to cleanse themselves and put on new clothing. They take new names by which they will be known

Explore more at
www.myanthrolab.com

henceforth, and return to the village, where relatives and neighbors greet them joyously. The boys have become men. They have learned their superior status to women and uninitiated boys, and have developed ties of loyalty and camaraderie with the other initiates.

In addition to marking the departure of the deceased, funerals serve to underscore family solidarity and allow for people's expression of sorrow and loss. Funerals are usually followed by a period of mourning during which close relatives of the deceased may wear special clothing, eat or avoid eating certain foods, refrain from engaging in some activities, and act out their grief in culturally prescribed ways. The duration of the mourning period varies widely. In some patriarchal cultures, widows may be expected never to remarry.

Healing or Curing

In every culture, people have theories about health maintenance, causes of disease, and strategies for treatment. In many cultures, health is thought of as a state of harmony or balance. Health depends on the orderly functioning of a person's body, a person's relations with other people, the environment in which a person lives, and the spirit beings and forces with which a person interacts. When this balance is disturbed, illness and misfortune may follow.

Most people make a distinction between illnesses with natural causes and those caused by spirit beings or forces. Natural illnesses include minor aches and pains, accidents, and transitory ailments such as the common cold. These ailments are typically treated with natural remedies, such as medicinal plants and animal or mineral substances. If problems persist or worsen, spiritual causes may be suspected that call for ritual diagnosis and treatment. Patients then seek the aid of religious specialists who can diagnose the cause and recommend or perform the cure. Diagnosis may be achieved through divination or revelation in a dream or vision. Spirit causes can include soul loss, object intrusion, spirit possession, or the violation of taboos.

Many Hispanic and Latino people living in North, Central, and South America believe that illness may be caused by the sudden departure of a person's soul, a condition known as *susto*. Because the soul is the activating, life-giving part of a person, soul loss is obviously a serious, potentially fatal, illness. Soul loss may cause fearfulness, listlessness, loss of appetite, loss of interest in social activities, and a general lack of enthusiasm and vitality (Rubel 1977). *Susto* is usually triggered by sudden fright resulting from natural disasters, such as earthquakes or thunderstorms, car accidents, or emotional shocks, such as the sudden and unexpected death of a loved one. In treating *susto,* a specialist, with the help of spirit messages from dreams or visions, is able to locate the missing soul and coax it back into the patient, thus effecting a cure.

Object intrusion may be the diagnosis when a person experiences a sudden, localized pain in some part of the body. It is believed that a spirit, witch, or malevolent person somehow shot a foreign object into the patient's body, causing pain and distress. The object may have a specific shape, such as a pebble, grain of sand, feather, or animal tooth, or it could be an amorphous substance or liquid. The specialist ritually extracts the foreign object by "cupping" (pressing with the hands) or by sucking at the site of the pain. After the object is extracted, it is ritually disposed of to prevent further harm.

Spirit possession may be welcomed as a positive experience or spiritual gift or as evidence of faith in some religions. In other religions, it is considered a symptom of illness. In all societies with this belief, signs of spirit possession commonly include convulsions or loss of muscular control, erratic and rapid changes in mood, or insomnia. People possessed by spirits seek treatment aimed at removing the spirit or enticing it to leave the person's body. Techniques of exorcism range from cajoling, bargaining with, threatening, or punishing the spirit to make it leave.

In Korea, women are most commonly the targets of spirit possession. When such a diagnosis is made, a shaman, also usually a woman, entreats the spirit to leave the afflicted person. The shaman gives offerings and promises that the patient will, in the future, erect a shrine in the spirit's honor and furnish it periodically with food and drink. Spirits choose to possess women who experience tension in their households, usually from conflicts over their roles as dutiful daughter, wife, and mother. These women may feel burdened by excessive demands, and spirit possession may be an outlet for them to express frustration about their life circumstances, as well as a means of extracting themselves from their daily burdens (Harvey 1979; Kendall 1984). The woman is not blamed for her predicament, but other members of her household may be held responsible for her unhappiness.

In Haiti, both men and women may be possessed. Male spirits generally possess women and female spirits possess men. The spirits are attracted to their targets by physical or personality characteristics. To persuade the spirit to leave the body, the afflicted person may agree to establish a lifelong conjugal relationship with the spirit. In some cases, a formal marriage ceremony is performed between the patient and the possessing spirit. Thereafter, a separate bed is kept to which the patient retires for one or two nights each week for conjugal visits with the spirit spouse (Lewis 1989).

Religious beliefs, such as spirit possession, allow for emotional release. Brazilian practitioners of macumba, which combines West African, Roman Catholic, and Native American beliefs and practices, enter a trance induced by a deity or *orisha,* a Yoruba term. In large public gatherings held several times a week, spirit mediums are serially possessed by four different deities. These include the Old Black Slave, the Indian, and two trickster deities, the Child and Eshu, a Yoruba trickster figure. In the macumba belief system, spirits possess people to impart advice and protection to the mediums as well as to their clients. Clients seek help making decisions or finding solutions for problems of illness, social tension, emotional distress, or difficulties such as unemployment. But possession also provides mediums with an outlet for behavior that would otherwise be deemed inappropriate. When possessed by "the child," for example, adults may act silly, play with toys, perform pranks, giggle for no reason, and express childish exuberance in other ways. It has been suggested (Lewis 1989) that, through the ecstatic experience, people give vent to their frustrations in a socially channeled and acceptable form. They are able to air their grievances in a way that does not disrupt or undermine the social order. Lewis (1989) has suggested that spirit possession and other ecstatic experiences are more common among women and marginalized men in stratified societies because powerless people may use the messages received from the spirit world to validate their claims for

spirit possession
Belief that spirits can enter a body and take over that person's thoughts and actions.

recognition and autonomy. Through these experiences, they can bring attention to themselves and make their voices heard. However, their frustrations are also contained because they are expressed in a socially acceptable, albeit unusual, form.

A study of the recent emergence of spirit possession episodes among Maasai women in Tanzania analyzes these experiences as responses to fundamental changes in Maasai social and economic life, especially as it affects women's roles (Hodgson 1997). The Maasai have an economy centered on the care of large herds of cattle. In the past, both men and women had rights to cattle and participated in decisions about their care and about their disposal as gifts in marriage exchanges and other ceremonial contexts. However, with the increasing focus on individual ownership and control of resources and on the growing market potential of cattle in the modern economy, women have gradually lost their rights to contribute to economic life because colonial and postcolonial government authorities have favored men's participation. Gender roles have become more rigid, disallowing women from many of the positive contributions that they have made in the past. As a consequence of British colonial influences during the span of the twentieth century, continued and compounded after independence by the Tanzanian government, incidents of spirit possession grew steadily. The Maasai themselves see this as a relatively recent phenomenon. In their view, foreign (nonlocal) spirits invade the target, causing a variety of initial symptoms including ". . . headaches, fevers, burning sensations, general listlessness and apathy, lack of appetite and insomnia. Later symptoms include wailing, shaking, thrashing, fits, and nightmares" (Hodgson 1997, 114). Most of the victims are women of childbearing age.

Through spirit possession, Maasai women enact their critique of changes to the core of indigenous culture that adversely affect their roles in their households and villages. In addition, women who are afflicted by spirits seek cures through Christian baptism and remain healthy by participating in group meetings with other victims. Christian baptism can, in this context, also be seen as a rejection of dominant male norms because men in particular have converted to Islam in the last century. As Hodgson concludes, "Orpeko [spirit possession] has emerged and spread alongside a particular historical, political-economic conjuncture between the increasing pressures and alienation produced by the intensifying economic, political, and social disenfranchisement of women, and the alternative possibilities for female community and solidarity provided by the Christian missions" (1997, 124–25). Although Christianity is itself founded in patriarchal cultures, Maasai women can at least find refuge through its "foreignness" and voice their opposition to changes in their lives.

> **How can spirit-caused illnesses give people outlets for expressing their needs for order, balance, and security in their lives? How do healers address those needs?**

Illness may result when a person commits some ritual transgression. For example, people become ill if they fail to adhere to taboos, trespass on territory protected by spirit beings, or come in contact with powerful ritual objects. To be cured, the patient needs to undergo purification and ritual rebalancing. Most spirit causes of disease are metaphors for imbalance or disorder.

Religious, ritual, and practical approaches to illness and health go hand in hand, even in societies with medical treatment models based on modern science. Spiritual and magical treatments are especially effective if people believe in them at the same time as other factors are at work, such as the use of pharmaceuticals, the therapeutic effects of receiving treatment, and the curative passage of time. A critical factor in the efficacy of ritual treatments is the patients' psychological state and beliefs. Patients become the center of attention of their family and community and benefit psychologically from the knowledge that people care about them and want them to recover. The patient's belief in the healer, whether shaman or physician, and in the treatment also affect the outcome of the cure.

Magic and Witchcraft

In addition to spirit causes of illness, witchcraft (also called sorcery) may be suspected in cases of illness, death, or misfortunes such as crop failure or infertility. Witches are people who employ spirit powers to cause harm to others, the opposite of healers. They are usually thought to be motivated by anger, jealousy, or simply the desire to see other people suffer. Their targets may be people with whom they have quarreled, but they may also harm someone randomly. As discussed in Chapter 12, witchcraft is also used as a form of social control and a means of achieving social justice. It is effective partly because people believe in it. For example, the literature cites many cases of healthy young people sickening and dying upon learning that a sorcerer has placed a curse on them.

IN THEIR OWN VOICES

Macumba, Trance and Spirit Healing

In these excerpts from the film Macumba, Trance and Spirit Healing, *two practitioners talk about their feelings when possessed by macumba orishas: the Old Black Slave, the Indian, and the Child. Moisir, a lawyer, and his daughter Beje, a schoolteacher, have been participating in macumba ceremonies several times each week for about ten years. In these group rites, dozens of mediums become possessed by four different spirits in succession. The mediums can then receive messages from the spirit world, giving advice to people who are sick, depressed, or in need. The experiences of Moisir and Beje reflect their direct contact with the spirit world, a contact that gives them emotional release and a prestigious role as healer or adviser in their community.*

MOISIR: Coming out of Senior Tupan (the Indian), my guide is annoyed, then I fall to the floor on the knees with one inside the other. He beats the floor twice with the hand opened and three times with the hand closed. They are strong blows, even violent enough to injure the hand. With this the recovery is complete.

BEJE: I feel that weight. Such a heavy weight. That once I am on my knees, as much as I want to, I can't get up. It's like I'm carrying something on my shoulders. Although the possession of the Old One is easy, coming out of it is a horrible thing. I think my head will leave my body. I begin to feel weak. Now, the Children are another story; they just say goodbye. With the Indian, the entrance and departure are equal. We feel tired to a degree but with a rested head. I have the impression of it being a little like a catharsis, you know, you get everything bad out and bring in a great deal of peace and tranquility.

MOISIR: The possession of the Old Black leaves the person very well. In spite of it being slow and difficult for the medium, it leaves the person feeling very well afterwards. Possession by the Old Black makes me feel very differently from the one by the Indian. In the possession of the Old Black, instead of feeling vibrations in the upper region, I feel it in both of my legs. My legs begin to get cold and a kind of pain comes into the knee and ends up knocking me on the floor. Upon feeling knocked down on the floor, I am nearly unconscious. I don't have the ability to reason, to talk for myself, to know people. I have a certain lack of consciousness in my work as the Old Black.

BEJE: The two possessions are totally different, not at all similar. For example, with the Indian, my hand begins to tremble, tremble, it keeps trembling, trembling, trembling until I feel the vibrations and fall to the knees. With the Old Black, I don't feel anything. Bam, bam, I'm on the floor.

MOISIR: As for coming out of the Old Black, it is very difficult. It really hurts when he leaves the medium. After, you feel a pleasant sensation as if you've come out of a sauna. You feel very tranquil, serene, without pain or preoccupations.

I don't like to call these "consultations" because we are not doctors. We simply give advice as to what people should do to better their spiritual and material lives. They look for jobs and they don't know what to do with all this desperation we are experiencing today. So we raise their morale. The Old Blacks have this objective, they are very much alive in material worlds.

Explore more at
www.myanthrolab.com

From *Macumba, Trance and Spirit Healing*, 1984. Written, produced, and directed by Madeleine Richeport. Richeport Films. Distributed by Filmakers Library, New York. © 1984. Reprinted by permission of Madeleine Richeport-Haley.

CRITICAL THINKING QUESTION

What are some emotional and social benefits to Macumba practices for the participants?

Witches employ different forms of magic to produce a specific and connected result. **Imitative magic,** for example, operates on the principle that "like causes like" or that "life imitates art." Thus, depictions and enactments of harmony may predispose a community toward harmony. Manipulating drawings or replicas of individuals may cause good or harm to come to those individuals in life. Witches may use imitative magic by cursing or damaging images or objects that represent their targets.

A practice known as *couvade* is an example of benign imitative magic. In Amazonian cultures, men leave the village when their wives are about to give birth, retiring to the forest. There they imitate the actions of women in labor. They may clutch their abdomens, writhe in pain, and scream out as though in physical distress. These actions are intended to attract evil spirits who lurk about in hopes of attacking newborns. These spirits are lured to the men, allowing the expectant mother to give birth in safety.

Contagious magic operates on the principle that positive and negative qualities can be transferred through proximity or contact, like an infection. Thus, one can become more sanctified or blessed by touching something holy. In pre-Christian Europe, contagious magic was used as a palliative for pain. The cure for a toothache, for example, was to nail

imitative magic
Magic that operates on the principle of "like causes like."

contagious magic
Magic that operates on the principle that positive and negative qualities can be transferred through proximity or contact.

a lock of one's hair to an oak tree, known for its strength, and then to pull one's head away. The pain of the toothache passed through the hair to the tree, where it remained. Gaining power or immunity by touching or wearing objects made powerful or immune through ritual, such as amulets or shrunken heads, are also examples of contagious magic. Witches use contagious magic by secretly collecting a victim's nail clippings, hair, urine, or excrement and saying a spell over it to harm their target.

In some cultures, witches are thought to sprinkle harmful substances in people's food or drink, on their bodies while they sleep, or along the thresholds of their houses. People may believe that witches are capable of extraordinary physical feats, making things appear or disappear, transforming themselves into animals to lurk near a victim's house, or transporting themselves great distances in an instant.

Witchcraft may be a vehicle for the conscious or unconscious expression of anger and envy. For example, patterns of witchcraft accusations may follow lines of social tensions. Among the Cewas of Zimbabwe, accusations of witchcraft are usually preceded by quarrels, especially among matrilineal kin (Marwick 1967). Cewa society has formal mechanisms for airing and resolving disputes between matrilineal groups but not within them. When conflict arises between members of the same matrilineal group, accusations about witchcraft may emerge as outlets.

> **Do you practice magic or magical thinking in your daily life? Are there principles or practices in a religion in your society that could be understood as magic?**

Thus, beliefs in witchcraft are also expressions of people's fears, revulsions, and suspicions about the unusual behavior of others and about the sources or causes of misfortunes. It is also an expression of people's desires and intentions in situations over which they have no direct control. Because of the secrecy of witchcraft, very little is known about its actual frequency. However, magic is not confined to societies with witchcraft. All religions incorporate principles or practices that can be understood as magic.

REVIEW Religious practices include ritual, prayer, and sacrifice—ways of mediating between people and their spirit world. Rituals, both sacred and secular, may include rites of renewal or intensification, **calendric rituals,** and rites of passage. Rituals are also used in curing ceremonies for illnesses with spirit causes, such as soul loss, object intrusion, spirit possession, or the violation of taboos. Imitative magic or contagious magic may be used in curing ceremonies and in other contexts, such as the couvade. Witchcraft or sorcery, which has complex social and psychological functions, also involves the use of magic.

THE ORIGINS AND FUNCTIONS OF RELIGION

It is impossible to know when or where religious beliefs first appeared in human societies. Archaeologists have discovered ancient human burials and can infer ritual practices that may have had religious meaning, such as the use of red ochre, grave goods, caches of ritual objects, and reliquaries or shrines. But we cannot know what was in the minds of those ancient peoples. Did they have some feeling of community and family ties that made them want to memorialize the burial places of their kin? Or did they have some beliefs in an eternal soul that made them want to give their relatives a respectable interment? Did they include grave goods with the burial so that the deceased could use them in an afterlife? Possible evidence of religious practices also comes from ancient cave paintings and rock paintings discovered in France, Spain, southern Africa, and Australia (Peregrine 2003). Most of the paintings in these venues are of animals. Why?

Explaining the World

People often turn to their religion to seek explanations for events whose causes seem unknown or uncontrollable. Their beliefs help them gain some sense of control over what is ultimately unexplainable, unpredictable, and uncontrollable. People may wonder why their efforts are sometimes successful and sometimes not, why the same effort on different occasions may lead to a positive outcome and sometimes not. Why are some hunting expeditions successful but others fail? Why are some babies born healthy but others are sickly? Why do people die? Through ritual, people attempt to impose order and control over the outcomes of their efforts. Through ritual, they appeal to spirit forces to aid them in their endeavors and to ensure successful outcomes and to avoid misfortune.

calendric rituals
Ceremonies performed at specific times during the year, for example, agricultural rituals performed for planting, growing, and harvesting crops.

The explanatory power of religious beliefs also helps people understand why the world is the way it is, why the earth has the shape it has, why the animals and plants have the form they have, and why people look and act the way they do. In most religions, there are thought to be creator or transformer deities who gave the world and all the creatures in it their present shape. These creator deities may also be responsible for imparting knowledge to people, teaching them how to plant, hunt, and organize their social life. They may be responsible for the origin of kinship groupings and of political structure. They may be responsible for setting out the kind of work that people do, the roles that men and women fill, and the values and ethics that people live by. In this way, religious beliefs are not only explanatory but also serve to legitimate a particular social or political system. For example, social inequality may be explained as part of a divine plan. A loved one's death may be explained as god's will.

Science and technology serve many of the same functions of explaining, predicting, and attempting to control the world. In science, however, the underlying premises about cause and effect are different. The scientific approach is based on empirical observation or modeling of effects that are believed to have physical causes. Religious interpretations of observations are based on the belief that ultimate causes are spiritual processes and forces.

Solace, Healing, and Emotional Release

Religious faith provides psychological support in times of anxiety and stress, and religious practices can be emotionally therapeutic for individuals and groups. Confession of wrongdoings enables people to express their remorse, shed their guilt, and feel rehabilitated in their own eyes, in the eyes of their community, and in the eyes of the deities who may see and judge their actions and bestow forgiveness or mercy. Psychological functions of religion may be seen, for example, in visionary experiences or spirit quests. The profound emotional catharsis that can result from prayer, participation in rituals, and contact with the spirit world may have a healing effect by comforting a sufferer, releasing tension and worry.

Social Cohesion

Religious beliefs and practices often function to support cohesive communities. Most rituals involve, in addition to individuals, their family, wider kinship grouping, and social networks that connect them to others. Some rituals, such as seasonal or annual celebrations, unite an entire local population or tribal group.

Religious beliefs and practices can further function to justify the existing social order. Relationships among deities may reflect the sociopolitical nature of the human society. In stratified societies, the leader (whether chief, emperor, or king) may be thought to be a descendant of the divinity, endowed with divine power, or chosen directly by the deities. In the Polynesian chiefdoms, central and southern African kingdoms, European monarchies, and the Inca Empire, the head of state was thought to rule by divine right.

Teachings conveyed by spirits, especially in stories of creation and transformation, also legitimate the existing social order. Gender roles, for example, and the relations between women and men may be mandated through divine teachings or modeled through the relationships of male and female deities. For example, in the Hindu pantheon of deities, gods and goddesses have important and powerful roles and are equally as likely to be worshipped by believers. However, married and unmarried goddesses have strikingly different personalities. When married, goddesses are nurturing, benevolent, and trustworthy; when unmarried, they are aggressive, dangerous, and unpredictable.

In contrast, Diné **cosmology**—a belief system concerning the origin and nature of the universe—presents many deities as interdependent and complementary male and female pairs. First Man and First Woman are important creator and transformer deities. Twilight Man and Twilight Woman and Dawn Man and Dawn Woman are deities of the daytime cycle. Although they play different roles, male and female deities have similar powers, personalities, and effects on the lives of humans.

Social Control

Rituals often function as formal and informal mechanisms of social control. In some stratified societies, codified criminal and civil laws, judicial processes, and punishments

cosmology
Religious worldview of a people, including beliefs about the origin of the world, the pantheon of deities that exist, and their relationships to the spirit realm.

What do texts in a religion with which you are familiar teach about gender roles and relationships? What social order do those teachings tend to support?

or penal sanctions are based on religious doctrines, customs, or texts. The function of social control can also be subtle, however. In some cultures, for example, the time of puberty is marked by role reversals in which socially disapproved behavior is permitted briefly in ritual context. Amish teenagers completing high school are permitted to drink beer and have noisy parties before settling down to a serious and devout life, for example. Similarly, central African teenagers are permitted to act in ways considered deviant— publicly speaking obscenities or acting lewd. They may also engage in gender reversals, boys dressing and acting like girls and girls mimicking the behavior and language of boys. Such ritualized permission to act inappropriately may temporarily ease tensions in societies where norms of proper behavior are strictly followed. They also serve to highlight social values through the transgression of norms.

Economic Adaptation

Another function of religion is to give people additional means to adapt to their environments and changes in their circumstances. Anthropologists using cultural materialist or ecological perspectives analyze religious practices as means of adapting to one's environment. Recall from Chapter 3, for example, Marvin Harris's interpretation of the sacred cow in India as protection against the slaughter of cattle in light of their central importance in the economy of farmers. In another classic study, Roy Rappaport (1969; 2000) demonstrates how a complex ritual cycle relates to the economy and environment of the Tsembaga of New Guinea.

CASE STUDY

Pigs for the Ancestors

Tsembaga Maring

The Tsembagas of New Guinea, numbering about 200 people, participate in an interrelated system of rituals, economic production, social activity, and warfare. The Tsembagas practice horticulture and animal husbandry. Women are the principal farmers, planting and harvesting yams that feed the people and the dozens of pigs that each family maintains. Tsembagas live in balanced competition with neighboring tribes. Intergroup relations involve mutually beneficial trade and social interactions that lead to marriage alliances and military support for raids. Raids help balance the ratio of people to land and resources. Raids also create buffer zones of uninhabitable land that is left fallow to regenerate. However, too frequent raiding would disturb people's ability to farm and raise their pigs. Therefore, a complex set of practices controls the frequency of warfare, and these practices are couched in beliefs about people's obligations to their ancestors and the spirit realm.

The cycle of practices may last twenty years. At the end of a period of hostilities, Tsembagas ritually plant a shrub, called a *rumbin,* in their territory. This act communicates the group's symbolic and real connection to their territory. An elaborate feast is then held, centered around the slaughter of nearly all the group's pigs. Only juvenile pigs are spared, to ensure future supplies. The pigs are slaughtered as a sacrifice to the ancestors who assisted the group to win the warfare with its neighbors.

No matter how many pigs are sacrificed, however, the people think that the obligations to the ancestors remain partly unfulfilled. People then solemnly promise the ancestors that they will offer future sacrifices. Until that time, hostilities must cease, because renewing hostilities is considered improper until all obligations to the ancestors have been discharged. Thus, episodes of warfare are regulated by the amount of time it takes to increase the pig population to the number needed for a proper sacrifice.

Complex factors are involved in people's judgments about whether they have enough pigs to offer to the ancestors. When the pig population is relatively small, the animals can be fed without too much effort, but after awhile, the women gardeners must use more land to grow food for pigs that would otherwise be used for human consumption. For instance, during Rappaport's fieldwork in the 1960s, about 36 percent of active farmland was used to feed the village's 170 pigs.

Eventually, a woman's complaints to her husband about the undue burdens on her labor reach a critical point, and he becomes willing to speak to other men. By that time, most of the men in the village are receiving similar complaints from their wives. Once people experience the burdens of maintaining a large number of pigs, they acknowledge their readiness to make sacrifices to the ancestors.

The next episode of the cycle commences with the uprooting of the *rumbin*, signaling the beginning of a yearlong festival. During the festival, they invite friendly neighboring groups to visit the village to socialize and feast on the sacrificed pigs. They may pursue social and economic goals during these festivals. They distribute pork to allies, and exchange other articles of trade. In addition, young men hold dances to signal their interest in and availability for marriage. Eligible young women attend the dances and observe the qualities of eligible men. The young men's presence is also interpreted as a willingness to aid the hosts as allies in future conflicts.

The final segment of the cycle begins after the festival period has ended. Raiding one's enemies (one's competitors for land) may now resume. When the hostilities have temporarily resolved tensions, the *rumbin* is replanted, marking the end of one cycle and the beginning of the next.

Explore more at
www.myanthrolab.com

Whatever their origins, religious beliefs and practices provide explanations for the world as it is, for how people are, and for major events in people's lives. Religion also provides solace in times of trouble and sorrow, allowing for emotional release and providing emotional support. Religious beliefs and practices also bind communities into cohesive networks. As ideologies, they can both support and change the existing social order and people's adaptations to their environment.

RELIGION AND CULTURE CHANGE

Religious beliefs and practices, like every other aspect of culture, are responsive to changes in society. Social, economic, political, and historical developments have an impact on religions. Changes in other areas of their lives may cause people to think about their relationship with the spirit world in different ways, altering some practices or even abandoning them altogether. People may begin to rethink the roles of religious practitioners, possibly changing the criteria for choosing them or how they are trained. Ritual practice may change as people adopt new ceremonies and modify or discard older ones. Although religion seems like a timeless tradition, it is subject to transformation like any other system of ideology and practice.

Religions are dynamic systems, incorporating new ideas either from external sources or from the innovative creativity of believers. Some religions may be inherently more receptive to change. Polytheistic religions, for example, usually do not have a single standardized doctrine. They allow for additions of new ideas or ritual elements that appear to be effective and the elimination of those that no longer achieve desired results. People might borrow new rituals from neighbors or from the religions of more distant people met in travel or trade. People observe one another's rituals, listen to religious narratives, and adopt practices that they find beautiful, compelling, or effective. New deities may be incorporated into a local pantheon as believers find them appealing or useful. This process is more common in religions that lack central texts whose interpretation can be argued or even fought over. People tend to borrow stories and mythic characters readily, often changing details to suit their own circumstances and attitudes. This process of

What is an example of a belief or practice in a religion that you know about that has been changed or abandoned?

GLOBALIZATION

Syncretism is a common result of political processes, especially in situations of conquest and colonization. As state societies have expanded throughout history, conquerors have imposed their religious beliefs and practices on defeated populations.

prophets
Religious leaders who receive divine inspiration, often in a vision or trance.

nativistic movements
Revitalization movements attempting to rid society of foreign elements and return to what is conceived to be a prior state of cultural purity.

revivalistic movements
Revitalization movements focused on bringing back cultural and religious practices that express core values that have been largely abandoned.

millinerian movements
Revitalization movements incorporating apocalyptic themes, prophesying an abrupt end to the world as we know it, leading to the establishment of a new way of life or form of existence.

messianic movements
Revitalization movements stressing the role of a prophet or messiah as a savior for people.

cargo cults
Revitalization movements arising in Melanesia in the early twentieth century with the aim of obtaining material wealth through magical means.

combining and modifying elements from different religions is called *syncretism,* a term first defined in Chapter 2, and is a process inherent to all religions.

Defeated populations, seeing the conquerors' gods as superior, may willingly adopt their religious systems. In many situations, however, conquered people resist change and resist abandoning their own religious beliefs and practices. They may hold even more tightly to their own traditions, keeping their rituals as acts of resistance and self-empowerment. In this context, new religious traditions may arise that give former practices new meanings and interpretations.

Revitalization Movements

A source of new religious traditions is revitalization movements—religion-based responses to societal crises. Revitalization movements arise in times of social and political upheaval, often in situations of invasion, conquest, and control, when people are confronted by a loss of their rights and restrictions on their freedom. Such movements may also arise as a response to increasing social and political inequalities within a society among people who lack rights or advantages. They are aimed at restructuring power relationships within a society or between conquered peoples and their rulers.

Revitalization movements frequently begin after individuals receive direct messages from the spirit world telling them to convey divine teachings to the community. Referred to as **prophets,** such individuals become the conduits for communication between the spirit world and ordinary people. Essentially, the messages point out how people have become demoralized by straying from the right path and abandoning their traditional values and ethics. Although external forces may be causing people's suffering, the people themselves contribute to their troubles. The prophets teach that the people must return to traditional ways, stressing the values of hospitality or civility, generosity, cooperativeness, and solidarity with relatives and community members. Leaders of revitalization movements proselytize others, always seeking to enlarge the community of followers and establish a network of believers.

There are several kinds of revitalization movements. **Nativistic movements** attempt to rid the society of foreign elements, returning to what is conceived to be a prior state of cultural purity. The late nineteenth-century Ghost Dance cult of the Plains Indians (see Chapter 2) is an example of a nativistic movement, inspired by the prophet Wovoka. **Revivalistic movements** stress the importance of reviving cultural and religious practices that express core values but have been marginalized or abandoned. **Millinerian movements** incorporate apocalyptic themes, prophesying an abrupt end to the world as we know it by a specific time or date in the future, leading to the establishment of a new way of life or form of existence. **Messianic movements** stress the role of a prophet or messiah as a savior. Some religion-based social movements combine aspects of these revitalization themes.

Although revitalization movements are religious, they also have social and political messages. They are always at least potentially revolutionary and can develop into direct challenges to the established order with the aim of transforming or overturning social and political systems. Historical factors affect whether political movements develop. If authorities recognize the political potential of revitalization themes, for example, they may brutally suppress the movement. However, the leaders of the movement may direct people's energies away from political action to protect them from attack. Messages might call for accommodating external situations, or they might postpone the rewards for faith to some distant time in the future, even until after death. These kinds of messages also direct people away from political rebellion.

Cargo Cults

A different kind of revitalization movement arose in Melanesia in the early twentieth century. Referred to as **cargo cults,** these movements were a response to British colonial control, the expropriation of native land, and the relegation of indigenous peoples to roles as menial laborers and second-class citizens. Cargo cults arose at various times and in various places in Melanesia, most notably in New Guinea (Worseley 1967; 1968). Prophets received spirit messages telling people to perform rituals, based on traditional principles of magical cause and effect, that were supposed to result in the arrival of material wealth ("cargo") for the native people.

Cargo cult followers built loading docks along the coast and, later, landing strips for airplanes in the bush, intending to make landing sites for ships and airplanes. They had seen these vehicles bringing in goods for the colonial Europeans, and they believed that if they acted as if the goods were coming, life would imitate art. On this principle of magic, the people imitated European behavior that they thought was responsible for the arrival of the cargo: They wore European-style top hats, neckties, and jackets, and sat around tables and scribbled on pieces of paper that they then put into boxes—all in imitation of having meetings and sending orders for goods.

Members of the John Frum cargo cult in Vanuatu blend traditional Pacific beliefs with Christian practices. The red cross may be a symbol borrowed from the United States military medical units during World War II.

Cargo cult activities appeared foolish to the Europeans, but these activities were consistent with the native worldview. According to Melanesian principles, wealth was obtained by a combination of hard work and ritual. Native people never saw Europeans doing what the Melanesians regarded as work, yet the foreigners received wealth from across the ocean or from the sky, so, clearly, their rituals were powerful. The preliterate Melanesians imitated what they took to be European rituals involving costumes and actions such as writing. Eventually, rituals were abandoned as they failed to attract cargo, until another prophet came with a new set of instructions on what to do. Waves of cargo rituals emerged and dissipated in the 1930s and 1940s. In contrast to the repressive responses to the Ghost Dance of the American Plains, however, the colonial government in New Guinea ignored the cargo cults because they posed no threat to colonial power. Eventually, the cargo movements dissolved because they failed to achieve the desired results. Note that cargo cults and the imitation of European behavior also demonstrate the political message underlying revitalization movements.

Role of Founders in Buddhism, Christianity, and Islam

Some of the most widely practiced religions in the world today began as revitalization movements. Buddhism, Christianity, and Islam originated with individuals who received divine inspiration. These founders essentially reacted against human suffering and the social and political inequalities in their societies, giving as their message the need for all people to establish freedom, equality, justice, and peace. These messages ultimately became institutionalized in formal religions under the control of ecclesiastical elites who serve as intermediaries and interpreters of divine messages.

Siddhartha Gautama, later referred to as Buddha, or "Enlightened One," was born about 563 B.C. in India, the eldest son of a local prince, destined to inherit his father's position. But Gautama rejected the privilege to which he was entitled by birth, choosing instead to leave his parents, wife, and son to seek inner wisdom and the end to physical and spiritual suffering (Koller 1982). Buddha's message was in part a reaction against inequities in the caste system maintained through Hinduism. That system consigned people at birth to specific inherited occupations, social standing, and degrees of ritual purity. Hinduism also emphasized people's roles in an inescapable cycle of reincarnation with its inescapable cycle of suffering. The message of Buddhism is that people can escape caste duty through right thinking and right action to achieve spiritual enlightenment, equality, and oneness with the universe. Eventually people can escape the cycle of reincarnation by attaining perfect knowledge and self-control.

Jesus, whose teachings led to the founding of Christianity, was born sometime after the death of Herod around 4 B.C. Biblical scholars have different interpretations of the life of Jesus, and those interpretations reflect the social and political beliefs of the analysts (Meier 1991). Some scholars emphasize Jesus's role as a prophet of "restoration theology," predicting the divine destruction of the imperial order imposed by Rome on

Israel and the establishment of a world of justice and mercy (Sanders 1985). In this view, Jesus's spiritual prophecy was central and within the tradition of Jewish law and interpretation. Other scholars emphasize his role as a teacher and somewhat subversive commentator on the life of his times (Mack 1988). Still others stress the social context of Jesus's life and see his message as relating fundamentally to sociopolitical conditions (Borg 1994; Crossan 1994). According to this view, like Buddha, Jesus was appalled by inequalities in the prevailing social system of his day. He was also angered by the cooperation of some members of the inner circles of power in the Hebrew state with their Roman invaders and conquerors. Although the common people chafed under increased control and demands for labor and tribute, the local secular and religious elites benefited from their favored positions as puppets of Roman colonial rule. This dynamic is not unique to that area but, rather, occurs in most colonized societies.

According to one modern interpretation (Crossan 1994), Jesus's critique of his own society focused on inequalities within the family, particularly the privileged role of the father in a patriarchal system of male dominance. Because hierarchical relations begin with lessons on dominance and subordination within the family, Jesus advocated the equality of women and men (Fiorenza 1983). Jesus used the metaphor of "open commensality"—the practice of eating at the same table—to undermine norms that segregated people according to rank and gender (Crossan 1994). The "open table," where everyone—men and women, beggars, lepers, and all types of social outcasts—were welcome and could eat together, became a powerful symbol of the egalitarian society Jesus envisioned. In addition, Jesus urged his followers to create the kingdom of God on earth through social and religious transformation.

The founder of Islam, Muhammad, was born in Mecca around A.D. 570 of a poor family. The Arabian Peninsula at the time was home to many small tribal groups who practiced polytheistic religions with an array of nature deities (Guillaume 1986). During a solitary meditation, Muhammad experienced a vision of the angel Gabriel, who told him that God is the one and only God whom people must obey. Muhammad began to preach his message of a monotheistic religion, initially attracting only a small following of mostly slaves and poor people. He was attacked as a sorcerer, but he continued to proclaim his message for all Arabs. His mission, then, was to unite the Arab world under the mantle of one religion with its one God. However, unity came with the price of war: If people did not join the faith on their own, they had to be compelled through force to believe, thus unleashing a holy war of proselytizing religion through conquest.

In Buddhism, Christianity, and Islam, disciples or followers began to spread the faith to others following the deaths of the founders. Over the centuries, increasingly centralized "churches" were organized to pull together a body of worship, setting out practices and doctrine. Eventually, ecclesiastical elites took control not only of priestly functions but also of standardized religious doctrines. People who had divergent interpretations of religious texts were deemed dissidents, and religious authorities harassed and punished dissidents as heretics at various times in the history of Buddhism, Christianity, and Islam. According to some views, these authorities moved away from the original messages, replacing them with doctrines of obedience to the state, hierarchical family systems, and a controlling priesthood.

Religion and Globalization

As state societies expand their borders and influence throughout many parts of the world far from their centers of origin, they have spread their religious beliefs through proselytism. **Proselytism** is the attempt to convert a person or group from one religion to another. State societies throughout history have brought their religions to the people they have conquered. Various denominations of Buddhism, Christianity, and Islam have gained millions of converts through this process. As missionaries spread their religions to all parts of the world, some locally indigenous religious beliefs and practices have been modified and others have been abandoned and replaced by the new religions. In some cases, people have modified foreign rituals and developed different interpretations of standard beliefs.

Diffusion of beliefs and practices and their absorption by distant peoples have resulted in marked contrasts between local practices and those in the centers of origin. For example, in Africa and the Caribbean, Roman Catholic saints are identified with tribal

proselytism
The attempt to convert a person or group from one religion to another.

African deities, and rituals dedicated to indigenous deities are merged with Roman Catholic practice. Spirit possession, a phenomenon marginalized in mainstream Roman Catholic doctrine, is given central importance in Haiti, Brazil, and many African indigenous churches. Similarly, Native American Christians may incorporate traditional practices, especially prayers to the Great Creator and such offerings as the burning of sage or cedar.

Buddhism, Christianity, and Islam, the major proselytizing religions, have been successful in part because their practice is not tied to a specific locale. They can be transplanted anywhere and incorporate local beliefs and practices. This characteristic contrasts with religions whose cosmologies are tied to specific places, such as those of the Diné or Australian Aborigines.

In the world today, as in the past, global economic and political processes have affected religious practices and interpretations of sacred texts. Some revitalization movements within Christianity and Islam have led to an increase in religious fundamentalism. **Fundamentalism,** a term coined in the United States in 1920, means a commitment to do battle to defend traditional religious beliefs. In the United States, members of some Christian fundamentalist movements advocate a return to both religious and social orthodoxy. They keep to a literal interpretation of the Bible and tend to believe in the divine origin of gender roles differentiating the work and family roles of women and men. They also tend to support an ideologically conservative political agenda and to place religious authority above secular authority in life matters. Fundamentalists organize against abortion rights, for example, and against gay marriage. They oppose the teaching of evolution in schools. Some fundamentalist groups have become associated with beliefs in white supremacy.

fundamentalism
A term coined in the United States in 1920 meaning a commitment to do battle to defend traditional religious beliefs.

CULTURE CHANGE

THE DEVELOPMENT OF RELIGIOUS DENOMINATIONS

The major world religions have changed many times and continue to change. The development of various Hindu, Buddhist, Judaic, Christian, and Islamic denominations follows local practices and beliefs. People in different places at different times interpret central texts in their own ways, adapting them to their cultures and their circumstances. Religions also change because philosophical or ethical issues become important to their followers. As times change, as social norms are transformed, religions respond by altering emphases in their practices and beliefs.

Some current controversies demonstrate these processes. Among Jews, the distinction among Orthodox, Conservative, and Reformed branches focuses partly on issues of dietary rules and gender roles. Orthodox Jews, for example, adhere strictly to biblical dietary restrictions, principally taboos on eating pork and shellfish. Kosher rules also prescribe the separation of meat and dairy foods, necessitating separate cooking utensils, dishes, and cutlery for each type of food. In contrast, Reformed and some Conservative Jews do not adhere to kosher dietary regulations. In Orthodox synagogues, men sit on the main level of the building, while women sit in a balcony, symbolizing and enacting the segregation of the genders. Rules of ritual purity and contamination also demand that women take purifying baths, called *mikvas,* at the end of their menstrual periods. Reformed Judaism and many Conservative Jews have abandoned these practices, which highlight gender differences and the polluting effects of women. In addition, Reformed and some Conservative Jews ordain women as rabbis whereas the Orthodox will not.

Christian churches and denominations are distinguished on the basis of doctrine and practice. One major doctrinal difference between Roman Catholics (and Eastern Orthodox churches) and many Protestants concerns the meaning of the rite of communion. Roman Catholicism and Eastern Orthodoxy teach that the bread and wine taken at communion have inner forms that become the body and blood of Jesus when blessed and consumed. Most Protestants treat the bread and wine only symbolically as representing but not actuating Christ's body. Protestants also tend to believe that individuals and groups are free to read and interpret the Scriptures for themselves rather than receive correct interpretations from the clergy. In addition, women may be ordained as ministers in many Protestant denominations but are barred from the Roman Catholic and Orthodox priesthood.

In Islam, the major Shi'ite and Sunni branches, among others, differ in their acceptance of religious authority, interpretation of the Qur'an, and application of religious law to secular activities. Sunnis, the majority, believe that any devout man can become a religious leader and that the Qu'ran should be taken at face value and not be subject to interpretation. Shi'ites, on the other hand, believe that religious leaders, imams, must be descended from Muhammad or divinely appointed and duly praised scholars, and that they are authorities on interpreting the Qur'an to address current events.

Strict adherence to religious doctrines is strongest in countries such as Saudi Arabia, where Islam began and is the only religion allowed by law, and among groups such as the Taliban, a militant Islamic group that took over Afghanistan from 1995 to 2001 and enforced a strict Muslim code of behavior. In regions far from the centers of Islamic origins, beliefs, practices, local traditions, and worldviews temper Islamic beliefs and practices. For example, in Indonesia, the most populous Muslim country, people rarely conform to strict interpretations of Islamic law.

GLOBALIZATION

In 2008, the number of adherents of Christian denominations worldwide was estimated at more than 2.1 billion, about a third of the world population. European state expansion, missionism, colonialism, economic and political hegemony, and imperialism have contributed to what some observers refer to as the globalization of Christianity. Islam, another strongly proselytizing religion historically associated with state expansion and consolidation and with economic and political domination, has about 1.3 billion adherents worldwide.

Fundamentalist organizations and lobbies have become a powerful influence in American politics. Other church groups, such as Americans United for Separation of Church and State, advocate separation between religious and political agendas. Some religious organizations work for progressive social and political change and are outspoken members of peace and antinuclear movements. Within the Roman Catholic Church, clergy and lay workers associated with liberation theology have been in the forefront of movements for social, economic, and political justice and equality, particularly in Central and South America.

Islamic fundamentalism has become increasingly popular and dangerous. In some countries of the Middle East and Africa, Islamic fundamentalists have taken over local or national governments, imposing a strict interpretation of the Qur'an on social and political policies. In Iran, for example, and in several states in Nigeria, public laws must conform to Islamic principles, and crimes and punishments are defined according to sacred texts. Religious authorities double as political leaders, whether by election or proclamation. In other Middle Eastern countries—for example, Iraq, as well as in Indonesia and the Philippines—Islamist movements have contributed to the destabilization of local and central governments and are attempting to overthrow elected or appointed authorities and institute Islamic law.

Some analysts attribute the upsurge in Islamic fundamentalism to the global spread of Western influence, chiefly from the United States. American social behaviors and social values are seen as immoral. Fundamentalist movements have gained popularity as proponents claim to resist American influence on internal affairs and foreign policies. This resistance has become increasingly violent. Al Qaeda, a terrorist network with cells in more than fifty countries, is an extreme expression of Islamic fundamentalism. Its members are both anti-Western and opposed to Arabic governments that do not espouse its own version of strict Islamic principles. On September 11, 2001, members of al Qaeda killed more than 3,000 people by flying aircraft into the twin towers of the World Trade Center in New York City.

REVIEW Internal and external forces change religious practices and beliefs over time. In syncretism, new religions are created by combining parts of older ones. Revitalization movements emphasize core beliefs and values as a means of adapting to undesired changes. Nativistic, revivalistic, millinerian, and messianic movements, as well as cargo cults, are all forms of religion-based adaptations to change. Major world religions such as Buddhism, Christianity, and Islam began as revitalization movements. Religions have spread through forces of globalization and the practice of proselytism. Religious fundamentalism has become a powerful force.

ANTHROPOLOGY APPLIED

Medical Anthropology and Ethnomedicine

Medical anthropologists apply the holistic and cross-cultural approaches of anthropology to understand and respond to questions of human well-being, health, and disease. How are illnesses caused, experienced, and spread, and how can they be prevented and treated? What healers, healing substances, and healing processes do people use, and what beliefs and values inform those uses? How is human health related to social structure, the health of other species, and the environment?

Medical practitioners use information from medical anthropology in treating their culturally diverse patients. For example, reaching a diagnosis and prescribing effective treatment are not based strictly on the scientific model but involve understanding people's perceptions and interpretations of their bodies and bodily processes and their beliefs about illness. Those perceptions, interpretations, and beliefs are culturally constructed because what is considered pathological is culturally defined. Some diseases are even culture-specific.

At a broader level, medical anthropologists may study epidemics, endemic diseases that persist in a society, or disease vectors that cause the spread of disease. They may study the distribution of disease in the world and the disparities in

health among different populations. Some focus on the relationships between people's health and health care and the political and economic factors in societies. Others focus on problem areas, such as child and maternal health, eating habits and nutrition, or sanitation in a world where 1,400 children die each day from diarrhea.

Ethnomedicine is the study of traditional medicine in cultural groups or in preindustrial societies. Beliefs and practices in different human groups include ideas about hygiene, disease prevention, and healing properties of objects in their environment. For example, the Maasai use an infusion of the bark from a kind of acacia tree as a digestive aid during ceremonies that call for consuming huge quantities of meat. The Maasai also use the bark from a kind of albizia tree as an emetic. The root can be boiled and mixed with milk to get rid of or prevent intestinal parasites in people and animals (Ryan 2000).

According to the World Health Organization (2004), 80 percent of Africans rely on traditional medicine for daily health. In Asia and Latin America as well, reliance on traditional medicines and practices may be more culturally acceptable and psychologically satisfying than those based on the Western scientific medical model. In addition, modern medicine, which is also the subject of ethnomedical research, may be inaccessible to most people in a developing country. Traditional medicines and practices may be just as effective. Plants that preindustrial people used to treat illness include the sources of aspirin, morphine, ephedrine, and penicillin.

CRITICAL THINKING QUESTIONS

What are some of your beliefs and values about health and illness? Where do those beliefs and values come from?

379

CHAPTER SUMMARY

What Is Religion?

- Religion is actions and feelings based on beliefs in spirit beings and supranormal (or superhuman) forces. Religious beliefs and practices give people ways to contact spirit beings and forces, show them honor and respect, and invoke their protection. Anthropologists use comparison and cultural relativism to analyze religious beliefs and behaviors. They try to understand people's ideas about the spirit realm from the people's own point of view. They also focus on how religious beliefs and practices are consistent with other aspects of culture.

Spirit Beings and Forces

- Spirit entities and forces have extraordinary powers. They are typically eternal or indestructible. They know more than a person can know and can act in ways that humans cannot. Thus, people seek to gain their protection and aid.

- One nearly universal form that spirit takes is the soul—the eternal aspect of living things. In some beliefs, only humans have souls. Souls are seen as the animating aspect of living things. When the body dies, souls escape and exist eternally in another form. The belief in souls is called animism; the belief that all things are endowed with some spirit essence is animatism.

- Some religious traditions have many spirit beings in human form with specific attributes, powers, and functions. Polytheism, belief in numerous deities, is widespread. In monotheistic religions, people believe in one supreme deity who affects all aspects of life, although there may also be lesser spirits and moral heroes.

- Mana is a spirit power or essence that endows people, animals, objects, or events with special qualities or powers. In some cultures of Australia and North America, people believe that they are descended from human or animal spirit beings called totems, the primordial protectors of the people.

- Spirit beings and forces are dangerous if contacted in the wrong way, in the wrong place, or at the wrong time. Restrictions on places or objects are called taboos. A tabooed object or place can cause harm because the spirit power within it can become dangerous.

Religious Practitioners and Specialists

- Most religions have individuals or groups who function as either part-time or full-time religious specialists. In some cases, a person receives a calling from the spirit world to become a religious specialist or inherits spiritual powers. In other cases, a person decides to become a religious practitioner for personal reasons.

- Mediums make contact with spirit beings or spirits of the dead. Diviners have the power to predict or shape the future through messages and omens they receive and interpret from the spirit world. Healers diagnose the spirit cause of illness and effect cures through rituals. Shamans receive visions and messages from the spirit realm and may serve as diviners and healers. Priests are full-time religious practitioners who lead religious organizations and officiate at rituals but are not expected to be able to communicate directly with the spirit world.

Religious Practice

- Rituals are a fundamental aspect of all religious practices and include prayer and offerings. Rituals mark events in religious and secular calendars.

- People also perform rituals to celebrate transitions in an individual's life cycle. Such rites of passage mark birth, puberty, marriage, and death. Rites of passage ritualize three aspects of a change in life status: separation, transition, and reincorporation. Puberty rites mark sexual maturity and the transition from childhood to adulthood. Funerals mark the departure of the deceased and reinforce family and community solidarity.

- Health is often thought of as a state of harmony or balance among a person's body, relations with others, the health of the environment, and relations with spirit beings and forces. When this balance is disturbed, illness and misfortune may follow. Serious illness is often attributed to spiritual causes needing ritual diagnosis and treatment by religious specialists. Spirit causes can include soul loss, object intrusion, spirit possession, or the violation of taboos. Curative rituals attempt to restore balance through magic, practical remedies, therapeutic effects, social validation, and the passage of time.

- Witchcraft may be suspected in cases of illness, death, or misfortune. Witches or sorcerers employ spirit powers to harm others. Witchcraft can be a form of social control and a means of achieving social justice. Witches, like healers, employ imitative and contagious magic. Magic is an expression of people's desires and intentions in situations over which they have no direct control.

The Origins and Functions of Religion

- Specific origins of religious beliefs are unknown. Religions give people solace, and religious beliefs and practices bind communities together. They give ideological support for the social structures, including family organization, social stratification, and political inequalities. Anthropologists using cultural materialist or ecological perspectives analyze religious practices as a means of adapting to one's environment.

- Social, economic, political, and historical developments affect religions. Changes may cause people to think about their relationship with the spirit world in different ways, altering practices or even abandoning them altogether. Religions incorporate new ideas from external sources or the innovations of believers.

Religion and Culture Change

- Revitalization movements are religion-based responses to societal crises. Revitalization movements are aimed at restructuring power relationships within a society or between conquered peoples and their rulers. They are begun by individuals who receive direct messages from the spirit world telling them to convey divine teachings. Nativism is aimed at ridding society of foreign elements, returning to what is thought to be a state of cultural purity. Revivalism stresses the importance of reviving cultural and political practices. Millinerian movements incorporate apocalyptic themes and an abrupt end to the present world and establishment of a new world. Messianic movements stress the role of a prophet or messiah as a savior.

- The major world religions have changed many times. As times change and social norms are transformed, religions alter their practices and beliefs. These changes can lead to the development of distinctive sects and denominations within the world religions.

- State societies have spread their religious beliefs through proselytism. Revitalization movements within Christianity and Islam have increased religious fundamentalism. Christian fundamentalists advocate a literal interpretation of the Bible and tend to support a conservative political agenda and to place religious authority above secular authority. Islamic fundamentalism includes terrorism and rejection of Western influences.

KEY TERMS

religion   354
religious speech   355
animism   356
animatism   356
polytheism   356
monotheistic
   religions   356
ancestor worship   357
mana   357
totemism   357

secret societies   358
mediums   359
diviners   359
healers   359
shamans   360
priests   360
rituals   361
sacred rituals   361
rites of renewal   362
prayer   362

sacrifice   362
puberty rites   364
funerary rights   364
spirit possession   367
imitative magic   369
contagious magic   369
calendric rituals   370
cosmology   371
prophets   374
nativistic movements   374

revivalistic
   movements   374
millinerian
   movements   374
messianic
   movements   374
cargo cults   374
proselytism   376
fundamentalism   377

REVIEW QUESTIONS

1. What questions do all religions answer?
2. How are animism, animatism, and deism different? How are these belief systems expressed?
3. How do different religions define and treat spirits of the dead?
4. How is a shaman different from a priest?
5. What are other types of religious practitioners? What roles and functions do they play in their societies?
6. How do people make distinctions between the sacred and the secular? How are concepts such as mana, taboo, and blessing used to bestow sacredness?
7. How is religion expressed through symbolic culture and religious speech?
8. In what ways is religion expressed through behavior? What religious concepts do people use to explain human behavior?
9. What types of secular and sacred rituals do people everywhere perform?
10. Why do people sometimes use magical thinking?
11. What are some social and cultural functions of sorcery or witchcraft?
12. What are some examples of the relationship between religion and other social systems in a society?
13. What five basic functions does religion serve for people?
14. How do religions change in response to social and culture change?
15. How do syncretisms reveal adaptations to cultural contact and the diffusion of ideas?
16. What are the types and characteristics of revitalization movements?
17. What is the impact of globalization on world religions?

PEARSON myanthrolab EXERCISES

To complete the following exercises and activities, you must log in to www.myanthrolab.com and select your current textbook.

1. In the **Explore** tab of Chapter 14, click on *Video* and watch the slide show on *The Emergence of Fundamentalism*. Complete the short answer exercise that accompanies the slide show.

2. While in the *Video* section of the **Explore** tab, watch the video on *Death – Native American Burial*. Complete the short answer exercise that accompanies the video.

3. In the **Explore** tab, click on the *NPR Audio Programs Broadcast* tab and go to *Theme 25: Religion*. Listen to one of the programs in this section and complete the short answer exercise that accompanies the program.

4. Enter the **MyAnthroLibrary** section on the home page to read more about topics and cultures that are discussed in this chapter. Suggested readings include:

Iroquios: The Tree of Peace and the War Kettle by Thomas Abler

Tlingit: Chiefs Past and Present by Kenneth Tollefson

THE ARTS

- How do anthropologists define art?

- What can we learn about people by examining their art?

- How is art embedded in culture? How do cultures shape artistic expression and the aesthetic principles on which it is based?

- What are some universal and culturally specific forms of art? How do those forms of art express or create symbolic culture?

- How does art reflect society and social realities?

- What cultural, social, and personal functions does art serve?

After a long time Mataora became jealous of his elder brother Tau-toru; he saw that he ardently desired his wife. In consequence he thrashed his wife Niwareka; which caused her to flee away to the underworld to the home of her ancestors and parents. A great sorrow fell on Mataora, and he deeply lamented his beautiful wife.

And now Mataora started off to search for his wife. When Mataora arrived at the guard-house of the underworld, he asked of the guard "Did you not see a woman pass this way?" "Ah, yes! She has gone on long ago; she was crying as she came along." Mataora then said, "Cannot I go to where she is?"

Mataora then descended, and went on until he came to a shed, at the village of Ue-tonga, where were many people. He found Ue-tonga engaged in tattooing; he sat down there to see the operation, and saw the blood descending from the cuts in the face. He called out, "Your system of tattooing the face is all wrong! It is not done in that manner up above." Ue-tonga said, "This is the custom below here; that above is quite wrong. That system is called by us 'painted.' That kind of moko [or face tattooing] is used in house building." Mataora replied, "That is called carving with us." Then Ue-tonga placed his hand on Mataora's face and rubbed it—and all the moko came off! The people all burst out laughing, and then Ue-tonga called out, "O ye above! O ye people of above! Ye are quite wrong in calling it carving. Behold the face is quite clean from rubbing. That is only painting."

Mataora now said to Ue-tonga, "You have destroyed the moko on my face; you must tattoo me." Ue-tonga replied, "It is well! Lie down!" Then Ue-tonga called on the artists to delineate the pattern on Mataora's face. Then Ue-tonga sat down by the side of Mataora with his chisel and commenced to tattoo him. Great was his pain and his groans. He then sang his song:

> Niwareka! that is lost, where art thou?
> Show thy self, O Niwareka! O Niwareka!
> 'Twas love of thee that dragged me down here below,
> Niwareka! Niwareka! love eats me up!
> Niwareka! Niwareka! thou has bound me tight.
> Niwareka! Niwareka! Let us remain in this world,
> Niwareka! Niwareka! Leave behind this underworld,
> Niwareka! Niwareka, and thus end my pain.

When Ue-kuru, the younger sister of Niwareka, heard this, she ran off to where Niwareka was engaged in weaving a garment. Ue-kuru said to her sister, "There is a man over there who is being tattooed; a very handsome man; who, whilst the operation was going on, was crying and singing. The words of the song often repeated your name." The female companions of Niwareka all said, "Let us all go and see!"

So Mataora was led off. Then was heard the welcome of Niwareka and her lady companions, who became enamored with the appearance of Mataora. She said to her friends, "His bearing is that of Mataora." When Mataora had sat down on the mats, Niwareka asked, "Art thou Mataora?" He bowed his head and held out his arms towards Niwareka, asking her to draw near. Niwareka then knew it was indeed Mataora.

Mataora now said to Niwareka, "Let us both return to the Earth." She replied, "The customs of the upper world are bad. Rather let us remain below, and gather our thoughts and turn them from the evils of the upper world." So Niwareka told her father and brothers the reason of Mataora's visit—to take her back to the Earth. Upon hearing this, her father said, "You go back, O Mataora! Leave Niwareka here. A custom of the upper world is to beat women, is it not?"

At this, Mataora was consumed with shame. The brother of Niwareka said to him, "Mataora! Abandon the upper world—the home of evil—altogether, and let us both live down here. Cut off all above and its evil ways, let all below with its better customs be separate." Mataora replied, "I will in future adopt your methods in the upper-world." Then the father said to him, "Mataora! Do not let a repetition of the evil repute of the upper-world, reach here below." Mataora replied, "Look on my moko; if it had been painted it might be washed off, but as it is a moko cut in the flesh by you it is permanent and cannot be washed out. I will adopt in future the ways of this lower world and its works."

From S. Percy Smith, *The Lore of the Whare-Wananga.* © 1913. New Plymouth, New Zealand, http://www.sacred-texts.com/pac/lww/index.htm.

In this story, the Maoris of New Zealand tell the origin of one of their prominent arts, tattooing on the face and body. According to tradition, the art was learned in primordial times from sacred beings that inhabited the underworld. This story gives a divine license to an artistic and aesthetic style. By the early twentieth century, few Maoris were getting tattoos because of pressure from European colonial authorities who regarded the practice as savage. But by the late twentieth century, the art had become popular again, partly as a sign of ethnic pride and identity.

WHAT IS ART?

Like the word *culture, art* is a word that we use in everyday speech but for which we have difficulty formulating a precise definition. Even anthropologists often describe the arts of the people they study without defining what they mean, taking for granted that the meanings are understood. In a study of American arts and **aesthetics**—philosophies about what has beauty and value in art—anthropologist Richard Anderson (2000, 8) proposed that the key characteristics of **art** are

- artifacts of human creation;
- created through the exercise of exceptional physical, conceptual, or imaginative skill;
- intended to affect the senses; and
- share stylistic conventions with similar works.

Let us explore these characteristics. Art objects are made by human beings. This seems straightforward, despite occasional museum exhibitions of the "artwork" of gorillas, chimpanzees, and even elephants. Although it might be said that some paintings by our primate relatives look similar to the works of modern artists, most would dismiss these as "not art" because of the lack of intentionality, at least as we attribute intentionality to human beings. That is, a human artist produces work intended to be art, with a preconceived plan of working through a specific medium. We assume that other animals lack this type of volition and intentionality, even though they may delight in the process of producing new objects.

Second, art is work stimulated by an exceptional creative concept and produced with exceptional physical skill. This suggests that paintings produced by some people may be defined as art, whereas paintings made by others may not. The concept of "skill" is embedded in the word art, which derives from the Latin *artem,* meaning "skill of any kind." The fact that art continues to mean skillful or a skill is reflected in such expressions as "the healing arts" or "the evil arts."

Artistic productions appeal to the human senses, stirring our minds and imaginations as well as our feelings. Some arts appeal primarily to the visual senses (painting, sculpture), whereas others appeal to the senses of hearing (music, song, prayer, oratory, poetry), touch (sculpture, carvings), and the sense of movement (dance). These sensual characteristics differentiate art objects from mundane utilitarian utensils, tools, or clothing.

Finally, artistic work is influenced by aesthetic conventions that are primarily cultural. In all societies, people have cultural assumptions about the media used to make art and

aesthetics
Philosophies about what has beauty and value in art.

art
Artifacts of human creation created through the exercise of exceptional physical, conceptual, or imaginative skill, and produced in a public medium and intended to affect the senses, sharing stylistic conventions with similar works.

How does the definition of art in this chapter apply to this piece of twentieth-century American art?

the styles of painting, sculpting, decoration, oral traditions, and dance movements that are considered appropriate. These conventions may be more or less rigid or flexible, depending on cultural attitudes. In certain media, strict adherence to formal conventions may be necessary, whereas greater flexibility and latitude are given to artists or performers in other realms of artistic work. In other words, people in every society have ideas about what they consider to be art, based on their interpretation of the criteria in Anderson's definition. Of course, artistic conventions may change. For example, Western musical styles heard today, both in classical and popular music, are vastly different from those appreciated during earlier centuries or even earlier decades.

In addition to cultural variability in what is considered art, there are similarities and differences in the meanings attributed to artistic production and the purposes that they serve. In some societies, artistic production is primarily destined to serve ritual or religious purposes. In other societies, secular functions of artistic production are paramount. In both cases, artistic work serves emotional or psychological needs, expressing the creativity of the artist and stimulating emotional responses in the viewers or users of art.

REVIEW — All societies have aesthetic values. From an anthropological perspective, art is made by the human hand using exceptional skill. It is intended to affect the senses of people who view it, and it refers to culture-based stylistic conventions. Art has meaning and serves important needs of both individuals and their societies.

CULTURAL AESTHETICS

mimetic
Art that portrays the world accurately.

representational
Art that imitates, idealizes, or symbolizes form and experience.

instrumental
Art that attempts to have a beneficial effect on society, enriching people's lives, teaching moral lessons, and providing insights for improving and changing the world.

formalist
Abstract art that focuses on the formal qualities of art—color, composition, sound, words, or movements.

Not only do cultures differ in the ways in which they express artistic impulses, but they also differ in their aesthetics or philosophies of art. In a cross-cultural study of aesthetic principles, Richard Anderson (1990) demonstrates the variety of cultural attitudes toward art and artists. Although cultural attitudes and philosophies of art are not all the same in his sample of nine societies, many of the foragers and horticulturalists share an understanding of art as a means of improving the world and life experiences or of serving primarily spiritual functions. For example, the Yoruba of Nigeria use art mainly to attract and show respect to spirit beings that then bestow prosperity, happiness, and fertility on the people who honor them.

In Western art, according to one analysis, four aesthetic paradigms or models have developed: mimetic, instrumental, emotionalist, and formalist (Anderson 2000, 201–02). The **mimetic** paradigm focuses on the ability of art to portray the world around us. Art may be **representational**, either imitating, idealizing, or symbolizing form and experience. Or it may be **instrumental**, transforming the world, enhancing our experience, or making the world a better place. In the instrumental paradigm, art should have a beneficial effect on society, enriching our lives, teaching us moral lessons, and providing us with the insights and abilities to improve and change our world. Emotionalist paradigms focus on the role of art to connect to our inner experience and feelings. In this view, art is expressive of the artist's emotions, but it can also serve to release emotions in the viewers of art. In fact, both artists and viewers are linked in the emotional catharsis stimulated by the creative process. Finally, the **formalist** aesthetic centers on the formal qualities of art—color, composition, sound, words, or movements. Qualities of form and the medium are more important than a true representation of the subject. Thus, art can be abstract.

CASE STUDY

Yoruba Art

Much of Yoruba art from West Africa is concerned with the body, either decorating and adorning the body to make it more beautiful or representing it in statuary and masks. Yoruba artists specialize in wooden sculptures that are idealized in their beauty. According to Yoruba aesthetics, carved figures should look like people but not show the physical flaws of ordinary mortals. Statues should depict people in full maturity, strength, and energy. These characteristics summarize the values of Yoruba principles of beauty (Anderson 1990, 127–28). Strength and energy are consistent with Yoruba valuation of youth and the power that comes from youthful vitality and vigor (Thompson 1974, 6–7).

Art for the Yorubas is, therefore, a projection and encapsulation of their beliefs about goodness, beauty, and morality. Yoruba statues are often carved with straight postures and slightly bent knees, to suggest both stability and the kinetic energy that can lead to movement. The contrasting themes in the statues are consistent with Yoruba philosophies of life, emphasizing both stability and change through the storage and release of strength and energy.

Yoruba art also indicates social status. The Yoruba kings' regalia included a royal stool, a beaded crown, umbrellas, whisks, scepters, gowns, and slippers. These garments, decorations, and gear were richly decorated and carved.

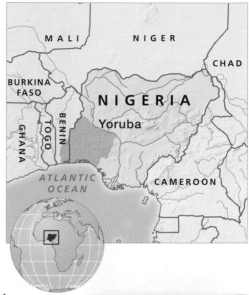

Only the king could wear the royal costume. His palace was decorated with carvings unlike those of any other person. The Yoruba believed the king was chosen and installed with divine blessing, so these artworks were displays of his wealth, and of his closeness to the spirit world.

PEARSON
myanthrolab

**Explore more at
www.myanthrolab.com**

Among the Yoruba, body scarification, as shown on this young girl, traditionally was for both beauty and social status.

This statue of a Sango priestess kneels and holds her breasts as signs of respect, like a young bride. Her strands of waist beads signify virginity.

These paradigms may not be foremost in our minds as we view art or as we live our lives in the midst of artworks, but thinking about them can help us understand the different functions of art. Art is part of symbolic culture—that is, art has meaning. Through art, we can learn about the world and be stimulated to make changes in our lives as we understand the messages transmitted through art. Messages may be transmitted through social and political art, for example, which reflects the instrumental potential in artworks. Artistic creations also serve as emotional expression for both the artist and the viewer. We are moved when we see paintings and sculptures, when we hear music and song, and when we participate in or watch performances of dance and drama. When we view art, we appreciate that art objects in any medium require skill of execution and conform to principles of style and form that are culturally appropriate in context, time, and place.

How might an anthropologist study this street mural? How is it an example of political art?

REVIEW
◉ Art conveys important messages. Mimetic art attempts to portray the world accurately, whereas representational art portrays the world in an ideal or symbolic way. Instrumental art attempts to change the world or people's experiences of it or to enrich people's lives. Emotionalist art attempts to express the artist's feelings or release the feelings of viewers. Formalist art is abstract art that focuses on color, form, texture, medium, or technique rather than on particular subjects, ideas, or feelings.

BODY ART

Do you practice any body arts? Why?

One of the most common media for the display of art is the human body, as in Maori tattooing and Yoruba **scarification**—piercing the skin to make patterns or designs of healed scars. Although societies differ in the degree to which they employ the human body as a canvas, all peoples take pleasure in the use of body decoration, hairstyles, clothing, and jewelry to enhance one's appearance and to display one's personal and cultural identity. Nomadic peoples are particularly likely to emphasize the use of the body in artistic production. Because they do not have permanent settlements and need to carry with them whatever objects they own, they keep their possessions to a minimum. The human body in this context becomes a sort of movable canvas for painting, tattooing, or decorating with jewelry.

Aboriginal foraging peoples of Australia used elaborate body painting, especially in ritual occasions when people painted themselves with lines, dots, and other designs as they prepared to participate in ceremonies. Nomadic foragers of the Kalahari Desert in Africa decorated their hair and bodies with beads cut from ostrich eggshells. They also fashioned their hair in decorative styles, cutting the hair in rows and patterns to make lines and other designs. And they used facial tattooing. The Inuit of Arctic Alaska and Canada also used **tattooing,** resulting when ink or dyes are injected under the skin at piercing sites, to enhance their appearance. Inuit tattooing was done mainly on the face, hands, and wrist. In their cold climate, these are the parts of the body that are exposed to the view of other people. Other parts of the body (chest, back, arms, and legs) were nearly always covered with clothing because of the cold temperatures. The fact that the Inuit tattooed those parts of the body exposed to people's view demonstrates one of the uses of personal art, namely, to announce one's identity, embellish one's appearance, and make oneself attractive to others.

In warm climates, where much of the body is routinely exposed, body tattooing may be much more elaborate, as described for the Maoris in the narrative that opened this chapter. In Samoa and other South Pacific societies, young men had much of their bodies, including their face, arms, hands, back, chest, and legs, emblazoned with intricate tattoos as they prepared themselves for marriage. The higher the social status of the individual, the more elaborate the tattooing. Tattooing, therefore, was a signal not only of personal inclination and artistic display but was also a validation of one's social status. Differences

scarification
Artistic and ritualistic scarring of the face or other parts of the body in particular designs, commonly used to mark transitions to adulthood.

tattooing
Injecting inks or dyes under the skin to produce designs.

in tattooing were correlated with a social system that emphasized rank and distinctions in the social standing of people ordered in a hierarchical system of stratification.

Tattooing and other body decoration may be indicators of age and identity. In the United States, tattoos and facial and body piercings have come to be almost necessities for teenagers in some social circles. The practice of multiple piercings may also be a gesture of defiance against parental authority and values. Although defying adult standards and practices, it also unites teenagers and reinforces their group identity through conformity to youth culture and values.

Throughout the world, people fashion beads, stones, and metals into jewelry that beautifies their appearance. In societies where there are differences in status and wealth, higher-ranked and wealthier people are able to accumulate more elaborate and more valuable jewelry for display on their bodies. Thus, they enhance their appearance and attractiveness, advertise their social status and identity, and display their wealth. In addition, jewelry may be a repository of wealth, convertible into other goods through trade or sale. Clothing functions in the same way. Although clothes are culturally necessary body coverings, the fineness of their materials and intricacies of design serve to transmit messages about social standing and wealth.

Clothing may be used to differentiate ethnic populations within complex, multiethnic societies. Wearing ethnically marked clothing may be a voluntary choice on the part of the wearer. In modern multiethnic states, people may prefer to wear the clothing of their region as a sign of their belonging to an identifiable community. Immigrants may choose to wear clothing typical of their native land to feel comfortable and as a sign of emotional loyalty to their homeland. For example, Indian women living in the United States may continue to wear saris even after otherwise assimilating.

In the past, some state societies used clothing and ornamentation as a means of dramatizing elite power. For example, in the Aztec Empire of Mexico, only high-ranking people were permitted to wear certain kinds of clothing or jewelry (Soustelle 1961, 138–39). Denying access to specific types of clothing and ornaments was not simply a matter of wealth, of being able to afford finery, but was a means of formally differentiating the population. Only the emperor was permitted to wear turquoise nose ornaments. Members of the military had the privilege of wearing particular jewels and feather adornments, depending on their rank. They also had the right to wear distinctive high-back sandals. Any man who was caught wearing an ornament or article of clothing to which he had no right was likely to be punished by death.

Hairstyles, body decoration, clothing, and jewelry are also indications of gender identity in nearly all societies. Women and men may wear their hair at different lengths or arrange it in different styles. They may use body painting or tattooing in different places or employ contrasting patterning and designs. Body adornments such as clothing and jewelry are also often styled differently for women and men. Although some of these differences in clothing style may be a response to anatomical or practical differences in work roles, they also highlight and dramatize the social roles of gender and gender identity.

Body art is universal in humans and includes clothing, jewelry, hairstyles, painting, piercing, and tattooing. Body art communicates individual identity, group affiliation, and social standing. **REVIEW**

ORIGINS AND FUNCTIONS OF ART OBJECTS

In many societies, utilitarian objects are sometimes embellished with coloration, designs, carvings, paintings, or other decoration to enhance their beauty or impart magical or spiritual properties. Objects usually referred to as crafts, such as those made of pottery, basketry, wood, or stone, may have ornamental designs that demonstrate people's aesthetic sense and awareness of the ways that human effort and skill can add to the beauty of an object. In many foraging and small farming societies, nearly everyone is a producer of some kind of tool, utensil, or craft necessary for their work. Some individuals may make such objects with only a utilitarian purpose in mind. Other individuals, those more skilled or more imaginative, may add to the basic utilitarian object through the creative use of design and color. Other members of the community may collect their work because of its beauty.

IN THEIR OWN VOICES

Artists Talk About Art

In these excerpts, modern artists write about the meaning of art, their techniques, and their aesthetic philosophies.

Barnett Newman, from *The Plasmic Image*

The subject matter of creation is chaos. It is now a widespread notion that primitive art is abstract, that the strength in the primitive statement arises from this tendency for abstraction. An examination of primitive cultures, however, shows that many traditions were realistic . . . [and] there always existed . . . a strict division between the geometric abstraction used in the decorative arts and the art of that culture. . . . [T]he practicing artist always employed a symbolic, even a realistic, form of expression. One of the serious mistakes made by artists and art critics has been the confusion over the nature of distortion, the easy assumption that any distortion from the realistic form is an abstraction of that form. . . . In primitive tribes distortion was used as a device whereby the artist could create symbols. It is also very important to try to draw a sharp line between art and the decorative arts. . . . In primitive tribes this separation was well defined.

Helen Frankenthaler from Artforum

When I judge my own pictures, I determine if they work in a certain kind of space through shape or color. I think all totally abstract pictures have tremendous space; perspectives space despite the emphasis on flat surface. And the ones that go dead and static can't be read that way; they don't move. In my work, because of color and shape a lot is read in the landscape sense. I will sometimes start a picture feeling "What will happen

The abstract expressionist Helen Frankenthaler was influenced by Robert Motherwell, Jackson Pollack, and other artists of her time. (Helen Frankenthaller [b. 1928] © Small's Paradise, 1964. Acrylic on canvas, 100 × 93⅜ in. [254 × 237.7 cm]. Smithsonian American Art Museum, Washington, DC/Art Resource, NY).

if I work with three blues and another color, and maybe more or less of the other color than the combined blues?" And very often midway through the picture I have to change the basis of

---

These **artisans** may become part-time specialists, exchanging their work either in barter or sale to others, thereby raising their status and increasing their wealth.

Societies differ in the degree to which they stress individuality or conformity to artistic styles. Although we value originality and denigrate an artist or craftsperson whose work is derivative and imitative, members of other societies appreciate an artist who adheres to particular artistic conventions. Such artists demonstrate their creativity and inspiration by the level of their skill and variation within specific parameters. Therefore, an archaeologist who unearths a clay pot in Mexico can tell by its style whether a Maya or an Aztec made it.

In the Suriname Maroon society of Saramaka, descendants of slaves who escaped from their masters, women carve and decorate the hard surfaces of calabash gourds as they fashion them into bowls, ladles, and other types of dishes. Men decorate the surfaces of covered calabash containers, but these containers are also considered to be the property of women. There are gender differences in the equipment used to execute the carvings, and there are differences in features of style and design as well (Price 1984). Men use chisels and compasses that they obtain in the world outside their remote communities, whereas women use pieces of broken glass to etch their designs. Men's work emphasizes symmetry and clear boundaries, but women's designs are more free-flowing and slightly unbalanced, sometimes with marks that disturb a central symmetry. All Saramaka women

artisans
Specialists in the production of works of art.

the experience. I used to try to work from a given, made shape. But I'm less involved now with the shape as such. I'm much more apt to be surprised that pink and green within the shapes are doing something. I'd rather risk an ugly surprise than rely on things I know I can do. The whole business of spotting; the small area of color in a big canvas; how edges meet; how accidents are controlled; all this fascinates me.

Mark Rothko, from *I Paint Very Large Pictures*

I paint very large pictures. I realize that historically the function of painting large pictures is painting something very grandiose and pompous. The reason I paint them, however—I think it applies to other painters I know—is precisely because I want to be very intimate and human. To paint a small picture is to place yourself outside your experience, to look upon an experience as a stereopticon view with a reducing glass. However you paint the larger pictures, you are in it. It isn't something you command.

Louise Bourgeois from Artforum

What modern art means is that you have to keep finding new ways to express yourself, to express the problems, that there are no settled ways, no fixed approach. This is a painful situation, and modern art is about this painful situation of having no absolutely definite way of expressing yourself. This is why modern art will continue, because this condition remains; it is the modern human condition. It is about the hurt of not being able to express yourself properly, to express your intimate relations, your unconscious, to trust the world enough to express yourself directly in it. It is about trying to be sane in this situation, of being tentatively and temporarily sane by expressing yourself. All art comes from terrific failures and terrific needs that we have. It is about the difficulty of being a self because one is neglected. Everywhere in the modern world there is neglect, the need to be recognized, which is not satisfied. Art is a way of recognizing oneself, which is why it will always be modern.

Robert Motherwell, from *Beyond the Aesthetic*

[If] a work is not aesthetic, it is not art by definition. But in this stage of the creative process, the strictly aesthetic—which is the sensuous aspect of the world—ceases to be the chief end in view. The function of the aesthetic instead becomes that of a medium, a means for getting at the infinite background of feeling in order to condense it into an object of perception. We feel through the senses, and everyone knows that the content of art is feeling.

Feelings must have a medium in order to function at all; in the same way, thought must have symbols. It is the medium, or the specific configuration of the medium that we call a work of art that brings feeling into being, just as do responses to the objects of the external world.

Explore more at www.myanthrolab.com

From Kristine Stiles and Peter Selz, *Theories and Documents of Contemporary Art: A Sourcebook of Artists' Writings.* © 1996. The Regents of the University of California. Reprinted by permission.

● CRITICAL THINKING QUESTION

What do these artists' statements tell us about Western notions of art and the role of the artist?

carve and decorate some of their own calabashes, but some women are known to be experts and others collect their work.

Saramakas have names for various calabash designs. Some styles are traditional, but others are the result of innovation. The people value both conformity to a standard aesthetic and the originality of individual artisans. Regional differences, village by village, are also recognized. These, too, are the result of personal innovations that become popular.

In addition to calabash carvings, women's art includes embroidery and patchwork with which they embellish rectangular cotton capes and cloths. Again, following a traditional aesthetic, both adherence to standard forms and innovation in design are appreciated. Among the compositional principles for these works are bilateral symmetry, sharp contrasts in colors but avoidance of domination by any one color, and avoidance of combining patchwork pieces taken from different grades of cotton (Price 1984, 157).

In most societies, objects used in rituals are embellished with either representational or abstract designs, painting, or beads, feathers, and jewels. These artistic works may add not only to the beauty of the object but also to its effectiveness in ceremonies. Works of art may attract spirit beings, please them, and make them more likely to bestow their blessings on the community. For example, as part of curing rituals performed by Diné (Navajo) healers, practitioners may construct sandpaintings to attract spirit beings and gain their beneficial powers. The **sandpaintings** are stylized representations of the Holy People, the

sandpaintings
Paintings made by sprinkling fine, colored sand to make stylized representations of spirit beings, in particular for use in Navajo curing ceremonials.

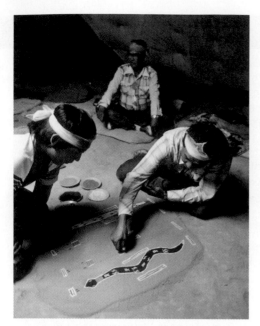

The designs in this Navajo medicine man's sandpainting are part of a healing ritual.

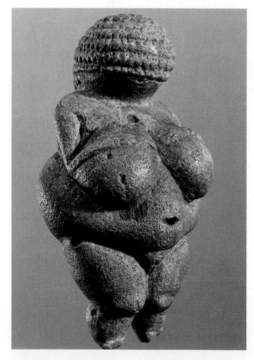

This four-inch figurine of a woman, found in Willendorf, Austria, dates to between 26,000 and 24,000 years ago.

Venus figurines
Sculptures made in Europe about 30,000 years ago, thought to represent pregnant women.

Diné's spirit beings. During the ritual, practitioners, called singers, and their helpers make a sandpainting on the floor of the ceremonial hogan or house by trickling ground bits of red, yellow, and white sandstone and charcoal through their fingers. The patient sits on one of the figures depicted. The singers then moisten their palms with herbal medicines, take up sand from the painting, and apply it to the corresponding parts of the patient's body. This act identifies the patient with the Holy People and allows the patient to absorb their protective powers and exchange evil for good.

When the ceremonial is completed, the sandpainting is ritually destroyed. The designs are methodically erased, trampled into the dirt by the healer. Once mixed back into the earth, the sand is taken up, removed from the ceremonial house, and disposed of to the north, the direction of power and danger. Although the Diné recognize and appreciate the beauty of the painting, its purpose is not to remain a frozen design but, rather, to create power. The act of creation and the use to which it is put make the painting powerful and effective. But its power also makes it dangerous. Therefore, it must be destroyed to protect human beings from the effects of too much contact with too great a spirit force.

The earliest known works of art date to about 30,000 to 40,000 years ago in Europe and Africa and to about 30,000 to 50,000 years ago in Australia (Peregrine 2003). Most of these are paintings in caves or on rocks. The most famous European examples come from caves in southern France and northern Spain. There, people used paint to depict animals and hunting gear. Because of the association between the animals and the weapons, anthropologists believe that the paintings were intended to bring about a successful hunt. This is a form of association called imitative magic, discussed in Chapter 14. Perhaps people believed that, by drawing pictures of animals being hunted, they were increasing the likelihood of a successful outcome. Although this is a reasonable hypothesis, it is impossible to know what people living so long ago believed or intended by their actions.

Cave paintings and rock paintings of animals have also been discovered in Africa dating to about the same time as those in Europe. Even older examples have been found in Australia. Some of the Australian examples include outlined and stick-figure drawings of animals and human beings, as well as stenciled outlines of human hands. These paintings and etchings, as well as those found in Europe and Africa, may be reflections of images connecting the artists to the spirit world and to experiences of spiritual power obtained through prayer, trance, and shamanic performances. Again, we will never know what these drawings and etchings meant to the people who created them, but we do know that modern Aboriginal Australians intend their paintings and drawings to represent spirit beings alive in the Dreaming, a primordial time when the world was being formed (Hume 2000). These spirits arose from inside the earth and then crossed the Australian continent, performing works and creating features of the landscape as they went. They also created human beings and taught the people important elements of their culture and beliefs.

Ancient stone sculptures have been discovered in Europe, dating to about 30,000 years ago. These sculptures, known as **Venus figurines,** are thought to represent pregnant women with enlarged breasts and hips. As in the case of cave and rock paintings, several theories attempt to explain the meaning of the carvings (Peregrine 2003, 15). Some researchers suggest that they were fertility objects, intended through principles of imitative magic to promote human fertility. Others suggest that they were meant as erotic representations of women. Still others analyze them as self-portraits made by women to depict their own bodies (McDermott 1996). All of these views focus on the disproportionate size of the breasts and hips of the sculpted figurines. By emphasizing secondary sexual characteristics, the figurines could be representations of fertility or of erotic sexual pleasure.

Male figurines with enlarged penises have also been found in Europe and elsewhere. These date from earliest farming communities and may, along with female symbols, be representations of generative impulses and powers (Gimbutas 1982).

CONTR O VERSIES

Interpreting "Art": The Case of Inca Quipus

It can be difficult to understand the objects ancient peoples produced. We may infer that sculptures or paintings produced by ancient Egyptians, Aztecs, or Greeks had representational or symbolic meaning. We assume that the designs used to decorate objects or the paints applied to their surfaces had symbolic or expressive meaning to their creators. We may not be sure what that meaning was, but we generally assume that they intended to produce a work of art. But what can we know about objects such as the Inca quipu?

Quipu means "knot" in Quechua, an indigenous Andean language. It was a device made out of knotted strings that was used for record keeping in the Inca Empire. All complex state societies need to keep track of their population, their economic output, trade, military service, and tribute or taxes. The Inca quipus served to enumerate objects or people and as records of events (Urton 2003).

Quipus present us with a number of dilemmas. First, although archaeologists and historians believe that they

Inca Empire

Quipus were constructed of strings, thickly spun and interwoven.

understand the counting system the Inca used in constructing the quipus, they do not know what was being counted or recorded. Second, we may find the quipus beautiful; we appreciate the use of color, texture, and design. But we do not know if the people who created them intended them to be works of art as well as utilitarian objects for record keeping. This problem touches on the issues of artistic intentionality and interpretation. Because quipus are no longer used for record keeping, we see them as objects of human creation detached from their utilitarian context. We can value them for their skill and ingenuity of construction and for the beauty of their textures and colors. But we will never know what was in their creators' minds. This is a problem that arises in comparing different artistic traditions. If we are studying the aesthetic principles and artistic traditions of living peoples, we can always ask them what they think about their work. With prehistoric cultures, that is impossible.

● CRITICAL THINKING QUESTIONS

Were quipus art? What about utilitarian objects in our own society? Would an anthropologist from the distant future consider an automobile, a stapler, or a light switch art?

Art is human and ancient, but we cannot know the intentions of prehistoric artists or distinguish ● utilitarian art (crafts and decorative arts) from high art or fine art. All art may be seen as utilitarian in some way. Cave art and fertility figurines suggest the importance of art in magic, religion, and ritual.

THE ARTS OF SOUND AND MOVEMENT

Artistic impulses also find expression in the sounds of music and song. In many cultures, music and singing are means of expressing religious themes or making contact with the spirit world. Through the power of song and sound, people attract spirit beings and transmit messages to the spirit realm. In some societies, religious songs must be sung according to prescribed patterns; in others, people compose their songs spontaneously as they make direct contact with the spirit world.

Do you ever find yourself singing spontaneously? What are the occasions? What are the songs?

Among the Gitksan of British Columbia, songs come spontaneously to people when they are called by the spirits to be healers or other religious practitioners. Isaac Tens, a Gitksan healer, had such an experience when he began to receive messages from the spirit world. In the midst of a vision from an Owl Spirit, he reported, "My body was quivering. While I remained in this state, I began to sing. A chant was coming out of me without my being able to do anything to stop it. Many things appeared to me presently: huge birds and other animals. They were calling me" (Barbeau 1975, 5).

Secular songs and spontaneous singing often accompany everyday activities. For example, the Diné of the American Southwest have "riding songs, walking songs, grinding songs, planting songs, growing songs, and harvesting songs" (Witherspoon 1977). These songs are sung not to entertain the singer but to enhance the beauty and harmony of the activity. According to Gary Witherspoon, the Diné, "count their wealth in songs they know, especially in the songs they have created" (p. 155). It is, therefore, the acts of creation and of artistic expression that make the songs beautiful and meaningful. In the words of a Diné singer quoted by ethnomusicologist David McAllester, "If it's worthwhile, it's beautiful" (1954, 71). Artistic expression is one means of creating and living in beauty and harmony.

The Inuit understand artistic expression in songs as a creative impulse that allows people to convey their inner feelings in ways that ordinary words cannot. As an Inuit man in Arctic Canada explained:

> Songs are thoughts, sung out with the breath when people are moved by great forces and ordinary speech no longer suffices. Man is moved just like the ice floe sailing here and there out in the current. His thoughts are driven by a flowing force when he feels joy, when he feels fear, when he feels sorrow. Thoughts can wash over him like a flood, making his breath come in gasps and his heart throb. And then it will happen that we, who always think we are small, will feel still smaller. And we will fear to use words. But it will happen that the words we need will come of themselves. When the words we want to use shoot up of themselves—we get a new song. (Rasmussen 1929)

In the Trobriand Islands of Melanesia, mourning is accompanied by intense singing by men. Groups of men gather in the evening outside the house after a death and spend the night singing. Some of these men are residents of the village of the deceased, but others come from neighboring settlements to participate in the burial and mourning practices. The men sit together in groups with others from their own village. The singing then takes on a competitive air as each group of men sings their distinctive songs. However, the outcome is not hostile but rather creates calm and alleviates the tension aroused by death (Weiner 1976, 65). Trobrianders use song to avert tension and conflict in other situations as well. For example, anthropologist Annette Weiner was once present at a situation when several men sitting together in a group became angry with each other. The other men in the group began to sing loudly until everyone joined in, including the men who were angry, thus avoiding a confrontation (ibid.).

Among the Kaluli of Papua New Guinea, human song is associated with the music of birds. Birds are thought to be the spirit reflections of people after death. That is, the invisible spirits of humans are manifested in the visible world as birds (Feld 1990, 30–31). Although singing can take place in many contexts, the most elaborate songs are performed on sad occasions such as after a death, the destruction of a house by fire, or loneliness after the departure of a close relative or friend (Feld 1990, 32). In these contexts, people conceive of song as derived from the "muni bird," through an origin story that tells of a sister and brother who were out fishing. The sister repeatedly caught fish while the brother caught none. Each time the brother asked the sister for some fish, she rejected the request, saying that the fish was intended for a different relative. Each time the brother whined and cried. Finally, he caught a fish and gradually turned into a muni bird. As he flew away, he sang a plaintiff song while his sister begged him to return.

Although both Kaluli men and women are expert singers, women's singing is more complex and sustained. On sad occasions, both men and women first react by wailing and weeping, quickly giving way to song melodies, usually of three or four notes in imitation of the muni bird. Men's singing starts and ends abruptly whereas women's singing continues for a longer time and is accompanied by text. The texts begin with a formulaic start naming the deceased or the reason for their sadness. Then the words of the songs are improvised. In the Kaluli view, ". . . while sadness moves both men and women to weeping, it is weeping that moves women to song" (Feld 1990, 33).

Yoruba musical styles, and West African music generally, are consistent with their aesthetic emphases on strength, energy, and youthful vigor. The rhythmic impulse puts equal stress on every note, resulting in a steady outpouring of tone and sound (Thompson 1974, 7). By Western standards, music and singing sound equally loud, but this loudness and unity of musical components conveys the essence of the Yoruba aesthetic.

Ethnomusicology is the study of music and musical performances, such as dance, in past or present cultural contexts. Ethnomusicologists study music systems, instruments, aesthetic values, symbols (including language), expression (including lyrics and costumes), and communication (including folklore). Although ethnomusicology is associated with recording and videotaping traditional or tribal musicians, it is really about studying any music from an anthropological perspective. How do people define, create, and use music in their lives and in the life of their community?

Dance is an art that is truly universal, appearing as a form of individual and group expression in all cultures. As Anya Royce notes, "Dance has been called the oldest of the arts. It is perhaps equally true that it is older than the arts. The human body making patterns in time and space is what makes the dance unique among the arts. Perhaps it explains its antiquity and universality" (1977, 3). Furthermore, Royce says, dance shares with other "social dramas" the characteristic of an "intensification or exaggeration of ordinary behavior. These kinds of events allow an outsider to see values stated forcefully" (p. 27).

In most cultures, dance is a central or key aspect of many rituals. Dance styles and movements may express sacred meanings handed down from ancient traditions or believed to indicate the movements of spirit beings. The intricate hand gestures of Balinese and Indian dancers refer specifically to characters or events in sacred narratives and folktales.

Artistic aesthetics influence styles of dance. The Yoruba emphasis on youthful vitality is reflected in dance as well as in sculpture and music. According to this tradition, dancers must be strong and use all parts of their bodies with equal strength and emphasis. The shoulders, the torso, the hips, and the feet are all driven by a percussive force that parallels the rhythms of the music and singing. With this force there is flexibility. All movements are linked together, with an emphasis on central balance. Finally, movements have clear boundaries marking beginnings and endings. Many of these elements, linking together movement, sound, and overall aesthetic design, have been carried into African American artistic styles, especially in dance and music (Thompson 1983).

Dance is everywhere important as a means of using the human body in the process of creating art. It involves movement of the body in ways not typically found in daily mundane activities. Dance is a complex artistic form because it generally combines many other arts as well. It is usually accompanied by the sounds of music, chanting, or singing. Dancers often adorn their bodies with special paint, costumes, and other body decorations. Dance also sometimes tells a story or expresses a narrative either in literal or symbolic form. Participation in or observation of a dance performance, therefore, is not only artistically complex but stimulates an appreciation through many realms of the senses. This appeal is a significant factor for an audience, even when observing ritual performances. So, for example, Zuni audiences often request encores of public sacred dances that they find beautiful (Bunzel 1932).

Cultural attitudes vary concerning the kinds of movements and configurations that are properly displayed in dance. And there are cultural norms about the degree of individual innovation permitted to dancers. In some societies, dancers must conform to an already established pattern, contributing very little of their own artistic sense except in some personal aspects of style and performance. In other societies, individual dancers are encouraged to innovate, creating new steps, new movements, and new configurations. There are also differences in whether people dance alone, in couples, or in groups. Gender may be a factor influencing the kinds of dancing that people do, or even whether they are permitted to dance in public at all.

As an ethnomusicologist, how might you design a study of blues, ragtime, country and western, or banjo music?

ethnomusicology
The study of the musical styles and traditions of a people.

How might you compare and contrast the cultural contexts of a tap dance, a line dance, and a disco dance?

oral literature
Stories that people tell about their sacred past, their secular histories, and their personal lives.

folktales
Secular stories that relate events that teach moral lessons or entertain listeners.

As in all aspects of behavior, context is significant. Some dances are reserved for sacred events, others for secular contexts, emphasizing the social element of dance and its entertainment values both for the dancer and the audience. Royce points out that social and recreational dances are usually relatively simple in their steps and movements so that everyone can participate (1977, 81). Dances that require greater skill tend to be performed by specialists. These specialized dances are more often restricted to particular contexts and serve other functions. They may celebrate ritual occasions, or they may be performed by specialists for an audience's entertainment. Dance may also provide emotional catharsis both for the dancer and onlookers.

Styles of dance, like all other aspects of culture, are subject to change both from innovation and influence. The kinds of social and recreational dance styles popular in the United States today differ vastly from their European, African, and other predecessors. Dances today are far removed in pattern and tempo from the courtly dances popular in Europe in the seventeenth and eighteenth centuries. Today, popular dancing may be done in groups rather than pairs, and unique movements may be preferred over the set steps of dance styles of the twentieth century, such as jazz and ballroom dancing, which called for specific steps and patterns of movement. Nevertheless, as in all other aspects of our behavior, dancers are influenced by cultural norms that dictate appropriateness in particular contexts. Today's hip-hop dancers conform to contemporary values and expectations just as their parents and grandparents conformed to the practices of their eras.

REVIEW ⊸—⊙ Music, song, and dance are universal in humans and serve critical individual and social functions, such as personal expression, group solidarity, and religious speech. Performances and their meanings must be understood through the cultural contexts in which they occur.

ORAL LITERATURE AND WRITTEN TEXTS

Another universal domain of artistic expression is **oral literature.** All peoples tell stories about their sacred past, their secular histories, and their personal lives. These narratives conform to cultural patterns of content and organization.

Sacred narratives recounting the creation or transformation of the world and the exploits of spirit beings form the central core of oral literature. Sacred stories tell of a primordial world that existed before this one and of the events that led to the formation of our present world. Such narratives present a blueprint for life, giving an understanding of how things are and how things ought to be. They may set out the roles that men and women ought to have, the relationships that people ought to have with other living creatures, and the responsibilities that people have to other members of their communities. Sacred stories present moral issues, giving guidance as to what is right and what is wrong. They may also be interpreted to validate or justify the prevailing social order, teaching people their place in society.

Folktales of a secular nature relate events that teach moral lessons or simply entertain. Like sacred narratives, folktales also have stylistic features that set them apart. For example, the oral literature of the Zuni begins with the incantation "So'nahchi," a form without a specific translation in English. The stories end with a phrase translated as "lived long ago" (Tedlock 1972; 1983). The recurrence of these phrasings alerts Zuni listeners that they are hearing a particular type of story.

A traditional Zuni performance style sets the stories off as an artistic event. The performance style includes changes in speaking volume from louder to softer, changes in voice quality, such as raspiness, tightness, and breaks, and pausing both within and between words. The dramatic shifts of pause and voice evoke different emotional states, not only on the part of the speaker but on the part of the listeners as well.

The narratives of the Western Apaches of New Mexico also have distinct stylistic features that convey cues about the type of

Storytellers, like this one at a Kwanza celebration in Chicago, often have a special role in the socialization of children.

artistic event being performed. Apache narratives, referred to as "historical tales," recount events occurring at specific, named places involving people a long time ago (Basso 1990). The stories teach moral lessons by pointing out mistakes that people made in the past and the unfortunate and sometimes humorous consequences that followed. They are morality tales, teaching and transmitting the wisdom of the ancestors and making them relevant to people today. The tales begin and end with the phrase "It happened at (named place)." This device frames the narrative, signaling to listeners both the beginning and ending.

Proverbs can be used to instruct, amuse, praise, or criticize, their particular meaning depending on the situation. Among the Akan of Ghana, people can use proverbs to indirectly give advice, make requests, or criticize someone's behavior. These are all actions that are considered rude if done directly. For example, a mother can ask her adult son to send money home to contribute to the support of his aged parents by reminding him of his familial responsibilities, quoting proverbs from the "elders." In one recorded conversation, the mother admonished her son (the researcher!) by saying "It is the elders who said, '*If someone looks after you when you're teething, you should also look after him when he loses his teeth.*' You're aware of your father's illness. Now he's incapable of working. Life is hard these days" (Obeng 1996, 532).

In many African cultures, proverbs are an important repository of traditional advice and admonitions. They, too, adhere to stylistic patterns. Here are some examples.

The eyes of the wise person see through you. (Haya)
If nothing touches the palm leaves, they do not rustle. (Ashanti)
The house-roof fights with the rain, but he who is sheltered ignores it. (Wolof)
His opinions are like water in the bottom of a canoe, going from side to side. (Efik)
A bird is in the air but its mind is on the ground. (Mandinka)
Between true friends even water drunk together is sweet enough. (Zimbabwe)
Words are spoken with their shells; let the wise man come to shuck them. (Mossi)
A family is like a forest, when you are outside it is dense, when you are inside you see that each tree has its place. (Akan)
The hunter in pursuit of an elephant does not stop to throw stones at birds. (Uganda).
Until lions have their own historians tales of the hunt will always glorify the hunter. (Igbo)
Even the Niger River must flow around an island. (Hausa)
A bird will always use another bird's feathers to feather its own nest. (Southern Sotho)
Where there is no jealousy, a small hare's leather is enough to cover four people. (Burundi)
An egg never sits on a hen (a child is never greater than its parents). (Kiswahili)
If the foot doesn't go (to the place of the quarrel), the mouth won't interfere. (Dagbani)
When they gossip about someone listen as if it were about you. (Ethiopia)
Everybody, even he who has a bad character, can be softened by kind conversation. (Sumbwa)
If a hen crows, kill it. (Northern Sotho)
All bent things, as days go by, will be straightened. (Kaonde)
Wisdom is like termite-hills: each one puts out new earth in its own way. (Luganda)
Where there is no shame, there is no honor. (Congo)
Sticks in a bundle are unbreakable. (Bondei)
He who hates, hates himself. (Zulu)

Riddles are another way of imparting cultural knowledge and wisdom through an artistic form. Riddles ask questions and provide answers that rely on wordplay, metaphor, and imagery. For example, fifteenth- and sixteenth-century Aztec children and adults tested one another with riddles as a means of both play and instruction. Following are some examples (Carrasco 1998, 168–69).

What is a little blue-green jar filled with popcorn? Someone is sure to guess our riddle: It is the sky.
What is that which is a stone offered ochre which goes jumping? The flea.
What is a mountainside that has a spring of water in it? Our nose.

What proverbs and riddles can you recall from your childhood enculturation? Which folktales may have had the greatest impact on your social or moral development?

What is that which says: You jump so that I shall jump? This is the drum stick.
What is that which is a small mirror in a house made of fir branches? Our eye.
What is it that goes along the foothills of the mountain patting [us] with its hands?
A butterfly!
What is it that has a tight shift? The tomato.
What is that which we enter in three places and leave by only one? It is our shirt.
What is a tiny colored stone sitting on the road? Dog excrement.
What is it that bends over us all over the world? The maize tassel.

Although we more readily think of artistic components of sacred and folk narratives, personal stories may also be produced by gifted storytellers with stylistic features that make them art.

For example, in an influential study of the structure of personal narratives told by ordinary people, William Labov collected the following story in response to his question, "Have you ever been in danger of dying? Have you ever said to yourself, 'This is it?'" The storyteller, a man named Harold Shambaugh, told about events that occurred to him when he was in South America. In addition to dialect, his story contains features that produce drama and tension (Labov 1997, 398).

Oh I w's settin' at a table drinkin'
And—this Norwegian sailor came over
an' kep' givin me a bunch o' junk about I was sittin' with his woman
An' everybody sittin' at the table with me were my shipmates.
So I jus' turn aroun'
an' shoved 'im
an' told 'im, I said, "Go away.
I don't even wanna fool with ya"
An' nex' thing I know I'm layin' on the floor, blood all over me,
An' a guy told me, says, "Don't move your head.
Your throat's cut."

Shambaugh's story is deceptively short and simple, but it contains all of the basic features of personal narrative. The events are recounted in chronological order with a bare minimum of detail, concentrating on the critical features of context, setting, significant characters, and dramatically relevant moments: the arrival of the Norwegian sailor, Shambaugh's responses (physical and verbal), and the result of the Norwegian's actions. But Shambaugh's skill as a storyteller is in his simplification and streamlining of events, with the effect of heightening the drama. He leaves out important details, not describing the Norwegian's actions directly but leaving it to the listener's imagination to reconstruct what happened. Only the violent consequences are stated. We contribute to the narrative ourselves by using our knowledge and imagination to fill in the empty spaces. This involves the listener as an active participant in the construction of the story.

Notice, too, the use of direct quotation: Shambaugh first quotes himself making what he presumably thought was an appropriate response to the Norwegian's accusations but evidently provoking the latter to retaliate. Then Shambaugh quotes a companion who reported the dramatic conclusion of events with the frightening warning, "Don't move your head" because "your throat's cut." Although the narrative recounts an occurrence of undoubtedly intense emotion for Shambaugh, it is told in objective, dispassionate language. The story is the product of a skilled narrator using the art of verbal construction to create a scene that he and his listeners would not soon forget.

> **What are some examples of skilled narratives you have read or heard? What literary devices contributed to their effectiveness?**

Written texts also have structural principles that reveal cultural norms and allow readers to follow, and, indeed, to anticipate the content and the plot's development. When reading novels, for example, we expect certain background facts to be made known to us, such as principal characters, physical settings, and motivations. We generally expect the plot to be about some tension or crisis in the main character's life that she confronts, deals with, or resolves. We expect some change in the character's circumstances, thoughts, or attitudes. In other words, we want the story to be about "something" where something "happens." Distinct genres of novels have their own structures and expectations. Think about the differences between Gothic romance, detective stories, and science fiction.

Some written texts are made to be visually beautiful in addition to their verbal content. For instance, ancient sacred texts produced in India combine the elegance of Sanskrit writing and the intricate beauty of illustrations embossed in gold and silver. Illustrated texts describe real as well as imagined events. Several decades after the fall of the Inca Empire, for example, Felipe Guaman Pomo de Ayala, a native Peruvian of the Andes, organized a 1,200-page handwritten manuscript around his 400 original drawings of life under the Spanish colonial government. His illustrated manuscript was essentially an account of the Spanish conquest and a letter to King Philip III of Spain asking him to reform the colonial government to save the Andean peoples from destruction (Adorno 2004).

Oral literature includes folktales, fairy tales, riddles, proverbs, poetry, rhymes, and recitations of history and myth. Written texts preserve these forms in genres that reveal the cultural norms, beliefs, values, and styles on which they are based.

ART AND GLOBALIZATION

Global processes have influenced the kinds of artworks produced, displayed, and performed. In some cases, arts originating in one country have become popular in far distant places. When a particular art form or art product is borrowed, it may keep its identification with its source, functioning as a symbol of the original ethnic or national identity. Sometimes people adopt art forms because they are associated with a dominant group and, therefore, can be interpreted as status symbols. However, people also acquire the artwork of small, relatively powerless groups in appreciation of its beauty. In the process of diffusion, art is like any other cultural form, changing both the donor and the receiver. Some indigenous communities have been able to prosper through the sale of pottery, basketry, carvings, and clothing that they formerly made for their own use and currently make for sale as well.

Performers of dance and music travel around the world, disseminating their styles and influencing one another. The current world music movement brings musicians and dancers from Asia, Africa, the Middle East, and Latin America to North American and European audiences. Not only is the music of a different style than Western forms, but the blending of music, dance, and song takes place in both sacred and secular contexts. In contrast, the performance practices of Western styles, where music is played in large concert halls, often removes ethnic musical traditions from their lived contexts (Shannon 2003). However, audiences can become sensitive to the cultural meanings of the music they hear by being exposed to new sounds and new styles.

Through colonialism and globalization, the arts of Europe and the United States have spread throughout the world. As in all diffusion, art forms carry with them cultural values and practices that contribute to culture change. Western art has also been influenced by the artistic content and styles of other peoples. For example, African music and stylistic features of sound and song have informed American musical traditions for centuries. Gospel singing, jazz, and rock and roll would not be what they are without African melodies and singing styles. African and Asian artistic traditions in music, painting, and sculpture have influenced Western art forms significantly since the nineteenth century.

Contacts between different peoples and cultures have always included introductions to one another's material and performing arts. In the twentieth century, Western art connoisseurs became fascinated with what they referred to as "primitive art," art produced by indigenous or tribal peoples. Such art was unsigned, anonymous to the Western viewer and often stereotyped as expressing a universal unconscious or innocence that modern "civilized" people have lost (Price 1989). The styles and genres of "primitive art" had a significant influence on the works of many modern painters and sculptors, including Picasso, Gauguin, and Pollock. Together, this influence is sometimes referred to as "primitivism" (McEvilley 1992).

Art and Identity

Art objects and art styles can serve as carriers of cultural identity. This is particularly true in multiethnic states where each group strives to maintain its uniqueness. Language, kinship systems, religion, and ethical values may be used to transmit and maintain cultural identity. However, the arts, both art objects and performing arts, can also carry meaning by identifying a particular ethnic group. In modern markets for indigenous

GLOBALIZATION

European classical music is taught and played in every country of the world. While maintaining national musical styles, countries such as Japan, India, and China also play European orchestral compositions. Influences on musical traditions are also evident in pop music, as American and British popular songs are sung throughout the world. All over the world, people have translated songs and musical styles into their languages from English and have translated their own songs into English as well.

What art do you display in your home? What does it say about who you are and the cultural groups you belong to?

"primitive art," the people making the art often come to see themselves through their products as symbols that represent them culturally (Graburn 1976). This connection between arts and ethnicity led some colonial and national governments to ban certain arts to impose control or enforce unity. For example, the Asmat of the part of New Guinea now absorbed by Indonesia as the province of West Irian were forbidden to continue their traditional styles of decorated house building and wood carvings, which incorporated human forms. These were seen as graven images, barred by Islamic principles.

Dance is also a marker of cultural identity. Particular types of dance styles may come to be associated both by in-group members and by outsiders as archetypal or symbolic of that cultural group. For example, we may think of the Mexican hat dance, the Hawaiian hula, and the Plains Indian war dance as representative of their respective cultural groups. This iconic use of a dance style often originates in situations of culture contact, with outsiders looking at "the other" and reinforcing stereotypes. In some situations of culture contact, people may accept others' views of them and associate their art styles with their ethnic identity.

For example, dance style is used to transmit Zapotec ethnic identity in southern Mexico. In the city of Juchitan, Zapotecs are the majority ethnic group (Royce 1977, 166). On social occasions where all the participants are Zapotec, people engage in popular Mexican dances of all types. But when non-Zapotecs are present, especially for celebrations of marriages between Zapotec and non-Zapotec, the Zapotec participants display their own ethnic dance style, emphasizing their Zapotec identity so that "the friends and relatives of the outsider spouse will be impressed with the extravagance and richness of the Zapotec heritage, which can more than hold its own in competition with anything else Mexico has to offer" (p. 170).

Art in the Global Economy

In all times and places, incorporation of indigenous peoples into regional, national, and global networks has an impact on artistic production. Local artisans become specialists, creating particular types of work destined for wider markets. These products then become symbols of their ethnic identity. For example, in Panama, women of the indigenous Kuna communities produce embroidered blouses and other items called *molas*, made of cotton appliquéd and embroidered with bright colors and bold designs. Molas were first made as blouses worn by the artisan and female members of her family. Then, in the 1960s, the influx of tourists visiting Kuna communities helped promote and broaden artistic production. Since then, production of molas has rapidly increased and diversified. Now women may sew and embroider privately in their homes or in cooperative workshops where they produce molas as blouses, wall hangings, table coverings, pillows, and numerous other household and personal items. The designs are often adapted according to market demands. Organizers of the cooperatives have contacts with retail outlets in Panama, North America, and elsewhere. These contacts influence styles and motifs by contracting for particular designs.

Through wide dissemination and popularity inside and outside of Panama, molas have become symbols of Kuna uniqueness and autonomy. The women's incorporation into the global economy helps sustain their families, contributing substantially to their income. An activity that was once part of women's domestic work has now become central to their families' economies. Many Kuna families are able to maintain other aspects of their traditional subsistence patterns and their land base, because the women bring in needed cash to purchase goods that are no longer made at home.

Similarly, in Canada, Inuit sculpture and other artworks are major sources of income in many small communities. Traditional sculptures were made from soapstone and whalebone, carved and etched to represent people, animals, and spirit beings. In the traditional view of artistic creativity, Inuit artists do not create the sculptures from their own imaginations but, rather, release the form hidden yet inherent in the medium that they are using. Thus, the soapstone releases its form through the work of the artists rather than the artists imposing their creation on the stone. Market forces have led to a diversification of Inuit artwork since the middle of the twentieth century.

In addition to sculpture, Inuit artisans now make prints and calendars for sale throughout North America and the world. The artworks and styles of carving and stenciled prints have become iconic symbols of Inuit culture.

GLOBALIZATION

In the United States and Canada, the Native American powwow has come to symbolize pan-Indian culture and heritage for the participants and for Indian and non-Indian spectators alike. Costumes worn by the dancers and the styles of dancing have spread from reservation to reservation, merging and blending formerly distinctive artistic expressions. Powwows thus symbolize both a local tribal identity and an international native identity.

Art and Tourism

In conjunction with other global processes linking distant places through trade and communication, tourists from North America, Europe, and Asia have traveled throughout the world looking for new experiences. In addition to visiting major cities that house museums, theaters, and stores, people increasingly travel to indigenous communities to learn about other cultures and collect unique arts and crafts. Indigenous peoples have taken advantage of this trend in ecotourism (a subject taken up in more detail in Chapter 17) to earn money and widen the market for their products. Many indigenous groups benefit economically from allowing tourists to explore their territories and even their homes, but others resent this attention or wish to avoid the risk of being viewed as curiosities. Some indigenous peoples use tourism as an opportunity to educate the public and gain support for political causes.

Arts made or performed for tourists often omit traditional intentions and symbolic meanings. In Hawaii, for example, the female hula dancer symbolizes tourist entertainment, a projection of tourists' ideas about the South Pacific. With her dark, flowing hair, warm, sunny smile, and alluring gestures and movements, she entices the tourist into a sensual experience. This imagery distorts Hawaiian culture, however, specifically the movements and purposes of Hawaiian dance. As Haunani-Kay Trask observed, "In the hotel version of the hula, the sacredness of the dance has completely evaporated while the athleticism and sexual expression have been packaged like ornaments. The purpose is entertainment for profit rather than a joyful and truly Hawaiian celebration of human and divine nature" (2001, 399). Yet the Hawaiian dance form "hula kahiko" is traditionally dedicated to a celebration of indigenous spirit beings, honoring them for their role in the creation of the Hawaiian Islands and the culture of indigenous peoples. The state of Hawaii has come to rely heavily on income from tourism. By 2000, tourists outnumbered state residents six to one and outnumbered Native Hawaiians by thirty to one (p. 394).

CULTURE CHANGE

DINÉ ART RESPONDS TO MARKET FORCES

The Diné (Navajo) of the American Southwest are skilled weavers of blankets and rugs and makers of silver and turquoise jewelry. They learned both of these arts from other peoples. When the Diné's ancestors migrated to the Southwest from western Canada in the fourteenth century, they settled near Pueblo peoples who had lived in the region for centuries. The Diné adopted many cultural practices from the Hopis and Zunis.

Although weaving is a man's job among Pueblo peoples, Diné women became the weavers in their families. Pueblo cloth was made from cotton, an art originally diffused from the Aztecs of Mexico. By the time Diné learned to weave, Spanish colonizers and settlers had introduced sheep into the Southwest, and Diné weavers began to work with wool. The earliest woolen blankets date from the late eighteenth century (Kahlenberg and Berlant 1972).

There were no artist specialists among the Navajo. Every woman wove blankets for her family's personal use. People draped the blankets over their shoulders as coverings. Women also made dresses, fashioned shirts and leggings for the men in their family, and made saddle blankets, sashes, and cords for their hair. Blankets were also thrown on the floor for sitting and sleeping and were hung in doorways to keep out cold and wind. But they were not used as decorative rugs, a use that became popular later in non-Indian homes.

In the 1870s, shortly after the Navajos returned to their own territory after four years of confinement in New Mexico at a U.S. army base, the people became involved in commerce, trading wool and animal skins. Within a decade, Navajo women were supplying regional markets and Anglo communities with woolen blankets. The Anglo purchasers, including the American military, used the blankets mainly as bed coverings, prompting Navajo women to make larger sizes. This was their first adaptation to market demands.

By the 1880s, Diné blankets were reaching national trade networks, finally arriving in the homes of eastern buyers. By that time, aniline dyes provided new colors in addition to the traditional white, black, and brown. A further innovation of the 1880s was machine-spun, dyed yarn that made a weavers' work much easier because they no longer had to spin the yarn from wool sheared from their own sheep.

The establishment of trading posts on the Diné reservation facilitated commercial expansion. Traders operated as middlemen, buying rugs woven by independent producers and then selling them to the American domestic market. Although commercial dyes and machine-made yarn increased production and lightened workload, these innovations also cheapened the product. Soon, wholesale houses became the primary suppliers of Diné blankets to American cities (Weiss 1984). The market for Navajo commodities also diversified. Weavers produced blankets, saddle blankets, sash belts, garters, saddle cinches, women's dresses, and knitted socks and leggings.

In addition to the blankets that women wove, men sold silver and turquoise jewelry, an art they learned from Mexican Indians. As the tourist trade grew, national companies began to sell the jewelry. Companies sent raw materials (silver, turquoise, and other jewels) to traders on the reservation, who farmed out supplies and ordered particular designs. Diné jewelers were paid by the ounce for the finished product (Weiss 1984). Silverwork included buttons, bracelets, bridle ornaments, concha belts, tobacco cases, and jewelry with turquoise stones (Bailey and Bailey 1986). When trading posts on the reservation started accepting silver ornaments in exchange for goods, people began to regard their jewelry as a form of savings. Meanwhile, crafts such as pottery and basketry declined because these products had little or no commercial value and could be replaced by store-bought items.

People prospered initially through their integration into the national economy with outlets for the sale of wool, woven products, and silverwork. However, that integration proved disastrous at the end of the nineteenth century because the people were vulnerable to fluctuations in prices for their goods. Moreover, non-Indian establishments off-reservation were producing imitation rugs and jewelry. In response, some companies established workshops on the reservation where they oversaw the production process (Weiss 1984). Although this aided sales against inauthentic competitors, it undermined the creative and autonomous role of the artists, turning them into wage workers.

Commercial interests also influenced color and design. Early Diné designs were of plain stripes, a style borrowed from their Pueblo neighbors. New motifs were introduced in the 1880s, especially diamond shapes and pictorial representations of horses, cows, birds, bows and arrows, knives and forks, shovels, houses, trains, and alphabet letters (Kahlenberg and Berlant 1972).

Copying from patterns and following instructions conflicted with traditional ways of weaving in which weavers created their own designs. Diné weaving was a spiritual, not just a utilitarian or even artistic, act. The entire process, from building the loom, carding and spinning the yarn, and weaving the pattern, was one of creative enlightenment, reenacting mythic narratives of world creation. The following is according to Diné sacred narratives:

> Spider Woman instructed the Navajo women how to weave on a loom which Spider Man told them how to make. The cross poles were made of sky and earth, the warp sticks of sunrays, the healds of rock crystal and sheet lightening. The batten was a sun halo, white shell made the comb. There were four spindles: one a stick of zigzag lightning with a whorl of cannel coal; one a stick of flash lightning with a whorl of turquoise; a third had a stick of sheet lightning with a whorl of abalone; a rain streamer formed the stick of the fourth, and its whorl was white shell. (Kahlenberg and Berlant 1972, 6)

And then, after Spider Man made the loom, he told the women:

> Now you know all that I have made for you. It is yours to work with and to use following your own wishes. But from now on when a baby girl is born you shall go and find a spider web woven at the mouth of some hole; you must take it and rub it on the baby's hand and arm. Thus, when she grows up she will weave, and her fingers and arms will not tire from the weaving. (Kahlenberg and Berlant 1972, 19)

Diné weavers and jewelers now sell their work to retail outlets on the reservation and throughout the United States and the world and via the Internet. But jewelry makers in particular have become increasingly concerned about imitation jewelry that is passed off as American Indian products. Laws ban false marketing claims by imitation jewelry, but these statutes are rarely enforced. Fake jewelry undercuts Diné (and other Native American) markets. They are made cheaply in mass production factories in foreign countries where wages are low. In comparison, authentic Diné crafts are expensive.

The Diné and other Southwestern native artisans have appealed to federal and state authorities to crack down on the illegal sale of fake jewelry, forming the Council for Indigenous Arts and Culture. In 1990, Congress passed the Indian Arts and Crafts Act (Public Law 101-644). This law makes it illegal to sell any art or craft product "in a manner that falsely suggests it is Indian produced, an Indian product, or the product of a particular Indian or Indian tribe or Indian arts and crafts organization." The act is aimed at protecting Native American artisans and the authenticity of their work.

CASE STUDY

Tourists Among the Toraja

In Indonesia, the Torajas, a farming people of Sulawesi, have attracted foreign visitors who photograph their elaborate funeral rituals and intricate carved effigies of the dead. Funeral ceremonies can go on for days and include water buffalo fights, after which the animals, sometimes more than a dozen of them, are killed as sacrifices to the ancestors. Funerary rites are based on animism and ancestor worship, with influences from Christianity derived from Dutch and British colonial agents. After the animal sacrifices, the deceased person is placed in a coffin and interred in a cave hollowed out of a high cliff containing the remains of Toraja ancestors. Sometimes the remains are suspended from the cliff wall as a hanging grave. Lifelike statues, called Tau-Tau, house the spirits of the ancestors and guard the grave sites, looking out from balconies high over the living.

The Torajas, who number approximately 350,000, have been inundated with tourists. In 1973, only 422 foreigners came to Toraja territory, but by 1991, more than 215,000 foreign and domestic tourists visited the region annually (Adams 1995a; 1995b). The Indonesian government has promoted the tourism to attract foreign dollars. The Torajas are marketed through travel brochures, postcards, T-shirts, hotel deals, and videos. They themselves purchase these commodities, becoming both viewer and viewed, observer and observed.

Tourism intensified conflict and competition among the Torajas. Torajas live in a ranked society, with status differences based on three ranks (high, middle, and low). High-status people claim descent from ancestral spirit beings who imparted the charter for Torajan society; middle-status Torajas are tradespeople; and lower-status people, the majority, are farmers and laborers.

With the influx of tourism, lower-status Torajas competed with higher-ranking groups. They began to construct elaborate carved decorations and perform funeral dances for the public, ignoring or disguising status differences in their society. This trend benefited lower-status Torajas, but it bred conflict between elite and nonelite members. The Toraja example demonstrates that outsiders, whether anthropologists or tourists, affect the inner workings of indigenous societies.

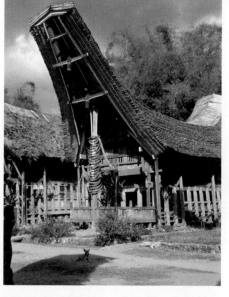

A Toraja house and granary, Sulawesi, Indonesia.

PEARSON
myanthrolab

Explore more at
www.myanthrolab.com

ANTHROPOLOGY APPLIED

Ethnomusicology

Ethnomusicologists point out that music is more than expressive or entertaining in popular culture. It can play a central role in religious, political, and economic systems. For example, Javanese gamelan ensembles accompany puppet dramas called *wayang*, which tell stories from the Hindu epics. Gamelan polyphonal music is made with bronze

keyed instruments; gongs; a xylophone, lute, zither, and flute; and choral and solo voices (Knight 2002). Traditional Mandinka drummers and kora players in Gambia, West Africa, are involved in healing ceremonies; and Tswana boys in Botswana play thumb pianos to calm the family cattle. In many societies, music marks rites of passage and is also a medium of social protest and social action (Chernoff 1981).

Some ethnomusicologists study the globalization of music and the emergence of world music. Zouk, for example, like reggae and calypso before it, is French Creole music of the West Indies. Combining African, Caribbean, and French colonial influences, zouk has gained global popularity (Guibault et al. 1993). Thus, new and emerging music, such as zouk or benga (Kenyan pop), is as much a legitimate subject of study as ancient, traditional, or folk music, such as cajun (southern Louisiana, United States).

⊙ CRITICAL THINKING QUESTIONS

What aspect or type of music might you study as an ethnomusicologist, and why? How would you apply an anthropological perspective?

Tourism and the appeal of **ethnic art**—art produced by a particular ethnic group—can make economic changes in people's lives and in village life. An example is the marked increase since the 1980s of interest in wooden carvings called *alebrijes,* produced since the 1950s by villagers in the Oaxaca Valley in Mexico. As tourism has increased, residents of the towns of Arrazola, San Martin, Tilcajete, and La Union Tejalapan have significantly raised their standard of living through sales of the carvings. The *alebrijes* are fanciful representations of lizards, cats, serpents, panthers, and other animals. Most of them are made of a soft wood, called copal, that is easy to carve but also vulnerable to insect infestations. Some artisans work instead with cedar, which is harder and longer-lasting but more costly, thus making the carvings more expensive. Many of the *alebrijes* have elaborate detailed decoration and are painted in dazzling colors.

At first, townspeople sold their work to individual buyers, mostly tourists. Then galleries in Mexico and elsewhere began to send in orders for particular designs. In addition, wealthy collectors and their agents descended on the towns to buy the most intricate and skillful of the carvings. Today, an estimated one-fifth of all of the families in the three major art-producing towns are involved in the work (Do 2004). Men and women, Zapotec Indians and mestizos—all participate. Artwork is often a family affair involving parents and their children. Adults do the carving and decorating, and children help paint the finished product, or different families may cooperate in different phases of the work.

Whatever the level of sophistication of the artist, the appeal of the *alebrijes* in national and international markets has changed the quality of life in the villages. Individual standards of living have improved as people spend their earnings on enlarging their houses and purchasing household goods that make their lives easier. In addition, the towns spend money on paving roads, bringing in electricity, and building and renovating schools. Fewer families are involved in farming, the traditional occupation and subsistence strategy of Oaxaca villagers. Many are now able to devote their time to producing ethnic arts, an occupation that earns them a greater income and is also less arduous. However, the unpredictability of the tourist art market makes the future of the Oaxacan carvers unpredictable as well. One response has been to diversify. Zapotec weavers incorporate motifs and designs from paintings by European masters such as Picasso and Miró as well as from Navajo blankets.

ethnic art

Art produced by a particular group of people that comes to express and symbolize their ethnic identity.

Ethnic arts have become commodities in the global economy, which influences art forms and alters the relationships between artists and their work and between artworks and the life of the community because art responds to market forces and tourist interests. Revenues from sales or performances of art have become important sources of income for indigenous peoples and cultural minorities.

CHAPTER SUMMARY

What Is Art?

- Anthropologists study arts and artistic principles to understand how artworks are produced, by whom, in what context, and for what purposes. They also study cultural aesthetics, or the philosophies of what has beauty and value in art. In some societies, art is meant to imitate or represent the natural world. In others, art is used to express spirituality, attract spirit beings, and honor the spirit realm.

Cultural Aesthetics

- In Western art, five aesthetic models have developed: mimetic (the ability of art to portray the world around us), representational (imitating, idealizing, or symbolizing form and experience), instrumental (transforming or improving the world, or enhancing our experience), emotionalist (connecting to our inner experience and feelings), and formalist (focusing on the formal qualities of art, the use of color, composition, sound, words, or movements).

Body Art

- Body art includes body decoration, hairstyles, clothing, and jewelry. Nomadic peoples are particularly likely to emphasize the use of the body in artistic production.

Origins and Functions of Art Objects

- The earliest known works of art date to about 30,000 to 40,000 years ago in Europe and Africa and about 30,000 to 50,000 years ago in Australia. Most of these are paintings in caves or on rocks. Many have been interpreted as sympathetic magic, connecting animals hunted with weapons used.

The Arts of Sound and Movement

- In many cultures, music and singing are means of expressing religious themes or contacting the spirit world. Songs and spontaneous singing also often accompany everyday activities.

- Dance is a form of individual and group expression in all cultures. In most cultures, dance is a key aspect of rituals. Dance uses the human body to create art.

Oral Literature and Written Texts

- Another universal domain of artistic expression is oral literature. Oral literature includes sacred narratives told about the spirit world or used in rituals and secular folktales that teach moral lessons or entertain. Proverbs, riddles, and other wordplay also instruct, amuse, advise, praise, or criticize listeners. Cultural styles of storytelling allow speakers to recount personal events and experiences.

Art and Globalization

- Styles of art are, like all aspects of culture, subject to change both from innovation and influence. Art can also function as a marker of cultural identity, particularly in multiethnic states where each group strives to maintain and dramatize its uniqueness.

- Incorporating indigenous peoples into regional, national, and global networks influences artistic production. Local artisans have become specialists creating work for wider markets. These products then become symbols of their ethnic identity. Like any goods or services, artworks respond to market forces.

- Indigenous peoples have become tourist attractions, marketing and selling their products and performances to a national and international audience. Tourism brings income to remote and marginalized communities. As ethnic art objects become popular, artisans can improve their standard of living and the community as a whole.

KEY TERMS

aesthetics 385	instrumental 386	artisans 390	oral literature 396
art 385	formalist 386	sandpaintings 391	folktales 396
mimetic 386	scarification 388	Venus figurines 392	ethnic art 405
representational 386	tattooing 388	ethnomusicology 395	

REVIEW QUESTIONS

1. How do anthropologists distinguish among types or categories of art?

2. On what different aesthetic principles can art be based?

3. How do Venus figurines and Inca quipus illustrate the problems of defining art?

4. How do individuals and groups use art to signify their identity and status?

5. What is body art? What are other universal art forms?

6. What are some social functions of art forms, such as oral literature?

7. How does art relate to social institutions?

8. What are some ethnographic examples of the use of art in healing?

9. What do ethnomusicologists contribute to our understanding of being human?

10. What is the role and impact of arts and crafts in economies?

11. How is art a part of global culture?

myanthrolab EXERCISES

To complete the following exercises and activities, you must log in to www.myanthrolab.com and select your current textbook.

1. In the **Explore** tab of Chapter 15, click on *Video* and watch the video on *Artistic Expression*. Complete the short answer exercise that accompanies the slide show.

2. While in the **Explore** tab of Chapter 15 click on the *NPR Audio Programs Broadcast* tab and go to *Theme 26: Arts*. Listen to one of the programs in this section and complete the short answer exercise that accompanies the program.

3. In the **Research Tools** section on the home page, click on the *Research Navigator*™ link and enter the Anthropology database to find relevant and recent scholarly and popular press publications. For this chapter enter the following keywords: *mimetic, aesthetic/aesthetics, artisans,* and *ethnomusicology.*

4. Enter the **MyAnthroLibrary** section on the home page to read more about topics and cultures that are discussed in this chapter. Suggested readings include:

Pride Against Prejudice: Haitians in the United States by Alex Stepick (edited by Nancy Foner)

COLONIALISM AND CULTURAL TRANSFORMATIONS

- What is colonialism, and what types of colonies were established?

- What are the patterns of relationships between colonists and their countries of origin and between colonists and indigenous peoples?

- How did the European slave trade differ from traditional forms of African slavery?

- How did the European slave trade change African societies and cultures?

- How does the history of the North American fur trade illustrate culture change?

- How did the buffalo trade and the horse change the Lakota way of life?

- How were patterns of colonization and change different in North and South America?

- How did plantations, missions, mines, and epidemics change indigenous South American societies?

- Who were the agents of change, and what were their goals?

- How did native peoples react to colonialism?

- How did native peoples lose their lands, and how did Europeans justify their land seizures?

- How did colonialism and the postcolonial era help set the stage for present-day globalization?

The commerce which may be carried on with the people inhabiting the line you will pursue, renders a knowledge of those people important. You will therefore endeavour to make yourself acquainted, as far as a diligent pursuit of your journey shall admit, with the names of the nations and their numbers;

The extent and limits of their possessions;
Their relations with other tribes or nations;
Their language, traditions, monuments;
Their ordinary occupations in agriculture, fishing, hunting, war, arts, and the implements for these;
Their food, clothing, and domestic accommodations;
The diseases prevalent among them, and the remedies they use;
Moral and physical circumstances which distinguish them from the tribes we know;
Peculiarities in their laws, customs, and dispositions;
And articles of commerce they may need or furnish, and to what extent.

And, considering the interest which every nation has in extending and strengthening the authority of reason and justice among the people around them, it will be useful to acquire what knowledge you can of the state of morality, religion, and information among them; as it may better enable those who may endeavour to civilize and instruct them, to adapt their measures to the existing notions and practices of those on whom they are to operate. . . .

In all your intercourse with the natives, treat them in the most friendly and conciliatory manner which their own conduct will admit; allay all jealousies as to the object of your journey; satisfy them of its innocence; make them acquainted with the position, extent, character, peaceable and commercial dispositions of the United States; of our wish to be neighbourly, friendly, and useful to them, and of our dispositions to a commercial intercourse with them; confer with them on the points most convenient as mutual emporiums, and the articles of most desirable interchange for them and us. If a few of their influential chiefs, within practicable distance, wish to visit us, arrange such a visit with them, and furnish them with authority to call on our officers on their entering the United States, to have them conveyed to this place at the public expense. If any of them should wish to have some of their young people brought up with us, and taught such arts as may be useful to them, we will receive, instruct, and take care of them. Such a mission, whether of influential chiefs, or of young people, would give some security to your own party.

From Thomas Jefferson letter to Meriwether Lewis, 1803, http://www.mt.net/~rojomo/landc.htm.

Thomas Jefferson's 1803 letter to Meriwether Lewis at the start of what came to be called the Lewis and Clark expedition reveals the thinking behind a common pattern of state expansion. The newly independent United States was expanding the territory it perceived itself as owning in North America. That thinking also helped Europeans and Americans rationalize colonialism and aggression against native populations on a global scale.

Recall from Chapter 12 that state societies are driven to expand their borders or spheres of influence, thus requiring a continuous influx of wealth, either as goods or laborers to produce more goods. The steady and growing supply of wealth enriches the elites and allows them to increase their control within their own territories and to exert influence outside. Conquest and colonialism are the results.

The early state societies in the Middle East, North Africa, China, Peru, and Mexico gained their wealth by conquering neighboring territories and incorporating the defeated peoples into their empires. Of these, the most long-lasting societies have been the Chinese state and Arabs in the Middle East and North Africa. The extent to which conquerors forced defeated groups to alter their indigenous cultures varied in different parts of the world and at different times. This chapter focuses on processes of state expansion that originated in Europe in the fifteenth and sixteenth centuries.

EUROPEAN COLONIALISM

colonies
Settlements of foreign nationals with controlling interests in indigenous territories.

imperialism
Empire building through state expansion in both commerce and territory.

European states did what earlier states elsewhere in the world had done before them, but the Europeans were in many ways the most successful. Other states enlarged their borders through expansion into adjacent lands, continuously increasing conquered territory as their borders were extended bit by bit. People who lived at great distances from the center of the state saw the space between them and the state shrink until they were the next group to be engulfed. European expansion eventually reached worldwide not only by expanding the borders of their countries but also by increasing their control over societies hundreds or thousands of miles from their shores. Arab influence also has extensive reach in large regions of the world, especially through the spread of Islam.

Technological advances unique to Europe enabled this expansion and control. The ability to travel long distances was made possible by improvements in sailing vessels, navigation, and mapmaking, enabling European explorers, traders, soldiers, and missionaries to venture to all parts of the world. Technological improvements in armaments also allowed Europeans to threaten or kill people who resisted them.

Although colonialism as a consequence of economic and political expansion was a characteristic of many developing state societies, this chapter focuses specifically on European colonialism because Europeans were able to establish, at one time or another, the most far-flung and extensive system of colonies throughout the world. In addition, the legacies of European colonialism(s) have affected and are affecting many countries in the contemporary world. However, we should be mindful of the fact that colonial and neocolonial policies emanate from other parts of the world today, as in the past.

Colonialism Defined

European powers, specifically Great Britain, France, Spain, Portugal, and Holland, endeavored to solidify their control and influence in far-flung regions through the establishment of **colonies**—settlements of foreign nationals with controlling interests in indigenous territories. Colonies were intimately tied to the host country, but colonists remained politically and economically subordinate to their home countries. Residents of the colonies did not have equal legal or social standing with the residents of the home country. Their purpose was to produce wealth that could be extracted from the territories they occupied to enrich the home country as the colonial power. A complex system of trade tied the colonies to the home country. The home country's policies governed the ways that colonial subjects had to behave.

As Jurgen Osterhammel defines it: "A colony is a new political organization created by invasion (conquest and/or settlement colonization) but built on pre-colonial conditions. Its alien rulers are in sustained dependence on a geographically remote (mother country) or imperial center, which claims exclusive rights (possession) of the colony" (1997, 10). Osterhammel defines colonialism, then, as the following:

> [a] relationship of domination between an indigenous (or forcibly imported) majority and a minority of foreign invaders. The fundamental decisions affecting the lives of a colonized people are made and implemented by the colonial rulers in pursuit of interests that are often defined in a distant metropolis. Rejecting cultural compromises with the colonized population, colonizers are convinced of their own superiority and of their ordained mandate to rule. (1997, 16–17)

Colonialism is often linked with **imperialism**, or empire building—an extension of nation building using other people's lands and resources. Osterhammel defines imperialism as the following:

> a concept that comprises all forces and activities contributing to the construction and the maintenance of trans-colonial empires. Imperialism presupposes the

This wall painting of the Chinese attacking the Tibetans during the T'ang Dynasty (A.D. 618–907) shows that empire building is not a recent European phenomenon. China's territory and influence on other Asian peoples reflect thousands of years of state expansion and colonization.

exploitation colonies
Colonies established by military conquest for the purpose of exploiting the economic and natural resources of a region.

maritime enclaves
Colonies established as a result of sea trade and coastal exploration for the purpose of controlling trade at foreign ports.

settlement colonies
Permanent colonies established through exploration or conquest for the purpose of occupying land and controlling labor.

resettlement policies
Efforts of colonial authorities to relocate indigenous people to permanent settlements, usually on less desirable land, to control and influence them.

will and the ability of an imperial center to define as imperial its own national interests and enforce them worldwide in the anarchy of the international system. Imperialism thus implies not only colonial politics, but international politics for which colonies are not just ends in themselves, but also pawns in global power games. (1997, 21)

There were both similarities and differences in the tactics and policies of the various European states as they imposed their will and controlled the peoples of distant lands.

Types of Colonies

There are three main types of colonies, depending on the purpose of contact or conquest: exploitation colonies, maritime enclaves, and settlement colonies. **Exploitation colonies** usually result from military conquests in which the colonial power seeks to exploit the economic resources of the region. The power usually sends a relatively small number of its citizens to invade as soldiers. Then it continues to control the colony through government functionaries and traders. In exploitation colonies, the home country exerts complete dominance over the political functioning of the colony and over its soldiers, bureaucrats, and traders.

Maritime enclaves develop from sea trade and coastal exploration. Their purpose is to control trade at the ports of foreign lands and to have an indirect control over internal trade in foreign territories. The colonized country remains formally independent, but the colonizing power has some degree of influence over the political and commercial policies of the supposedly independent state through its maritime enclaves.

Settlement colonies result from military invasions that support permanent settlement by the invader's citizens. By encouraging settlement, the home country aims to acquire abundant cheap land and labor. In establishing a permanent presence, foreign settlers appropriate land from indigenous inhabitants.

Colonial governments attempt to settle nomadic people in more permanent communities—a common policy in North America in the nineteenth century. In North Africa and the Middle East, where nomadic pastoralists use vast tracts of land for grazing their animals, modern governments institute policies restricting people's access to territory, thus compelling them to abandon their traditional economies and settle in towns and villages. Resettlement policies continue today in other parts of the world, for example among native peoples of the Arctic Circle in the former USSR. As in the past, **resettlement policies** make controlling and influencing indigenous peoples easier for central government authorities.

In settlement colonies, colonists have some degree of self-rule, although the home country wields ultimate control. The rights of the indigenous population may be disregarded, and their land taken. Where they resist, they may be killed and, sometimes, whole groups may be exterminated. Different strategies develop for controlling the labor supply and acquiring land in the colony. In colonial New England and the later United States, indigenous peoples were displaced or killed if they refused to move. After an initial period of coexistence, indigenous peoples were seen as economically unnecessary.

In contrast, colonial settlers in Africa remained economically dependent on the indigenous population. Because their labor was needed on plantations and in mines, colonists could not afford to entirely displace or annihilate them. In the Caribbean and parts of North and South America, slaves were imported from Africa as the indigenous populations began to die off. Slaves performed the vital economic functions of producing crops and manufactures in colonial cities and plantations.

In the 1990s, 250,000 Tatars who had been deported in 1944 by the former USSR returned to their Crimean homeland and gathered here to honor those who died.

In Africa and elsewhere, Europeans sought to instill their values both directly and indirectly through **missionism**—settlement for the purpose of religious conversion—and education, as well as through social, economic, and political control. For example, a 1919 French reader proclaimed: "It is an advantage for a native to work for a white man, because the whites are better educated, more advanced in civilization than the natives, and because, thanks to them, the natives will make more rapid progress. . . . and become one day really useful men. . . . You who are intelligent and industrious, my children, always help the Whites in their tasks. This is a duty" (Buell 1928, 63). In East African colonies under Italian control, African children read textbooks that contained such sayings as "I am happy to be subject to the Italian government and I love Italy with the affection of a son," or "Help me, oh God, to become a good Italian!" (DeMarco 1943, 36, 40)

Christian missionaries competed with one another for influence and converts to their particular sect. Missionaries of Islam and Buddhism vied for converts as well. Islam and its cultural influences have spread, especially to North and Central Africa and Asia, from its Middle Eastern origins. More recently, it has spread to Europe and North America. Buddhist missionaries have been primarily successful in Asia. These religions have also aided processes of state consolidation and cultural transformation.

missionism
Settlement for the purpose of religious conversion.

slave trade
Buying and selling of people into servitude.

REVIEW

Imperialism, or empire building, in state societies is achieved through conquest and absorption of neighboring peoples and the establishment of colonies in distant lands. Colonialism involves the domination and exploitation of indigenous peoples. Colonies were also established as military enclaves and settlements. Settlement colonies involved forcing native peoples to relocate. Motivations for colonization included enriching the home country, gaining religious converts, and extending power and influence.

THE EUROPEAN SLAVE TRADE

GLOBALIZATION

The scope in numbers alone of the European **slave trade** is staggering. Between 1451 and 1600, about 275,000 Africans were forcibly sent to Europe and the Americas. During the seventeenth century, about 1,341,000 Africans were enslaved, sent mainly to sugarcane plantations in the Caribbean (Wolf 1982, 195–96). In the eighteenth century, more than 6 million people were taken from Africa, two-thirds to the Caribbean and most of the rest to other European colonies in the Americas. Even though Great Britain banned the slave trade in 1807, an additional 2 million Africans were sold into slavery in the nineteenth century. These figures combine to a total of about 10 million people who were stolen from their communities in Africa and sent to labor for the rest of their lives on plantations many thousands of miles away. The wealth produced by slaves in the Americas contributed to the accumulation of capital and resources in Europe, directly and indirectly leading to the Industrial Revolution in the late eighteenth and early nineteenth centuries (Williams 1944).

The slave trade was instrumental in developing a globalized system of economic and political networks from which Europeans directed and profited. The slave trade both benefited from and accelerated the growth of manufacturing in Europe, which led to the Industrial Revolution and the worldwide dominance of European commerce for centuries to come.

The Portuguese initiated the European international slave trade along the western coast of Africa. At first, they were interested in obtaining gold and spices, but then they shifted to a focus on extracting people to work on the plantations that they were developing in South America, principally in Brazil. Competition soon began as Dutch slave traders were supplying their sugar plantations in the Caribbean. By the late seventeenth century, the British and the French were deeply involved in the slave trade as well. The purchase of slaves was made possible by a rise in production of goods in Europe.

Slavery in Africa

Slavery was practiced in Africa and the Middle East long before European powers arose. Slavery was seen as a source of labor, a means of absorbing conquered peoples, and a solution for people who became destitute for any reason. The growth in the international slave trade depended on preexisting indigenous systems of slavery in West Africa that contributed to the capture and transshipment of other Africans.

This slave family living in Savannah in the 1860s contributed to their master's wealth but did not share his standard of living. In contrast, slaves in Africa lived with their masters and had similar comforts.

CULTURE CHANGE

IMPACTS OF THE EUROPEAN SLAVE TRADE ON AFRICAN STATES

The effects of the European slave trade were borne primarily by its direct victims, but it also deprived people who survived in their home communities of family members to aid in their subsistence and welfare. The slave trade tore apart households and disturbed networks of people who shared rights and responsibilities toward one another. Some Africans also benefited economically and politically from the slave trade.

The elites in West African chiefdoms and kingdoms, which existed before European contact, amassed wealth and power by participating in the European slave trade and acting as intermediaries and distributors of European goods, which they gained from selling slaves, to other members of their communities.

Elite accumulation of wealth and power contributed to the formation of state societies in West Africa whose rulers gained even more control, particularly in Nigeria and in the Congo. The Ashantis in the Gold Coast (modern Ghana) and Nigeria extended their power both locally and regionally. Ashanti slave traders gained from Europeans in exchange for slaves. The Yorubas subjugated small states and demanded slaves as tribute from conquered tribes. Through successful campaigns, they extended their trading networks into Central Africa (Wolf 1982). In contrast, the precolonial kingdom of the Kongo dissolved because competing elites vied for control of the slave trade.

The political consequences of the European slave trade for African societies, therefore, depended on the access to slaves and the role of local elites. Some states were founded; others consolidated their power; still others broke apart during the centuries of upheaval that slave trade caused. As the trade intensified, West Africans moved from their coastal villages inland to escape slave-raiding expeditions. Raiders targeted small autonomous societies that lacked strong centralized governments or armed militaries. As people moved eastward, however, they sometimes came into contact with newly emerging states that took part in slave trading in their regions. Thus, the trade that began in West Africa radiated throughout the continent. In East Africa, Arab traders took slaves to supply demands for labor in the Middle East and Asia.

The slave trade strengthened principles of patrilineal descent. In precolonial times, some Western and Central African societies reckoned descent patrilineally whereas others were based on matrilineal kinship. However, men gained greater power and authority through involvement in the slave trade and by using the sons of their slave women as warriors against other groups (Wolf 1982). This shift may have strengthened patrilineal kinship in previously matrilineal societies.

Many societies in West Africa had extensive networks of long-distance trade that could be used to funnel people forced into slavery or coerced labor. War captives were often taken from enemy communities and forced to work for their captors. Some West African societies also had systems of indenture in which people pawned themselves if they became indebted to another person and were unable to repay a loan. Selling children into slavery or service to prevent their starvation was also an option. In addition, a period of indentured labor was often used as a punishment for wrongdoing in traditional systems of justice.

From a cross-cultural perspective, how would you define the social functions of slavery? How would you account for the continuation of an international slave trade in Africa and the Middle East today?

Slavery in the Americas

Europeans and colonists saw African slaves as racially inferior. In the Americas, slaves were completely cut off from their kin and home communities. Their duration of enslavement was indefinite, with no hope of release and return. They were not seen as economic partners, though they certainly were economic assets. They could be, and were, bought and sold as possessions with no regard to their well-being, family ties, or their personal autonomy and feelings. They could be subjected to whatever treatment or maltreatment their owners decided to heap upon them.

The European Industrial Revolution was built on the African slave trade and on colonial materials and markets. The internationalization of the slave trade had profound human costs; in Africa, it led to the consolidation of kingdoms, greater competition and conflict between groups (as well as greater cooperation), and changes in families and kinship. The European slave trade contributed to the globalization that we see today.

 REVIEW

TRADE AND SETTLEMENT IN NORTH AMERICA

The colonial enterprise in North America took the form of both trading and settler colonies. Europeans first came to North America in the late fifteenth century when Portuguese, Spanish, and French fishermen caught fish in the ocean off the coast of Newfoundland and Québec. The first European to make an official landfall on the northeastern coast of North America, however, was John Cabot, who arrived in 1497 and promptly declared Newfoundland a possession of England. By 1550, approximately fifty fishing boats from each of the European countries (England, France, Portugal, Spain) were making annual visits to the Atlantic waters. By the end of the sixteenth century, the numbers had tripled (Sauer 1971).

Intermittent commercial relations in the northeast soon expanded to become the focus of European activities there. Native peoples gradually became enmeshed in trading networks that had far-reaching effects on their cultures and histories. At the same time that French, British, and Dutch traders were establishing commercial ties with indigenous nations in the northeast, Spanish adventurers were invading and plundering

At first, native peoples were often eager to trade furs, such as these beaver pelts, for metal European tools and utensils. (North Wind Picture Archives)

Mexico in the south and northward into what later became the southern United States. Although the early history of regional contact in the Western Hemisphere reveals different colonial motives, the eventual impact of European contact followed similar patterns throughout the continent. Trade, conquest, and colonization spread everywhere, and all native peoples were engulfed and their cultures transformed within a few centuries.

The Fur Trade

The involvement of Native Americans in the **fur trade,** at first peripheral to their economies, transformed their societies materially as durable metal goods became mainstays of material culture. Dependence on trade also had unforeseen negative effects. Native trappers could not control the market for furs, which made them vulnerable to changes in demand. When demand was high, people abandoned some traditional practices in an effort to keep pace. They overtrapped nearby territories, leading to a rapid depletion of beaver, otter, and other animals. People had to travel greater distances from their communities to find the desired resource, often entering territories of others who were similarly engaged in trapping and trading. Competition sometimes led to open conflict. When the demands of the fur market declined, people were left without the ability to acquire desired goods. In addition, some desired European products, such as guns and liquor, had negative effects on indigenous communities.

Involvement in the fur trade also led to other changes. As early as the seventeenth century in some eastern nations, trapping and trading became men's central economic activities. Among farming people where farmwork was the responsibility of women, food supplies were maintained; however, among foragers who depended more heavily on the meat and fish brought in by hunters, traditional food resources were not exploited as fully as previously. Many people then traded with Europeans for food as well as for manufactured goods. This process eventually led to increased dependence on traders, further deepening the need to spend even more time trapping animals.

Women were also involved in the fur trade because their labor was necessary to prepare the pelts for market. As the economic roles of both men and women focused more on tasks related to the fur trade, people grew more dependent on trade to supply their needs and wants. Economic systems shifted from subsistence to a focus on trapping and trading. Thus, the shift in gender roles and a new emphasis on acquiring personal wealth and private property also developed.

Through indigenous peoples' contact with Europeans, the concept of personal private property developed, which contrasted fundamentally with most traditional beliefs about ownership of resources either communally or by kinship groups as collective entities. As people lost access to their own territory, competition grew to own or control lands and resources that remained, often leading to warfare. In addition, formerly nomadic communities gradually established temporary and then permanent settlements near trading posts. This change was most marked in Canada and the Arctic. Small groups began to camp near riverbanks and coastal trading posts for access to European goods. Other demographic changes included great losses in population.

Westward Expansion and Depopulation

fur trade
Exchange of animal pelts or hides between Native Americans and colonists in exchange for European trade goods.

As trade and European settlement moved steadily westward in the eighteenth and nineteenth centuries, intense wars of survival pitted native groups against one another. Conflicts were often prompted and made worse by Europeans, who forged commercial and military alliances with native peoples in opposition to other European nations and their respective indigenous allies. In this new form of warfare, thousands of people were killed, and thousands more were routed from their homes or forced to flee to safety.

The Europeans' desires for settlement intensified competition over land. The British were most successful in establishing growing communities in North America, but French settlements remained comparatively small and isolated along the rivers and ports of their primary dominance in what is now Québec and New Orleans. The Spanish foothold in North America was concentrated in Mexico, and in what is now the southern United States and California. Beginning in the early seventeenth century, English colonists established villages from the Atlantic coast moving steadily westward. In doing so, they expropriated indigenous lands and dispersed, annihilated, or assimilated the original inhabitants.

European expropriation was aided by the spread of diseases of European origin that had never been seen in North America, especially smallpox, measles, and influenza. Native peoples had no natural resistance or immunities to these diseases. In the early 1600s, the Powhatan chief, Wahunsonacock, told John Smith in Virginia: "I have seen two generations of my people die. Not a man of the two generations is alive now but myself" (Hariot 1972). In Massachusetts, Massasoit, a Wampanoag chief, concluded, "Englishmen, take that land, for none is left to occupy it" (Brasser 1978, 66). As settlers moved westward, carrying their diseases with them, they caused untold numbers of deaths when they settled in the plains in the early and mid-nineteenth century. As Little Wolf of the Cheyenne noted, "Many have died of diseases we have no name for" (Thornton 1987, 134).

Estimates for the indigenous population of North America vary widely. Today, accepted figures range from more than 2 million (Ubelaker 1976) to more than 7 million (Thornton 1987). Whatever the number, rates of decline from the sixteenth through the nineteenth centuries were undoubtedly enormous. By the end of the nineteenth century, only about 250,000 Native Americans survived in the United States. This steep **depopulation** had significant social, economic, and political consequences, in addition to the human tragedy. Whole families—sometimes entire lineages or clans—were wiped out in just a few years. Not only did the most vulnerable, such as young children and elders, die in great numbers, but men and women in their prime also succumbed. Their deaths left survivors without the farmers, gatherers, hunters, artisans, and leaders they needed to sustain themselves and their ways of life.

GLOBALIZATION

Depopulation was a global phenomenon, not limited to European colonies in the Americas. European colonies in Indonesia and the Pacific islands and in Australia also led to depopulation among indigenous peoples.

REVIEW

European trade and settlement in North America began with the fur trade and led to the depopulation of Native Americans through displacement, warfare, and disease. Participation in European trading networks transformed native peoples' subsistence activities, settlement patterns, land use, gender relations, political organization, and economic systems.

SPANISH COLONIZATION IN THE AMERICAS

The Spanish began their invasions and conquests in Mexico and Central and South America in the early sixteenth century. Their goal was originally to find gold and other precious metals. It later shifted to acquiring territory to establish large plantations for growing domestic and imported crops. Spain lost Brazil to Portugal, but the Spanish took land and resources elsewhere on the continent. At first, both groups confiscated indigenous people's land and forced them to work on plantations. Other native people were forced to work in mines, extracting silver and other precious minerals.

An early catastrophic effect of European invasion was loss of life through disease. Reliable figures are not available for the pre-Columbian populations of South America, but estimates for Mexico suggest a native population of approximately 30 million at the time of the Spanish invasions in 1519. The indigenous population of Mexico fell to 3 million in 1568, a loss of 90 percent in barely fifty years (Cowley and Talbot 2001, 281).

In the Andes as well, Spanish invasions took a toll as a result of direct military conflict and the spread of European diseases. Examination of Inca skeletal samples from Ecuador indicates that, just prior to contact, the health of native populations was beginning to deteriorate (Ubelaker 1994). These health deficits resulted from sedentary lifestyles and higher population densities associated with farming as the Inca Empire

depopulation
Reduction in population size as a result of war, conquest, colonization, or disease.

expanded. Recall from Chapter 7 the benefits and risks of agriculture as a mode of subsistence. These conditions accelerated in the period following the Spanish invasions. Life expectancy dropped further, especially for people under the age of 15, and maximum longevity in years also declined. These health effects were directly caused by trauma and exposure to infectious diseases. As mentioned earlier, one consequence of this die-off of Native Americans was the importation of African slaves to Spanish and Portuguese colonial plantations.

CASE STUDY

Lakota Trade and the Consequences of Change in Economic Production

The Lakotas were a loose alliance of nations whose original homeland was in central Minnesota. Their economy combined farming and foraging. Women did the planting and gathered wild foods, and men were hunters. Lakotas also exchanged meat and hides for crops from settled farming peoples.

Although Lakotas were well adapted to their prairie environment, the arrival of European settlers and traders made their stay in that region difficult. Eastern Indians fled toward the west and entered territories inhabited by other nations, leading to competition for land and resources. In the early eighteenth century, Lakotas crossed west into the Great Plains where they became nomadic foragers, extending into the Dakotas, Nebraska, and Wyoming.

The most important innovation in eighteenth-century native culture was horses, originally obtained through trading networks from Spanish sources in the Southwest. Plains Indians immediately realized these animals' potential for travel and transport. Horsemen continued their roles as traders and hunters, especially for buffalo, which became important in European and American trade.

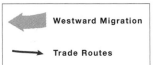

Westward Migration

Trade Routes

European trade increased the people's fortunes. Trade between Lakotas and the French began in the late seventeenth century when the people still inhabited lands in Minnesota. After the people migrated into the plains, they obtained European goods through intermediary nations such as the Mandans, Hidatsas, and Arikaras living along the Missouri River. Then, in the early 1800s, Americans from St. Louis traded with Lakotas for animal hides and meat. Lakota soon became middlemen between American traders and other native peoples living in the plains, thereby asserting economic dominance in the region.

As trade deepened, both men and women spent more time procuring and preparing animal products for market. Hunters killed many more animals than their subsistence required. Women spent more time processing buffalo meat into dried pemmican and tanning hides for trade (Klein 1980).

Economic changes promoted shifts in cultural values and social relations. In contrast to traditional ethics of equality and generosity, greater differences in wealth and rank emerged. The number of horses people owned became a symbol of their fortunes, as the accumulation of property became a desired goal. People increased the number of their horses by buying them, or, more commonly, by raiding other peoples. Wealthy families enhanced their social prestige by being generous to others. However, unlike past practices, when successful people gave away all or most of their surplus abundance, now wealthy families kept more of their personal goods, thereby leading to differences in standards of living.

A complex relationship developed between gender and wealth. To accumulate property and increase status, a man needed women's services to transform raw products into marketable items. However, one woman working alone could not keep pace with the supply of animals that a man could hunt. Three to ten days of work were probably required to tan one buffalo hide, yielding a seasonal rate of twenty to thirty hides (Klein 1983, 155). Thus, men sought to have more than one wife. Age at marriage rose for men, therefore, as only experienced hunters and warriors could acquire enough horses to give as obligatory gifts to a woman's parents upon proposal of marriage. Marriage for women declined, as fathers agreed to daughters' unions in exchange for the horses they would receive. The widening gap in age between spouses strengthened husbands' control because seniority conferred prestige in Lakota society.

Interaction with American traders destabilized power relations among the Lakotas. Traders and government officials established ties with individuals who they thought could control hunters and warriors, shifting the economic balance in favor of hunting and trapping for the market. Although the "chiefs" that Americans contacted did not traditionally dominate their communities, "the more the agents treated them as powerful, the more powerful they became" (Schusky 1994, 263–64). As native leaders became the conduit for wealth to their nation, they used the situation to their material and social advantage.

Thus, trade had complex, interconnected consequences for the Lakotas and other indigenous nations of North America (and elsewhere). Changes in subsistence strategies, settlement patterns, gender relations, and the social order were mutually reinforcing in transforming indigenous ways of life.

Explore more at
www.myanthrolab.com

encomiendas
Spanish landholding system in the American colonies that granted the use of land and the labor of any indigenous people on that land to soldiers, priests, and settlers.

haciendas
Estates made up of lands directly owned by Spanish settlers.

Indigenous depopulation as a direct or indirect consequence of colonialism has been estimated for a number of countries worldwide, such as those shown in Table 16.1.

Spanish Landholding in the Colonies

The Spanish crown gave land grants, called **encomiendas,** to soldiers, priests, and settlers. Encomiendas gave the holder rights to use the land and the labor of the native people residing on that land. The native people were essentially conscripted laborers, forced to work for others on the very land that they once held themselves. Another landholding system was the estates, or **haciendas,** direct ownership of land by Spanish settlers. Native people on haciendas worked as sharecroppers, owing part of their produce to the owners. A third type of landholding was the mission village, populated by Spanish priests and their forced converts. People in surrounding communities were compelled to relocate to the missions and to provide labor on mission farms. New Spanish settlers promptly confiscated land vacated by the indigenous population.

TABLE 16.1 ESTIMATED DEPOPULATION IN THE AMERICAS AND THE PACIFIC

	Precontact Population	Population Low Point	Depopulation
United States and Canada	7,000,000	390,000	6,610,000*
South America	8,500,000	450,000	8,050,000
Oceania/Polynesia	1,100,000	180,000	920,000
Micronesia	200,000	83,000	117,000
Melanesia/Fiji	300,000	85,000	215,000
New Caledonia	100,000	27,000	73,000
Australia	300,000	60,500	239,500

*According to the 2000 U.S. Census, Native American and Alaskan native populations have rebounded to nearly 2.5 million people, about a third of the original estimated population. Native Hawaiians, Samoans, Tongans, Tahitians, and other Pacific Islanders numbered 398,000 in 2000.

*Source: John Bodley, Victims of Progress, 5th ed. © 2008. Altamira Press, p. 50. Reprinted by permission of Rowman & Littlefield.

mita
Traditional Incan system of conscripted labor for public works, adapted by the Spanish for use in obtaining indigenous workers for their mines.

Mining Quotas

Mining interests were activated by the discovery of silver in Bolivia in 1545. At first, the Spanish obtained indigenous workers for their mines using the model of community service already present in the Inca Empire. In this system, called **mita,** each community was obligated to provide a specified number of workers for state projects. Under Incan control, men worked on public construction projects such as roads and irrigation works, and both men and women worked on farms owned by the Incan elite and priesthoods. The Spanish used the same system of labor but for Spanish profit rather than public works. The system became increasingly brutal as people died from disease and the rigors of the work. Burdens on each worker increased as the population shrank and service quotas for each community remained constant. The Spanish also obtained workers for their mines by dispossessing people from their land, turning them into "free" laborers. Unable to earn a living from their land, free laborers found it necessary to take whatever work they could find, essentially consigning themselves to the mines. Later, African slaves were used in the mine industry, especially in the processing of silver with mercury (Wolf 1982).

Intermarriage

In both South America and Mexico, Spaniards replaced the indigenous social elites but also used some elites to control local populations. Local elites were permitted to continue receiving tribute in produce and labor from members of the common classes. They functioned as supervisors of local populations, helping to keep rebellion in check in their own interests as well as those of Spanish colonists.

Marriage customs reinforced this social system. In Mexico, for example, the Spanish government encouraged intermarriage between Spanish men and native women, often through capture and rape. Because most of the Spanish immigrants into Mexico were men, they needed the services, sexual and domestic, of indigenous women. In addition, Spanish authorities believed that intermarriage would create a mixed-race class of people that would stabilize social tensions created by invasion and conquest.

The Mission System

In the southwestern United States and California, the building of missions and military forts more directly destroyed indigenous culture. By the end of the eighteenth century, colonists had enslaved tens of thousands of native people, who were rounded up, removed from their homes, compelled to convert to Roman Catholicism, and forced into labor. Mission Indians typically lived in virtual slavery. Infractions or resistance were often punished by beatings, solitary confinement, mutilation, branding, or execution (Castillo 1978; Jackson and Castillo 1995). The brutal treatment, as well as malnutrition, led to a precipitous decline in the native population. As elsewhere in North America, disease was the most significant cause of death, accounting for about one-half of deaths (Cook 1976; 1978).

REVIEW ──⊙ Spanish colonization of Mexico, Central America, the Caribbean, and South America was based on plantation farming and mining using forced native labor and the mita system. Encomiendas, haciendas, and the mission system removed land and resources from indigenous access or control. Intermarriage created a unique system of social stratification with Native Americans at the bottom of the hierarchy.

AGENTS OF DIRECTED CULTURE CHANGE

Colonial authorities attempted to subdue indigenous populations through military actions and the establishment of law and order in the colonies. They also applied social, economic, and political pressures on indigenous peoples to persuade them to change their cultural practices to be more consistent with European values and behaviors. Indoctrination was achieved through the work of missionaries, teachers, and enforcers of the rule of law.

Missionaries

Missionaries were a powerful force for cultural transformation in indigenous communities. From the sixteenth century, missionaries preceded, accompanied, and followed military and exploratory campaigns into the Americas. At first, they generally saw their role as compatible with their country's goals, which included converting, civilizing, and, they thought, helping pagan inhabitants, while at the same time exploiting any resources that might benefit their home country and the church. In later periods, though, missionaries sometimes came into conflict with civilian authorities, whose actions and policies toward native people became increasingly brutal at a time when European moral standards had begun to change.

Different groups of missionaries had different approaches to conversion. Many thought that indigenous people were subhuman and should be controlled as one would control animals. As soon as they entered a region and gained control, they forced the people to build churches, destroyed traditional ceremonial structures and paraphernalia, and beat and tortured native religious leaders into submission.

A Spanish hacienda in Tarahuasi, Peru.

Others assumed that indigenous people were fully human and capable of intelligent thought and reasoning (Vecsey 1997). Jesuits, for example, believed that pagan religious and intellectual errors resulted from the powers that the devil had over them or from the control exerted by native people who masqueraded as shamans and religious practitioners. Many missionaries saw their role as enlightening misguided but sincere people. They also made use of economic and political arguments to gain converts. Trading posts gave favorable terms and provided guns to Christian Indians but not to pagans (Bonvillain 1986).

Later, British missionaries came to convert indigenous people to Protestantism. They emphasized the spiritual rewards of Christianity along with advantages of protection supposedly bestowed upon converts by the British crown. Christian Indians were favored through trade and military alliances. Missionaries taught people, directly or indirectly, to be ashamed of their culture, their heritage, and themselves. They transferred the Christian notion of sin to people who had no concept of innate sinfulness. In the words of a modern Coast Salish Catholic from the state of Washington, "The priests said, 'You are sinful, vile,' and the Indians wondered, 'What have I done?'" (Hilbert 1987, quoted in Vecsey 1997, 351).

The missionaries advocated changes in native settlement patterns and systems of leadership and social control. They encouraged people who were previously nomadic to settle permanently, preferably near European ports and trading posts, where they were more easily contacted and controlled. The priests tried to convince their converts to obey laws, their superiors, and colonial government personnel. Many tried to supplant indigenous child-rearing practices that they saw as lenient with more authoritarian measures, including corporal punishment as a means of controlling a child's will and compelling obedience. Missionaries also condemned native ethics concerning sexuality, which generally regarded premarital sexual relations as normal and natural. They also criticized marital flexibility and the relative ease of divorce found in most indigenous societies. Lastly, they attempted to transform the basically egalitarian gender relations that they observed in most native societies into the system of patriarchal dominance and authority that was typical of Europe.

Schoolteachers

In all countries under colonial control, authorities used education as a means of reorienting indigenous cultures. Forced attendance at boarding schools, for example, separated children from their parents and communities, with the result that children lost touch with traditional ways of interacting, sacred knowledge and rituals, and even their native languages. Values inculcated in schools encouraged children to identify with their teachers

GLOBALIZATION

Throughout the world, European colonizers banned ceremonial practices they saw as contrary to Christian beliefs and ethics. Also, missionaries, teachers, and government officials distributed clothing to native peoples in the Americas, Africa, and the Pacific. They especially insisted that women wear blouses or dresses to cover their breasts and that men wear shorts or pants instead of traditional clothing styles that revealed all or part of their genitals. Today, the same type of native clothing may be found on an Amazonian Indian and a Belgian tourist in New York City or Tokyo.

while at the same time making them ashamed of their parents and their heritage. They were taught that their people's customs were backward, immoral, and irrational. They were made to believe that civilization, as reflected in European customs, was desirable, if not fully attainable. These lessons were taught subtly in the context of general education, religious instruction, and industrious work. The values of hard work and obedience to authority (whether it be teacher, administrator, or king) were transmitted as necessary attributes of a civilized and educated person.

Missionaries, teachers, and government officials also condemned indigenous religious ceremonies and practitioners. Some practices, especially shamanism, were seen as backward, ignorant, and dangerous. In North America, the U.S. government outlawed the Sun Dance ceremony of the Plains Indians, and the Canadian government outlawed the potlatch ceremonial complex of the Pacific Northwest peoples.

Government Officials

Colonial administrators imposed Eurocentric patterns of law and social control in indigenous and tribal societies, which they saw as essentially disorderly. European jurisprudence, based solely on the facts in a criminal case or civil dispute, was antithetical to native justice, which was based on social context. This social context included common knowledge about the parties in a dispute and the reciprocal obligations that people have toward one another in relatively small, face-to-face communities. To indigenous peoples, the goal of adjudication was conflict resolution—a negotiated settlement that repairs social relations. To colonial administrators, the goal of adjudication was the determination of guilt or fault and its assignment to one of the parties in a dispute.

By imposing European concepts and systems of law, colonial authorities disturbed traditional systems of social relationships and ethical values, creating far-reaching changes in behavior and attitudes. Law has been described as "the cutting edge of colonialism" (Chanock 1985, 4) because of its effect on the fabric of indigenous society. Furthermore, by establishing courts and judicial systems based on European principles, the problems of indigenous people were reinterpreted in a language of law that distorted the indigenous experience. Concepts such as "equality under the law" and "innocent until proven guilty," for instance, were not traditional in native justice.

In some regions, colonial authorities recognized "native courts" that enforced "customary law" (Merry 1991, 893). However, **customary law** was often an inaccurate creation of colonial regimes. For example, in Zambia and Malawi, colonial authorities transformed indigenous systems of adjudication that were flexible and adaptable to different contexts and different social needs into a system of customary law that was based on a rigid written code (Chanock 1985). Enshrining a particular set of indigenous practices in a written code privileges some practices over others and creates an artificial "tradition" that then becomes identified as part of indigenous culture. Colonial authorities manipulated this process to reflect their interests in the region. When countries in Africa and elsewhere gained their independence, they sometimes used these codes of customary law to establish judicial procedures. These borrowed procedures then became central ingredients in developing statehood, a national culture, and nationalistic pride.

A Cash Economy

Colonial law and administrative control benefited elites and their wealth in both the colonies and the home country. Imposed taxes obtained income for the state and compelled changes in indigenous economic systems. In Africa, both British and French administrations used taxation. Households were required to pay taxes in cash, but people's access to money was limited, because their economies were based on subsistence farming or cattle herding. Access to manufactured goods, foods, and luxury items also required cash. As a result, some members of the family, usually men, had to obtain work outside of their local communities for which they would be paid in cash. In some areas, women sold milk and home-brewed beer for cash.

In Africa, most of the work available was on plantations producing crops for export or in mines extracting valuable mineral resources. Migration from rural areas to plantations, mines, and towns disturbed the social cohesiveness of local communities; families were splintered by the need for employment to buy the goods that had come to

customary law
Selected aspects of native justice and jurisprudence codified into law by colonial authorities, mainly to secure greater control over indigenous populations.

symbolize the good life. Women who remained in the local communities were burdened by additional responsibilities in their households and in subsistence farming that supported their families. Colonial **cash economies** and systems of taxation thus continued the household and community fracturing that had occurred during the slave trade era.

Agents of directed culture change included missionaries, schoolteachers, and government officials. They discouraged or outlawed traditional ways of life, changing how people ate, dressed, and raised their children. They also imposed European values. Finally, they introduced a cash economy, which led to labor migration and changes in family relations and replaced traditional systems of reciprocity and redistribution.

JUSTIFICATIONS FOR COLONIAL RULE

Throughout the eighteenth and nineteenth centuries, European control increased in many parts of the world. The colonial presence of the Portuguese, Spanish, and Dutch was gradually replaced by that of Great Britain, France, Germany, Italy, Belgium, and the United States. As they set up colonial regimes in Africa, Asia, and the Pacific, they developed new justifications for their rule to replace the earlier rationale that Europeans could take lands they conquered simply by self-declared "right of discovery."

The British used the model of European landholding patterns and practices to claim that, in order to "own" land, one had to transform it through labor. This agrarian model did not always fit indigenous economies in other parts of the world. Thus, British authorities recognized that indigenous people "used" land but questioned whether they "owned" it. Lack of proof of ownership thus became a rationale for ignoring indigenous claims to land and resources.

The same principle of landownership through farming was used in the United States to justify settler expansion in the plains and the West in the nineteenth century. Many indigenous peoples were nomadic foragers without fixed or permanent settlement sites. American authorities viewed hunting territories as open and unsettled because they did not find permanent villages and plowed fields. In Australia as well, the British and, later, Australian governments ignored the rights of Aborigines to their accustomed territories. They claimed that the land was "unoccupied wasteland" and therefore could be appropriated by the Australian state (Bodley 1999, 88).

White Man's Burden

European colonizers also justified their control of indigenous peoples by claiming cultural and moral superiority. Administering to these people responsibly was the **"white man's burden."** Various versions of the white man's burden were used to justify the eradication of indigenous practices and their replacement with behaviors, values, and attitudes more consistent with those of Europeans. Missionaries working in North and South America in the sixteenth and seventeenth centuries embodied the idea that they were saving the natives and doing God's work by converting them.

In Africa, Asia, and the Pacific, educators and government officials spoke the same Eurocentric and essentially racist attitudes in a language of science and reason. For example, Herman Merivale, a British professor of political economy, wrote in 1861 that the natives deserved protection from the excesses of colonial settlers and also deserved to be civilized by the guidance and superiority of the white men. As Merivale advocated, "Colonial authorities should act upon the assumption that they have the right, in virtue of the relative position of civilized and Christian men to savages, to enforce abstinence from immoral and degrading practices" such as cannibalism, infanticide, and wife abuse (1988, 101). Furthermore, "[T]here should be no hesitation in acting on the broad principle that the natives must, for their own protection, be placed in a situation of acknowledged inferiority, and consequently of tutelage" (p. 103).

In 1841, the British House of Commons Select Committee on South Australia issued an official report (*British Parliamentary Papers*, 1841, vol. IV, no. 394) generally deploring

cash economies
Systems of exchange based on the use of currency in modern markets.

white man's burden
Paternalistic, racist, colonial attitude that treated colonized peoples as inferiors in need of protection and instruction on how to live.

In your opinion, should Europeans have refrained from interfering in native practices of cannibalism, infanticide, and domestic abuse? Why, or why not?

the harsh treatment of Aborigines by colonial authorities. It observed that government policy "has thrown impediments in the way of successful colonization; it has engendered wars, and it has vanished from our confines, or exterminated, the native, who might have been profitable workmen, good customers, and good neighbors" (quoted in Bodley 1988, 68). British colonial authorities in the twentieth century elaborated on the white man's burden. In the words of Sir Hubert Murray, lieutenant governor of Papua New Guinea, in the 1930s, colonial governments have a duty "towards subject races"—the duty of "association and collaboration." As he stated, "We are not trying to make the brown man white; we are trying to make him a better brown man than he was before" (Murray 1933, in Bodley 1988, 43).

A Sacred Trust

The British colonial attitude of "sacred trust" toward indigenous peoples justified their efforts to "civilize" them. Murray advocated a policy of "peaceful pacification" of indigenous peoples through "indirect rule." As he said, a "scientific method of **pacification**" rests on "knowledge of the people whom you propose to pacify, and some idea of what you are going to do with them when they are pacified" (1988/1933, 43).

Murray emphasized that "native races are no longer deliberately exterminated" and that colonial governments should refrain from punitive attacks on native villages as a punishment for rebellious acts. Such a policy, he said, was both morally untenable and impractical because it led to hostility on the part of indigenous peoples and therefore thwarted colonial efforts at "peaceful pacification." Instead, Murray advocated the establishment of a local police force made up of members of the indigenous community. This would foster loyalty to the government and help administer indigenous regions. The police would develop "pride in their uniform." This tactic proved to be divisive in indigenous communities, however, as native police upheld colonial authority and sometimes abused their powers.

Murray also advocated winning over local leaders who would then convince members of their communities to support or at least not oppose colonial authority. This strategy, too, caused divisions within indigenous communities, pitting one faction against another. Colonial administrators were advised

- To establish posts in interior districts in order to deepen their control and create multiple centers of influence;
- To demonstrate benevolence and create goodwill, for example by returning prisoners to their communities as "ambassadors of peace"; to bring gradual rather than abrupt change to the lives of indigenous people;
- And to permit the preservation of indigenous customs so long as they did not contribute to disorder and resistance (1988, 49).

The Reservation System

In the nineteenth century in the United States and Canada, the federal governments obtained land from native peoples through ostensibly legal means, replacing the outright confiscation of territory and annihilation of indigenous peoples. The U.S. government was consistent in its goal of removing native peoples to lands outside areas of American settlement. The philosophy of manifest destiny was at the heart of these efforts, as Americans believed that the land was rightfully theirs. They acquired land through the procedural legality of signing treaties with native leaders and establishing reservations (or reserves, as they are called in Canada) for native peoples.

Reservations consisted of land guaranteed by treaty for native residents' ownership and control. Treaty language promised that the government would protect reservations from confiscation or settlement by nonnative people. In exchange, people agreed to cede their territory for protection and the perpetual right to live on their remaining land. Through these treaties, the United States acquired millions of acres of native land and created hundreds of reservations.

However, settlers nevertheless frequently intruded on these protected lands. Once this happened, government officials, claiming they were powerless to stop the settlers, urged the indigenous people to abandon their lands and move farther west, out of the

pacification
Colonial goal of forcing indigenous people to be peaceful and nonresistant so that settlers could safely inhabit their lands.

reservations
Land guaranteed by treaty for native residents' ownership and control.

These Apache children were photographed before (left) and after (right) they entered a boarding school to learn new values.

way. Some native groups moved three or four times before finally ending up in "Indian territory," now Oklahoma.

When people resisted giving up their homelands, however, Americans resorted to intimidation and threat of military force, and no justifications were offered. For example, speaking in 1831 to a delegation of Sauk leaders who balked at moving from their Illinois villages, General Edmund Gaines told them: "I came here neither to beg nor hire you to leave your village. My business is to remove you, peaceably if I can, but forcibly if I must" (Jackson 1964, 111–12). In 1851, Luke Lea, the federal commissioner of Indian Affairs, told Santee delegates in South Dakota, "Suppose your Great Father wanted your land and did not want a treaty for your good, he would come with 100,000 men and drive you off to the Rocky Mountains" (Meyer 1993, 78).

CASE STUDY

Captive Societies of Australia and Tasmania

In Australia, Aboriginal ownership of land had been denied from the outset of British colonization. Because Aborigines were nomadic foragers, their entitlement to the territories they inhabited and where they gathered and hunted resources was invisible to British farmers, sheep ranchers, and government officials. The people traditionally lived in small, scattered, seasonal encampments. Their presence was barely acknowledged by colonial administrators, who saw them as nuisances to be pushed away from the newly founded and growing towns and cities of colonial Australia. White officials took young Aboriginal children from their families. The children were placed in institutions or in white foster homes as servants and denied contact with their families. Ironically, this practice was seen as a humane way to assimilate natives into colonial society and culture. According to Australian government reports, 10 percent to 33 percent of Aboriginal children were part of this "Stolen Generation." This policy was not officially rescinded until 1969 (Johnston 2008).

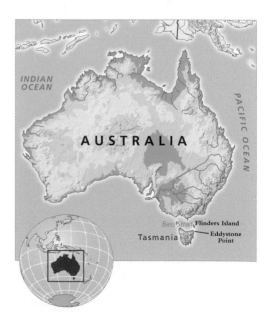

In response to pressure from Aboriginal communities and their supporters, Prime Minister Kevin Rudd apologized to Aboriginal peoples in February 2008 (BBC News 2008). He also acknowledged the gap between contemporary Aboriginal and non-Aboriginal Australians in their "life expectancy, educational achievement, and economic opportunity." Indeed, Aboriginal life expectancy averages seventeen years less than for non-Aboriginal Australians, while their unemployment rate is three times that of non-Aboriginals (Johnston 2008). Although many Aboriginal leaders welcomed Rudd's apology and its recognition of past injustices, they also point out that the government is not willing to compensate members of the Stolen Generation or their communities.

In Tasmania, an island off the southeastern coast of Australia, nineteenth-century British colonial policies led to the near extinction of the Tasmanian people. When Tasmanians resisted attempts to confiscate their settlement and hunting areas, Australian settlers killed or captured whole villages and communities. The native people retaliated against Anglo ranchers and farmers.

In 1828, Governor Sir Arthur Lawley warned settlers to cease attacking Tasmanians, but he also ordered Tasmanians to keep clear of Anglo settlements unless they had received official passports allowing them entry. When he was ignored, Lawley ordered his soldiers to round up the natives and remove them for their own safety. Rewards were offered for natives taken alive, but many more were killed than captured. In the end, the few hundred native Tasmanians who survived were taken to Flinders Island, off the coast of Tasmania. By 1854, it was reported that only sixteen Tasmanians were left, and only one was left by 1870. She died in 1876 (Howells 2001, 263).

However, some of the people's descendants had eluded the settlers and soldiers. Today native Tasmanians, preferring their own name, Palawa, are demanding recognition of their rights to some of their land and sacred sites. In particular, they are reclaiming Eddystone Point, a traditional trading base and ceremonial center. When the Australian government offered the site for public bidding, the Palawa held demonstrations. The government then stopped the bidding process. Meanwhile, Aboriginal peoples from Tasmania and Australia use the site as a place to express their solidarity and perform sacred rituals (*Cultural Survival Quarterly* 2002, 13). In 2006, the Tasmanian government formally apologized for the treatment of the Tasmanians.

PEARSON
myanthrolab

Explore more at
www.myanthrolab.com

Another land-grabbing strategy, popular through the 1870s, was collusion between government and traders to force native representatives to sign land-cession agreements in exchange for the forgiveness of debts that their community members incurred. Traders gave credit to indigenous families that amounted to more than they could ever repay. Officials then demanded land in exchange for the debts owed. Bribing and intoxicating indigenous delegates to treaty negotiations was another strategy in which leaders signed away their people's land without even knowing what they were doing.

Once native people were settled on reservations and reserves, the U.S. and Canadian federal governments implemented policies aimed at "civilizing" them. "Civilized" native people were sedentary farmers who lived in nuclear family households, wore Anglo clothing, spoke English, and attended church. Missionaries often took control of local education and merged religious doctrines with secular training in farming, manual skills, and domestic duties. Participation in traditional religious ceremonies was forbidden.

REVIEW European justifications for their treatment of indigenous peoples in colonized lands were based on Eurocentric and racist ideas. These ideas, such as the right of discovery, the white man's burden, and the sacred trust, made Europeans the stewards of people they viewed as racially "inferior," culturally "primitive," or simply "wild." "Pacification" was followed by the establishment of the reservation system designed to "civilize" the natives.

REACTIONS OF INDIGENOUS PEOPLES TO EUROPEAN COLONIZERS

When indigenous peoples first encountered Europeans sailing in the waters off their shores or arriving in their territories, they reacted in different ways. Coastal peoples were amazed at the sight of strange-looking, pale, absurdly dressed men atop huge moving sailing vessels that looked to them like "floating houses" or "hovering clouds" (Bitterli 1989, 21). The open and friendly manner of many indigenous peoples struck European explorers as simple and straightforward. The following is from the journals of Christopher Columbus, writing in October 1492 about his first contact with indigenous people in Hispaniola, now known as Santo Domingo:

> I, in order that they might feel great amity towards us, because I knew they were a people to be delivered and converted to our holy faith rather by love than by force, gave to some among them some red caps and glass beads, which they hung round their neck, and many other things of little value. At this they were greatly pleased and became so entirely our friends that it was a wonder to see. Afterwards they came swimming to the ship's boats, where we were, and brought us parrots and cotton thread in balls, and spears and many other things. (Vigneras 1960, 23)

Columbus also remarked that the residents of the territory would make good slaves.

Slightly more than a century later, Samuel de Champlain described his meeting with Algonquian Indians in Maine in 1604, which began with speeches of friendship. Champlain referred to the desire of the French to visit the country and trade with the inhabitants:

> They signified their great satisfaction, saying that no greater good would come to them than to have our friendship, . . . and we should dwell in their land, in order that they might in future more than ever before engage in hunting beavers, and give us a part of them in return for our providing them with things which they wanted. After he finished his discourse, we presented them with hatchets, caps, knives, and other little knick knacks. (Champlain 1907, 50)

Trade Goods and Gods

Indigenous peoples were usually willing, and often eager, to acquire goods of European manufacture. These were utilitarian objects, especially made of metal, or decorative objects, which Europeans thought of as relatively worthless baubles and trinkets. The eagerness with which natives sought foreign goods confirmed the Europeans' sense of superiority and their view of indigenous peoples as somewhat childish.

Some indigenous peoples had to make compromises between their desire for trade goods and their wariness of the strangers. In some cases, they managed this compromise through indirect or distant exchanges, as in the following example, reported by a French trader exploring the West African coast of Guinea:

> These barbarous people would not venture close to us in order to exchange their fish and water for our tobacco and ship's biscuit. They behaved rather as we behave towards victims of the plague; our people were obliged to take the goods they wanted to exchange for fish some distance from the ship and then turn back. After the natives had observed this, they approached to what had been brought to them, put their fish in the same place, and returned to their huts. (Jannequin 1643, 43–44)

Native North Americans typically saw Europeans as childish, stupid, and cruel. They were shocked at what they perceived as coldness toward human suffering and unwillingness to be generous to people in need. They saw foreigners as stupid for always getting lost in the woods and failing to notice features of the landscape. They were also dismayed by the Europeans' tendency to complain about discomfort, hunger, and pain (Thwaites 1906).

In other parts of the world, native peoples endowed Europeans with supernatural powers. Their awe may have exaggerated Europeans' feelings of cultural superiority and self-importance. For the Aztecs and Incans, the timing of contact happened to coincide with prophecies of the return of divine beings or strange creatures with supernatural powers. One of these prophecies concerned the Incan creator god Viracocha, who was a bearded white man, just like the Spaniards. When Cortés arrived in Mexico in 1519 and Pizarro came to Peru in 1526, they, with their horses, were greeted and welcomed as returning gods.

People soon realized their mistake, however. The following are the words of an Incan chronicler, recorded by a Spanish monk in Peru soon after the conquest of the Inca Empire:

> I thought they were kindly beings sent (as they claimed) by Tecsi Viracocha, that is to say, by God; but it seems to me that all has turned out the very opposite from what I believed; so let me tell you, brothers, from proof they have given me since their arrival in our country, they are the sons not of Viracocha, but of the devil. (Wachtel 1977, 22)

These words reveal not only the Incan attitude but also the Spaniards' manipulation of native beliefs. The Spanish claimed to be kindly beings sent by God, giving greater importance to indigenous prophecies as a cause of the conquest than was the case. Native peoples later reinterpreted their histories to fit their circumstances, using concepts from Christianity to explain events.

Guns and Other Technological Wonders

How is the theme of technologically superior strangers with unknown intentions played out in American popular culture today?

Europeans used their technology to instill awe, confusion, and sometimes fear. For example, Jesuit missionaries working among the Hurons in Ontario in the 1630s used clocks to inspire awe. The Hurons were surprised by the "voice" that the clock made when it struck on the hour. They interpreted this "voice" as the sound of the spirit of the clock and were amazed that the missionaries could order the clock to use its voice at will. The Hurons did not know that the Jesuits could predict when the clock would strike because they could tell the time. The Hurons interpreted European behavior in their own terms, as all peoples do. As animists, believing that objects may be imbued with spirit power and may have voices and wills, the Hurons interpreted the new objects in terms of their prior beliefs.

Guns had more damaging effects. They created fear when fired into the air as a display or directly at animals or people, causing injury and death. The arbitrary, random, and unforeseen manner in which the Europeans used their weapons also instilled fear. In 1606, in the waters off the coast of New Guinea, for example, Luis Baez de Torres had his soldiers shoot at people in their canoes as they were rowing toward him in a friendly greeting. According to de Torres, "On reaching them, we saluted them with our arquebuses and killed some, and when any fell dead they gave them blows with their clubs to make them get up, thinking that they were not dead" (Hilder 1980, 28).

The Aztecs are reported to have recoiled in horror at the display of Spanish artillery: "[I]t was as if one had lost one's breath; it was as if for the time being there was stupefaction, as if one were affected by mushrooms. Fear prevailed. It was as if everyone had swallowed his heart. Even before it had grown dark, there was terror, there was astonishment, there was apprehension, there was a stunning of the people" (Sahagun 1975, 47).

IN THEIR OWN VOICES

Nelson Mandela on the Struggle Against Apartheid in South Africa

In this excerpt, Nelson Mandela discusses the beginnings of the antiapartheid movement. This movement was part of the struggle against colonial rule in Africa in the 1950s and 1960s. In South Africa, it took decades to achieve victory but, finally, in 1992, with all South Africans able to vote, a new government led by the African National Congress (ANC) was elected. Nelson Mandela was its first president.

Since 1912 and year after year thereafter, in their homes and local areas, in provincial and national gatherings, on trains and buses, in the factories and on the farms, in cities, villages, shanty-towns, schools and prisons, the African people have discussed the shameful misdeeds of those who rule the country.

Year after year they have raised their voices in condemnation of the grinding poverty of the people, the low wages, the acute shortage of land, the inhuman exploitation, and the whole policy of white domination. But instead of more freedom, repression began to grow in volume and intensity and it seemed that all their sacrifices would end in smoke and dust.

Today the whole country knows that their labours were not in vain, for a new spirit and new ideas have gripped our people. Today the people speak the language of action: there is a mighty awakening among the men and women of our country and the year 1952 stands out as the year of this upsurge of national consciousness. In June 1952, the African National Congress and the South African Indian Congress, bearing in mind their responsibility as the representatives of the downtrodden and oppressed people of South Africa, took the plunge and launched the campaign for the Defiance of the Unjust Laws. . . . It spread throughout the country like wildfire. Factory and office workers, doctors, lawyers, teachers, students, and the clergy; Africans, Coloureds, Indians, and Europeans, old and young, all rallied to the national call. . . .

The Campaign called for immediate and heavy sacrifices. Workers lost their jobs, chiefs and teachers were expelled from the service, doctors, lawyers, and businessmen gave up their practices and businesses and elected to go to jail. Defiance was a step of great political significance. It released strong social forces which affected thousands of our countrymen.

It was an effective way of getting the masses to function politically; a powerful method of voicing our indignation against the reactionary policies of the government. It was one of the best ways of exerting pressure on the government and extremely dangerous to the stability and security of the State. It inspired and aroused our people from a conquered and servile community of "yes-men" to a militant and uncompromising band of comrades-in-arms. . . .

The entire continent is seething with discontent, and already there are powerful revolutionary eruptions in the Gold Coast, Nigeria, Tunisia, Kenya, the Rhodesia, and South Africa. The oppressed people and the oppressors are at loggerheads. The day of reckoning between the forces of freedom and those of reaction is not very far off. I have not the slightest doubt that when that day comes truth and justice will prevail.

**Explore more at
www.myanthrolab.com**

From Nelson Mandela, *No Easy Walk to Freedom.* © 1965. Reprinted by permission of the Nelson Mandela Foundation.

CRITICAL THINKING QUESTIONS

How does Nelson Mandela suggest that oppressed peoples can achieve political and social justice? Why did the ANC succeed in defeating apartheid?

Native Resistance and Retaliation

Indigenous peoples tended to treat Europeans with generosity and friendliness, until they learned from experience that the strangers were not to be trusted and that they desired their land, resources, and labor. From most reports, attacks on Europeans seem to have been well motivated, as friendliness turned to retaliation, against either a particular offending group or the next party of European intruders. In Spanish colonies in the Americas, for example, residents of marginal regions in Central Mexico resisted foreign control. This resistance was most marked in the north among the Yaqui and Apache in Sonora, the northernmost Mexican state. Not until the middle and late nineteenth century were these two groups "pacified" with the help of the U.S. military.

Farther north, the Pueblo peoples (Hopi, Zuni, Cochiti, Tewa, and others), living along the Rio Grande in what is now New Mexico, staged a revolt in 1680. After more than a century of rule by Spanish colonizers and priests, the various communities united

GLOBALIZATION

Since the 1940s, as dozens of countries have won their independence, much of the world has become free of direct colonial rule. Independence movements spread through forces of globalization are still at work in the world today.

to oust the foreigners, killing 21 priests and about 400 settlers out of a population of 2,500 (Dozier 1970, 59). Then, 12 years later, the Spanish sent another invading force and reestablished control in 1692. Eventually, this region became part of the United States after the Mexican-American War ended in 1846 with the signing of the Treaty of Guadalupe-Hidalgo.

In the south of Mexico, Spanish authorities also had a difficult time establishing permanent control, especially in Chiapas. There, members of indigenous Tzotzil and Tzeltal communities put up active resistance through military defense as well as passive resistance through retreat to remote mountain areas. Even in later centuries, their resistance simmered, most recently manifested in the Zapatista movement of the 1990s.

REVIEW ⊸ Indigenous reactions to European colonizers were diverse, but a common pattern was awe, friendship, interest in trade goods, treaties, acts of resistance or aggression, and ultimate defeat in armed conflict. Some resistance movements have persisted to the present day.

GLOBALIZATION IN THE POSTCOLONIAL ERA

In 1947, India was one of the first large colonized countries to free itself of European control from Great Britain. The independence movement accelerated in the 1950s and 1960s, when many African countries became independent of Great Britain, France, and Belgium. Similar processes occurred in Asia and in the Pacific in the following decades. Indigenous peoples nevertheless seldom obtained equal social, economic, or political rights in their new nations. They often remained marginalized groups under pressure from newly formed central governments to conform to national practices and values. Central authorities justified this pressure in the name of **nationalism,** focusing on the importance of building a common culture to strengthen national unity. In the process of nation building, cultural diversity was often a casualty, as indigenous ways were targeted as backward and obstacles to growth.

Land grabbing did not end with independence. National governments in Peru, Bolivia, Colombia, Venezuela, Brazil, and Chile, for example, changed land policies that had favored Indians' rights and permitted outside interests to exploit native lands and resources. In the United States today, successes in Native American land claims are balanced against the appropriation of resources on those lands, such as oil, uranium, and platinum.

Similar patterns developed in Africa and the Middle East, sometimes contributing tragically to internal competition and intertribal genocide. In **xenophobic** reactions, the governments of newly independent states sought to selectively expel or decimate tribes, ethnic minorities, foreign laborers, merchant elites, or former colonial overlords. Issues over land and resources aggravated these conflicts.

Table 16.2 summarizes data on indigenous populations in selected countries and the land under their control during the height of the colonial period, prior to 1960.

Colonialism began a process of global transformation in all areas of society and culture, affecting economic systems, social life, political organization, and more. In the **postcolonial era,** processes have continued to integrate national societies throughout the world. Migration of peoples from rural to urban areas within their own countries and migration to foreign lands have contributed to the creation of a very different world than existed in 1500. As people have traveled from one place to another, they have brought with them their cultural practices and beliefs, their languages, and their expectations for a new way of life. They have also brought with them some of the plants and animals native to their home regions. This process, begun on a worldwide scale many centuries ago, has had a global impact on environments and economic systems, as well as on an emerging global culture.

When Christopher Columbus made his second voyage to Hispaniola (now the Dominican Republic) in 1493, he brought seeds and cuttings for planting wheat, chickpeas, melons, onions, radishes, greens, grapevines, sugarcane, and fruit stones (Crosby 1972, 67). Not all of these plants were successfully grown in that region, but many did prosper. Sugar, in particular, came to dominate the economies of Central and South America, and wheat is grown all over North and South America. According to Crosby,

Which nations can be characterized as xenophobic today? Why?

nationalism
Movement in independent states to build national identity, pride, and unity.

xenophobic
Having to do with fear, hatred, and envy of strangers, outsiders, or foreign-born minorities within the society.

postcolonial era
Period (roughly since 1965) following the independence of the last former European colonies as new nations under indigenous leadership and control.

TABLE 16.2	AMOUNT OF LAND RESERVED FOR INDIGENOUS POPULATIONS IN DIFFERENT COUNTRIES	
	Native Population as Percentage of Total Population	Native Lands as Percentage of Total Area
Bechuanaland	99+	38
Swaziland	98	48
New Guinea	98	97
Zimbabwe	95	33
Botswana/Namibia	87	25
Canada	3	0.2
Chile	2	0.6
United States	0.3	1

Note: These figures are pre-1960. As countries gained independence, native lands as a percentage of total land area rose, by definition, to nearly 100 percent (depending on the amount of foreign-owned land). Most African countries achieved independence with majority rule by 1970. For example, Bechuanaland, a British protectorate, became the Independent Republic of Botswana in 1966. Papua New Guinea achieved independence in 1975, but the western part of the island, Irian Jaya, was annexed by Indonesia in 1968. In Canada, the United States, and South America, both native population as a percentage of total population and native lands as a percentage of total land area generally rose, the latter through recent successful land claims.

Source: John Bodley, *Victims of Progress*, 5th ed. © 2008. Altamira Press, p. 107. Reprinted by permission of Rowman & Littlefield.

although many of the European plants and animals that were transplanted to the Americas were brought deliberately, many seeds also came inadvertently, "in the folds of textiles, in clods of mud, in dung, and in a thousand other ways" (p. 73). Many weeds and grasses that are now common in North America are European in origin, including bluegrass, daisies, and dandelions.

Indigenous peoples in the Americas gradually adopted European livestock. Sheep and goats were incorporated into the economies of southwestern peoples, who utilized the animals' wool, milk, and meat. Cattle, chickens, and pigs were also kept as sources of food.

In turn, Native American plants have been carried to the other continents as well. Among the most important food crops are maize, beans, peanuts, potatoes, sweet potatoes, manioc (cassava), squashes, pumpkin, papaya, avocado, pineapple, tomato, chili pepper, and cocoa (Crosby 1972, 170). Many of these crops, particularly potatoes, maize, manioc, beans, and peanuts, have contributed to population growth in Europe and Africa, as well as in the Americas. Today, some native foods of the Americas are major export crops of other countries. For example, India is one of the world's largest producers of peanuts, and China produces more sweet potatoes than any other country. Peanuts and cocoa are important export crops for countries in West Africa, whereas maize and manioc are critical for domestic consumption there. Finally, national cuisines make us realize the impact that worldwide exploration and exchange have made. For instance, the pasta and tomato sauces so common in Italian recipes are the gifts of China and Mexico.

In what other ways can present-day globalization be attributed to European colonialism? In what sense, according to some, is colonialism still going on today?

Since the 1940s, as people gained independence from colonial rulers, nationalism and globalization continued the legacies of colonialism. Newly independent nations evicted foreigners and competed internally for power. Ethnic or tribal minorities were often persecuted, marginalized, or pressured to sacrifice their ways of life. The global economy has transformed production and resource use in the new nations.

REVIEW

ANTHROPOLOGY APPLIED

Establishing the Xingu National Park

In the Amazon, national governments have vacillated between recognizing and guaranteeing indigenous peoples' rights to land and uprooting them to make way for settlement and economic development. In Brazil, constitutions written between 1891 and 1946 respected native peoples' rights to their lands, and some Brazilian states set aside lands under the guardianship of the Indian Protection Service. By 1961, however, settlers and land speculators had reduced the largest of these reserves from 33,000 square miles to 8,500 square miles. At that time, the reserve, later expanded to 11,500 square miles, became the Xingu National Park

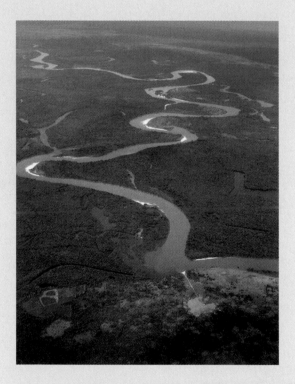

(Bodley 1999, 83). The Brazilian National Indian Foundation (FUNAI) supposedly protects this park and other native reserves, but Brazilian governments have permitted mining on native lands (Gray 1990).

Anthropologists helped establish the Xingu National Park and work today to protect the people who live there. Ethnographies of the Amazonian people date back to the 1880s and 1930s. In the early 1960s, anthropologists Robert Carneiro and Gertrude Dole supported the efforts of the Brazilian champion of Indians, Claudio Villas-Boas, and his brothers to save the indigenous peoples of the Xingu River valley by creating a preserve. In 1965, only an estimated 542 people remained, but today more than 6,000 people in 30 villages representing 17 nations live in the Xingu National Park.

CRITICAL THINKING QUESTION

Why do governments decide to protect indigenous peoples or exploit protected lands?

European Colonialism

- Conquest and colonialism have occurred in many parts of the world as state societies expanded their borders or spheres of influence. In the process, conquerors and colonizers changed the cultures of indigenous peoples. Europeans established colonies, that is, settlements of foreign nationals with controlling interests in indigenous territories, on every continent. These colonies were tied to the home country both politically and economically. The home country governed how colonial subjects behaved and extracted resources.

- There were three major types of colonies: exploitation colonies (resulting from military conquests in which the colonial power exploits economic resources), maritime enclaves (resulting from sea trade and coastal exploration to control trade at foreign ports and territories), and settlement colonies (resulting from military invasion that supports permanent colonial settlement).

The Slave Trade

- The slave trade took West Africans to work on plantations in the Caribbean, South America, and the United States. About 10 million people were taken from Africa by the time the slave trade ended in the nineteenth century.

- The wealth the slaves in the Americas produced enriched their owners and contributed to the accumulation of capital and resources that led to the Industrial Revolution.

- Many African societies had systems of slavery or coerced labor.

- Conditions of slavery in the Americas were likely worse than those in traditional African societies. European colonists typically saw African slaves as racially inferior. They were the property of the masters, who could treat them any way them decided.

- The slave trade changed West African societies. Some African elites were able to centralize their wealth and power, but other African societies fell apart because rival factions competed for war captives who could be sold as slaves.

Trade and Settlement in North America

- In North America, settler colonies relegated indigenous peoples to small portions of their ancestral homelands or to unknown lands.

- European and American settlers benefited from the spread of epidemic diseases such as measles and smallpox. The destruction of resources and military intervention persuaded native leaders to cede most of their land to the U.S. government.

- European powers focused their economic interests in North America on the fur trade. Most native communities participated in the fur trade to procure European manufactured goods.

- Native people could not control the market for furs, which made them vulnerable to changes in demand. They overtrapped their territories and then competed with other indigenous groups. As settlers pushed west, indigenous peoples fled, increasing competition and warfare.

Spanish Colonies in the Americas

- Spanish colonization in the Americas was focused on exploiting resources, especially precious metals, and on establishing plantations that would produce marketable crops, principally sugarcane, in the Caribbean and South America.

- At first, indigenous inhabitants of the regions were compelled to work in mines and on plantations, but African slaves replaced them due to depopulation in some regions. Landholding patterns included encomiendas, haciendas, and mission villages.

- The Spanish intermarried with indigenous peoples, creating a social class of mixed ancestry. This group functioned as intermediaries and as an elite class.

Agents of Directed Culture Change

- Throughout the world, colonial authorities have pressed indigenous peoples to change their cultural practices to be more consistent with European values and behaviors. Missionaries aided in this process by attempting to convert indigenous peoples to Christianity. Schoolteachers inculcated European values and norms. Native children in boarding schools lost touch with their traditional ways, religious beliefs, and languages.

- Colonial administrators imposed Eurocentric patterns of law and social control, disturbing traditional social relationships and ethical values. The introduction of cash economies based on market principles changed economic relationships.

Justifications for Colonial Rule

- Europeans believed that they could take land they conquered simply by their self-declared "right of discovery." Lack of proof of ownership was also a rationale for ignoring indigenous claims to land and resources. Nationalism and imperialism helped to justify colonialism.

- European colonizers claimed a "white man's burden" of cultural, moral, and racial superiority. Europeans believed that they had a "sacred trust" to pacify and civilize the natives.

Indigenous Reactions to European Colonizers

- Some indigenous peoples were awed by European technology and manufactures or believed that Europeans were gods.

- Indigenous communities differed in their attitudes toward Europeans. Many were eager trading partners. Once people realized Europeans wanted to control their lands and lives, however, disagreements often arose.

Globalization in the Postcolonial Era

- Since the 1940s, much of the world has been freed from direct colonial control. Competition for power

and authority among tribes or elites has led to violence. Indigenous peoples often remain marginalized in the newly established nations. Nationalism is hard to achieve in culturally diverse societies.

- Indigenous foragers and nomadic pastoralists have been encouraged or compelled to settle permanently in one area and farm or work for wages. Efforts to spread a national language have lessened cultural diversity.

KEY TERMS

colonies 409	resettlement	encomiendas 417	pacification 422
imperialism 409	policies 410	haciendas 417	reservations 422
exploitation	missionism 411	mita 418	nationalism 428
colonies 410	slave trade 411	customary law 420	xenophobic 428
maritime enclaves 410	fur trade 414	cash economies 421	postcolonial era 428
settlement colonies 410	depopulation 415	white man's burden 421	

REVIEW QUESTIONS

1. What were European motivations for colonialism and patterns of colonization?

2. How did the European slave trade spread colonialism and undermine African states?

3. How did indigenous peoples of North America become involved in European trading networks? How did that affect their modes of subsistence?

4. How did systems of Spanish landholding and mining affect native peoples?

5. Why was intermarriage between Spaniards and indigenous people encouraged? What role did their descendants have in colonial society?

6. What were the three principal agents of directed culture change, and what impacts did they have on indigenous peoples?

7. How did Europeans justify colonial rule? What are some legacies of colonialism in postcolonial nations today?

8. How did indigenous peoples react to European colonizers?

PEARSON myanthrolab EXERCISES

To complete the following exercises and activities, you must log in to www.myanthrolab.com and select your current textbook.

1. In the **Explore** tab of Chapter 16, click on *Video* and watch one of the videos available in this section. Complete the short answer exercise that accompanies the video.

2. While in the **Explore** tab, click on the *NPR Audio Programs Broadcast* tab and go to *Theme 27: Colonialism.* Listen to one of the programs in this section and com-

plete the short answer exercise that accompanies the program.

3. Enter the **MyAnthroLibrary** section on the home page to read more about topics and cultures that are discussed in this chapter. Suggested readings include:

Yuqui: Fighting the Odds for Cultural Survival by Allyn MacLean Stearman

Kiowa: An Emergent People by Nancy P. Hickerson

LIVING IN A GLOBAL WORLD

PREVIEW

- How is migration changing national and world demographics?
- How does migration affect local, national, and global economies?
- How have new nations re-created themselves in the postcolonial era, and how have they adapted to their own cultural diversity?
- Why can ethnogenesis reflect both a colonial past and a globalized future?
- What is transnationalism and the emerging "global identity"?
- What is the status of cultural minorities in the world today? How are they threatened, and how can they protect themselves?

Maran Kai Ra
Female, age 28.
From: Sumprabum, Kachin State.
Occupation: family grocery store and distributing medicine.
Education: BA, Myitkyina University.
Ethnicity: Kachin.
Religion: Baptist.
Left Burma: September 2000.

Q: Why did you leave Burma?

A: Because of the political movement. Since 1988, I started to be involved in the student movement, and after that, when Aung San Suu Kyi came to Myitkyina, I welcomed her with flowers. After she left, I was asked to come to the MI for interrogation, and after that I had a record. I was also involved with the 1996 student movement and continuously I was involved in the political movements and organizing and distributing political pamphlets. Most recently they suspected me of involvement with Aung San Suu Kyi's party and the underground student movement. My name was on their list.

Q: What was political organizing like as a student?

A: We had to do it as an underground movement, through the religious groups and the Kachin literature and the cultural organizations. We don't have formal organizations like student unions.

Q: How did you get information?

A: News from abroad we get from BBC, VOA and AIR, but within Burma, within the student organization we have a kind of representative or student leader from Myitkyina or Rangoon and they travel and give information to each other.

Q: Were many university students involved in politics?

A: About 60% of the students were interested in politics.

Q: What education was available in Sumprabum?

A: There's only up to 8th grade [standard] in Sumprabum. So mostly they have to go to Myitkyina or Rangoon for higher education.

Q: What were the health conditions in Sumprabum?

A: There's no proper clinic or hospital, there's not a single doctor. And there's plenty of health problems, especially malaria. The local people in Sumprabum are taught by the nurses, not by the doctors, how to avoid the diseases. As far as I know, there's no HIV positive in the area, but some TB. The people who have TB have to go to Myitkyina for treatment, there's no clinic.

Q: Are there traveling doctors in the area?

A: There's a kind of doctor who goes around checking villagers, almost once a year.

Q: What is the food situation in the Sumprabum area?

A: Mostly everything is locally grown. But salt and oil . . . they bring from Myitkyina. There's not enough rice. Because of the hill cultivation we cannot produce enough rice for the local people.

Q: Is there much government army in the area?

A: Yes, they have an army base there.

Q: Do they ever ask people to work for them?

A: Yes, many times. In the past, there's plenty of portering. People were forced to work as porters. But now, there's almost no more portering. But still people are forced to do forced labor to build their army camp or to build roads or such things. There's no payment. Every household has to do it one by one. If this week it's this household, next week it will be the other to help the military.

Q: Is there logging in that area?

A: Yes, the government gives the permit to businessmen, mostly Chinese, to cut the wood, and taking the gold and cane for trading. They hire the local people and people who come from Myitkyina, not just Kachin, everyone. Because of that permission to cut the tree and do the gold mining and other stuff, most of the mountains and the hillsides have been emptied of forests. And the way of the streams, they also changed it to dig the gold. So everything's changed, and also the wildlife. In the past we heard the sound of the wildlife. But no more. They all ran away.

Q: What about fishing?

A: In the past the villagers, the local people only used nets for fishing. But the people from the city, when they arrived, they used the mines [explosives] for the fishing. That's why now there is almost no more fish at all.

Q: How is the water for drinking?

A: The water's very good.

Q: In Sumprabum, in the last two years before you left, was life for the local people getting better?

A: There's not much change, but I would say slightly better because of the cease-fire between the KIA [Kachin Independence Army] and the government, since there is no fighting. So it's a little bit safer than before.

Q: Is the gold mining or logging improving people's economic status?

A: Slightly better, but I believe that for the long term it won't be good.

Q: Are people able to freely practice their religion there?

A: They are allowed to, if they get the permission from the military authorities. In advance they have to ask for permission. How many days the Christian festival or religious festival will take place, how many people will come to the festival.

An Interview with a Kachin Activist Refugee from Burma is reprinted by permission of the author, Edith Mirante.

Maran Kai Ra was interviewed in Guam, where she was seeking political asylum in the United States. In this interview, she discusses some of the conditions that led her to leave her country, Burma, also called Myanmar. Her experiences are fairly typical of political refugees. Although refugees account for many people who move from one country to another, many more voluntarily enter new countries to obtain education or employment. This pattern is not unique to our times, but global processes of change and interaction have accelerated migration throughout the twentieth and into the twenty-first century. The present-day global economy, although initiated centuries ago, has accelerated the transfer of goods, services, and peoples around the world. International migration has brought people far from their homes. As they settle into their new countries, they adopt new cultural practices, often blending them with their own values and perspectives. They contribute their labor and spend their money in their new countries. They also add cultural diversity and richness to their immigrant communities.

Political processes have also strengthened ties among countries. International organizations such as the United Nations, the World Health Organization, and many regional groups coordinate activities; set economic, social, and environmental policies; and resolve conflicts. The success of these organizations varies. Although, in principle, countries are equals, in practice, the voices of larger, richer, and more powerful countries drown out those of smaller and poorer ones. The rich and powerful countries exert greater influence because they can promise economic rewards, political support, and military aid to those who follow their lead, while they threaten to withdraw aid or retaliate against those who defy them.

All of these factors are part of the process of globalization. Globalization includes the movement of people and the exchange of cultural practices, goods and services, and

cultural minorities
Members of ethnic or cultural groups who have become minorities in their native lands due to migrations of other peoples into their territories or due to the historical configuration of a nation-state made up of diverse groups.

labor migration
Migration of people from one area of a country to another or across national borders in search of jobs.

GLOBALIZATION

As a result of present-day globalization, international organizations and multinational corporations have tremendous impacts on nations and on cultural minorities living in those nations, as well as on global interrelationships among nations.

The Nenets, Samoyeds of western Siberia, are nomadic foragers, fishers, and reindeer herders. They inadvertently consume deadly heavy metals from pollution when they eat mosses and reindeer meat.

attitudes worldwide. Through global exchanges, people learn from one another, obtain goods made elsewhere, and share information through media outlets and technological advances such as the Internet. This chapter explores some of the characteristics and consequences of these processes.

The ways of life of **cultural minorities** have come under increasing threat. Their lands and resources are vulnerable to encroachment and exploitation by the governments of the countries in which they live and by multinational corporations that covet their minerals, forests, and other natural products. In the last quarter of the twentieth century, however, indigenous peoples began to protect their lands and their cultures.

MIGRATION

Temporary travel and permanent migration have been features of human life for millennia, but the last several centuries have witnessed an acceleration of these processes both in the numbers of people who leave their native countries and in the distances that they travel. In addition to voluntary migrants, some people become refugees because of war and other turmoil. Indeed, wars in the Middle East and Africa have created the largest number of refugees in the world. In 2006, for example, 2.1 million Afghans, who made up 21 percent of the world's refugee population, were refugees in more than 70 asylum countries, mainly Pakistan, Iran, and Saudi Arabia. Iraqis accounted for the second-largest group, with 1.5 million people leaving to find shelter in neighboring countries. Many people from the African countries of Sudan, Somalia, the Democratic Republic of the Congo, and Burundi also fled (see Tables 17.1 and 17.2).

Rural-to-Urban Migration

Migration takes place within a country as well. Urban centers attract people from rural areas who seek better employment and income. In Europe and the United States, rural-to-urban migration intensified after the Industrial Revolution of the early nineteenth century, but it also accelerated in the last century. Industrial development led to the creation of jobs in manufacturing and service occupations, attracting people from the countryside. In addition, advances in agricultural technology meant that fewer people were needed to grow the food sustaining larger urban populations. The spread of industrial agriculture, particularly in the United States, led to wealthy and efficient corporations buying out small family farmers. After World War II, many thousands of African Americans left the predominantly rural South, heading north for work and a less overtly racist social and political environment. These are all patterns of **labor migration.**

Similar trends in labor migration take place in Asia and Africa. In Malaysia, for example, rural peasant families send some of their children to work in electronics and other factories owned by multinational corporations, especially from Japan and Korea (Ong 1983). As in Mexico, Malaysian peasants adapt to poverty by sending their daughters to work in factories (see the Case Study).

Do you know anyone who has come to this country to work? What circumstances made them come?

TABLE 17.1 MAIN ORIGIN OF REFUGEES, 2006

Origin	Beginning of 2006	End of 2006	Share of Total (End of Year Percent)
Stateless	3,192,000	5,819,000	18
Colombia (Internal Displaced)	2,540,000	3,562,000	11
Iraq	1,765,000	3,519,000	11
Afghanistan	3,192,000	2,751,000	8
Sudan	1,568,000	2,125,000	6
Democratic Republic of the Congo	526,000	2,040,000	6
Uganda	39,000	1,914,000	6
Somalia	840,000	890,000	3
Azerbaijan	816,000	816,000	2
Lebanon	20,000	786,000	2

Source: 2008 UNHCR Statistical Yearbook, Table 11A.

TABLE 17.2 MAIN COUNTRIES OF ASYLUM, 2007

Country of Asylum	People Granted Asylum
Pakistan	2,033,100
Syria	1,503,800
Iran	963,500
Germany	758,900
Jordan	500,300
Tanzania	435,600
China	301,100
United Kingdom	299,700
Chad	294,000
United States	281,200

Source: 2008 UNHCR Statistical Yearbook, Figure 3.

Industrial work is divided by class and world region. The high-tech skilled jobs in research and development are centered in developed countries, whereas the low-skilled assembly-line tasks are performed in peripheral areas. The Malaysian government grants tax benefits and reduces tariffs for multinationals because jobs are needed for people who are displaced from their lands, especially in a country experiencing high population growth. Lack of health and safety regulations, no minimum wage, and restrictions on union membership also attract companies. For example, to join a union, a worker must be employed in the same job for a minimum of three years, but most of the workers in multinational industries are hired on six-month contracts, resulting in high turnover and little job security. The Malaysian government's goals are both economic (providing jobs) and political (forestalling political unrest) (Ong 1983).

CASE STUDY

Labor Migration in Mexico

Patterns of labor migration reveal the complex causes of people's relocations and dislocations as a consequence of globalization. A significant trend in Latin America and Asia is the migration of workers from rural areas to factories owned by multinational corporations in development or free trade zones. Companies are attracted to the zones because they receive tax exemptions for capital investment and find a large labor pool. Moreover, these zones have low wages, weak or nonexistent unions, and few environmental or health and safety regulations (Fuentes and Ehrenreich 1983).

The young women who make up most of the work force are relatively unskilled. They are literate but are rarely graduates of secondary schools and, therefore, tend to lack higher aspirations. For example, Mexico has seen an enormous growth in manufacturing jobs since the 1960s, when its government embarked on a policy of industrial development in conjunction with multinational corporations, principally based in the United States. Mexico hoped the program would attract investment, create jobs, and alleviate its soaring rates of unemployment and poverty.

Before the North American Free Trade Agreement (NAFTA) eliminated tariffs on products traded among the United States, Mexico, and Canada, foreign companies established what was known as the maquiladora system in Mexico. Maquiladoras assembled electronics parts and precut garment pieces made in the United States or in other foreign factories that then entered the United States at low tariff rates. The companies leased or acquired land near the U.S. border at low prices and paid little or no local taxes. They had access to a constant supply of workers willing to work for low wages with few, if any, job benefits (Fernandez-Kelly 1983).

By the 1990s, over 500 maquiladora companies were employing more than half a million people. About 85 percent of those workers were young women with some, but low, education. About one-third of the workers were single parents and heads of households (Fernandez-Kelly 1997, 526). Women were favored as employees because of their willingness to do monotonous work, accept low wages, and follow orders. Men, in contrast, were not recruited as assembly-line workers because, quoting an electronics plant manager, "The man in Mexico is still the man. This kind of job is not doing much for his macho image. It's just a little quirk of a different culture. They'd rather run a factory" (Fuentes and Ehrenreich 1983, 30).

Because of widespread poverty in Mexico, young women, like the one shown here, have left their villages to work in maquiladora plants.

Since the beginning of the twenty-first century, economic changes due to NAFTA have eliminated many maquiladora jobs. Although, the maquiladoras still employed more than 200,000 people in 2008, the economic downturn that began that year has resulted in the loss of more than 90,000 factory jobs in the Mexican city of Juarez alone, and even larger numbers of people are unemployed or underemployed because businesses that catered to the workers have also suffered (Kolenc 2008).

The Mexican experience is just one example of a familiar pattern. Because of the prevailing landholding tradition in Latin America, young men tend to work on and inherit family lands. Peasant women whose families own little or no land may migrate to urban centers to seek jobs and relieve their families of the burdens of supporting them. Many of these young women initially work in domestic service, later leaving for other kinds of jobs or to marry and become housewives. In addition, both male and female migrants often work in the "informal sector," selling food, crafts, and other goods on the streets. Although most would prefer factory work, there are not enough jobs, which creates a marginal population who try to earn a living as best they can.

PEARSON
myanthrolab

Explore more at
www.myanthrolab.com

TABLE 17.3 U.S. FOREIGN-BORN POPULATION BY WORLD REGION, 2007	
Total:	38,059,555
Europe:	4,990,294
Asia:	10,184,906
Africa:	1,419,317
Oceania:	216,701
Latin America and Caribbean:	21,248,337
Canada:	830,388

Source: 2007 American Community Survey, US Census Bureau, Place of Birth for the Foreign-Born Population.

Transnational Migration

International migration has had a profound effect on people in both the countries of origin and of settlement. Poor countries lose citizens to wealthier countries with better job opportunities. Although population loss might relieve economic burdens within a poor country in theory, many of the people who leave are among the better educated and more skilled in practice. Thus, the possibilities of economic recovery are undermined in their home countries. However, today's migrants often send a portion of their earnings back to their families, money that makes its way into the local and national economies. Still, the loss of people's skills, experience, and knowledge is more significant and has greater long-term effects than the loss of money alone. Table 17.3 tallies the foreign-born population in the United States in 2007 by region of origin.

Until the middle of the twentieth century, the vast majority of migrants were people leaving poor countries that had few jobs, particularly in the industrial sector, when manufacturing and service industries were concentrated in Europe, North America, and Japan. Many initially thought of themselves as temporary residents of their new countries, hoping to save enough money to return home and use their savings to live better. This goal was usually unfulfilled, however. Although the wages that they received were higher than what they could have expected at home, their cost of living was also greater and far exceeded their ability to save. Although some eventually abandon their desire to return, they may face difficulties adjusting to the countries where they settle.

Some of these difficulties result from the marginalization of migrants within their new countries. They are often segregated in poor neighborhoods, a spatial division that

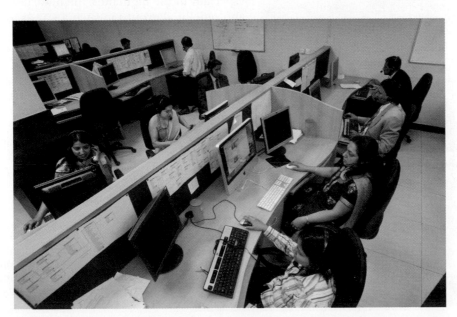

A call center in India.

tribalization
A process of identification with one's tribal origins.

dramatizes and reinforces their separation from the dominant society. Cultural differences of language, religion, and values also set them apart. Eventually, immigrants form "ethnic groups" based on markers of cultural identity, a process called ethnogenesis first defined in Chapter 2. Ethnic groups are also formed because of rejection from members of the dominant culture, creating "a generalized culture of ethnic inequality in which immigrants are perceived in stereotypical terms by the indigenous population, whatever their actual attributes, as a race apart, as primitives" (Worsley 1984, 239).

REVIEW — ◉ Migration patterns include international or transnational migration to escape persecution, war, or poverty; rural-to-urban migration in developing countries; and labor migration to take advantage of new economic opportunities. Refugee and immigrant groups affect the communities or countries they leave, as well as the ones they join. Often, they become tolerated but isolated ethnic minorities.

ETHNOGENESIS AND ETHNIC IDENTITIES

Ethnic identity is context-bound but changeable, an adaptation to circumstances. Although we may think of an ethnic identity as a single, stable concept, in fact, people can have various identities, depending on the way they see themselves in relation to others. Ethnic groups are formed and transformed in response to interactions with other people. As with other social identities, ethnic labels are applied as conditions arise that favor their use. People may think of themselves as members of groups based on one set of criteria but may find themselves categorized as members of other groups based on different criteria.

Group identity based on a political stance as well as an ethnic or tribal identity complicates social relations, even in comparatively homogeneous societies. An example is Papua New Guinea. Its colonial history began in the nineteenth century, when the British and the Germans divided the eastern portion of the island of New Guinea between themselves. (The western portion was formerly a Dutch colony, invaded and annexed by Indonesia in 1975.) At the end of World War I, the two colonial regions were united under Australian administration as Papua New Guinea, becoming an independent country in 1975. Although independence has led to some detribalization as the central government attempts to form a national identity, other factors led to **tribalization,** or the formation of tribal identities. One of the consequences of the competition for access to political power and economic benefits has been a resurgence of "tribal" warfare, especially in the highlands. Such warfare "has defined and redefined groups in such a way as to re-create, in part, an earlier tribal structure—a structure uncomfortably at odds with its own national government" (Strathern 1992, 232).

Even though government agencies have attempted to quell the fighting, people's respect for state authority has declined. Instead, local businessmen vie for economic advantages and political power, very much in the traditional model of the Melanesian "big men." These men attract armed fighters who support them and are in return protected by them. The central government occasionally sends in police and military patrols to keep order, but they are largely unsuccessful in eliminating violence.

Pakistani Brahmin immigrants to the United Kingdom who may think of themselves as white and as superior to dark-skinned South Indians are shocked to find out that the British may think of them as "black" or "coloured," in the same category as immigrants from the West Indies.

CASE STUDY

Ethnic Identity in Sudan

In a study of Sudanese agricultural production, Jay O'Brien (1986) details how ethnic identities were formed as different groups of people were incorporated into the work force. Their roles in production became linked to their ethnic identity. In the early 1900s, farmers and pastoralists began to work on plantations that produced cotton for export. These plantations were in what came to be known as the Gezira Scheme, a large area of irrigated fields. As elsewhere in the British Empire, indigenous people had to pay taxes in cash, but their sources of obtaining money were limited because they had few markets for their subsistence crops, and the importation of cheap manufactured goods undermined home craft production.

Sudanese farmers and pastoralists continued to maintain their traditional productive strategies but were available for seasonal work on the plantations when needed. They received wages but remained marginal actors in the new economy. Then, as the plantation system expanded, workers from other countries were recruited, especially Muslim Hausa from West Africa. These landless immigrants were a ready pool of cheap wage labor. Other West African Muslims also provided seasonal labor. They came from several ethnic groups and spoke different languages, although many learned Hausa as a second language (O'Brien 1986, 901).

Nearly as soon as the immigrants arrived, distinctions developed between them and their indigenous coworkers. The immigrants came to be known as *Fellata,* a term with negative connotations that obliterated their own, separate tribal distinctions. In response to their new cultural environment, the West Africans adopted some outward traits of their Sudanese neighbors, especially styles of dress and housing. However, to differentiate themselves from the Sudanese, they also intensified some of their own cultural practices, emphasizing fundamentalist Islamic practices in contrast to the animistic beliefs in spirit possession and trance found among Arabs in North Africa. They began to apply the word *Takari* to themselves, a respectful term signifying "pilgrims." Although they replaced a negative term (Fellata) with a positive one, they essentially accepted the view of themselves as members of an ethnic group different from their hosts. Thus, they participated in the formation of an ethnic identity, initially imposed on them but then adopted as part of their self-definition.

A third group, the Joamas, were also incorporated into plantation production. The Joamas of central Sudan became known as efficient and hardworking cotton pickers. They earned a high reputation and a relatively stable income. Gradually, migrants from West Africa settled on the outskirts of Joama communities and were also hired as seasonal cotton pickers. By their own hard work and commitment to the region, they came to refer to themselves and to be referred to as *Joama.* They thus adopted an ethnic identity that was theirs only by assertion and lifestyle. It was an identity that they had to earn.

myanthrolab

Explore more at
www.myanthrolab.com

Transnationalism

Although migrants adjust to and adapt to their country of settlement, they all do not necessarily focus solely on developing their lives in their new environment. Rather, they also maintain emotional and cultural ties with their homeland. Because of increased ease of communication and travel, a new phenomenon of transnationalism is developing. **Transnationalism** is the constellation of "processes by which immigrants build social fields that link together their country of origin and their country of settlement, connecting them to two or more societies simultaneously" (Schiller, Basch, and Blanc-Szanton 1992, 1–2).

transnationalism
Processes by which immigrants maintain social, economic, religious, and political ties to both their immigrant communities and their communities back home.

The Internet features many transnational sites like this one, which embraces all people with roots in India living anywhere in the world, including those who have become citizens of other countries.

GLOBALIZATION

Transnationalism is a phenomenon in which migrants create new sociocultural networks and identities for themselves that link their country of origin and their country of settlement. Although not new, transnationalism has redeveloped in the context of the spread of global capitalism, which has shifted populations across borders.

Transmigrants maintain complex social, economic, religious, and political ties linking them to their immigrant communities and to their communities back home.

Transnationalism has developed in the context of the spread of global capitalism that has shifted capital and labor across borders. As capital investments flow from high-wage countries to low-wage regions, labor shifts take place in both developed and developing countries. A transnational identity based on transnational commitments is a sensible and appropriate response to economic vulnerability and possible job displacement. In addition, transmigrants are important players in the creation of ethnic identities in their countries of settlement, forming connections among people who identify as a group on the basis of shared activities, values, beliefs, and goals.

Nationalism and Pluralism

In addition to analyzing the ways that people create themselves as ethnic groups, anthropologists also look at the ways that ethnic groups are formed as structural features that support social, economic, and political systems. Ethnic groupings are especially significant in state societies composed of peoples of disparate origins and traditions. They are also "inherently political, shaped by and shaping the politics of 'us versus them' in political systems" (Ferguson and Whitehead 1992, 15).

At the same time, states also generate nationalistic views of themselves as overriding ethnic differences in the formation of a national identity. Peter Worsley describes nationalism as a form of ethnicity that is the "institutionalization of one particular ethnic identity by attaching it to the State" (1984, 247). Nationalism, though, is more than identifying with a state as a political institution. It is also an allegiance to the nation as a symbolic identity, as a people associated with a particular way of life and sets of values. As members of a state develop a national identity, they ignore their differences and concentrate on achieving commonly shared goals and interests. Nationalism also involves the process of selective memory and the construction of a fictive past, as the past is formulated according to contemporary values and goals. As Worsley points out, "They project the values of the present onto a past which does not always sustain them" (p. 274).

States utilize various processes to resolve relationships between a central identity and disparate ethnic groups. A dominant ethnic group may assert itself as the only legitimate identity, equating the national culture with its own. Also, a state may assert a uniformity of culture, subsuming and homogenizing differences. Finally, a state may maintain a pluralistic attitude toward cultural differences, allowing secondary identities to coexist along with a national one (Worsley 1984, 252).

A state's strategies may change over time. A state often chooses a dominant identity as it embarks on consolidation and expansion, exerting control over its constituent

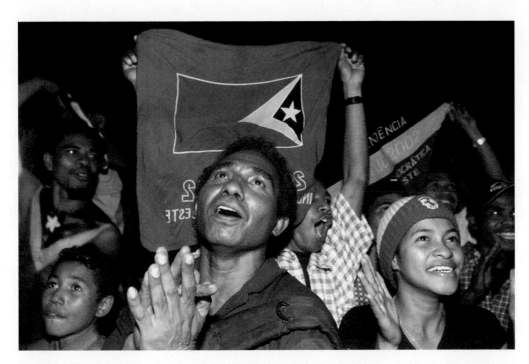

On May 20, 2002, these East Timorese celebrated their independence after 24 years of Indonesian rule and centuries of Portuguese colonization.

populations. An emphasis on uniformity then becomes prominent as states become secure and attempt to eliminate ethnic boundaries. Recognition of cultural pluralism often emerges with the formation of ethnically diverse nation-states as older colonial empires crumble. The rise of ethnic pluralism, therefore, was often a product of decolonization, giving legitimacy to the strivings of disparate groups within a country for recognition and some degree of social and political autonomy. As in the past, however, newly independent states vary in the approaches that they take to ethnic diversity.

CULTURE CHANGE

IMPACTS OF INDONESIAN STATE EXPANSION

Indonesia is an instructive example of a central government's attempts to create a national identity that privileges one ethnic group, the Javanese, as the national norm (Perry 1996). Javanese cultural traditions are exported to other Indonesians through formal education, the media, and public discourse. Following a process of **Islamization**, Islam is imposed on others, either obliterating or subsuming local beliefs. A national language called Indonesian (based on a dialect of Malay) is taught throughout the country and is used in all public contexts. The Indonesian government has embarked on an aggressive policy of creating and imposing cultural uniformity while giving some recognition to ethnic diversity.

However, for Indonesia, as Bernard Nietschmann (1988) puts it, "nation-building" sometimes is state expansion by "nation-destroying." Authorities developed a program of forced internal migration, sending Javanese to outlying regions inhabited by tribal groups who, in turn, were sent to live elsewhere. The program of intense directed culture change is in the service of national unity. But it is also an attempt to wrest lands rich in resources from indigenous peoples. Multinational corporations allied with the state can then exploit the resources. The Indonesian policy is also aimed at dissipating

Islamization
The process of imposing the Islamic religion and associated cultural values within a nation to foster cultural uniformity.

indigenous resistance movements. The army is often deployed to indigenous territories, ostensibly to fight terrorism and insurgencies.

Just one year after Indonesia gained its independence from the Netherlands in 1949, the central government embarked on policies of state expansion by invading and annexing independent islands. In 1950, the army took over the South Moluccas, followed by the annexation of West Papua (renamed Irian Jaya) in 1962, and the invasion of East Timor in 1975.

In West Papua, the Indonesian government implemented its program of transmigration to "redistribute overpopulation" by importing 5 million people from Java (Nietschmann 1988). Indigenous peoples were displaced, and their lands and resources were appropriated to accelerate economic development and national unity. The region is especially rich in timber, minerals, and offshore oil. The World Bank, the United Nations, the Islamic Development Bank, and several countries, including the United States, Germany, France, and the Netherlands helped finance the program. The government also established "assimilation camps," in which cultural minorities were taught the official national Indonesian language and Islam. These were also called "centers for social development" with the aim of "cultivating national pride and defending the state." People who resisted Indonesian political control and cultural hegemony were branded "terrorists," justifying military action against them.

The eastern half of the island of Timor became a battleground where the struggles of the indigenous East Timorese erupted in violence after decades of clandestine resistance. The Indonesian government had forced many East Timorese from their homes, transporting them to Sumatra and other majority Javanese islands while importing Javanese to East Timor. Between 1975 (when the Indonesian army invaded and unilaterally annexed East Timor) and 1990, an estimated 200,000 East Timorese (about one-third of the population) were killed. The international community ignored the situation until the 1990s, when world public opinion shifted to support independence for East Timor. In 2002, a referendum monitored by the United Nations resulted in independence, but East Timor still struggles with poverty, poor infrastructure, and political upheaval, all legacies of Indonesian colonial rule.

Genocide? The Case of Rwanda

Some postcolonial conflicts have centered on internal competition for power rather than independence from expanding new states. Conflicts in many countries in Africa, for example, are often portrayed as ethnic or tribal genocide, but they are more appropriately seen as struggles for power between groups with different interests and loyalties. The 1994 civil war in Rwanda that took the lives of some 800,000 people at first glance looks like a conflict between the majority Hutus (about four-fifths of the population) and the minority Tutsis (about one-fifth). In addition, about 1 percent or 2 percent of the population belongs to a tribal group called Twa, who are considered aboriginal and marginal to Rwandan society (Maybury-Lewis 1997, 100).

Although the Tutsis and Hutus are now thought of as ethnic groups, they represented political strata before Belgian colonial rule was established in 1916. The name *Tutsi* was applied to lineages that controlled wealth and chiefly power, whereas Hutu were lineages without wealth whose members formed a majority peasantry. Although the hierarchical system was relatively stable, particular individuals could rise or fall in status. If members of Tutsi lineages lost wealth and prestige, they would be considered Hutu, and Hutus who acquired wealth could become Tutsis. Hutus allied themselves as clients of particular Tutsi chiefs, giving political support and gaining protection.

During the colonial period, lasting until 1962, the Belgian government administered the territory through indirect rule, essentially using Tutsi chiefs as their surrogates. The chiefs who cooperated enhanced their power. Belgian policies led to an increased rigidity in the system of status and power, fomenting hostility between the Tutsi and Hutu "ethnic groups."

After independence, in 1962, the former Belgian colony split into two countries, Rwanda and Burundi. Civil wars in both countries ensued out of struggles for power. In Burundi, the Tutsi minority persevered and were able to hold on to their positions of power, but Hutu rebels maintained pressure on the Tutsi minority, and between 100,000 and 200,000 were killed in 1972. In Rwanda, the Hutu majority took control. Many Tutsis fled the country, forming a resistance movement with the aim of returning to Rwanda and regaining power. After many years of conflict, both sides agreed to form a coalition government in Rwanda in 1993. Then, a few months later, members of the Tutsi-dominated army assassinated the newly elected Hutu president of Burundi. As civil war erupted there, about 200,000 Hutus fled into Rwanda, where they joined anti-Tutsi militias that were trying to undermine the peace accords.

In 1994, on their way back from Tanzania to attend a United Nations–sponsored meeting discussing implementation of the agreements, the airplane carrying the presidents of both Rwanda and Burundi was shot down by still unknown assailants. At the news, Hutu militias in Rwanda began genocidal campaigns against Tutsis and moderate Hutus who advocated peace and accommodation, including the moderate Hutu prime minister and many other government officials. Estimates put the number of deaths at about 800,000. The Tutsi-controlled army finally defeated the Hutus, many of whom then fled into neighboring Zaire, where most still remain in refugee camps. These tragic events show the influence of policies that rigidify "collective identities . . . [that are] reactivated, mythologized and manipulated for political advantage" (Lemarchand 1994, 31).

Although indigenous Rwandans directly caused the violence in the country, the historical roots of the conflict can be traced to the period of Belgian colonization. Belgian policies had and continue to have their legacy in creating and/or exacerbating tensions among different segments of the population.

Reactions Against Pluralism

In many Western countries, ethnic identities have become significant vehicles for the development, channeling, and recruitment of individuals for social and political action. This rise in cultural identities is coincident with large increases in immigration throughout the twentieth century. Perhaps the worldwide movement toward decolonization since the end of World War II is a contributing factor because it champions political and cultural independence and autonomy.

In addition, large numbers of people immigrating from the same country or region are more likely to maintain ties among themselves. These bonds can create cohesion and solidarity that can be used to achieve social and political goals. They also allow immigrants to resist social and political pressures toward assimilation. For instance, the influx into the United States of people from Central and South America since the 1970s has led to the development of a strong power base wielding political influence both regionally and nationally. In Europe, the rise in immigration from the Caribbean, Africa, and South Asia has brought to the foreground issues of nationality and national identity. For example, the multiracial and multicultural makeup of the populations of the United Kingdom or France must redefine what it means to be "British" or "French."

Cultural pluralism is usually tolerated as long as members of disparate ethnic groups do not attempt to build political power blocs. However, at the same time as the complexion (both literally and figuratively) of American and European countries is changing, internal political movements opposing immigration have strengthened. Members of some anti-immigration movements claim that immigrants threaten national unity because they do not share prevailing heritage, values, and attitudes. These claims are based on a view of a nation that has been "mythologized and manipulated" for political purposes. In addition, a rise of xenophobic sentiments—as defined in Chapter 16, the fear and hatred of out-groups—is stimulated by economic shifts and the perceived downward mobility of members of the middle and lower classes who then blame their misfortunes on the newcomers. Thus, xenophobia and anti-immigration movements are two common reactions to cultural pluralism.

Ancestors of these nomadic Rom "Gypsies" originated in northern India and were victims of xenophobia in every country they entered on their long-distance treks.

Malaysia, Singapore, and Indonesia are examples of countries with complex histories that, in postcolonial times, have led to the establishment of multicultural societies (Hefner 2001). Prior to the European presence in Southeast Asia, these countries had a long history of maritime trade that brought in people from elsewhere, particularly from China and India. Ethnic differences were recognized, but people cooperated in the formation of pluralistic societies. However, the Dutch and the British treated the inhabitants as segregated groups to assert control and foster competition for access to influence and rewards. When the countries became independent in the mid-twentieth century, their constituent ethnic groups then vied for control of the newly emerging states. Competition for the benefits of economic development programs contributed to intergroup tensions.

In Malaysia and Indonesia, social and political distinctions were maintained between indigenous peoples and the ethnic Chinese descended from merchants who prospered from trade even before European colonial powers came to dominate the region. However, treatment of the Chinese differs in Malaysia and Indonesia. In Malaysia, the Chinese have been permitted to send their children to Chinese-language schools if they wish to maintain their culture. Still, Malaysian political parties are organized along ethnic lines and, although pluralism is part of the social and political fabric of society, ethnic Malays have ascendancy over people of Chinese, Indian, and other origin. Also, although religious differences are protected, Islam is the state religion of Malaysia. In Indonesia, however, the Chinese have faced discrimination despite official statements of ethnic inclusion and pluralism. Cultural and religious distinctions are used to promote Javanese interests and claims to power over those of the Chinese and other groups.

Globalization and Cultural Identities

GLOBALIZATION

Anthropologists and other social scientists have been studying the global marketplace as a kind of borderless society. The shared beliefs, values, expectations, and behaviors of members of this society constitute a global culture. This culture has emerged as a result of rapid changes in technology and the political and economic process known as globalization. Researchers seek to make sense of what may be called a global culture of consumerism.

Globalization is popularly thought of as an economic and cultural process that spreads wealth and investment throughout the world. However, as in the past, wealth and investment are concentrated regionally and in the hands of elites. Today, much of the world's wealth comes from Europe and the United States, but investment increasingly goes elsewhere, such as Asia and the Pacific Rim. European companies account for twenty-one of the world's top fifty largest corporations, whereas the rest are Asian (Friedman 1999). Since the 1960s, the centers of manufacturing have shifted to Japan and other Asian countries, particularly Hong Kong, Taiwan, Korea, and China. The United States has been a major importer of goods from these and other countries (Friedman 1999, 187–88).

A Global Identity?

These economic shifts have contributed to what some theorists see as the re-creation of an international or **global identity** based on social class. That is, in North America and Europe, regions that Jonathan Friedman (1999) calls "declining hegemonies," members of elite classes have a global identity that links them to elites in other countries on the basis of class. Characteristics include sharing privileges, interests, leisure activities, locations, and tastes. This global identity is different from the global popular culture in which the world's middle classes increasingly participate, in which they eat food from McDonald's, watch the same movies, listen to the same music, discuss the same topics on the Internet, and buy the same books and other consumer goods.

A global identity has developed as middle and lower classes have tended to fragment along ethnic lines, with groups asserting their own interests. In addition, the power of the state to "manufacture consent" (to use the term from Herman and Chomsky [1988]) and to create and transmit a national identity tends to decline as the nation's economic and political elites focus their activities elsewhere. At the same time, immigrants tend to remain identified with their countries of origin or with emigrants residing in other countries. Thus, some theorists see both a rise in ethnic pluralism and an increasing gap between the classes as major factors in the process of globalization and the invention of a global identity.

The mass media contribute to, and reflect, a growing global identity. People throughout the world watch many of the same movies and television programs, listen to much of the same music, and read the same magazines translated into dozens of languages. These

global identity
An identity of shared interests, practices, and values across international borders, uniting people worldwide.

sources of information and entertainment disseminate people's activities, attitudes, and tastes, contributing to shared experiences and frames of reference. Although there are and will continue to be local variations, the media provide outlets for creating global identities. The Internet is also a powerful and increasingly utilized forum through which people in many countries can communicate, learn from one another, and share ideas. The global spread of the English language, now the most common second language of the world, facilitates this exchange. Although English will presumably continue to be the world's dominant international language for some time to come, other languages have begun to challenge its role in personal communication. For example, in 1990, an estimated 75 percent of all mail and 80 percent of computer data sent worldwide were written in English (Baron 1990). However, by 2008, English's dominance on the Internet was approached by that of Chinese. That is, 29.4 percent of all Internet users employed English whereas 18.9 percent used Chinese (Internet World Statistics 2008). Rounding out the top-five Internet languages are Spanish, Japanese, and French, although these three combined for slightly less than 20 percent. In all, the top-ten Internet languages accounted for 84.9 percent of all Internet users, leaving all of the other thousands of languages spoken in the world with only 15.1 percent of user share.

Ethnogenesis involves a group's creation of a new ethnic identity through both self-definition and definition by other groups. Proliferating identities can lead to tribalization rather than national unity. In transnationalism, however, groups identify across nationalities, based on their shared country or culture of origin. Nationalism calls for minimizing differences to achieve national rather than group unity and loyalty. In pluralistic or culturally diverse societies, ethnic minorities may become marginalized or forced to conform to majority culture. Ethnic minorities, like immigrant groups, are also often victims of xenophobic reactions against outsiders, and conflicts between groups based on their cultural identities can lead to genocide. A global identity may be developing, based on social class.

CULTURAL MINORITIES IN A GLOBAL WORLD

The mid- and late twentieth century saw a revitalization of indigenous communities in many countries and a new energy and focus in their struggles for self-determination. An estimated half of the world's conflicts are now fought over lands and resources of foragers, horticulturalists, and pastoralists (Nietschmann 1988). As defined in Chapter 1, the term *indigenous* refers to comparatively homogeneous peoples or small-scale societies who share the same culture and are "native" to their territory or have occupied it for a long time. Defining who is indigenous is a complex matter, however, and depends also on historical and cultural contexts. In countries with a history as a settler colony (the United States, Canada, Australia, Mexico, and all the countries of modern Central and South America), the term *indigenous* refers to the peoples who lived in these regions prior to the arrival of Europeans, beginning in the late fifteenth century. In these countries, descendants of the original settlers and later immigrants now dominate.

> **Are you or any of your friends members of cultural minorities or indigenous peoples?**

State policies toward indigenous peoples vary considerably in the Western Hemisphere. In the United States and Canada, treaties were negotiated between colonial powers and indigenous peoples, guaranteeing some rights to land and certain rights to limited forms of sovereignty. However, in both countries, federal governments are empowered to override treaty rights in some circumstances, despite the fact that the treaties were legally ratified agreements backed by the force of international law. It should be noted that the U.S. and Canadian governments are "empowered" by their own laws or constitutions. That is, they unilaterally grant themselves the power to break treaties without the consent of the peoples affected. The following sections survey the state of indigenous peoples in the Americas and Africa.

United States and Canada

In the United States and Canada, the federal governments recognize the sovereignty of native tribes (or First Nations, as they are called in Canada), although the people's exercise of sovereignty is limited either by federal law or by judicial rulings. In each country, the specific history of treaty signing and of legislation affecting native peoples varies, but the general trends are similar. Since the 1960s, native peoples in both countries have won important advances in their quest for sovereign powers.

Congress passed the Indian Self-Determination and Education Assistance Act in 1975, establishing principles of self-government for native reservations. Indian tribes have used these principles to broaden their claims of sovereignty and to extend tribal jurisdiction in planning and implementing educational, medical, and social services, as well as to gain control over their territories, economic development plans, and tax immunity.

Do you think native people living and working on reservations should not have to pay taxes? Why or why not?

Tax immunity is a critical issue for native peoples in both Canada and the United States. The concept refers to the fact that Indian lands are immune, not exempt, from all forms of state, provincial, or federal taxation. This means that Indians living on reservations do not pay property taxes, sales taxes on goods purchased on the reservation, or income tax on wages earned on reservations. The tax-immune status of reservations has become especially contentious in New York State since 1997, when the state government first attempted to collect sales taxes on gasoline and cigarettes sold to nonnative people by Native Americans at reservation stores. Because of objections by the native governments, the state delayed its move until 2003, two years after the terrorist attacks of September 11, 2001, in New York City caused a sharp decline in state revenues. Then, New York Governor George Pataki again announced his plan to impose sales taxes on goods purchased by nonnative people from stores on reservations. In 2004, the state legislature authorized collection of those taxes, but in a reversal, Pataki vetoed the bill.

Congress has dealt several times with the issue of Native American religious practices. In 1978, it passed the American Indian Religious Freedom Act, extending protection for Native Americans to "believe, express, and exercise" their traditional religions, granting access to sacred sites and objects, and guaranteeing rights to perform ceremonies. Subsequently, the Native American Religious Freedom Restoration Act of 1993 furthered these protections, with an added amendment in 1994 that specifically protects the use of peyote in religious services. The Restoration Act itself has been declared unconstitutional by the U.S. Supreme Court, but the Court has not ruled on the amendments.

Although most economic activities of native tribes are not specifically addressed by legislation, Congress has enacted laws dealing with casino gambling on Native American reservations. The Indian Gaming Regulatory Act of 1988 sets standards for gambling on reservations and requires agreements between tribes and their state governments that stipulate the kinds of gaming permitted and the percentage of revenues that the tribes agree to give to the states.

Some twenty-seven years after the Florida Seminoles opened the first tribal bingo hall in 1981, there were 423 casinos operated by 225 tribal governments (some governments operate more than one casino). Native people in Canada operate other casinos. In 2006, the total U.S. tribal government revenue from gaming amounted to $25.7 billion (National Indian Gaming Association 2008). Although casinos run by Native Americans account for a mere 5 percent of gambling revenue in the United States, one of the most lucrative is Foxwoods, owned by the Pequots in eastern Connecticut (*American Indian Report* 1999). With more than 11,000 employees, they are one of the ten largest employers in the state. Their profits, amounting to about $1 billion a year, have been invested in reinvigorating their community and the surrounding area. They have built new housing and roads and provide job training, scholarships, and health services to tribal members. The casino and its accompanying resort generate additional income for nearby hotels, restaurants, and stores (Harvey 1996). In the rest of the United States, approximately 670,000 jobs have been created through Indian gaming. Nationwide, Native Americans held 25 percent of these jobs whereas people of other races and ethnicities held 75 percent (National Indian Gaming Association 2008). Therefore, nonnative people, both as workers and as owners of businesses catering to casino customers, profit as much or more from Indian gaming as do Native Americans.

The presence of a casino can boost income for all residents of an area, but it can also bring changes to the community that all residents do not desire. The work that casinos create tends to be low-wage jobs with little future. Some people do not approve of gambling on moral grounds or because of its historical connection with organized crime.

In the state of Hawaii, some Native Hawaiians are asking for recognition of their claims to ancestral territories and their desire to have a legal status somewhat comparable to that of Native Americans living in the other forty-nine states. In 1978, the state created an Office of Hawaiian Affairs with responsibility for administering 1.8 million acres of royal land held in trust for Native Hawaiians. This land was exempt from annexation when Hawaii became a state. The office collects revenues generated by the natural resources, minerals, and use of these lands for the benefit of Native Hawaiians. It also formulates policies regarding social, economic, and health services applicable to native people.

In Canada, the new Constitution Act of 1982 included a short section that affirmed the existing rights of the country's aboriginal peoples. Subsequently, both the federal and provincial governments concluded government-to-government agreements with native reserves covering and expanding indigenous control over health, education, and social services, as well as economic development.

Finally, land claims cases continue to be of paramount importance, enlarging reservation territory and establishing indigenous rights to self-government. Recent settlements in both Canada and the United States usually stipulate some degree of sovereign native control over economic, social, and cultural policies. Hundreds of cases are pending, with outcomes most likely to be decided in the first few decades of the twenty-first century. Some analysts expect large amounts of land and monies to be transferred to native sovereignty, especially in Canada. According to Canadian government estimates, settlements of more than 210 claims may give First Nations (the term used in Canada to refer to indigenous people) control over about 10 percent of the country, an increase from the current native land base of 0.3 percent (Brooke 1999). In the United States, native peoples now control about 2 percent of the country's territory. The increase in their land base is not expected to rise very much because monetary compensation settlements are more the norm in the United States.

Mexico and *Indigenismo*

The Mexican government, like several others in South America, has vacillated in its policies toward indigenous peoples throughout its history since independence from Spain in 1821. At times, some indigenous peoples had recognized rights to land that they held communally, but these rights were ignored and the state appropriated indigenous land at other times. The constitution of 1993 acknowledged the rights of indigenous peoples in a policy known as *indigenismo* that guarantees protection of native customs. However, the actual living conditions of native peoples have not improved, particularly in the southernmost state of Chiapas with its majority Mayan population. There, some indigenous people maintain their traditional land-use patterns, holding their land communally in *ejidos*. Others had been forced off their land by intruding settlers and multinational companies. Some retreated farther into the highlands, where they cleared new farmland, many growing coffee for sale and export.

In the early 1990s, the Mexican government embarked on policies to exploit its vast oil deposits. As an adjunct to this strategy, the government abandoned its stated intentions to grant additional indigenous groups the right to their communal *ejidos*. The government also eliminated price supports to small farmers, another policy that harmed the Mayan farmers of Chiapas. As well, the government allowed wealthy ranchers to expand their holdings, buying up the land of poor farmers. In addition, public projects to develop and generate electricity from hydropower led to the flooding of indigenous lands. Finally, the Mexican government has begun to develop biodiversity projects, concluding agreements with pharmaceutical companies for the exploitation of forests and plants for research into the manufacture of drugs. As a result of these policies, Mayans often become landless wage workers, but their wages are so low that they need to maintain links to strong family networks in traditional communities to survive (Barreda and Cecena 1998).

Mayans suffer discrimination because they have become a cultural minority within their traditional territories. They are outnumbered by Ladino settlers whose incomes and levels of education far exceed those of the Mayans. The Ladinos—an ethnic term for Mexicans with an appearance, language, and identity that are more Spanish than Indian—feel justified in their negative attitudes toward the Mayans, because the indigenous people are poor and lack the education or job skills that would suit them for the modern sector. But the Indians' poverty is a result, not a cause, of their marginalization.

CONTR⊙VERSIES

Who "Owns" the Past? NAGPRA and American Anthropology

In the past century, anthropologists and archaeologists have contributed to the "cultural dispossession" of Native Americans. Archaeologists could excavate sites without permission on the grounds of scientific interest alone. Some collected artifacts and human remains for study without much concern for their relationship to present-day native peoples in the region, and a few looted those sites for sales to collectors. Despite successive migrations, artifacts and remains found in an area could belong to ancestors of living people. This is especially true for finds from recent eras.

Native Americans have spoken out against the desecration of Indian burial grounds. According to Walter and Roger Echohawk, Native Americans have had to witness the destruction of their burial grounds and removal of the remains of their ancestors (Echohawk and Echohawk 1994). In 1989, for example, an "Indian burial pit" was opened in Salina, Kansas, displaying skeletons as a tourist attraction.

In 1979, Congress passed the Archaeological Resources and Protection Act of 1979, which required the consent of a Native American tribe before archaeologists could get a federal permit to excavate on or remove material from tribal lands. In 1990, Congress passed the Native American Graves Protection and Repatriation Act (NAGPRA), which requires that skeletal remains and certain cultural items uncovered on federal or tribal land must be returned to the nation concerned upon request, including materials uncovered in construction sites. In addition, human remains, sacred objects, and other artifacts of "cultural patrimony" held in museums

receiving federal funds must be returned to the appropriate tribal group, if requested.

NAGPRA also requires that any group or individual making a claim first satisfy federal officials that they are part of a recognized Native American group. Then they must demonstrate "cultural affiliation" with the people whose objects or remains they are claiming. The law defines cultural affiliation as "a relationship of shared group identity that can be reasonably traced historically or prehistorically between a present-day

---

The issue of indigenous rights in Mexico became nationally and internationally visible because of the efforts of a group of Mayans in Chiapas to mobilize for their collective rights in land and resources. Their organization, called the Zapatista Army for National Liberation (named after the Mexican revolutionary leader Emiliano Zapata), burst upon the world scene on January 1, 1994. On this date, they took up arms against the Mexican military, a move that was timed to coincide with the implementation of the North American Free Trade Agreement (NAFTA) signed by the United States, Canada, and Mexico.

During the crisis that followed the insurrection of January 1994, the army entered their territory and attempted to arrest their leaders and squelch the resistance. However, the government softened its approach because of the media publicity that drew attention to the conflict, generating generally positive support from the international community. The government then agreed to enter into negotiations with the Zapatistas to settle some of these issues without further violence. However, the government has not yet agreed to anything other than minor concessions.

After decades of conflict, Zapatistas have gained international support for their struggle to gain autonomy in their region of Mexico.

Indian tribe and an identifiable earlier group." Thus, the older the objects or remains are, the harder it is to establish an unambiguous affiliation between them and a present-day group.

Some of the fiercest controversies generated by the law involve objects thousands of years old. In 2004, courts upheld the right of scientists to study skeletal remains excavated from a riverbed in Kennewick, Washington. These remains are nearly 10,000 years old, far too early in the history of occupation of North America for any present-day native group to be able to claim them.

The desire of Native American groups to reclaim masks, figurines, and other ritual paraphernalia is an expression of their sense of the sacred. Under NAGPRA's provisions, once a tribe gains possession, it may keep or dispose of the item as it sees fit. Between 1978 and 1992, the Zunis repatriated sixty-nine wooden sacred figures from museums, art galleries, and collectors (Merrill, Ladd, and Ferguson 1993), including two of their most sacred wooden sculptures, Twin War Gods, from the Smithsonian Institution in Washington, DC. The War Gods have subsequently been used in ceremonies that expose them to the elements. As a result, they will eventually decompose, a natural process in keeping with Zuni practices.

The archaeological community has not been uniformly in favor of NAGPRA. Although most archaeological associations support the moral principles underlying the act, many argue about the law's effects on research and the discovery of knowledge. The clash between the native and archaeological communities reveals underlying tensions and differences in perspectives on science and the past. By letting their War

Gods deteriorate through use and exposure, for example, the Zunis are asserting the precedence of their ethical and religious claims on the sculptures over the scientific and aesthetic claims of scholars who want them preserved as art objects and objects of study. Similarly, groups that rebury remains of their ancestors assert the priority of their beliefs over whatever knowledge further study of those remains might have revealed. Even when impoverished groups sell repatriated objects, they are disposing of them as they see fit (Killhefer 1995).

Many archaeologists and anthropologists have begun to confront their own status as privileged experts who, until recently, framed the discourse about the past and ownership of cultural artifacts in the terms that suited their needs for research. Many welcome the opportunity to rethink their assumptions. As archaeologist Tamara Bray noted, "We must acknowledge that archeology, like all other social and natural sciences, is legitimately subject to criticism on the level of 'values,' not just 'facts'" (1996, 444). According to anthropologist T. J. Ferguson, despite restrictions and loss of research materials, archeologists may find "new opportunities available . . . if they work in partnership with Native Americans" (1996, 64).

◉ CRITICAL THINKING QUESTIONS

Should archaeologists be able to examine cultural, even skeletal, remains from Native American archaeological sites? Why, or why not? What "new opportunities" do you think researchers may find in working with Native Americans?

The Zapatistas have been particularly effective in utilizing sophisticated communication technologies, especially the Internet, to publicize their movement and to forge alliances with other indigenous and marginalized groups striving for social, economic, and political justice. They have used these communication channels to gain international support.

Brazil and the "Indian Problem"

Due to the establishment of plantations by the Portuguese in the seventeenth century, the immigration of many Portuguese and Spanish settlers, and the importation of millions of African slaves, the indigenous population of Brazil is relatively small, currently about 300,000 people, only 0.2 percent of the total population. Estimates of the number of inhabitants in 1500 range from 1 million to 6 million. Although enormous population losses occurred in the early centuries of European colonization, about one hundred indigenous nations disappeared in the first seventy years of the twentieth century (Ribeiro 1971). Most remaining indigenous communities are located in isolated regions in the Amazon. They are generally small settlements, each consisting of a few hundred residents.

Brazil's policies toward its indigenous peoples have wavered between protecting native lands and cultures and allowing intrusions into native territories by ranchers, settlers, and multinational corporations exploiting their resources. Earlier in the twentieth century, the Brazilian government had established a federal agency to protect Indian rights to maintain their lands and their cultures. The agency was to be guided by the motto of

Guarani Indians in Paraguay and Brazil today focus on establishing strong communities based on village life. This Guarani Indian family rides a horse-drawn cart on one of the ranches they reclaimed as ancestral land.

GLOBALIZATION

Brazil's "Operation Amazonia" was a direct response to the global economy and the globalization of industries that exploit natural resources. To encourage economic development, this government program granted tax credits to foreign companies and exempted them from paying import or export duties.

"Die if need be, but never kill" (quoted in Maybury-Lewis 1997, 22). In the 1960s, however, the government changed course and instituted aggressive efforts to develop remote regions. Settlers and ranchers took this as permission to go into indigenous territories and either push out or kill the residents. Although the government did not officially condone their actions, it did little to stop them. In fact, it permitted cattle ranchers in particular to invade the region in large numbers and clear the forests for their herds.

Operation Amazonia. In a program called Operation Amazonia, the Brazilian government granted tax credits and exempted companies from paying import or export duties. By 1980, more than $1 billion were invested in cattle ranching in the Brazilian Amazon (Schmink 1988, 168). Forest timber and minerals, especially tin, copper, uranium, iron, gold, and diamonds, are found in rich deposits as well. Finally, Brazil and the other countries that share the Amazon have recently attracted investment in biodiversity projects. Of the estimated 500,000 species of plants currently existing in the world, about 16 percent (35,000 to 50,000 species) are located in the Amazon (Tyler 1996, 7). Brazil in particular is home to about 22 percent of the world's "higher" plant species, as well as about 24 percent of primate species and between 10 million and 15 million species of insects (Elisabetsky 1996, 405).

To develop these resources, the Brazilian government has set aside some fourteen "extractive reserves," together containing more than 49 million acres of land (Barrionuevo 2008, 14). These reserves are defined as "forest areas inhabited by extractive populations granted long-term usufruct rights to forest resources which they collectively manage" (Elisabetsky 1996, 403). The term *extractive populations* refers to rubber tappers, miners, timber workers, and settlers, but the territories set aside are often also claimed by indigenous peoples, groups whose use of the land is not protected. Instead of protecting Indians' interests in their resources, officials drew up policies aimed at "civilizing" them, attempting to solve the "Indian problem" through assimilation, with the hope of eventually phasing out the government's national Indian Service that oversees native land.

However, despite the efforts of the Brazilian government to assimilate Indian nations, formerly unknown communities of indigenous peoples are "discovered" from time to time. In 1999, a group known as the Korubu was found deep in the Amazonian region of northwestern Brazil, near the borders with Colombia and Peru. Brazilian officials have documented at least fifty sites of Indian habitation that were previously unknown (Schemo 1999). When new groups are found, authorities working for the National Indian Foundation (FUNAI) attempt to have further contact by placing tools, utensils, and clothing in forest clearings. This is done with the assumption that the Indians will continue to return to the clearings to obtain more goods and can eventually be convinced to leave the region or settle in supervised communities. Lands claimed by indigenous peoples can then be opened for development of their timber, mineral, and pharmaceutical resources.

Yanomami at Risk. Because of pressure exerted on the Brazilian government by indigenous peoples and their advocates, a number of reservations have been set aside where lands are under indigenous control and given government protection. The largest of these, and, indeed, the largest indigenous reservation in the world, is an area of 20.5 million square acres inhabited by some 23,000 Yanomamis, the largest indigenous nation in the Amazon (Schemo 1999, 72).

Traditional Yanomami territory had been made vulnerable in the early 1980s, when the Brazilian government permitted road construction cutting through their lands. Although the road was never completed, the initial projects brought a number of deadly diseases to the people, including measles, influenza, and malaria. These diseases killed many hundreds of Yanomamis, decimating 90 percent of some communities (Gorman 1991). The government also conducted aerial surveys that revealed valuable deposits of gold, tin, and radioactive materials.

In particular, gold has brought about 50,000 miners to the region. They have illegally built some 120 airstrips hidden in the jungle and dammed dozens of rivers to obtain water pressure to make prospecting easier. In addition, the use of mercury in gold prospecting has polluted many of the rivers, contaminating the fish that Yanomamis eat, in turn leading to birth defects and nerve disorders (ibid.). New waves of epidemic diseases have stricken the communities. In addition, the miners killed hundreds of people, burned their houses, and destroyed forestland (Wiessner 1999, 77).

Infringements on their lands, the spread of diseases, and competition over resources had the further effect of creating or exacerbating internal conflicts between neighboring Yanomami settlements and within the communities as well (Ferguson 1992). Therefore, what might look to an outsider as endemic warfare was actually, at least in part, a response to turmoil caused by external forces.

The plight of the Yanomamis came to international public awareness in 1987, when four Yanomamis and one miner were killed in a clash (Gorman 1991). Brazilian authorities then drew up plans to reduce the size of Yanomami lands, giving the Indians nineteen separate "islands of habitation" and creating state parks and national forests in which gold mining was permitted. However, an indigenous advocacy group called Survival International brought a lawsuit to the Brazilian High Court, which ruled the government's plan to be unconstitutional and instead ordered the expulsion of the gold miners. In the following year, the government reached a compromise that would return most of the confiscated land to the Yanomamis, keeping about 3,000 square miles for mining operations.

The establishment of reservations throughout Brazil grants the Indians their rights to control their own destinies, living according to their own cultural norms and absorbing as much external influences as they choose. However, despite the intentions of FUNAI, ranchers and resource developers continue to encroach on Indian lands. They often operate in remote regions far from contact with government officials. In addition, although reservation lands are formally protected, most have unclear and unmarked boundaries, making it difficult for Indians to assert claims over particular acreage. So far, about 80 percent of the lands in Brazil officially defined as indigenous territory have been mapped, although even their boundaries are vulnerable to encroachment by settlers, miners, and resource companies (Wiessner 1999, 79). These territories amount to approximately 12 percent of Brazil's total land and about 21 percent of the Amazonian region (Barrionuevo 2008, 14).

Brazil's "Urban Indians." In addition to the indigenous communities officially recognized by the Brazilian government, many more self-identified Indian people live in small villages, towns, and cities throughout the country, even in the densely settled northeast. Some estimates suggest that urban Indians account for about one-quarter of Brazil's Indian population (Warren 2001, 16). And their numbers are increasing. In Brazil, as in the United States and Canada, the number of people who self-identify as Indian has steadily risen in the last several decades. Part of the increase can be explained on the basis of natural growth, but the numbers far exceed that process. Most of the increase results from the easing of people's reluctance to identify themselves as indigenous because of prevailing racism and social stigma.

Many Indians living in rural or urban settings are oriented to indigenous traditions that have been transformed or destroyed over the past five centuries. Still, they "define indigenous ancestral roots as essential to [their] identity, to make them the anchor of [their] dreams and future, and to work toward their recovery" (Warren 2001, 21). They have an orientation that is "post-traditional" in the sense that they look to traditions but also mold and adapt these traditions in a way that is meaningful today. And many face negative attitudes held in Brazilian society toward Indians and Indianness. Some are denied social recognition as Indians because they are the products of racial mixtures, and their appearance, therefore, does not conform to stereotypical images of Indians. Their behavior similarly combines practices and attitudes of their multiple ancestries. However, although they recognize their complex past, they gravitate most toward their Indian identity. They feel most comfortable associating with

In 1991, Brazil established a protected reservation in Yanomami territory. Here, a Brazilian doctor aids the Yanomami.

As an anthropologist, to what extent do you think you would get involved in the political, economic, or medical problems or struggles of the people you were studying? What ethical dilemmas would you face in deciding this question?

other Indians, living in Indian communities or neighborhoods, and decorating their homes with symbols of their indigenous heritage (Warren 2001, 254–59).

Brazilian Indians and their supporters are active in forming organizations that advocate for their lands and their rights. Some of these organizations are backed and funded by members of the Catholic clergy, espousing "liberation theology," which looks to the church to ally itself with the struggles of indigenous and other poor people who are fighting for social, economic, and political justice (Ramos 1997). Although they do not represent the dominant or mainstream church, they do constitute a vocal and active faction. In addition, Brazilian Indians forge alliances among themselves, as well as with other indigenous peoples in South, Central, and North America, learning from one another's experiences and working together to accomplish their common goals.

Costs of Economic Development in Ecuador and Bolivia

Do you think the indigenous people of Ecuador have the right to block oil drilling on their property? How would you resolve the conflict of interest in this situation?

Indigenous peoples in Ecuador and Bolivia are in the forefront of movements to organize opposition to government policies that encroach on their lands, harm their environments, and destroy their cultures. Both countries have a majority population of indigenous people, the descendants of powerful and complex societies. Today, their territories are the targets of oil exploration and extraction. In Ecuador, for example, the government is focusing on oil as the basis of its projected economic development. Ecuador has the largest petroleum reserves in Latin America, equal to those of Mexico and Nigeria (Forero 2003). Most of the oil is located in remote areas of the Amazon inhabited primarily by indigenous communities. Many of these communities oppose the oil companies because of the environmental pollution and destruction that follow oil drilling and pipelines, interfering with the people's ability to maintain their traditional economies that rely on horticulture and foraging. In addition, the people do not receive monetary benefits from the resources because profits from the oil are rarely reinvested in their communities. Instead, the resources benefit wealthy investors and consumers elsewhere in Ecuador, as well as in foreign countries.

Indians have organized protests against government policy and have also occasionally sabotaged the drilling equipment and pipelines. The Ecuadorian government responded by sending military patrols to protect oil company gear and personnel. In addition, representatives of the indigenous Kichwa, Achuar, and Shuar have sent delegations to the capital Quito and to meetings of the Organization of American States and of petroleum company shareholders. They have also forged coalitions with environmental groups. They have filed lawsuits against giant petroleum companies such as Texaco, suing for compensation for damages to the environment, especially leakage of black sludge into rivers, destroying the waterways (Taxin 2003). The government of Ecuador has promised aid to those communities that permit oil development. However, although some indigenous people favor the development, hoping that they will reap economic benefits, the majority opposes petroleum extraction. As a result of the instability in the Amazon, major foreign companies have been reluctant to invest in the region.

In Bolivia, indigenous peoples led protests against government policies in 2003, which eventually led to the resignation of the president, Gonzalo Sanchez de Lozada (Rohter 2003). In 2005, they organized protests calling for nationalizing oil and gas resources. The proportion of indigenous peoples in Bolivia is the highest of all in South America, constituting 55 percent of the total population (Wiessner 1999, 83). Since the 1980s, Indians in Bolivia have gained recognition of their rights to land, obtaining ownership of 1 million hectares of territory in the Andes. In 1994, an addendum to the Bolivian constitution officially designated the country as a "multiethnic, pluricultural society" (p. 84). However, despite favorable political and legal status, indigenous peoples occupy the lowest stratum economically and socially.

Indigenous activism in Bolivia continued to affect national and international policies. Then, in December 2005, an indigenous socialist candidate, Evo Morales, was elected president in a landslide victory. He is an Aymara Indian, with close ties to native communities. Coming to office with a reformist agenda, Morales has embarked on policies to nationalize some gas and oil industries and to redistribute wealth to aid the overwhelmingly poor indigenous and nonindigenous sectors of society in a country where 60 percent of the residents are indigenous and 70 percent are living in poverty (Chavez 2006). Morales has promised not to interfere with property rights of land under production but pledges to redistribute nonproductive land to landless farmers. His policies have come under criticism by the United States and by members of the Bolivian elite, but they have galvanized political participation among the poor and indigenous populations.

Developments in Africa

The situation for indigenous peoples in Africa shares some similarities with, and yet differences from, that of peoples in North and South America. Most European colonial efforts in Africa did not include large numbers of settlers. Therefore, in contemporary Africa, the delineation of who is "indigenous" or "tribal" is more complex than in the settler colonies of the Americas and Australia. After former colonies gained their independence, the new countries developed policies that affected various groups within their borders. In general, members of large and powerful groups came to dominate the governments and benefited from political, economic, and social policies, whereas members of small, isolated groups received far fewer advantages. In many cases, they remain marginalized in their own countries and face various forms of discrimination and control. These factors are reflected in various definitions of "indigenous" proposed by scholars of international law. However, a consensus summary states the following:

> Indigenous communities are best conceived of as peoples traditionally regarded, and self-defined, as descendants of the original inhabitants of lands with which they share a strong, often spiritual bond. These peoples are, and desire to be, culturally, socially and/or economically distinct from the dominant groups in society, at the hands of which they have suffered, in past or present, a pervasive pattern of subjugation, marginalization, dispossession, exclusion and discrimination. (Wiessner 1999, 115)

Central governments in the East African countries of Sudan, Kenya, and Tanzania have continued colonial policies aimed at encouraging or forcing nomadic pastoral societies to become sedentary farmers or wage workers. Colonial and postcolonial governments prefer sedentary citizens because they are more easily supervised and controlled. In addition, nomadic pastoralists rely on large tracts of land to graze their animals. Gaining access to these lands allows national governments to proceed with economic development projects. Also, the governments often phrase their policies in terms of building national unity through cultural uniformity. In some cases, pastoralists are forced to change their economic systems by the unilateral confiscation of their territory. For example, in the 1970s, the Sudanese government undertook the construction of canals on the Nile River that would control flooding but disrupted the traditional economies of the Dinkas, cattle pastoralists of southern Sudan (Lako 1988).

Sudan and the Dinka. The Dinkas rely on floodwaters to irrigate pastureland for their cattle, but the Sudanese authorities claim that such use of water is wasteful. Instead, the government diverts floodwaters for the use of farmers and urban dwellers in the populous northern Sudan. These choices have political implications as well because Sudanese society is split between the predominantly Muslim north and the predominantly Christian south. The two regions are frequently at odds, a conflict that periodically erupts in sectarian violence. The government's plan was to build the Jonglei Canal at a part of the Nile that is in the heart of Dinka territory. They claimed that the Dinkas would benefit from the changes as the people became incorporated into the modern economy. The authorities tried to convince the Dinkas that they would be able to maintain their cattle as sedentary ranchers rather than as nomadic pastoralists. They held out the promise of health care, educational services, and agricultural training as incentives to living in stable villages. In response to Dinkas' complaints that the canal would disrupt animal migration routes, the government established crossing points on the canal. However, the crossing points created a further problem because animals would be concentrated in these areas, leading to depletion of resources through heavy use. In addition, the amount of fish available to the Dinkas would be diminished, curtailing an important source of food.

Given their awareness of the potential negative effects, most Dinkas feared the loss of their traditional way of life. Although they objected to the presence of the canal in their territory, opposition was relatively weak, and a minority of canal supporters consisting mainly of traders, businessmen, and civil servants proved to be more vocal. The Jonglei Canal project uncovered latent class distinctions and contrasts in class interests in Dinka society. Many Dinkas were forced to move, although they did receive some financial compensation.

Sudan and Darfur. Since 2003, a civil war in the southern Sudan has resulted in what the United Nations has termed "violations of international humanitarian and human rights law." After many years of economic and political neglect, factions from several African tribes in the Darfur region, especially the Zaghawa, Massalit, and Fur, took up arms against the central Sudanese government in an attempt to establish autonomy or independence. In response, the government has fought on two fronts, first by sending military units against the rebels, especially using air campaigns, and second by supporting Arab-dominated militias, called the Janjaweed (from an Arabic term meaning "horse and gun") to terrorize civilians. Hundreds of villages have been destroyed and the residents either killed or forced to flee. In 2004, the United Nations Security Council demanded that the Sudanese government disarm the Janjaweed militias and allow humanitarian aid to reach the civilian population. However, the Sudanese government has not heeded the United Nations demands and continues to deny the severity of the conflict and its own support of the Janjaweed militias. According to United Nations data, corroborated by other international sources, at least 200,000 people had been killed in Darfur by the end of 2007, and at least 2.5 million (out of a total Darfur population of 6 million) were made homeless (CNN 2008). Many of these victims have fled, often seeking shelter in refugee camps in neighboring Chad. People unable to leave Darfur are victims of attacks, rapes, and destruction of their meager subsistence base.

The media and public discourse have tended to portray the conflict in Darfur as the result of ethnic divisions, but economic inequalities and social discrimination have also led to policies by the Sudanese government that are more complex than ethnic tensions. Disputes over valuable resources have also contributed to these conflicts.

Kenya and Tanzania: The Maasai and the Barabaig. The Maasai, a group of fourteen independent tribal entities of about 375,000 people, have seen their grazing lands in Kenya and Tanzania decreased, first by actions of British and German colonial authorities and then by postcolonial governments. In the early nineteenth century, European settlers encroached on Maasai lands, taking about half of their acreage (Fratkin and Wu 1997). Then, in the mid-twentieth century, the Kenyan and Tanzanian governments took additional land to create wildlife parks and reserves. In addition, the Maasais have lost grazing territories to small-scale independent farmers and large-scale corporate estates. Governments and international funding sources claim that the Maasai and other pastoralists are inefficient utilizers of the land, which could be better used for producing cash crops and commercial beef (ibid.). In Tanzania, Maasai grazing lands have been confiscated to make way for commercial rice farms and irrigation projects.

However, the Maasais are no longer willing to see their way of life deteriorate. In Kenya, the Loita Maasais have organized the Loita Naimina Enkiyio Conservation Trust to help protect their legal rights to lands in Narok County against a plan to turn some of their acreage into a wildlife reserve that would include the construction of roads and a hotel for tourists.

In Tanzania, the Barabaigs, a group of cattle pastoralists numbering about 30,000, are fighting government and private projects that will turn much of their land into commercial wheat farms. In an important decision, the Tanzanian High Court supported the Barabaigs' suit on the basis of customary use rights. However, the decision was overturned in 1986, after the government filed an appeal on the grounds that not all of the plaintiffs in the case were "native" according to official definitions, because some were not indigenous Barabaigs but instead were descendants of Somali immigrants.

The Kenyan and Tanzanian governments took thousands of square miles of land from the Maasais when they created one of the world's largest and most visited wildlife reserves and national parks. When the British originally established the Serengeti National Park in 1929, Maasais lost resource-rich grazing and farming territory. In response to protests, the British granted the tribes access to the nearby Ngorongoro Conservation Area (NCA). However, by 1975, the Kenyan government prohibited farming in the NCA, even though Maasais had come to rely on maize as a necessary supplement to their shrinking herds. Malnutrition is becoming an increasingly serious problem. Restrictions on access to lands now turned into game parks have also created and exacerbated intertribal tensions as various groups compete for scarcer territories and resources.

What do you predict for the future of pastoralism as a mode of human subsistence?

IN THEIR OWN VOICES

Viktor Kaisiepo on the International Decade of the World's Indigenous People

In this excerpt, Viktor Kaisiepo, a Papuan activist and member of the Presidium Dewan Papua (an organization of indigenous people in Papua), reflects on some of the goals and accomplishments of indigenous people involved in activities related to the International Decade of the World's Indigenous People (1994–2004), declared by the United Nations. Kaisiepo assesses the gains indigenous peoples made during that decade.

Sometimes I wish I were a carpenter, because if I were a carpenter, at the end of two or three days I could say, "Here's a chair." But in the field of human rights how do you measure success? Some people feel empowered by being part of the U.N. process, and others say, well I've been here 10 years but still nothing has changed. So there has been a huge progress when you look back over the years. Let me put it this way: If I am a member of the liberation movement, 22 years down the road I'm still occupied. Is that success? Is that failure? According to my own objectives it is a failure because I am still occupied, but in terms of building international networks and support I've gained a lot. Like I said, when you throw the stone in the Pacific Ocean, one day down the road the waves will come to the shore. So, I think, the people that are here, they will gain a lot of experience, a lot of knowledge.

I don't think this first International Decade of the World's Indigenous People will be a clear indicator of the success of the indigenous movement, but during this decade we will have accumulated a lot of information, and generated a lot of interaction. The best way to see whether there are big results or not is to wait for the second decade. Whether it's declared

a second International Decade by the United Nations or not, the results of the first International Decade will be seen in the next 10 years. Some people become involved in the beginning, some a quarter of the way down the road, some halfway down the road, some three quarters down the road.

You need capacity-building processes for indigenous peoples. Do I understand my rights properly; do I understand the mechanisms made available to me? How do I utilize them, when am I supposed to utilize them, and whom do I have to address? When people come to the United Nations, they think, well, when I address them, that's the end of the story. No, it's the beginning of the story. Things are changing for the better and you must appreciate that. When you meet moments like we did, in 1993, when we asked for the establishment of the Permanent Forum, and in 2002 it was established—within 10 years—then that is a great success. And you have to celebrate it.

The United Nations has declared a Second International Decade of the World's Indigenous People (2005–2015).

**Explore more at
www.myanthrolab.com**

From: Viktor Kaisiepo, "We've Gained a Lot," *Cultural Survival Quarterly* 28, 3 (Fall 2004), pp. 19–20. Copyright © 2004. Reprinted by permission.

CRITICAL THINKING QUESTIONS

According to Kaisiepo, what gains have indigenous peoples made? What still needs to be done?

Nigeria and the Ogoni. Indigenous lands are confiscated elsewhere in Africa so that economic development can proceed apace. For example, the Nigerian government has granted licenses to the Shell Oil Company for drilling on land claimed by the Ogonis, a group of about 500,000 people (Beveridge 2003, 9). Most of the oil drilled in Nigeria is located in Ogoni territory, land that has been harmed by toxic emissions and oil leakages from ruptured pipelines. A group of eight Ogoni activists and one of their supporters, the internationally known writer Ken Saro-Wiwa, were arrested, charged with murder, and executed in 1995, despite vigorous protests from the United Nations and from many countries in the world.

Biodiversity prospecting is becoming big business in parts of Africa, as in Asia and the Pacific (Reid et al. 1996). However, the issue of ownership is a contentious problem in many countries (Iwu 1996). Africa, for example, is rich in plants and animals containing medicinal properties that could be used to treat many ailments. A research project in Nigeria identified several plants that could be used for the treatment of viral infections, and other agents that have antiparasitic, antiplaque, and antifungal properties, as well as a greaseless body oil (Iwu 1996, 243). Management of these and other resources is complicated by competing needs. Conservation of biodiversity resources is critical to their continuation but, at the same time, the intense poverty many Africans suffer drives the governments to allow rapid harvesting even though this policy threatens future supplies.

REVIEW — ◉ In the United States, issues have centered on indigenous peoples' control of land and resources and gaming, while in Canada, efforts have also focused on achieving sovereignty. In Mexico, the policy of *indigenismo* has granted rights to natives, but cultural minorities continue to struggle for independence. South American governments vacillate between protecting indigenous peoples and exploiting the natural resources in their homelands. In Africa, pastoralists struggle to retain grazing land, while people try to keep commercial oil interests at bay.

LEGAL RIGHTS AND INTERNATIONAL RECOGNITION

To protect themselves and their lands, indigenous peoples have formed coalitions to place their concerns on the agendas of international organizations. In the international forum, the question of who is "indigenous" becomes politically and legally significant. Self-identification and community cohesiveness are some of the relevant factors. However, historical changes, migrations of individuals and groups, and intermarriage with members of other communities blur identities and social cohesion. In 1993, a United Nations working group proposed a Draft Declaration on the Rights of Indigenous Peoples that contains forty-five articles outlining international recognition of their rights. Among these are the right to self-determination (to determine their political status and identity), to maintain their cultures, and to be protected from genocide, ethnocide (cultural genocide), or forced relocation. In addition, the document recognizes indigenous peoples' right to practice, develop, and teach their traditions, histories, languages, and religions. They have the right of access to all forms of media, and they are protected in their rights to fully participate in the development of policies and decisions that affect them through their own chosen representatives. Fourteen years after it was first introduced, the Declaration on the Rights of Indigenous Peoples was finally passed by the United Nations General Assembly in 2007. The resolution to accept the Declaration won overwhelming international support. However, four countries voted against the Declaration: the United States, Canada, Australia, and New Zealand. There were eleven abstentions. Significantly, the four countries voting in opposition are all the historical descendents of settler colonies, each having a history of violence toward its indigenous peoples and of policies aimed at eradicating these peoples and their cultures.

CASE STUDY ◉

Papua New Guinea's Customary Law

Legal practice in Papua New Guinea has vacillated between formal jurisprudence and customary procedures. Although the country consists of numerous and diverse populations, the traditions of most communities stress the responsibility of kin groups to redress wrongs committed against their members, either by demanding compensation or by physical retaliation against the perpetrators. People resort to personal redress with or without the approval of informal councils who hear complaints and attempt reconciliation. These councils have no coercive authority, only the force of public opinion. Kinship groups may try to facilitate agreements through negotiation and compromise to resolve problems and reconstitute social harmony.

During most of the colonial period, British and, later, Australian authorities did not recognize customary practices in state legal settings. The adversarial system of due process was imposed through the courts and the laws. In the villages, away from official view, people continued seeking to resolve disputes through traditional means, either by consulting village councils or by calling on their kinship groups to act as mediators. In the 1960s, colonial jurisprudence began to accept defenses or reduce sentences based on customary practices and attitudes.

The courts nevertheless regarded customary law as illegitimate, a product of the "primitive culture and environment of the accused, which made it impossible for the accused to understand and accept Australian values" (Ottley and Zorn 1983, 265). For example, people accused of assault, manslaughter, or murder might claim that cultural expectations led them to commit the offense after the victim had provoked them. If the accused were members of a remote community where traditional practices and attitudes prevailed, they might be acquitted or receive light sentences. However, if the accused were, in the court's judgment, sufficiently assimilated, cultural defenses might not be accepted.

In addition, the Australian Supreme Court denied defenses based on retaliation for sorcery, even though beliefs in sorcery are widespread in Papua New Guinea. The court did not acknowledge that Papuans consider a belief in sorcery to be "reasonable" but imposed its own cultural and legal standards. The court would allow Australian defendants, but not Papuans, to plead insanity for killing someone they believed was a sorcerer. In the court's opinion, "In Papua New Guinea, although most people believe in sorcery, and most sane people do so, no reasonable person would" (Ottley and Zorn 1983, 276).

Following independence in 1975, the Papua New Guinea Law Reform Commission formulated a system of law emphasizing customary law consistent with traditional principles of conflict resolution (Ottley and Zorn 1983). These principles were based on provisions of the new constitution that aimed to legitimate customary practices where possible. However, customary principles and procedures have only been marginally and inconsistently incorporated into the country's legal system. The supreme court has relied heavily on colonial statutes in cases involving customary practices. For example, the court ruled as unconstitutional a statute called the Inter-Group Fighting Act, passed in 1973, in response to a perceived escalation of fighting in tribal areas. That statute was consistent with customary attitudes that hold each member of a group responsible for the actions of the group as a whole. The act was aimed at limiting fighting by permitting the legal system to punish all members of a group engaged in fighting, even though each person may not have been involved in a particular incident. In declaring the act to be unconstitutional, the Supreme Court referred to the Western tradition of individual responsibility rather than the Papuan tradition of collective responsibility for criminal acts. The court also continues to base its judgments on rulings made before independence, again impeding the establishment of customary law.

The actions of the Papua New Guinea courts highlight resistance to custom as a legitimate source of judicial and political processes. This resistance suggests the desire of the state to retain control over competing local interests. Central control and consistency are impossible if communities have their own mechanisms of solving disputes and punishing wrongdoers. The postindependence government is also concerned with establishing a national identity distinct from its colonial past and with attracting foreign investment. It also sees customary law not as an aspect of society that is uniquely Papuan but as a threat to its power.

Explore more at
www.myanthrolab.com

In economic spheres, the United Nations Declaration on the Rights of Indigenous Peoples guarantees the right to own and control "the total environment of their traditional territories," including the conservation, development, and protection of their lands and resources. In politics, indigenous peoples have the right to autonomy or self-government, to maintain their own systems of justice and conflict resolution, to maintain "traditional relationships with peoples across international borders," and to protect their rights agreed in treaties. Finally, the United Nations is charged with creating a special indigenous body to oversee implementation of the Declaration of the Rights of Indigenous Peoples.

International law supports the claims of indigenous peoples to their lands, resources, and cultural heritage. In North America, treaties signed between representatives of native peoples and European or American colonial powers have the force of international law. Because treaties are documents signed by sovereign countries, they either explicitly or implicitly recognize the basic sovereignty of native nations. The fact that subsequent governments in the United States and Canada have unilaterally abrogated provisions of these treaties does not alter the underlying principles of international law.

However, in most countries, treaties were never signed between governments and native populations. Therefore, the rights of indigenous peoples rest on other principles, especially on the principle of **customary international law.** Customary rights include the right to respect traditional lands; to maintain languages and cultural practices; to obtain welfare, health, educational, and social services; and the right to self-determination (Wiessner 1999, 98–99). Indigenous peoples, therefore, have both individual rights and collective rights that need to be protected by international organizations as well as by domestic laws. However, as noted in Chapter 12, domestic laws often fail to capture the spirit and intent of native customs.

Recognizing their relatively low numbers worldwide and the low priority that their interests have within their own countries, indigenous peoples are increasingly seeking to establish alliances among themselves to exert more pressure on national and international policies. For example, representatives of hundreds of indigenous groups from eleven countries of Latin America met in 2008, to establish the International Alliance of Forest Peoples, aimed at having a voice in international climate change policy. Their meeting, also attended by representatives from Indonesia and Africa, proposed the establishment of a fund donated by wealthy countries (principally the United States and Europe) that would pay developing countries for not cutting down trees in forestlands such as the Amazon (Barrionuevo 2008, 14.).

REVIEW — To protect themselves and their lands, indigenous peoples have formed transnational coalitions to place their concerns on the agendas of international agencies and nongovernment organizations. International law supports the claims of indigenous peoples to their lands, resources, and cultural heritage, as well as to basic human rights. The legal systems of newly independent countries, however, tend to be based on colonial rather than customary law.

ECOTOURISM AND INDIGENOUS LANDS

In addition to projects aimed at economic development, increasing numbers of countries in Africa, Asia, and Latin America are infringing on indigenous lands to set up national parks and wildlife reserves (Colchester 2004). **Ecotourism** has created great demand for these areas worldwide. Approximately 12 percent of the earth's landmass currently has been set aside as conservation protected areas. An unlikely coalition has formed between government agencies and conservation organizations that often oppose the people's attempts to secure the resources that they and their ancestors have depended upon for generations.

In an international meeting of the World Parks Congress, held in South Africa in 2003, representatives of indigenous groups issued an appeal protesting their "dispossession and resettlement, the violation of rights, the displacement of peoples, the loss of sacred sites, and the slow but continuous loss of cultures, as well as impoverishment. First we were dispossessed in the name of kings and emperors, later in the name of State development and now in the name of conservation" (MacKay and Caruso 2004, 14). Their position brings them into conflict with conservation groups who favor preserving "wilderness areas" kept "primitive and natural," that is, uninhabited (Colchester 2004, 18).

customary international law
Traditional practices of dispute and conflict resolution, involving mechanisms for mediation and negotiation and principles for punishment or restoration of community relations.

ecotourism
Visiting wildlife sanctuaries and national parks to enjoy a more pristine environment than found in urban life.

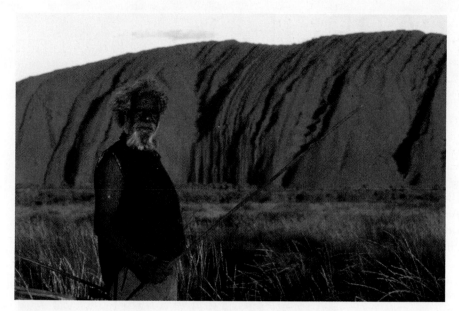

Walter Pukitiwara walks near Uluru (Ayers Rock) in Australia, which is a sacred site to Aborigines.

Although firm statistics are unavailable, some estimates suggest that indigenous peoples actually inhabit 85 percent of reserved and protected lands in Latin America and some 600,000 "tribal peoples" living in India have been forced to relocate in order to establish protected areas.

However, some countries are attempting to reconcile the needs of indigenous peoples and the desire to conserve natural resources. For example, the Peruvian government has established what it calls "communal reserves" to be managed jointly by indigenous communities and conservation agencies (Newing and Wahl 2004, 38). Indigenous peoples maintain legal title to the land and are guaranteed protection against encroachment by loggers, miners, and settlers. However, government agencies also monitor activities of indigenous people to ensure that their land use does not conflict with the goals of "biodiversity conservation."

In South Africa, government commissions staffed by representatives from indigenous groups and conservation agencies work out equitable management policies that recognize the people's rights to their lands. The San, an indigenous people whose traditional lands are located in the Kalahari Desert spanning Namibia and Botswana, have concluded agreements with the Namibian government that establishes the Nyae Nyae Conservancy to oversee the people's communal lands with control over management and utilization of natural resources (Hitchcock and Biesele 2002, 9). Other groups of San have won recognition of their rights to land and, importantly, to water, the most critical resource in the desert.

Income from ecotourism potentially supports people, parks, and species, an attractive prospect for developing countries. Some hail this trend as a positive adaptation to irrevocable change, but others argue, at what price? Revenues from tourism often go to governments and commercial interests rather than directly benefiting the people.

Ecotourism offers a means of protecting native populations and lands but also encroaches on those lands and the people. The double-edged sword of ecotourism is a metaphor for the complexity of human problems in our postcolonial and increasingly postmodern and globalized world.

REVIEW

FUNAI Anthropologists

Anthropologists work both for the Brazilian government and for indigenous communities to protect or extend Indian rights while furthering government policies and national goals—a balancing act that is often difficult. Anthropologists have played crucial roles in (1) mapping aboriginal lands to support Indian claims to ancestral territories; (2) contacting new groups deep in the Amazon to help them prepare for contact with the outside world; (3) reporting abuses of Indians; (4) representing Indians in disputes with settlers, prospectors, and government agents; (5) educating indigenous communities about their political and economic rights and interests; and (6) advocating on behalf of indigenous Amazon peoples.

In March 2003, for example, indigenous leaders from across Brazil, politicians, anthropologists, and officials from the National Indian Foundation (FUNAI) met in Brasilia to discuss indigenous rights. Topics included proposals to improve the quality of life of indigenous populations and strategies to prevent the invasion of indigenous lands. They also discussed the corruption of FUNAI officials and the murder of indigenous leaders (Radiobras 2003).

In 2004, anthropologists helped prevent bloodshed when 3,000 Guarani Indians invaded fourteen ranches near the Paraguayan border that they claim as part of their ancestral land. In negotiations through FUNAI, the Guaranis agreed to leave eleven of the farms, but continued to occupy the

three largest ranches to press FUNAI to expand their tribal reserve by incorporating the land on which the ranches are located.

Anthropologists say that the indigenous community has a legitimate ancestral claim to this property. Rubem Almeida, one of the two anthropologists who wrote the report that will serve as the basis for FUNAI's demarcation of the Guarani territory, said the Guaranis are legally entitled to the land. Almeida presented testimony and material evidence that the Guaranis traditionally lived on the property, as well as "specific documents from 1927" that confirm their legal claim to the land. Despite the ranchers' protests, the local indigenous community has a right to that land under the Brazilian constitution, which cancels out the land titles held by the ranchers. Although a law the Brazilian government passed in 2005 guaranteed the Guarani territory, called Nanderu Marangatu, ranchers still occupy most of the land. This continuing conflict was the subject of a Great Assembly called by the Guarani in 2008, demanding an end to the illegal occupation of their territory (Survival International 2008).

◉ CRITICAL THINKING QUESTIONS

Why is being a government anthropologist a balancing act in Brazil? How might this compare with being an anthropologist in the Bureau of Indian Affairs in the United States?

CHAPTER SUMMARY

Migration

- The global economy accelerates the transfer of goods, services, and peoples from one part of the world to others. International migration has increased cultural diversity. Political processes have strengthened ties among countries.

- Processes of internal migration particularly from rural to urban areas have also accelerated, often because people seek job opportunities. Factories run by multinational corporations in development or free trade zones in Asia and Latin America have increased internal migration. Young women make up most of the work force in labor-intensive factories.

- International migration has shifted populations to wealthier countries with better job opportunities. As transnational migrants, people are increasingly maintaining ties with their native countries and communities. The ease of transportation and communication makes a transnational identity more likely.

- Although many international migrants assimilate into their new countries, others develop an identity based on their origin and ethnicity. However, ethnic identities are context-bound and adaptable to circumstances. People may think of themselves as members of groups based on one set of criteria but may find themselves categorized as members of other groups based on different criteria. Ethnic groups may develop strong political influence on the basis of their relative numbers and cohesiveness as a social and political community.

Ethnogenesis and Ethnic Identity

- Multiethnic states may employ various strategies to resolve relationships between central identities and disparate ethnic groups. One ethnic group may equate national culture with its own. A state may seek to assert cultural uniformity. A state may allow secondary identities to coexist along with a national identity. Ethnic

strife may lead to tension and conflict within a multiethnic country. As well, cultural pluralism may spawn xenophobic sentiments.

- An international or global identity based on social class has developed among elites. A popular global culture has also developed as people throughout the world eat the same foods, watch the same movies, listen to the same music, and purchase the same consumer goods.

Cultural Minorities in a Global World

- Policies toward indigenous peoples vary considerably. In the United States and Canada, treaties and court rulings support limited sovereignty for native communities. In Mexico, federal policies have vacillated between recognizing and ignoring the land rights of indigenous peoples. In South America, although indigenous communities have gained some recognition to land rights, resources, and their cultural practices, their lands have also been the target of resource extraction.

- In many African states, indigenous peoples remain marginalized and face discrimination and control. In Sudan, Kenya, and Tanzania, governments have attempted to force nomadic pastoralists to adopt a sedentary lifestyle.

Legal Rights and International Recognition

- To protect themselves and their land, indigenous peoples have formed coalitions to assert their rights under international law. The United Nations is formulating a Declaration on the Rights of Indigenous Peoples.

Ecotourism and Indigenous Lands

- In addition to projects aimed at economic development, many countries are infringing on indigenous lands to create national parks and wildlife reserves for ecotourism. However, in some countries, indigenous residents have gained protections.

KEY TERMS

cultural minorities   436
labor migration   436
tribalization   440

transnationalism   441
Islamization   443
global identity   446

customary international law   460
ecotourism   460

REVIEW QUESTIONS

1. What are the distinguishing features and effects of forced migration, urban migration, and labor migration?

2. What difficulties can transnational migration cause for cultural minorities? How might they participate in a culture of transnationalism?

3. What are some examples of ethnogenesis?

4. How have postcolonial states treated cultural minorities in the process of nation building?

5. How has globalization affected cultural identities and consumerism?

6. What challenges do cultural minorities face around the world? How do situations in Canada, Brazil, Nigeria, and other countries show how those challenges play out?

7. How has the law worked both against and for cultural minorities?

8. What role could ecotourism play for cultural minorities?

myanthrolab⁕ EXERCISES

To complete the following exercises and activities, you must log in to www.myanthrolab.com and select your current textbook.

1. In the **Explore** tab of Chapter 17, click on *Video* and watch the video on *Reclaiming Indian Heritage*. Complete the short answer exercise that accompanies the video.

2. While in the *Video* section of the **Explore** tab, watch the video on *Migration: A Profile of the U.S.* Complete the short answer exercise that accompanies the video.

3. While in the **Explore** tab, click on the *NPR Audio Programs Broadcast* tab and go to *Themes 28, 29 and 30 on Globalization*. Listen to one of the programs in this section and complete the short answer exercise that accompanies the program.

4. Enter the **MyAnthroLibrary** section on the home page to read more about topics and cultures that are discussed in this chapter. Suggested readings include:

Badagas: Sometime Refugees in a New Land by Paul Hockings

Gaining Ground?: Evenkis, Land, and Reform in Southeastern Siberia by Gail A. Fondahl

GLOSSARY

acculturation Process by which a group adjusts to living within a dominant culture while at the same time maintaining its original cultural identity.

achieved status A social position attained by a person's own efforts and skills.

aesthetics Philosophies about what has beauty and value in art.

affines People related through marriage.

African American Vernacular English (AAVE) A dialect of English spoken by some, but not all, Americans of African descent.

age grade (age set) A sociopolitical association of people of more or less similar age who are given specific social functions.

agriculture A subsistence strategy focusing on intensive farming, investing a great deal of time, energy, and technology.

ambilineal descent Principle of descent in which individuals may choose to affiliate with either their mother's or their father's kinship group.

ancestor worship Belief in the importance of ancestors as they affect the lives of their survivors, protecting their descendants in return for rituals of honor performed to show them respect.

animatism Belief that all things are endowed with some spirit form or essence.

animism Belief in the existence of souls.

anthropology The study of humanity, from its evolutionary origins millions of years ago to its current worldwide diversity.

applied anthropology An area of anthropology that applies the techniques and theories of the field to problem solving outside of traditional academic settings.

archaeology The study of past cultures, both historic cultures with written records and prehistoric cultures that predate the invention of writing.

arranged marriages Marriages that are arranged by the parents or other relatives of the bride and groom.

art Artifacts of human creation created through the exercise of exceptional physical, conceptual, or imaginative skill, and produced in a public medium and intended to affect the senses, sharing stylistic conventions with similar works.

artisans Specialists in the production of works of art.

ascribed status A social position that a person attains by birth. A person is born into an ascribed status.

assimilation Process by which a less numerous and less powerful cultural group changes its ways and cultural identity to blend in with the dominant culture.

associations Sociopolitical groups that link people in a community on the basis of shared interests and skills.

avoidance relationships Patterns of behavior between certain sets of kin that demonstrate respect and social distance.

avunculocal residence Patterns of residence after marriage in which the couple lives with or near the husband's mother's brother.

balanced reciprocity Exchange of goods and services of a specified value at a specified time and place.

bands Small, loosely organized groups of people held together by informal means.

barter An exchange of products in which one person gives one type of product in exchange for another type of product.

berdaches Male Two-Spirits in some Native American societies who adopted some of the economic and social roles of women.

bilateral descent Principle of descent in which people think of themselves related to both their mother's kin and their father's kin at the same time.

bilocal residence Patterns of residence after marriage in which the couple alternates between living with the wife's kin and the husband's kin.

biological, or physical, anthropology The study of human origins and biological diversity.

blood feud Ongoing conflict between kin groups or communities, based on vengeance.

body language The meanings people communicate through their posture, stance, movements, expressions, gestures, and proximity to other communicants.

brideservice A period of months or years before or after marriage during which the husband performs labor for his wife's parents.

bridewealth Presents given by the husband's family to the wife's kin before, during, or after the wedding ceremony.

calendric rituals Ceremonies performed at specific times during the year, for example, agricultural rituals performed for planting, growing, and harvesting crops.

call systems (signal systems) Animal communication systems that consist of a relatively small number of sounds to express moods and sensations, like fear, delight, contentment, anger, or pain.

capital Land, money, factories, and the like that support and supply the materials needed for production.

capitalism An economic mode of production in which the goal is to amass wealth in the form of money in order to gain control over the means of production and then use this control to accumulate even greater wealth.

cargo cults Revitalization movements arising in Melanesia in the early twentieth century with the aim of obtaining material wealth through magical means.

carrying capacity The number of people who can be sustained by the resources and environment in which they live.

cash economies Systems of exchange based on the use of currency in modern markets.

caste Social grouping whose membership is determined at birth and is generally inflexible.

chiefdoms Stratified societies organized by kinship.

child-rearing practices Methods used to take care of infants and young children, including ways of feeding, playing with, carrying, and sleeping arrangements.

clans Named groups of people who believe that they are relatives even though they may not be able to trace their actual relationships with all members of their group.

class Social grouping usually determined on the basis of a combination of birth and achievement.

cognates Words in different languages that are derived from the same word in their parent language.

colonialism Policies in which countries establish colonies in distant places to exploit their resources and labor, and possibly to establish settlements of their own citizens abroad.

colonies Settlements of foreign nationals with controlling interests in indigenous territories.

commodity A product that can be sold or traded in return for money or other products.

comparative perspective An approach in anthropology that uses data about the behaviors and beliefs in many societies to document both cultural universals and cultural diversity.

componential analysis A technique of analyzing the similarities and contrasts among words in a particular category, such as kinship terms or animal names.

confederacy A form of political organization in which tribes and bands join together under common leadership to face an external threat.

conflict avoidance Prosocial behaviors, such as reconciliation, consolation, politeness, or apology, to repair social relationships without aggression.

conflict perspectives Understanding cultural differences as a consequence of conflict in the interests and goals of various groups within a society and focusing on issues of power and resistance.

consanguines People related by blood.

consumerism Culture of consumption of goods and services.

consumption The use of subsistence resources, including outcomes of production.

contagious magic Magic that operates on the principle that positive and negative qualities can be transferred through proximity or contact.

contract archaeology The application of archaeology to assess the potential impact of construction on archaeological sites and to salvage archaeological evidence.

cosmology Religious worldview of a people, including beliefs about the origin of the world, the pantheon of deities that exist, and their relationships to the spirit realm.

counterculture An alternative cultural model within a society that expresses different views about the way that society should be organized.

courtship Period prior to marriage when a couple tests attraction to and compatibility with each other.

creoles Languages that have historic roots as an amalgamation of vocabulary and grammar derived from two or more independent languages.

cross-cousin A child of one's mother's brother or of one's father's sister.

cross-cultural comparisons Means of understanding cultural differences and similarities through data analysis rather than direct observation.

Crow system Kin terms used by some matrilineal peoples that extend the term for father and father's sister to include cross-cousins on the paternal side.

cult of domesticity A constellation of beliefs popular in the late nineteenth and early twentieth centuries that promoted the notion that women were, by nature and biology, suited to the domestic tasks of nurturing and caring for their husbands and children.

cultural anthropology The study of cultural behavior, especially the comparative study of living and recent human cultures.

cultural constructs Models of behavior and attitudes that a particular culture transmits to its members.

cultural core Practices by which people organize their work and produce food and other goods necessary for their survival.

cultural ecology Field that studies cultures as dynamic wholes based on the satisfaction of human needs through cultural behaviors.

cultural evolution Belief of early anthropologists that cultures evolve through various stages from a simpler and more primitive state to a complex and more culturally advanced state.

cultural integration Tendency for people's practices and beliefs to form a relatively coherent and consistent system.

cultural knowledge Information that enables people to function in their society and contributes to the survival of the society as a whole.

cultural materialism Explanations of cultural differences as the results of cultural adaptations through economic production.

cultural minorities Members of ethnic or cultural groups who have become minorities in their native lands due to migrations of other peoples into their territories or due to the historical configuration of a nation-state made up of diverse groups.

cultural models Shared assumptions that people have about the world and about the ideal culture.

cultural pluralism Condition in a stratified society in which many diverse cultural groups ideally live together equally and harmoniously without losing their cultural identities and diversity.

cultural presuppositions Shared knowledge and unspoken assumptions that people have as members of their culture.

cultural relativism An approach in anthropology that stresses the importance of analyzing cultures in their own terms rather than in terms of the culture of the anthropologist.

cultural resource management The application of archaeology to preserve and protect historic structures and prehistoric sites.

culture The learned values, beliefs, and rules of conduct shared to some extent by the members of a society that govern their behavior with one another.

culture change Changes in peoples' ways of life over time through both internal and external forces.

culture contact Direct interaction between peoples of different cultures through migration, trade, invasion, or conquest.

culture history Ongoing culture change in which people respond and adapt to their environment.

culture shock Feeling an anthropologist may have at the start of fieldwork of being out of place in unfamiliar surroundings.

culture-specific psychological disorders Psychological disorders that seem to occur with some frequency in certain cultures but are rare or absent in others.

culture wars Internal disagreements in a society about cultural models or about how society or the world should be organized.

customary international law Traditional practices of dispute and conflict resolution, involving mechanisms for mediation and negotiation and principles for punishment or restoration of community relations.

customary law Selected aspects of native justice and jurisprudence codified into law by colonial authorities, mainly to secure greater control over indigenous populations.

deference Nonthreatening verbal and nonverbal behaviors that convey respect or subordination to others.

depopulation Reduction in population size as a result of war, conquest, colonization, or disease.

deviance Behaviors that violate cultural norms and expectations.

dialect A variety of a language spoken by a particular group of people, based on regional differences or social differences such as gender, class, race, or ethnicity.

diffusion Spread of ideas, material objects, and cultural practices from one society to another through direct and indirect culture contact.

displacement Ability to communicate about something that is not happening at the moment.

diviners People with the power to predict the future through messages and omens from the spirit world.

dominance hierarchies In primate groups, social hierarchies established on the basis of sex and age.

double descent Kinship principle in which people belong to kinship groups of both their mother and father.

dowry Gifts given by the wife's family to the married couple or to the husband's kin before, during, or after the wedding ceremony.

Ebonics Another name for African American Vernacular English.

economic anthropology Subdiscipline of anthropology that focuses on subsistence strategies and economic systems.

economic system Cultural methods of allocating natural resources, the means of exploiting the resources through technology, the organization of work, and the production, distribution, consumption, and exchange of goods and services.

ecotourism Visiting wildlife sanctuaries and national parks to enjoy a more pristine environment than found in urban life.

egalitarian societies Societies in which all members have equal access to valued resources, including land, social prestige, wealth, and power.

elites Members of a social group in a stratified society who have privileges denied to the majority of the population.

emblems Nonverbal actions with specific meanings that substitute for spoken words.

emic Subjective, based on insiders' views, as in explanations people have for their own cultural behavior.

empires States expanded into larger units through conquest and the occupation or annexation of new territories.

empiricism The practice of conducting studies through direct observation and objective description.

encomiendas Spanish landholding system in the American colonies that granted the use of land and the labor of any indigenous people on that land to soldiers, priests, and settlers.

enculturation Process of learning one's culture through informal observation and formal instruction.

endogamy Marriage principle in which people marry members of their own group.

Eskimo system Kin terms making distinctions between the nuclear family and all other types of relatives and on gender.

ethical relativism The belief that all rights and wrongs are relative to time, place, and culture, such that no moral judgments of behavior can be made.

ethnic art Art produced by a particular group of people that comes to express and symbolize their ethnic identity.

ethnicity Social category based on a complex mix of ancestry, culture, and self-identification.

ethnocentrism The widespread human tendency to perceive the ways of doing things in one's own culture as normal and natural and that of others as strange, inferior, and possibly even unnatural or inhuman.

ethnogenesis Ongoing process in which people develop, define, and direct their own cultural and ethnic identities.

ethnography Aspect of cultural anthropology involved with observing and documenting peoples' ways of life.

ethnography of communication Study of communication as it occurs within a particular cultural context, considering such features as settings, participants, and participants' attitudes and goals.

ethnohistory Field of study for reconstructing and interpreting the history of indigenous peoples from their point of view as well as the points of view of ethnohistorians.

ethnology Aspect of cultural anthropology involved with building theories about cultural behaviors and forms.

ethnomusicology The study of the musical styles and traditions of a people.

ethnosemantics Study of culture through people's use of language to categorize and classify people, objects, activities, and experiences.

etic Objective, based on outsiders' views, as in explanations of people's behavior by anthropologists or other observers.

evolutionism View held by early social philosophers that human differences can be accounted for by different rates of progress, leading to different levels of cultural achievement.

exogamy Marriage principle in which people cannot marry members of their own lineage or clan but instead must forge alliances with members of other groups.

exploitation colonies Colonies established by military conquest for the purpose of exploiting the economic and natural resources of a region.

extended family Family formed with three or more generations, for example, parents, children, and grandparents.

external warfare Warfare that takes place at some distance from home communities, requiring warriors' absence from their homes for extended periods of time.

factionalism The tendency for groups to split into opposing parties over political issues, often a cause of violence and a threat to political unity.

family A married couple or other group of adult kinfolk who cooperate economically and in the upbringing of children, and all or most of whom share a common dwelling.

fictive kin Unrelated individuals who are regarded and treated as relatives.

fieldwork In anthropology, living and interacting with the people or group under study.

folklore Texts that relate traditional stories, the exploits of cultural heroes and characters handed down from generation to generation.

folktales Secular stories that relate events that teach moral lessons or entertain listeners.

food producers Users of a subsistence strategy that transforms and manages the environment to obtain food.

foragers Early peoples whose subsistence pattern was hunting and gathering.

forensic anthropologists Biological anthropologists who analyze human remains in the service of criminal justice and families of disaster victims.

formalist Abstract art that focuses on the formal qualities of art—color, composition, sound, words, or movements.

formal sanctions Rewards and punishments administered by persons in authority, the state, or the law.

functionalism View that cultural traits have social functions that contribute to the smooth operation of the whole society.

fundamentalism A term coined in the United States in 1920 meaning a commitment to do battle to defend traditional religious beliefs.

funerary rites Rituals performed to mark a person's death and passage to the afterworld.

fur trade Exchange of animal pelts or hides between Native Americans and colonists in exchange for European trade goods.

gender The roles that people perform in their households and communities and the values and attitudes that people have regarding men and women.

gender construct (gender model) The set of cultural assumptions about gender roles and values and the relations between the genders that people learn as members of their societies.

gender equality A constellation of behaviors, attitudes, and rights that support the autonomy of both women and men.

gender gap The difference in wages and income earned by men and women for comparable work.

gender identity The way that people think about themselves in terms of their sex, how they present themselves as men or women.

gender inequality The denial of autonomy and equal rights to one group of people based on their gender.

gender relations Norms of interaction between men and women, which may reflect differences in the relative status, prestige, and power of women and men.

gender roles Constellations of rights, duties, attitudes, and behaviors that are culturally associated with each gender.

generalized reciprocity The exchange of goods and services without keeping track of their exact value, but often with the expectation that their value will balance out over time.

Ghost Dance movement Nineteenth-century revitalization movement of the Plains Indians of North America.

ghost marriage Marriage practice among the Nuer of Sudan in which a widow marries her dead husband's brother and in which the children ensuing from the second marriage are said to be the children of the first, dead husband.

global culture A constellation of technologies, practices, attitudes, values, and symbols that spread internationally from one broad cultural origin, most recently from the Anglo-European-American cultural complex.

global identity An identity of shared interests, practices, and values across international borders, uniting people worldwide.

globalization The rapid transformation of local cultures around the world in response to the economic and other influences of a dominant culture.

haciendas Estates made up of lands directly owned by Spanish settlers.

Hawaiian system Kin terms making distinctions only of generation and gender.

healers Religious practitioners who acquire spirit power to diagnose the spirit cause of illness and effect cures.

historical linguistics The study of changes in language and communication over time and between peoples in contact.

holistic perspective A perspective in anthropology that views culture as an integrated whole, no part of which can be completely understood without considering the whole.

horticulture A subsistence strategy that focuses on small-scale farming using a relatively simple technology.

household A group of people occupying a common dwelling.

imitative magic Magic that operates on the principle of "like causes like."

imperialism Empire building through state expansion in both commerce and territory.

incest taboo A ban on sexual relations or marriage between parents and their children and between siblings.

independent self Concepts of individuals as self-contained, independent agents with a focus on their own thoughts, feelings, and achievements.

indigenous societies Peoples who are now minority groups in state societies but who were formerly independent and have occupied their territories for a long time.

industrial agriculture Application of industrial technology and chemicals to farming to increase productivity.

industrialism The use of machines to produce products and foods.

informal sanctions Rewards and punishments expressed through praise, ridicule, gossip, and the like.

informed consent The full disclosure to research participants of the research goals, methods, types of analyses, and reporting procedures.

inheritance rules Rules for the passage of land, wealth, and other property from one generation to the next.

initiation rites Rituals that mark a person's transition from childhood to adulthood.

innovation Process by which new technologies and systems of knowledge are based on or built from previous tools, knowledge, and skills.

instrumental Art that attempts to have a beneficial effect on society, enriching people's lives, teaching moral lessons, and providing insights for improving and changing the world.

intensive agriculture Application of technology and intensive labor to farming, such as the plow and irrigation.

intercultural communication The communication of meanings between people of different languages and cultures.

interdependent self Concepts of individuals as connected to others, related to other people, with a focus on group needs rather than individual inner feelings, opinions, and attitudes.

internal warfare Warfare between closely situated villages or communities.

interpretive anthropology View that cultural differences can be understood as complex webs of meaning rather than through forms.

inventions New technologies and systems of knowledge.

Iroquois system Kin terms that emphasize the difference between one's parents' same-sex siblings and parents' opposite sex siblings, classifying parallel cousins with one's own siblings.

Islamization The process of imposing the Islamic religion and associated cultural values within a nation to foster cultural uniformity.

joint family Family consisting of siblings with their spouses and children, sharing work and resources.

joking relationships Patterns of behavior between certain sets of kin that involve reciprocal joking, teasing, and playfulness, sometimes taking the form of flirtation and sexual innuendo.

kindred Kinship group consisting of known bilateral relatives with whom people interact, socialize, and rely on for economic and emotional assistance.

kingdom A centralized political organization with the king as the paramount leader.

kinship system System of determining who one's relatives are and what one's relationship is to them.

kinship terminology system System of terms used to address and refer to relatives.

labor migration Migration of people from one area of a country to another or across national borders in search of jobs.

language Any form of communication that involves symbols, displacement, and productivity.

language family A group of languages that are historically related, descendants of a common ancestral form.

leveling mechanisms Cultural practices designed to equalize access to food, resources, and social prestige through a community so that no one individual can amass greater wealth or greater prestige than other people.

levirate Marriage preference rule in which a widow marries her deceased husband's brother.

life histories A research methodology focusing on collecting narratives of the life experiences of research participants, including their places of residence, work, family composition, social interactions, and roles within their communities.

lineage A set of relatives tracing descent from a known common ancestor.

lingua francas Languages used in particular areas by speakers of many different languages in order to communicate with each other.

linguistic anthropology The study of language and communication and the relationship between language and other aspects of culture and society.

linguistic relativity The concept that people perceive objects, events, and relationships in time and space based on the grammatical forms provided by their language.

loanwords Words borrowed from one language into another.

male dominance A constellation of behaviors and attitudes that grant men access to roles of prestige and reward and deny the same to women.

mana A force, power, or essence that endows people, animals, other living things, and possibly inanimate objects with special qualities or powers.

maritime enclaves Colonies established as a result of sea trade and coastal exploration for the purpose of controlling trade at foreign ports.

market economy Economic system in which products are traded in impersonal exchanges between buyers and sellers using an all-purpose currency.

marriage A socially recognized, stable, and enduring union between two adults that publicly acknowledges their rights and obligations and forms a new alliance between kin groups.

material culture The tools people make and use, the clothing and ornaments they wear, the buildings they live in, and the household utensils they use.

materialist perspectives Explanations of cultural differences that emphasize environmental adaptation, technologies, and methods of acquiring or producing food.

matriclans Clans formed through descent and inheritance from women of their group.

matrilineal Descent system in which kinship group membership and inheritance pass through the female line.

matrilocal residence Pattern for residence after marriage in which the couple lives with or near the wife's family.

medical anthropology A discipline that bridges cultural and biological anthropology, focusing on health and disease in human populations.

mediums People having special gifts to make contact with the spirit world, often in a state of trance.

messianic movements Revitalization movements stressing the role of a prophet or messiah as a savior for people.

millinerian movements Revitalization movements incorporating apocalyptic themes, prophesying an abrupt end to the world as we know it, leading to the establishment of a new way of life or form of existence.

mimetic Art that portrays the world accurately.

missionism Settlement for the purpose of religious conversion.

mission system Pattern of Spanish colonization of the Americas in the name of the Roman Catholic Church.

mita Traditional Incan system of conscripted labor for public works, adapted by the Spanish for use in obtaining indigenous workers for their mines.

mobility A principle that people can move from membership in one social group to another.

modernization Complex culture change, both internal and external, based on industrialism and a transnational market economy.

moieties Groups of linked clans that divide a society into two halves, usually exogamous.

monogamy Marriage rule that stipulates a union between two people.

monotheistic religions Belief systems that hold to the existence of one supreme deity who has powers and knowledge that affect all aspects of life.

morpheme A unit of sound and meaning, either a separate word or a meaningful part of a word.

morphology The study of the internal structure of words and the combination of meaningful units within the words.

narratives Stories and myths that dramatize actual memories or events in symbolic form consistent with cultural practices of storytelling.

national character A constellation of behaviors and attitudes thought to be characteristic of a modal personality type prevalent in a particular country.

nationalism Movement in independent states to build national identity, pride, and unity.

nativistic movements Revitalization movements attempting to rid society of foreign elements and return to what is conceived to be a prior state of cultural purity.

naturalization The process of learning and incorporating attitudes, values, and behaviors so that they seem natural or part of one's nature rather than learned cultural behavior.

naturalized concepts Ideas and behaviors so deeply embedded in a culture that they are regarded as universally normal or natural.

negative reciprocity Exchange of goods and services in which each party seeks to benefit at the expense of the other, thus making a profit.

negative sanctions Punishments for offending social norms.

neolocal residence Pattern of residence after marriage in which the couple establishes a new, independent household separate from their relatives.

nomads People who do not have permanent homes but travel to sources of food as the food becomes seasonally available.

nonverbal communication Communication through gestures, facial expressions, body posture, use of space, and touch.

norms Sets of expectations and attitudes that people have about appropriate behavior.

nuclear family Family consisting of parents and their children.

Omaha system Kin terms used by some patrilineal peoples that extend the term for mother and mother's brother to include cross-cousins on the maternal side.

optimal foraging theory Application of animal studies and decision theory to human foraging.

oral literature Stories that people tell about their sacred past, their secular histories, and their personal lives.

oral traditions Cultural narratives that have validity as artifacts of culture and experience.

pacification Colonial goal of forcing indigenous people to be peaceful and nonresistant so that settlers could safely inhabit their lands.

paleoanthropology The study of the fossil record, especially skeletal remains, to understand the process and products of human evolution.

parallel cousin A child of one's mother's sister or of one's father's brother.

parallel descent Kinship principle in which descent and inheritance follow gender-linked lines so that men consider themselves descended from their fathers and women consider themselves descended from their mothers.

pastoralism A subsistence strategy focusing on raising and caring for large herds of domesticated animals.

patriarchy Social system in which men occupy positions of social, economic, and political power from which women are excluded.

patriclans Clans formed through descent and inheritance from men of their group.

patrilineal Descent system in which kinship group membership and inheritance pass through the male line.

patrilocal residence Pattern of residence after marriage in which the couple lives with or near the husband's relatives.

peacemakers Individuals with a specialized social role of preventing conflict from erupting into dangerous combat.

personality A constellation of behavioral traits and dispositions. Some features of personality emerge at birth while others are acquired in the process of enculturation and psychological and cognitive growth.

phoneme A minimal unit of sound that differentiates meaning in a particular language.

phonemics Analysis of the use of sounds to differentiate the meanings of words.

phonetics Study of the articulation and production of human speech sounds.

phonology Study of sound systems in language, including phonetics and phonemics.

phratries Groups of linked clans that are usually exogamous.

pidgins Rudimentary languages that have a simplified grammar and a limited vocabulary.

politeness strategies Behaviors designed to mute antagonisms and avoid overt hostility by affirming common bonds and recognizing another person's rights and feelings.

political anthropology The study of the ways that communities plan group actions, make decisions affecting the group, select leadership, and resolve conflicts and disputes both within the group and with other groups.

political organization The ways in which societies are organized to plan group activities, make decisions affecting members of the group, select leadership, and settle disputes both within the group and with other groups.

poll taxes Taxes levied on households.

polyandry Marriage between a woman and two or more men.

polygamy Marriage in which the marital unit consists of three or more people.

polygyny Marriage between a man and two or more women.

polyphony The many voices of people from all the different segments and groups that make up a society; a quality of ethnographic writing today that presents multiple views of a culture.

polytheism Belief in the existence of numerous deities that have specific attributes, powers, and functions.

positive sanctions Recognition and rewards for observing social norms.

postcolonial era Period (roughly since 1965) following the independence of the last former European colonies as new nations under indigenous leadership and control.

postconflict reconciliation Patterned behavior that occurs immediately after conflict has erupted and taken its course, to restore some measure of social harmony.

potlatch Ceremonial feast, characteristic of indigenous Pacific Northwest coast societies, during which hosts distributed to guests a great deal of food and goods that had been accumulated over many months or years.

power The ability to exert control over the actions of other people and to make decisions that affect them.

prayer Religious speech or thought through which believers transmit messages to spirit beings.

prestige A social resource reflected in others' good opinions, respect, and willingness to be influenced.

priests Full-time religious practitioners who lead a religious organization and officiate at rituals but are not expected to be able to communicate directly with the spirit world.

primogeniture A system of inheritance of leadership in which the eldest child (usually the eldest son) automatically inherits the position of leadership from his or her parent.

private self One's inner feelings and concepts of oneself.

production System of extracting resources and utilizing labor and technology to obtain foods, goods, and services.

productivity Ability to join sounds and words in theoretically infinite meaningful combinations.

prophets Religious leaders who receive divine inspiration, often in a vision or trance.

proselytism The attempt to convert a person or group from one religion to another.

psychological anthropology A subfield of cultural anthropology that studies the psychological motivations of behavior and the personality types prevalent in a society.

puberty rites Rituals performed to mark the passage of an individual from childhood to adulthood; also called initiation rites.

public self The self that one projects in public, in interactions with others.

qualitative data Information obtained through personal interviews, life histories, observation, and interaction with community members.

quantitative data Statistical information about population, employment and income figures, census reports on births and mortality, and so on, that reflect trends and processes within a community.

race A cultural category that groups people according to so-called "racial" distinctions.

ranked societies Societies in which people or, more usually, kinship groups are ordered on a continuum in relation to each other.

reactive adaptation Coping response of captive, conquered, or oppressed peoples to loss and deprivation.

reciprocity Principles of mutual gift giving.

redistribution The gathering together and then reallocation of food and resources to ensure everyone's survival.

redistributive networks Economic systems in which food and other goods are amassed by an organizer and then distributed to community members or guests at large public gatherings.

reflexive anthropology The anthropology of anthropology, which focuses on the labels that anthropologists use, the impacts of anthropologists on the people they study, and professional ethics.

religion Thoughts, actions, and feelings based on belief in the existence of spirit beings and supranormal (or superhuman) forces.

religious speech Invocations, prayers, prophecies, songs of praise, and curses that are powerful means of transmitting messages about the world and also creating the world.

representational Art that imitates, idealizes, or symbolizes form and experience.

republics State societies with elected rather than inherited leadership.

reservations Land guaranteed by treaty for native residents' ownership and control.

resettlement policies Efforts of colonial authorities to relocate indigenous people to permanent settlements, usually on less desirable land, to control and influence them.

residence rules Rules that stipulate where a couple will reside after their marriage.

revitalization movement Type of nonviolent reactive adaptation in which people try to resurrect their culture heroes and restore their traditional way of life.

revivalistic movements Revitalization movements focused on bringing back cultural and religious practices that express core values that have been largely abandoned.

revolution   Process by which people try to change their culture or overturn the social order and replace it with a new, ideal society and culture.

rites of passage   Rituals that mark culturally significant transitions throughout the life cycle, including birth, puberty, marriage, and death.

rites of renewal   Rituals performed with the goal of renewing the bounty of the earth.

rituals   Activities, including religious speech, ceremonies, and behaviors, that are demonstrations of belief.

rules of descent   Social rules that stipulate the nature of relationships from one generation to another.

sacred rituals   Activities, places, or objects that are connected to the spirit realm and are imbued with power.

sacrifice   Offerings made to spirit beings to show gratitude and honor.

sagamore   A leader of a Mi'kmaq band who had some degree of control over a small territory and had some role in economic redistribution.

same-sex marriage   Marriage between two men or two women.

sandpaintings   Paintings made by sprinkling fine, colored sand to make stylized representations of spirit beings, in particular for use in Navajo curing ceremonials.

Sapir-Whorf hypothesis   The assertion that the form and content of language influence speakers' behaviors, thought processes, and worldview.

scarification   Artistic and ritualistic scarring of the face or other parts of the body in particular designs, commonly used to mark transitions to adulthood.

secret societies   Organizations that control the use of special objects used in religious rituals.

sedentary communities   Settlement pattern involving long-term, permanent settlements.

segmentary lineages   Lineages organized in a hierarchical structure, ranked according to the number of generations they encompass.

self-concepts   Attitudes that people hold about themselves.

semantics   Study of systems of meaning in language.

serial monogamy   Marriage pattern that stipulates that a person can be married to only one person at a time, although individuals may have two or more spouses during their lifetime.

settlement colonies   Permanent colonies established through exploration or conquest for the purpose of occupying land and controlling labor.

settlement pattern   The way people distribute themselves in their environment, including where they locate their dwellings, how they group dwellings into settlements, and how permanent or transitory those settlements are.

sex   Biological differences between males and females.

shamans   Part-time religious practitioners who make contact with the spirit world through prayer, ritual, and trance.

single-parent family   Family consisting of one parent (either mother or father) and her or his children.

slash-and-burn (swidden) cultivation   A farming technique for preparing new fields by cutting down trees and bushes and then burning them in order to clear the land and enrich the soil with nutrients.

slavery   An ascribed status forced on a person upon birth or through involuntary servitude.

slave trade   Buying and selling of people into servitude.

social birth   Social recognition of the transition to personhood.

social control   Informal and formal mechanisms in society through which people's actions are controlled and social norms or laws are enforced.

social Darwinism   Early belief that cultures compete for survival of the fittest, as in the process of natural selection in biological evolution.

social fatherhood   The status of a man who fulfills the responsibilities of parenting, a role that may or may not be the same as biological paternity.

socialization   A similar process to enculturation that emphasizes social rather than cultural factors in learning one's culture.

social reproduction   The care and sustenance of people who will be able to contribute productively to society.

social stratification   Division of society into two or more groups, or strata, that are hierarchically ordered.

societies   Populations of people living in organized groups with social institutions and expectations of behavior.

sociolinguistics   Study of the impacts of socioeconomic and cultural factors, such as gender and class, on language and communication within a society.

song duels   Inuit contests in which conflict is expressed and resolved through public response to music.

sororal polygyny   Marriage between a man and two or more women who are sisters.

sororate   Marriage between a widower and his deceased wife's sister.

specialization of labor   System of allocating work in which different people perform different tasks.

spirit possession   Belief that spirits can enter a body and take over that person's thoughts and actions.

Standard English   Dialect of English chosen as normative, a reflection of the social, economic, and political standing of its speakers.

states   Highly organized, centralized political systems with a hierarchical structure of authority.

status   The position or rank that one occupies in a group or society that carries certain role expectations.

stratified societies   Societies in which people have differential access to valued resources, including land and property, social prestige, wealth, and political power.

stress   Phonemic use of accented sounds or syllables.

structuralism   View that cultural differences can be explained by differences in forms or conceptual categories rather than in meanings.

subculture   A group whose members and others think of their way of life as in some significant way different from that of other people in the larger society.

subsistence patterns   Methods of obtaining food using available land and resources, available labor and energy, and technology.

Sudanese system   Kin terms that give separate words for all kin relationships.

surplus   Food and other goods that are produced at a level greater than that needed for survival.

surplus value   The amount of value produced by workers in capitalist production that is greater than the wage paid to them.

survey research   Use of formal questionnaires, administered to a random sample of subjects, eliciting social data that can be analyzed statistically.

symbol   A word, image, or object that stands for cultural ideas or sentiments.

symbolic culture   The ideas people have about themselves, others, and the world, and the ways that people express these ideas.

symbolic feature   A feature of language based on symbols or on the arbitrary association of sounds with meanings.

syncretism   Process by which a cultural product is created when people adapt a cultural item selectively borrowed from another culture to fit their existing culture.

syntax   The rules that generate the combination of words to form phrases and sentences.

taboos   Norms specifying behaviors that are prohibited in a culture.

tattooing   Injecting inks or dyes under the skin to produce designs.

terrorism   Acts of violence perpetrated by private citizens against groups within their own country or against a foreign country without the cover and sanction of a state-declared war.

theocracies   Societies ruled by religious leaders, in which the social order is upheld through beliefs in its divine origin or sanction.

totem   An animal or plant believed by a group of people to have been their primordial ancestor or protector.

totemism   Belief system in which people believe they are descendants of spirit beings.

trade   System of exchange in which goods are exchanged for either other goods or for money.

transhumance   The practice among pastoralists of moving to new pastureland on a seasonal basis.

transnationalism   Processes by which immigrants maintain social, economic, religious, and political ties to both their immigrant communities and their communities back home.

transvestism   Dressing in the clothes usually worn by members of the opposite gender.

tribalization   A process of identification with one's tribal origins.

tribes   Societies with some degree of formalization of structure and leadership, including village and intervillage councils whose members regularly meet to settle disputes and plan community activities.

Two-Spirits   In Native American societies, males who adopted some of the social and economic roles of women, and females who adopted some of the social and economic roles of men.

unilineal descent   Principle of descent in which people define themselves in relation to only one side, either their mother's side or their father's side.

universal grammar   Abstract rules that underlie the structure of phrases and sentences in all languages, generally thought to be an innate capacity of human thought.

urban anthropology   Field that focuses on studying the lives of people living in cities or urban neighborhoods.

uxorilocal   Living with or near the wife's parents.

vengeance   Aggression against others, based on the principle of revenge.

Venus figurines   Sculptures made in Europe about 30,000 years ago, thought to represent pregnant women.

virilocal   Living with or near the husband's parents.

warfare   Armed aggression and hostilities between groups.

wealth   Economic resources, whether in land, goods, or money.

white man's burden   Paternalistic, racist, colonial attitude that treated colonized peoples as inferiors in need of protection and instruction on how to live.

witchcraft   A belief system that functions as a mechanism of social control by channeling anger toward others.

worldview   Culture-based, often ethnocentric, way that people see the world and other peoples.

xenophobic   Having to do with fear, hatred, and envy of strangers, outsiders, or foreign-born minorities within the society.

REFERENCES

Aberle, David. 1961. "Matrilineal Descent in Cross-Cultural Perspective." In *Matrilineal Kinship*, ed. D. Schneider and K. Gough, 655–727. Berkeley: University of California Press.

Abrahams, Roger. 1983. *African Folktales*. New York: Pantheon.

Abu-Lughod, Lila. 1986. *Veiled Sentiments*. Berkeley: University of California Press.

Abu-Lughod, Lila. 1990. "The Romance of Resistance: Tracing Transformations of Power through Bedouin Women." *American Ethnologist* 17:41–55.

Adams, Kathleen. 1995a. "Cultural Commoditization in Tana Toraja, Indonesia." *Cultural Survival Quarterly* 14:31–36.

Adams, Kathleen. 1995b. "Making Up the Toraja? The Appropriation of Tourism, Anthropology and Museums for Politics in Upland Sulawesi, Indonesia." *Ethnology* 34:143–154.

Adams, Robert. 1982. "Property Rights and Functional Tenure in Mesopotamian Rural Communities." In *Societies and Languages of the Ancient Near East*, 1–14. Warminster, UK: Aris & Phillips.

Adorno, Rolena. 2004. *Nueva corónica y buen gabierno* (c. 1615) by Pomo de Ayala, Felipe Gauman. Yale University. http://base.kb.dk/pls/hsk_web (accessed August 24, 2004).

Aguilar, Mariano. 2000. "Pastoral Disruption and Cultural Continuity in a Pastoral Town." In *Rethinking Pastoralism In Africa: Gender, Culture and the Myth of the Patriarchal Pastoralist*, ed. Dorothy Hodgson, 249–63. Athens: Ohio University Press.

Ahmadu, Fuambai. 2000. "Female Circumcision." In *Africa: Culture, Controversy, and Change*, ed. B. Shell-Duncan and Y. Hernlund. London: Lynne Rienner.

Alexander, Alex E. 1975. *Russian Folklore: An Anthology in English Translation*. Belmont, CA: Nordland.

Almroth, L., S. Elumsharaf, and N. El Hadi. 2005. "Primary Infertility After Genital Mutilation in Girlhood in Sudan." The Lancet, July 29, 2005 #366.

American Anthropological Association. 1998. *Code of Ethics*.

American Anthropological Association. 2001. El Dorado task force papers. http://www.aaanet.org/edtf/.

American Civil Liberties Union. 2005. Briefing Paper No. 6: "English Only." http://www.lectlaw.com/files/con09.htm.

American Indian Report. 1999. "No Dice for Problem Gamblers: Tribes Team Up to Tackle Compulsive Gambling." 2:20–21.

Amott, Teresa, and Julie Matthaei. 1991. *Race, Gender and Work: A Multicultural Economic History of Women in the United States*. Boston: South End Press.

Anderson, Richard. 1990. *Calliope's Sisters: A Comparative Study of Philosophies of Art*. Upper Saddle River, NJ: Prentice Hall.

Anderson, Richard. 2000. *American Muse: Anthropological Excursions into Art and Aesthetics*. Upper Saddle River, NJ: Prentice Hall.

Andrews, George. 1992. "Racial Inequality in Brazil and the United States: A Statistical Comparison." *Journal of Social History* 26 (2):22–63.

Appel, Rene, and Pieter Muyskcn. 1987. *Language Contact and Bilingualism*. London: Edward Arnold.

Arias, Oscar. 1997. "Esquipulas II: The Management of a Regional Crisis." In *Cultural Variation in Conflict Resolution: Alternatives to Violence*, ed. D. Fry and K. Bjorkqvist. Mahwah, NJ: Lawrence Erlbaum.

Aries, Phillippe. 1962. *Centuries of Childhood*. Harmondsworth: Penguin.

Armstrong, Sue. 1991. "Female Circumcision: Fighting a Cruel Tradition." *New Scientist* 2:42–47.

Arnold, Fred, and Liu Zhaoxiang. 1986. "Sex Preference, Fertility, and Family Planning in China." *Population and Development Review* 12:221–46.

Associated Press. 2008. "Census Will Not Record Same-Sex Marriages." July 18, 2008.

Aylwin, Jose. 2007. "Land and Resources." *Cultural Survival Quarterly* 30(4):14–15.

BBC News. 2006. If the "Global Child Labour Figures Fall." May 4, http//news.bbc.co.uk.

BBC News. 2008. "Australia Apology to Aborigines." February 13, http://news.bbc.co.uk/2/hi/asia-pacific/7241965.stm.

Babb, Florence. 1989. *Between Field and Cooking Pot: The Political Economy of Marketwomen in Peru*. Austin: University of Texas Press.

Bacheller, John. 1997. *A Native American Source Book*. New York: McGraw-Hill.

Bailey, Garrick, and Roberta Bailey. 1986. *A History of the Navajos: The Reservation Years*. Santa Fe, NM: School of American Research Press.

Baker, Lee. 1998. *From Savage to Negro: Anthropology and the Construction of Race, 1896–1954*. Berkeley: University of California Press.

Bakhtin, Mikhail. 1981. *The Dialogic Imagination, Four Essays*. Austin: University of Texas Press.

Balick, M., and P. Cox. 1996. *Plants, People, and Culture: The Science of Ethnobotany*. New York: Scientific American Library.

Ballard, Chris. 2002. "The Denial of Traditional Landrights in West Papua." *Cultural Survival Quarterly* 26 (3):40–43.

Barbeau, Marius. 1975. "The Career of a Medicine Man." In *Teachings from the American Earth*, ed. D. Tedlock and B. Tedlock, 3–12. New York: Liveright.

Barlett, Peggy. 1989. "Industrial Agriculture." In *Economic Anthropology*, ed. S. Plattner, 253–91. Palo Alto, CA: Stanford University Press.

Baron, Dennis. 1990. *The English-Only Question*. New Haven, CT: Yale University Press.

Barreda, Andres, and Ana Cecena. 1998. "Chiapas and the Global Restructuring of Capital." In *Zapatista! Reinventing Revolution in Mexico*, ed. John Holloway and Eloina Pelaez, 39–63. London: Pluto Press.

Barrionuevo, Alexei. 2008. "Amazon's 'Forest Peoples' Seek Role in Climate Talks." *New York Times*, April 6, 14.

Barth, Frederick. 1964. *Nomads of South Persia*. Oslo: Universitetsforlaget.

Basso, Keith. 1970. *The Cibecue Apache*. New York: Holt, Rinehart & Winston.

Basso, Keith. 1979. *Portraits of "The Whiteman."* New York: Cambridge University Press.

Basso, Keith. 1989. "Southwest: Apache." In *Witchcraft and Sorcery of the American Native Peoples*, ed. D. Walker, 167–90. Moscow: University of Idaho Press.

Basso, Keith. 1990. *Western Apache Language and Culture: Essays in Linguistic Anthropology*. Tucson: University of Arizona Press.

Baugh, John. 1984. *Black Street Speech*. Austin: University of Texas Press.

Behzadi, K. G. 1994. "Interpersonal Conflict and Emotions in an Iranian Cultural Practice: Qahr and Ashti." *Journal of Culture, Medicine, and Psychiatry* 18:321–59.

Bender, Barbara. 1978. "Gatherer-Hunter to Farmer: A Social Perspective." *World Archeology* 10:361–92.

Benedict, Ruth. 1934. *Patterns of Culture*. Boston: Houghton Mifflin.

Benedict, Ruth. 1946. *The Chrysanthemum and the Sword*. Boston: Houghton Mifflin.

Beneria, Lourdes, and Gita Sen. 1986. "Accumulation, Reproduction, and Women's Role in Economic Development: Boserup Revisited." In *Women's Work: Development and the Division of Labor by Gender*, ed. E. Leacock and H. Safa, 141–57. Cambridge, MA: Bergin & Garvey.

Berch, Bettina. 1982. *The Endless Day: The Political Economy of Women and Work*. New York: Harcourt Brace.

Berlitz, Charles. 1982. *Native Tongues*. New York: Grosset & Dunlap.

Berreman, Gerald. 1989. *Social Inequality: Comparative and Developmental Approaches.* New York: Academic Press.

Beveridge, Sydney. 2003. "Human Rights Commission Condemns Mistreatment of Ogoni." *Cultural Survival Quarterly* 26 (3):9.

Binford, Lewis. 1971. "Post-Pleistocene Adaptations." In *Prehistoric Agriculture,* ed. S. Struever. Garden City, NY: Natural History Press.

Bitterli, Urs. 1989. *Cultures in Conflict.* Stanford, CA: Stanford University Press.

Blackman, Margaret. 1982. *During My Time: Florence Edenshaw Davidson, a Haida Woman.* Seattle: University of Washington Press.

Blackman, Margaret. 1989. *Sadie Brower Neakok: An Inupiaq Woman.* Seattle: University of Washington Press.

Bledsoe, Caroline. 1976. "Women's Marital Strategies among the Kpelle of Liberia." *Journal of Anthropological Research* 32:372–89.

Boas, Franz. 1897. *The Social Organization and the Secret Societies of the Kwakiutl Indians.* Report of the U.S. National Museum of 1895. Washington, DC, pp. 311–738.

Boas, Franz. 1966. *Kwakiutl Ethnography,* ed. H. Codere. Chicago: University of Chicago Press.

Boddy, Janice. 2001. "Spirit Possession and Gender Complementarity: Zar in Rural Northern Sudan." In *Gender in Cross-Cultural Perspective,* 3rd ed., ed. C. Brettell and C. Sargent, 397–408. Upper Saddle River, NJ: Prentice Hall.

Bodenhorn, Barbara. 1988. "Whales, Souls, Children, and Other Things That Are 'Good to Share': Core Metaphors in a Contemporary Whaling Society." *Cambridge Anthropology* 13(1):1–19.

Bodenhorn, Barbara. 1993. "Gendered Spaces, Public Places: Public and Private Revisited on the North Slope of Alaska." In *Landscape: Politics and Perspectives,* ed. B. Bender, 169–203. Providence, RI: Berg.

Bodley, John, ed. 1988. *Tribal Peoples and Development Issues: A Global Overview.* Mountain View, CA: Mayfield.

Bodley, John. 2008. *Victims of Progress,* 5th ed. Lanham, MD: Altamira Press.

Bohannan, Laura. 1966. "Shakespeare in the Bush." *Natural History* 75:28–33.

Bones, Jah. 1986. "Language of the Rastafaris." In *Language & the Black Experience,* ed. D. Sutcliffe and A. Wong. London: Blackwell.

Bonvillain, Nancy. 1978. "Linguistic Change in Akwesasne Mohawk: French and English Influences." *International Journal of American Linguistics* 46:31–39.

Bonvillain, Nancy. 1980. "Iroquoian Women." In *Studies on Iroquoian Culture,* ed. N. Bonvillain. *Man in the Northeast,* 47–58. Occasional Publications in Northeastern Anthropology No. 6.

Bonvillain, Nancy. 1986. "The Iroquois and the Jesuits: Strategies of Influence and Resistance." *American Indian Culture and Research Journal* 10:29–42.

Bonvillain, Nancy. 2001. *Native Nations: Cultures and Histories of Native North America.* Upper Saddle River, NJ: Prentice Hall.

Bordo, Susan. 2004. *Unbearable Weight: Feminism, Western Culture, and the Body,* rev. ed. Berkeley: University of California Press.

Borg, Marcus. 1994. *Jesus in Contemporary Scholarship.* Valley Forge, PA: Trinity Press International.

Bose, Christine. 1987. "Dual Spheres." In *Analyzing Gender,* ed. B. Hess and M. Ferree, 267–85. Newbury Park, CA: Sage.

Boserup, Ester. 1970. *Women's Role in Economic Development.* London: Allen & Unwin.

Bourdieu, Pierre. 1991. *Language and Symbolic Power.* Cambridge, MA: Harvard University Press.

Bowers, Alfred. 1992. *Hidatsa Social and Ceremonial Organization.* Lincoln: University of Nebraska Press.

Brasser, T. J. 1978. "Early Indian-European Contacts." In *Northeast,* ed. B. Trigger, vol. 15, *Handbook of North American Indians,* 78–88. Washington, DC: Smithsonian Institution Press.

Bray, Tamara. 1996. "Repatriation, Power Relations, and the Politics of the Past." *Antiquity* 70 (268):440–443.

Brazelton, T. B. 1990. *Touch: The Foundation of Experience.* Madison, WI: International Universities Press.

Brewer, Terri. 2000. "Touching the Past, Teaching Ways Forward: The American Indian Powwow." In *Indigenous Religions: A Companion,* ed. Graham Harvey, 255–68. New York: Cassell.

Briggs, Jean. 1982. "Eskimo Women: Makers of Men." In *Many Sisters,* ed. C. Matthiason, 261–304. New York: Free Press.

Broadwell, George. 1995. "1990 Census Figures for Speakers of American Indian Languages." *Language in Society* 61:145–49.

Broch-Due, Vigdis. 2000. "The Fertility of Houses and Herds: Producing Kinship and Gender Amongst Turkana Pastoralists." In *Rethinking Pastoralism in Africa: Gender, Culture and the Myth of the Patriarchal Pastoralist,* ed. Dorothy Hodgson, 165–86. Athens: Ohio University Press.

Brooke, James. 1999. "Indian Affairs Heat Up (Witness the Lobster War)." *New York Times,* December 30, A1, A22.

Brooke, James. 2003. "Dowry Too High, Lose Bride and Go to Jail." *New York Times,* February 3.

Brown, Judith. 1975. "Economic Organization and the Position of Women among the Iroquois." In *Toward an Anthropology of Women,* ed. R. Rieter, 235–51. New York: Monthly Review Press.

Brown, Penelope, and Stephen Levinson. 1987. *Politeness: Some Universals in Language Usage.* New York: Cambridge University Press.

Buell, Raymond. 1928. *The Native Problem in Africa.* 2 vols. New York: Macmillan.

Bunzel, Ruth V. 1932. *Introduction to Zuni Ceremonialism. Bureau of American Ethnology, Annual Report No. 47.* Washington, DC, 467–544.

Burger, Richard L. 1992a. *Chavin and the Origins of Andean Civilization.* London: Thames & Hudson.

Burger, Richard L. 1992b. "The Sacred Center of Chavín de Huantar." In *The Ancient Americans, Art from Sacred Landscapes,* ed. Richard F. Townsend. Art Institute of Chicago/Prestel Verlag, Munich.

Callender, Charles, and Lee Kochems. 1983. "The North American Berdache." *Current Anthropology* 24:443–470.

Carneiro, Robert. 1970. "A Theory of the Origin of the State." *Science,* August, 733–38.

Carrasco, David. 1998. *Daily Life of the Aztecs: People of the Sun and Earth.* Westport, CT: Greenwood Press.

Carter, Jennifer. 2008. "Thinking Outside the Framework: Equitable Research Partnerships for Environmental Research in Australia." *The Geographical Journal* 174(1):63–76.

Castillo, Edward. 1978. "The Impact of Euro-American Exploration and Settlement." In *California,* ed. R. Heizer, Vol. 8, 99–127. *Handbook of North American Indians.* Washington, DC: Smithsonian Institution Press.

Castro, A. 2004. "Anthropologists as Advocates: Power, Suffering and AIDS." *Anthropology News,* October, 9, 11.

Center for Strategic and International Study. 2003. HIV/AIDS Task Force. "Botswana's Strategy to Combat HIV/AIDS, Empowering Women and People Living with HIV/AIDS," November 12.

Chagnon, Napoleon. 1973. "The Culture-Ecology of Shifting Cultivation among the Yanomamo Indians." In *Peoples and Cultures of Native South America,* ed. D. Gross, 126–42. New York: Doubleday/Natural History Press.

Chagnon, Napoleon. 1997. *Yanomamo: The Fierce People,* 5th ed. New York: Holt, Rinehart & Winston.

Champlain, Samuel de. 1907. *Voyages of Samuel de Champlain, 1604–1618,* ed. W. L. Grant. New York: Scribner's.

Chance, Norman. 1990. *The Inupiat and Arctic Alaska: An Ethnography of Development.* New York: Holt, Rinehart & Winston.

Chanock, Martin. 1985. *Law, Custom, and Social Order: The Colonial Experience in Malawi and Zambia.* Cambridge: Cambridge University Press.

Chavez, Franz. 2006. "Bolivia's Morales Predicts 500 Years of Indigenous Rule." Inter-Press Service, IPS News. IPSNews.net.

Chernoff, J. M. 1981. *Aesthetics and Social Action in African Musical Idioms.* Chicago: University of Chicago Press.

Cheshire, Jenny. 1982. "Linguistic Variation and Social Function." In *Sociolinguistic Variation in Speech Communities,* ed. S. Romaine, 153–66. London: Edward Arnold.

China Statistical Yearbook. 2005. National Bureau of Statistics Plan to the Report.

Chitnis, Suma. 1988. "Feminism: Indian Ethos and Indian Convictions." In *Women in Indian Society,* ed. R. Ghadially, 81–95. Newbury Park, CA: Sage.

Chomsky, Noam. 1968. *Language and Mind.* New York: Harcourt Brace Jovanovich.

Clancy, Patricia. 1986. "The Acquisition of Communicative Style in Japanese." In *Language Socialization Across Cultures,* ed. B. Schieffelin and E. Ochs, 213–50. Cambridge: Cambridge University Press.

Clark, Ella. 1953. *Indian Legends of the Pacific Northwest.* Berkeley: University of California Press.

Clifford, James, and George Marcus, ed. 1986. *Writing Culture: The Poetics and Politics of Ethnography.* Berkeley: University of California Press.

CNN.com/world. "U.N. Report: Darfur Attacks Broke Human Rights Law." http://edition.cnn.com/2008/WORLD/africa/03/20/sudan.report/.

Codere, Helen. 1950. *Fighting with Property: A Study of Kwakiutl Potlatching and Warfare, 1872–1930.* Monographs of the American Ethnological Society, No. 18. New York.

Cohany, Sharon, and Emy Sok. 2007. "Trends in Labor Force Participation of Married Mothers of Infants." *Monthly Labor Review,* February 2007: 9–16.

Colchester, Marcus. 2004. "Conservation Policy and Indigenous People." *Cultural Survival Quarterly* 28 (1):17–22.

Cook, Sherburne. 1976. *The Conflict Between the California Indian and White Civilization.* Berkeley: University of California Press.

Cook, Sherburne. 1978. "Historical Demography." In *California,* ed. R. Heizer, Vol. 8, 91–98. *Handbook of North American Indians.* Washington, DC: Smithsonian Institution Press.

Costello, Cynthia, Shari Miles, and Anne Stone. 1998. *The American Woman 1999–2000: A Century of Change—What's Next?* New York: Norton.

Coulmas, Florian. 1981. "Poison to Your Soul: Thanks and Apologies Contrastively Viewed." In *Conversational Routine,* ed. F. Coulmas, 69–91. The Hague: Mouton.

Cowley, Geoffrey, and Mary Talbot. 2001. "The Great Disease Migration." In *Anthropology: Contemporary Perspectives,* 8th ed., ed. P. Whitten, 280–83. Needham Heights, MA: Allyn & Bacon.

Croll, Elizabeth. 1982. "The Sexual Division of Labor in Rural China." In *Women and Development: The Sexual Division of Labor in Rural Societies,* ed. L. Beneria, 223–74. New York: Praeger.

Croll, Elizabeth. 1986. "Rural Production and Reproduction: Socialist Development Experiences." In *Women's Work: Development and the Division of Labor by Gender,* ed. E. Leacock and H. Safa, 224–52. Cambridge, MA: Bergin & Garvey.

Crosby, Alfred. 1972. *The Columbian Exchange: Biological and Cultural Consequences of 1492.* Westport, CT: Greenwood.

Crossan, John. 1994. *Jesus: A Revolutionary Biography.* New York: HarperCollins.

Crossette, Barbara. 1987. "New Generation Finds Strength in Borneo's Past." *New York Times,* October 18.

Cultural Survival Quarterly. 2002. "The Fight for Tasmania." 26 (2):13.

Cushing, Frank H. 1979. *Zuni: The Selected Writings of Frank Hamilton Cushing.* Lincoln: University of Nebraska Press.

D'Anglure, Bernard Saladin. 1984. "Inuit of Quebec." In *Arctic,* vol. 5, 476–507. *Handbook of North American Indians.* Washington, DC: Smithsonian Institution Press.

Dannaeuser, Norbert. 1989. "Marketing in Developing Urban Areas." In *Economic Anthropology,* ed. S. Plattner, 222–52. Palo Alto, CA: Stanford University Press.

Deloria, Vine, Jr. 1995. *Red Earth, White Lies: Native Americans and the Myth of Scientific Fact.* Golden, CO: Fulcrum.

DeMarco, Roland. 1943. *The Italianization of African Natives: Government Native Education in the Italian Colonies 1890–1937.* Teachers College Contributions to Education No. 880. New York: Columbia University.

Demos, John, ed. 1972. *Remarkable Providences 1600–1760.* New York: George Braziller.

Denny, J. P. 1982. "Semantics of the Inuktitut (Eskimo) Spatial Deictics." *International Journal of American Linguistics* 48:359–84.

Department of Defense. 2008. "Report on Search for Human Radiation Experiment Records 1944–1994." Washington DC.

DeVos, George, and Hiroshi Wagatsuma. 1995. "Cultural Identity and Minority Status in Japan." In *Ethnic Identity: Creation, Conflict, and Accommodation,* 3rd ed., ed. L. Romanucci-Ross and G. DeVos, 264–97. London: Sage.

de Waal, Frans. 2000. "The First Kiss: Foundations of Conflict Resolution Research in Animals." In *Natural Conflict Resolution,* ed. F. Aureli and F. de Waal, 15–20. Berkeley: University of California Press.

Diamond, Jared. 1995. "The Worst Mistake in the History of the Human Race." In *Peoples of the Past and Present,* ed. J.-L. Chodkiewicz, 114–17. New York: Harcourt Brace.

Diamond, Norma. 1975. "Collectivization, Kinship and the Status of Women in Rural China." In *Toward an Anthropology of Women,* ed. R. Reiter, 372–95. New York: Monthly Review Press.

Dillehay, Tom, Jack Rossen, Thomas Andres, and David Williams. 2007. "Preceramic Adoption of Peanut, Squash, and Cotton in Northern Peru." *Science* 316(5833):1890–93.

Dirks, Nicholas. 2001. *Castes in Mind: Colonialism and the Making of Modern India.* Princeton, NJ: Princeton University Press.

Do, Anh. 2004. "Art Brings Creature Comforts to Villages." http://kicon.com/anhdo/artbrings.html.

Dorson, Richard. 1975. *Folktales Told around the World.* Chicago: University of Chicago Press.

Dozier, Edward. 1970. *The Pueblo Indians of North America.* New York: Holt, Rinehart & Winston.

Draper, Patricia. 1975. "!Kung Women: Contrasts in Sexual Egalitarianism in Foraging and Sedentary Contexts." In *Toward an Anthropology of Women,* ed. R. Reiter, 77–109. New York: Monthly Review Press.

Dugger, C. W. 1996. "U.S. Grants Asylum to Woman Fleeing Genital Mutilation Rite." *New York Times,* June 14.

Echohawk, Walter, Jr., and Roger C. Echohawk. 1994. *Battlefields and Burial Grounds: The Indian Struggle to Protect Ancestral Graves in the United States.* Minneapolis, MN: Lerner.

Edelstein, Stuart J. 1986. *The Sickled Cell: From Myth to Molecules.* Cambridge, MA: Harvard University Press.

Eggan, Fred. 1966. *The American Indian: Perspectives for the Study of Social Change.* Chicago: Aldine.

Ehrenberg, Margaret. 1989. *Women in Prehistory.* Norman: University of Oklahoma Press.

Eiselen, W. M. 1934. "Christianity and the Religious Life of the Bantu." In *Western Civilization and the Natives of South Africa,* ed. I. Schapera, 65–82. London: Rutledge.

Elisabetsky, Elaine. 1996. "Community Ethnobotany: Setting Foundations for an Informed Decision on Training Rain Forest Resources." In *Medicinal Resources of the Tropical Forest: Biodiversity and Its Importance to Human Health,* ed. M. Balick and E. Elisabetsky, 402–08. New York: Columbia University Press.

Elmi, Asha, Dekha Ibrahim, and Janice Jenner. 2000. "Women's Roles in Peacemaking in Somali Society." In *Rethinking Pastoralism in Africa: Gender, Culture and the Myth of the Patriarchal Pastoralist,* ed. Dorothy Hodgson, 121–37. Athens: Ohio University Press.

Ember, Carol. 1981. "A Cross-Cultural Perspective on Sex Differences." In *Handbook of Cross-Cultural Human Development,* ed. Ruth H. Munroe, Robert L. Munroe, and Beatrice B. Whiting, 531–80. New York: Garland.

Ember, Melvin, and Carol Ember. 1971. "The Conditions Favoring Matrilocal vs. Patrilocal Residence." *American Anthropologist* 73: 571–94.

Ember, Melvin, and Carol Ember. 1996. *Comparing Cultures: What Have We Learned from Cross Cultural Research,* vol. 2, no. 2, 1–5. Washington, DC: Council for General Anthropology, General Anthropology Division.

Encyclopedia of New York State. 2008. Syracuse: Syracuse University Press. www.syracuseuniversitypress.syr.edu/enclyclopedia/entries/african-burial-ground.

Erchak, Gerald. 1977. *Full Respect: Kpelle Children in Adaptation.* New Haven: HRAF Press.

Eriksen, Christine. 2007. "Why Do They Burn the 'Bush'? Fire, Rural Livelihoods, and Conservation in Zambia." *The Geographical Journal* 173(3): 242–57.

Ervin-Tripp, S. M., M. C. O'Connor, and J. Rosenberg. 1984. "Language and Power in the Family." In *Language and Power,* ed. M. Schulz and C. Kramerae, 116–35. Belmont, CA: Sage.

Etienne, Mona, and Eleanor Leacock, ed. 1980. *Women and Colonization.* New York: Praeger.

Evans-Pritchard, E. E. 1940. *The Nuer.* Oxford: Oxford University Press.

Evans-Pritchard, E. E. 1951. *Kinship and Marriage Among the Neur.* Oxford: Oxford University Press.

Evans-Pritchard, E. E. 1955. *Kinship and Marriage Among the Nuer.* Oxford: Clarendon.

Fagan, Brian M. 1984. *The Aztecs.* New York: Freeman.

Farnell, Brenda. 1995. *Movement and Gesture.* In *Encyclopedia of Cultural Anthropology,* ed. D. Levinson and M. Ember. New Haven, CT: Human Relations Area Files.

Fears, Darryl. 2003. "Latinos or Hispanics? A Debate about Identity." *Washington Post,* August 25, A1.

Federal Reserve. 2008. "Consumer Credit: Federal Reserve Statistical Release." http://www.federalreserve.gov/release (February 7, 2008).

Fedigan, Linda 1986. "The Changing Role of Women in Models of Human Evolution." *Annual Review of Anthropology* 15:25–66.

Feld, Steven. 1990. *Sound and Sentiment: Birds, Weeping, Poetics, and Song in Kaluli Expression,* 2nd ed. Philadelphia: University of Pennsylvania Press.

Fenton, William, ed. 1968. *The Constitution of the Five Nations.* Syracuse, NY: Syracuse University Press.

Ferguson, R. Brian. 1992. "A Savage Encounter: Western Contact and the Yanomami War Complex." In *War in the Tribal Zone: Expanding States and Indigenous Warfare,* ed. R. Ferguson and N. Whitehead, 199–227. Santa Fe, NM: School of American Research Press.

Ferguson, R. Brian, and Neil Whitehead. 1992. "The Violent Edge of Empire." In *War in the Tribal Zone: Expanding States and Indigenous Warfare,* ed. R. Ferguson and N. Whitehead, 1–30. Santa Fe, NM: School of American Research Press.

Ferguson, T. J. 1996. "Native Americans and the Practice of Archaeology." In *Annual Review of Anthropology* 25:63–79.

Fernandez-Kelly, Maria. 1983. "Mexican Border Industrialization, Female Labor Force Participation, and Migration." In *Women, Men, and the International Division of Labor,* ed. J. Nash and M. Fernandez-Kelly, 205–23. Albany: State University of New York Press.

Fernandez-Kelly, Maria. 1997. "Maquiladoras: The View from the Inside." In *Gender in Cross-Cultural Perspective,* 2nd ed., ed. C. Bretell and C. Sargent, 525–37. Upper Saddle River, NJ: Prentice Hall.

Fiorenza, Elisabeth. 1983. *In Memory of Her: A Feminist Theological Reconstruction of Christian Origins.* New York: Crossroad Press.

Firth, Raymond. 1970. *Rank and Religion in Tikopia.* London: Allen & Unwin.

Fishman, Joshua. 1981. "Language Policy: Past, Present and Future." In *Language in the USA,* ed. C. Ferguson and S. Heath, 516–26. New York: Cambridge University Press.

Flannery, Kent. 1973. "The Origins of Agriculture." *Annual Review of Anthropology* 2:274.

Forbes, Jack. 1990. "Undercounting Native Americans: The 1980 Census and the Manipulation of Racial Identity in the United States." *Wicazo Sa Review* 6:2–26.

Forero, Juan. 2003. "Seeking Balance: Growth vs. Culture in the Amazon." *New York Times,* December 10.

Foster, George, and Barbara Anderson. 1978. *Medical Anthropology.* New York: Wiley.

Foucault, Michel. 1976. *Madness and Civilization: A History of Insanity in the Age of Reason.* New York: Pantheon.

Foulks, Edward. 1972. "The Arctic Hysterias of the North Alaskan Eskimo." *Anthropological Studies No. 10.* Washington, DC: American Anthropological Association.

Fouts, Roger. 1997. *Next of Kin: What Chimpanzees Have Taught Me About Who We Are.* New York: Simon & Shuster.

Fox, Mary, and Sharlene Hesse-Biber. 1984. *Women at Work.* Mountain View, CA: Mayfield.

Fox, Robin. 1984. *Kinship and Marriage: An Anthropological Perspective.* New York: Cambridge University Press.

Fratkin, Elliot, and Tiffany Wu. 1997. "Maasai and Barabaig Herders Struggle for Landrights in Kenya and Tanzania." *Cultural Survival Quarterly* 21 (3).

Freeman, Derek. 1970. "The Iban of Western Borneo." In *Cultures of the Pacific,* ed. Thomas Harding and Ben Wallace, 180–200. New York: The Free Press.

Freidenberg, Judith. 2000. *Growing Old in El Barrio.* New York: New York University Press.

French, Laurence. 2003. *Native American Justice.* Chicago: Burnham.

Fried, Morton. 1967. *The Evolution of Political Society.* New York: Random House.

Friedl, Ernestine. 1975. *Women and Men.* New York: Holt, Rinehart & Winston.

Friedman, Jonathan. 1999. "Class Formation, Hybridity and Ethnification in Declining Global Hegemonies." In *Globalisation and the Asia-Pacific,* ed. Kris Olds, Peter Dicken, Philip Kelly, Lily Kong, Hanry Wai-chung Yeung, 183–201. London: Routledge.

Frisancho, A. R. 1981. "Principles and Definitions in the Study of Human Adaptation." In *Human Adaptation: A Functional Interpretation,* 1–10. Ann Arbor: University of Michigan Press.

Fry, Douglas. 2000. "Conflict Management in Cross-Cultural Perspective." In *Natural Conflict Resolution,* ed. F. Aureli and F. deWaal, 334–51. Berkeley: University of California Press.

Fuentes, Annette, and Barbara Ehrenreich. 1983. *Women in the Global Factory.* Cambridge MA: South End Press.

Gailey, Christine. 1980. "Putting Down Sisters and Wives: Tongan Woman and Colonization." In *Women and Colonization,* ed. M. Etienne and E. Leacock, 294–322. New York: Praeger.

Gailey, Christine. 1987a. "Evolutionary Perspective on Gender Hierarchy." In *Analyzing Gender,* ed. B. Hess and M. Ferree, 32–67. Newbury Park, CA: Sage.

Gailey, Christine. 1987b. *Kinship to Kingship: Gender Hierarchy and State Formation in the Tongan Islands.* Austin: University of Texas Press.

Galliland, Mary Kay. 1995. "Nationalism and Ethnogenesis in the Former Yugoslavia." In *Ethnic Identity: Creation, Conflict, and Accommodation,* 3rd ed., ed. L. Romanucci-Ross and G. DeVos, 197–221. London: Sage.

Geertz, Clifford. 1973. *The Interpretation of Cultures.* New York: Basic Books.

Gergen, Kenneth. 1991. *The Saturated Self: The Limits of Identity in Contemporary Life.* New York: Basic Books.

Ghadially, Rehana, and Pramod Kumar. 1988. "Bride Burning: The Psycho-Social Dynamics of Dowry Deaths." In *Women in Indian Society,* ed. R. Ghadially, 167–77. Newbury Park, CA: Sage.

Ghazi, P. 2004. "Unearthing Controversy at the Ok Tedi Mine." In *World Resources 2002–2004: Decision for the Earth.* World Resources Institute. http://www.ionteraction.org/library/ (accessed November 2, 2004).

Gibbs, James. 1965. "The Kpelle of Liberia." In *Peoples of Africa,* ed. J. Gibbs. New York: Holt, Reinhart & Winston, 197–240.

Gill, Sam. 1982. *Native American Religions.* Belmont, CA: Wadsworth.

Gimbutas, Marija. 1982. *Goddesses and Gods of Old Europe: 6500–3500 BC.* Berkeley: University of California Press.

Gleason, Jean. 1987. "Sex Differences in Parent-Child Interaction." In *Language, Gender and Sex in Comparative Perspective,* ed. Susan Philips, Susan Steele, and Christine Tanz, 189–99 New York: Cambridge University Press.

Glick, J. 1975. "Cognitive Development in Cross-Cultural Perspective." In *Review of Child Development Research,* ed. F. D. Horowitz. Vol. 4, 595–654. Chicago: University of Chicago Press.

Goetz, Deila and Sylvanus Griswold Morley. 1954. The Book of the People : Popol Vuh: the national book of the ancient Quiche Maya. Los Angeles: Plantin Press.

Goffman, Erving. 1971. *Relations in Public.* New York: Basic Books.

Goldfield, David, Carl Abbott, Virginia Anderson, and JoAnn Argersinger. 2004. *The American Journey,* 3rd ed. Upper Saddle River, NJ: Prentice Hall.

Goodale, Jane. 1971. *Tiwi Wives: A Study of the Women of Melville Island, North Australia.* Seattle: University of Washington Press.

Goodman, Felicitas. 1990. *Where the Spirits Ride the Wind: Trance Journeys and Other Ecstatic Experiences.* Bloomington: Indiana University Press.

Gorman, Peter. 1991. "A People at Risk: The Yanomami of Brazil." *Culture-Crossroads,* November, 670–81.

Gough, Kathleen. 1961. "Nayar: Central Kerala." In *Matrilineal Kinship,* ed. David Schneider and Kathleen Gough, 298–384. Berkeley: University of California Press.

Gough, Kathleen. 1968. "Anthropology, Child of Imperialism." In *Monthly Review,* April.

Gough, Kathleen. 1975. "The Origin of the Family." In *Toward an Anthropology of Women,* ed. R. Reiter, 51–76. New York: Monthly Review Press.

Government of India. 2006. Crime in India, Chapter Three: Violent Crimes. www .mppolice.gov.in/mpphq/crimeinindia/ table-htm.

Graburn, Nelson. 1969. *Eskimos without Igloos: Social and Economic Development in Sugluk.* Boston: Little, Brown.

Graburn, Nelson, ed. 1976. *Ethnic and Tourist Arts: Cultural Expressions from the Fourth World.* Berkeley: University of California Press.

Gray, Andrew. 1990. "Indigenous Peoples and the Marketing of the Rainforest." *The Ecologist* 20 (6):223.

Gratton, Nancy. 1991. "Kaluli." *Encyclopedia of World Cultures, vol. 2: Oceania,* ed. Terence Hays, 101–04. Human Relations Area Files, Inc. Boston: G.K. Hall.

Grosjean, Francois. 1982. *Life with Two Languages.* Cambridge, MA: Harvard University Press.

Grossman, A. 2000. "Napoleon Chagnon's Waterloo: Anthropology on Trial." *Dartmouth Review,* October 30.

Gruenbaum, Ellen. 1993. "The Movement against Clitoridectomy and Infibulation in Sudan: Public Health Policy and the Women's Movement." In *Gender in Cross-Cultural Perspective,* ed. C. Brettell and C. Sargent, 411–22. Upper Saddle River, NJ: Prentice Hall.

Guibault, J., G. Averill, E. Benoit, and G. Rabess. 1993. *Zouk: World Music in the West Indies.* Chicago: University of Chicago Press.

Guillaume, Alfred. 1986. *Islam.* New York: Viking/Penguin.

Hafner, Katie. 1999. "Coming of Age in Palo Alto." *New York Times,* June 10.

Hager, Lori. 1991. "The Evidence for Sex Differences in the Hominid Fossil Record." In *The Archaeology of Gender,* ed. Dale Walde and Noreen Willows, 46–49. Calgary: The University of Calgary, Archaeological Association.

Haile, Berard. 1954. "Property Concepts of the Navajo Indians." *Anthropological Series No. 17.* Washington, DC: Catholic University of America.

Hall, Judith. 1984. *Non-Verbal Sex Differences: Communication, Accuracy and Expressive Style.* Baltimore: Johns Hopkins University Press.

Halle, Morris, and G. N. Clements. 1983. *Problem Book in Phonology.* Cambridge, MA: MIT Press.

Halperin, Rhoda. 1990. *The Livelihood of Kin: Making Ends Meet (The Kentucky Way).* Austin: University of Texas Press.

Hardman, Charlotte. 2000. "Rites of Passage among the Lohorung Rai of East Nepal." In *Indigenous Religions,* ed. G. Harvey, 204–18. London: Cassell.

Hariot, Thomas. 1972/1590). *A Briefe and True Report of the New Found Land of Virginia,* ed. P. Hulton. New York: Dover.

Harris, Grace. 1986. *Casting Out Anger: Religion among the Taita of Kenya.* Prospect Heights, IL: Waveland.

Harris, Marvin. 1970. "Referential Ambiguity in the Calculus of Brazilian Racial Identity." *Southwestern Anthropology* 26:1–14.

Harris, Marvin. 1974. *Cows, Pigs, Wars and Witches: The Riddles of Culture.* New York: Random House/Vintage.

Harris, Marvin. 1979. *Cultural Materialism: The Struggle for a Science of Culture.* New York: Random House.

Hart, C. W. M., and Arnold Pilling. 1960. *The Tiwi of Northern Australia.* New York: Holt, Rinehart & Winston.

Hartmann, Heidi. 1979. "Capitalism, Patriarchy, and Job Segregation by Sex." In *Capitalist Patriarchy and the Case for Socialist Feminism,* ed. Z. Eisenstein, 206–47. New York: Monthly Review Press.

Harvey, Sioux. 1996. "Two Models to Sovereignty: A Comparative History of the Mashantucket Pequot Tribal Nation and the Navajo Nation." *American Indian Culture and Research Journal* 20:147–94.

Harvey, Youngsook Kim. 1979. *Six Korean Women: The Socialization of Shamans.* St. Paul, MN: West.

Hassrick, Royal. 1964. *The Sioux, Life and Customs of a Warrior Society.* Norman: University of Oklahoma Press.

Hays, Sharon. 1996. *The Cultural Contradictions of Motherhood.* New Haven, CT: Yale University Press.

Heath, Shirley. 1977. "Language and Politics in the United States." In *Linguistics and Anthropology,* ed. M. Saville-Troike, 267–96. Georgetown University Round Table on Languages and Linguistics. Washington, DC: Georgetown University Press.

Hefner, Robert. 2001. "Multiculturalism and Citizenship in Malaysia, Singapore and Indonesia." In *Politics of Multiculturalism: Pluralism and Citizenship in Malaysia, Singapore and Indonesia,* ed. R. Hefner, 1–58. Honolulu: University of Hawaii Press.

Heine, S. J., D. Lehman, H. Markus, and S. Kitayama. 1999. "Is There a Universal Need for Positive Self-Regard?" *Psychological Review* 106 (4):766–94.

Henley, Nancy. 1977. *Body Politics: Power, Sex and Non-Verbal Communication.* Englewood Cliffs, NJ: Prentice Hall.

Herdt, Gilbert. 2006. *The Sambia: Ritual, Sexuality, and Change in Papua New Guinea,* 2nd ed. Belmont, California: Thomson/ Wadsworth.

Herman, Edward, and Noam Chomsky. 1988. *Manufacturing Consent: The Political Economy of the Mass Media.* New York: Pantheon.

Hewlett, Barry. 1991. *Intimate Fathers: The Nature and Context of Aka Pygmy Paternal Infant Care.* Ann Arbor: University of Michigan Press.

Hilder, B. 1980. *The Voyage of Torres.* St. Lucia: University of Queensland Press.

Hill, A. 2002. Tryptamine Based Entheogens of South America. http://students.whitman .edu/~hillap/tryptamine%20based%20 Entheogens.htm.

HimRights, International Himalayan Human Rights Monitors (INHURED). www.inhured .org/download/HimRights_brochure.pdf (accessed November 2, 2004).

Hitchcock, Robert, and Megan Biesele. 2002. "Controlling Their Destiny: Ju/'Hoansi of Nyae Nyae." *Cultural Survival Quarterly* 26 (1):13–15.

Hodgson, Dorothy. 1997. "Embodying the Contradictions of Modernity: Gender and Spirit Possession among Maasai in Tanzania." In *Gendered Encounters: Challenging Cultural Boundaries and Social Hierarchies in Africa,* ed. Maria Grosz-Ngate and Omari Kokole, 111–28. New York: Routledge.

Hodgson, Dorothy. 1999. "Pastoral, Patriarchy and History: Changing Gender Relations Among Maasai in Tanganyika, 1890–1940." *The Journal of African History* 40(1):41–65.

Hoebel, E. Adamson. 1978. *The Cheyennes: Indians of the Great Plains.* New York: Holt, Rinehart & Winston.

Hollan, Douglas. 1997. "Conflict Avoidance and Resolution among the Toraja of South Sulawesi, Indonesia." In *Cultural Variation in Conflict Resolution: Alternatives to Violence,* ed. D. Fry and K. Bjorkqvist, 59–68. Mahwah, NJ: Lawrence Erlbaum.

Holland, Killian. 1996. *The Maasai on the Horns of of Dilemma: Development and Education.* Nairobi, Kenya: Gideon S. Were Press.

Holton, Robert. 2000. "Globalization's Cultural Consequences." Annals of the American Academy of Political and Social Science. Volume 570:140–152.

Holtzman, J. 2000. *Nuer Journeys, Nuer Lives.* Boston: Allyn & Bacon.

"Honoring Native Languages, Defeating the Shame." 2000. *Tribal College Journal of American Indian Higher Education.* Spring.

Howells, William. 2001. "Requiem for a Lost People." In *Anthropology: Contemporary Perspectives,* 8th ed., ed. P. Whitten, 268–74. Needham Heights, MA: Allyn & Bacon.

Hu, Huiting. 2002. "Family Planning Law and China's Birth Control Situation." China Internet Information Center. October 18.

Hua, Cai. 2001. *A Society without Fathers or Husbands: The Na of China.* Cambridge, MA: Zone Books/MIT Press.

Hulbert, Ann. 2003. *Raising America: Experts, Parents, and a Century of Advice about Children.* New York: Knopf.

Hume, Lynne. 2000. "The Dreaming in Contemporary Aboriginal Australia." In *Indigenous Religion,* ed. G. Harvey, 125–38. London: Cassell.

Hursey, Charlotte. 2001. Watching the Anthropologists: Reflections on Ethnography as Practice within NGOs. INTRAC (International NGO Training and Research Centre). http://www.intrac.org/ (accessed November 2, 2004).

Hutchinson, Sharon. 1996. *Nuer Dilemmas: Coping with Money, War, and the State.* Berkeley: University of California Press.

Hymes, Dell. 1974. *Foundations in Socio-Linguistics: An Ethnographic Approach.* Philadelphia: University of Pennsylvania Press.

Indian Time. 2003. "Minnesota's Indian Bands Bringing Back Banishment." December.

International Labour Office. 2006. *The End of Child Labour: Within Reach.* Report of the Director General, International Labour Organization.

International Women's Democracy Center. 2008. Fact Sheet: Women's Political Participation. http://www.iwdc.org/resources/fact_sheet.

Internet World Statistics. 2008. "Internet World Users by Language." www.internetworldstats.com.

Intrator, Kira. 2007. "For the Love of Furniture." *Cultural Survival Quarterly* 30(4):26–31.

Itoh, Shinji. 1980. "Physiology of Circumpolar People." In *The Human Biology of Circumpolar Populations,* ed. F. A. Milan. Cambridge: Cambridge University Press.

Iwu, Maurice. 1996. "Resource Utilization and Conservation of Biodiversity in Africa." In *Medicinal Resources of the Tropical Forest: Biodiversity and Its Importance to Human Health,* ed. M. Balick et al., 233–50 New York: Columbia University Press.

Jablow, Joseph. 1950. *The Cheyenne in Plains Indian Trade Relations 1795–1840.* Monographs of the American Ethnological Society No. 19. Seattle: University of Washington Press.

Jackson, Donald, ed. 1964. *Black Hawk: An Autobiography.* Urbana: University of Illinois Press.

Jackson, Robert, and Edward Castillo. 1995. *Indians, Franciscans, and Spanish Colonization: Impact of the Mission System on California Indians.* Albuquerque: University of New Mexico Press.

Jacobs, Andrew. 2008. "One-Child Policy Lifted for Parents of China Quake Victims." *New York Times,* May 27, A8.

Jefferson, Thomas. 1803. Letter to Meriwether Lewis. http://www.mt.net/!rojomo/landc.htm.

Johnson, Allen. 1978. "In Search of the Affluent Society." *Human Nature,* September, 50–59.

Johnson, Gregory. 1973. *Local Exchange and Early State Development in Southwestern Iran.* Anthropological Papers No. 51. Ann Arbor: University of Michigan, Museum of Anthropology.

Johnston, Tim. 2008. "Australia to Apologize to Aborigines for Past Mistreatment." *New York Times,* January 31.

Jolly, Alison. 1985. *The Evolution of Primate Behavior,* 2nd ed. New York: Macmillan.

Jones, Barbara. 1998. "Infighting in San Francisco: Anthropology in Family Court, Or: A Study in Cultural Misunderstanding." *High Plains Applied Anthropologist* 18(1):37–41.

Kahlenberg, Mary, and Anthony Berlant. 1972. *The Navajo Blanket.* New York: Praeger/Los Angeles County Museum of Art.

Kaisiepo, Viktor. 2004. "We've Gained a Lot." *Cultural Survival Quarterly* 28(3):19–20.

Katz, Richard. 1982. *Boiling Energy: Community Healing among the Kalahari !Kung.* Cambridge, MA: Harvard University Press.

Kehoe, Alice. 1989. *The Ghost Dance: Ethnohistory and Revitalization.* New York: Holt, Rinehart & Winston.

Kellman, Shelly. 1982. "The Yanomamis: Their Battle for Survival." *Journal of International Affairs* 36:15–42.

Kelly, Raymond. 1976. "Witchcraft and Sexual Relations: An Exploration in the Social and Semantic Implications of the Structure of Belief." In *Man and Woman in the New Guinea Highlands,* ed. P. Brown and G. Buchdinder, 36–53. Special Publication No. 8. Washington, DC: American Anthropological Association.

Kendall, Laurel. 1984. "Korean Shamanism: Women's Rites and a Chinese Comparison." In *Religion and the Family in East Asia,* ed. G. DeVos and T. Sofue, 185–200. Berkeley: University of California Press.

Kershaw, Sarah, and Monica Davey. 2004. "Plagued by Drugs, Tribes Revive Ancient Penalty." *New York Times.* January 18, A1, 25.

Killhefer, Robert. 1995. "Reburying the Past." *Omni* 17:30–36.

Kirsch, Stuart. 2006. *Reverse Anthropology: Indigenous Analysis of Social and Environmental Relations in New Guinea.* Stanford: Stanford University Press.

Kirsch, Stuart. 2007. "Indigenous Movements and the Risks of Counterglobalization: Tracking the Campaign Against Papua New Guinea's Ok Tedi Mine." *American Ethnologist* 34(2):303–21.

Klein, Alan. 1980. "Plains Economic Analysis: The Marxist Complement." In *Anthropology on the Great Plains,* ed. W. R. Wood and M. Liberty, 129–40. Lincoln: University of Nebraska Press.

Klein, Alan. 1983. "The Political-Economy of Gender: A 19th-Century Plains Indian Case Study." In *Hidden Half: Studies of Plains Indian Women,* ed. P. Alvers and B. Medicine, 143–73. Lanham, MD: University Press of America.

Kluckhohn, Clyde, and Dorothea Leighton. 1946. *The Navaho.* Cambridge, MA: Harvard University Press.

Knight, R. 2002. Ethnomusicology. http://www.oberlin.edu/faculty/rknight/ (accessed November 18, 2004).

Kolenc, Vic. 2008. "Maquilas Feel Pinch: 20,000 Jobs Lost in Juarez." *El Paso Times,* November 18.

Koller, John. 1982. *The Indian Way.* New York: Macmillan.

Kopytoff, Igor. 1961. "The Suku of Southwestern Congo." In *Peoples of Africa,* ed. J. Gibbs, 441–78. New York: Holt, Rinehart & Winston.

Koso-Thomas, Olayinka. 1992. *The Circumcision of Women: A Strategy for Eradication.* London: Zed Books.

Kottak, Conrad. 1999. *Assault on Paradise: Social Change in a Brazilian Village,* 3rd ed. New York: McGraw-Hill.

Krauss, Michael. 1992. "The World's Languages in Crisis." *Language* 68:4–10.

Kroeber, Alfred, and Clyde Kluckhohn. 1952. *Culture: A Critical Review of Concepts and Definitions.* New York: Random House.

Kruks, Sonia, and Ben Wisner. 1989. "Ambiguous Transformations: Women, Politics and Production in Mozambique." In *Promissory Notes: Women in the Transition to Socialism,* ed. Sonia Kruks, Rayna Rapp, and Marilyn Young, 148–71. New York: Monthly Review Press.

Kumar, Radha. 1995. "From Chipko to Sati: The Contemporary Indian Women's Movement." In *The Challenge of Local Feminisms: Women's Movement in Global Perspective,* ed. A. Basu. Boulder, CO: Westview.

Labov, William. 1966. *The Social Stratification of English in New York City.* Washington, DC: Center for Applied Linguistics.

Labov, William. 1972a. *Language in the Inner City.* Philadelphia: University of Pennsylvania Press.

Labov, William. 1972b. *Sociolinguistic Patterns.* Philadelphia: University of Pennsylvania Press.

Labov, William. 1982. "Objectivity and Commitment in Linguistic Science: The Case of the Black English Trial in Ann Arbor." *Language in Society* 11:165–201.

Labov, William. 1997. "Some Further Steps in Narrative Analysis." *Journal of Narrative and Life History* 7:395–415.

Labov, William. 2004. "Can Reading Failure Be Reversed? A Linguistic Approach to the Question." In *Literacy among African American Youth,* ed. V. Gadsden and D. Wagner. Cresskill, NJ: Hampton Press.

Lacey, Mark. 2004. "Genital Cutting Shows Signs of Losing Favor in Africa." *New York Times,* June 8.

Lafitau, Joseph. 1974/1724. *Customs of the American Indians.* Toronto: Champlain Society.

Lako, George. 1988. "The Impact of Jonglei Scheme on the Economy of the Dinka." In *Tribal Peoples and Development Issues,* ed. J. Bodley, 137–50. Mountain View, CA: Mayfield.

Lakoff, George, and Mark Johnson. 1980. *Metaphors We Live By.* Chicago: University of Chicago Press.

Lamphere, Louise. 2001. "The Domestic Sphere of Women and the Public World of Men: The Strengths and Limitations of an Anthropological Dichotomy." In *Gender in Cross-Cultural Perspective,* 3rd ed., ed. C. Brettell and C. Sargent, 100–10. Upper Saddle River, NJ: Prentice Hall.

Lancaster, Jane. 1983. "Evolutionary Perspectives on Sex Differences in the Higher Primates." In *Gender and the Life Course,* ed. Alice Rossi. Hawthorne, New York: Aldine.

Lancaster, Jane, and Philip Whitten. 1993. "Sharing in Human Evolution." In *Anthropology: Contemporary Perspectives,* 7th ed., ed. P. Whitten and D. Hunter, 70–74. New York: HarperCollins.

Leacock, Eleanor. 1954. "The Montagnais 'Hunting Territory' and the Fur Trade," vol. 56, no. 5, pt. 2, Memoir No. 78.

Washington, DC: American Anthropological Association.

Leacock, Eleanor. 1981. *Myths of Male Dominance.* New York: Monthly Review Press.

LeClercq, Chretien. 1968/1691. *New Relation of Gaspesia.* New York: Greenwood.

Lee, Richard. 1982. "Politics, Sexual and Nonsexual, in an Egalitarian Society." In *Politics and History in Band Societies,* ed. E. Leacock and R. Lee, 37–60. New York: Cambridge University Press.

Lee, Richard. 2003. *The Dobe Ju/'hoansi,* 3rd ed. New York: Harcourt Brace.

Leibowitz, Lila. 1983. "Origins of the Sexual Division of Labor." In *Women's Nature: Rationalizations of Inequality,* ed. M. Lowe and R. Hubbard, 123–47. Elmsford, NY: Pergamon.

Lemarchand, Rene. 1994. "The Apocalypse in Rwanda." *Cultural Survival Quarterly* 18 (2/3):29–33.

Levine, Nancy E. 1988. *The Dynamics of Polyandry. Kinship, Domesticity, and Population on the Tibetan Border.* Chicago: University of Chicago Press.

Lévi-Strauss, C. 1949. *Elementary Structures of Kinship.* Paris: Preses Universitaires de France.

Lewis, I. M. 1989. *Ecstatic Religion: A Study of Shamanism and Spirit Possession,* 2nd ed. London: Routledge.

Lindenbaum, Shirley. 1979. *Kuru Sorcery: Disease and Danger in the New Guinea Highlands.* Palo Alto, CA: Mayfield.

Lindenfeld, Jacqueline. 1969. "The Social Conditioning of Syntactic Variation in French." *American Anthropologist* 71:890–98.

Lindfors, Bernth, and Oyekan Owomoyela. 1973. "Yoruba Proverbs: Translation and Annotation." Papers in International Studies: Africa Series No. 17. Athens: Ohio University Center for International Studies.

Linton, Sally. 1971. "Women the gatherer: male bias in anthropology." In *Women in Perspective —A Guide for Cross-Cultural Studies,* ed. S. E. Jacobs, 9–21. Urbana: University of Illinois Press.

Lockwood, Victoria. 1997. "The Impact of Development on Women: The Interplay of Material Conditions and Gender Ideology." In *Gender in Cross-Cultural Perspective,* 2nd ed., ed. C. Brettell and C. Sargent, 504–17. Upper Saddle River, NJ: Prentice Hall.

Loeb, Edwin. 1926. "Pomo Folkways." In *American Archeology and Ethnology,* Vol. 19, No. 2, 149–405. Berkeley: University of California.

Lucy, John. 1996. "The Scope of Linguistic Relativity: An Analysis and Review of Empirical Research." In *Rethinking Linguistic Relativity,* ed. John Gumperz and Stephen Levinson, 37–70. New York: Cambridge University Press.

Lutz, Ellen. 2006. "Indigenous Peoples and Water Rights." *Cultural Survival Quarterly* 29(4):11–13.

MacArthur, R. H., and E. R. Pianka. 1966. "On the Optimal Use of a Patchy Environment." *American Naturalist* 100: 603–09.

Mack, Burton. 1988. *A Myth of Innocence: Mark and Christian Origins.* Philadelphia: Fortress Press.

MacKay, Fergus, and Emily Caruso. 2004. "Indigenous Lands or National Parks." *Cultural Survival Quarterly* 28 (1):14–16.

Mackey, W. C. 1985. *Fathering Behaviors: The Dynamics of the Man-Child Bond.* New York: Plenum.

Makino, Catherine. 2008. "Indigenous People: Japan Officially Recognises Ainu." www.ipsnews.net.

Malinowski, Bronislaw. 1922. *Argonauts of the Western Pacific.* London: Routledge & Kegan Paul.

Malinowski, Bronislaw. 1929. *The Sexual Life of Savages in North-Western Melanesia.* New York: Halcyon House.

Malinowski, Bronislaw. 1935. *Coral Gardens and Their Magic.* New York: American Book Company.

Malkin, Elisabeth. 2008. "Ways of Ancient Mexico Reviving Ancient Lands." *New York Times,* May 13, A7.

Mandela, Nelson, ed. 1965. *No Easy Walk to Freedom.* London: Heinemann.

Mann, Barbara, and Jerry Fields. 1997. "A Sign in the Sky: Dating the League of the Haudenosaunee." *American Indian Culture and Research Journal* 21:105–64.

Marable, Manning. 1995. "Beyond Racial Identity Politics: Towards a Liberation Theory for Multicultural Democracy." In *Race, Class, and Gender,* 2nd ed., ed. M. Andersen and P. Collins, 363–66. Belmont, CA: Wadsworth.

Marcus, George. 1992. *Lives in Trust: The Fortunes of Dynastic Families in Late Twentieth Century America.* Boulder, CO: Westview.

Markus, Hazel R., and Shinobu Kitayama. 1991. "Culture and the Self: Implications for Cognition, Emotion, and Motivation." *Psychological Review* 98 (2):224–53.

Marwick, M. G. 1967. "The Sociology of Sorcery in a Central African Tribe." In *Magic, Witchcraft, and Curing,* ed. J. Middleton, 101–26. New York: Natural History Press.

Marx, Karl. 1967. Capital: A Critique of Political Economy. New York: Modern Library.

Mataira, Peter. 2000. "Mana and Tapu: Sacred Knowledge, Sacred Boundaries." In *Indigenous Religions,* ed. G. Harvey, 99–112. New York: Cassell.

Matt, Susan. 2002. "Children's Envy and the Emergence of the Modern Consumer Ethic, 1890–1930." *Journal of Social History* 36(2):283–302.

Matthaei, Julie. 1982. *An Economic History of Women in America.* New York: Schocken.

Maybury-Lewis, David. 1997. *Indigenous Peoples, Ethnic Groups, and the State.* Boston: Allyn & Bacon.

McAllester, David. 1954. *Enemy Way Music.* Cambridge, MA: Peabody Museum.

McBrearty, Sally, and Marc Moniz. 1991. "Prostitutes or Providers? Hunting, Tool Use, and Sex Roles in Early Homo." In *The Archaeology of Gender,* ed. Dale Walde and Noreen Willows, 71–82. Calgary: The

University of Calgary, Archaeological Association.

McDermott, LeRoy. 1996. "Self-Representation in Female Figurines." *Current Anthropology* 37:227–75.

McElroy, Ann, and Patricia Townsend. 1989. *Medical Anthropology in Ecological Perspective.* Boulder, CO: Westview.

McEvilley, Thomas. 1992. *Art and Otherness: Crisis in Cultural Identity.* Kingston, NY: McPherson.

McWhorter, John. 1997. "Wasting Energy on an Illusion." *Black Scholar* 27 (1):9–14.

Meggers, Betty. 1971. *Amazonia: Man and Culture in a Counterfeit Paradise.* New York: Free Press.

Meier, John. 1991. *A Marginal Jew: Rethinking the Historical Jesus.* New York: Doubleday.

Mencher, Joan. 1965. "The Nayars of South Malabar." In *Comparative Family Systems,* ed. M. E. Nimkoff, 162–91. Boston: Houghton Mifflin.

Merivale, Herman. 1988/1861. "Policy of Colonial Government Towards Native Tribes, as Regards Their Protection and Civilization." In *Tribal Peoples and Development Issues,* ed. J. Bodley, 95–105. Mountain View, CA: Mayfield.

Merrill, William, Edmund Ladd, and T. J. Ferguson. 1993. "The Return of the Ahayu:da: Lessons for Repatriation from Zuni Pueblo and the Smithsonian Institution." *Current Anthropology* 34 (5):523–66.

Merry, Sally. 1991. "Law and Colonialism." *Law and Society Review* 2:889–918.

Meyer, Roy. 1993. *History of the Santee Sioux: United States Indian Policy on Trial,* rev. ed. Lincoln: University of Nebraska Press.

Michelson, Truman. 1920. *Autobiography of a Fox Woman.* Fortieth Annual Report of the Bureau of American Ethnology for the years 1918–1919, 291–349. Washington, DC.

Miller, Peggy, and Barbara Moore. 1989. "Narrative Conjunctions of Caregiver and Child: A Comparative Perspective on Socialization Through Stories." *Ethos* 17(4):428–49.

Mills, C. Wright. 1956. *The Power Elite.* New York: Oxford University Press.

Mina, Hanna. 1993. *Fragments of Memory: A Story of a Syrian Family.* Austin: University of Texas Press, Center for Middle Eastern Studies.

Mintz, Sydney. 1996. *Tasting Food; Tasting Freedom: Excursions into Eating, Culture, and the Past.* Boston: Beacon Press.

Molony, Carol. 1977. "Recent Relexification Processes in Philippine Creole Spanish." In *Sociocultural Dimensions of Language Change,* ed. B. Blount and M. Sanches, 131–59. New York: Academic Press.

Mooncy, James. 1965. *The Ghost Dance Religion and the Sioux Outbreak of 1890.* Chicago: University of Chicago Press.

Moore, Henrietta. 1988. *Feminism and Anthropology.* Minneapolis: University of Minnesota Press.

Morelli, Gilda A., Barbara Rogoff, David Oppenheim, and Denise Goldsmith. 1992. "Cultural Variation in Infants' Sleeping

Arrangements: Questions of Independence." *Developmental Psychology* 38:604–613.

Morgan, Lewis Henry. 1877. *Ancient Society.* Cambridge, MA: Harvard University Press.

Morioka, Kiyomi. 1984. "Ancestor Worship in Contemporary Japan: Continuity and Change." In *Religion and the Family in East Asia,* ed. G. DeVos and T. Sofue, 201–16. Berkeley: University of California Press.

Morris, Craig, and Donald Thompson. 1985. *Huanuco Pampa: An Inca City and Its Hinterland.* London: Thames & Hudson.

Munroe R. M., and R. H. Munroe. 1975. "Levels of Obedience among U.S. and East African Children on an Experimental Task." *Journal of Cross-Cultural Psychology* 6:498–503.

Murphy, Jane. 1981. "Abnormal Behavior in Traditional Societies: Labels, Explanations and Social Reactions." *Medical Anthropology,* pp. 809–26.

Murray, Sir Hubert. 1988/1933. "The Scientific Aspect of the Pacification of Papua." In *Tribal Peoples and Development Issues,* ed. J. Bodley, 42–52. Mountain View, CA: Mayfield.

Namahoe, Luwahiwa, and Kaimana Barcarse. 2007. "I ka'olelo no ke ola, I ka yolelo no ka make: In Language There Is Life, in Language There Is Death." *Cultural Survival Quarterly* 31(2):44–47.

Nanda, Serena. 1990. *Neither Man Nor Woman: The Hijras of India.* Belmont, CA: Wadsworth.

National Indian Gaming Association. 2008. "Indian Gaming Facts." www.indiangaming.org/liba\rary/indian-gaming-facts.

Navajo Nation. 1972. *The Navajo Ten Year Plan.* Windowrock, AZ: The Navajo Tribe.

Navarro, Mireya. 2008. "Who Are We? New Dialogue on Mixed Race." *New York Times,* March 31, A1, A15.

Neihardt, John. 1961. *Black Elk Speaks: Being a Life Story of a Holy Man of the Oglala Sioux.* Lincoln: University of Nebraska Press.

Nettle, Daniel, and Suzanne Romaine. 2000. *Vanishing Voices: The Extinction of the World's Languages.* New York: Oxford University Press.

New York Times. 2008. "Beijing to Raise Fines on Elites Who Violate the One-Child Rule." January, 22.

New York Times. 2008. "Clashes Over Caste Lines Kill 2 Dozen in Northwest India." May 25, A8.

Newing, Helen, and Lissie Wahl. 2004. "Benefiting Local Populations? Communal Reserves in Peru." *Cultural Survival Quarterly* 28 (1):38–42.

Newman, Katherine. 1989. *Falling from Grace: Experience of Downward Mobility in the American Middle Class.* New York: Random House.

Nietschmann, Bernard. 1988. "Third World Colonial Expansion: Indonesia, Disguised Invasion of Indigenous Nations." In *Tribal Peoples and Development Issues,* ed. J. Bodley, 191–208. Mountain View, CA: Mayfield.

Njoku, John Eberegbulam. 1990. *The Igbos of Nigeria: Ancient Rites, Changes and Survival.* Lewiston: The Edwin Mellen Press. African Studies, volume 14.

Nongovernmental Organizations Research Guide 2004. http://docs.lib.duke.edu/igo/guides/ngo/, October 10 (accessed November 2, 2004).

Obeng, Samuel Gyasi. 1996. "The Proverb as a Mitigating and Politeness Strategy in Akan Discourse." *Anthropological Linguistics* 38:521–549.

O'Brien, Jay. 1986. "Toward a Reconstitution Ethnicity: Capitalist Expansion and Cultural Dynamics in Sudan." *American Anthropologist* 88 (4):898–907.

Ochs, Elinor, and Caroline Taylor. 1995. "The 'Father Knows Best' Dynamic in Dinnertime Narratives." In *Linguistic Anthropology: A Reader,* ed. A. Duranti, 431–49. Malden, MA: Blackwell.

Ong, Aihwa. 1983. "Global Industries and Malay Peasants in Peninsula Asia." In *Women, Men, and the International Division of Labor,* ed. J. Nash and M. Fernandez-Kelly, 426–39. Albany: State University of New York Press.

Orme, Nicholas. 2002. *Medieval Children.* New Haven: Yale University Press.

Osterhammel, Jurgen. 1997. *Colonialism: A Theoretical Overview.* Princeton, NJ: Markus Wiener.

Ottenberg, Phoebe. 1965. "The Afikpo Ibo of Eastern Nigeria." In *Peoples of Africa,* ed. J. Gibbs, 3–39. New York: Holt, Rinehart & Winston.

Ottenberg, Simon, and Phoebe Ottenberg. 1962. "Afikpo Market 1900–1960." In *Markets in Africa,* ed. P. Bohannan and G. Dalton, 117–69. Evanston, IL: Northwestern University Press.

Ottley, Bruce, and Jean Zorn. 1983. "Criminal Law in Papua New Guinea: Code, Custom and the Courts in Conflict." In *American Journal of Comparative Law* 31:251–300.

Parr, Lisa, Bridget Walter, and Sarah Vick. 2007. "New Developments in Understanding Emotional Facial Signals in Chimpanzees." *Current Directions in Psychological Science* 16(3):117–22.

Peluso, Nancy. 1992. *Rich Forests, Poor People: Resource Control and Resistance in Java.* Berkeley: University of California Press.

Peregrine, Peter. 2003. *World Prehistory: Two Million Years of Human Life.* Upper Saddle River, NJ: Prentice Hall.

Perry, Richard. 1996. *From Time Immemorial: Indigenous Peoples and State Systems.*" Austin: University of Texas Press.

Philips, Susan. 1978. "Participant Structures and Communicative Competence: Warm Springs Children in Community and Classroom." In *A Pluralistic Nation,* ed. M. Lourie and N. Conklin, 390–407. Rowley, MA: Newbury House.

Platt, John, Heidi Weber, and Ho Minn Lian. 1984. *The New Englishes.* London: Routledge & Kegan Paul.

Plattner, Stuart. 1989. Economic Anthropology. Stanford: Stanford University Press.

Price, Sally. 1984. *Co-wives and Calabashes.* Ann Arbor: University of Michigan Press.

Price, Sally. 1989. *Primitive Art in Civilized Places.* Chicago: University of Chicago Press.

Pyles, Thomas, and John Algeo. 1982. *The Origins and Development of the English Language,* 3rd ed. New York: Harcourt Brace Jovanovich.

Rabinow, Paul. 1977. *Reflections on Fieldwork in Morocco.* Berkeley: University of California Press.

Radiobras. 2003. http://forests.org/articles/reader.asp?linkid=21266 (accessed March 18).

Raheja, Gloria Goodwin, and Ann Grodzins Gold. 1994. *Listen to the Heron's Words: Reimagining Gender and Kinship in North India.* Berkeley: University of California Press.

Ramos, Alcida. 1997. "The Indigenous Movement in Brazil: A Quarter Century of Ups and Downs." *Cultural Survival Quarterly* 21 (2).

Rappaport, Roy. 1969. "Ritual Regulation of Environmental Relations among a New Guinea People." In *Environment and Cultural Behavior,* ed. A. Vayda, 181–201. Garden City, NY: Natural History Press.

Rappaport, Roy. 2000. *Pigs for the Ancestors: Ritual in the Ecology of a New Guinea People,* 2nd ed. New Haven, CT: Yale University Press.

Rasmussen, Knud. 1929. *Intellectual Culture of the Iglulik Eskimo.* Vol. 7, No. 1, of the Report of the Fifth Thule Expedition, 1921–1924. Copenhagen: Clydendalske Boghandel.

Rathje W., and Murphy C. 1992. "Five Major Myths about Garbage and Why They're Wrong." *Smithsonian,* July.

Reid, Walter, Sarah Laird, Carrie Meyer, and Rodrigo Gámez. 1996. "Biodiversity Prospecting." In *Medicinal Resources of the Tropical Forest: Biodiversity and Its Importance to Human Health,* ed. M. Balick, E. Elisabetsky, and S. A. Laird, 142–73. New York: Columbia University Press.

Rensberger, Boyce. 2001. "Racial Odyssey." In *Anthropology: Contemporary Perspectives,* 8th ed., ed. P. Whitten, 81–89. Boston: Allyn & Bacon.

Ribeiro, Darcy. 1971. *The Americas and Civilization.* New York: Dutton.

Richeport, Madeleine. 1984. *Macumba Trance and Spirit Healing.* Richeport Films.

Richmond, John. 1986. "The Language of Black Children and the Language Debate in the Schools." In *Language and the Black Experience,* ed. D. Sutcliffe and A. Wong, 123–35. Oxford: Blackwell.

Rickford, John. 1997. "Unequal Partnership: Sociolinguistics and the African American Speech Community." *Language in Society* 26:161–198.

Ries, Paula, and Ann Stone, eds. 1992. *The American Woman 1992–1993: A Status Report.* New York: Norton.

Robarchek, Clayton. 1997. "A Community of Interest: Semai Conflict Resolution." *Cultural Variation in Conflict Resolution: Alternatives to Violence,* ed. D. Fry and K. Bjorkqvist, 52–58. Mahwah, NJ: Lawrence Erlbaum.

Robbins, Jim. 2004. "Ice Age Floodwaters Leave a Walkable Trail across the Northwest." *New York Times,* August 24.

Roberts, Sam. 2008. "Most Children Still Live in Two-Parent Homes, Census Bureau Reports." *New York Times,* February 21.

Rodman, Margaret. 1993. "Keeping Options Open: Copra and Fish in Rural Vanuatu." In *Contemporary Pacific Societies: Studies in Development and Change,* ed. V. Lockwood, T. G. Harding, and B. J. Wallace, 171–84 Upper Saddle River, NJ: Prentice Hall.

Rohrlich-Leavitt, Ruby, Barbara Sykes, and Elizabeth Weatherford. 1975. "Aboriginal Woman: Male and Female Anthropological Perspectives." In *Toward an Anthropology of Women,* ed. R. Reiter, 110–26. New York: Monthly Review Press.

Rohter, Larry. 2003. "Bolivia's Poor Proclaim Abiding Distrust of Globalization." *New York Times,* October 17.

Romero, Simon. 2008. "Armed with a Pen, and Ready to Save the Incas' Mother Tongue." *New York Times,* June 7, A6.

Rosaldo, Michelle. 1974. "Women, Culture and Society: A Theoretical Overview." In *Women, Culture and Society,* ed. M. Rosaldo and L. Lamphere, 17–42. Stanford, CA: Stanford University Press.

Rowe, John. 1950. "The Inca Culture at the Time of the Spanish Conquest." In *Handbook of South American Indians,* ed. J. Steward. Smithsonian Institution, Bureau of American Ethnology, Bulletin 143, Vol. 2, 183–330. Washington, DC.

Royce, Anya. 1977. *The Anthropology of Dance.* Bloomington: Indiana University Press.

Rubel, Arthur. 1977. "The Epidemiology of a Folk Illness: Susto in Hispanic America." In *Culture, Disease, and Healing: Studies in Medical Anthropology,* ed. D. Landy, 119–28. New York: Macmillan.

Rumbaugh, Duane, and E. Sue Savage-Rumbaugh. 1994. "Language Research with Animals." In *Animal Learning and Cognition,* ed. N. J. McIntosh, 307–33. New York: Academic Press.

Russian Federation State Statistics Service. 2006. Employment by Sex and Occupation in 2006. Table 6.4. http://www.gks.ru/free_doc/2007.

Ryan, K. 2000. "Edible Wild Plants as Digestive Aids: Ethnoarchaeology in Maasailand. Science and Archaeology." *Expedition* 42 (3):7–8.

Sahagun, Bernardino de. 1975/1938. *Florentine Codex: General History of the Things of New Spain.* Santa Fe, NM.

Sahlins, Marshall. 1961. "The Segmentary Lineage: An Organization of Predatory Expansion." *American Anthropologist* 63: 332–345.

Sakajiri, N. 2004. "Japan Cited in Human Trafficking." *Asahi Shimbun,* June 16.

Sanday, Peggy. 1981. *Female Power and Male Dominance.* New York: Cambridge University Press.

Sanders, E. P. 1985. *Jesus and Judaism.* Philadelphia: Fortress Press.

Sanderson, Lilian Passmore, and Neville Sanderson. 1981. *Education, Religion & Politics in Southern Sudan 1899–1964.* London: Ithaca Press.

San Francisco Chronicle. 1996. "EU to Help Pay for Cow Slaughter, Nations Back Plan to Eradicate Disease, Restore Trust." April 3, A5.

Sano, Mariko, and Toshiyuki Sano. 2001. *Life in Riverfront: A Middle Western Town Seen Through Japanese Eyes.* Fort Worth, TX: Harcourt Brace.

Sapir, Edward. 1949. "Language and Environment." In *Selected Writings of Edward Sapir,* ed. E. Mandelbaum, 89–103. Berkeley: University of California Press.

Sapiro, Virginia. 1986. *Women in American Society.* Palo Alto, CA: Mayfield.

Sasson, Jack. 1995. *Civilizations of the Ancient Near East, I-IV.* New York: Scribner's.

Sauer, Carl. 1971. *Sixteenth Century North America: The Land and the People as Seen by the Europeans.* Berkeley: University of California Press.

Saussure, Ferdinand de. 1916. *A Course in General Linguistics.* Paris: Editions Payot.

Schemo, Diana. 1999. "The Last Tribal Battle." *New York Times,* October 31, 70–77.

Scheper-Hughes, Nancy. 1989. "The Human Strategy; Death without Weeping." *Natural History Magazine,* October, 8–16.

Scheper-Hughes, Nancy. 1992. *Death without Weeping: The Violence of Everyday Life in Brazil.* Berkeley: University of California Press.

Scheper-Hughes, Nancy. 2004. *Parts Unknown: Undercover Ethnography of the Organs-Trafficking Underworld.* Thousand Oaks, CA: Sage. http://eth.sagepub.com/cgi/reprint/5/1/29.pdf (accessed November 2, 2004).

Schieffelin, Bambi. 1990. *The Give and Take of Everyday Life: Language Socialization of Kaluli children.* New York: Cambridge University Press.

Schiller, Nina Glick, Linda Basch, and Cristina Blanc-Szanton, ed. 1992. "Transnationalism: A New Analytic Framework for Understanding Migration." In *Towards a Transnational Perspective on Migration: Race, Class, Ethnicity, and Nationalism Reconsidered.* Annals of the New York Academy of Sciences, Vol. 645, pp. 1–24. New York: New York Academy of Sciences.

Schmink, Marianne. 1988. "Big Business in the Amazon." In *People of the Tropical Rain Forest,* ed. Julie Denslow and Christine Padoch, 163–74. Berkeley: University of California Press.

Schmink, Marianne, and Charles Wood. 1992. *Contested Frontiers in Amazonia.* New York: Columbia University Press.

Schneider, David. 1961. "The Distinctive Features of Matrilineal Descent Groups." In *Matrilineal Kinship,* ed. D. Schneider and K. Gough, 1–32. Berkeley: University of California Press.

Schneller, Raphael. 1988. "The Israeli Experience of Cross-Cultural Misunderstanding: Insights and Lessons." In *Cross-Cultural Perspectives in Non-Verbal Communication,* ed. F. Poyatos, 153–71. Lewiston, NY: C. J. Hogrefe.

Schusky, Ernest. 1994. "The Roots of Factionalism Among the Lower Brule Sioux." In *North American Indian Anthropology: Essays on Society and Culture,* ed. R. De Mallie and A. Ortiz, 258–77. Norman: University of Oklahoma Press.

Seattle Times. 1996. "British Agree to Destroy Beef in Mad-Cow Scare, Europeans to Help Pay for Industry Losses." April 3, A3.

Segall, Marshall. 1979. *Cross-Cultural Psychology: Human Behavior in Global Perspective.* Monterey, CA: Brooks/Cole.

Service, Elman. 1962. *Primitive Social Organization: An Evolutionary Perspective.* New York: Random House.

Seyfarth, Robert, and Dorothy Cheney. 2007. "Primate Social Knowledge and the Origins of Language." *Mind and Society* 7(1):129–42.

Shannon, Jonathan. 2003. "Sultans of Spin: Syrian Sacred Music on the World Stage." *American Anthropologist* 105:266–277.

Sharff, Jagna. 1998. *King Kong on 4th Street: Family and the Violence of Poverty on the Lower East Side.* Boulder, CO: Westview.

Shostak, Marjorie. 1983. *Nisa: The Life and Words of a !Kung Woman.* New York: Vintage.

Silverblatt, Irene. 1978. "Andean Women in the Inca Empire." *Feminist Studies* 4:7–61.

Silverblatt, Irene. 1980. "Andean Women under Spanish Rule." In *Women and Colonization,* ed. M. Etienne and E. Leacock, 149–185. New York: Praeger.

Silverblatt, Irene. 1987. *Moon, Sun, and Witches: Gender Ideologies and Class in Inca and Colonial Peru.* Princeton, NJ: Princeton University Press.

Siskind, Janet. 1973. "Tropical Forest Hunters and the Economy of Sex." In *Peoples and Cultures of Native South America,* ed. D. Gross, 226–40. New York: Doubleday/Natural History Press.

Smith, S. Percy. 1913. "The Lore of the Whare-Wananga." New Plymouth, N.Z., http://www.sacredtexts.com/pac/lww/index.

Smitherman, Geneva, and Sylvia Cunningham. 1997. "Moving Beyond Resistance: Ebonics and African American Youth." *Journal of Black Psychology* 28:227–232.

Smitherman, Geneva. 2003. "Toward a National Public Policy on Language." In *The Skin that We Speak: Thoughts on Language and Culture in the Classroom,* ed. Lisa Delpit and Joanne Dowdy, 164–78. Oakland: CES National.

Smuts, Barbara. 1985. *Sex and Friendship in Baboons.* Hawthorne, New York: Aldine.

Smuts, Barbara. 2001. "What are Friends For?" In *Anthropology: Contemporary Perspectives,* ed. P. Whitten, 49–55. Needham Heights, Massachusetts: Allyn & Bacon.

Snow, Marguerite Ann, John Hyland, Lia Kambi-Stein, and Janet Harclerode Yu. 1996. "U.S. Language Minority Students: Voices from the Junior High Classroom." In *Voices from the Language Classroom: Qualitative Research in Second Language Education,* ed. Kathleen Bailey and David Nunan, 304–17. New York: Cambridge University Press.

Sofue, Takao. 1984. "Family and Interpersonal Relationships in Early Japan." In *Religion and the Family in East Asia*, ed. G. DeVos and T. Sofue, 201–16. Berkeley: University of California Press.

Soustelle, Jacques. 1961. *Daily Life of the Aztecs: On the Eve of the Spanish Conquest*. Stanford, CA: Stanford University Press.

Southwold, Martin. 1965. "The Ganda of Uganda." In *Peoples of Africa*, ed. J. Gibbs, 81–118. New York: Holt, Rinehart & Winston.

Soyinka, Wole. 1981. *Ake, the Years of Childhood*. New York: Vintage.

Spencer, Herbert. 1877. *Principles of Sociology*. Chicago: University of Chicago Press.

Spencer, Paul. 1988. *The Maasai of Matapato: A Study of Rituals of Rebellion*. Bloomington: Indiana University Press.

Spencer, Paul. 1993. "Becoming Maasai, Being In Time." In *Being Maasai: Ethnicity and Identity in East Africa*, ed. Thomas Spear and Richard Waller, 140–56. Athens: Ohio University Press.

Spencer, Robert. 1984. "North Alaska Coast Eskimo." In *Arctic*, Vol. 5, pp. 320–337. *Handbook of North American Indians*. Washington, DC: Smithsonian Institution Press.

Spradley, James. 1972. *Guests Never Leave Hungry: The Autobiography of James Sewid, a Kwakiutl Indian*. Montreal: McGill Queens University Press.

Stack, Carol. 1975. *All My Kin: Strategies for Survival in a Black Community*. New York: Harper Torchbooks.

Statistical Abstracts. 2002. Washington, DC.

Stearns, Peter. 2003. *Anxious Parents: A History of Modern Childrearing in America*. New York: New York's University Press.

Stephens, D. W., and J. R. Krebs. 1986. *Foraging Theory*. Princeton, NJ: Princeton University Press.

Stiles, Kristine, and Peter Selz. 1996. *Theories and Documents of Contemporary Art: A Sourcebook of Artists' Writings*. Berkeley: University of California Press.

Stone, Linda. 2006. *Kinship and Gender*, 3rd ed. Boulder Colorado: Westview Press.

Strathern, Andrew. 1992. "Let the Bow Go Down." In *War in the Tribal Zone: Expanding States and Indigenous Warfare*, ed. R. Ferguson and N. Whitehead, 229–50. Santa Fe, NM: School of American Research Press.

Survival International. 2008. "Guarani Demand Justice in 'Great Assembly.'" November 4.

Taxin, Amy. 2003. "Battle Rages with Ecuador Indians Over Jungle Oil." Reuters, Ltd. December 19.

Tedlock, Dennis. 1972. *Finding the Center: Narrative Poetry of the Zuñi Indians*. Dennis Tedlock, trans.; from performances in the Zuñi by Andrew Peynetsa and Walter Sanchez. Lincoln: University of Nebraska Press.

Tedlock, Dennis. 1983. *The Spoken Word and the Work of Interpretation*. Philadelphia: University of Pennsylvania Press.

Thompson, Robert. 1974. *African Art in Motion*. Berkeley: University of California Press.

Thompson, Robert. 1983. *Flash of the Spirit: African and Afro-American Art and Philosophy*. New York: Random House.

Thornton, Arland, and Linda Young-DeMarco. 2001. "Four Decades of Trends in Attitudes Toward Family Issues in the United States: The 1960s Through the 1990s." *Journal of Marriage and Family* 63:1009–37.

Thornton, Russell. 1987. *American Indian Holocaust and Survival: A Population History Since 1492*. Norman: University of Oklahoma Press.

Thwaites, R. G., ed. 1906. *Jesuit Relations and Allied Documents, 1610–1791*. 73 vols. Cleveland, OH: Burrows Brothers.

Titiev, Mischa. 1992. *Old Oraibi: A Study of the Hopi Indians of Third Mesa*. Albuquerque: University of New Mexico Press.

Trask, Haunani-Kay. 2001. "Lovely Hula Hands: Corporate Tourism and the Prostitution of Hawaiian Culture." In *Native American Voices: A Reader*, 2nd ed., ed. Susan Lobo and Steve Talbot, 393–401. Upper Saddle River, NJ: Prentice Hall.

Triandis, Harry. 1989. "The Self and Social Behavior in Differing Cultural Contexts." *Psychological Review* 96 (3):506–20.

Tronick, Edward, Gilda Morelli, and Paula Ivey. 1992. "The Efe Forager Infant and Toddler's Pattern of Social Relationships: Multiple and Simultaneous." *Developmental Psychology* 28 (4):568–77.

Trudgill, Peter. 1972. "Sex, Covert Prestige and Linguistic Change in the Urban British English of Norwich." *Language in Society* 1:179–95.

Trudgill, Peter. 1974. *The Social Differentiation of English in Norwich*. New York: Cambridge University Press.

Trudgill, Peter. 1983. *Sociolinguistics*. New York: Penguin.

Tsing, Anna. 2005. *Friction: An Ethnography of Global Connection*. Princeton: Princeton University Press.

Tucker, Richard. 2007. *Insatiable Appetite: The United States and the Ecological Degradation of the Third World*. Lanham, Maryland: Rowman & Littlefield.

Tyler, Varro. 1996. "Natural Products and Medicine: An Overview." In *Medicinal Resources of the Tropical Forest: Biodiversity and Its Importance to Human Health*, ed. M. Balick, M. Balick, and E. Elizabetsky, 3–10. New York: Columbia University Press.

Tylor, Edward Burnett. 1871. *Primitive Culture*. London: J. Murray.

U.S. Bureau of the Census. 2001, 2003. *Statistical Abstracts*.

U.S. Department of Justice, Federal Bureau of Investigation. 1999. *Thirty Years of Terrorism: A Special Retrospective*, p. ii. http://www.fbi.gov/publications/terror/terror99.pdf (accessed March 2, 2005).

U.S. Department of Labor. 2002. Bureau of Labor Statistics.

U.S. Department of State. 2004. *2004 Trafficking in Persons Report*. http://www.state.gov/g/tip/rls/tiprpt/2004/ (accessed March 2, 2005).

U.S. English, Inc. 2007. Fact Sheet.

Ubelaker, Douglas. 1976. "Prehistoric New World Population Size: Historical Review and Current Appraisal of North America." *American Journal of Physical Anthropology* 45:661–66.

Ubelaker, Douglas. 1994. "The Biological Impact of European Contact in Ecuador." In *In the Wake of Contact: Biological Responses to Conquest*, 147–60. New York: Wiley-Liss.

Uchendu, Victor. 1995. "The Dilemma of Ethnicity and Polity Primacy in Black Africa." In *Ethnic Identity: Creation, Conflict, and Accommodation*, 3rd ed., ed. L. Romanucci-Ross and G. DeVos, 125–35. London: Sage.

Ukwu, I. U. 1969. "Markets in Iboland." In *Markets in West Africa*, ed. B. W. Hodder and I. U. Ukwu, 113–250. Ibadan, Nigeria: Ibadan University Press.

UNICEF. 2007. Papua New Guinea, At a Glance. http://www.unicef.org/infocountry/papuang.

Union of Concerned Scientists. 2008. Food and Environment. http://www.ucsusa.org/food.and.environment/sustainable.food.

United Nations. 2007. *Declaration on the Rights of Indigenous Peoples*. New York.

United Nations. Department of Economic and Social Affairs. 2004. http://www.unstats.un.org/unsd/cdb.

United Nations, Division for the Advancement of Women. 2001. http://www.unstats.un.org/unsd/cdb.

United Nations, Statistics Division: Demographic and Social Statistics. 2007. http://unstats.un.org/demographic.

Urton, Gary. 2003. "Quipu Knotting Account in the Inka Empire." Santiago: Chilean Museum of Pre-Columbian Art.

van den Broeck, Jef. 1977. Class Differences in Syntactic Complexity in the Flemish Town of Maaseik. *Language in Society* 6:149–181.

van Gennep, Arnold. 1961. *Rites of Passage*. Chicago: University of Chicago Press.

Vecsey, Christopher. 1997. *The Paths of Kateri's Kin*. Notre Dame, IN: University of Notre Dame Press.

Vigneras, L. A. 1960. *The Journal of Christopher Columbus*. London: The Hakluyt Society.

Wachtel, Nathan. 1977. *The Vision of the Vanquished: The Spanish Conquest of Peru through Indian Eyes, 1530–1570*. New York: Gordon Willey.

Wallace, Anthony F. C. 1956. "Revitalization Movements." *American Anthropologist* 58:264–81.

Wallace, Anthony F. C. 1961. *Culture and Personality*. New York: Random House.

Wallace, Anthony F. C. 1966. *Religion: An Anthropological View*. New York: Random House.

Walraven, B. 1994. *Songs of the Shaman: The Ritual Chants of the Korean Mudang*. New York: Columbia University Press.

Wardhaugh, Ronald. 1977. *Introduction to Linguistics*. New York: McGraw-Hill.

Warren, Jonathan. 2001. "Racial Revolutions: Antiracism and Indian Resurgence in Brazil." Durham, NC: Duke University Press.

Waters, Elizabeth, and Anastasia Posadskaya. 1995. "Democracy Without Women Is No Democracy: Women's Struggles in Post Communist Russia." In *The Challenge of Local Feminisms: Women's Movement in Global Perspective*, ed. A. Basu, 351–73. Boulder, CO: Westview.

Watson, Ruby. 1986. "The Named and the Nameless: Gender and Person in Chinese Society." *American Ethnologist* 13 (4):619–31.

Weber, Max. 1968. *Max Weber on Charisma and Institution Building*, ed. S. N. Eisenstadt. Chicago: University of Chicago Press.

Weber, Max. 1981. *General Economic History*. New York: Collier Books.

Weiner, Annette. 1976. *Women of Value, Men of Renown: New Perspectives in Trobriand Exchange*. Austin: University of Texas Press.

Weiner, Annette. 1988. *The Trobrianders of Papua New Guinea*. New York: Holt, Rinehart & Winston.

Weiss, Lawrence. 1984. *The Development of Capitalism in the Navajo Nation: A Political-Economic History. Studies in Marxism*, Vol. 15. Minneapolis: MEP Publications.

Wellington, John. 1967. *South West Africa and Its Human Issues*. Oxford: Clarendon/Oxford University Press.

White, Richard. 1983. *The Roots of Dependency: Subsistence, Environment, and Social Change among the Choctaw, Pawnees, and Navajos*. Lincoln: University of Nebraska Press.

Whiting, John W. M., and Irvin L. Child. 1953. *Child Training and Personality*. New Haven, CT: Yale University Press.

Whorf, Benjamin. 1956. "The Relation of Habitual Thought and Behavior to Language." In *Language, Thought and Reality*, ed. J. B. Carroll, 134–59. Cambridge, MA: MIT Press.

Wiessner, Siegfried. 1999. "Rights and Status of Indigenous Peoples: A Global Comparative and International Legal Analysis." *Harvard Human Rights Journal* 12:57–128.

Williams, Eric. 1944. *Capitalism and Slavery*. Chapel Hill: University of North Carolina Press.

Williams, Michael. 2003. *Deforesting the Earth: From Prehistory to Global Crisis*. Chicago: University of Chicago Press.

Williams, Robert. 1997. "The Ebonics Controversy." *Journal of Black Psychology* 23: 208–213.

Williams, Walter. 1986. *The Spirit and the Flesh: Sexual Diversity in American Indian Culture*. Boston: Beacon Press.

Wilson, Gilbert. 1981. *Waheenee: An Indian Girl's Story Told by Herself to Gilbert L. Wilson*. Lincoln: University of Nebraska Press.

Witherspoon, Gary. 1972. *Navajo Kinship and Marriage*. New York: Cambridge University Press.

Witherspoon, Gary. 1977. *Language and Art in the Navajo Universe*. Ann Arbor: University of Michigan Press.

Wittfogel, Karl. 1957. *Oriental Despotism: A Study of Total Power*. New Haven, CT: Yale University Press.

Wolf, Eric. 1982. *Europe and the People without History*. Berkeley: University of California Press.

Wolf, Marjorie. 1974. "Chinese Women: Old Skills in a New Context." In *Women, Culture and Society*, ed. M. Rosaldo and L. Lamphere, 157–72. Stanford, CA: Stanford University Press.

Wong, Aline. 1974. "Women in China: Past and Present." In *Many Sisters*, ed. C. Matthiasson. New York: Free Press.

Wong, Aline. 1986. "Planned Development, Social Stratification, and the Sexual Division of Labor in Singapore." In *Women's Work: Development and the Division of Labor by Gender*, ed. E. Leacock and H. Safa, 207–23. Cambridge, MA: Bergen & Garvey.

World Health Organization. 2004. Traditional Medicine Fact Sheet. http://www.who.int/mediacentre/factsheets/fs134/en/ (accessed November 18, 2004).

Worsley, Peter. 1967. "Millenarian Movements in Melanesia." In *Gods and Rituals*, ed. J. Middleton, 337–52. Garden City, NY: Natural History Press.

Worsley, Peter. 1968. *The Trumpet Shall Sound: A Study of Cargo Cults in Melanesia*. New York: Schocken.

Worsley, Peter. 1984. *The Three Worlds: Culture and World Development*. Chicago: University of Chicago Press.

Wynne, Clive. 2008. "Aping Language: A Skeptical and Analysis of the Evidence for Nonhuman Primate Language." *Skeptic* 13(4):10–15.

Yap, P. M. 1969. "The Culture-Bound Reactive Syndromes." In *Mental Health Research in Asia and the Pacific*, ed. W. Caudill and T. Y. Lin, 33–53. Honolulu: East-West Center Press.

Yazzie, R. 1992. *The Navajo Peacemaker Court: Contrasts of Justice*. Windowrock, AZ: Navajo Tribe.

Yeoman, L. 1987. "Universal Primary Education: Factors Affecting the Enrollment and Retention of Girls in Papua New Guinea Community Schools." In *The Ethics of Development: Women as Unequal Partners in Development*, ed. S. Stratigos and P. J. Hughes, 108–55. Port Moresby: University of Papua New Guinea.

Young, Robert, and William Morgan. 1987. *The Navajo Language*, rev. ed. Albuquerque: University of New Mexico Press.

Youngstedt, Scott. 2004. "Creating Modernities Through Conversation Groups: The Everyday Worlds of Hausa Migrants in Niamey, Niger. African Studies Review, vol. 47, no.3, 91–118.

Zentella, Ana. 1985. "The Fate of Spanish in the U.S.: The Puerto Rican Experience." In *Language of Inequality*, ed. N. Wolfson and J. Manes, 41–59. The Hague: Mouton.

Zihlman, Adrienne. 1981. "Women as Shapers of the Human Adaptation." In *Woman the Gatherer*, ed. Frances Dahlberg, 75–120. New Haven: Yale University Press.

Zolbrod, Paul. 1984. *Dine Bahane: The Navajo Creation Story*. Albuquerque: University of New Mexico.

CREDITS

Chapter 1   Page 1: Marilyn "Angel" Wynn/Native Stock Pictures; p. 3: Walt Disney/Storyline/Citadel/Picture Desk, Inc./Kobal Collection; p. 4: Craig Stanford/Jane Goodall Research Center; p. 4: Aijaz Rahi/AP Wide World Photos; p. 7: David Waters/CORBIS ALL RIGHTS RESERVED; p. 10: Natalie Fobes/CORBIS ALL RIGHTS RESERVED; p. 12: John Reader/Photo Researchers, Inc.; p. 13: Dave Mercado/AP Wide World Photos; p. 14: Eye of Science/Photo Researchers, Inc.; p. 16: Cultural Survival, Inc., www.culturalsurvival.org; p. 16: © Richard T. Nowitz/CORBIS All Rights Reserved; p. 16: © Kazuyoshi Nomachi/CORBIS All Rights Reserved

Chapter 2   Page 19: Alison Wright/CORBIS ALL RIGHTS RESERVED p. 21: Topham/The Image Works; p. 22: Imapress/Charreire/The Image Works; p. 23: Kike Calvo/The Image Works; p. 23: Alain Keler/Sygma/Corbis/Sygma; p. 24: Ariel Skelley/CORBIS ALL RIGHTS RESERVED; p. 26: Jack K. Clark/The Image Works; p. 29: Geri Engberg/The Image Works; p. 31: Getty Images Inc. - Hulton Archive Photos; p. 31: Michael Ventura/PhotoEdit Inc.; p. 33: John Van Hasselt/CORBIS ALL RIGHTS RESERVED; p. 36: Photofest; p. 36: A Band Apart/Miramax/Andre Cooper/Picture Desk, Inc./Kobal Collection; p. 40: Z. Bzdak/The Image Works; p. 41: Desmond Kwande/AF/Getty Images; p. 41: © Yann Arthus-Bertrand/CORBIS All Rights Reserved; p. 41: Friedrich Stark/DAS FOTOARCHIV/Peter Arnold, Inc.

Chapter 3   Page 44: © Natalie Fobes/CORBIS ALL RIGHTS RESERVED; p. 46: Father James Driscoll; p. 47: Bettman/Corbis p. 50: © Earl & Nazima Kowall/Corbis/Bettmann; p. 51: Alamy Images; p. 52: Photolibrary.com; p. 53: Elisha P. Renne; p. 57: Photos.com; p. 58: © Mark Peterso/CORBIS ALL RIGHTS RESERVED; p. 64: David McLain/Contributor/Getty Images; p. 64: Alamy Images; p. 64: Jacques Jangoux/Photo Researchers, Inc.

Chapter 4   Page 67: © Ed Kashi/CORBIS CORBIS All Rights Reserved; p. 69: © Anna Clopet/CORBIS All Rights Reserved; p. 72: © Ariel Skelley/CORBIS All Rights Reserved; p. 73: Karen Huntt/CORBIS ALL RIGHTS RESERVED; p. 74: AP Wide World Photos; p. 74: Michael Gibson/Paramount Picture Desk, Inc./Kobal Collection; p. 75: Photos.com; p. 81: David Young-Wolf/PhotoEdit Inc.; p. 86: Moodboard Micro/Corbis RF; p. 88: Regien Paassen/Shutterstock; p. 90: B.A. Stewart & J.E. Fletcher/Getty - National Geographic Society; p. 90: Lawrence Migdale/Lawrence Migdale/Pix

Chapter 5   Page 93: © Paul Almasy/CORBIS All Rights Reserved; p. 97: Jason Laure/The Image Works; p. 99: Steve Winn/Anthro-Photo File; p. 103: © Diego Goldberg/CORBIS All Rights Reserved; p. 104: Jose Luis Pelaez, Inc. CORBIS ALL RIGHTS RESERVED; p. 109: Ariel Skelley/CORBIS ALL RIGHTS RESERVED; p. 118: © Nik Wheeler/CORBIS All Rights Reserved; p. 123: Condon/Anthro-Photo File; p. 124: Philip de Bay/Corbis/Bettmann; p. 124: © Erwin Patzelt/dp/CORBIS All Rights Reserved; p. 124: © Wayne Lawler; Ecoscen/CORBIS All Rights Reserved

Chapter 6   Page 127: © Tibor Bognar /CORBIS All Rights Reserved; p. 129 © Ludo Kuipers/CORBIS All Rights Reserved; p. 130: Michael Freeman/IPNstock/Nielsen Business Media; p. 131: Joy May Hilden; p. 132: © Layne Kennedy/CORBIS All Rights Reserved; p. 135: GIANLUIGI GUERCIA/AF/Getty Images; p. 136: © Lowell Georgia/CORBIS All Rights Reserved; p. 139: The Image Works; p. 143: Jon Holtzman; p. 144: Victor Englebert; p. 147: Bobby Yip/Reuter/CORBIS ALL RIGHTS RESERVED; p. 151: Craig Morris. Courtesy, Division of Anthropology, American Museum of Natural History; p. 151: Reuters/Rickey Roger/Corbis/Reuters America LLC; p. 151: © Danny Lehman/CORBIS All Rights Reserved

Chapter 7   Page 154: Irven DeVore/Anthro-Photo File; p. 156: © Robert van der Hilst/CORBIS All Rights Reserved; p. 157: David Cavagnaro/Peter Arnold, Inc.; p. 161: © Owen Franken/CORBIS All Rights Reserved; p. 163: Courtesy Azerbaijan International—AZER.com; p. 164: Bojan Brecelj/CORBIS ALL RIGHTS RESERVED; p. 165: © Phillippe Lissac/Godong/CORBIS All Rights Reserved; p. 166: Fujifoto/The Image Works; p. 168: Dinodia Picture Agency; p. 170: © Steve Crise/Transtock/CORBIS All Rights Reserved; p. 170 © Frans Lanting/CORBIS All Rights Reserved; p. 173: © Steve Raymer/CORBIS All Rights Reserved; p. 177: © Benjamin Lowy/CORBIS All Rights Reserved; p. 177: Alamy Images

Chapter 8   Page 180: © Bettman/CORBIS All Rights Reserved; p. 182: © Susana Raab/CORBIS All Rights Reserved; p. 184: © Peter Johnson/CORBIS All Rights Reserved; p. 186: © Doranne Jacobson/International Images; p. 187: Bell/Anthro-Photo File; p. 189: Jon Burban/The Image Works; p. 192: Topham/The Image Works; p. 196: © Ludo Kuipers/CORBIS All Rights Reserved; p. 202: © Brian A. Vikander/CORBIS All Rights Reserved; p. 205: National Gallery of Art, Washington DC, USA/The Bridgeman Art Library; p. 205: © Morton Beebe/CORBIS All Rights Reserved; p. 205: © Martin Harvey/CORBIS All Rights Reserved

Chapter 9   Page 209: © Benjamin Lowy/CORBIS All Rights Reserved; p. 210: © Dex Image/CORBIS All Rights Reserved; p. 211: © Danny Lehman/CORBIS All Rights Reserved; p. 212: Elizabeth Crews/The Image Works; p. 213: David Grossman/The Image Works; p. 217: © Doranne Jacobson/International Images; p. 219: Lauren Goodsmith/The Image Works; p. 221: © Ann Johansson/CORBIS All Rights Reserved; p. 222: © Peter Johnson/CORBIS All Rights Reserved; p. 225: Bob Daemmrich/The Image Works; p. 226: © John Van Hasselt/CORBIS All Rights Reserved; p. 229: Adrian Arbib/Anthro-Photo File; p. 232: Hideo Haga/The Image Works; p. 235: Tont Savino/Sygma/Corbis/Sygma; p. 235: Reuters/Jason Reed/Corbis/Reuters America LLC

Chapter 10   Page 239: Werner Forman/Art Resource, N.Y.; p. 241: © Steve Raymer/CORBIS All Rights Reserved; p. 244: Charles Walker/Topfot/The Image Works; p. 247: Art Resource/Smithsonian American Art Museum/Art Resource, NY; p. 250: Bob Daemmrich/The Image Works; p. 251: © Steven Vidler/Eurasia Pres/CORBIS All Rights Reserved; p. 254: © Wendy Stone/CORBIS All Rights Reserved; p. 259: © David Sutherland/CORBIS All Rights Reserved; p. 260: James Marshall/The Image Works; p. 262: © CORBIS All Rights Reserved; p. 268: © Craig Lovell/CORBIS All Rights Reserved; p. 272: Tor Richardsen, Scanpix/AP Wide World Photos; p. 272: AP Wide World Photos; p. 272: © Unic Yangon/epa/CORBIS All Rights Reserved; p. 272: © Justin Guariglia/CORBIS All Rights Reserved

Chapter 11   Page 275: The Bridgeman Art Library International; p. 277: Reuters/Jason Reed/Corbis/Reuters America LLC; p. 282: Rachel Epstein The Image Works; p. 283: © The Art Archive/CORBIS All Rights Reserved; p. 283: Andrew Holbrooke/The Image Works; p. 285: © Atlantide Phototravel/CORBIS All Rights Reserved; p. 286: Abd Rabbo-Niviere/SIPA Press; p. 287: © David Orr/CORBIS All Rights Reserved; p. 288: © J. Patrick Forden/CORBIS All Rights Reserved; p. 290: Hideo Haga/The Image Works; p. 296: Obama For America/Handout/Reuter/Corbis/Reuters America LLC; p. 297: © David Turnley/CORBIS All Rights Reserved; p. 298: © Galen Rowell/CORBIS All Rights Reserved; p. 298: © Warrick Page/CORBIS All Rights Reserved; p. 298: Frederic Pitchal/Sygm/Corbis/Sygma

Chapter 12   Page 301: Native Stock Pictures; p. 303: © Ali Abbas/ep/CORBIS All Rights Reserved; p. 306: Nova Scotia Musuem, Halifax, N.S. - Ethnology Collection; p. 311: K. Hympendahl/Peter Arnold, Inc.; p. 314: © Bettmann/CORBIS ALL RIGHTS RESERVED; p. 314: Image Works/Mary Evans Picture Library Ltd; p. 316: Victor Englebert; p. 320: Philippe Colombi/Photodisc Getty Images; p. 323: Jeff Christensen/REUTER/Corbis/Reuters America LLC; p. 324: © Howard Davies/

CORBIS ALL RIGHTS RESERVED; p. 324: © Jean-Marc Bernard/Realis Agenc/CORBIS All Rights Reserved; p. 324: © Karen Kasmauski/CORBIS ALL RIGHTS RESERVED

Chapter 13   Page 327: Lars Smith/Anthro-Photo File; p. 329: OSF/BROMHALL, CLIV/Animals Animals/Earth Scenes; p. 330: David Young-Wolff/PhotoEdit Inc.; p. 335: © Peter Johnson/CORBIS ALL RIGHTS RESERVED; p. 336: Lynsey Addario/CORBIS ALL RIGHTS RESERVED; p. 338: Malcolm Linton/Getty Images; p. 340: George Catlin (1796–1872). "Eagle Dance, Choctaw". Oil on canvas, 19 ½ × 27 ½ in. Gift of Mrs. Joseph Harrison Jr. Smithsonian American Art Museum, Washington, DC. Photo Credit: Smithsonian American Art Museum, Washington, DC/Art Resource, NY.; p. 344: Greg Wahl-Stephens/AP Wide World Photos; p. 345: © Paul Colangelo/CORBIS ALL RIGHTS RESERVED; p. 349: © CORBIS All Rights Reserved; p. 349: Peter Bowater/Alamy Images; p. 349: AP Wide World Photos

Chapter 14   Page 352: © Geoffrey Clements/CORBIS ALL RIGHTS RESERVED; p. 354: Embassy of Italy; p. 355: Frèdèric Solta/CORBIS ALL RIGHTS RESERVED; p. 355: © Bob Sacha/CORBIS ALL RIGHTS RESERVED; p. 357: Shimizu Teruyo/Photo Japan; p. 358: Lawrence Migdale/Lawrence Migdale/Pix; p. 360: Cedar Bough Photography; p. 361: Christopher D. Roy; p. 362: © Christophe Boisvieux/CORBIS ALL RIGHTS RESERVED; p. 362: © Edward S. Curtis/CORBIS ALL RIGHTS RESERVED; p. 364: Raghu Rai/Magnum Photos, Inc.; p. 365: © Frans Lemmens/zef/CORBIS ALL RIGHTS RESERVED; p. 371: © Anders Ryman/CORBIS ALL RIGHTS RESERVED; p. 379: Zsolt Nyulaszi/Shutterstock; p. 379: © George Shelley/CORBIS ALL RIGHTS RESERVED; p. 379: Alamy Images

Chapter 15   Page 383: Topham/The Image Works; p. 386: Kim Grant/Lonely Planet Images/Photo 20-20; p. 387: Victor Englebert; p. 387: Used by permission of Lakeview Museum of Arts and Sciences, Peoria, IL.; p. 388: © Michael Christopher Brown/CORBIS ALL

RIGHTS RESERVED; p. 389: Helen Frankenthaler (b.1928) © Small's Paradise, 1964. Acrylic on canvas, 100 × 93 ⅜ in. (254 × 237.7 cm). Smithsonian American Art Museum, Washington, CD/Art Resorce, NY; p. 390: Knoedler & Company; p. 392: Martha Cooper/Peter Arnold, Inc.; p. 392: Archivo Iconografico, S.A. Corbis/Bettmann; p. 393: Werner Forman/CORBIS ALL RIGHTS RESERVED; p. 396: Lawrence Migdale/Lawrence Migdale/Pix; p. 403: © Robert Harding/Robert Harding World Imagery/CORBIS ALL RIGHTS RESERVED; p. 404: SuperStock, Inc.; p. 404: Alamy Images; p. 404: Joel Jean-Pierre/AP Wide World Photos

Chapter 16   Page 407: Bettmann Corbis/Bettmann; p. 409: The Bridgeman Art Library International; p. 410: © Gleb Garanich/CORBIS ALL RIGHTS RESERVED; p. 412: © CORBIS ALL RIGHTS RESERVED; p. 414: North Wind Picture Archives; p. 419: © Michael and Patricia Fogden/CORBIS ALL RIGHTS RESERVED; p. 423: John N. Choate/Hulton Archive/Getty Images; p. 423: John N. Choate/Hulton Archive/Getty Images; p. 426: Knud Petersen/Art Resource/Bildarchiv Preussischer Kulturbesitz/Art Resource NY; p. 430: © Gregg Newton/CORBIS ALL RIGHTS RESERVED; p. 430: © Marc Lecureuil/CORBIS ALL RIGHTS RESERVED

Chapter 17   Page 433: AP Wide World Photos; p. 436: © Staffan Widstrand/CORBIS ALL RIGHTS RESERVED; p. 438: Jack Kurtz/The Image Works; p. 439: © Nevada Wier/CORBIS ALL RIGHTS RESERVED; p. 440: © Michael Nicholson/CORBIS ALL RIGHTS RESERVED; p. 442: Courtesy of Hindustan Times; p. 443: © Reuters/Lirio da Fonsec/CORBIS ALL RIGHTS RESERVED; p. 445: © Barry Lewis/CORBIS ALL RIGHTS RESERVED; p. 450: Josh Reynold/The Image Works; p. 452: © Andrew Hay/Reuter/CORBIS ALL RIGHTS RESERVED; p. 453: FOTOGRAF/Still Picture/Peter Arnold, Inc.; p. 461: © Catherine Karnow/CORBIS ALL RIGHTS RESERVED; p. 462: REUTERS/STR/Landov Media; p. 462: Stephen Ferry/Liaison/Getty Images

INDEX

A

Aberle, David, 185
Abnormal behavior, 121–23
  and cultural norms, 22
  culture and response to, 121–22
  See also Psychological disorder
Aboriginal Family History Project, 52
Abrahams, Roger D., 240, 328
Abu-Lughod, Lila, 32
Acculturation, 33
Achieved status
  defined, 277
  social class as, 286
Achuar (Ecuador), 454
Adamson, E., 302
Adaptation to culture, 26
  of colonized peoples, 37–38
  maladaptive, examples of, 27–28
  reactive adaptation, 37
  See also Enculturation
Adesanya, Dr. Aderonke, 53
Adolescents, rites of passage.
    See Initiation rites
Adorno, Rolena, 399
Adultery, and culture, 244–45
Aesthetics, 385
Affines, 182, 210
Afghanistan
  refugees from, 437
  Taliban, 378
Africa
  biodiversity prospecting, 457
  civil wars, 345, 444–45
  economic development, effects
    on indigenous, 457
  ethnic identity, complexity of,
    294–95, 441
  indigenous defined, 455
  missionism, 411
  patrilineal descent, shift to, 413
  proverbs, 397
  sickle-cell trait, 14–15
  slavery in, 411–13
  women and HIV/AIDS, 267
  See also South Africa; specific countries
    and specific groups of indigenous
    people
African Americans
  African-American Vernacular English
    (AAVE), 81–84
  child schooling, 115–16
  civil rights movement, 323

kinship groups, 184
marginalized in U.S., 290–91
segregation of, 288
sickle-cell anemia, 14–15
slavery era, 287, 413
sleeping arrangements, 99
South to North migration, 436
African-American Vernacular English
    (AAVE), 81–84
  Bridge program, 82–83
  Ebonics, 82–83
  examples of, 82
  political/legal issues, 82–84
African National Congress (ANC), 346–48
Afro-Caribbeans
  Afro-Lingua, 30
  child schooling, 115–16
  music of, 404
  Santeria, 33
  slave era, 410–11
Age
  and division of labor, 131
  and status, 106–7, 278
Age grades/sets
  defined, 307
  Hidatsa (Native Americans), 308–9
  Maasai (Kenya/Tanzania), 309–10
  and tribes, 307–10
Aggression
  prevention of. *See* Conflict avoidance
  primates, 329–30
  See also Warfare
Agrarian societies. *See* Agricultural
    societies
Agribusiness, 169–70
Agricultural societies
  child labor, 158–59
  and craft specialization, 148, 157
  division of labor, 131
  gender status, 259–60
  health status decline, 148, 176
  land ownership, 156, 176
  lifestyle pros/cons, 148, 176, 179
  population size, 131
  residence patterns, 229–30
  settlement patterns, 131, 156, 176
  sharecropping, 162–63
  surplus redistribution, 162–64
Agriculture
  defined, 130
  earliest crops, 147
  industrialization of, 169–72
  intensive, methods/tools, 149–50

irrigation systems, 145
as modern economic sector, 174–75
negative social impact, 26, 169–72
origin of, 147–48
Ahmadu, Fuambai, 8
Ainu (Japan)
  extinction of language, 90
  social status of, 290
Akan (Ghana), proverbs, 397
Aklla (Inca women), 151
Alebrijes (carvings), 405
Alexander, Alex, 276
Algeo, John, 88
Algonkians (Canada)
  Champlain meeting with, 425
  windigo (spiritual possession), 123
Amazon
  deforestation, 171
  economic development, effect on
    indigenous, 451–54
  Operation Amazon, 452
Ambilineal descent, 190
Ambler, Marjane, 77
American Anthropological Association,
  Code of Ethics, 62
American Indian Religious Freedom Act
  (1978), 448
American Revolution, 323
American Sign Language (ASL), primate
  learning of, 69
American society. *See* United States
Amok (intense outbursts), 122–23
Amott, Teresa, 263
Ancestor worship, 357
Ancestral spirits
  Hopi kachina, 357
  Ju/'hoansi (Kalahari Desert), 357
Andeans
  biological differences of, 13
  depopulation and colonialism, 415–16
  economic development, effects on
    indigenous, 454–55
  societal stratification of, 23
  See also Inca
Anderson, Barbara, 14
Anderson, Richard, 385–87
Andrews, George, 291
Animal communication, call
  systems, 69–70
Animal herding, pastoralists, 138–43
Animal sacrifice, 362
  Melanesians, 146
  Tsembaga (New Guinea), 372–73

Animatism, 356–57
Animism, 356, 426
Anthony, Susan B., 263
Anthropological approaches
    conflict perspectives, 49, 51
    cultural ecology, 48–49
    cultural materialism, 49–50
    empiricism, 47–48
    evolutionism, 46–47
    fieldwork, 47, 48, 51–61
    functionalism, 48
    interpretive anthropology, 49, 50–51
    structuralism, 49, 50
Anthropology
    archaeology, 11–13
    biological, 13–14
    careers in, 7
    cultural, 6–10
    defined, 3
    ethical issues, 62
    holistic perspective, 4–5
    labeling issues, 62
    linguistic, 10–11
    paleoanthropology, 13
    study, elements of, 3–4, 6, 46
    study methods. *See* Anthropological
        approaches
    See also Applied anthropology
Apache
    historical tales, 396–97
    nai'es puberty rite, 365–66
    native language speakers, 80
    witchcraft accusations, 335
Apartheid, South Africa, 31, 323, 427
Apocalypse, millinerian movements, 374
Apologies
    and conflict avoidance, 331–32
    Japan, 331–32
Applied anthropology, 15–17
    economic, 128–29
    forensic, 15
    industrial, 17
    legal, 349
    linguistic, 10–11
    medical, 14, 17, 379
    political, 302–3
    psychological, 116–20
    reflexive, 61
    urban, 57–61
Applied archaeology
    contract archaeology, 15
Archaeological sites, Native American,
        protection and repatriation, 450
Archaeology, 11–13
    applied, 15
    evidence in, 11–12
    focus of study, 11–12
Arctic indigenous. *See* Inuit; Inupiaq;
        Yup'iks
Arias, Oscar, 345
Arizona Garbage Project, 12–13
Armstrong, Sue, 8
Arnold, Fred, 262

Arranged marriage, 226–27
    India, 223–24
    Kwakwaka'wakw (British Columbia),
        226–27
    Lohorung Rai (Nepal), 225
    personal accounts of, 226–27
Art
    body art, 388–89
    cave paintings, 365, 370, 392
    characteristics of, 385–86
    and cultural change, 36
    and cultural identity, 399–400
    dance as, 385–86, 395–96, 400
    defined, 385
    earliest known, 392
    emotionalist art, 386
    ethnic art, 405
    formalist art, 386
    in global economy, 400
    instrumental art, 386
    interpretation issues, 393
    mimetic art, 386
    narratives as, 396–99
    objects, decoration of, 389–92
    representational art, 386
    songs and music as, 394–95
    as symbolic communication, 32
    tourists as consumers, 401–3, 405
    Yoruba (Nigeria), 386–88
Artisans, 390–92
Ascribed status
    defined, 277
    slavery as, 287
Ashanti (Nigeria), as slave traders, 412
Ashti (end of war), 332
Assimilation process, 33, 292–93
Associations
    age grade, 307–10
    defined, 307
    of tribes, 307–10
Assumptions, cultural, 22, 30–31
Athabascan language family, 11
Atomic bomb survivors, Japanese
        discrimination, 290
Australia
    Great Britain colonialism, 33, 52,
        421, 423–24
    See also Australian aborigines; Tiwi
Australian aborigines
    body art, 388
    and colonial policies, 33, 52, 421,
        423–24
    Dreamtime, 358, 392
    ethnohistory database on, 52
    genocide of, 52
    government apology to, 52
    polygyny, 219–20
    rites of passage, 109–10
    rock paintings, 392
    stolen generation, 33, 423
    taboos, 358
Avoidance relationships, 199
Avunculocal residence, 228–29

Awaba Aborigines (Australia),
        ethnohistory database on, 52
Ayahuasca (hallucinogen), 124
Ayllus (Inca kinship groups), 321–22
Aztec (Mexico)
    clothing/jewelry of elite, 389
    education of children, 111–12
    Europeans, view of, 425–26
    human sacrifice, 362
    riddles, 397–98
    ritual bloodletting, 112

B

Baez de Torres, Luis, 426
Bailey, Garrick, 402
Bailey, Roberta, 402
Baker, Lee, 297
Bakhtin, Mikhail, 63
Balanced reciprocity, 160
Bands, 303–6
    conflict avoidance, 337–38
    cultural features of, 303–6
    defined, 303
    size of groups, 303
    subsistence pattern, 304
    Tiwi (Australia), 305–6
Bani Hamida (Jordan), division
        of labor, 131
Banishment, Native American
        punishment, 343
Bantu (Somalia), refugees, 7
Baptism, 97, 364, 368
Barabaig (Tanzania), territory, loss
        of, 456
Barbeau, Marius, 394
Bar mitzvah/bat mitzvah, 364
Baron, Dennis, 447
Barreda, Andres, 449
Barter, defined, 161
Basseri (Iran), as pastoralists, 139–41
Basso, Keith, 30, 104, 335, 365–66,
        396–97
Baugh, John, 82
Becharaa' (conflict resolution
        meeting), 333
Behavior, socially appropriate
        learning of, 104
Behavioral science, and forensic
        anthropology, 15
Behzadi, K. G., 332
Belgium, African colonialism, 444–45
Beliefs, and religion, 354–56
Benedict, Ruth, 47, 120
Beneria, Lourdes, 266
Benga (Kenyan pop music), 404
Berch, Bettina, 263
Berdaches (transgenders), 246
Berlant, Anthony, 401–2
Berreman, Gerald, 278, 291–92
Beveridge, Sydney, 457
Biehl, Amy, 346–47
Biesele, Megan, 461

Big men, Melanesian, 440
Bikini Atoll, 349
Bilateral descent, 183–84
    Cheyenne, 200–1
    defined, 182
    in foraging societies, 183, 193
    in industrial societies, 183–84
    kindred groups, 183–84
    and nuclear family, 212
Bilocal residence, 229
Bin Abdul Aziz, king of Saudi Arabia, 323
Binford, Lewis, 147
Biodiversity prospecting, 457
Biological anthropology, 13–14
    medical anthropology, 14
    paleoanthropology, 13
Biopiracy, 124
Bipedalism, 95
Birale language, 90
Birdsell, Joseph, 52
Bison hunting, Native Americans, 139
Bitterli, Urs, 424
Black Elk, Oglala spiritual leader, 121
Blackman, Margaret, 136–37, 226
Black Mouth Society (Hidatsa), 309
Blankets, Navajo, 401–2
Blood feuds, 338
Boas, Franz, 220
    contributions of, 47–48
Boddy, Janice, 251
Bodenhorn, Barbara, 136, 255
Bodley, John, 417, 421–22, 429–30
Body art, 388–89
    jewelry, 389
    scarification, 388
    and social status, 387, 389
    tattoos, 388–89
Body language. *See* Nonverbal
    communication
Bohannan, Laura, 33–35
Boissoneau, Doris, 77
Bolivia
    indigenous rights, 454–55
    silver mines exploitation, 418
    See also Andeans; Inca
Bones, Jah, 30
Bonvillain, Nancy, 196, 217, 258
Boorana (Kenya), 257
Bordo, Susan, 122
Borg, Marcus, 376
Bose, Christine, 263
Boserup, Ester, 266
Bourdieu, Pierre, 81
Bowers, Alfred, 309
Bowers v. Hardwick, 245
Boyer, Paul, 77
Brahmins, 217, 284–85
Brasser, T. J., 415
Bray, Tamara, 451
Brazelton, T. B., 99
Brazil
    economic development, effects
        on indigenous, 451–54

Guarani land rights, 462
    indigenous preservation, 452–53
    racial system, 291
    slave era, 411
    tribal extinction, 451
    urban Indians, 453–54
    Waika psychotropic plant use, 124
    Xingu National Park, 430
    See also Yanomamo
Brazilian National Indian Foundation
    (FUNAI), 430
Breastfeeding, and population
    control, 144
Brideservice
    defined, 223
    Kpelle (Liberia), 234, 236
Bridewealth
    defined, 222–23
    Keplelle (Liberia), 234, 236
Briggs, Jean, 256
British Columbia. *See* Gitksan;
    Kwakwaka'wakw
Broadwell, George, 80
Broken Hill Proprietary (BHP), 349
Brown, Judith, 258
Brown, Penelope, 331
Broz, Josip, 295
Buddha (Enlightened One), 375–76
Buddhism
    founding of, 375
    missionaries, 411
Bull Society (Hidatsa), 309
Bunzel, Ruth, 96, 117, 395
Burakumin, 289–90
Bureaucrats, 317, 320
Burger, Richard L., 12
Burundi
    independence of, 444
    refugees from, 436

C

Cabot, John, 413
Calabash designs, Saramaka
    (Suriname), 390–91
Caldwell, Alan, 76
Calendric rituals, 370
Callendar, Charles, 246
Call systems, animal communication,
    69–70
Calmecas (Aztec schools), 111–12
Canada
    First Nations, 447–49, 453
    indigenous of. *See* Native Americans;
        specific bands
    indigenous rights legislation, 449
Cannibalism, and *kuru*, 27–28
Capital, 165
Capitalism, 164–66
    colonialism and spread of, 166–68
    cultural/ideological supports for,
        165–66
    defined, 165

naturalized concepts in, 31
    production, attributes of, 165
    social classes, necessity of, 165, 282–83
    and social inequalities, 173–75
CARE, 324
Careers in anthropology, 7
Cargo cults, 374–75
Caribbean
    slave labor, 410
    See also Afro-Caribbeans
Carneiro, Robert, 37, 319, 430
Carrasco, David, 397–98
Carrying capacity
    defined, 130
    and food production, 130
Caruso, Emily, 460
Casas, Bartolemé de las, 46
Caste,
    defined, 216
    economic functions of, 284–85
    endogamy in, 217–18, 284
    India, 218, 284–85, 375
    and political power, 286
    compared to race, 288
Castillo, Edward, 167, 418
Castro, A., 324
Cave paintings, 365, 370, 392
Cayuga, in Iroquois Confederacy,
    308, 312
Cecena, Ana, 449
Central Identification Laboratory-Hawaii
    (CILH), 15
Cewa (Zimbabwe), witchcraft accusations
    in, 370
Chagnon, Napoleon, 63, 145, 259
Chamberlain, Joseph, 168
Champlain, Samuel de, 425
Chance, Norman, 255
Change and culture. *See* Cultural change
Changing Woman, 365–66
Channeled aggression, 331–32
Chanock, Martin, 420
Chavín de Huántar (Peru), 12
Chernoff, J. M., 404
Cherokee, native language speakers, 80
Cheshire, Jenny, 116
Cheyenne
    bilateral descent, 200–1
    as horse pastoralists, 139
    Two-Spirits, 246, 247
Chiefdoms, 310–16
    cultural features of, 310–14
    defined, 310
    examples of, 311
    Tonga (Polynesia), 315–16
Chiefs
    Iroquois Confederacy, 308,
        312–13
    leopard-skin (Nuer), 338–39
    redistribution of resources by,
        311–12
    role/powers of, 196, 198, 310–14
Child, Irvin, 98

Childbirth
  couvade, 369
  healer assisted, 360
  indigenous practices, 95, 189, 360
  pregnancy taboos, 358–59
Child labor
  extent of, global statistics, 158–59
  forced labor/human trafficking,
    159, 298
  and globalization, 101
  hazardous work, 159
  horticulturalists, 145
  modern categories of, 158–59
Child rearing, 97–102
  behavioral expectations, learning, 104
  collectivist versus individualist society,
    117–19
  contact with caregivers, 99, 101
  feeding/weaning practices, 98
  skills/values, transmission of, 103–4
  sleeping arrangements, 98–99
  teaching methods, 97–98
Children, enculturation of, 25–26
China
  culture change, 260
  division of labor, 261
  foot binding, 261–62
  gender preference, 108, 261
  male dominance, 261–62
  marriage/divorce, 261–62
  Na marital forms, 221
  naming practices, 108
  patrilocal residence, 261
  population control, 262
  T'ang Dynasty empire building, 409
Chitnis, Suma, 230
Choctaw
  raids/warfare, 340
Chomsky, Noam, 71, 72, 446
Christening, 364
Christianity
  founding of, 375–76
  fundamentalism, 377–78
  missionaries, 411
Chrysanthemum and the Sword, The
    (Benedict), 120
Circumcision
  Female, 8–9
  as initiation rite, 110, 309, 366
  Suku (Congo), 366
Cities
  rural migration to, 436–37
  and states, 318
  urban Indians, Brazil, 453–54
Clam diggers, 157
Clancy, Patricia, 105
Clans, 192–98
  chiefs, 196, 198
  decision making/problem solving,
    193–94
  defined, 192
  economic functions of, 193–94
  exogamy, 191, 193, 195

Ganda (Uganda), 194–95
  matriclans and patriclans, 192
  Mohawks, 196
  phratries and moieties, 195
  segmentary lineages, 193–94
  totems and taboos, 192–93
Clark, Ella, 45
Class
  defined, 216
  See also Social class; Social stratification
Class mobility
  and caste, 286
  defined, 286
  downward in U.S., 296–99
  in ranked societies, 278–79
Clifford, James, 61
Clothing
  and cultural identity, 389
  and gender identity, 244, 389
  and social status, 387, 389
Cocopa, Two-Spirits, 246
Code of Ethics, of anthropologists, 62
Codere, Helen, 161
Cofee Alliance, 16
Cognates
  defined, 88
  Indo-European examples, 89
Cognition and culture, 119–20
  context-bound thought, 119–20
  intellectual functioning, 120
  spatial task mastery, 119
Cohabitation, 215
Colchester, Marcus, 460
Collectivist society, child rearing in,
    117–19
Colonialism, 408–28
  and cultural change, 36–38, 166–69,
    316, 323, 340, 416–17
  cultural change agents, 418–21
  defined, 166
  and economic systems, 166–69
  and gender inequality, 252,
    256–57
  guns, impact of, 426
  justifications for, 421–24
  and nation building, 167, 409
  native resistance/revolts, 427–28
  pacification as goal, 422
  plants/animals exchange, 428–29
  poll taxes, 167
  postcolonial era, 428–29
  resettlement policies, 410
  and slavery, 411–13
  and taxation, 420–21
  white man's burden, 421–22
  See also Great Britain; Native
    Americans and colonialism; Spanish
    colonialism
Colonies
  defined, 409
  types of, 410
Columbus, Christopher, 424–25
Commodity, functions of, 164

Communication
  animals, 69–70, 73
  ethnography of, 85–86
  style, gender differences, 107
  See also Language; Linguistic
    anthropology; Nonverbal
    communication
Comparative perspective
  of culture, 5
  globalization process, 5
Competition
  in plural marriages, 336
  in ranked societies, 279
  in siblings, 337
Componential analysis, language,
    84–85
Confederacy, 308, 312–13
  cultural features of, 308
  defined, 308
  Iroquois Confederacy, 196, 308,
    312–13
Confirmation, 364
Conflict
  in bands, 337–38
  blood feuds, 338–39
  family violence, 336–37
  tribal societies, 337–39
  warfare, 339–42, 344–48
Conflict avoidance, 330–35
  and apologies, 331–32
  channeled aggression, 331–32
  defined, 330
  Japan, 331–32
  Nuer (Sudan), 338
  and parent-child relationship, 332
  politeness, 331
  and reciprocity, 334
  self-control, 330
  Semai (Malaysia), 332–33
  Toraja (Indonesia), 334
  witchcraft in, 335–36, 370
Conflict perspectives
  on cultural diversity, 49
  focus of, 51
  and Marxist theory, 51
Confucianism, 261
Congo. *See* Democratic Republic
    of Congo
Consanguines, 182, 210
Conservation policies, anti-indigenous,
    460–61
Consumerism, 171, 173–74
  defined, 173
  in developing countries, 174
  and globalization, 39–40
  time as commodity, 173
Consumption, 173
Contagious disease, Native American
    depopulation, 14, 415–16
Contagious magic, 369–70
Contract archaeology, focus of, 15
Cook, Sherburne, 418
Copra production, 268, 316

Corn, Native American diet, 150
Corporations
    downsizing, 297
    outsourcing, 174
Cortes, Hernan, 425
Cosmology, Diné, 371
Costa Rica, military, lack of, 345
Costello, Cynthia, 29
Cottage industry, 168
Coulmas, Florian, 331
Councils
    chiefdoms, 314
    Iroquois Confederacy,
        312–13
    tribal, 306
Countercultures, 31
Courtship, 227
Cousin marriage
    cross-cousins, 191
    as joking relationship, 199
    parallel cousins, 191
Couvade, 369
Cowley, Geoffrey, 415
Cox, P., 124
Coya (Inca queen), 321
Craft specialization
    and agricultural communities,
        148, 151, 157
    artisans, 390–92
    Inca, 151
Creation myths
    Diné, 353
    Native American, 45, 353
    Tibetan, 20
Creoles, 87
Creutzfeld-Jakob disease, 28
Crimea, Tatars, resettlement of, 410
Criminal investigation, and forensic
        anthropology, 15
Croll, Elizabeth, 261, 269
Crosby, Alfred, 428–29
Crossan, Joh, 376
Cross-cousin marriage, 191–92
Cross-cultural comparisons, and
        ethnohistory, 52, 53
Crow, as horse pastoralists, 139
Crow system, kinship terminology,
        203–4
Cult of domesticity, 260, 262
Cultural anthropology, 6–10
    applied, 17
    ethnographic research, 6–9
    ethnology, 6
    focus of study, 6
Cultural constructs
    gender identity as, 243–44
    meaning of, 243
    race as, 287
Cultural diversity, anthropological
        theories of, 46–51
Cultural ecology
    on cultural diversity, 49
    focus of, 49

Cultural evolution, 33
    defined, 33–34
    evolutionism, 46–47
Cultural identity
    and art, 399–400
    and clothing, 389
    ethnogenesis, 35–36, 440
    See also Ethnic identity
Cultural materialism, 49–50
    on cultural diversity, 49
    emic and etic views, 49–50
    focus of, 49
    and Marxist theory, 49
Cultural minorities
    defined, 436
    ethnic identity, 440–60
    indigenismo policy, 449–51
    xenophobia against, 428, 445
    See also Indigenous cultures; specific
        groups, e.g. Maori
Cultural pluralism
    development of, 33, 443
    xenophobia as reaction, 428, 445
Cultural presuppositions, in
        languages, 85
Cultural relativism, 8–9
    Boas concept of, 47–48
    defined, 8
    female genital mutilation issue
Cultural resource management
        (CRM), 15
Cultural Revolution,
Cultural Survival
Culture
    adaptation to, 26
    anthropological study of. See
        Anthropological approaches
    aspects of, 20–21
    changes in. See Cultural change
    comparative perspective, 5
    countercultures, 31
    cultural core, 26, 32
    cultural integration, 29–29
    cultural knowledge, 21
    cultural models, 22, 31
    defined, 4, 20–21
    global culture, 38–40
    learning of. See Enculturation
    maladaptive adaptations to, 26–28
    meaning of, 4
    naturalized concepts in, 30–31
    as shared assumptions/norms, 22–24,
        34–35
    subcultures, 23
    symbolic and material, 4
    symbols of, 30
    and worldview, 31, 32
Culture change, 33–38
    and colonialism, 36–38, 166–69, 316,
        323, 340, 416–17
    and cultural evolution, 33–36
    and economic development, 452–57
    external forces in, 36–38

    internal forms of, 33–36
    and religion, 373–78
    and subsistence patterns, 150
    syncretism process, 33
Culture history, 35–36
Culture shock, meaning of, 54
Culture wars, U.S., examples of, 31
Cupping, 367
Curacas (Inca elite), 321–22
Cushing, Frank H., 96
Customary law
    defined, 420
    international law, 460
    Papua New Guinea, 458–59

D

Dakota, native language speakers, 80
Dale, Jennifer, 77
Dalmatian language, 90
Dance, 385–86, 395–96, 400
    hula, 400–1
    Native Americans, 395, 400
    Yoruba (Nigeria), 395
D'Anglure, Bernard Saladin, 136
Dani (New Guinea), internal
        warfare, 229
Darfur, the Sudan, 456
Data, fieldwork gathering/reporting,
        55–57
Daughter from Danang, 24
Davidson, Florence Edenshaw, 226
Day of the Dead, 211
Death
    ancestor worship 357
    ancestral spirits, 357
    funerary rites, 364–66
    infants, 96–97
Decision making
    and clans, 193–94
    and families, 211
Deference, 331
Deforestation, 170–72
de las Casas, Bartolemé, 46
DeMarco, Roland, 411
Democratic Republic of the Congo
    refugees from, 436–37
    Suku initiation rites, 364, 366
Demographic studies, linguistic
        anthropology, 78
Demos, John, 181
Denny, J. P., 119
Denominations, development of, 377–78
Dependency, childhood, 95–96
Depopulation, Native Americans,
        14, 414–15, 417
Descent groups, 181–98
    ambilineal descent, 190
    bilateral descent, 182–84
    double descent, 189–90
    inheritance rules, 187
    lineage, 190–91
    matrilineal descent, 185–86

Descent groups (*continued*)
  parallel descent, 190
  patrilineal descent, 185–86
  rules of descent, meaning of, 182–83
  unilineal descent, 182–83, 184–85,
    190–98
Developing countries, consumerism
    in, 174
Developmental anthropology
  goals/mission of, 41
Deviance
  defined, 121
  See also Abnormal behavior
De Vos, George, 289–90
De Waal, Frans, 329–30
Dialects, 78–84
  African Americans, 81–84
  American English (map), 78
  defined, 78–79
Diamond, Jared, 148, 261
Diffusion, and culture change, 37
Diné
  avoidance relationships of, 199
  clans, 193
  cosmology, 371
  creation myth, 353
  divorce, 233
  matrilineal society, 187–88
  Peacemaker conflict resolution,
    343–44
  See also Navajo
Dinka (Sudan), Jonglei Canal, effects
    of, 455
Dirks, Nicholas, 285
Discrimination and inequality. *See*
    Cultural minorities; Gender
    inequality; Racial inequality; Social
    stratification
Disease; *See* Illness
Displacement of language, 69–70
Divination, 363
Divine rights, 371
Diviners, 359
Division of labor
  and age, 131, 157, 176
  and children. *See* Child labor
  foragers, 131, 133, 134–35, 249–50,
    254–56
  and gender, 131, 133, 134–35, 136, 140,
    145–46, 157, 176, 248–50, 257–60
  horticultural societies, 145–46, 257–59
  pastoralists, 140, 142–43, 256–57
Divorce, 232–33
  Kpelle (Liberia), 234, 235
  Native Americans, 233
  patrilineal versus matrilineal societies,
    186, 232–33
  religious rules, 233
  and subsistence patterns, 233
Do, Anh, 405
Dobe. *See* Ju/'hoansi
Dobu Islanders (Melanesia), national
    character of, 120

Dole, Gertrude, 430
Dominance hierarchies, primates, 329
Dominican Republic, Columbus
    landing, 428–29
Dorson, Richard, 94, 155, 209
Double descent, 189–90
Double standard, and patriarchy, 245
Downsizing, 297
Dowry, 223–24
  defined, 223
  dowry deaths, 223–24, 337
Dozier, Edward, 427–28
Draft Declaration on the Rights of
    Indigenous Peoples, 458
Dreamtime, 358, 392
Drugs, native plants, 124, 449, 457
Du Bois, W. E. B., 292–93
Duggar, C. W., 9

E

EarthRights International, 272
East Timor, indigenous resistance
    movement, 444
Eating disorders, as American
    disorder, 122
Ebonics. *See* African-American
    Vernacular English
Economic anthropology
  applied to corporate research, 177
  focus of, 128–29
  subsistence patterns, 129–51
Economic development, effects on
    indigenous, 451–57
Economic sectors, global breakdown,
    174–75
Economic systems
  agriculture as, 169–70
  capitalism, 164–66
  and colonialism, 166–69
  and consumerism, 173–74
  defined, 156
  exchange of products/services, 160–64
  industrial economies, 168–69
  labor, 157–59
  land/resource allocation, 156
  market economy, 164
  and production of goods, 157
  and subsistence patterns, 156
Ecotourism, 460–61
Ecuador
  economic development, effect on
    indigenous, 454–55
  indigenous groups of, 454
Eddystone Point, 423–24
Edelstein, Stuart J., 14
Education. *See* Schooling
Efe (Zaire), infant/adult contact, 101
Egalitarian societies, 278
  chiefdoms, 311
  defined, 278
  features of, 278
  of foragers, 136–37

Eggan, Fred, 200
Egypt, female genital mutilation, 8–9
Ehrenreich, Barbara, 438
Eiselen, W. M., 168
Ejidos (communal lands), 449
El Barrio (New York City), Puerto
    Ricans, 58–59
Elisabetsky, Elaine, 452
Elites
  clothing/ornaments of, 387, 389
  defined, 282
  power of, 282
  and states, 318–19
Ember, Carol, 53, 107, 230
Ember, Melvin, 53, 230
Emblems, 73
Emic views, 49
Emotionalist art, 386
Empires, formation of, 317, 409–10
Empiricism, anthropological approach,
    47–48
Encomiendas (land grants), 417
Enculturation
  age and status of person, 106–7
  behavior, appropriate learning, 104
  child-rearing practices, 97–102
  and colonized people, 36–38
  gender socialization, 107–9
  infant/child learning, 95–96
  versus maladaption, 26–28
  and naming, 97
  naturalization process, 116
  process of, 24–26, 30, 95–96
  rites of passage, 109–10
  schooling, 110–16
  social birth practices, 96–97
  values, learning of, 103–4
Endogamy
  and caste system, 217–18, 284
  defined, 191, 216
  and race, 288
  social organization, impact on, 217–18
Energy sources, and industrialization, 169
English language, 78–84
  African-American Vernacular English
    (AAVE), 81–84
  changes over time, 87
  creole languages of U.S., 87
  dialect map, 78
  versus language diversity in U.S., 79–80
  loanwords in, 88–89
  phonology of, 71
  Standard English, 81, 82–84
Enlightenment, 46–47
Entheogens, psychotropic effects, 124
Environmental circumscription, state
    formation, 319
Equality
  and women. *See* Gender equality
  See also Egalitarian societies
Ervin-Tripp, Susan, 106
Eskimo system, kinship terminology,
    202–3

Esposito, Anita, 106
Ethical issues, Code of Ethics in anthropology, 62
Ethical relativism, 10
Ethiopia, female genital mutilation, 8–9
Ethnic art, 405
Ethnic identity, 440–47
  Africa, ethnic issues, 294–95, 441
  assimilation, 292–93
  ethnogenesis, 35–36, 440
  and nationalism, 442–43
  and transnationalism, 441–42
  tribalization, 440
  Yugoslavia, ethnic issues, 295–96
  See also Cultural identity
Ethnicity, 291–96
  basis of, 291–93
  defined, 291
  ethnics in U.S., 294–96
Ethnobotany, psychotropic substances of plants, 124
Ethnocentrism
  versus cultural relativism, 8–10
  defined, 8
  evolutionism, 46–47
  and naturalized concepts, 30–31
  and social Darwinism, 33–35, 47
Ethnogenesis
  defined, 35–36
  See also Ethnic identity
Ethnography, 6–10
  applied use of, 6
  of communication, 85–86
  defined, 6, 53
  information gathering methods, 6–7
  and polyphony, 62
  See also Fieldwork
Ethnohistory, 52, 53
  and cross-cultural comparisons, 53
  focus of, 53
  Human Relations Area Files (HRAF), 52–53
Ethnology, defined, 6
Ethnomedicine, 379
Ethnomusicology, 395
Ethnosemantics, 84–86
  componential analysis in, 84–85
  cultural presuppositions, 85
  ethnography of communication, 85–86
  focus of study, 84
Etic views, 49
Etienne, Mona, 252
Etoro (New Guinea), homosexual practices, 245
European colonies. *See* Colonialism
Evans-Pritchard, E. E., 63, 142, 193, 220
Evolutionism
  anthropological approach, 46–47
  conflict, view of, 329–30
  and social Darwinism, 47
Evo Morales, 454–55
Exchange systems, 160–64
  barter, 161

market exchange, 163–64
  reciprocity, 160–61
  redistribution, 162–63
  trade, 163
Exogamy
  and clans, 193, 195
  defined, 191, 216
  and social organization, 216–17
Exorcism, 367
Expert witnesses, anthropologists as, 235
Exploitation colonies, 410
Extended family
  defined, 213
External warfare, 230
Extinction
  of indigenous, 424, 451
  of languages, 10–11, 90
Eyak (Alaska)
  extinction of language, 90
  last native, 10–11

F

Facial expressions, universality of, 73–74
Facial tattoos, 388
Factionalism, 322
Factories
  maquiladora system, 438
  See also Industrialization
Fagan, Brian M., 111
Family
  American Anthropological Association on, 210–11
  cohabitation, 215
  conflict resolution, Iran, 332
  defined, 210
  as economic unit, 211
  extended family, 213
  family values issue, 210
  functions of, 211
  joint family, 216
  maternal employment, 264
  nuclear family, 212–13
  single-parent family, 213
  See also Kinship; Marriage
Family size
  decrease in, 214–15
  foragers, 212–13
Family violence
  causes of, 336–37
  dowry deaths, 223–24, 337
  ethnological male bias, 67
Fantan, Tsetsele, 267
Farming. *See* Agricultural societies; Agriculture; Horticultural societies; Horticulture
Fathers
  couvade, 369
  patrilineal descent, 184–86
  social fatherhood, 212
  See also Child rearing
Fears, Darryl, 294
Feeding, infants, 98

Fellata (Sudanese minority), 441
Female genital mutilation (FGM), 8–9
Fenton, William, 313
Ferguson, R. Brian, 442, 453
Ferguson, T. J., 451
Fernandez-Kelly, Maria, 438
Fictive kin, 182
Fields, Jerry, 308
Fieldwork, 51–61
  and culture shock, 54
  defined, 51
  empirical approach, 47
  funding, 54
  participant observation, 54, 58
  steps/activities in, 54–57
  survey research, 58
Fiorenza, Elizabeth, 376
First Nations, 447–49, 453
Fishman, Joshua, 80
Flannery, Kent, 147
Flinders Island, 423–24
Floods, Native American narratives, 45
Floodwater irrigation, 145
Folklore, 104
Folktales
  defined, 396
  See also Narratives
Food production
  and population size, 148–49
  producers versus foragers, 129–30
  and women, 131, 133, 145–46
  See also Agriculture; Horticulture
Foods
  food taboos, 25, 358–59
  irradiation, 169
  of Native Americans, 429
Foot binding, 261–62
Foragers, 132–38
  as bands, 303–5
  bilateral descent, 183, 193
  division of labor, 131, 133, 134–35
  family size, 212–13
  versus food producers, 129–30
  gender status, 254–56
  Inuit and Inupiaq (Arctic), 136–37
  Ju/'hoansi (Kalahari Desert) as, 135
  kinship relations, 182–83
  land/resources management, 133, 156
  leveling mechanisms, 132, 135
  lifestyle, pros/cons of, 176
  as nomads, 132
  optimal foraging theory, 133
  and patrilineal descent, 185–86
  population control methods, 133–34
  population size, 133–34
  residence patterns, 229
  and sharing, 136
  social equality among, 136–37
  time spend foraging, 133
Foraging, defined, 129
Forbes, Jack, 294
Fore (New Guinea), *kuru*, 27–28
Forensic anthropology, focus of, 15

Forero, Joan, 454
Formalist art, 386
Formal sanctions, 329
Foucault, Michel, 121
Foulks, Edward, 123
Fox, Mary, 29, 264
Fox, Robin, 190, 210
Foxwoods casino, 448
France, North American colonies, 415
Frankenthaller, Helen, 390
Fratkin, Elliot, 456
Free trade zones, 438
Freidenberg, Judith, 58–59
French, Laurence, 342–43
Freud, Sigmund, 217
Fried, Morton, 277
Friedl, Ernestine, 250, 252
Friedman, Jonathan, 446
Fry, Douglas, 330–31
Fuentes, Annette, 438
Functionalism
    anthropological approach, 48
    on social stratification, 282–83
Fundamentalism
    Christian, 377–78
    defined, 377
    Islamic, 346–47, 378
Funding for fieldwork, 54
Funerary rites, 364–66
    defined, 364
    India, 364
    Mohawks, 365
    Toraja (Indonesia), 403
    Turkana, 365
Fur trade, 414
Future, diviner prediction of, 359

G

Gailey, Christine, 315–16
Gaines, Edmund, 423
Gajdusek, Carlton, 27–28
Galliland, Mary Kay, 295–96
Gambling casinos, Native Americans, 448
Ganda (Uganda)
    clans, 194–95
    as patrilineal society, 194–95
Gangwasi (ancestral spirits), 357
Gautama, Siddhartha, 375
Gays, same-sex marriage, 221–22
Geertz, Clifford, 49–51
Gender
    defined, 240
    evolutionary perspectives,
        241–43
Gender construct
    gender identity, 240–41
    ideology, impact on, 240
    meaning of, 240
Gender differences
    communication style, 107
    and cultural norms, 23
    language usage, 80–81, 244

nonverbal behaviors, 74
    schooling opportunities, 112–13
Gender equality
    advocacy groups, 272
    defined, 251
    in hunting-gathering communities, 51
    Mohawks, 251
    and patrilineal societies, 186
    Semai (Malaysia), 332–33
    societal features, 251–53, 278
Gender identity
    clothing/hairstyle/body art, 244,
        247, 389
    as cultural construct, 240–41
    defined, 107
    and naming, 108–9
Gender inequality
    and colonialism, 252
    defined, 251
    gender gap, 260, 264
    occupational segregation, 260
    and patriarchy, 251
    and religion, 251, 368, 377–78
Gender preference, and culture, 108
Gender relations, defined, 248
Gender roles
    changes and ideology, 250, 255
    and cultural integration, 28
    defined, 248
    division of labor, 131, 133–36, 140,
        145–46, 157, 176, 248–50, 254–66
    men as house-husbands, 271
Gender socialization, 107–9
    and family interaction, 109
    gender and expected behaviors, 107
Gender status, 253–63
    and agricultural societies, 259–60
    and culture change, 255
    foragers, 254–56
    horticultural societies, 257–59
    pastoralists, 256–57
    See also Gender equality; Gender
        inequality
Genealogy, LINKAGES project, 205
Generalized reciprocity, 160
Genetic engineering, agricultural
        products, 169
Genocide
    of Australian aborigines, 52
    and language extinction, 90
    of Tasmanians, 423–24
    of Tutsi (Rwanda), 444–45
Germany
    Papua New Guinea colonialism,
        440, 444
    refugees in, 437
Gettysburg Address (1863), 276
Gezira Scheme (Sudan), 441
Ghadially, Rehana, 223–24
Ghana, Akan proverbs, 397
Ghost Dance movement, 37–38, 374
Ghost marriage, 232
    defined, 220

as levirate, 232
    of Nuer (Sudan), 220
Ghosts, 357
Gibbs, James, 234
Gill, Sam, 189
Gimbutas, Marija, 392
Gitksan (British Columbia)
    oral histories, validity of, 46
    songs of, 394
Gleason, Jean, 106–7
Glick, J., 119
Global culture, 38–40
    defined, 38
Global identity
    defined, 446
    and mass media, 446–47
Globalization
    agents of, 39–40
    and art, 399–405
    and child labor, 101
    and comparative perspective, 5
    and consumerism, 38–39
    defined, 5, 435–36
    economic sectors, 174
    global identity, 446–47
    historical view, 39
    and international organizations,
        435–36, 458–60
    and Internet, 442, 446–47
    and language loss, 90
    and mass communication, 40,
        446–47
    and migration, 436–40
    multinational corporations, 39–40,
        436–38
    and nonverbal gestures, 73
    postcolonial era, 428–29
    and religion, 376–78
    and service jobs, 174
    and tourism, 460–61
    and warfare, 340–44
    women in labor force, 266–71, 438
Gods and goddesses
    polytheism, 356
    Roman, 355
Goffman, Erving, 331
Goodale, Jane, 305
Goodall, Jane, 13
Goodman, Felicitas, 360
Goose Society (Hidatsa), 309
Gorman, Peter, 452–53
Gough, Kathleen, 63, 210, 212,
    220, 229
Graburn, Nelson, 255, 400
Great Britain
    Australian colonialism, 33, 52, 421,
        423–24
    dark-skinned immigrant status, 440
    India independence, 428
    industrialization, 168–69, 260
    land grabs, 421
    missionaries, 419
    North American colonies, 413–15

Papua New Guinea colonialism, 440, 444, 458–59
Tasmanians, genocide of, 423–24
Grosjean, Francois, 79
Grossman, A., 64
Guadalupe-Hidalgo, Treaty of (1846), 428
Guarani (Paraguay, Brazil), land rights, 462
Guibault, J., 404
Guillaume, Alfred, 376
Gullah, 78, 87
Gypsies, xenophobia toward, 445

H

Haciendas (estates), 417
Hafner, Katie, 17
Haida (Canada)
    arranged marriage, 226
    pregnancy taboo, 359
Haiti, spirit possession, 367, 377
Hall, Judith, 74, 91
Hallucinogens, ritual use of, 124
Halperin, Rhoda, 184
Hardman, Charlotte, 96, 225
Hariot, Thomas, 415
Harris, Grace, 335
Harris, Marvin, 49, 259, 291, 372
Hart, C. W. M., 220
Hartmann, Heidi, 260
Harvey, Youngsook Kim, 367
Hasidic Jews (New York), 23
Hassrick, Royal, 233
Hawaii
    hula dance, 400–1
    Office of Hawaiian Affairs, 448–49
Hawaiian Creole, 79, 87
Hawaiian system, kinship terminology, 202–3
Hazardous work, child labor in, 159
Healers, 359–60
    childbirth attendants, 95
    healing rituals, 359–60, 366–68
    role of, 359–60
    shamans, 360
Healing rituals, 366–70
    cupping, 367
    Macumba trance, 367, 369
    magic, 368–70
    spiritual treatments, 367–68
Health status
    agriculture, impact of, 148, 176
    See also Illness
Heath, Shirley, 79
Hefner, Robert, 446
Helplessness, infants, 95
Henley, Nancy, 74
Herding, pastoralists, 138–43
Herman, Edward, 446
Hesse-Biber, Sharlene, 29, 264
Hibakusha (atomic bomb survivors), 290

Hidatsa
    age grades, 308–9
    naming practices, 97
Hijras (transgenders), 245
Hilder, 426
HimRights, 298
Hindi, 88, 89
Hinduism
    Buddhism as reaction to, 375
    and caste, 284–85, 375
    cows as sacred, 49–50
    spirits in, 356
    See also India
Hindustani language, 88
Hispanic Americans, marginalized in U.S., 290–91
Hispaniola, 424–25, 428
Historical linguistics, 10, 87–91
    focus of study, 88
    language families, study of, 88–91
Historical particularism, 47–48
Historical tales, 396–97
Hitchcock, Robert, 461
HIV/AIDS, African women, 267
Hoebel, E. Adamson, 302
Holistic perspective
    elements of, 4–5
    ethnography as, 6
Hollan, Douglas, 334
Holtzman, Jon, 143
Holy People, 391–92
Home languages, Native American speakers, 80
Homestead, defined, 210
Hominids, 241–42, 249
Homosexuality
    and cultural norms, 245
    same-sex marriage, 221–22
Hopi
    faction, 322
    as horticulturalists, 145
    kachinas, 357
    language, Sapir-Whorf hypothesis, 76
Horse pastoralism, Native Americans, 139
Horticultural societies, 144–47
    division of labor, 144–46
    gender status in, 257–59
    kinship relations, 182–83
    and leisure time, 173
    lifestyle, pros/cons of, 176
    matrilineal descent, 185–86
    population size, 131
    residence patterns, 229
    settlement pattern, 131, 144–45
    social equality, 278
    surplus in, 144
Horticulture
    defined, 130, 144
    slash-and-burn, 144–45
    tools used, 144
Hotevilla, 322

Household
    defined, 210
    See also Family
House-husbands, 271
Howells, William, 424
Hua, Cai, 221
Huánuco Pampa (Peru), craft production, 151
Huitzilopochtli, Aztec god, 362
Hula dance, 400–1
Human evolution, and primates, 13
Humanity, anthropology as a study of, 3
Human Relations Area Files (HRAR), 52–53
Human relationships
    avoidance relationships, 199
    descent groups, 181–98
    joking relationships, 199
    kinship, 181–85
    marital. *See* Marriage
    sexuality, 244–45
Human sacrifice
    Aztec, 362
    Inca, 151
Human trafficking
    children, 159, 298
    countries involved, 298
    prevention of, 298
Hume, Lynne, 358, 392
Humor, as symbolic communication, 30
Hunt, George, 220
Hunter, Ruby, 33
Hunting-gathering communities and gender equality, 51
    See also Foragers
Hurons (Canada), 426
Hursey, Charlotte, 324
Hutus (Rwanda), genocide of Tutsis, 444–45
Hydraulic hypothesis of state, 319
Hymes, Dell, 85

I

Iban (Western Borneo), residence pattern, 231–32
Identity. *See* Cultural identity; Ethnic identity; Gender identity; Global identity
Ideology
    and gender constructs, 270–71
    of inequality, 282
    transmission of, 282
Igbo (Nigeria), 252, 258–59
    credit associations, 164
Illness
    contagious, native depopulation, 14, 415–16, 418
    healers, 359–60
    healing rituals, 359–60, 366–68
    HIV/AIDS and African women, 267
    as maladaptive adaptation, 27–28
    organ trafficking, 298

Illness (*continued*)
  sickle-cell anemia, 14–15
  spiritual causes of, 366–68
  witchcraft as cause, 368–70
Il-rah (tribal road), 141
Imams, 378
Imitative magic, 369
Imperialism
  defined, 409–10
  See also Colonialism
Inbreeding, incest taboo, 217
Inca (Peru/Bolivia)
  craft specialization, 151
  Europeans, view of, 425–26
  human sacrifice, 151
  Machu Picchu, 320
  mita (conscripted labor), 418
  parallel descent, 190
  quipu (knot), 393
  redistribution, 162
  sibling marriage, 321
  state, features of, 321–22
  See also Andeans
Incest taboo
  and marriage rules, 216
  origin of, 217
Independent self, 118
India
  arranged marriage, 230–31
  caste system, 218, 284–85
  cows as sacred, 49–50
  dowry deaths, 223–24, 337
  female infanticide, 223
  funerary rites, 364
  gender inequality, 251
  hijras (transgenders), 245
  Hindustani language, 88
  independence of, 428
  industrialization of, 168
  land ownership, 167
  Nayar marital forms, 220–21
  patrilineal system, 186–87
  polyandry, 218–19
  residence rules, rural North,
    230–31
  See also Hinduism
Indian Arts and Crafts Act (1990), 403
Indian Crimes Act (1976), 342–43
Indian Gaming Regulatory Act
  (1988), 448
Indian Self-Determination and
  Education Act (1975), 448
Indigenismo policy, 449–51
Indigenous cultures
  anthropologists as advocates, 15
  contemporary reparations. *See* Cultural
    minorities, modern policies
  customary law, 420, 458–60
  defined, 7, 455
  depopulation and colonialism, 14,
    414–17
  dispossession for land reserves, 456,
    460–61

economic development, effects of,
  451–57
ethnography of, 6–7
extinction of, 451
and forces of change. *See* Culture
  change
genocide of, 52, 428, 444–45
International Decade of
  (1994–2004), 457
and international law, 460
legal rights of, 458–60
protection policies, 447–57
tribalization, 440
See also specific groups by name, e.g.,
  Australian aborigines
Individualistic society, child rearing
  in, 118
Indonesia
  deforestation, 171
  female genital mutilation, 8–9
  Islamization of, 443–44
  Javanese, redistribution of, 443–44
  See also Toraja (Indonesia)
Industrial agriculture, 169–72
  features of, 169
  negative aspects of, 169–72
Industrialization, 168–69
  Asian centers of, 446
  defined, 168
  historical view, 168–69, 260
Industrial Revolution, negative effects
  of, 26
Industrial societies
  bilateral descent, 183–84
  and consumerism, 173–74
  gender status, 260, 262–63
  nuclear family in, 212–13
  residence patterns, 229
Industry, applied anthropology, 17
Inequality
  religious rationale, 371
  See also Cultural minorities; Gender
    inequality; Racial inequality; Social
    stratification
Infanticide
  female, India, 223
  and population control, 134, 144
Infants
  child-rearing practices, 97–102
  death, parental grief, 96–97
  social birth practices, 96–97
Informal sanctions, 329
Informed consent, 62, 64
Inheritance rules, 187–90
  and ambilineal descent, 190
  defined, 187
  and gender preferences, 108
  matrilineal societies, 187
  Nuer pastoralists, 142
  and parallel descent, 190
  primogeniture, 317
Initiation rites, 364
  Apache, 365–66

Christian, 364
circumcision as, 110, 309, 366
forms of, 109–10
Jewish, 364
puberty, 364–66
Suku (Congo), 366
Innovation, and culture change, 36
Institute for Developmental
  Anthropology (IDA), mission of, 41
Instrumental art, 386
Intensive agriculture, methods/
  tools, 149
Intercultural communication, 73–74
Interdependent self, 118
Inter-Group Fighting Act (1973), 459
Internal warfare, 229, 230
International Center for Research on
  Women, 272
International Decade of the World's
  Indigenous People (1994–2004), 457
International Fund for Agricultural
  Development (IFAD), 272
International law, and indigenous
  cultures, 460
International organizations, goals of,
  435–36
Internet, and globalization, 446–47
Interpretive anthropology
  on cultural diversity, 49
  focus of, 50–51
Inuit (Arctic)
  abnormal behavior (*nuthkavihak*), 121
  biological differences of, 13
  culture change, effects on, 255
  division of labor, 253
  as foragers, 132, 135, 136, 253, 254–56
  marriage/residence pattern, 254
  pibloktoq (Arctic hysteria), 123
  pregnancy taboo, 358–59
  sculptures/artwork of, 400
  social incorrigibles (*arankan*), 122
  song duels, 331–32
  songs, 394
  spatial tasks, mastery of, 119
  spiritual beliefs, 255
  tattoos, 388
  women, status of, 254–56
Inupiaq (Alaska)
  as foragers, 136–37
Inventions, and cultural change, 36
Iran
  Basseri pastoralists, 139–41
  family conflict mediation, 332
  refugees in, 436–37
Iraq
  marriage folktale, 209–10
  refugees in, 436–37
Iroquois
  chief, selection/role of, 196
  division of labor, 253
  gender preference at birth, 108
  as horticulturalists, 230
  matrilocal residence, 230

polyandry, 218
women, status of, 253
Iroquois Confederacy
colonialism, effect on, 340–41
constitution, 312–13
features of, 308, 312–13
origin of, 308
tribes of, 308, 312
Iroquois system, kinship terminology, 201–2
Irradiation of foods, 169
Irrigation
floodwater system, 145
Islam
denominations of, 378
on divorce, 233
founding of, 376
fundamentalists and conflicts, 346–47, 378
Islamization of Indonesia, 443–44
spread of, 409, 411
Islamic Development Bank, 444
Israel-Palestine conflict, 345–46
Itel'men (Siberia), preservation of language, 90
Itoh, Shinji, 13
Iwu, Maurice, 457

J

Jackson, Donald, 418
Jackson, Robert, 167, 423
Jannequin, C., 425
Japan
Ainu people, 90, 290
ancestor worship, 357
apologies, 331–32
Burakumin, 289–90
child socialization in, 105–6
discrimination in, 289–90
and human trafficking, 298
mother/child bond, 189
national character, 120
Jargons, study of, 84
Javanese (Indonesia), redistribution of population, 443–44
Jefferson, Thomas, 408
Jesus Christ, 375–76
Jewelry
Navajo, 401–2
and social status, 389
Jews. *See* Judaism; Orthodox Judaism
Jivaro (Peru), women and food production, 145
Joama (Sudanese minority), 441
Johnson, Allen, 173
Johnson, Mark, 173
Joint family, 216
Joking relationships, 199
Jones, Barbara, 235
Jordan, Bani Hamida division of labor, 131

Judaism
denominations of, 377
naming practices, 97
puberty rites, 364
Orthodox. *See* Orthodox Judaism
Ju/'hoansi (Kalahari desert)
ancestral spirits, 357
childbirth practices, 95
conflict avoidance, 330
division of labor, 133, 253
as foragers, 133, 134–35, 254–57
hours in workweek, 133
marriage/residence pattern, 254
naming of children, 97
women, status of, 254–57
Juju (sorcery), 121

K

Kachinas, 357
Kahlenberg, Mary, 401–2
Kaisiepo, Victor, 457
Kalahari Desert
Nyae Nyae Conservancy, 461
See also Ju/'hoansi
Kaluli (Papua New Guinea)
as horticulturalists, 146–47
songs, 394–95
Kaska, Two-Spirits, 246
Katz, Richard, 95
Kehoe, Alice, 38
Kellman, Shelly, 259
Kelly, Raymond, 245
Kendall, Laurel, 367
Kennewick man, 451
Kenya
benga pop music, 404
Luo, colonialism, impact on, 37
Taita conflict resolution ritual, 334–35
See also Maasai
Kia (trance), 95
Kichwa (Ecuador), 454
Kindred groups, 183
Kingdom
defined, 316
primogeniture, 317
Kinship, 181–85
anthropological study of, 47, 50, 55
bands, 303–6
change, effects on, 199–201
clans, linkages to, 195
defined, 182
descent rules. *See* Descent groups
family roles, 50
fictive kin, 182
relationships by blood, 182, 210
relationships by marriage, 182, 210
and subsistence patterns, 185–86
tribes, 306–7
See also Family
Kinship terminology systems, 201–4
Crow system, 203–4
Eskimo system, 202–3

Hawaiian system, 202–3
Iroquois system, 202
Omaha system, 204
Sudanese system, 204
Kitayama, Shinobu, 118
Kiver, Dr. Eugene, 45
Klein, Alan, 416
Kluckhohn, Clyde, 21
Knight, R., 404
Kochems, Lee, 246
Koller, John, 284, 375
Koloa (women's valuables), 316
Kopytoff, Igor, 366
Korea
shamanism in, 360
spirit possession, 360, 367
Koreans, discrimination in Japan, 290
Koro (fear of penile retraction), 123
Korubu (Brazil), 452
Koso-Thomas, Olayinka, 8–9
Kottak, Conrad, 291
Kpelle (Liberia)
content-bound thought, 119
divorce, 234, 236
marriage options, 234, 236
rites of passage, 110
Krebs, J. R., 133
Kroeber, Alfred, 21
Kshatriyas, 284
Kumar, Pramod, 223–24
Kuna (Panama), *molas* (embroidered items), 400
Kuru, and cannibalism, 27–28
Kwakiutl (British Columbia). *See* Kwakwaka'wakw
Kwakwaka'wakw (British Columbia)
ambilineal descent, 190
arranged marriage, 227
lineages, 191
marital forms among, 220
national character of, 120
potlatch, 160–61
as sedentary foragers, 160
slavery, 287

L

Labeling issues, in anthropology, 62
Labor
and children. *See* Child labor
colonial exploitation of, 167–68
and industrialization, 168–69
labor migration, 436–40
maquiladora system, 438
organizing. *See* Division of labor
and social status, 159
specialization of, 157, 282–83, 317
women in global work force, 266–69, 438
women in U.S. work force, 263–66
Labov, William, 81–84, 116, 286, 398
Lactose intolerance, 13
Ladd, Edmund, 451

Lafitau, Joseph, 252, 258
Lakoff, George, 173
Lako, George, 455
Lakota
  divorce, 233
  as horse pastoralists, 139
  native language speakers, 80
  trade with whites, cultural conse-
    quences, 416–17
  Two-Spirits, 247–48
Lamphere, Louise, 251
Land-cession agreements, 424
Land ownership. *See* Property ownership
Language, 67–91
  African-American dialect, 81–84
  anthropological study of. *See* Linguistic
    anthropology
  creoles, 87
  defined, 68–69
  dialects, 78–84
  diversity in U.S. *See* English language
  extinction of, 10, 90
  features of, 68–70
  gender differences in use, 80–81, 244
  jargons, 84
  lingua franca, 87
  linguistic diversity of U.S., 79–80
  morphology, 71
  Native American. *See* Native American
    languages
  nonverbal communication, 73–74
  phonology, 70–71
  pidgins, 87
  production, physical aspects, 69–71
  semantics, 71–72
  social class differences, 81, 286–87
  sociolinguistics, 75
  syntax, 71
  as system of symbols, 30–31, 32, 68–69
  universal grammar, 71
Language families
  cognates in, 88
  loanwords, examples of, 88–89, 91
  study of, 88–91
Lankard, Dune, 11
La Salle, Sieur de, 200
Latah (startle reaction), 122
Latin America
  women migrant laborers, 438
  See also specific countries
Lawal, Amina, 245
Lawley, Sir Arthur, 424
Laws
  customary law, 420, 458–60
  and states, 318
  white, imposition on indigenous, 420
Lea, Luke, 423
Leacock, Eleanor, 51, 252
Leadership
  bands, 303–4
  divine right, 371
  tribes, 306
  See also Chiefs

Learning Lodge Institute, 76–77
Lebra, Sugiyama, 331
Lee, Richard, 97, 133, 134–35, 253, 330
Legal anthropology
  expert witnesses, anthropologists
    as, 235
  and international disputes, 349
Leibowitz, Lila, 249
LeJeune, Paul, 219
Lemarchand, Rene, 445
Lesbians, same-sex marriage, 221–22
Leveling mechanisms
  defined, 132
  foragers, 135
Levinson, Stephen, 331
Levirate, widowhood in, 232
Lévi-Strauss, Claude, 49, 50
Lewis, I. M., 252, 367
Lewis, Meriwether, 408
Lewis and Clark Expedition, 408
Liberation theology, 454
Lincoln, Abraham, 276
Lindenbaum, Shirley, 27
Lindenfeld, Jacqueline, 81
Lindfors, Bernth, 104
Lineages, 190–92
  defined, 190
  endogamy, 191
  exogamy, 191
  Kwakwaka'wakw
    (British Columbia), 191
Lingua francas, 87
Linguistic anthropology, 10–11, 75–86
  applied, 17
  demographic studies of language, 78
  ethnography of communication, 85–86
  ethnosemantics, 84–86
  focus of, 10–11, 75
  historical linguistics, 10–11, 87–91
  language change, study of, 87–91
  Sapir-Whorf hypothesis, 75–78
LINKAGES project, 205
Literature. *See* Narratives
Little Wolf, Cheyenne chief, 415
Liu Zhaoxiang, 262
Loanwords, 88–89
Lockwood, Victoria, 269
Loeb, Edwin, 341
Lohorung Rai (Nepal)
  arranged marriage, 225, 226
  social birth rites, 96
  wedding ceremony, 225
Loita Naimina Enkiyio Conservation
  Trust, 456
Louisiana Creole, 87
Luo (Kenya), colonialism, impact on, 37

M

Maasai (Kenya/Tanzania)
  advocacy organizations of, 456
  age grades, 309–10
  education, 113

medical practices of, 379
  spirit possession, 368
  territory, loss of, 456
MacArthur, R. H., 133
Machiguenga (Peru), horticultural
  societies, hours worked, 173
Machu Picchu (Peru), 320
Mack, Burton, 376
MacKay, Fergus, 460
Macumba trance, 367, 369
Mad cow disease, cause of, 28
Magic, 368–70
Maidus, as foragers, 138
Major Crimes Act (1885), 342
Malaria, and sickle-cell trait, 14–15
Malaysia
  female genital mutilation, 8–9
  labor migration, 436–37
  multiculturalism of, 446
  See also Semai
Male concubinage, Kpelle (Liberia), 234
Male dominance, 252, 278
  China, 261–62
  defined, 251
  universality of, 252
  See also Patriarchy
Mali, female genital mutilation, 8–9
Malinowski, Bronislaw, 47–48, 217
Mana (spiritual power), 314, 357
Mandela, Nelson, 348, 427
Manifest destiny, 422
Mann, Barbara, 308
Manus (New Guinea), Mead's study
  of, 47
Maori (New Zealand)
  facial tattoos, 384–88, 388
  language revitalization, 78
  mana (spirit power), 314
Maquiladora system, 438
Marable, Manning, 291
Marcus, George, 61
Maritime enclaves, 410
Market economy
  capitalism, 165–66
  colonialism and spread of, 166–68
  elements of, 164–65
Market exchange, defined, 163–64
Markus, Hazel, 118
Marquesas (South Pacific), infant
  feeding, 98
Marriage
  arranged marriage, 226–27
  bridewealth and brideservice, 222–23
  cousin marriage, 191–92
  cultural differences, 48, 53
  defined, 211
  divorce, 232–33
  dowry, 224–24
  endogamy, 191, 217–18
  exogamy, 191, 216–17
  functions of, 211–12
  ghost marriage, 232
  incest taboo, 216–17

levirate pattern, 232
monogamy, 218
in patrilineal versus matrilineal
    societies, 186, 211–12
plural marriage, 218
polyandry, 218–19
polygamy, 218
polygyny, 218–20
rare forms of, 220–21
residential patterns, 228–30
same-sex, 221–22
sibling marriage, 217, 315, 321
social organization, impact on,
    216–18
sororate pattern, 232
wedding as rite of passage,
    225–28
widowhood, 232
Martin, Sidney, 77
Marwick, M. G., 370
Marxist theory
    and conflict perspectives, 51
    and cultural materialism, 49
    and social class, 286
    and social stratification, 283
Massasoit, Wampanoag chief, 415
Mass communication
    and global identity, 446–47
    and globalization, 39–40,
        446–47
    Internet, 446–47
Mataira, Peter, 314
Material culture, 4
Materialist approaches
    to cultural diversity, 49
    cultural materialism, 49–50
    cultural ecology, 48–49
    focus of, 48
Mate selection
    arranged marriage, 226–27
    courtship, 227
Matriclans, 192
Matrilineal societies, 184–89
    avoidance relationships of, 199
    characteristics of, 184–86
    defined, 185
    emotional bonds, 186, 188–89
    and horticultural societies, 184
    inheritance rules, 187–89
    marriage/divorce in, 186, 211–12,
        232–33
    Mohawk society, 196
    prevalence of, 185–86
    residence patterns, 228–30
Matrilocal residence, 228
Matthaei, Julie, 260, 263
Maya (Mexico, Central America)
    discrimination against, 449–50
    infant sleeping arrangements, 100
Maybury-Lewis, David, 444, 451–52
Mbuti Pygmy (Zaire), gender
    equality, 254
McAllester, David, 394

McDermott, LeRoy, 392
McElroy, Ann, 13
McEvilley, Thomas, 399
McWhorter, John, 83
Mead, Margaret, 47
Medical anthropology
    applied, 17
    ethnomedicine, 379
    focus of, 14, 379
Medicinal plants
    biodiversity prospecting, 457
    psychotropic effects of, 124
Mediums, 359, 367, 369
Meggers, Betty, 145
Meier, John, 375
Melanesia
    big men, 440
    cargo cults, 374–75
    Dobu Islanders' national
        character, 120
    See also Trobriand Islanders
Mencher, Joan, 220
Menomini language, 90
Mental illness. See Psychological
    disorders
Merrill, William, 451
Merivale, Herman, 421
Merry, Sally, 420
Messianic movements, 374
Mexican-American War, 428
Mexican Revolution (1910), 323
Mexico
    alebrijes (carvings), 405
    depopulation of natives, 415
    indigenismo policy, 459–61
    maquiladora system, 438
    native resistance/revolts, 427–28,
        450–51
    Spanish colonialism, 415, 418
    Zapatistas, 450–51
    Zapotec dance, 400
    See also Aztec; Maya
Meyer, Roy, 423
Miami, Two-Spirits, 247
Michelson, Truman, 360
Middle East
    regional warfare, 345–48
    See also Islam; specific countries
Migration,
    labor migration, 436–40
    refugees, 143, 436–37
    rural-to-urban, 436–37
    transnational, 439–40
Mikvas (purifying baths), 377
Millinerian movements, 374
Mills, C. Wright, 318
Mimetic art, 386
Mina, Hanna, 162–63
Mind, theory of, 50
Minority groups. See Cultural
    minorities
Mintz, Sidney, 130
Mirante, Edith, 434–35

Missionaries, practices against
    indigenous, 418–19
Missionism, defined, 411
Mission system, Spanish, 418
Mistaken Chief, Duane, 76
Mita (conscripted labor), 418
Miwoks, as foragers, 138
Mixtec (Mexico), 172
Mobility. See Class mobility
Modernization, and cultural
    change, 33
Mohammed VI, king of Morocco, 323
Mohave, Two-Spirits, 246
Mohawks
    clans, 196
    divorce, 233
    funerary rites, 365
    gender equality, 251
    gender preference at birth, 108
    in Iroquois Confederacy, 196, 308,
        312–13
    marriage/wedding, 228
    as matrilineal society, 196
Moieties
    defined, 195
    Mohawks, 196
Molas (embroidered items), 400
Money, functions of, 164
Mongolians, as pastoralists, 139
Mono, Two-Spirits, 247
Monogamy
    defined, 218
    serial monogamy, 218
Monotheism, 356, 375–76
Montagnais (Canada), 51
Mooney, James, 37
Moore, Henrietta, 268
Morality tales, 94–95
Morelli, G. A., 98, 100, 120
Morgan, Frank, 76
Morgan, Lewis Henry, 47
Morioka, Kiyomi, 357
Morocco, Sidi Lahcen fieldwork
    experience, 56–57
Morphemes, 71
Morphology, 71
Morris, Craig, 151
Mothers
    Japanese, 189
    Native American, 99
Mothers
    infant death, 96–97
    infant sleeping arrangements,
        98–99, 100
    maternal employment, 264
    See also Childbirth; Child
        rearing
Motherwell, Robert, 390–91
Mott, Lucretia, 263
Muhammad, 376
Multiculturalism
    and cultural pluralism, 33, 443
    xenophobia against, 428, 445

Multinational corporations
    and globalization, 39–40
    outsourcing, 438
Munroe, R. H., 117, 119–20
Munroe, R. M., 117, 119–20
Murphy, C., 12
Murphy, Jane, 121–22
Murray, Sir Hubert, 422
Music, 394–95
    ethnomusicology, 395
Muslims. *See* Islam
Myanmar, and human trafficking, 298
Mygatt, Jacob, 181
Myths, cultural connections among, 50

N

Na (China), marital forms among, 221
Nai'es (puberty rite), 365–66
Namias, June,
Naming
    cultural practices, 97
    and gender identity, 108
    in rites of passage, 110
Narratives, 396–99
    and child rearing, 95, 98, 104
    creation myths, 20, 45, 353
    and culture specificity, 2–3
    defined, 45
    on diversity of language, 67–68
    on economic systems, 155
    folktales, 396
    food crops, origin of, 128
    on gender roles, 240
    on governance systems, 302
    morality tales, 94–95
    on new bride and mother-in-law, 209
    oral, 45–46, 396–98
    on origin of art, 384–85
    proverbs as, 397
    riddles, 397–98
    sacred, 396
    on societal conflict, 328
    on status and wealth, 276
    storytelling, 398
    values transmitted by, 104
    written, 398–99
Naskapi (Labrador), 51
Natchez, classes of, 216–17
Nation building, and colonialism,
    167, 409
National character
    Benedict on, 120
    defined, 119
National Foundation for the Indian
    (FUNAI), 453–53, 462
Nationalism, 428, 442–43
Native American Graves Protection and
    Repatriation Act (NAGPRA) (1990),
    450–51
Native American languages
    Athabascan language family, 11
    communication style, 30

cultural presuppositions in, 85
    extinction of, 10
    home languages, statistics on, 80
    preservation of, 17, 76–78, 90
    Sapir-Whorf hypothesis, 75–78
Native American Religious Freedom
    Restoration act (1993), 448
Native Americans
    burial ground protection, 450–51
    casino operations, 448
    child education, 114–15
    colonialism, impact. *See* Native
        Americans and colonialism
    conflict resolution, 340–44
    criminal acts, federal jurisdiction,
        342–44
    dances of, 395, 400
    divorce, 233
    food crops of, 429
    gender preference at birth, 108
    as horticulturalists, 145
    infant/mother contact, 99
    kinship terminology systems, 201–4
    marginalized in U.S., 290–91
    and matrilineal societies, 185, 187,
        189, 193, 196, 216–17
    as pastoralists, 139
    potlatch, 9, 160–61
    religion, freedom to practice, 448
    rites of passage, 110
    same-sex marriage, 221
    self-government of, 448–49
    tax immunity, 448
    treaties/legislation related to (1960s-
        present), 447–49
    Two-Spirits (third gender), 246–48
    U.S. Census on (2001), 294
    warfare, 340–42, 344
    See also specific tribes, e.g. Mohawks
Native Americans and colonialism
    Anglicization, 419–20, 424
    culture change, 416–17, 419–20
    depopulation, 14, 415–17
    European disease, 14, death from,
        415–16
    explorers' impressions, 424–25
    food crops, expansion of, 428–29
    Ghost Dance movement, 37–38,
        374–75
    land-cession agreements, 424
    laws/social controls imposed on, 420
    manifest destiny, 422
    missionary practices, 418–19
    mission system, 419
    reservation system, 422–24
    resettlement policies, 410
    resistance and revolts, 427–28
    schooling by whites, influence of,
        419–20
    trade, 414, 416–17, 425–26
    view of Europeans, 425–26
    Wounded Knee Creek massacre, 38
Nativistic movements, 374

Naturalization, 116
Naturalized concepts, and culture, 30–31
Navajo
    blankets, 401–2
    child learning, 103
    native language speakers, 80
    sandpainting, 391–92
    Two-Spirits, 247
    See also Diné
Nayar (India), marital forms among,
    220–21
Nazism, 345
Neakok, Sadie Brower, 136–37
Negative reciprocity
    defined, 161
    potlatch as, 160–61
Negative sanctions, 328–29
Neihardt, John, 121
Neolocal residence, 229
Nepal. *See* Lohorung Rai
Netherlands, slave trade, 411
Networks, for redistribution, 162–63
New Guinea
    British colonialism, 440, 444, 458–59
    German colonialism, 440, 444
    redistribution of population, 443–44
    See also Papua New Guinea
Newing, Helen, 461
Newman, Barnett, 390
Newman, Katherine, 297
New Zealand. *See* Maori
Ngorongoro Conservation Area
    (NCA), 456
Nietschmann, Bernard, 443–44, 447
Nigeria
    economic development, effects on
        indigenous, 457
    Igbo women, status of, 258–59
    See also Ashanti; Yoruba
Nineteenth Amendment, 263
Nomads
    and body art, 388
    foragers as, 132–33, 134
    lifestyle, pros/cons, 176
    pastoralists as, 140–41
Nongovernmental organizations
    (NGOs), 324
Nonverbal communication, 73–74
    cultural differences, 73–74
    intercultural communications, 73
    as status indicator, 74
Norms
    defined, 22, 32
    learning. *See* Enculturation
    sanctions, 328–29
    See also Culture
North America
    colonialism. *See* Colonialism; Native
        Americans and colonialism
    See also Canada; Mexico; United States
North American Free Trade Agreement
    (NAFTA), 438, 450
North Korea, and human trafficking, 298

Norway, Sami reindeer herding, 21
Nuclear family, 212–13
   and bilateral descent, 212
   defined, 212
   functions of, 212–13
Nuclear weapons, 348–49
Nuer (Sudan)
   bridewealth, 222
   child learning, 103
   conflict avoidance, 338
   economic change, effects of,
      142–43
   domestic violence, 63
   ghost marriage, 232
   inheritance rights, 142
   as pastoralists, 140, 142–43
   as refugees, 143
   same-sex marriage, 221
Nuthkavihak (mentally ill person), 121
Nyae Nyae Conservancy, 461
Nyanga (Zaire), narratives on
   economic system, 155

O

Oaxacan Valley (Mexico), *alebrijes*
   (carvings), 405
Obeng, Samuel Gyasi, 397
Object intrusion, 367
Objective views, etic, 49
O'Brien, Jay, 441
Observation, and enculturation, 24
Occupational segregation, 260
Ochs, Elinor, 109
Office of Hawaiian Affairs, 448–49
Oglala, Black Elk, 121
Ogoni (Nigeria), economic
   development, effects of, 457
Ojibwe, native language speakers, 77
Okinawans (Japan), discrimination
   against, 290
Ok Tedi mine, effects on indigenous, 172
Omaha, Two-Spirits, 247
Omaha system, kinship terminology, 204
Oneida, in Iroquois Confederacy, 308,
   312–13
Ong, Aihwa, 268, 436–37
Onondaga, in Iroquois Confederacy, 308,
   312–13
Operation Amazonia, 452
Optimal foraging theory, 133
Oracles, 363
Oral traditions, as historical record,
   45–46, 396–97
Organ transplantation, organ
   trafficking, 298
Orthodox Judaism
   on divorce, 233
   gender inequality among, 251
   Hasidic Jews, 23
   practices of, 377
Osage, Two-Spirits, 247
Osterhammel, Jurgen, 409

Otomac (Venezuela), psychotropic plant
   use, 124
Ottenberg, Phoebe, 146
Ottenberg, Simon, 146, 258
Ottley, Bruce, 459
Outsourcing
   by multinationals, 438
   service jobs, 174
Owomoyela, Oyekan, 104
Oxfam, 324

P

Pacification, 422
Pacific Islanders
   amok (intense outbursts), 122–23
   depopulation of, 417
Paiute language, Sapir-Whorf
   hypothesis, 75
Pakistan, refugees in, 436–37
Palawa, 424
Paleoanthropology, focus of, 13
Palestine
   Israel-Palestine conflict, 345–46
Panama, Kuna *molas* (embroidered
   items), 400
Papago, native language speakers, 80
Papua New Guinea
   cannibalism and *kuru*, 27–28
   cargo cults, 374–75
   colonialism, 440, 444, 458–59
   customary law, 458–59
   Dani internal warfare, 229
   economic development, effects on in-
      digenous, 172
   Etoro homosexual practices, 245
   Kaluli, 146–47
   kuru, 27–28
   Manus, Mead's study, 47
   post-independence tribal warfare, 440
   Tsembaga animal sacrifice, 372–73
Papua New Guinea Sustainable
   Development Program
   Company, 349
Paraguay, Guarani land rights, 462
Parallel cousin marriage, 191–92
Parallel descent, 190
Parent-child relationship, Iran, conflict
   avoidance, 332
Participant observation, elements of, 58,
   60–61
Partners in Health (PIH), 324
Pastoralism, defined, 130
Pastoralists, 138–43
   Basseri (Iran) as, 139–41
   combined subsistence strategies
      of, 139
   division of labor, 140, 256
   gender status, 256–57
   kinship relations, 182
   land/resource management,
      139–40, 156
   lifestyle, pros/cons of, 176

   nomadic pattern, 140–41
   Nuer (Sudan) as, 140, 142–43
   patrilineal descent, 185
   sharing, 140
   social status, 140
   transhumance practice, 140
Pataki, George, 448
Patriarchy
   defined, 186
   and double standard, 245
   and dowry, 223–24
   and family violence, 336–37
   and female genital mutilation, 8
   and gender inequality, 251
   male dominance, 252, 261–62
   and polygyny, 219
Patriclans, 192
Patrilineal societies, 184–89
   Africa, shift to, 413
   avoidance relationships of, 199
   characteristics of, 185–86
   cousin marriage, 191–92
   defined, 185
   divorce in, 233–34
   emotional bonds, 186, 188–89
   and foraging/pastoral societies, 185
   Ganda (Uganda), 194–95
   and gender equality, 186
   marriage, importance of, 186, 211–12
   residence patterns, 228–30
Patrilocal residence, 228
Patterns of Culture (Benedict), 120
Peacemakers, role of, 330, 343–44
Pequots, Foxwoods, 448
Peregrine, Peter, 26, 392
Perry, Richard, 443
Personality, 116–18
   defined, 116
   development and culture, 116–17
   independent/interdependent self,
      118–19
   private/public self, 117–18
   self-concept, 118–19
Personhood, social birth, 96–97
Peru
   Chavín de Huántar, 12
   communal reserves, 461
   Huánaco Pampa craft production, 151
   Jivaro women and food
      production, 145
   Machiguenga, working hours of, 173
   Machu Picchu, 320
   See also Andeans; Inca
Pharmaceutical companies, native plants,
   use of, 124
Philips, Susan, 114
Phoneme, 71
Phonemics, 70
Phonetics, 70
Phonology, 70–71
   voiced/voiceless sounds, 71
Phratries, 195
Pianka, E. R., 133

Pibloktoq (Arctic hysteria), 123
Pidgins, 87
Pilling, Arnold, 220
Pima, native language speakers, 80
Pizarro, Francisco, 425
Plains Indians
    Ghost Dance Movement, 37–38,
      374–75
    self-torture sacrifice, 362
Plants
    contraceptive effect, 134
    psychotropic substances from, 124
Play, toys and cultural roles, 103
Pluralism. *See* Cultural pluralism
Plural marriage, 218
Politeness, and conflict avoidance, 331
Political anthropology, focus of, 302–3
Political movements
    factionalism, 322–23
    revolutions, 323
Political organization
    bands, 303–6
    chiefdoms, 310–16
    confederacy, 308, 312–13
    defined, 303
    states, 317–22
    tribes, 306–7
Pollution, and agricultural
    chemicals, 171
Polyandry, 218–19
Polygamy, 218
Polygyny, 218–20
    functions of, 218–20
    Maasai (Kenya/Tanzania), 310
    sororal polygyny, 218
    Tiwi (Australia), 219–20, 305–6
Polynesia
    Marquesas infant feeding, 98
    women in work force, 268–69
    See also Melanesia; Tonga
Polyphony, and ethnographic studies, 62
Polytheism, 356
Pomo
    territory claims, 338
    tribal warfare, 341
Pomo de Ayala, Felipe Guaman, 399
Population control
    China, 262
    foragers' methods, 133–34
Population growth, and food
    production, 148
Population size
    of foragers, 133–34
    and subsistence patterns, 131
Poro (initiation rites), 110
Portugal, slave trade, 411
Posadskaya, Anastasia, 269
Positive sanctions, 328
Possession. *See* Spirit possession
Postcolonial era, 428–29
    indigenous land reserves, 429–30
    nationalism, 428
    time frame of, 428

Postindustrial economy, services,
    growth of, 174
Potlach
    communal function of, 9
    defined, 160
    Kwakwaka'wakw, 160–61
    as negative reciprocity, 160–61
Poverty
    in capitalist societies, 166–67,
      282–83
    and single-parent families, 213,
      297, 299
    white Americans, 290–91
Power
    conflict perspective, 49, 51
    defined, 277
    of elites, 282
    in stratified societies, 279, 282
Prayer, as ritual, 355–56, 362–63
Prayer flags, Tibet, 362
Pregnancy taboos, 358–59
Prehistoric art, 392–93
Prestige
    defined, 277
    in stratified societies, 279, 282
Price, Sally, 390–91, 399
Priests, 360
Primates
    aggression/conflict, 329–30
    dominance hierarchies, 329
    facial expressions, 73
    and human evolution, 13
    sign language learning, 73
Primitive Culture (Tylor), 20
Primogeniture, 317
Private self, cultural notions of,
    117–18
Productivity, of language, 69
Profits, and capitalism, 165
Property ownership
    agricultural societies, 176
    chiefdoms, 313
    tribes, 307
Prophets
    defined, 374
    and revitalization movements, 374
Proselytism, defined, 376
Proselytizing religions
    major religions as, 376–77
    and missionism, 411
    revitalization movements, 374
Prostitution, child, 159
Protestantism
    beliefs of, 377–78
    missionaries to Indians, 419
Proverbs, 397
    for child rearing, 104
Psychological anthropology, 117–20
    abnormal behavior, 121–23
    cognition and culture, 119–20
    focus of, 116
    personality traits, 116–18
    self-concepts, 118–19

Psychological disorders, culture-specific,
    122–23
    amok, 122–23
    defined, 122
    eating disorders, 122
    koro, 123
    latah, 122
    pibloktoq, 123
    windigo, 123
Psychological support, religion
    as, 371
Psychotropic substances, plant-derived,
    types of, 124
Puberty rites
    Apache, 365–66
    defined, 364
    Suku, 366
    See also Initiation rites
Puerto Ricans, El Barrio (New York City)
    study, 58–59
Pyles, Thomas, 88

Q

al Qaeda
    recruitment by, 347
    September 11 attacks, 378
Qahr (family conflict), 332
Questionnaires, survey research, 58
Quetzalcoatl, Aztec god, 112
Quipu (knot), 393
Qur'an (Koran), 378

R

Ra, Maran Kai, 434–35
Rabinow, Paul, 51, 56–57
Race, 287–91
    as American societal issue,
      296–97, 299
    Brazilian system, 291
    compared to caste, 288
    as cultural construction, 287
    defined, 287
Racial inequality
    apartheid, 31, 323, 346–48, 427
    Japan, 289–90
    United States, 288, 290–91
Radcliffe-Brown, A. R., 48
Raids, as tribal warfare, 339–40
Ramos, Alcida, 454
Ranked societies
    defined, 277
    features of, 278–79
    mobility in, 279
Rappaport, Ray, 146, 372–73
Rasmussen, Knud, 394
Rathje, William, 12
Reactive adaptation
    of colonized people, 37–38
    and revitalization movements,
      37–38
Real Bird, Lanny, 76–77

Reciprocity, 160–62
  and conflict avoidance, 334
  defined, 131
  balanced, 160
  generalized, 160
  negative, potlatch as, 160–61
  and subsistence patterns, 131
  See also Sharing
Red Crow Community College, 76
Redistribution, 162–64
  chief, role of, 311–12
  networks of, 162–63
  potlatch as, 162
  and subsistence patterns, 131–32
Reflexive anthropology, elements of, 61
Refugees
  African, 7, 143, 445
  global population of, 436–37
Reid, Walter, 457
Reindeer herding, Sami (Norway), 21
Relationships. *See* Human relationships
Religion
  church/organization as product, 376
  components of, 354–56
  and cultural change, 373–78
  cultural significance of, 355
  defined, 354
  denominations, development of,
    377–78
  freedom to practice, Native
    Americans, 448
  fundamentalism, 376–77
  functions of, 370–73
  and globalization, 376–78
  as integrative system, 28–29
  monotheistic, 356, 375–76
  polytheistic, 356
  practices. *See* Rituals
  practitioners. *See* Religious
    practitioners
  proselytizing/conversions, 376–77,
    411, 418–19
  religious speech, 355–56
  revitalization movements, 37–38, 374
  spirit beings, 356–57
  and symbols, 28
  syncretism, 33, 373–74
  theocracies, 320
  and transmission of ideology, 282
Religious practitioners,
  calling, methods of, 359
  diviners, 359
  healers, 359–60
  mediums, 359
  priests, 360
  prophets, 374
  shamans, 360
Renewal rituals, 362
Renne, Elisha, 53
Rensberger, Boyce, 14
Repatriations, Native Americans, 450–51
Representational art, 386
Republics, 317

Reservations
  Brazil, 452–53
  Native Americans, 422–24
  self-government on, 448–49
  tax immunity of, 448
Resettlement policies, 410
Residence rules, 228–32
  avunculocal, 228–29
  bilocal, 229
  defined, 228
  India, 230–31
  matrilocal, 228
  neolocal, 229
  patrilocal, 228
  and subsistence patterns, 229–30
  uxorilocal, 228
  virilocal, 228
  and warfare frequency, 230
  West Borneo, 231–32
Resource allocation
  and social stratification, 282–83
  and subsistence patterns, 156
Revitalization movements, 37–38, 374–75
  cargo cults, 374–75
  defined, 37
  Ghost Dance, 37–38, 374–75
  messianic, 374
  millinerian, 374
  nativistic, 374
  revivalistic, 374
Revolution
  and cultural change, 36, 323
  defined, 36
  and revitalization movements, 374
Ribeiro, Darcy, 451
Richeport, Madeleine, 369
Richmond, John, 116
Rickford, John, 82–83
Riddles, 397–98
Ries, Paula, 270
Rites of passage, 109–10, 364–66
  adolescents. *See* Initiation rites
  birth rituals, 95, 189
  funerary rites, 364–66
  weddings as, 225–28
Rites of renewal, 262
Rituals, 361–70
  bloodletting, 112
  calendric, 370
  chiefs, role of, 314
  for conflict avoidance, 370
  defined, 361
  healing, 366–70
  life transitions. *See* Rites of passage
  objects as artistic works, 391–92
  prayer, 362
  psychotropic substances, use in, 124
  and redistribution, 162
  rites of renewal, 362
  sacred rituals, 361–62
  sacrifice, 362, 372–73
  secular rituals, 361–62
  of social birth, 96–97

  and spirit possession, 367–68
  and witchcraft, 368–70
Roach, Archie, 33
Robarchek, Clayton, 332–33
Robinson, Gene, 245
Rock paintings, 392
Rodman, Margaret, 268
Rogoff, Barbara, 120
Rohrlich-Leavitt, Ruby, 252
Rohter, Larry, 454
Roman Catholicism
  cross-cultural blends of, 367, 376–77
  denominations, development of,
    377–78
  on divorce, 233
  liberation theology, 454
  missionaries, practices of, 418–19
  mission system, 418
  priests, 360
  puberty rites, 364
Rome, ancient
  and Christianity, 375–76
  gods and goddesses, 355
Rosaldo, Michelle, 252
Rothko, Mark, 391
Rowe, John, 321
Royce, Anya, 395–96, 400
Rubel, Arthur, 367
Rules of descent, 182
Rural dwellers, kinship groups, 184
Russian Revolution (1917), 323
Rwanda
  independence of, 444
  refugees from, 445
  Tutsi/Hutus civil war, 444–45
Ryan, K., 379

S

Sacred narratives, 396
Sacred rituals, 361–62
Sacrifice
  animal, 362, 372–73
  human, 151, 362
  objects/forms of, 362
  ritual bloodletting, 112
  self-torture, 362
Sahagun, Bernardino de, 112
Sahlins, Marshall, 193
Sakajiri, N., 298
Sambia (Papua New Guinea), 340,
    341–42
Same-sex marriage
  gay/lesbian couples, 221–22
  legal aspects, 245
  Native Americans, 221
  Nuer (Sudan), 221
  U.S. Census data on, 215
Sami (Norway)
  language, 90
  reindeer herding, 21
Samoan Islanders, 279–81
  matai (titles), 280

San (Kalahari Desert), Nyae Nyae Conservancy, 461
Sanchez de Lozada, Gonzalo, 454
Sanctions
    formal and informal, 328–29
    positive and negative, 329
    and social control, 330
Sanday, Peggy, 251, 255
Sanders, E. P., 376
Sandpainting, Navajo, 391–92
Sano, Mariko Fujita, 60–61
Sano, Toshiyuki, 60–61
Santeria, 33
Santo Domingo (Dominican Republic), 424–25
Sapir, Edward, 75–78, 87
Sapir-Whorf hypothesis, 75–78
Saramaka (Suriname), calabash designs, 390–91
Saro-Wiwa, Ken, 457
Sasson, Jack, 26
Saudia Arabia
    divorce in, 232
    refugees in, 436
    royals, power of, 286
    as theocracy, 378
Sauer, Carl, 413
Saussure, Ferdinand de, 50
Save the Children, 324
Scarification
    as initiation rite, 110
    Yoruba (Nigeria), 387–88
Schemo, Diana, 452
Scheper-Hughes, Nancy, 96, 298
Schiller, Nina Glick, 441
Schmink, Marianne, 26
Schneider, David, 187
Schneller, Raphael, 74
Schooling, 110–16
    African-Americans, 115–16
    Aztec children, 111–12
    Native American children, 114
    Nigerian children, 114–15
    opportunities and gender, 112–13
Sculptures
    Inuit (Arctic), 400
    male figurines, 392
    Venus figurines, 392
    Yoruba (Nigeria), 387
Sea mammals, Inuit/Inupiaq hunting of, 136–37
Seasonal disorders, *pibloktoq* (Arctic hysteria), 123
Seasonal rituals, 362, 371
Secret societies, 358
Secular rituals, 361–62
Sedentism
    and agricultural societies, 148, 156
    and horticultural societies, 144
    and tribes, 306
Segall, Marshall, 119
Segmentary lineages, division of, 193–94

Self-concept, 118–19
    independent versus interdependent self, 118–19
Self-control, and conflict avoidance, 330
Selz, Peter, 391
Semai (Malaysia)
    conflict avoidance, 332–33
    cultural climate of, 332–33
Semantics, 71–72
Seminoles, bingo halls, 448
Sen, Gita, 266
Seneca, in Iroquois Confederacy, 308, 312–13
Seneca Falls Convention (1848), 263
Senegal, developmental anthropology projects in, 41
Sentences, syntax, 71
September 11 attacks
    forensic anthropology application, 15
    and al Qaeda, 378
    and symbols, 30
Serengeti National Park, and Maasai land loss, 456
Serial monogamy, 218
Service, Elman, 303
Service jobs, in postindustrial economy, 174
Settlement colonies, 410
Settlement pattern, and subsistence, 131
Sewid, James, 227
Sex, defined, 240
Sexual abstinence, for population control, 133–34
Sexual dimorphism, 241
Sexuality
    cultural attitudes/norms, 244–45
    homosexuality, 245
    third gender, 246–48
Shamans, 360
    Korea, 360, 367
    psychotropic substance use, 124
Shambaugh, Harold, 398
Shannon, Jonathan, 399
Sharecropping, 162–63
Sharff, Jagna, 59, 61
Sharing
    and foragers, 135, 136
    and horticulturalists, 145
    and pastoralists, 140
Shi'ite Muslims, 378
Shuar (Ecuador), 454
Shudras, 284
Siberia
    Itel'men language preservation, 90
    latah (abnormal startle reaction), 122
Siblings
    competition among, 337
    ghost marriage, 232
    incest taboo, 216–17
    joint family, 216
    levirate and sororate marriages, 232
    sibling marriage, 217, 315, 321

sororal polygyny, 218
Sickle-cell anemia
    diet and symptom reduction, 15
    evolution of trait, 14–15
Sidi Lahcen (Morocco), fieldwork experience, 56–57
Silverblatt, Irene, 321
Singapore, multiculturalism of, 446
Singlehood, never marrieds, 214
Single-parent family, 213
    U.S. Census data on, 214–15
Siskind, Janet, 259
Sistine Chapel, 354
Skeletal remains, archaeological study of, 12–13
Skin color, as physical adaptation, 13
Slash-and-burn horticulture, 144–45
Slavery, 287, 411–13
    African, 411–13
    American, 287, 413
    Caribbean, 411
    child, forms of, 159, 298
    defined, 287
    European, extent of, 411
    features of system, 287
    human trafficking, 159, 298
    Kwakwaka'wakw (British Columbia), 287
    and mission system, 418
    Sudan, 287
Sleeping arrangements, and culture, 98–99, 100
Smith, John, 415
Smith, S. Percy, 385
Smith-Jones, Marie, 10–11
Snohomish, narrative, 68
Social birth, enculturation practices, 96–97
Social class, 284, 286–87
    as achieved status, 286
    as American societal issue, 296–97, 299
    determinants of, 284, 286
    and language usage, 81, 286–87
    Marxist theory, 283, 286
    and mobility, 286
Social control
    defined, 318
    and religion, 371–72
    in small communities, 330
    in states, 318
Social Darwinism
    and evolutionism, 47
    meaning of, 34
Socialist societies, women's status in, 269
Socialization
    defined, 95
    and family, 211
    See also Child rearing; Enculturation
Social mobility. *See* Class mobility
Social regulation, by states, 319–20

Social reproduction, role of women, 264–66
Social status
    and body art, 387, 389
    and capitalist societies, 165–66
    and clothing/jewelry, 387, 389
    and labor, 159
    pastoralists, 140
    and surplus, 147–48
Social stratification, 282–87
    American society, 296–97, 299
    apartheid, 31, 323, 346–48, 427
    caste, 284–86
    defined, 282
    elite, resources of, 282
    endogamy as practice, 217–18
    exogamy as practice, 216–17
    features of, 279, 282
    and race, 287–91
    slavery, 287
    social class, 284, 286–87
    and states, 318, 321–22
    theories of, 282–83
Societies
    defined, 3
    egalitarian, 278
    ranked, 278–79
    stratified, 279, 282–287
Sociolinguistics, focus of, 75
Somalia
    female genital mutilation, 8–9
    refugees from, 9, 436–37
Song duels, Inuit, 331–32
Songs, 394–95
Sororate, widowhood, 232
Soul, belief in, 356
Sounds, phonology, 70–71
Soustelle, Jacques, 111, 389
South Africa
    apartheid, 31, 323, 346–48, 427
    crime rate, 348
    indigenous rights policies, 460–61
    internal disputes, 348
    Truth and Reconciliation Hearings (1998), 346–47
South America
    Spanish colonialism, 415–18
    See also specific countries and specific groups of indigenous people
Southeast Asians, latah (startle reaction), 122
South Moluccas, 444
Southwold, Martin, 194–95
Soyinka, Wole, 114–15
Spanish colonialism, 415–18
    Bolivia, mining quotas, 418
    de las Casas account, 46
    and depopulation of natives, 415–17
    encomiendas (land grants), 417
    haciendas (estates), 417
    mission system, 418

native resistance/revolts, 427–28
    Spanish/Indian intermarriage, 418
Spatial learning, and culture, 119–20
Specialization
    crafts, 148, 151, 157
    labor, 157, 282–83, 317
    and states, 317, 320
Spencer, Herbert, 47
Spencer, Paul, 309–10
Spencer, Robert, 136
Spirit beings,
    ancestral, 357
    animatism, 356
    animism, 356
    ghosts, 357
    mana (spiritual power), 314, 357
    in polytheism, 356
    secret societies, 358
    specialists in. See Religious practitioners
    and taboos, 358–59
    totemic ancestors, 357–58
Spirit possession, 367–68
    Macumba trance, 367, 369
    windigo of Algonquians, 123
Spradley, James, 227
Stack, Carol, 184
Standard English
    defined, 81
    See also English language
Stanton, Elizabeth Cady, 263
States, 317–23
    characteristics of, 317–20
    cultural pluralism, rise of, 33, 443
    defined, 317
    Inca (Peru/Bolivia), 321–22
    nationalism, 442–43
    origin of, 319
    political movements of, 322–23
    theocracies, 320
    warfare, 317, 320, 344–48
Status
    achieved, 277
    and age, 106–7, 278
    ascribed, 277
    and cultural norms, 22–23
    defined, 106
    and gender, 250–53
    nonverbal communication as indicator of, 74
    and prestige, 277
    See also Social status
Stephens, D. W., 133
Steward, Julian, 49
Stiles, Kristine, 391
Stolen Generation, 33
Stone, Anne, 270–71
Storytelling, 398
Strathern, Andrew, 440
Stratified societies
    chiefdoms, 310–16

defined, 279
    See also Social stratification
Structuralism
    on cultural diversity, 49
    focus of, 50
Subcultures
    characteristics of, 23
    defined, 23, 32
Subjective views, emic, 49
Subsistence patterns, 129–50
    agriculture, 130, 147–50, 156
    and carrying capacity, 130
    combined patterns, 139
    comparison of, 156, 176–78
    and cultural change, 150
    defined, 129
    and distribution of settlement, 131
    and division of labor, 131, 157
    and divorce, 233
    and economic systems, 156
    foraging, 129, 132–38
    and gender status, 253–60
    horticultural societies, 130, 144–47
    and kinship patterns, 183–83, 185–86
    land/resources allocation, 156
    pastoralists, 130, 138–43
    and population size, 131
    and residence rules, 229–30
    and social relations, 131–32, 278
    surplus, handling of, 131, 140, 144, 145, 147–50, 157
Sudan
    female genital mutilation, 8–9
    Gezira Scheme, 441
    and human trafficking, 298
    Jonglei Canal, effect on Dinka, 455
    minorities, ethnic identity, 441
    refugees from, 143, 436–37
    slavery, 287
    See also Nuer
Sudanese system, kinship terminology, 204
Suffrage movement, 263
Suku (Congo), initiation rites, 366
Sumatra, 444
Sumerians, agriculture of, 26
Sun Dance, 362, 420
Sunni Muslims, 378
Suriname, Saramaka calabash designs, 390–91
Surplus
    and capitalism, 165
    defined, 144
    distribution by chief, 311–12
    social functions of, 148, 157, 176
    and subsistence patterns, 131, 140, 144, 145, 147–50, 157, 176
Survey research, elements of, 58
Sustainable development, 171–72
Susto (soul loss), 367

Swidden cultivation, 144–45
Symbolic culture, defined, 4
Symbols
  cultural creation of, 30–31
  defined, 30, 32
  and language, 30–31, 68–69
Syncretism
  and cultural change, 32, 33
  defined, 32
Syntax, 71

T

Taboos
  of clan, 192
  and culture, 25
  defined, 25
  food taboos, 25, 358–59
  incest taboo, 216–17
  pregnancy taboo, 358–59
Taita (Kenya), conflict resolution ritual,
    334–35
Taiwan, naming practices, 108
Taiwanese, discrimination in Japan, 290
Takari (Sudanese minority), 441
Talbot, Mary, 415
Taliban, 378
Talismans, 357
Tanzania
  Barabaig territory loss, 456
  refugees in, 437
  See also Maasai
Tasmanians
  genocide of, 424
  reclamation of sacred land, 424
Tatars (Crimea), resettlement of, 410
Tattoos
  Inuit (Arctic), 388
  Maori (New Zealand), 384–85, 388
Taxation
  imposed by colonialism, 420–21
  Native American tax immunity, 448
  poll taxes, 167
Taylor, Caroline, 109
Tedlock, Dennis, 2, 396
Telpochcalli (Aztec school), 112
Terrorism, defined, 320
Tewa, patrilineal society, 186
Theocracies
  defined, 320
  Saudi Arabia as, 378
  states as, 320
Thinking, cognition and culture,
    119–20
Third gender
  berdaches, 246
  hijras, 245
  Two-Spirits, 246–48
Thompson, Donald, 151
Thompson, Robert, 387, 395
Thornton, Russell, 415
Thought, language relationship, 75–78

Thwaites, R. G., 219, 258
Tibet
  creation myths, 20
  prayer flags, 362
Time, as commodity, 173
Tindale, Norman, 52
Titiev, Mischa, 322
Tiwi (Australia)
  as band, 305–6
  polygyny, 219–20, 305–6
Tlingit, matrilineal descent, 187
Tonga (Polynesia)
  as chiefdom, 315–16
  colonialism, impact on, 315–16
  koloa (women's valuables), 316
  marriage customs, 315
Toraja (Indonesia)
  conflict avoidance, 334
  funerary rites and tourism, 403
Totemism
  and clans, 192
  defined, 357
  totem poles, 358
Totems, defined, 192
Tourism
  ecotourism, 460–61
  indigenous art collecting, 401–3, 405
Townsend Patricia, 13
Toys, and cultural roles, 103
Trade
  defined, 163
  Native Americans and colonists, 414,
    416–17, 425–26
Trance state
  mediums, 359
  oracles, 363
  shamans, 360
  spirit possession, 367–68
Transgender persons. *See* Third
  gender
Transhumance, of pastoralists, 140
Transnational migration
  elements of, 439–40
  and transnationalism, 442
Transvestism, defined, 244
Trask, Haunani-Kay, 401
Triandis, Harry, 117–18
Tribalization, 440
Tribes, 306–10
  age grades, 307–10
  associations of, 307
  conflict resolution, 337–39
  councils, 306
  cultural features of, 306–7
  defined, 306
  examples of, 307
  warfare, 339–44
Trobriand Islanders (Melanesia)
  Malinowski's study of, 48
  kinship and descent, 197–98
  matrilineal descent, 197
  songs, 394

Trudgill, Peter, 81, 286
Truth and Reconciliation Hearings
    (1998), 346–47
Tryptamines, psychotropic effects, 124
Tsalagi language, preservation/learning
  of, 90
Tsembaga (New Guinea), animal
  sacrifice, 372–73
Turkana (Kenya), 257, 365
Tutsi (Rwanda), genocide of, 444–45
Twa (Rwanda), 444
Twin War Gods (Zuni sculpture), 451
Two-Spirits (third gender), 246–48
  defined, 246
  features of, 246–48
  sexual lives of, 247
Tyler, Varro, 452
Tylor, Edward B., 20, 33–34, 47
Tzeltal (Mexico), 428
Tzotzil (Mexico), 428

U

Ubelaker, Douglas, 415
Ubykh language, 90
Uchendu, Victor, 293, 295
Uganda
  clans, 194–95
  Ganda patrilineal society, 194–95
Ukwu, I. U., 259
Umialik (leader), 136
Uncles, avunculocal residence, 228–29
Unemployment, in U.S., 297
Unilineal descent, 184–98
  clans, 192–98
  defined, 184
  exogamy and endogamy, 191
  lineages, 190–92
  matrilineal societies, 184–89
  patrilineal societies, 184–89
United Kingdom, refugees in, 437
United Nations
  Commission on Human Rights, 298
  Draft Declaration on the Rights of
    Indigenous Peoples, 458
  Inter-African Committee (IAC), 8
United States
  American Dream myth, 296–97
  Christian fundamentalism, 377–78
  colonialism. *See* Colonialism; Native
    Americans and colonialism
  consumerism, 171, 173–74
  debt of Americans, 173–74
  downward mobility in, 297, 299
  eating disorders, 122
  foreign-born population in, 294, 439
  household composition
    (1970–200), 271
  indigenous of. *See* native Americans;
    specific tribes
  individualism and personality, 100,
    117–18

industrialization, 169, 260
intellectualism, stress on, 101–2, 120
linguistic diversity of, 79–80. *See also*
    English language
marital status statistics, 214–15
naming practices, 108
racial system, 288, 290–91
refugees in, 437
same-sex marriage, 221–22, 245
single-parent families, 213
slavery, 287, 413
social stratification, 296–97, 299
tattoos and body piercing, 389
time as commodity, 173
women in labor force, 266–71
Universal grammar, 71
Untouchables, 284–85
Urban anthropology, 57–61
    El Barrio example, 58–59
    focus of, 57–58
Urbanization, and states, 318
Urton, Gary, 393
Uxorilocal residence, 228

V

Vaishyas, 284
Values, transmission of, 103–4
van den Broeck, Jef, 81, 286–87
Van Gennep, Arnold, 364
Vanuatu Islands, copra production, 268
Vecsey, Christopher, 419
Venezuela, Otomac psychotropic
    plant use, 124
Vengeance, blood feuds, 338–39
Venus figurines, 392
Vigneras, L. A., 425
Violence
    terrorism, 320
    See also Conflict; Family violence;
        Warfare
Violent Criminal Apprehension Program
    (ViCAP), 15
Viracocha, Inca god, 425
Virilocal residence, 228
Visual arts. *See* Art
Voting rights, women in the U.S., 263

W

Wachtel, N., 425
Waffle gardens, 145
Wagatsuma, Hiroshi, 289–90
Wahl, Lissie, 461
Wahunsonacock, Powhatan chief, 415
Waika (Brazil), psychotropic plant
    use, 124
Wallace, Anthony F. C., 37, 123
Warfare, 339–40
    defined, 339
    and gender status, 253, 259
    and globalization, 340–44

internal and external, 229, 230
    and residence rules, 229, 230
    and state societies, 317, 320, 344–48
    tribal, 339–44
Warren, Jonathan, 453–54
Waters, Elizabeth, 269
Watson, Ruby, 108
Wealth and wealthy
    in capitalist societies, 165, 282
    defined, 277
    kinship network, 183–84
    in stratified societies, 279, 282
Weaning, and culture, 98
Weatherwax, Marvin, 76–77
Weavers, Navajo, 401–2
Weber, Max, 277
Wedding ceremony
    Lohorung Rai (Nepal), 225
    Mohawks, 228
    as rite of passage, 225–28
Weiner, Annette, 198
Weiss, Lawrence, 402
Wellington, John, 168
Were (mentally ill person), 121–22
West Papua, redistribution of
    population, 444
Whitehead, Neil, 442
White man's burden, 421–22
Whiting, John, 98
Whiting, Sarah, 181
Whorf, Benjamin, 75–76
Widowhood
    in levirates/sororates, 232
Wiessner, Siegrief, 453–55, 460
Williams, Eric, 411
Williams, Robert, 82
Williams, Walter, 247–48
Windigo (spiritual possession), 123
Winnebago Tribal Diabetes Project
    Director, 76
Wintus, as foragers, 138
Witchcraft, 368–70
    accusations, function of, 35, 370
    in conflict avoidance, 334–35, 370
    defined, 335
    magic, types of, 369–70
Witherspoon, Gary, 199, 394
Wittfogel, Karl, 319
Wolf, Eric, 411–13, 418
Wolf, Marjorie, 252, 261
Womankind Kenya, 9
Women
    anthropological study, absences of, 63
    as artisans, 390–91
    cult of domesticity, 260, 262
    cultural integration, impact on
        role, 29
    and division of labor, 131, 133, 134–35,
        136, 140, 145–46
    dowry deaths, 223–24
    factory workers, 438
    female genital mutilation, 8–9

and food production, 131, 133,
    145–46
    in global labor force, 266–69
    human trafficking, 298
    Inca sacrifice of, 151
    maquiladora system, 438
    matrilineal descent, 184–89
    in polygynous marriages, 218
    roles and culture, 22
    in single-parent families, 213,
        297, 299
    in socialist societies, 269–70
    social reproduction, role in, 264–66
    suffrage movement, 263
    in U.S. Labor force, 264–66
    See also Mothers; entries under *Gender*
Women's Environment and
    Development Organization, 272
Women's Rights Project, 272
Wong, Aline, 30, 261–62, 268
Wood, Charles, 26
Words
    morphology, 71
    semantics, 71–72
Work force. *See* Labor
World Parks Congress, 460
Worldview, 31, 32
    defined, 31, 32
    societal challenges to norm, 31
World War II, 345, 348
Worsley, Peter, 374, 440, 442
Wounded Knee massacre, 38
Wovoka, Paiute prophet, 38
Written narratives, 398–99
Wu, Tiffany, 456

X

Xenophobia, 428, 445
Xingu National Park (Brazil), 430

Y

Yakuza (organized crime), 298
Yanas, as foragers, 138
Yanomamo (Brazil)
    domestic violence, 63
    economic development, effects of,
        452–53
    as horticulturalists, 145, 230
    male prestige, 259
    marriage, 259
    patrilineal society, 187–88
    patrilocal residence, 228, 259
    territorial protection measures, 453
    warfare, 229, 230, 259
    women, status of, 259
Yap, P. M., 122
Yazzie, Robert, 343–44
Yeoman, I., 113
Yin and *yang*, 244
Yokuts, as foragers, 138

Yonggum (Papua New Guinea), 172
Yopo (hallucinogen), 124
Yoruba (Nigeria)
    arankan social incorrigibles, 122
    art of, 387
    body art, 387–88
    child education, 114–15
    child-rearing proverbs, 104
    dance of, 395
    music of, 395
    scarification of, 387–88
    as slave traders, 412
    were (abnormal behavior), 121–22
Young, Robert, 85, 91
Yugoslavia, interethnic issues, 295–96

Yup'iks (Arctic)
    native language speakers, 80

Z

Zaire
    Efe child rearing, 99, 101
    Mbuti Pygmy gender equality, 254
    Nyanga narratives, 155
    refugees in, 445
Zambia, 172
Zapatista Army for National Liberation,
    450–51
Zapotecs (Mexico), dance of, 400
Zar (spirits), 251–52

Zimbabwe, Cewa witchcraft
    accusations, 370
Zolbrod, Paul, 353
Zorn, Jean, 459
Zouk (French Creole music), 404
Zuni
    birth rituals, 189
    dance of, 395
    as horticulturalists, 145
    narratives of, 2–3, 396
    national character of, 120
    personality traits
        encouraged, 117
    repatriations of, 451
    social birth rites, 96